A CATHOLIC INTRODUCTION TO THE BIBLE

Volume 1

"The study of the Sacred Scriptures must be
a door opened to every believer."

—Pope Francis
Apostolic Exhortation *Evangelii Gaudium* 175
November 24, 2013

John Bergsma and Brant Pitre

A CATHOLIC INTRODUCTION TO THE BIBLE

Volume I

The Old Testament

IGNATIUS PRESS   SAN FRANCISCO

Nihil Obstat: Rev. James M. Dunfee, M.A., S.T.L.
Censor Librorum

Imprimatur: The Most Reverend Jeffrey M. Monforton
Bishop, Diocese of Steubenville

Cover art:
The Hospitality of Abraham and the Sacrifice of Isaac
6th century mosaic
Basilica San Vitale, Ravenna, Italy
Photograph by Petar Milošević/CC SA-BY 4.0

Cover design by Riz Boncan Marsella

CONTENTS

THE PROPHETIC LITERATURE

1. THE VISION OF THIS BOOK

A Catholic Introduction to the Old Testament

The world of publishing offers an amazingly wide spectrum of introductions to the Old Testament. Many books adopt a completely secular approach, subjugating the claims of any religious confession to the supposed "objectivity" of a critical method. Others proceed from a Protestant world view, whether mainstream or evangelical, and reflect the questions, debates, and theological outlooks that prevail in their own ecclesial communities. Still others are written for an ecumenical classroom setting, where faith is not opposed, but no particular faith is privileged. All these approaches have their own value, and we will draw on many of their insights throughout this work.

However, it is also important for there to be an in-depth introduction to Scripture that is both thoroughly informed by contemporary scholarship and explicitly written from a *Catholic* perspective of faith and reason, embracing what might be called an "ecclesial" method of biblical exegesis. In particular, at the beginning of the twenty-first century, there is a real need for an up-to-date Catholic introduction to the Bible that is truly *integrated*, uniting exegesis and theology, faith and reason, Scripture and Tradition, and the Old and New Testaments. As we will see in a moment, just such an approach was called for by Pope Benedict XVI in the first major papal document on the Bible in over fifty years and the longest papal document on Scripture ever written: his Apostolic Exhortation on the Word of God, *Verbum Domini*.[1] In the wake of the publication of *Verbum Domini*, and in the light of the many exciting advances taking place in contemporary biblical studies, now seems a very fitting time to provide a fresh introduction to the Old and New Testaments that takes into account the significant developments in the study of Scripture both in biblical scholarship and in recent magisterial teaching. That is what this volume—*A Catholic Introduction to the Bible: The Old Testament*—and the next volume—*A Catholic Introduction to the Bible: The New Testament*—are designed to provide.

Therefore, this book has been written for anyone who wants to gain an in-depth understanding of the Old Testament from a Catholic perspective. In particular, the text was designed with two key audiences in mind:

1. *Catholic Seminarians, Graduate Students, and Ordained Ministers*: The present volume was written first and foremost to serve as a robustly historical, literary, and theological introduction to the Old Testament for Catholic seminarians and

---

[1] Pope Benedict XVI, Post-Synodal Apostolic Exhortation *Verbum Domini*, On the Word of God in the Life and Mission of the Church (September 30, 2010; hereafter abbreviated *VD*).

lay students in graduate programs in religion and theology. As such, it is ideally suited for a standard single-semester course on the Old Testament. However, the book was also deliberately designed to be thorough enough to be utilized in courses on the various parts of the Old Testament: (1) the Pentateuch, (2) the historical books, (3) the wisdom literature and Psalms, and (4) the prophetic literature. (In this format, it could be supplemented by other readings.) Finally, the text was also designed to serve as a "refresher" course for ordained ministers, both priests and deacons, who are no longer in the classroom but who may want to brush up on what ancient interpreters as well as contemporary scholars have discovered about the books of the Old Testament.

2. *College Students, Directors of Religious Education, Scripture Teachers, and Interested Lay People*: Although intended primarily to be a graduate-level textbook, this introduction does not presuppose any previous study of the Old Testament. Instead, it is written as clearly as possible in order to be accessible to anyone interested in learning more about the Bible. It is our hope, then, that it could also be used as a reference work for undergraduate students, directors of religious education, Bible study leaders, and any interested lay people. Indeed, the text covers every book of the Old Testament precisely so that the teacher or reader has the freedom to select those parts of the canon (and those portions of the book) that he or she deems most important, whether it be the introductions, the sidebars, the sections on theological issues, or the sections on the living tradition. In particular, the sections in each chapter on how that particular Old Testament book is utilized in the Lectionary will prove extremely valuable for pastors and ministers who preach the Scriptures regularly. Finally, in terms of personal Scripture study, each chapter has been designed to be long enough so that it could even be utilized as a short individual "Bible study" on that particular book of the Old Testament.

In sum, there is something for everyone in this introduction to the Old Testament. Although one might wonder at the accuracy of referring to a book of this length as an "introduction", as the reader will soon discover—and as the bibliographies "for further reading" that are attached to each chapter make clear—this book only scratches the proverbial surface of the sacred library of forty-six books known as the "Old Testament".

An Integrated Approach to Scripture

Before diving into the text of the Old Testament itself, it is important first to say a few words about what we mean by an "integrated" Catholic approach to the Old and New Testaments. To be precise: inspired by the teachings of Pope Benedict XVI in *Verbum Domini*, this introduction aims to bring together the following aspects of scriptural study: historical exegesis and theology, faith and reason, Scripture and Tradition, and the Old and New Testaments. As we will see, taken together, these will culminate in a distinctly liturgical approach to Scripture, one that is tied to the contemporary Lectionary of the Catholic Church. In what follows, we will take a few moments to reflect on each of these principles as guideposts to how the rest of the book will proceed.

1. Historical Exegesis and Theology

It is critical to emphasize: this introduction is self-consciously both historical and theological in its approach.

The reason for the emphasis on *history* in a Christian introduction to the Bible is simple: Christianity is a historical religion, and divine revelation is inextricably bound up with the "deeds and words" performed by God "in the history of salvation".[2] In his Apostolic Exhortation on the Word of God, Pope Benedict reiterated the reasons for a historical approach to Scripture when he wrote:

> Before all else, we need to acknowledge the benefits that historical-critical exegesis and other recently developed methods of textual analysis have brought to the life of the Church. *For the Catholic understanding of sacred Scripture, attention to such methods is indispensable, linked as it is to the realism of the Incarnation*: "This necessity is a consequence of the Christian principle formulated in the Gospel of John 1:14: *Verbum caro factum est.* ["The Word became flesh."] The historical fact is a constitutive dimension of the Christian faith. *The history of salvation is not mythology, but a true history, and it should thus be studied with the methods of serious historical research.*" The study of the Bible requires a knowledge of these methods of enquiry and their suitable application. (*VD* 32 [emphasis added])

Notice here that the pope describes historical-critical exegesis of Scripture not only as helpful but as "indispensable". For Benedict, this need for historical exegesis is rooted in the historical reality of the Incarnation itself. Because the Word became flesh and dwelt in history (Jn 1:14), any Catholic approach to Scripture must give serious attention to the historical-critical and textual questions surrounding the Bible. As a result, in this book, we will have constant recourse to contemporary historical-critical studies and literary-critical analyses of each book of the Old Testament. Each chapter will focus on the literary structure and the historical issues raised by that particular book. It will also examine what scholars are saying about the historical origins of the various books of the Old Testament and the historicity of the events depicted therein. We hope that in this way the book can help serve as a corrective to what Pope Benedict calls "the fundamentalist interpretation of sacred Scripture", which has wreaked such havoc in recent times, leading many Catholics to leave the Church (*VD* 44). According to the pope, one major problem with the fundamentalist interpretation of the Bible is that it refuses "to take into account the historical character of biblical revelation" and thereby "makes itself incapable of accepting the full truth of the incarnation itself" (*VD* 44).

At the same time, this historical approach to the Scriptures will be balanced by a theological approach. The reason for this is equally straightforward: according to the Catholic faith, Sacred Scripture is not just a human book; it is also "inspired by God" (2 Tim 3:16). In the final analysis, this means that "God is the author of Sacred Scripture" and that "the divinely revealed realities, which

---

[2] Second Vatican Council, Dogmatic Constitution on Divine Revelation *Dei Verbum* (November 18, 1965; hereafter abbreviated *DV*), 2, in Austin Flannery, O.P., ed., *Vatican Council II*, vol. 1, *The Conciliar and Postconciliar Documents*, new rev. ed. (Northport, N.Y.: Costello, 1996), 751.

are contained and presented in the text of Sacred Scripture, have been written down under the inspiration of the Holy Spirit."[3] As Pope Benedict points out, one implication of the truth of inspiration is that Scripture must be interpreted not only from a historical-critical or literary perspective, but also from a theological perspective:

> On the one hand, the [Second Vatican] Council emphasizes the study of literary genres and historical context as basic elements for understanding the meaning intended by the sacred author. On the other hand, since Scripture must be interpreted in the same Spirit in which it was written, the Dogmatic Constitution indicates three fundamental criteria for an appreciation of the divine dimension of the Bible: 1) the text must be interpreted with attention to *the unity of the whole of Scripture*; nowadays this is called canonical exegesis; 2) account is be taken of *the living Tradition of the whole Church*; and, finally, 3) respect must be shown for *the analogy of faith*. "Only where both methodological levels, the historical-critical and the theological, are respected, can one speak of a theological exegesis, an exegesis worthy of this book." (*VD* 34)

In this book, we will attempt to engage in this kind of "theological exegesis", following the three criteria of Vatican II, by paying close attention to (1) the content and unity of the whole Bible, both Old and New Testaments, (2) the living tradition of the Church, and (3) the analogy of faith. For example, in the "Living Tradition" section in each chapter, we will examine how key passages from the Old Testament are interpreted in the New Testament, in the writings of the Church Fathers and Doctors, as well as in the teachings of the Magisterium.

In this way, we will try to help realize Vatican II's goal of making "the study of the sacred page" the "soul of sacred theology" (*DV* 24). As many contemporary biblical scholars and theologians have noted, this reintegration of historical exegesis and theological interpretation is desperately needed. Pope Benedict puts it strongly when he writes: "In a word, '*where exegesis is not theology, Scripture cannot be the soul of theology*, and conversely, where theology is not essentially the interpretation of the Church's Scripture, such a theology no longer has a foundation'" (*VD* 35 [emphasis added]).

2. Faith and Reason

Of course, in order to integrate exegesis and theology, one must also interpret Scripture from the perspective of faith and reason. As mentioned above, many contemporary introductions to the Bible, often written for a secular university context, take the approach of "bracketing" or prescinding from faith, in order to study the Scriptures from the vantage point of human reason alone. Although such studies have their value, they are intrinsically *secular* in character and, as a result, can never be properly theological. In *Verbum Domini*, the

---

[3] *Catechism of the Catholic Church*, 2nd ed. (Vatican City: Libreria Editrice, 1997; Washington, D.C.: United States Catholic Conference, 1997; hereafter abbreviated *CCC*), 105, quoting *DV* 11.

pope called for an interpretation of Scripture that utilizes all of the tools of natural human reason (such as historical-critical exegesis) but unites them to supernatural faith:

> [A] hermeneutical approach to sacred Scripture inevitably brings into play *the proper relationship between faith and reason*. Indeed, the secularized hermeneutic of sacred Scripture is the product of reason's attempt structurally to exclude any possibility that God might enter into our lives and speak to us in human words. Here too, we need to urge a broadening of the scope of reason. *In applying methods of historical analysis, no criteria should be adopted which would rule out in advance God's self-disclosure in human history.* The unity of the two levels at work in the interpretation of sacred Scripture presupposes, in a word, *the harmony of faith and reason*. On the one hand, it calls for a *faith* which, by maintaining a proper relationship with right reason, never degenerates into fideism, which in the case of Scripture would end up in fundamentalism. On the other hand, it calls for a *reason* which, in its investigation of the historical elements present in the Bible, is marked by openness and does not reject *a priori* anything beyond its own terms of reference. In any case, the religion of the incarnate *Logos* can hardly fail to appear profoundly reasonable to anyone who sincerely seeks the truth and the ultimate meaning of his or her own life and history. (*VD* 36 [emphasis added])

In this book, we will strive to maintain such a "harmony" of faith and reason, recognizing that "though faith is above reason, there can never be any real discrepancy between faith and reason. Since the same God who reveals mysteries and infuses faith has bestowed the light of reason on the human mind, God cannot deny himself, nor can truth ever contradict truth" (*CCC* 159). Therefore, in each chapter, we will use reason to examine openly the historical and exegetical questions that are raised by the text, while at the same time taking into account what we also know from faith, avoiding a viewpoint that is ultimately based on the outlook that the Divine does not intervene in human history or one that would explain away all of the divine elements in Scripture (cf. *VD* 35). This is no secular introduction to the Bible, but one animated by "faith seeking understanding" (Latin *fides quaerens intellectum*).

3. Scripture and Tradition

A third distinctive aspect of this book is that it will study the Old Testament from the perspective of both the Sacred Scripture, which is the biblical text, and Sacred Tradition, which is how that text has been interpreted in the "doctrine, life, and worship" of the Church (cf. *CCC* 77–78). In the words of the Second Vatican Council:

> Sacred Tradition and sacred Scripture, then, are bound closely together, and communicate one with the other. For both of them, flowing out from the same divine well-spring, come together in some fashion to form one thing, and move towards the same goal. Sacred Scripture is the speech of God as it is put down in writing under the breath of the Holy Spirit. And Tradition transmits in its entirety the Word of God which has been entrusted to the apostles by Christ the Lord and the Holy Spirit. It transmits it to the successors of the apostles so that, enlightened by the Spirit of truth, they may faithfully preserve, expound

and spread it abroad by their preaching. *Thus it comes about that the Church does not draw her certainty about all revealed truths from the holy Scriptures alone.* Hence, *both Scripture and Tradition* must be accepted and honored with equal feelings of devotion and reverence.[4]

In light of such teaching, Pope Benedict has stressed that knowledge of the Tradition is not just helpful for interpreting Scripture, but *essential*: "The living Tradition is essential for enabling the Church to grow through time in the understanding of the truth revealed in the Scriptures" (*VD* 17).

In this book, we will attend to the relationship between Scripture and the "living tradition" of the Church by giving special attention to how the text of the Old Testament has been interpreted by the early Church Fathers, the medieval Doctors, the living Magisterium, and, above all, the *liturgy* of the Church. With regard to this last element, a liturgical approach is justified by the historical fact that the Christian canon of Scripture itself was gathered, edited, and canonized to serve *as a liturgical text*. Indeed, the "canon" of Scripture is nothing other than the collection of sacred books authorized to be read publicly in the liturgy. As a result, the privileged place for the proclamation, interpretation, and actualization of the Scriptures is and remains the liturgical celebration, especially the Eucharist. At the very outset of his discussion of biblical interpretation, Pope Benedict XVI stresses that a "fundamental criterion" of biblical hermeneutics is that the "primary setting for scriptural interpretation is the life of the Church" (*VD* 29). Later on, he makes clear that in a special way this refers to the proclamation and interpretation of Scripture in the liturgy:

> In considering the Church as "the home of the word", attention must first be given to the sacred liturgy, for *the liturgy is the privileged setting in which God speaks to us in the midst of our lives*; he speaks today to his people, who hear and respond. Every liturgical action is by its very nature steeped in sacred Scripture. In the words of the Constitution *Sacrosanctum Concilium*, "sacred Scripture is of the greatest importance in the celebration of the liturgy. From it are taken the readings, which are explained in the homily and the psalms that are sung. From Scripture the petitions, prayers and liturgical hymns receive their inspiration and substance. From Scripture the liturgical actions and signs draw their meaning." ... *A faith-filled understanding of sacred Scripture must always refer back to the liturgy*, in which the word of God is celebrated as a timely and living word. (*VD* 52 [emphasis added])

One of the most unique elements of this introduction is its close attention to the reception of Scripture within the liturgical texts and rites of the Catholic Church. For example, in the final section of each chapter on the individual books of the Old Testament, we will examine how that particular book is utilized (or not utilized) in the contemporary Lectionary (*Roman Missal*, 3rd ed.). This makes the book particularly useful for ministers who have the task of preaching the Scriptures to congregations of the faithful on a weekly or even daily basis. In addition, this emphasis on the Lectionary should also prove relevant to non-Catholic readers who may be familiar with the Revised Common

---

[4] *DV* 9, in Flannery, *Vatican Council II*, 1:755 (emphasis added).

Lectionary (1983), which is used in many Protestant communities and which was originally based on the Roman Catholic Lectionary published in 1969.

4. The Old Testament and the New Testament

As anyone who has spent any time reading the Old Testament already knows, one of the greatest difficulties that arises is the question: How does the Old Testament relate to the New? Is the God of the Old Testament the same as the God of the New? If so, how do we explain the significant differences between the two Testaments?

In light of such questions, the fourth and final notable aspect of this book is its deliberate attempt to integrate the Old and New Testaments. Once again, this emphasis on the unity of the two Testaments is described by Pope Benedict XVI:

> From apostolic times and in her living Tradition, *the Church has stressed the unity of God's plan in the two Testaments through the use of typology*; this procedure is in no way arbitrary, but is intrinsic to the events related in the sacred text and thus involves the whole of Scripture. Typology "discerns in God's works of the Old Covenant prefigurations of what he accomplished in the fullness of time in the person of his incarnate Son". *Christians, then, read the Old Testament in the light of Christ crucified and risen.* While *typological interpretation* manifests the inexhaustible content of the Old Testament from the standpoint of the New, we must not forget that the Old Testament retains its own inherent value as revelation, as our Lord himself reaffirmed (cf. Mk 12:29–31). Consequently, "*the New Testament has to be read in the light of the Old.* Early Christian catechesis made constant use of the Old Testament (cf. 1 Cor 5:6–8; 1 Cor 10:1–11)". For this reason the Synod Fathers stated that "the Jewish understanding of the Bible can prove helpful to Christians for their own understanding and study of the Scriptures." (*VD* 41 [emphasis added])

As we will see many times in the course of this book, one of the most exciting aspects of studying the Old Testament from the perspective of faith and reason and through the lens of Scripture and Tradition is the way in which typological interpretation does indeed open up "the inexhaustible content of the Old Testament". To be sure, typology must not be "arbitrary", but must flow from the events and realities described by the text itself. As we will see, when this is done, the ancient Christian saying will prove true: "The New Testament lies hidden in the Old and the Old Testament is unveiled in the New."[5]

Invitation to the Old Testament

With these basic principles of interpretation in mind, we now invite the reader to enter (or reenter) the amazing world of the Old Testament. It is our hope that, with the help of this introduction, readers will not only learn more about the Old Testament but encounter the truth that "the books of the Old Testament bear witness to the whole divine pedagogy of God's saving love"

---

[5] See Augustine, *Questions on the Heptateuch* 2.73; cited in *CCC* 129.

(*CCC* 122). Indeed, these writings "are a storehouse of sublime teaching on God and of sound wisdom on human life, as well as a wonderful treasury of prayers; in them, too, the mystery of salvation is present in a hidden way."[6]

For Further Reading

The Interpretation of Scripture

Andrews, James A. *Hermeneutics and the Church: In Dialogue with Augustine*. ND Reading the Scriptures. Notre Dame, Ind.: University of Notre Dame Press, 2012.

Augustine, Saint. *Teaching Christianity (De Doctrina Christiana)*. Translated by Edmund Hill. Hyde Park, N.Y.: New City Press, 2002.

Bechard, Dean P. *The Scripture Documents: An Anthology of Official Catholic Teachings*. Collegeville, Minn.: Liturgical Press, 2002.

Benedict XVI, Pope. *Verbum Domini* (Post-Synodal Apostolic Exhortation, the Word of the Lord). Boston: Daughters of Saint Paul, 2010.

Daniélou, Jean. *From Shadows to Reality: Studies in the Biblical Typology of the Fathers*. Translated by Dom Wulstan Hibberd. Westminster, Md.: Newman Press, 1960.

De Lubac, Henri. *Medieval Exegesis: The Four Senses of Scripture*. 3 vols. Grand Rapids, Mich.: Eerdmans, 1997–2009.

Farkasfalvy, Denis, O. Cist. *Inspiration and Interpretation: A Theological Introduction to Sacred Scripture*. Washington, D.C.: Catholic University of America Press, 2010.

Hahn, Scott. *Letter and Spirit: From Written Text to Living Word in the Liturgy*. New York: Image, 2005.

———, ed. *Promise and Fulfillment: The Relationship between the Old and New Testaments*. Letter & Spirit 8. Steubenville, Ohio: St. Paul Center for Biblical Theology, 2013.

Johnson, Luke Timothy, and William S. Kurz, S.J. *The Future of Catholic Biblical Scholarship: A Constructive Conversation*. Grand Rapids, Mich.: Eerdmans, 2002.

Levering, Matthew J. *Participatory Biblical Exegesis: A Theology of Biblical Interpretation*. Notre Dame, Ind.: University of Notre Dame Press, 2008.

Pontifical Biblical Commission. *The Inspiration and Truth of Sacred Scripture*. Collegeville, Minn.: Liturgical Press, 2014.

———. *The Interpretation of the Bible in the Church*. Boston: Pauline Press, 1993.

———. *The Jewish People and Their Sacred Scriptures in the Christian Bible*. Boston: Pauline Press, 2003.

Ratzinger, Joseph Cardinal. *God's Word: Scripture, Tradition, Office*. Edited by Peter Hünermann and Thomas Söding. Translated by Henry Taylor. San Francisco: Ignatius Press, 2008.

Shökel, Luis Alonzo. *A Manual of Hermeneutics*. London: T&T Clark, 1998.

Smith, Steven. *The Word of the Lord: Seven Essential Principles for Catholic Scripture Study*. Huntington, Ind.: Our Sunday Visitor, 2012.

A Note on Frequently Used Texts and Translations

Unless otherwise noted, all translations of the Bible, the writings of the early Church Fathers, ancient Jewish writings, the *Summa Theologica*, and Vatican II contained herein are from the editions listed below. Note: from a pedagogical perspective, it is essential to highlight key elements of scriptural passages and

---

[6] *DV* 15, in Flannery, *Vatican Council II*, 1:759.

other ancient texts. For this reason we will frequently *italicize* key portions of ancient texts quoted herein for the sake of emphasis. Thus, *all emphasis in quotations of Scripture and other ancient texts is our own.* When emphasis is added to modern texts cited herein, it will be duly noted.

The Bible

Holy Bible. *Revised Standard Version. Second Catholic edition.* San Francisco: Ignatius Press, 2006.

Ancient Jewish Writings

Charlesworth, James H., ed. *The Old Testament Pseudepigrapha.* 2 vols. New York: Doubleday, 1983–1985.

Danby, Herbert. *The Mishnah.* New York: Oxford University Press, 1933.

Epstein, Isidore, ed. *The Babylonian Talmud.* Soncino edition. 35 vols. London: Soncino, 1935–1952.

Josephus. *Works.* Edited and translated by H. St. J. Thackeray, Ralph Marcus, and Louis Feldman. 10 vols. Loeb Classical Library. Cambridge, Mass.: Harvard University Press, 1926–1965.

Philo. *Works.* Edited and translated by F. H. Colson and G. H. Whitaker. 10 vols. Loeb Classical Library. Cambridge, Mass.: Harvard University Press, 1929–1943.

Early Church Fathers

Eusebius of Caesarea. *Ecclesiastical History.* Books 1–5 translated by Kirsopp Lake. Books 6–10 translated by J. E. L. Oulton. 2 vols. Loeb Classical Library. Cambridge, Mass.: Harvard University Press, 1926, 1932.

Roberts, A., and J. Donaldson, eds. *Ante-Nicene Fathers.* 10 vols. 1885–1887. Repr., Peabody, Mass.: Hendrickson, 1994.

Schaff, Philip, et al., eds. *A Select Library of Nicene and Post-Nicene Fathers.* 2 series. 14 vols. each. 1886–1900. Repr., Peabody, Mass.: Hendrickson, 1994.

Summa Theologica

Aquinas, Saint Thomas. *Summa Theologica.* Translated by the Fathers of the English Dominican Province. 5 vols. 1948. Westminster, Md.: Christian Classics, 1981.

Vatican Council II

Flannery, Austin, ed. *Vatican Council II.* Vol. 1, *The Conciliar and Post Conciliar Documents.* New rev. ed. Northport, N.Y.: Costello, 1975.

2. INTRODUCING THE OLD TESTAMENT

Most readers of the Old Testament today encounter it as the first part of one two-part "book" we know as "the Bible"—from the ancient word for "book" or "scroll" (Greek *biblos*). Yet the Old Testament is in fact an enormous *library* of books that were written by human beings and gathered together over the course of centuries. Unlike many ancient books, it was preserved through time and continues to be the object of intense study up to our own day. Therefore, before diving into the text of Scripture itself, it is important to address topics such as the formation of the Bible as a collection of sacred books (the canon), the transmission of the words of each of its component books (the text), and various modern theories about the composition of the Bible as a human endeavor (critical theories).

The Canon of the Old Testament

Most people today never give a thought to the question of what books should be included in the Bible. The typical modern-day reader who wants a Bible, for example, simply goes to a bookstore and asks for one. Decisions about which books are included have already been made. Protestant Christians will be directed to racks and racks of various English translations of a book consisting of the thirty-nine sacred volumes from the Jews bound together along with the twenty-seven documents of the New Testament. Catholic Christians will be directed to a single rack displaying two or three different translations of the forty-six books of the Christian Old Testament and the twenty-seven books of the New. The Eastern Orthodox Christian will likely have even fewer options from which to choose but would find still more books in the Old Testament of the Bible he eventually purchases.

Why the difference in the number and order of the books of the Old Testament between these different communities? Who made those decisions, and when? The answers to these questions are what is known as the *canon* of Scripture, which is defined as either (1) the list of inspired and authoritative books or (2) the collection of books themselves—that is, the Bible.

The term "canon" is Latin, derived from the Greek *kanon*, which itself stems from the Hebrew *qaneh*, meaning a "cane" or "reed". Since reeds were used as measuring sticks in antiquity, the word "canon" in early Christianity came to mean a rule, measure, or authoritative standard against which to evaluate doctrine. Although Origen first used the term with respect to Scripture in the late second century A.D., it was Saint Athanasius in the mid- to late fourth century A.D. who popularized it. During this same period (late fourth and early fifth centuries), a number of early Church Fathers and councils were called to discuss and proclaim decisions regarding the canonical status of different biblical and nonbiblical books.

When discussing the scriptural canons of Judaism and Protestantism, care must be taken not to impose on these other faith communities concepts that apply only within the Catholic Church. For example, neither Judaism nor Protestantism (as a whole) has a central hierarchy or authoritative body (such as an ecumenical council) invested with infallible authority on matters of faith. Therefore, while the canonization of the Scriptures in the Catholic Church can be identified with formal decisions of Church councils, canonization in Judaism and Protestantism took place differently, often without formal decisions.

The Contents of the Old Testament

The Jewish, Catholic, Protestant, and Eastern Orthodox communities all have different traditions concerning the order and divisions of the books of the Old Testament.

The Jewish Bible is often called the *Tanakh*. This word is an acronym formed from the first letters of the three divisions of the Jewish Scriptures: the *Torah* ("Law"), the *Nevi'im* ("Prophets"), and the *Ketuvim* ("Writings") (cf. Lk 24:44). The Law corresponds to the Books of Moses, or the Pentateuch. The Prophets are divided into the "Former", corresponding to the historical books Joshua through 2 Kings, and the "Latter", corresponding to Isaiah through Malachi. The Writings embrace all the other books that do not fall into the previous two categories.

The divisions and order of the Christian Old Testament have been considerably more diverse through history and currently differ between Catholic, Protestant, and Orthodox Bibles. The Jewish division of the canon exerted some influence on the Church's views, especially for Saint Jerome, yet was never fully embraced. More often, the canonical ordering has been arranged according to the historical sequence of events and/or the literary genres of the various books. The result is that the Christian Old Testament in its various forms is arranged according to literary genres: the Pentateuch, historical books, wisdom literature, and prophets (see chart on next page).

Given the diversity of canonical order and contents in the Christian Old Testament, scholars have adopted different strategies for

The Law *Torah*			Genesis Exodus Leviticus Numbers Deuteronomy
The Prophets *Nevi'im*	Former		Joshua Judges 1–2 Samuel 1–2 Kings
	Latter	Major	Isaiah Jeremiah Ezekiel
		Minor	Hosea Joel Amos Obadiah Jonah Micah Nahum Habakkuk Zephaniah Haggai Zechariah Malachi
The Writings *Ketuvim*			Psalms Job Proverbs Ruth Song of Solomon Ecclesiastes Lamentations Esther Daniel Ezra Nehemiah 1 Chronicles 2 Chronicles
Jewish Canonical Order of the "TaNaK"			

Jewish (24 books)	Protestant (39)	Catholic (46)	Greek Orthodox (49)[a]
TORAH	PENTATEUCH	PENTATEUCH	PENTATEUCH
Genesis	Genesis	Genesis	Genesis
Exodus	Exodus	Exodus	Exodus
Leviticus	Leviticus	Leviticus	Leviticus
Numbers	Numbers	Numbers	Numbers
Deuteronomy	Deuteronomy	Deuteronomy	Deuteronomy
PROPHETS	HISTORICAL BOOKS	HISTORICAL BOOKS	HISTORICAL BOOKS
Former			
Joshua	Joshua	Joshua	Joshua
Judges	Judges	Judges	Judges
	Ruth	Ruth	Ruth
Samuel (2 volumes)	1–2 Samuel	1–2 Samuel	1–2 Samuel
Kings (2 volumes)	1–2 Kings	1–2 Kings	1–2 Kings
Latter	1–2 Chronicles	1–2 Chronicles	1–2 Chronicles
Isaiah	Ezra	Ezra	*1 Esdras*
Jeremiah	Nehemiah	Nehemiah	2 Esdras (Ezra-Neh)
Ezekiel	Esther	Tobit	Esther (with additions)
"The Twelve"		Judith	Judith
(1 book)		Esther (with additions)	Tobit
Hosea		1–2 Maccabees	1–2 Maccabees
Joel			*3 Maccabees*
Amos			
Obadiah			
Jonah	WISDOM BOOKS	WISDOM BOOKS	WISDOM BOOKS
Micah	Job	Job	Psalms (+*Psalm 151*)
Nahum	Psalms	Psalms	*Prayer of Manasseh*
Habakkuk			Job
Zephaniah	Proverbs	Proverbs	Proverbs
Haggai	Ecclesiastes	Ecclesiastes	Ecclesiastes
Zechariah	Song of Solomon	Song of Solomon	Song of Solomon
Malachi		Wisdom of Solomon	Wisdom of Solomon
		Sirach	Sirach
WRITINGS	PROPHETS	PROPHETS	PROPHETS
Psalms	Isaiah	Isaiah	Hosea
Proverbs	Jeremiah	Jeremiah	Amos
Job	Lamentations	Lamentations	Micah
Song of Solomon		Baruch	Joel
Ruth	Ezekiel	Ezekiel	Obadiah
Lamentations	Daniel	Daniel (with additions)	Jonah
Ecclesiastes			Nahum
Esther	Hosea	Hosea	Habakkuk
Daniel	Joel	Joel	Zephaniah
Ezra-Nehemiah	Amos	Amos	Haggai
(1 vol.)	Obadiah	Obadiah	Zechariah
Chronicles	Jonah	Jonah	Malachi
	Micah	Micah	Isaiah
	Nahum	Nahum	Jeremiah
	Habakkuk	Habakkuk	Baruch
	Zephaniah	Zephaniah	Lamentations
	Haggai	Haggai	Ezekiel
	Zechariah	Zechariah	Daniel (with additions)
	Malachi	Malachi	

[a] There are variations in the canons of various Eastern and Oriental Orthodox churches.

introducing these books. Some follow the Jewish divisions and order, treat-ing those books that are in the Christian Old Testament but not in the Jewish Tanakh—known as "deuterocanonical books"—at the end. Others arrange the books according to a chronological reconstruction of their dates of composi-tion or according to the book's claimed chronological setting or according to a hybrid compromise between canonical order and chronological order. All these systems have both advantages and disadvantages. To follow the Jewish canonical divisions, however, seems to privilege the Jewish theological appropriation of the Scriptures, which is different from a Christian one. Likewise, to follow a purely historical arrangement unduly privileges prevailing historical reconstruc-tions (which are always in flux) over the canonical form of the sacred text.

In light of the present volume's commitment to interpreting Scripture within the context of the liturgy, we will follow the canonical order that has become standard in the Catholic Church, which is largely that of the Latin Vulgate (see *CCC* 120). Again, in this canon, the biblical books are arranged by genre: (1) the Pentateuch, (2) the historical books, (3) the wisdom literature, and (4) the prophetic literature. The one exception to this rule consists of the books of Maccabees, which are sometimes placed at the end of the historical books and at other times placed at the end of the Old Testament, after the book of Mala-chi, as an indication of the transitional period before the arrival of the Messiah and the inauguration of the New Covenant.

The Development of the Old Testament Canon

The Bible's own account of its origins begins with references to Moses writing down the laws of God at Sinai (Ex 24:4; 34:27–28) and receiving from God tablets of stone containing the Ten Commandments (Ex 24:12; 31:18; 32:15; 34:1; Deut 5:22; 9:10). These holy documents were stored in the Ark of the Covenant (Deut 10:2–4; 1 Kings 8:8), revealing from the very first the close proximity between the preservation of sacred writings and the liturgical worship of ancient Israel.

At the end of the wilderness wanderings, there are further references to Moses writing down the laws that comprise the book of Deuteronomy in a "book" or "scroll" (Deut 28:58, 61; 29:20–21, 27; 30:10; 31:19, 22) and entrusting it to the Levitical priests (Deut 31:9), who were to store it next to the ark (Deut 31:24–26). Significantly, Moses instructed the Levitical priests to read the "Book of the Law" (Hebrew *sepher hattorah*) to the people of Israel every seven years, during the Feast of Booths, when the covenant was renewed (Deut 31:9–13). This "Book of the Law" was the first "Bible" in Israel's religious history, and its function is both significant and paradigmatic: it was intended as a guide for faith and morals, to be proclaimed in the context of the liturgy, as an integral part of the renewal of God's covenant with his people. This continues to be the function of the Scriptures in the New Covenant. The Christian Bible continues to be a covenant document (in two divisions, the Old and the New) proclaimed publicly in the celebration of the covenant-renewing liturgy.

According to Moses' command (Deut 27:3–8), Joshua wrote a publicly acces-sible copy of the "Book of the Law" on tablets of stone on Mount Ebal in a covenant-making ceremony with the people of Israel after entering the Promised Land (Josh 8:32). At the end of his life, Joshua added supplementary material to the "Book of the Law" (Josh 24:26), presumably the copy kept by the Levites next to the ark. Following the ministries of Moses and Joshua, there is a long hiatus in references to sacred writing in the Scriptures. Samuel wrote the laws of the kingship in a book to be kept in the sanctuary (1 Sam 10:25), and later mention is made of chronicles that he kept (1 Chron 29:29). Roughly half the psalms are attributed to David; presumably these were composed orally and reduced to writing by royal scribes. Likewise, Solomon is remembered for having uttered 3,000 proverbs and composed 1,005 songs (1 Kings 4:32). Thus, during the reign of these two great kings (ca. 900s B.C.), the Psalms and wisdom literature begin to take shape.

The middle of the eighth century B.C. witnessed the rise of the "literary prophets". While we have no evidence that the early prophetic figures such as Elijah and Elisha left any written materials, the eighth-century prophets Amos, Hosea, Isaiah, and Micah did write down at least some of their oracles, recorded in the books that bear their names. The seventh century B.C. saw the ministries of Habakkuk (Hab 2:2) and Zephaniah, but it is especially the prophets Jeremiah and Ezekiel, ministering at the end of the Judean monarchy and the beginning of the exile (ca. 630–570 B.C.), who provide us the most information about the literary activity of the prophets. Both Jeremiah and Ezekiel are filled with clear references to texts that we now find in the books of the Pentateuch, Jeremiah being strongly influenced by material from Deuteronomy and Ezekiel by material from Leviticus (although both prophets allude to various passages scattered throughout the entire Pentateuch). It is clear, therefore, that these Mosaic texts were available and authoritative in the late Judean monarchy—indeed earlier, since references to them are not lacking in the older prophets as well. The book of Jeremiah, in particular, abounds with references to the writing down of Jeremiah's prophecies (Jer 25:13, 30:2, 36:2; 51:60), which took place by Jeremiah's dictation to his scribe Baruch (Jer 36:4, 6, 17–18; 45:1). An initial copy of Jeremiah's prophecies was burned by the king (Jer 36:27) and then rewritten and expanded (Jer 36:28–32). Far fewer explicit references to Ezekiel's writing down of his own prophecies are extant, but the prophetic book of Ezekiel is, in its style and structure, notable for its written rather than oral style. Ezekiel also contains the greatest evidence of intentional reuse of older written sources, particularly the second half of the book of Leviticus (Lev 17–27), called the "Holiness Code" by contemporary scholars.

Sometime during the Babylonian exile (sixth century B.C.), it appears that an unknown scribe undertook to compose a history of the people of Israel from the entrance to the land until the exile, comprising what we now know as the historical books Joshua through Kings. This scribal historian used preexisting written sources, which he occasionally mentions: the Book of Jashar (Josh 10:13; 2 Sam 1:18), the Book of the Acts of Solomon (1 Kings 11:41), and the Books of the Chronicles of the Kings of Israel and Judah (for example, 1 Kings 14:19, 29; 2 Kings 1:18; 8:23).

After the Persians conquered Babylon (539 B.C.), the priest Ezra led a large group of Babylonian exiles back to the land of Judah and was heavily invested in teaching the postexilic Judean community to live according to the law of Moses (Ezra 1–6). Later Jewish and Christian tradition, as well as some modern scholars, credit Ezra with editing the Books of Moses into their present form. Ezra's younger contemporary Nehemiah also led the postexilic community and left literary remains, as did the prophets Nahum, Haggai, Zechariah, Joel, Obadiah, and Malachi.

The conquest of the Near East by Alexander the Great (333 B.C.) ushered in the final cultural epoch of the Old Testament. In the last three centuries before Christ, additional wisdom books were written (for example, the Wisdom of Solomon, Sirach) that show the influence of Greek thought. The books of Maccabees, recording the battle for the freedom of the Jews against the Hellenistic king Antiochus IV, who ruled over one of Alexander's successor kingdoms centered in Syria, were perhaps the last of the Old Testament books to be written.

No "Closed Canon" of Jewish Scripture in the Days of Jesus

In the development of a canon of Scripture, two steps need to be distinguished: the *composition* of the sacred books and the *collection* of these same books together into a sacred library that would later come to be known as "the Bible". Although the composition of the books that constitute what we now know as the Old Testament was likely complete before the turn of the first century A.D., the process of their collection and canonization was long and complex.

On the one hand, we have clear evidence that by the second century B.C., the collections of Jewish Scriptures were being gathered together into three main groups: (1) the Law (the five Books of Moses); (2) the Prophets (books such as Joshua, Judges, 1–2 Samuel, and 1–2 Kings, as well as works of major and minor prophets like Isaiah, Jeremiah, Ezekiel, Hosea, and so on); and (3) other Writings. For example, during the late Second Temple period— sometime around the composition of the book of Sirach in 150 B.C.—we begin to find evidence that these three collections were widely recognized as inspired and authoritative. As the prologue to Sirach states:

> [M]any great teachings have been given to us through *the law* and *the prophets* and *the others that followed them*, on account of which we should praise Israel for instruction and wisdom.... [M]y grandfather Jesus, after devoting himself especially to the reading of *the law* and *the prophets* and *the other books of our fathers*, and after acquiring considerable proficiency in them, was himself also led to write something pertaining to instruction and wisdom.... You are urged therefore to read with good will and attention, and to be indulgent in cases where, despite our diligent labor in translating, we may seem to have rendered some phrases imperfectly. For what was originally expressed in Hebrew does not have exactly the same sense when translated into another language. *Not only this work, but even the law itself, the prophecies, and the rest of the books differ not a little as originally expressed.*

Notice here that the book of Sirach provides clear evidence of an accepted body of Jewish Scriptures consisting of three parts as well as the translation of the Hebrew Scriptures into Greek—a distinct reference to the ancient Greek translation later known as the Septuagint (LXX).

On the other hand, although certain parts of the Jewish Scriptures were widely agreed upon, other parts were the subject of continuing debate, with the result that by the time of Jesus in the first century, there was still no "closed" canon of Scripture, demarcating *exactly* which books were inspired and which were not. Instead, different sects within Judaism had divergent views of exactly which books were inspired and authoritative. For example, the *Samaritans* and the *Sadducees*, although very different in their religious views and practice, were agreed that only the five Books of Moses were divinely inspired Scripture. The first-century Jewish historian Josephus tells us that the Sadducees "own no observance of any sort apart from the laws",[1] and the early Christian biblical scholar Origen further clarifies: "the Samaritans and Sadducees ... receive the books of Moses alone."[2]

The *Pharisees*, on the other hand, accepted a larger canon very close to that of modern Jews and Protestants. One of the earliest witnesses to this canon is Josephus himself, who was a follower of the Pharisees and a contemporary of Saint Paul, and who has this to say about the Jewish Scriptures:

	Josephus' Canon: One Proposal
For we have not an innumerable multitude of books among us, disagreeing from and contradicting one another [as the Greeks have], *but only twenty-two books, which contain the records of all the past times; which are justly believed to be divine*; and of them five belong to Moses, which contain his laws and the traditions of the origin of mankind till his death. This interval of time was little short of three thousand years; but as to the time from the death of Moses till the reign of Artaxerxes, king of Persia, who reigned after Xerxes, the prophets, who were after Moses, wrote down what was done in their times in thirteen books. The remaining four books contain hymns to God, and precepts for the conduct of human life. It is true, our history hath been written since Artaxerxes very particularly, but hath not been esteemed of the like authority with the former by our forefathers, because there hath not been an exact succession of prophets since that time; and how firmly we have given credit to those books of our own nation, is evident by what we do; *for during so many ages as have already passed, no one has been so bold as either to add anything to them, to take anything from them, or to make any change in them; but it becomes natural to all Jews, immediately and from their very birth, to esteem those books to contain divine doctrines*, and to persist in them, and, if occasion be, willingly to die for them.[3]	Genesis Exodus Leviticus Numbers Deuteronomy
	Joshua Judges Ruth? 1–2 Samuel 1–2 Kings Isaiah Jeremiah Lamentations? Ezekiel Daniel The Twelve 1–2 Chronicles Ezra Nehemiah?
	Job Psalms Proverbs Song of Solomon?

Unfortunately, it is not at all clear which books Josephus meant by his "thirteen books of the prophets" and "four

[1] Flavius Josephus, *Jewish Antiquities, Books XVIII–XIX*, trans. Louis Feldman, Loeb Classical Library 9 (Cambridge, Mass.: Harvard University Press, 1965), 18.16, pp. 13–14.

[2] Origen, *Against Celsus* 1.49, in *Ante-Nicene Fathers*, ed. Alexander Roberts and James Donaldson, vol. 4 (1885; repr., Peabody, Mass.: Hendrickson, 1994), 418.

[3] Josephus, *Against Apion* 1.38–42, in *The Works of Josephus: Complete and Unabridged*, trans. William Whiston, rev. ed. (Peabody, Mass.: Hendrickson, 1987), 776.

books of hymns . . . and precepts". Several different reconstructions are possible. Moreover, the list of Scriptures to which Josephus refers is that of his own sect, the Pharisees.

Moreover, after the discovery of the Dead Sea Scrolls in the 1940s and 1950s, it is now apparent that the group known as the *Essenes*—a large sect of Jews given to asceticism, prayer, and rigorous observance of the law—accepted an even larger body of Scriptures than that given by Josephus. The Essenes esteemed as divinely revealed certain apocryphal works like the *Book of Jubilees* and various books that are now found together in *1 Enoch*. They may even have viewed the deuterocanonical book of *Tobit* as inspired, along with some sectarian works like *The Temple Scroll*. Furthermore, the large numbers of Greek-speaking Jews scattered around the Mediterranean outside the land of Israel read the Scriptures almost exclusively in the Greek translation later known as the Septuagint (see below) and, based on the extant Greek manuscripts we possess, seem to have accepted as inspired a larger collection than that of the Pharisees, one that roughly corresponds with the books of the Old Testament eventually accepted by the Catholic Church.

When the Jewish community did reach consensus on their canon of Scripture is a matter of dispute. "Canon" and "canonization" are Christian ecclesiastical terms that presuppose a single teaching authority (Latin *magisterium*) competent to make formal decisions on religious matters that are universally binding. The Jewish tradition does not have any such hierarchy or magisterium and does not claim to hold infallible councils. In 1871, the German scholar Heinrich Graetz suggested that the Jews may have reached closure on their biblical canon in A.D. 90 at the "Council of Jamnia [Jabneh]", a city on the coast of Israel to which the Sanhedrin relocated after the destruction of Jerusalem. This theory was popular for about a century but has now been discredited due to a lack of evidence.[4] The Mishnah records debates about the status of the Song of Solomon and Ecclesiastes still ongoing in the second century A.D., but there is simply no evidence that there was ever a "council" of Jamnia in which the first-century rabbis promulgated an authoritative ruling on which books belong to the Jewish canon of Scripture and which do not.

In short: during the life of Jesus and at the time of the birth of the early Church, there was significant and widespread disagreement within Judaism over exactly which ancient Jewish writings were inspired Scripture, and this was just one of many disputed religious questions that were expected to be resolved by the coming of the Messiah (cf. Jn 4:25).

The New Testament Evidence for a Developing Canon

Although the New Testament does not record Jesus communicating a list of inspired books to the apostles, some indication of what books were considered inspired can be seen in those books cited as Scripture by Jesus and his disciples. Many of the books of the Jewish Scriptures are quoted in the New

---

[4] See Jack Lewis, "Jamnia Revisited", in *The Canon Debate*, ed. Lee Martin McDonald and James A. Sanders (Peabody, Mass.: Hendrickson, 2002), 146–62.

Testament, almost always according to the Greek translation now known as the Septuagint (abbreviated LXX, Latin for "Seventy"). However, several undisputed books of the Old Testament (such as Esther and Lamentations) are *never cited* in the New Testament, whereas some non-canonical books (like the *Book of Enoch*) *are* quoted (see Jude 14–15). Therefore, New Testament quotation cannot be a criterion for canonicity, as is sometimes proposed by non-Catholics. If it were, *1 Enoch* would be in the Bible, but Esther would not.

The Development of the Canon in the Early Church

In the first three centuries, the exact boundaries of the canon did not constitute a pressing theological issue. Of much greater concern were questions like the manner of inclusion of Gentiles into the Church (Acts 15), the relationship of the law to salvation in Jesus Christ (Romans; Galatians), and maintaining the visible unity of the Church (see *1 Clement* and the Letters of Ignatius of Antioch).

The second and third centuries witnessed frequent persecutions of the Church that threatened her very survival. This probably explains why it is not until after the legalization of Christianity by Constantine in the early fourth century that we begin to have extant lists of the canon of Scripture from various Church Fathers and councils. By the end of the fourth century, the Churches in communion with Rome settled on the canon recognized by the Catholic Church today, as can be seen from the Councils of Rome (382), Hippo (383), and Carthage (397 and 419) and by Augustine (see chart on pp. 26–27).

It is important to stress here that for the early Church, the fact that a book was "biblical" or "canonical" did not mean that it was printed "between the covers" of a leather-bound, gold-leafed "Bible". These would not be invented for many centuries. Canonicity was not a *literary* reality as much as it was a *liturgical* reality. For the early councils and Church Fathers, canonical books were those which were authorized by legitimate apostolic authority *to be read publicly in worship*. Non-canonical (sometimes called "apocryphal") texts were, by contrast, not approved for public proclamation. Notice the liturgical character of the decrees of these early councils on the biblical books:

> No psalms composed by private individuals *nor any uncanonical books may be read in the church*, but *only the Canonical Books of the Old and New Testaments*. (Canon 59, Council of Laodicea, A.D. 364)[5]

> ITEM, that besides the Canonical Scriptures *nothing [is to] be read in church* under the name of divine Scripture. (Canon 24, Council of Carthage, A.D. 419, citing Canon 36, Council of Hippo, A.D. 383)[6]

Therefore, the designation of "canonical" versus "apocryphal" referred not only to a theological difference but to a liturgical one. The canon defines the books approved for the Church's worship; the Bible is the Church's liturgical book.

---

[5] In *Nicene and Post-Nicene Fathers*, 2nd series, ed. Philip Schaff and Henry Wace, vol. 14 (1900; repr., Peabody Mass.: Hendrickson, 1994), 158 (emphasis added; hereafter abbreviated *NPNF2*).

[6] Ibid., 453.

Further insight into the thought of the early Church on the issue of canon is provided by Saint Augustine in *On Christian Doctrine*. Since Saint Augustine holds such authority in Western Christendom, not only in the Catholic Church but also among Christians in the Lutheran and Calvinist traditions, it is well worth quoting his views on canon in full:

> Now, in regard to the canonical Scriptures, [one] must follow the judgment of the greater number of catholic churches; and among these, of course, a high place must be given to such as have been thought worthy to be the seat of an apostle and to receive epistles. Accordingly, among the canonical Scriptures he will judge according to the following standard: to prefer those that are received by all the catholic churches to those which some do not receive. Among those, again, which are not received by all, he will prefer such as have the sanction of the greater number and those of greater authority, to such as are held by the smaller number and those of less authority. If, however, he shall find that some books are held by the greater number of churches, and others by the churches of greater authority (though this is not a very likely thing to happen), I think that in such a case the authority on the two sides is to be looked upon as equal.
>
> Now the whole canon of Scripture on which we say this judgment is to be exercised, is contained in the following books:—Five books of Moses, that is, Genesis, Exodus, Leviticus, Numbers, Deuteronomy; one book of Joshua the son of Nun; one of Judges; one short book called Ruth, which seems rather to belong to the beginning of Kings; next, four books of Kings, and two of Chronicles,—these last not following one another, but running parallel, so to speak, and going over the same ground. The books now mentioned are history, which contains a connected narrative of the times, and follows the order of the events. There are other books which seem to follow no regular order, and are connected neither with the order of the preceding books nor with one another, such as Job, and Tobias, and Esther, and Judith, and the two books of Maccabees, and the two of Ezra, which last look more like a sequel to the continuous regular history which terminates with the books of Kings and Chronicles. Next are the Prophets, in which there is one book of the Psalms of David; and three books of Solomon, viz., Proverbs, Song of Songs, and Ecclesiastes. For two books, one called Wisdom and the other Ecclesiasticus, are ascribed to Solomon from a certain resemblance of style, but the most likely opinion is that they were written by Jesus the son of Sirach. Still they are to be reckoned among the prophetical books, since they have attained recognition as being authoritative. The remainder are the books which are strictly called the Prophets: twelve separate books of the prophets which are connected with one another, and having never been disjoined, are reckoned as one book; the names of these prophets are as follows:—Hosea, Joel, Amos, Obadiah, Jonah, Micah, Nahum, Habakkuk, Zephaniah, Haggai, Zechariah, Malachi; then there are the four greater prophets, Isaiah, Jeremiah, Daniel, Ezekiel. The authority of the Old Testament is contained within the limits of these forty-four books.[7]

Augustine's teachings on the canon are noteworthy for a number of different reasons.

---

[7] Augustine, *On Christian Doctrine* 2.12–13, in *Nicene and Post-Nicene Fathers*, 1st series, ed. Philip Schaff, vol. 2 (1887; repr., Peabody, Mass.: Hendrickson, 1994), 538–39 (hereafter abbreviated *NPNF1*).

Canonical Lists of the Early Local Councils and Fathers		
Cyril of Jerusalem A.D. 350	Council of Laodicea A.D. 364	St. Athanasius A.D. 367
1. Genesis	1. Genesis	1. Genesis
2. Exodus	2. Exodus	2. Exodus
3. Leviticus	3. Leviticus	3. Leviticus
4. Numbers	4. Numbers	4. Numbers
5. Deuteronomy	5. Deuteronomy	5. Deuteronomy
6. Joshua	6. Joshua	6. Joshua
7. Judges and Ruth	7. Judges and Ruth	7. Judges
8. 1–2 Sam (one)	8. Esther	8. Ruth
9. 1–2 Kings (one)	9. 1–2 Sam. (one)	9. 1–2 Sam (one)
10. 1–2 Chronicles	10. 1–2 Kings (one)	10. 1–2 Kings (one)
11. Ezra–Nehemiah	11. 1–2 Chronicles	11. 1–2 Chronicles
12. Esther	12. Ezra–Nehemiah	12. Ezra–Nehemiah
13. Job	13. Psalms	13. Psalms
14. Psalms	14. Proverbs	14. Proverbs
15. Proverbs	15. Ecclesiastes	15. Ecclesiastes
16. Ecclesiastes	16. Song of Solomon	16. Song of Solomon
17. Song of Solomon	17. Job	17. Job
18. The Twelve	18. The Twelve	18. The Twelve
19. Isaiah	19. Isaiah	19. Isaiah
20. Jeremiah + Lam, Bar, Letter	20. Jeremiah + Lam, Bar, Letter	20. Jeremiah + Lam, Bar, Letter
21. Ezekiel	21. Ezekiel	21. Ezekiel
22. Daniel	22. Daniel	22. Daniel

(continued)

First and foremost, it is significant that for a criterion of canonicity Augustine does *not* propose (1) the personal experience of the believer, (2) the opinions of scholars, (3) the beliefs of the Jews, (4) the quotation of a book by the New Testament, or (5) any abstract principle like "prophetic character". Instead, Augustine states clearly that *the judgment of the Church* is the principal criterion of canonicity. With that said, it is also important to stress that Augustine does not endorse the view that the Church *confers* inspired status on a book, much less that approval by the Church *makes* the book inspired. Rather, the Church *recognizes* or, to use his terms, "receives" books as sacred and inspired. The Scriptures do not require the approval of the Church to *become* inspired; they were

Canonical Lists of the Early Local Councils and Fathers (*continued*)		
Council of Rome A.D. 382[a]	Council of Africa A.D. 383	St. Augustine A.D. 397
1. Genesis	1. Genesis	1. Genesis
2. Exodus	2. Exodus	2. Exodus
3. Leviticus	3. Leviticus	3. Leviticus
4. Numbers	4. Numbers	4. Numbers
5. Deuteronomy	5. Deuteronomy	5. Deuteronomy
6. Joshua	6. Joshua	6. Joshua
7. Judges	7. Judges	7. Judges
8. Ruth	8. Ruth	8. Ruth
9. 1 Kings (= 1 Sam)	9. 1 Kings (= 1 Sam)	9. 1 Kings (= 1 Sam)
10. 2 Kings (= 2 Sam)	10. 2 Kings (= 2 Sam)	10. 2 Kings (= 2 Sam)
11. 3 Kings (= 1 Kings)	11. 3 Kings (= 1 Kings)	11. 3 Kings (= 1 Kings)
12. 4 Kings (= 2 Kings)	12. 4 Kings (= 2 Kings)	12. 4 Kings (= 2 Kings)
13. 1 Chronicles	13. 1 Chronicles	13. 1 Chronicles
14. 2 Chronicles	14. 2 Chronicles	14. 2 Chronicles
15. Psalms	15. Job	15. Job
16. Proverbs	16. Psalms	16. Tobias (Tobit)
17. Song of Songs	17. Proverbs	17. Esther
18. Ecclesiastes	18. Ecclesiastes	18. Judith
19. Wisdom (of Solomon)	19. Song of Solomon	19. 1 Maccabees
20. Ecclesiasticus (= Sirach)	20. Wisdom of Solomon	20. 2 Maccabees
21. Isaiah	21. Sirach	21. 1 Ezra (= Ezra)
22. Jeremiah + Lam (+ Bar?)	22. The Twelve (separated)	22. 2 Ezra (= Nehemiah)
23. Ezekiel	Hosea—Malachi	23. Psalms
24. Daniel	34. Isaiah	24. Proverbs
25. The Twelve (separated)	35. Jeremiah (+ Lam & Bar?)	25. Song of Solomon
Hosea—Malachi	36. Daniel	26. Ecclesiastes
37. Job	37. Ezekiel	27. Wisdom (of Solomon)
38. Tobit	38. Tobit	28. Ecclesiasticus (= Sirach)
39. 1 Ezra (= Ezra)	39. Judith	29. The Twelve (separated)
40. 2 Ezra (= Nehemiah)	40. Esther	Hosea—Malachi
41. Esther	41. 1 Ezra	41. Isaiah
42. Judith	42. 2 Ezra (= Nehemiah)	42. Jeremiah (+ Lam & Bar?)
43. 1 Maccabees	43. 1 Maccabees	43. Daniel
44. 2 Maccabees	44. 2 Maccabees	44. Ezekiel

[a] Disputed by some, because the list is only found appended to a fifth-century document, the *Decree of Gelasius*.

inspired by God during their composition. However, the individual believer does require the guidance of the Church in order to know which books are inspired. In other words, the Church has an epistemological, not ontological, role with respect to Scripture; she does not make the Scriptures inspired, but she does *make known* which Scriptures *are* inspired.

Secondly, and equally importantly, already in the fifth century A.D., Augustine gives the complete Catholic canon of Scripture, including the so-called "deuterocanonicals". Although he does not explicitly mention Baruch and Lamentations, these were widely regarded as part of Jeremiah, as made explicit by Cyril of Jerusalem, Athanasius, and the Council of Laodicea. Some of the earlier

Church Fathers and the Council of Laodicea (A.D. 364) were influenced by Jewish views of canon and felt constrained to restrict the list of Old Testament books to twenty-two only—a pious Jewish tradition related to the twenty-two letters of the Hebrew alphabet. Significantly, however, even these early decrees included at least one book—Baruch—considered "deuterocanonical" by Jews and Protestant Christians today. Nonetheless, perusal of the table of patristic use of the deuterocanonicals below shows that all of them were used, and frequently affirmed, as Scripture by various Church Fathers. As the discussion of the canon developed, the late fourth-century Councils of Rome, Hippo, and Carthage clarified that the Church was not restricted to the twenty-two books of the Pharisees but, rather, affirmed as Scripture all those books which had been employed as such by the Church for centuries, as the following chart demonstrates (see chart on next page).

The canon of Scripture endorsed by the late fourth-century councils became the standard for churches in communion with Rome through the rest of antiquity and the Middle Ages. The question of canon did not become pressing again until the Ecumenical Council of Florence in the mid-fifteenth century A.D., during attempts to heal the schism between the Western (Latin Catholic) and Eastern (Greek Orthodox) Churches. The Council of Florence, with the full participation of the pope, the ecumenical patriarch, and the emperor of Constantinople, arrived at a common statement of faith, including a common canon of Scripture, in 1441. The canon proposed was the same affirmed by the late fourth-century councils and repeated afterward by the ecumenical Council of Trent (A.D. 1546). It is important for ecumenical dialogue to be aware that the Roman Catholic canon was established by an ecumenical council that included ample Eastern representation about a century prior to the outbreak of the Protestant Reformation.

The So-Called "Deuterocanonical" Books

The Old Testament canon of the Catholic Church includes seven books not found in the Jewish canon of Scripture or in the Protestant Old Testament: the books of Tobit, Judith, the Wisdom of Solomon, Sirach (traditionally known as Ecclesiasticus), Baruch, 1 Maccabees, and 2 Maccabees. For the sake of convenience, we will follow common scholarly parlance and refer to these seven books as the "deuterocanonical books", although, as we will see momentarily, this terminology is misleading. Indeed, these seven books are subject to several misconceptions that need to be dispelled:

1. *The deuterocanonical books do not, and did not, form a discrete, recognized collection within Scripture.* The deuterocanonical books are not a genre division like the Pentateuch or the Prophets. Instead, they fall under different genre categories. Baruch is considered part of the prophets; Tobit, Judith, and 1–2 Maccabees are narratives or histories; Wisdom and Sirach are wisdom books.

There is a widespread notion, especially among Protestant writers, that the deuterocanonical books constituted a discrete collection of books that were

The Patristic Use and Affirmation of the Deuterocanonical Books							
	Baruch	Wisdom	Sirach	Tobit	Judith	1 Mac	2 Mac
Pope St. Clement of Rome (d. ca. 99)					*		
St. Polycarp (d. 155)	*						
St. Irenaeus (d. 202)	!						
St. Clement of Alexandria (d. 215)	!	!	!	!	*		
Tertullian (d. 220)	!	!					
St. Hippolytus (d. 236)						*	
Pope Callixtus (d. ca. 202)				!			
Origen (d. 254)		!	!	!			!
St. Cyprian of Carthage (d. 258)	!	!	!	!		!	*
St. Dionysius of Alexandria (d. 265)		*	!	*			
St. Methodius of Olympus (d. 311)	!	!	*				
Lactantius (d. ca. 330)	*	*	*				
Aphraates			*				*
St. Hilary of Poitiers (d. 368)	!	!					!
St. Athanasius (d. 373)	!	!	!	*			
St. Basil the Great (d. 379)	*	*	!		*		*
St. Cyril of Jerusalem (d. 386)	!	*	*				
St. Gregory the Theologian (d. 390)	*	*	*		!		*
St. Gregory of Nyssa (d. ca. 395)	!	!					
St. Ambrose of Milan (d. 397)	!	!	*	*	*	*	*
St. John Chrysostom (d. 407)	*	!	!		*	*	*
St. Jerome (d. 420)	!	!	!	*	!a		
St. Augustine (d. 430)	!	!	!	!	!	!	!

* = *uses* (quotes, cites, or alludes to) the book as though it were Scripture
! = *affirms explicitly* that the book is Scripture or the equivalent (e.g., prophetic, divine, the word of God, etc.) when quoting it.
a St. Jerome personally disputes Judith but reports that the Ecumenical Council of Nicaea received it as canonical Scripture.

accepted or rejected as a group in antiquity. Thus, it is not hard to find scholars who will claim that one or another of the Church Fathers rejected "the deuterocanonicals" as a group, while others accepted them.

In point of fact, the deuterocanonical books differ from one another in their individual canonical histories, and the Fathers and ancient councils treated them *book by book*, and not as a collection. For example, there is no evidence that Baruch was disputed by any Father or council in antiquity: the entire book was considered, along with Lamentations, as part of the book of Jeremiah. On the other hand, certain Church Fathers, particularly Saint Jerome, did express doubts about, or even deny, the canonicity of some or all of the other deuterocanonical books. Even then, however, there was frequently inconsistency, for Saint Jerome can be found quoting Wisdom and Sirach as Scripture in his various writings, although in his prefaces to the Vulgate he relegates them to a non-canonical status. The situation is similar with Saint Athanasius.

2. *The deuterocanonicals do not have a secondary level of inspiration.* The term "deuterocanonical" comes from the Greek words *deuteros* ("second") and *kanon* ("canon" or "rule"), hence meaning "second canon". Although widely used today, this can be a misleading expression, because it implies that these books are secondary to the other canonical books and are perhaps less inspired or authoritative. In Catholic doctrine, however, there is only *one* canon of Scripture, of which these books are part (see *CCC* 120). Hence, according to the teaching of the Church, these seven books of the Old Testament are fully inspired by God and are no less a part of Scripture than any of the other biblical books.

3. *The deuterocanonicals are not the same as the "apocrypha".* The term "apocrypha" (Greek for "hidden") refers to books that might be studied privately but were not to be read in the public liturgy. Which books are considered apocryphal varies in different religious communities. Jews and Protestants consider the deuterocanonicals as apocryphal. The Eastern Orthodox generally accept as canonical certain books considered apocryphal by the Catholic Church, including *1 Esdras* and *3 Maccabees*, sometimes also *4 Maccabees* and the *Odes of Solomon*. The Ethiopic Orthodox accept *1 Enoch* and the *Book of Jubilees*, both of which are considered apocrypha by Jews, Protestants, Catholics, and Orthodox alike. The category "apocrypha" is therefore broader than the "deuterocanonicals".

4. *The deuterocanonicals were included in manuscripts of the Septuagint, but this does not necessarily mean that they were part of a "Greek canon".* It is sometimes said that the deuterocanonical books were included in the "Greek canon" of Jewish Scripture reflected in the Septuagint, but excluded from the "Hebrew canon" of Scripture used by Jews in the Holy Land. The statement is not quite accurate, however.

It is true that the Aramaic-speaking Jews of Palestine tended to follow the Pharisees in holding to a smaller canon of Scripture, which eventually became the modern Jewish canon, or "Hebrew Bible". It is also true that Greek-speaking Jews of the diaspora seem to have accepted a larger number of books as inspired, including most of those included in ancient manuscripts of the Septuagint, the ancient translation of the Bible into Greek. This larger body of books, translated into Greek, is roughly approximate to the Catholic canon of the Old Testament.

However, it must be kept in mind that recent research has shown that there was no exact "canon" of the Septuagint, nor was there a set order of the biblical books in the Septuagint. The origin of the Septuagint will be discussed below; for now we will just point out that no ancient manuscript of the Septuagint has exactly the same number of Old Testament books in exactly the same order.

5. *The deuterocanonicals were not added by the Catholic Church to the Bible during the sixteenth-century Council of Trent in order to produce scriptural support for "unbiblical" doctrines.* The problems with this assertion should be apparent already. As we have seen, the deuterocanonical books were used as Scripture by the Fathers, endorsed by local councils in antiquity, and reaffirmed by the Ecumenical Council of Florence in 1441. All seven of these books are received also by the Eastern Orthodox Churches, which broke from Rome in 1054. It should go without saying that since the Eastern Orthodox do not recognize the authority of the Council of Trent, it is patently false to claim that the Catholic Church only added the deuterocanonical books to the canon at Trent.

Longer Editions of Some Old Testament Books

In addition to the deuterocanonical books, the Catholic Church accepts as canonical the *longer editions* of certain biblical books, such as the book of Daniel, which includes the Prayer of Azariah and the Song of the Three Young Men (found within Dan 3) as well as Susanna (Dan 13) and Bel and the Dragon (Dan 14). Apparently, the book of Daniel circulated in antiquity in longer and shorter editions. Similarly, the Greek translation of Esther received by the Church is considerably longer than the Hebrew text that eventually became standard within the Jewish community. Although these longer editions of the Old Testament books of Daniel and Esther were composed and translated by Jews and circulated among Jewish communities in antiquity, they are not accepted as inspired by contemporary Judaism or Protestantism.

The Process of Canonization from the Perspective of Catholic Faith

The exact limits of the canon of Scripture were a disputed point in ancient Judaism at the time of Jesus. While the New Testament does not provide a list of canonical books, it does make clear that Jesus authorized the apostles to make authoritative judgments about religious law. The most pointed example is to be found in Jesus' declaration to Peter at Caesarea Philippi:

> And I tell you, you are Peter, and on this rock I will build my Church, and the gates of Hades shall not prevail against it. I will give you the keys of the kingdom of heaven, and *whatever you bind on earth shall be bound in heaven, and whatever you loose on earth shall be loosed in heaven.* (Mt 16:18–19)

Leaving aside for the moment the significance of the "keys of the kingdom of heaven", let us focus on the concept of "binding" and "loosing". In first-century Judaism, the terms "bind" and "loose" referred to authoritative decisions about religious law. Religious law was (and is) called *halakhah*, from the verb *halakh*, "to walk". *Halakhah* is, then, the way one "walks"—that is, how one behaves. To "bind" meant to prohibit a behavior; to "loose" meant to permit it. In practice, the Pharisaic scribes generally bound and loosed for the common people of Israel: Jesus refers to their exercise of religious authority (and even partially endorses it!) elsewhere:

> The scribes and the Pharisees sit on Moses' seat; so practice and observe whatever they tell you, but not what they do; for they preach, but do not practice. They *bind* heavy burdens, hard to bear, and lay them on men's shoulders; but they themselves will not move them with their finger. (Mt 23:2–3)

The point of Jesus' declaration at Caesarea Philippi, then, is that he is investing Peter—and, later, the apostles with him (Mt 18:18)—with the authority to make "binding" decisions concerning religious law for the people of God. One such question of religious law was the correct list of inspired books—that is, the canon. Jesus taught the apostles by word and example which books were part of authoritative Jewish Scripture, and they, in turn, passed down this tradition, along with the authority to "bind and loose", to their successors, the bishops of the Church, who began to address the canon question explicitly in the second half of the fourth century, when circumstances were favorable to the clarification of Church doctrine. Their decisions about canon concerned which books were suitable to be read in public worship.

Should there be any doubt about the important role played by the successor of Peter in this process, consider the example of the Council of Carthage in A.D. 419. After declaring that only the "canonical scriptures" were to be read "in church" under "the name of divine Scripture" and giving an authoritative list, the council also declared that its canon of Scripture should be *submitted to the bishop of Rome*—Boniface I, the forty-second successor of Peter—for confirmation of their decision:

> *Let this be sent to our brother and fellow bishop, Boniface, and to the other bishops of those parts, that they may confirm this canon,* for these are the things which we have received from our fathers to be read in church.[8]

In other words, the bishops and Fathers of the fourth-century councils discerned the limits of the canon on the basis of tradition, especially liturgical tradition, and under the guidance of the successor of Peter, the bishop of Rome. They did not innovate; rather, they approved those books which had been used by the Church of the apostles as inspired Scripture for centuries.

Since the canon of Scripture was discerned by the Magisterium of the Church on the basis of liturgical tradition, it makes little sense to interpret Scripture apart from its relationship to the Magisterium, the liturgy, and the Church's tradition. Although the development of the canon is part of the historical process of the development of ancient Judaism and Christianity, in the final analysis, it is the Holy Spirit who guides the Church to the certainty of faith that the

---

[8] Council of Carthage, A.D. 419, canon 24, in *NPNF2* 14:454.

seventy-three books of the Catholic canon of Scripture, and these alone, are inspired by God: "When the Spirit of truth comes, he will guide you into all the truth" (Jn 16:13).

The Text of the Old Testament

The Original Languages of the Old Testament

The original language of a large majority of the Old Testament books is *Hebrew*, the ancestral language of the people of Israel. It is a *Semitic* language—that is, one of a family of Near Eastern languages that share certain features such as tri-literal word roots (that is, words formed from a root consisting of three consonants), the absence of true verbal tenses, and a paratactic syntax (that is, the logical relationships between words, phrases, and clauses are often simply implied by juxtaposition, rather than clearly indicated by a hierarchical syntactical structure, as in Greek). In ancient times, Hebrew was (and continues to be) written from right to left without vowels. In its most ancient form, it was written using a script now called *paleo-Hebrew*, an example of which is illustrated here, from a ninth-century B.C. inscription found in northern Israel.

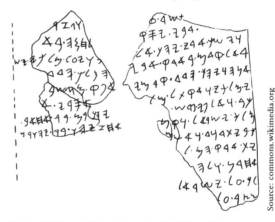

Paleo-Hebrew Script from the Tel Dan Stele

Source: commons.wikimedia.org

A radical linguistic and literary shift occurred for the people of Israel when much of the population of Judah was deported to Babylon in 597 and 587 B.C. During the decades the Judeans spent in Babylon, they began to speak *Aramaic*, the international language of the day. Aramaic is the mother tongue of ancient Aram (modern Syria), and it is closely related to Hebrew. The two languages are almost mutually intelligible. Not only did the Jews begin to use Aramaic as their spoken language; they also adopted the Aramaic square script, which continues to be the font used for copying and printing the Hebrew Scriptures to this day (see illustration).

The very nature of the ancient Hebrew language reveals the essential role of sacred tradition in ancient Judaism. Because ancient Hebrew was written without vowels, it was not possible to interpret the ancient texts of Scripture accurately without first learning the *oral tradition* of the community from those responsible for the preservation and interpretation of the documents—usually the priests and scribes. There is some theological significance in

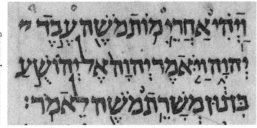

Source: en.wikipedia.org

An example of Hebrew Square Script

this fact, inasmuch as it demonstrates the reciprocal, complementary relationship that has always existed between Sacred Scripture and Sacred Tradition, both in Judaism and Catholicism.

The Hebrew language did change during the centuries in which the books of the Bible were being composed, so not all biblical books are written in the same kind of Hebrew. A distinction between Classical (or Standard) Biblical Hebrew and Late Biblical Hebrew is widely recognized by scholars. *Classical Biblical Hebrew* is a preexilic form of the language, while *Late Biblical Hebrew* reflects a greater influence of Aramaic and other linguistic changes introduced during the trauma of the exile. A good contrast between the two forms of the language can be seen between the Classical Biblical Hebrew of the historical books Genesis–Kings (the "primary history") and the Late Biblical Hebrew of the books of Chronicles, which employ the earlier books as a source.

It may have been possible for ancient scribes to write documents in an older form of the Hebrew language in a procedure called "archaizing"—think here of the way modern poets will sometimes imitate the English language of Shakespeare or the King James Bible. It was also possible systematically to rewrite an older document in a more contemporary form of the language. Hence, the use of linguistic data to assign the *composition date* of biblical documents remains a point of debate among biblical scholars.

Besides Hebrew, two other languages are employed in the Old Testament: *Aramaic*, the international language of the Near East under the Assyrian, Babylonian, and Persian Empires (eighth–fourth centuries B.C.), and *Greek*, the language spread throughout the ancient Mediterranean world by the conquests of Alexander the Great (fourth century B.C.). Portions of Daniel and Ezra and probably all of Tobit were originally written in Aramaic. The Wisdom of Solomon and 2 Maccabees seem to have been composed in Greek originally. All other books of the Old Testament, including 1 Maccabees and Esther, were first written in Hebrew.

The Oldest Manuscripts of the Old Testament

The original manuscripts written by the sacred authors themselves—commonly known as the *autographs*—are no longer extant for any book of the Bible. The oldest partial copies of the text of any biblical book are to be found among the Dead Sea Scrolls (see below). However, the oldest complete manuscript of the Hebrew books of the Old Testament accepted by medieval Jews is a *codex* (a book formed by leaves of paper stitched on one side—that is, the form of book most familiar to us) called the *Leningrad Codex*, or *Leningradensis*, held in the National Library of Russia in Saint Petersburg (formerly Leningrad). *Leningradensis* is a complete copy of the *Masoretic Text* written in Galilee around A.D. 1000.

The Masoretic Text

The *Masoretic Text* is the standard Hebrew form of the books of the Jewish Bible, the form used for chant and proclamation in traditional Jewish synagogues to this day. It takes its name from the *Masoretes*, a school of Jewish scribes that flourished between A.D. 700 to 1000. The Masoretes raised the reproduction of the Hebrew Scriptures to a high art. Among other innovations, they devised a system of markings (called "points") placed above and below the Hebrew consonants to indicate the vowel to be pronounced after the consonant. In this way, they were able for the first time to put down in writing the Jewish oral tradition of the pronunciation of the Hebrew Scriptures. The Masoretes also introduced various quality-control measures for the reproduction of manuscripts, such as painstakingly tabulating the exact number of words and letters in each biblical book, so that scribes could check their work and be certain they had not missed a single letter! Subsequently, every newly written copy was carefully counted to verify its accuracy.

Leningradensis is almost universally regarded as the oldest and best copy of the Masoretic Text, the name given to the precise form the Hebrew developed by the Masoretes as their standard. When translating or studying the Old Testament today, scholars typically begin from the Hebrew of the Masoretic Text, usually a printed (or, increasingly, an electronic) edition of *Leningradensis*.

The Greek Septuagint

When translating the Old Testament, scholars also consult the readings of the *Septuagint*, the ancient Greek translation of the Old Testament books.

According to the ancient Jewish writing known as the *Letter of Aristeas*, the Septuagint translation was begun when the Hellenistic king of Alexandria in Egypt, Ptolemy II (283–246 B.C.), brought Jewish scribes from Jerusalem to Alexandria in order to translate the sacred books of the Jews into Greek for the Library of Alexandria in the third century B.C. This tradition is the origin of the name *Septuagint* (Greek for "seventy")—commonly abbreviated with the Roman numeral "LXX"—after the seventy Jewish scholars commissioned to make the translation. In the words of the *Letter of Aristeas*:

> [King] Ptolemy, the son of Lagus, being very anxious to adorn the library, which he founded in Alexandria, with all the best extant writings of all men, asked from the inhabitants of Jerusalem to have their Scriptures translated into Greek. They ... sent to Ptolemy seventy elders, the most experienced they had in the Scriptures and in both languages, and God thus wrought what he willed. But Ptolemy, wishing to make a trial of them in his own way, and being afraid lest they should have made some agreement to conceal by their translation the truth in the Scriptures, separated them from one another and commanded them all to write the same translation. And this they did in the case of all the books. But when they came together to Ptolemy, and compared each his own translation, God was glorified and the Scriptures were recognized as truly divine, for they all rendered the same things in the same words and the same names, from beginning to end, so that even the heathen who were present knew that the Scriptures had been translated by the inspiration of God.[9]

---

[9] Eusebius of Caesarea, *Ecclesiastical History* 5.8.11–14, in vol. 1, trans. Kirsopp Lake, Loeb Classical Library (Cambridge, Mass.: Harvard University Press, 1926), 459–61.

Although this account is widely regarded as embellished and semi-legendary in character, the basic historicity of King Ptolemy II commissioning a Greek translation of the Pentateuch for his library is plausible and fits the known data. The translation of the Pentateuch was the first and perhaps best and dates to ca. 250 B.C. The other Jewish Scriptures were translated progressively over the next two centuries, under circumstances unknown to us. As far as we can tell from our extant manuscripts, the Septuagint translation began to circulate in a collection that was broader than the Hebrew canon mentioned by Josephus (see above), including works later regarded as deuterocanonical and/or apocryphal.

The quality and style of translation exhibited in the Septuagint can vary quite widely from book to book. The Septuagint translation of Daniel, for example, was so loose that the Church replaced it with a better translation attributed to Theodotion (ca. A.D. 150–200), a Hellenistic Jew. Other books, such as Genesis, were much more literal in translation. All in all, the Septuagint carried enormous prestige in the ancient world. Jewish scholars like the philosopher Philo and the historian Josephus regarded it as virtually inspired, a view shared by some Church Fathers, such as Saint Augustine.[10] For the millions of Greek-speaking Jews living in the Roman Empire outside of Palestine, it was the only form of the Scriptures they used. The majority of the Old Testament quotations in the New Testament are taken from the Greek Septuagint, since the apostles and other New Testament authors typically wrote for a broad audience, rather than just the Jews of Palestine. As Christianity grew and became the leading religion of the Roman Empire, however, a reaction set in, especially among Jews in Palestine. Increasingly, Jews rejected the Septuagint, calling it inaccurate and misleading. At least three Greek-speaking Jewish scholars published *recensions* (revised versions) of the Septuagint that were closer to the Hebrew in use in Palestine: Aquila (ca. A.D. 130), Theodotion (ca. A.D. 150?), and Symmachus (ca. A.D. 170).

By the fourth century A.D., the Church, with the newly acquired support of the Roman government, had the resources to produce *codices* (bound books, not scrolls) of the entire Bible for use in major churches (for example, cathedrals). Our oldest more-or-less complete manuscripts of the entire Bible come from this century and consist of the Septuagint plus the New Testament in Greek. The three most important are named for the places where they were found or now reside: *Vaticanus*, the best manuscript of the complete Greek Bible, Old and New Testaments, stored in the Vatican Libraries at least since the Middle Ages; *Alexandrinus*, an excellently preserved Greek Bible from Alexandria, now stored in the British Library; and *Sinaiticus*, another Septuagint + Greek New Testament found in the nineteenth century in Saint Catherine's Monastery on Mount Sinai and now also residing in the British Library. The Septuagint remains the official version of the Old Testament in use by the Greek Orthodox Church as well as by the Eastern rites of the Catholic Church that use Greek in their liturgies. To this end, it is important to stress that the Second Vatican Council speaks of the Septuagint with special affection: "The Church, from the

---

[10] Augustine, *On Christian Doctrine* 2.15, in *NPNF1* 2:539.

very beginning, *made her own* the ancient translation of the Old Testament called the septuagint."[11]

The Latin Vulgate, Other Ancient Versions, and the Cairo Geniza

Also of value to Old Testament scholars and translators is the *Vulgate*, the Latin translation of the Catholic Scriptures executed (largely) by Saint Jerome in the late fourth and early fifth centuries. Saint Jerome translated most of the biblical books of the Old Testament directly from the best Hebrew copies he was able to procure. On the one hand, this makes his translation worthy of consultation as an important witness to the ancient manuscripts available to him in his day— manuscripts to which we no longer have access. On the other hand, as far as we can tell, the Hebrew text used by Saint Jerome tends, by and large, to resemble closely the Hebrew of the Masoretic Text that we now possess. For this reason, when the Masoretic Text is itself unclear or appears disturbed, Saint Jerome's Vulgate is often not helpful in resolving the textual issues.

Scholars also consult other ancient *versions* (that is, translations) of the Old Testament, such as the ancient Syriac translation known as the *Peshitta*, as well as versions in ancient Coptic (a form of Egyptian) and Ethiopic (the language of Ethiopia). In the nineteenth century, fragments of biblical books dating to the medieval period were also found in the *genizah* (a storeroom for worn biblical scrolls) of the oldest synagogue in Cairo. Many of these *Cairo Genizah* texts have been published and are of some interest to biblical scholars, especially since there is some overlap with books found among the Dead Sea Scrolls.

Important Ancient Texts of the Old Testament			
Name	Language	Date Translated	Date of Oldest Surviving Complete Copies
Masoretic Text (MT)	Hebrew	Not a translation; standardized A.D. 700–1000	11th cent. A.D. (ca. 1000)
Septuagint (LXX)	Greek	250–100 B.C.	4th cent. A.D. (late 300s)
Vulgate	Latin	A.D. 382–405	8th cent. A.D. (mid-700s)
Peshitta	Syriac	A.D. 100s	6th–7th cent. A.D. (500s–600s)

The Dead Sea Scrolls

Of far greater interest to textual scholars of the Old Testament are *the Dead Sea Scrolls*, the remains of an ancient Jewish library—widely believed to belong to the group known as the "Essenes"—found in caves at the northwest end of the Dead Sea in the late 1940s at a site called Qumran. The Dead Sea Scrolls

---

[11] *DV* 22, in Austin Flannery, O.P., ed., *Vatican Council II*, vol. 1, *The Conciliar and Postconciliar Documents*, new rev. ed. (Northport, N.Y.: Costello, 1996), 762–63 (emphasis added).

provide our oldest copies of any portion of Scripture, including texts that date to the second century B.C. Copies of all the undisputed books of the Old Testament were found among the Dead Sea Scrolls except for Esther and Nehemiah. However, apocryphal books like *1 Enoch* and *Jubilees* are better represented than most biblical books, and just as many copies of Tobit were discovered as of Jeremiah, Ezekiel, and Job (six copies each). For this reason, as mentioned above, most scholars believe the collection of sacred writings used by the Essenes— what would later be called a "canon"—was significantly larger than that of the Pharisees and later rabbinic Judaism.

Fragmentary remains of about a thousand scrolls were found at Qumran, of which some 250 were copies of biblical books, almost all in Hebrew. About a third of the Hebrew biblical texts found among the Dead Sea Scrolls closely follow the textual form that we now know as the Masoretic Text. The other biblical texts display differences in wording, including some that agree closely with the Septuagint (about 5 percent of the texts; see below on Septuagint), some that agree with the form of the Pentateuch used by the Samaritans (also 5 percent), and a large number that had *unique readings* (differences of wording) in many biblical passages.

The Dead Sea Scrolls changed how scholars viewed the history of the text of the Old Testament. It became clear that in antiquity, around the time of Jesus, the text of the Jewish Scriptures varied from Hebrew manuscript to Hebrew manuscript. Over time, the Jewish rabbinical tradition, culminating in the work of the Masoretes, settled on a standard form of the text. This Masoretic Text is, by and large, an ancient and generally reliable form of the text—but still only one of those that circulated in antiquity.

The discovery among the Dead Sea Scrolls of ancient Hebrew biblical texts that agree closely with the Greek Septuagint also changed the way scholars viewed the reliability of the LXX. Certain books of the Septuagint—most notably Jeremiah and 1 Samuel—had long been known to differ significantly from the Hebrew Masoretic Text. Many scholars suspected that the Septuagint translators were responsible for these differences because of a lack of fidelity to their Hebrew originals. The Dead Sea Scrolls made it clear, however, that the Septuagint translators had, for the most part, translated the Hebrew in front of them straightforwardly. The more significant differences between portions of the Septuagint and the Masoretic Text were due to variations in the Hebrew editions of the biblical books, not to the activity of the Septuagint translators.

While the study of the Dead Sea Scrolls did change the way scholars understand the development of the Hebrew text of the Bible, it has not fundamentally changed the translations in use among modern believers, whether Christian or Jewish. The variant readings found in the Scrolls were, and are, of great interest to biblical scholars who specialize in *textual criticism* (the study of the exact wording of Scripture), but theologians and lay people often find them of less interest. The vast majority of variations in wording are trivial (a few missing or additional words, the substitution of synonyms, changes in declension or conjugation); and of those that are significant, it is usually easy to distinguish the original reading from errors or intentional changes in some manuscripts.

The Text of the Bible and Modern Catholic Translations

Prior to the encyclical *Divino Afflante Spiritu*,[12] Catholic translations of the Bible into English were based on the text of the Latin Vulgate. Pius XII clarified that Trent's declaration of the Vulgate as the "authentic" translation was meant to establish the Vulgate as the official *Latin* translation (among many Latin translations in circulation) and to provide a common biblical text for use in public theological discussion and education. The decree of Trent was not meant to enshrine the Vulgate as more authoritative than the original Hebrew, Greek, or Aramaic texts composed by the sacred authors. In the words of Pope Pius XII:

> And if the Tridentine Synod wished "that all should use as authentic" the Vulgate Latin version, this, as all know, *applies only to the Latin Church and to the public use of the same Scriptures; nor does it, doubtless, in any way diminish the authority and value of the original texts.* For there was no question then of these texts, but of the Latin versions, which were in circulation at that time.... Hence this special authority or, as they say, authenticity of the Vulgate was not affirmed by the Council particularly for critical reasons, but rather because of its legitimate use in the Churches throughout so many centuries; by which use indeed the same is shown, in the sense in which the Church has understood and understands it, to be free from any error whatsoever in matters of faith and morals; so that, as the Church herself testifies and affirms, it may be quoted safely and without fear of error in disputations, in lectures and in preaching; and *so its authenticity is not specified primarily as critical, but rather as juridical.*
>
> Wherefore this authority of the Vulgate in matters of doctrine by no means prevents—nay rather today it almost demands—either the corroboration and confirmation of this same doctrine by *the original texts* or the having recourse on any and every occasion to the aid of these same texts, by which the correct meaning of the Sacred Letters is everywhere daily made more clear and evident. (*DAS* 21–22 [emphasis added])

In the wake of this papal encyclical, modern English translations of the Catholic Old Testament—such as the 1966 Revised Standard Version, Catholic Edition (RSVCE), or the 1970 New American Bible (NAB)—have been based on the best original language texts available. This ordinarily means the Masoretic Text for the Hebrew books of the Old Testament, supplemented by consultation with the ancient versions and the Dead Sea Scrolls. The Vulgate remains the official version of the Latin rite of the Catholic Church, which represents, in certain places, an authoritative interpretive tradition of the Church that should be given weighty consideration in the process of translation.

Contemporary Study of the Old Testament

With these principles from Catholic tradition in mind, we bring this chapter on interpretation to a close by briefly surveying contemporary methods of biblical

---

[12] Pius XII, Encyclical on Promoting Biblical Studies *Divino Afflante Spiritu* (September 30, 1943; hereafter abbreviated *DAS*).

study. In biblical scholarship, these are often referred to as "critical" methods, though the term "criticism" is a neutral term simply meaning "analysis". In what follows, we describe the origin and practice of the various forms of biblical criticism, beginning with the uncontroversial "lower", or textual, criticism and proceeding through the stages of what used to be called "higher" criticism but is now usually called the "historical-critical method".

Textual Criticism

Textual criticism is the careful comparison and analysis of the ancient manuscripts of the Bible in order to reconstruct, insofar as possible, the original wording of the biblical document under consideration.

Due to human error, no two ancient manuscripts (handwritten copies) of the Bible are exactly alike. Textual criticism attempts, by careful comparison of texts, to correct obvious *errors*, such as misspellings or wrong words; to remove *additions* to the text, whether unintentional or theologically motivated; and to restore *lacunae*—that is, missing words, phrases, and verses.

Textual criticism was undertaken already by the early Church Fathers. Origen was the greatest text critic of the patristic era. He produced a celebrated work called the *Hexapla*, in which he arranged, in six columns, the Hebrew text of the Old Testament, a Greek transliteration of the Hebrew, the recension (= revision of the Septuagint) by Aquila, the recension of Symmachus, Origen's own recension, and the recension of Theodotion. The *Hexapla* was an enormous work, said to comprise fifty volumes, and was kept in Caesarea until being lost during the Muslim invasions of the seventh century A.D.

The economic and political duress of the Middle Ages prevented much progress in the area of textual criticism, but the revival of classical learning in the Renaissance and Reformation period led to renewed efforts to produce accurate editions of Scripture in the original languages. Erasmus produced a critical text of the New Testament in the early sixteenth century. Francisco Cardinal Jimenez de Cisneros, famous for his work in renewing the Church in Spain, sponsored one of the finest achievements of textual criticism in the sixteenth century: the *Complutensian Polyglot*, a critical edition of the Bible in Hebrew, Latin, and Greek. The Old Testament was published in 1517, with the Masoretic Text, Vulgate, and Septuagint in three parallel columns.

In modern times, the textual criticism of the Old Testament has mostly involved making slight adjustments to the Masoretic Text based on the ancient versions in other languages and, since the 1950s, the Hebrew copies of the Jewish Scriptures found among the Dead Sea Scrolls. Rudolf Kittel, a German Old Testament scholar (1853–1929), was probably the most influential Old Testament textual critic in modern times. His critical edition of the Masoretic Text developed ultimately into the *Biblia Hebraica Stuttgartensia*, the standard printed edition of the Hebrew Bible published by the United Bible Societies in Stuttgart, Germany, and used as an international standard by Bible scholars and translators worldwide.

The Rise of the Historical-Critical Method

The basic patristic approach to Scripture remained functional into the period of the Reformation. The Protestant Reformers tended not to elaborate on hermeneutical methodology, but accepted the paradigm that a virtuous life, sound philosophy, and liberal education—especially grammar, logic, and rhetoric—were necessary and sufficient to interpret the Scriptures. The Reformers, however, did begin to part ways with the Catholic tradition over the use of typology; they did so for various reasons, including the following: (1) some commentators had overused typology and argued for fanciful typological associations, which discredited the method; (2) typological interpretations were often used to support "Roman" doctrines the Reformers opposed; (3) lacking a magisterium, the Reformers were uncomfortable with the recognition of multiple senses in Scripture and sought for a interpretive methodology that would consistently yield the same, single meaning each time it was applied to a given text, regardless of who applied it.

Increasingly, then, the Reformers began to move away from the spiritual sense of Scripture and to emphasize the literal sense and the literary tools needed to obtain that sense: a command of the original languages and literatures and—increasingly—historical study. The Reformers' increased emphasis on the grammatical and historical aspects of the text, combined with new movements in philosophy (for example, those of Baruch Spinoza and René Descartes) and a general loss of faith in the institutional Church due to the religious wars ravaging Europe, contributed to the development of the "historical-critical method", a secular approach to Scripture that became increasingly influential during the Enlightenment and dominated the academic study of Scripture from the end of the nineteenth century to the end of the twentieth.

Source Criticism

"Higher" or "historical" criticism proper began in earnest in the mid-eighteenth century with the rise of *source criticism*, the effort to distinguish the sources used by the biblical authors. Literary clues—such as the use of distinct terminology or names and the presence of apparent "doublets" or recurrences of a similar story—were used to isolate the different (hypothetical) sources of a biblical book.

Influenced by the work of the Jewish philosopher Baruch Spinoza (1632–1677), some of the first practitioners of source criticism were the French Catholics Richard Simon, an Oratorian priest (1638–1712), and Jean Astruc, a lay physician (1684–1766). Simon published a work, *Critical History of the Old Testament* (French *Histoire critique du Vieux Testament*) in 1678, arguing that Moses had written only the legal portions of the Pentateuch and that later chroniclers had added the narratives piecemeal, producing the apparent doublets and repetitions in parts of Genesis and Exodus. His arguments were not well-received by orthodox Catholics or Protestants at the time. A generation later, Jean Astruc attempted (ironically) to defend the intelligibility of the Pentateuch against rationalist critics by separating out different documents from which it was supposed to have been compiled. Based on different names used for God—the Hebrew words *YHWH* ("Lord") and *Elohim* ("God")—Astruc separated apparent doublets (repeated stories), repetitions, and inconsistencies into at least two distinct documents arranged in parallel columns. Astruc argued that Moses himself had composed the Pentateuch in this way and that a later editor had combined the documents to produce the supposed inconsistencies noted by Thomas Hobbes (1588–1679), Spinoza, and other skeptics and rationalists.

Scholar	Date of Publication of Seminal Work	Contribution
Jean Astruc	1753	Suggested two sources in Genesis distinguishable by the divine names YHWH or Elohim
Johann Gottfried Eichhorn	1780	Applied Astruc's views to the entire Pentateuch; abandoned Mosaic authorship completely
Wilhelm de Wette	1805	Identified Deuteronomy as a separate source; nothing dates earlier than David
Friedrich Bleek	1822	Extended the source documents to the book of Joshua
Hermann Hupfeld	1853	Split the Elohist (E) into two sources (E^1 and E^2)
Karl Heinrich Graf	1866	Tried to prove that E^1 was the last of the sources.
Julius Wellhausen	1877–1878	Identified E^1 as the Priestly source (P) and arranged the sources chronologically JEDP

While Simon and Astruc did not question the substantial Mosaic authorship of the Pentateuch, as source criticism developed, any substantial contribution of the historical Moses to the first five books of the Bible was eventually eliminated. A succession of German scholars continued to advance and develop Astruc's source analysis, including J. G. Eichhorn (1752–1827), Wilhelm de Wette (1780–1849), Friedrich Bleek (1793–1859), Hermann Hupfeld (1796–1866), Karl Heinrich Graf (1815–1869), and ultimately Julius Wellhausen (1844–1918).

Source criticism is generally regarded as reaching a high point in the late 1800s, when Julius Wellhausen advanced his classic *Documentary Hypothesis* of the Pentateuch. Wellhausen's views achieved a virtual consensus among Old Testament scholars at the major universities of Europe, and dissenting voices were suppressed or ignored. Although resisted by the Church's Magisterium in the late nineteenth and early twentieth century, the Documentary Hypothesis was regnant in Protestant and secular universities, and finally also in Catholic ones, for about a hundred years, from the time of Wellhausen until the 1980s.

The classic Documentary Hypothesis, as advanced by Wellhausen, held that the Pentateuch was composed by combining four older sources. According to the theory, the *Yahwist* source (abbreviated "J" for the German "Jahwe") was composed by a Judean around 850 B.C., used the Hebrew name YHWH for God almost exclusively, and included simple narratives of the patriarchs in which God has very human, personal qualities. A second document was composed by the *Elohist* ("E") about a century later. Written by a northern Israelite, the E source retells many of the stories of J in a more distant, formal style, depicting a transcendent deity. Around 650 B.C., the *Deuteronomist* ("D") composed the bulk of the book of Deuteronomy to provide the basis for a religious reform under King Josiah of Judah (ca. 650–610 B.C.), which was fused by himself or a later editor to the end of the combined JE narrative during the period of the exile (587–537 B.C.). Finally, sometime in the fifth century B.C., the priests of postexilic Judah composed a large body of ritual and moral law, the bulk of the books of Leviticus and Numbers and the end of Exodus. According to the theory, this *Priestly source* ("P") was placed in the center and surrounded with older narratives by some unknown editor or *redactor* ("R") of the fifth or fourth century B.C. This basic form of the Documentary Hypothesis has been so influential in the history of Old Testament studies that a separate excursus will be devoted to it later in this text.

Form Criticism

At the end of the nineteenth century, Wellhausen's work on source criticism seemed so definitive that scholars began to look for new avenues of biblical analysis. Wellhausen's younger German contemporary Hermann Gunkel (1862–1932) is associated with the development of *form criticism* of the Old Testament. Form criticism—in German, *Formgeschichte* ("history of forms")—attempts to identify and label the "form" or genre of the individual literary units called "pericopes" (pronounced *per-IH-koh-peez*) of the Old Testament text and then assign the unit a historical-cultural "life-setting" (in German, *Sitz-im-Leben*) that may have provided its origin. Gunkel assumed that different literary genres were clearly identifiable with certain historical eras and social contexts: the royal court, the Temple, the tribal campfire, and so on. Thus, identifying the genre was the key to discovering the time and place of a pericope's origin.

It is no coincidence that Gunkel's most influential form-critical work focused on the book of Psalms, in which the "life-setting" of the various hymns and songs that constitute the Psalter can often be deduced from the headings attached to the psalms—such as the "love song" (Psalm 45) or the liturgical "Songs of Ascent" sung going up to the Temple to offer sacrifice (Psalm 120)—or the contents of the psalms themselves—such as the royal enthronement psalms (for example, Psalm 2), psalms of repentance (for example, Psalm 51), or psalms of lamentation for those undergoing persecution (for example, Psalm 69). However, over time, it became clear that not every biblical book lends itself as well to form criticism as does the Psalter.

Tradition Criticism

Gunkel's work was further developed by two German Old Testament scholars who dominated the field in the mid-twentieth century, Gerhard von Rad

(1901–1971) and Martin Noth (1902–1968). Moving beyond form criticism, these scholars advanced a methodology that came to be known as *tradition criticism*. This critical approach focused its attention on the development over time of the hypothetical original oral "forms" of the pericopes standing behind the text of the Old Testament, and especially their transition into written form and inclusion into the larger biblical narrative. Hence, in German, this method was known somewhat more accurately as *Traditionsgeschichte*—the "history of traditions". When applied to the Pentateuch, tradition criticism de-emphasized the four literary documents that the source critics had theorized were running through the length of the Pentateuch and focused instead on the hypothetical development of individual narratives or blocks of narrative in the oral stage of tradition behind the final text. In a sense, tradition criticism thus attempted to serve as a kind of theoretical "bridge" between form criticism and source criticism.

Redaction Criticism

For his part, Martin Noth is also associated with the development of *redaction criticism* of the Old Testament. The word "redaction" comes from *Redaktor*, the German word for "editor". Redaction criticism—in German, *Redaktionsgeschichte*, "history of redaction"—is the study of the editorial process that combined the individual text units into the "final form" of the narrative now found in the biblical text. Although basic forms of redaction criticism were practiced by Wellhausen and other older scholars, Noth became renowned for his redaction-critical study of the historical books of the Old Testament. Noth argued that the books of Joshua through 2 Kings were redacted or edited together by a single scribe in the seventh or sixth century B.C. in order to emphasize the need for the descendants of Israel to remain faithful to the Mosaic covenant recorded in Deuteronomy. Since the publication of Noth's work in the 1940s, scholars have taken to calling the historical books Joshua through Kings "the Deuteronomistic history" to reflect this redaction-critical conclusion about the final form of these books.

The Composite Historical-Critical Method

Taken together, source criticism, form criticism, tradition criticism, and redaction criticism are usually considered essential steps of a composite method now known as the *historical-critical method*, or "historical criticism". This method is understood as a unified process that begins with the sources and ends with the final editing in order to present a complete history of the composition of the text. In the words of the Pontifical Biblical Commission:

> When this last method [redaction criticism] was brought into play, the whole series of *different stages characteristic of the historical-critical method* became complete: from *textual criticism* one progresses to *literary criticism*, with its work of dissection in the quest for sources [source criticism]; then one moves to a *critical study of forms* [form criticism] and, finally, to *an analysis of the editorial process* [redaction criticism],

which aims to be particularly attentive to the text as it has been put together. All this has made it possible to understand far more accurately the intention of the authors and editors of the Bible as well as the message which they addressed to their first readers. The achievement of these results has lent the historical-critical method an importance of the highest order.[13]

It is important to emphasize this composite character of the historical-critical method, since, in the final analysis, it is not in fact a single method, but a cluster of several critical methods aimed at reconstructing the *history behind the final form of the biblical text*. As practiced in biblical studies, the "historical-critical method" is not the same as the "historical method" that might be used by an ancient historian. When it comes to source, form, tradition, and redaction criticism, the "history" that the historical-critical method aims to reconstruct is not history in the usual sense, *but the history of the composition of the text*. This is much clearer in the German descriptions of these critical methods than in their English translations.

Beginning in the last quarter of the twentieth century, scholars began to find fault with various aspects of the historical-critical method as practiced since the seventeenth century. Some scholars pointed out that historical-criticism was almost entirely concerned with the process of the composition of the text, and not with discovering the *meaning of the text as we have it*. This leaves the method noticeably incomplete, insofar as so much energy and time is expended in speculating about the prehistory of the text, it often never arrives at the goal of *exegesis*: drawing out the meaning of the text in its final form.

Other scholars pointed out that many of the historical and literary assumptions utilized by source critics were often products of their own time and culture and were anachronistic when applied to ancient documents. For example, there is abundant evidence that ancient authors delighted in the kinds of repetitions, doublets, tensions, and wordplays that modern source critics deemed incontrovertible signs of multiple literary sources. Although such features in a modern literary work might be signals of multiple authorship or faulty editing, this is not necessarily the case in ancient texts.

Another criticism had to do with certain questionable *philosophical* and *theological tendencies* that pervade the works of major source, form, and redaction critics. For example, almost all the most influential contributors to the development of the historical-critical method were German liberal Protestants. On the one hand, this tradition was widely noted for its scholarly rigor and penchant for encyclopedic and exhaustive collection of data. On the other hand, many Jewish scholars have pointed out that certain biases of liberal Protestantism often skew some of the major conclusions of the method.[14]

In recent years, still other American and European scholars have felt that even Wellhausen's work was not radical enough in its delimitation and late dating of

---

[13] Pontifical Biblical Commission, *The Interpretation of the Bible in the Church* (April 23, 1993) (Boston: St. Paul Books & Media, 1993), I.A.1, pp. 37–38 (emphasis added).

[14] See Jon D. Levenson, *The Hebrew Bible, the Old Testament, and Historical Criticism: Jews and Christians in Biblical Studies* (Louisville, Ky.: Westminster John Knox Press, 1993), and Moshe Weinfeld, *The Place of the Law in the Religion of Ancient Israel* (Leiden: Brill, 2004).

sources. Thus, contemporary source criticism of the Old Testament, particularly the Pentateuch, is in a state of vigorous controversy between camps with widely differing views concerning the existence and dating of the various hypothetical sources.

In addition to source criticism, form criticism and tradition criticism have also been the subjects of scholarly controversy. Scholars have called into question the idea that the life-setting (*Sitz-im-Leben*) and historicity of a pericope can be reliably identified simply by its genre or that the development of *oral* forms can be confidently reconstructed hundreds or thousands of years later solely on the basis of an existing *written* text. In other words, form criticism and tradition criticism, by their very nature, are extremely *speculative* enterprises, because we do not have any direct access to the forms and traditions behind the text. For this and other reasons, form criticism and tradition criticism have been abandoned by many contemporary scholars, and those who still practice them do so more cautiously than in previous generations.

Finally, redaction criticism—the study of the final editing process—has probably weathered the contemporary upheaval in biblical studies the best, because it, unlike the other historical-critical methods, works directly with the final form of the biblical text. Nevertheless, to the extent that it hypothesizes about the reasons *behind* various authorial and editorial choices, certain aspects of redaction criticism can also be quite speculative in nature, since we lack direct access to the authors' or editors' thought process and can only ever infer reasons from the final text. However, because of its additional emphasis on this final form, redaction criticism is in many ways similar to the synchronic methods that have now become more widespread in their application (see below).

Synchronic Methods of Biblical Study

While the historical-critical forms of analysis developed in the seventeenth through twentieth centuries continue to be used in Old Testament studies today, many scholars have turned their attention elsewhere, to kinds of biblical analysis concerned with the biblical text as we have it. These methods, which analyze the meaning of the "final stage" of the biblical text, are usually called *synchronic* ("at the same time") to distinguish them from the more *diachronic* ("through time") forms of analysis associated with the historical-critical methods, which study the prehistory and composition of the text as it developed through time. We will mention three of the most important methodologies for our purposes: rhetorical, narrative, and canonical criticism.

Rhetorical criticism is a study of the rhetorical features of the text: how the author uses words to communicate meaning and persuade his audience or readership. Rhetorical criticism is not always distinguishable from a general literary criticism of the Bible. In other words, it tends to analyze the biblical text in much the same way a literary critic would analyze a classic work like Dostoevsky's *Crime and Punishment* or Shakespeare's *Macbeth*. The brilliant Italian-Jewish rabbi and polymath Umberto Cassuto (1883–1951) was an early rhetorical critic who argued already in the first half of the twentieth century that the literary features used by source critics to delineate separate sources—such as doublets, repetitions, and variations in divine names—had literary or rhetorical explanations that could be illuminated by parallels in other classic world literature, from the Homeric epics to medieval ballads to Dante's *Divine Comedy*. Other Jewish scholars pursued similar lines of thought (H. C. Brichto, Meir Sternberg), and the influential American Old Testament scholar James Muilenburg is credited with starting a rhetorical-critical movement within English-speaking biblical scholarship in the late 1960s.

Narrative criticism may be considered a sub-discipline of rhetorical or literary criticism that examines the narrative features of the text, such as plot, theme, characterization, character dynamics, climax, denouement, and so on. A seminal work in this area was Robert Alter's *The Art of Biblical Narrative* (1981). Although Alter (1935–) did not contest the work of source criticism, his examination of the Pentateuch as a story line caused many of the traditional source divisions to recede from view and revealed a remarkably unified final composition.

Canonical criticism is a movement within biblical scholarship associated especially with the American scholar Brevard Childs (1923–2007) and the German Rolf Rendtorff (1925–2014), the student and successor of Gerhard von Rad. Independently of one another in the 1970s, Childs and Rendtorff began to call for a return to scholarly focus on the meaning of the final, received form of the biblical text. This kind of criticism is "canonical" in two senses. First, the object of study is the *canonical form* of the text, not some hypothetical form or putative source from an earlier stage of the text. Thus, the canonical critic studies the book of Leviticus as we have it, not "P" as it exists in the imagination of historical-critics. Second, this kind of criticism studies the *canonical context* of the biblical passage or book—that is, in its place within the entire body of biblical literature. The canonical critic asks the question, "What does Leviticus mean, now that it is viewed as the third book in the canon, an authoritative, inspired collection of books that spans Genesis through Revelation?" Thus, canonical criticism attends to the ways in which biblical books interact with one another and how the placement of a book within the wider collection of biblical books shapes the way in which it is perceived and understood.

Besides rhetorical, narrative, and canonical criticism, there are other forms of synchronic criticism as well as a wide variety of ideological criticisms (feminist, womanist, Marxist, postcolonialist, and so on) of the Bible being practiced today. An excellent overview from the late twentieth century may be found in the document of the Pontifical Biblical Commission, *The Interpretation of the Bible in the Church* (1993; see *For Further Reading*).

Conclusion

The discipline of biblical studies is currently in a state of flux, with a wide variety of different camps or schools of thought attempting to develop the discipline in different and often contradictory directions simultaneously. To engage the contemporary culture, the Church cannot ignore any mode of biblical scholarship and requires scholars who are familiar with, or have mastered, the various modern methodologies. However, the Church's interpretation cannot be based solely on one method or even a confluence of them. Instead, an ecclesial interpretation must take the best aspects of these various methods and integrate them into an approach to the biblical text that is both rigorously exegetical and theologically fruitful. In this regard, the return of scholarly interest to the text as we have it, rather than to the hypothetical history of composition, leads much more naturally to a properly theological interpretation of Scripture, because it is only the canonical, received form of the text that the Church holds to be inspired, true, and authoritative for faith and morals. As we will see, the canonical form of the text often displays a compelling unity and coherence, even while showing signs of development.

For Further Reading

The Canon of Scripture

Collins, John J. "Before the Canon: Scriptures in Second Temple Judaism". Pages 225–41 in *Old Testament Interpretation: Past, Present, and Future: Essays in Honor of Gene M. Tucker*. Edited by J. L. Mays, D. L. Peterson, and K. H. Richards. Nashville: Abingdon Press, 1995.

Josephus, Flavius. *The Works of Josephus: Complete and Unabridged*. Translated by William Whiston. Rev. ed. Peabody, Mass.: Hendrickson, 1987.

Leiman, Shnayer Z. *The Canonization of Hebrew Scripture: The Talmudic and Midrashic Evidence*. Hamden, Conn.: Archon Books, 1976.

McDonald, Lee Martin. *The Biblical Canon: Its Origin, Transmission, and Authority*. Grand Rapids, Mich.: Baker Academic, 2007.

———, and James A. Sanders, eds. *The Canon Debate*. Peabody, Mass.: Hendrickson, 2002.

Sundberg, Albert C. *The Old Testament of the Early Church*. Cambridge, Mass.: Harvard University Press, 1964.

Von Campenhausen, Hans. *The Formation of the Christian Bible*. Philadelphia: Fortress Press, 1977.

The Text of the Old Testament

Hengel, Martin. *The Septuagint as Christian Scripture: Its Prehistory and the Problem of Its Canon*. Grand Rapids, Mich.: Baker Academic, 2004.

Müller, Mogens. *The First Bible of the Church: A Plea for the Septuagint*. The Library of Hebrew Bible/Old Testament Studies 206. London: T&T Clark, 2009.

Tov, Emanuel. *Textual Criticism of the Hebrew Bible*. 3rd rev. and enl. ed. Minneapolis: Fortress Press, 2011.

Ulrich, Eugene. *The Dead Sea Scrolls and the Origins of the Bible*. Grand Rapids, Mich.: Eerdmans, 1995.

Contemporary Study of the Old Testament

Collins, John J. *The Bible after Babel: Historical Criticism in a Postmodern Age*. Grand Rapids, Mich.: Eerdmans, 2005.

Gignilliat, Mark S. *A Brief History of Old Testament Criticism: From Benedict Spinoza to Brevard Childs*. Grand Rapids, Mich.: Zondervan, 2012.

Hahn, Scott W., and Benjamin Wiker. *Politicizing the Bible: The Roots of Historical Criticism and the Secularization of Scripture 1300–1700*. New York: Crossroad, 2013.

Levenson, Jon D. *The Hebrew Bible, the Old Testament, and Historical Criticism: Jews and Christians in Biblical Studies*. Louisville, Ky.: Westminster John Knox Press, 1993.

Morrow, Jeffrey L. *Three Skeptics and the Bible: La Peyrère, Hobbes, Spinoza, and the Reception of Modern Biblical Criticism*. San Jose, Calif.: Pickwick, 2016.

Pontifical Biblical Commission. *The Interpretation of the Bible in the Church*. Boston: Pauline Books and Media, 1993.

———. *The Jewish People and Their Sacred Scriptures in the Christian Bible*. Boston: Pauline Books and Media, 2003.

Weinfeld, Moshe. *The Place of the Law in the Religion of Ancient Israel*. Vetus Testamentum Supplements 100. Leiden and Boston: Brill, 2004.

The Pentateuch

3. WHAT IS THE PENTATEUCH?

The Pentateuch, traditionally known as the five "Books of Moses", comprises the first part of the Jewish and Christian canons of Scripture. These five books enjoy the distinction of having their inspired status recognized by every sect of ancient Judaism (Samaritans, Sadducees, Pharisees, Essenes) as well as by all major Christian communities. The five books of the Pentateuch have pride of place in the liturgy of the Jewish synagogue in very much the way that the four Gospels have pride of place in the Christian Liturgy of the Word.

The word "Pentateuch" comes from the Greek words *pente* ("five") and *teuchos* ("roll", later coming to mean "scroll") and began to be used by both Greek-speaking Jews and Christians in the early centuries to refer to the "five scrolls" or "five books" of Moses.[1] In the Jewish tradition, the Pentateuch is usually called "the Torah", from the Hebrew *torah*, meaning variously "law", "instruction", "teaching", or "doctrine". In the New Testament, the Pentateuch is often referred to as "the law" (Greek *ho nomos*; Mt 5:17) or "the law of Moses" (Greek *ho nomos Mouseōs*; Lk 2:22) or "the law of the Lord" (Greek *ho nomos kuriou*; Lk 2:23).

Over the course of its long history, the authority of the Pentateuch has been denied by various Christian heresies. Perhaps the most influential of these was spread by *Marcion*, a bishop in Italy in the second century A.D. who rejected the Pentateuch along with the rest of the Old Testament as being the work of a false god, not the God revealed by Jesus Christ. Much later in Christian history, certain groups with roots in the Protestant Reformation would dismiss the authority of the Pentateuch by characterizing it as "law" opposed to the "Gospel" that comes through Jesus Christ. Thus, the famous nineteenth-century liberal Protestant theologian Friedrich Schleiermacher considered the Pentateuch and, indeed, the whole Old Testament as theologically worthless except as a background for understanding Jesus and the apostles.

In contrast, the Church has always defended and upheld the importance of these books, based on the teaching of the New Testament. On more than one occasion in the Gospels, Jesus asserts the inspired character of the Torah down to the smallest Hebrew letters (the "iota" = the letter *waw* or "w", and the "dot" = the letter *yod* or "y"):

> Do not think that I have come to abolish *the law* and the prophets; I have come not to abolish them but to fulfil them. *For truly, I say to you, till heaven and earth pass away, not an iota, not a dot, will pass from the law until all is accomplished.* (Mt 5:17)

> But it is easier for heaven and earth to pass away, than for one dot of *the law* to become void. (Lk 16:17)

---

[1] See *Letter of Aristeas* 189; Epiphanius, *Against Heresies* 33.4; Tertullian, *Against Marcion* 1.10.

Indeed, after the Psalms and Isaiah, Genesis and Deuteronomy are the books most quoted in the New Testament, and the books of the Pentateuch have continued to be foundational to Christian theology and worship: the theology of creation, the body, and marriage are deeply rooted in Genesis; Eucharistic theology rests on the celebration of Passover in Exodus; the Christian doctrine of sin, sacrifice, and merit has roots in Leviticus; the wilderness wanderings of Numbers have always been understood as a type of the Christian journey toward the new Promised Land; and Moses' great exhortation in the book of Deuteronomy to "love the LORD your God with all your heart, and with all your soul, and with all your might" (Deut 6:5) is identified by Jesus as "the first of all" commandments (Mk 12:28; cf. Mt 22:38).

Synopsis of the Pentateuch

The narrative of the Pentateuch covers an enormous span of time, from the beginning of the world to the death of Moses (ca. 1450 or 1250 B.C., depending on the date of the exodus [see below]), including such momentous events as the creation of the world, the Flood, the call of Abraham, the sojourn of the people of Israel in Egypt, the exodus at the time of Moses, the covenant between the Lord and Israel at Sinai, and the wanderings in the wilderness up to the entry into the Promised Land. The establishment of four foundational covenants are recounted in these books: the covenants with Adam, Noah, Abraham, and Israel (at Sinai). The world view presented in the Pentateuch is presupposed by every other biblical book.

The book of *Genesis* recounts the history of the world from its creation to the birth of Abraham (Gen 1–11), and then follows in great detail the lives of the three patriarchs of the people of Israel: Abraham, Isaac, and Jacob (Gen 12–36); and finally the life of Jacob's favorite son, Joseph, who is largely responsible for relocating the family of Jacob (Israel) in Egypt in the second millennium B.C. (Gen 37–50).

The book of *Exodus* begins with the background of the birth of Moses (Ex 1–2) and then follows the ministry of Moses in leading the people of Israel out of Egypt into the desert, to the holy mountain called Sinai (Ex 3–23), where God establishes a covenant with the twelve tribes of Israel, grants them laws, forgives their rebellion against him in their idolatrous worship of the Golden Calf, and guides them in the construction of a house of worship, the Tabernacle (Ex 24–40).

The book of *Leviticus* describes in great detail the laws given by God to Israel after the Golden Calf incident and the establishment of the Levites as the priestly tribe: laws concerning sacrifice, worship, and ritual cleanliness (Lev 1–16) followed by certain social and civil laws (Lev 17–27) to guide the life of the people as a nation in the land of Israel.

The book of *Numbers* recounts two censuses of the Israelites (Num 1 and 26) taken before and after a period of approximately forty years spent wandering in the desert due to Israel's refusal to enter the land of Canaan (Num 14). This period of wilderness wandering is depicted as one of continuous rebellion against God, his representatives, and his laws—ten such rebellions are recorded in the book. Intermixed with these historical narratives are laws added to the covenant relationship after leaving Sinai.

Finally, the book of *Deuteronomy* constitutes a well-organized treaty-covenant document between God and Israel, sharing the structure of typical treaty-covenant texts between lords and vassals in the ancient Near East. Written as the first-person discourse of Moses, it also comprises the "last will and testament" of the greatest prophet in Israel's historical memory, as he warns the people to obey God's covenant law, restates that law with further additions, and utters prophecies about the future history of God's people (Deut 1–33). The book concludes with Moses' death, prior to the people's entrance into the land of Canaan (Deut 34).

Literary Structure of the Pentateuch

Tetrateuch or Hexateuch?

For over two millennia, the Pentateuch has been considered a discrete collection or literary unit by Jews and Christians. However, in modern scholarship there have been some movements toward conceiving the Books of Moses as either a Tetrateuch (Genesis–Numbers) or Hexateuch (Genesis–Joshua).

The *tetrateuch* (Greek for "four scrolls") concept was advocated by the twentieth-century scholar *Martin Noth* (1902–1968) and his followers, on the basis of the fact that the historical books Joshua through Kings are strongly influenced by the language and theology of Deuteronomy, and that Deuteronomy can be understood as a preface to this historical collection. However, because the book of Numbers fails to provide adequate closure in its final chapters, it serves as a very poor ending to the narrative arc beginning in Genesis, and this theory has not been widely adopted.

On the other hand, many scholars have noticed that certain themes and even patterns of language from the Pentateuch continue into the book of Joshua. Indeed, many of the promises made in the Pentateuch—most notably the possession of the land—are not fulfilled until the end of Joshua. Thus, *Gerhard von Rad* (1901–1971), Noth's contemporary, argued for a *hexateuch* (Greek for "six scrolls"). However, most scholars have continued to feel that the death of Moses at the end of Deuteronomy, which declares: "There has not arisen a prophet since in Israel, whom the LORD knew face to face" (Deut 34:10), is a particularly strong literary disjunction that marks off the five preceding books from what follows as having a unique authority within the canon, the authority of this great prophet Moses. While Joshua does serve well as a *denouement* of several Pentateuchal themes, the book itself does not seem to share the character of authoritative instruction (Hebrew *torah*) claimed for the first five books.

Therefore, even in modern scholarship, the Pentateuch continues to be studied as a discrete—and almost certainly intentional—literary unity.

Structure of the Pentateuch

Viewed as a unity, it is not hard to perceive a kind of balanced structure to the books of the Pentateuch. The first and last books (Genesis and Deuteronomy) are the most unique and may be understood as a prologue and epilogue, respectively. While quite different from each other in literary style, in other ways these two books share features not found to the same degree in the other three. Genesis and Deuteronomy both have *retrospective* (backward-looking) as well as *prospective* (forward-looking) elements:

	Retrospective Elements	Prospective Elements
Genesis	Relates the prehistory of the world (Gen 1–11) and Israel (Gen 12–50)	Instructs Israel through living example (throughout) Prophesies Israel's future (Gen 15:12–21; 17:5–8; 22:15–18) Concludes with blessings of the tribes (Gen 49)
Deuteronomy	Recaps the history of the world and Israel (Deut 1–11)	Instructs Israel through law (Deut 12–26) Prophesies Israel's future (Deut 30–32) Concludes with blessings of the tribes (Deut 33)

On the one hand, Genesis can be regarded as the background and anticipation for the life of Moses, whereas Deuteronomy is a retrospective on the career of Moses. On the other hand, both books include narratives of historical review and oracles of prophetic anticipation. Both books end with the blessing of the twelve tribes (by Jacob/Israel in Genesis 49 and by Moses himself in Deuteronomy 34), which is perhaps the clearest sign of an intentional literary balance between them.

The middle three books, Exodus, Leviticus, and Numbers, are closely tied to one another and together cover the entire life of Moses with the exception of his last few days on the plains of Moab (= Deuteronomy). Exodus begins with the people of Israel on the banks of the Nile and moves with them to Sinai. All of Leviticus is situated at Sinai. Numbers begins with the people still at Sinai and moves with them to the banks of the Jordan. Thus the central movement of the Pentateuch is to and from Sinai, the mountain of God. Leviticus—with its extensive instructions on holy liturgy (Lev 1–16) and holy living (Lev 17–27)—forms the centerpiece of the Pentateuch, suggesting that the goal of the Mosaic instruction is the communion of God and his people through the liturgy and a liturgically-shaped lifestyle.

The structure of the Pentateuch, therefore, can be represented as a *chiasm*—that is, a literary structure in which the first and last elements balance, the second and second-to-last balance, and so on, all the way down to a central point in the text. The word "chiasm" is derived from the Greek *chi*, the name of the letter X, because, when arranged as a visual outline, a chiasm resembles one side of the letter X, as in the chart below:

Genesis: Prologue—Israel's past (and future)
    Exodus 1–19: Israel from the fields of Egypt to Sinai

Exodus 20–40: Israel at Sinai, preparing for the liturgy
Leviticus: Israel's liturgy established at Sinai
Numbers 1–10: Israel at Sinai, preparing to leave
Numbers 11–36: Israel from Sinai to the plains of Moab
Deuteronomy: Epilogue—Israel's future (and past)

Of course, this simplified structure omits many other parallels and structuring devices between the books, and flattens certain unique features of each. For example, Genesis covers an immense span of time unparalleled by any other book; whereas the literary style of Deuteronomy—a set of speeches given by Moses in the first person—is utterly singular. Nonetheless, this outline conveys in a basic form the movement of the Pentateuch to and from Sinai, bracketed by a retrospective prologue (Genesis) and a prospective epilogue (Deuteronomy).

The World of the Pentateuch

The Pentateuch covers an enormous historical time span, from the creation of the world until the death of Moses, which is given variously as around 1450 B.C. or 1250 B.C. Almost all the events recounted take place within the ancient Near East, specifically within the Fertile Crescent (see map).

The events in the Pentateuch for which there exists an identifiable historical-geographical context therefore take place within *the second millennium B.C.* During that time period, the following were the major civilizations influential in the Fertile Crescent and relevant to understanding the biblical narrative:

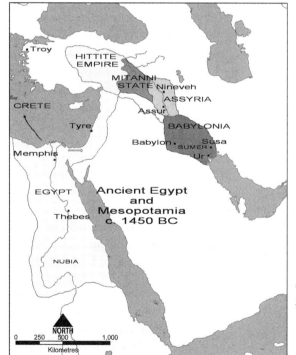

Second Millenium B.C. ANE Empires

Source: en.wikipedia.org

Mesopotamia

The Bible records Abraham's city of origin as "Ur of the Chaldeans", a city in southeast Mesopotamia. This reference is the first of many pieces of biblical evidence that point to the influence on the people of Israel of the great cultures that arose in what is modern-day Iraq.

Mesopotamia comes from the Greek *meso*, "middle", and *potamos*, "river", referring to the "Land of the Two Rivers", the Tigris and Euphrates. The first

---

Language Families

Hebrew and most of the languages of ancient Israel's neighbors belong to the *Semitic* language family, so named because the speakers of these languages are, for the most part, descendants of Shem according to the genealogies of Genesis. Semitic languages are characterized by word roots consisting of three consonants. Different words are produced by changing the vowels between the consonants or adding prefixes and suffixes.

The root for "write": *k-t-b*

"Writer" = *kōtēb*

"Written" = *kātûb*

"He will write" = *yiktōb*

Most Semitic languages in antiquity were written without vowels, which makes translation difficult.

Important Semitic languages for the study of the Bible and the ancient Near East include Hebrew, Phoenician, Ugaritic, Aramaic, and Akkadian. Egyptian is a more distant relative of the Semitic languages.

A few languages of the ancient Near East were not Semitic but *Indo-European*. These languages were brought by invading populations with roots in Europe and, like English, follow the patterns typical of European languages. Some examples include Hittite and Sumerian.

---

civilization to arise in this region was that of the Sumerians, whose base of power was in southern Babylonia, in the city-states of Eridu, Uruk, Nippur, and Ur. The Sumerians were a people of uncertain ethnicity, who spoke a non-Semitic language written ideographically using pictograms. The Sumerians flourished from the middle of the fourth to the end of the third millennium B.C. By the beginning of the second millennium B.C., the dawn of the history of the patriarchs, the Sumerians were no longer a political force, but their language and literature were considered "classical"—something akin to the "Latin" of the ancient Near East. They continued to be studied and transmitted into the first century A.D. The Sumerian accounts of a primeval flood and their genealogical lists of ancient kings pose intriguing parallels as well as contrasts with similar material in Genesis 1–11.

The Sumerians and their culture were eventually conquered and assimilated by the Akkadians, a Semitic population who migrated to Mesopotamia from the west. The name of the ethnic group and their language is taken from the city of Akkad, the capital of their first great ruler, Sargon I (ca. nineteenth century B.C.), who overcame the Sumerians and established Akkadian hegemony in the region. By the second millennium B.C., the Akkadian culture had broken into two regions with separate cultural and political development: Assyria in the northwest and Babylonia to the southeast. Akkadian was a Semitic language written phonetically, usually on clay tablets using a wedge-shaped stylus, a mode of writing called *cuneiform*. Akkadian became the *lingua franca* (international language) of the ancient Near East from the middle of the third (ca. 2500 B.C.) to the middle of the first millennium (ca. 500 B.C., by which time it was overtaken by Aramaic.) The phonetic character set was also used to transcribe non-Akkadian languages, like Ugaritic and Hittite.

An immense literature in Akkadian remains extant, exhumed by archaeologists on clay tablets or cylinders or inscribed in stone. Notable among this literature for its relevance to the Pentateuch are the following three documents:

1. The *Enuma Elish*, an extensive Babylonian creation myth
2. The *Epic of Gilgamesh*, the story of a mythical semi-divine hero named Gilgamesh, which includes a global flood story strikingly similar to the account of Noah's flood
3. The *Code of Hammurabi*, a compilation of laws promulgated by Hammurabi, king of Babylon (ca. 1810–1750 B.C.)

Source: dreamstime.com

An Example of Cuneiform Script

These three documents both compare and contrast with the Pentateuchal accounts of the creation, Flood, and laws of Moses, respectively. For much of the second millennium B.C., the Akkadian-speaking populations of Assyria and Babylonia were unable to free themselves from the dominance of foreign invaders such as the Amorites, Hurrians, Kassites, so despite the cultural influence, the political influence of Mesopotamia is generally not visible in the Pentateuch.

Mesopotamian religion was a polytheistic paganism focused around the gods considered patrons of the major city-states. Marduk, patron of Babylon itself, was the high god. Other chief gods included the sky-god Anu, the earth-goddess Ki, the creator/craftsman god Ea, the air-god Enlil, and the love-goddess Ishtar (the Mesopotamian equivalent of the Roman goddess Venus). Mesopotamian religion was a melting pot of religious traditions from the several important Mesopotamian city-states, which often had different names and different myths associated with various deities. In a sense, Mesopotamian religion was politics mythologized.

Ancient Egypt

The other great "river civilization" of the ancient Near East, the civilization of *Egypt*, grew up along the banks of the Nile. Classic Egyptian culture already experienced its formative stage (known as the Old Kingdom, ca. 2650–2150 B.C.) during the middle of the third millennium B.C., when most of the pyramids were probably being built and the foundations of Egyptian religion were established. The dawn of the second millennium B.C. found Egypt experiencing the prosperity of the Middle Kingdom (ca. 2000–1700 B.C.).

The middle of the millennium, however, was a time of turmoil in Egypt known among scholars as the Second Intermediate Period. Mysterious Asiatic invaders called the *Hyksos* invaded the country and overthrew the native aristocracy. The second half of the millennium witnessed a resurgence of Egyptian power, as a dynasty from southern Egypt expelled the Hyksos. This dynasty included a string of colorful pharaohs remembered even to this day, including the great monotheist *Akhenaten* (reigned ca. 1353–1336 B.C.), who suppressed all worship save that of the sun-god Aten and was considered a heretic by his successors; his immediate heir, *Tutankhamun* (reigned ca. 1332–1323 B.C.), known to the West as "King Tut" from his famous and fortuitously preserved funerary remains; and *Ramesses II* (reigned ca. 1279–1213 B.C.), the great tyrant often suggested as the pharaoh of the exodus. The Pentateuch describes an extended

Years	Name	Description	Famous Pharaohs	Bible Narrative
2700–2200 B.C.	Old Kingdom	Classical period of Egyptian culture; pyramids built; writing system and religion crystalized	*Cheops* (Khufu; 2589 to 2566 B.C.), builder of the Great Pyramid	—
2200–2000 B.C.	First Intermediate Period	Cultural and political confusion and instability	—	—
2000–1700 B.C.	Middle Kingdom	A dynasty from Thebes in Upper (Southern) Egypt unifies the country; feudalism, peace, and prosperity; literature flourishes	*Amenemhet I*, great conqueror and administrator *Sesostris III*, first pharaoh to invade Canaan	Patriarchal Period: Abraham, Isaac, Jacob
1700–1550 B.C.	Second Intermediate Period	Asiatic Semites from Canaan, the *Hyksos*, conquer and rule Egypt	—	Joseph and the start of the Egyptian sojourn?
1550–1100 B.C.	New Kingdom	Theban dynasty expels the Hyksos; advances in military technology and tactics; centralized state and bureaucracy; Egyptian control over Canaan; international relations with Asia Minor (Hittites) and Mesopotamia	*Thutmose III* (1479–1425 B.C.), expands empire to the Euphrates *Akhenaton* (ca. 1328–1335 B.C.), colorful monotheist "heretic" *Ramesses II* (1279–1213 B.C.), great warrior, pharaoh of the exodus? *Merneptah* (1213–1203 B.C.), mentions defeating Israel on an inscription	Egyptian sojourn; Moses; the Exodus

sojourn of the people of Israel in Egypt, starting with Joseph and ending with Moses (Gen 37–50). It is often suggested that Joseph's career is set in the period of the Hyksos, and Moses led the exodus near the end of the New Kingdom. We will return to this question in our treatment of the book of Exodus.

The Egyptians had a well-developed and elaborate polytheistic religion with numerous gods associated with aspects of the environment such as the sun

Source: alamy.com

Souls presented before Egyptian Deities, from the Book of the Dead

(*Amon-Rē*), the sky (*Nut*), the earth (*Geb*), the Nile (*Hapi*), and so on. These localized deities were often represented by images of an animal or a human-animal hybrid. Belief in the afterlife, especially for the pharaoh and members of the upper nobility, was very strong, as was also the notion of a personal judgment before the gods. As we will see, certain formal aspects of Israelite religion (such as the Ark of the Covenant) appear to be based on Egyptian prototypes, while at the same time much of Israelite cult and cultic law are distinctly anti-Egyptian. The language of Ancient Egyptian is only distantly related to Hebrew and was written primarily with hieroglyphs (pictographs) but also in simplified, more phonetic scripts. The immense extant Egyptian literature includes liturgical texts, historical chronicles, historical romances (novels or novellas), biographies, wisdom litera-ture, and mercantile records. Among the more significant are the *Tale of Sinuhe*, a semi-fictional account of an Egyptian royal courtier who flees court intrigue in Egypt for Canaan, rises to greatness among the barbaric Canaanites, and even-tually is invited back to Egypt with pomp and honor. Another is *The Song of the Harper*, a minstrel's song about the fleetingness of life, the certainty of death, and the wisdom of a "carpe diem" attitude: eat, drink, and be merry.

Source: alamy.com

Hittite chariot in combat, c. 1274 B.C.

The Hittites

To the northwest of the land of Canaan lay the empire of another formative culture for the background of the Pentateuch: the *Hittites*. Located in Asia Minor (modern Turkey), with its capital at Hattusas (near modern Ankara), the Hittite Empire flourished from about 1800 B.C. to 1200 B.C., before disinte-grating due to civil war and possibly pressure from unknown foreign invaders. The Hittites were Europeans whose language and myths had closer connections to the Greeks than those of other ancient Near Eastern cultures.

They raised horses, built chariots, pioneered the use of iron, and helped introduce all these innovations to the rest of the ancient Near East.

The Hittite literary remains include tens of thousands of cuneiform tablets written in Hittite using Akkadian script or sometimes in Akkadian itself. Mesopotamian literature was known and emulated by Hittite scribes. These scribes also corresponded extensively with the Egyptian royal court as well as with their own vassals in the northern Levant. Among the literary remains of the Hittites are a number of extensive ritual texts that have many formal parallels with the priestly legislation in the Pentateuch, law codes that compare and contrast with Mosaic law, and several celebrated covenant-treaty texts between the Hittite emperor and one of his vassals or with the pharaoh. Significantly, all of these Hittite documents seem to predate the exodus from Egypt and bear strong structural resemblance to covenant codes in the Pentateuch, especially the book of Deuteronomy. Hence, they shed a great deal of light on the concept, structure, language, and rituals of covenants and covenant-making in the ancient Near East. Indeed, the era of the patriarchs—Abraham, Isaac, and Jacob—seems to be set during the flourishing of the Hittite Empire, as when Abraham is described as purchasing land in Canaan from Hittites who controlled it (Gen 23).

> ### The Levant
>
> The eastern Mediterranean coastland between modern-day Turkey (ancient Asia Minor) and Egypt is called *the Levant* and in modern times includes the nations of Israel and Lebanon as well as the western coastal region of Syria.

The Canaanites

During the second millennium B.C., there were many city-states with a high level of culture in the territories within and surrounding the modern-day land of Israel. The peoples of these lands were known as the *Canaanites*. Although many Canaanite city-states are mentioned in documents from Egypt and Mesopotamia throughout the second millennium, our best sources for Canaanite culture come from the latter half of the fourteenth century B.C.: the Amarna tablets and the remains of Ugarit.

The *Amarna tablets* are a collection of mostly Akkadian (that is, Babylonian) cuneiform documents from the reign of Amenhotep IV, better known as Akhenaten (ca. 1353–1336 B.C.), the monotheistic pharaoh who was deemed a "heretic" for only worshipping the sun-god Aten. Akhenaten moved the capital of Egypt up the Nile to a site now known as Tell el-Amarna. There, a collection of Akhenaten's diplomatic records were discovered. Most consisted of letters between Akhenaten and his vassal kings of

Source: metmuseum.org

Cuneiform Tablet

the city-states in Canaan. Interestingly, the common language of diplomacy was Babylonian Akkadian, not Egyptian or Canaanite. The letters show a great deal of petty infighting among the small kings of Canaan, almost all of whom were nominal vassals either of the pharaoh or of the Hittite emperor to the northwest. These vassal kings complain about each other, about the lack of military assistance from Egypt, and about the threat of raids from the 'Apiru, a landless people or peoples whom various scholars have suggested should be identified with the biblical "Hebrews" (Ex 1:15–22). In the Amarna letters, we see a highly literate civilization in Canaan, heavily influenced by, and in contact with, the "great" civilizations in Asia Minor, Egypt, and Mesopotamia. Canaan was a land bridge for trade between the three great civilizations, so it formed virtually the hub of ancient Near Eastern culture.

An even better window on the culture of Canaan is afforded by the archaeological remains at Ugarit (modern Ras Shamra on the coast of Syria, north of Lebanon). This extreme northern Canaanite city first appears in historical records around 1800 B.C. and flourished from around 1400–1200 B.C., until it was destroyed by invading "Sea Peoples". The city was burned to the ground by these mysterious invaders, fortuitously baking and preserving all the clay tablets on which their literature was written. Royal, temple, and private libraries have been recovered, with religious, diplomatic, political, economic, and literary texts, written in at least four different languages and seven different scripts. The language of Ugarit is very similar to Hebrew, and Ugaritic and biblical literature share many formal similarities, especially in the book of Psalms. Perhaps the most interesting Ugaritic texts for biblical research are the cycles of myths that shed light on Canaanite religion, which revolved especially around the worship of *Baal*, the storm-god, and his consort *Asherah*, who are mentioned on more than one occasion in the Pentateuch (Ex 34:13; Num 25:5; Deut 7:5; 12:3). Other important deities included *El*, the father of the gods, who was worshipped with idols in the form of a bull; Anat, a hunter-goddess like the Roman Diana; and Dagon, god of grain. As in the Greek myths, the Canaanite gods were often violent, unscrupulous, and sexually perverse, which helps explain the extremely negative perspective that the Bible maintains toward Canaanite religion, which posed a constant temptation for the people of Israel throughout their history.

In sum, the historical activity of the Pentateuch is set in the Fertile Crescent in the second millennium B.C. This was a tumultuous, active, vibrant era that saw the rise and fall of many highly developed, highly literate civilizations that maintained strong cultural, diplomatic, and economic ties with one another. From Abraham's origins in Mesopotamian Ur to his purchase of land from the Hittites to Israel's sojourn in Egypt, historical references to the *realia* of the ancient Near East will be found throughout these books. Perhaps more importantly, the influence of Mesopotamian, Egyptian, Hittite, and Canaanite cultures will be seen in the concepts and language of the Pentateuch, even as Greek, Roman, and Jewish literary and cultural influences are seen in the New Testament. Nonetheless, the sacred author of the Pentateuch, while sharing in the common ancient Near Eastern cultural "language", conveys a message and world view often radically at odds with those of his contemporaries, a message and world view that remain challenging and controversial into our own day.

Themes in the Pentateuch

The central theme of the Pentateuch is the *covenant* between God and his people. A covenant may be defined as the extension of kinship by an oath[2] or as a *sacred family bond*: (1) a bond, because it unites two parties in a permanent way; (2) family, because the united parties become *kin* to one another; (3) sacred, because the relationship is solemnized and enforced by oaths taken in the name of God.[3] A covenant is distinct from a *contract*—an agreement between two persons that is not necessarily sacred, familial, or permanent, usually concerned with the exchange or disposition of goods.

A constellation of other realities cluster around the central idea of covenant in the Old Testament. Covenants were solemnized by an oath, and the oath was frequently ritualized as a sacrifice celebrated by a priest or one who had priestly authority at a sacred place or sanctuary, often associated with a holy mountain. Often a sign—either a mark or a customary practice—was linked to a covenant in order to distinguish covenant members from outsiders. When one of the parties to a covenant was a group of people, one person could step forward to represent the group and undertake the rituals on their behalf; such a person may be termed a mediator. A familial meal typically followed, which consumed the sacrificial animal and expressed the covenant kinship that had just been established by means of the oath. Laws expressing the obligations of the newly created kinship relationship were often included at some point in the covenant-making rituals.

The Pentateuch recounts a series of covenants between God and mankind. Although the term "covenant" (Hebrew *berith*; Greek *diathēkē*) does not occur in Genesis 1–3, there are exegetical reasons for believing that the sacred author presents Adam as created as a *mediator* of God's covenant relationship with all creation. By virtue of this covenant, Adam enjoyed the status of a son of God, with certain privileges and obligations that arose from that status.

Adam eventually rejects the privileges and obligations of his role, which causes the estrangement of mankind from God, leading to the judgment of the Flood, after which God reestablishes the covenant with Noah, although the original perfection of the covenant relationship is lost. Noah and his sons, however, also show themselves to be imperfect, and a cycle of human estrangement from God starts again.

The third covenant recorded in the Pentateuch is with Abraham, whose covenant relationship with God is built up in successive stages, in Genesis 15,

---

[2] G. P. Hugenberger, *Marriage as a Covenant: A Study of Biblical Law and Ethics Governing Marriage, Developed from the Perspective of Malachi* (Leiden and New York: Brill, 1994); Frank Moore Cross, "Kinship and Covenant in Ancient Israel", in *From Epic to Canon: History and Literature in Ancient Israel* (Baltimore: Johns Hopkins University Press, 1998).

[3] See Scott W. Hahn, *Kinship by Covenant: A Canonical Approach to the Fulfillment of God's Saving Promises*, Anchor Yale Bible Reference Library (New Haven, Conn.: Yale University Press, 2009).

17, and 22. In the final form of God's covenant relationship to Abraham, God promises unilaterally to bless all the nations of the world through Abraham's "seed", meaning "descendants" (Gen 22:18). This becomes a foundational promise of redemption throughout the rest of the Pentateuch.

These first three covenants are all described within Genesis. The fourth covenant of the Pentateuch, the covenant of God with Israel mediated through Moses, occupies the bulk of the remaining four books of the Pentateuch. Acting to fulfill his covenant obligations to the "descendants" of Abraham, God leads Israel out of Egyptian slavery by the prophet Moses and establishes a covenant with them at the holy mountain Sinai, complete with oath, sacrificial ritual, familial meal, and laws. Israel breaks the covenant relationship by worshipping a golden calf, however, necessitating the remaking of the covenant in the later chapters of Exodus and in Leviticus (Ex 32–Lev 27). Again in the wilderness, Israel breaks the covenant multiple times (Num 11–25), making it necessary to remake it prior to entering the Promised Land (Deuteronomy).

Several other themes are of significance to the Pentateuch, but these are always related to the central theme of the covenant. For example, *divine blessing* forms an important motif, as the book of Genesis shows God bestowing a comprehensive blessing ("be fruitful and multiply") on Adam and Eve and this same essential blessing being communicated to the patriarchs Abraham, Isaac, and Jacob and transmitted through them to the sons of Israel (blessed in Gen 49) and ultimately the tribes of Israel (blessed in Deut 33). *Blessing* represents the favor bestowed by God on those in covenant relationship with him, who follow the laws of the covenant relationship, which foster communion with God and peace (*shalom*) with God's creation.

The motif of the *land* is also of great significance. Adam and Eve are ejected from their paradise home in Genesis 3, and thereafter mankind is scattered over the face of the earth (Gen 11), and even the patriarchs, who are at the center of God's saving purposes for mankind, wander about in anticipation of God's gift of the land. They never possess it within their lifetimes, and the promise is transmitted to their children. However, Moses' attempt to lead them to that promised inheritance is unsuccessful, and the Pentateuch ends with Israel still awaiting the Promised Land.

Significantly, the land functions in the Pentateuch as a kind of "sacrament" of paradise. Paradise (Eden) itself was a sanctuary, a kind of primordial garden-temple for the worship of God and communion with him. Therefore the land is not an end in itself, nor is it primarily a geographical or economic reality. The land is a space for worship; and worship—or, more specifically, *sacrificial liturgy*—is the means by which the covenant relationship with God is renewed and maintained and communion with God is actualized and experienced. The land, then, provides the space, safety, and material resources for God's people to live a life of liturgical communion with him, unimpeded by the spiritual and material interference of other peoples who are not yet a party to the covenant relationship. We will examine each of these themes of covenant, land, divine blessing, and liturgy when we turn to the books of the Pentateuch proper.

For Further Reading

Literary Structure of the Pentateuch

Alter, Robert. *The Art of Biblical Narrative*. 2nd ed. New York: Basic Books, 2011.

Sailhamer, John H. *The Pentateuch as Narrative: A Biblical-Theological Commentary*. Grand Rapids, Mich.: Zondervan, 1995.

The World of the Pentateuch

Coogan, Michael D., and Mark S. Smith, eds. *Stories from Ancient Canaan*. 2nd ed. Louisville, Ky.: Westminster John Knox Press, 2012.

Dalley, Stephanie. *Myths from Mesopotamia*. Oxford: Oxford University Press, 1989.

Hallo, William W., and K. Lawson Younger, eds. *Canonical Compositions from the Biblical World*. Vol. 1 of *The Context of Scripture*. Leiden and Boston: Brill, 1997.

Pritchard, James B., ed. *Ancient Near Eastern Texts*. 3rd ed. Princeton, N.J.: Princeton University Press, 1969.

Sasson, Jack M., ed. *Civilizations of the Ancient Near East*. 4 vols. New York: Scribner's; Peabody, Mass.: Hendrickson, 1995.

Walton, John H. *Ancient Near Eastern Thought and the Old Testament: Introducing the Conceptual World of the Hebrew Bible*. Grand Rapids, Mich.: Baker Academic, 2006.

Themes in the Pentateuch

Alexander, T. Desmond. *From Paradise to the Promised Land: An Introduction to the Pentateuch*. 3rd ed. Grand Rapids, Mich.: Baker Academic, 2012.

Campbell, Anthony F., S.J., and Mark A. O'Brien, O.P. *Rethinking the Pentateuch: Prolegomena to the Theology of Ancient Israel*. Louisville, Ky.: Westminster John Knox Press, 2005.

Clines, David J. A. *The Theme of the Pentateuch*. Sheffield: Sheffield Academic Press, 1978.

Hahn, Scott W. *Kinship by Covenant*. Anchor Yale Bible Reference Library. New Haven, Conn.: Yale University Press, 2009.

Lohfink, Norbert. *Theology of the Pentateuch: Themes of the Priestly Narrative and Deuteronomy*. Minneapolis: Fortress Press, 1994.

4. THE ORIGINS OF THE PENTATEUCH

No introduction to the Pentateuch would be complete without a discussion of its origins. As is well known, in Jewish and Christian tradition, the first five books of the Bible were attributed to the figure of Moses. As is equally well known, in modern times, especially since the nineteenth century, biblical scholars have largely abandoned the idea that the Pentateuch originated with Moses in the late second millennium B.C. Why? Why did ancient Jews and Christians believe that the Pentateuch had originated with Moses? What are biblical scholars saying today about the origins of the Pentateuch? And what has the Catholic Church said about this question?

This chapter will answer these questions by providing a brief overview of the origins of the Pentateuch from ancient to modern times. Before beginning, however, it is important to stress that the purpose of this chapter is not to *settle* the many complex questions surrounding the origins of the Pentateuch. Instead, the goal is to *inform* the reader about what has been said about the origins of these books in ancient Jewish and Christian tradition, in contemporary biblical scholarship, and by the Catholic Church.

Ancient Jewish and Christian Tradition

The ancient Jewish and Christian tradition associating Moses with the origins of the book of the Pentateuch has its roots in the texts of Jewish Scripture. Indeed, the primary reason that both Jewish and Christian tradition regarded Moses as the principal author of the first five books of the Bible is the witness of various passages in the Pentateuch and historical books that speak about Moses engaging in literary activity with regard to what would later come to be known as the Torah.

Moses and the Pentateuch in the Torah

For example, on one occasion, the book of Exodus states that Moses wrote down a "memorial" of a successful battle in which the Israelites triumphed over the Amalekites (Ex 17:14). Elsewhere, it describes Moses transcribing "the words of the LORD" on tablets after the revelation at Mount Sinai (Ex 24:4; 34:27). Along similar lines, the book of Numbers says that Moses kept a written account of the various stages of the Israelites' journey through the desert (Num 33:2). Finally, and perhaps most influential of all, a passage in the book of Deuteronomy speaks of the entire "law" (Hebrew *torah*) given in that book as being "written" (Hebrew *katab*) by Moses:

> And *Moses wrote this law*, and gave it to the priests the sons of Levi, who carried the ark of the covenant of the LORD, and to all the elders of Israel.... *When Moses had finished writing the words of this law in a book, to the very end*, Moses commanded

the Levites who carried the ark of the covenant of the LORD, "Take this book
of the law, and put it by the side of the ark of the covenant of the LORD your God,
that it may be there for a witness against you." (Deut 31:9, 24–26)

Notice two key aspects of this material. First, contrary to what one might assume
at first glance, this passage does *not* attribute the Pentateuch as a whole to Moses.
Instead, read in context, it seems to refer specifically to the "book" or "scroll"
(Hebrew *sepher*) of Deuteronomy—the law delivered by Moses to the second
generation of Israelites on the plains of Moab (cf. Deut 1:1). Second, it is significant that it describes the *liturgical* preservation of the scroll of Deuteronomy:
Moses gives the scroll to "the Levites" to be placed beside the ark in the Tabernacle, in order to be handed down to future generations by the authoritative
tradents of the Levitical priesthood.

Moses and the Pentateuch in the Old Testament

In addition to those passages in the Pentateuch which speak of Moses authoring
certain parts of the Pentateuch, there are also a number of other texts in Jewish
Scripture outside the Pentateuch that link the first five books with him in various ways.

For example, the book of Joshua describes Joshua, as Moses' prophetic successor, inscribing onto tablets of stone "the law of Moses, which he had written" (Josh 8:32; cf. 24:25–26). Along similar lines, the books of Kings describe
David (ca. tenth century B.C.) as admonishing his son Solomon to keep what
is "written in the law of Moses" (1 Kings 2:3). Likewise, the same books elsewhere describe a quotation from the book of Deuteronomy as something "written in the book of the law of Moses" (2 Kings 14:6; see Deut 24:16). In the
context of the return from the Babylonian exile (sixth century B.C.), the book of
Ezra attributes the sacrificial and sacerdotal laws found in the book of Leviticus
to Moses when it speaks of the Jews offering burnt offerings and sacrifices "as it
is written in the law of Moses" (Ezra 3:2) and arranging the priests and Levites
in their divisions "as it is written in the book of Moses" (Ezra 6:18). From a
roughly contemporary period, the book of Nehemiah describes the postexilic
Jewish community as reading from "the book of the law of Moses which the
LORD had given to Israel" (Neh 8:1), specifically mentioning "the law that
the LORD had commanded by Moses" regarding observance of the festival of
Tabernacles (Neh 8:14; cf. 9:13–18; Lev 23; Deut 16). Finally, such attributions
of portions of the Pentateuch to Moses continue in the books of Chronicles (see
2 Chron 25:4; 35:12).

In light of such texts both in and outside the Pentateuch, it is easy to understand why ancient Jewish tradition came to associate the origins of the Torah
with the literary activity of Moses.

Moses and the Pentateuch in the New Testament

In terms of Christian tradition, by far the most influential texts associating Moses
with the Pentateuch come from the writings of the New Testament.

For example, on various occasions in the Gospels, Jesus ties portions of Genesis, Exodus, Leviticus, and Deuteronomy to the figure of Moses:

> Jesus answered them.... "If on the sabbath a man receives circumcision, so that *the law of Moses* may not be broken, are you angry with me because on the sabbath I made a man's whole body well?" (Jn 7:23; cf. Gen 17:1–14)

> "For *Moses said*, 'Honor your father and your mother'; and, 'He who speaks evil of father or mother, let him surely die.'" (Mk 7:10; cf. Ex 20:12; 21:17)

> And Jesus said to him, "See that you say nothing to any one; but go, show yourself to the priest, and offer the gift *that Moses commanded*, for a proof to the people." (Mt 8:4; Mk 1:44; cf. Lev 14:2)

> For your hardness of heart *Moses allowed you* to divorce your wives, but from the beginning it was not so. (Mt 19:7; Mk 10:3–4; cf. Deut 24:1–4)

Perhaps the most influential passage of all occurs when Jesus not only speaks of Moses "writing" (Greek *graphō*) about him in the Torah, but makes belief in the writings of Moses a precondition for belief in him:

> If you believed *Moses*, you would believe me, *for he wrote of me. But if you do not believe his writings, how will you believe my words?* (Jn 5:46–47)

In all likelihood, this passage is alluding to certain texts from Genesis and Deuteronomy that were interpreted in Jewish tradition as prophecies of the Messiah and the future age of salvation (Gen 3:15; 22:18; 49:10; Deut 18:15). If this is correct, then the teaching of Jesus in the Gospels links four out of the five books of the Pentateuch to Moses: Genesis, Exodus, Leviticus, and Deuteronomy.

The same is true of the New Testament writings taken as a whole, which attribute portions of each book of the Pentateuch (with the exception of Numbers) to Moses. Following the order of the books in the Pentateuch, these passages can be tabulated as follows:

Genesis 17:10–14	attributed to Moses in John 7:22–23
Exodus 3:6	attributed to Moses in Luke 20:37
Exodus 20:12	attributed to Moses in Mark 7:10
Exodus 21:17	attributed to Moses Mark 7:10
Leviticus 12:2–8	attributed to Moses in Luke 2:22
Leviticus 14:2	attributed to Moses in Matthew 8:4; Mark 1:44; Luke 5:14
Leviticus 18:5	attributed to Moses in Romans 10:5
Leviticus 20:10	attributed to Moses in John 8:5
Deuteronomy 17:2–6	attributed to Moses in Hebrews 10:28
Deuteronomy 18:18	attributed to Moses in Acts 3:22; Acts 7:37
Deuteronomy 24:1–4	attributed to Moses in Matthew 19:7; Mark 10:3–4
Deuteronomy 25:4	attributed to Moses in 1 Corinthians 9:9
Deuteronomy 25:5–10	attributed to Moses in Matthew 22:24; Mark 12:19; Luke 20:29
Deuteronomy 32:21	attributed to Moses in Romans 10:19
The Law	attributed to Moses in John 1:17; 7:19; Acts 13:39; Acts 15:5

Notice here that there is no explicit attribution of the entire Pentateuch—the "five books" of the law—to Moses in the New Testament. On the other hand, it seems clear that, by the first century A.D., the contents of the Pentateuch were being ascribed to Moses without qualification because the tradition was firmly in place that the books of the Torah originated with him.

The Pentateuch in Ancient Jewish and Patristic Tradition

Before turning to what contemporary scholarship has had to say about the origins of the Pentateuch, it is worth noting that some significant developments regarding the relationship of Moses to these books took place in ancient Jewish and Christian writings outside the Bible.

On the one hand, there were some ancient Jews who interpreted the traditional attribution of the books of the Pentateuch to Moses in the strictest possible sense. For example, in the first century A.D., the Jewish historian Josephus asserts that Moses even wrote the account of his own death at the end of the Pentateuch:

> As [Moses] was going to embrace Eleazar and Joshua, and was still discoursing with them, a cloud stood over him on the sudden, and he disappeared in a certain valley, *although he wrote in the holy books that he died, which was done out of fear, lest they should venture to say that, because of his extraordinary virtue, he went to God.*[1]

Clearly, for some Jews, like Josephus, the Mosaic authorship of the Pentateuch was interpreted to mean that he personally wrote every single line in the Torah in the form that it had come down to them.

On the other hand, there were some ancient Jews—such as the rabbinic authors of the Babylonian Talmud (third–fifth centuries A.D.)—who interpreted the tradition about the Mosaic origins of the Pentateuch in a broader sense. For example, unlike Josephus, the later rabbis admitted the presence of at least some "post-Mosaic material" in the Pentateuch:

> Who wrote the Scriptures?—*Moses wrote his own book* and the portion of Balaam and Job. *Joshua wrote the book which bears his name and [the last] eight verses of the Torah.*[2]

This particular tradition is significant because it shows that in antiquity, the rabbis were aware of the fact that some verses of the Pentateuch were probably not written by Moses himself but by later editors (in their view, Joshua).

When we turn to ancient Christian writers outside the Bible, we find an even more nuanced interpretation of the tradition of Mosaic authorship of the Pentateuch. Like the rabbinic authors of the Talmud, Saint Jerome was also open

---

[1] Josephus, *Antiquities* 4.326, in *The Works of Josephus: Complete and Unabridged*, trans. William Whiston, rev. ed. (Peabody, Mass.: Hendrickson, 1987), 125.

[2] Babylonian Talmud, *Baba Bathra* 14b, in Isidore Epstein, ed., *The Babylonian Talmud*, 35 vols. (London: Soncino, 1935–1952).

to the presence of post-Mosaic material in the Pentateuch and even suggested that the priest Ezra may have edited the book hundreds of years after the time of Moses:

> The word of God says ... at the end of Deuteronomy, "So Moses the servant of the Lord died there in the land of Moab.... And he buried him in the valley, in the land of Moab over against Beth-peor: but no man knoweth of his sepulchre unto this day." *We must certainly understand by* this day *the time of the composition of the history, whether you prefer the view that Moses was the author of the Pentateuch or that Ezra re-edited it. In either case I make no objection.*[3]

Notice here the nuance of Jerome's position. On the one hand, he seems to subscribe to the traditional belief in the Mosaic authorship of the Pentateuch. On the other hand, unlike Josephus, Jerome does not think that this tradition precludes the possibility that the Pentateuch was "re-edited" by the scribe Ezra in the fifth century B.C., almost a millennium after the (traditional) date of Moses' lifetime (fifteenth century B.C.).

In sum, when ancient Jewish and Christian Scripture and tradition are taken together, we find both a strong affirmation of the Mosaic authorship of the books of the Pentateuch and a developing openness to the possibility of post-Mosaic additions and later editorial activity. Such developments will in some sense set the stage for the eventual formulation in the modern period of much more complex theories of origins, the most famous of which is known as the "Documentary Hypothesis".

The Rise of the Documentary Hypothesis

As we saw in an earlier chapter, one of the most significant developments that took place in the modern period was the rise of *source criticism*, which attempted to reconstruct the various sources, literary and oral, that lay behind the current text of the Old Testament (see chapter 2). In no area of research did source criticism expend more energy than in the question of the origins of the Pentateuch. Although early source critics such as Jean Astruc and Richard Simon (eighteenth century) did not question the substantial Mosaic authorship of the Pentateuch, as time went by, modern scholars began to raise doubts about the Mosaic origins of the Pentateuch, for a number of reasons.

Scholarly Doubts about the Mosaic Origins of the Pentateuch

First, scholars contended that the Pentateuch contains material that would have to have been written after the lifetime of Moses himself. For example, there are passages about Moses that clearly reflect *a post-Mosaic time period*. The premier examples of this used by scholars are the account of Moses' own death, burial, and succession by Joshua that we find at the end of the book of Deuteronomy and the extolling of Moses' meekness in the book of Numbers:

---

[3] Jerome, *On the Perpetual Virginity of Mary* 7, in *NPNF2* 6:337.

So Moses the servant of the LORD *died there in the land of Moab,* according to the word of the LORD, *and he buried him in the valley in the land of Moab opposite Beth-peor; but no man knows the place of his burial to this day.... And there has not arisen a prophet since in Israel like Moses, whom the* LORD *knew face to face,* none like him for all the signs and the wonders which the LORD sent him to do in the land of Egypt, to Pharaoh and to all his servants and to all his land, and for all the mighty power and all the great and terrible deeds which Moses wrought in the sight of all Israel. (Deut 34:5–6, 10–12)

Now the man Moses was very meek, *more than all men that were on the face of the earth.* (Num 12:3)

Clearly such passages in the Pentateuch are the work of a later, non-Mosaic writer, reflecting back on the greatness of the prophet Moses.

Second, modern scholars also pointed to *chronological glosses* in the text of the Pentateuch that seem to suggest that a substantial portion of time has passed since the lifetime of Moses himself and the exodus from Egypt:

Abram passed through the land to the place at Shechem, to the Oak of Moreh. *At that time the Canaanites were in the land.* (Gen 12:6)

These are the kings who reigned in the land of Edom, *before any king reigned over the Israelites.* (Gen 36:31)

And the sons of Israel ate the manna forty years, *till they came to a habitable land;* they ate the manna, till they came to the border of the land of Canaan. (Ex 16:35)

Each of these passages seems to have been written after the lifetime of Moses, whether after the completion of the wilderness journey (Ex 16:35); after the time of the Israelite conquest of the land (Gen 12:6); or even after the time of the rise of the Israelite kings Saul, David, Solomon, and their successors (Gen 36:31). In light of such materials, it is difficult to deny that there are passages in the Pentateuch as we now have it that come from centuries after the lifetime of Moses.

Third, source critics also highlighted passages in the Pentateuch that seem to have been written from the perspective of someone living *within the Promised Land,* even though Moses himself, according to the Pentateuch, died outside the land. Consider the following:

Then the sons of Israel set out, and encamped in the plains of Moab *beyond the Jordan* [east of the Jordan] at Jericho. (Num 22:1)

These are the words that Moses spoke to all Israel *beyond the Jordan* [east of the Jordan] in the wilderness. (Deut 1:1)

These and other passages of similar vantage point (see also Gen 50:10; Num 32:32; 34:15; 35:15; Deut 1:5; 3:8; 4:41–49) suggested to modern scholars that the Pentateuch as we have it has been revised and updated by an editor (or editors) writing from a different chronological and geographical vantage point than Moses himself.

Fourth, modern source critics also began to argue that not only individual verses but large portions of the material in the Pentateuch could be dated to *the post-Mosaic period*, thereby ruling out the possibility of a literary origin with Moses. Of the many arguments used to date the hypothetical sources of the Pentateuch to the post-Mosaic period, three in particular stand out:

1. *Hebrew Language*: The Hebrew of the Pentateuch is the classical Hebrew of the monarchic period, not the archaic Hebrew of Moses' day.

2. *Legal and Social Material*: The narratives and laws of the Pentateuch are thought to reflect social and historical realities of a later age, not the time period they purport to describe.

3. *Lack of Pentateuch Citations in Preexilic Books*: Expected references to the laws or narratives of the Pentateuch are claimed to be absent from later biblical narratives until the time after the Babylonian exile (post 587 B.C.).

In the light of these and other observations, modern Old Testament scholarship eventually replaced the traditional view of Mosaic authorship with the theory of multiple sources and authors of the Pentateuch—a theory commonly associated with the figure of Julius Wellhausen (1844–1918) and known as the "Documentary Hypothesis". It is to that theory that we now turn.

Julius Wellhausen and the "Documentary Hypothesis"

The German liberal Protestant Bible scholar Julius Wellhausen is arguably the most influential figure in the history of Pentateuchal criticism and theories of its origins. In stark contrast to the traditional Jewish and Christian views of the origins of the Pentateuch (even those nuanced by the admission of some post-Mosaic material), Wellhausen did not even believe Moses was a historical figure or that writing had been developed at the time period in which Moses was purported to have lived. According to Wellhausen, the Pentateuch was produced after the return of the Jews from exile in Babylon (the postexilic period, ca. fifth century B.C.) by an editor or editors who combined four source documents: those of the Yahwist (J), the Elohist (E), the Deuteronomist (D), and the Priestly source (P). As we saw in an earlier chapter, a theory of multiple sources behind the Pentateuch had been developing for over a century, but Wellhausen was able to formulate the theory in a way that won the assent of the majority of his contemporaries. The description of the four sources, along with their hypothetical provenance and date as proposed by various prominent scholars, including Wellhausen, can be shown by the table on the next page.

The Success of Wellhausen's Theory in the Nineteenth Century

As one can see from the table below, the Documentary Hypothesis is complex and, because of its hypothetical character, subject to marked disagreements about dating and authorship even among its most prominent scholarly

The Documentary Hypothesis				
	Yahwist	Elohist	Deuteronomist	Priestly Source
Date	9th cent. (Wellhausen) 10th (von Rad, others) 5th (Schmid, Van Seters)	8th cent. (Wellhausen) No "E" (Volz/ Rudolph, many others)	7th–6th cent. (Wellhausen, many others) 10th cent. (Gordon, Rendsburg, Tigay [for parts]) 13th cent. (Kitchen)	5th cent. (Wellhausen) 8th cent. (Kaufmann) 12th cent. for parts (Milgrom)
Divine Name	"Yahweh" (יהוה), even in Genesis	"Elohim" (אלהים) and other titles until Exodus 3	"Yahweh our God" יהוה (אלהינו), "Yahweh your God" (יהוה אלהיכם)	"Elohim" (אלהים) or "El-Shaddai" (אל שדי) until Exodus 6
Provenance	Judah	Northern Israel	Israel (Levitical and/or prophetic reformers who fled to Judah after 722 B.C.)	Judah (postexilic priestly community)
Extent	Continuous narrative Genesis–Numbers	Episodic and supplemental; begins with Abraham	Deuteronomy; some edits or insertions in earlier books.	Most of Exodus 35–Numbers 36, including all of Leviticus
Source Profile	a. Epic and vibrant style; master storyteller b. Depiction of God as anthropomorphic (also represented by "the angel of the LORD") c. Interest in the promise to the patriarchs and its fulfillment in the Davidic kingdom d. Includes revised Covenant Code (Ex 34:1–28) e. Uses "Sinai", not "Horeb"; "Canaanites", not "Amorites"	a. Less vibrant than J b. Stress on "the fear of God" b. God is distant—mediated through dreams, visions, and angels c. Interest in northern locations (Shechem, Bethel) d. Includes Aqedah (Gen 22); Decalogue/ Covenant Code (Ex 20–23); Golden Calf (Ex 32) e. Speaks of "Horeb", not "Sinai"; "Amorites", not "Canaanites"	a. Moralistic and homiletic b. Most distinct of the five books c. Strong influence on historical books (Joshua-Kings) d. Interest in "all Israel" (all 12 tribes) e. "Horeb", not Sinai f. Is the "Book of the Law" used for Josiah's reform in 622 B.C. (2 Kings 22:8)	a. Unadorned, formulaic, repetitious b. God is exalted and transcendent c. Interest in genealogies, census lists, sacred calendar, covenants, purity, ritual d. Mostly non-narrative material, but a few stories (e.g., creation, Flood, Noah covenant) e. Preserves ancient elements, but mainly reflects worship of postexilic Jerusalem

advocates.[4] How, then, did it come to be the dominant theory about the sources of the Pentateuch?

On the one hand, the Documentary Hypothesis was extremely influential because, in the wake of the widespread modern collapse of confidence in the tradition of Mosaic authorship, it offered a historical reconstruction of the origins of the Pentateuch that took into account the presence of *implicit internal evidence* for multiple sources in the Pentateuch, especially the following:

1. *Variations in Language and Style*: The use of different names for the Deity—primarily the Hebrew *YHWH* ("the Lord") versus the Hebrew *'Elohim* ("God")—or the different terminology of the laws—such as those of Leviticus versus those in Deuteronomy—is understood as being too different to have come from the hand of a single author such as Moses.

2. *Duplications and Repetitions*: Duplications—such as the two creation narratives in Genesis 1 and 2—are seen as incompatible with a single author. Likewise, repetitions—such as the different explanations in which Moses himself (Num 20:12) or the people of Israel (Deut 1:37) were primarily responsible for his being unable to enter the Promised Land—are viewed as too inconsistent to be reconciled with a single author.

3. *Different Theological Perspectives*: For the strongly anthropomorphic depiction of *YHWH* found in Genesis 2–3 (deemed "J" material) is thought to conflict with the transcendent depiction of *Elohim* who is above all creation found in Genesis 1.

In light of its ability to explain such apparent internal inconsistences, the Documentary Hypothesis as formulated by Wellhausen quickly spread and established dominance in the universities of Western Europe at the end of the nineteenth century and continued to be the standard account for the composition of the Pentateuch into the late twentieth century.

On the other hand, in addition to the brilliance and forcefulness of Wellhausen's writings, there are some sociological reasons for the theory's quick rise to success and continued dominance that should be noted. First, scholars at the end of the nineteenth century—under the influence of the philosopher Georg W. F. Hegel (1770–1831) and the naturalist Charles Darwin (1809–1882)—were starting to view all of reality from an evolutionary perspective. Wellhausen presented a coherent and apparently scientific account of the *evolutionary* development of Israelite religion, from the simple, personal faith of Abraham recounted by the Yahwist ("J"), to the more formal, distant God of the Elohist ("E"), to Deuteronomy's stringent imposition of covenant categories and law ("D"), to the immense complexity of the rituals, regulations, and liturgical apparatus of the Priestly source ("P"). This simple-to-complex view of development fit the prevailing Darwinian world view and received an extremely favorable reception by many scholars of the day who were interested in establishing a "scientific" approach to Scripture based on the methods that were being utilized to great success in the natural sciences.

---

[4] See John Ha, *Genesis 15: A Theological Compendium of Pentateuchal History*, BZAW 181 (Berlin and New York: Walter de Gruyter, 1989).

Frank Moore Cross on Julius Wellhausen

Frank Moore Cross (1921–2012), late professor of Hebrew Bible at Harvard University, comments:

"For Wellhausen, the relationship between God and Israel in premonarchical times and in early prophecy was 'natural,' spontaneous, free, interior (individualistic). Such language is his inheritance from a philosophic milieu created by idealism and romanticism, borrowed immediately from Vatke, and congruent with Protestant antinomianism. That early covenant forms were sociocentric, mutual, and expressed in legal institutions (kinship-in-law) was unthinkable. Law—static, petrified, exterior, abstract—was the creation of the Judaic spirit, hence late and perverse. That such views persist in the face of new knowledge of the ancient Near East, the history of religion and law, and advances in social anthropology is a testimony, not to the soundness of the Wellhausenist synthesis, but to the power and perversity of ... anti-Judaic dogma."[a]

[a] Frank Moore Cross, "Kinship and Covenant in Ancient Israel", in *From Epic to Canon: History and Literature in Ancient Israel* (Baltimore: Johns Hopkins University Press, 1998), 15–16.

Furthermore, the academic study of the Bible in the universities of Wellhausen's day, as well as long afterward, was dominated by the thought of *liberal Protestantism*, especially as formulated in post-Enlightenment Germany. As opposed to Judaism and Catholicism, liberal Protestantism had virtually no liturgy or religious law; in fact, it was opposed in principle to both these realities. Liberal Protestantism held (and holds) to a narrative about the origin of Christianity in which the original religion of Jesus, which was essentially a simple teaching concerning the fatherhood of God and the brotherhood of all people, was gradually complicated and encumbered until it became the antithesis of the Gospel—namely, medieval Catholicism. In the nineteenth century, Wellhausen's view of the development of the Pentateuch fit well with liberal Protestant scholars' preexisting understanding of the development of Christianity. Just as Jesus' Gospel became complicated and overlaid by the accretions of early Catholicism in the New Testament era, so the original message of the Yahwist became complicated and overlaid by the rules and regulations of the Priestly source, which itself became the basis for what liberal Protestants used to refer to as "late Judaism". Thus, from the viewpoint of nineteenth-century liberal Protestants, both Jews and Catholics practice encumbered, obscured religions. The liberal Protestant Bible scholar, on the other hand, is cast as a kind of Promethean liberator of humanity, who removes and discards the accumulated debris of the centuries to reveal the original simplicity of the religious message of Jesus in the Gospels and the Jahwist in the Pentateuch. Such a theory had an obvious appeal for Wellhausen's liberal Protestant colleagues in universities throughout Western Europe, so the widespread embrace of the Documentary Hypothesis is easily understood. Many Jewish scholars, however, recognized a latent anti-Judaism in the structure of Wellhausen's theory and protested against it.[5] The theory had the effect of removing almost all basis for the Jewish religion in history and

---

[5] See Moshe Weinfeld, *The Place of the Law in the Religion of Ancient Israel, Vetus Testamentum* Supplements 100 (Leiden: Brill, 2004).

revelation, reducing the core texts of Jewish faith (the Pentateuchal laws) to late, ideologically motivated documents composed by a self-centered and reactionary priesthood. No wonder, then, that Rabbi Solomon Schechter, the founder of American Conservative Judaism, famously quipped that the "Higher Criticism" was actually a "Higher Anti-Semitism" that had the effect of "denying all our claims for the past, and leaving us without hope for the future".[6]

Of course, the fact that Wellhausen's theory agreed well with his own world view and that of most of his international peers in academic biblical study does not mean his theory is false. To argue so would be to commit a genetic fallacy. The truth or falsehood of the theory needs to be adjudicated on the evidence and arguments for and against it. In this regard, Pentateuchal criticism continued to develop after Wellhausen, in different, often conflicting, directions. Here, we will focus briefly on just a few of the major movements or "trajectories" that scholarship has taken since the nineteenth century: the *tradition-historical* school, some *Jewish-Israeli* approaches, the "American School", and some prominent *independent voices*.

The Tradition-Historical School

Hermann Gunkel (1862–1932), a younger contemporary of Wellhausen, rose to the forefront of Pentateuchal studies after Wellhausen's death. Although Gunkel did not dispute Wellhausen's basic source theory, Gunkel himself was more interested in analyzing the genres of individual textual units (form criticism) and speculating about their development over time, as they were passed down orally or in written form (tradition criticism). Gunkel's *tradition-critical* approach was taken up and advanced by the next generation of German scholars, Martin Noth (1902–1968) and Gerhard von Rad (1901–1971), but again, without taking any exception to the standard form of Wellhausen's Documentary Hypothesis.

Finally, however, von Rad's student and successor Rolf Rendtorff (1925–2014) announced, at the end of the twentieth century, his conviction that the results of tradition criticism of the Pentateuch ultimately contradicted the Documentary Hypothesis. According to Rendtorff, there was no "P" source or any other continuous literary documents (like "J") running through the Pentateuch. Rather, he proposed that large complexes of traditions focused around a certain number of pivotal events—such as the adventures of the patriarchs, the covenant at Sinai, the wilderness wanderings, and so on—had grown up and been collected independently of one another and then were joined together by editors at a late stage in Israel's history. For Rendtorff, the whole Pentateuch was ultimately unified by two *redactions* (processes of editing): first, a "Deuteronomistic" redaction that added the book of Deuteronomy and, then, a "Priestly" redaction that produced the final form of the text. Rendtorff's student and successor Erhard Blum (1950–) has focused his work on distinguishing the "Deuteronomistic" from the "Priestly" redactional layers. In his work, Rendtorff's

---

[6] Solomon Schechter, "Higher Criticism—Higher Anti-Semitism", delivered at the Judaean Banquet, given in honor of Dr. Kaufman Kohler, March 26, 1903, in *Seminary Address and Other Papers* (Cincinnati: Ark Publishing, 1915), 37.

concepts have almost been turned into a new kind of documentary hypothesis, but now with just two sources, D and P.

Jewish and Israeli Scholarship on the Pentateuch

Many Jewish scholars did accept and continue to accept the basic form of the Documentary Hypothesis. Among other Jewish scholars, especially those living in the land of Israel, however, there has been a tendency to critique at least some aspects of the theory. These can be grouped into two major movements: the *Kaufmann school* and the *literary-critical school.*

Yehezkel (Ezekiel) Kaufmann (1889–1963) was a brilliant and prolific Israeli philosopher and biblical scholar who spent the end of his career as a professor at the influential Hebrew University in Jerusalem. His best-known work is *The Religion of Israel,* a massive four-volume *tour de force* published in Hebrew in 1960. Kaufmann accepted three sources in the Pentateuch (JE, P, D), but he dated P much earlier than D and argued that it truly reflected the early religion and worship of preexilic Israel. Kaufmann, like Wellhausen, tied his source analysis of the Pentateuch to an account of the development of Israelite religion, but, unlike Wellhausen, he did not seek purely natural and evolutionary explanations. For Kaufmann, Israelite monotheistic religion was simply a *novum,* an innovation (not a development) that was part of the identity of the people of Israel from the beginning of their existence as an identifiable nation. Kaufmann did not believe that human history developed smoothly according to simple evolutionary principles: to cite just one counterexample, the great fourteenth-century Pharaoh Akhenaten had abruptly converted Egypt to monotheism during his reign, and his successor, Tutankhamun, with equal abruptness, reverted to polytheism.

Kaufmann shaped a generation of influential and brilliant Israeli biblical scholars, including Moshe Weinfeld (1925–2009), Moshe Greenberg (1928–2010), Jacob Milgrom (1923–2010), and others. Unlike Kaufmann himself, his students published much of their scholarship in English, so the views of the Kaufmann school began to influence biblical studies worldwide, especially in the United States. His students continued to argue that P was earlier than D and received support from some Jewish scholars in America (for example, Richard E. Friedman, 1946–). Milgrom, in fact, asserted that the heart of the Priestly material (Lev 1–16) goes back to the sanctuary the Israelites established at the town of Shechem in the twelfth century B.C. Kaufmann's students have also stressed a division of P into two sub-sources, P proper (primarily Lev 1–16 and parts of Numbers) and H, the Holiness Source (primarily Lev 17–26). According to them, P and H represent earlier and later historical stages in the development of Priestly thought. This distinction and chronological ordering are now widely accepted even in European scholarship, where it is becoming popular to regard H as the final redactor(s) of the Pentateuch.

Another trajectory within Jewish-Israeli scholarship on the Pentateuch has been characterized by *literary criticism.* These scholars apply to the biblical narrative the same forms of analysis used on other great world literature, in order to highlight the subtle art of the biblical author. Such scholars include Umberto

Cassuto (1883–1951), Meir Sternberg (1944–), Michael Fishbane (1943–), Robert Alter (1935–), H. C. Brichto (1925–1966), and many others. They vary in their attitude toward the Documentary Hypothesis from vocal rejection (U. Cassuto, H. Brichto) to indifference (R. Alter, M. Fishbane). What they share in common, however, is the conviction that many of the features of the biblical text that have been taken as evidence for sources or redactions are in fact *intentional literary features*—such as repetition, repetition with variation, *chiasm*, or palistrophe, and so on—that are employed by the ancient authors to enhance the narrative.

For example, the great Jewish archaeologist and Near Eastern historian Cyrus Gordon (1908–2001) defended the literary unity of the Pentateuch by appealing to a broad range of ancient Near Eastern documents, from Homer's *Iliad* to the *Code of Hammurabi*. These ancient documents exhibit literary features similar to the Pentateuch, such as apparently duplicate but variant accounts of the same (or similar) event(s) and passages of very different genres within the same document. Gordon was convinced that the Pentateuch, on the whole, greatly resembled the other literary masterpieces of the ancient Near East characteristic of the historical eras the Pentateuch purports to describe. Gordon's approach has been perpetuated by his students Nahum Sarna (1923–2005) and Gary Rendsburg (1954–).

The "American" or "Albright" School

American Old Testament scholarship began to become an international force largely under the leadership and influence of William Foxwell Albright (1891–1971), generally considered the dean of American biblical scholarship in the mid-twentieth century. Albright, the son of Methodist missionaries, was trained and taught for most of his career at Johns Hopkins University in Maryland. He devoted most of his scholarly efforts to the archaeology of the land of Israel and felt that many of his discoveries, as well as those of his colleagues working in other areas of the Near East, served to confirm the substantial historicity of the biblical narratives.

Although Albright never took issue with Wellhausen's Documentary Hypothesis *per se*, he did hold that the essential contents of the different sources had been passed down faithfully for generations before being committed to writing and were historically reliable in their broad outlines, starting with the call of Abraham (Gen 12). In contrast to Wellhausen, who dismissed any connection with reality behind the Pentateuchal narratives, Albright's approach greatly softened the impact of the Documentary Hypothesis on Jewish and Christian faith. To a greater or lesser degree, Albright's attitudes were maintained by his more prominent students, G. E. Wright (1909–1974), John Bright (1908–1995), David Noel Freedman (1922–2008), and Frank Moore Cross (1921–2012). Albright was ecumenical in spirit and worked closely with Catholic scholars (Roland de Vaux, 1903–1971) and taught others (Raymond Brown, 1928–1998), thus helping to shape the "mainstream" of international biblical studies, both Protestant and Catholic, during the middle of the twentieth century. This mainstream was above all reflected in the monumental series of critical commentaries on the Old and New Testaments edited by W. F. Albright and David Noel Freedman, the famous *Anchor Bible Commentary*.

The end of the twentieth century, however, saw the rise of "Biblical Minimalism", a school of thought, extremely skeptical of any historical veracity in the Old Testament, associated with Niels Peter Lemche (1945–), Philip R. Davies (1945–), Thomas L. Thompson (1939–), and the University of Copenhagen, where some of these scholars taught. Members of this school regarded most if not all of the Pentateuch as fiction composed by Jewish scribes after the Babylonian exile in order to create a religious and cultural identity for postexilic Judah.

Independent Voices

Very few among the scholars who continued to devote themselves to source criticism of the Pentateuch in the wake of Wellhausen simply reproduced his conclusions exactly. Many have argued for novel variations on his theory but have not established a lasting "school" or movement.

For example, Scandinavian scholar Sigmund Mowinckel (1884–1965) emphasized the role of oral tradition and argued that there was no real distinction between J and E. He shaped a generation of Scandinavian Bible scholars who were critical of the Documentary Hypothesis and emphasized oral tradition, but the movement has declined. Otto Eisfeldt (1887–1973), an influential German scholar who wrote a widely used *Introduction* published in the middle of the twentieth century, felt Wellhausen had not gone far enough, divided the sources into finer layers denoted by superscripts, and included an "L" ("Lay") source out of parts of "J". Some felt that Eisfeldt's work represented the *reduction ad absurdum* of the source-critical method. So many sources were distinguished that it amounted to a "fragmentary" rather than "documentary" hypothesis. Likewise, the Swiss scholar H. H. Schmid (1937–2014) argued that the Yahwist source should be divided into two, J^1 and J^2, one early (tenth century) and one late (postexilic). Canadian scholar John Van Seters (1935–) advanced Schmid's theory by identifying all of J as a late source, possibly the latest of the Pentateuchal sources and devoid of all historical content.

Finally, in the late twentieth century, Ronald N. Whybray (1923–1997), a prominent British Old Testament scholar, published a landmark study criticizing the entire methodology undergirding the Documentary Hypothesis. While such criticisms had been made before by conservative Jews and Christians, Whybray was neither and had no particular religious motivation. He simply pointed out the inconsistencies of the method. For example, in documentary source criticism, it is always assumed that authors of sources (J, E, P, and so on) do not repeat themselves and are always consistent. At the same time, it is assumed that the ancient redactors were not bothered by repetitions and inconsistencies. Why, asks Whybray, do we assume that the standards of the ancient authors were different from those of the redactors? If the redactors were comfortable with repetition with variation, why not the authors themselves? At the end of the twentieth century, at around the same time Whybray's study was published (1987), Rolf Rendtorff also published his *Introduction to the Old Testament* (1991), in which he announced the final incompatibility of tradition criticism with Wellhausen's Documentary Hypothesis. Both these critiques had a large impact on Old Testament studies and marked the end of the period of dominance of the Documentary Hypothesis in its classic form.

Some Difficulties with the Documentary Hypothesis

Given the fact that currently the scholarly discussion regarding the origins of the Pentateuch and the classic Wellhausian Documentary Hypothesis is in a state of flux, it is important here to take a few moments to outline some of the internal difficulties with the Documentary Hypothesis. To be sure, the hypothesis still has strong defenders.[7] Nevertheless, there remain certain difficulties with the hypothesis in its classical form that have been highlighted by its critics and that are worth cataloguing here before bringing our chapter to a close.

No Consensus on the Dates of the Pentateuchal Sources

First, as noted above, unlike the situation a century ago, there is no longer one dominant paradigm for understanding the composition of the Pentateuch within the academy. The dates, extent, and even existence of almost all the hypothetical sources have been disputed by scholars at the top of the profession from an array of religious and theological backgrounds. In the words of British Pentateuchal critic Ronald N. Whybray:

> There is at the present moment no consensus whatever about when, why, how and through whom the Pentateuch reached its present form, and opinions about the dates of composition of its various points differ by more than five hundred years.[8]

Since Whybray penned these words more than twenty years ago, the field of Pentateuch criticism has become more—not less—diverse, and there continues to be no consensus about the authorship and date of sources of the Pentateuch,[9] despite the appearance of consensus often given by textbooks.

Consider, for example, the following ranges of dates proposed for each of the standard sources of the Documentary Hypothesis.:

The Jahwist Source (J):
tenth century B.C. (G. von Rad)
ninth century B.C. (J. Wellhausen; R. E. Friedman)
sixth century B.C. (J. Van Seters)

The Elohist Source (E):
eighth century B.C. (J. Wellhausen)
ninth–eighth centuries B.C. (R. E. Friedman)

---

[7] See Joel S. Baden, *The Composition of the Pentateuch: Renewing the Documentary Hypothesis*, Anchor Yale Bible Reference Library (New Haven, Conn.: Yale University Press, 2012).

[8] Ronald N. Whybray, *An Introduction to the Pentateuch* (Grand Rapids, Mich.: Eerdmans, 1995), 12.

[9] For a recent survey, see T. Desmond Alexander, *From Paradise to the Promised Land: An Introduction to the Pentateuch*, 3rd ed. (Grand Rapids, Mich.: Baker Academic, 2012).

The Deuteronomist Source (D):
seventh century B.C. (J. Wellhausen, R. E. Friedman)
fifth–third centuries B.C. (postexilic period) (T. Thompson)

The Priestly Source (P):
eighth century B.C. (Y. Kaufmann)
seventh century B.C. (R. E. Friedman)
sixth century B.C. (J. Wellhausen)
fifth century B.C. (T. Römer, C. Nihan)
third century B.C. (T. Thompson)

As this list makes clear, despite the appearance of a consensus among Old Testament scholars that the Documentary Hypothesis frequently holds in the popular imagination, the reality of the situation is that scholarly theories about the dates of the hypothetical sources J, E, D, and P vary widely, often by *centuries*. Since no manuscripts of a source have ever been found, their date and existence remain a hypothetical construct.

The Absence of Certain Post-Mosaic Elements in the Pentateuch

Second, in terms of the overall contents of the Pentateuch, there is a striking absence of certain post-Mosaic elements that we would expect to find if the Documentary Hypothesis were correct in positing that Pentateuchal material in large part originated hundreds of years after Moses, between the eighth and fifth centuries B.C.

For example, if the substance of the Pentateuch did in fact originate between the eighth and fifth centuries B.C., one would expect to find some references embedded therein justifying the authority of the kingdom of David and the primacy of the city of Jerusalem. *And yet, neither the Priestly material (P) nor the book of Deuteronomy (D) mentions or reflects any hint of the Davidic monarchy, the theology of Zion, the city of Jerusalem, or the Jerusalem Temple.* To the contrary, the Pentateuch—in striking contrast to the prophetic literature from the time of the divided monarchy on—is deafeningly silent about "Jerusalem" or "Zion" or the "Temple". Instead, the so-called Priestly materials focus on the construction and liturgy of the Tabernacle, the portable sanctuary of Israel while in the desert. Certain aspects of the Tabernacle, not least its portable character, pose a potential challenge to the later sacred texts (in the Psalms, for example) that associated God's presence almost exclusively with Zion, Jerusalem, and the Temple.[10] Furthermore, although Deuteronomy mandates a central sanctuary, it never specifies *where* that sanctuary was to be, despite the fact that throughout both the First *and* Second Temple period there were serious and problematic rival claimants to the role of preferred sanctuary for the people of Israel. If Deuteronomy did in fact originate during the late monarchic period, it could have easily justified the centrality and primacy of Jerusalem and its Temple by even a single explicit reference; yet no such reference exists.

---

[10] T. Fretheim, "The Priestly Document: Anti-Temple?" *Vetus Testamentum* 18, no. 3 (1968): 313–29.

Do the Laws of the Pentateuch Demand a Late Setting?

Wellhausen and his followers insisted that the law codes of the Pentateuch, especially the priestly laws, were too complex to have arisen in early Israel and reflected instead Second Temple reality. Frank Moore Cross, professor emeritus of Harvard University, pioneer of Dead Sea Scroll research, and one of the most distinguished American Bible scholars of the late twentieth century, disagreed. He explained the anachronism of the Pentateuchal laws with monarchic, exilic, and postexilic society as due to a "revival" of ancient traditions:

"Late in the monarchy and in the Exile there was a revival of covenantal ideology, law, and cultic practice. Drawing on surviving elements of league and kinship structures, as well as traditional religious and legal lore, the tradents of the school of Deuteronomy and of the Priestly school made a stalwart effort to reconstruct and resurrect the covenantal institutions of the 'Mosaic Age', that is, the era of the league.... I should assert that the Pentateuchal tradents, D and P, were more successful in their reconstructions of the covenantal institutions of early Israel than we critical historians have supposed, and that their traditionalist approaches are often less doctrinaire and closer to historical reality than the unilinear historical schemes imposed by scholars of yesteryear."[a]

[a] Frank Moore Cross, *From Epic to Canon: History and Literature in Ancient Israel* (Baltimore: Johns Hopkins University Press, 2000), 21.

Moreover, if the substance of the Pentateuch had indeed originated between the eighth and fifth centuries B.C., one would also expect to find *legal material* justifying a centralized monarchic state with a standing army, royal taxation, and royal bureaucracy. Instead, what we find in the so-called Priestly and Deuteronomic portions of the Pentateuch are law codes reflecting a decentralized tribal society ruled primarily by elders and religious leaders (priests). One looks in vain through these law codes for any clear indication of a royal administration governing Israelite society; in fact, many of the laws "are a survival of prestate tribal societies" and "run counter to the claims and interests of monarchy" and are "in some sense antistate".[11] It is the case, then, that the law codes of the Pentateuch are, in fact, at odds with a Second Temple setting and even a First Temple setting. Efforts by scholars to read these codes as reflective of the monarchic, exilic, or postexilic periods always involve a certain *allegorical reading* in which elements of the text (for example, the Tabernacle) are taken as allegories or ciphers of their *actual* referents (for example, the Temple). None of the anachronisms with a monarchic, exilic, or postexilic setting are ever allowed to count as evidence against such a setting. Instead, they are invariably attributed to the "literary fiction" of Mosaic authorship. It should go without saying that such a hermeneutic—in which (1) all material that lends itself to allegorical application to a later sociohistorical time period is taken as truly indicative of the date of composition, and (2) all material that is anachronistic to a later sociohistorical time period is attributed to the "fictional" Mosaic setting—can never fail to conclude that the Pentateuch is a "late" composition, because the method presupposes its own conclusions from the outset.

---

[11] Frank Moore Cross, *From Epic to Canon: History and Literature in Ancient Israel* (Baltimore: John Hopkins University Press, 1998), 19.

Lastly, if the substance of the Pentateuch did indeed originate during the period of the divided Davidic kingdom (ca. eighth–fifth centuries B.C.), then one would expect to find multiple *warnings about the religious or political threats of Syria (Aram), Assyria, or Babylon*—Israel's antagonists during the monarchy and the exile. In stark contrast, the nations portrayed by the Pentateuch as a threat to Israel's existence and identity—"the Hittites and the Amorites, the Canaanites and the Perizzites, the Hivites and the Jebusites" (Deut 20:17, and so on)—are those which, for the most part, had already ceased to pose a threat to Israel during the reigns of Saul and David (tenth century B.C.), when the military focus was almost entirely on the defeat of the Philistines. Now, it is true that the curses of the covenant (Lev 26 and Deut 27) warn of exile, which is taken by many scholars to be a "prophecy after the fact" (Latin *vaticinium ex eventu*). However, the biblical curses of exile include no specifics concerning by whom or to where the threatened exile will be, and the threat of exile is a typical covenant curse attested in other ancient Near Eastern treaty-covenants that are manifestly not prophecies after the fact.[12]

The Pentateuch and Second-Millennium Ancient Near Eastern Literature

Third, some scholars have recently argued that much of the material in the putative sources of the Pentateuch can be reasonably associated with the time in which Moses lived—the late second millennium B.C.[13] This evidence is particularly significant for reexamining the question of dating the Pentateuchal material, since the archaeological data and literary parallels upon which the following observations are based had not yet been discovered in the nineteenth century, when Julius Wellhausen and others were giving the Documentary Hypothesis its classic shape. We will consider each of the major portions of the Pentateuch in its canonical order.

1. *The Primeval History (Gen 1–11) and Pre-Mosaic Cosmogonies.* The Primeval History (Gen 1–11) shows striking formal parallels with other ancient Near Eastern cosmogonies and primeval histories, especially (but not limited to) Mesopotamian ones, such as the *Enuma Elish*, the *Epic of Gilgamesh*, and the *Sumerian King List*. All these documents long predate any estimate of the lifetime of Moses, even conservative ones. Already in the mid-second millennium B.C., ancient Near Eastern culture was remarkably cosmopolitan, with a great exchange of language and literature. Mesopotamian language and literature were held in such esteem that in the fifteenth century B.C., the pharaoh was using a form of the language of Babylon to correspond with his own vassals in Canaan. Competent familiarity with the languages and literatures of the ancient Near East could have been available to any educated person throughout the region, including someone trained in the court of the pharaoh.

2. *The Patriarchal Narratives and Second-Millennium Mesopotamian Culture.* The narratives of the patriarchs (Gen 12–50) reflect the culture and ambiance of

---

[12] Kenneth A. Kitchen, *On the Reliability of the Old Testament* (Grand Rapids, Mich.: Eerdmans, 2003).
[13] See ibid., 159–447.

Canaan in the early second millennium B.C., when the Hittite Empire still stood and held sway in parts of Canaan (cf. Gen 23). Repeatedly the patriarchs are identified culturally with "Padan-Aram", or northwest Mesopotamia (Gen 25:20; 28:2–7; 31:18; 33:18; 35:9,26; 46:15; 48:7). It is precisely from this region that archaeologists have discovered a set of texts that provide more numerous and striking parallels with the patriarchal narratives than any others, from the ancient city of Nuzu (or Nuzi), destroyed at or slightly after the patriarchal age (fifteenth–fourteenth centuries B.C.), which has been called "the single society closest to the life of the patriarchs".[14] This surprising correlation between the cultural, geographical, and temporal claims of the patriarchal narratives and the literary remains of this ancient northwest Mesopotamian city constitute a strong argument for the antiquity of the core narrative of the patriarchal cycle, since the correlations involve fundamental plot elements and not superficial glosses or editorial comments.

3. *The Exodus and Late Second-Millennium Egyptian Culture.* The basic premise of the exodus (Ex 1–19) of a Semitic tribal group enslaved in Egypt that escapes to the desert is widely acknowledged as fitting the time period of New Kingdom Egypt (ca. 1550–1077 B.C.), from which we have extant texts recording several instances of escaped Asiatic slaves as well as military patrols along the border that attempted to prevent such excursions. Numerous features of the exodus narrative come to life against the background of Egyptian culture of the late second millennium; specific examples will be discussed below in the chapter on the exodus.

4. *The Sinai Legislation and Second-Millennium Legal Codes.* The civil legislation given to Israel at Sinai in Exodus through Numbers, most of which is attributed to the "Priestly source", can usually be paralleled by legal material extant from the Hittite Empire (ca. 1600–1180 B.C.), Egypt, or Mesopotamia, most of which predates the exodus by centuries, including the codes promulgated by Hammurabi (eighteenth century B.C.), Ur-Nammu (ca. twenty-first century B.C.), Ammisaduqa (seventeenth or sixteenth century B.C.), Lipit-Ishtar (nineteenth century B.C.), and other monarchs of the second millennium. The design of the Tabernacle and the Ark of the Covenant strongly resemble Egyptian royal and ritual tents and vessels from the New Kingdom period, to the point that examination of ancient Egyptian ark-like objects elucidate some biblical passages otherwise difficult to interpret.[15] Israel's cultic and sacrificial regulations are simpler than those of the Hittite religious texts of the second millennium, indicating that no long period of development was necessary to attain the supposed "complex" system presented in the Pentateuch. On the whole, Israel's cultic regulations are simpler than those of its neighbors for all periods during the second and first millennia B.C. Several cultic laws and prohibitions seem directly aimed against aspects of Egyptian and Canaanite religion, as later attested in the religious documents from Ugarit dated to the thirteenth century B.C., about the time of the exodus according to some scholars.

---

[14] Cyrus Gordon and Gary Rendsburg, *The Bible and the Ancient Near East* (New York and London: W.W. Norton, 1999), 111.

[15] Raanan Eichler, "The Meaning of *zēr*", *Vetus Testamentum* 64 (2014): 196–210.

5. The Book of Deuteronomy and Ancient Hittite Treaties. Some of the strongest parallels between any part of the Bible and ancient Near Eastern literature are those between the treaty (covenant) literature of the Hittites from the fourteenth century B.C. and the book of Deuteronomy. Some of the Hittite treaties were with the pharaoh, others with vassal kings in the northern Levant, so it seems plausible that the form of these treaties was known throughout the western Near East. Many scholars have pointed out the similarity in structure between these second-millennium treaties and Deuteronomy.

The Structural Parallels of Second-Millennium Hittite Covenants and Deuteronomy	
1. Prelude: ("These are the words of X")	1. Prelude (Deut 1:1–5)
2. Historical Prologue (history of relations)	2. Historical Prologue (Deut 1–4)
3. Obligations of the Vassal toward Suzerain	3. Obligations (Deut 4–26)
4. Provision for Deposit and Public Reading	4. Deposit/Public Reading (Deut 27, 31)
5. List of Divine Witnesses to Treaty	5. Witnesses for Renewal (Deut 29–34)
6. Curses and Blessings (obedience or failure)	6. Curses and Blessings (Deut 27–28)

The parallels, however, are not limited to macrostructure but also include various particulars, such as the microstructure and phrasing of the prohibitions of covenant infidelity in Deuteronomy 13.[16] While certain aspects of the structure and style of these covenant documents are perpetuated in the covenant-treaty tradition of the ancient Near East and recur at a later period as well (that is, the seventh-century Assyrian treaties), the greatest number of structural and stylistic parallels are to be found between Deuteronomy and the earlier Hittite literature.

The Pentateuch and the Preexilic Old Testament Books

Fourth, one of the major arguments for the late origins of the Pentateuch is the supposed absence of references to Pentateuchal materials in preexilic books of the Bible (such as the writings of the eighth-century prophets).

However, as we will see later, several preexilic biblical books refer to the materials of the Pentateuch. There are in fact a number of instances in the major and minor prophets, as well as the Psalms and historical books, that either refer to or presume knowledge of the wording, narratives, laws, or *realia* of the Pentateuch. The claim to the contrary by Wellhausen and his followers was only successful due to a combination of (1) ignoring some evidence, (2) explaining other evidence away by classifying it as a late interpolation into a preexilic text, or (3) claiming that the order of literary dependence should be reversed—in other words, an apparent quote of the Pentateuch in the prophets is actually a quote of the prophets in the Pentateuch.

---

[16] Joshua Berman, "CTH 133 and the Hittite Provenance of Deuteronomy 13", *Journal of Biblical Literature* 130 (2011): 25–44.

Wellhausen and the Book of Leviticus

Although many scholars have pointed out that there is no good reason to attribute any part of the book of Ezekiel to a time period much later than the life of the prophet himself (in other words, later than about halfway through the Babylonian exile),[a] Ezekiel extensively quotes and reuses the priestly materials of the Pentateuch, especially the second half of Leviticus, called the Holiness Code (chaps. 17–26). Wellhausen and his followers explained this literary relationship by claiming that Ezekiel showed an early stage of the development of the priestly materials, but they never made a *careful* and *comprehensive* study of the parallel passages in Leviticus and Ezekiel. Such studies of these passages have been undertaken recently[b] and demonstrate compellingly that it is *Ezekiel* who is making use of *Leviticus*, not vice versa. Ezekiel quotes and reuses Leviticus and other parts of the Pentateuch extensively. Thus, if the Book of Ezekiel was composed in the early exile, as Wellhausen and many others have held, then the priestly materials of the Pentateuch must have been extant already in the pre-exilic period.

[a] See Lawrence Boadt, "Do Jeremiah and Ezekiel Share a Common View of the Exile?", in *Uprooting and Planting: Essays on Jeremiah for Leslie Allen*, Library of Hebrew Bible/Old Testament Studies 459 (New York: T&T Clark, 2007), 14–31.

[b] Risa Levitt Kohn, *A New Heart and a New Soul: Ezekiel, the Exile, and the Torah*, Journal for the Study of the Old Testament 358 (London and New York: T&T Clark, 2002); Michael A. Lyons, *From Law to Prophecy: Ezekiel's Use of the Holiness Code*, Library of Hebrew Bible/Old Testament Studies 507 (London: T&T Clark, 2009).

With that said, it is nevertheless true that there is a lack of *explicit citation* of the Pentateuch in most preexilic Scriptures. What are we to make of this? In this instance, the evidence in the Old Testament itself provides a plausible explanation for why some of its books might not allude to the Pentateuch. According to the book of Kings, "the book of the Torah"—presumably a reference to the Pentateuch as a whole, or at least the book of Deuteronomy—was in fact *lost* for an extended period of time and only rediscovered by a priest in the Temple in the late seventh century B.C.:

> In the eighteenth year of King Josiah [ca. 622 B.C.], the king sent Shaphan the son of Azaliah, son of Meshullam, the secretary, to the house of the LORD.... *And Hilkiah the high priest said to Shaphan the secretary, "I have found the book of the law in the house of the LORD."* And Hilkiah gave the book to Shaphan, and he read it.... Then Shaphan the secretary told the king, "Hilkiah the priest has given me a book." And Shaphan read it before the king.
>
> And when the king heard the words of the book of the law, he tore his clothes. And the king commanded Hilkiah the priest, and Ahikam the son of Shaphan, and Achbor the son of Micaiah, and Shaphan the secretary, and Asaiah the king's servant, saying, "Go, inquire of the LORD for me, and for the people, and for all Judah, concerning the words of this book that has been found; for great is the wrath of the LORD that is kindled against us, because our fathers have not obeyed the words of this book, to do according to all that is written concerning us."
> (2 Kings 22:3, 8, 10–13)

Ironically, the very text that Wellhausen and his followers used to argue that the Deuteronomic source was "invented" by Josiah in the late seventh century

B.C. is the very same text that provides us with a plausible explanation for why some preexilic books of the Old Testament—such as the writings of certain prophets—do not manifest extensive knowledge of the Pentateuch.

Other explanations can be found for the relative "Pentateuchal silence" of some preexilic Scriptures. For example, the *Code of Hammurabi*, a comprehensive law code in many ways comparable to the Pentateuch or at least to portions of it, is known to have been promulgated by Hammurabi around 1750 B.C., and yet there is not a single reference to it in the judicial literature of Babylon subsequently.[17] In fact, our records of Babylonian court cases show that its laws were not followed in practice. Therefore, even if it were true that the preexilic biblical books do not mention the laws of the Pentateuch, it would prove nothing. The lack of correspondence between ANE law codes and the actual practice of law is a well-known problem in ANE research.[18] Strangely, however, new evidence has come to light showing at least that many of the cultic laws of the Pentateuch *were* actually followed in the monarchic period. Excavations of temple sites in northern Israel from the period of the divided monarchy have recently revealed that several cultic laws usually identified with the Priestly source of the Pentateuch were in fact enforced at this early period, even in the "schismatic" or "heterodox" northern kingdom.[19]

The Dating of Hebrew Language and Date of Composition

Fifth and finally, the Pentateuch appears to be written in classical Hebrew of the monarchic period (tenth–sixth centuries B.C.).[20] This is both later than the presumed era of Moses, which is usually placed somewhere within the fifteenth–thirteenth centuries B.C., but also earlier than the postexilic period (ca. 537–332 B.C.) in which Wellhausen and others have placed much of the composition of the Pentateuch. Yet, when evaluating ancient texts, one cannot always equate the *date of language* with the *date of composition*. The reason is, of course, that in the case of a text passed down over the course of many centuries, it is very difficult (if not impossible) to rule out later scribal revision of the language of the text in order to remove archaisms and clarify its meaning.

In the history of texts, especially sacred texts, these kinds of comprehensive revisions do take place. Think, for example, of the revision of classic archaic English texts such as the King James Version of the English Bible. Although the KJV was originally written in A.D. 1611, it was updated and revised according to current English standards as the Revised Version (1880s), the Revised Standard Version (1950s–1960s), and the New Revised Standard Version (1989). Now, it

[17] Bruce Wells, "What Is Biblical Law? A Look at Pentateuchal Rules and Near Eastern Practice", *Catholic Biblical Quarterly* 70 (2008): 223–43.

[18] Fritz R. Kraus, "Ein zentrales Problem des altmesopotamischen Rechtes: Was ist der Codex Hammurabi?" [A central problem of old Mesopotamian law: What is the Code of Hammurabi?], *Geneva* 8 (1960): 283–96.

[19] Jonathan Samuel Greer, *Dinner at Dan: Biblical and Archaeological Evidence for Sacred Feasts at Iron Age II Tel Dan and Their Significance*, Culture and History of the Ancient Near East 66 (Leiden and Boston: Brill, 2013).

[20] William Schniedewind, *How the Bible Became a Book: The Textualization of Ancient Israel* (Cambridge: Cambridge University Press, 2004).

would of course be erroneous to argue from the contemporary language of the NRSV that the contents of the English Bible were composed in the 1980s. In like manner, scholars cannot rule out the ancient origins of the material in the Pentateuch on the basis of Hebrew language analysis alone.

On the other hand, the classical Hebrew of the Pentateuch seems incompatible with a view of its composition in the exilic or postexilic period. Some scholars are convinced that the linguistic evidence is sufficient to conclude that the bulk of the Pentateuch cannot have been composed later than the end of the Judean monarchy.[21] Others hold open the possibility that later authors composed in archaic Hebrew, imitating language forms of an earlier, "classical" period.

In short, despite the widespread acceptance of some form of the Documentary Hypothesis in nineteenth- and twentieth-century scholarship, there remain serious difficulties with the overall hypothesis. Given the positive evidence for multiple correspondences between the Pentateuch and ancient Near Eastern culture of the second millennium B.C., it will be fascinating to see where contemporary Pentateuchal criticism goes in the near future as scholars continue to debate the origins of the first five books of the Bible.

The Catholic Church and the Origins of the Pentateuch

Before bringing this chapter to a close, it important to take a few moments to document what the Catholic Church's official response to the modern discussion of the origins of the Pentateuch has been. This response has two key moments worth highlighting. The first took place at the beginning of the twentieth century, with the 1906 response of the Pontifical Biblical Commission on the question of Mosaic authorship of the Pentateuch. The second occurred at the beginning of the twenty-first century, with the remarks of then Cardinal Joseph Ratzinger in his 2002 address to the Pontifical Biblical Commission. We will take a few moments to examine each of these in turn.

The Pontifical Biblical Commission and the Pentateuch (1906)

In the early twentieth century, in the wake of the formulation and growing influence of the Documentary Hypothesis, the Catholic Church promulgated her first official response to questions about the origins the Pentateuch. The response was given by the Pontifical Biblical Commission—an organ of the Magisterium founded by Pope Pius X in order to answer biblical questions—which crafted a "reply" to the "question" (Latin *dubium*) of the Mosaic origins of the Pentateuch. This response, which was published in 1906, affirmed Moses as author of the Pentateuch but attached certain qualifications to this conclusion. In so doing, it formulated its views in terms similar to those of Jerome, and not according to the strict view of Mosaic authorship that we saw witnessed above in the writings of Josephus.

On the one hand, the Pontifical Biblical Commission affirmed the "Mosaic authorship" of the Pentateuch, based on several reasons:

---

[21] Ibid.

1. "The many statements ... in both Testaments taken together";
2. "The persistent consensus of the Jewish people";
3. "The constant tradition of the Church";
4. "and the internal evidence coming from the text itself".[22]

On the other hand, the commission also stated that upholding "the Mosaic authorship of the Pentateuch" does *not* require that "everything in it was written by Moses with his own hand or dictated to secretaries".[23] Instead, the commission granted that:

> *Moses made use of sources in producing his work,* namely written documents or oral traditions from which he took some things and inserted them in the work, either word for word or substantially, abridged or amplified, as suited his special purpose and under the influence of divine inspiration.[24]

Finally, the commission even allowed that "in the long course of centuries *a number of modifications* happened to it [the Pentateuch]", such as:

1. "Additions after the death of Moses by an inspired author";
2. "glosses and explanations interspersed in the text";
3. "some words and grammatical forms translated from an ancient language into a more recent one";
4. "finally, incorrect readings to be blamed on copyists."[25]

In other words, like Jerome before it, the Pontifical Biblical Commission did not see the clear evidence for post-Mosaic material in the final form of the Pentateuch as a problem for following the Jewish and Christian tradition that such later alterations and additions could be accepted while "safeguarding substantially the Mosaic authorship and integrity of the Pentateuch".[26]

As should be clear from what we have seen so far, however, over the course of the twentieth century, the vast majority of biblical scholars, including Catholic scholars, did not come to the same conclusions as the Pontifical Biblical Commission. Instead, the Documentary Hypothesis came to be widely (if not universally) held as the more plausible explanation for the origins of the Pentateuch.

Cardinal Ratzinger's 2002 Address to the Pontifical Biblical Commission

Almost a century after the publication of the 1906 statement and exactly one hundred years after the establishment of the Pontifical Biblical Commission, in the year 2002, then Cardinal Joseph Ratzinger, the acting president of the

[22] Pontifical Biblical Commission. "Reply concerning Mosaic Authorship of the Pentateuch (1906)", I.1, in *The Church and the Bible: Official Documents of the Catholic Church*, 2nd ed., ed. Dennis J. Murphy, M.S.C. (Bangalore: St. Paul's/Alba House, 2007), 99.

[23] Ibid., II.1, p. 99.

[24] Ibid., III (emphasis added), p. 99.

[25] Ibid., IV, p. 99.

[26] Ibid.

commission, addressed the status of the early decrees regarding Mosaic authorship in his address to the members of the Pontifical Biblical Commission.

In that address, Cardinal Ratzinger gives an overview of the history of the commission and refers to the early twentieth-century responses as follows:

> Meanwhile, not only those decisions of the Biblical Commission which had entered too much into the sphere of merely historical questions were corrected; we have also learned something new about the methods and limits of historical knowledge.[27]

With regard to such historical topics as the attribution of the Pentateuch to Moses, Cardinal Ratzinger asserts that "there will always be room for discussion" and stresses that certain questions often remain open:

> What we have learned in the meantime, moreover, is that many questions in their particulars must remain open-ended and be entrusted to a conscious interpretation of their responsibilities.[28]

This "open-ended" approach reflects the current state of the question on the part of the Magisterium of the Church. With this guidance in mind, we can now finally turn to the text of the Pentateuch itself.

For Further Reading

The Origins of the Pentateuch

Alexander, T. Desmond. *From Paradise to the Promised Land: An Introduction to the Pentateuch.* 3rd ed. Grand Rapids, Mich.: Baker Academic, 2012.

Assmann, Jan. *Moses the Egyptian: The Memory of Egypt in Western Monotheism.* Cambridge, Mass.: Harvard University Press, 1998.

Baden, Joel S. *The Composition of the Pentateuch: Renewing the Documentary Hypothesis.* Anchor Yale Bible Reference Library. New Haven, Conn.: Yale University Press, 2012.

Berman, Joshua. "CTH 133 and the Hittite Provenance of Deuteronomy 13". *Journal of Biblical Literature* 130 (2011): 25–44.

Blenkinsopp, Joseph. *The Pentateuch: An Introduction to the First Five Books of the Bible.* Anchor Yale Bible Reference Library. New Haven, Conn.: Yale University Press, 2000.

Cassuto, Umberto. *The Documentary Hypothesis and the Composition of the Pentateuch.* Jerusalem: Shalem Press, 2006.

Eichler, Raanan. "The Meaning of *zēr*". *Vetus Testamentum* 64 (2014): 196–210.

Friedman, Richard Elliott. "Torah". Pages 605–61 in vol. 6 of the *Anchor Bible Dictionary.* Edited by D. N. Freedman. New York: Doubleday, 1991.

Greer, Jonathan Samuel. *Dinner at Dan: Biblical and Archaeological Evidence for Sacred Feasts at Iron Age II Tel Dan and Their Significance.* Leiden and Boston: Brill, 2013.

Ha, John. *Genesis 15: A Theological Compendium of Pentateuchal History.* BZAW 181. Berlin and New York: Walter de Gruyter, 1989.

---

[27] Joseph Cardinal Ratzinger, "Address to Pontifical Biblical Commission on the Centenary of Its Establishment (October 30, 2002)", in Murphy, *Church and the Bible,* 993–94.

[28] Ibid, 993.

Harrison, R. K. *Introduction to the Old Testament.* Repr., Peabody, Mass.: Hendrickson, 2004.

Hengstenberg, E. W. *Dissertations on the Genuineness of the Pentateuch.* Repr., Eugene, Ore.: Wipf and Stock, 2004.

Kitchen, Kenneth A. *On the Reliability of the Old Testament.* Grand Rapids, Mich.: Eerdmans, 2003.

Kline, Meredith G. *Treaty of the Great King: The Covenant Structure of Deuteronomy.* Grand Rapids, Mich.: Eerdmans, 1963.

Kraus, Fritz R. "Ein zentrales Problem des altmesopotamischen Rechtes: Was ist der Codex Hammurabi?" (A central problem of old Mesopotamian law: What is the Code of Hammurabi?), *Geneva* 8 (1960): 283–96.

Lyons, Michael A. *From Law to Prophecy: Ezekiel's Use of the Holiness Code.* Library of Biblical Studies 507. Sheffield: Sheffield Academic Press, 2009.

Nicholson, Ernest. *The Pentateuch in the Twentieth Century: The Legacy of Julius Wellhausen.* Oxford: Clarendon Press, 2003.

Noth, Martin. *A History of Pentateuchal Traditions.* Translated and edited by Bernhard W. Anderson. Englewood Cliffs, N.J.: Prentice Hall, 1971.

Pontifical Biblical Commission. "On the Mosaic Authorship of the Pentateuch". Page 188–89 in *The Scripture Documents: An Anthology of Official Catholic Teachings.* Edited by Dean P. Béchard. Collegeville, Minn.: Liturgical Press, 2002.

Rendtorff, Rolf. *The Problem of the Process of Transmission in the Pentateuch.* Translated by John J. Scullion. Journal for the Study of the Old Testament Supplement 89. Sheffield: JSOT Press, 1990.

Sailhamer, John H. *The Meaning of the Pentateuch: Revelation, Composition, Interpretation.* Downers Grove, Ill.: IVP Academic, 2009.

Schechter, Solomon. "Higher Criticism—Higher Anti-Semitism", delivered at the Judaean Banquet, given in honor of Dr. Kaufman Kohler, March 26, 1903. Pages 35–39 in *Seminary Address and Other Papers.* Cincinnati: Ark Publishing, 1915.

Schniedewind, William. *How the Bible Became a Book: The Textualization of Ancient Israel.* Cambridge: Cambridge University Press, 2004.

Weinfeld, Moshe. *The Place of the Law in the Religion of Ancient Israel. Vetus Testamentum* Supplements 100. Leiden and Boston: Brill, 2004.

Wellhausen, Julius. *Prolegomena to the History of Ancient Israel.* 1885; Atlanta: Scholars Press, 1994.

Wells, Bruce. "What Is Biblical Law? A Look at Pentateuchal Rules and Near Eastern Practice". *Catholic Biblical Quarterly* 70 (2008): 223–43.

Whybray, R. N. *An Introduction to the Pentateuch.* Grand Rapids, Mich.: Eerdmans, 1995.

———. *The Making of the Pentateuch: A Methodological Study.* London: T&T Clark, 1987.

The Catholic Church and the Origins of the Pentateuch

Pontifical Biblical Commission. "Reply concerning Mosaic Authorship of the Pentateuch (1906)". Pages 98–100 in *The Church and the Bible: Official Documents of the Catholic Church.* 2nd ed. Edited by Dennis J. Murphy, M.S.C. Staten Island, N.Y.: Saint Paul's/Alba House, 2007.

Ratzinger, Cardinal Joseph. "Address to Pontifical Biblical Commission on the Centenary of Its Establishment (October 30, 2002)". Pages 985–94 in *The Church and the Bible: Official Documents of the Catholic Church.* 2nd ed. Edited by Dennis J. Murphy, M.S.C. Staten Island, N.Y.: Saint Paul's/Alba House, 2007.

5. GENESIS 1–11
(THE PRIMEVAL HISTORY)

Introduction

The name Genesis is from the Greek word *geneseōs* (birth, lineage, generation). This Greek word is derived from the root *gen-*, associated with "becoming" or "origination", as in the English word *generate*. Genesis seems to have been the Greek translation of the Hebrew word *toledoth* (generations), which is part of an important formula that occurs ten times in the book at key junctures in the narrative: "these are the generations of" (Gen 2:4; 5:1; 6:9; 10:1; and so on). Eventually, it became the title of the book in the Septuagint translation (ca. 250 B.C.).

In Hebrew, the name of the book is its first word, *Bereshit* (literally, "In the beginning"). It is the book of origins. As such, its significance for Christian theology and Western literature, culture, and history can scarcely be exaggerated. Indeed, the importance of the book of Genesis is remarkably out of proportion to the length of the book, because it presents in a unique way the fundamental account of the origin of creation, mankind, and the people of God. It also gives the account of more covenants between God and mankind than any other biblical book. In the course of its fifty chapters, it covers the divine covenants with Adam, Noah, and Abraham: three of the five main covenants recounted in the Old Testament as a whole. From a literary perspective, the book of Genesis sets up the tensions that will drive the plot of the rest of the Bible.

The narrative of the book of Genesis covers a larger time frame than any other biblical book: from the creation of the world to the sojourn of the twelve tribes of Israel in Egypt in the second millennium B.C. In the first eleven chapters, vast periods of time are passed over quickly, by means of schematic genealogies and a few carefully chosen, illustrative stories about the early ancestors of the human family. The pace of the story slows dramatically in chapter 12, the beginning of the account of Abraham. From chapter 12 to the end of the book, the sacred author follows in some detail the lives of the three patriarchs, Abraham, Isaac, and Jacob, whose descendants will constitute the people of Israel, through whom God swears to bless all of mankind.

Literary Structure of Genesis 1–11

The literary structure of Genesis can be analyzed in different ways. In terms of content, the most obvious division of the book is between Genesis 1–11, often called the *Primeval History*, and Genesis 12–50, the *Patriarchal*

The Fundamental Division of Genesis	
Gen 1–11	Primeval History: The Origin of Humanity
Gen 12–50	Patriarchal History: The Origin of Israel

History. The first eleven chapters describe the origin of humanity as a whole; the next thirty-nine chapters describe the origin of Israel as a people.

Each of the two halves of the book may be further divided. Within the *Primeval History* of Genesis 1–11, there is a disjunction roughly between Genesis 1–5 and Genesis 6–11. The first five chapters focus on the Adam and his sons (Cain, Abel, Seth); the next six focus on Noah and his sons (Shem, Ham, Japheth).

The Primeval History	
Gen 1–5	Adam and Sons
Gen 6–11	Noah and Sons

Likewise, the second half of the book falls into two major parts. Genesis 12–36 gives the accounts of the lives of the three patriarchs, Abraham, Isaac, and Jacob. While the focus shifts from father to son over the course of the narrative, the lives of the fathers obviously overlap with those of their sons, making it difficult to observe clean divisions of the narrative. However, Genesis 37–50, often called

The Patriarchal History	
Genesis 12–36	The History of the Three Patriarchs
Genesis 37–50	The History of Twelve Sons of Jacob

the *Joseph Cycle*, exhibits a strong literary unity and is focused on the life of Joseph, Jacob's favored son, with his eleven brothers as an important supporting cast. These chapters describe fundamental dynamics in the relationships between the twelve sons of Jacob that later would be reflected in the relationships of the twelve tribes throughout Israel's history. They also explain pivotal events that

The *Toledoth* ("Generations") Structure of Genesis		
1	2:4	"These are the generations of the heavens and the earth" (Followed by the Adam Cycle)
2	5:1	"This is the book of the generations of Adam" (Part of a transition to the Noah Cycle)
3	6:9	"These are the generations of Noah" (Followed by the Noah Cycle: Flood, Fall, Aftermath)
4	10:1	"These are the generations of the sons of Noah" (Part of a transition to the Abraham Cycle)
5	11:10	"These are the descendants of Shem" (Also transitioning to the Abraham Cycle)
6	11:27	"These are the descendants of Terah" (Followed by the Abraham Cycle)
7	25:12	"These are the descendants of Ishmael" (A transition to the Jacob Cycle)
8	25:19	"These are the descendants of Isaac" (Followed by the Jacob Cycle)
9	36:19	"These are the descendants of Esau" (A transition to the Joseph Cycle)
10	37:2	"This is the history of the family of Jacob" (Followed by the Joseph Cycle)

lead to the sojourn in Egypt, an experience that permanently shaped the character of the people of Israel.

There are other legitimate ways to understand the literary structure of the book. When analyzed formally, it appears the sacred author has employed genealogical formulas to mark what he considered key divisions of his text. The word for "generations" or "genealogy" in Hebrew is *toledoth*, but it has a much broader range of meaning, including "history", "origin", "narrative", and related concepts. The stock phrase "these are generations of" (Hebrew *'elleh toledoth*) or a variation thereof is used at the junctures between blocks of narrative called "cycles" that largely follow one of five dominant figures in the book: Adam, Noah, Abraham, Jacob, and Joseph (see table). Thus, when we combine a *formal* analysis of the book with a *material* analysis of its content, we discover that Genesis appears to have been compiled as five major cycles, each distinguished—and, at the same time, joined—by *toledoth* formulas. This five-cycle structural analysis is presented in the following table and will be used as the basis for our comments on Genesis in this chapter and the next.

The Structure of Genesis: The Five Cycles Marked by *Toledoth* Formulae		
The Adam Cycle	Gen 1:1—6:8	Includes a prologue (1:1—2:4a); begins in earnest after the *toledoth* of the heavens and the earth (2:4a); joined to the Noah Cycle by the *toledoth* of Adam (chap. 5) plus a brief narrative of mankind's sin (6:1–8)
The Noah Cycle	Gen 6:9—11:26	Begins with the *toledoth* of Noah (6:9); connected to the following Abraham Cycle by the *toledoth* of his son Shem (11:10–26)
The Abraham Cycle	Gen 11:27—25:18	Begins with the *toledoth* of Abraham's father Terah; ends with the account of Abraham's death (25:7–11) and connected to the following Jacob Cycle by the *toledoth* of his son Ishmael (25:12–18)
The Jacob Cycle	Gen 25:19—36:43	Begins with the *toledoth* of Jacob's father, Isaac (25:19), and the account of Jacob's birth (25:20–26); ends with the death of his father, Isaac (35:27–29), and connected with the following Joseph Cycle by the *toledoth* of his brother Esau (chap. 36)
The Joseph Cycle	Gen 37–50	Begins with the *toledoth* of Joseph's father, Jacob (37:1–2); ends with Joseph's own death (50:22–26)

Overview of Genesis 1–11

The Creation of the Heavens and the Earth (Genesis 1)

The book of Genesis begins with a grand prologue giving the account of the creation of the heavens and the earth within the framework of six days. This magnificent narrative, called the *Hexaemeron* ("Six Days") by the Church Fathers, is one of the finest and most influential pieces of world literature and has lost none

---

"In the Beginning?" (Gen 1:1)

The first verse of the Bible is usually translated: "In the beginning, God created the heavens and the earth." However, the grammar of Genesis 1:1 is somewhat unusual. The word "beginning" lacks the article, so the Hebrew is literally "In beginning". The word is also not in the expected grammatical case for its position in the sentence. For this reason, some scholars in recent years have advocated taking Genesis 1:1 as a subordinate clause introducing Genesis 1:2, giving the following in English: "When God began to create the heavens and the earth, the earth was formless." However, while this alternative translation solves some grammatical problems in v. 1, it creates others in vv. 2–3 by producing a sentence without a finite verb in the proper form. The traditional translation is supported by the vocalization and punctuation of the standard Jewish text of Scripture, the Masoretic Text, as well as every ancient translation (the Vulgate, Septuagint, Syriac Peshitta, and others). It is also reflected in the adaptations of the wording of Genesis found in non-canonical literature (the *Book of Jubilees*) and the Gospel of John, which imitates Genesis with "In the beginning was the Word", not "When God began to create, there was the Word." Therefore, although Genesis 1:1 displays some grammatical irregularity, there is no evidence that its meaning was in doubt in antiquity.

---

of its dignified beauty to the passing of the years, as anyone who has witnessed it read well during the Easter Vigil can attest.

People naturally want to know how the six days of creation are to be understood in light of the claims of modern science, which views the origin of the universe as the matter of vast ages of time and an evolutionary process (see sidebar on p. 100). However, scientific concerns—at least as we moderns understand science—are not the primary interest of the sacred author. It is best to read the narrative in light of other ancient *cosmogonies* (accounts of the origin of the cosmos) and according to its own literary structure. When we do so, it becomes apparent that the sacred author has composed an elegantly balanced *temple-building* account that points to the *liturgical orientation of creation*.

The opening line of Genesis reads, according to the Hebrew Masoretic Text and all ancient versions: "In the beginning God created the heavens and the earth" (Gen 1:1). The Hebrew language has no exact word for "cosmos" or "universe". "The heavens and the earth" expresses the same concept by means of a *merism*—a figure of speech by which the parts are used to refer to the whole. (Interestingly, in all of ancient Near Eastern literature, the merism of "heavens and earth" as a reference to the cosmos finds a parallel only in ancient Egyptian texts.) This grand opening line serves as a summary statement and suggests the calling into existence of the cosmos without the presence of any preexisting substance. Indeed, the Hebrew word *bara'*, "to create" (Gen 1:1), is only ever used in the Bible with God as its subject and never with an accusative of material indicating a substance from which he created. However, the newly existent creation is not called into existence in a finished state; the sacred author notes that it was "without form and void" (Gen 1:2). In the Hebrew language, "without form and void" is an onomatopoeic phrase, *tohu wabohu* ("formless and empty"). These two privations—lack of form and lack of content—will be addressed systematically in the succession of six days.

In the first sequence of three days, God creates the forms of day and night (time), sky and seas (spaces), dry land and vegetation (habitat). Over the following three days, he populates these three *realms* with appropriate *rulers*: the sun, moon, and stars (markers of time); the birds and fish (who traverse the great spaces); animals (who dominate the land); and finally man (who rules over all). This process can be diagrammed as follows:

The Six Days of Creation as Temple-Building

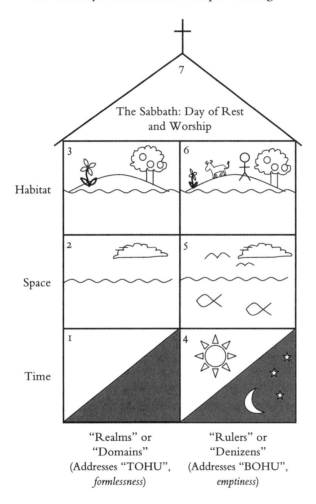

Within this overarching framework, the creation of man is special. The narrative slows, and more is said about man than about anything else God has made. Man is said, first of all, to be made in the *"image"* and *"likeness"* of God (Gen 1:26). What does it mean to be in the "image" and "likeness"? Scholars have rightly pointed out that "images" (Hebrew *tzelamim*) of the emperors of the ancient Near East used to be placed throughout their realms to represent their authority. So the sacred author is suggesting that man is the representative of God's royal rule on earth and the bearer of God's authority. He is the divine vice-regent.

On the other hand, if we look ahead briefly in Genesis for insight, we read, "(Adam) became the father of a son *in his own likeness, after his image*" (Gen 5:3). Taking this knowledge back to Genesis 1, we realize that "image" and "likeness" is also the implicit language of *sonship*. Adam is, in some sense, created as the *son of God*—a fact that will eventually be explicitly asserted in the New Testament (Lk 3:38). But in what sense is he a son? Antiquity knew two kinds of sonship: natural and adoptive. Is Adam the natural son of God? Apparently not, because, in sharp contrast to other ancient Near Eastern creation myths, there is no notion of man arising from some kind of sexual process among the gods or of being birthed from a goddess. Adam is not, therefore, a son of God in any natural sense: instead, he is a creature. Therefore, the sonship of Adam, described as "image" and "likeness", can only be *adoptive* sonship. Significantly, in antiquity, adoptive sonship was established by means of a *covenant*. This is one of many reasons why, although the term "covenant" (Hebrew *berith*) is not explicitly used in Genesis 1–2, there are good reasons to suggest that an original covenant between God and Adam is implied by the creation narrative (see excursus on p. 104).

As the adopted son of God, Adam is blessed: "Be fruitful and multiply!" (Gen 1:28). He is also commissioned explicitly with vice-royal activity: "Fill the earth and *subdue* [Hebrew *kavash*] it; and *have dominion* [Hebrew *radah*] over the fish of the sea" (Gen 1:28). When these Hebrew words are compared with the same expressions used elsewhere to refer to the kingship of David and that of Solomon (2 Sam 8:11; 1 Kings 4:24), there are good reasons to conclude that Adam is being established as *the first visible king over creation*, who acts as representative of the invisible divine King (cf. Ps 8). This royal status and original blessing of Adam will continue to be an important theme throughout Genesis. Indeed, it is precisely this blessing and status that will be transmitted through the patriarchs and ultimately to Israel.

While the creation of man is dramatic, it is not the climax of the account of creation in Genesis 1. All things culminate on the seventh day, the *Sabbath*: the day of divine "rest", the fundamental day of worship in Israel's later liturgical calendar. This suggests all creation was ordered to the divine rest and worship of the Sabbath. Indeed, understood against the ancient Near Eastern background in which the cosmos was understood as a great temple and earthly temples were often built as a representation of the cosmos, the seven days of creation can be perceived as a temple-building account. The clear parallels between the creation of the cosmos in Genesis 1 and the building of the Tabernacle (Ex 35–40) and the Temple (1 Kings 6–8) will be explored later.

Genesis and Ancient Near Eastern Cosmogonies

The full significance of the Genesis 1 creation account comes into fuller relief when contrasted with other ancient Near Eastern accounts of the origin of the world, known as *cosmogonies*.

In one Mesopotamian cosmogony, the *Enuma Elish*, the creation of the world is the unintended consequence of a battle among the gods. Marduk, patron god of Babylon, slays Tiamat, the goddess of the depths of the sea, and forms

Source: commons.wikimedia.org

Babylonian God Marduk Slaying the Chaos Demon Tiamat in the Process of Creation

the world from her dead corpse. Later, Tiamat's husband, Kingu, is also slain, and human beings are formed from his blood, as slaves of the gods, to perform menial tasks so the gods may take their ease.

We have fewer cosmogonies from ancient Egypt, but the Egyptians did leave an abundance of iconography representing their understanding of the universe. In this illustration, for example, the female sky god Nut is seen arched over the male earth god Geb. The sun-god, Amon-Rē (or Amun-Rā), is seen ascending Nut's body in the east in his ship and also descending in the west. Other gods are represented performing supportive tasks. For the ancient Egyptian, the entire cosmos was deified: every aspect of the natural realm was divine, a god or goddess.

The contrast with the biblical account is easy to see. In Genesis, God creates without conflict with any competing gods. In peace and with supreme authority, he speaks, and the elements of the cosmos come into existence. The various aspects of the visible world—earth, sea, sky, sun—are not divine, but obedient creatures of God, each made for its own proper purpose or function. Mankind, too, is a creature, not a piece of dead divinity, created not as a slave but as an adopted son and vice-regent. The concept of

Source: commons.wikimedia.org

The Egyptian "Theological" view of the cosmos: Detail from a papyrus image of Geb and Nut and Ra's divine boat from the Third Intermediate Period (ca. 500 B.C.E.)

God, man, and their relationship one to the other is inherently more positive and optimistic in the biblical account than in those of Israel's neighbors.

The Creation of Adam and Eve (Genesis 2)

Genesis 2:4a says, "These are the generations of the heavens and the earth when they were created." Most English Bibles now mark this verse as the beginning of a new unit, but the unit that follows describes the creation, not of the heavens and earth, but of man and his domestic environment. Accordingly, while

---

Genesis, Creation, and Evolution

It is natural to seek to understand the relationship between the creation accounts and modern science.

On the one hand, the *Catechism of the Catholic Church* describes Scripture as presenting "the work of the Creator symbolically as a succession of six days of divine 'work,' concluded by the 'rest' of the seventh day" (*CCC* 337), as expressing the "corporeal and spiritual" nature of the human person in "symbolic language" (*CCC* 362).

At the same time, the Catechism also teaches that "all of nature" and "all human history are rooted in this primordial event" of creation (*CCC* 338) and that the account of the Fall "uses figurative language, but affirms a primeval event, a deed that took place *at the beginning of the history of man*" (*CCC* 390).

In other words, the Church recognizes that the creation accounts use figurative or symbolic language but describe real events that happened in history. Therefore, not all theories of origins may be compatible with scriptural teaching on creation. Certain fundamental parameters of interpretation were laid down in the encyclical *Humani Generis* (1950) of Pius XII (nos. 35–37). Theories that claim, for example, that science *proves* that matter, chance, and necessity *alone* (apart from divine providence) are sufficient explanation for all reality, including the human soul, are not compatible with Scripture and the Church's faith. Certain truths about origins are non-negotiables, including

1. initial creation from nothing (*ex nihilo*) (*CCC* 327);
2. the infusion of a spiritual soul into the first man, thus differentiating him from the animals (*CCC* 362–66);
3. a historical first human couple, from which all people are descended (i.e., not polygenism) (*CCC* 360);
4. the state of original holiness, constituted by "harmony between the first couple and all creation" as well as a condition in which "man would not have to suffer or die" (*CCC* 376);
5. a historical fall of the first human couple—a decision of our first parents to reject God (*CCC* 389–90);
6. the transmission of original sin "*by propagation* to all mankind" from the first man and woman (*CCC* 404 [emphasis added]).

Apart from these and any related teachings that are *de fide*, the Church permits wide discussion on the issue of origins but urges that the discussion be balanced.

Genesis 2:4a certainly marks a literary "seam" or "joint", it probably functions more as a conclusion of the seven-day account of Genesis 1.

The account that begins in Genesis 2:4b is often called "Another Account of Creation", "The Second Creation Story", or a similar title. Modern source criticism identifies it as the "Yahwistic" creation account (J), as opposed to the "Priestly" account of Genesis 1:1–2:3 (P). The differences between the accounts could be explained as the result of different sources, but they can also be explained as the result of a shift in perspective by the sacred author. In any event, the interpreter must attempt to understand the relationship of the two accounts as we have them now, joined together. Genesis 1 and 2 should be viewed, not as competing, but as complementary scenes. Just as many movies begin with a "panoramic" shot that scans the horizon in order to establish the mood and the environment, followed by a "close-up" on the main character of the story, so Genesis 1:1—2:4a functions as a *panorama* or overview of the creation of the entire cosmos, while Genesis 2:4b–25 functions as a *close-up*, focusing the reader's attention on the creation of man and woman in the Garden of Eden.

The account begins, "*In the day* that the LORD God made the earth and the heavens" (Gen 2:4b). The phrase "in the day" is a Hebrew idiom meaning simply "when" and has no specific reference to a single day. The sacred author continues by noting the absence of cultivated plants ("plant *of the field* . . . herb *of the field*") because agriculture had not yet started ("there was no man to till the ground") (Gen 2:5 [author's trans.]).[1] This forms an *inclusio* that functions as a literary "bookend" with the conclusion of chapter 3, when Adam will be "sent . . . forth . . . to till the ground from which he was taken" (Gen 3:23).

Genesis 2–3 forms a strong literary unit, unified by many themes, one of which is *agriculture* (see following table).

The Beginnings of Agriculture	
An Important Theme in Genesis 2–3	
2:5	Absence of "farmers" of cultivated plants in the beginning
2:8	God "plants" a garden
2:9	God makes *domestic* trees ("good for food") to grow
2:10	Rivers useful for irrigation flow from Eden
2:15	Adam placed in garden to "till" and "keep" it; Adam is first "gardener" or "farmer"
2:19	God makes *domestic* animals: animals that are potential "helpers" for Adam
3:17–19	Adam's "farming" is cursed—his relationship with the soil will be forever frustrating
3:23	Adam sent out to "till the soil", i.e., to farm
The Theme Continues through Genesis	
4:2	Cain follows in Adam's footsteps as a farmer ("tiller of the ground")
4:12	Cain's relationship to the soil also cursed
9:20	Noah also begins to farm (to be a "tiller of the soil")

Whereas the creation of Adam in Genesis 1 emphasized God's *transcendence*, in Genesis 2 the emphasis is on God's *immanence* or closeness to humanity. "The LORD God formed man [Hebrew *ādām*] of dust from the ground [Hebrew *'adāmāh*], and breathed into his nostrils the breath of life; and man became a living soul" (Gen 2:7). The Hebrew for "formed" is the word *yātzar*, which is commonly used of pottery and the work of a potter, giving rise to the common image in the Scriptures and tradition of God as a potter forming Adam from the clay of the earth.

---

[1] See Umberto Cassuto, *A Commentary on the Book of Genesis, Part One: From Adam to Noah*, trans. Israel Abrahams (Jerusalem: Magness, 1961), 101–3.

"And the LORD God planted a garden in Eden, in the east; and there he put the man whom he had formed" (Gen 2:8). Eden has an important but frequently overlooked function in the narrative. Eden is not simply synonymous with the "garden" (Greek *paradeisos*, from which we get the English word "paradise") planted by God for Adam. Eden is described as a mountain or mountaintop— this can be deduced from the fact that all four primary rivers of the earth (from an Israelite perspective) flow out *from* Eden. That would make Eden the highest point of the known world, and this accords with Ezekiel's reference to Eden as "the mountain of God" (Ezek 28:14, 16) and a great deal of ancient Near Eastern iconography and textual evidence for the belief in a primordial divine garden on the top of the "cosmic mountain" or central mountain of the world.[2]

The Creation of Plants and Animals

In Genesis 1, the plants and animals are created before man; in Genesis 2, they appear to be created after man. How is this to be understood? First of all, one should recognize the *agricultural* focus of Genesis 2–3 (see table above). Genesis 2 is concerned with domestic plants and animals, not all living things *per se*. Genesis 2:15 notes the absence of cultivated plants, not all vegetation. Likewise, the animals created and brought to Adam (2:18–20) appear to be domestic animals, because their purpose is to be a "help" to him. Dogs and horses are potential "helpers"; sharks and vultures are not. Secondly, one should understand the ancient Near Eastern symbolic genre of these accounts, which emphasizes the nature of things over strict chronology. An example of this may be seen in the Egyptian icon of the cosmos (given above). Notice that the sun (= the god Amon-Rē) is depicted both rising in the east and setting in the west and, indeed, shining at high noon in the middle! Where is the sun at the time this picture was "taken"? The ancient artist was not portraying chronology but what he viewed as the essences of the elements of the natural world: namely, that they were gods in relationship with one another. In a certain sense, Genesis 2 is an "iconographic" text as well. The loose chronology is facilitated by the fact that, strictly speaking, the Hebrew language does not have tenses, and the perception of tense is often simply derived from the context. If the ancient reader even noticed the difference in order concerning the animals between Genesis 1 and 2, he could have resolved it by taking the action of 2:19 in a past perfect sense: "So out of the ground the Lord God *had formed* every beast."[a]

[a] See Umberto Cassuto, *The Documentary Hypothesis and the Composition of the Pentateuch* (1961; repr., Jerusalem and New York: Shalem Press, 2006), 87–94.

At the same time, there are clear signs that point to Eden and its garden as the original sanctuary or "temple" of God. First of all, there is a general ancient Near Eastern association between temples and the primordial cosmic mountain. Temples in many parts of the ancient world were built in part to represent the original "mountain of God". Secondly, the sacred author notes the presence near Eden of gold as well as precious stones, such as "onyx" and "bdellium" (Gen 2:12). These materials were necessary for the decoration and ornamentation of temples: we will see them in large quantities in the Tabernacle and Temple. Onyx in particular was a "sacred stone" much used for liturgical vessels and

---

[2] G. K. Beale, *The Temple and the Church's Mission: A Biblical Theology of the Dwelling Place of God*, New Studies in Biblical Theology 17 (Downers Grove, Ill.: InterVarsity Press, 2004), 93, 149.

vestments. The water flowing out of Eden is also an image associated elsewhere with the Temple mount (see Ezek 47:1–12). Notice also the presence of angelic beings known as *cherubim* by the garden (Gen 3:24). Images of cherubim also protect the later Tabernacle (Ex 25:18–20; 26:1) and Temple (1 Kings 6:23–29). Finally, the garden has only one east-facing entrance (Gen 3:24), something also true of the eastward-facing Tabernacle as well as the Temple in Jerusalem. Significantly, the temple nature of Eden was recognized in ancient Jewish interpretation, as in the *Book of Jubilees*, which portrays Adam and Eve following the purity regulations appropriate for the Temple when they are in Eden (see *Jubilees* 3:8–14).

"The LORD God took the man and put him in the garden of Eden to *till it* and to *keep it*" (Gen 2:15). Adam's mission in the garden, to "till" and to "keep", has a double meaning. In Hebrew, the words are literally "work" (*'ābad*) and "guard" (*shāmar*). On one level, they refer to horticultural duties: Adam is to tend the garden and make it grow. On the other hand, this combination of verbs—"work" and "guard"—is not used elsewhere in the Pentateuch until the same two words are found in a description of the duties of the Levitical priests in the Tabernacle (Num 3:7–8; 8:26; 18:7). Thus the second level of meaning is that Genesis is also depicting Adam as a *priestly* figure, commissioned to serve in Eden, the primordial garden-sanctuary.

As discussed in the excursus, it is likely that the sacred author viewed Adam as the mediator of a covenant between God and creation. Covenants typically included an element of law that governed the covenant relationship, accompanied by sanctions: blessings for covenant fidelity and curses for covenant infidelity. In this vein, the blessings of the covenant relationship were already bestowed in Genesis 1:28–29. In Genesis 2:16–17, the sacred author emphasizes the simplicity of the initial covenant with mankind. There is only one prohibition: "Of the tree of the knowledge of good and evil you shall not eat" and one sanction: "in the day that you eat of it, you shall die" (Gen 2:17).

Adam's first task is to name the animals (Gen 2:18–20), a duty that rightfully belongs to God the Creator but is deputed to Adam as vice-regent. This activity has Adam speaking for the first time and, indeed, speaking on behalf of God, because God recognizes and confirms whatever Adam, his vice-regent and priest, says: "Whatever the man called every living creature, that was its name" (Gen 2:19). Thus, Adam is the first prophet.

However, none of the animals are "fit" for Adam, so the story builds toward its climactic moment. Adam is put into a deep sleep, and God takes from his flesh a "rib"—literally, one of his "sides" (Hebrew *tzela'*) (Gen 2:21)—and from Adam's "side" he "builds" (Hebrew *bānah*) a woman and brings her to the awakened man. At this point we have the first recorded words of Adam in Scripture and also the first lyrical poetry: "Bone of my bones and flesh of my flesh; she shall be called Woman [Hebrew *'ishāh*] because she was taken out of Man [Hebrew *'ish*]" (Gen 2:23). The sacred author marks this climactic moment, the revelation of the woman-bride, with a literary flourish. Significantly, as scholars have noted, "bone of my bones and flesh of my flesh" is covenant-making language, repeated elsewhere in the Old Testament in the context of covenant-making between David and Israel (2 Sam 5:1). It is not so

---

Is There a Covenant with Adam?

The presence of a covenant with Adam can be debated. Although the Jewish and Christian traditions have affirmed the existence of such a covenant, the actual word *berith*, "covenant", is lacking in Genesis 1–3. Nonetheless, since ancient times, the book was interpreted as *implying* a covenant, and the following considerations lead us to support this conclusion:

1. Not all covenant texts use the word "covenant" (Hebrew *berith*). Most scholars recognize 2 Samuel 7:4–17 as the fundamental description of the Davidic covenant, but the word *berith* is absent (compare Ps 89).

2. Elsewhere in the Pentateuch, the Sabbath is understood as the "sign" of God's "covenant" (Ex 31:16–1). But the Sabbath is established, not at Sinai, but at creation. This suggests that already from creation, a covenant is in place.

3. One of the earliest of the prophets, Hosea, compares Israel and Adam, both sons of God, in terms of their breach of covenant fidelity: "But they, like Adam, transgressed the covenant" (Hos 6:7, Masoretic Text). Likewise Sirach, in an obvious reference to Genesis 2:17, says, "The covenant [Greek *diathēkē*] from of old is, 'You must surely die!'" (Sir 14:17).

4. As mentioned above, the creation narratives understand Adam as a son of God, but not a natural son, the only alternative to which is covenant sonship (cf. Gen 1:26; 5:3).

5. As mentioned above, the narratives also understand Adam as God's vice-regent. But vice-regents in the ancient Near East, as is apparent from numerous extant treaty texts, were regarded as the covenant "sons" of their father the emperor, or "great king".

6. When the covenant is established with Noah (Gen 8:20–9:17), the language used echoes the creation narrative (Gen 1:26–30). The verb employed (Hebrew *heqîm*) usually denotes confirmation or renewal rather than initiation (Hebrew *karat*), suggesting that the covenant with Noah is a *renewal* of a previously existing covenant with Adam.

7. In the living tradition, the presence of an Adamic or original covenant with man is affirmed by the Church Father Irenaeus (*Against Heresies* 3.11.8), Pope John Paul II (*Redemptor Hominis*, no. 7), and the *Catechism of the Catholic Church*, which states that God manifested himself to "our first parents" and "offered them his covenant" (*CCC* 70). Likewise, liturgical texts recognize this: "With everlasting love you renewed with your servant the covenant you made with Adam" (*Roman Ritual*, no. 72).

8. Even critical scholars like Julius Wellhausen have recognized that the author of Genesis intends to portray Adam in a covenant relationship.

Even if one were to deny the existence of a covenant with Adam, there are sound reasons for understanding Adam to be in a *filial relationship* with God that forms the model or prototype of subsequent divine-human covenants.

---

much a simple observation as a *declaration of kinship*: Adam is formally declaring Eve to be his wife and, hence, his family. The sacred author proceeds to an explanation of marriage: "Therefore a man leaves his father and his mother and clings to his wife, and they become one flesh" (Gen 2:24).

The sacred author has joined the accounts of Genesis 1 and 2, thereby inviting us to read them together. Accordingly, it is possible to view Adam as being depicted as created on the sixth day, put into a sleep, and awaking on the seventh to be greeted by his bride. In such a way, the seventh or Sabbath day becomes a climactic event that marks the culmination of the creation narrative. In sacred time (the Sabbath, the "sign" of the covenant) and sacred space (Eden), the priestly man (Adam) establishes the sacred covenant of marriage with his bride

(Eve). Thus we find a convergence of covenantal, nuptial, and liturgical themes at the climax of the combined creation accounts.

The Fall of Adam and Eve (Genesis 3)

With Genesis 3, we turn to what is perhaps one of the momentous chapters in the entire Old Testament: the account of the Fall. With this narrative, Genesis reveals to us the sin that lay at the origins of mankind and, therefore, the root cause of all moral evils with which human history has been inundated. This chapter is tightly integrated with the previous account of the creation of Adam and Eve, in such a way that most of the verses in Genesis 3 reflect one or more verses of Genesis 2 and the information contained there.

A general theme of chapter 3 is the *inversion of norms*. Everything is turned upside down. In the divinely established order in Genesis 1–2, Adam, God's vice-regent, is to obey God. He is to communicate God's will to Eve, his spouse, and together they are to rule over the animals. In the course of Genesis 3, the animal (the serpent) is going to rule over Eve, Eve is going to communicate the animal's will to Adam, and together all three will defy God.

The account begins by focusing on the figure of *the serpent*, which is described as being "more subtle than any other wild creature that the LORD God had made" (Gen 3:1). How should we interpret this figure? With regard to the language of the text, the word "serpent" (Hebrew *nāhāsh*) has a wide range of meaning. On the one hand, it can refer to the animal we know as a "serpent" or "viper", that "bites ... horse's heels" (Gen 49:17). On the other hand, the same Hebrew word is also used to describe the great "dragon" known as "Leviathan the twisting serpent" (Is 27:1), who was considered the embodiment of evil and chaos (cf. Amos 9:3). In either case, serpents almost always bear negative connotations in Scripture (perhaps in part because the Hebrew verb form spelled with the same consonants, *nāhash*, means "sorcery", "divination"). In Egyptian mythology, the sun-god (Rā or Rē) descended into the west each evening and did battle until dawn with the chaos-serpent Apep (Greek *Apophis*), the chief demon or malevolent deity in Egyptian religion, the embodiment of evil and chaos.[3] Thus, the identification of the serpent as the symbol of the chief personification of evil predates the composition of the Hebrew Scriptures by centuries. With this ancient Near Eastern background in mind, it is easy to understand how eventually, by the time we reach the New Testament period, the creature in Genesis 3 is explicitly identified as "that ancient serpent, who is called the Devil and Satan, the deceiver of the whole world" (Rev 12:9). As one of the "wild creatures" that God had made (Gen 3:1), despite all the malevolence and power that the "serpent" would eventually display in human history, he was and is not divine, but a created being ultimately subject to God's will.

The serpent, whose motivation is not explained, begins his assault on the human pair by *casting doubt on the truth of God's word*: "Did God say, 'You shall

---

[3] Richard E. Averbeck, "Ancient Near Eastern Mythography as It Relates to Historiography in the Hebrew Bible: Genesis 3 and the Cosmic Battle", in *The Future of Biblical Archeology: Reassessing Methodologies and Assumptions*, ed. James K. Hoffmeier and Alan Millard (Grand Rapids, Mich.: Eerdmans, 2004), 328–56.

not eat of any tree of the garden'?" (Gen 3:1). After Eve's response, he proceeds to outright denial of the veracity of God's warning, in effect calling God a liar: "You will not die" (Gen 3:4). He then establishes what we might call a "herme-neutic of suspicion" toward the divine command by suggesting that God's will for Adam and Eve—which up till now they have had every reason to believe was benevolent—is in fact deceptive, hypocritical, and aimed at suppressing the true realization of Adam and Eve's potential: namely, divinity itself. "For God knows that when you eat of it your eyes will be opened, and you will be like God"—or "like gods"; the Hebrew 'elohim can be translated either way—"knowing good and evil" (Gen 3:5).

What is the meaning of the "knowledge of good and evil" upon which everything in the account hangs? At least three interpretations are possible, none of which are mutually exclusive. The expression may refer to (1) the awaken-ing of *moral knowledge*—that is, the awakening of the consciences of Adam and Eve; (2) the gift of *supernatural knowledge*, since "good and evil" may be taken as a merism for "all knowledge", in the sense of "to know (everything from) good (to) evil"—that is, "from the best to the worst, from high to low, from A to Z"; and (3) the *self-determination* of what constitutes "good and evil". This would refer to the ability for Adam and Eve to decide, apart from God's word, what is good and what is evil in the moral order, since to "know" sometimes connotes to "decide" or "determine" elsewhere in the Pentateuch (Ex 33:5; cf. *CCC* 1850).

With this in mind, the question remains: Why do Adam and Eve choose to eat of the fruit of the tree? What are the *reasons for the Fall*? Although the point is often overlooked by readers of Genesis, it is important to emphasize that the text explicitly states *why* they break God's command, listing *three* specific motives. After listening to the words of the serpent, Eve observes that the tree was "good for food", a "delight to the eyes", and "desired to make one wise" (Gen 3:6). In its immediate context, the first two of these descriptions harks back to the description of all the trees in Eden, which God had made "pleasant to the sight" and "good for food"—including the "tree of life" (Gen 2:9). Pre-sumably this allusion is meant to point out the insufficiency of these motives; Adam and Eve need not have broken God's command in order to satisfy the first two desires listed. Likewise, the power of the fruit "to make one wise" seems to allude directly to the desire to be "like God, knowing good and evil" (Gen 3:5)—that is, the desire for some form of *divinization* apart from commu-nion with God.

It is worth noting here that although Genesis emphasizes Eve's role initiating the act of eating, she is not alone. According to Genesis, "She took of its fruit and ate; and she also gave some to her husband *who was with her* and he ate" (Gen 3:6 [author's trans.]). Many translations omit the Hebrew phrase "who was with her" (Hebrew *'immāh*), but the phrase is important, emphasizing that Adam is present for this whole dialogue yet has been strangely and culpably silent and passive. He has not performed his priestly duty of "guarding" (Hebrew *shāmar*) the garden from threats to its sanctity. Furthermore, together with Eve, he breaks the one prohibition of their covenant relationship to God. In this sense, the Fall is truly that of both Adam and Eve.

With the account of the Fall out of the way, Genesis quickly turns to the immediate *effects* of Adam and Eve's transgression: "Then the eyes of both were opened, and they knew that they were naked" (Gen 3:7). The result is darkly humorous, in light of the grandiose promises from the serpent of supernatural knowledge. After the Fall, the only particular piece of knowledge Adam and Eve seem to gain from their Promethean effort is ... that of their own nakedness! The man and woman's quest for God-like power and omniscience ultimately leads only to the revelation of their weakness and vulnerability. Their response, to sew fig-leaf garments, is clearly inadequate, even pathetic, illustrating the fact that they have gotten themselves into a predicament that is beyond their meager resources to resolve.

In the midst of this broken covenant situation, a disordered *fear of God* now enters in. In the wake of the Fall, the Lord has to pursue the human couple, who hide from him: "Where are you? ... Have you eaten of the tree?" (Gen 3:9, 11). Adam's response: "The woman whom *you* gave to be with me, *she* gave me fruit of the tree" (Gen 3:12), is a remarkably efficient evasive maneuver, simultaneously blaming both his wife and God, who gave her to him. Eve is somewhat less evasive, declaring: "The serpent beguiled me, and I ate" (Gen 3:13). However, neither she nor Adam breathes one word of repentance for the transgression. The narrative does not speculate about what would have been the result had either of them repented. Instead, the result of covenant breaking, here and throughout Scripture, is the experience of covenant punishments (Gen 3:14–19), which are distinctively adapted to the roles and culpability of each of the three parties. Even in the midst of the application of these curses, we may note three signs of God's mercy on Adam and Eve.

First and foremost, *before God ever pronounces a word of punishment toward the man and woman, he promises the eventual triumph over the serpent by the "seed" of the*

Who Will Crush the Serpent's Head?

Most modern English translations of Genesis 3:15 read, "*He* shall crush your head", referring to the "seed of the Woman", understood to be Jesus Christ. However, the Douay-Rheims and Vulgate read, "*She* shall crush your head", which has always been understood as a reference to the Blessed Virgin. This has often been depicted in iconography. The difficulty probably lies in the fact that the Hebrew male and female pronouns are written similarly and easily confused: St. Jerome's Hebrew text evidently had a feminine pronoun in this place. The stronger linguistic case, however, can be made for an original masculine pronoun. Theologically, there is no difficulty, since it is true that both the *seed* (Jesus Christ) and the *woman* (the Virgin Mary) crush the head of the serpent: the *woman* crushes the head *by means of* her seed.

"Crush", "Bruise", "Strike at"?

Will the serpent's head be "crushed" (Douay-Rheims) or "bruised" (RSVCE) or "struck" (NAB)? The Hebrew verb *shûph* is very rare, occurring elsewhere only in Psalm 139:11 and Job 9:17. Its use in Genesis 3:15 is theologically controversial because of the significance of the verse, and translations vary widely. However, in the relatively uncontroversial passage Job 9:17, almost all English versions translate "crush" or "break". Therefore, the traditional translation "crush" in Genesis 3:15 (following the Latin Vulgate) is justified.

woman. To the serpent, God declares: "I will put enmity between you and the woman, and between your seed and her seed; he shall bruise (Hebrew *shûph*) your head, and you shall bruise (Hebrew *shûph*) his heel" (Gen 3:15). This remarkable verse, which was regarded as a prophecy of the Messiah in ancient Jewish tradition[4] and later referred to as the *Protoevangelium* ("first gospel") in Christian tradition, suggests hope for mankind when the "seed" will mortally wound the *nāhāsh*, understood against the ancient Near Eastern context as an embodiment of evil. It is a mysterious verse, since, in antiquity, women were not considered to have "seed" (Hebrew *zerah*); thus, the phrase "seed of the woman" is exceptional.

Second, although the serpent is cursed (Gen 3:14), *neither the woman nor the man is said to be accursed.* Instead, with respect to the man, it is the "ground" that is "cursed ... because of you" (Gen 3:17). Nevertheless, it is true that the man and the woman are both made to feel the *effects* of the divine curse, though God does not curse them directly. This and the obvious fact that they are not put to death, as Genesis 2:17 ("in the day that you eat of it you shall die") implied they would be, are clear literary pointers to an expression of divine mercy. In contrast to the widespread and erroneous depiction of the "God of the Old Testament" as unforgiving and vengeful, in the very first pages of Genesis, the Lord is merciful, mitigating the punishment deserved by the human pair.

Third and finally, *although suffering and death make their entrance into human history, God does not abandon Adam and Eve.* To be sure, as a result of the Fall, both the woman and the man will experience suffering. On the one hand, the woman's "pain in childbearing" will be exceedingly great, and she will experience both desire and domination in her relationship with her husband (Gen 3:16). On the other hand, the man will experience fruitless toil in trying to grow food from the ground that has been cursed (Gen 3:17–18). Remarkably, both of these effects of the Fall are ordered toward family life: the woman will suffer in her body and her relationship with her husband in order to give life to her offspring, and the man will suffer in his labor in order to give life to his family by feeding them. Although directed to the man alone, the final effect of breaking the covenant is death: "you are dust, and to dust you shall return" (Gen 3:19). Nevertheless, in the midst of these pronouncements, it is surely significant that the Lord is solicitous for Adam and Eve's welfare, replacing their inadequate leaf garments with "garments of skins" (Gen 3:21). This verse implicitly depicts the Lord as killing an animal on behalf of the man and woman and, as such, constitutes the very first case in the Hebrew Scriptures of *animal sacrifice* for sin. From this point of view, God takes the role of acting as priest (something Adam was supposed to do) and supplying the victim—a role that, as we will see, will prove central to the liturgy throughout the rest of the Old Testament. Although Adam and Eve do not experience physical death immediately, another life is offered on their behalf, in order to clothe them and cover the "nakedness" they have experienced as a result of their transgression (cf. Gen 3:7).

---

4 Joseph Klausner, *The Messianic Idea in Israel*, trans. W. F. Stinespring (London: George Allen & Unwin, 1956), 26, citing *Targum Pseudo-Jonathan* on Gen 3:15 and *Targum Neofiti* 1 on Gen 3:15.

At the conclusion of the account of the Fall, the Lord exiles Adam and Eve from the garden sanctuary. The breaking of the covenant means the forfeiture of the priestly role, and Adam is therefore no longer able to dwell in the sanctuary. "Behold, the man has become like one of us ... and now, lest he put forth his hand and take also of the tree of life, and eat, and live for ever ..." (Gen 3:22). God does not wish Adam and Eve to become immortal in a state of covenant separation from him, thus rendering them permanently alienated. Because the process of dying leads to humility (Ps 90:3–10) and repentance (Ps 90:11–13) and ultimately reconciliation (Ps 90:14–17), it is a natural antidote to the pridefulness and self-sufficiency of sin. Therefore, death is not merely a punishment but also a remedy for sin. As in the later sanctuary of Israel, the *cherubim*—the first angelic beings mentioned in the Hebrew Scriptures— permanently guard the way to the tree of life (Gen 3:24). The rest of the Bible will, in a sense, be a long story of mankind's journey back to a state in which it can once again eat from the fruit of the "tree of life" and "live for ever" (see Jn 6:51; Rev 22:2).

The Generations of Adam (Genesis 4:1–6:8)

The sin introduced into humanity by Adam and Eve quickly metastasizes into murder, as we see in the account of Cain and Abel (Gen 4:1–16). Foreshadowing similar strife between elder and younger sons that will take place in the history of salvation (Ishmael vs. Isaac, Jacob vs. Esau, Joseph vs. his elder

---

Where Did Cain Get His Wife?

"Cain knew his wife, and she conceived" (Gen 4:17). People naturally want to know where this wife came from. Some have speculated that there were other humans present at the dawn of creation who were not descendants of Adam and Eve. This "pre-Adamite" theory has always been rejected by the Church. It undermines the doctrine of unity of the human race, which stems from "one ancestor" (Acts 17:26; *CCC* 360), as well as the doctrine of original sin, which teaches that "Adam and Eve committed a *personal sin* ... transmitted *by propagation* to all mankind" (*CCC* 404). Historically, the pre-Adamite theory has also been used to support racist ideologies, in which those in social control will tend to label socially marginalized ethnic groups as "pre-Adamite" in descent, in order to deny them full human dignity and civil rights.

In stark contrast, the Christian and Jewish traditions have always recognized that the first generations of the human race had to have married close relations, based on the evidence that Adam had "other sons and daughters" besides the three sons named in Scripture (Gen 5:4). For example, one early extra-biblical Jewish writing, the *Book of Jubilees*, explicitly states that Cain married a sister and provides her with a name (*Jub.* 4:8). Likewise, in the patristic era, Augustine argued that marriage between siblings in the first generation was "dictated by necessity" in order that the human race "might multiply". Augustine goes on to point out that this would have required only one generation: "the grandchildren of the first pair" would have been "able to choose their cousins for wives"—the standard practice throughout biblical times.[a]

---

[a] See Augustine, *City of God* 15.16, in *NPNF1* 2:297–98; he is followed by Thomas Aquinas, *Summa Theologica* II–II, q. 154, a. 9.

brothers), Abel, the righteous son, is persecuted and slain by the less righteous, Cain. As he did with Adam and Eve, God again mitigates the punishment warranted by the actions of the sinner. As Genesis will later make clear, although Cain's murder of another human being merits his own death (cf. Gen 9:6), God shows mercy and spares Cain's life, and, ironically, his line of descent is responsible for the early development of human civilization (Gen 4:17–26). This culture is not without its shadows, however: its degeneration is suggested by the fact that Lamech, in the sixth generation from Cain, is a violent braggart and inventor of bigamy who intimidates his wives by boasting of his murders (Gen 4:23–24). In keeping with the method of the sacred author of Genesis, the text does not explicitly condemn the sexual license (*bigamy*) and violence (*murder*) of Lamech but, rather, suggestively associates these developments in human history with the family of Cain, the first murderer. Thus Cain's descendants are worse than Cain himself (Gen 4:24). Some hope is introduced into this picture by the announcement of the birth of Seth (Gen 4:25), who is associated with worship and the time when human beings "began to call upon the name of the LORD" (Gen 4:26). At this point, the text traverses the long time between Adam and Noah by means of the first of many *toledoth* ("generation") sections in Genesis (Gen 5:1–32). In contrast to the line of Cain, Adam's genealogical line, traced through Seth, is marked by extremely long life-spans, righteous figures such as Enoch, who "walked" (Hebrew *halak*) with God (Gen 5:21–22), and Noah, who is prophetically described as a kind of deliverer figure who will bring "relief" (Hebrew *nuach*) to the world (Gen 5:29).

Unfortunately, in the end we discover that the sin of Cain's descendants spreads throughout all mankind, apparently infecting and influencing even the more righteous line of Seth. The "sons of God"—in other words, the heirs of Adam's adoptive divine sonship (the line of Seth; cf. Gen 5:3)—saw that the "daughters of men [the line of Cain] were fair; and they took to wife such of them as they chose" (Gen 6:2).

This last line implies: "as many as they wanted". Bigamy, invented by Lamech, has developed into *polygamy*, now being practiced even among the sons of Seth, who in their earlier generations were marked by calling on the name of the Lord and walking with God. The result is social chaos: the violence of the Lamech and the Cainite family spreads to all mankind, and the earth is "filled with violence" (Gen 6:11). At this point, the forbearance of punishment that God demonstrated with Adam (Gen 3:21) and Cain (Gen 4:15) alike comes to its end, and the Lord decides to bring judgment: the great Flood, which is the beginning of the Noah Cycle.

It is worth noting at this point the *implicit critique of polygamy* that runs throughout Genesis and other parts of the Hebrew Scriptures. Although the Old Testament nowhere explicitly forbids polygamy, nonetheless the biblical narrative does not portray it in a favorable light. First of all, the pre-Fall state of perfection is clearly one of monogamy: only one woman is made for Adam (Gen 2:22), and the paradigm established by God is that a man should cling to his "*wife*", not his *wives*, and that they become "*one flesh*", not *many*

Who Are the "Sons of God" and "Daughters of Men"?

"The sons of God saw that the daughters of men were fair; and they took to wife such of them as they chose" (Gen 6:2). Who are these mysterious "sons of God"? Three interpretations have been proposed:

1. The *fallen angels* interpretation was very popular in antiquity and is reflected in ancient Jewish writings outside the Bible such as *Jubilees* and *1 Enoch*. According to this view, angels left heaven to cohabitate with human women and bore monstrous children. Despite its popularity, this theory, from a theological perspective, is impossible, since angels are "spiritual, non-corporeal beings" (*CCC* 328); this means that they do not have bodies and hence cannot reproduce with human beings. From a literary perspective, a major weakness of this theory is that these angelic beings would never be mentioned elsewhere in Genesis. Moreover, in the narrative, the Flood is the result of the sin of the "sons of God", yet it is not angelic beings but "man" who is blotted out from the earth (Gen 7:4). This view turns Genesis 6:1–4 into a philosophically incredible and literarily inexplicable fragment in which these supposed angelic beings come out of nowhere and then immediately disappear from the narrative.

2. The *ancient kings* theory can be supported by the biblical and ancient Near Eastern practice of calling kings and other rulers "sons of God" (Ps 2:6–7; 82:6–7). From this point of view, Genesis 6:2 describes the growth of royal harems. Parallels for this concept can be found in other ancient Near Eastern literature.

3. The *sons of Seth* interpretation, adopted here, is the common view of the Catholic tradition. Scripture and ancient Near Eastern literature employ "son" as a covenant category (Ps 2:7; 89:26–28; Ex 4:22). In the narrative of Genesis, the "sons of God" are Sethites, heirs of the covenant of adoptive divine sonship from Adam. The "daughters of men" would be the women descended from Cain, the line that has turned its back on the presence of God (Gen 4:16).

From a literary perspective, the Sethite interpretation is supported by the fact that the Pentateuch repeatedly depicts intermarriage between men of the covenant line and women from other peoples who do not worship the Lord as something to be avoided (e.g., Gen 16, 24, 26:34–35; 28:6–9; Num 25:1–5, etc.). It also makes much more sense of the Flood that follows: as a result of intermarriage, the covenant people become so corrupted that all the world is violent like Cain's descendants, with the sole exception of Noah and his family, the righteous "remnant" of the line of Seth. The Sethite interpretation is also taught by Augustine, *City of God* 15.23, and Thomas Aquinas, *Summa Theologica* I, q. 51, a. 3.

---

fleshes (Gen 2:24). Bigamy is invented by Lamech, a man seven times more evil than Cain (Gen 4:19). Polygamy (Gen 6:1) gives rise to the violence on the earth (Gen 6:11–12) that provokes the Flood. Later in Genesis, Abraham's polygamous marriages with Hagar and Keturah only succeed in producing the forefathers of the enemies and persecutors of Israel (the Ishmaelites). Jacob does not initially desire polygamy but is duped into the situation by Laban, his unscrupulous uncle (Gen 29:21–30). The rivalry between Jacob's wives (and concubines) quickly leads to sadness, tension, and outright conflict in the home, with Jacob becoming the sexual object of warring wives trying to outdo one another in the bearing of children (Gen 29:31–30:24), as well as murderous conflict between his twelve sons and the tribes that come from them (for example, Gen 37:2–4).

The Generations of Noah and the Flood (Gen 6:9–11:26)

The Noah Cycle largely repeats the fundamental elements of the Adam Cycle. The sacred author has composed the Primeval History (Gen 1–11) as an elegant literary unity in which mankind twice progresses through the following sequence: creation—covenant—fall—curse—expansion—rebellion, as in the following chart:

	Adam Cycle (Gen 1:1—6:8)		Noah Cycle (Gen 6:9—11:26)
A	Creation and Covenant (chaps. 1–2)	A'	Re-creation (6:9—8:19) and Renewal of Covenant (8:20—9:17)
B	Sin of Adam (chap. 3) and His Son (4:1–16)	B'	Sin of Noah and His Son (9:18–28)
C	Expansion of Adam's Sons (4:17–26)	C'	Expansion of Noah's Sons (chap. 10)
D	Adam to Noah: Ten Generations to Three Sons (5:1–32) ↘	E'	Collective Sin of Mankind: Tower of Babel (11:1–9)
E	Collective Sin of Mankind: "Sons of God" with "Daughters of Men" (6:1–8) ↗	D'	Shem to Terah: Ten Generations to Three Sons (11:10–26)

Adapted from Gary Rendsburg, *The Redaction of Genesis* (Winona Lake: Eisenbrauns, 1996), 7–25.

Whatever approach one may take with respect to possible sources, it is clear that the text as we have it is a carefully arranged unity. The one alteration in the sequence occurs at the end of the second cycle, where the account of the collective sin of mankind and the ten generations are in reverse order from the first cycle. This may have been done to create a better segue into the account of Abraham in Genesis 12.

In any case, Noah is introduced already at the end of the genealogy starting from Adam (Gen 5:32) as one who brings hope for mankind, despite the curse on the earth and the proliferation of sexual perversion and violence (Gen 5:29, 6:2, 11–12). The Lord's forbearance is at an end: he decides to send judgment in the form of a flood and begin anew with Noah (Gen 6:7–8).

The Flood narrative itself is often said to be a composite of two accounts, that of the Yahwist ("J") and the Priestly source ("P"). According to the J narrative, the Flood lasts for forty days and nights, and seven pairs of every animal are brought onto the ark, but according to P, the Flood lasts for 150 days and only one pair of each animal is brought.[5] The two sources may be distinguished by different names used for God: "The Lord" (Hebrew *YHWH*) in J and "God" (Hebrew *Elohim*) in P.

As noted above in the discussion of the authorship and date of the Pentateuch, it may well be the case that the sacred author combined information from two or more sources, perhaps oral traditions about the great Flood of the ancient past.

[5] John J. Collins, *Introduction to the Hebrew Bible* (Minneapolis: Fortress Press, 2004).

However, the traditional source-critical analysis of the Flood narrative is not completely satisfactory. A close reading of the text reveals that the forty days and nights commonly assigned to J are not the total duration of the Flood but the duration of the *rain* (Gen 7:12). Likewise, the 150 days do not pertain to the rain but to how long it takes the waters to recede from the earth (Gen 7:24). Moreover, Noah is not commanded to bring seven pairs of *every* animal onto the ark, but seven pairs of *clean* animals and birds (Gen 7:2–3), in addition to the male and female of every other kind of animal (Gen 6:19–22). The reason for this is simple: Noah is to bring "seven pairs of all clean animals" into the ark "to keep their kind alive upon the face of the earth" (Gen 7:3), since it is precisely these animals— "every clean animal and ... every clean bird"—that he will offer as sacrifices immediately after departing from the ark (Gen 8:20).

Traditional Source Analysis of the Flood Narrative	
J	6:5–8
P	6:9–22
J	7:1–5
P	7:6–16a
J	7:16b–23
P	7:24—8:5
J	8:6–12
P	8:13–19
J	8:20–22

Moreover, source-critical analysis leads to some counterintuitive results for the standard Documentary Hypothesis. For example, the command of the Lord to Noah to take seven pairs of clean animals onto the ark (Gen 7:1–5) as well as the account of Noah's ritual sacrifice of those same animals after the Flood (Gen 8:20–22) are attributed to the Yahwist (J) on the basis of the use of the divine name "YHWH" in these passages, despite the fact that the distinction between "clean" and "unclean" animals is primarily a Priestly concern in the Bible (for example, Lev 10:10; 13:16), and the account of Noah's sacrifice employs terminology that only occurs elsewhere in Priestly material in the Pentateuch (for example, the "pleasing odor" of the sacrifice, in Hebrew, *rêach nîchōach*; a Priestly term; Ex 29:18). So, according to the Documentary Hypothesis, the Priestly authors, who left us almost all the material in the Pentateuch concerning sacrifice and food laws, originally wrote an account in which Noah did not bring along enough clean animals for sacrifice or for food and did not offer sacrifice after the Flood. The Yahwist, however, *did* remember to attend to this issue (Gen 7:2–5; 8:20–22) and after the Flood records Noah making a priestly sacrifice of clean animals, using language associated with the Priestly materials. This result seems unconvincing, so it is clear that, for the source analysis of this passage to be successful, a much more detailed dissection of sources would be necessary.

Several scholars have abandoned the source-critical approach to this passage and suggested that the present Flood narrative is carefully constructed as a *chiasm* or palistrophe, where repetitions of key numbers such as seven, forty, and 150 are used, along with other literary devices and key words, to create balance between the accounts of the escalation of the Flood (Gen 6:10–7:24) and its *denouement* (Gen 8:1–9:19).[6] Sometimes time indications are "unnecessarily" repeated, simply to achieve the rhetorical and poetical effect of balance. To modern readers, unused to ancient literary conventions, the story can sound

---

[6] Gordan Wenham, *Genesis*, 2 vols., Word Biblical Commentary 1 (Dallas: Word, 1987).

redundant. Nonetheless, the narrative in its present form can be understood as a unity.

From a theological perspective, the Flood needs to be understood as an act of *re-creation*, whereby God plunges the world (almost) back to the original state of *tohu wabohu* ("formless and void"), with the earth below the surface of the deep, and then raises it back up again.

From this point of view, Noah, likewise, is a kind of *new Adam* figure, a new father of the human race, who is given almost the exact same commands as the first Adam: "Be fruitful and multiply, and fill the earth" (Gen 9:1). The ark may be seen as a floating (zoological) garden, a kind of *new Eden*, that comes to rest on a new holy mountain, Ararat. Like the Solomonic Temple, the ark is built on three levels (Gen 6:16; 1 Kings 6:6). There are also parallels with the construction of the Tab-

Parallels between Creation and the Flood		
	Creation	Flood
Waters over the Earth	1:2, 6–7	7:19–20
Spirit of God over the Waters	1:2	8:1
Emergence of the Dry Land	1:9–10	8:5
Emergence of Plants	1:11–12	8:11
Emergence of Animals and Man	1:20–27	8:13–19
Blessing: Be Fruitful and Multiply	1:28	9:1

ernacle: the ark and the Tabernacle are the only two passages of instruction from God concerning the construction of a dwelling in the Bible. The accounts end similarly: "Noah did this; he did all that God commanded him" (Gen 6:22); "Moses saw all the work, and behold, they had done it; as the Lord had commanded, so had they done it" (Ex 39:43).

The Covenant with Noah

Genesis 9:1–17 recounts the establishment of the covenant with Noah. Significantly, the covenant renewal is associated with Noah's sacrifice (Gen 8:20–22). The relationship of sacrifice and covenant is a consistent theme in Scripture (Ps 50:5) and will be seen clearly again in the description of the covenant with Abraham (Gen 15) and with all Israel at Sinai (Ex 24).

Moreover, the extensive *linguistic parallels with the creation account* have led interpreters both ancient and modern to see the covenant with Noah as a renewal of the relationship between God and Adam. Indeed, the terms of the *explicit* covenant with Noah include significant changes from the terms of the *implicit* covenant with Adam.

For example, with regard to food, whereas Adam is given only the "green plants" to eat (Gen 1:29), to Noah "every moving thing that lives"—that is, all the *animals*—are given as food: hence the "fear" or "dread" of man that now falls on the animals (Gen 9:2–3). This signifies that the original harmony of creation prior to the Fall has been marred by man's violence, and thus the renewed covenant, when compared to the original creation before the Fall, is imperfect and affected by man's sinfulness. Along similar lines, whereas Adam was originally permitted to eat from the fruit of "the tree of life" (Gen 2:9) and then

---

The Interpretation of the Flood Narrative

How are we to understand the account of the Flood in Genesis 6–9? In terms of the history of interpretation, three views stand out:

1. *Global Flood.* This view stems from the passages that state that God destroyed "all flesh in which is the breath of life from under heaven" (Gen 6:17; 7:15–17) and that "all the high mountains ... were covered" with water so that "all flesh died that moved upon the earth" except Noah and those with him (Gen 7:19–23). Moreover, after the Flood, the point of the "Table of Nations" is to show that all the peoples of the world are descended from the sons of Noah (Gen 10:1–32). This interpretation is taken by the New Testament, which repeatedly interprets the Flood at the time of Noah as a cosmic destruction (Mt 24:37–44; Lk 17:26–27; 1 Pet 3:20–22; 2 Pet 3:1–13). It is because of texts such as these that Jewish and Christian tradition from ancient times treated the Flood as a global catastrophe (e.g., Augustine, *City of God* 15:27).

2. *Local Flood.* This view is more difficult to accommodate to the wording of the Genesis narrative, but it allows the Flood to be identified with a number of water events that appear to have struck the Near East in ancient times. It has in its favor the fact that all the peoples of the ancient Near East remembered a singular flood that almost wiped out mankind. Some scholars see this as evidence that a very real, traumatic flood did strike the region at an early stage in human history, even marshalling archaeological and geological evidence to support their claims.

3. *Mythical Flood.* This view holds that there is no historical event whatsoever behind the Flood narrative but that Genesis is simply one among many ancient Near Eastern myths of origins, such as those found in the *Epic of Gilgamesh* or the *Enuma Elish*. It has in its favor the striking literary parallels between the Flood account in Genesis and other ancient texts.

In recent magisterial documents, the *Catechism of the Catholic Church* treats Noah and the Flood as a real part of salvation history when it teaches that God made a covenant with Noah "after the flood" and that "the covenant with Noah remains in force" (*CCC* 56, 58, 71), but leaves the precise interpretation of the event open.

---

later prohibited from doing so (Gen 2:22), so now Noah is commanded not to consume blood, because the blood is "life" (Gen 9:4). Moreover, God will no longer forbear to punish the one who sheds blood, as he did with Cain. In obvious reference to the Cain and Abel story, we read, "of every man's brother I will require the life of man" (Gen 9:5). On pain of death, Noah and his descendants are prohibited from shedding the blood of another person: "Whoever sheds the blood of man, by man shall his blood be shed" (Gen 9:6). Here we find the very first reference to capital punishment in Scripture, for the sin of murder. Finally, just as the creation account concluded with the Sabbath (Gen 2:1–3)—identified elsewhere in the Pentateuch as the "sign of the covenant" (see Ex 31:16–17)—so the rainbow is explicitly described by God as "the sign of the covenant" (Gen 9:12–13), which some understand as an image of the war-bow of God, a sign of his judgment, now hung harmlessly in the sky, no longer "pointed" toward the earth. Thus, at the conclusion of the Flood narrative, the earth has experienced judgment and renewal. A "new creation" has emerged, and mankind's covenant relationship with God, albeit in an imperfect form, has been renewed.

The Sin of Noah and Ham

The enigmatic story of the sin of Noah and Ham (Gen 9:18–27) brings together themes and language from the account of the Fall of Adam and Eve and the murder of Abel by Cain. Like Adam (Gen 2:7; 3:19) and Cain (Gen 4:2), Noah is a "tiller of the soil" (Gen 9:20).

What follows is a story in which Noah consumes fruit (in the form of wine), gets naked, is shamed by his son, and curses him. The motifs of *fruit*, *nakedness*, *shame*, and *curse* are clear echoes of the Fall narrative. The conflict between the righteous offspring (Shem and Japheth) and an unrighteous son (Ham) also connects the story with the Cain and Abel account. Just as in earlier chapters we saw Adam and his son offend God and experience a curse, so now history repeats itself. We discover that, even though God has cleansed the earth and started over with the most righteous man, even in this man and his family, there is a seed of sin that will bear evil fruit as history unfolds. In sum, the account of Noah's drunkenness is the "Fall of Noah", and the cursing of Ham serves as background for the coming genealogy of Noah's descendants, in which Ham's offspring will be identified with some of the Hebrew people's worst persecutors and enemies: Egypt, Canaan, Assyria, Nineveh, the Amorites, and the peoples of Sodom and Gomorrah (Gen 10:6–20).

> ### What Was the Sin of Ham?
>
> The account of Ham's sin is compressed and enigmatic (Gen 9:20–27). What was Ham's sin? A full discussion would be too technical, but, in brief, "to uncover the nakedness of your father" is a Hebrew idiom for a serious sexual offense that falls under the general prohibitions of incest (see Lev 18:7; 20:11, 17). Why is Canaan cursed and not Ham himself (Gen 9:25)? Perhaps because Noah's sons, including Ham, were already covered by divine blessing (Gen 9:1). Other explanations are also possible.

The Table of Nations and the Tower of Babel (Genesis 10–11)

The three sons of Noah give rise to *seventy nations* that populate the entire earth. The following genealogy, which incorporates notes about various remarkable descendants, is parallel to, if larger than, the genealogy of Cain's descendants and Seth (Gen 4:17–26). The record of the seventy nations descended from Noah is significant: they are not forgotten, and God's salvific purpose, even under the Old Covenant, always has *all of mankind* in view. As we will see, the call of Abram (Gen 12:1–3) will be for the purpose of blessing "all the families of the earth" recorded here in Genesis 10.

The Tower of Babel incident represents a widespread, collective rebellion of mankind against God similar to the sons of God/daughters of men episode. The tower is like a synthetic or man-made "holy mountain". It functions as a substitute for the now lost Eden mountain sanctuary, but it is a shrine to the pride of human beings who say "let us make a name [Hebrew *shem*] for ourselves" (Gen 11:4) rather than following their righteous ancestors by calling on the "name" (Hebrew *shem*) of God (cf. Gen 4:26). In order to prevent this, God "confuse[s]" (Hebrew *balal*) their speech (Gen 11:7). This confusion is necessary to compel mankind to fulfill the divine mandate to "fill the

---

The Long Life-Spans in the Genealogies

Almost all the ancient Near Eastern cultures remembered an ancient flood that divided human history into a "pre-modern" period beforehand and the "modern" period afterward. Kings and heroes had enormous life-spans before the Flood, but death came more quickly for those who lived afterward. Mesopotamian king lists give reigns of tens of thousands of years for their pre-Flood rulers![a] The Hebrew life-spans of hundreds of years for the patriarchs seem modest in comparison. Nonetheless, how are these to be understood? There are three dominant interpretations:

1. *Literal*: mankind in its early stages lived much longer than modern humanity
2. *Honorific*: the long life-spans are not meant literally but are to show the importance and honor due to ancestors
3. *Genealogical*: the life-span of the patriarch is a reference to the duration of his dynasty or family line.

Uncertainty over how to interpret the genealogies precludes making precise calculations about the date of the Flood or creation itself. Intriguingly, debates over the interpretation of the genealogies go back to ancient times. For example, Augustine once wrote: "They are by no means to be listened to who suppose that in those times years were differently reckoned, and were so short that one of our years may be supposed to be equal to ten of theirs. So that they say, when we read or hear that some man lived 900 years, we should understand ninety, ten of those years making but one of ours, and ten of ours equaling 100 of theirs." Augustine rejects this view, since in the Hebrew manuscript Kenan begat his son Mahalalel when he was seventy years old. If seventy years in those times meant only seven of our years, what man seven years old begets children?[b]

---

[a] See Kenneth A. Kitchen, *On the Reliability of the Old Testament* (Grand Rapids, Mich.: Eerdmans, 2003), 443–45.
[b] See Augustine, *City of God* 15.12, in *NPNF1* 2:293.

---

earth" (Gen 9:1), but it also sows disunity and division in the human family. Significantly, this confusion will not be overcome until the New Testament at Pentecost, when people from many nations will once again understand one another's language. At Pentecost, however, the overcoming of the language barrier takes place through the power of the Holy Spirit, not the pride of human beings (Acts 2:1–11).

The Tower of Babel is thus a kind of "Fall of the Nations", which sets the stage for the call of Abram, through whom the divisions introduced at Babel will ultimately be undone, when "all the families of the earth" are blessed (Gen 12:3). The call of Abram is God's solution to the problem of Babel.

Genesis 1–11 in the Living Tradition

The Primeval History is not only foundational to the Pentateuch as a whole and the book of Genesis in particular; it also plays a key role in the living tradition of the Church. Indeed, with regard to Genesis 1–11 and its history of interpretation—referred to by some scholars as the *Nachleben* (German for "afterlife")—the early Church Fathers, the medieval doctors, and magisterial teachings provide us with an enormous amount of material—far too much to cover here.[7] In fact, in the early centuries of the Church, it was popular to preach on this portion of Scripture during the seasons of Lent and Holy Week (for example, Ambrose, John Chrysostom). In what follows, we will give an extremely brief sampling of how Genesis 1–11 has been interpreted since New Testament times as well as of the meaning that it continues to have in the living tradition of the Church.

The Six Days of Creation

Contrary to what some contemporary readers may assume, the debate over whether to interpret the "six days" of creation in Genesis 1 as a historical account of how the world was made or as a symbolic account using figurative language actually goes back to ancient times. In the early centuries of the Church, the account of creation in Genesis 1, known as the *Hexaemeron* (Greek for "six days"), was an extremely popular text and gave rise to a number of lengthy "commentaries" by figures such as Origen of Alexandria, Basil the Great, John Chrysostom, Ephrem the Syrian, Augustine of Hippo, and many others.[8]

On the one hand, the majority of early Church Fathers and medieval writers interpreted the six days of Genesis 1 as a historical account of how the world was made. Consider, for example, the words of Ephrem the Syrian and Basil the Great, the latter of whom wrote perhaps the most influential commentary on the *Hexaemeron* in the early Church:

> So let no one think that there is anything allegorical in the works of the six days. No one can rightly say that the things that pertain to these days were symbolic, nor can one say that they were meaningless names or that other things were symbolized for us by their names. Rather, let us know in just what manner heaven and earth were created in the beginning.[9]

> There are those truly, who do not admit the common sense of the Scriptures, for whom water is not water, but some other nature, who see in a plant, in a fish, what their fancy wishes, who change the nature of reptiles and of wild beasts to suit their allegories, like the interpreters of dreams who explain visions in sleep to make them serve their own ends. For me grass is grass; plant, fish, wild beast, domestic animal, I take all in the literal sense. "For I am not ashamed of the gospel" [Rom 1:16].[10]

---

[7] See Andrew Louth and M. Conti, *Genesis 1–11*, Old Testament 1, Ancient Christian Commentary on Scripture, ed. Thomas C. Oden (Downers Grove, Ill.: InterVarsity Press, 2001), and Joy A. Schroeder, *The Book of Genesis*, The Bible in Medieval Tradition (Grand Rapids, Mich.: Eerdmans, 2015).

[8] See Louth and Conti, *Genesis 1–11*, xxxix–lii.

[9] Ephrem the Syrian, *Commentary on Genesis* 1.1, in Saint Ephrem the Syrian, *Selected Prose Works*, trans. Edward G. Matthews Jr. and Joseph P. Amar, The Fathers of the Church 91 (Washington, D.C.: Catholic University of America Press, 1994), 74.

[10] Basil the Great, *The Hexaemeron* 9.1, in *NPNF2* 8:101.

This literal or historical interpretation of Genesis 1 can also be found in the writings of other figures, such as Ambrose of Milan, John Chrysostom, John Damascene, Leo the Great, and the later writings of Thomas Aquinas.[11]

On the other hand, there were other Church Fathers and medieval writers who interpreted the six days of Genesis 1 as only symbolic or figurative. Consider, for example, the words of Origen of Alexandria and Augustine of Hippo:

> To what person of intelligence, I ask, will the account seem logically consistent that says there was a "first day" and a "second" and a "third," in which also "evening" and "morning" are named, without a sun, without a moon, and without stars, and even in the case of the first day without a heaven?[12]

> The creator, after all, about whom scripture told this story of how he completed and finished his works in six days, is the same as the one about whom it is written elsewhere, and assuredly without there being any contradiction, that "*he created all things simultaneously together*" (Sir 18:1 [Latin]). And consequently, the one who made all things simultaneously together also made simultaneously together these six or seven days, or rather this *one day* six or seven times repeated. So then, what need was there for the six days to be recounted so distinctly and methodically? It was for the sake of those who cannot arrive at an understanding of the text, "he created all things together simultaneously," unless scripture accompanies them more slowly, step by step, to the goal to which it is leading them.[13]

In other words, for Augustine, although the world was actually created all at once—in "one day", as he puts it—God reveals the creation as taking place over six distinct days for the sake of the readers' comprehension. Although the minority position, this kind of symbolic or figurative interpretation of Genesis 1 in Origen and Augustine can also be found in the early writings of Thomas Aquinas.[14]

In recent years, the Magisterium of the Church has clearly emphasized the symbolic meaning of the six days. Consider, for example, the treatment of the *Hexaemeron* in the 1992 *Catechism of the Catholic Church*:

> God himself created the visible world in all its richness, diversity, and order. *Scripture presents the work of the Creator symbolically as a succession of six days of divine "work,"* concluded by the "rest" of the seventh day. On the subject of creation, the sacred text teaches the truths revealed by God for our salvation, permitting

---

[11] See, for example, Ambrose, *Hexaemeron* 1.37; John Chrysostom, *Homilies on Genesis* 7.9–10; John Damascene, *On the Orthodox Faith* 2.7; Leo the Great, *Sermon* 27.5; Thomas Aquinas, *Summa Theologica* I, q. 70, a. 2; q. 74, a. 2.

[12] Origen, *On First Principles* 4.3.1, in Origen, *An Exhortation to Martyrdom, Prayer, First Principles: Book IV, Prologue to the Commentary on the Song of Songs, Homily XXVII on Numbers*, trans. Rowan A. Greer (New York: Paulist Press, 1979), 189.

[13] Augustine, *The Literal Meaning of Genesis* IV.52, in Augustine, *On Genesis*, trans. Edmund Hill et al. (Hyde Park, N.Y.: New City Press, 2002), 273.

[14] Cf. Origen, *Homilies on Genesis*; Augustine, *On Genesis*; Thomas Aquinas, *Commentary on the Sentences* II, XII, q. 1, art. 2; see also Peter C. Bouteneff, *Beginnings: Ancient Christian Readings of the Biblical Creation Narratives* (Grand Rapids, Mich.: Baker Academic, 2008).

us to "recognize the inner nature, the value, and the ordering of the whole of creation to the praise of God." (*CCC* 337 [emphasis added])

The Resurrection on the Eighth Day

In contrast to these disagreements over the literal or allegorical interpretation of the six days, from the earliest times, the beginning of creation on the "first day" of the week (= Sunday) and the "resting" of God on the seventh day (= Saturday) was seen as pointing forward to the Resurrection of Christ on Easter Sunday. From this point of view, the Resurrection—the beginning of the new creation—took place on Sunday, the same day on which the world was made. As one early Christian writer put it:

> [God said:] "That sabbath which I have made, in which, after giving rest to all things, I will make the beginning of the eighth day, that is, the beginning of another world. Therefore, we also celebrate with joy the eighth day on which Jesus also rose from the dead after his rest, was made manifest and ascended into heaven."[15]

This emphasis on Sunday as both the day of the Resurrection and the beginning of the new creation continues down to our own day (see *CCC* 349). It reveals how in the living tradition of the Church, the early chapters of Genesis were not only studied for insights into the mysteries of *protology* (the study of origins or "beginnings"), but also read as containing prefigurations of the mysteries of *eschatology* (the study of the "end" of history).

The Creation of Man and the Image of the Trinity

Another key text that was richly mined by the living tradition was the mysterious statement: "Let *us* make man in *our image, after our likeness*" (Gen 1:26). For the early Church Fathers, this text proved that human beings were different from other creatures, since God did not speak of anything else in creation as being made in his "image".[16] Even more, though, some of them saw in the implicit plurality of persons mentioned in this decree a hint of the mystery of the Trinity:

> For how can He say "to our image," since the Son is the image of the Father alone. But ... man is said to be "to the image" on account of an imperfect likeness, and, therefore, *"to our image,"* in order that man might be the image of the Trinity, not equal to the Trinity as the Son to the Father, but approaching it, as has been said, by a kind of similarity.[17]

This is an excellent example of how the early Church Fathers interpreted the Scriptures in light of the principle that "the New Testament is concealed in the Old and the Old Testament is revealed in the New."

---

[15] *Letter of Barnabas* 15.8, in Louth and Conti, *Genesis 1–11*, 46.

[16] For example, Gregory of Nyssa, *On the Origin of Man* 8.

[17] Augustine, *On the Trinity* 7.6.12, in Augustine, *The Trinity*, trans. Stephen McKenna, The Fathers of the Church 45 (Washington, D.C.: Catholic University of America Press, 2002), 241.

The Creation of Woman and the Origin of the Church

Another aspect of Genesis 1–11 that was a favorite focus of the living tradition was the mysterious account of the "woman" being fashioned from the "side" or "rib" of the first man, after God put him into a deep "sleep".[18] For example, in one of his homilies, Saint Jerome writes:

> "God took a rib from the side of Adam and made it into a woman." Here Scripture said *aedificavit* [built].... We have heard about the first Adam; let us come now to the second Adam and see how the Church is made [*aedifcetur*] from His side. The side of the Lord Savior as He hung on the cross is pierced with a lance and from it there comes forth blood and water. Would you like to know how the church is built up from water and blood? First, through the baptism of water, sins are forgiven; then, the blood of the martyrs crowns the edifice.[19]

Many centuries later, in his famous *Summa Theologica*, Saint Thomas Aquinas saw this mystery both as teaching the dignity of the woman and as prefiguring the origin of the Church from the side of Christ crucified:

> It is written (Genesis 2:22): "God built the rib, which He took from Adam, into a woman.".... It was right for the woman to be made from a rib of man. First, to signify the social union of man and woman, for the woman should neither *use authority over man*, and so she was not made from his head; nor was it right for her to be subject to man's contempt as his slave, and so she was not made from his feet. Secondly, for the sacramental signification; *for from the side of Christ sleeping on the Cross the Sacraments flowed—namely, blood and water—on which the Church was established.*[20]

Even up to this day, a similarly typological interpretation of the making of woman can be found in the *Catechism of the Catholic Church*: "As Eve was formed from the sleeping Adam's side, so the Church was born from the pierced heart of Christ hanging dead on the cross" (*CCC* 766).

Before the Fall: Original Holiness in Genesis

One of the most intriguing aspects of the book of Genesis is its account of human life *before* sin and death enter into human history. Indeed, one of the most common questions readers of Genesis over the centuries have asked is: *What was life like before the Fall?*

In a remarkable example of synthesizing the interpretation of Scripture with the living tradition of the Church, the 1992 *Catechism of the Catholic Church* answers this question by repeated reference to the text of Genesis. (We have put the scriptural texts from the footnotes in brackets so that the biblical bases of the teaching is explicit.)

---

[18] See Louth and Conti, *Genesis 1–11*, 66–73.

[19] Jerome, *Homilies 66*, in *The Homilies of Saint Jerome*, trans. Marie Liguori Ewald, The Fathers of the Church 57 (Washington, D.C.: Catholic University of America Press, 1966), 65.

[20] Saint Thomas Aquinas, *Summa Theologica* I, q. 92, a. 4, trans. the Fathers of the English Dominican Province (1947; repr., Allen, Tex.: Christian Classics, 1981), 1:468 (emphasis added).

The first man was not only created good, but was also established in friendship with his Creator and in harmony with himself and with the creation around him, in a state that would be surpassed only by the glory of the new creation in Christ.

The Church, interpreting the symbolism of biblical language in an authentic way, in the light of the New Testament and Tradition, teaches that our first parents, Adam and Eve, were constituted in an original "state of holiness and justice." This grace of original holiness was "to share in ... divine life."

By the radiance of this grace all dimensions of man's life were confirmed. *As long as he remained in the divine intimacy, man would not have to suffer or die* [cf. Gen 2:17; 3:16, 19]. *The inner harmony of the human person, the harmony between man and woman* [cf. Gen 2:25], *and finally the harmony between the first couple and all creation, comprised the state called "original justice."*

The "mastery" over the world that God offered man from the beginning was realized above all within man himself: *mastery of self.* The first man was unimpaired and ordered in his whole being because he was free from the triple concupiscence that subjugates him to the pleasures of the senses, covetousness for earthly goods, and self-assertion, contrary to the dictates of reason.

The sign of man's familiarity with God is that God places him in the garden [cf. Gen 2:8]. There he lives "to till it and keep it." *Work is not yet a burden* [Gen 2:15; cf. 3:17–19], but rather the collaboration of man and woman with God in perfecting the visible creation.

This entire harmony of original justice, foreseen for man in God's plan, will be lost by the sin of our first parents. (*CCC* 374–79 [emphasis added])

Notice here how the Church's *doctrine* of original holiness is expressly founded on and rooted in an interpretation of *Scripture*, interpreted in the light of Tradition. From it, the Church derives the remarkable doctrine of original holiness, which teaches that the state of human life before sin and death entered human history was one of immortality, perfect intimacy with God, freedom from suffering and the burden of labor, and harmony between the first man and woman and all of creation.

The Protoevangelium: The Old Eve and the New Eve

In the interpretation of the early chapters of Genesis, perhaps no verse has garnered more attention than the mysterious oracle about the "enmity" between the "woman" and the "serpent" and how the woman's "seed" would bruise the serpent's head (Gen 3:15). This text—which came to be known as the *Protoevangelium*, or "First Gospel" (Gen 3:15)—was widely interpreted as a cryptic prophecy of the virginal conception of Jesus. Moreover, it also helped to establish a typological connection between the woman Eve and the woman Mary, who came to be recognized as the "new Eve". Consider, for example, the words of Irenaeus of Lyons, writing in the second century A.D.:

As Eve was seduced by the word of a [fallen] angel to flee from God, ... so Mary by the word of an angel received the glad tidings that she would bear God by obeying his word. The former was seduced to disobey God [and so fell], but the latter was persuaded to obey God, so that the Virgin Mary might become advocate of the virgin Eve. As the human race was subjected to death through the act of a virgin, so was it saved by a virgin, and thus the disobedience of one virgin was precisely balanced by the obedience of another.[21]

Over time, this Eve-Mary typology developed and led the living tradition to see in the prophecy about the "woman" and her "seed" a prophecy of Mary's identity as the new Eve:

> This passage in Genesis [3:15] is called the *Protoevangelium* ("first gospel"): the first announcement of the Messiah and Redeemer, of a battle between the serpent and the Woman, and of the final victory of a descendant of hers.
>
> The Christian tradition sees in this passage an announcement of the "New Adam" who, because he "became obedient unto death, even death on a cross," makes amends superabundantly for the disobedience of Adam. *Furthermore many Fathers and Doctors of the Church have seen the woman announced in the Protoevangelium as Mary, the mother of Christ, the "new Eve."* Mary benefited first of all and uniquely from Christ's victory over sin: she was preserved from all stain of original sin and by a special grace of God committed no sin of any kind during her whole earthly life. (*CCC* 410–411 [emphasis added])

Notice here how the teaching about Mary's Immaculate Conception, though not explicitly taught in Scripture, flows directly out of a typological interpretation of her as the new Eve.

Noah's Flood and the Waters of Baptism

In the Gospels, Jesus employs the Flood at the time of Noah as a type of the eschatological judgment, through which sin will be dealt with in a definitive way (Mt 24:37–38; Lk 17:26–27). In the early Church, however, the biblical Flood was interpreted typologically as a prefiguration of baptism. This is already present in the New Testament itself, in the first epistle of Peter:

> God's patience waited in the days of Noah, during the building of the ark, in which a few, that is, eight persons, were saved through water. *Baptism, which corresponds to this, now saves you*, not as a removal of dirt from the body but as an appeal to God for a clear conscience. (1 Pet 3:20–21)

Indeed, this image of Christian baptism as having been prefigured by the Flood was a favorite among the early Church Fathers.[22] In our own day, it is also preserved in the blessing of the water from the contemporary rite of baptism in the *Roman Missal*, which declares:

> The waters of the great flood
> you made a sign of the waters of Baptism,
> that make an end of sin and a new beginning of goodness.
> (*Roman Missal*, Easter Vigil 42; Blessing of Water, quoted in *CCC* 1219)

---

[21] Irenaeus, *Against Heresies* 5.19.1, in Louth and Conti, *Genesis 1–11*, 78–79.
[22] See Louth and Conti, *Genesis 1–11*, 136–40.

Genesis 1–11 in the Lectionary

Before bringing our discussion of Genesis 1–11 in the living tradition to a close, it is important to recognize that this section of Scripture has not only figured prominently in the writings of various Fathers and Doctors of the Church. On the contrary, the Primeval History also takes a central place in the contemporary Roman Lectionary. Consider the following chart, which provides an overview and brief explanation of the readings from Genesis 1–11 used on Sundays, feast days, and other occasions in the Lectionary:

Readings from the Primeval History (Gen 1–11) for Sundays, Feast Days, and Other Occasions
MSO = Masses for Special Occasions; *OM* = Optional Memorial; *VM* = Votive Mass; *Rit* = Ritual

Scripture	Description	Place in Calendar	Explanation
1:1–2:2	The seven days of creation	*Easter Vigil Reading 1*	Lays down the fundamental doctrine of creation and prepares for the celebration of baptism as a "new creation" through the Spirit and the water
1:11–12	The creation of the dry land	MSO: For Productive Land	Recalls God's initial creation of the soil and his blessing of it
1:14–18	The creation of the heavenly bodies to serve as markers for the seasons	MSO: Beginning of the Civil Year	Recalls the establishment of the cycles of time and the "seasons". In particular, the heavenly bodies mark the "liturgical seasons", reminding us that time is to be sanctified by worship
1:26–2:3	The creation of man in God's image, the mandate to rule the earth, the Sabbath day	OM: St. Joseph the Worker (May 1); MSO: Various Civil Needs and Blessing of Human Labor	Recalls the dignity of man in the image of God and man's exalted role as king of creation as well as his need to sanctify his time and labor through the Sabbath of rest and worship of God
2:4b–9, 15	Creation of man, placement in Eden to till and keep the ground	MSO: Blessing of Human Labor	Recalls work as part of the initial perfection of creation. Labor is not a result of the Fall.
2:7–9; 3:1–7	Creation of Adam, the Fall	*1st Sunday of Lent (A)*	Begins the brief recitation of the pivotal points of salvation history during the Sundays of Lent: recalls the Fall, including the threefold concupiscence that led to Eve's sin and that is overcome by prayer, fasting, and almsgiving

(continued)

Readings from the Primeval History (Gen 1–11) for Sundays, Feast Days, and Other Occasions *(continued)*			
MSO = Masses for Special Occasions; *OM* = Optional Memorial; *VM* = Votive Mass; *Rit* = Ritual			
Scripture	Description	Place in Calendar	Explanation
2:18–24	Creation of Eve, first marriage	*27th Sunday of OT (B)*; *Rit*: Sacrament of Marriage	Recalls the purpose and intention of marriage
3:9–15	Curse on the Serpent + *Protoevangelium*	*10th Sunday of OT (B)*; Solemnity of the Immaculate Conception; Common of BVM; *VM*: BVM Mother of the Church	The *Protoevangelium*, promising victory over the serpent by the "seed of the woman", is seen as one of the most important prophecies of the role of the BVM in salvation history.
4:3–10	Cain and Abel	*MSO*: In Time of War or Civil Disturbance	Recalls that we are to be our "brother's keeper"
9:8–15	Covenant with Noah	*1st Sunday of Lent (B)*	Begins a brief recitation of the pivotal points of salvation history in the first readings of Lent, and also prepares for the celebration of baptism by recalling the Flood, one of the primary types of baptism
11:1–9	Tower of Babel	*Vigil of Pentecost Reading 1, Option 1*	Provides the background for understanding Pentecost as a reversal of Babel, a reintegration of the human family by the reestablishment of a common language, the language of the Spirit

Several aspects of this chart stand out and provide us with significant windows into the interpretation of Genesis 1–11 in the living tradition expressed by the liturgy.

1. *The Hexaemeron and the Easter Vigil*: First and foremost, it is striking to note that while Genesis 1 has often played little to no role in much contemporary theology and catechesis,[23] the biblical account of the six days of creation, the *Hexaemeron* (Gen 1:1—2:2), constitutes the very first of seven Old Testament readings for the most solemn liturgy of the Church's calendar: the Easter Vigil. Indeed, the proclamation of Genesis 1 during the contemporary Easter Vigil grounds the life of the Church in the fundamental doctrine

---

[23] See Joseph Cardinal Ratzinger, *"In the Beginning . . .": A Catholic Understanding of the Story of Creation and the Fall*, trans. Boniface Ramsey, O.P. (Grand Rapids, Mich.: Eerdmans, 1995).

and reality of *creation*, by answering the perennial questions: "Where do we come from?" "Where are we going?" "What is our origin?" "What is our end?" (*CCC* 282). Genesis 1 asserts a world view in which the one God creates the entire cosmos in a well-ordered manner and in a state of goodness, with man—himself the "image and likeness" of God—as the pinnacle of creation and ordered to the seventh day, the Sabbath of rest and worship.

2. *The Water and Spirit of Creation and Baptism*: The reading of Genesis 1 during the Easter Vigil is also meant to ground the celebration of baptism that ordinarily takes place during that liturgy in the biblical description of the first creation, when the "spirit" (Hebrew *ruah*) of God hovered about over the face of the "waters" (Gen 1:2). In both the New Testament and the early Church Fathers, this connection between the spirit and the water of the old creation in Genesis is revealed as a foreshadowing of the new creation, which will be inaugurated by the descent of the "Spirit of God" upon Jesus in the waters of the Jordan River at his baptism (Mt 3:16) and fulfilled in the life-giving waters of Christian baptism, by which human beings become a "new creation" in Christ (Gal 6:15). In other words, the readings of the Easter Vigil begin with the creation account because the Resurrection is nothing less than the beginning of a new creation in Christ and baptism is the entry into that new creation (cf. *CCC* 281). The *Hexaemeron* is, therefore, the very first Scripture to echo in the ears of the newly baptized.

> "Once the elements of the world were set in order ... it was the primordial waters which were commanded to produce living creatures. The primordial water brought forth life, so that no one should be astonished that in Baptism the waters are able to give one life."[a]
>
> [a] Tertullian, *On Baptism* 2, as quoted in Jean Daniélou, S.J., *The Bible and the Liturgy* (Notre Dame, Ind.: University of Notre Dame Press, 2009), 72.

3. *The Creation of Woman and the Origin of Matrimony*: The account of the creation of woman (Gen 2:18–24) is read on the Twenty-Seventh Sunday in Ordinary Time (Year B), during which the Gospel of Mark is being read semi-continuously. In this case, the selection of Genesis reflects what is known as the "principle of harmony", in which the Old Testament reading is selected because of its connections with the New Testament reading for that day. The Gospel on this Sunday recounts the famous discussion between Jesus and the Pharisees over the indissolubility of marriage, in which Jesus prohibits remarriage based on the testimony of Genesis regarding the first marriage established by God "from the beginning" (Mk 10:2–16). The juxtaposition of these two texts reflects the ancient and widespread understanding that marriage is not a purely human institution but is authored by God himself and, as such, is an indissoluble lifelong covenant, breakable only by death (see *CCC* 1603, 1614). Here we see, then, both the New Testament and later Church Tradition drawing out one of the *moral* implications of Genesis regarding God's original purpose and intent for the relationship between man and woman and the matrimonial covenant. It is also one of the optional first readings for the celebration of the sacrament of matrimony.

4. *The Fall of Adam and Eve and the Triple Concupiscence*: Fourth, the accounts of the creation of Adam from the dust of the earth and the Fall of Adam and Eve (Gen 2:7–9 and 3:1–7) together constitute the first reading for the First Sunday

of Lent, Year A. The formation of Adam from the dust (Gen 2:7) is meant to recall the distribution of ashes from Ash Wednesday of the previous week, accompanied by the words, "You are dust, and to dust you shall return" (Gen 3:19). Along similar lines, the recitation of the account of the Fall in Genesis 3 is meant to call to mind the fallenness of human nature and the reality of sin. From the perspective of the entire canon of Scripture, the three desires enumerated in Genesis would eventually be identified with what the New Testament describes as the threefold "lust" of those who love the world more than God (1 Jn 2:16). In Christian tradition, these three reasons will eventually come to be identified as "the triple concupiscence", the three disordered desires that lie at the root of all human sinfulness (see *CCC* 377). Perhaps most striking of all, the three reasons given by Genesis for the Fall of Adam and Eve—the lust of the flesh, the lust of the eyes, and the pride of life—are directly tied to the three key disciplines of the Lenten season.

The Fall of Adam and Eve	*The Triple Lust*	*Lenten Disciplines*
1. Good for food	1. Lust of the flesh	1. Fasting
2. Delight of the eyes	2. Lust of the eyes	2. Almsgiving
3. To make one wise	3. The pride of life	3. Prayer
(Gen 3:6)	(1 Jn 2:16)	(cf. *CCC* 1438)

From this spiritual reading of Genesis, the rationale of Lent becomes clear: fasting, which mortifies the lust of the flesh; almsgiving, which mortifies the lust of the eyes; and prayer, which humbles our pride by acknowledging our dependence on God.

5. *The Protoevangelium and the Immaculate Conception*: This passage in Genesis 3:15 constitutes the first reading for the Solemnity of the Immaculate Conception and an optional reading for other Marian Masses. In the living tradition, the "enmity" between the serpent and the mysterious figure of the "woman" (Gen 3:15a) is reflected in the New Testament vision of the "woman clothed with the sun" (Rev 12:1), who is not only the mother of the Messiah but also at war with the devil, who is identified as "the great dragon ..., that ancient serpent" (Rev 12:9). Because of such connections, the *Protoevangelium* has been applied in a singular way by the Church to the Blessed Virgin, whose "enmity" with Satan is so comprehensive that it begins from the first moment of her conception; indeed, she is preserved immune from the stain of original sin, to which Adam and Eve subjected themselves by failing to do battle with the serpent (cf. *CCC* 491).

6. *Noah's Flood and the Mystery of Baptism*: The account of the covenant with Noah after the Flood (Gen 9:8–15) is the first reading for the First Sunday of Lent in Year B. This selection has two significant implications. For one thing, it highlights the importance given above to the concept of the "covenant" (Hebrew *berith*) as an important framework not only for the book of Genesis itself, but for the shape of salvation history made present in the liturgy. The Year B Lenten reading cycle progresses through the various covenantal stages of salvation history: the covenant with Noah (First Sunday), the covenant with Abraham (Second Sunday), the covenant with Israel at Sinai (Third Sunday), the account of Israel's covenant infidelity and exile in 2 Chronicles 26 (Fourth

Sunday), and the promise of a New Covenant in Jeremiah 31 (Fifth Sunday). This is meant to complement the catechesis of those preparing to enter into the New Covenant through baptism at Easter, and it reminds the whole Church of her fundamental narrative identity.

7. *The Tower of Babel and the Feast of Pentecost*: Finally, the Tower of Babel narrative (Gen 11:1–9) is the first of four optional first readings for the Vigil Mass of Pentecost. The Tower of Babel, as mentioned above, forms an important backdrop for understanding the significance of Pentecost. The Acts of the Apostles notes that representatives of all nations were present to witness the apostle's preaching (Acts 2:5) and notes their ironic bewilderment at being able to understand one another's "languages" or "tongues" (see Acts 2:6). Moreover, the Acts of the Apostles then enumerates a lengthy list of the nations from which those who experience the miracle are drawn (Acts 2:9–11), almost as if deliberately alluding to (although abbreviating) the so-called "Table of Nations" in Genesis 10. By placing the Feast of Pentecost against the backdrop of the descent of the Holy Spirit at Pentecost and the gift of "tongues", the Lectionary is reflecting the ancient Christian tradition that views the event of Pentecost as nothing less than *the undoing of the Tower of Babel* that will begin the reunification of the human family through the mission and witness of the apostolic Church.

Conclusion

Genesis 1–11 established the background for salvation history by describing God's sovereign creation of the cosmos as a temple for worship of himself, with mankind at the pinnacle of a hierarchy of good creatures over which man serves as king, priest, and mediator of the covenant by virtue of his status as son of God. Mankind's subsequent rejection of the privileges of divine sonship by rebellion against the paternal command launches a sad history of progressively increasing defiance of God and the natural order, necessitating God's intervention through the Flood and the confusion of languages at the Tower of Babel.

The initial covenant with Adam reveals the roles that God intended for all of mankind: sonship, kinship, priesthood, prophethood, and nuptial (or spousal) relationship. The celebratory account of matrimony at the conclusion of the creation accounts points to the significance of this mystery in the economy of salvation, since it provides an icon of the covenant relationship between God and his people.

The covenant with Noah is a restoration of the Adamic filial relationship, but in an impaired form in which the initial *shalom* that characterized man's interaction with the creation has been lost. However, Noah offends against even this impaired covenant, and mankind once more falls into a pattern of rebellion against God (Gen 11:1–9). This sets up the biblical narrative for the introduction of Abraham, the one through whom a more definitive solution for the alienation of mankind from communion with God will come (Gen 22:18; Gal 3:29).

For Further Reading

Commentaries and Studies on Genesis 1–11

Cassuto, Umberto. *From Adam to Noah.* Pt. 1 of *A Commentary on the Book of Genesis.* Translated by Israel Abrahams. Jerusalem: Magnes Press, 1961.

Currid, John. *Ancient Egypt and the Old Testament.* Grand Rapids, Mich.: Baker Books, 1997. (See pp. 33–73.)

Hamilton, Victor P. *The Book of Genesis: Chapters 1–17.* The New International Commentary on the Old Testament 1. Grand Rapids, Mich.: Eerdmans, 1990.

———. *Handbook on the Pentateuch.* Grand Rapids, Mich.: Baker Academic, 2005. (See pp. 19–80.)

Hess, Richard S., and David Toshio Tsumura. *I Studied Inscriptions from Before the Flood: Ancient Near Eastern, Literary, and Linguistic Approaches to Genesis 1–11.* Winona Lake, Ind.: Eisenbrauns, 1994.

Klausner, Joseph. *The Messianic Idea in Israel, from Its Beginning to the Completion of the Mishnah.* Translated by W. F. Stinespring. New York: Macmillan, 1955.

L'Heureux, Conrad E. *In and Out of Paradise: The Book of Genesis from Adam and Eve to the Tower of Babel.* New York: Paulist Press, 1983.

Martin, R. A. "The Earliest Messianic Interpretation of Genesis 3:15". *Journal of Biblical Literature* 84 (1965): 425–27.

Ratzinger, Joseph Cardinal. *"In the Beginning ...": A Catholic Understanding of the Story of Creation and the Fall.* Translated by Boniface Ramsey, O.P. Grand Rapids, Mich.: Eerdmans, 1995.

Walton, John H. "Genesis". Pages 1–68 in *Genesis, Exodus, Leviticus, Numbers, Deuteronomy.* Vol. 1 of *Zondervan Illustrated Bible Backgrounds Commentary.* Edited by John H. Walton. Grand Rapids, Mich.: Zondervan, 2009.

———. *Genesis 1 as Ancient Cosmology.* Winona Lake, Ind.: Eisenbrauns, 2011.

Wenham, Gordon J. *Genesis.* 2 vols. Word Biblical Commentary 1. Dallas: Word Books, 1987.

Westermann, Claus. *Genesis 1–11: A Commentary.* Translated by J. J. Scullion. Minneapolis: Fortress Press, 1984.

Genesis 1–11 in the Living Tradition

Ambrose, Saint. *Hexameron, Paradise, and Cain and Abel.* Translated by John J. Savage. The Fathers of the Church 42. Washington, D.C.: Catholic University of America Press, 1961.

Anderson, Gary A. *The Genesis of Perfection: Adam and Eve in Jewish and Christian Imagination.* Louisville, Ky.: Westminster John Knox Press, 2001.

Aquinas, Saint Thomas. "Treatise on the Work of the Six Days". *Summa Theologica* I, qq. 65–74. Translated by the Fathers of the English Dominican Province. 1948. Repr., Westminster, Md.: Christian Classics, 1981. (See vol. 1, pp. 325–59.)

Augustine, Saint. *The City of God.* Translated by Marcus Dods. In *Nicene and Post-Nicene Fathers,* 1st series. 1887. Repr., Peabody, Mass.: Hendrickson, 1994. (See books 13–15; 2: 245–314.)

———. *On Genesis.* Translated by Edmund Hill et al. Hyde Park, N.Y.: New City Press, 2002.

———. *The Trinity.* Translated by Stephen McKenna. The Fathers of the Church 45. Washington D.C.: Catholic University of America Press, 2002.

Basil the Great, Saint. "The Hexaemeron". In *Exegetic Homilies*. Translated by Agnes Clare Way. The Fathers of the Church 46. Washington, D.C.: Catholic University of America Press, 1967.

Bede, Venerable. *On Genesis*. Translated by Calvin Kendall. Translated Texts for Historians 48. Liverpool: Liverpool University Press, 2008. (See pp. 1–271.)

Bonaventure, Saint. *The Breviloquium*. Vol. 2 of *The Works of Bonaventure*. Translated by José de Vinck. Paterson, N.J.: Saint Anthony Guild Press, 1963. (See pp. 69–125.)

Bouteneff, Peter C. *Beginnings: Ancient Christian Readings of the Biblical Creation Narratives*. Grand Rapids, Mich.: Baker Academic, 2008.

Catechism of the Catholic Church. 2nd ed. Washington, D.C.: USCCB, 1997. (See nos. 279–421.)

Chrysostom, Saint John. *Homilies on Genesis 1–17*. Translated by Robert C. Hill. The Fathers of the Church 74. Washington, D.C.: Catholic University of America Press, 1986.

———. *Homilies on Genesis 18–45*. Translated by Robert C. Hill. The Fathers of the Church 82. Washington, D.C.: Catholic University of America Press, 1990. (See pp. 1–236.)

Daniélou, Jean, S.J. *The Bible and the Liturgy*. Notre Dame, Ind.: University of Notre Dame Press, 1956. (See pp. 70–85, 222–41.)

———. *From Shadows to Reality: Studies in the Biblical Typology of the Fathers*. Translated by Dom Wulstan Hibberd. Westminster, Md.: Newman Press, 1960. (See pp. 1–112.)

Ephrem the Syrian, Saint. *Selected Prose Works*. Translated by Edward G. Mathews Jr. and Joseph P. Amar. Edited by Kathleen E. McVey. The Fathers of the Church 91. Washington, D.C.: Catholic University of America Press, 1994. (See pp. 67–148.)

Greer, Rowan A. *Origen*. New York: Paulist Press, 1979.

Jerome, Saint. *The Homilies of Saint Jerome*. Translated by Marie Liguori Ewald. The Fathers of the Church 57. Washington, D.C.: Catholic University of America Press, 1966.

Kugel, James L. *Traditions of the Bible: A Guide to the Bible as It Was at the Start of the Common Era*. Cambridge, Mass.: Harvard University Press, 1997. (See pp. 44–242.)

Louth, Andrew, and Marco Conti. *Genesis 1–11*. Old Testament 1 of Ancient Christian Commentary on Scripture. Edited by Thomas C. Oden. Downers Grove, Ill.: InterVarsity Press, 2001.

Origen. *Homilies on Genesis and Exodus*. Translated by Ronald E. Heine. The Fathers of the Church 71. Washington, D.C.: Catholic University of America Press, 1982.

Pius XII, Pope. Encyclical Letter *Humani Generis* (1950), nos. 35–40.

Schroeder, Joy A. *The Book of Genesis*. The Bible in Medieval Tradition. Grand Rapids, Mich.: Eerdmans, 2015.

Theodoret of Cyrus. *On Genesis and Exodus*. Vol. 1 of *The Questions on the Octateuch*. Translated by Robert C. Hill. The Library of Early Christianity 1. Washington, D.C.: Catholic University of America Press, 2007.

6. GENESIS 12–50
THE PATRIARCHAL HISTORY

Introduction

If Genesis 1–11 provided the early history of mankind as a whole, Genesis 12–50 provides the early history of Israel in particular. The two are related: in the Pentateuch, Israel is a microcosm of mankind, and the hopes for all people are tied to the fortunes of this one family and the promises God makes to them.

Genesis 12–50 tells the story of the three great patriarchs, the ancestors of Israel—Abraham, Isaac, and Jacob—as well as the stories of the twelve sons of Jacob from whom the twelve tribes will descend, especially Joseph. The covenant God establishes with Abraham, which is passed down to his heirs Isaac and Jacob and ultimately to the twelve tribes, becomes the foundation for the plan of salvation for mankind throughout the rest of biblical history. As a result, it is difficult to overemphasize the significance of these chapters in Genesis for both history and theology. Indeed, as we will see, the entire history of salvation, from the election of Abraham to the blessing of "all the peoples of the earth", is present in seed form in three brief verses of this section of the Pentateuch (Gen 12:1–3).

Literary Structure of Genesis 12–50

The literary structure of the entire book of Genesis was discussed in the previous chapter. Here, we are dealing with the three cycles of the lives of the patriarchs, which are both distinguished and joined by the headings marked by the Hebrew word *toledoth* (generations) and other literary markers of transition (for example, birth and death announcements).

Outline of Genesis 12–50

1. Abraham Cycle	Gen 11:27—25:18	Begins with the *toledoth* of Abraham's father, Terah; ends with the account of Abraham's death (25:7–11) and is connected to the following Jacob Cycle by the *toledoth* of his son Ishmael (25:12–18)
2. Jacob Cycle	Gen 25:19—36:43	Begins with the *toledoth* of Jacob's father, Isaac (25:19), and the account of Jacob's birth (25:20–26); ends with the death of his father, Isaac (35:27–29), and is connected with the following Joseph Cycle by the *toledoth* of his brother Esau (chap. 36)
3. Joseph Cycle	Gen 37–50	Begins with the *toledoth* of Joseph's father, Jacob (37:1–2); ends with Joseph's own death (50:22–26)

Isaac alone among the patriarchs does not have a clearly marked literary cycle. Although Isaac is an extremely important character historically and theologically, his *literary* position in the book of Genesis serves largely to join his father Abraham with his son Jacob.

Each cycle shows a roughly *chiastic* internal structure, in which the first and second half of the cycle are balanced around a center point. For example, *the Abraham Cycle* has been analyzed by some scholars as a literary *chiasm*:

A. Genealogy of Terah (Gen 11:27–32)
    B. Start of Abraham's Spiritual Journey (Gen 12:1–9)
        C. Sarai Threatened in Foreign Palace; Abram and Lot Part (Gen 12:10—13:18)
            D. Abram Intervenes on Behalf of Sodom and Lot (Gen 14:1–24)
                E. Covenant with Abraham; Birth of Ishmael (Gen 15:1—16:16)
                E'. Covenant with Abraham; Birth of Isaac Announced (Gen 17:1—18:15)
            D'. Abraham Intervenes on Behalf of Sodom and Lot (Gen 18:16—19:38)
        C'. Sarah Threatened in Foreign Palace; Abraham and Ishmael Part (Gen 20:1—21:34).
    B'. Climax of Abraham's Spiritual Journey (Gen 22:1–19)
A'. Genealogy of Nahor (Gen 22:20–24)

The parallelism is not rigidly enforced by the author of Genesis; moreover, the Abraham Cycle does continue with three accounts of the wives of the patriarchs: Sarah (chap. 23), Rebekah (chap. 24), and Keturah (Gen 25:1–6), before relating Abraham's death (Gen 25:7–11) and segueing into the Jacob Cycle (Gen 25:12–19).

Along similar lines, as several scholars have shown,[1] the *Jacob Cycle* also proceeds according to a balanced pattern:

A. Oracle Sought; Struggle in Childbirth; Jacob Born (Gen 25:19–34)
    B. Interlude: Rebekah in Foreign Palace; Covenant with Foreigners (Gen 26:1–34)
        C. Jacob Fears Esau and Flees (Gen 27:1—28:9)
            D. Messengers (Angels) from/to God (28:10–22)
                E. Arrival at Haran (Gen 29:1–30)
                    F. Jacob's Wives Are Fertile (Gen 29:21—30:24)
                    F'. Jacob's Flocks Are Fertile (Gen 30:25–43)
                E'. Departure from Haran (Gen 31:1–54)
            D'. Messengers from/to Esau and the Messenger of the Lord (Gen 32:1–32)

---

[1] For example, Michael Fishbane, "Composition and Structure in the Jacob Cycle (Gen. 25:19—35:22)", *Journal of Jewish Studies* 26 (1975): 15–38, and Gary A. Rendsburg, *The Redaction of Genesis* (Winona Lake, Ind.: Eisenbrauns, 1986), 53–69.

       C'. Jacob Returns and Fears Esau (Gen 33:1–32)
     B'. Interlude: Dinah in a Foreign Palace; Covenant with Foreigners (Gen 34:1–31)
  A'. Oracle Fulfilled; Struggle in Childbirth; Jacob Becomes Israel (Gen 35:1–22)

Again, the structuring is not rigid, but a general balanced pattern, centered on the fertility of Jacob (chap. 30) in fulfillment of the Genesis blessing "be fruitful and multiply", is hard to deny once it is seen.

Finally, a similar literary pattern holds true for the third and final cycle in the book of Genesis: the *Joseph Cycle*. Again our sacred author has produced a balanced narrative:

A. Tension between Joseph and His Brothers; Jacob and Joseph Are Parted (Gen 37:1–36)
  B. Interlude: Joseph Not Present, Focus on Another Brother (Gen 38:1–30)
    C. Reversal: Joseph Guilty, Potiphar's Wife Innocent (Gen 39:1–23)
      D. Joseph Becomes Hero of Egypt (Gen 40:1—41:57)
        E. Two Trips to Egypt (Gen 42–43)
          F. The Climactic Test (Gen 44)
          F'. The Climactic Resolution (Gen 45)
        E'. Two Accounts of the Descent to Egypt (Gen 46:1–27; 46:28—47:12)
      D'. Joseph Becomes Hero of Egypt (Gen 47:13–26)
    C'. Reversal: Ephraim Firstborn, Manasseh Second-born (Gen 47:28—48:22)
  B'. Interlude: Joseph Minimally Present, Focus on Other Brothers (Gen 49:1–28)
A'. Tension between Joseph and His Brothers; Jacob and Joseph Part (Gen 49:29—50:26)

The connection between some units in this structure are very loose (for example, B and B', two units most unlike all the others), but the basic balanced pattern is undeniable. We begin and end with accounts of Joseph and the tension in his relationship with his brothers (Gen 37:2–28; 50:15–21) and with Jacob and Joseph being parted: on the one hand, Jacob weeping for Joseph (Gen 37:35), on the other, Joseph weeping for Jacob (Gen 50:1). Likewise, it is undeniable that the narrative thread of Genesis 40–41, which recounts Joseph's rise to the viziership and his rule over Egypt, is resumed in Genesis 47:13–26, and these two narrative blocks wrap or surround the emotional heart of the story (Gen 42:1—47:12), the interactions between Joseph and his brothers while he is ruler of Egypt.

In sum, with such deliberate literary structures and strategies at work, it is little wonder that the Patriarchal History contains some of the most memorable and dramatic narratives in all of world literature.

Overview of Genesis 12–50

The Abraham Cycle (Genesis 11:27—25:18)

The end of the Primeval History showed the growth of human sin once again after the re-creation that was the Flood and the eventual dispersion and disunity of the human family by means of the confusion of languages after their rebellion against God at the Tower of Babel. The biblical narrative quickly narrows in Genesis 11 to one family line and then to one man: Abram.

However, the sad fate of dispersed, disunified, and disgraced mankind is not forgotten: this one man will become the source of blessing for all the nations, whose origins are rooted in the three sons of Noah: Shem, Ham, and Japheth (Gen 10–11). Indeed, should there be any doubt about the universal significance of Abram's particular call, it is precisely this universal dimension that is stressed from the moment God first speaks to him, in what is arguably one of the most consequential texts in the entire Hebrew Bible:

> Now the LORD said to Abram, "Go from your country and your kindred and your father's house to the land that I will show you. And I will make of you a great nation, and I will bless you, and make your name great, so that you will be a blessing. I will bless those who bless you, and him who curses you I will curse; and *by you all the families of the earth shall be blessed.*" (Gen 12:1–3 [RSVCE, slightly adapted])

The "families of the earth" that shall be blessed are those listed in the long genealogy of the descendants of Noah in Genesis 10, who lose communion with God and one another in the tragic Tower of Babel account in Genesis 11. The goals mankind tried to achieve by its own power at Babel—a great "name" (Gen 11:4) and a single great nation (Gen 11:6)—are now promised to Abraham, not as the result of collective human effort, but as gifts of God's grace. Significantly, these verbal connections establish an important salvation-historical link between the Primeval History (Gen 1–11) and the Patriarchal History (Gen 12–50) as *one single history* of the salvation of mankind by God's grace and not human grasping.

The Threefold Promise to Abraham

This opening call of Abram (Gen 12:1–3) is programmatic for the Abraham Cycle and, in a sense, contains the outline of salvation history in the Old Testament and, later, of the Gospel in the New Testament, in embryonic form. Three specific blessings may be isolated in these verses: nation (v. 2a), name (v. 2b), and universal blessing (v. 3). These three blessings are given to Abram at the beginning of his walk with God as divine *promises* but over the course of the Abrahamic Cycle will be transformed by God into three solemn *covenants* in three subsequent chapters:

1. *The great nation*: the sacrifice of the animals (Gen 15)
2. *The great name*: the circumcision of Abraham (Gen 17)
3. *The universal blessing*: the sacrifice of Isaac (Gen 22)

The Figure of Lot in the Abraham Cycle

When the Abraham Cycle opens, Lot is Abraham's heir apparent, since he is his nephew and Abraham has no sons (Gen 12:5). However, Lot's separation from Abram (Gen 13:9–11) seems to end this relationship. Thereafter, the heir apparent becomes Abram's steward (chief servant), Eliezer (Gen 15:2), until Ishmael is born. Abraham is always loyal to Lot and intervenes for his welfare, but Lot only entangles Abraham in danger. Lot is not a wholly bad character: he shows hospitality to the angels (Gen 19:2–3), a clear display of virtue. Nonetheless, he is flawed by selfishness, sloth, and intemperance (Gen 13:10–11; 19:16, 30–38) and ultimately becomes the unwitting father of Israel's hostile rivals and enemies, the Ammonites and Moabites.

These chapters constitute the backbone of the Abraham Cycle. They are surrounded by narratives that describe various threats or challenges to the fulfillment of these covenant promises through God's intended heir, Isaac: (1) the endangerment of Isaac's mother, Sarah, in foreign palaces (Gen 12:10–20; 20:1–18); (2) familial strife and shortage of resources (Gen 13:1–18; 21:22–34); (3) the birth of hostile rivals to Isaac (Gen 16:1–16; 19:30–38; 25:1–6); (4) possible inability to find a suitable bride for Isaac (Gen 24:1–67). For the most part, these threats and challenges to the fulfillment of the covenant through Isaac are avoided and/or overcome; in some instances, however, the attentive reader knows that the present peace is only temporary and that the seeds of future turmoil have been sown.

The chiastic structure outlined above for the main part of the cycle (Gen 12–22) does accurately show how the covenant-making ceremonies are central (Gen 15, 17); they are surrounded by stories of the endangerment of Sarah and Lot and begin and end with two closely related narratives of God's call to Abraham initially (Gen 12:1–9) and then again at Mount Moriah (Gen 22:1–18). It is most important to understand the two covenant-making episodes (Gen 15, 17) and the narrative climax, the sacrifice of Isaac (Gen 22:1–18), which is also a covenant-making episode, so we will focus on those three units.

Nationhood and the Animal Sacrifices of Abram (Genesis 15)

Abraham has already survived a number of adventures by the time we reach Genesis 15: his foolish endangerment of his wife, Sarai, in the pharaoh's court (Gen 12:10–20); strife and separation from his heir apparent Lot (Gen 13); outright warfare in order to fulfill his familial obligation to Lot (Gen 14). Just before Genesis 15, he is blessed in the name of God Most High by the mysterious priest-king Melchizedek in the wake of his defeat of the various pagan kings in the Promised Land (Gen 14:14–18).

At the beginning of Genesis 15, God appears to Abram to confirm the divine blessing most recently articulated by Melchizedek (Gen 15:1). But Abram protests that he has no descendants, and, with Lot gone, his steward Eliezer will be his heir (Gen 15:2–5). Strikingly, God responds to Abram's anxiety by bringing him outside and telling him to "look toward heaven" and "number the stars", declaring, "So shall your descendants be" (Gen 15:5). It is Abram's response to this divine declaration regarding his descendants that constitutes the foundation of the role he would go on to play as a figure of faith: "And he believed the LORD; and he reckoned it to him as righteousness [Hebrew *tsedaqah*]" (Gen 15:6).

Unfortunately, Abram's reaction to the divine promise of *the land* is not so faith-filled as his reaction to the promise of *descendants*. Immediately following the positive depiction of Abram's faith in God regarding the heir of his house, Genesis describes another divine decree, in which the Lord declares that he is going to give Abram "this land to possess" (Gen 15:7). In this instance, Abram responds: "O Lord GOD, how am I to *know* that I shall possess it?" (Gen 15:8). Notice the doubt implicit in Abram's response; the obvious answer to the question of how Abram is to "know" that he will possess the land is because the Lord has just said so! Nevertheless, this is not how God responds to Abram's doubt about the promise of land. Instead, the Lord responds by saying: "Bring me a heifer three years old, a she-goat three years old, a ram three years old, a turtle-dove, and a young pigeon" (Gen 15:9). The meaning of this otherwise-bizarre list is simple when read in its literary context: by commanding Abram to acquire animals for sacrifice, the Lord is in essence instructing Abram to transform the promise of the land into a solemn covenant by means of *blood sacrifice*. Indeed, after Abram lays out the split carcasses of the animals and falls into a deep sleep, the presence of God appears in the form of "a smoking fire pot and a flaming torch", moving between the pieces and promising Abram the land of Canaan for his descendants (Gen 15:17–20).

The strange ritual that Abram and God perform in this chapter is a classic ancient Near Eastern covenant-making ceremony, for which close parallels can be found elsewhere in Scripture and in ancient Near Eastern texts (see Jer 34). To move between the pieces while uttering promises was a ceremonial way of stating: "If I do not keep my commitments, may I be slain like these animals." Note well that the content of God's covenant commitments to Abram in this covenant sacrifice is limited to numerous descendants and the land (Gen 15:5, 14, 18–21). In other words, by means of animal sacrifice, *the first promise* of Genesis 12:1–3, that Abram would become a "great nation", is transformed into a solemn covenant.

The Great Name and the Covenant of Circumcision (Genesis 17)

The intervening narrative between Genesis 15 and 17 is significant for understanding why, in Genesis 17, we have a covenant-making episode that, at first glance, appears to duplicate what took place in the earlier chapter.

In Genesis 16, Abram and Sarai attempt to hasten the fulfillment of God's slow-to-be-realized promise of descendants through their own natural power, by means of recourse to ancient forms of "reproductive technology": the well-attested ancient Near Eastern practice of

> *Royalty and the "Great Name"*
>
> "Great name" was associated with kingship in the ancient Near East, as can be seen from the inscription from Shamshi-Adad I, king of Assyria, ca. 1800 B.C.: "I erected a stela in my *great name* in the land of Lebanon, on the shore of the Great Sea [= Mediterranean]."

using servant women as surrogate mothers. So Sarai gives Hagar to Abram as a secondary wife, and she bears Ishmael.

There can be no doubt that the author of Genesis does not view this incident favorably. For one thing, the sacred author writes, "Abram *listened to the voice of Sarai*" (Gen 16:2), which is an intertextual echo of God's words of rebuke to Adam, "Because you have *listened to the voice of your wife*, and have eaten of the tree" (Gen 3:17). The repeated phrase draws the parallel between two covenant mediators who follow the advice of their spouse instead of the commands or promises of God, with the results leading them both into an

---

What Is the Sin of Sodom and Gomorrah?

Sodom and Gomorrah, the cities of the plain of the Jordan, play an important role in the life of Abraham (Gen 14, 18, 19) but never again in the history of Israel. The Bible describes the men of these cities as "wicked, great sinners" (Gen 13:13). In contemporary scholarship, the question has been raised: What exactly is the sin of Sodom and Gomorrah? Is it homosexual relations? Or is it, as some scholars have suggested, a sin of inhospitality toward strangers, or is it some other kind of sin, such as social injustice?

After telling us that the "sin" of Sodom and Gomorrah is "very grave" (Gen 18:20), Genesis then goes on to describe a situation that is clearly focused on homosexual relations. After discovering that Lot has two male visitors, the men of the city of Sodom demand: "Bring them out to us, that we may *know* them" (Gen 19:5). In this case, the word "know" (*yada'*) is a Hebrew euphemism for sexual relations. This is made explicit immediately after, when Lot insists on protecting his two male visitors and despicably offers the men of Sodom instead his two daughters who "have not known (*yada'*) man" (Gen 19:8).

In recent times, based on later references to Sodom and Gomorrah in the prophetic literature, some argue that the sin of Sodom has nothing to do with homosexual relations but, rather, is focused on inhospitality or some other form of injustice. And indeed, the prophets associate Sodom and Gomorrah with a lack of social justice (Is 1:9; 3:9), disregard for the poor (Ezek 16:46–51), and widespread immorality (Jer 23:14). However, a close reading of these texts in the prophets reveals that these are prophetic *applications* of the proverbial depravity of Sodom to the contemporary city of Jerusalem. They are not *redefinitions* of the sin of Sodom as presented in Genesis. Indeed, the New Testament itself explicitly identifies the sin of Sodom as sexual in nature when it refers to the "licentiousness" of the citizens (2 Pet 1:6–7).[a]

In response to this debate, the Magisterium of the Catholic Church has clarified that the account of Sodom does in fact refer to "homosexual relations" and continues to teach, on the basis of Genesis 19 and other texts in Sacred Scripture, that while "homosexual persons" must be "accepted with respect, compassion, and sensitivity", "homosexual acts" are acts of "grave depravity" and are "intrinsically disordered".[b]

In closing, it is worth noting that the cities of Sodom and Gomorrah have, at times, been considered mythical, the invention of the biblical author. However, recent archaeological excavations have made a strong case for identifying Sodom and Gomorrah with *Tall-el-Hammam*, a site in what is now the state of Jordan, near the entrance of the river Jordan to the Dead Sea. If the identification is correct, the archaeological record shows that Sodom and Gomorrah were extremely powerful and wealthy cities in the early second millennium B.C., but were destroyed suddenly by a natural disaster by mid-millennium and remained uninhabited for about 700 years.

[a] See Robert A.J. Gagnon, *The Bible and Homosexual Practice: Texts and Hermeneutics* (Nashville: Abingdon Press, 2002), 269.

[b] CCC 2357–58; Congregation for the Doctrine of the Faith, Letter *On the Pastoral Care of Homosexual Persons* (1986), 4–7.

imprudent, covenant-endangering course of action. Moreover, from the perspective of Genesis as a whole, the practice of *polygamy* begins with the negative figure of Cain's descendent, Lamech (Gen 4), and such polygamous situations generally lead to short- and long-term familial strife in the Old Testament, as in the story of the strife between the two wives and two concubines of Jacob (see Gen 29–30). In this regard, Genesis 16 is no exception: the peace of Abram's household is destroyed by conflict between Sarai and Hagar. Finally, the ancient reader would have been aware that this son, Ishmael, would be the ancestor of hostile rivals and persecutors of the people of Israel down through the centuries (Gen 16:12; 17:11). In the present case, Abram's acquiescence to Sarai's plan shows a lack of faith on his own part that God's promises will be fulfilled without human assistance, and it produces an unintended heir who complicates the line of covenant succession.

This situation necessitates God's intervention, and so in the very next chapter, the Lord appears to Abram again and issues what may be an implicit rebuke of Abram's behavior: "I am God Almighty; walk before me, and *be blameless*" (Gen 17:1). God then reaffirms to Abram the covenant relationship, but not without important changes and qualifications, all of which are focused on the second part of God's initial promise to Abram: *the promise of a great name* (Gen 12:2).

This connection to the promise of a great name is evident in several aspects of Genesis 17. The most obvious of these is the divine *change of Abram's name*. Up to this point in Genesis, his name has been *Abram* (Hebrew for "exalted father"); from now on, his name shall be *Abraham* (Hebrew for "father of a multitude") (Gen 17:5). Throughout the Hebrew Scriptures, whenever God changes someone's name, it is invariably a significant moment, signaling to the reader not only who that person is in the eyes of God, but what role he will play in the history of salvation (cf. Gen 3:20; 25:26; chaps. 29–30; and so on). Moreover, the promise of nationhood contains within itself an implicit forecast of *royalty* from Abram's line. This promise of royalty is at the heart of the blessing of the "great name", because the concept of "great name" was associated with kings both in Scripture (2 Sam 7:9) and in ancient Near Eastern texts. The promise here of a "great name" or royalty is intrinsically linked to the concept of "father of a multitude of nations", because it is not primarily in a physical sense that Abraham will become the father of a multitude. Physically, only Israel, Edom, and the Arab tribes descend from him: several nations, but not a multitude. However, ancient Near Eastern emperors or "great kings" were typically termed "fathers" of the vassal kings who ruled individual nations under them. As we will see, in the course of the Old Testament as a whole, Abraham's "fatherhood" over a multitude of nations will be fulfilled in his descendants David and Solomon, who become, in essence, Israelite *emperors*, "fathers" of all the kings and their peoples from the Euphrates to the border of Egypt (1 Kings 4:21). Then representatives of all the subject peoples would gather in Jerusalem for worship: "The princes of the peoples gather as the people of the God of Abraham" (Ps 47:9).

Should there be any doubt about this next stage of God's promise being transformed into a covenant, it is critical to note that God not only reaffirms his commitment to bring his promise of a great name to pass; he once again gives Abram assurance by means of a covenant sacrifice to perform. In this case,

---

Oath and Covenant in Scripture

Since a covenant was formed by either a verbal or a ritual oath (or both), "covenant" and "oath" are often synonymous in Scripture:

"There both of them swore an *oath*. So they made a *covenant* at Beer-sheba" (Gen 21:31–32).

"Let there be an *oath* between you and us, and let us make a *covenant* with you" (Gen 26:28).

"As I live, surely *my oath* which he despised, and *my covenant* which he broke, I will repay upon his head" (Ezek 17:19).

"To remember his holy *covenant*, the *oath* which he swore to our father Abraham" (Lk 1:72–73). This last quote is a direct reference to the covenant-oath of the *Aqedah* (Gen 22:16–18), the only time God explicitly swears to Abraham. It shows a canonical recognition of the oath of the *Aqedah* as a solemn formulation of the Abrahamic covenant.

---

however, the sacrifice demanded is not simply the blood of bulls and goats, but Abram's own flesh: the covenant of *circumcision*. The ritual removal of "the flesh of your foreskins" will be "a sign of the covenant between me and you" (Gen 17:11). Although this ritual may seem bizarre, even irrational, when taken in isolation, when circumcision is located within *its narrative context* in the Abrahamic Cycle, it makes sense. In Genesis 16, Abram attempts to bring God's promise of descendants to pass by means of his own sexual power, by lying with Hagar; in Genesis 17, God reaffirms his promise of descendants, but in the wake of Abram's action, obliges him and his descendants to perform, as a sign of the covenant, a sacrificial and penitential act directly tied to the member of his body with which he deviated from God's will. From this point of view, the covenant has an implicit but intrinsically *penitential* symbolism. In Genesis 15, Abram cut animals to solemnize the covenant of nationhood; in Genesis 17, he must cut his foreskin to solemnize the covenant of great name. Therefore, there does seem to be an escalation in the intensity of the covenant commitment: it becomes both more costly and more personal.

Finally, it is important to note that the Lord specifies that the heir of the covenant is to be Isaac, not Ishmael, despite Abraham's protest (Gen 17:18). This is perhaps the key reason for the renewal and revision of the covenant relationship in this chapter, because, in the intervening time, Abraham has produced an heir outside of God's intention. Ishmael remains a party to the first covenant (Genesis 15), which promised great nationhood for Abraham; therefore God will make Ishmael into a "great nation" and grant him "princes" (Gen 17:20), but not kings. However, the present covenant, promising kingship and "fatherhood of many nations", is restricted to Isaac and his line.

Universal Blessing and the Sacrifice of Isaac (Genesis 22)

The third and final stage in the three-stage development of the Abrahamic covenant comes in the famous passage known in Jewish tradition as the "binding" of Isaac (Hebrew *Aqedah*). Although Christians ordinarily refer to this text as the "Sacrifice of Isaac", in point of fact, Isaac is bound but not slain. In this episode, the third and final aspect of the threefold promise to Abraham—the promise of "universal blessing" for all families—is elevated to the status of a covenant by means of Abraham's willingness to offer his only beloved son in sacrifice.

The removal of all potential back-up heirs and the drama surrounding the long-awaited birth of Isaac contribute to the heart-rending intensity of the test Abraham undergoes in this chapter. First, Abraham's nephew, Lot, is distanced from him (Gen 18:16—19:38), and then, Ishmael, his son by Hagar the concubine, likewise departs from him (Gen 21:8–21). Some twenty-four years after the initial call of Abram at the age of seventy-five, the promise of a son for Abram and Sarai is finally realized when he is ninety-nine years old (Gen 18:1–15, 20:1–18; 21:1–7). Then, after an unspecified amount of time has elapsed, God "tests" Abraham by commanding him to take Isaac, "your only son, whom you love", and offer him as a "burnt offering" upon a mountain chosen by God (Gen 22:1–2). At least four aspects of the binding of Isaac are worth highlighting here.

First, Abraham is commanded to sacrifice his *only beloved son*. Three times in Genesis 22 Isaac is called the "one and only" son of Abraham (Hebrew *yahid*) and identified as the "son ... whom you love" (Gen 22:2). The rare Hebrew term *yahid* literally means "unique, singular", but was translated "beloved" (Greek *agapētos*) in the Septuagint. Later on in the New Testament, Jesus Christ will be identified with two similar terms: he is the "only-begotten" (Greek *monogenēs*) son of God (Jn 3:16), the "beloved [Greek *agapētos*] Son" with whom God is well-pleased (Mt 3:17).

Second, contrary to many artistic renderings of the scene, in the Genesis account, *Isaac is not a child* but a young man. For one thing, the same Hebrew term is used for Isaac and for Abraham's servants: he is a "young man" (Hebrew *na'ar*) (see Gen 22:3). Even more telling, Isaac carries sufficient wood up the mountain to burn up the body of a sacrificial animal. Such a heavy load would be impossible for a child to carry and much heavier than that of his father, who has only the fire and the knife. Already in antiquity Jewish interpreters deduced from these narrative clues that Isaac was no longer a child but a young man, stronger than his elderly father.[2] As a young man, then, as soon as he realized what his father was about to do, he could have overpowered the frail Abraham. However, Isaac voices no objection and makes no effort to resist; hence, although he is not killed, he does willingly offer himself in sacrifice. It is a death Isaac freely accepts (thus justifying the expression, "sacrifice" of Isaac, even though he lives).

Third, Genesis makes quite clear that *God never actually intends for Isaac to be put to death*. Instead, the entire drama is meant to test the faith of Abraham. For example, God's opening command to Abraham to "Go ... to a mountain I will tell you" reuses Hebrew words of his earlier call: "Go ... to a land I will show you" (Gen 22:1; 12:1 [author's trans.]). In this way, the Hebrew text signals that the sacrifice of Isaac is a kind of microcosm of Abraham's entire faith journey begun in his call from Ur of the Chaldeans. In contrast to the moments of

---

[2] See James Kugel, *Traditions of the Bible: A Guide to the Bible as It Was at the Start of the Common Era* (Cambridge, Mass.: Harvard University Press, 1997), 304–5.

doubt and hesitation in the intervening years, when the test of sacrificing Isaac comes, Abraham obeys without question, as at the beginning of his journey. In Genesis 12, he undertook a journey that parted him from the family of his past; here in Genesis 22, he undertakes a journey that will part him from his family of the future, his descendants through Isaac. Abraham journeys three days to the land of Moriah, then climbs a mountain there with Isaac, but is stopped by the angel of God from killing Isaac at the very last moment. Because Abraham passes the test of faith, God elevates the final promise of universal blessing to the level of a covenant:

> By myself I have sworn, says the LORD, *because you have done this, and have not withheld your son, your one and only* [Hebrew *yahid*] *son*, I will indeed bless you, and I will multiply your seed as the stars of heaven and as the sand which is on the seashore. And your seed shall possess the gate of his enemies, and *in your seed shall all the nations of the earth be blessed, because you have obeyed my voice*. (Gen 22:16–18 [author's trans.])

This is the final form of the covenant with Abraham. Because the word "covenant" does not explicitly appear in this passage, the covenant significance of this narrative is often overlooked. However, when we understand that covenants are established by means of an *oath*—as demonstrated quite clearly in the previous chapter (Gen 21:21–32)—we recognize the full import of God's self-sworn oath as a response to the binding of Isaac. Genesis 22 is a covenant-solemnization account on a par with Genesis 15 and 17. In these previous chapters, Abraham had been called, in order to solemnize the covenant, to sacrifice (1) animals, then (2) his own flesh, now finally (3) his only son

---

The Patriarchs and the "Philistines"

Both Abraham (Gen 21:22–34) and Isaac (Gen 26:26–33) make a covenant with Abimelech, the Philistine king of Gerar. Are the stories confused duplicates of one another? Not necessarily: it was not uncommon for an ancient Near Eastern king to make a covenant with a neighboring ruler and then renew it with his successor(s); several such covenant-treaties are extant (e.g., between the king of Aleppo Talmi-sharruma and two Hittite kings, Mursil II and his successor Muwatallis II). As for the term "Philistine", the Hebrew author appears to use it broadly to cover any of the Aegean seafaring peoples related to the Greeks, who had a long history of trade and colonization in Canaan. The cordial "Philistines" of the patriarchs, located in Gerar, are not the same as the hostile "Philistines" of Saul and David, located in the five coastal cities: Gaza, Ashdod, Ashkelon, Ekron, and Gath. These later "Philistines" did not invade the coast of Palestine until around 1200 B.C., long after the patriarchs.

---

and heir, Isaac. So there is an intensification in each instance. Genesis 15 had promised great nationhood to Abraham; Genesis 17 included kingship and fatherhood over a multitude of nations; now in Genesis 22:18 the final promise of universal blessing mentioned in Genesis 12:3 is incorporated into a covenant-oath: "*in your seed* shall all the nations of the earth be blessed" [author's trans.]. The difference between Genesis 12:3 and 22:18 is that now the blessing shall be not simply "*in you*" but "*in your seed*"—that is, through your *descendant* or *descendants*, since "seed" is ambiguously singular or plural, in Hebrew (*zerah*) as in English.

Fourth and finally, it is important not to overlook the significance of the fact that Isaac is sacrificed, not just anywhere, but *on one of the mountains of Moriah* (Gen 22:2–4). In the Hebrew Scriptures, this will later be identified as the site upon which King Solomon would build the Temple in Jerusalem: "Then Solomon began to build the house of the LORD in Jerusalem on *Mount Moriah*" (2 Chron 3:1). The reason this cultic and geographical connection with the Temple is important is because in the Genesis account itself, there is an explicit emphasis on the significance of the mountain where Isaac is sacrificed as the place of future covenant blessing. Indeed, in the wake of the binding of his only beloved son, Abraham gives the locale a prophetic name:

> So Abraham called the name of that place The LORD will provide [Hebrew *YHWH yireh*]; as it is said to this day, *"On the mount of the LORD it shall be provided."* (Gen 22:14)

As the Hebrew Scriptures will later make clear, the "mount of the LORD" here is the Jerusalem Temple mount; there is a wordplay on "Jerusalem" (Hebrew *yiru-shalem*) and the Hebrew word for "see to it" or "provide" (*yireh*) (compare Ps 76:1–2). In some streams of later Jewish tradition, the animal sacrifices offered at the Jerusalem Temple were regarded as memorials or re-presentations of the sacrifice of Isaac, the rationale being that the blood of bulls and goats was not effective in itself but symbolized the truly meritorious self-offering of the forefather of the entire nation.[3]

The *Aqedah*, the "Calvary of the Old Testament", brings the career of Abraham to a stunning climax. Although Abraham is an imperfect character who has shown imprudence, vacillations in faith, and differences with the will of God, when put to the ultimate test, he demonstrates faith at the most profound level. The oath of God in response to Abraham's (and Isaac's) willingness to sacrifice everything establishes the final form of the Abrahamic covenant. Indeed, although the circumcision covenant (Gen 17) is formulated as dependent on Abraham's fulfillment of covenant obligations, the violation of which will result in breech of the covenant (Gen 17:14), the covenant that stems from the sacrifice of Isaac (Gen 22) is formulated as a pure grant from God ("by myself I have sworn ... I will indeed bless you"). It is dependent, not on the fulfillment

---

Types of Covenant in the Ancient Near East

Covenants were solemnized by a verbal or ritual oath. Scholars distinguish different types of covenant by observing which of the two covenanting parties swears the oath. If both parties swear, it is a "parity" or "kinship" covenant, which emphasizes mutuality and familial relationship. If only the inferior party swears, it is a "vassal" covenant, usually imposed by the superior party to control the behavior of the inferior. If only the superior party swears, it is a "grant" covenant, a unilateral promise of benefit from the superior to the inferior, usually as a reward for notable fidelity.[a]

[a] See Scott W. Hahn, *Kinship by Covenant*, Anchor Yale Bible Reference Library (New Haven, Conn.: Yale University Press, 2009), 29.

---

[3] See Jon D. Levenson, *The Death and Resurrection of the Beloved Son: The Transformation of Child Sacrifice in Judaism and Christianity* (New Haven, Conn.: Yale University, 1993), 173–74 *et passim*.

of obligations (none are given, nor are any sanctions), but solely on the basis of Abraham's demonstrated obedience ("because you have done this" Gen 22:16). Such a covenant in which the superior party swears unilaterally to uphold its conditions is termed by scholars a "grant" covenant, as opposed to a "vassal" covenant in which the inferior party is placed under obligations. Dependent no longer on the weakness of human performance but solely on divine commitment, the threefold Abrahamic covenant will become a continuous source of hope and mercy for the "seed" (descendants) of Abraham and the families of the world (see Ex 32:13).

The Jacob Cycle (Genesis 25:19—35:29)

After the binding of Isaac and the covenant of universal blessing, the Abraham Cycle begins a *denouement* with three narratives about the wives of the patriarchs, (1) the death of Sarah (Gen 23); (2) the acquisition of Rebekah (Gen 24); and (3) the concubine Keturah (Gen 25:1–6), preceding the account of Abraham's own death (Gen 25:7–11). The genealogy of the "cadet line" of Ishmael links the Abraham Cycle to the Jacob Cycle. Jacob is born to Rebekah, the younger of a set of twins, and given the Hebrew name *yakob*, "he grasps (the heel)", meaning "he deceives" (compare the English expression, "he's pulling your leg"). In a pivotal moment in the covenant history of Abraham's family, Jacob buys the right of the firstborn, under a sworn oath, from his brother Esau for a pot of stew (Gen 25:27–34). At the instigation of his mother, Rebekah (and against his better

> ### "Cadet Lines" in Genesis
>
> "Cadet lines" are non-inheriting lines of a dynasty, usually the descendants of daughters and younger sons. Due to role reversals, frequently the descendants of *older* sons in Genesis turn out to be "cadet lines". Although they are not in the direct line of the covenant, the "cadet lines" in Genesis are still important to God and will ultimately share in the universal blessing to all the nations/families of the earth that lies at the heart of the covenant with Abraham (Gen 22:18). Therefore, to connect the major narrative cycles, several cadet-line genealogies are given in Genesis: of the sons of Noah (Gen 10); of Nahor (Gen 22:20–24); of Ishmael (Gen 25:12–18); of Esau (Gen 36).

judgment), Jacob then tricks his father, Isaac, into giving him the blessing that should have accompanied that birthright (Gen 27). After Esau realizes what has happened to him, Jacob is forced to flee from his enraged brother to his mother's brother Laban in Paddan-Aram—that is, northwest Mesopotamia (Gen 28). On the way, God appears to him in a dream at Bethel, reaffirming to him the Abrahamic blessing and explicitly renewing the covenant of nation, name, and universal blessing that was made with Abraham and Isaac (Gen 28:13–15). In response to this vision, Jacob builds a shrine there and then continues to Paddan-Aram, where he falls in love with Laban's daughter Rachel, but is tricked by Laban into marrying both Rachel and her older sister Leah, whom he did not find attractive (Gen 29:17). Jacob serves Laban fourteen years as a bride-price for the two daughters (Gen 29:20, 30) and another six years to gain flocks and herds of his own (Genesis 31:41). At the end of this time, not surprisingly, the relationship with Laban has soured, and Jacob flees back to Canaan with his family, only to be hunted down by Laban and saved from harm by divine intervention alone (Gen 31). The uncle and nephew make peace by means of a "covenant" (Gen 31:43–55), but Jacob must then face the wrath of his brother Esau, who has heard of his homecoming. The imminent approach of Esau with a small army leads to a personal and spiritual crisis for Jacob involving intense prayer (Gen 32:9–12) and even a mysterious wrestling with the angel of the Lord, the climax of his entire biography (Gen 32:22–32). Emerging from this struggle with a divine blessing strangely mixed with a permanent physical injury (Gen 32:29–32), Jacob reconciles with Esau, settles in the land, and returns to worship at Bethel, the place where he had seen God as a young man (Gen 33, 35). The deaths of Rachel (Gen 36:16–21) and Isaac (Gen 35:27–29) conclude the narrative cycle focused on him.

In contrast to Abraham and Isaac, Jacob produces no "cadet lines". All his sons are heirs to the covenant promises, all twelve tribes of Israel. As a result, Jacob-Israel is the distinctive embodiment of the nation that springs from him, and so his narrative cycle is significant for its portrayal of Jacob's character, which is the national character. Jacob's character is most notable for his *desire to be heir of the covenant*, or, in other words, *his desire for God's blessing*. Jacob is not the "firstborn" or the natural choice for this role, and the story of his career is one of struggle against others, especially his family, and even against God himself, in an effort to receive the blessing. In this he contrasts with his brother Esau, who is not wholly bad, and is even a sympathetic character at times, and yet, in the final analysis, is indifferent to the covenant patrimony of his status as firstborn son, preferring the earthly good of a meal to the spiritual blessing won from him by his younger brother (Gen 25:34).

Throughout the Jacob Cycle, there is a decided moral growth on his part, so that, by the end, he has learned that he is "not worthy" in the least of all the steadfast love shown him by the God of Abraham and Isaac (Gen 32:9–12)

Does God Condone Jacob's Deceit?

Jacob's name can be translated "trickster", and so he is remembered. But does God condone trickery and bless those who deceive? The Jacob narrative is not so simple. First of all, Jacob's "deceit" is often exaggerated. His purchase of Esau's birthright involved no deception and was legal according to the customs of the day. With the birthright should have come the blessing, but, for whatever reason, Isaac intends to confer the blessing on Esau anyway. It is Rebekah, not Jacob, who invents and executes the plan to "steal" the blessing through deception. Jacob cooperates against his better judgment in this effort to take back what should have been his by purchase of the birthright. Forced afterward to flee to Laban, Jacob finds himself tricked and cheated with respect to his wives (Gen 29:20–30) and his flocks (Gen 30:35–36). He does try some measures to fight back (Gen 30:37–43), but these would have been completely ineffective without divine intervention (Gen 31:1–12). In sum, Jacob is not the habitual cheater he is sometimes thought to be. Moreover, as the ancients saw already in antiquity, he is made to do penance for his deception of his father by being deceived by Laban and suffering through twenty years of strenuous outdoor labor (Gen 31:38–42), though he himself preferred a comfortable indoor life-style (Gen 25:27). God thoroughly punishes and humbles Jacob for his deceptions but, nonetheless, blesses him for his desire to *claim the covenant promise*, a desire of great value in God's eyes.

and that it was God who delivered him in his distress and has been with him wherever he went (Gen 35:2–3). Thus he wins the name "man-who-strives-with-God" (Hebrew *Ish-ra-el*). Although the sacred author does not wish the people of God to emulate everything about Jacob (see sidebar on p. 144), his passionate desire to *claim the covenant* and *receive the blessing* are held up as models for the national character.

The Joseph Cycle (Genesis 37–50)

The Joseph Cycle is a well-integrated, discrete narrative that has been described by some scholars as a kind of short novel (*novella*) and recognized by many as a masterpiece of world literature. It is largely set in Egypt, and, as one might expect, it reflects Egyptian culture and literature, sharing themes with classic Egyptian literary works from the second millennium B.C., notably the *Tale of Sinuhe*.

In keeping with the earlier narratives of creation, Noah, and the former patriarchs, the Joseph Cycle begins with a *toledoth* marker: "This is the *toledoth* of Jacob", and then immediately launches into the biography of Joseph (Gen 37:2). This is yet another literary clue that the genre of Genesis is a sacred family history. Joseph, as the favored son of Jacob, is too free in sharing his dreams of grandeur and so alienates his brothers, who plot to kill him, but ultimately settle on selling him into slavery in Egypt (Gen 37).

Joseph rises in the house of his Egyptian master, only to be falsely denounced by his master's lustful wife and sent to prison. Once again he rises among the ranks of prisoners until he exercises all the authority of the warden (Gen 39). A chance to interpret the favorable dreams of the pharaoh's imprisoned butler seems to present an opportunity to leave the prison, but these hopes are dashed (Gen 40). It is not until the pharaoh himself is disturbed by his dreams that

---

What Was the Sin of Onan?

Genesis 38:1–11 tells the story of Onan, the son of Judah, who marries Tamar, the wife of his deceased brother, according to the law of "levirate marriage" (Deut 25:5–10). However, in the act of marital intercourse, Onan "spilled the semen on the ground" so that he would not give offspring to his brother (Gen 38:9). As a result, "What he did was displeasing in the sight of the LORD, and he slew him" (Gen 38:10).

Interpreters debate the question: What was the sin of Onan? On the one hand, some argue that Onan's sin was his *refusal to give children to his brother's wife*. The problem with this interpretation, however, is that the punishment for failing to carry out the levirate duty was *not death*, but a public act of shaming the widow involving taking off the man's sandal and spitting in his face (see Deut 25:7–11).

The more plausible interpretation is that Onan is killed for *the deliberately contraceptive sexual act* of spilling his semen on the ground and thereby willfully rendering procreation impossible. This is supported by the fact that elsewhere in the Pentateuch, sexual acts that render procreation impossible are also capital crimes punishable by death (e.g., Lev 20:13, 15–16).

In the eighteenth century, the term "onanism" was coined and sometimes misleadingly used as a euphemism for masturbation. This led to some confusion in interpreting this text, since what is in view in Genesis 38 is not masturbation but a deliberately interrupted sexual act (Latin *coitus interruptus*).

the butler remembers Joseph and recalls him from prison. Joseph successfully interprets the pharaoh's dreams as foretelling a coming famine, and the pharaoh makes him the vizier (prime minister) of Egypt because of his apparent mystic insight. Joseph quickly sets about preparing Egypt for the seven years of famine foretold by the dreams (Gen 41).

Meanwhile, Joseph's brothers are suffering from famine in the Promised Land of Canaan. As a result of the shortage of food, they are compelled to travel to Egypt to buy food, where they find themselves—unwittingly—begging for entrance to Egypt before their own brother (Gen 42)! Hiding his identity, Joseph harasses them as spies, but he quickly relents and sends them back to Canaan well-provisioned, on the condition that if they come again, they must bring his full brother, Benjamin, with them.

Jacob, however, is most reluctant to part with Benjamin, so the return trip to Egypt is delayed until starvation is imminent. At last, Benjamin is entrusted to the care of his older brother Judah, and the brothers return to Egypt to encounter Joseph once more (Gen 43). Joseph entertains them for a few days, then sends them on their way—but not before planting stolen goods in Benjamin's packs. Benjamin is "discovered", and Joseph purports to detain him in Egypt permanently. Finally Judah, the very brother who had intially proposed to sell Joseph to Egypt, steps forward and gives an impassioned speech in which he offers his own life on behalf of his half brother Benjamin, for the sake of the peace of their father, Jacob (Gen 44). Joseph is overcome with emotion and reveals his identity to his shocked brothers. He sends them, well-stocked, back to Canaan to fetch their father, Jacob, and their families (Gen 45). The extended family arrives in Egypt, is granted a royal audience with the pharaoh, and is assigned a share of the best pasture land in the country. Joseph successfully sees the nation through the years of famine and does so in such a way that the people are grateful but the pharaoh is also enriched (Gen 46–47). Elderly Jacob blesses the sons of Joseph and then all twelve of his own sons before dying and receiving a burial fit for a king (Gen 48–49). At last, Joseph himself dies, but not before making his surviving kinfolk swear to bring his body back to Canaan when they leave Egypt (Gen 50).

As can be seen from this brief overview, the narrative tension in the Joseph Cycle builds, develops, and intensifies up to Judah's tear-jerking monologue (Gen 44:18–33); then the tension is released with Joseph's tearful yet joyous self-revelation (Gen 45:1–14), and for the remainder of the narrative, one tension after another is resolved with peace and success far better than could have been anticipated.

The Joseph Cycle and the Providence of God

The overarching theme of the Joseph Cycle is that of God's *providence*. Despite the evil intentions and actions of the human players in the drama, God is constantly working out his plan of salvation, including the fulfillment of his covenant promises. Thus Joseph sums up the moral of the entire narrative when he says to his brothers: "As for you, *you meant evil against me; but God meant it for good*, to bring it about that many people should be kept alive, as they are today" (Gen 50:20). So we see that the Abrahamic covenant promise of universal

The Joseph Cycle and Egyptian Literature

The Joseph Cycle is largely set in Egypt and has an authentically Egyptian flavor. Scholars have noted several thematic parallels with ancient Egyptian literature. These include the *Tale of Sinuhe*, an apparently authentic account of an Egyptian civil servant who is forced to leave Egypt against his will (ca. 1960 B.C.), almost dies in Canaan, is saved by a chieftain of a nomadic clan, rises to power in Canaan, and then is invited back to the Egyptian royal court, where he is scarcely recognizable in his Canaanite garb. He lives out his last days in Egypt, grateful to die in his beloved homeland. Thus it is almost an inverted image of the Joseph Cycle; compare Joseph's desire to be buried in Canaan (Gen 50:25). Another relevant text is the *Story of Two Brothers*, a folktale about an upright younger brother falsely accused of adultery with his older brother's wife, often compared with the Potiphar's wife incident (Gen 39). Egyptians were much concerned with the interpretations of dreams, and at least one fragmentary copy of a handbook of dream interpretation is still extant from ca. 1300 B.C. Also, an Egyptian inscription found on the banks of the Nile claims to transmit an ancient tradition of a seven-year famine once sent as punishment by the gods. The sacred author of Genesis 37–50 knew Egyptian culture and tells the biography of Joseph highlighting its Egyptian features.

blessing for all the nations of the earth finds an initial fulfillment, inasmuch as Joseph, Abraham's "seed" or descendant, becomes the source of blessing not only for Egypt but for "all the earth" that comes to Egypt to be fed during the famine (Gen 41:57).

In fact, one of the important functions of the Joseph Cycle is to explain the origin of the various relationships that will ultimately take shape between the tribes that descend from the twelve brothers. For example, Reuben is the oldest brother, and yet his tribe never exercises leadership. The narrative explains how this came about: Reuben offended his father by having relations with his father's concubine (Gen 35:22) and thereby fails to receive the blessing of kingship that would have been rightfully his as firstborn son (Gen 49:3–4). Likewise, Simeon and Levi, though next in line biologically, also suffer a loss of covenant blessing status because of the injustice they perpetrated by deceiving the men of Shechem into circumcising themselves and then slaughtering the Shechemites while they were recovering from the procedure (Gen 34). In the course of the story, we see that Reuben tries to exercise leadership in the family but is always unsuccessful (Gen 37:22–30; 42:37–38). Instead, the family trusts and follows the leadership of Judah (Gen 37:26–28; 43:8–15). Although behind Reuben, Simeon, and Levi in birth order, Judah is the eldest son who is not cursed by his father for some grave offense (Gen 49:3–7), and so to him falls the "scepter" of rightful kingship (Gen 49:10).

On the other hand, Joseph, the eldest son of Jacob's beloved wife Rachel, also obviously exercises leadership in the family and receives the most profuse blessing (Gen 49:22–26). Remarkably, it is upon the heads of his sons—who bear the blood of an Egyptian mother—that the covenant blessings are conferred (Gen 48:15–16). In this way, Jacob's blessing sets up a tension between these two brothers and the tribes that will come from them by granting the "scepter" (kingship) to Judah (Gen 49:10) and yet calling Joseph the "prince" among his brothers (Gen 49:26 NABRE). It is from these two tribes, Judah and Joseph (= Ephraim) that the kings of southern Judah and northern Israel, respectively, will be provided. Other future relationships between the tribes are also foreshadowed in this cycle: for example, the close relationship between Judah and Benjamin that develops, with Judah offering himself as protection for Benjamin, will manifest itself in tribal history, as Benjamin alone among the other tribes stays loyal to the Judean monarchy and thereby finds itself preserved as a tribe all the way into the Christian era, as, for example, in the self-proclaimed "Hebrew of Hebrews"—the apostle Paul—who is himself a Benjaminite (Rom 11:1).

Historical Issues in Genesis 12–50

In both ancient Jewish and Christian tradition, the substantial historical truth of the accounts of the patriarchs has never been subject to doubt. For example, in its overview of salvation history, recent magisterial teaching appears to assume the historicity of the call of Abraham, the existence of the patriarchs, and the formation of the people of Israel from their descendants (see *CCC* 59–60, 62). In modern times, however, the pendulum of scholarly views concerning the historicity of these narratives has swung back and forth repeatedly and continues to do so.

Debates over the Historicity of the Patriarchal Narratives

At the end of the nineteenth century, Julius Wellhausen asserted his influence with the view that the patriarchal narratives were pure fiction written during the period of the Judean monarchy (tenth century B.C.) or later. In the mid-twentieth century, the pendulum swung back again toward confidence in the historical accuracy of the narratives under the influence of W. F. Albright and the "American school", bolstered by a number of archaeological finds that illuminated the cultural background of many aspects of the patriarchal stories. Toward the end of the century, the rise of biblical "minimalism" among scholars such as Thomas L. Thompson produced another swing and a return of the "fictional" perspective of yesteryear. This minimalism has itself spurned a reaction in the early years of the twenty-first century from scholars with expertise in archaeology such as Kenneth A. Kitchen, who argue that the minimalists are ignoring entire swaths of cultural evidence from Egypt and the Ancient Near East that supports the contextual plausibility of the accounts of Abraham, Isaac, and Jacob.

On one side of the ledger, scholars who argue against the historicity of the patriarchal narratives make the following points: (1) there is no direct archaeological confirmation of the specific characters in the narratives; (2) the presence of dialogue with God and some miraculous elements indicates the genre of the narratives is that of *legend*; (3) the presence of certain elements, such as camels and Philistines in Canaan, and some late name-forms like *Potiphar* are anachronistic and hence point to the legendary character of the tales; and (4) the presence of foreshadowing or prophetic elements (like the scepter to Judah, Gen

49:10) suggest a date of composition in the monarchic period or even much later yet.[4]

On the other hand, scholars arguing for the historicity of the patriarchal narratives respond as follows: (1) the archaeological record of the ancient Near East is quite haphazard, and direct archaeological evidence for private, nomadic individuals like the patriarchs is not to be expected;[5] (2) the literary genre of the patriarchal narratives best fits ancient Near Eastern *biography*, which recounts actual history but also typically includes assertions of interaction with the gods, due to the strong theological world view of the ancients;[6] (3) camels as well as Aegean foreigners (= "Philistines") are attested for an early date in Canaan, and other anachronisms may be light retouches by editors in later centuries; (4) the presence of some prophetic elements is not a problem for those with a theistic world view.

Are the Patriarchal Narratives an Idealized Account from a Later Period?

Indeed, many elements in the accounts of the patriarchs are hard to explain as the inventions of an Israelite author at a later period, given the tendency for cultures to idealize (or "whitewash") ancient heroes and founders as the centuries pass. Among the elements that would *not* have been invented later, we may mention the following:

- Abraham's marriage to a half sister (Gen 20:12), contrary to Mosaic law (Lev 18:9)
- The prominence of Sodom and Gomorrah (Gen 13–14, 18–19), which were destroyed by the mid-second millennium B.C. and played no role in later Israelite history
- Jacob, father of all Israel, duped into marrying a woman (Gen 29:23–27) and her sister (Gen 29:28), contrary to Mosaic law (Lev 18:18)
- Judah, forefather of the royal tribe, marrying a Canaanite woman (Gen 38:2) and producing the majority of his heirs through unwitting incest with his Canaanite daughter-in-law (Gen 38:24–30), contrary to Mosaic law (Lev 18:15), thus making the tribe of Judah half-Canaanite
- Ephraim and Manasseh being half-Egyptian through their mother, Asenath, daughter of a pagan priest (Gen 41:50)
- Reuben as *firstborn* son (Gen 29:32), despite the fact that his tribe was never prominent
- Levi, the forefather of the holy priestly tribe, as a violent killer (Gen 34:25), cursed by his father (Gen 34:30; 49:5)
- The traditional enemies of Israel—Ishmael, Edom, the "Philistines", and the pharaoh—portrayed sympathetically (Gen 13:10–20; 17:20; 20:1–18; 21:8–21, 21:22–34, 26:6–11, 26:31; 33:1–16; 47:7–11)

[4] John J. Collins, *Introduction to the Hebrew Bible* (Minneapolis: Fortress Press, 2004), 84–88.
[5] James K. Hoffmeier, *The Archaeology of the Bible* (Oxford: Lion Hudson, 2008), see 33–48.
[6] Kenneth A. Kitchen, *On the Reliability of the Old Testament* (Grand Rapids, Mich.: Eerdmans, 2003), 313–72.

- The patriarchs worshipping at groves and setting up stone pillars, without the benefit of priests, all contrary to Mosaic law (Lev 26:1; Deut 12:12; 16:22)
- The patriarchs never worshipping in Jerusalem, but instead worshipping at all manner of sites in Canaan, some of which became heterodox rival sanctuaries later in Israel's history, like Bethel (1 Kings 12:29)

Ancient Near Eastern Law and the Patriarchs

One piece of evidence that has convinced some scholars of the basic authenticity of the patriarchal narratives is the striking correspondence between many of the unusual customs in the biblical stories and those reflected in ancient Near Eastern law codes from at or about the same time period.

For example, law tablets recovered from Nuzi, a city in northwest Mesopotamia (biblical Paddan-Aram), the very region from which the patriarchs acquire their wives, attest at least nine customs found in the biblical accounts that otherwise seem puzzling:

1. The adoption of a servant as heir of a householder (Gen 15:2)
2. A wife supplying her husband with a surrogate mother in the case of infertility (Gen 16:2)
3. Legal clauses preventing the expulsion of the second wife's children upon the birth of children to the first wife (Gen 21:11)
4. The sale of an inheritance to a brother in exchange for provisions to avoid starvation (Gen 25:29–34)
5. The legally binding nature of a father's deathbed blessing (Gen 27:33)
6. A prospective son-in-law paying the bride-price for a man's daughter by means of labor (Gen 29:18)
7. A son-in-law becoming the primary heir of his father-in-law (Gen 31:1, 43)
8. The possession of the family's household gods (idols) as legal basis for primary inheritance rights (Gen 31:19)
9. Handmaids as paternal wedding gifts to daughters (Gen 29:24, 29)

The Nuzi tablets date from a few generations after the patriarchs (ca. 1500 B.C.) but undoubtedly reflect long-standing common law in their homeland. Similar laws can be found in other older ancient Near Eastern law codes, although the Nuzi tablets provide the most parallels from a single source. In short: *the accounts of the patriarchs in Genesis 37–50 reflect the culture of the time period in which the biblical chronology places them* and are unlikely to be the free creations of a much later Israelite author.

Contextual Plausibility of the Description of Canaan

In addition, those who would affirm the historicity of the patriarchs would stress that the sociopolitical situation in Canaan depicted in the narratives only fits the early second millennium B.C., the same time frame to which the biblical accounts date the patriarchs. For example, in the Canaan of the patriarchs,

Source: commons.wikimedia.org

This tomb-wall painting from Egypt, ca. 1900 B.C., depicts a clan of nomadic "Asiatics" (Syro-Palestinians) under the leadership of their chief "Ab-sharru" (cf. Ab-raham) visiting Egypt to sell their goods. The clans of the patriarchs would have been similar.

nomadic clans are able to move freely through the land; there is political influence from Mesopotamia (Gen 14) and the Hittites (Gen 23) but not from Egypt; there is easy access to Egypt and its delta capital; Sodom and Gomorrah are still standing. The general picture is very similar to the early second-millennium Egyptian account *The Tale of Sinuhe*, about an Egyptian civil servant who flees political trouble in Egypt and escapes to Canaan, where he is saved from starvation by a nomadic clan chief very much like one of the patriarchs.

However, by the mid-second millennium B.C., passage through the land for nomadic groups became very difficult due to the Egyptian military presence and petty warfare between the Canaanite city-states. Mesopotamian and Hittite influence in Canaan had waned or disappeared. Egypt had adopted a hostile attitude toward Semitic migrants and had moved its capital to a more inaccessible location up the Nile. Sodom and Gomorrah were no longer in existence, having suddenly been destroyed at least by the mid-second millennium. Other incidental information in Genesis 12–50, such as the name-forms of the patriarchs, the slave-price of Joseph, and the absence of Baal-worship in Canaan, also better fit the first half of the second millennium B.C. rather than a later time period. Fuller discussion is

Names and Slaves

Small pieces of incidental data often point to the antiquity of the patriarchal narratives. For example, biblical names beginning with "I" or "J" in English (like *Isaac, Jacob,* and *Joseph*) usually reflect a type of Hebrew name based on the imperfective form of the verb. Sometimes called "Amorite imperfectives", these name-forms made up about 40 percent of all names in the Near East in the early second millennium B.C., but nearly disappeared in the first millennium. Similarly, the price of slaves (twenty shekels of silver, Gen 37:28) recorded in Genesis reflects second-millennium prices, not the radically inflated prices found later in the first millennium.

available elsewhere,[7] but here we may summarize by emphasizing that recent scholarship shows that the sociopolitical picture of Canaan in the accounts of the patriarchs (Gen 37–50) fits best with the known situation in Palestine ca. 1800–1600 B.C., *and neither before nor after*. This cultural convergence is hard to explain if the text originated centuries later, when the cultural and political scene had dramatically changed in the ancient Near East and in the land of Canaan, but is easy to explain if the narratives present authentic historical memories from the second millennium B.C.

Genesis 12–50 in the Living Tradition

Given the foundational role of Abraham, Isaac, and Jacob in salvation history as a whole, it should come as no surprise that the section of Genesis dealing with the lives of the patriarchs has played a prominent role in the living tradition of the Church. In what follows, we will once again give a brief sampling of the way in which these texts have been interpreted in the Christian tradition.[8]

Abraham as a Model of Faith

From the very earliest days of the Church, Abraham was held up as a model of faith in many ways, with three in particular standing out: his willingness to leave behind all that he knew when he set out from Ur of the Chaldeans in response to God's call to journey with his family to the land of Canaan, even though he was already at an advanced age (Gen 11:31; Acts 7:2–4); his act of believing God's promise of a multitude of descendants, even though he was old and Sarah was barren (Gen 15:1–6; Rom 4:3); and his willingness to offer up his only beloved son, Isaac, in sacrifice, trusting that, somehow, God would nevertheless fulfill his promise of descendants and, if necessary, raise Isaac from the dead (Gen 22; Heb 11:19). In the Christian tradition, the faith of Abraham is summed up in the classic text from the letter to the Hebrews:

> By faith Abraham obeyed when he was called to go out to a place which he was to receive as an inheritance; and he went out, not knowing where he was to go. By faith he sojourned in the land of promise, as in a foreign land, living in tents with Isaac and Jacob, heirs with him of the same promise. For he looked forward to the city which has foundations, whose builder and maker is God.... By faith Abraham, when he was tested, offered up Isaac, and he who had received the promises was ready to offer up his only-begotten son, of whom it was said, "Through Isaac shall your descendants be named." He considered that God was able to raise men even from the dead; hence he did receive him back and this was a symbol. (Heb 11:8–10, 17–19)

The apostle Paul declares that Abraham had a righteousness that came from faith in God, and not from external obedience to the law of Moses (Gal 3:6).

---

[7] Ibid.

[8] See Mark Sheridan, ed., *Genesis 12–50*, Old Testament 2, Ancient Christian Commentary on Scripture, ed. Thomas C. Oden (Downers Grove, Ill.: InterVarsity Press, 2002); Kugel, *Traditions of the Bible*, 243–500.

While this truth can be exaggerated into the Protestant notion of *sola fide*, or salvation by faith alone, nonetheless, Abraham does provide us a model and example of relationship with God based on deep trust rather than legalism. On the other hand, as the letter of James emphasizes, Abraham's faith does not exclude works but expresses itself through them:

> Was not Abraham our father justified by works, when he offered his son Isaac upon the altar? You see that faith was active along with his works, and faith was completed by works, and the Scripture was fulfilled which says, "Abraham believed God, and it was reckoned to him as righteousness." (Jas 2:21–23)

The initial call of Abraham—the beginning of the patriarchal narratives (Gen 12:1–3)—is understood by the Church as the model or paradigm of each person's call to walk with God through life in a relationship of faith. It is the model of the Christian vocation generally as well as of particular vocations to lives of service within the Church: to holy orders or to religious or consecrated life. As a result—as we will see below when we turn to the Lectionary—the call of Abram is read at Masses concerned with Christian initiation or entrance to a particular vocation.

Melchizedek, the Priesthood, and the Eucharist

The encounter between the patriarch Abram and the mysterious figure of Melchizedek is one of the primary typological texts in the patriarchal narratives in the New Testament, the writings of the Church Fathers, and later Christian tradition. This typological significance revolves around both the identity of Melchizedek and the sacrifice of bread and wine.

Although Genesis itself is quite enigmatic regarding the identity of Melchizedek, several points of interest emerge. For one thing, Melchizedek is Abraham's superior. Although Abraham defeats the coalition of Mesopotamian kings, who in turn had just subjugated the primary kings of the land of Canaan (Gen 14:1–7), he does not establish himself as king but, rather, recognizes the kingship—and priesthood—of Melchizedek, king of Salem, who emerges into the narrative suddenly at this point and disappears again just as suddenly. In Hebrew, *Melchizedek* means "king of righteousness", and *Salem* literally means "peace" and was the original and archaic name for the city of "Jerusalem" both in the Bible and in ancient Near Eastern texts (see Ps 76:1–2). In other words, Abram is paying his tithe of war to the ancient king of Jerusalem, who is named for his righteousness.

In order to explain why Abram showed such deference, later Jewish and Christian tradition almost unanimously identified Melchizedek as *Shem*, the oldest son of Noah, who, according to the biblical genealogies, lives well into the lifetime of Abraham and, hence, would have been his patriarch and superior (see Gen 11:10–32). From this point of view, "Melchizedek" was regarded as the royal name of Shem (much like kings and popes in our own time will have both a birth name and a throne name). This Shem-Melchizedek identification is found already in the ancient Aramaic translations of Genesis known as the

Targums (*Targum Neofitii* on Gen 14:18) and later rabbinic tradition (*Genesis Rabbah* 43:6; *Leviticus Rabbah* 25:6). It was also adopted in Christian interpretation by the Fathers and Doctors in ancient and medieval times (appearing in the *Glossa Ordinaria*) up to the time of the Reformation. For example, the fourth-century Church Father Ephrem the Syrian writes:

> This Melchizedek is Shem, who became a king due to his greatness; he was the head of fourteen nations. In addition, "he was a priest." He received this from Noah, his father, through the rites of succession. Shem lived not only to the time of Abraham, as Scripture says, but even to [the time of] Jacob and Esau.[9]

Following this patristic tradition, the medieval *Glossa Ordinaria* puts it this way: "The Hebrews say this Melchizedek was Shem son of Noah, who lived until Isaac; and [they also say] that every primogenitor, from Noah to Aaron, was a priest."[10]

According to this tradition, then, the blessing Shem receives from Noah is not lost but, rather, passed on to Abram (Gen 9:26; 14:19–20). Likewise, the priesthood of Melchizedek/Shem is a *natural priesthood* passed from father to firstborn son, through the genealogies, from Adam to Shem to Abram. This would explain why the New Testament identifies the priesthood of Jesus Christ as being "according to the order of Melchizedek" (Heb 5:6, 10). From this point of view, the priesthood of Christ in the New Covenant is not a complete *novum* but, rather, a restoration and transformation of the natural priesthood of the firstborn son, a form of priesthood exercised during the period of the patriarchs and which prevailed prior to the sin with the Golden Calf and the restriction of the priesthood to the tribe of Levi (see Ex 32:25–29).

With all of this in mind, the *sacrifice of Melchizedek* takes on new significance (Gen 14:18). As "priest of God Most High", Melchizedek, the *king of Jerusalem*, offers a sacrifice of *bread and wine* in thanksgiving to God. It does not take much to see in such an act a type or foreshadowing of Jesus Christ, the true "king of righteousness", offering his own sacrifice of bread and wine at the Last Supper, in the city of Jerusalem. Indeed, the Eucharistic symbolism of this event is recalled in Eucharistic Prayer 1, also known as the Roman Canon:

> Be pleased to look upon these offerings with a serene and kindly countenance, and to accept them, as once you were pleased to accept the gifts of your servant Abel the just, the sacrifice of Abraham, our father in faith, and the offering of your high priest Melchizedek.[11]

In light of such connections in the living tradition of the Church, the account of Melchizedek is read at Masses devoted to Eucharistic veneration: the Feast of Corpus Christi and votive Masses to the Most Holy Eucharist (see below).

---

[9] Ephrem the Syrian, *Commentary on Genesis* 11.2, in Sheridan, *Genesis 12–50*, 26.

[10] J.P. Migne, *Patrologia Latina* 198.1094–95 (author's trans.).

[11] Eucharistic Prayer I, from *Daily Roman Missal*, ed. James Socias, 3rd ed. (Woodridge, Ill.: Midwest Theological Forum, 2010), 777.

The Sacrifice of Isaac and the Passion of Christ

In the history of the patriarchs, perhaps no passage stands out more in terms of its typological significance for the Christian tradition than the so-called "sacrifice of Isaac" (Gen 22).[12] From ancient times, this dramatic and difficult account of God's "test" of Abraham's faith was seen as a foreshadowing of the Passion and death of Christ on the Cross. Indeed, in the ancient Christian tradition, a number of parallels between Genesis 22 and the accounts of Jesus in the Gospels stand out:

Sacrifice of Isaac	Sacrifice of Christ
Father Abraham offers his "only-begotten son" as a sacrifice. (Gen 22:2)	God the Father offers his "only-begotten Son" as a sacrifice. (Jn 3:16)
Isaac carries "the wood" of his own sacrifice up the mountain. (Gen 22:4–6)	Jesus the Son carries the wood of his Cross up to Golgotha. (Jn 19:17)
Isaac says "My Father" (Hebrew *Abi'*) in face of his sacrifice. (Gen 22:7)	Jesus prays "Father" (Aramaic *Abba*) in face of his sacrifice. (Mk 14:36)
Abraham declares that "God will provide himself the lamb" for sacrifice. (Gen 22:8)	Jesus is "the Lamb of God, who takes away the sin of the world". (Jn 1:29)
Isaac willingly offers himself in sacrifice in obedience to his father. (Gen 22:9)	Jesus willingly offers himself in sacrifice in obedience to the Father. (Jn 10:18)
God provides a "ram" caught by his horns in a "thicket" instead of Isaac. (Gen 22:13)	God provides his Son wearing a crown of thorns on his head. (Mt 27:29)
The sacrifice of Isaac takes place on Mount Moriah (= Jerusalem). (Gen 22:2, 4; 2 Chron 3:1)	The sacrifice of Jesus takes place in Jerusalem (= Mount Moriah). (Mt 27:33; cf. 2 Chron 3:1)

In light of these and other parallels between the binding of Isaac and the sacrifice of Christ, the early Church Fathers did not hesitate to see in this mysterious test of Abraham a kind of divine "pre-enactment" of the Passion of Jesus.

For example, in his homily on the binding of Isaac, Saint John Chrysostom writes: *"All these things were types of the cross.* That is why Christ said: Abraham rejoiced that he might see My day: he saw it, and was glad. How did he see it, considering that he was born so many years before? In type (*typos*) and in shadow (*skia*).... *The reality had to be depicted beforehand in type."*[13] Along similar lines, Saint Augustine writes:

---

[12] Jean Daniélou, S.J., *From Shadows to Reality: Studies in the Biblical Typology of the Fathers*, trans. Dom Wulstan Hibberd (Westminster, Md.: Newman Press, 1960), see 115–30.

[13] John Chrysostom, *Homilies on Genesis* 47.3, in ibid., 129.

In whose similitude but His of whom the apostle says, "He that spared not His own Son, but delivered Him up for us all?" *And on this account Isaac also himself carried to the place of sacrifice the wood on which he was to be offered up, just as the Lord Himself carried His own cross.* Finally, since Isaac was not to be slain, after his father was forbidden to smite him, who was that ram by the offering of which that sacrifice was completed with typical blood? For when Abraham saw him, he was caught by the horns in a thicket. *What, then, did he represent but Jesus, who, before He was offered up, was crowned with thorns . . .?*[14]

This typological reading provides a powerful explanation for the otherwise inexplicable and unique occurrence of the God of Israel appearing to command *human sacrifice*. Seen in the full light of the New Testament and living tradition, we discover that God does not desire the death of Isaac but does desire for Abraham and Isaac to *enact within salvation history* the kind of self-sacrificial donation that God himself, as a Trinity of persons, will carry out in order to bring about the salvation of mankind. Because Abraham the father and Isaac the son are both willing to submit to the test, they win for themselves arguably the most solemn oath of blessing from God in the entire Old Testament (Gen 22:15–18) and become models of faith even for the New Covenant.

The Sin of Onan and the Teaching on Contraceptive Sexual Acts

In addition to typological interpretation, the second part of Genesis also had consequential implications for the moral teaching of Christianity, with specific reference to its teachings on human sexuality. Perhaps the most significant of these regards the account of the sin of Onan, who "spilled the semen on the ground" in the course of relations with Tamar and, as a result, was slain by God (Gen 38:9–10). In the living tradition of the Church, Onan's sin was identified as a deliberately contraceptive sexual act and in this way became the key biblical foundation for the Christian rejection of contraception. Consider, for example, the words of Jerome:

> But I wonder why he [the heretic Jovinianus] set Judah and Tamar before us for an example, unless perchance even harlots give him pleasure; or Onan who was slain because he grudged his brother seed. Does he imagine that we approve of any sexual intercourse except for the procreation of children?[15]

In more recent times, the most significant expression of this tradition was given in the early twentieth century by Pope Pius XI in his Encyclical Letter on Christian Marriage, *Casti Connubii* (1930). This papal encyclical—which was published in the immediate wake of the 1930 Anglican Lambeth Conference, which altered the traditional Christian teaching and permitted the use of

---

[14] Augustine, *The City of God* 16.32.1, in *NPNF1* 2:329.
[15] Jerome, *Against Jovinian* 1.20, in *NPNF2* 6:361.

"methods of conception control" other than abstinence—reiterated the Christian teaching about the gravely sinful character of contraceptive sexual acts by appealing directly to the story of Onan in Genesis 38:

> No reason, however grave, may be put forward by which anything intrinsically against nature may become conformable to nature and morally good. Since, therefore, the conjugal act is destined primarily by nature for the begetting of children, those who in exercising it deliberately frustrate its natural power and purpose sin against nature and commit a deed which is shameful and intrinsically vicious.
>
> *Small wonder, therefore, if Holy Writ bears witness that the Divine Majesty regards with greatest detestation this horrible crime and at times has punished it with death.* As St. Augustine notes, *"Intercourse even with one's legitimate wife is unlawful and wicked where the conception of the offspring is prevented. Onan, the son of Juda, did this and the Lord killed him for it"* [Augustine, *De coniug. adult.* 2.12; Gen 38:8–10].
>
> Since, therefore, openly departing from the uninterrupted Christian tradition some recently have judged it possible solemnly to declare another doctrine regarding this question, the Catholic Church, to whom God has entrusted the defense of the integrity and purity of morals, standing erect in the midst of the moral ruin which surrounds her, in order that she may preserve the chastity of the nuptial union from being defiled by this foul stain, raises her voice in token of her divine ambassadorship and through Our mouth proclaims anew: any use whatsoever of matrimony exercised in such a way that the act is deliberately frustrated in its natural power to generate life is an offense against the law of God and of nature, and those who indulge in such are branded with the guilt of a grave sin.[16]

Few issues have been more consequential or controversial than the modern debate over the Catholic Church's teaching on sexuality. Here we see how Genesis 38 played a direct role in shaping the Church's teaching that "every action which, whether in anticipation of the conjugal act"—as in the case of Onan—"or in its accomplishment, or in the development of its natural consequences, proposes, whether as an end or as a means, to render procreation impossible" is "intrinsically evil".[17]

The "Passion" of Joseph and the Life of Jesus

The final figure from the patriarchal narratives who stands out in both the book of Genesis and in the living tradition is that of Joseph, who garners more chapters than any other character in the entire book of Genesis (chaps. 37–50). Although the parallels between the life of Joseph and the life of Jesus are less well known, they too were part of the typological reading of Genesis in the Christian tradition. Indeed, when seen in the light of the New Testament with Joseph as a type of Christ, one can even speak of Genesis 37–50 as a kind of foreshadowing of the Passion, death, Resurrection, and exaltation of Jesus:

---

[16] Pius XI, Encyclical on Christian Marriage, *Casti Connubii* (1930), 54–56.
[17] Paul VI, *Humanae Vitae* 14; *CCC* 2370.

Life of Joseph	*Life of Jesus*
Joseph is firstborn son of Rachel and beloved son of Jacob. (Gen 30:22–24; 37:3)	Jesus is firstborn son of Mary and beloved son of God. (Mt 1:25; 3:17)
Joseph is sold to Gentiles for twenty silver pieces by Judah and eleven brothers. (Gen 37:25–36)	Jesus is sold to Gentiles for thirty silver pieces and abandoned by eleven disciples. (Mt 26:15, 30)
Joseph is with two condemned men (cupbearer and baker), one of whom is pardoned and given physical life. (Gen 40:1–23)	Jesus is with two condemned men, one of whom is forgiven by Jesus and given everlasting life. (Lk 23:32, 39–43)
Joseph is exalted to the right hand of the Pharaoh and rules over kingdom of Egypt. (Gen 41:40–44)	Jesus is exalted to the right hand of God and rules over kingdom of heaven. (Acts 2:32–33)
Joseph saves Israel and Gentiles from death and feeds them life-giving wheat. (Gen 41:55–57)	Jesus saves Israel and Gentiles from spiritual death and feeds them eternal life-giving bread. (Jn 6:1–71)
Joseph gives special honor to Benjamin, youngest of the twelve, at a banquet. (Gen 43:33–34)	Jesus gives special place of honor to John, the Beloved Disciple, at the Last Supper. (Jn 13:23)
Joseph is revealed to his brothers, who do not recognize him at first, after he is exalted to the throne of Egypt. (Gen 42:8)	Jesus is revealed to his disciples, who do not recognize him at first, after he is raised from the dead. (Lk 24)

In light of such parallels, early Church Fathers such as Saint Ambrose saw in the life of Joseph a prefiguration of the life of Christ and the sufferings and trials of Joseph as a "symbolic representation of the Lord's passion".[18] Indeed, as the offspring of Abraham, Joseph feeds the nations all with "the gift of finest wheat", so that Joseph becomes a type of the one betrayed by his "brother" Judah (= "Judas") for pieces of silver, who descends into the pit of death and yet is raised up and seated at the right hand of the king, there becoming the source of blessing for the whole world.

Genesis 12–50 in the Lectionary

Once again, a brief chart of the readings from the Patriarchal History (Gen 12–50) in the contemporary Lectionary helps us to hone in on certain aspects of this portion of Sacred Scripture as they have been interpreted by the Church in the living tradition. Significantly, most of the connections we have made above are represented in the selections used in the Lectionary (see chart on the following pages).

---

[18] Ambrose, *On Joseph* 3.14, in Sheridan, *Genesis 12–50*, 239.

Readings from the Patriarchal History (Gen 12–50) for Sundays, Feast Days, Liturgical Seasons, and Other Occasions			
MSO = Masses for Special Occasions; OM = Optional Memorial; VM = Votive Mass; Rit = Ritual			
Scripture	Description	Place in Calendar	Explanation
12:1–4a	The initial call of Abraham; the threefold promise of blessing; Abraham's obedient departure	*2nd Sunday of Lent (A)*; also Common of Holy Men and Women, opt. 1; *Rit*: Entrance into the Order of Catechumens; *Rit*: Consecration of Virgins and Religious Profession; *MSO*: For Vocations to Holy Orders or Religious Life	In Lent, Year A, this text functions as part of a review of salvation history through the Sundays of Lent following the sequence Adam–Abraham–Moses–David–Prophets–Christ. On other Eucharistic observances, this call of Abraham provides the *quintessential* paradigm of God's *vocation* or call to the believer, both generally to every Christian as well as specifically to those with a particular vocation within the Church. The saints are those who responded to this call with the fidelity of Abraham.
12:1–7	See above; plus Abraham's worship in the land of Canaan	Common of the BVM, opt. 2	The Blessed Virgin is remembered as one who shared the faith of Abraham and responded to God's calling with similar fidelity; also, she became the means of the fulfillment of the promises to Abraham, particularly the promise of blessing to all the families of the earth.
14:18–20	Melchizedek's offering of bread and wine, and the blessing of Abraham	*Corpus Christi (C)*; *VM*: The Most Holy Eucharist; *Rit*: Institution of Acolytes	Melchizedek's offering is one of the primary Old Testament types of the Eucharist. His priesthood is intrinsically related to the Davidic covenant centered on Salem/Jerusalem and is fulfilled in Christ's priesthood shared with the Church's clergy.
15:1–6; 21:1–3	The promise of descendants to Abram plus the birth of Isaac	*Feast of the Holy Family (B)*	This duo of texts points to the centrality of the family in God's plan of salvation; the Holy Family is the icon and embodiment of the family of Abraham and the family of God.
15:1–6; 18a	The initial covenant with Abraham	*Rit*: Christian Initiation apart from Easter Vigil, opt. 1	Baptism is understood as entrance into the New Covenant, which is the fulfillment of the covenant with Abraham initiated so long ago.
15:5–12, 17–18	See above; plus description of the covenant ritual	*2nd Sunday of Lent (C)*	The sequence of 1st readings of Year C in Lent includes a loose gathering of key events from salvation history. This theophany of God to Abraham

(continued)

Readings from the Patriarchal History (Gen 12–50) for Sundays, Feast Days, Liturgical Seasons, and Other Occasions *(continued)*

MSO = Masses for Special Occasions; OM = Optional Memorial;
VM = Votive Mass; Rit = Ritual

Scripture	Description	Place in Calendar	Explanation
			by blazing torch (Gen 15:17) pairs with the Gospel account of the Transfiguration (Lk 9:28–36), another theophany of the same God in blazing light.
17:1–8	The covenant of circumcision with Abraham	*Rit*: Christian Initiation apart from Easter Vigil, opt. 2; also Thurs., 5th Week of Lent (17:3–8)	Baptism (Christian initiation) is the New Covenant analogue and fulfillment of circumcision, as St. Paul affirms (Col 2:11–12).
18:1–10a	Abraham and Sarah serve a meal to the angel of the Lord and receive the promise of a son.	*16th Sunday in Ordinary Time (C)*	In Year C, Ordinary Time, the Gospel of Luke is read *ad seriatim*. This 1st reading is chosen as a typological parallel to the Gospel, the account of Martha and Mary entertaining the Lord in Bethany (Lk 10:38–42). Martha's busy preparation of food for Jesus is like Sarah's efforts to entertain the angel of the Lord.
18:20–32	Abraham's intercession for mercy for the city of Sodom	*17th Sunday in Ordinary Time (C)*	*See previous*. The 1st reading pairs with the Gospel, Luke 11:1–13, Luke's account of the Lord's Prayer and Jesus' teaching on prayer generally. Abraham is held up as one who "asked, sought, and knocked" in prayer with the Lord and whose prayers were heard for his persistence.
22:1–18	The *Aqedah*, the sacrifice of Isaac on Mount Moriah	*Easter Vigil (ABC) (2nd reading);* 2nd Sunday of Lent (B)	The Old Testament readings of the *Easter Vigil* recite the covenant history of salvation, beginning with creation and extending to the prophetic promises of a New Covenant. This text recalls the climax of Abraham's covenant relationship with God, including God's solemn oath of universal blessing to mankind. *Lent of Year B* includes a rehearsal of covenant history following the sequence Noah–Abraham–Moses/Sinai–Sinai–CovenantInfidelity–Prophecyof the New Covenant. This momentous OT text provides opportunity to explain the typology

(continued)

Readings from the Patriarchal History (Gen 12–50) for Sundays, Feast Days, Liturgical Seasons, and Other Occasions *(continued)*			
MSO = Masses for Special Occasions; *OM* = Optional Memorial; *VM* = Votive Mass; *Rit* = Ritual			
Scripture	Description	Place in Calendar	Explanation
			of the Cross and the new, Eucharistic covenant that fulfills the covenant-oath to Abraham in Genesis 22:18.
24:48–51; 58–67	The courtship of Isaac and Rebekah	*Rit*: For the Conferral of the Sacrament of Marriage, opt. 3	The marriage of Isaac and Rebekah is the most affectionate of any of the patriarchal marriages and was a necessary link in the fulfillment of the plan of salvation. It provides a model for Christian matrimony, which continues to play a role in God's salvific plan for mankind.
28:11–18	Jacob's vision of the "ladder" of angels ascending to God at Bethel	*MSO*: Dedication of an Altar	Jacob consecrates the rock on which he slept when he dreamed of the "ladder" ascending to heaven and later builds the first permanent shrine to God at that site (35:14).
37:3–28	Joseph dreams of greatness and is sold into slavery by his brothers.	Fri., 2nd Week of Lent	The Gospel reading (Mt 21:33–41), the parable of the tenants, recalls Israel's rejection and persecution of all the prophets preceding Christ. Joseph is portrayed here as a prophet, whose oracles are rejected by the sons of Israel because of their jealousy. The typology with Christ is unmistakable.
49:2, 8–10	Jacob's blessing of Judah, including the Messianic promise of the "scepter".	Advent Weekday: December 17	This messianic prophecy of the "scepter" to the "one to whom it belongs" of the tribe of Judah is paired with the genealogy of Jesus (Mt 1:1–17), which shows him to be the royal descendant of Judah.

An examination of the Church's Lectionary shows her preference for three texts in particular from the patriarchal narratives: the initial call of Abraham (Gen 12:1–4 or 1–7); the offering of Melchizedek (Gen 14:18–20); and the *Aqedah*, or binding, of Isaac (Gen 22:1–18). Indeed, the sacrifice of Isaac (Gen 22:1–18) is read at two prominent places in the Church's liturgy: (1) the Easter Vigil and (2) the Second Sunday of Lent in Year B. Both the Easter Vigil and the cycle of first readings for Lent in Year B present a review of salvation history through a series of carefully chosen Old Testament texts. In both of these series, Genesis 22:1–18 is used to recall God's covenant with Abraham, confirmed by God's solemn oath after the near-sacrifice of Isaac and ultimately fulfilled in

		Reading of the Patriarchal History (Gen 12–50) for Daily Mass: Ordinary Time, Year I: Weeks 12–14	
Week	Day	Reading	Description
12	M	12:1–19	Abram's call to journey in faith; Abram and Sarai in Egypt
12	Tu	13:2, 5–18	Abram and Lot part; God reaffirms his promises to Abram
12	W	15:1–12, 17–18	The first covenant, "between the pieces"
12	Th	16:1–12, 15–16	Sarai gives Hagar to Abram, Ishmael born
12	F	17:1, 9–10, 15–22	The second covenant, marked by circumcision
12	Sat	18:1–15	Abraham entertains angels; Isaac promised; Sarai laughs
13	M	18:16–33	Abraham intercedes for Sodom
13	Tu	19:15–29	Sodom and Gomorrah destroyed; Lot flees with daughters
13	W	21:5, 8–20a	Isaac born; Hagar and Ishmael sent away, yet saved and blessed
13	Th	22:1b–19	The binding (*Aqedah*) of Isaac; the covenant confirmed by oath
13	F	23:1–4, 19; 24:1–8, 62–67	The death of Sarah; the marriage of Isaac and Rebekah
14	Sat	27:1–5, 15–29	Jacob deceives Isaac, gains Esau's blessing
14	M	28:10–22a	Jacob's "Ladder": the angelic dream at Bethel
14	Tu	32:23–33	Jacob wrestles with the angel at Peniel
14	W	41:55–57; 42:5–7a, 17–24a	Joseph's brothers appear before him to buy grain in Egypt
14	Th	44:18–21, 23b–29; 45:1–5	Judah pleads for Benjamin; Joseph reveals himself to his brothers
14	F	46:1–7, 28–30	Jacob brings his family to Egypt and settles in Goshen
14	Sat	49:29–32; 50:15–26a	The deaths of Jacob and Joseph

the Passion, death, and Resurrection of Christ, which is prepared for during Lent and celebrated during Easter. Also significant is the selection of Joseph's betrayal (Gen 37:3–28) during the Friday of the Second Week of Lent.

Conclusion

The Primeval History (Gen 1–11) showed us two covenants of creation: the original "creation covenant" with Adam as mediator and the "re-creation covenant" with Noah after the Flood. Unfortunately, the Flood does not eradicate the human sinfulness that traces its origin to the disobedience of Adam and Eve; mankind still lives in opposition to God, as the Tower of Babel incident makes clear (Gen 11:1–9). The patriarchal narratives (Gen 12–50) show God's plan to address the issue of human sin and its consequences (estrangement from God and loss of divine blessing) by working within the human family, starting with one man and his descendants to spread blessing outward to the rest of mankind.

This plan is summarized already in the initial call to Abraham (Gen 12:1–3) and unfolds in a progression of covenants with Abraham in Genesis 15, 17, and 22, each of which involves subtle adjustments of the covenant relationship and the progressive inclusion of each of the three specific blessings mentioned in Genesis 12:1–3 (nationhood, name/royalty, and universal blessing). *The whole history of salvation is typologically summarized already in the life of Abraham.* The three covenants made with him foreshadow three subsequent covenants made with his descendants: (1) the Sinai or Mosaic covenant, which will establish Israel as a great nation; (2) the Davidic covenant, which will establish Abraham's "seed", David, as a "great name" (2 Sam 7:9) and everlasting king (2 Sam 7:16); and finally (3) the New Covenant (Lk 22:20), through which blessing (the Holy Spirit) will be poured out over all the earth (Gal 3:14).

The fact that Abraham's life journey of faith encapsulates the history of salvation explains why Saint Paul returns again and again to the stories of Abraham in order to demonstrate to his Jewish readers that the New Covenant is actually present in the Scriptures of Israel (Rom 4; Gal 3–4; cf. Heb 6–7) and why the Lectionary privileges the Abraham Cycle over other patriarchal narratives. The Jacob and Joseph Cycles also have their importance, primarily in showing the divine blessing, first bestowed on Adam and reaffirmed to Noah, then transmitted from Abraham to the heirs of his covenant, Isaac and Jacob, and thus ultimately to the people of Israel, especially the sons of Joseph.

Why does Genesis focus the blessing ultimately on Joseph and his descendants, when it is Judah from whom the Messiah will come? And why is it Judah who retains the identity and heritage of Israel, whereas Joseph's descendants will be dispersed and assimilated among the nations (2 Kings 17:21–23)? In biblical theological perspective, Judah and his tribe are the "older brother" who is faithful to the father, whereas Joseph and his tribe are the prodigal who wanders into a foreign land (Lk 15:11–32). Yet, even though the Messiah (Mt 1:1–16) and his apostles come from Judah, for salvation is from the Jews (Jn 4:22), yet the Messiah will encounter resistance from the descendants of Judah (Jn 8:48–59) and acceptance among the Gentiles (Jn 12:20–21) among whom the tribes of Joseph were scattered. Such was also the experience of the apostles (Acts 28:23–31). This may explain Paul's mysterious statement that "a hardening has come upon part of Israel [that is, Judah], until the full number of the Gentiles come in, and *so all Israel* will be saved" (Rom 11:26). All Israel—including the tribes of Joseph, scattered among the Gentile nations—will be saved by the incoming of those Gentile nations. By their dispersal among the nations, the tribes of Joseph assimilate God's covenantal promises of blessing among the nations as well, so that the Church's universal mission becomes the fulfillment of God's promise both to the nations and to the descendants of Israel.

For Further Reading

Modern Commentaries and Studies on Genesis 12–50

Cross, Frank Moore. *Canaanite Myth and Hebrew Epic: Essays in the History of the Religion of Israel.* Cambridge, Mass.: Harvard University Press, 1973.

Gagnon, Robert A.J. *The Bible and Homosexual Practice: Texts and Hermeneutics.* Nashville: Abingdon Press, 2002. (See pp. 71–91.)

Gunkel, Hermann. *The Stories of Genesis.* Translated by John J. Scullion. Vallejo, Calif.: BIBAL Press, 1994.

Hahn, Scott. *Kinship by Covenant: A Canonical Approach to the Fulfillment of God's Saving Promises.* Anchor Yale Bible Reference Library. New Haven, Conn.: Yale University Press, 2009. (See pp. 101–35.)

Hamilton, Victor P. *The Book of Genesis.* 2 vols. Grand Rapids, Mich.: Eerdmans, 1995.

Redford, Donald B. *A Study of the Biblical Story of Joseph (Genesis 37–50).* Vetus Testamentum Supplements 20. Leiden and Boston: Brill, 1970.

Westermann, Claus. *Genesis 12–36: A Commentary.* Translated by John J. Scullion. Minneapolis: Augsburg, 1985.

———. *Genesis 37–50: A Commentary.* Translated by John J. Scullion. Minneapolis: Augsburg, 1986.

Historical Issues in Genesis 12–50

Collins, John J. *Introduction to the Hebrew Bible.* Minneapolis: Fortress Press, 2004. (See pp. 84–90.)

Hoffmeier, James Karl. *The Archaeology of the Bible.* Oxford: Lion Hudson, 2008. (See pp. 33–48.)

———. *Israel in Egypt: The Evidence for the Authenticity of the Exodus Tradition.* Oxford: Oxford University Press, 1999. (See pp. 77–106.)

Kitchen, Kenneth A. "Genesis 12–50 in the Near Eastern World". Pages 67–92 in *He Swore an Oath: Biblical Themes from Genesis 12–50.* Edited by R. Hess, P.E. Satterthwaite, and G.J. Wenham. Carlisle: Paternoster Press; Grand Rapids, Mich.: Baker Book House, 1994.

———. *On the Reliability of the Old Testament.* Grand Rapids, Mich.: Eerdmans, 2003. (See pp. 313–72.)

Walton, John H. "Genesis". Pages 68–159 in *Genesis, Exodus, Leviticus, Numbers, Deuteronomy.* Vol. 1 of *Zondervan Illustrated Bible Backgrounds Commentary.* Edited by John H. Walton. Grand Rapids, Mich.: Zondervan, 2009.

Genesis 12–50 in the Living Tradition

Bede, Venerable. *On Genesis.* Translated by Calvin Kendall. Translated Texts for Historians 48. Liverpool: Liverpool University Press, 2008. (See pp. 244–322.)

Chrysostom, Saint John. *Homilies on Genesis.* Translated by Robert C. Hill. 3 vols. The Fathers of the Church 74, 82, and 87. Washington, D.C.: Catholic University of America Press, 1986–1992. (See Vol. 2, pp. 237–483; Vol. 3, pp. 3–278.)

Daniélou, Jean, S.J. *From Shadows to Reality: Studies in the Biblical Typology of the Fathers.* Translated by Dom Wulstan Hibberd. Westminster, Md.: Newman Press, 1960. (See pp. 115–49.)

Ephrem the Syrian, Saint. *Selected Prose Works.* Translated by Edward G. Mathews Jr. and Joseph P. Amar. Edited by Kathleen E. McVey. The Fathers of the Church 91. Washington, D.C.: Catholic University of America Press, 1995. (See pp. 148–213.)

Kugel, James L. *Traditions of the Bible: A Guide to the Bible as It Was at the Start of the Common Era.* Cambridge, Mass.: Harvard University Press, 1997. (See pp. 243–500.)

Melito of Sardis. *Fragments on Genesis 22.* In vol. 8 of *Ante-Nicene Fathers.* Edited by Alexander Roberts and James Donaldson. 1886. Repr., Peabody, Mass.: Hendrickson, 1994. (See p. 759.)

Origen. *Homilies on Genesis and Exodus.* Translated by Ronald E. Heine. The Fathers of the Church 71. Washington, D.C.: Catholic University of America, 1982. (See pp. 89–224.)

Sheridan, Mark, ed. *Genesis 12–50.* Old Testament 2 of Ancient Christian Commentary on Scripture. Edited by Thomas C. Oden. Downers Grove, Ill.: InterVarsity Press, 2002.

Theodoret of Cyrus. *On Genesis and Exodus.* Vol. 1 of *The Questions on the Octateuch.* Translated by Robert C. Hill. The Library of Early Christianity 1. Washington, D.C.: Catholic University of America Press, 2007.

7. EXODUS

Introduction

The book of Exodus recounts the liberation of the people of Israel from Egyptian slavery, their entrance into a covenant with God at Mount Sinai, and the building of their first sanctuary, the Tabernacle. As with Genesis, it is almost impossible to overestimate the significance of the book of Exodus for the rest of the biblical canon, for ancient Judaism, early Christianity, and world history and culture. In this book we have (1) the historical basis and liturgical regulations for the Passover, the central ritual celebration of Judaism and the primary prefiguration of the Christian Eucharist (Ex 12–13); (2) the giving of the Ten Commandments, the basis of all Judeo-Christian morality and Western law (Ex 19–20); and (3) the solemn establishment of the covenant with Israel through Moses at Mount Sinai (Ex 24), which Jews regard as the birth of their faith and nation and Christians regard as the prototype for the new and everlasting covenant between Christ and the Church.

The word *exodus* derives from two Greek words: *ex*, "out, out of", and *hodos*, "road, way", and is derived from the Greek title of the book in the Septuagint (LXX). Hence, the title means "the way out, exit, departure", referring to the central action of the book: the departure of Israel from Egypt. In contrast, the Hebrew name for the book is *Shemōth*, from the opening phrase of the book: "And these are the names" (Hebrew *ve-elleh shemoth*), thus introducing us to and focusing on the fact that the book begins with the descendants of the twelve sons of Jacob who arrived in Egypt (Ex 1:1).

Although in literary style and content Exodus sometimes differs markedly from Genesis, there are strong elements of continuity between the two books. First of all, the opening unit of Exodus, "These are the names of the sons of Israel who came to Egypt" (see Ex 1:1–5), is a summary of the longer list near the end of Genesis (see Gen 46:8–27). Secondly, the opening notice that "the descendants of Israel were fruitful and increased greatly; they multiplied and grew exceedingly strong; so that the land was filled with them" (Ex 1:7) picks up the creational blessing of the first man and woman: "And God blessed them, and God said to them, 'Be fruitful and multiply, and fill the earth and subdue it'" (Gen 1:28), indicating that this blessing has found fulfillment in the people of Israel. Thirdly, the text of Exodus explicitly grounds God's redemption of Israel from Egyptian bondage in the Abrahamic covenant: "And God heard their groaning, and God remembered his covenant with Abraham, with Isaac, and with Jacob" (Ex 2:24). Likewise, God reveals himself to Moses as the God of the three patriarchs: "the God of Abraham, the God of Isaac, and the God of Jacob" (Ex 3:6). Therefore, God's covenant with Israel in Exodus is laid firmly on the foundation of his covenant with Abraham in Genesis.

Literary Structure of Exodus

The structure of Exodus may be perceived in different ways, based on geography, theme, or other factors. A geographical analysis gives a three-part structure: Israel in Egypt (Ex 1–15), Israel in the Wilderness (Ex 16–18), Israel at Sinai (Ex 19–40). A thematic perspective gives a slightly different structure: *liberation* from Egypt (Ex 1–18); *legislation* at Sinai (Ex 18–24); and a place for *liturgy*, the Tabernacle (Ex 25–40):

Different Perspectives on the Structure of Exodus	
Geographical Focus	Thematic Focus
Israel in Egypt (1–15)	Liberation: Israel Redeemed (1–18)
Israel in the Wilderness (16–18)	
Israel at Sinai (19–40)	Legislation: The Covenant Given (19–24)
	Liturgy: The Tabernacle Constructed (25–40)

The central theme of the book is "Israel is my first-born son, and I say to you, 'Let my son go that he may *serve* me'" (Ex 4:23). The Hebrew word "serve" (*'abad*) can mean either *work* or *worship*. At the beginning of Exodus, the Israelites are *serving* (Hebrew *'abad*) the pharaoh in Egypt, but by the end, they are *serving* (Hebrew *'abad*) the Lord in the Tabernacle. Thus there is strong movement in the book from *work* to *worship*, from *labor* to *liturgy*.

In the first part of the book, God delivers his "son" Israel (Ex 4:22) from bondage and brings him to Sinai. There he formally "adopts" Israel by solemnizing a covenant with them through Moses at the mountain. Finally, God makes possible a *filial communion* with Israel in the last chapters (Ex 25–31, 35–40) by providing for Israel a sanctuary, where communion may take place through worship. It is important to recognize that the activity of the whole book is oriented toward the communion-through-worship enabled by the construction of the Tabernacle at the end. Neither the deliverance of the exodus (Ex 1–15) nor the law given at Sinai (Ex 19–24) are ends in themselves. The exodus liberation brings the people to a place where they can worship, which they could not do in Egypt for fear of being slain (Ex 8:26). The covenant at Sinai, with its attendant laws, is oriented toward forming Israel into a holy people able to commune with God through worship. Finally, the Tabernacle is the place for that communion-through-worship which is the filial privilege of Israel. In light of this literary form, we may truly speak of the *liturgical orientation* of the book of Exodus: the initial deliverance is about worship, the conflict between the pharaoh and Israel centers on worship, and the overall "exodus" from Egypt culminates in worship (Ex 25–40). Indeed, just as Genesis is the creation account of the world as a place for worship, Exodus may be understood as the creation account of Israel as a people of worship.

Focusing on God's drawing of "son Israel" out of Egypt in order to enter into a filial relationship of communion through worship enables us to summarize the

tripartite structure of the book by the terms *call, covenant,* and *communion.* The
detailed structure is as follows:

Outline of the Book of Exodus

I. "Call": The Exodus from Egypt (Ex 1–18)
    A. The Call of Moses, the Liberator (1–4)
    B. The Call of Israel, the Liberated (5–18)
       1. The Deliverance from Egypt (5–15)
          a. The Plagues (5–12)
          b. The Passover (12–13)
          c. The Parting of the Sea (14–15)
       2. Signs and Wonders in the Wilderness (16–18)
          a. Provision of Bread (16)
          b. Provision of Water (17)
          c. Provision of Leadership (18)

II. "Covenant": The Mount Sinai Revelation (Ex 19–24)
    A. Rituals of Preparation (19)
    B. Primary Covenant Law: The Ten Commandments (20)
    C. Secondary Covenant Law: The "Covenant Code" (21–23)
    D. The Solemnization of the Covenant (24)

III. "Communion": The Tabernacle of Moses (Ex 25–40)
    A. The Instructions for the Tabernacle (25–31)
     B. Covenant Rejected: The Golden Calf (32)
     B'. Covenant Renewed: Moses' Intercession (33–34)
    A'. The Construction of the Tabernacle (35–40)

It will be noted that the concluding account of the instructions and the construction of the Tabernacle (Ex 25–31, 35–40) are "wrapped around" the account
of the covenant-breaking worship of the Golden Calf. The sacred author intends
a contrast between the false worship of the people (Ex 32) and the prescriptions
for true worship in the surrounding chapters (Ex 25–31, 35–40). Moreover, the
account suggests that the atoning liturgy that will take place in the Tabernacle-
sanctuary is the "bandage" that wraps the "wound" of the people's sin: that is,
the remedy and antidote—at least temporarily—for the sinfulness of the people.
Nonetheless, as we will see below, the covenant-breaking at the Calf has some
irremediable effects, and, despite the covenant renewal (Ex 33–34), Exodus ends
on a bittersweet note.

Overview of Exodus

The Infancy and Early Years of Moses (Exodus 1–2)

As noted above, the opening of Exodus summarizes the descendants of Israel
and notes the fulfillment of the divine creational blessing of fruitfulness and
multiplication in the people of Israel (Ex 1:7). However, just as this blessing

was continually threatened in Genesis by maternal barrenness or foreign kings, so there is a threat here in Exodus: a new Egyptian king comes to power who is threatened by Israel and attempts to kill the people through forced labor and infanticide (Ex 1:8–14, 15–22). The pharaoh's genocidal intentions toward Israel at the beginning of the narrative are an important moral counterbalance to the tenth plague, the death of the Egyptian firstborn males; initially, it is Egyptian policy that attempts to bring about the death of *all* Israelite males.

The pharaoh's genocide is thwarted through the Hebrew midwives, but the lot of Israel in Egypt is nonetheless made miserable: "They made the sons of Israel *serve* with rigor" (Ex 1:13). This initial verse establishes the theme of *service* (Hebrew *'abad*) in the book of Exodus. Once again, Israel will move in the course of the book from serving the pharaoh, which is slavery, to serving God, which is the true freedom of worship; the word "serve" (Hebrew *'abad*) has both meanings and is used interchangeably throughout the text to heighten the drama of whether Israel will "serve" the pharaoh or "worship" God.

Just as threats to the continuity of the covenant in Genesis were often resolved by a providential birth, so in Exodus a note of hope is sounded with the announcement of the birth of a "goodly" child of the tribe of Levi (Ex 2:2). The name of Moses (Hebrew *mosheh*)—which appears to parallel other famous Egyptian names such as the pharaohs Ah*mose*, Thut*mose*, and Ra*messes* (sixteenth–twelfth centuries B.C.)—is explained by reference to the expression "to draw out" (Hebrew *mashah*) (Ex 2:10).[1] To circumvent the royal policy of infanticide, Moses' mother floats him down the Nile in a waterproofed basket, which may have been an ancient way of handling children whose parents could not provide for them (similar to the modern practice of leaving a baby on a doorstep). Particularly in Egypt, where the Nile was divinized, one could hope that whoever found the child washed up on the bank might consider him to be a gift of Hapi the Nile god and raise him with care. In this case, the mother's plan succeeds splendidly, and the pharaoh's own daughter discovers the child and commissions Moses' mother herself as a wet nurse at royal expense (Ex 2:9–10). As a result, Moses is raised in the court as the pharaoh's grandson, which suggests a providential opportunity: if Moses waits until his generation comes to power, he may well be in a position to influence royal policy and attain the freedom of his people in a peaceful manner.

However, this happy prospect is quickly destroyed by an exercise of rash temper: Moses slays an Egyptian for beating one of his fellow Hebrews (Ex 2:11–15). While the reader may sympathize with Moses' indignation, this is clearly an overreaction and miscarriage of justice, which breaks two of the laws Moses himself will later give to Israel: "You shall not kill" (Ex 20:13) and "eye for eye, tooth for tooth"—the *lex talionis*, or law of proportional punishment (Ex 21:23–25). Moreover, he carries out the murder incompetently, hiding the body in sand. Unsurprisingly, the deed is discovered, and Moses is forced to flee to the desert country of Midian, where he ends up as a shepherd, a vocation detestable to Egyptians and therefore certainly not in keeping with his royal status as an adopted son of the pharaoh's daughter (compare Gen 46:34).

---

[1] Victor Hamilton, *Handbook on the Pentateuch* (Grand Rapids, Mich.: Baker, 2005), 139–40.

Jethro or Reuel?

Moses' father-in-law is known as both Reuel (Ex 2:18) and Jethro (Ex 3:1). How does one explain this? In the ancient Near East, it was very common for a person or place to have more than one name or title. There are many examples in Scripture, such as Abram/Abraham, Jacob/Israel, Esau/Edom, Sinai/Horeb, Jebus/Salem/Jerusalem, etc. "Reu-el" is a name meaning "friend of God". "Jethro" may be a title meaning "His Excellency".[a]

[a]Cyrus H. Gordon and Gary A. Rendsburg, *The Bible and the Ancient Near East*, rev. ed. (New York: W. W. Norton, 1997).

At this point the sacred author notes that God heard the "groaning" of Israel and "*remembered* his covenant with Abraham" (Ex 2:24), which recalls the statement in Genesis during the Flood, "God *remembered* Noah" (Gen 8:1). In the Old Testament, to "remember" (Hebrew *zakar*) is seldom if ever a passive activity limited to calling something to mind. Instead, in most contexts, *zakar* refers to *taking positive action*, usually on the basis of a covenant established in the past, with a view to fulfilling the covenant obligations. In this way, God declares that when he sees the rainbow he will "remember" his covenant with Noah and all creation (Gen 9:15), and, later on, the Israelites are commanded to "remember" the Sabbath day, the sign of God's covenant with mankind (Ex 20:8). In the New Testament, this same Hebrew concept will ultimately stand behind Jesus' injunction at the Last Supper to the disciples: "Do this ... in *remembrance* of me" (1 Cor 11:25).

God's "remembrance" of Israel takes the form of calling Moses to be their liberator. He reveals himself in the form of a burning bush in the desert to Moses and equips him for leadership by communicating to him the divine name (Ex 3:13–22; see excursus on p. 171), supernatural powers (Ex 4:1–9), and the assistance of Aaron (Ex 4:10–17). Moses' continued resistance to his call is not admirable (Ex 3:11, 13; 4:1, 10, 13) and finally compels God to enlist Aaron as Moses' spokesman. In light of Aaron's later involvement in the Golden Calf debacle, the reader wonders if this trouble could have been avoided if Moses had complied more quickly with God's commission.

The Burning Bush and the Revelation of the Divine Name (Exodus 3–4)

One of the most theologically significant passages in the entire Old Testament is the description of the call of Moses and the revelation of the divine name to him on Mount Sinai.

The event takes place during Moses' sojourn as a fugitive from justice and a shepherd. During the (presumably somewhat dull) act of shepherding his sheep, Moses perceives the first of several wonders in the book of Exodus: the "bush" that, though burning, is not consumed (Ex 3:1–2). Turning aside to see the site, he experiences what scholars refer to as a *theophany*: an extraordinary "appearance" or "vision" of God. In the midst of this theophany, God calls Moses to lead the people of Israel out of servitude to the pharaoh in Egypt in order, once again, to bring them to "serve" or "worship" (Hebrew *'abad*) him

---

The Divine Name in Exodus

"I appeared to Abraham, to Isaac, and to Jacob, as God Almighty [Hebrew *El Shaddai*], but by my name the LORD [YHWH] I did not make myself known to them" (Ex 6:3).

J. Wellhausen and other source critics attributed this verse to the Priestly source and argued that the Priestly author did not believe God used the name YHWH with the patriarchs. Therefore, no text of Genesis that employed YHWH could be from the Priestly source: even texts that had strong Priestly themes (Gen 7:1–5; 8:20–22).

Other scholars doubt that this verse really means to say the patriarch did not know the phonetic unit "YHWH" as an identification of God. In biblical thought, the concept of a "name" is so much more significant than phonetics. To know the "name" is to know the essence, character, or nature of a person. If a person has different names, they represent different aspects of his nature. When there is a substantial change in a person's identity, there is also a change of name (Gen 17:5; 32:28). While the patriarchs knew the phonetics "YHWH", they did not know what the name meant or what aspect of God's nature it revealed. It can scarcely be accidental that, not once, but twice God reveals to Moses what his name YHWH means and what dimension of his character it represents: at the burning bush (Ex 3:13–15) and at Sinai (Ex 34:5–7). It may be that Exodus 6:3 refers to these sublime events of self-revelation by YHWH experienced by Moses but not previously by the patriarchs.

---

on Mount Sinai (sometimes called Mount Horeb) (Ex 3:12). In response to the marvelous divine vocation, Moses reacts by objecting that he is ignorant of the deity's name: "If . . . they ask me, 'What is his name?' what shall I say to them?" (Ex 3:13).

Although it is generally understood that in response to this question God reveals his *name* to Moses, a closer examination shows that God reveals *two distinct names* to Moses. First and foremost, he declares: "I AM WHO I AM" (Hebrew *ehyeh asher ehyeh*) (Ex 3:14). This mysterious expression is based on the verb "to be" (Hebrew *hayah*) and can also be translated "I Am What I Am" or "I Will Be What I Will Be." The ancient Greek Septuagint translates it as "I Am He Who Is" (Greek *ego eim ho ōn*) (Ex 3:14 LXX). However one translates the expression, in every case, the emphasis is on the mystery of who God is in himself: he is the eternal God who simply *is*—he has no beginning, no end; he has been, is, and always will be. In later theological terms, this passage may be the most "metaphysical" in all of Scripture, revealing that God is not "a being" among beings but, rather, he who is *being itself*. It is a revelation of who God is in himself (Latin *in se*).

Indeed, by revealing himself as "I AM", God distinguishes himself from the other gods of the nations, which "are not". He is the only God who truly is. Furthermore, the name "I AM" stresses that God exists of himself; unlike all other beings, he does not take his existence from some other cause. Later philosophical language will describe God as the one necessary being. While lacking technical philosophical language, the ancients did have the concept of self-existence: in Egyptian religion, the sun-god Amon-Rē "came into being by himself", and all other beings took their existence from him. However, God reveals to Moses that it is he, the Lord—not Amon-Rē or any other Egyptian god—who is the ground of being and the source of existence.

The Tetragrammaton: YHWH or Jehovah?

The Hebrew language was written without vowels until the Middle Ages, when the Jewish scribes known as the Masoretes developed a vowel-writing system. At this time, the form YHWH, however, was written with the vowels for the Hebrew word *adonai* (meaning "Lord"), the word that ancient Jews would pronounce in place of the holy tetragrammaton.

When the English translators of the King James Version encountered this punctuation in the seventeenth century, they did not understand the Masoretic system of pronunciation with reference to YHWH and in a few instances combined the Hebrew consonants of YHWH with the Hebrew vowels of *adonai* to form the erroneous pronunciation "Jehovah".

Catholic tradition addresses God neither with the ancient pronunciation YHWH nor the mistaken pronunciation Jehovah but, rather, with the word "Lord" (Greek *kyrios*), following the Greek Septuagint translation of the word YHWH (see Ex 3:14–15 LXX). This is also in keeping with the practice of the New Testament writers, who always render YHWH as "Lord" (*kyrios*).

In most English Bibles, "LORD" in caps represents YHWH in the Hebrew text, while "Lord" in lower case represents the actual Hebrew word *adonai*.

On the other hand, in the very next verse, God also gives a different name to Moses: "Say this to the sons of Israel, '*The LORD, the God of your fathers, the God of Abraham, the God of Isaac, and the God of Jacob*, has sent me to you': this is my name for ever, and thus I am to be remembered throughout all generations" (Ex 3:15). In this passage, God provides another name deriving from the verb "to be" (Hebrew *hayah*): "the Lord" (Hebrew *Yhwh*), often pronounced as "Yahweh" and best translated as "He Is". This is the famous *tetragrammaton* (meaning "four letters"). Notice, however, that in this instance God qualifies this being-focused name by also revealing that he is *the God of the covenant*: a God in relation with the patriarchs Abraham, Isaac, and Jacob. In addition to the revelation of who God is in himself (Latin *in se*), we also find a revelation of who God is for us creatures (Latin *pro nobis*), the God who not only is, but who speaks and acts in salvation history, above all through the covenants. Once again, this establishes a direct link between the acts of God in Exodus and the patriarchal narratives in Genesis.

The Plagues, the Gods of Egypt, and the Pharaoh's Heart (Exodus 5–12)

Once this revelation to Moses is accomplished, God sends him back to the pharaoh with this important message: "Israel is my *first-born son*.... Let my son go that he may serve [Hebrew *'abad*] me" (Ex 4:22–23). Once again, we see the *covenant* shape and the *liturgical* goal of the exodus from the very beginning: Israel is in a filial relationship with YHWH, and, as a result, Moses and Aaron appeal to the pharaoh to let the people of Israel go into the wilderness to celebrate a "feast" and "sacrifice" to their God (Ex 5:1, 3). The pharaoh does not "know" the Lord and thus refuses to let Israel go. In fact, he increases their labor and persecution, which provokes the Israelites to reject Moses and Aaron and their intercessory efforts (Ex 5:4—6:13). God promises, however, that what is about to ensue will cause not only the pharaoh but all Egypt to "know that I am the LORD" by a display of his "great acts of judgment" (Ex 7:4–5).

One of the more difficult aspects of the account of the exodus for contemporary readers is the account of the plagues against Egypt. Why does God take such drastic measures against the pharaoh and the kingdom of Egypt? How are we to understand the striking plagues unleashed against the Egyptians but not against the Israelites? As a number of contemporary scholars have shown, a strong case can be made that, in its ancient Near Eastern context, the ten plagues should be understood as a form of *theomachy*, or "divine combat", between the one true God of Israel and the many gods of Egypt.[2] As is well known, the ancient Egyptians divinized nature and worshipped various elements of their environment—the sun, the moon, the sky, the earth, the river Nile, their livestock, and various wild animals—as *gods*. It was the responsibility of these gods to maintain the life, health, and prosperity of Egypt and the responsibility of Egyptians to give them worship and honor.

Indeed, there are several remarkable parallels between the ten plagues in Exodus and specific ancient Egyptians deities:

Plagues as Divine Combat: The God of Israel vs. the Gods of Egypt (Ex 12:12; Num 33:4)	
Plague	Egyptian God
(1) The Nile to Blood	Hapi, god of the Nile
(2) Frogs	Hekhet, frog-goddess of fertility
(3) Gnats and (4) Flies	Kephrer, beetle-god and sun-symbol; Uatchit, a fly-god
(5) Death of Livestock	Apis, bull-god; Hathor, cow-goddess; other gods represented by livestock
(6) Boils and Sores	Sekhmet, goddess of healing
(7) Hail, Killing the Crops	Nut, goddess of the sky; Shu, god of the air; Tefnut, goddess of rain
(8) Locusts	Senehem, god of crops
(9) Three Days of Darkness	Amon-Rē, the sun-god
(10) Death of the Firstborn	Pharaoh himself, believed to be a god; Osiris, god of life, resurrection, and patron of Pharaoh

Seen in this light, the plagues are not just remarkable displays of divine power over nature by the God of Israel. Even more, they are a systematic and public display of divine power over the Egyptian gods, designed to show that the Lord is God and that the gods of Egypt are not. In support of this interpretation of the plagues as the defeat and humiliation of the Egyptian gods, it is critical to note that this is precisely how the Pentateuch itself speaks of the plagues in the

[2] See James K. Hoffmeier, "Egypt, Plagues in", in *Anchor Bible Dictionary*, ed. D.N. Freedman (New York: Doubleday, 1992), 2:374–78; John J. Davis, *Moses and the Gods of Egypt* (Grand Rapids, Mich.: Baker, 1971).

past tense: "Upon their gods also the LORD executed judgments" (Num 33:4; cf. Ex 12:12).

Alongside this emphasis on the Egyptian gods also runs the theme of the hardness of the pharaoh's heart. Once again, contemporary readers often find troubling the repeated statements "the LORD hardened Pharaoh's heart" (Ex 7:3; 9:12; 10:1; 11:10; 14:4, 8, 17), seeming to emphasize divine sovereignty to the exclusion of human freedom and rendering the pharaoh inculpable for his actions. However, in order to understand these statements correctly, equal emphasis must be given to the fact that on several occasions, the text explicitly states that "*Pharaoh ... hardened his [own] heart*" (Ex 8:15, 32; 9:34) or describes the situation passively: "Pharaoh's heart was hardened" (Ex 7:13, 14, 22; 8:19; 9:7, 35).

The obvious tension between these phrases is allowed to stand in the final text, emphasizing *both* the sovereign providence of God *and* the pharaoh's willful rejection of God's command: that is, both divine providence and human freedom. On the one hand, the formula "the LORD hardened Pharaoh's heart" affirms the *providence of God* in the face of human evil: the inexplicable and unreasonable stubbornness of the pharaoh does not derail the plan of God but is in fact only serving to further God's purposes, to reveal his power to Israel, Egypt, and all the world. On the other hand, the affirmation "Pharaoh hardened his heart" acknowledges that sin is, nonetheless, truly the result of human free will exercised in opposition to God. Finally, the passive construction "Pharaoh's heart was hardened" recognizes that there is always something mysterious and irrational about sin, what the apostle Paul will later call "the mystery of lawlessness" (2 Thess 2:7).

Thus the theme of the hardness of the pharaoh's heart is related to another theme through the plagues, the more positive theme of the *self-revelation of God*, almost a form of "proclamation" or even "evangelism" through the wonders God displays in Egypt. As God says to the pharaoh: "for this purpose have I let you live, *to show you my power*, so that my name may be declared throughout all the earth" (Ex 9:16). Indeed, Israel comes to recognize the Lord as the true God through the experience of the plagues (Ex 14:31; 15:1–3), but this is also the experience of many of the Egyptians as well (Ex 8:19; 9:20; 10:7; 11:3) and even peoples in distant lands (Ex 18:11; Josh 2:10). The wonders in Egypt thus function as motives for belief in the reality and sovereignty of the one true God of Israel and creation.

The Passover Sacrifice and Meal (Exodus 12–13)

The tenth plague is surrounded by instructions for the observation of the Passover sacrifice and meal, perhaps *the* fundamental observance of Israelite religion and later Judaism. This sacrifice is intended to commemorate the definitive historical event that established the identity of the people of Israel on the basis of God's singular saving act of deliverance.

In this regard, several aspects of the Passover sacrifice stand out as significant. First, the word "Passover" (Hebrew *pesah*) stems from a verb meaning "to pass over" (Hebrew *pasah*), as in God's promise to Israel that, on the night of the final plague, the destroying angel will "pass over" the houses of all those marked with the blood of the sacrificial lambs (Ex 12:27). Second, the people of Israel are commanded by God to perform a *ritual sacrifice*, which consists of several specific steps and instructions (Ex 12:1–14):

1. Kill an unblemished male lamb, one year old.
2. Not a bone of the lamb is to be broken; it is to be sacrificed whole.
3. Dip a branch of hyssop in the blood of the lamb.
4. Sprinkle the blood of the lamb on the doorposts and lintel of the home.
5. Eat the flesh of the lamb roasted, with unleavened bread and bitter herbs.
6. Perform this ritual every year as a "remembrance" of the original Passover.

Notice several distinctive aspects of this initial Passover ritual: in contrast to the later period, when Israel enters the land, the original Passover is a domestic sacrifice, in which the *father* of each Israelite home functions as priest over his family. In other words, we are still in the period of the primordial priesthood going back to the patriarchs, Noah, and Adam. The tribe of Levi has not yet been established as the sole legitimate priests, and the Tabernacle has not yet been set up as the sole place of sacrifice. Second—and this is important—the Passover sacrifice is completed by a sacred meal, in which the flesh of the lamb must be eaten. In other words, the Passover is completed, not by the death of the lamb, but by the consumption of its flesh in a sacrificial feast: Passover is hence both a sacrifice and a banquet.

Third and finally, the Passover is to be celebrated annually, in conjunction with the subsequent seven-day feast of "Unleavened Bread" (Hebrew *mazzot*) (Ex 13:1–10). In this way, the original deliverance effected by the Passover is not a one-time event that ends with the dawn of Israel's deliverance from Egypt but is, rather, an event that is continually made present each year to subsequent generations of Israelites through the memorial celebration. Its saving significance for Israel endures throughout time through the process of "remembering", and thereby making present, the initial Passover (Ex 12:14).

The Crossing of the Sea of Reeds (Exodus 14–15)

The parting of the Red Sea, while not one of the ten plagues, is the last of the great "wonders" (Ex 3:20; 15:11) that God performs in Egypt and brings to an end the first section of the book. After crossing the sea, Israel is no longer in Egyptian territory and neither the pharaoh nor the Egyptians pose a physical threat to Israel for the remainder of the Pentateuch.

Scholars debate the exact location of the body of water that the Israelites crossed in the exodus. To this day, the common understanding that the Israelites crossed the "Red Sea" goes back to the ancient Septuagint translation, which indeed states that the Israelites crossed the "Red Sea" (Greek *erythra thalassa*) (Ex 15:22 LXX). However, in the original Hebrew, the sea is actually called the "sea of reeds" (Hebrew *yam suph*), which appears to be a freshwater body, not the saltwater body later known to us as the Red Sea (Ex 15:22). From this point of view, the "Sea of Reeds" probably refers to one of the marshy lakes that lie along the present course of the Suez Canal. This clarification of the original name, however, in no way detracts from the miraculous nature of the event. Despite the attempts of some to suggest that the "Sea of Reeds" is a shallow body of water that could be crossed on foot, there is no way to reconcile such a revision with the actual account in Exodus, which incontrovertibly describes one of YHWH's supernatural "wonders" (Ex 15:11), in which "the waters" are "a wall" to the Israelites "on their right hand and on their left" (Ex 14:22) and in which the "Sea of Reeds" is clearly deep enough to drown "Pharaoh's chariots and his host" (Ex 15:4).

Like other events in the book of Exodus, the crossing of the Sea of Reeds contains echoes of the book of Genesis. The blowing of the "wind" or "spirit" (Hebrew *ruah*) over the water of the sea (Ex 14:1) recalls the movement of the "spirit" (Hebrew *ruah*) of God over the waters of the deep at creation (Gen 1:2). Likewise, the splitting of the sea (Ex 13:22) recalls the division of the waters on the second day (Gen 1:6), and the "dry ground" on which the Israelites walk (Ex 14:29) recalls the creation of the dry land on the third (Gen 1:9). In light of these parallels, the parting of the sea can be viewed as a kind of a "re-creation", much like the Flood, although in this case the people of Israel themselves are the "new creation" that emerges from the waters.

From another point of view, modern scholars have also drawn attention to parallels between the account of the parting of the sea and the creation myths of the Mesopotamians.[3] These myths tell of Marduk creating the world by defeating the monster of the deep sea and dividing his (or her) body in order to build the heavens and the earth as a temple-palace for the worship of Marduk. The key difference, of course, is that the battle of Marduk is a myth set in an unknown distant past, whereas the Hebrew Scriptures claim that Israel's crossing of the sea takes place in history, in which the one true God of Israel splits the sea and defeats the historical personification of evil and chaos (the pharaoh), leading his new creation-people into the wilderness to build him a sanctuary (the Tabernacle).

The Miracles on the Way to Mount Sinai (Exodus 16–18)

The Song of the Sea (Ex 15:1–21) marks the definitive end of the first section of Exodus with its focus on Egypt and the Egyptians. The next section describes Israel's journey in the desert on the way to Sinai (Ex 16–18) and has strong literary parallels with the wilderness wanderings of the second generation (see Num 11–21). Thus, accounts of Israel's travels in the wilderness, characterized by God's gracious provision despite Israel's ungrateful complaining, bracket the narrative of God's grant of a covenant to Israel at Sinai (Ex 19–Num 10) that stands at the center of the Pentateuch.

In this journey to Sinai, God enacts several more "wonders", showing his providential care for the tribes of Israel in the wilderness. In this regard, five miracles in particular stand out: (1) the transformation of the bitter water at Marah (Hebrew for "bitterness") to sweet when Moses throws the wood of a "tree"

---

[3] Frank Moore Cross, *Canaanite Myth and Hebrew Epic* (Cambridge, Mass.: Harvard University Press, 1997).

What Is the Manna from Heaven?

The food God provides in the wilderness is the famous manna, whose name derives from the Hebrew expression "What is it?" (*man-hu*) (Ex 16:15). Efforts have been made to identify the manna with the congealed sap of a desert shrub that grows in the Sinai peninsula or the emission of one of the insects living in the desert. However, neither these shrubs nor the insects suggested would ever produce enough of this sap to feed any sizable population for any length of time. Even more importantly, the text of Exodus clearly states that the manna was a supernatural phenomenon, since twice the usual amount appears on Friday, and none appears on the Sabbath (Ex 16:27). If the substance were purely natural, one would have to posit quite a different kind of miracle, in which the Lord gets the insects and/or plant life in the region to keep the Sabbath! Finally, it is critical to note that the manna is a temporary miracle: its appearance is limited to the forty-year period Israel wanders in the wilderness (Ex 16:35). There is no need to explain this rationalistically as a purely natural phenomenon; it is clearly one of several miracles or "wonders" (Hebrew *niphloth*) (Ex 3:20) performed by YHWH in the deliverance of Israel.

---

into the water (Ex 15:22–25); (2) the provision of "bread" (manna) and "flesh" (quail) from heaven when Israel cries out for food (Ex 16:1–36); (3) the flow of water from the rock at Meribah (Hebrew for "contention") or Massah (Hebrew for "testing") (Ex 17:1–7); (4) the miraculous overthrow of the Amalekites through the intercession of Moses and his outstretched arms (Ex 17:8–16). The presence of so many miracles in such a concentrated way in this period is remarkable and unique in the Old Testament. Although modern readers are sometimes prone to think of the Old Testament as rife with divine "interventions" and miracles, the reality is that miracles and wonders are unusual and restricted to two periods in Israel's history: the life and ministry of the prophet Moses and the lives of Elijah and Elisha. Apart from these (and perhaps the accounts of the creation of the first man and woman in Genesis), miracles are relatively rare in the Hebrew Scriptures.

Mount Sinai and the Ten Commandments (Exodus 19–20)

By Exodus 19:1, Israel has arrived at Mount Sinai, and the following five chapters give the account of the first covenant made between God and Israel at Sinai through the ministry of Moses. Two chapters describing covenant rituals and the divine theophany (Ex 19, 24) bracket the statement of the laws governing the covenant relationship (Ex 20–23), which are divided into (1) a primary or basic law, the Ten Commandments, called "the Words" (Hebrew *debarim*) (Ex 20:1–17), and (2) a secondary or derived law, the Covenant Code, styled "the Ordinances" (Hebrew *mishpatim*) (Ex 21:1–23:33).

The preface to the giving of the covenant is tremendously important for understanding the theological and salvation-historical significance of the first Sinai covenant:

And Moses went up to God, and the LORD called to him out of the mountain, saying, "Thus you shall say to the house of Jacob, and tell the sons of Israel: You have seen what I did to the Egyptians, and how I bore you on eagles' wings and brought you to myself. Now therefore, if you will obey my voice and keep my covenant, you shall be my own possession among all peoples; for all the earth is mine, and you shall be to me a kingdom of priests and a holy nation. These are the words which you shall speak to the children of Israel." (Ex 19:3–6)

In these words, we see the orientation of the whole exodus process toward communion with God: "I bore you on eagles' wings and *brought you to myself.*" Next we observe a promise, contingent on Israel's covenant fidelity: "If you ... keep my covenant, ... you shall be to me a *kingdom of priests* and a holy nation." The phrase "kingdom of priests" (Hebrew *mamlekhet kohanim*) is critical (Ex 19:6). The Hebrew *mamlekhet* can be rendered "kingdom" or "kingship"; here the *mamlekhet kohanim* may have the force of "a *kingship* of priests": in other words, a *royal* priesthood, which is how the phrase is rendered in the Septuagint (Greek *basileion hierateuma*) and the New Testament (Ex 19:6 LXX; 1 Pet 2:9).

We saw in the creation narratives that Adam is described as king (Gen 1:26, 28) and priest in Eden (Gen 2:15). His role as king and priest derived from his status as son of God (Gen

> ### Who Served as Priests before the Levites?
>
> Exodus makes mention of Israelite "priests" (Hebrew *kohanim*) at the foot of Sinai prior to the Ten Commandments (Ex 19:22–24) and also speaks of young men performing priestly duties during the Sinai covenant solemnization (Ex 24:5). However, the Israelite priesthood was limited to the tribe of Levi (Ex 32:29), and not even Aaron the high priest was ordained until Leviticus 9. Who, then, are these pre-Levitical priests at Sinai?
>
> Jewish tradition identifies them with *the firstborn sons of the tribes of Israel* for good reason. The Passover experience involved the "consecration" of Israel's firstborn sons (Ex 13:2), using a word that usually means "ordination" (Hebrew *qaddesh*; e.g., Ex 28:3; 30:30) when applied to men. In Numbers, there is a formal ritual in which God accepts the Levites *in place of* Israel's firstborn (Num 3:44). The implication would be that the priestly duties of the firstborn are taken over by the Levites, who ordained themselves by their zeal during the Golden Calf debacle (Ex 32:29). Therefore, the pre-Levitical priests at Sinai (19:22–24; 24:5) were Israelite firstborn sons.

1:26; cf. 5:3). Along similar lines, in Exodus God identifies the people of Israel as his "first-born son" (Ex 4:22). In offering to Israel the covenant at Sinai, God is formally adopting Israel and granting to the nation the filial privileges of royalty and priesthood once exercised by Adam. In other words, Israel is corporately *a new Adam.* Moreover, the covenant offered to Israel at Sinai has the potential to fulfill all the promises of the Abrahamic covenant, including great nationhood, great name (royalty), and universal blessing. The covenant at Sinai provides a fundamental law or constitution for Israel's civil life (Ex 20–23), thus forming it into a "great nation". The whole nation is called to be kingly or royal—presumably exercising authority and leadership within the community of nations (cf. Deut 15:6), fulfilling the promise of a "great name". Furthermore, the nation will be priestly, and one of the primary functions of priesthood is to dispense divine blessing (cf. Num 6:22–27). Presumably Israel is supposed to dispense blessing to the community of nations, thus fulfilling the climactic promise to Abraham: In your seed shall all the families of the earth be blessed (see Gen 12:3; 22:18). All of this is contingent on Israel's covenant fidelity: "*If* you will obey my voice and keep my covenant" (Ex 19:5). As we will see, Israel will *not* keep the covenant, and the Abrahamic promises will only be partially fulfilled through the Mosaic covenant.

Exodus 20 relates the giving of the Ten Commandments, Israel's fundamental law. "Law" and "covenant" are not synonymous. A covenant establishes a familial relationship, but *all families and all relationships are governed by certain rules*; otherwise familial life would be chaos. Therefore, both biblical and extrabiblical covenant documents from the ancient Near East included lists of stipulations or laws intended to specify the privileges and obligations of "family members" (= covenant partners) toward one another.

How Do We Count the Ten Commandments?

The Hebrew text of the Bible is very clear that there are "ten commandments", or fundamental laws given by God at Sinai/Horeb (Ex 34:28; Deut 4:13; 10:4). It is much less clear, however, about how these ten are to be divided and counted. Two traditions have arisen.

First, there is the method of counting in Judaism and most of Protestantism. Following the text of Exodus 20:1–17, Jews separate the commandment against other gods (Ex 20:3) from the prohibition of idols (Ex 20:4) to form *two* commandments. Likewise, they combine the prohibitions against coveting wives and property into one (Ex 20:17), forming one final commandment.

Second, there is the Catholic (and Lutheran) method of counting, going back at least as far as Augustine. Following the text of Deuteronomy 5:7–21, Catholic tradition understands the prohibition of worship of other gods and idolatry as one command (Deut 5:7–10), but distinguishes the prohibition of lust (Deut 5:21a) from the prohibition of avarice (Deut 5:21b) to form the ninth and tenth commandments. In support of this distinction, it is worth noting that in the Deuteronomic form of the Decalogue, two different words are used to describe the coveting in question: "Neither shall you covet [Hebrew *hamad*] your neighbor's wife; and you shall not desire [Hebrew *'awa*] your neighbor's house" (Deut 5:21).

In the Ten Commandments, the first three commands (Ex 20:3–8) govern the relationship of the "children" (Israel) toward their "father" (God), whereas the next seven (Ex 20:9–17) govern the relationship of the "siblings" (fellow Israelites) toward each other. Moreover, each of the specific commandments can be linked back to God's call to the people of Israel on Mount Sinai to be "holy" or "set apart" (Hebrew *qadosh*), as illustrated in the following chart demonstrating how each commandment revolves around the sanctity/holiness of some aspect of the relationships between God and man:

Tablet 1: Relationship with God

1. Sanctity of God
2. Sanctity of the Divine Name
3. Sanctity of Time

Tablet 2: Relationship with Neighbor

4. Sanctity of Paternity and Maternity
5. Sanctity of Life
6. Sanctity of Marriage
7. Sanctity of Private Property
8. Sanctity of Speech/the Truth
9. Sanctity of Another's Spouse
10. Sanctity of Another's Property

Seen in this light, each of the commandments in the Decalogue is meant to "spell out" exactly what it means for the people of Israel to be holy, in relationship to both God and other human beings. The prohibition of *idolatry* (first commandment) upholds the holiness of God the Creator, who is set apart and above all creatures and is alone worthy of worship (Ex 20:2–6). For this reason, the "service" or "worship" (Hebrew *abodah*) given to God alone can be given to no other creature, much less to a graven image. Likewise, the prohibition of *blasphemy* (second commandment) upholds the holiness of God's name, which is not to be taken in "vain" (Hebrew *shawe'*), meaning not to be treated as if it were "empty" or "vain" (Ex 20:7). Third, the command to remember the "Sabbath" (Hebrew *Shabbath*) upholds the holiness of time, some of which is to be set apart for "rest" (Hebrew *nuch*) in the Lord in imitation of the One who made the world in six days but rested on the seventh (Ex 20:8–11).

With regard to relationships with one's neighbor, there is the command to "honor"—literally, to "glorify" (Hebrew *kabod*)!—one's parents (Ex 20:12; cf. Ps 22:23; Is 24:15). This command upholds the sanctity of procreation and the home by emphasizing the glory due to the givers of natural life, notably, both father *and* mother, and focusing on the very first relationship with "neighbors" experienced by all human beings: the parent-child relationship. Next we find the prohibition "You shall not kill" (Ex 20:13) (fifth commandment). It must be emphasized in this regard that the traditional translation fails to capture the precise meaning of the Hebrew command, which actually uses, not the word "kill" (Hebrew *hemît*), but the more specific term "slay" (Hebrew *ratzah*). This word is used elsewhere in the Pentateuch to describe what we would call "murder" (see Num 35:16–28). In this way, the Decalogue is not absolutely prohibiting *all* forms of killing but, rather, the "murder" or "slaying" of the innocent. The prohibition against *adultery* (sixth commandment) is likewise a specific prohibition of illicit sexual relations with a married person other than one's spouse. The outlawing of *theft* emphasizes the fact that another person's property is "set apart" for them, and they cannot be forcibly deprived of it without committing an injustice. The forbidding of *false witness*, although applied in later tradition to all lying whatsoever, envisages the specific context of public "testimony" in a juridical situation. Finally, and intriguingly, the commandments against coveting one's neighbor's wife or property (ninth and tenth commandments) take the law regarding relationship with one's neighbor into the interior of the human person, anticipating Jesus' own later teaching that all sins ultimately find their root cause in the disordered desires of the human "heart" (Mk 7:21–23). Because of this distinction, these are the only commandments of the Decalogue that are not elsewhere described as being punishable by death: all other violations of the Decalogue are cases of capital crime and, therefore, subject to capital punishment (see, for example, Ex 21:15, 16; 22:20; 31:15; Deut 19:18; 22:22).

The Covenant Code and the Liturgy at Mount Sinai (Exodus 21–24)

It is typical of ancient Near Eastern covenant documents to include a statement of basic laws as well as a longer section of more specific applications or stipulations, and the laws of the covenant at Mount Sinai are no exception. The Ten Commandments are followed by the "ordinances" (Ex 21–23), a unit called the "Covenant Code" by biblical scholars and traditionally attributed to the

---

The Covenant Code and Ancient Near Eastern Law Codes

Scholars have long noted peculiar and striking parallels between the Covenant Code (Ex 21–23) and ancient Near Eastern law codes, especially the Code of Hammurabi (CH). The CH was written ca. 1700 B.C. but was studied and recopied as part of the education of scribes throughout the Near East for well over a millennium. The laws in it address common legal cases in ancient Near Eastern society and probably represent judicial precedent or custom even older than Hammurabi himself.

There is no need to posit direct dependence of the Covenant Code on the Code of Hammurabi. Both are part of an ancient Near Eastern legal tradition and share some similarities. However, even when the situation both codes address is virtually identical, the legal remedy is often quite different. Moreover, the Covenant Code is substantially shorter than the Code of Hammurabi and reflects a simpler, less stratified, less urbanized society—as one might expect for Israel, a new nation composed of poor ex-slaves. The Covenant Code knows no social distinctions except that between slave and free and has no laws concerning priesthood, temple, palace, king, or royal administration.

Yahwist ("J") by source critics. In canonical context, these laws apply the general principles of morality laid down in the Ten Commandments to specific life situations in the ancient world. In this way, the Covenant Code consists of two primary kinds of laws: (1) *apodictic laws*: that is, laws that stipulate general principles or prohibitions, usually formulated in an absolute way; and (2) *casuistic laws*, which focus on specific situations. For example, the command against sorcery is apodictic: "You shall not permit a sorceress to live" (Ex 22:18). On the other hand, the command regarding breaking and entering is more casuistic in form: "If a thief is found breaking in, and is struck so that he dies, there shall be no bloodguilt for him; but if the sun has risen upon him, there shall be bloodguilt for him" (Ex 22:2–3).

Modern readers are distressed by the inclusion of laws concerning slavery in this biblical code (Ex 21:1–11, 20–21, 26–27, 32), but for the ancient peoples, including Israel, slavery was simply an unquestioned reality and a part of life. When the laws of the Covenant Code are compared with other ancient Near Eastern law codes, it is worth noting that they emphasize limiting the duration of slavery (Ex 21:1–6), protecting the marital rights of female slaves (Ex 21:7–11), and providing sanctions against the abuse of slaves (Ex 21:20, 26–27).

Ancient Near Eastern covenant documents typically end with a statement of blessings for covenant fidelity and curses for covenant infidelity, as is found at the conclusion of the Covenant Code: Exodus 20:20–33. What follows is an actual description of the rituals by which the covenant was *solemnized*—that is, actualized or officially established (Ex 24:1–11). The details of the ritual are all significant: Moses reads the terms of the covenant from "the book of the covenant" to the people and gains their consent (Ex 24:3). Then, with the assistance of some "young men of the sons of Israel", traditionally understood as Israelite firstborns, who served as ministerial priests prior to the Golden Calf incident, Moses offers animal sacrifice (Ex 24:5). He takes half the blood and sprinkles it on the altar, and—having gained the people's consent one more time—he sprinkles the rest on the people themselves, declaring: "Behold the blood of the covenant which the LORD has made with you in accordance with all these

---

Differences between Ancient and Modern Law

Modern readers, used to contemporary "statutory law" legal systems, often misunderstand the nature of law in the ancient Near East, which operated according to a different system, known as "common law". Statutory law systems function by the strict application of the written code; common law systems allow freedom to the individual judge, who consults unwritten tradition as well as written codes and judicial precedents to derive principles to apply to the particular case at hand.

The legal system established by Moses is a "common law" system: the judiciary is formed by Jethro's advice (Ex 18). In this way, the "Covenant Code" in Exodus 21–23 is by no means exhaustive and is not meant to be. Its interpretation and application in any given case would be guided by unwritten tradition and common sense on the part of the judge. It is a collection of precedents that embody the principles of morality and civil law to guide the particular judge in dispensing justice. Thus, there are often unwritten assumptions behind the formulations of particular laws.

What applies to the rest of Scripture also applies especially to the Covenant Code: God does not communicate his will exhaustively by Scripture alone (*sola scriptura*). The written word is always delivered to a society that already has a tradition and religious authorities (e.g., Moses, the elders, and judges) (Ex 18) to interpret and apply that "word" or "law" properly.

---

words" (Ex 24:8). The blood of the covenant ritual has a twofold sense. On the one hand, it both represents and establishes a *familial relationship with God*, who is represented by the altar. Because the blood is thrown on both the altar (God) and the people (Israel), the Israelites are now the family of God. On the other hand, the blood represents *covenant sanction*, a ritual statement to this effect: "May my blood be shed like the blood of these animals if I do not fulfill my covenant obligations!" It is important to note that, although the Lord is clearly the superior party in the covenant, nonetheless the covenant ritual at Sinai is, at first, one of mutuality: both God and the people share equally in the blood.

It is important to emphasize that the covenant at Mount Sinai, like the Passover before it, is completed, not by the sacrifices alone, but rather with the *heavenly banquet* with which the covenant comes to its climax (Ex 24:9–11). After the blood sacrifice is offered at the foot of the mountain, the representatives of the people journey up to the top of the mountain and, indeed, into God's very presence in heaven: "They beheld God, and ate and drank" (Ex 24:11). Once again, this heavenly banquet points out the liturgical nature of the covenant: shared meals typically followed ritual sacrifice, since in most forms of sacrifice only part of the animal was burned on the altar, the rest eaten. Furthermore, the meal also signifies the familial relationship between God and Israel, since in antiquity, as today, one of the distinctive marks of the family is that family members eat together (Gen 31:44–54). On the other hand, as Exodus makes abundantly clear, this is no ordinary banquet but, rather, is a *theophanic covenant banquet*: a sacrificial feast in which God appears and reveals himself to his people.

The Tabernacle of Moses (Exodus 25–31)

Up to this point in the narrative of Exodus, the pace of events has been remarkably engaging; all this changes, however, as the book shifts focus to a painstakingly detailed description of the furnishings of the place of worship known as "the tent of meeting": or, in more popular parlance, the "Tabernacle of Moses". Indeed, with the exception of a brief but important interlude involving the worship of the Golden Calf (Ex 32–34), the divinely revealed description of the Tabernacle (Ex 25–31) and the narrative account of the construction of the Tabernacle (Ex 35–40) constitute over one-fourth of the entire book of Exodus. Obviously, this material, however dull it may be for some contemporary readers—this is where many who nobly set out to read the Bible "from cover to cover" stop!—was considered of extreme importance by the sacred author of Exodus.

For our purposes several aspects of the description of the Tabernacle stand out as important. First and foremost, it is critical to note that the description of how God wishes to be worshipped by Israel is *divinely revealed*: Moses obtains the instructions for the construction of the Tabernacle while in the glory cloud atop Mount Sinai (Ex 25:31). Seen in this light, the liturgy of the Tabernacle is presented, not as something constructed by human beings according to human preferences, but as something constructed according to instructions from God.

Second, when analyzed carefully, it becomes very clear in context that the Tabernacle is intended to function as a *portable Mount Sinai*. As Moses is explicitly told by God: "And see that you make them [the furnishings of the Tabernacle] after the pattern for them, *which is being shown you on the mountain*" (Ex 25:40; cf. 25:9). In other words, what happens to Israel in the covenant ceremony of Mount Sinai (Ex 19–20, 24) is meant to be represented in the liturgy of the Tabernacle. Consider, for example, the following parallels between the events on Mount Sinai and the symbols in the Tabernacle:

Mount Sinai	*The Tabernacle of Moses*
"Feet"/Throne of God (Ex 24:10)	Ark of the Covenant (Footstool) (Ex 25:10–22)
Heavenly Banquet with God "Eat and Drink" (Ex 24:11)	Golden Table of the Bread (and Wine) of the Presence (Ex 25:23–30)
Cloud of Fire (Ex 24:17–18)	Golden Lampstand of Fire (Ex 25:31–40)
Blood Sacrifices on the Altar at the Foot of Mount Sinai (Ex 24:4–6)	Bronze Altar of Sacrifices in the Outer Court (Ex 27:1–8)
Washing with Water before Coming to Mount Sinai (Ex 19:10–15)	Bronze Laver of Water, in the Outer Court (Ex 30:17–21)

As should be clear from this brief chart, not only does the Tabernacle correspond to Mount Sinai as a whole, but the sacred furnishings of "pure gold" in the Holy Place seem to recapitulate the events at the *top* of the mountain, whereas the sacred furnishings of "bronze" in the outer court of sacrifice recapitulate the events at the *bottom* of Mount Sinai. In this way, passage through the various parts of the Tabernacle becomes a kind of symbolic "ascent" into

God's presence. By means of the sacrificial liturgy of the Tabernacle, the priests and people of Israel are enabled to experience, in sign and symbol, the "heaven" of Mount Sinai on earth while traveling through the desert toward the Promised Land.

The Golden Calf and the Broken Tablets (Exodus 32–34)

Most unfortunately, while Moses is atop Mount Sinai communing with God and receiving these instructions on how he is to be worshipped, the people of Israel at the foot of the mountain grow impatient—Moses is, after all, gone for "forty days and forty nights" (Ex 24:18)!—and fall away from God before they ever even get to hear what God has in store for them in the liturgy of the Tabernacle.

During this time, the people waiting at the foot of the mountain for Moses' return grow impatient and give up on Moses and the new religion to which he introduced them. Needing religious sanction for their continued journey and entrance to Canaan, they prod Aaron to make an idol or idols for them, so they can perform sacrifices and continue their journey (Ex 32:1). A curiously passive (or intimidated) Aaron constructs for them a golden bull-calf, which may plausibly be identified either with the Egyptian god Apis or with the Canaanite deity El; since they have just come from Egypt, perhaps the first is more probable. In any event, the people hail the idol as a deity: they worship it with "burnt offerings" and "peace offerings", sit down to a sacred meal, and then rise up "to play" (Ex 32:6). The latter expression is a Hebrew euphemism for the kind of non-marital sexual activity that accompanied the "worship" of pagan deities, many of whom were associated the powers of virility or fertility. From a canonical perspective, the association of *idolatry* with a form of spiritual *adultery* here is not accidental. As we will see when we get to the prophets, the covenant with the Lord is frequently framed in matrimonial terms; hence, infidelity to the covenant is likewise frequently associated with acts of physical infidelity to the covenant of marriage (see Hos 1–2; Is 1–2; Ezek 16).

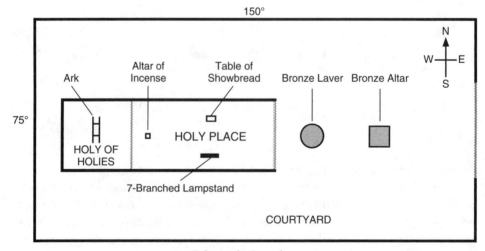

Tabernacle Complex

In response to Israel's infidelity, God declares to Moses that he will execute the curses on Israel for breech of their covenant: "Let me alone, that ... I may consume them" (Ex 32:10). It is important to stress that God's declaration that he will punish Israel here is not arbitrary or vengeful but, rather, the enforcement of the commitment made by the Israelites in the covenant at Sinai, in which, as we saw above, the sacrificial blood symbolized death for covenant infidelity (Ex 24:8). In point of fact, however, the Lord's warnings to Moses about the impending punishment (Ex 32:7–10) are actually intended to provide Moses the opportunity to intercede for the people, which he does to a remarkable degree, even offering his own life in exchange for theirs (Ex 32:11–14, 30–34). Given our focus on the centrality of the covenant, it is worth underscoring here that Moses' plea for mercy appeals directly to the oath-bound, unilateral covenant with Abraham: "Remember Abraham, Isaac, and Israel, your servants, to whom you swore by your own self, and said to them, 'I will multiply your descendants' " (Ex 32:13). Taken in context, Moses' words are a direct reference to the divine oath sworn *after the sacrifice of Isaac*, the only place in Scripture where God explicitly *swears by himself* to any of the patriarchs (Gen 22:15–18). Hearing this argument, the Lord relents, confirming our earlier suggestions that God's covenant-oath at the sacrifice of Isaac functions as a kind of "Calvary" of the Old Testament, insofar as it is a font of mercy and a firm foundation of grace that preserves Israel even when she violates her covenant with God.

Moses' response to Israel's apostasy is equally fiery: after realizing what the people have done, he descends from Mount Sinai and smashes the tablets of the covenant law out of anger and as a sign that the covenant relationship has been broken (Ex 32:15–20). The scene at the foot of the mountain is chaotic—like a pagan riot or orgy—so Moses rallies the Levites around him and sends them through the camp to execute some three thousand of the men of Israel, who are apparently the leaders of the rebellion (Ex 32:28). By this act, the Levites "*ordain*" themselves "for the service of the LORD" (Ex 32:29)—that is, they gain

> ### What Was the Law of the Renewed Sinai Covenant?
>
> When God renews the Sinai covenant with Israel through Moses in Exodus 34:10–28, the text includes a short list of laws (Ex 34:11–26). This is not intended to be exhaustive but is, rather, a "representative sampling" of laws for the renewed covenant. In fact, a great body of additional legislation—the entire book of Leviticus—is added into the covenant relationship after the Golden Calf.

a priestly status by both defending and enforcing the covenant at Sinai, the first commandment of which was "You shall have no other gods before me" (cf. Ex 20:1–3).

Moses then returns to the mountain in order to intercede for Israel. What follows is an extensive dialogue between God and Moses, in which Moses reaches a greater level of intimacy with God than he has ever had previously. God shows him his glory and proclaims his name once more, as at the bush (Ex 34:5). In response to this theophany, Moses' face becomes illumined with the divine presence (Ex 34:29). Theologically, the Calf incident provides Moses with an opportunity to rise above mere intercession to the level of *self-sacrificial mediation*, in which Moses offers his own life before God in exchange for the lives of the sinful people of Israel (Ex 32:20–34), a state that, mysteriously, he would not have attained were it not for the people's sin. Nonetheless, as close as Moses comes to God, he only ever sees God's "back" (Ex 33:23), which indicates that salvation history still awaits a more perfect mediator, who not only *sees* the face of God but *shows* the face of God (cf. Jn 14:9).

In response to Moses' self-sacrificial act, God deigns to renew the covenant with Israel because of Moses' intercession (Ex 34:10–28), but the covenant relationship is restructured in important ways that represent an increase in mediation between God and Israel. The two forms of the covenant, before and after the apostasy with the Golden Calf, may be distinguished from one another as (1) the *Sinaitic* covenant and (2) the *Levitical* covenant. Before the Golden Calf, the covenant relationship is directly between God and Israel: Moses says, "Behold the blood of the covenant which the LORD has made with you" (Ex 24:8). After the Golden Calf, the covenant relationship is triangulated, and Moses is included as a party: the Lord says, "In accordance with these words I have made a covenant *with you* [Moses] and *with Israel*" (Ex 34:27). Before the Calf, the firstborn sons of all twelve tribes served as priests (see above); after the Calf, the tribe of Levi alone takes over priestly duties (Ex 32:29). Before the Calf, the covenant laws were quite brief and basic (Ex 20–23). After the Calf, a much larger body of cultic and civil law is added to the covenant relationship, which will be expressed in the book of Leviticus (Lev 1–27). Before the Calf, the tablets were written with "the finger of God" (Ex 31:18); after the Calf, Moses writes the tablets himself (Ex 34:28). The contrasts between the Sinaitic and Levitical covenants are summarized in this table:

	Sinaitic Covenant (Ex 19–24)	Levitical Covenant (Ex 32–Lev 27)
Priesthood	Firstborn (Ex 13:1; 24:5)	Levites are priestly tribe (Ex 32:29)
Covenant Configuration	Covenant is direct; Lord + Israel (Ex 24:8)	Covenant is indirect, mediated through Moses: Lord + Moses + Israel (Ex 34:27)
Laws	Few laws: Ex 20–23	Many laws: Ex 34–Lev 27 (cf. Gal 3:19)
God's Revelation	Tablets written by God (Ex 31:18)	Tablets written by Moses (Ex 34:28)
Summary	*Covenant is light and direct*	*Covenant is burdened and mediated*

In light of the Adamic role to which Israel was called in the first Sinai covenant (Ex 19:5–6), we may say that what the forbidden fruit of the Tree of Knowledge was to Adam, the Golden Calf was to Israel. Indeed, both Adam and Aaron try to pass the blame for their transgressions to others: Adam to Eve ("The woman ... she gave me fruit of the tree, and I ate") (Gen 3:12) and Aaron to the people of Israel ("So they gave it to me, and I threw it into the fire, and there came out this calf") (Ex 32:24).[4] Both Adam and Israel are "first-born

---

[4] Hamilton, *Handbook on the Pentateuch*, 221.

sons" who broke their filial covenants with God almost immediately after those covenants were made.

The Construction of the Tabernacle (Exodus 35–40)

Nonetheless, it is a sign of God's mercy toward Israel that the construction and erection of the Tabernacle, planned before the Calf, continues after the covenant breaking and renewal. Somewhat unexpectedly, the people bring a generous donation of materials (Ex 35:4–29)—perhaps their piety was spurred on by the three thousand who died!—and Bezalel and Oholiab set about constructing the Tabernacle proper (Ex 35:30—36:38). When the work is finished (Ex 39:32–43), Moses erects the Tabernacle and the cloud of God's glory comes down to cover it (Ex 40:1–38).

We saw earlier that the instructions for making the Tabernacle parallel certain features of the events at Mount Sinai. Along similar lines, modern scholars have pointed out that the narrative of the construction of the Tabernacle contains several remarkable parallels with the account of the creation of the world in the book of Genesis. Compare the following parallels from the sixth and seventh days in the Hexaemeron with the account of Moses' completion of the Tabernacle in the book of Exodus:[5]

The Creation of the World	The Building of the Tabernacle
And God saw everything that he had made, and behold, it was very good. (Gen 1:31)	And Moses saw all the work, and behold, they had done it; as the LORD had commanded. (Ex 39:43)
Thus the heavens and the earth were finished. (Gen 2:1)	Thus all the work of the tabernacle of the tent of meeting was finished. (Ex 39:32)
God finished his work which he had done. (Gen 2:2)	So Moses finished the work. (Ex 40:33)
So God blessed the seventh day. (Gen 2:3)	And Moses blessed them. (Ex 39:43)

From this point of view, it seems clear that for the author of Genesis and Exodus, the Tabernacle of Moses is not only a "new Sinai" but also a kind of *new Eden* for Israel, a *new Adam*. Indeed, not only does the account of the construction of the Tabernacle echo the days of the Hexaemeron, but even its decorations contain echoes of the Garden of Eden: precious metals (especially gold) and stones (Gen 2:11–12; Ezek 28:13; Ex 35:4), particularly onyx (Gen 2:12; Ex 35:9); flowering, fruiting trees (Gen 2:9; Ex 25:31–40); plentiful water (Gen 2:10; Ex 30:17–21); and cherubim (Gen 3:24; Ezek 28:14; Ex 25:18–20).[6] These same motifs will also be observed later in the Jerusalem Temple.

---

[5] Ibid.

[6] See G. K. Beale, *The Temple and the Church's Mission: A Biblical Theology of the Dwelling Place of God*, New Studies in Biblical Theology 17 (Downers Grove, Ill.: IVP Academic, 2004).

Historical Issues in Exodus

As with the accounts of the patriarchs in the book of Genesis, for the vast majority of Jewish and Christian history, the accounts of the events in the book of Exodus were accepted as substantially historical. Even in recent times, the *Catechism of the Catholic Church* assumes the basic historicity of God "freeing" the Israelites from "slavery in Egypt" (*CCC* 62). With that said, when it comes to the details of the exodus, modern scholarship has raised a number of important historical questions regarding the event. For our purposes here, the three main issues that deserve attention are (1) the historicity of the basic exodus event, (2) the question of the date of the exodus, and (3) the historicity of the Tabernacle as a place of worship.

Regarding the historical truth of the exodus event, modern scholarly opinions on the issue vary widely, from those who regard the exodus as a late post-exilic myth invented to create a communal identity for the people of Israel (for example, J. Wellhausen, T. Thompson) to those who uphold the substantial historicity of the biblical account (for example, K. A. Kitchen, J. K. Hoffmeier).

The Debate over the Historicity of the Exodus

On the one hand, scholars who deny the historicity of the exodus call upon several arguments in their favor. First and foremost is the argument that the exodus of the Israelites is "not attested in any ancient nonbiblical source".[7] From this point view, although there are numerous references to the exodus in the Hebrew Scriptures themselves, what is needed to substantiate these accounts is some ancient, non-Israelite testimony, of which we have none. Second, and even more important, is the contention that the literary genre of the accounts in Exodus is "legendary and folkloristic", not "historiography".[8] Significantly, the primary reason given for this conclusion is not literary but philosophical: the accounts of the exodus are "replete with miraculous incidents", and therefore, for some scholars, they must be unhistorical.[9] A third major argument against the historicity of the exodus is that there is no explicit *archaeological evidence* for the passage of the Israelites through the Sinai peninsula. Surely if such a massive event took place, there must be some imprint left in the archaeological record? Fourth and finally, there are the problems that revolve around dating the event of the exodus and whether it is to be placed in the fifteenth or thirteenth century B.C. (see discussion below). For more skeptical scholars, one reason a date of the exodus cannot be resolved is because the event never happened.

On the other hand, scholars who uphold the basic historicity of the exodus give several reasons. First and foremost, both internal and external evidence support the basic historicity of the exodus. When it comes to the text itself, even a cursory reading of Exodus reveals that standard genre cues of ancient

---

[7] John J. Collins, *Introduction to the Hebrew Bible* (Minneapolis: Fortress Press, 2004), 108.
[8] Ibid., 109.
[9] Ibid.

history—such as a focus on geography, places names, exact dates, and such—abound.[10] Perhaps because of such cues, the book of Exodus was universally treated as historical by all known ancient Jewish writers as well as by the authors of the New Testament and the early Church Fathers (see, for example, Philo, *Life of Moses*; Josephus, *Antiquities of the Jews*; Acts 7; and so on). In this regard, it is worth noting that the lack of references to the exodus in contemporary Egyptian literature is not difficult to explain. Egyptian historiographers never recorded the defeats or mistakes of any of the pharaohs—Egyptian history was essentially pro-pharaonic propaganda, and thus the exodus, if it was anything like what the Bible describes, would never have been recorded in Egyptian annals. However, with that said, it is simply *not true* that no extra-biblical evidence whatsoever exists supporting the historicity of the exodus. To the contrary, according to Josephus, the ancient Egyptian historian *Manetho*, even though he was thoroughly anti-Jewish, affirmed the historicity of the exodus of the Israelites from Egypt in the fourth century B.C.[11]

Second, although it is true that there is no explicit archaeological evidence for the exodus, this is also true of the vast majority of historical events in ancient Near Eastern history—especially events that did not take place in long-standing urban areas (that is, cities), the primary locales where archaeological investigation is even possible. If, as the Pentateuch claims, the exodus from Egypt was a transitory event across the shifting sands of the Sinai peninsula, then the absence of evidence is easily explained by recognizing that such evidence may still be in the ground or else has been permanently lost due to erosion (a major problem in seas and deserts), decay, and human activity. Moreover, the phenomenon of disagreement between ancient historical documents and the reconstructions of archaeology is widely attested and should caution against too quickly assuming that a lack of direct archaeological evidence indicates that the biblical text is legendary or fictional.[12] For example, the southern Judean cities of Dibon (Num 21:30; 32:3) and Hebron (Josh 10:36) feature significantly in the account of the exodus and conquest; however, archaeology has not turned up evidence of the existence of cities at these locations during any plausible time period for those events. Nonetheless, the annals of Pharaoh Ramesses II, often thought to be the pharaoh of the exodus, *also* mention Dibon and Hebron as being present in this time period—in fact, Ramesses fought against and sacked Dibon. Now, clearly the annals of Ramesses II are contemporary historical documents, not fiction—despite the discrepancy with current archaeological findings.

Third, while direct evidence for the exodus is lacking, there is a great deal of indirect evidence that creates a *contextual plausibility* for the exodus. Large-scale exoduses of whole ethnic groups are not at all unknown in human history (for example, the Huns whom Attila would rule), and several other major exoduses (beside the Israelite) are attested in the ancient Near East in the second

---

[10] Kenneth A. Kitchen, *On the Reliability of the Old Testament* (Grand Rapids, Mich.: Eerdmans, 2003), 241–312.

[11] Josephus, *Against Apion* 1.228–52.

[12] Charles R. Krahmalkov, "Exodus Itinerary Confirmed by Egyptian Evidence", *Biblical Archeology Review* 20:5 (1994): 54–62, 79.

millennium B.C. (for example, the Philistines vacating their Mediterranean islands to settle the coast of Palestine by military force). So the scenario of a large ethnic group being forced to vacate its original territory and settle in a different location is not historically anomalous. The general phenomenon of Semitic slaves employed by the Egyptians for monumental building projects is well-attested in different periods through the second millennium B.C. We also have records of small bands of these slaves fleeing Egypt into the Sinai peninsula as well as efforts by the Egyptian military to halt these escapes. Slaves making bricks from clay with straw (Ex 5) is an attested practice in Egyptian records: the straw contained chemicals making the clay more malleable and also increased the tensile strength of the resultant brick. Many of the plagues describe known natural calamities that occasionally struck the Egyptian environment; in particular, the sequence of plagues seems to follow the known ancient Egyptian agricultural year. The biblical descriptions of Egyptian and Sinai environment and living conditions agree with known historical reality in numerous minor details (for example, Egyptian taskmasters over Semitic foremen [Ex 5:15–21], the description of the Egyptian diet [Num 11:5], the presence of quail in the Sinai peninsula [Num 11:31–35]). The itinerary of the Israelites on their exodus route from Egypt (Numbers 33) also seems to agree with Egyptian itineraries in the Sinai region from the second millennium B.C.[13] These and other pieces of evidence creating a historical plausibility for the exodus have been collected by different scholars.[14]

Fourth and finally, it is important to stress that the argument from the impossibility of miracles is not a historical argument at all but, rather, a philosophical one. Whether or not modern scholars believe that works of history should contain affirmations of miraculous events, the fact of the matter is that ancient Near Eastern historical accounts outside the Bible also attribute historical events to divine causality. For example, victories are typically attributed to the divine intervention of the patron deity of the triumphant king. Seen in this light, the presence of "supernatural" events in the Exodus narrative does *not* automatically classify the document as legendary or mythical. Indeed, as mentioned above, the book of Exodus was, after all, universally considered a historical document by ancient writers, even by those unfavorable to the Jews.

When Did the Exodus Take Place?

Scholars who affirm the historical truth of the exodus continue to debate exactly when it took place, with some proposing a date in the fifteenth century B.C. and others suggesting a date in the thirteenth century B.C.

On the one hand, *the fifteenth-century date of the exodus* has both internal and external evidence in support of it. In terms of internal biblical evidence, a

---

[13] Ibid.

[14] James K. Hoffmeier, *Ancient Israel in Sinai: The Evidence for the Authenticity of the Wilderness Tradition* (Oxford: Oxford University Press, 2005); Hoffmeier, *Israel in Egypt: The Evidence for the Authenticity of the Exodus Tradition* (Oxford: Oxford University Press, 1996); Kitchen, *Reliability of the Old Testament*, 241–312.

straightforward reading of the dates provided in Scripture places the exodus around 1450 B.C., under the reign of Thutmose III. The key piece of evidence in this regard is the testimony that Israel dwelt for more than "three hundred years" in the land of Canaan (Judg 11:26) and that it was after almost five centuries that the Jerusalem Temple was built:

> *In the four hundred and eightieth year after the sons of Israel came out of the land of Egypt,* in the fourth year of Solomon's reign over Israel, in the month of Ziv, which is the second month, *he began to build the house of the LORD.* (1 Kings 6:1)

In terms of external evidence, the so-called "Amarna letters", a large body of correspondence between the court of Pharaoh Akhenaten and his Canaanite vassal kings in the mid-1300s B.C., give ample evidence that the kings of Canaan were panicked in this time period by military pressure from an ill-defined group of landless people (or peoples) called the *Apiru*, who lived in the countryside and attacked the Canaanite city-states. If the exodus took place in the mid-1400s B.C., then the Amarna letters would reflect the situation like that described in the book of Judges and 1 Samuel, in which Israel was struggling against continued Canaanite presence in the land. Moreover, if the exodus took place in the fifteenth century, it may be possible to correlate the conquest of the land under Joshua with the archaeological evidence for the destruction of a large number of Canaanite cities at the end of the Middle Bronze Age, although the end of the Middle Bronze II Age would have to be brought down somewhat (from around 1550 B.C. to around 1420 B.C.)

On the other hand, the *thirteenth-century date of the exodus* is supported by a larger number of contemporary scholars for several reasons. First and foremost, the reference to the Israelite slaves being forced to build the cities of "Pithom" and "Raamses" (Ex 1:11) is tied to the reign of the Egyptian Pharaoh Ramesses II (ca. 1303–1213), under which the city of Ramesses (Egyptian spelling) was made his capital. Ramesses II was a powerful and oppressive pharaoh who made widespread use of Semitic slave labor for his building projects and thus fits the profile of the hard-hearted pharaoh in the book of Exodus. Moreover, it is Ramesses II's successor, the Egyptian Pharaoh Merneptah, who provides us with the first extra-biblical attestation of the nation of Israel. The famous *Merneptah Stele*—an inscribed stone from his reign—mentions "Israel" along with a number of Canaanite city-states as defeated by Merneptah in his various military campaigns.[15] Since Ramesses II's successor provides us with our first direct evidence of Israelites living in the land of Canaan, the presumption is they must have left Egypt under Ramesses himself. The stele indicates that "Israel" is neither a city nor a land but an ethnic group—which some take to indicate they had only recently arrived and had not yet established permanent settlements. Finally, according to certain archaeologists, a large number of Canaanite cities were also destroyed in the late thirteenth century, which may correlate with the account of the conquest under Joshua.

---

[15] See Kitchen, *Reliability of the Old Testament*, 219–20.

The Historicity of the Tabernacle

In addition to the debate over the historicity of the exodus from Egypt, there is also a debate over the historicity of the detailed account of the Tabernacle of Moses that takes up so much of the book of Exodus (Ex 25–31, 35–40). Scholarly skepticism in this regard goes back once again to Julius Wellhausen, who popularized the view that the Tabernacle was a fictional invention of the postexilic priesthood, who retrojected their own views of the Temple and its liturgy back into the Mosaic period. In this way, the Tabernacle became a cypher for the postexilic Temple. In support of this contention, Wellhausen argued that without the benefit of corroborative archaeological data, the description of the Tabernacle sounded too elaborate to have been the creation of the newly escaped Israelite slaves. Unfortunately for Wellhausen—who was arguing well before the explosion of artifacts and information about ancient Egypt and the Near East that took place in the twentieth century—far from being an argument against the historicity of the exodus, the detailed description of the Tabernacle provides one of the stronger arguments *for* the historicity of the book of Exodus.

Indeed, as recent historical and archaeological research on the Tabernacle has demonstrated, the dimensions, decoration, arrangement, materials, and construction techniques of the Tabernacle and the ark have clear and undeniable analogues with *ancient Egyptian tent-shrines and sacred vessels from the second*

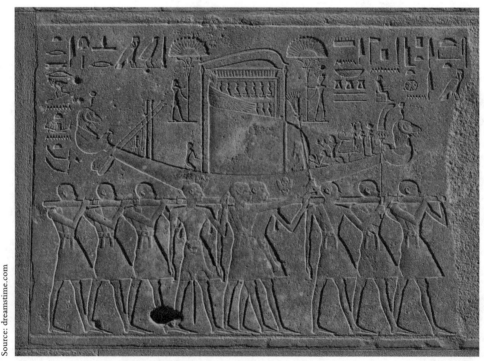

Source: dreamstime.com

A typical scene of an Egyptian funeral procession. The shrine being carried on poles is a canopic chest, similar in concept to the biblical Ark of the Covenant.

millennium B.C., especially from the New Kingdom period (ca. 1500–1000 B.C.).[16] The closest known analogue to the ark is an Egyptian sacred or royal chest with poles from the reign of Pharaoh Tutankhamun ("King Tut", 1341–23 B.C.; see image of Egyptian priests transporting a golden "ark" on poles, from the temple of Ramesses II in Abydos, Egypt). Likewise, the closest analogue to the Tabernacle layout as a whole is the war-tent and precinct of Ramesses II (who considered himself divine) used during his military campaigns. The correspondence between the Egyptian and biblical data is so close that some of the surviving Egyptian ark-like objects have enabled scholars to clarify the meaning of some obscure parts of the Hebrew text describing the ark.[17]

For example, the Tabernacle narratives (Ex 25–31; 35–40) describe a rectangular tent in the middle of a rectangular precinct formed by curtains on frames. This is precisely the pattern used by Ramesses II for his royal tent and court while leading military excursions. It may not be coincidental, then, that in Numbers 1–10, the people of Israel are arranged as military units encamped in order around the Tabernacle. The whole layout resembles the pattern of the Egyptian army on campaign. The message to the Israelites would be: "Your king and god is no longer Pharaoh, but the LORD, who will lead you to victory over your enemies in Canaan."

This Egyptian archaeological data presents a considerable challenge to Wellhausen's view that the Tabernacle was a mythical construct of the Second Temple period. For one thing, the dimensions and decorations of the Tabernacle do not correspond exactly to those of either the Solomonic or the Second Temple. If the Tabernacle was invented as a retrojection of either, why do the dimensions not match? Furthermore, would not the claim that God authorized Moses to build a portable tent-shrine not actually *delegitimize* the Temple by raising the obvious question: "If God said to build a *Tabernacle*, why are we worshiping at this stone *Temple*?"[18] Indeed, the Tabernacle narrative poses serious problems for the legitimacy of the Second Temple, especially since the Tabernacle was focused around the Ark of the Covenant, a sacred object that was no longer present in the Second Temple period. Finally, given the parallels between second-millennium Egyptians shrines and the Mosaic Tabernacle, is it really plausible to suggest that priests in the land of Israel after the Babylonian exile (sixth century B.C.) could have known or re-created construction techniques and patterns of mid- to late second-millennium Egyptian tent-shrines? Or is it more likely that the reason the description of the Tabernacle in the book of Exodus parallels a second-millennium Egyptian tent-shrine is because the description stems from someone who lived in and was familiar with second-millennium Egyptian worship? In the light of recent discoveries, the description of the Tabernacle is, in fact, one of the best pieces of evidence that ties the book of Exodus to the time period and culture it claims to represent.

---

[16] See Hoffmeier, *Ancient Israel in Sinai*, 193–222.

[17] Raanan Eichler, "The Meaning of Zēr", *Vetus Testamentum* 64 (2014): 196–210, esp. 202–7: "Extant chests from ancient Egypt reveal parallels to almost every detail of the ark as described in priestly and other biblical texts" (203).

[18] T. Fretheim, "The Priestly Document: Anti-Temple?" *Vetus Testamentum* 18, no. 3 (1968): 313–29.

Exodus in the Living Tradition

Perhaps even more than the book of Genesis, the account of the exodus from Egypt has played a central role in the living tradition of the Christian faith. In particular, the accounts of the exodus from Egypt and the Tabernacle of Moses have provided rich fodder for the ancient method of reading Scripture known as *typology*, by which events and realities in the Old Testament prefigure fulfillments in the New Testament (*CCC* 128). Several passages in Exodus have been recognized since the apostolic age as sacramental types: the Passover, the crossing of the sea, the manna, the water from the rock, the covenant ceremony on Sinai, and the Bread of the Presence. We will take a few moments to examine each of these in order to highlight the theological role that the book of Exodus has played in the living tradition of the Church.

The Passover Lamb and the Passion of Christ

As we saw above, the deliverance of the twelve tribes of Israel from Egypt was not achieved by the first nine plagues but only by the final wonder of the Passover. During this climactic act of God, the Israelites secured their redemption through the sacrifice and consumption of the flesh of the Passover lamb (Ex 12–13). From the very beginnings of the early Church, following the actions of Jesus himself at his final Passover meal (Mt 26; Mk 14; Lk 22), the Passover became the preeminent foreshadowing of the deliverance from slavery to sin and death that would be effected by the new Passover inaugurated by the Passion, death, and Resurrection of Jesus. This Passover typology was based on several striking points of correspondence between the original Passover and the Last Supper and Passion of Jesus:

The Passover of Egypt	*The Passover of Jesus*
Unblemished male lamb, one year old. (Ex 12:5)	Jesus is the "lamb of God" who is without sin/blemish. (Jn 1:29; 1 Pet 4:15)
Sacrificed during 14/15 Nisan. (Ex 12:6)	Sacrificed during 14/15 Nisan. (Mt 26:1–2; Jn 13:1–2)
Not a bone of the lamb is to be broken. (Ex 12:46)	Not one of Jesus' bones is broken during his crucifixion. (Jn 19:36)
Spread blood on wood of doorposts and lintel with hyssop. (Ex 12:7)	Crucified on the wood of the cross; given wine on hyssop. (Jn 19:17–18, 29)
Eat the flesh of the lamb with unleavened bread. (Ex 12:8)	Disciples must "eat" his "flesh" in order to have eternal life. (Jn 6:53–58)
A day of "remembrance" forever. (Ex 12:14)	Last Supper: "Do this in remembrance of me." (Lk 22:19–20; 1 Cor 11:23–25)

In light of such parallels, it is not surprising that early Christian tradition went on regularly to cite the account of the Passover in the book of Exodus as one of the preeminent foreshadowings of the Passion and death of Christ. In the words of Saint Augustine: "So now that prophetic figure has been fulfilled in truth when Christ is led as a sheep to the slaughter. By his blood, after our doorposts have been smeared [with it], that is, by the sign of his cross, after our foreheads have been marked [with it], we are freed from the ruin of this world as though from the captivity or destruction in Egypt. And we effect a most salutary passing over when we pass over from the devil to Christ and from this tottering world to his most solidly established kingdom."[19]

The Crossing of the Red Sea and Baptism

Along similar lines, the Church Fathers universally understood the miraculous crossing of the sea as a type of baptism, with the latter understood as a passing through the water under the power of God's "spirit" (Hebrew *ruah*) that marks the transition from slavery to sin and to the freedom of the children of God. Such an understanding is first attested in the writings of the apostle Paul, when he says to the Corinthians:

> I want you to know, brethren, that our fathers were all under the cloud, and *all passed through the sea, and all were baptized into Moses in the cloud and in the sea*, and all ate the same supernatural food and all drank the same supernatural drink. (1 Cor 10:1–2)

Following Paul, the later Christian tradition takes the crossing of the sea as one of the preeminent types by which the mystery of baptism is explained to the catechumens during the Easter celebration of initiation. For example, in the powerful words of Saint Cyril of Jerusalem, in his fourth-century catecheses to the newly baptized, we read:

> For when Pharaoh, that most bitter and cruel tyrant, was oppressing the free and high-born people of the Hebrews, God sent Moses to bring them out of the evil bondage of the Egyptians.... Now turn from the old to the new, from the figure to the reality. There we have Moses sent from God to Egypt; here, Christ, sent forth from His Father into the world: there, that Moses might lead forth an afflicted people out of Egypt; here, that Christ might rescue those who are oppressed in the world under sin ... *there, the tyrant was pursuing that ancient people even to the sea; and here the daring and shameless spirit, the author of evil, was following thee even to the very streams of salvation*. The tyrant of old was drowned in the sea; and this present one disappears in the water of salvation.[20]

---

[19] Augustine, *Tractate on the Gospel of John* 55.1, in Joseph T. Lienhard, "Exodus", in *Exodus, Leviticus, Numbers, Deuteronomy*, Old Testament 3, Ancient Christian Commentary on Scripture, ed. Thomas C. Oden (Downers Grove, Ill.: InterVarsity Press, 2001), 63.

[20] Cyril of Jerusalem, *Five Catechetical Lectures* 19.2–3, in *NPNF* 7, 144–45.

And this is but one of dozens of examples from the early Church Fathers of the typological understanding of Christian baptism in relation to the exodus from Egypt. Indeed, this may be the most popular understanding of baptism in the writings of ancient Christianity.[21] Notice here that for the early Church Fathers, the sacraments of the Church not only communicate the saving power of Christ's Passion, death, and Resurrection; they also prolong and make present in a certain way the "wonders" (Greek *thaumata*) of the Old Testament, which events are actions of one and the same spirit of YHWH, the God of history and creation.

The Manna from Heaven and the Bread of Life

But this kind of typological reading can be traced back beyond the works of the apostle Paul to the words and deeds of Jesus in the four Gospels. In this regard, there is perhaps no more explicit typological understanding of the "wonders of God" (*mirabilia Dei*) in the exodus than that found in the Bread of Life discourse of Jesus in the Gospel of John. Strikingly, when Jesus gives his most explicit and realistic teaching on the Eucharist, he uses the manna from heaven as the primary event for unlocking the mystery:

> "I am the bread of life. *Your fathers ate the manna in the wilderness, and they died. This is the bread which comes down from heaven, that a man may eat of it and not die.* I am the living bread which came down from heaven; if any one eats of this bread, he will live for ever; and the bread which I shall give for the life of the world is my flesh."
>
> The Jews then disputed among themselves, saying, "How can this man give us his flesh to eat?" So Jesus said to them, "Truly, truly, I say to you, unless you eat the flesh of the Son of man and drink his blood, you have no life in you; he who eats my flesh and drinks my blood has eternal life, and I will raise him up at the last day. *For my flesh is food indeed, and my blood is drink indeed.* . . . This is the bread which came down from heaven, not such as the fathers ate and died; he who eats this bread will live for ever." (Jn 6:48–55, 57–58)

Note here an important principle of the typological interpretation of Exodus: there is both continuity and discontinuity between the saving actions of God in the past and the saving actions of God in the New Covenant. In terms of continuity, if the manna of the exodus was miraculous bread from heaven, then the Eucharist of Jesus cannot be just a symbol, but rather, truly is his saving flesh and blood. In terms of discontinuity, the manna of the exodus was only able to communicate physical life: the "fathers ate it and died" (Jn 6:58)—whereas the new manna of the Eucharist gives eternal life: he who eats will "live for ever" (Jn 6:51). Once again, Saint Augustine sums up the tradition well when he writes: "The manna also came down from heaven; *but the manna was only a shadow, this is the truth.*"[22]

---

[21] See Jean Daniélou, S.J., *The Bible and the Liturgy* (Notre Dame, Ind.: University of Notre Dame Press, 1956), 86–98.

[22] Augustine, *Homilies on John* 26.13, in *NPNF1*, 7:172.

The Water from the Rock and the Sacraments

Still another wonder of the exodus that drew the attention of the living tradition was the memorable occasion of Moses striking the rock at Horeb in order to provide water for the thirsty Israelites (Ex 17:1–5). As we have already seen, the apostle Paul spoke of this wonder as providing "supernatural drink" or "spiritual drink" for the Israelites in the desert, identifying "the rock" as "Christ" (1 Cor 10:1–4).

The Fathers continued to make this identification, but went even farther, emphasizing the fact that God mediates the wonders of the New Covenant through the ministry of New Covenant priests. Consider the words of Saint Ambrose from the fourth century:

> What do we learn from the type which was prefigured in the time of Moses? That when the people of the Jews thirsted and murmured because they had no water God bade Moses strike the rock with his rod. He struck the rock and the rock poured forth a flood of water, as the Apostle says: "They drank of that spiritual rock which followed them; and that Rock was Christ" [1 Cor 10:4]. Do you also drink, that Christ may follow you. You see the mystery. Moses is the prophet; the rod is the word of God. *The priest strikes the rock with the word of God: the water flows and the people of God drink. And the priest touches the cup, waters streams into the cup, springing up into eternal life.*[23]

Once again, we see how the early Christian interpretation of the sacraments as miracles—as supernatural acts of God, and not just symbols—was directly related to the interpretation of the wonders of the exodus as types of the sacramental mysteries.

The Bread of the Presence and the Eucharist

But it is not only the miracles of Exodus that were interpreted typologically; it is also the liturgy of the Tabernacle. In this regard, the various sacred furnishings of the Tabernacle were often interpreted typologically and symbolically in the Christian tradition, especially in the Middle Ages.[24] In this regard, one of the most intriguing types can be found in the mysterious "Bread of the Presence", sometimes erroneously translated into English as the "showbread" (see Ex 25:23–30). This bread, which was set out in the Tabernacle and meant to be an earthly sign of the heavenly banquet atop Sinai (Ex 24:9–11), was early on recognized as a type of the real presence of Christ in the bread and wine of the Eucharist. Once again, it is Cyril of Jerusalem who highlights this mystery:

> In the Old Testament also there was shew-bread [= the Bread of the Presence]; but this, as it belonged to the Old Testament, has come to an end; but in the New

---

[23] Ambrose, *On the Sacraments* 5.1, in Jean Daniélou, *From Shadows to Reality: Study in the Typology of the Fathers*, trans. Dom Wulstan Hibbard (Westminster, Md.: Newman Press, 1960), 194.

[24] See Bede, *On the Tabernacle*, trans. Arthur G. Holder (Liverpool: Liverpool University Press, 1994), and Thomas Aquinas, *Summa Theologica* I–II, q. 102, a. 4.

Testament there is Bread of heaven, and a Cup of salvation, sanctifying soul and body.... *Consider therefore the Bread and the Wine not as bare elements, for they are, according to the Lord's declaration, the Body and Blood of Christ*; for even though sense suggests this to thee, yet let faith establish thee. Judge not the matter from the taste, but from faith be fully assured without misgiving, that the Body and Blood of Christ have been vouch-safed to thee.... Having learnt these things, and been fully assured that the seeming bread is not bread, though sensible to taste, but the Body of Christ; and that the seeming wine is not wine, though the taste will have it so, but the Blood of Christ.[25]

Although many of the early Church Fathers did not know Hebrew, their typological understanding of the Bread of the Presence takes on an added depth when we recall that the Hebrew name for the Bread of the Presence literally means "the bread of the face" (Hebrew *lehem ha-panim*). In this way, the heavenly meal in the divine presence that follows the Sinai covenant-making (Ex 24:9–11) also finds fulfillment in the Eucharist.

Mount Sinai and the Heavenly Worship

Although many more types from Exodus could be singled out and highlighted, for our purposes here, in closing, it is important to note that certain aspects of Exodus were interpreted not only *typologically*—as pointing forward to New Covenant realities—but also *anagogically*—as pointing "upward" to heavenly realities. In this regard, the assembly of Israel at Mount Sinai for the covenant worship is already interpreted in the letter to the Hebrews as a foreshadowing of New Covenant worship, as heaven on earth. Once again, note both the similarity and dissimilarity:

> *For you have not come to what may be touched*, a blazing fire, and darkness, and gloom, and a tempest, and the sound of a trumpet, and a voice whose words made the hearers entreat that no further messages be spoken to them.... *But you have come to Mount Zion and to the city of the living God, the heavenly Jerusalem, and to innumerable angels in festal gathering, and to the assembly of the first-born who are enrolled in heaven....* Therefore let us be grateful for receiving a kingdom that cannot be shaken, and thus let us offer to God acceptable worship, with reverence and awe; for our God is a consuming fire. (Heb 12:18–19, 22–23, 28–29)

With these words, the author of Hebrews calls his audience to recognize that the *visible* wonders that took place in the theophany to the assembly of Israelites at Mount Sinai are now both transcended and fulfilled in the *invisible* heavenly realities into which Christians enter when they offer God "acceptable worship" through the blood of Jesus (Heb 12:28).

The Book of Exodus in the Lectionary

The book of Exodus is liturgical in its very nature. The purpose of the exodus was to provide the freedom the Israelites needed to "serve" or "worship" (Hebrew

---

[25] Cyril of Jerusalem, *Catechetical Lectures* 22.5–6, 9, in *NPNF2* 7:152.

'abad, Ex 4:23) God by a proper liturgy (Ex 5:1–3; 8:25–27; 10:9, 24–26; and so on). Key points in the narrative are marked by liturgical rituals: the Passover (Ex 12–13), the solemnization of the covenant (Ex 24), the consecration of the Tabernacle (Ex 40). Instructions for the building of the sanctuary and the account of its construction dominate the end of the book (Ex 25–40). The narrative arc of the book moves from Israel "serving" (slave labor) the pharaoh and the Egyptian gods to Israel "serving" (worshipping) the Lord God in the Tabernacle, a newly constructed "portable Eden", where the communion with God denied to man since the expulsion from the garden is partially restored. Thus, one could rightly say that Exodus is a book about the restoration of proper worship for the people of God. It is appropriate, then, that the book of Exodus continues to be proclaimed frequently in the Church's liturgical celebrations.

Given everything we have seen so far, it is unsurprising that when we turn to the contemporary Lectionary's use of the book of Exodus, we find a pronounced emphasis on and selection of the very passages that the living tradition has emphasized as signs and foreshadowings of the sacraments in the New Covenant.

As can be seen from the table below, the crossing of the sea (Ex 14–15) and the water from the rock (Ex 17) are read on liturgical celebrations oriented toward baptism, whereas various Passover selections (Ex 12–13), the manna (Ex 16), and the covenant ritual at Sinai (Ex 24:1–8) are read on those oriented toward the Eucharist. The account of the theophany at Sinai (Ex 19) is also read on Pentecost, which was and is a Jewish feast fifty days after Passover, commemorating God's self-revelation and gift of the law at Sinai.

The Lectionary also values the two accounts of the proclamation of God's name to Moses, at the bush in Exodus 3:13–15 and after the Golden Calf in Exodus 34:5–7. The Lectionary ties these accounts to forms of God's name in the New Covenant: the Most Holy Name of Jesus, and the Most Holy Trinity. In a few places, it also emphasizes Moses as a moral example of one called by God to shepherd God's people (Ex 3:1–12), as one who perseveres in prayer (Ex 17:8–13), and as a good pastor who intercedes for his flock before God (Ex 32:7–14). Finally, but by no means least significantly, the words of the Decalogue are read on the Third Sunday of Lent (Ex 20:1–17), echoing the central place that the Ten Commandments played in the catechetical formation of converts to Christianity in the ancient Church.

Key selections from Exodus are read semi-continuously during daily Mass in Year 1, weeks 15–17, according to the table on the following pages.

Conclusion

The book of Exodus recounts the foundational historical events by which God formed the people of Israel into a nation and entered into covenant with them. These events are commemorated, celebrated, and sacramentally experienced in the liturgy of the people of Israel as well as in the New Covenant liturgy. If Genesis recounts the creation of the world, Exodus recounts the creation of Israel, the first manifestation of the people of God in salvation history. Its significance for biblical theology, Catholic faith, moral teaching, and sacramental catechesis can hardly be exaggerated.

Readings from Exodus 3–34 for Sundays, Feast Days, Liturgical Seasons, and Other Occasions			
MSO = Masses for Special Occasions; OM = Optional Memorial; VM = Votive Mass; Rit = Ritual			
Scripture	Description	Occasion	Explanation
3:1–6, 9–12	The burning bush; God commissions Moses to lead Israel	MSO: For Vocations to Holy Orders or Religious Life, opt. 2	Moses is held up as a model of religious leadership, called by God to meet the grave needs of the people of Israel.
3:1–8a, 13–15	The theophany at the burning bush and the revelation of the divine name "I AM"	3rd Sun. of Lent (C)	Year C of Lent presents a selection of key texts from salvation history in the sequence of first readings. This reading reminds the congregation of God's covenant with Israel through Moses.
3:11–15	The revelation of the divine name	VM: Most Holy Name of Jesus, opt. 1	In the New Covenant, the name Jesus succeeds the name YHWH and acquires its sanctity.
12:1–8, 11–14	The regulations for the Passover	Holy Thursday: Mass of the Lord's Supper; VM: Mystery of the Holy Cross, opt. 1	The Passover is the primary Old Testament type of the Eucharist as well as the bloody sacrifice on the Cross.
12:21–27	A description of the Passover and its celebration	VM: The Most Holy Eucharist, opt. 2; The Most Precious Blood, opt. 1	See above.
14:15—15:1; 15:1–6, 17–18	The parting of the sea; the "Song of Moses"	Easter Vigil (rdg. 3 & resp. 3)	The Easter Vigil is the privileged time for the celebration of baptism and Christian initiation. The parting of the sea is a critical Old Testament type of baptism.
16:2–4, 12–15	The manna in the wilderness	18th Sun. in OT (B); Rit: Institution of Acolytes, opt. 2; VM: The Most Holy Eucharist opt. 3	John 6 is read over the course of several weeks in Year B, while the first readings represent key Old Testament types of the Eucharist. Here, the manna pericope pairs with the Gospel (Jn 6:24–35) describing Jesus as the true manna.
17:3–7	The water from the rock	3rd Sun. of Lent (A); also 3rd Week of Lent Optional Mass; Rit: Conferral of Infant Baptism	Lent is focused on preparation for Christian initiation; Cycle A surveys salvation history in the sequence Adam-Abraham-Moses-David-New Covenant. This reading conveys a key type of baptism associated with the Mosaic covenant.

(continued)

	Readings from Exodus 3–34 for Sundays, Feast Days, Liturgical Seasons, and Other Occasions (*continued*)		
	MSO = Masses for Special Occasions; *OM* = Optional Memorial; *VM* = Votive Mass; *Rit* = Ritual		
Scripture	Description	Occasion	Explanation
17:8–13	The defeat of Amalek by Moses' arms uplifted in prayer	*29th Sun. in OT (C)*	Moses serves as an example of perseverance in prayer, paired with Luke 18:1–8, the parable of the persistent widow, with application to prayer.
19:2–6a	The promise of royal priesthood if Israel will obey the covenant	*11th Sun. in OT (A)*	Cycle A reads Matthew *ad seriatim*; Exodus 19:2–6 pairs with Matthew 9:36–10:8, the calling of the apostles and their commissioning. The twelve apostles are the core of the New Israel, commissioned in the New Covenant like the twelve tribes were by Moses at Sinai.
19:3–8a, 16–20b	See above; plus the account of the theophany at Sinai	*Pentecost: Vigil Mass (opt. 2)*	The Jewish feast of Pentecost celebrated the theophany and giving of the law at Sinai. Pentecost is the new Sinai, a new storm of wind and fire that brings a New Law: the Holy Spirit.
20:1–17	The giving of the law (Ten Commandments) at Sinai	*3rd Sun. of Lent (B)*	Cycle B of Lent recounts salvation history in the sequence Noah-Abraham-Moses-Covenant Failure-New Covenant. This reading recalls the covenant with Moses as a stage of salvation history.
22:20–26	A selection of laws concerning God and neighbor from the Covenant Code	*30th Sun. in OT (A)*	Cycle A reads Matthew *ad seriatim*. This pericope pairs with Matthew 22:34–40, the Lord's summation of the law as love of God and neighbor. The selected laws from Exodus clearly fit this bipartite division.
23:20–23	The angel of the Lord sent into Canaan to prepare the way for Israel	Feast of the Guardian Angels	Perhaps the first passage of Scripture to describe an angel in a defensive or protective role toward God's people.
24:3–8	The solemnization rite of the covenant at Sinai	*Corpus Christi (B); Rit*: Institution of Acolytes, opt. 3; *VM*: The Most Holy Eucharist, opt. 4; The Most Precious Blood, opt. 3	The Sinai ritual is a central but often overlooked prototype of the Eucharistic covenant, but the text and its significance are highlighted on the Feast of Corpus Christi.

(continued)

Readings from Exodus 3–34 for Sundays, Feast Days, Liturgical Seasons, and Other Occasions (*continued*)			
MSO = Masses for Special Occasions; *OM* = Optional Memorial; *VM* = Votive Mass; *Rit* = Ritual			
Scripture	Description	Occasion	Explanation
32:7–11, 13–14	The Golden Calf incident; Moses intercedes, pleads the covenant with Abraham; God relents	*24th Sun. in OT (C)*; also Thurs., 4th Week of Lent; Common of Pastors, opt. 1	This text pairs with the Gospel reading of Luke 15:1–32, the parables of lost sheep, coin, and prodigal son. God's forgiveness of Israel after the Calf incident is recalled as an example of his long-suffering and mercy.
34:4b–6, 8–9	The proclamation of the divine name to Moses after the Calf	*Holy Trinity (A)*; *VM*: The Most Sacred Heart, opt. 1	The title "Holy Trinity" describes God's nature; this first reading is the fullest proclamation of God's nature in the Old Testament.

Reading of Exodus for Daily Mass: Ordinary Time, Year I: Weeks 15–17			
Week	Day	Reading	Description
15	M	1:8–14, 22	The oppression of the Israelites under Pharaoh; infanticide
15	Tu	2:1–15a	Birth of Moses; slaying the Egyptian; flight from Egypt
15	W	3:1–6, 9–12	The burning bush and God's commissioning of Moses
15	Th	3:13–20	The revelation of the divine name "I AM"
15	F	11:10—12:14	The regulations for Passover and warning of the last plague
15	Sat	12:37–42	The hasty departure from Egypt
16	M	14:5–18; resp. 15:1bc–2, 3–4, 5–6	The Egyptian army pursues and traps Israel by the sea; the "Song of the Sea" as response
16	Tu	14:21—15:1; resp. 15:8–9, 10–12, 17	The parting of the sea and the drowning of the Egyptians; the "Song of the Sea" as response
16	W	16:1–5, 9–15	The manna account
16	Th	19:1–2, 9–11, 16–20b	The preparations and theophany before the Sinai covenant
16	F	20:1–17	The giving of the Ten Commandments
17	Sat	24:3–8	The covenant solemnization rite at Sinai
17	M	32:15–24, 30–34	The Golden Calf incident
17	Tu	33:7–11; 34:5b–9, 28	Moses' intercession and covenant renewal after the Calf
17	W	34:29–35	The shining face of Moses
17	Th	40:16–21, 34–38	The completion and consecration of the Tabernacle

For Further Reading

Commentaries and Studies on Exodus

Cassuto, Umberto. *A Commentary on the Book of Exodus*. Jerusalem: Magnes Press, 1967.

Childs, Brevard S. *The Book of Exodus: A Critical, Theological Commentary*. Old Testament Library. Philadelphia: Westminster Press, 1974.

Currid, John. *Ancient Egypt and the Old Testament*. Grand Rapids, Mich.: Baker Books, 1997. (See pp. 83–157.)

Davis, John J. *Moses and the Gods of Egypt: Studies in Exodus*. Grand Rapids, Mich.: Baker Book House, 1971.

Hamilton, Victor P. *Exodus: An Exegetical Commentary*. Grand Rapids, Mich.: Baker Academic, 2011.

Haran, Menahem. "Priestly Vestments". Volume 13, pages 1063–69 in *Encyclopaedia Judaica*. Edited by Cecil Roth. Jerusalem: Keter, 1972.

———. "Shewbread". Volume 14, pages 1394–96 in *Encyclopaedia Judaica*. Edited by Cecil Roth. Jerusalem: Keter, 1972.

Hoffmeier, James K. "Egypt, Plagues in". Volume 2, pages 374–78 in *Anchor Bible Dictionary*. Edited by D. N. Freedman. New York: Doubleday, 1992.

Levenson, Jon D. *Sinai and Zion: An Entry into the Jewish Bible*. Minneapolis: Winston Press, 1985. (See pp. 15–86.)

Mendenhall, George E. *Law and Covenant in Israel and the Ancient Near East*. Pittsburgh: Biblical Colloquium, 1955.

Propp, William H. C. *Exodus 1–18: A New Translation with Introduction and Commentary*. Anchor Bible 2. New York: Doubleday, 1999.

Segal, Ben-Zion, ed. *The Ten Commandments in History and Tradition*. Jerusalem: Magnes Press, 1985.

Historical Issues in Exodus

Assmann, Jan. *Moses the Egyptian: The Memory of Egypt in Western Monotheism*. Cambridge, Mass.: Harvard University Press, 1997.

Frerichs, Ernest S., and Leonard H. Lesko, eds. *Exodus: The Egyptian Evidence*. Winona Lake, Ind.: Eisenbrauns, 1997.

Fretheim, T. "The Priestly Document: Anti-temple?" *Vetus Testamentum* 18.3 (1968): 313–29.

Halpern, Baruch. "Eye-witness Testimony: Parts of Exodus Written with Living Memory of the Event". *Biblical Archaeology Review* 29 (2003): 50–57.

Hoffmeier, James Karl. *Ancient Israel in Sinai: The Evidence for the Authenticity of the Wilderness Tradition*. Oxford: Oxford University Press, 2005.

———. *Israel in Egypt: The Evidence for the Authenticity of the Exodus Tradition*. Oxford: Oxford University Press, 1996.

Kitchen, K. A. *On the Reliability of the Old Testament*. Grand Rapids, Mich.: Eerdmans, 2003. (See pp. 241–312.)

Walton, John. "Exodus, Date of". In *Dictionary of the Old Testament: Pentateuch*. Edited by T. Desmond Alexander and David W. Baker. Downers Grove, Ill.: InterVarsity Press, 2003.

Wells, Bruce. "Exodus". Pages 181–283 in *Genesis, Exodus, Leviticus, Numbers, Deuteronomy*. Vol. 1 of *Zondervan Illustrated Bible Backgrounds Commentary*. Edited by John H. Walton. Grand Rapids, Mich.: Zondervan, 2009.

Exodus in the Living Tradition

Aquinas, Saint Thomas. "Whether Sufficient Reason Can Be Assigned for the Ceremonies Pertaining to Holy Things?" *Summa Theologica* I–II, q. 102, art. 4. Translated by the Fathers of the English Dominican Province. 1948. Repr., Westminster, Md.: Christian Classics, 1981.

Bede, Venerable. *On the Tabernacle*. Translated by Arthur G. Holder. Liverpool: Liverpool University Press, 1994.

Catechism of the Catholic Church. 2nd ed. Washington, D.C.: USCCB, 1997. (See nos. 2052–557 for an exposition of the Ten Commandments.)

Cullmann, Oscar. *Early Christian Worship*. Translated by A. Stewart Todd and James B. Torrance. London: SCM Press, 1956.

Cyril of Alexandria, Saint. *Commentary on the Book of Exodus: First Discourse*. Translated by Evie Marie Zachariades-Holmberg. Rollinsford, N.H.: Orthodox Research Institute, 2010.

Daniélou, Jean, S.J. *The Bible and the Liturgy*. Notre Dame, Ind.: University of Notre Dame Press, 1956. (See pp. 86–95, 162–76.)

———. *From Shadows to Reality: Studies in the Biblical Typology of the Fathers*. Translated by Dom Wulstan Hibberd. Westminster, Md.: Newman Press, 1960. (See pp. 153–226.)

Ephrem the Syrian, Saint. "Commentary on Exodus". Pages 217–65 in *Selected Prose Works*. Translated by Edward G. Mathews Jr. and Joseph P. Amar and edited by Kathleen E. McVey. The Fathers of the Church 91. Washington, D.C.: Catholic University of America Press, 1995.

Kugel, James L. *Traditions of the Bible: A Guide to the Bible as It Was at the Start of the Common Era*. Cambridge, Mass.: Harvard University Press, 1997. (See pp. 501–774.)

Lienhard, Joseph T. "Exodus". Pages 1–162 in *Exodus, Leviticus, Numbers, Deuteronomy*. Old Testament 3 of Ancient Christian Commentary on Scripture. Edited by Thomas C. Oden. Downers Grove, Ill.: InterVarsity Press, 2001.

Origen. "Homilies on Exodus". Pages 225–387 in *Homilies on Genesis and Exodus*. Translated Ronald E. Heine. The Fathers of the Church 71. Washington, D.C.: Catholic University of America, 1982.

Pitre, Brant J. *Jesus and the Jewish Roots of the Eucharist: Unlocking the Secrets of the Last Supper*. New York: Image, 2011.

Pontifical Biblical Commission. *The Bible and Morality: Biblical Roots of Christian Conduct*. Vatican City: Libreria Editrice Vaticana, 2008.

Theodoret of Cyrus. *On Genesis and Exodus*. Vol. 1 of *The Questions on the Octateuch*. Translated by Robert C. Hill. The Library of Early Christianity 1. Washington, D.C.: Catholic University of America Press, 2007. (See pp. 222–345.)

8. LEVITICUS

Introduction

The name Leviticus is derived from a Greek adjective meaning "pertaining to the Levites" (Greek *leuitikos*) because the book was perceived as being primarily concerned with cultic regulations for the Levitical priests, such as the laws of sacrifice (Lev 1–7) and the laws regarding the ordination of priests (Lev 8–10). Along similar lines, in ancient Jewish tradition, the book came to be known as the "law/instruction for priests" (Hebrew *torat kohanim*). With this in mind, however, it should be emphasized that the majority of passages in Leviticus actually address the Israelite lay people, such as the laws about ritual purity (Lev 11–16), holiness (Lev 17–26), and vows (Lev 27).

Although the book of Leviticus is arguably one of the least read and least popular books among contemporary Christians, from the point of view of its literary position, it stands at the very heart of the Pentateuch. In our own day, Leviticus is typically the first book of the Bible used in teaching Hebrew to Jewish boys, and its system of cleanliness and holiness is the basis for the religious life-style of contemporary orthodox Jews. Although, as we will see, much of the legislation of Leviticus is not binding on Christians in the New Covenant (see Acts 15), the concepts of sacrifice, priesthood, cleanliness, and holiness embodied in the book establish the cultic and liturgical matrix in which the life and ministry of Jesus—and above all, his sacrificial act of redemption—were understood by the early Church. Hence, Leviticus remains a critical source for understanding both the Old and New Testaments.

Literary Structure of Leviticus

Leviticus contains less historical narration than any other book in the Pentateuch. There are only two narrative units: the account of the ordination of Aaron and his sons (Lev 8–10) and the account of a blasphemer and his punishment by stoning (Lev 24:10–23). Otherwise, the book consists entirely of laws and regulations, with one chapter of blessings and curses (Lev 26). However, since all the laws and regulations are presented within thirty-seven direct speeches of God to Moses, the book does, technically, have a narrative structure: it is the account of a series of divine monologues given to Moses at Mount Sinai before the Israelites set out on their journey through the desert to the Promised Land (see Num 1–25):

Outline of the Book of Leviticus

I. The Sacrifices (Leviticus 1–7)
   A. The Whole Burnt Offering (chap. 1)
   B. The Grain Offering (chap. 2)
   C. The Peace Offerings (chap. 3)

D. The Sin Offering (4:1—5:13)
E. The Guilt Offering (5:14—6:7)
F. Special Instructions to the Priests about the Offerings (6:8—7:38)
   1. Burnt Offering (6:8–13)
   2. Grain Offering (6:14–17)
   3. Consecration Offering (6:19–23)
   4. Sin Offering (6:24–30)
   5. Guilt Offering (7:1–10)
   6. Peace Offerings (7:11–38)

II. The Priesthood (Leviticus 8–10)
   A. The Ordination of the Priests (chap. 8)
   B. The Inauguration of the Priestly Ministry (chap. 9)
   C. The Seriousness of the Priestly Ministry: Violations and Warnings (chap. 10)

III. The Cleanliness Code (Leviticus 11–15)
   A. Food (Animals) (chap. 11)
   B. Childbirth (chap. 12)
   C. Skin (= Surface) Diseases (chaps. 13–14)
   D. Bodily Discharges (chap. 15)

IV. The Day of Atonement (Leviticus 16)

V. The Holiness Code (Leviticus 17–25)
   A. Holy People (chaps. 17–20)
      1. Holiness in Worship (chap. 17)
      2. Holiness in Sexuality (chap. 18)
      3. Holiness in Life-Style (chap. 19)
      4. Penalties for Violations (chap. 20)
   B. Holy Priesthood (chaps. 21–22)
      1. Holiness in Life-Style (chap. 21)
      2. Holiness in Worship (chap. 22)
   C. Holy Times (chaps. 23–25)
      1. Annual Holy Seasons: The Yearly Feasts (chap. 23)
      2. Continuous Holy Time (24:1–9) in the Tabernacle: Lamp and Bread
   D. A Violation of Holiness: The Blasphemer (24:10–23)
   E. Super-Annual Holy Seasons: Sabbatical and Jubilee Years (chap. 25)

VI. Covenant Blessings and Curses (Lev 26)

VIII. Epilogue: Voluntary Dedications to the Sanctuary (Lev 27)

With a few exceptions, the structure of Leviticus follows a logical progression. The book of Exodus ends with the erection and consecration of the Tabernacle, and Leviticus opens with God calling to Moses from the newly erected sanctuary. Throughout Leviticus, God will speak to Moses *from the Tabernacle*. This is significant, because it reveals that the Tabernacle has replaced Mount Sinai as the locus of revelation. In other words, the Tabernacle is a kind of "portable Sinai": just as Mount Sinai itself was a successor of Eden as the mountain of God, so now in Leviticus the Tabernacle is also a kind of new Eden.

Because the Tabernacle will be the place where the priests offer sacrifices, it is entirely logical that the first major section of Leviticus gives the stipulations for sacrifices, first for the three types of sacrifice that were already known (burnt, grain, and peace), then for the two types of sacrifice that were particular to the Tabernacle: the *sin* and *guilt* sacrifices. Sacrifices require priests to officiate, so following the description of the sacrifices (Lev 1–7) we have the account of the inauguration of the priesthood (Lev 8–10).

In the aftermath of Aaron's ordination, the rationale for most of the rest of the structure of Leviticus is provided by the emphasis on the distinction between "the holy" and "the common", between "the clean" and "the unclean" (Lev 10:10–11). Much of the book of Leviticus revolves around these two category distinctions: holy vs. common and clean vs. unclean. The distinction between *clean and unclean* is detailed in Leviticus 11–16, culminating in the Day of Atonement, the primary cleansing rite for the entire nation. However, the Day of Atonement not only *cleanses* but *consecrates* (makes holy) the nation once again, so it serves as a good hinge or joint to Leviticus 17–25, which deals with the distinction between *holy and profane* (or "common"), culminating in the holiest year of the Israelite calendar, the Year of Jubilee, which—in parallelism with Leviticus 16—is proclaimed on the Day of Atonement.

Leviticus 26, a chapter of blessings for covenant fidelity and curses for covenant infidelity, concludes the main body of the book of Leviticus. Lists of blessings and curses virtually always conclude a covenant document in biblical and ancient Near Eastern literature. Leviticus 26, then, is clearly a conclusion of a covenant document—what is unclear, however, is where that covenant document begins. Perhaps the best narrative solution is to take Leviticus 26 as the conclusion of a new body of covenant law introduced after the laicization of the eleven tribes and the ordination of the Levites as the sole priestly tribe by Moses after the worship of the Golden Calf (Ex 34). Leviticus 26 brings the covenant renewal after the Golden Calf to completion, promising covenant blessing or curse respectively for fidelity or infidelity to all the laws and ordinances given in the books of Exodus and Leviticus. The final chapter, Leviticus 27, is an epilogue to the book, dealing with voluntary offerings to the sanctuary. This chapter falls *outside* the blessings and curses of Leviticus 26 because the offerings dealt with are not *mandatory* for the covenant relationship and therefore evoke neither the blessings of Leviticus 26 for fulfillment nor the curses for omission.

Overview of Leviticus

The Five Kinds of Sacrifice (Leviticus 1–7)

One of the most puzzling and difficult aspects for contemporary readers of the Old Testament in general and the book of Leviticus in particular is its description of and emphasis on ritualized animal and vegetable *sacrifice*. Why does the God of the universe demand all of these sacrifices from the Israelites? What do they mean? And why are there so many? Does each of the sacrifices have a distinct meaning, or are they all just different ways of expressing the same thing?

In order to answer these questions, it is important first to emphasize that the basic meaning of all sacrifices, of whatever kind, is that of a kind of *ritualized self-offering*.[1] By means of the sacrificial gift—be it bloody or unbloody, animal, food, or drink—the worshipper symbolically offers himself to God. Although the offerings listed in Leviticus 1–7 are typically called "sacrifices" in English, in the original language they are ordinarily called "gifts" or "offerings" (Hebrew *qorban*). The word "sacrifice" (Hebrew *zebah*), which is used much less frequently, emphasizes more the fact that in order for them to be offered to God, the gifts must be transformed through slaughter (as with the animal sacrifices) and/or through burning (as with the animal and vegetable sacrifices).

The five sacrifices listed in the opening chapters of Leviticus can be divided into two overarching groups: sacrifices that *express* communion with God— (1) the burnt offering, (2) the cereal offering, and (3) the peace offering—and sacrifices that *restore* communion with God—(4) the sin offering and (5) the guilt offering. Intriguingly, the first three kinds of sacrifice (burnt, cereal, and peace offerings) are described in the Pentateuch as being offered *prior* to the construction of the Tabernacle and would continue to be offered on free-standing altars apart from the Tabernacle late in Israel's history (for example, 1 Kgs 3:4), whereas the last two kinds of sacrifice (sin and guilt offerings) are only introduced with the erection of the Tabernacle and are specific to the Tabernacle cult (and, later, the Temple). In addition to these basic divisions, each of the five kinds of sacrifice is given a clear delineation and appears to have a distinct purpose, meaning, occasion, and ritual, as follows:

1. *The Burnt Offering*: (Hebrew *'olah*; Greek *holocaust*). The Hebrew name for this offering literally means "ascending" (Hebrew *'olâ*), because the entire animal "ascends" or "goes up" in smoke. In the Greek Septuagint, this Hebrew name was translated as the "burnt whole" or "whole burnt offering" (Greek *holocaust*), emphasizing, not the movement of the sacrifice upward, but its complete consumption by the fire. In contrast to other sacrifices, nothing of the burnt offering is eaten; everything "goes up" to God. In order to signify that the animal symbolizes the offerer, hands are laid on the head of the animal, thereby establishing a transferal of identity or symbolic representation. In this way, the burnt offering is the most basic of all offerings: on behalf of the offerer, the animal is completely given to God, thereby representing the offerer's own self-donation to the Lord, in a fundamental act of worship.

2. *The Grain Offering* (Hebrew *minhah*). Although this offering is commonly translated as "cereal" offering, it has nothing to do with what readers today think of as breakfast "cereal" but, rather, is an unbloody sacrifice consisting of

---

[1] See Roland de Vaux, *Ancient Israel: Its Life and Institutions*, trans. John McHugh (1961; repr., Grand Rapids, Mich.: Eerdmans, 1997).

some form of grain, whether baked as a cake or not. The Hebrew name means "gift" or "tribute" (Hebrew *minhah*) to the Lord and once again expresses the communion between the offerer and God in the form of a kind of "meal" being presented to the deity—though the Bible elsewhere discourages any literalistic interpretation of this symbolism (see Ps 50). Only a portion of the cereal offering was burned on the altar—the rest was consumed by the priests.

3. *The Peace Offerings* (Hebrew *shelamim*). The name of these sacrifices stems from the word for "peace" or "wholeness" (Hebrew *shalom*), thus signifying the state of communion between God and the worshipper. The fat of the animal (considered a delicacy) was offered to God, but priest and people ate the rest of the animal in a celebratory feast together with the grain offerings that accompanied it. Because the peace offering was a communal meal with God and his servants (the priests), it always followed any other offerings (burnt, sin, or guilt). While the sin and guilt offerings serve to restore peace or *shalom* with God, the peace offering both recognizes and celebrates it. It is a sacrifice of joy and thanksgiving.

4. *Sin Offering* (Hebrew *hattat*). Although in English we speak of a sin "offering", the Hebrew name of this sacrifice is simply the Hebrew word for "sin" (Hebrew *hattat*). Hence, the purpose of this sacrifice is to restore communion with God through the forgiveness of sin (it literally "de-sins" or purifies a person or object). In this way, the sin offering serves to cleanse the worshipper—and sometimes also the sanctuary or other objects—from ritual uncleanness, which could be brought about by unwitting moral or ritual violations.

5. *Guilt Offering* (Hebrew *asham*). Although the fifth and final offering also serves to restore communion with God, scholars continue to debate exactly what the difference is between the sin offering and the guilt offering. The most likely explanation is that while the sin offering *restores the relationship* with God and the offerer through forgiveness, the guilt offering makes *reparation or restitution* for the damage done by sin.[2] In other words, sin has a kind of double consequence: forgiveness and reparation are not the same thing, and the two final kinds of sacrifice are meant to deal with each of them respectively.

Once again, while burnt, grain, and peace offerings have been offered since the time of Noah, the *sin* and *guilt* offerings are introduced here for the first time in salvation history, because God has come down to dwell continually in the presence of Israel, and there must be a system in place to deal with the inevitable violations of the divine standards that will take place in this arrangement.

The Inauguration of the Levitical Priesthood (Leviticus 8–10)

The last element that needs to be installed in the Tabernacle system is the priesthood itself. Intriguingly, Moses serves as a kind of "supreme" priest and prophet, performing the sacrifices and actions necessary to ordain Aaron and his sons to the post–Golden Calf Levitical priesthood (Lev 8). Significantly, the ordination ritual consists of several steps:

---

[2] Victor Hamilton, *Handbook on the Pentateuch* (Grand Rapids, Mich.: Baker, 2005), 233.

Priestly Ordination Rite of Aaron and Sons

1. Washing with water (Lev 8:5–6)
2. Vesting of Aaron, the high priest (Lev 8:7–9)
3. Anointing with oil of priests, Tabernacle, altar, and utensils (Lev 8:10–14)
4. Vesting of Aaron's sons as priests (Lev 8:10–13)
5. Ordination sacrifices (Lev 8:14–31)
6. Ordination banquet of "flesh and bread" (Lev 8:31–35)

Although English translations use the word "ordain" to refer to the ritual by which Aaron and his sons are installed as priests, the actual Hebrew expression literally means to "fill your hand(s)" (Lev 8:33 [author's trans.]). Indeed, throughout Jewish Scripture, the Hebrew expression "to fill the hand" is used whenever a man is ordained a priest (see Ex 28:41; Num 3:3; Judg 17:5; 1 Kings 13:33). Although scholars continue to debate exactly what the expression signifies, the most likely meaning is that by means of ordination, the priests' hands are consecrated to offer sacrifice, as Leviticus itself states when it says of the priest: "And he presented the cereal offering, and filled his hand [Hebrew *wayemalle' kappo*] from it, and burned it upon the altar" (Lev 9:17; cf. 2:2). Through the filling of his hands, the priest offers his first sacrifice.

After his ordination, Aaron performs his first priestly duties on behalf of the entire community, and God shows his favor by a dramatic theophany at the end of the ritual celebration, when the "fire" of God descends from heaven to consume the sacrifice (Lev 9). This high point in the relationship between God and Israel is short-lived, however, because Aaron's sons Nadab and Abihu treat their priestly status carelessly by offering "unholy fire"— perhaps using fire from some other source than the altar—and are slain (Lev 10:1–3). This sad event lends a somber mood to the account of the inauguration of the priesthood, a pivotal section that emphasizes the gravity of the ministerial priesthood of Aaron: priests are to avoid "wine" and "strong drink" (Lev 10:9) while ministering and have the privilege and duty of teaching the people the difference between "the holy and the common, and between the unclean and the clean" (Lev 10:10). Indeed, the text goes so far as to describe the priests as sin-bearers, who are not only to consume the celebratory peace offerings but even the flesh of the "sin offering", so that they might "bear the iniquity of the congregation, to make atonement for them before the LORD" (Lev 10:17).

The "Cleanliness Code": Laws of Clean and Unclean (Leviticus 11–15)

The next section in Leviticus shifts its focus to one of its most puzzling aspects for contemporary readers: the laws regarding the distinction between "clean" (Hebrew *tahor*) and "unclean" (Hebrew *tame'*).

In order to understand these laws, it is important to underscore that the cultic system of Leviticus is based on two complementary but distinct categories of evaluation: (1) the *cleanliness* spectrum, which evaluates things on the range from "clean" to "unclean", with gradations; and (2) the *holiness* spectrum, which evaluates things on the range from "holy" to "common", again with gradations.

On the one hand, cleanliness is a measure of *the suitability of something to be in the presence of God.* Unclean things are not suitable to be in the divine presence, whereas clean things are. On the other hand, holiness is a measure of *the presence of God itself.* A holy thing is somehow imbued with, or mediates, the divine presence, whereas a common thing does not.

Because of this distinction, certain rules follow. For example, a *clean* thing may be either holy or common. Likewise, a common thing may be either clean or unclean. However, a *holy* thing may never be unclean, nor an unclean thing holy. Indeed, an unclean thing will *defile* (render unclean) a clean thing and *desecrate* (render common or profane) a holy thing. In short, the ritual system of Leviticus emphasizes the need to keep the holy apart from the unclean. Since God has

Defilement → (*ṭimmēʾ*)	Unclean and Common → (*ṭāmēʾ*)	Cleansing (*ṭihēr*) ↓
Clean and Common (*ṭāhôr*) ↑	The Cleanliness/ Holiness Cycle	Clean and Common (*ṭāhôr*) ↓
Profanation ← (*ḥillēl*)	Clean and Holy (*qōdeš*)	← Sanctification (*qiddaš*)

come to dwell with Israel in the Tabernacle, all the people of Israel must maintain themselves and their camp in a state of cleanliness—that is, suitability to be in the divine presence, the presence of holiness. Within this system of thought it is important to realize that there are gradations of holiness, and certain precincts (like the Tabernacle courts) require stricter standards of cleanliness than others. With these concepts in mind, we can turn to the laws of clean and unclean themselves.

Perhaps the most famous of these are the laws of clean and unclean animals (Lev 11:1–47), which in later Jewish tradition come to be known as the laws of *kosher* foods, from the word meaning "to be suitable" (Hebrew *kasher*). (This word does not appear in Leviticus 11 itself.) Although a number of kinds of animals are forbidden to the people of Israel, the most well-known are the prohibitions against eating pigs, or "the swine" (Lev 11:7), and shellfish—that is, "anything in the seas or the rivers that has not fins and scales" (Lev 11:10).

How are we to explain the laws of clean and unclean animals? Why does the Lord at this point in Israel's history prohibit the consumption of animals that in earlier times have been permitted? After the Flood, God allows Noah to eat *any* kind of animal—"Every moving thing that lives"—with the only stipulation being that they shall not eat the flesh with the blood (Gen 9:3–4). Why this restriction of the Noahic food laws? What rationale, if any, can be given to the laws of clean and unclean foods in Leviticus? Over the years, commentators have provided a spectrum of explanations, including the following:

1. *Hygenic Explanation*: The animals declared "unclean" are bad for human health and prohibited by God to ensure the physical well-being of the Israelite people. The food laws prohibit unhealthy meat such as pork, which is notorious for the spread of trichinosis, and shellfish, which are filter feeders and concentrate any environmental toxins in their tissues. This view remains extremely

popular in contemporary explanations of the laws of clean and unclean animals and can be found in the influential work of the medieval Jewish philosopher Moses Maimonides.[3]

2. *Aesthetic Explanation*: The animals declared "unclean" are prohibited because they are repugnant to human beings (such as animals that "creep" and "swarm") and therefore unworthy of consumption.

3. *Ethical Explanation*: From this point of view, the curbing of appetites with regard to certain foods is meant to assist the Israelites in growing in self-control and abstention from violence and bloodshed. According to this view, which is very ancient, the animals symbolize various human passions (such as lust, envy, anger, and so on). It can be found in the ancient Jewish text known as the *Letter of Aristeas* (first century A.D.) as well as in patristic writings such as that of Novatian of Rome on *Jewish Foods* (third century A.D.).[4]

4. *Anatomical Explanation*: The animals declared "unclean" are forbidden because they are anatomically anomalous and represent the mixing of categories that should not be combined. From this point of view, mammals should have parted hoofs and chew the cud; any that lack one of these characteristics or mix them with other features (like the pig) is forbidden. Likewise, water creatures should have both fins and scales; any that lack one of these (like shellfish) are forbidden. This view is forwarded by the modern sociologist Mary Douglas.[5]

5. *Liturgical Explanation*: Animals designated as "unclean" were associated with the Gentiles, their pagan culture and religion. In this way, the cultic prohibition of certain animals serves the social function of separating the people of Israel from the Gentile nations, so that they might be "holy" (set apart) and not fall back into the idolatry of the culture from which they came (Egypt) or into the idolatry of the cultures among which they will settle (Canaan). This view is forwarded by Thomas Aquinas.[6]

Although none of these explanations have completely convinced the majority of scholars, a form of the last interpretation seems to be espoused by the New Testament, which treats the unclean animals as symbols of the Gentile nations from which Israel was separated for a time (see Acts 10). Moreover, it is supported by a long tradition attested in Jewish, Christian, and pagan authors in antiquity and throughout the Middle Ages, which identifies the animals selected for Israelite sacrifice as those sacred to various Egyptian gods. For example, the ram was sacred to the sun-god Amon-Rē, the bull to Apis, the cow to Hathor, and so on. Therefore, God was commanding Israel to sacrifice to him the animals sacred to, and representative of, the Egyptian gods, as a process of religious de-Egyptianizing of the people of Israel.

Now, some object to this explanation because the Egyptians did, in fact, sacrifice these animals to their gods—that the ram was sacred, for example, to

---

[3] Moses Maimonides, *Guide to the Perplexed* 3.48.

[4] See Joseph T. Lienhard, *Exodus, Leviticus, Numbers, Deuteronomy*, Old Testament 3, Ancient Christian Commentary on Scripture, ed. Thomas C. Oden (Downers Grove, Ill.: InterVarsity Press, 2001), 177.

[5] Mary Douglas, *Purity and Danger: An Analysis of Concepts of Pollution and Taboo* (London: Routledge and Kegan Paul, 1966).

[6] Thomas Aquinas, *Summa Theologica* I–II, q. 102, a. 6.

Amon-Rē could make that animal an acceptable sacrifice to Amon-Rē. While this is true, it needs to be kept in mind that the Israelites were sacrificing Amon-Rē's sacred animal to the *Lord (YHWH)*, not Amon-Rē! By taking the animals sacred to the Egyptian gods and killing them in worship to the Lord, an effective religious inversion of Egyptian religion was created. Indeed, several other laws are clearly aimed at prohibiting or frustrating pagan rituals or superstition among the Israelites, including the prohibitions against the offering of honey (Lev 2:11, attested in Canaanite paganism), the boiling of a kid in its mother's milk (Ex 23:19, a Canaanite magic ritual), ritual shavings or mutilations (Lev 21:5, also common in pagan religio-magical practice, cf. 1 Kings 18:28), and the practice of divination or witchcraft (Lev 19:26).

With this explanation of clean and unclean foods in mind, there appears to be a somewhat distinct rationale behind the next set of laws of cleanliness and uncleanliness, which deal with the purification of women after childbirth (Lev 12:1–8), various skin diseases (Lev 13:1–59), the cleansing of leprosy (Lev 14:1–56), and the bodily discharges of men and women (Lev 15:1–31). Once again, the question arises: What is the reason for the distinction between clean and unclean?

Although scholars have yet to offer a complete and wholly satisfactory explanation, a couple of points are helpful. First and foremost, the idea of clean and unclean being espoused in this section is primarily a *cultic* category rather than a *moral* impurity. All of the laws are geared toward the question of participation in the sanctuary:

> Thus you shall keep the sons of Israel separate from their uncleanness, lest they die in their uncleanness *by defiling my tabernacle* that is in their midst. (Lev 15:31)

From this cultic point of view, then, a *clean* thing is something suitable to be brought into the divine presence, even if it is not itself holy. A clean thing has at least the potential to be consecrated and made holy. The opposite of "unclean" is "whole, integral, healthy, normal"—these adjectives together are a good approximation of the category "clean" in the system of Leviticus. Hence, diseases of the skin and discharges from the body are signs of "abnormality" or imbalance rather than wholeness, health, and integrity—they render the person unclean.

Second, and perhaps even more important, when the various forms of contact that make one "unclean" are placed side by side, there is one common thread that unites them: all of them involve *contact with death* or some kind of *loss of life*. Consider the following:

1. *Childbirth*: loss of blood, in which is "the life" (Lev 12:1–8)
2. *Leprosy*: loss of blood and body fluids in decaying flesh (Lev 14:1–56)
3. *Emission of Semen*: loss of "seed", containing life (Lev 15:1–12)
4. *Menstruation*: loss of blood, in which is "the life" (Lev 15:19–30)
5. *Marital Intercourse*: loss of "seed", containing life (Lev 15:16–18)

If this connection with death/loss of life is the common link between these otherwise strangely conjoined laws of becoming "unclean"—and it finds support in the later Pentateuchal text that explicitly states that contact with a corpse renders a person "unclean" (Num 19:11–19)—then it appears that the pedagogical rationale of the laws is to teach the people of Israel that *death has no place in the sanctuary of the Lord*. If this is correct, it would cohere with what we have seen earlier in the Pentateuch, in which death comes into the world through the Fall of Adam and Eve (Gen 3:1–22) and which depicts the Garden of Eden before the Fall as a kind of prelapsarian sanctuary.

Thus, the laws of Leviticus taught certain spiritual principles in a symbolic fashion, encouraged the separation of Israel from surrounding cultures, fostered the health and flourishing of the Israelite community, and frustrated the practice of pagan religion. Nonetheless, the fact that such laws were not given to Noah, to the patriarchs, or even to Israel prior to the Calf indicates that these laws were not strictly necessary for a covenant relationship between God and man; therefore, one could reasonably expect that at some point these laws would have served their purpose and that the covenant relationship between God and his people would be rearranged more closely to resemble one of the earlier covenant forms. In fact, since the laws of Leviticus are added after the sin of the Golden Calf and more laws are added in Numbers and Deuteronomy following various rebellions in the wilderness, these laws may be regarded as having a *penitential* aspect: that is, they are given to God's people as practices to help rehabilitate the nation from a state of sin and rebellion.

The Laws of Clean and Unclean in Their Ancient Near Eastern Context

In support of a cultic explanation of the laws of clean and unclean, it is worth noting that these laws would have completely frustrated some key religious practices of the Egyptians and Canaanites. In the "Cleanliness Code" (Lev 11–15), virtually any contact with a dead thing or any sexual activity rendered a person unclean and, therefore, unable to enter the sanctuary and unable to worship.

The Canaanites, however, included sexual activity within the ritual worship of their gods and in their myths spoke of their gods engaged in incest, extra-marital sexuality, and bestiality. For their part, the Egyptians worshipped their dead pharaohs and built temples or chapels over or near the tombs of their deceased kings. In fact, the tombs of the pharaohs were major sites of religious pilgrimage.

Furthermore, the pharaohs were considered gods and typically married incestuously (within the "divine" lineage), so that, for example, King Tutankhamun (1341–1323 B.C.) was the son of Pharaoh Akhenaten and one of Akhenaten's younger sisters and, in turn, married his own half sister Ankhesenamun, herself the daughter (and perhaps briefly, wife) of Akhenaten.

From the perspective of Israelite religion, however, all of this was abhorrent: sexuality and contact with the dead were strictly excluded from worship of the Lord, and all forms of deviant sexuality were contrary to the holiness of the one God. The cleanliness laws of Leviticus, therefore, create a religious culture that is completely antithetical to that of Egypt and Canaan.

The Day of Atonement (Leviticus 16)

If the book of Leviticus stands at the center of the Pentateuch, the description of the sacrifices for the Day of Atonement stands at the center of Leviticus itself, surrounded by the "Cleanliness Code" (Lev 11–15) and the "Holiness Code" (Lev 17–25). Although contemporary Jewish tradition refers to this day as *Yom Kippur* ("The Day of Atonement"), the book of Leviticus itself actually uses a plural form, referring in its liturgical calendar to the "day of atonements" (Hebrew *yom hakippurim*) (Lev 23:27 [author's trans.]). The Hebrew word *kippur*, and its related verb *kapar*, although translated "atonement", actually means something closer to "purgation, purification, or expiation", which indeed *brings about* "atonement"—literally, "at + one + ment", that is, reconciliation—between God and man, through the sprinkling of the blood of the sacrifices on the "mercy seat" (Hebrew *kapporet*) of the Ark of the Covenant. Next to the Feast of Passover, the Day of Atonement gets the most detailed description of any liturgical feast in the Pentateuch. It was the definitive ritual that both *cleansed* and *reconsecrated* (made holy) the priests, the people, and the sanctuary.

According to the book of Leviticus, the sacrificial rituals for the Day of Atonement consisted of several key elements. First, the high priest would enter into the innermost sanctum of the Tabernacle, known as the "Holy of Holies"—something done but once a year, on this feast day (Lev 16:1–14). Second, he was to offer a bull as a sin offering for himself, presumably as a kind of penance hearkening back to the worship of the Golden Calf by his sacerdotal ancestor, Aaron (Lev 16:6). Third, and most memorable of all, the priest was to take two goats: (1) one goat "for the LORD" that would be sacrificed as a sin offering and (2) a second goat, "for *Azazel*", that would not be sacrificed in the sanctuary but "sent away into the wilderness" (Lev 16:6–10). On this day Aaron (and his successors) was commanded to enter the Tabernacle "in the cloud" of incense, "make atonement" for the people, and then symbolically communicate the sins of the people to the scapegoat by laying hands on its head so that it might "bear all their iniquities" (Lev 16:22). In prepa-

> ### Where Do We Get the Concept of the "Scapegoat"?
>
> The biblical origin of the concept of a scapegoat comes from the description of the two goats of the Day of Atonement: one offered to "the LORD", and the other designated in Hebrew as "for Azazel" (Lev 16:6–10).
>
> Although modern scholars tend to translate the Hebrew word *Azazel* as the name of a kind of goat-demon living in the desert to whom the second goat is offered, this is not the way the term was understood in earlier times.
>
> For example, the Greek Septuagint and the Latin Vulgate both translate the word as "the one sent away" or the goat "sent away for release". For example, the Douay-Rheims translation of the Latin term speaks of the "emissary goat" (Lev 16:6–10). The English word "scapegoat" comes from the Protestant William Tyndale's translation of the Scriptures into English (1530), in which he rendered the Hebrew term *azazel* as "escapegoat".[a]
>
> ---
> [a] Victor Hamilton, *Handbook on the Pentateuch* (Grand Rapids, Mich.: Baker Book House, 2005), 278.

ration for such an awesome and solemn occasion, the people were to "afflict" themselves through fasting, penance, and abstention from sexual relations (Lev 16:29). Indeed, in the whole Mosaic law, the Day of Atonement is the only day on which fasting is required of the people of Israel. It is the most solemn day of the Israelite liturgical calendar.

The Holiness Code and the Liturgical Calendar (Lev 17–26)

Prior to the grant of the covenant at Mount Sinai, God promised that obedience to the covenant would result in Israel becoming a "kingdom of priests" and "holy nation" (Ex 19:5–6). Every Israelite, therefore, was called to be "holy" (Hebrew *qadosh*)—that is, "set apart" *from* sin and uncleanness and "set apart" *for* the presence of God. As the Lord says to the people: "Consecrate yourselves therefore, and be holy, for I am holy" (Lev 11:44). Of course, there are gradations of holiness. Different standards of holiness were designated for priests, who were directly associated with God's presence in the sanctuary, than for the Israelite laity.

The final portion of the book of Leviticus is so focused on the concept of the "holy"—words based on the Hebrew root *q-d-sh* occur some eighty-five times—that modern scholars refer to it as "the Holiness Code" (Lev 17–25). This final section describes in detail the behaviors necessary for Israelites to maintain their status as a "holy" people in several key ways. First, they are to maintain holiness by offering *holy sacrifices* (Lev 17). Significantly, it is here that we find the famous prohibition against consuming blood, explained by the fact that "the life [Hebrew *nephesh*] ... is in the blood" (Lev 17:10–16). Second, the Israelites are to avoid unholy *sexual relations*, which would defile the land. Such illicit relations include sexual practices of the Canaanites, incest, sexual intercourse during menstruation, adultery, homosexual intercourse, and bestiality (Lev 18). Third, the people are to practice *holy actions*, such as leaving food for "the poor and for the sojourner" (Lev 19:9–10), providing just wages, and not keeping day wages "all night" (Lev 19:13). Particular concern is shown in this regard for the elderly (Lev 19:32) and the immigrant, toward the latter of which God commands: "You shall love him as yourself" (Lev 19:34). They are also to avoid illicit activities associated with the occult, such as augury (reading "signs"), witchcraft, self-mutilation, and tattoos (Lev 19:27–28). Violations of any of these rules of holiness are subject to punishments, whether in the form of the death penalty (for adultery, cursing mother or father, bestiality, and sodomy) or exclusion from the community (for incest) (Lev 20). These same standards are even more stringent for priests, since they handle the holy things of the Lord directly (Lev 21–22).

Frequency of Key Terms in the "Cleanliness" and "Holiness" Codes			
	Lev 11–15: "Clean vs. Unclean" The "Cleanliness Code"	Lev 17–25: "Holy vs. Profane" The "Holiness Code"	Ratio of Occurrences
tahor (clean)	12 times	only 4 times	3 to 1
tamē' (unclean)	104 times	only 26 times	4 to 1
qōdesh (holy) and derivatives	only 5 times	49 times	1 to 10
hillēl (to profane)	no occurrences (0 times)	18 times	0 to 18

Significantly, at the heart of the Holiness Code stands what may be the most systematic description of the ancient Israelite liturgical year found in Scripture (Lev 23). According to this section, the holiness of life was not just a moral ideal to be striven for, but a liturgical reality lived out through various daily, weekly, and annual feasts. Indeed, by laying out the annual liturgical calendar—based on the weekly Sabbath, and the annual feasts of Passover, First Fruits, Weeks, Trumpets, Atonement, and Booths—the Holiness Code reveals that *time itself* is also holy. The following chart is based on the description given in Leviticus 23, with certain additions from elsewhere in the Pentateuch:

Regular Feasts

The Daily Sacrifice (Tamid)
Morning and Evening Sacrifice
(Ex 29:38–46; Num 28:1–8)

Every Morning and
Evening

The Sabbath (Shabbat)
Day of Rest and Worship
(Gen 1; Ex 20; 31:12–17; Lev 23:1–3; Num 28:9–10)

Friday Evening to
Saturday Evening

Spring Feasts

Passover (Pesach)
Memorial of Passover
(Ex 12–13; Lev 23:4–5; Num 28:16; Deut 16:1–7)

14 Nisan
(March-April)

Unleavened Bread (Hamazzot)
7-Day Festival Following Passover
(Ex 12–13; Lev 23:6–8; Num 28:17–25; Deut 16:8)

15–21 Nisan
(March-April)

First Fruits (Bikkurim)
Very First Sheaf of Ripe Barley
(Lev 23:9–14; Deut 16:9–12; cf. Deut 26)

16 Nisan or First Sunday
after Passover Sabbath

Pentecost (Shebuoth)
First Fruits of Grain Harvest
(Ex 23:16; Lev 23:15–22; Num 28:26–31; Deut 16:9–12)

6 Sivan
(May-June) (7 Weeks
from First Fruits)

Fall Feasts

Trumpets (Shoferim)
Festival of New Moon
(Lev 23:23–25; Num 29:1–6)

1 Tishri
(September-October)

Day of Atonement (Yom Kippurim)
Annual Atonement for Sin
(Lev 16; 23:26–32; Num 29:7–11)

10 Tishri
(September-October)

Tabernacles (Sukkoth)
Final Fall Harvest: Grapes, Olives
(Ex 23:17; Lev 23:33–43; Num 29:12–39; Deut 16:13–15)

15–22 Tishri
(September-October)

Significantly, although later texts and traditions would go on to develop associations between these various feasts and historical acts of deliverance by God (such as the giving of the law at Mount Sinai and Pentecost, or the wilderness wandering and the feast of Tabernacles), at this point, the primary meaning given to most of the feasts is *agricultural* or, perhaps more properly, *cosmic*. From the ancient Israelite perspective, the rhythm of the life of worship (which theologians will later call the "order of redemption") moves in time with the rhythm of the cosmos (which theologians will later refer to as "the order of creation"). Apparently, grace builds on nature in ancient Israel as well as in later Christian tradition.

A brief historical narrative about the stoning of a blasphemer (Lev 24:10–23) interrupts the treatment of holy time. While it is difficult to account for the placement of this narrative here, the themes of the narrative are certainly directly pertinent to the Holiness Code (Lev 17–25), because the offense involved the profanation or cursing (Hebrew *qillēl*) of the Name, and the holiness of the Name is a major concern of the Holiness Code. In any case, the final section of Leviticus concerns holy seasons that occur in the longest time cycles: (1) the *Sabbatical Year*, which is celebrated every seven years (Lev 25:1–7), and (2) the *Year of Jubilee*, which occurs every fifty years (Lev 25:8–55). According to these laws, every seventh year was to be observed as a Sabbath, on which no agricultural work was to be done, and the Israelites, the land, animals, and vegetation were all to observe a solemn rest. And every seventh Sabbath (the forty-ninth year) was to be followed by a Jubilee, during which the same "rest" as the Sabbath was observed, but in addition, on the Day of Atonement, the blast of a trumpet or "ram's horn" (Hebrew *yobel*) throughout the land announced the remission of all debts and the return of all ancestral land. During the Jubilee, anyone enslaved for debt was to return to his family and any land sold for debt was likewise returned to its original owner. This effectively "reset" or "rebooted" the economy and was meant to prevent the permanent impoverishment of any Israelite family. Embedded in the rules for the Jubilee Year are the regulations for the *go'ēl*, the "kinsman-redeemer", or nearest male relative, who was responsible to relieve debt slavery or the alienation of land before the Jubilee, if possible. This is the fundamental biblical description of the *redeemer*, but the role and title will be applied extensively to the Lord himself in the book of Isaiah, with a permanent effect on the language and conceptualization of God's salvific work in the New Covenant.

The book of Leviticus concludes with a small number of blessings promised for covenant fidelity (Lev 26:3–12) and a large number of curses threatened for infidelity (Lev 26:13–45), culminating in the ultimate curse: expulsion from the Promised Land by means of exile (Lev 26:39). Notably, hope is held out for God's mercy to be expressed to Israel in exile (Lev 26:44–45), but a return from exile is not predicted in this book. An epilogue covers votive offerings: persons, places, or things voluntarily consecrated to the Lord (Lev 27). The value of such things is computed on the basis of the Jubilee Year, which returns vowed property to its original owner, even if it was dedicated to the Lord and the sanctuary.

Historical Issues in Leviticus

When did the laws written in the book of Leviticus originate? Can they be plausibly attributed to the time of Israel's origins? If not, how and when should the material in this book be dated?

Julius Wellhausen's Theory of a Postexilic Leviticus

Prior to Wellhausen, the "Priestly source" (P), believed to be much of the content of Leviticus, was regarded as the oldest of the Pentateuchal sources. For example, Wellhausen's contemporary, the noted German Orientalist and Bible scholar August Dillmann (1823–1894), advanced this position and continued to defend it to the end of his life. Wellhausen, however, reversed this and insisted P was the last of the sources of the Pentateuch, assigning it a postexilic date. He drew this conclusion for the following reasons: (1) the prophets and preexilic historical sources do not show the influence of P; (2) P's view of the cult is the most complex of any of the Pentateuchal sources and, therefore, the last; and (3) since P assumes the centralization of the cult established by D, P is after D. Since, for Wellhausen, the Deuteronomic material (D) is late preexilic, P must be exilic or more likely postexilic. At the same time, it is frequently forgotten that Wellhausen conceded that individual parts of P could reflect very ancient traditions. This concession by Wellhausen made his position virtually impossible to challenge, because whenever critics of his position have presented evidence for the antiquity of one or more of the textual units or historical *realia* of P, his defenders have responded by conceding the antiquity of that element, but still maintaining the late date of the composition of the final form of P.

Any one of Wellhausen's arguments is a matter of debate. The preexilic historical sources do, for example, trace the history of the Tabernacle and Ark of the Covenant and give testimony to the practice of certain other cultic rituals more or less unique to P, like the role of the Nazirite and the oracular use of the Urim and Thummim (Ex 28:30; Lev 8:8; Num 27:21; 1 Sam 14:14; 28:6). Moreover, the prophets, some more and some less, do reflect the language and concepts of P in various places. Ezekiel is the best example. Writing in the late monarchic and early exilic era, Ezekiel reflects extensive knowledge of the language of Leviticus, especially the "Holiness Code" (Lev 17–26). Wellhausen, without making any careful study of the issue, explained the connections of language between Ezekiel and Leviticus by arguing that Ezekiel represented an early stage of Priestly literature—in other words, Leviticus used Ezekiel. However, more systematic studies of the literary characteristics of Ezekiel and its literary relations to Leviticus have not supported this view.[7] The Hebrew of Ezekiel is a later form than that of Leviticus,[8] and the literary connections between the two books are much easier to explain as Ezekiel's use of Leviticus than vice versa. A commonsense interpretation of the literary relationship between Leviticus and Ezekiel would be that much of Leviticus, especially chapters 17–26, was in written form when the prophet wrote.[9] This would make the bulk of Leviticus

---

[7] Michael A. Lyons, *From Law to Prophecy: Ezekiel's Use of the Holiness Code*, Library of Hebrew Bible/Old Testament Studies 507 (New York and London: T&T Clark, 2009).

[8] Avi Hurvitz, *A Linguistic Study of the Relationship between the Priestly Source and the Book of Ezekiel: A New Approach to an Old Problem*, Cahiers de la Revue biblique 20 (Paris: J. Gabalda, 1982); Jacob Milgrom, "The Antiquity of the Priestly Source: A Reply to Joseph Blenkinsopp", *Zeitschrift für die alttestamentliche Wissenschaft* 111 (1999): 10–22.

[9] Lyons, *From Law to Prophecy*; Risa Levitt Kohn, *A New Heart and a New Soul: Ezekiel, the Exile, and the Torah*, Library of Hebrew Bible/Old Testament Studies 358 (London and New York: Sheffield Academic, 2002); Jacob Milgrom, "Leviticus 26 and Ezekiel", in *The Quest for Context and Meaning: Studies in Biblical Intertextuality in Honor of James A. Sanders* (Leiden: Brill, 1997), 57–62.

preexilic. Instances of literary borrowing from P may also be found in Jeremiah, Isaiah, and other prophets, but the examples are less prevalent and have typically been ignored.[10]

Problems with a Late Date for Levitical Legal Material

The idea that P's view of the cult is supposedly more complex than that of other Pentateuchal sources, and therefore late and postexilic, rests on several assumptions.

First of all, it is an example of circular reasoning, because interest in—and the complexity of—the cult are criteria for identifying the source "P" in the first place. Second, it assumes that "more complex" means "later", even though one could cite many historical examples—from Akhenaten to Vatican II—of reform or simplification of religious rituals resulting in a *later* but nonetheless *simpler* cult. Third, and what is the most probable explanation: the texts assigned to "P" are more concerned with cult and ritual than those assigned to D or any other biblical source or author and therefore give the *fullest account* of any of them. Therefore P's cult is not the *latest*, but the most *detailed description*. Fourth, Wellhausen's assumption that P drew on Deuteronomy's centralization of the cult in Jerusalem—which he identified with the reign of Josiah (ca. 627 B.C.)—and therefore was composed at a later period, has been challenged on a number of grounds. It is by no means clear that P assumes the centralization of the cult described in Deuteronomy 12, and some recent scholarship has argued that it does not.[11]

Fifth and finally, there are certain texts in the book of Leviticus that make much more sense as having originated *before*—not after—the book of Deuteronomy. Consider, for example, the contradictory laws concerning whether or not animals can be slaughtered anywhere other than the sanctuary:

> If any man of the house of Israel kills an ox or a lamb or a goat in the camp, or kills it outside the camp, and does not bring it to the door of the tent of meeting, to offer it as a gift to the LORD before the tabernacle of the LORD ... that man shall be cut off from among his people. (Lev 17:3–4)

> If the place which the LORD your God will choose to put his name there is too far from you, then you may kill any of your herd or your flock, which the LORD has given you ... and you may eat within your towns as much as you desire. (Deut 12:21)

As we see here quite clearly, what Leviticus prohibits—the sacrifice of animals anywhere other than the sanctuary—Deuteronomy allows. As scholars have pointed out, the standard JEDP theory, which places P after D, would have to

---

[10]John S. Bergsma, *The Jubilee from Leviticus to Qumran: A History of Interpretation* (Vetus Testamentum Supplements 115; Leiden: Brill Academic, 2007), 56–60, 157–76, 190–203. For Priestly/Holiness texts in Jeremiah, see Dalit Rom-Shiloni, " 'How Can You Say, "I Am Not Defiled ..."?' (Jeremiah 2:20–25): Allusions to Priestly Legal Traditions in the Poetry of Jeremiah", *Journal of Biblical Literature* 133.4 (Winter 2014): 757–75. For P/H in Isaiah, see Benjamin C. Sommer, *A Prophet Reads Scripture: Allusion in Isaiah 40–66* (Contraversions: Jews and Other Differences; Stanford: Stanford University Press, 1998).

[11]Jacob Milgrom, "Does H Advocate the Centralization of Worship?", *Journal for the Study of the Old Testament* 88 (2000): 59–76.

posit that postexilic priestly editors composed a law for people living in the land of Israel that effectively banned the consumption of all meat anywhere outside the sanctuary (= the Jerusalem Temple).[12] However, the apparent contradiction is easily explained if the Levitical laws originated *before* the book of Deuteronomy, when the Israelite community was very small and lived within easy distance of the sanctuary, and the Deuteronomic material originated *later*, when the Israelite tribes spread out over the land of Canaan but worship of YHWH remained centralized. In fact, the narrative of the Pentateuch contextualizes these two laws of sacrifice appropriately: the prohibition of profane slaughter away from the sanctuary is in force during the period of wilderness wandering (Lev 17:2–4), when the community is encamped around the Tabernacle; but the permission for profane slaughter is granted prior to the conquest and settlement of the Promised Land (Deut 12:21) in anticipation of the territorial expansion that is about to occur.

As noted above, the Tabernacle, the ark, and other sacred vessels at the heart of P are demonstrably Bronze Age artifacts with strong connections to Egyptian New Kingdom practice and technology. The cultic principles and practices reflected in P are comparable to cultic practices of other ancient Near Eastern nations of the second millennium—in fact, P's system is *simpler* than the temple cults of the second-millennium-B.C. Hittites and Mesopotamians.[13] Wellhausen maintained that Jewish priests developed the complex system of sacrifice, cleanliness, and holiness due to an increased sense of guilt in the period of the exile. This position no longer has any force in light of the similarities of Israel's rituals with those of its neighbors. The cult of the Lord in Leviticus employs the common "ritual language" of the ancient Near East from at least the second millennium B.C. onward. So no argument based on the development of human culture would force one to place P in the postexilic period. In fact, recent archaeology of sanctuaries in northern Israel attest compliance with many of P's cultic regulations during the period of the divided monarchy.[14] Finally, there are no clear cultural or historical references in P to the *realia* of the postexilic period or even the exilic or monarchic periods. Granted, Leviticus 26 does threaten exile as a punishment for breech of the covenant; however, exile as a covenant curse can be attested also in nonbiblical ancient Near Eastern covenant documents (for example, Hittite treaties).[15]

In sum, then, there is very little hard evidence to place the date of Leviticus in the postexilic period and a variety of evidence—language, literary relationships with the prophets, archaeology of Israelite sanctuaries, parallels with late second-millennium Egyptian *sancta*—as well as the claims of the text itself that point to an earlier historical period.[16]

---

[12] Hamilton, *Handbook on the Pentateuch*, 372–75.

[13] Yitzhaq Feder, *Blood Expiation in Hittite and Biblical Ritual*, Writings from the Ancient World Supplements 2 (Atlanta: Society of Biblical Literature, 2011).

[14] Jonathan S. Greer, *Dinner at Dan: Biblical and Archaeological Evidence for Sacred Feasts at Iron Age II Tel Dan and Their Significance*, Culture and History of the Ancient Near East 66 (Leiden: Brill, 2013).

[15] See Kenneth A. Kitchen, *On the Reliability of the Old Testament* (Grand Rapids, Mich.: Eerdmans, 2003), 292–303.

[16] Ibid., 241–312; Jacob Milgrom, *Leviticus 1–16: A New Translation with Introduction and Commentary* (Anchor Bible 3; New York: Doubleday, 1991), 3–41.

Leviticus in the Living Tradition

The book of Leviticus is the heart of the Pentateuch. Therefore it is significant that the book is largely taken up with the prescriptions for and inauguration of the Tabernacle liturgy of the people of Israel (Lev 1–10, 16), together with the laws that will enable Israel to maintain "cleanness", a state of readiness for worship (Lev 11–15), and "holiness", a state in which they participate in the divine presence (Lev 16–27). Leviticus is all about the *communion* of God with his people through the liturgy and the necessary life-style to maintain that communion. *Liturgical communion is the heart of the Pentateuch, of Israel's Law?*

While the book presents, from one perspective, a beautiful picture of a holy God dwelling with a holy people, we also recognize that the regulations for the liturgy and life of the people have become more burdensome and demanding than they originally were (cf. Ex 20–23) due to the sin of the people (Ex 32:1–10). Due to the hardness of the Israelites' hearts (Mt 19:8) and their "stiff neck" (Ex 32:9; 33:3, 5; 34:9), these extensive regulations have become necessary if God is going to dwell in their midst and "go up among them" (Ex 33:3, 5; 34:9) into the Promised Land.

Although the book of Leviticus is little used in the Christian liturgy, the theology of the New Covenant is in several ways more indebted to the world view of Leviticus than is commonly recognized. Before bringing this chapter to a close, then, we will take a few moments to highlight some of the ways in which this much-neglected book has functioned in the living tradition of Christianity.

The Laws of Leviticus and the New Covenant

The book of Leviticus presents as divine law a large number of regulations, some of which Christians continue to follow and others of which are no longer considered in force. Thus Leviticus has always posed something of a challenge for the Christian tradition: Are there legitimate, non-arbitrary criteria by which we determine that some of these laws but not others are still valid? And if some of these laws are not valid, why were they given in the first place?

Although these questions might not seem very pressing to contemporary Christians, for whom the laws of Leviticus are often unknown and certainly not binding, it was an extremely important issue for the first generation of Christians—the vast majority of whom were ethnically Jewish. The most visible example of this comes from the Acts of the Apostles, in its account of how the apostle Peter came to realize that the food laws of Leviticus 11 were no longer binding on disciples of Jesus:

> Peter went up on the housetop to pray, about the sixth hour. And he became hungry and desired something to eat; but while they were preparing it, he fell into a trance and saw the heaven opened, and something descending, like a great sheet, let down by four corners upon the earth. *In it were all kinds of animals and reptiles and birds of the air.* And there came a voice to him, "Rise, Peter; kill and eat." But Peter said, *"No, Lord; for I have never eaten anything that is common or unclean."* And the voice came to him again a second time, *"What God has cleansed, you must not*

call common." This happened three times, and the thing was taken up at once to heaven. (Acts 10:9–16)

Significantly, this vision of Peter's directly concerns the food laws from the book of Leviticus and even employs the language from Leviticus of "common" (Greek *koinon*) and "unclean" (Greek *akatharton*) (Acts 10:14). Peter is in essence saying, "I've never broken the laws of Leviticus!" In response to his objection, however, God reveals that the animals in the vision have somehow been "cleansed" (Greek *ekatharisen*), so that it is no longer fitting to refer to them as unclean (Acts 10:15). After encountering the Gentile Cornelius and witnessing his faith, Peter interprets the unclean animals in the vision as symbols for the Gentile peoples: "God has shown me that I should not call any man common or unclean" (Acts 10:28). Implicit in this declaration is an explanation of the food laws that is both symbolic and social: the unclean animals represent the (formerly) unclean pagan peoples of the world, who have been cleansed through the Passion and death of Christ, who offered his life as a sacrifice "for many" (Mt 20:28; Mk 10:45). Once the paschal mystery has been accomplished, therefore, there is no longer any need for the food laws that were *temporarily* put in place in order to separate the "Jew" from "any one of another nation" (cf. Acts 10:28). From this point onward, Christians in communion with the apostle Peter and his successors have treated the food laws of Leviticus as no longer binding; thus returning, in a sense, to the earlier period in salvation history, when all foods were permitted, as at the time of Noah (see Gen 9; Acts 15).

There are, however, many more laws in Leviticus than just the laws of the clean and unclean. Over the centuries, Christian theologians have offered various explanations for distinguishing between those laws in Leviticus which are no longer binding (such as the *kosher* laws) and those which continue to bind members of the New Covenant. One particularly prominent apologist for the Levitical laws was Thomas Aquinas, who devotes an enormous amount of time and attention to the status of the Old Law in the *Summa Theologica* I–II, 98–105. In these questions, Aquinas distinguishes, at the outset, three categories of law in Leviticus as well as the Pentateuch generally:

1. *Civil laws*: These are laws given for the governing of Israel as a sovereign nation, such as the death penalty for blasphemy (Lev 24:10–23) or other transgressions (Lev 20). The application of the death penalty is the prerogative of the government, not individuals. Such laws could only be enacted when Israel was a sovereign nation capable of making and enforcing its own laws. They no longer apply, because the people of God are organized, no longer as a civil state, but as a Church.

2. *Ceremonial laws*: These laws are concerned with ritual worship, such as the regulations for the five kinds of sacrifice (Lev 1–7), the laws of cleanness and uncleanness (Lev 11–15), and the celebration of the regular and annual feasts, such as the Day of Atonement (Lev 16, 23).

3. *Moral laws*: These laws stem from what later philosophers and theologians refer to as "the natural law"—that is, the basic moral order. They are often

extensions or applications of the laws in the Decalogue, such as the prohibition against adultery and other illicit sexual acts (Lev 18); against stealing, false dealing, and lying (Lev 19:11); and the command not to retain wages unjustly from a worker (Lev 19:13).

With these categories in mind, Aquinas taught that the *civil* law was only applicable to the nation of Israel as a civil state in antiquity. The *ceremonial* law, which consisted of types and foreshadowings, has been fulfilled in Christ's one definitive sacrifice on the Cross and hence has fulfilled its purpose. From a Christian point of view, therefore, the *moral* law alone continues to have validity in the New Covenant, and even this is subject to interpretation within the wider framework of what Aquinas calls "the Law of the Gospel" or "the New Law".[17] Significantly, these kinds of distinctions may help explain why the Church accepts the moral law of Leviticus against the illicit nature of homosexual relations without insisting upon the civil penalty of capital punishment for the act (Lev 20:18).

Still, the question arises: Why did God give civil and ceremonial legislation that was not permanently binding? The apostle Paul both articulated this question and provided an answer: "Why then the law? *It was added because of transgressions*, till the seed should come to whom the promise had been made" (Gal 3:19 [author's trans.]). The "seed" is Jesus Christ, the seed of Abraham promised by God: "By your seed shall all the nations of the earth be blessed" (Gen 22:18 [author's trans.]). Until Jesus Christ arrived, the law was added, Paul says, *because of transgressions*. Saint Paul here is interpreting the literary structure of the Pentateuch. We have already seen that the first covenant made at Sinai had very little law attached to it: only the Ten Commandments and three chapters of civil application of them (Ex 20–23). The great bulk of the law, consisting of the book of Leviticus, is added *after the transgression of the Golden Calf*. This suggests that the Levitical law is a response to Israel's sin and, therefore, in some sense *penitential*. Indeed, the fact that the Levitical law is in *response* to the sin of the people of Israel is suggested in a literary fashion by the way that the Tabernacle narrative (Lev 25–31; 35–40) forms a literary envelope around the Golden Calf episode, suggesting that the Tabernacle and its liturgy (that is, the book of Leviticus) is the means of rehabilitation of Israel that, if put into practice, will neutralize Israel's tendency to rebellion.

The Love Commandment and the Concept of Holiness

With these distinctions between the civil, ceremonial, and moral precepts of Leviticus in mind, it is worth emphasizing that the moral laws of this book have left a powerful impact on the living tradition of the Christian faith. In particular, two stand out: the command to love one's neighbor as oneself (Lev 19:18) and the distinct emphasis in the book of Leviticus on being "holy" as God is "holy" (Lev 11:44–45; 19:2; 20:7, 26).

[17] See *Summa Theologica* I–II, qq. 106–8.

With regard to the former, it is Jesus himself who identifies this as the second of the two greatest commandments:

> And one of them, a lawyer, asked him a question, to test him. "Teacher, which is the great commandment in the law?" And he said to him, "You shall love the Lord your God with all your heart, and with all your soul, and with all your mind" [Deut 6:5]. This is the great and first commandment. *And a second is like it*, "You shall love your neighbor as yourself" [Lev 19:18]. *On these two commandments depend all the law and the prophets*. (Mt 22:35–40)

Notice that Jesus does not quote the Decalogue for the "great commandment"; he draws instead on the books of Deuteronomy and Leviticus. And the writers of the New Testament followed suit: the command to love one's neighbor is quoted in some form eight other times in the New Testament (see Mt 5:43; 19:19; Mk 12:31, 22; Lk 10:27; Rom 13:9; Gal 5:14; Jas 2:8). Although one wonders how many Christians today realize that Jesus was mining the book of Leviticus for one of his most famous teachings, the antiquity of this second "great commandment" was not lost on Saint Augustine when he wrote: "*Long before Christ it had been said* ... 'You shall love your neighbor as yourself' [Lev 19:18], a phrase which, as the apostle says, expresses the fulfillment of the whole law."[18]

Equally influential is the emphasis of the book of Leviticus on holiness as a goal for the people of God. Consider, for example, how the apostle Peter's description of the Christian life is in distinctively Levitical terms:

> Come to him, to that living stone, rejected by men but in God's sight chosen and precious; and like living stones be yourselves built into a spiritual house, to be a *holy priesthood*, to offer *spiritual sacrifices* acceptable to God through Jesus Christ....
>
> But you are a chosen race, *a royal priesthood*, a *holy nation*, God's own people, that you may declare the wonderful deeds of him who called you out of darkness into his marvelous light. (1 Pet 2:4–5, 9)

Likewise, the apostle Paul uses the language of clean and unclean to call the Christians at Corinth to spiritual purity when he writes: "Since we have these promises, beloved, let us *cleanse* ourselves from every *defilement* of body and spirit, and make *holiness* perfect in the fear of God" (2 Cor 7:1).

In short: the teaching of the New Testament asserts that Jesus Christ is our *high priest*, who makes *atonement* for *sins* by the *sacrifice* of himself, with the result that his blood effects the *cleansing* of those who believe in him and *consecrates* them to a *priestly* status within the Church, communicating to them God's own *holiness* via his Spirit. Our theological vocabulary would be severely impoverished without the matrix provided by Leviticus and its religious world view. Even if it is the case, for example, that in the New Covenant all foods are declared "clean", the concept of "cleanness" is redefined but not abolished: our Lord and the apostles continue to employ the term and concept and urge

---

[18] Augustine, *Letter* 177, in Lienhard, *Exodus, Leviticus*, 189.

Christians to avoid what is unclean. Thus, Christian theology is more indebted to Leviticus than is commonly realized. Moreover, meditation on the system and principles of sacrifice, cleanliness, and holiness in Leviticus continues to have enduring value for the light such meditation sheds on the significance of these and related concepts in the economy of the New Covenant.

The Day of Atonement and the Scapegoat

The enduring theological value of Leviticus is not, however, limited to its moral precepts. It also plays a major role in the typological Christology of the Christian tradition—in particular, with reference to its detailed description of the sacrificial liturgy of the Day of Atonement (Lev 16).

In the New Testament itself, the rites of *Yom Kippur* are taken up in the stunning theological vision of the letter to the Hebrews, which uses the book of Leviticus as a primary template for describing how Christ is the true High Priest, who enters into the heavenly Holy of Holies to secure an eternal redemption for the people of God:

> These preparations having thus been made, the priests go continually into the outer tent, performing their ritual duties; *but into the second only the high priest goes, and he but once a year, and not without taking blood which he offers for himself and for the errors of the people.* . . .
>
> But when Christ appeared as a high priest of the good things that have come, then through the greater and more perfect tent (not made with hands, that is, not of this creation) *he entered once for all into the Holy Place, taking not the blood of goats and calves but his own blood, thus securing an eternal redemption.* For if the sprinkling of defiled persons with the blood of goats and bulls and with the ashes of a heifer sanctifies for the purification of the flesh, how much more shall the blood of Christ, who through the eternal Spirit offered himself without blemish to God, purify your conscience from dead works to serve the living God. (Heb 9:6–7, 11–14)

In later Christian tradition, it was not only the figure of the high priest on the Day of Atonement who functioned as a type of the Messiah, but the two goats of *Yom Kippur* that pointed forward to Christ as well. Evidence for this tradition can be found in the writings of Justin Martyr (second century A.D.), who argues from the typology of both the Passover lamb and the scapegoat in his famous defense of Christianity to the Jewish man named Trypho:

> The mystery, then, of the lamb which God enjoined to be sacrificed as the passover, was a type of Christ; with whose blood, in proportion to their faith in Him, they anoint their houses, i.e., themselves, who believe in Him. . . . And *the two goats which were ordered to be offered during the fast, of which one was sent away as the scape [goat], and the other sacrificed, were similarly declarative of the two appearances of Christ*: the first, in which the elders of your people, and the priests, having laid hands on Him and put Him to death, sent Him away as the scape [goat]; and His second appearance, because in the same place in Jerusalem you shall recognise Him whom you have dishonoured, and who was an offering for all sinners willing to repent. . . . And further, you are aware that the offering of the two goats, which

were enjoined to be sacrificed at the fast, was not permitted to take place similarly anywhere else, but only in Jerusalem.[19]

In other words, it was the book of Leviticus that provided early Christians with one of the primary matrices by which they understood the mystery of their redemption accomplished in the Passion, Resurrection, and Ascension of Christ into heaven. Indeed, without the conceptual matrix of Leviticus— including key terms such as sin, atonement, sacrifice, holiness, cleansing, consecration, priesthood, redemption—the theology of the New Testament would be inexplicable.

The Book of Leviticus in the Lectionary

Unfortunately—perhaps because of the difficulty in explaining how the laws and rituals of Leviticus, the second Sinai covenant, continue to apply in the New Covenant—Leviticus is the least-read Pentateuchal book in the Lectionary: indeed, one of the least-read of the entire canon.

Only two readings from Leviticus are found on Sundays or feast days. An excerpt from the laws of leprosy (Lev 13:1–2, 44–46) is read on the Sixth Sunday in Ordinary Time in Cycle B, where it provides the background for the Gospel reading of the cleansing of the leprous man (Mk 1:40–45). Unsurprisingly, it is the command to love one's neighbor as oneself (Lev 19:1–2, 17–18) that features more prominently: it is read on the Seventh Sunday in Ordinary Time in Cycle A, where it is paired with the Lord's explication of this command and his exhortation to moral perfection in the Sermon on the Mount (Mt 5:38–48). A longer reading from this same chapter, including more laws of social justice (Lev 19:1–2, 11–18), is heard in the Common of Holy Men and Women (opt. 2) and on Monday of the First Week of Lent, complementing the parable of the sheep and the goats, where the nations are judged on the basis of their charity toward the "least brethren" of the Lord. Finally, in the Seventeenth Week of Year I of the weekday cycle, two readings from Leviticus occur between the *lectio continua* reading of Exodus and Numbers. The two passages are the introduction of the festival cycle (Lev 23:1–11) and the description of the Jubilee Year (Lev 25:1, 8–17). In light of the almost complete absence of Leviticus from the Lectionary, Christians interested in learning about the text will almost certainly have to open it and study it for themselves.

For Further Reading

Commentaries and Studies of Leviticus

Bergsma, John S. *The Jubilee from Leviticus to Qumran: A History of Interpretation*. Vetus Testamentum Supplements 115. Leiden and Boston: Brill, 2007.

Cody, Aelred. *A History of Old Testament Priesthood*. Analecta Biblica 35. Rome: Pontifical Biblical Institute, 1969.

---

[19] Justin Martyr, *Dialogue with Trypho* 40, in *Ante-Nicene Fathers*, ed. Alexander Roberts and James Donaldson, vol. 1 (1885; repr., Peabody, Mass.: Hendrickson, 1994), 214–15.

de Vaux, Roland. *Ancient Israel: Its Life and Institutions*. Translated by John McHugh. Repr., Grand Rapids, Mich.: Eerdmans, 1997. (See pp. 173–77, 345–57, 415–56, 507–10.)

Gagnon, Robert A.J. *The Bible and Homosexual Practice: Texts and Hermeneutics*. Nashville: Abingdon Press, 2002. (See pp. 111–45.)

Gerstenberger, Erhard S. *Leviticus: A Commentary*. Old Testament Library. Louisville, Ky.: Westminster John Knox Press, 1996.

Hamilton, Victor P. *Handbook on the Pentateuch*. Grand Rapids, Mich.: Baker Academic, 2005. (See pp. 229–99.)

Klawans, Jonathan. *Impurity and Sin in Ancient Judaism*. Oxford: Oxford University Press, 2000.

Milgrom, Jacob. *Leviticus*. 3 vols. Anchor Bible 3–3B. New York: Doubleday, 1991–2001.

Historical Issues in Leviticus

Gane, Roy E. "Leviticus". Pages 285–337 in *Genesis, Exodus, Leviticus, Numbers, Deuteronomy*. Vol. 1 of *Zondervan Illustrated Bible Backgrounds Commentary*. Edited by John H. Walton. Grand Rapids, Mich.: Zondervan, 2009.

Hoffmeier, James Karl. *Ancient Israel in Sinai: The Evidence for the Authenticity of the Wilderness Tradition*. Oxford: Oxford University Press, 2005.

Hurvitz, Avi. *A Linguistic Study of the Relationship between the Priestly Source and the Book of Ezekiel: A New Approach to an Old Problem*. Cahiers de la Revue biblique 20. Paris: J. Gabalda, 1982.

Levitt Kohn, Risa. *A New Heart and a New Soul: Ezekiel, the Exile and the Torah*. Journal for the Study of the Old Testament Supplement Series 358. Sheffield: Sheffield Academic, 2002.

Lyons, Michael A. *From Law to Prophecy: Ezekiel's Use of the Holiness Code*. Library of Hebrew Bible/Old Testament Studies 507. New York: T&T Clark, 2009.

Milgrom Jacob. "The Antiquity of the Priestly Source: A Reply to Joseph Blenkinsopp". *Zeitschrift für die alttestamentliche Wissenschaft* 111 (1999): 10–22.

———. "Does H Advocate the Centralization of Worship?" *Journal for the Study of the Old Testament* 88 (2000): 59–76.

Leviticus in the Living Tradition

Aquinas, Saint Thomas. "The Old Law". *Summa Theologica* I–II, qq. 98–105. Translated by the Fathers of the English Dominican Province. 1948. Repr., Westminster, Md.: Christian Classics, 1981. (See pp. 1025–103.)

Lienhard, Joseph T. "Leviticus". Pages 163–204 in *Exodus, Leviticus, Numbers, Deuteronomy*. Old Testament 3 of Ancient Christian Commentary on Scripture. Edited by Thomas C. Oden. Downers Grove, Ill.: InterVarsity Press, 2001.

Origen. *Homilies on Leviticus 1–16*. Translated by Gary Wayne Barkley. The Fathers of the Church 83. Washington, D.C.: Catholic University of America Press, 1990.

Theodoret of Cyrus. *On Leviticus, Numbers, Deuteronomy, Joshua, Judges, and Ruth*. Vol. 2 of *The Questions on the Octateuch*. Translated by Robert C. Hill. The Library of Early Christianity 2. Washington, D.C.: Catholic University of America Press, 2007.

9. NUMBERS

Introduction

The book of Numbers is a little less neglected than Leviticus among modern Christian readers, if only because, unlike its predecessor, it combines its long lists of laws with a number of dramatic narratives about the rebellions of Israel against God in the wilderness. Nevertheless, it still has against it the title "Numbers", which suggests anything but an interesting story! Like other books of the Pentateuch, its English title is derived from manuscripts of the Greek Septuagint, in which the book is called "Numbers" (Greek *Arithmoi*), referring to the two *numberings* of the first and second generations in the wilderness. These censuses form the pillars of the literary structure of the book (Num 1 & 26). In terms of its narrative contents, the Hebrew name for this book is more accurate: "In the Wilderness" (Hebrew *Bamidbar*), derived from the opening line of the text: "The LORD spoke to Moses in the wilderness of Sinai" (Num 1:1). As we will see, this is an accurate description of both the geographical and *spiritual* location of Israel throughout most of the narrative.

The book of Numbers has a strong literary relationship with its neighbors in the Pentateuch. In many ways it corresponds with the book of Exodus. Exodus begins with the people staying in Egypt (Ex 1–13), then describes their journey through the desert (Ex 14–19), and ends with them stationary at Sinai (Ex 20–36). Numbers begins with the people staying at Sinai (Num 1–10), describes their journey through the desert (Num 11–25), and ends with them stationary on the plains of Moab. Sinai and the plains of Moab correspond: at each location the people will receive a covenant (see below on Deuteronomy). Furthermore, there are strong literary connections between the journeys through the wilderness to and from Sinai (Ex 14–19; Num 11–25). Both these sections are dominated by accounts of the people of Israel "murmuring" (Hebrew *lôn*), "rebelling" (Hebrew *mārāh*), or "striving" (Hebrew *rib*) against the Lord and/or Moses, together with Moses' need for additional help to rule an unruly people (Ex 18; Num 11:16–39) and God's miraculous provision for the people's physical needs (Ex 15:22—17:7; Num 11:31–34; 20:1–13). This is evidence of careful literary artistry: the central Sinai narrative (Ex 20–Num 10) is surrounded by the unruly behavior of the people wandering in the desert (Ex 14–19; Num 11–25).

Numbers also has a close relationship with the books that follow it. If Leviticus established a sacred "constitution" for the life of Israel, exhibiting a logical, systematic order that concluded, like a good covenant document, with a listing of blessings and curses (Lev 26), Numbers is more like a list of "amendments" to the constitution, together with accounts of the historical circumstances that led to their enactment. And like the lists of amendments on many state and national constitutions, the laws have an *ad hoc*, circumstantial character, with little logical connection between successive "amendments". Finally, Numbers "sets the stage" for the book of Deuteronomy, providing us the necessary information about the geographical and moral condition of the people of Israel when they arrived at the "plains of Moab beyond the Jordan at Jericho" (Num 22:1) in order to appreciate the extended homily and renewal of the covenant that Moses will deliver at this site in the final book of the Pentateuch (Num 36:13; cf. Deut 1:5, 29:1).

Literary Structure of Numbers

The book of Numbers has been accused of being the most disorganized of the Pentateuchal books—indeed, one of the most chaotic in the Bible. This is largely due to the abrupt juxtaposition of narratives of Israel's rebellions with lengthy sections of legislation. However, this apparently awkward juxtaposition of law and narrative so characteristic of Numbers actually has a theological point, which we will address momentarily. Moreover, there are clear signs of literary structuring in the book, and its major divisions and subsections can be readily identified.

First, as the name suggests, the book of Numbers divides neatly into parts based on the two *numberings* or censuses in the book: the First Generation (chap. 1) and the Second Generation (chap. 26):

The Fundamental Structure of the Book of Numbers		
Part 1	1–25	The First Generation in the Wilderness
Part 2	26–36	The Second Generation in the Wilderness

The first census is of the Israelites at Sinai a year after the exodus; the second census is of their children forty years after the exodus, just prior to the entry into the land. Since none of the first generation are left alive at the time of the second census (Num 25:64), chapter 26 marks the "turning over of a new leaf" in the history of Israel.

The two parts of the book can be broken down further. Part 1, the account of the First Generation, breaks neatly at the end of Numbers 10. In Numbers 1–10, the First Generation is at Sinai, getting organized and prepared to leave. In Numbers 11–25, the First Generation is traveling through the wilderness in a virtual constant state of rebellion, from Sinai to Moab:

The First Generation in the Wilderness		
Part A	Num 1–10	The First Generation in Good Order at Sinai
Part B	Num 11–25	The First Generation in Disorder in the Wilderness

However, Numbers 1–10, the account of the First Generation preparing to leave Sinai and enter the Promised Land, also has strong literary parallels with Numbers 26–36, the Second Generation preparing to leave the wilderness and enter the Promised Land. This gives us a tripartite structure for the book, which can be outlined as follows:

Part A. The 1st Generation Prepares to Enter the Land (chaps. 1–10)
Part B. The 1st Dies Out, the 2nd Grows Up in the Wilderness (chaps. 11–25)
Part A'. The 2nd Generation Prepares to Enter the Land (chaps. 26–36)

Thus the central section of the book (Num 11–25) is framed by two accounts of preparation to enter the land (Num 1–10 and Num 26–36). The two outer sections occur in the space of a few months at the beginning and the end of the forty years in the wilderness; the central section covers the majority of the forty years in a brief fourteen chapters.

The whole book may be outlined as follows:

Outline of the Book of Numbers

I. The First Generation Prepares to Enter the Land (Numbers 1–10)
- A. The Census of the First Generation (1)

Inclusio: Israel as a War Camp [B–H]
- B. *The Arrangement of Israel at Sinai as a War Camp* (2)
- C. Assignment of the Levites to Transport the Tabernacle (3–4)
- D. Various Laws (5–6)
  1. Expulsion of Unclean Persons (5:1–4)
  2. Confession and Restitution for Sins (5:5–10)
  3. The Unfaithful Wife or Jealous Husband (5:11–31)
  4. The Nazirite Vow (6:1–21)
  5. The Priestly Blessing (6:22–27)
- E. Tribes Offer Gifts to Transport and Adorn the Tabernacle (7)
- F. The Levites Ordained and Installed at Their Duties (8)
- G. The Departure from Mount Sinai (9–10)
  1. The Departure Feast: The Passover (9:1–14)
  2. The Departure Sign: The Movement of the Cloud and Fire (9:15–23)
  3. The Departure Signal: The Silver Trumpets (10:1–10)
- H. *The Departure Arrangement: Israel as a War Camp* (10:11–36)

II. The First Dies Out, the Second Grows Up in the Wilderness (Numbers 11–25)
- A. Rebellion 1: Complaint and Fire at Taberah (11:1–3)
- B. Rebellion 2: Complaint, Quails, and Plague at Kibroth-hattaavah (11:4–35)
- C. Rebellion 3: Miriam and Aaron Challenge Moses at Hazeroth (12:1–16)
- D. Rebellion 4: Israel Revolts at the Spies' Report at Kadesh (13:1—14:38)
- E. Rebellion 5: The People Disobey and Invade the Land Anyway (14:39–45)

  Block of Laws in Response to Israel's Sin:
  1. Increased Cereal and Drink Offerings for Sacrifices (15:1–21)
  2. Sacrifices for Unwitting Sins (15:22–31)

3. Capital Punishment for Sabbath Breaking (15:32–36)
4. Tassels on Garments as Reminders of Obedience (15:37–41)

F. Rebellion 6: The Revolt of Korah, Dathan, Abiram at Kadesh (16:1–40)

G. Rebellion 7: Revolt of the People after Korah, Dathan, and Abiram's Death (16:41—17:13)

Block of Laws in Response to Israel's Sin:
1. Clarification of the Duties of Priests vs. Levites (18:1–7)
2. Clarification of Privileges of Priests vs. Levites (18:8–32)
3. Ritual for Making Water to Cleanse from Corpse Defilement (Red Heifer Ceremony) (19:1–10)
4. Ritual for Handling Corpses (19:11–22)

H. Rebellion 8: The People Murmur for Water at Meribah (20:1–13)
1. Passage through Edom Refused (20:14–21)
2. Aaron Dies at Mount Hor (20:22–29)

I. Rebellion 9: Plague of Snakes and Bronze Serpent near Mount Hor (21:1–9)
1. Journey to Moab and Digging of Well at Be'er (21:10–20)
2. Sihon and Og Defeated, Transjordan Conquered (21:21–35)
3. The Balaam Cycle (chaps. 22–24):
   a. Balak Summons Balaam; the Donkey Incident (22:1–40)
   b. Balaam's First Oracle (22:41—23:12)
   c. Balaam's Second Oracle (23:13–30)
   d. Balaam's Third Oracle (24:1–9)
   e. Balaam's Fourth Oracle and Messianic Prophecy (24:10–25)

J. Rebellion 10: Idolatry and Fornication at Beth-Peor (25:1–16)

III. *The Second Generation Prepares to Enter the Land* (Numbers 26–36)
A. The Census of the Second Generation (26)
B. *The Inheritance of Zelophehad: His Daughter's Rights Protected* (27:1–11)
C. Joshua Appointed to Succeed Moses (27:12–23)
D. Further Laws (28–30)
   1. Expanded Liturgical Calendar with Increased Offerings (28–29)
   2. Vows of Women (30)
E. The Conquest and Settlement of Transjordanian Lands (31–32)
F. Recap of Israel's Wilderness Wanderings (33)
G. The Conquest and Settlement of the Cisjordanian Lands (34–35)
H. *The Inheritance of Zelophehad: His Tribe's Rights Protected* (36).

Inclusio: Inheritance in the land

There is an abrupt shift of mood between the end of the first generation's stay at Sinai (Num 10) and the beginning of its travels toward the Promised Land (Num 11). Whereas all had been peaceful obedience to God at Sinai in the first section (Num 1–10), as soon as the Israelites enter the wilderness, the grumbling begins and continues almost unabated throughout their travels.

The second major section (Num 11–25) is the real narrative heart of the book: the ten accounts of rebellion in the wilderness. These accounts of rebellion are broken up by the insertion of two blocks of law (15:1—16:30; 18:1—19:22), illustrating the principle of the apostle Paul: the law "was added because of transgressions" (Gal 3:19). Just as many ceremonial laws in the book of Leviticus were added into the covenant economy after the debacle of the Golden Calf, so too as Israel sins in the wilderness, more laws are added as "amendments" to the covenant. In some cases, a rationale or relationship may be seen between the laws and the surrounding narratives of rebellion. For example, after the initial five rebellions (Num 11–14), God increases the requirements for sacrifices and mandates tassels on garments as a reminder for the Israelites to obey the covenant laws (Num 15). Again, after the revolt of the Levite Korah over the rights of the priesthood, which resulted in many corpses of those slain by a plague (Num 16), God provides additional laws clarifying the distinction of roles between the priests and the Levites and the procedure for making a "holy water" that purifies uncleanness from contact with corpses (Num 19). The Balaam Cycle, which interrupts the accounts of rebellion right before the tenth and final debacle, is a unique literary unit and will be discussed below.

Overview of Numbers

The Census of Israel (Numbers 1)

The first section of the book is dominated by a sense of optimism. The Calf debacle and the attitudes that prompted it seem to have been overcome by means of the covenant renewal at Sinai and the institution of the Levitical priesthood (Exodus 34–Leviticus 27). The initial census reveals an extremely numerous nation—"their whole number was six hundred and three thousand five hundred and fifty" (Num 1:46). Within the context of the Pentateuch as a whole, this estimate clearly indicates a fulfillment of the creational and patriarchal blessing, "be fruitful and multiply" (Gen 1:28), despite the fact that the people are living in the desert rather than Eden or the Eden-like Promised Land.

The War Camp of Israel and the Levites (Numbers 2–4)

Significantly, the arrangement of the people of Israel is not haphazard; as scholars have noted, it is the arrangement of an ancient war camp (see figure on p. 234). In the center of this camp stands the Tabernacle of the Lord, with four groups of three tribes each surrounding it on the east (Judah, Isaachar, Zebulun), south (Reuben, Simeon, Gad), west (Ephraim, Manasseh, Benjamin), and north (Dan, Asher, Naphtali) (Num 2). While the image of the thousands of Israelites arranged in battle companies leads to optimism about the imminent conquest of the land, the extensive attention paid to the tribe of Levi is a reminder of the people's sin at the Golden Calf.

The change in covenant economy between the original Sinai covenant (Ex 20–23) and the later Levitical covenant included a marked increase in mediation between God and Israel. Now Israel needs to be "buffered" from God because of its inclination to sin. This "buffering" is also visible in the arrangement of the Tabernacle war camp: between the twelve tribes of the Tabernacle stand groups

---

The War Camp of Israel

Israel's arrangement as a war camp (Num 2–3) is interesting for several reasons. First, it bears striking resemblance to the war camps of the pharaohs, particularly that of Ramesses II, often thought to be the pharaoh of the exodus. Ramesses II arranged his army on campaign in a huge rectangle, with the royal tent pitched in the center, surrounded by a large rectangular precinct marked off by poles and curtains. The similarity with the Tabernacle and its precinct is obvious. Since the pharaoh was considered both king and god, the theological point of Israel's encampment seems to be, "The Lord is now your king and God, whom you will serve, and he will fight for you!"

Apart from special roles for the tribes of Judah (as vanguard) and Levi (surrounding the Tabernacle), the rest of the tribal arrangements are curious, because they do not reflect the tribal associations or alliances of any later time period in premonarchic, monarchic, or postexilic Israel. This may be evidence of an authentic ancient tradition.[a]

[a]See James K. Hoffmeier, *Ancient Israel in Sinai: The Evidence for the Authenticity of the Wilderness Tradition* (Oxford: Oxford University Press, 2005).

Source: commonswikimedia.org

The war camp of Ramesses II, showing the royal tent in a rectangular precinct cordoned off by curtains, which lay in the center of the camp, surrounded by the pharaoh's battalions. Note the two cherubim-like beings flanking the pharaoah's inner sanctuary, like the Ark of the Covenant.

of priestly mediators on the east (Moses and the priests), south (Kohathite Levites), west (Gershonite Levites), and north (Merarite Levites) (Num 3). In other words, by the time we get to the book of Numbers, these men are ensconced around the Tabernacle in the center of the camp to protect the Tabernacle from incursions by the "lay" tribes. The Levites are a defensive barrier to God's holiness. Their primary duty is the handling of the Tabernacle items and their transportation, although they also serve as secondary clergy in a kind of "diaconal" role, assisting the priests with the extensive manual labor involved in the sacrificial liturgy (Lev 4:47).

Of particular note is the careful census of the Levites and the Israelite firstborn and the intentional sacral substitution of the Levites for the firstborn (Num 3:40–51). This implies that the clerical ministry that the Levites will henceforth perform was originally the privilege of the firstborn sons of Israel. For this reason, ancient Jewish tradition has typically understood the men engaged in priestly ministry prior to the Golden Calf as the firstborn sons of the different tribes. Therefore, as a result of the idolatrous worship of the Golden Calf, the eleven tribes are in effect "laicized"—their firstborn may no longer serve in clerical ministry but are redeemed (bought back) from God and replaced by Levite men. The other tribes no longer fully participate in the call to be a royal priesthood (Ex 19:5–6). Although the covenant has been renewed (Ex 34:27), there is now, as a result of sin, an increased distance between God and Israel.

Confession, the Suspected Adulteress, and Blessings (Numbers 5–6)

The laws that follow the assignment of the Levites provide further reminders of Israel's unworthiness before God. All unclean persons must be put outside the camp (Num 5:1–4). Provision is made for the confession and restitution of moral offenses against other Israelites (Num 5:5–10). Significantly, in the description of these acts of confession, not only is "oral confession indispensable", but so is the idea of penance, with "full restitution plus 20 percent more than the value of what was taken or stolen" being commanded.[1] The law for the testing of the suspected adulteress (Num 5:11–31) has a deeper narrative significance: at the Golden Calf, Israel was like an unfaithful wife who broke her covenant with her "jealous" husband, the Lord (Ex 20:3–5). Israel's journey through the wilderness will provide a "test" of its faithfulness to him. Although the eleven tribes of Israel have been "laicized", provision is made for the individual Israelite to consecrate himself to the Lord on a personal basis: the Nazirite vow of abstention from contact with corpses, strong drink, and the cutting of hair, which functions as the most ancient Israelite prototype of all later religious or consecrated life and, significantly, is something that could be carried out by both Israelite men and women (Num 6:1–21). It is a life of being "holy" or "set apart" (Hebrew *qadosh*) in a special way (Num 6:8). Provision is also made for the priests to

---

The Law of the Jealous Husband and Suspected Wife

Modern readers often feel that the ritual for testing a wife accused of unfaithfulness (Num 5:11–31) was unfair or prejudicial toward women. This modern perspective overlooks the fact that according to the Pentateuch—unlike other ancient Near Eastern codes of law—the wife is presumed innocent until proven guilty. Compare, for example, the Code of Hammurabi, which states: "If a citizen charges a woman with adultery, but has no evidence, then she is to be tried by ordeal in the river to restore the honor of her husband. If she survives she must pay a fine."[a] Moreover, the entire ritual in the Pentateuch takes the judgment of the woman's faithfulness completely out of the hands of her husband or other male authorities and entrusts it completely to God, who alone knows her guilt or innocence. Thus, the ritual functioned to protect the woman from fickle judgment and mistreatment by a suspicious husband.

In ancient societies, infidelity could be grounds for a husband to free himself of his obligation to support his wife. On the other hand, dissolving the marriage relationship left a wife without support. Thus, there was economic motivation for a husband to accuse a wife of infidelity, but not vice versa. This may be why the Pentateuch provides a ritual for one situation, but not the other.

[a] *Law 132*, cited in R. Dennis Cole, "Numbers", in *Genesis, Exodus, Leviticus, Numbers, Deuteronomy*, vol. 1 of *Zondervan Illustrated Bible Backgrounds Commentary*, ed. John H. Walton (Grand Rapids, Mich.: Zondervan, 2009), 348.

---

[1] Victor Hamilton, *Handbook on the Pentateuch* (Grand Rapids, Mich.: Baker Academic, 2005), 310.

bless the people in the name of the Lord (Num 6:22–27), an act that communicates the "name" (Hebrew *shem*) and thus something of the presence and
holiness of God to the people (Num 6:27).

Further Preparations for Departure (Numbers 7–10)

The remaining narratives in the first section are focused on the last preparations for the people to depart. The tribal princes donate six wagons and twelve
oxen to the Levites in order to assist in the transportation of the Tabernacle
(Num 7:3), but the narrative digresses to describe additional gifts brought by
each prince on behalf of the twelve tribes over a period of twelve days. This
twelve-day ceremony presents a beautiful picture of perfect equality between
the twelve tribes of Israel in devotion to the Lord, and it concludes with the
blessing of a theophany to Moses in the Tabernacle (Num 7:89). The Levites
are then ordained and installed in their diaconal ministry (Num 8) so that
they may begin packing up and transporting the Tabernacle. Significantly, the
departure of Israel from Mount Sinai is marked by the celebration of the Passover (Num 9:1–14), just as the first Passover marked its departure from Egypt.
God gives the signal when to depart by lifting the glory cloud of his presence
from off the Tabernacle (Num 9:15–23, esp. 17), and silver trumpets blown by
the priests give the signal to all Israel (Num 10:1–10). At last, the preparations
are complete, and Israel sets off for the Promised Land in battle array (Num
10:11–35).

The First Three Rebellions in the Wilderness (Numbers 11–12)

As soon as the people begin their journey through the wilderness, however, a
massive shift takes place: the sense of optimism is lost, and the spirit of "murmuring" or complaint that characterized the initial journey toward Sinai returns
(cf. Ex 15:22–17:7). In fact, the stories of the journey *to* Mount Sinai and the
journey *from* Mount Sinai have many similarities: the manna, the water from
rock, and Moses' inability to rule the people by himself.

A brief initial rebellion results in a plague of fire at Taberah (Num 11:1–3).
Next, and even more significant, the Israelites begin to complain about their
diet of manna, not only desiring the sumptuous fare of Egypt, but even going
so far as to despise the heavenly gift: "there is nothing at all but this manna to
look at" (Num 11:6). Likewise, Moses also complains to the Lord about his
inability to handle the unruly mob (Num 11:10–15), and God responds to both
complaints by providing the people with quail and Moses with seventy (or
seventy-two) spirit-inspired under-prophets (Num 11:16–30). Despite God's
acquiescence to the people's request, his wrath is kindled against the grumblers,
and the very flesh they preferred to the manna proves death to them when a
plague breaks out after partaking of the quail (Num 11:33–34).

The complaining spirit is not limited to the Israelite laity. There is even
dissent and jealousy among the leaders of the people, who resent the fact that
Moses is, in the words of one Protestant scholar: "God's vicar on earth, a kind of

papal figure".[2] Indeed, Moses' own older sister, Miriam, and his young brother, Aaron, turn against him and challenge his authority as the sole mediator of God's revelation: "Has the LORD indeed spoken only through Moses?" (Num 12:2). The precipitating cause of resentment is Moses' "Cushite" wife, although it is unclear why this was considered an issue of conflict. Some commentators think it was a question of Moses' wife being of Ethiopian ethnicity, others simply that of negative tribal associations with her origins in Midian or Cushan (see Hab 3:7). It is clear, however, that Miriam was the

> ### Moses' "Cushite" Wife
>
> Numbers 12:1 speaks of Moses' "Cushite" wife. Cush was the ancient name of Ethiopia; "Cushite" = "Ethiopian". The only named wife of Moses in Scripture is Zipporah, the daughter of Reuel/Jethro, the priest of Midian. It is possible that Moses was polygamous, and his "Cushite" wife was in addition to Zipporah. Another possibility is that "Cushite" is being used here in a figurative sense. Ethiopians were very dark; "Cushite" may have been used figuratively to describe any dark person. Zipporah may have had a dark complexion that distinguished her from most of the Israelites, and Miriam may have pointed to Moses' marriage to a foreigner as weakening his claim to authority over Israel.

primary protagonist in the attempted coup—the original Hebrew is a feminine verb, "And she spoke, Miriam and Aaron, against Moses" (Num 12:1 [author's trans.])—and God punishes her by making her skin white with leprosy.[3] This punishment appears to function as an ironic inversion of her aspersions against Moses' dark-skinned wife. Moses intercedes on his sister's behalf, and after a week the punishment is lifted and Miriam is restored to her role as leader of Israel's women (Num 12:9–15).

The Revolt at the Spies' Report and Its Aftermath (Numbers 13–14)

We now come to the central crux of the plot of the book of Numbers: the revolt of Israel at the report of the spies. After Israel has reached Kadesh, in the southern wilderness below the Promised Land, Moses chooses twelve spies, one from each tribe, and sends them out to reconnoiter the Canaanite territory. Ten of the spies bring back a "majority report" that recommends a return to Egypt; two spies (Joshua of Ephraim and Caleb of Judah) present a "minority report" advocating immediate conquest. The people adopt the "majority report" and attempt to stone Moses and choose another leader to take them back to Egypt (Num 13).

What ensues is a virtual recapitulation of the Calf incident, with the Lord threatening punishment of the people (Num 14:11; cf. Ex 32:9–10) and offering Moses the opportunity to become a "great nation" through his own progeny (Num 14:12; cf. Ex 32:10b). Moses again intercedes for Israel, employing one of the same arguments he used on Mount Sinai (Num 14:13–19; cf. Ex 32:11–12) and making reference to the revelation of the divine name as a manifestation of mercy in the aftermath of the Calf incident (Num 14:18–19; cf.

---

[2] Ibid., 325.
[3] Ibid.

Ex 34:6–7). Moses' intercession is effective: the Lord pardons, but there is an important qualification:

> Then the LORD said, "I have pardoned, according to your word; but truly, as I live, and as all the earth shall be filled with the glory of the LORD, *none of the men who have seen my glory and my signs which I wrought in Egypt and in the wilderness, and yet have put me to the proof these ten times* and have not hearkened to my voice, *shall see the land which I swore to give to their fathers;* and none of those who despised me shall see it. . . .
>
> But your little ones, who you said would become a prey, I will bring in, and they shall know the land which you have despised." (Num 14:20–23, 31)

This is the succinct statement of the premise of the plot of Numbers, which recounts the dying out of the exodus generation and the rising up of their children in the wilderness. The resonances with the event of the Golden Calf are not accidental: the message is that the lesson of the Golden Calf has not been learned by this generation, and despite everything they remain ungrateful and unfaithful. Yet the Lord's mercy is still demonstrated, and they are not disinherited. Their children will see the Promised Land from which they have allowed the spirit of grumbling and complaint to keep them.

The Lord makes mention of the "ten times" the people have "put me to the test" and "not heeded my voice" (Num 14:22 [author's trans.]). This is a reference to ten rebellions against Moses and God, starting from Moses' first attempt to free the people in Egypt and extending to the present insurrection:

The Ten Times Israel "Tests" the Lord in Exodus and Numbers		
1	Ex 5:15—6:9	The people of Israel reject Moses and his message when his initial efforts backfire.
2	Ex 14:10–12	Israel complains, loses faith, and wants to give up on the shores of the Red Sea.
3	Ex 15:22–25	Israel "murmurs" against Moses because the water is bitter at Marah.
4	Ex 16:1–36	Israel "murmurs" because of hunger; God provides manna, but the people ignore Moses' word about not keeping it overnight (16:20) or gathering on the Sabbath (16:27).
5	Ex 17:1–19	Israel "murmurs" and "tests" the Lord at Massah; God provides water from the rock.
6	Ex 32:1–35	The Golden Calf incident.
7	Num 11:1–3	Complaint against God and fire-plague at Taberah.
8	Num 11:4–35	The demand for meat, the provision of quail, and an ensuing plague.
9	Num 12:1–16	Miriam and Aaron try to rally the people against Moses, claiming equal prophetic gifts.
10	Num 14:1–38	General revolt and mutiny after the bad report from the spies: "none of the men who have . . . put me to the proof these *ten times* . . . shall see the land" (Num 14:22–23).

The significance of God's response to these ten rebellions should not go unnoted. First and foremost, it demonstrates that, far from being malevolent or vicious, the Lord is extremely patient with his people, forgiving them time and time again after major acts of transgression and even apostasy. Second, and equally important, God's punishment of the Israelites in the book of Numbers is a mysterious combination of irony, justice, and mercy. The irony can be found in the biblical principle that God punishes his people by *giving them what they want*, when what they desire is not him and his will:

> And the LORD said to Moses and to Aaron, "How long shall this wicked congregation murmur against me? I have heard the murmurings of the sons of Israel, which they murmur against me. *Say to them, 'As I live,' says the LORD, 'what you have said in my hearing I will do to you*: your dead bodies shall fall in this wilderness; and of all your number, numbered from twenty years old and upward, who have murmured against me, not one shall come into the land where I swore that I would make you dwell, except Caleb the son of Jephunneh and Joshua the son of Nun. But your little ones, who you said would become a prey, I will bring in, and they shall know the land which you have despised. But as for you, your dead bodies shall fall in this wilderness. And your children shall be shepherds in the wilderness forty years, and shall suffer for your faithlessness, until the last of your dead bodies lies in the wilderness. *According to the number of the days in which you spied out the land, forty days, for every day a year, you shall bear your iniquity, forty years*, and you shall know my displeasure.'" (Num 14:26–34)

This single passage may be one of the most consequential turning points in the entire Hebrew Bible, both historically and theologically. For it is the Israelites themselves who prayed, "Would that we had died in this wilderness!" (Num 14:2), and so now will their own words come to pass, when they are condemned to die without entering the Promised Land (Num 14:32). Likewise, their cry, "Why does the LORD bring us into this land ...?" (Num 14:3), meets with the decree that no one of them shall enter the land except Joshua and Caleb (Num 14: 30). Nevertheless, God is merciful as well as just, and he responds to their faithless prediction concerning their children that "our little ones will become a prey" (Num 14:3) by declaring that while the children will suffer for their faithlessness—forty years of suffering, to be exact—they will not die in the desert but will be brought into the land (Num 14:31).

Remarkably—stunningly—even in the face of such a decree, the people do not learn obedience; the following day they stubbornly attempt to invade the land despite Moses' warning, and the result is disaster (Num 14:41–45).

Laws for Unintentional and Intentional Grave Sins (Numbers 15)

The narrative flow is interrupted by a block of laws, but we may discern a narrative reason for the insertion of the laws at this point.

First, the Lord specifies and increases the requirements for sacrificial offerings (Num 15:1–21). Most of the standard offering must now be accompanied by cereal offerings of fine flour mixed with oil and a libation of wine (that is, high-quality food of greater expense). Second, the text goes on to make the important distinction between two kinds of sins and their effects: (1) *inadvertent grave sins*: that is, those committed "unwittingly", which can be atoned for by means of sacrificial sin offerings (Num 15:22–29), and (2) *deliberate grave sins*: that is, those committed "with a high hand", which evidently cannot be atoned for and whose only punishment is being "cut off" from the people (Num 15:30–31). This last expression is presumably a reference to the death penalty, since this law is directly followed by the troubling story of a man who was stoned to death by the congregation for breaking the Sabbath by "gathering sticks on the sabbath day" (Num 15:32–35). Indeed, the account of the execution of the Sabbath breaker emphasizes that during the time of ancient Israel, deliberate violations of the Ten Commandments (here, the honoring of the Sabbath) were literally *mortal* sins: the punishment for such transgression was physical death.

Indeed, it is precisely in response to the gravity of this situation that a new development is instituted by God: the Israelites are to sew "tassels" (Hebrew *tzitzit*) on the corners of their garments as visible reminders to "remember all the commandments of the LORD, to do them, not to follow after your own heart and your own eyes, which you are inclined to go after wantonly" (Num 15:38–39). This custom would remain in place up to the time of Jesus and is mentioned in the Gospels, which speak of "the fringe" of Jesus' "garment" (Mt 9:20) as well as the ostentatiously long and visible tassels of the Pharisees, worn out of spiritual pride (Mt 23:5). In short, taken together, the laws of Numbers 15 show an escalation of the "penitential" ceremonial legislation of the people of Israel, along with a concerted emphasis on the gravity of obedience to God's law.

Korah's Rebellion and Its Aftermath (Numbers 16–17)

Moses and Aaron now face a combined challenge from members of the tribes of Levi and Reuben against their religious and civil leadership. Levites under the leadership of a certain Korah—himself a Levite, but of the Kohathite group, and not of the priestly sons of Aaron—are dissatisfied with their "diaconal" (non-priestly) role and wish to usurp the rights of the Aaronic priesthood (Num 16:9–10). They attempt to gather popular support for their movement by employing a slogan roughly equivalent to the concept of the "priesthood of all believers" as it has functioned in historical Protestantism, with its rejection of any ministerial priesthood at all. In the words of Korah: "You have gone too far! *For all the congregation are holy, every one of them*, and the LORD is among them; why then do you exalt yourselves above the assembly of the LORD?" (Num 16:3).

However, in this case, Korah's intention is not so much to eradicate the ministerial "priesthood" (Hebrew *kehunah*) of the sons of Aaron as it is to gain it for himself and the other Levites who support him (Num 16:10). In order to carry out this plan, Korah attracts the political support of Dathan and Abiram, leaders of the tribe of Reuben. This tribe, descended from the firstborn of Israel, had a natural claim to civil leadership over Israel—though it had always been denied them due to Reuben's offense against his father (Gen 35:22; 49:3–4). They object not so much to the Aaronic priesthood as to Moses making himself "prince" (Hebrew *sar*) of the people (Num 16:13). In other words, their

---

Were the Levites Really "Priests"?

The Levites are often called "the priestly tribe", but several parts of the Pentateuch make a clear distinction between priests (Aaron and his sons) and Levites and their different roles. Other parts, however, like the book of Deuteronomy, simply speak of "the Levitical priests" (Hebrew *hakkohanim halevi'im*).

Source critics explain this by an appeal to different biblical sources arising from different communities within Israel at different times in its history, each with their own views on the difference—if any—between priests and Levites.

Another explanation would be that the Hebrew term *kohanim* had a range of meaning, not unlike the English word "cleric". Sometimes all clerics are called *kohanim*—this is the practice in the book of Deuteronomy. At other times, a clear distinction is made between Levites and the *kohanim* proper, the sons of Aaron.

Something analogous happens in modern Catholic culture. Persons unfamiliar with Church structure will refer to any cleric in a roman collar—whether he is a seminarian, deacon, or priest—as "Father", because they make no distinction between "priest" and "cleric".

---

desire is to form "political" or civil authority, rather than spiritual. This dual revolt requires the supernatural intervention of God to be suppressed: "The earth opened its mouth and swallowed them up, with ... all that belonged to them [and they] went down alive into Sheol"—the Hebrew name for the realm of the dead (Num 16:31–35).

Amazingly, however, because Korah, Dathan, and Abiram had broad popular support, their followers are not impressed by the supernatural judgment against their leaders. Instead, they blame Moses and Aaron for the whole affair and are even ready to stone them (Num 16:41–42)! This time it is precisely the coveted priesthood of Aaron that is necessary to atone for the people's sin and stop the plague God sends on them (Num 16:46–50). The following day Aaron's cultic leadership of the people is supernaturally confirmed: all the tribal leaders place their "rods" (or staffs) before God in the Tabernacle, and Aaron's alone blossoms and buds—thereby signifying by means of a sign and wonder that the priesthood has indeed been restricted to his family alone (Num 17:8). Nevertheless, the people continue to grumble, ensuring that further rebellions are on the way (Num 17:13).

Laws for Levites, Priests, and Corpse Impurity (Numbers 18–19)

The block of laws that follows the revolt of Korah, Dathan, and Abiram has a strong narrative connection to the preceding material. Korah's revolt concerned a usurpation of the rights of the priesthood proper by the Levites generally. Therefore, the laws that follow the death of Korah and his followers very explicitly define distinctions in the responsibilities of the priests as opposed to those of the Levites (Num 18).

Likewise, the plagues that were necessary to put down the insurrections led by Korah, Dathan, and Abiram resulted in many dead bodies. Therefore, God provides a ritual for the making of a "holy water" that will serve to cleanse the Israelites from corpse defilement (Num 19). Intriguingly, the water is given the power to cleanse by being united with the mysterious sacrifice of the "red heifer" (Num 19:1–10), which can then be sprinkled using a branch of "hyssop" upon the Tabernacle, the furnishings, and the persons who may have become unclean through contact with a corpse (Num 19:14–19).

The Waters of Meribah and the Fiery Serpents (Numbers 20–21)

The narrative picks up again with the people of Israel still continuing to refuse to change their attitude. Now they begin to grumble once more about the lack of water. In response to their complaint, God commands Moses and Aaron to speak to a rock that it might pour forth water; in disobedience to God's com-

---

What Was Moses' Sin?

In Numbers 20:11, Moses strikes the rock instead of speaking to it, as God had commanded. Although he was technically disobedient, his action does not seem grave enough to merit the punishment God imposes on him: never to enter the Promised Land. Therefore, since antiquity readers have puzzled to identify the nature of Moses' sin and the rationale for his punishment.

We should note that this is, in fact, not the first time in Moses' career when he expresses doubt about God's will or even opposes it. Furthermore, we will find out in the book of Joshua that Moses was negligent about certain matters, such as ensuring that the Israelite children were circumcised according to the covenant (Josh 5:5).

A superficial reading of the biblical text will miss the fact that Moses' relationship with God had not only high points but also tensions and complications all along. At Meribah in Numbers 20:11, these issues come to the surface. God's judgment on Moses is based less on the gravity of his exterior actions than on the state of his heart, which is seen only by God (cf. 1 Sam 16:7). The sacred author does not give us a full explanation but intentionally leaves ambiguity about the exact reason for the gravity of Moses' punishment.

---

mand, Moses strikes the rock "twice" (Num 20:11–12). The water comes forth, but God is not pleased with the apparent lack of faith on the part of Moses and Aaron. At this point, they receive the (presumably devastating) news that they, too, will not enter the Promised Land:

> And the LORD said to Moses and Aaron, "*Because you did not believe in me*, to sanctify me in the eyes of the sons of Israel, therefore you shall not bring this assembly into the land which I have given them." These are the waters of Meribah [Hebrew for "contention"], where the sons of Israel contended with the LORD, and he showed himself holy among them. (Num 20:12–13)

Although the text does not make explicit exactly what aspect of God's word Moses and Aaron failed to believe, the context suggests that perhaps they did not believe that it was possible for their prophetic word to be enough to bring forth water miraculously from the rock. They thought it necessary to strike the rock, as Moses had done before, shortly after the departure from Egypt (see Ex 17). In any case, the general rebelliousness against God characteristic of the whole people had finally manifested itself in Moses and Aaron as well: the spirit of ingratitude, it seems, was contagious.

Forcefully turned away from Edom, the people journey from Kadesh to Mount Hor, where Aaron dies and is succeeded as high priest by his son Eleazar (Num 20:22–29). Again there are complaints about conditions in the desert, and God sends another plague upon the people: this time, a plague of "fiery serpents" (Hebrew *hannehashim hasseraphim*) (Num 21:6). Intriguingly, the language used to describe these serpents is evocative both of the angelic beings known as *seraphim* (Hebrew for "the burning ones") as well as the "serpent" (Hebrew *nahash*) in the Garden of Eden (Gen 3:1). Once again, Moses steps into the breach, acting as intercessor for the people, and is given a way of escape by God: he is to make a graven image of a "fiery serpent"—literally, in Hebrew, a *saraph*—and set it on a pole, so that "every one who is bitten, when he sees it, shall live" (Num 21:8). (This may be the origin of the later Christian tradition that Satan was one of the angels known as *seraphim*.) Here we have further evidence, in addition to the golden cherubim above the ark (Ex 25), that the first commandment of the Decalogue was not an absolute prohibition of all graven images. In the case of the Bronze Serpent, the graven image is directly commanded by God and is, moreover, a necessary, visible, material instrument of divine salvation and grace—something that later theology would come to refer to as a "sacramental".

Despite the people's rebelliousness, signs of God's favor to them are not lacking: the digging of an abundant well (Num 21:16–20) and military successes (Num 21:1–3, 21–35) suggest hope for the future.

The Balaam Cycle (Numbers 22–24)

The following chapters continue this unexpected theme of hopefulness. The king of Midian, Balak, hires a Mesopotamian seer by the name of Balaam to place a curse on the people of Israel (Num 22). Balaam consents to attempt this four times: in each case, he is compelled to bless Israel and not curse (Num 23–24). These accounts pick up an important theme from the patriarchal narratives, first articulated in the promise to Abraham: "I will bless those who bless

---

The Puzzle of the Balaam Cycle

The Balaam account has puzzled interpreters since antiquity. How can he be a true prophet and yet a Gentile? Why does he seem to vacillate in his obedience to God? Why does God use a talking donkey to speak to him? Why does he bless the Israelites, then advise the Moabites on how to ensnare them (Num 31:16)?

The donkey incident has generally been taken literally in the interpretive tradition, although some noted Jewish sages (Saadyah Gaon and Maimonides) regarded it as a dream sequence that Balaam experienced, which would explain some of the surreal aspects of the story. In the Christian tradition, Thomas Aquinas interpreted it as an example of angelic dominion over all visible creatures, considering the voice of the donkey as in fact that of the angel of the Lord (*Summa Theologica* I, q. 110, a. 1).

In the end, Balaam is a complex and conflicted character who illustrates both that Gentiles outside of the visible confines of Israel can have "the Spirit of God" come upon them (Num 24:2) and that these same spiritual gifts can be granted to morally weak persons who ultimately fall away.

you, and him who curses you I will curse; and by you all the families of the earth shall be blessed" (Gen 12:3 [author's trans.]). Thus we find, despite the sin of the Israelites, God's covenant with them prevents them from being cursed. Despite themselves, they will be blessed and be the conduit of blessing for the rest of the world: "By your descendants shall all the nations of the earth bless themselves" (Gen 22:18). In Balaam's fourth and climactic oracle, there is even a specifically messianic prophecy:

> I see him, but not now;
>   I behold him, but not near:
> *a star shall come forth out of Jacob,*
>   *and a scepter shall rise out of Israel*;
> it shall crush the forehead of Moab,
>   and break down all the sons of Sheth. (Num 24:17)

This oracle takes up and advances two promissory blessings from Genesis: the promise of the scepter (representing international dominion) falling to Judah (Gen 49:10) and the promise of the "seed" of the woman who will crush the head of the serpent (Gen 3:15). In light of these previous prophecies, Balaam's oracle points toward a king arising from Judah who will crush the heads of those who manifest the evil of the serpent—in this case, some of the surrounding nations like Moab and Edom (Num 24:17–18). In ancient Jewish tradition, this prophecy would later come to be understood as referring in the first place to David and ultimately to the Messiah.

The Apostasy of Israel at Beth-Peor (Numbers 25)

What Balaam cannot do by divination he almost accomplishes through seduction. For, as we learn later in Numbers, it is he who counsels the Midianites to encourage their daughters to lure the men of Israel into the sexual rites involved in the worship of local Midianite deities—in particular, a certain "god" or "lord" (Hebrew *ba'al*) associated with the location Peor, whose shrine was called "Beth-peor" (lit. "House of [the god of] Peor") (Num 31:16). This plan succeeds, and the men of Israel commit both physical immorality and spiritual adultery (two realities often linked in the Bible) by consorting with the Midianite women and worshipping the Baal of Beth-peor (Num 25:1–3). A plague breaks out and is only stopped by Aaron's son Phinehas, who alone is willing to take firm action by executing a tribal chief who flaunts his idolatry and fornication by taking a Midianite woman into the "tent" (Hebrew *qubbah* Num 25:8)—possibly the Tabernacle—in "the sight of Moses and in the sight of the whole congregation of the sons of Israel, while they were weeping at the door of the tent of meeting" (Num 25:6).

The seriousness of the apostasy of Israel on the plains of Moab at Peor is often overlooked. In many ways, it is another recapitulation of the Golden Calf incident, this time with the wilderness generation rather than the exodus generation. Both events involve idolatry combined with sexual misconduct (Ex 32:6; Num 25:1, 8). In both cases, one or more Levites rise up to execute judgment and stop the plague on God's people and win for themselves a clerical role (Ex 32:29; Num 25:10). After the Golden Calf, the Levites become the "clerical" tribe. After the worship of Baal at Peor, Phinehas wins the high priesthood for himself and his descendants.[4] The obvious parallels with the Golden Calf point to the gravity of this event as does the fact that it is the *tenth wilderness rebellion* recorded in the literary structure of Numbers (see outline on pp. 231–32).

Indeed, Beth-peor, the geographical location of this promiscuous idolatry on the plains of Moab, will be the site of Israel's encampment *for the entire remainder of the Pentateuch*, including the whole duration of Moses' lengthy and often severe discourses in the book of Deuteronomy. This is significant: the location is associated with the spiritual failing of the people of Israel, including members of the second generation. The location of Beth-peor will cast a shadow over the close of the Pentateuch and partly explain the severity of some of Moses' laws and exhortations in the "farewell discourse" that is the book of Deuteronomy.

> ### Who Dies at Beth-Peor?
>
> Because the Beth-peor debacle takes place days before the second census, which reveals no survivors of the first generation, many consider this debacle simply as the "last gasp" of the exodus generation, which dies out and leaves its innocent children to be counted a few days later (Num 26).
>
> But since the incident at Beth-peor occurs after the death of Aaron, which was in the fortieth year after the exodus (Num 33:38), any remaining men of the first generation were sixty years old at the youngest by this time.
>
> In view of the fact that the offending activity was with the young women of Moab/Midian (Num 25:1, 6, etc.), it seems highly unlikely that the only or even primary offenders were the geriatrics from the first generation. Moreover, the plague that breaks out on the offenders is halted by Phinehas' zeal (Num 25:8)—it does not run its course, and the implication is that not all who sinned with the Moabite women died in the plague (Num 25:8–9).

The Second Generation Prepares to Enter the Land (Numbers 26–36)

Immediately after the plague on the plains of Moab, Moses and the high priest Eleazar take another census of the people of Israel and discover that none of the men of the first (exodus) generation remain (Num 26). Again, this does not exonerate the second (or wilderness) generation from participation in the Beth-peor affair; instead, it rather implies that few of the elderly men of the first generation were even left in the preceding days when the fornication with the Moabite women took place. Therefore, the Beth-peor affair was primarily the responsibility of the *second* generation, whose men were already in the prime of life (twenty to fifty-nine years of age). In this light, the literary parallels between the Golden Calf (Exodus 32) and the idolatry of Baal of Peor (Num 25) become quite significant: what the Calf was to the exodus generation, the Baal of Peor was to the wilderness generation.

With this generational shift in mind, the final section of the book of Numbers is a mixture of hope with a continuing awareness of the recalcitrance of the people. Most of these last chapters will be taken up with necessary preparations

---

[4] Jacob Milgrom, *Numbers*, JPS Torah Commentary 4 (Philadelphia: Jewish Publication Society, 2003).

for the conquest and settlement. This material is "wrapped" by an *inclusio* involving the person of Zelophehad of the tribe of Manasseh, who died in the wilderness without a son (Num 27:1–11; Num 36:1–13). Moses rules that his inheritance should pass to his five daughters and thus be preserved in his family line (Num 27:1–11), with the proviso that the daughters must marry within the tribe of Manasseh, so that their land is not alienated from their tribe. The daughters comply (Num 36:1–13). There can be no doubt that this *inclusio* at the end of Numbers is meant to strike a note of hope for the people of Israel: despite all their sin and rebellion, the Lord takes care to ensure that the memory and posterity of those who died in the wilderness are preserved. The preservation of the "name" of Zelophehad in the Promised Land (Num 27:4) is a foretaste of the richer concept of eternal life, which is implied but not yet clearly articulated in the Pentateuch.

The initial account of the daughters of Zelophehad (Num 27:1–11) is followed by a block of laws concerning the transition of leadership from Moses to Joshua (Num 27:12–23), increased offering requirements for the liturgical calendar (Num 28:1–29:40), and the regulation of vows, especially those of women (Num 30:1–16). These laws may all be seen as responses to the failure of Israel in its covenant relationship in the wilderness. Even Moses partook of this failure (Num 27:14), and so he is replaced by Joshua (Num 27:22). The ceremonial laws and sacrificial requirements imposed on Israel are again increased, producing the most extensive and demanding liturgical calendar yet listed in the Pentateuch (Num 28–29; cf. Lev 23).

The regulations concerning a woman's vows need to be compared to the law for the suspected unfaithful wife (Num 5:11–31). These two laws near the beginning and end of Numbers have a certain correspondence: they both concern potential conflicts between a husband and a wife and prescribe a way to resolve them. Indeed, in light of the fact that the breaking of the covenant at Beth-Peor is described as Israel beginning to "play the harlot" (Num 25:1), these chapters may have a second level of meaning. Israel is, in fact, the "wife" whose fidelity is suspect at the beginning of the narrative (Num 5:11–31), and the "testing" in the wilderness proves her infidelity; nonetheless, she has vowed herself irrevocably to the Lord (Ex 24:8), and her vows will stand because they are confirmed by the Lord her husband (Num 30:1–16).

The rest of Numbers consists of an account of the conquest and settlement of territory outside the land of Canaan, such as Midian (Num 31) and the Transjordan (Num 32). These accounts are paired with anticipatory instructions for the conquest and settlement of the land of Canaan itself—that is, the Cisjordan (Num 34–35). These accounts surround a recapitulation of the itinerary of the key stages of the people of Israel through the exodus and wilderness wanderings (Num 33).

Two narratives in this final section of Numbers indicate that the second generation is not the moral superior of its parents. First, Moses is very angry with the Israelite soldiers for not being thorough in their punitive war against Midian (Num 31:12–20). Second, Moses is indignant with the tribes of Reuben and Gad, perceiving in their request to settle in the Transjordan a desire to avoid the rigors of combat that will fall to the rest of the tribes:

"Why will you discourage the heart of the sons of Israel from going over into the land which the LORD has given them? Thus did your fathers, when I sent them from Kadesh-barnea.... And behold, you have risen in your fathers' stead, a brood of sinful men, to increase still more the fierce anger of the LORD against Israel!" (Num 32:7–8, 14)

Thus, at the end of Numbers, Moses compares the actions of Gad, Reuben, and Manasseh to that of the unfaithful spies who discouraged Israel from entering the land—the pivotal failure of the first generation. Although the tribes work out a compromise with Moses that assuages his anger, the narrative raises (and does not fully resolve) serious questions about whether the second generation is any better than the first. These nagging doubts will continue through the book of Deuteronomy. Nonetheless, the conclusion of Numbers with the preservation of the inheritance of Zelophehad within the tribe of Manasseh provides hope for Israel, based not on its own righteousness but only on the promises of the Lord (Num 36:1–13).

Historical Issues in Numbers

Because of its heavy emphasis on historical narrative (in addition to legal material), there are several historical issues in the book of Numbers that are worthy of our attention.

The Six Hundred "Thousands" of Israelites

Above all stands the question of the historical plausibility of *the large number of Israelites* revealed in the opening census, from which the book itself takes its title in the Greek Septuagint.

The two censuses in the book place the number of fighting men of Israel at around 600,000, not including dependents, the addition of which would bring the total number of Israelites to around two to four million (see Num 1:19–46; 25:19–26:51). For many contemporary scholars, these numbers are simply too large to be believable, and as a result they are written off as unhistorical hyperbole. For others, such a large number of Israelites seems in tension with aspects of the biblical text itself as well as with archaeological and historical data. For example, the entire population of Egypt during this time period is estimated at only 3.5 million, and the Egyptian army at 20,000–25,000 soldiers. The entire population of Canaan was probably less than one million persons.[5] If the Israelite host included 600,000 fighting men, it is difficult to explain how the pharaoh's army—outnumbered by more than ten to one—could have seriously threatened them at the sea (Ex 14) or why the Israelites felt they were too weak to conquer the inhabitants of Canaan (Num 13:31).

[5] Gary A. Rendsburg, "An Additional Note to Two Recent Articles on the Number of People in the Exodus from Egypt and the Large Numbers in Numbers I and XXVI", *Vetus Testamentum* 51 (2001): 392–96; and Kenneth A. Kitchen, *On the Reliability of the Old Testament* (Grand Rapids, Mich.: Eerdmans, 2003), 241–312.

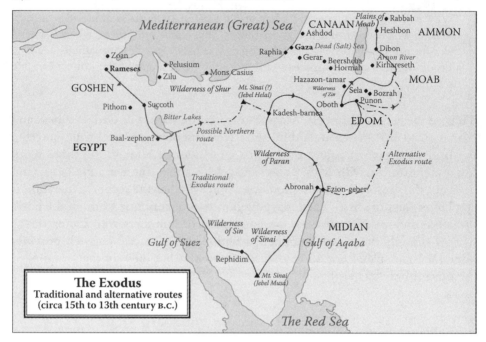

Possible routes of the Exodus

One solution to this tension offered by scholars stems from the Hebrew word for "thousand" (Hebrew *'eleph*, pl. *'elaphim*). In certain passages in the Jewish Scriptures, this word can also mean "military unit", "clan", or (with different vowels) "commander", "tribal chief", or "armed warrior" (see Num 1:16; Josh 22:14, 21, 30; 1 Sam 23:23; Zech 9:7; 12:5–6). Consider, for example, the following:

> And [Gideon] said to him, "Please, Lord, how can I deliver Israel? Behold, my clan [Hebrew *'eleph*] is the weakest in Manasseh, and I am the least in my family." (Judg 6:15)

> Now therefore present yourselves before the LORD by your tribes and by your thousands [Hebrew *'eleph*]. (1 Sam 10:19)

In light of such parallels, some scholars have proposed that this word became misunderstood at some point in transmission history of the Hebrew text of the Pentateuch.[6] From this perspective, the statement that the tribe of Reuben consisted of "forty-six *'elaphim*, five hundred" may have originally meant "forty-six 'fighting units' [totaling] five hundred men" (Num 1:21). At some point in the transmission (recopying) of the Hebrew text, *'elaphim* was misunderstood as "thousands", leading to an inflated figure of the Israelite population. Based on

---

[6] James K. Hoffmeier, *Ancient Israel in Sinai: The Evidence for the Authenticity of the Wilderness Tradition* (Oxford: Oxford University Press, 2005), 153–59.

a correction of the meaning of *'eleph*, scholars have made different proposals for the actual number of Israelites, usually falling within the range of 5,000 to 20,000 persons—a large number indeed, but comparable to the populations and fighting forces of the ancient Near East at that time and according well with the accounts of Israel as a formidable but not invincible military presence (for example, Ex 17:8–13).[7]

With that said, some scholars continue to defend the straightforward interpretation of the large numbers, whether as an accurate count of a people "too many and too mighty" for the pharaoh and the chariots of Egypt (Ex 1:9) or as a form of deliberate rhetorical hyperbole on the part of the author.[8]

Contextual Plausibility of the Wilderness Traditions

Other issues of historical and contextual plausibility associated with Numbers revolve primarily around the geography of the route described by the book and the details of the wilderness sanctuary.

With regard to the exact route of the wilderness wanderings, there continues to be healthy debate. Not all the locations listed in the "wilderness itinerary" given by Numbers (Num 33) can be identified with confidence. Moreover, there is no direct archaeological evidence of the Israelite encampments in the Sinai peninsula. On the other hand, given the fact that archaeological evidence is often only preserved in urban areas where centuries of population presence make possible multiple strata of material remains, it is unclear how much or what kind of archaeological evidence of a tent-dwelling, nomadic people we should expect to find after thousands of years of erosion and scavenging.[9]

Certain of the historical narratives of Numbers seem to reflect the environment and ecology of the Sinai peninsula as opposed to the land of Judea or Samaria, where many modern scholars imagine these accounts to have been written.[10] For example, to this day, the Sinai peninsula is known for phenomena such as periodic large flights of quail (Num 11:31–35), unstable and dangerous land surfaces (Num 16:31–33), and springs bursting forth from rock formations (Num 20:11).[11] Moreover, various stretches of the wilderness itinerary run parallel to second-millennium Egyptian itineraries of routes from Egypt through Sinai to Canaan, which speaks to their authenticity.[12] Finally, with

---

[7] Cf. Kitchen, *Reliability of the Old Testament*, 264–65.

[8] D. M. Fouts, "Another Look at Large Numbers in Assyrian Royal Inscriptions", *Journal of Near Eastern Studies* 53 (1994): 205–11, and Fouts, "A Defense of the Hyperbolic Interpretation of Large Numbers in the Old Testament", *Journal of the Evangelical Theological Society* 40 (1997): 377–87.

[9] Hoffmeier, *Ancient Israel in Sinai*, 149–53.

[10] Kitchen, *Reliability of the Old Testament*, 241–312.

[11] Cf. R. Dennis Cole, "Numbers", in *Genesis, Exodus, Leviticus, Numbers, Deuteronomy*, vol. 1 of *Zondervan Illustrated Bible Backgrounds Commentary*, ed. John H. Walton (Grand Rapids, Mich.: Zondervan, 2009), 355–56, 371.

[12] Charles R. Krahmalkov, "Exodus Itinerary Confirmed by Egyptian Evidence", *Biblical Archeology Review* 20:5 (1994): 54–62, 79.

Source: en.wikipedia.org

Egyptian Silver Trumpets; cf. Numbers 10:2

regard to the wilderness sanctuary, Numbers adds the details of oxcarts donated to transport the Tabernacle (Num 7:3) and silver trumpets made to announce battle alarms and liturgical feasts (Num 10:1–10). Oxcarts used for transporting tent-shrines are attested in Egyptian iconography from the New Kingdom period, as are silver trumpets as battle bugles. In fact, both a copper and a silver trumpet were recovered from the tomb of Pharaoh Tutankhamun ("King Tut", 1341–1323 B.C.) (see image).[13] In light of these and other culturally contextual parallels between the book of Numbers and the second millennium B.C., archaeologist and biblical scholar James K. Hoffmeier concludes his massive study of the historicity of the wilderness tradition with these words:

> It seems to me easier to believe that the Bible accurately preserves an authentic picture of the travels and life in the Sinai wilderness than to suppose that authors six to seven hundred years later, writing in ignorance of the past and using creative imagination, got so much certifiably correct.... If one jettisons the wilderness tradition, as some have done, we are left with too many unanswered questions about ancient Israel's origin, her religion, the covenant, and most significantly about the divine name Yahweh.[14]

Numbers in the Living Tradition

In light of the many dramatic historical narratives and the deliberate depiction of the spiritual degeneracy of the exodus and wilderness generations in the book of Numbers, certain episodes from the book have figured quite prominently in the living tradition of the Christian faith, from its earliest years up to and including our own day.

The Sin of the Wilderness Generation

One of the most prominent uses of the book of Numbers in the later writings of the New Testament and the later Christian tradition is a decidedly negative one: the picture of the wilderness generation as an example of how *not* to walk in the presence of God.

One of the most striking examples of this can be found in the apostle Paul's first letter to the Church at Corinth. In the course of his many moral and spiritual exhortations, Paul uses the various punishments of the wilderness generations

---

[13] Cole, "Numbers", 353.
[14] Hoffmeier, *Ancient Israel in Sinai*, 249.

as a warning to Christians against spiritual presumption, sexual immorality, and ingratitude, when he writes:

> I want you to know, brethren, that our fathers were all under the cloud.... Nevertheless with most of them [the exodus generation] God was not pleased; for they were overthrown in the wilderness.
>
> Now these things are warnings for us, not to desire evil as they did.... We must not indulge in immorality as some of them did, and twenty-three thousand fell in a single day. We must not put the Lord to the test, as some of them did and were destroyed by serpents; nor grumble, as some of them did and were destroyed by the Destroyer. Now these things happened to them as a warning [Greek *typikos*], but they were written down for our instruction, upon whom the end of the ages has come. (1 Cor 10:1, 5–6, 8–11)

In this dense but powerful passage, Paul draws out both the typological and moral senses of the book of Numbers, alluding in a few sentences to the condemnation of the first generation to death in the wilderness (Num 14:29–30), the sexual immorality that accompanied the apostasy on the plains of Moab with the Baal of Peor and the devastating plague that resulted (Num 25:1–18), the plague of fiery serpents by which thousands of Israelites were killed for rejecting the manna (Num 21:5–6), and the "murmuring" of the rebellious Israelites who participated in Korah's rebellion and its aftermath (Num 16:41–49). Indeed, this may be the densest compilation of scriptural allusions to Numbers in the entire New Testament. It is not, however, the only one, since the epistle to the Hebrews uses the wilderness generation in the exact same fashion, citing the "fathers" who put God "to the test" for "forty years" as an example of spiritual hard-heartedness, rebellion, rejection of legitimate spiritual authority, and sin (Heb 2:7–18). Indeed, the author of Hebrews uses the fact that the wilderness generation was "unable to enter [the Promised Land] because of unbelief" as a warning to all Christians about failing to enter eternal life because of the same kind of sinfulness (Heb 3:19—4:13).

Given the prominence of these New Testament references to Numbers, it is not surprising that the early Church Fathers continued to use the punishments of the wilderness generation as a warning to all Christians who would neglect the real consequences of immorality, ingratitude, and rebellion against authority. Consider, for example, the reflections of Caesarius of Arles (fifth century A.D.), who reflects on the forty years' punishment in this way:

> For my part I am afraid to examine the secrets of this mystery, for I see comprehended in it the calculation of sins and punishment. If each sinner is assigned punishment for the sin of one day and according to the number of days he sins must spend so many years in punishment, I fear that perhaps for us who sin daily and spend no day of our life without offense, even ages and ages will not suffice to pay our penalties. In the fact that for forty days of sin those people were afflicted in the desert for forty years and not permitted to enter the holy land, a kind of similarity to the future judgment seems to be evident.[15]

---

[15] Caesarius of Arles, *Sermon* 108.2, in Joseph T. Lienhard, S.J., *Exodus, Leviticus, Numbers, Deuteronomy*, Old Testament 3, Ancient Christian Commentary on Scripture, ed. Thomas C. Oden (Downers Grove, Ill.: InterVarsity Press, 2001), 225.

The Bronze Serpent and the Mystery of the Cross

In addition to the typological interpretation of the wilderness generation's sins, there is also the typological tradition of the mechanisms of their redemption. One of these particularly stands out since it goes back to the words of Jesus himself in the Gospel of John, when he alludes to the book of Numbers in order to illustrate the mystery of his redemptive Passion and death on the Cross:

> As Moses lifted up the serpent in the wilderness, so must the Son of man be lifted up, that whoever believes in him may have eternal life. (Jn 3:14-15)

Although these words may seem unsurprising to readers familiar with the New Testament, they are, upon further reflection, a rather strange way to speak about the Cross, since they imply the identification of Jesus himself with the serpent. As a result, Christian tradition did not fail to offer further explanation using the details from Numbers to clarify the meaning of the typology at work in Jesus' word. For example, Venerable Bede (seventh century A.D.) had this to say:

> In the raising up of the bronze serpent (when those who were stricken beheld it, they were cured) is prefigured our Redeemer's suffering on the cross, for only by faith in him is the kingdom of death and sin overcome. The sins which drag down soul and body to destruction at the same time are appropriately represented by the serpents, not only because they were fiery and poisonous [and] artful at bringing about death but also because our first parents were led into sin by a serpent, and from being immortal they became mortal by sinning. *The Lord is aptly made known by the bronze serpent, since he came in the likeness of sinful flesh.* Just as the bronze serpent had the likeness of a fiery serpent but had absolutely none of the strength of harmful poison in its members—rather by being lifted up it cured those who had been stricken by the [live] serpents—so the Redeemer of the human race did not merely clothe himself in sinful flesh but entered bodily into the likeness of sinful flesh, in order that by suffering death on the cross in [this likeness] he might free those who believed in him from all sin and even from death itself.[16]

Similar comments can be found in other Church Fathers, who regularly appealed to the Bronze Serpent both as a defense of images and as a typological sign of "the cross" of Christ.[17]

The Seventy Elders and the Order of Presbyters

One final example of a popular typological interpretation of Numbers revolves around the appointment of the "seventy men of the elders" to assist Moses (Num 11:16-23).

The connection between these seventy and the leaders of the early Christian movement goes back to the public ministry of Jesus himself, when he

---

[16] Bede, *Homilies on the Gospels* 2.18, in Bede the Venerable, *Homilies on the Gospels*, bk. 2: *Lent to the Dedication of the Church*, trans. Lawrence T. Martin and David Hurst, O.S.B. (Kalamazoo, Mich.: Cistercian Publications, 1991), 184-85.

[17] For example, Justin Martyr, *Dialogue with Trypho* 94.

"appointed seventy others, and sent them on ahead of him, two by two, into every town and place where he himself was about to come" (Lk 10:1). This act alone establishes not only Jesus as a kind of New Moses but his disciples as new leaders of the eschatological Israel. Significantly, many ancient Greek manuscripts of Luke read "seventy-two" instead of "seventy", showing that while ancient Christian scribes were somewhat confused about the exact number of disciples chosen by Jesus, they were clear that Jesus' act of appointing hearkened back to Numbers' account of the seventy elders appointed by Moses (Num 11:16–26), with the additional two figures of Eldad and Medad, upon whom the spirit fell inside the camp (Num 11:27–30).

In this light, it is perhaps unsurprising that the Greek word used to translate "the elders of Israel [Greek *tōn presbyterōn Israel*]" (Num 11:16 LXX) came to be used multiple times in the New Testament to describe early Christian "elders" (Greek *presbyteroi*) appointed through the laying on of hands (for example, Acts 1:30; 14:23; 1 Tim 5:19; Tit 1:5; Jas 5:14; 2 Jn 1:1; 3 Jn 1:1). Indeed, it is because of such connections that in the contemporary Roman rite of ordination to the priesthood (Latin *presbyterate*), the prayer of consecration for priests makes direct allusion to Numbers when the bishop prays:

> When you had appointed high priests to rule your people, you chose other men next to them in rank and dignity to be with them and to help them in their task; and so there grew up the ranks of priest and the offices of Levites, established by sacred rites. *In the desert you extended the spirit of Moses to seventy wise men who helped him to rule the great company of his people.* You shared among the sons of Aaron the fullness of their father's power, to provide worthy priests in sufficient number for the increasing rites of sacrifice and worship.... *Lord, grant also to us such fellow workers.... Almighty Father, grant to these servants of yours the dignity of the priesthood.*[18]

The Book of Numbers in the Lectionary

Much like Leviticus, Numbers is a book shaped by a liturgical vision. The "war camp" of Israel formed at Sinai to march into the Promised Land is simultaneously a liturgical procession of the tribes of the Lord gathered around the Tabernacle and the ark. God's intention for Israel was for them to process into the land as an act of worship, and the land itself was to provide space and sustenance for Israel to live a life centered around the cult of the Lord. This plan is derailed in the wilderness wanderings, however, by Israel's rejection of the Lord as its God in successive rebellions, culminating in the worship of a foreign god at Beth-peor.

Despite the liturgical shape of the book and the popularity of its typological interpretation in the New Testament and Church Fathers, Numbers appears infrequently in the Lectionary. By far the most treasured and prominent reading is the priestly benediction of Aaron (Num 6:22–27), which is always the first reading on the Solemnity of Mary, Mother of God, which coincides with the beginning of the civil year in most Western nations (January 1). This reading

---

[18] From *The Rites of the Catholic Church*, vol. 2 (Collegeville: Liturgical Press, 1991), 60–61.

expresses the Church's desire to invoke the blessing of the Triune God on herself and on the nations in which she resides over the entire coming year.

Given the typological tradition involving the serpents in the wilderness, the Church also reads the account of the Bronze Serpent (Num 21:4–9) on a few liturgical occasions where meditation on the Cross is particularly appropriate. Finally, other texts of Numbers that concern the appointing of leaders to assist Moses and Aaron (Num 3:5–9; 11:11–25) are employed at Masses for the Conferral of Holy Orders, where they demonstrate the continuity of divinely appointed leadership for the people of God in the Old Covenant and in the New:

Readings from Numbers for Sundays, Feast Days, Liturgical Seasons, and Other Occasions			
MSO = Masses for Special Occasions; *OM* = Optional Memorial; *VM* = Votive Mass; *Rit* = Ritual			
Passage	Description	Occasion	Explanation
3:5–9	The "diaconal" duties of the Levites specified, as they are presented to Aaron and his sons	*MSO*: Conferral of Holy Orders, opt. 1	The account of the presentation of the Levites to the priests (Aaron and his sons) as a "gift" to them to assist them in their ministry is particularly appropriate for Masses solemnizing diaconal ordination.
6:22–27	The Priestly Blessing of God's people with the triple invocation of the divine name, once used annually on the Day of Atonement (*Yom Kippur*) when the Temple stood	Jan. 1: Mary Mother of God (ABC); also *MSO*: For a Country or City, etc., opt. 4; For the Beginning of the Civil Year, opt. 2	The Church treasures this much-beloved priestly triple-blessing with the divine name (YHWH) and invokes it at the beginning of the civil year and at other times when there is a need to implore God's blessing on the entire civil community. In conjunction with the Solemnity of Mary Mother of God, we are reminded of Mary's role as the conduit of blessing from the Trinity to mankind.
11:11–25 (*excerpted*)	Moses unable to lead the people alone; God bestows the Spirit also on the seventy "elders"	*MSO*: Conferral of Holy Orders, opt. 2	The relationship of Moses to the seventy elders who share God's prophetic spirit and assist him in governance of God's people is analogous to the relationship of a bishop and his priests (*presbyteroi*): thus this reading is particularly appropriate for ordination to the priesthood.
11:25–29	The prophesying of Eldad and Medad outside the camp; Moses desire for all God's people to be prophets	*26th Sun. in OT (B)*	This account is chosen to complement the Gospel (Mk 9:38–49), which recounts a man not of the disciples who is casting out demons but who is not stopped by our Lord. Both texts illustrate a desire for the generous distribution of the gifts of God's spirit among all people.

(*continued*)

Readings from Numbers for Sundays, Feast Days, Liturgical Seasons, and Other Occasions (*continued*)
MSO = Masses for Special Occasions; *OM* = Optional Memorial; *VM* = Votive Mass; *Rit* = Ritual

Passage	Description	Occasion	Explanation
21:4–9	The plague of serpents; Moses raises the Bronze Serpent on the pole	Sept. 14: Exaltation of the Cross; *also* Tues., 5th Week of Lent	The Bronze Serpent is an important OT type of the Cross; thus this reading is paired with John 3:15 in the Gospel on the Feast of the Exaltation and also late in Lent, as the liturgical focus moves increasingly toward contemplation of the Passion.
24:2–7, 15–17a	Balaam's third and fourth oracles of blessing on Israel	Mon., 3rd Week of Advent	This reading is chosen for the sake of Balaam's fourth oracle: "a star shall come forth out of Jacob, and a scepter shall rise out of Israel." This important oracle was a source of great hope for Jews awaiting the coming of the Messiah—an experience the Church relives in Advent.

In terms of the principle of *lectio continua*, key selections from Numbers are read during daily Mass in Year 1, Week 18, according to the following table. The daily Mass readings provide the daily communicant with a representative selection of the ten rebellions against the Lord and Moses during the wilderness wanderings:

Reading of Numbers for Daily Mass: Ordinary Time, Year I: Week 18		
Day	Passage Read	Description
M	11:4b–15	The second rebellion after leaving Sinai: the people demand meat, and Moses complains to the Lord that he is not able to lead the people alone.
Tu	12:1–13	The third rebellion after leaving Sinai: Miriam and Aaron speak against Moses and his "Cushite" wife; Miriam is struck with leprosy.
W	13:1–2, 25–14:1, 26a–29a, 34–35	The fourth rebellion: the mutiny after the bad report of the spies; God swears the first generation will die in the wilderness.
Th	20:1–13	The eighth rebellion: the people demand water at Meribah; Moses strikes the rock rather than speaking to it, and God denies him entrance to the land.

Conclusion

Numbers tells the history of God's people under the economy of the renewed or Levitical covenant (Ex 34–Lev 27) as they journey through the wilderness to take possession of the Promised Land of Canaan. Although the preparation of the nation to depart from Sinai goes smoothly (Num 1–10), the journey through the wilderness is a disaster, a nadir in the relationship between the Israelites and their God consisting of ten rebellions involving every element and sector of Israelite society. The generation of the exodus dies out in the wilderness, largely due to retributive plagues. The second generation grows up in the wilderness, but the narratives implicate the second generation in some of the rebellions and cast serious doubt on whether there has been a significant change in the heart of God's people. Nonetheless, the positive oracles of Balaam the foreign prophet and the laws that guarantee the inheritance of those who died in the wilderness are clear literary indicators that there remains hope for Israel, based not on its own merit but on the oath-bound promise of God.

For Further Reading

Commentaries and Studies of Numbers

Budd, Philip J. *Numbers*. Word Biblical Commentary 5. Waco, Tex.: Word Books, 1984.
Coats, George W. *Rebellion in the Wilderness: The Murmuring Motif in the Wilderness Traditions of the Old Testament*. Nashville: Abingdon Press, 1968.
de Vaux, Roland. *Ancient Israel: Its Life and Institutions*. Translated by John McHugh. Repr., Grand Rapids, Mich.: Eerdmans, 1997. (See pp. 358–71, 415–56, 466–67.)
————. *The Early History of Israel*. Translated by David Smith. 2 vols. London: Darton, Longman, and Todd, 1978. (See vol. 2, pp. 551–92.)
Hamilton, Victor. *Handbook on the Pentateuch*. Grand Rapids, Mich.: Baker Academic, 2005. (See pp 303–64.)
Levine, Baruch A. *Numbers 1–20* and *Numbers 21–36*. Anchor Bible 4 & 4a. New York: Doubleday, 1993–2000.
Milgrom, Jacob. *Numbers*. JPS Torah Commentary 4. Philadelphia: Jewish Publication Society, 2003.
Noth, Martin. *Numbers: A Commentary*. Translated by James D. Martin. Old Testament Library. Philadelphia: Westminster Press, 1968.

Historical Issues in Numbers

Cole, R. Dennis. "Numbers". Pages 340–417 in *Genesis, Exodus, Leviticus, Numbers, Deuteronomy*. Vol. 1 of *Zondervan Illustrated Bible Backgrounds Commentary*. Edited by John H. Walton. Grand Rapids, Mich.: Zondervan, 2009.
Hoffmeier, James Karl. *Ancient Israel in Sinai: The Evidence for the Authenticity of the Wilderness Tradition*. Oxford: Oxford University Press, 2005. (See pp. 153–59, 193–249.)

Numbers in the Living Tradition

Catechism of the Catholic Church. 2nd ed. Vatican City: Libreria Editrice Vaticana, 1997. (See nos. 1541–42.)
Kugel, James L. *Traditions of the Bible: A Guide to the Bible as It Was at the Start of the Common Era*. Cambridge, Mass.: Harvard University Press, 1997. (See pp. 775–826.)
Lienhard, Joseph T. "Numbers". Pages 205–74 in *Exodus, Leviticus, Numbers, Deuteronomy*. Old Testament 3 of Ancient Christian Commentary on Scripture. Edited by Thomas C. Oden. Downers Grove, Ill.: InterVarsity Press, 2001.

The Rites of the Catholic Church. Vol. 2. Collegeville, Minn.: Liturgical Press, 1991. (See pp. 60–61.)

Theodoret of Cyrus. *On Leviticus, Numbers, Deuteronomy, Joshua, Judges, and Ruth.* Vol. 2 of *The Questions on the Octateuch.* The Library of Early Christianity 2. Washington, D.C.: Catholic University of America Press, 2007.

10. DEUTERONOMY

Introduction

"Deuteronomy" derives from the Greek word *deuteronomion*, meaning "second law" (Greek *deuteros* + *nomos*). The Septuagint translators coined the term to render the phrase "a copy of this law" (Hebrew *mishnēh hattorah*) (Deut 17:18), and it became the name of the book. Although not an exact translation of the Hebrew, Deuteronomy or "Second Law" is an apt title for the book, since it repeats the Ten Commandments (Deut 5:6–21) and presents itself as "another covenant" law in addition to the one God made with Israel at Sinai (Deut 29:1).

In Jewish tradition, as with the other books of the Torah, the title is taken from the first words of the book; hence, Deuteronomy is named "These are the words" (Hebrew *'ēlleh haddebarîm*) (Deut 1:1) and, ultimately, just "words" (Hebrew *debarîm*). This title, too, is apt, since it conveys the sense of Deuteronomy as the parting speech of Moses, addressed to the second generation of Israelites on the plains of Moab just before his death (Deut 1:1–2).

The importance of Deuteronomy to the canon of Scripture and the tradition of both Judaism and Christianity can scarcely be exaggerated. The only other Old Testament books that can claim to rival it in theological significance are Genesis, the Psalms, and Isaiah; yet, in important ways, the Psalms and Isaiah are both dependent on Deuteronomy. Among the Dead Sea Scrolls, more copies of Deuteronomy were found than of any other biblical book except the Psalms. In the New Testament, Deuteronomy is third after the Psalms and Isaiah in the number of quotations and allusions. It has rightly been called the "linchpin" of the Old Testament. It serves as a hinge or pivot joining the Pentateuch to the historical books, and its influence can be felt in all the books of history, most of the prophets, and even into the wisdom literature. This is because, as the final and definitive form of God's covenant with Israel through Moses, it was the theological and political "constitution" of Israel for the rest of its history, even if it was seldom (if ever) fully implemented.

Literary Structure of Deuteronomy

There are three complementary ways of understanding the structure of Deuteronomy: (1) as a series of speeches of Moses, (2) as a literary chiasm, and (3) as an ancient covenant document.

If Deuteronomy is viewed primarily as the speeches—or better, *sermons*—of Moses, then a tripartite structure emerges, followed by an epilogue of concluding materials:

Outline of the Book of Deuteronomy

I. Moses' First Sermon (Deut 1:1—4:43; roughly chaps. 1–4):
Looking Back: A Recap of the Exodus and Wanderings

II. Moses' Second Sermon (Deut 4:44—26:19; roughly chaps. 5–26):
Looking at the Present: The Laws Israel Must Obey

III. Moses' Third Sermon (Deut 27:1—31:30; roughly chaps. 29–31):
Looking Ahead: Provisions and Prophecies for Israel's Future

IV. Concluding Material
   a. Moses' Song (Deut 32)
   b. Moses' Blessing (Deut 33)
   c. Moses' Death (Deut 34)

On the other hand, commentator Duane Christenson,[1] looking at larger structures in the composition of Deuteronomy, has identified a chiastic pattern wrapped around the central law code of the book (Deut 12–26):

A. The Outer Frame: A Look Backward (Deut 1–4)
   B. The Inner Frame: The Covenant Summary (Deut 5–11)
      C. The Central Core: Covenant Stipulations (Deut 12–26)
   B'. The Inner Frame: The Covenant Solemnization (Deut 27–30)
A'. The Outer Frame: A Look Forward (Deut 31–34) (*adapted*)

Finally, since the pioneering work of George E. Mendenhall[2] and Meredith G. Kline,[3] many scholars have recognized that Deuteronomy follows the basic outline of a second-millennium "vassal treaty"—that is, a binding covenant imposed by a high king on a subordinate (vassal) king. The typical outline of such treaties was as follows:

1. Preamble
2. Historical Prologue (the relationship of the covenant partners to date)
3. Stipulations (laws governing the covenant relationship)
4. Instructions for Storage and Periodic Reading of the Covenant Document
5. The Calling of Witness (various gods) to Enforce the Covenant
6. Blessings and Curses

In Deuteronomy, not just some but *all* the same elements are present, although the order varies slightly:

---

[1] Duane L. Christenson, *Deuteronomy 1–11*, Word Biblical Commentary 6A (Dallas: Word Books, 1991).

[2] George E. Mendenhall, *Law and Covenant in Israel and the Ancient Near East* (Pittsburgh: Presbyterian Board of Colportage of Western Pennsylvania, 1955).

[3] Meredith G. Kline, *Treaty of the Great King: The Covenant Structure of Deuteronomy* (Grand Rapids, Mich.: Eerdmans, 1963).

1. Preamble (Deut 1:1–5)
2. Historical Prologue (Deut 1:6—3:29)
3. Stipulations
   a. Basic (Deut 4:1—11:32)
   b. Specific (Deut 12:1—26:19)
4. Curses and Blessings
   a. Curses (Deut 27:1–26; 28:15—30:10; 32:1–52)
   b. Blessings (Deut 28:1–14; 33:1–29)
5. The Calling of Witnesses ("heaven and earth", Deut 30:11–20)
6. Instructions for Storage and Periodic Reading (Deut 31)

In light of such parallels, it is clear that Deuteronomy has strong affinities with second-millennium treaty documents, and yet it does not follow them slavishly. It may well be that the core of Deuteronomy was a treaty-covenant, which the text records Moses as writing down (Deut 31:24). However, the form of Deuteronomy as we now have it does not follow the treaty structure exactly, because an editor has inserted historical and homiletic materials by or about Moses into the outline at key points. So, for example, after a listing of blessings and curses in typical ancient Near Eastern covenant form (Deut 28), we have a lengthy exhortation from Moses on the theme of blessing and curse (Deut 29–30). Likewise, the instructions for deposition and reading of the covenant document (Deut 31:9–13, 24–26) are surrounded by more Mosaic "homiletical" material (Deut 31:1–8, 14–23). At the end of the book, we find narratives that would not normally be in a covenant document (Moses' song, blessing, and death, Deut 32–34) but are obviously important to the larger biblical narrative and fit well at the end of this canonical book.

All the different ways of analyzing the structure of Deuteronomy have something to contribute. Observing the chiastic structure of Deuteronomy highlights its role as a *literary hinge* that links the Pentateuch with the next major canonical grouping, the historical books (Joshua—2 Kings). The technical literary term for such a hinge is a *janus* (from the Roman god of beginnings and endings, who had two faces, one forward and the other backward). Thus Deuteronomy, in its early chapters (Deut 1–5), recounts much of the material from Exodus through Numbers concerning the wilderness wanderings and even makes pointed references to material in Genesis, such as the creation (Deut 4:32) and the patriarchal covenant (Deut 9:5). On the other hand, in its later chapters (Deut 28–33), it looks forward to Israel's future, usually offering dire predictions of Israel's fate (Deut 28:15–54; 31:14—32:47) but also holding out the hope of divine blessing and mercy (Deut 30:1–10; 33:1–29). At the center of the book is Moses' last and definitive legislation for Israel's civil and religious life (Deut 12–26). So, Deuteronomy recaps Genesis through Numbers and previews Joshua through 2 Kings, while repeating the divine covenant law in an authoritative fashion. It is, therefore, *the* key link in joining Israel's prehistory (Genesis—Numbers) with its national history (Joshua—2 Kings).

Finally, recognizing the vassal-treaty structure of Deuteronomy also gives us a true window onto the meaning of the book. While not *merely* a covenant document, Deuteronomy certainly *is* a covenant document. As recent scholarship has demonstrated, the form of the Deuteronomic covenant document is significant: it is a kind of *vassal-treaty*, which was generally imposed by a high king on a lesser king who had been rebellious.[4] Indeed, Israel was an excessively rebellious vassal during the wilderness wanderings in Numbers. The vassal-treaty form was not clearly recognizable during the stay at Sinai (Ex 20–24), where the covenant had a more familial and personal character; in the book of Deuteronomy, however, it is everywhere in evidence. Israel's relationship with God has degenerated from what scholars call a "parity" or "kinship" covenant in the book of Exodus, where the emphasis was on mutual loyalties (Ex 24), to a "vassal" covenant in Deuteronomy, where the emphasis is strongly on Israel's obligation to obey its covenant Lord under the dire threat of mortal curses (Deut 27:11–26; 28:14–54; 32:1–43). While Israel remains the "son" of God, Deuteronomy suspends filial privileges and treats Israel more as a servant than as a son.

Overview of Deuteronomy

Moses' Overview of the History of Israel (Deuteronomy 1:1—4:43)

This first section consists of a short introduction by the narrator (Deut 1:1–5) followed by an unbroken first-person discourse by Moses in which he recounts the wilderness wanderings up to the present, summarizing material from Exodus and Numbers for the second generation of Israelites as they stand before him on the plains of Moab (Deut 1:6—4:40). The purpose of this retrospective history is to make a homiletical point: reflection on God's faithfulness and their own infidelity during the wanderings in the wilderness should motivate the Israelites to gratitude and obedience.

Significantly, the narrator's introduction stresses the distinction in *time* and *location* from the covenant established at Mount Sinai. When Deuteronomy opens, it is now in "the fortieth year, on the first day of the eleventh month" since Israel left Egypt, and the location is "beyond the Jordan, in the land of Moab" (Deut 1:3,5). Later notices will specify the location more exactly as "the valley opposite Beth-peor" (Deut 3:29; 4:46), thus echoing the earlier apostasy committed by the second generation at the end of the book of Numbers (see Num 25).

The difference in time and location is of critical importance to the proper interpretation of Deuteronomy. This book does not simply give an alternative or competing account of the events that took place at Sinai. Rather, as the book itself expressly emphasizes, this is in fact a different covenant:

> These are the words of the covenant which the Lord commanded Moses to make with the sons of Israel in the land of Moab, *besides the covenant which he had made with them at Horeb.* (Deut 29:1)

Hence, thirty-eight consequential years have passed since the Sinai covenant was made at the mountain of God—here called "Horeb" (Deut 1:6). The lapse

---

[4] Scott W. Hahn, *Kinship by Covenant: A Canonical Approach to the Fulfillment of God's Saving Promises*, Anchor Yale Bible Reference Library (New Haven, Conn.: Yale University Press, 2009), 62–83.

of time and the events that have transpired in the meanwhile help to explain the different laws and emphases of Deuteronomy over against earlier covenant legislation in both the original Sinaitic (Ex 20–24) and later Levitical covenants (Ex 34–Lev 27). Significantly, whereas the earlier covenant(s) are ratified on a holy mountain, Deuteronomy takes place on "the plains"—indeed, the "valley opposite Beth-peor" (Deut 3:29; 4:46). A valley in Gentile territory in view of the site of one of Israel's greatest apostasies (the worship of Baal at Beth-peor, Num 25:1–18) is a far cry from the holy mountain of God. Deuteronomy is the only major biblical covenant established in such an inauspicious location. In fact, it is the only major biblical covenant not delivered on a mountaintop (though it will be linked with Mounts Gerizim and Ebal later in the book; cf. Deut 11:26–32). The bad omen of the location points to the fact that Israel's sinful rebellion hangs heavily over the book: Deuteronomy is a covenant designed for a rebellious, not a righteous, people (Deut 31:27).

The first-person exhortation with which the book opens is a novelty in the Pentateuch (Deut 1:6), which up till now has largely consisted of third-person narration. In Deuteronomy, we hear Moses' own "voice", and we get his personal perspective on events that were described somewhat differently in the earlier books. This "Mosaic perspective"—or even "Mosaic spin", if one may say so—must be taken into account for the proper interpretation of the book. For example, we know from earlier in the Pentateuch that it was particularly Moses' lack of faith at the waters of Meribah that resulted in his exclusion from the Promised Land (Num 20:12). Yet in Moses' first sermon, there is a decidedly different emphasis: "The LORD was angry with me *on your account*, and would not listen to me" (Deut 3:26; cf. 1:37). It is true, in a qualified sense, that the Israelites caused Moses and the Lord to have a "falling out": the stress of dealing with the people pushed Moses to the point of acting erratically and ultimately disobediently. Nonetheless, one detects a note of self-justification in Moses' own retelling of these events!

Another characteristic of Deuteronomy, as Moses' first-person speech, is its "homiletical" rhetoric. For rhetorical effect, Moses uses exaggerations and hyperbole: for example, he declares that every offender was wiped out in the plague at Beth-peor (contrary to Num 25:8) and that "not with our fathers did the LORD make this covenant, but with us, who are all of us here alive this day" (Deut 5:3). In fact, every Israelite under forty—probably a majority of the congregation Moses was addressing—was not even alive when the Sinai covenant was given. Nonetheless, Moses makes these rhetorical assertions for a purpose: he aims to sting their conscience concerning the event of the Baal of Peor, and to stress that the covenant is just as binding on this generation as it was on their parents.

Sometimes Moses' accounts of events in the book of Deuteronomy differ from earlier narratives in various ways without an obvious theological or rhetorical reason. This should not surprise us. Parallel accounts of the same events in ancient literature invariably show differences. For example, in a very close parallel with Deuteronomy, we have extant successive covenant-renewal documents between Hittite kings and their vassals, in which the successive historical prologues retell, with variation and differences, the same history of the covenant relationship between the suzerain and his vassal.[5] With this in mind, at the end of his recitation of salvation history from the exodus to the present, Moses drives home the point of his first sermon: "Know therefore this day, and *lay it to your heart*, that the LORD is God in heaven above and on the earth beneath; there is no other. Therefore you shall keep his statutes and his commandments" (Deut 4:39–40). In other words, before diving into the legal material proper, he stresses meditation on sacred history, which should lead the Israelites to reverence and obedience to God.

Moses' Exposition of the Decalogue (Deuteronomy 4:44—11:32)

The sacred author marks the beginning of Moses' second sermon with an introduction similar to the first that restates the time and place of Moses' speech (Deut 4:44–49). What follows is one of the most passionate exhortations to exclusive love and fidelity to the Lord in all the Old Testament. This is the most-quoted portion of Deuteronomy in the New Testament: for example, Jesus will cite from this section three times during the wilderness temptations (see Mt 4:4, 7, 10, citing Deut 6:13, 16; 8:3).

Moses begins by retelling the story of the giving of the Decalogue, restating the commandments themselves, with some slight alterations (Deut 5:6–21). The rest of the sermon is loose in structure, a rambling exhortation largely focused on the first commandment and fidelity to the Lord. There is a general narrative movement from the first giving of the law at Sinai (Deut 5) to the second giving of the law after the Calf (Deut 10), but along the way Moses makes generous use of examples of Israel's failure and rebellion in the wilderness as foils for the fidelity he commends and repeated reference to the "covenant sworn to your fathers"—that is, the patriarchal covenant, the oath after the sacrifice of Isaac, the only explicit oath from God to any of the patriarchs (Gen 22:15–18). The Mosaic covenant, which can be broken, is ultimately grounded in a deeper and older covenant, the Abrahamic, which is guaranteed by divine oath.

Moses Reminds Israel of Its Failures		
Incident	Found in:	Cited in:
Murmuring at Massah	Ex 17	Deut 6:16; 9:22
The Calf Incident	Ex 32	Deut 9:9–21; 9:25–10:11
Murmuring at Taberah and Kibroth-hatta'avah	Num 11	Deut 9:22
Rebellion at the Spies' Report	Num 14	Deut 9:23–24
Revolt of Dathan and Abiram	Num 16	Deut 11:6

Two passages within this sermon have particular theological importance. The first is Moses' restatement and exposition of the first commandment:

"*Hear, O Israel: The LORD our God is one LORD; and you shall love the LORD your God with all your heart, and with all your soul, and with all your might.* And these words

[5] Joshua Berman, "Histories Twice Told: Deuteronomy 1–3 and the Hittite Treaty Prologue Tradition", *Journal of Biblical Literature* 132.2 (2013): 229–50.

which I command you this day shall be upon your heart; and you shall teach them diligently to your children, and shall talk of them when you sit in your house, and when you walk by the way, and when you lie down, and when you rise. And you shall bind them as a sign upon your hand, and they shall be as frontlets between your eyes. And you shall write them on the doorposts of your house and on your gates." (Deut 6:4–9)

These lines, especially the opening verse, have become the central prayer and creed of Judaism, called the *Shema*, from its first Hebrew word, meaning "Hear!" (Deut 6:4). Together with the following verses (Deut 6:6–9) and two other Torah passages (Deut 11:13–21; Num 15:37–41), the *Shema* from ancient times was recited aloud by faithful Jews at least twice a day and continues to be prayed in this way to this day. It is little wonder, then, that in the New Testament, this verse is singled out by Jesus as the greatest commandment of the law (Mt 22:34–40), a sort of summation of the whole law. Note it well: it is Deuteronomy in particular that reveals that the heart of all divine law is not mechanical obedience but a personal, covenantal relationship of love with the God of Israel, the God of the covenant.

A second passage from this section of Deuteronomy drives home a similar point. Near the end of the second sermon, Moses exhorts Israel: "*Circumcise therefore the foreskin of your heart*, and be no longer stubborn" (Deut 10:16)! This passage indicates that already in the Old Testament there is an emphasis on the interior reality symbolized by visible, external signs: true circumcision is not merely outward and physical; it is an inward and spiritual reality. In the final analysis, the problem with the Israelites in Deuteronomy is an interior resistance to the will of God, a resistance they cannot overcome in their own power: ultimately, they cannot circumcise their own hearts. Later in the book, Moses will foresee a time when the Lord will do what they cannot: he will circumcise their hearts in an age to come (Deut 30:6).

The Deuteronomic Code (Deuteronomy 12–26)

These central chapters are often called the "Deuteronomic Code" (Deut 12–26), because they resemble other law codes found in the ancient Near East, such as the Code of Hammurabi, and in the Pentateuch itself, such as the Covenant Code (Ex 21–23) and the Holiness Code (Lev 17–26). In this new code of legal material, Moses moves from his more general exhortations of fidelity to the Lord to specific commandments on a wide variety of topics.

Scholars have long puzzled over the exact rationale behind this "second law" and debated the organizing principles behind it. Although a variety of explanations have been offered, perhaps the most compelling views the material in the Deuteronomic Code (Deut 12–26) as *an expansion and application* of the laws of the Ten Commandments, first given to Israel at Mount Sinai (Ex 20) and then reiterated by Deuteronomy itself on the plains of Moab (Deut 5).[6] Strikingly, these topics follow the order of the Ten Commandments as their organizing principle:

---

[6] See Victor Hamilton, *Handbook on the Pentateuch* (Grand Rapids, Mich.: Baker Academic, 2005), 404–5.

Ten Commandments (Deut 5)	Deuteronomic Code (Deut 12–26)
1. No Other Gods or Idols (Deut 5:6–10)	1. Licit Sacrifice and Central Sanctuary (Deut 12:1–28)
2. Prohibition of Blasphemy (Deut 5:11)	2. False Prophecy, Abominable Foods (Deut 13:1—14:21)
3. Observance of the Sabbath (Deut 5:12–15)	3. Appointed Feasts, Sabbatical Year (Deut 14:22—16:17)
4. Honoring Father and Mother (Deut 5:16)	4. Judges, Priests, Leaders, King, Levites (Deut 16:18—18:22)
5. Prohibition of Murder (Deut 5:17)	5. Manslayer, Murder, Herem, Capital Crime (Deut 19:1—21:23)
6. Prohibition of Adultery (Deut 5:18)	6. Rape, Adultery, Incest, Immorality (Deut 22:13—23:14)
7. Prohibition of Stealing (Deut 5:19)	7. Destructive Loans, Kidnapping, Just Wages (Deut 23:19—24:14)
8. Prohibition of False Witness (Deut 5:20)	8. False Witness, Perversion of Justice (Deut 24:17–18)
9. Coveting Neighbor's Wife (Deut 5:21a)	9. Levirate Marriage, Fighting over Wife (Deut 25:5–12)
10. Coveting Neighbor's Property (Deut 5:21b)	10. False Measures, Dishonest Sales (Deut 25:13–16)

Although there are several passages that do not fit neatly into this basic arrangement (such as Deut 22:1–12, 24:1–4), nevertheless, the fact that the Deuteronomic Code not only contains substantial topical parallels with the Decalogue but that these topical parallels occur *in the same order* as in the Decalogue strongly suggests that what we have in these chapters is nothing less than an "expanded Decalogue".[7] If this explanation of the ordering of many of the laws is correct, it provides a fascinating biblical precedent for later "moral theology", which in the catechetical tradition of Christianity would often be organized as an expanded commentary on the implications of the Decalogue (see, for example, part 3 of the *Catechism of the Council of Trent*, published in 1566, and part 3 of the *Catechism of the Catholic Church*, published in 1992, both of which are expansions and applications of the Ten Commandments).

In any case, the specific commandments of the Deuteronomic Code variously reaffirm, revise, rescind, or add to other commandments given previously in the Torah (see also Ex 21–23; Lev 17–26). The changes (revisions, recisions, and additions) usually have a narrative explanation. For example, certain laws in Deuteronomy tend to be *harsher and stricter* than previous law codes, which is a result of Moses' experience of the stubbornness and recalcitrance of Israel in the wilderness, amply illustrated by the ten rebellions (or more) in Numbers, to which Moses refers frequently in the opening chapters. In particular, Deuteronomy is very specific about which infractions merit the death penalty. Intriguingly, each of the crimes that are punishable by death can also be linked to the Decalogue and described as grave violations of one of the Ten Commandments:

---

[7] Stephen A. Kaufman, "The Structure of the Deuteronomic Law", *Ma'arav* 1.2 (1979): 105–58.

Capital Crimes in the Deuteronomic Code

1. False Prophecy (Deut 13:1–6; 18:20–22)
2. Disregard for Priests (Deut 17:12)
3. Murder (Deut 19:11–13)
4. False Witness in Capital Case (Deut 19:15–21)
5. Rebellious Son (Deut 21:18–21)
6. Adultery (Deut 22:22)
7. Kidnapping (Deut 24:7)

In light of such data, it is worth pointing out that although the Old Testament can sometimes be caricatured as sentencing death for the least possible infraction, the reality is that the *only* crimes punishable by death are precisely those that constitute grave violations of one of the Ten Commandments.

With that said, there is an increased rigor in certain laws of the Deuteronomic Code. The premier example is the legislation concerning *centralization of worship*, widely identified by scholars as a central theme in this section of the book (see especially Deut 12). The original law code at Sinai had envisioned Israel being able to worship freely in different locations, so long as the altar of sacrifice was properly built of unworked stones (Ex 20:24–26). Already in Leviticus, this freedom of worship was severely constrained because of the people's idolatry. All slaughter of animals had to be part of a liturgical ritual at the Tabernacle (Lev 17:1–9). This command of Leviticus was workable as long as Israel was a small community traveling in the desert close to the Tabernacle sanctuary, but it would be completely impractical once the people had settled in the land of Israel. Israelites settled several days' journey from the Tabernacle would not be able to slaughter any meat.

In Deuteronomy, Moses revises the earlier laws in light of a new situation: the imminent settlement of the land. Moses could have resolved the predicament in one of two ways: he could have authorized multiple sites for sacrificial worship (similar to the multiple cities of refuge, Deut 4:41–43), or he could have maintained a single site of worship and rescinded the prohibition on profane (non-liturgical) slaughter of animals (Lev 17:1–9). He opts for the latter, because he does not trust the people to operate multiple sanctuaries throughout the land without falling into syncretism and idolatry. He prefers that worship be centralized at one place in the land, in the presence of the ark (Deut 31:9), regulated by the law, under the watchful eye of the priesthood (Deut 31:25). This adaptation of centralization to the conditions in the land is the key novelty of Deuteronomy over against earlier law codes. It requires revision of certain laws given in the Holiness Code (Lev 17–27) on the assumption that the sanctuary would be close at hand for every Israelite. Thus, it is now possible to slaughter meat apart from cultic worship (Deut 12:20–22; cf. Lev 17:1–9) and to sell an animal at home and buy another for sacrifice at the place of worship (Deut 14:24–26; cf. Lev 27:10, 33), and the major liturgical feasts become mandatory pilgrimages (Deut 16:16–17; 26:1–15).

Another issue much more prominent in Deuteronomy than in earlier law codes is *the regulation of the conquest and settlement of the Promised Land*. Because of this emphasis, we have far more laws in Deuteronomy concerned with warfare and dealing with the native populations of Canaan than previously (Deut 7:1–5; 12:1–3, 29–31; 20:1–20; 21:10–14; 25:17–19). Moses' injunctions are, at times, quite harsh: he enjoins total warfare against the Canaanite inhabitants and total destruction of their material culture, especially religious structures or objects. Significantly, his explicit reason for this severe policy is fear that the Israelites will otherwise succumb to the temptations of Canaanite paganism:

> But in the cities of these peoples that the LORD your God gives you for an inheritance, you shall save alive nothing that breathes, but you shall utterly destroy them, the Hittites and the Amorites, the Canaanites and the Perizzites, the Hivites and the Jebusites, as the LORD your God has commanded; *that they may not teach you to do according to all their abominable practices which they have done in the service of their gods*, and so to sin against the LORD your God. (Deut 20:16–18)

Within the context of the Pentateuch narrative, Moses' fear is well-founded, since the Israelites quickly reverted to paganism at the Golden Calf (Ex 32) and, much more recently, at Beth-peor (Num 25). In fact, the people are currently encamped within sight of Beth-peor (Deut 4:46), so the potential for a quick slide into idolatrous worship appears to be one of, if not *the*, driving force(s) behind the Deuteronomic legislation.

A final major concern of Moses is the continuity of leadership and authority after his death and the settlement of the land. Therefore he establishes local judges and officers (Deut 16:18–20); reaffirms the authority of the priests and judges at the central sanctuary (Deut 17:8–13); provides for the eventual possibility of a king (Deut 17:14–20); and promises the rising of a prophet like himself who will guide the people authoritatively (Deut 18:15–22). This last promise was understood, in time, as a prophecy that shaped the later messianic hopes of Israel to look for a "new Moses".

Moses' Solemnization of the Covenant (Deuteronomy 27–30)

The conclusion of Moses' second sermon emphasized that a covenant was being formed between God and Israel on the very day of Moses' proclamation of the Deuteronomic Code: "You have declared *this day* concerning the LORD that he is your God, and that you will walk in his ways ... and the LORD has declared *this day* concerning you that you are a people for his own possession" (Deut 26:17–18).

Curiously, however, Moses does not perform a covenant solemnization ritual on the plains of Moab, but he provides for one to take place after Joshua has brought the people into the land (Deut 27:2–26). After the tribes have entered the land, Joshua is to write the law on stones at the top of Mount Ebal and then celebrate a sacrificial ritual (Deut 27:5–7). Half the tribes are to ascend Mount Gerizim "to bless", and half of them Mount Ebal "for the curse". (Between these mountains lay Shechem, a centrally located city that would eventually serve as the early base for Israel's conquest of the land.) Moses then provides a litany of twelve curses to be recited to solemnize the covenant but no corresponding blessing litany, as we would have every reason to expect.

The following chapter does contain blessings (Deut 28), but not in the form of a litany, and they correspond, not to the twelve curses of the ceremony for Mount Ebal (Deut 27:15–26), but rather with the curses enumerated afterward (Deut 28:15–68). The blessings (Deut 28:1–14) and curses (Deut 28:15–68) formally correspond to the blessing and curse lists that typically conclude an ancient Near Eastern treaty. Note, however, that the listing of curses (fifty-four verses) is three times longer than that of the blessings (only fourteen verses).

In sum, after the Deuteronomic law code, we have a description of a covenant ritual (Deut 27) and the conclusion of a formal covenant document (Deut 28). These are followed by yet another sermon, urging faithfulness to the covenant Moses has just offered Israel, especially in view of the curses he has just enumerated (Deut 30). At the end of this exhortation, he calls upon the "witnesses" of the covenant between God and Israel. In other ancient Near Eastern cultures, these "witnesses" would have been a host of gods, but here it is "heaven and earth" (Deut 30:19). In this way, remarkably, the whole cosmos is called to witness the fact that Israel is entering into a covenant relationship with God that promises life for obedience and death and destruction for infidelity (cf. Deut 4:26).

The Song of Moses and the Authority of Joshua (Deuteronomy 31–32)

Moses now turns his attention to three final vehicles that will perpetuate his legacy and authority in the generations to come.

The first is his successor, Joshua, who is reaffirmed as the personal bearer of Moses' mantle of authority (Deut 31:1–8, 14–23). The second is the Book of the Law (Hebrew Torah), the written form of the Deuteronomic covenant, which was placed beside the ark (Deut 31:9, 24–26) and ordained to be read aloud to Israel every seven years at the Feast of Booths (Tabernacles) (Deut 31:9–13). The third is the Song of Moses, a lengthy poem describing Israel's offenses against God and his application of curses to them (Deut 32:1–43). This he teaches to the people of Israel as a reminder, a historical-cultural "I told you so!" that would function as a rebuke when the events it described inevitably took place. Moses' successor, his law, and his song would perpetuate his memory and authority for the people of Israel into the next generation and beyond.

The Blessing and Death of Moses (Deuteronomy 33–34)

Deuteronomy concludes with the "deathbed" blessing of Moses on the twelve tribes (Deut 33) and the brief account of his death (Deut 34). The Mosaic blessing is clearly parallel in form to Jacob's "deathbed" blessing of his sons at the end of the book of Genesis (Gen 49:1–27). In Deuteronomy, Moses is a new Jacob figure: if Jacob was the father of Israel the family, Moses is the father of Israel the nation (Deut 33). Both Genesis and Deuteronomy close with the blessing of the tribes by a father figure and the account of his death. This lends literary closure to the Pentateuch and positions Genesis and Deuteronomy as bookends around the central historical narrative, Exodus through Numbers.

While Jacob privileged Joseph and Judah (the royal tribe) and bestowed "non-blessings" on Reuben, Simeon, and Levi (Gen 49), Moses privileges Joseph and Levi (the priestly tribe) and provides at least a modest blessing for all the tribes with the exception of Simeon (Deut 33). In this way, the Pentateuch closes without a clear focus on the hope of a ruler from the tribe of Judah (Gen 49:10). Instead, any hope for a Messiah is directed toward the promise of a prophet like Moses (Deut 18:18), who is, significantly, still to come according to the last lines of the book:

> *And there has not arisen a prophet since in Israel like Moses,* whom the LORD knew face to face, none like him for all the signs and the wonders which the LORD sent him to do in the land of Egypt, to Pharaoh and to all his servants and to all his land, and for all the mighty power and all the great and terrible deeds which Moses wrought in the sight of all Israel. (Deut 34:10–12)

With these words, the Pentateuch closes on a note of expectancy. Although Joshua has arisen as Moses' successor, it is Moses himself who remains enshrined as the towering figure in Israel's history, the prophet than whom none greater has arisen, who points beyond himself to some future figure who will recapitulate the signs and wonders of the man "whom the LORD knew face to face" (Deut 34:10).

Historical Issues in Deuteronomy

In modern critical scholarship, the book of Deuteronomy is typically associated in some way with the reforms launched by King Josiah of Judah (641–609 B.C.). According to the book of Kings, during Josiah's reign, "the Book of the Law" (Hebrew *sepher hattorah*) was found in the Temple during the reign of King Josiah (2 Kings 22:8–10). After hearing it, Josiah was deeply moved to repentance and immediately implemented sweeping religious reforms, including the destruction of all sanctuaries other than the Jerusalem Temple (2 Kings 22:11—23:28). Indeed, many scholars have accepted the theory that this Book of the Law was in fact not discovered by Josiah but, rather, composed *de novo* and put forward as a pious fraud in order to centralize the cultic authority of the Davidic king in Jerusalem. Others think the book was compiled of older materials and simply promulgated at the time of Josiah.

King Josiah and the Finding of the Book of the Law

Deist intellectuals and freethinkers of the eighteenth century first suggested that Deuteronomy was a composition of the Josianic period, based on the fact that the centralization of worship called for by Deuteronomy had not been fully implemented (according to them) by any previous king. At the beginning of the nineteenth century, the German liberal Protestant Bible scholar Wilhelm de Wette argued for identifying the "Book of the Law" found by Josiah as a copy of Deuteronomy and, further, that Deuteronomy was composed at that time,

not truly "found" or "rediscovered". A seventh-century B.C. date for Deuteronomy, at least for its final form, has been assumed by most professional biblical
scholars since.

Indeed, for Julius Wellhausen, the seventh-century Deuteronomist was the
fixed point around which he developed his theories of the development of
Israelite religion and the relative order of the Pentateuchal literary strata in the
JEDP hypothesis. He assumed that (1) the historical account of 2 Kings 22–23
was largely reliable; (2) Deuteronomy (or a substantial form thereof) was the
law book of Josiah's reform; (3) Deuteronomy was not "found" but actually
composed at that time; (4) biblical texts (including Deuteronomy itself) that
provided evidence against this theory were historically unreliable.[8]

Indeed, there are good reasons to think that the book found in the Temple
during Josiah's reign was (or included) some form of Deuteronomy. For example, many of Josiah's reforms reflect laws unique to, or emphasized in, this book:
(1) the centralization of worship and the elimination of rival sanctuaries (Deut
12; 2 Kings 23:4–20); (2) the observance of Passover in Jerusalem alone (Deut 16;
2 Kings 23:21–22); (3) the elimination of mediums and others who dabble in the
occult (Deut 18:14–22; 2 Kings 23:24); and (4) the conformity of the king's rule
to the Book of the Law (Deut 17:18–19; 2 Kings 22:11; 23:2–3).

However, identifying Deuteronomy as the law book found during the reign
of Josiah does not demonstrate that Deuteronomy was *composed* in order to
justify Josiah's reforms. By analogy, Martin Luther's "reform" of Catholic faith
and theology was inspired by the books of Galatians and Romans, but this does
not mean that those epistles were written in the sixteenth century. The account
in the book of Kings is perfectly plausible if taken at face value: after the utter
neglect of the law of God under the reign of King Manasseh (2 Kings 21), the
book of the Torah was in fact rediscovered in the Temple by Hilkiah the high
priest during his work in the sanctuary (2 Kings 22:8). It seems inconsistent to
take every aspect of the account in 2 Kings 22 as historical *except* for the explicit
claim that the Book of the Law had been lost but now was found.

Internal Evidence for the Antiquity of Deuteronomy

Moreover, while King Josiah's seventh-century reform does seem inspired by
Deuteronomy, internal features of the book suggest a time and place of composition different from seventh-century Jerusalem.

1. Deuteronomy has very little role for *the king* in public life. Although it certainly forecasts a future time when kings will have to follow certain rules (Deut
17:14–20), by and large, the laws of the book reflect a decentralized society
without any of the trappings or indications of a royal bureaucracy (for example,
a standing army, taxation, royal officials). Yet in Josiah's day, the monarchy
dominated Judean society.

2. Deuteronomy also does not reflect any of the ideas surrounding *the covenant
with David*—above all God's choice of *Jerusalem* as his dwelling place or the

---

[8] See Julius Wellhausen, *Prolegomena to the History of Israel* (1885; repr., Atlanta: Scholars Press, 1994),
32–34.

investment of the hopes of Israel in the Davidic dynasty (cf. Pss 2, 72, 89, 132). Yet there is no reason to doubt that by the time of Josiah, the theology of the Davidic covenant was an integral part of Judean culture, and so it appears as a central theme in the historical books (1 Kings 1:36, 39). The writer of 2 Kings highlights Josiah as an important heir of the Davidic covenant, and by the end of 2 Kings the hope for the nation is tied up with a final act of mercy toward Jehoiachin, the last heir of David and hope for the fulfillment of the Davidic covenant (2 Kings 25:27–30). If Deuteronomy is really entirely constructed as a seventh-century attempt to centralize power in Jerusalem and under a Davidic monarch, the failure to mention Jerusalem, Zion, or David is inexplicable.

3. The military and religious threats to Israel in Deuteronomy are *the seven indigenous Canaanite nations*: the Hittites, the Girgashites, the Amorites, the Canaanites, the Perizzites, the Hivites, and the Jebusites (Deut 7:1–11). None of these ethnic groups were even identifiable by the time of Josiah. Instead, in the seventh century B.C., the military threat to Israel was posed by the Egyptians and Babylonians, and the religious threat by the Sidonians, Moabites, and Ammonites (2 Kings 23:13).

"Priests" and "Levites" in Deuteronomy

The books of Exodus through Numbers make a clear distinction between the Levites descended from Aaron, who serve as priests proper, and non-Aaronic Levites, who have a diaconal role. In Deuteronomy, however, Moses shows no interest in the distinction but, instead, refers in a general way to "the Levitical priests" (Hebrew *hakkohanim halevi'im*).

Wellhausen and the majority of biblical scholars since have explained this by arguing that no distinction between priests and Levites was known at the time Deuteronomy was written (that is, during the reign of Josiah), that the distinction was introduced by Ezekiel, and that it was only implemented in the postexilic period. They dismiss all texts that indicate that the distinction is preexilic (Exodus, Leviticus, Numbers, 1 Kings 8:4, 1–2 Chronicles) as unhistorical.

A less drastic explanation would be that Moses is speaking to lay Israelites in Deuteronomy and is unconcerned with technical cultic matters dealt with extensively in previous legislation. Thus he employs the term "priests" (Hebrew *kohanim*) in a more general sense as "clergy" or "clerics", without bothering to distinguish the ranks or duties of the sons of Aaron from other Levites.

---

4. Josiah's Book of the Law was found by Hilkiah the high priest in the Temple (2 Kings 22:8), but Deuteronomy famously makes no mention of the Temple and never describes the role of the high priest. Wellhausen held that the author of Deuteronomy did not even know of the office of high priest, which makes the finding of Deuteronomy by Hilkiah the high priest quite ironic, since he must have been a party to the plot to promulgate the book as a pious fraud.

5. Three characteristics of Deuteronomy are highly unlikely to be the marks of a writer trying to centralize the cult in Jerusalem in the late seventh century B.C.: (a) the consistent identification of the site of the central sanctuary as "the place which the LORD your God will choose" (Deut 12:5) *rather than Jerusalem*; (b) the command at the end of Deuteronomy to build an altar and hold a covenant-renewal ceremony on Mount Ebal (Deut 27:1–8), in the territory of

northern Israel; and (c) the extensive blessings given to the northern Josephite tribes (Deut 33:13–17), while a minimal blessing is bestowed on Judah (Deut 33:7). In particular, Deuteronomy's failure clearly to identify "the place" chosen by God could lead to irresolvable disputes with those who might champion Gibeon (1 Kings 3:4), Bethel (Gen 28:10–22; 1 Kings 12:29), Dan (1 Kings 12:29), or some other traditional site as the "chosen place". In fact, this is precisely what happened: in time there was a schism with the Samaritans, who claimed that Mount Gerizim was the "chosen place" and built their temple there (Jn 4:20).

For these and many other internal reasons, a large number of scholars who work on Deuteronomy are convinced that the materials of the book are older than the time of Josiah, even if they believe a form of the book was promulgated at that time.[9] Indeed, as we saw in chapter 4, the book of Deuteronomy more closely resembles Hittite covenant documents from the late second millennium B.C.—the probable time of the exodus—than covenant documents from either earlier or later time periods.[10]

The Question of Cultic Centralization

However, if Deuteronomy is substantially old within the history of Israel as a nation, it is necessary to explain why the centralization of the cult required by the book is so sporadic until the time of Josiah. The Scriptures themselves actually provide a fairly coherent explanation of this development: Deuteronomy is quite clear that the centralization of the cult is tied to the nation experiencing "rest" from warfare (Deut 12:8–10). In other words, when travel is safe and easy, national worship should be centralized at the shrine where the ark resides (Deut 12:10). At times when there is not "rest" and safe pilgrimage is impossible, the implication seems to be that it is permissible to build altars in places other than the central location (compare Ex 20:24–26 with Deut 27:5–7).

In Israel's subsequent history, there was "rest" for a while under Joshua (Josh 21:43–45; 22:4; 23:1), and the central sanctuary was located in Shiloh (Josh 18:1; 21:2; 22:12; Judg 21:19; 1 Sam 1–4; Jer 7:12). The "rest" was lost again during the time of the Judges (Judg 2:14), and the Israelite cult was thrown into total disarray by the sack of Shiloh and the capture of the ark by the Philistines (1 Sam 4:1–7:2). The "rest" of the Lord was not regained until the time of David (2 Sam 7:1, 11), who again pursued a policy of cult centralization by bringing the ark to his capital, Jerusalem (2 Sam 6:1–19), and making plans for a permanent Temple there (2 Sam 7:1–3). This plan was carried out by Solomon (1 Kings 6–8), and after the building of the Temple, there is no indication of other sanctuaries of the Lord until the splitting of the kingdom between Rehoboam and Jeroboam (1 Kings 12). Jeroboam's policy of cult *decentralization*

---

[9]Jeffrey H. Tigay, *Deuteronomy*, JPS Torah Commentary 5 (Philadelphia: Jewish Publication Society, 2003).

[10]Kenneth A. Kitchen, *On the Reliability of the Old Testament* (Grand Rapids, Mich.: Eerdmans, 2003), 283–307; Kline, *Treaty of the Great King*; Joshua Berman, "CTH 133 and the Hittite Provenance of Deuteronomy 13", *Journal of Biblical Literature* 130.1 (2011): 25–44.

Do All Laws Reflect Their Time of Composition?

Older critical scholars such as de Wette and Wellhausen assumed that religious texts reflect the actual practice of their time of composition. Since centralization of the cult appeared not to have taken place until the time of Josiah, they assumed Deuteronomy 12:5–14 and similar laws were composed at that time. They also maintained a great deal of skepticism about the historical reliability of any of the biblical materials until near the end of the monarchy. Thus, Deuteronomy's own historical claims, as well as early testimonies to the existence of the ark and the Tabernacle, were dismissed (e.g., 1 Sam 1–4), whereas the account of Josiah's reform (2 Kings 22–23) was received as substantially accurate.

However, we now realize that religious and other legal texts often do not correspond to the actual practice at the time of their composition and sometimes implement ideal legislation that is never, or only much later, actualized. For example: (1) the Code of Hammurabi was promulgated ca. 1700 B.C., but it was virtually never followed in Mesopotamian law courts subsequently. (2) Plato's *Laws* did not reflect the structure of Athenian society and in fact have never been implemented in any society. (3) The Declaration of Independence of the United States declared in the late eighteenth century that "we hold these truths to be self-evident, that all men were created equal", yet the Constitution of the United States manifestly did not recognize the equality of persons of non-European descent. Full civil equality for persons of African descent was not a reality in the United States until the late twentieth century. Yet we cannot, for that reason, consider the Declaration of Independence, or parts of it, to have been written during or after the Civil Rights Movement of the 1960s. (4) In a similar way, ecclesiastical history is replete with examples of canonical legislation enacted by councils or promulgated by popes that was contrary to current practice in much of the Church and was only much later implemented on a consistent basis: the Council of Nicaea (A.D. 325) defined the divinity of Christ, but in fact Arianism continued to be politically dominant in the Church for generations.

(1 Kings 12:25–33) clearly indicates that the cult of the Lord had been centralized to some significant extent under Solomon. After Solomon, however, the "rest" was lost again (1 Kings 14:25–28), competing sanctuaries were rebuilt (1 Kings 14:23), and none of the successive kings had the political and religious resolve to remove them (1 Kings 15:14; 22:44; 2 Kings 12:3; and so on) until the time of Josiah and his reforms (2 Kings 22–23).

These considerations need to be brought to bear when evaluating the historical background of the book of Deuteronomy. There is no strong reason to assume that the laws of Deuteronomy can be matched with social, civil, or religious practice at the time of its composition: in fact, the book insists that such is not the case (see Deut 12:8)! The call for centralization of the cult (Deut 12:1–28) is not proof that the work was composed during or after the reforms of Josiah, nor is the law for the king (Deut 17:14–20) proof that it was composed after the establishment of the monarchy. Civil and ecclesiastical legislators can and do promulgate laws that are not immediately implemented or only inconsistently implemented or that anticipate situations that may arise in the future but are not of immediate concern (see sidebar).

Deuteronomy and Ancient Hittite Treaties

The similarity between Deuteronomy and the structure and contents of the fourteenth-century Hittite treaties (political covenants) is important for an evaluation of its date of composition. Although Deuteronomy does share some features with later covenant documents like the vassal treaties of Esarhaddon of Assyria (reigned 681–669 B.C.), these are mostly limited to some similar expressions in the curse sections of the documents. Otherwise, a better correspondence of structure, included elements, and several specifics are found with the earlier Hittite documents.[11] Moreover, there was extensive trade, communication, and diplomacy between the Hittite Empire and Egypt in the New Kingdom period (ca. 1550–1050 B.C.), and one of the best-preserved Hittite treaty-covenants is between the Hittite king Hattusilis III and Pharaoh Ramesses II, often thought to be the pharaoh of the exodus. Someone trained as a scribe or diplomat in the Egyptian royal court could have been familiar with this treaty-literature and its forms. This fact together with evidence discussed in previous chapters concerning the New Kingdom Egyptian cultural background of the ark and the Tabernacle combine to create a possible temporal and cultural setting for the origin of the Pentateuchal legal materials, which were subsequently edited in the course of Israel's history.

Deuteronomy in the Living Tradition

Like the other books of the Pentateuch, Deuteronomy plays a prominent role in both the writings of the New Testament and the living tradition of the Church. However, its role in Christian theology also presents us with a striking paradox.

On the one hand, Deuteronomy reaches great poetic and spiritual heights in its descriptions of the love of God for his people and the total, passionate devotion that should characterize the response of his people to that love. Because of this, it has functioned in a preeminent way as a source for moral and legal teaching and, in a special way, for what today we refer to as "social doctrine" (care for the poor, just wages, and so on). On the other hand, Deuteronomy also contains some of the strongest condemnations of the people of Israel, the harshest laws, the most severe punishments, and the most horrific curses of any biblical book. It also contains, for the first time in the Pentateuch, the permission to divorce and the command for *herem* warfare, in which Israel is to put to death all of the inhabitants of the Promised Land—men, women, and children. What are we to make of this complex juxtaposition of materials in a single book? How has the tradition dealt with this text?

In what follows, we will begin by highlighting a few of the more positive appropriations of Deuteronomy before turning to the way in which its morally difficult teachings have been handled.

Deuteronomy, Moral Teaching, and Love for the Poor

As mentioned above, the book of Deuteronomy has long functioned as a source of moral and spiritual teaching as well as of rules for social interaction that would

---

[11] Kitchen, *Reliability of the Old Testament*, 283–307; Berman, "CTH 133 and the Hittite Provenance of Deuteronomy 13", 25–44.

later come to be known as "social doctrine" or "social justice". It was one of the most popular books of Jewish Scripture in Jesus' day; Jesus himself quotes it in the accounts of his temptation in the wilderness (Mt 4:4, 7, 10; cf. Deut 6:13, 18; 8:3); and it is the source of the *Shema* (Deut 6:4–6), which Jesus identifies as the greatest of all the commandments (Mt 22:37–38).

In addition to these various elements, one aspect of Deuteronomy's social teaching in particular stands out: its declaration that *because* the poor will always exist, charity toward them is commanded of the people of Israel:

> For the poor will never cease out of the land; therefore I command you, You shall open wide your hand to your brother, to the needy and to the poor, in the land. (Deut 15:11)

Notice here that there is no place for the idea that, because it is impossible to eliminate poverty totally from human society, nothing should be done about it. To the contrary, it is precisely because of the insurmountable nature of the human condition that the chosen people must do everything in their power (with an "open hand") to ameliorate it.

Indeed, the singular character of Deuteronomy as a source for this particular social doctrine is highlighted in the *Catechism of the Catholic Church* when it teaches that the Old Testament juridical measures of the Jubilee forgiveness of debts, the prohibition of giving loans at interest (a.k.a. usury), the daily payment of laborers, and the right of the poor and marginalized to glean the edges of fields and vines all together "answer the exhortation of *Deuteronomy*" to open wide one's hands "to the needy and to the poor in the land" (*CCC* 2449, citing Deut 15:11). With these words, the Church recognizes the book of Deuteronomy as a foundational source for her teaching on social justice and love for the poor.

The Circumcision of the Heart and Interior Transformation

Along similar lines, Deuteronomy is also the principal source of the key notion of the "circumcision of the heart" (see Deut 10:16)—that is, the idea that the commands of God must be kept not only out of exterior duty but out of an interior motivation animated by love. However, it also implies that this circumcision is something that the Deuteronomic law itself does not yet bestow but that is held out for the future, which God himself will accomplish:

> And when all these things come upon you, the blessing and the curse, which I have set before you, and you call them to mind among all the nations where the LORD your God has driven you, and return to the LORD your God, you and your children, and obey his voice in all that I command you this day, with all your heart and with all your soul; then the LORD your God will restore your fortunes, and have compassion upon you, and he will gather you again from all the peoples where the LORD your God has scattered you. If your outcasts are in the uttermost parts of heaven, from there the LORD your God will gather you, and from there he will fetch you; and the LORD your God will bring you into the land which your fathers possessed, that you may possess it; and he will make you more prosperous

and numerous than your fathers. *And the* LORD *your God will circumcise your heart and the heart of your offspring, so that you will love the* LORD *your God with all your heart and with all your soul, that you may live.* And the LORD your God will put all these curses upon your foes and enemies who persecuted you. *And you shall again obey the voice of the* LORD, *and keep all his commandments which I command you this day.* (Deut 30:1–8)

In other words, the book of Deuteronomy in its canonical form places Israel under fearsome covenant curses that will be actualized inevitably. Israel will break the covenant, but in the aftermath of that disaster the Lord will intervene to "circumcise their hearts". Circumcision was a covenant-making ritual (Gen 17); "circumcision of the heart" would refer to a divine act of covenant-making effecting an interior transformation of God's people, empowering them to fulfill the law. Deuteronomy is paradoxical: although Moses himself sees clearly the heights of love that a covenant relationship with God requires (Deut 6:4–5), he simultaneously provides for Israel an accommodated legislation because he recognizes their incapacity to muster this love on their own (Deut 31:27–29). He knows their true transformation will require a divine act in the future (Deut 29:4; 30:6), the "circumcision of the heart".

In hindsight, we may say that Moses sees the necessity of the New Covenant and its future coming, even while providing the definitive form of the Old Covenant for the people of Israel (cf. Rom 2:28–29). Indeed, the apostle Paul will eventually identify this "spiritual circumcision" as something that takes place through the mystery of baptism, when he writes to the Church at Colossae: "In him also you were circumcised with a circumcision made without hands, by putting off the body of flesh in the circumcision of Christ; and you were buried with him in baptism, in which you were also raised with him" (Col 2:11–12). Baptism thus replaces circumcision as the covenant-making ritual of the New Covenant.

Deuteronomy and the Hardness of the Wilderness Generation's Heart

This idea of the circumcised heart provides an excellent segue into those aspects of Deuteronomy which are more morally problematic and seem to pose special difficulties for contemporary readers. How are we to deal with these passages?

Once again, recourse to the normative witness of the New Testament and the living tradition can provide us with reliable guides to the fact that not all of the legal material of the book of Deuteronomy has the same origin or enduring value. The premier example of this comes from the famous exchange between Jesus and the Pharisees over Moses' permission to divorce one's wife (Deut 24:1–4). In this exchange, Jesus responds to the Pharisees' objection that Moses commanded the Israelites to divorce their wives by declaring:

> They [the Pharisees] said to him [Jesus], "Why then did Moses command one to give a certificate of divorce, and to put her away?" [Deut 24:1–4] He said to them, "*For your hardness of heart Moses allowed you to divorce your wives, but from the beginning it was not so.* And I say to you: whoever divorces his wife, except for unchastity, and marries another, commits adultery." (Mt 19:7–8)

With these words, a case can be made that in at least three ways Jesus provides us with a hermeneutical key for unlocking the enigma of Deuteronomy when he addresses the issue of divorce.

First, Jesus attributes this command of Deuteronomy, *not to God, but to Moses* (Deut 24:1). In doing so, he follows literary indicators in the text itself. Whereas the laws of the first and second Sinai covenants are repeatedly prefaced by the phrase "The Lord spoke to Moses" or a similar phrase, almost all of Deuteronomy is presented as first-person speech of Moses. God does not speak to Moses until near the end of the book (Deut 31:16–23). None of the laws in the central legislation are prefaced by "The Lord spoke to Moses" (Deut 12–26). In Deuteronomy, Moses takes responsibility for the promulgation of its laws in a unique way, unlike the accounts in Exodus–Numbers:

> [Moses said:] "And now, O Israel, give heed to the statutes and the ordinances *which I teach you*, and do them; that you may live.... You shall not add to the word *which I command you*, nor take from it; that you may keep the commandments of the LORD your God *which I command you*.... Behold, *I have taught you statutes and ordinances*, as the LORD my God commanded me, that you should do them.... And what great nation is there, that has statutes and ordinances so righteous as all this law *which I set before you this day*?" (Deut 4:1–2, 5, 8)

To be sure, Moses is approved by God and bears divine authority, but the emphasis on Moses as commander, teacher, and lawgiver in Deuteronomy is distinct from earlier parts of the Pentateuch, where Moses is the passive scribe who hears God's word and communicates it to the people.

A text near the end of Deuteronomy suggests how to understand the difference between the relationship that exists between God, Moses, and the law in Deuteronomy from that in previous covenants:

> These are the words of the covenant *which the LORD commanded Moses to make with the sons of Israel* in the land of Moab, besides the covenant which he had made with them at Horeb. (Deut 29:1)

Here a clear distinction is made between the Deuteronomic covenant and the covenant at Mount Sinai, which we know was broken and renewed once (in the Levitical covenant). Whereas the first Sinai covenant was described as "the covenant which the LORD has made with you [Israel]" (Ex 24:8) and the renewed Sinai covenant was described as the covenant "I [the LORD] have made ... with you [Moses] and with the sons of Israel" (Ex 34:27), Deuteronomy is described as the covenant "the Lord commanded *Moses to make* with Israel" (Deut 29:1). These differences are not without significance. We are seeing an increased mediation and triangulation of the covenant relationship as it progresses through these three stages. At the Deuteronomic stage, it is phrased *almost* as if God is no longer a party to the covenant but has stepped aside while bestowing on Moses (his deputy or proxy) the authority to make a covenant with Israel. The opening words of the book capture its spirit: "These are the words that Moses spoke to all Israel" (Deut 1:1).

Thus, when Jesus attributes the Deuteronomic law of divorce *to Moses* rather than to God, his interpretation follows literary indicators present in the text that highlight Moses as lawgiver in this book. The theological significance of the literary distinction between the direct divine law-giving in Exodus through Numbers and the Mosaic promulgation in Deuteronomy is to create distance between the Lord and the Mosaic legislation. The laws of Deuteronomy do not always represent the divine ideals but in certain places are *accommodations* or *compromises* introduced by Moses.

Second, Jesus specifies the *reason* Moses introduced accommodations and compromises into Israel's sacred law: "for your hardness of heart" (Mt 19:8). The "hardness of heart" of Israel was thoroughly demonstrated during the wilderness wanderings in Numbers, which culminated in the apostasy with the Baal of Peor (Num 25). Moses, then, has tailored some of the laws of Deuteronomy as responses to the rebellious nature of the people, whose hearts remain hard and uncircumcised (Deut 10:16).

Third, Jesus specifies that certain divine ideals were expressed earlier in Scripture and salvation history, from which the Mosaic law degrades: "but from the beginning it was not so" (Mt 19:8). In this instance, the reference seems to be to the original state of the first married couple, Adam and Eve, in the garden prior to sin, who provide the model of the "one flesh" union of husband and wife, without any thought or hint of the possibility of a breaking of that bond (Gen 2).

Taken together, these principles derived from Jesus' response to the Pharisees constitute an important hermeneutical principle for interpreting some of the laws of Deuteronomy: *laws that seem disharmonious with principles expressed elsewhere in Scripture may be examples of Moses accommodating the divine ideals expressed earlier to the sinfulness of Israel.* It is another example of Saint Paul's hermeneutical principle: "[The law] was added because of transgressions" (Gal 3:19).

Deuteronomy as a Self-Retiring Witness to Israel's Sinfulness

This principle may be applied to more laws of Deuteronomy than simply the permission for divorce. Scanning the Deuteronomic Code (Deut 12–26), we find several laws besides the permission for divorce (Deut 24:1–4) that are novelties compared to earlier Pentateuchal legislation, including (1) the centralization of the cult (Deut 12:1–28); (2) the permission for a king (Deut 17:14–20); (3) the command of total (*herem*) warfare against the Canaanites (Deut 20:16–18); (4) the permission to marry captured foreign wives (Deut 21:10–14). Each of these represents accommodations of divine ideals to the moral state of Israel:

First, in the original Sinai covenant, Israel was allowed great freedom in the choice of place to worship (Ex 20:24–26), but such freedom was abused already in the wilderness, leading to a restriction of sacrifice to the Tabernacle (Lev 17:1–9). Moses adapts this principle to the settled conditions of the land in the Deuteronomic Code, providing for a single sacrificial sanctuary in Israel. This is not because of the moral rectitude of Israel, but expressly because he fears the heretical and syncretistic perversion of worship if shrines are permitted throughout the land (Deut 12:2–4, 8–9, 29–31).

Second, neither the first Sinai covenant (Ex 20–24) nor the second (Ex 34–Lev 27) foresaw any kind of royal institution in Israel. The only central authority provided was the priesthood, centered at the Tabernacle. *Theocracy* is the divine ideal in the Pentateuch; the whole narrative of the exodus to Sinai suggests that God alone is the king of Israel, not any human king (for example, the pharaoh). It is only in Deuteronomy for the first time that we find the possibility that Israel might appoint a human king (Deut 17:14–20), as long as his role is limited. One of Moses' successors, Samuel, will call marked attention to the drawbacks and pitfalls a human monarch poses for Israel (1 Sam 8:1–22); nonetheless Moses provides the possibility for one, because during the wilderness wanderings the people have not shown themselves capable of being governed by prophet and priest alone.

Third, in previous legislation, the people of Israel were commanded to destroy the altars of the false gods, make no covenant with them, and "drive out" the people of the land of Canaan (Ex 34:11–16; Num 33:50–56). Nothing at all is said of destroying them utterly. In Deuteronomy, however, after the apostasy on the plains of Moab (Num 25), Moses places the indigenous Canaanite populations under the "ban" (Hebrew *herem*). According to this rule of warfare, although Israel may spare the cities outside the Promised Land, within it they must destroy every Canaanite who does not flee, and all their goods as well (Deut 12:16–18). Theologically, this *herem* warfare is one of the most difficult issues in the Old Testament: an excursus will be devoted to it below (see chapter 11 on Joshua). Here we must limit ourselves to pointing out that Moses gives this command, not because of the righteousness of Israel, but because of its weakness and tendency to succumb to the temptations of paganism (Deut 20:16–18), already demonstrated at the Calf and at Beth-peor. Moses would rather that the debased Canaanites be destroyed than that Israel become like them and the covenantal plan of salvation for all the nations be derailed: "that they may not teach you to do according to all their abominable practices which they have done in the service of their gods, and so to sin against the LORD your God" (Deut 20:18).

Fourth, previous passages of the Pentateuch placed a high value on Israelites not intermarrying with foreigners who did not share their cult and culture (Gen 24:1–4; 26:34–35; 28:1–2; 34:14; Lev 21:13–14). However, in Deuteronomy Moses provides for Israelite men to find their wives among foreign captives (Deut 21:10–14). This is far from the ideal form of marriage. Instead, it is an accommodation to the desires of Israelite soldiers, while providing certain safeguards for the treatment of female prisoners of war that respect their human dignity (Deut 21:12–13) and guarantee them some legal rights (Deut 21:14), which is preferable to the abuses that otherwise would take place.

The presence of accommodated or compromised laws within Scripture is a complex issue that strikes many readers as counterintuitive. How can imperfections be part of Sacred Scripture, much less be considered inspired? In response, it is helpful to remember that Aristotle, later followed by Thomas Aquinas, points out that the wise legislator will not necessarily enact perfect laws if they are beyond the capacity of his people to follow; rather, he will accommodate his standards to a level practical for them.[12] Therefore, the presence of such laws in the book of Deuteronomy does not necessarily entail a wholesale endorsement of their principles. Indeed, already in the Old Testament various prophets were aware that certain Mosaic laws did not represent God's highest will for his people. Malachi famously rails against the permission of divorce: "I hate divorce, says the LORD the God of Israel" (Mal 2:16). Likewise, when Ezekiel recites the salvation history of Israel, he describes the law-giving to the second generation in the wilderness (that is, Deuteronomy) in these terms: "Moreover I gave them statutes that were not good and ordinances by which they could not have life" (Ezek 20:25).

Perhaps most important of all, *the book of Deuteronomy itself* suggests that the laws of Deuteronomy do not possess the same degree of holiness or permanence as the Ten Commandments when it describes Moses' commands to the Levites as to where the Book of the Law he has just given should be kept:

> When Moses had finished writing the words of this law in a book, to the very end, Moses commanded the Levites who carried the ark of the covenant of the LORD, *"Take this book of the law, and put it by the side of the ark of the covenant of the LORD your God, that it may be there for a witness against you.* For I know how rebellious and stubborn you are; behold, while I am yet alive with you, today you have been rebellious against the LORD; how much more after my death!" (Deut 31:24–27)

Notice here that, in contrast to the Ten Commandments, which are kept *inside* the Ark of the Covenant, the Book of the Law of Deuteronomy is put "by the side" of the ark, suggesting its impermanence and different status (Deut 31:26). Moreover, Moses reveals that this law is not merely prescriptive but is to function as a "witness against" the rebellious and stubborn people of Israel. It is therefore meant to function as a testament to just how hard the hearts of the wilderness generation have become. In that sense, we may say that the covenant of Deuteronomy, in its present canonical form, has a built-in obsolescence, or is designed to be self-retiring. Indeed, when Jesus expresses criticism of certain aspects of the Mosaic law, he is not inaugurating an evasive maneuver to circumvent difficult aspects of the Old Law, but is, rather, standing in a tradition rooted in the Law and Prophets themselves.

The Prophet Like Moses and the Messiah

One final aspect of Deuteronomy worth highlighting is its prophetic forecast of a "prophet like Moses" (Deut 18). In later Jewish and Christian tradition, this oracle came to be interpreted as a prophecy of the Messiah, who would perform signs and wonders akin to those of Moses himself, as a visible sign of his identity and authenticity. From the very beginning of the Church, the apostle Peter and

---

[12] *Summa Theologica* I-II, q. 96, a. 2, trans. the Fathers of the English Dominican Province (1948; repr., Westminster, Md.: Christian Classics, 1981).

others saw this oracle fulfilled in the words and deeds of Jesus, as the apostle himself declares before the Sanhedrin in the Acts of the Apostles:

> Repent therefore, and turn again, that your sins may be blotted out, that times of refreshing may come from the presence of the Lord, and that he may send the Christ appointed for you, Jesus, whom heaven must receive until the time for establishing all that God spoke by the mouth of his holy prophets from of old. Moses said, "The Lord God will raise up for you a prophet from your brethren as he raised me up. You shall listen to him in whatever he tells you. And it shall be that every soul that does not listen to that prophet shall be destroyed from the people." (Acts 3:19–23, citing Deut 18:19)

The Book of Deuteronomy in the Lectionary

Since Moses establishes that the book of Deuteronomy shall be read at the Feast of Tabernacles every seven years for all Israel's history (31:10–13), it stands in a perpetual liturgical "Today" (cf. Heb 3:7, 13; 4:7). Every generation of Israel that reads Deuteronomy, ever time they read it, is addressed as those who experienced the exodus, heard the divine voice at Sinai, entered the Sinai covenant, and are now—at this very moment—called to enter into the Deuteronomic covenant (Deut 5:1–5). The canonical Moses *re-presents* Sinai—which was itself a liturgical celebration (Ex 24:1–8)—in a liturgical manner for every successive generation of the people of Israel. Thus, since Deuteronomy is Moses' great homily composed for liturgical proclamation at periodic celebrations of covenant renewal down through the history of God's people, it is highly appropriate that the Church continues to proclaim Deuteronomy in the covenant-renewing liturgy of the Eucharist.

In contemporary times, the Roman Lectionary includes a modest number of readings from Deuteronomy. None of the specific laws in the Deuteronomic Code (Deut 12–26) are ever read in the regular course of the Lectionary. Because so many are accommodated to the particular situation of Israel about to enter the Promised Land, application of these laws to Christian life poses a homiletical challenge that the Lectionary avoids. Instead, the Church values most the many passages at the beginning and end of Deuteronomy that summarize the high points of salvation history as a motivation for both gratitude and obedience to God and/or succinctly summarize the essence of the covenant as a relationship of love with God.

The three passages of Deuteronomy read at solemnities fall into one or both of these categories. Thus, on Trinity Sunday, Moses' recitation of the great events of the exodus and wilderness wanderings is read, in which the Lord demonstrated vis-à-vis the gods of Egypt that he alone is the one, true God. Likewise, the recollection of God's great love in electing Israel (Deut 7:6–11) fits well with the theme of God's love that permeates the celebration of the Solemnity of the Most Sacred Heart; and Moses' exhortation not to forget God's mercy and love in sending the manna in the wilderness finds a Eucharistic application on the Feast of Corpus Christi. Another summary of salvation history, which

Moses prescribes for the Israelite pilgrim to recite on arrival at the sanctuary (Deut 26:4–10), is used to remind us of the history of God's pilgrim people at the beginning of Lent. The famous summary of the covenant obligation as the great commandment of love (the *Shema*, Deut 6:4–6) is used as a Sunday reading and for other occasions in the life of the Church.

Deuteronomy's version of the Ten Commandments is never read, except for the third commandment (Deut 5:12–15), which, unlike the Exodus version, provides a humanitarian motive for Sabbath observance and fits well with Jesus' humanitarian healings on the Sabbath in the Gospels. The only clear example of "messianic prophecy", the promise of the "prophet like Moses" (Deut 18:15–20), is read early in Year B. Almost all the rest of the readings from Deuteronomy in the regular cycle of the Lectionary are taken from passages at the beginning or end of the book where Moses urges obedience to the commandments of God, often by promising blessings and threatening curses (Deut 4, 11, 26, 30).

The Lectionary thus shows that the Church treasures Deuteronomy most, not for its specific laws, but because it preserves the voice of Moses the preacher, who calls the people of God to reflect on the Lord's faithfulness and enter more deeply into the total self-gift of love demanded by the covenant relationship.

Readings from Deuteronomy for Sundays, Feast Days, Liturgical Seasons, and Other Occasions			
MSO = Masses for Special Occasions; OM = Optional Memorial; VM = Votive Mass; Rit = Ritual			
Passage	Description	Occasion	Explanation
1:9–14	Moses recaps the appointment of the elders and judges (Ex 18; Num 11:16–30).	*Rit*: Admission to Candidacy for Diaconate/ Priesthood	Just as wise and experienced men were needed to help Moses lead the people of God in the wilderness, so the bishop requires worthy coworkers to assist him in his task: the deacons and priests.
4:1–2, 6–8	An exhortation by Moses to keep the law, that Israel may live in the land as a wise people	*22nd Sun. in OT (B)*	Emphasizing obedience to divine law, the epistle (Jas 1:17–27) will stress doing the law rather than hearing it only; in the Gospel reading (Mk 7:1–23), Jesus rebukes the Pharisees for observance of human custom rather than divine law.
4:1, 5–9	See above; plus a warning not to forget God's saving deeds	Wed., 3rd Week of Lent	This reading complements the Gospel (Mt 5:17–19) that Jesus has not come to abolish the law; during the season of Lent, we are reminded that obedience to divine command is still necessary for holiness.

(continued)

	Readings from Deuteronomy for Sundays, Feast Days, Liturgical Seasons, and Other Occasions (*continued*)		
	MSO = Masses for Special Occasions; *OM* = Optional Memorial; *VM* = Votive Mass; *Rit* = Ritual		
Passage	Description	Occasion	Explanation
4:32–34, 39–40	Only the Lord has performed the wonders of the exodus and Sinai; he alone is God.	*Holy Trinity Sunday (B)*	The mystery of the Trinity includes both God's unity and his triperson-ality. The first reading emphasizes God's unity and uniqueness: there are no other gods besides the Holy Trinity.
5:12–15	The third com-mandment, to rest on the Sabbath Day, since "you were slaves in Egypt"	*9th Sun. in OT (B)*	This passage complements the Gospel (Mk 2:23–3:6) in which Jesus heals on the Sabbath and teaches about its true meaning. Deuteronomy alone cites humanitarian reasons for the Sabbath (to provide rest for the oppressed), and Jesus performs humanitarian acts of mercy (healings) on the Sabbath.
6:1–7	Moses' introduc-tion of the law, plus the *Shema*: "Hear, O Israel: The LORD our God is one LORD."	*Rit*: Presentation of the Creed	The *Shema* serves as the "creed" of Judaism, and its central tenets continue to be affirmed in the creeds of the Church.
6:2–6	See above	*31st Sun. in OT (B)*	The passage complements the Gospel (Mk 12:28b–34) in which Jesus identifies the *Shema* as the greatest commandment, together with love of neighbor (Lev 19:18), serving as the foundation for all divine law.
6:3–9	The *Shema*, plus exhortations to talk about the laws of God to one's children, at all times and in all situations (vv. 7–9)	St. Stephen of Hungary (Aug. 16); Common of Holy Men and Women, opt. 3; *Rit*: Institution of Readers, opt. 1	St. Stephen of Hungary left a famous literary work consisting of admoni-tions to his son and heir St. Emeric to follow the law of God; thus he is remembered for fulfilling Deutero-nomy 6:7–9. To a lesser extent, many saints spoke constantly of the word of God in all situations. The office of Reader is particularly dedicated to the proclamation of divine revelation.
7:6–11	Israel was not chosen for its merit, but out of the great love of God, who is faithful to all who love him.	*Solemnity of the Sacred Heart (A)*; *VM*: Most Sacred Heart	The Sacred Heart readings focus on God's love for us and ours for him. The second reading is a discourse on the love of and for God (1 Jn 4:6–17); the Gospel highlights Jesus' tender compassion: "Come to me, all who labor and are heavy laden" (Mt 11:25–30).

(*continued*)

	Readings from Deuteronomy for Sundays, Feast Days, Liturgical Seasons, and Other Occasions (*continued*)		
	MSO = Masses for Special Occasions; *OM* = Optional Memorial; *VM* = Votive Mass; *Rit* = Ritual		
Passage	Description	Occasion	Explanation
8:2–3, 14b–16a	Exhortation not to forget God's gift of manna during the time of "testing" in the desert	*Corpus Christi (A)*; *Rit*: Institution of Acolytes; *VM*: Most Holy Eucharist	The Eucharist is the New Manna (Jn 6:58); we are reminded not to take it for granted during the "testing in the wilderness" that constitutes our earthly sojourn.
8:7–18	Exhortation not to forget God and take pride in self after enjoying a bountiful harvest in the good land	*MSO*: After the Harvest	The earth's bounty is a gift of God, which should inspire gratitude and humility, not pride and self-sufficiency.
10:8–9	Moses summarizes the setting aside of the Levites as the clerical tribe.	Common of Pastors, opt. 2; Common of Holy Men and Women, opt. 4	The consecration of the Levites for divine service is a type of the ordination of priests and the consecration of religious for dedicated service to God and his people.
10:12–22	Moses repeats the great commandment and speaks of the Lord "setting his heart in love" upon the people of Israel.	*VM*: Most Sacred Heart of Jesus, opt. 3	Already in the Old Covenant Israel was urged to a relationship of mutual love with the Lord; the Lord's loving heart for Israel is manifested in the Most Sacred Heart of Jesus.
10:17–19	Moses commands love for the "sojourner", since Israel was a "sojourner" in Egypt.	*MSO*: For Refugees and Exiles, opt. 1	The people of God had their origin as foreigners in a foreign land. Only later did they receive land of their own. The people of God must always show compassion for those driven from their homeland.
11:18, 26–28, 32	Fidelity to the covenant results in blessings, but infidelity in curses.	*9th Sun. in OT (A)*	This passage complements the Gospel (Mt 7:21–27), the parable of the wise and foolish builders at the end of the Sermon on the Mount. The pairing of texts suggests Jesus is offering a New Covenant to God's people, with new blessings and curses attached.
18:15–20	The promise of a "prophet like Moses" whom God will raise up at a future time	*4th Sun. in OT (B)*	In the Gospel (Mk 1:21–28) Jesus proves himself to be a prophet as powerful as Moses by publicly exorcising a man possessed by demons.

(*continued*)

Readings from Deuteronomy for Sundays, Feast Days, Liturgical Seasons, and Other Occasions (*continued*)			
MSO = Masses for Special Occasions; *OM* = Optional Memorial; *VM* = Votive Mass; *Rit* = Ritual			
Passage	Description	Occasion	Explanation
24:17–22	Because they were slaves and foreigners in Egypt, the Israelites should make an extra effort to show kindness to the vulnerable among them.	*MSO*: In Time of Famine; For Refugees and Exiles, opt. 2	The commands of social justice under the Old Covenant still oblige Christians to work for mercy and justice for marginal members of society.
26:4–10	The "creedal" recitation of salvation history to be said by every Israelite who brings his first fruits to the sanctuary	*1st Sun. of Lent (C)*	Lent is a time of reflection on the course of salvation history, culminating in the seven readings at the Easter Vigil. This text is helpful as a start to Lent, because it summarizes so much of sacred history (the patriarchal wanderings, the Egyptian sojourn, and the exodus, conquest, and settlement of the land).
26:16–19	Moses calls the people of Israel to obedience to the covenant at the end of the Deuteronomic Code.	Sat., 1st Week of Lent	In the Gospel (Mt 5:43–48), Jesus calls his hearers to "be perfect, even as your heavenly father is perfect." So there is an advance over the Mosaic covenant, which called only for obedience.
30:1–4	The promise of God's regathering of Israel after the tribes are scattered in exile	*MSO*: For the Unity of Christians	The breaking of the Church in the Great Schism and Reformation are analogous to the division of the kingdom of Israel, its decline, and its eventual dispersion. Yet just as God gathered Israel in Christ, he can regather the Church.
30:10–14	Moses insists it is possible to keep the law of God: "The word is very near you ... so that you can do it."	*15th Sun. in OT (C)*; *Rit*: Institution of Readers, opt. 2; *MSO*: For a Council, Synod or other Meeting	This reading complements the parable of the good Samaritan, where Jesus, too, teaches that obedience to the two great commandments is possible and leads to eternal life. But he makes us realize this way is more demanding than it seems; we realize we need God's strength to live out this love radically.

(*continued*)

	Readings from Deuteronomy for Sundays, Feast Days, Liturgical Seasons, and Other Occasions (*continued*)		
	MSO = Masses for Special Occasions; *OM* = Optional Memorial; *VM* = Votive Mass; *Rit* = Ritual		
Passage	Description	Occasion	Explanation
30:15–20	Moses sets blessing and curse, life and death, before the people and urges them to choose life.	Thurs. after Ash Wednesday; *Rit*: Christian Initiation apart from Easter Vigil, opt. 4	Right at the beginning of Lent, the daily worshipper is confronted with a call to decision and urged to decide for life by choosing the way of God. The choice to become a Christian is also a moment of crisis, when one chooses the path of life and baptism rather than the way of the world that leads to death.

	Reading of Deuteronomy for Daily Mass: Ordinary Time, Year I: Week 18–19	
Day	Passage Read	Description
F	4:32–40	Moses calls Israel to reflect on the mighty deeds of the Lord, acknowledge him as the only God, and obey his commandments.
S	6:4–13	This passage includes the *Shema*, plus exhortation not to forget the Lord when Israel experiences the blessings of the Promised Land.
M	10:12–22	Moses restates the great commandment and urges Israel to obedience by considering the goodness of God to his people through history.
Tu	31:1–8	Moses makes a farewell speech to Israel, then invests Joshua with authority as his successor.
W	34:1–12	Moses' final view of the Promised Land, his death, and eulogy at the end of the Pentateuch.

Conclusion

Deuteronomy is Moses' last will and testament to the people of Israel, couched in the form of a series of sermons that also follow, in rough sequence, the basic parts or topics of an ancient covenant-treaty document. As the final form of the Mosaic covenant—which had already been given in two forms previously—it formed the "constitution" of the people of Israel as a civil and religious body until the coming of the Messiah.

Deuteronomy is rightly regarded as a hinge or center point of the main Old Testament narrative, holding together the primary history (Genesis through 2 Kings). Since it recaps previous salvation history (Deut 1–11) and forecasts Israel's future (chaps. 30–33), Deuteronomy is almost an embodiment or synopsis of the whole Old Testament. Thus it is hard to exaggerate its importance to biblical theology.

In Deuteronomy, Moses sees the depth of intimacy that a covenant relationship with God entails and calls Israel to it, all the while quite aware that Israel will not maintain this covenant despite the accommodations he has introduced to the divinely authorized legislation. All hope is invested in the future, when God will affect an interior transformation of his people described as "the circumcision of the heart" (cf. Deut 10:16).

Because of its central role in the structure of the Old Testament canon, Deuteronomy's role as a liturgical document, intended to serve as the basis for a septennial covenant-renewal liturgy, suggests the entire Old Testament should be understood in a liturgical light. Every seven years, Deuteronomy was intended to rhetorically and ritually re-present God's appearance at Sinai to the people of Israel and compel them to enter once more into the covenant. But the limitations to this covenant already seen by Moses himself suggest that God's people await a better liturgy of a better covenant, which will re-present God's presence not only rhetorically and ritually, but tangibly.

For Further Reading

Commentaries and Studies on Deuteronomy

Christensen, Duane L. *Deuteronomy 1–11*. Word Biblical Commentary 6A. Dallas: Word Books, 1991.

Hahn, Scott W. *Kinship by Covenant: A Canonical Approach to the Fulfillment of God's Saving Promises*. Anchor Yale Bible Reference Library. New Haven, Conn.: Yale University Press, 2009. (See pp. 1–92.)

Hamilton, Victor. *Handbook on the Pentateuch*. Grand Rapids, Mich.: Baker Academic, 2005. (See pp. 365–464.)

Kaiser, Walter C., Jr. *Toward Old Testament Ethics*. Grand Rapids, Mich.: Zondervan, 1983. (See pp. 127–37.)

Kline, Meredith G. *Treaty of the Great King: The Covenant Structure of Deuteronomy*. Grand Rapids, Mich.: Eerdmans, 1963.

Tigay, Jeffrey H. *Deuteronomy*. JPS Torah Commentary 5. Philadelphia: Jewish Publication Society, 2003.

Weinfeld, Moshe. *Deuteronomy 1–11*. Anchor Bible 5. New York: Doubleday, 1991.

Wenham, Gordon J. "Deuteronomy and the Central Sanctuary". Pages 94–108 in *A Song of Power and the Power of Song: Essays on the Book of Deuteronomy*. Edited by Duane L. Christensen. Winona Lake, Ind.: Eisenbrauns, 1993.

Historical Issues in Deuteronomy

Berman, Joshua. "CTH 133 and the Hittite Provenance of Deuteronomy 13". *Journal of Biblical Literature* 130.1 (2011): 25–44.

———. "Histories Twice Told: Deuteronomy 1–3 and the Hittite Treaty Prologue Tradition". *Journal of Biblical Literature* 132.2 (2013): 229–50.

Carpenter, Eugene E. "Deuteronomy". Pages 418–547 in *Genesis, Exodus, Leviticus, Numbers, Deuteronomy*. Vol. 1 of *Zondervan Illustrated Bible Backgrounds Commentary*. Edited by John H. Walton. Grand Rapids, Mich.: Zondervan, 2009.

Kitchen, Kenneth A. *On the Reliability of the Old Testament*. Grand Rapids, Mich.: Eerdmans, 2003. (See pp. 283–312.)

Wellhausen, Julius. *Prolegomena to the History of Israel*. 1885. Repr., Atlanta: Scholars Press, 1994.

Patristic Commentaries and Studies on Deuteronomy

Aquinas, Saint Thomas. "The Old Law". *Summa Theologica*. I–II, qq. 98–105. Translated by the Fathers of the English Dominican Province. 1948. Repr., Westminster, Md.: Christian Classics, 1981. (See pp. 1025–103.)

Kugel, James L. *Traditions of the Bible: A Guide to the Bible as It Was at the Start of the Common Era*. Cambridge, Mass.: Harvard University Press, 1997. (See pp. 827–88.)

Lienhard, Joseph T. "Deuteronomy". Pages 275–341 in *Exodus, Leviticus, Numbers, Deuteronomy*. Old Testament 3 of Ancient Christian Commentary on Scripture. Edited by Thomas C. Oden. Downers Grove, Ill.: InterVarsity Press, 2001

Theodoret of Cyrus. *On Leviticus, Numbers, Deuteronomy, Joshua, Judges, and Ruth*. Vol. 2 of *The Questions on the Octateuch*. Translated by Robert C. Hill. The Library of Early Christianity 2. Washington, D.C.: Catholic University of America Press, 2007.

The Historical Books

11. JOSHUA

Introduction

The book of Joshua (Hebrew *sepher yehōshua'*) recounts the career of Moses' successor, Joshua, who led the people of Israel into the land of Canaan, defeated their enemies, and divided the land among the twelve tribes. Joshua is one of only several figures in the Bible whose name is changed to reflect his role in the history of salvation (for example, Abraham, Sarah, Peter). He was originally given the name Hosea (Hebrew *hoshea'*), meaning "salvation" (Num 13:8; Deut 32:44), but Moses changes his name to "Joshua" (Hebrew *yehōshua'*), meaning "the Lord saves", after he is chosen to be one of the twelve spies sent into the Promised Land (Num 13:16). Joshua is also unique in that he ascends Mount Sinai with Moses even higher than Aaron the priest and the other elders of Israel (Ex 24:13), is waiting for Moses when he descends (Ex 32:17), and is specially privileged to accompany Moses into the Tabernacle sanctuary itself (Ex 33:11). In light of such distinctive roles, it is perhaps unsurprising that God directly instructs Moses to commission Joshua as his successor (Num 27:18–23), which is described in the closing lines of the Pentateuch: "And Joshua the son of Nun was full of the spirit of wisdom, *for Moses had laid his hands upon him*; so the sons of Israel obeyed him, and did as the Lord had commanded Moses" (Deut 34:9).

In this way, the book of Joshua serves both as an epilogue to the Pentateuch and as a transition into the historical books of the Old Testament, known in Jewish tradition as the "Former Prophets". In particular, Joshua brings to resolution certain themes introduced already in Genesis, especially the possession of the land, although subsequent biblical books (such as Judges) will make clear that certain aspects of the resolutions effected by Joshua were provisional and temporary.

Literary Structure of Joshua

Joshua is a short book, and its literary structure is relatively simple. The opening chapters (Josh 1–5) recount Israel's spiritual and material preparations for the conquest of the Promised Land, while the heart of the book recounts the actual conquest of various cities and peoples (Josh 6–12). In the wake of these conquests, subsequent chapters provide a detailed account of how the various parts of the Promised Land were divided among the twelve tribes of Israel (Josh 13–21), and the closing chapters of the book contain exhortations by Joshua to the people about keeping the land through faithfulness to the covenant (Josh 22–24). This gives us the following four-part structure:

   I.   Preparations to Take the Land (1–5)
  II.   Taking the Land (6–12)
 III.   Dividing the Land (13–21)
 IV.   Keeping the Land (22–24)

The main narrative about the conquest (Josh 6–12) falls into three sections: (1) an initial central campaign that takes Jericho and Ai (Josh 6–8); (2) a southern campaign into the Judean Negeb (southern desert) (Josh 9–10); and (3) a northern campaign into the Galilee region (Josh 11), followed by summaries of the conquests of Moses and Joshua (Josh 12). The dividing of the land (chaps. 13–21) is arranged by tribe, beginning with the Transjordanian (east of the Jordan) tribes (Josh 13), then the largest Cisjordanian (west of the Jordan) tribes (Josh 14–17), and finally all the rest of the tribes (Josh 18–19). Significantly, two chapters are devoted to the allotment of the forty-eight cities set apart for the Levites, the only tribe not to receive any tribal territories (Josh 20–21). The conclusion of the book recounts the building of an altar to remind the Transjordanian tribes to be faithful to the Lord (Josh 22) and a final exhortation to covenant fidelity, whose words and actions strongly resemble those of Moses at the end of Deuteronomy (Josh 23–24).

Outline of the Book of Joshua

  I. Preparations to Take the Land (Josh 1–5)
     A. Practical Preparations (chaps. 1–3)
        1. Joshua Commissioned (1:1–9)
        2. Joshua Orders Israel to Pack Up (1:10–18)
        3. Joshua Sends Spies into Jericho (2:1–24)
        4. The People Cross the Jordan (3:1–17)
     B. Cultic Preparations (chaps. 4–5)
        1. Joshua Builds an Altar of Jordan River Stones at Gilgal (chap. 4)
        2. Joshua Circumcises Israel (5:1–9)
        3. The People Celebrate Passover (5:10–15)

  II. Taking the Land (Josh 6–12)
     A. The Central Campaign (chaps. 6–8)
        1. The Conquest of Jericho (chap. 6)
        2. The Conquest of Ai (7:1–8:29)
        3. Covenant Renewal at the End of the Campaign (8:30–35)
     B. The Southern Campaign (chaps. 9–10)
        1. The Ruse of the Gibeonites (chap. 9)
        2. Campaign to the South to Defend the Gibeonites (chap. 10)
     C. The Northern Campaign (chap. 11)
     D. Summary of Kings Conquered under Moses and Joshua (chap. 12)

 III. Dividing the Land (Josh 13–21)
     A. The Transjordanian Tribes
        1. Reuben (13:15–23)

Overview of Joshua

Preparations to Take the Land (Joshua 1–5)

The book of Joshua opens with a moving exhortation from the Lord to Joshua in the wake of Moses' death to rise up, be "strong and of good courage", and enter into the land that God has "given" to the people of Israel (Josh 1:1–9). Significantly, all of the events described in these opening chapters of the book are told in such a way that the close reader can hear echoes of similar events in the life of Moses, Joshua' predecessor. The commissioning of Joshua to lead the people of Israel (Josh 1:1–9) calls to mind the commissioning of Moses (Ex 3:1–4:17).

The sending of spies into Jericho (Josh 2:1–24) recalls the spies sent into the Promised Land (Num 13). The miraculous crossing of the Jordan River (Josh

3–4) strikingly resembles the miraculous crossing of the Red Sea (Ex
14–15), and the celebration of the
Passover feast in the Promised Land
(Josh 5:10–12) recapitulates the Passover feasts celebrated before leaving
Egypt (Ex 12–13) and before leaving
Sinai (Num 9:1–14). In each case,
the Passover is eaten before Israel
embarks on the next momentous
stage of its geographical and spiritual
journey. These similarities highlight
Joshua not just as Moses' faithful successor, who does all that the Lord
and Moses did and commanded, but
almost as a kind of *new Moses* figure.

In fact, Joshua even exceeds Moses
in some ways. In the opening chapters of the book, all of Joshua's actions,
such as the sending of spies into Jericho, succeed without difficulty (Josh
1–5), unlike those of Moses, who was
always confronted with grumbling
and rebellion from his people. Joshua
even performs a covenantal action
that Moses, for some reason, culpably

> ### Is Rahab Rewarded for Lying?
>
> Since ancient times, the story of Rahab's
> deception of her fellow Jerichoites in order
> to save the two Israelite spies and herself
> (Josh 2) has raised the moral question of her
> act of outright lying.
>
> During the patristic period, Augustine
> wrote on this question as follows: "No lie
> is just. Accordingly, when examples of lying
> are proposed to us from the sacred Scrip-
> tures, either they are not lies but are thought
> so for not being understood, or, if they are
> lies, they are not to be imitated because they
> cannot be just.
>
> "As for its being written that God dealt
> well with the Hebrew midwives and with
> Rahab the harlot of Jericho, he did not
> deal well with them because they lied but
> because they were merciful to the men of
> God. And so, it was not their deception that
> was rewarded, but their benevolence; the
> benignity of their intention, not the iniquity
> of their invention."[a]
>
> [a]Augustine, *Against Lying* 15.31–32, in John
> R. Franke, *Joshua, Judges, Ruth, 1–2 Samuel*, Old
> Testament 4, Ancient Christian Commentary on
> Scripture (Downers Grove, Ill.: InterVarsity Press,
> 2005), 10.

neglected: the circumcision of the people (Josh 5:2–7). In these opening chapters, we suddenly discover that the second generation of the wilderness wandering, who grew up under Moses' leadership in the desert, had *never been circumcised*. This was in obvious violation of the Abrahamic covenant, which stipulated
circumcision for all Israelite males on the eighth day after birth (Gen 17). One
dramatic result of this covenant negligence is that there are so many men who
need to be circumcised that the site where Joshua performed the circumcisions
is named "The Hill of the Foreskins" (Hebrew *Gibeath-haaraloth*)! This surprising revelation of Moses' neglect to enforce the covenant of circumcision curiously recalls the mysterious episode in which Moses finds his life in danger from
God because of his failure to circumcise his own son (Ex 4:24–26). It is hard to
know what to make of the fact that the second generation of Israelites have not
even kept the most basic requirement of the Abrahamic covenant; although it
reinforces the point made in the last chapter about the grave spiritual infidelity
manifested by the second generation of Israelites to which Moses gives the book
of Deuteronomy (see chap. 10). In certain ways, then, Joshua shows himself to
be a more effective leader, even if his status as a prophet never approaches that
of Moses (compare Deut 34:10–12).

Perhaps the best-known story from this opening section of the book is the
account of the Israelite spies being saved by Rahab the prostitute (Josh 2).
Although some scholars have raised doubts about whether Rahab is actually a

harlot (suggesting instead she is just an "innkeeper"), the Hebrew word *zōnah* (Josh 2:1) ordinarily means a "prostitute" (cf. Deut 23:18). Significantly, Rahab's actions on behalf of the spies stem not only from a desire to preserve her life and the lives of her family, but from a confession of faith in YHWH, the God of Israel, based on reports she has heard of the wonders performed for his people in the exodus from Egypt (Josh 2:9–13). This episode is key for evaluating the moral and theological significance of the conquest of Jericho and other Canaanite cities in the subsequent narrative, since it reveals the extent of the Canaanites' knowledge of Israel's recent history and the power of the Israelite God. If Rahab is in any way representative, the Canaanites are not sprung upon unawares; they *know* about the miracles YHWH has worked for Israel and his promise of the land to them. Nonetheless, by and large the Canaanites choose to oppose Israel and YHWH, usually through preemptive strikes (Josh 10:1–5; 11:1–5), rather than evacuate the land or sue for peace (Josh 11:19). Ultimately, their overthrow stems from their grave, conscious, and deliberate defiance of YHWH. Rahab, in stark contrast, makes a covenant with the people of God and, by means of that covenant, is delivered from death (Josh 2:12–14).

The Conquest of Jericho and the Land (Joshua 6–12)

After crossing the west bank of the Jordan River, the city of Jericho is the first major fortified city in the way of the advance of Israel. Its capture is described in greater detail than that of any other city in the book.

The defeat of Jericho exercised great influence in Jewish and Christian memory, because the manner of its overthrow was primarily *liturgical* and *miraculous*, rather than strategic and military (Josh 6:1–7). The people, led in liturgical procession by the Levitical priests carrying the Ark of the Covenant, are instructed by the Lord to march around the city once each day for seven days and seven times around on the seventh day. At the conclusion of all this marching, the people shout to the Lord, the walls of the city collapse, and the entire city is put to the sword:

> Joshua said to the people, "Shout; for the LORD has given you the city. And the city and all that is within it shall be devoted to the LORD for destruction [*herem*]; only Rahab the harlot and all who are with her in her house shall live, because she hid the messengers that we sent." (Josh 6:16–17)

We will discuss the question of total, or *herem*, warfare later (see below); for now, notice that the salvation of Rahab and her entire family out of the condemned populace of the city also contains echoes of the exodus under Moses. In particular, it bears striking parallels with the night of the Passover (Ex 12). Just as the Israelites marked the opening of their homes with the red blood of the lamb so that the angel of death would pass by harmlessly, so Rahab and her family huddle within her house, the window marked by a red cord, while the Israelite soldiers ("angels of death") pass by harmlessly outside (cf. Josh 2:18). In this way, she and her family enter into the people of Israel; in fact, according to the New Testament, Rahab goes on to become the wife of Salmon, the father of Boaz, the great-great-grandfather of King David himself (Mt 1:5). The example of Rahab shows that, despite the comprehensive sound of the "ban" (Hebrew *herem*) placed on the cities within the land of Canaan (Deut 20:16–18), those who feared the Lord and sought his protection were still able to enter his people by means of covenant.

The battle for the smaller city of Ai does not go as smoothly (Josh 7). Unknown to the rest of the Israelites, a certain man named Achan has violated the ban against taking loot from the defeated city of Jericho. As a result, God's power and presence do not accompany the Israelites in the battle against Ai, leading to defeat. By divine inquiry, Achan and his sin are discovered, and he and his entire family are executed. Once the sin of Achan is removed from the people, the Israelites are enabled to defeat the city of Ai (Josh 8).

With Jericho and Ai subdued, Joshua and the Israelites journey north to Mount Ebal and Mount Gerizim, the location specified by Moses for the covenant-renewal ceremony that is to be performed once the Israelites have entered the Promised Land (Deut 27:1–26). There, Joshua transcribes "a copy of the law of Moses" upon "the stones"—hearkening once again back to Moses' tablets of stone on Mount Sinai (Ex 34:29)—and performs the covenant renewal exactly as Moses commanded, thereby solemnizing and sealing the covenant between God and Israel in its Deuteronomic form (Josh 8:30–35).

The next cities in the way of Israel's central thrust belong to the Gibeonites, who differ strikingly from the people of Jericho and Ai in that they devise a clever ruse to save themselves through a covenant with Israel (Josh 9). Sending messengers with worn-out clothes and few provisions, they pretend to be immigrants from a land far away who wish to enter into an alliance with the Israelites. The Israelites comply, only to discover a few days later that they have been deceived. Angered but bound by their covenant-oath, the Israelites punish the Gibeonites by making them supply labor for the material needs of the sanctuary (water and wood; Josh 9:23). In this whole episode, the Gibeonites show themselves to be like Rahab, in that they attempt to enter into a relationship with Israel because they have heard "report" of "all that [the LORD] did in Egypt" and the exodus (Josh 9:9). On the other hand, they are also similar to the Israelites themselves, who are descended from Jacob, a man who deceived in order to enter into God's covenant (Gen 27:1–29) and was punished with hard labor (Gen 31:38–42), though permitted to retain the covenant blessing. As with Rahab, so with the Gibeonites: despite the laws of Deuteronomy (Deut 20:16–18), God permits those Canaanites who fear him to enter his covenant people. The "punishment" of the Gibeonites turns out to be a blessing for them: they become a race of Temple servants ("sacristans", so to speak), who provide the material needs such as wood and water for the worship of the Lord and so live and work more closely to the divine presence than most of the tribes of Israel themselves!

After making this covenant with the Gibeonites, the Israelites are soon drawn into battle to defend their new allies (Josh 10). Five Canaanite kings of the south band together against Joshua and the Israelites but are defeated by a surprise attack coupled with two more miracles: a providential hailstorm and prolonged daylight that enables Joshua to complete his victory. Having defeated the kings' armies, Joshua proceeds to attack and capture each of their cities, with the exception of Jerusalem. The army of Israel then returns to its base camp at Gilgal near Jericho, which remains its center of operations throughout its campaigns.

At this point, a coalition of northern Canaanite kings, headed by Jabin, king of Hazor, gathers together in opposition to Israel. Joshua marches north and again attacks by surprise, routing the northern coalition and capturing all their cities (Josh 11). This is the last campaign that the book of Joshua recounts in any detail. Many other battles are summarized in the phrase "Joshua made war a long time with all those kings" (Josh 11:18). However, he is ultimately victorious and emerges as master of the land of Canaan. In the fashion of other ancient Near Eastern lists of conquered cities and defeated lands, the book of Joshua summarizes the kings and cities conquered by the people of Israel (Josh 12).

Dividing the Promised Land (Joshua 13–21)

Although in many ways the conquest of the land under Joshua is effective, the book of Joshua itself makes very clear that there remain quite a number of cities and territories that neither Joshua nor the Israelites take. When Joshua "was old and advanced in years", the Lord declares to him: "there remains yet very much land to be possessed" (Josh 13:1). Joshua's campaigns have pacified the land, so that the remaining Canaanites do not pose a threat to drive out, much less exterminate, the people of Israel, as was feared at the beginning of the conquest (see Josh 7:7–9). Nonetheless, there remain Canaanite populations who have withdrawn to their fortified cities and are not yet dislodged.

Be that as it may, Joshua proceeds to divide up the land among the tribes, even if certain territories have yet to be fully conquered. He begins with a rehearsal of the tribal allotments of the Transjordanian tribes of Reuben, Gad, and the eastern half of Manasseh (Josh 13); proceeds to the larger Cisjordanian ones of Judah, Ephraim, and the western half of Manasseh (Josh 14–15); and concludes with the smaller tribes of Benjamin, Simeon, Zebulun, Issachar, Asher, Naphtali, and Dan (Josh 16–19). Last of all, he sets aside cities of refuge for those who commit unintentional manslaughter (as opposed to premeditated murder), all of which are designated from among the forty-eight cities given to the Levites (Josh 20–21).

Keeping the Land: Reminders to Remain Faithful (Joshua 22–24)

After the land is divided and the Transjordanian tribes return to their territory across the river, a controversy erupts over an altar that these three tribes decide to build along the banks of the Jordan (Josh 22). The other tribes interpret this as a provocative violation of the rule of the central sanctuary (Deut 12), a sign of a deliberate breach of the covenant. They gather for war with the Transjordanian tribes, but the offending tribes insist they meant no harm: the altar was only a monument to their fidelity to the Lord and inclusion within the people of Israel. The leaders of the other tribes accept this explanation, and there is peace. The altar remains, interpreted as a monumental reminder of the commitment of the tribes to worship the Lord. However, the reader is left wondering what the tribes' real motives were and whether this bodes ill for the future perseverance of the Transjordanian tribes as members of the covenant people of Israel.

The final two chapters of Joshua breathe the spirit of Deuteronomy. Joshua delivers two very "Deuteronomic" sermons to the people of Israel assembled at Shechem, located between Mounts Ebal and Gerizim, the two mountains used for the solemnization of the Deuteronomic covenant, and close to Shiloh, where the Tabernacle resided during the period of Joshua and the Judges (Josh 23:1–16; 24:1–15). As Moses did in Deuteronomy, Joshua speaks of his impending death, recounts the Lord's faithfulness and the people's sins in their recent history, and warns them to stay faithful to the Lord and his covenant. Although the fact is often overlooked, it is in the context of warning the twelve tribes of Israel against idolatry that Joshua pronounces his often-quoted words:

> And if you be unwilling to serve the LORD, *choose this day whom you will serve,* whether the gods your fathers served in the region beyond the River, or the gods of the Amorites in whose land you dwell; but *as for me and my house, we will serve the LORD.* (Josh 24:15)

After making this declaration, Joshua performs a covenant-renewal ritual and "wrote these words in the book of the law of God" (Josh 24:26). Unlike Moses, however, he neither blesses the people nor provides for a successor.

Historical Issues in Joshua

Do Joshua and the Israelites Completely Conquer the Land?

Joshua presents several historical problems, not the least of which is the apparent tension between some of the sweeping claims made about Joshua's victories and the subsequent indications that large numbers of cities and territories remained unconquered. Consider, for example, the following descriptions of Joshua's victories in the Promised Land:

> So Joshua took *all* that land, the hill country and all the Negeb and all the land of Goshen and the lowland and the Arabah and the hill country of Israel and its lowland from Mount Halak, that rises toward Seir, as far as Baal-gad in the valley of Lebanon below Mount Hermon. And he took *all* their kings, and struck them, and put them to death.... There was not a city that made peace with the sons of Israel, except the Hivites, the inhabitants of Gibeon; *they took all in battle.* (Josh 11:16–19)

> Now Joshua was old and advanced in years; and the LORD said to him, "You are old and advanced in years, and *there remains yet very much land to be possessed. This is the land that yet remains*: all the regions of the Philistines, and all those of the Geshurites ..., and those of the Avvim, in the south, all the land of the Canaanites, and Mearah which belongs to the Sidonians, to Aphek, to the boundary of the Amorites, and the land of the Gebalites, and all Lebanon." (Josh 13:1–5)

How do we reconcile the apparent discrepancy, in the same biblical book, between these comprehensive assertions of conquest and those passages which suggest that Joshua's campaign leaves much of the land unoccupied?

Hyperbole in Ancient Conquest Accounts[a]

"The great army of Mittani is overthrown in the twinkling of an eye. It has perished completely, as though they had never existed, like the ashes of a fire."

—from a victory stele of Thutmose III, ca. 1450 B.C.

"Yanoam made nonexistent, Israel is wasted, his seed is not."

— the "Israel Stele" of Pharaoh Merneptah, ca. 1210 B.C.

"But I saw my desire over him and his house, and Israel has utterly perished forever."

— the stele of Mesha, king of Moab, ca. 840 B.C.

"The soldiers of Hirimme, dangerous enemies, I cut down with the sword, and not one escaped."

— inscription of Sennacherib, king of Assyria, ca. 700 B.C.

"I made Mt. Asharpaya empty (of humanity).... I made the mountains of Tarikarimu empty (of humanity)."

— inscription of Hittite King Mursili II, ca. 1300 B.C.

[a] Adapted from K. Lawson Younger, *Ancient Conquest Accounts: A Study in Ancient Near Eastern and Biblical History Writing* (Sheffield: JSOT Press, 1990).

One way that scholars have approached this problem is by positing multiple sources in the book of Joshua. According to this theory, the passages containing all-encompassing claims of Joshua's victories come from a source that had an optimistic view of the conquest, whereas other passages indicating continued resistance are from a different, more "realistic" source.

What is surprising, however, is how little attention has been paid in the history of scholarship to other ancient Near Eastern conquest accounts in order to understand Joshua according to the rhetorical features of this genre. These conquest accounts were highly stylized and often employed *hyperbole*—a rhetorical device using deliberate exaggeration—understood as such by both the writers and readers in antiquity.

As we have seen before, the genre of Joshua needs to be taken into account to interpret properly the intended meaning of some of the statements. For example, at one point, Joshua presents a stylized account of the conquest of cities Joshua captured, following roughly this format: "The LORD gave it [the city] also and its king into the hand of Israel, and he [Joshua] struck it with the edge of the sword, and every person in it; he left none remaining in it" (Josh 10:30, and throughout). This indicates there were none remaining on the field of battle, and no inhabitants were left in the town afterward, as opposed to battles that resulted in (1) the subjugation of the town (cf. Josh 16:10) or

---

An Example of Egyptian Historiography

Pharaoh Ramesses III (1186–55 B.C.) recorded the following victories over the "sea peoples", usually identified with the Philistines:

> "I extended all the frontiers of Egypt and overthrew those who had attacked them from their lands. I slew the Denyen in their islands, while the Tjeker and the Philistines were made ashes. The Sherden and the Weshesh of the Sea *were made nonexistent*, captured all together and brought in captivity to Egypt like the sands of the shore. I settled them in strongholds, bound in my name. Their military classes were as numerous as hundred-thousands. I assigned portions for them all with clothing and provisions from the treasuries and granaries every year."[a]

Note that Ramesses III claims both that the sea peoples were "made nonexistent" and also that they were "captured all together", as numerous "as hundred-thousands." Yet there can be no question of multiple sources in this text; nor is the pharaoh attempting to dissimulate. He is simply employing the rhetorical idioms of ancient Near Eastern conquest accounts.

[a]James Pritchard, *Ancient Near Eastern Texts Relating to the Old Testament with Supplement*, 3rd ed. (Princeton, N.J.: Princeton University Press, 1969), 262.

---

(2) the capture of the inhabitants as slaves (cf. Num 31:9–12). Typically, however, unknown numbers of inhabitants, both combatants and non-combatants, would flee before, during, and after combat; and this fact is seldom reported in ancient Near Eastern conquest accounts, unless the fugitives figured significantly in a later battle. For example, Pharaoh Merneptah of Egypt and King Mesha of Moab reported what sounds like the complete extermination of Israel around 1210 B.C. and 840 B.C. respectively (see inset on p. 299). Obviously their reports were hyperbolic and indicated, rather, that all significant armed resistance had been killed or driven from the field of battle. It is extremely important to emphasize that the evidence for this phenomenon of deliberate hyperbole is indisputably present in the biblical text itself, when read as a whole. For example: in the account of Joshua's victory over the five southern kings of Canaan, on the one hand, the enemies of Israel are described as slain "with a very great slaughter" until they were "wiped out", and, on the other hand, the sacred author immediately recounts that the *"remnant which remained of them ... entered into the fortified cities"* (Josh 10:20)! Clearly, in this case, in the space of one verse, the text signals to the reader that the assertion about the comprehensive defeat of the enemies is not intended to be interpreted literally.

Along similar lines, when interpreting the accounts of the battles in the land in Joshua and Judges, it is important to keep in mind the distinction between sacking a city and defeating its leaders, on the one hand, and permanently *occupying* the city, on the other. In certain instances, Israel was able to capture and sack certain cities, but the expelled inhabitants would return later and refortify. The most obvious example of this is Jerusalem (a.k.a. Jebus), which was sacked once (Judg 1:8) but could not be held permanently (Josh 15:63; Judg 1:21). The same was probably also the case with other cities.

Finally, it also important to keep in mind that in ancient Near Eastern warfare, it was possible to defeat a *king* and his army in the open field without being able to take possession of the king's *city*. This was the case, for example, in the unusually well-documented Battle of Kadesh (ca. 1274 B.C.) between Pharaoh Ramesses II and the Hittite king Muwatalli. Ramesses II routed the Hittite forces in the field but could not dislodge them from the city, and he eventually returned to Egypt. This scenario also seems to explain the list of thirty-one "kings of the land" whom "the people of Israel defeated" (see Josh 12:7–24). In the case of these kings, it seems apparent from subsequent narratives in Joshua and Judges that while the various leaders may have been defeated, the Israelites were not able to take and hold all the associated royal cities of the defeated kings. This should come as no surprise to contemporary readers; even in modern-day warfare, it is one thing to conquer an enemy and very much another thing to occupy a conquered territory.

In short, when we read the text of Joshua carefully in the light of the rhetorical features of ancient Near Eastern conquest accounts, the apparent tension between the passages of Joshua that celebrate his successes and those that reflect the reality of continued occupation of the land by different Canaanite populations is greatly reduced, if not eliminated. Joshua led a series of fast campaigns in central, southern, and northern Canaan, returning every time to the Israelite base camp in Gilgal.[1] His campaigns eliminated organized resistance to the Israelite occupation and established certain areas—especially the central hill country—firmly within Israelite control. The Israelites typically did not burn the cities they captured (Josh 11:13), as they expected eventually to occupy the towns themselves (Deut 6:10–12). Finally, we should note that the literary style of the conquest narratives in Joshua 1–11 exhibits close parallels in style and structure to Egyptian New Kingdom (late second-millennium) military conquest texts, like the annals of Thutmose III.[2] This is another piece of evidence tying the biblical material concerning the exodus and conquest to this time period.

The Question of the Date of the Conquest and Settlement under Joshua

Because the date of the conquest under Joshua is ultimately tied to the date of the exodus under Moses, most of the arguments on this question have been discussed in a previous chapter. Among scholars who take the historicity of the conquest account of Joshua seriously, there are two main proposals: (1) an early fifteenth-century conquest of the land (high 1400s B.C.) or (2) a late thirteenth-century conquest (low 1200s B.C.).

On the one hand, the fifteenth-century conquest is supported by a straightforward reading of chronological indications in the Old Testament itself (see 1 Kings 6:1). Scholars who hold this view also identify destruction layers found at many sites in the land of Israel at the end of the Middle Bronze Age with the conquest of the land by the Israelites.[3] (Other scholars have associated these

---

[1] Kenneth A. Kitchen, *On the Reliability of the Old Testament* (Grand Rapids, Mich.: Eerdmans, 2003), 159–90.

[2] James K. Hoffmeier, "The Structure of Joshua 1–11 and the Annals of Thutmose III", in *Faith, Tradition, and History: Old Testament Historiography in Its Near Eastern Context*, ed. A. R. Millard, James K. Hoffmeier, and David W. Baker (Winona Lake, Ind.: Eisenbrauns, 1994), 165–79.

[3] John J. Bimson, *Redating the Exodus and Conquest* (Sheffield: Sheffield University Press, 1978).

destruction layers with the expulsion of the Hyksos from Egypt.) One weakness of the fifteenth-century conquest theory is that Egyptian documents from the next several centuries, including the Amarna correspondence of Pharaoh Akhenaten and the campaign records of Pharaoh Ramesses II, do not contain clear evidence of Israel occupying the land at that time.

On the other hand, the thirteenth-century conquest theory is supported by some archaeological evidence, above all the *Merneptah Stele*, which records the presence of Israel in the land of Canaan by around 1209 B.C. Also, archaeological remains show a rapid growth of villages in the hill country of Canaan in the twelfth century (1100s B.C.). Such rapid expansion of the population is very difficult to explain as the result of natural biological growth. It appears, then, to be the result of migration into the region, which could be easily explained by the Israelite migrations described in the book of Joshua. Significantly, the archaeological evidence at these settlements shows little or no evidence of pig bones, which appears to distinguish them as Israelite rather than Canaanite villages. The weakness of the thirteenth-century theory is that it requires the chronological data of the Bible itself to be interpreted in a figurative or non-literal way, without any clear indications from the text that it should be interpreted as such.

What about explicit archaeological evidence of battles in the major cities? Should there not be clear signs of destruction in the archaeological record? The evidence is disputed. The book of Joshua records the burning of only three Canaanite cities: *Jericho*, *Ai*, and *Hazor*. Excavations at Hazor have turned up destruction levels that might correlate with either the early or late conquest models, but Ai and Jericho pose greater difficulties. Many archaeologists believe neither site shows evidence of occupation or destruction that would correlate with either the early or the late date of the conquest. In response, other scholars argue that the traditional location of Ai (modern et-Tell) has been misidentified, and biblical Ai is actually Khirbet el-Maqatir, nine miles north of Jerusalem, which has a suitable destruction layer.

By contrast, the location of the city of Jericho is not disputed, but its archaeological interpretation is. The British archaeologist Kathleen Kenyon argued in the 1960s and '70s that Jericho was destroyed around 1550 B.C. and not reoccupied until the Iron Age (early Israelite monarchy, ca. 1000 B.C.). In the 1990s, Bryant G. Wood found evidence of the destruction of a settlement in the 1400s B.C. that would correspond to an early date of the conquest. A decade later, Kenneth Kitchen argued that the remains of the thirteenth-century city captured by Joshua have been lost to erosion.[4]

Alternative Theories of Conquest and Settlement of the Land

Observing the difficulties in getting a good match between the archaeological and textual data, a number of contemporary scholars have given up on the reality of a "conquest" at all. They propose that the biblical account in the book of Joshua is essentially fictitious. The most extreme among these argue that all preexilic biblical "history" is a literary invention from the Persian period (late

---

[4] See Kitchen, *Reliability of the Old Testament*, 187–88.

sixth–fourth centuries B.C.). Less extreme theorists propose one of two alternative models for the origin of Israel in Canaan:

1. *The Peaceful Immigration Theory*: According to this view, the Israelites were in fact nomads from east of the Jordan River (Transjordanian territory) who began to settle in the highlands west of the Jordan (Cisjordanian territory) in the twelfth century B.C. and then gradually spread westward. Originally, the cultural distinctions between the Canaanites of the land and these immigrants was not religious or cultic but agricultural, the forerunners of the Israelites being nomads and the natives being herders.

2. *The Peasant Revolt Theory*: According to this view, "Israel" is the final cultural identity of what began as an uprising of rural peasants in Canaan against the oppressive political and economic policies of the Canaanite city-states.[5] On the one hand, those we now call the "Canaanites" took the role of oppressors, practicing the religion of Baal, while the "Israelites" were the oppressed of the land, united under the religion of YHWH.

As should be clear, strictly speaking, these models are contrary to the biblical text, though elements of them may be found there. For example, the book of Joshua indicates that at least two Canaanite groups allied themselves with Israel: Rahab and her entire family, and the Gibeonites (Josh 2, 9). These groups intermarried and eventually assimilated with Israel. The Gibeonites were a large ethnic group occupying four major cities in the hill country of Judah (Josh 9:17; 10:2). Also, while Rahab is the only Canaanite mentioned who assisted the Israelites in the conquest of the cities, this may be because the attack of Jericho is described in great detail and the conquest accounts of most other cities are very brief. There may very well have been other "Rahabs" who entered Israel with their families, and whose stories are not recorded due to the brevity of the accounts. In other words, a careful reading of Joshua indicates that Israel did merge with some Canaanite clans or even whole cities who were sympathetic to them. When we move to the book of Judges, there will be even more evidence of assimilation, as the Israelites "dwelt among the Canaanites, the inhabitants of the land", without open hostility or warfare (Judg 1:32).

How are these proposals to be evaluated? First, there are issues of basic historical plausibility: Would tens of thousands of new, culturally distinct settlers (for example, who ate no pork) in the Canaanite highlands in the twelfth century really be welcomed without opposition from the native Canaanites on whose resources they were encroaching? And how probable is a Marxist-style revolution in thirteenth-century Canaan, especially in the absence of almost any archaeological or textual evidence for such an event? Thus, alternatives to the conquest model are not without difficulties in reconciling the biblical and archaeological data. Certainly the most radical, that biblical "Israel" is a Persian period fantasy, has the least to commend it. A minority view among scholars, it is difficult to sustain even prescinding from faith, because there is too much

---

[5] Norman K. Gottwald, *The Tribes of Yahweh: A Sociology of the Religion of Liberated Israel, 1250–1050 B.C.E.* (Maryknoll, N.Y.: Orbis, 1979).

archaeological data for Israel's existence in the land prior to the rise of the Persian Empire.[6] The "peaceful immigration" and "peasant revolt" models have as their major weakness that they are unable to explain the biblical data. If these really were the ways that Israel arose in Canaan, why did the Israelites not tell their history that way? Why did they not recall YHWH leading them westward across the Jordan where they were greeted by like-minded Semites who shared their values? Why not tell about YHWH calling them to rise up against their urban masters to establish a more egalitarian society? If these were their true origins, there were many ways that those origins could have been understood from a theological perspective. Why discard their true national history in favor of the one presented in the biblical text?

The book of Joshua is far more detailed—and includes many more unexpected, awkward, or embarrassing episodes—than we would expect from a work of pure fiction (for example, Achan's sin, the failure to conquer many areas, the Transjordanian altar fiasco, and so on). Its description of the land of Canaan shows an intimate familiarity with the late second- to early first-millennium geography of that region and displays no awareness of some important later developments, such as the city of Jerusalem becoming the capital of the nation: Jerusalem in Joshua is often called "Jebus" (Josh 15:8; 18:28; 19:10–11), and the sacred writer notes that Jebusites still controlled it at the time of writing ("to this day", Josh 15:63). We have already noted its similarities to contemporary Egyptian conquest narratives.[7] While it is difficult to get a perfect match between the events of the book and the archaeological record, this is not a problem unique to biblical history. Other historical conquests—the Anglo-Saxon conquest of Britain, the Norman of England, the Arab of Palestine—have also left little archaeological evidence. The archaeological record, by definition, is incomplete. It may be hoped that further excavations in Israel may clarify the date of the conquest. In the meantime, it is reasonable to conclude, from the perspective of both reason and faith, that the book of Joshua describes historical events in Canaan in the mid- to late second millennium B.C.

Theological Issues in Joshua

The Role of Liturgy in the Book of Joshua

Contrary to contemporary nationalistic or secular conceptions of warfare, the conquest of the Promised Land in the book of Joshua is presented as *liturgical action*. This is in continuity with ideas from the book of Numbers, where the war camp of Israel was also a liturgical procession gathered around the ark and the Tabernacle (Num 1–10).

For example, at the very onset of the conquest, the twelve tribes of Israel are led by the priests and the Ark of the Covenant in a liturgical procession across the river Jordan, where they set up an altar and twelve stones as a memorial of the event (Josh 3–4). Along similar lines, it is by means of a seven-day liturgical

---

[6] See Kitchen, *Reliability of the Old Testament*, 159–240.
[7] Hoffmeier, "Structure of Joshua 1–11", 165–79.

procession that the Israelites attack the city of Jericho, processing around the city in patterns of seven—the sacred number of the covenant (cf. Gen 21:25–34)—with the priests praising God upon trumpets made of ram's horns (Josh 6:1–21; cf. Ps 98:6; 150:3). With this liturgical context of conquest in mind, then, the book of Joshua depicts the cities of Canaan as being "dedicated" as offerings to the Lord (see below on *herem* warfare); the people do not engage in war for material gain, but in order to fulfill the will of the Lord. Finally, the object of the conquest is "rest"—a liturgical concept associated with the Sabbath day and the establishment of a central sanctuary within the land (Deut 12:10). At key points before, during, and after the conquest and division of the land, Joshua leads the people in covenant-renewal rituals or liturgies: circumcision (Josh 5:1–9), Passover (Josh 5:10–12), the reading of the law of Moses on Mount Ebal (Josh 8:30–35), and the covenant renewal at Shechem (Josh 23–24). The Promised Land is ultimately a place for worship; the exodus was oriented toward worship from the beginning (Ex 4:23; 5:3), and the land was described figuratively as God's "mountain" and "sanctuary" (Ex 15:17). Joshua participates in a biblical and ancient Near Eastern pattern in which a deity defeats his foes and builds a temple for himself to mark his victory. This pattern was seen in the book of Exodus, with the defeat of the Egyptians leading to the building of the Tabernacle. Now again, Joshua defeats the Canaanites and establishes the Tabernacle at the northern city of Shiloh, which is mentioned here for the first time in the Bible (Josh 19:51).

The Problem of Herem Warfare

The total, or *herem*, warfare against the Canaanites is one of the most difficult moral and theological issues in the Old Testament. It is not limited to one book, but concerns Deuteronomy, where the command of *herem* warfare is given, as well as Joshua, where it is carried out. Above all, it raises the question: How does one explain the presence of the command for the complete annihilation of the Canaanite peoples—men, women, and children—in Scripture? Before looking at various explanations, several historical and linguistic aspects of *herem* warfare should be highlighted.

First, it is important to note that there is a linguistic difficulty revolving around the very word *herem*. This is a significant issue, since the book of Joshua uses the Hebrew noun (*herem*) and verb (*haram*) more than any other book of the Old Testament, some twenty-seven times total.[8] What exactly does it mean? Although contemporary discussions of the issue frequently speak about "holy war" in the Bible, there is no such expression in Hebrew Scripture; it is a modern construction.[9] The Old Testament speaks only of the *herem*. With this in mind, most scholars agree that in a general sense, the Hebrew term *herem* means "devoted", and it was used in a liturgical context to describe persons, places, or things that were wholly given over to the use or service of God. However,

---

[8] Victor Hamilton, *Handbook on the Historical Books* (Grand Rapids, Mich.: Baker Academic, 2001), 33–34.

[9] See Heath A. Thomas, Jeremy Evans, and Paul Copan, *Holy War in the Bible: Christian Morality and the Old Testament Problem* (Downers Grove, Ill.: IVP Academic, 2013).

when it comes to exact translations of the term in a military context, English translations of the Bible vary widely on how to render it:

English Translations of Herem *in the Book of Joshua*

1. "To be accursed" (KJV)
2. "Devoted for destruction" (RSV)
3. "Under the LORD's ban" (NAB)
4. "Devoted under the curse of destruction" (NJB)

In a military context, *herem* referred to the dedication of a city as a sacrifice or offering to God. Since everything in the city was consecrated, it could not be taken as booty for the enrichment of the soldiers but had to be offered to God through destruction, on the analogy of a burnt offering (Josh 6:17–19).

Second, from a historical perspective, *herem* warfare was not unique to ancient Israel. For example, King Mesha of Moab, to the east of the Jordan, attacked certain Israelite towns and dedicated them to his pagan deity:

> Then Chemosh said to me: "Go, take Nebo from Israel!" (15) So I went by night and fought against it from the break of dawn until noon, taking it and slaying all, seven thousand men, boys, women, girls and maid-servants, for I had devoted them to destruction for (the god) Ashtar-Chemosh.[10]

The seven thousand slain probably represent an estimate of the total population of the town before the attack. Although the text describes all as slain, this means none were left alive in the town—the numbers of fugitives who fled from the battle are not recorded.

Third, from the literary point of view, the genre of the accounts of *herem* in the book of Joshua needs to be interpreted correctly, in light of the ancient Near Eastern convention of using hyperbole in descriptions of military conquest. From this perspective, the use of hyperbole urges caution in interpreting just how many Canaanites were actually put to death. In practice, the *herem* against the Canaanites was not carried out as thoroughly as Moses envisions in the last book of the Pentateuch (Deut 20:16–18). According to the book of Joshua itself, elements of the Canaanite population like Rahab and the Gibeonites did find ways to assimilate with Israel (Josh 2, 8). Indeed, while it is true that the Israelites left no one remaining alive in the cities they captured, there is good reason to believe that untold numbers fled alive before, during, and after the siege.[11] Despite the comprehensive sound of the description of Israelite victories mentioned above (Josh 10:28–41; 11:10–15), large numbers of the inhabitants must have fled and taken refuge elsewhere to return later, because some of the same cities, such as Hazor, arise once more to pose a threat in Israel's history (cf. Josh 11:10–11; Judg 4:2).

---

[10] James B. Pritchard, ed., *The Ancient Near Eastern Texts relating to the Old Testament*, 3rd ed. with Supplement (Princeton, N.J.: Princeton University Press, 1969), 320.

[11] See Paul Copan, *Is God a Moral Monster? Making Sense of the Old Testament God* (Grand Rapids, Mich.: Baker Academic, 2011), 169–85.

Fourth, as the book of Joshua indicates, the Canaanites could have avoided war with Israel, perhaps by vacating peacefully or converting to Yahwism (Josh 11:19). Instead, most of Joshua's campaigns began as *defensive* measures against coordinated Canaanite aggression (Josh 10:1–5; 11:1–5).

Nevertheless, even when we take into account these mitigating factors, the fact remains that according to both Deuteronomy and Joshua, the *herem* by its very nature entailed the death of some non-combatants, such as women and children. This fact requires a theological explanation: *How can God permit this?* In the history of biblical interpretation, from ancient until modern times, there are at least four major explanations of *herem* warfare:

1. *The Divine Pedagogy Explanation*: According to this point of view, the best way to explain the divine command to carry out *herem* warfare is to put it in the context of a "divine pedagogy" or progressive revelation. In essence, this consists in admitting that somewhere along the way—whether with the historical figures of Joshua and the Israelites themselves or with the human author(s) of the biblical text—those describing the actions of Israel "record for us what they *thought* God wanted them to carry out rather than what he has *actually* willed".[12] It is important to stress that the idea of a mistaken prophet can take very different forms: some assert that the Bible is simply in error when it claims that God commanded the Israelites to destroy the men, women, and children of Canaan. Others refuse to accuse the Scriptures of formal moral error. Instead, they assert that, in the absence of the fullness of divine revelation, the people of the Old Covenant "were not privy" to later "distinctions" between what was commanded by God (his "positive" will) and what was permitted by God (his "permissive" will).[13] This material limitation results in the biblical text describing God as the direct cause of a warfare that, in fact, he only allows as a result of human sin.

2. *The Allegorical Explanation*: Another solution, which dates at least as far back as the time of Origen of Alexandria (ca. A.D. 200), holds that the destruction of Jericho and the Canaanites should be explained according to the *spiritual sense* (or "allegorical" sense) of the biblical text rather than the literal sense, the latter of which seems irreconcilable with the goodness of God. For example, in his series of homilies on the book of Joshua, Origen argues that the conquest of the Promised Land by Joshua really serves only to foreshadow the spiritual warfare of the New Covenant.:

> If those things that were dimly sketched through Moses concerning the tabernacle or the sacrifices and the entire worship are said to be a "type and shadow of heavenly things" (Heb 8:5), doubtless *the wars that are waged through Jesus* [Greek for Joshua], *and the slaughter of kings and enemies must also be said to be "a shadow and type of heavenly things,"* namely, of those wars that our Lord Jesus with his army and officers—that is, the throngs of believers and their leaders—fights with the Devil and his angels.[14]

---

[12] Matthew J. Ramage, *Dark Passages of the Bible: Engaging Scripture with Benedict XVI and St. Thomas Aquinas* (Washington, D.C.: Catholic University of America Press, 2013), 185.

[13] See ibid., 189, 191.

[14] Origen, *Homilies on Joshua* 12.1, trans. Barbara Bruce, The Fathers of the Church 105 (Washington, D.C.: Catholic University of America Press, 2002), 120.

It is worth noting that Origen develops this explanation in response to early Christian heretics such as Marcion who rejected the Old Testament because of the "cruelty" of the "God of the Law" depicted in the historical books.[15] In response to such accusations, Origen insists that Joshua's destruction of the Canaanites is "not teaching cruelty through this, as the heretics think, but representing the future sacraments in these affairs".[16]

3. *The Divine Judgment Explanation*: According to this solution, the practice of *herem* at the time of Joshua was as a singular instance of divine punishment, in which God deputed the Israelite armies to carry out his judgment upon the cities of Canaan, including the non-combatants. From this point of view, God uses the Israelites as his instruments of justice to judge the Canaanites, even as he will later use Assyria and Babylon as instruments to judge Israel (cf. Josh 10:12–19). The oldest example of this explanation goes back to the Wisdom of Solomon, which recognizes the moral problem of total warfare but answers it by emphasizing the horrific evils being committed by the Canaanites (cf. Lev 18, Deut 18:9–14) as well as the unquestionable justice of the Creator:

> Those who dwelt of old in your holy land [that is, the Canaanites]
> you hated for *their detestable practices,*
> *their works of sorcery and unholy rites,*
> *their merciless slaughter of children,*
> *and their sacrificial feasting on human flesh and blood.*
> These initiates from the midst of a heathen cult,
> these parents who murder helpless lives,
> you wanted to destroy by the hands of our fathers,
> that the land most precious of all to you
> might receive a worthy colony of the servants of God.
> But even these you spared, since they were but men,
> and sent wasps as forerunners of your army,
> to destroy them little by little,
> though you were not unable to give the ungodly into the hands of
>   the righteous in battle,
> or to destroy them at one blow by dread wild beasts or your stern
>   word.
> But judging them little by little you gave them a chance to repent,
> though you were not unaware that their origin was evil
> and their wickedness inborn,
> and that their way of thinking would never change.
> For they were an accursed race from the beginning,
> and it was not through fear of any one that you left them unpunished
>   for their sins.
>
> *For who will say, "What have you done?"*
> *Or who will resist your judgment?*

[15] Ibid., 12.3, p. 123.
[16] Ibid., 11.6, p. 119.

Who will accuse you for the destruction of nations which you made?
Or who will come before you to plead as an advocate for unrighteous
     men?
For neither is there any god besides you, whose care is for all men,
to whom you should prove that you have not judged unjustly;
nor can any king or monarch confront you about those whom you
     have punished.
You are righteous and rule all things righteously,
deeming it alien to your power
to condemn him who does not deserve to be punished. (Wis 12:3–15)

In later centuries, the divine judgment explanation of the destruction of the Canaanites would go on to be proposed by both Augustine and Thomas Aquinas, who addressed the question of whether the commandment "You shall not kill" (Ex 20:13) was violated by the Israelites when they destroyed the Canaanites. According to Augustine:

[T]here are some exceptions made by the divine authority to its own law, that men may not be put to death. These exceptions are of two kinds, being justified either by a general law, or by a special commission granted for a time to some individual. And in this latter case, he to whom authority is delegated, and who is but the sword in the hand of him who uses it, is not himself responsible for the death he deals. And, accordingly, they who have waged war in obedience to the divine command, or in conformity with His laws, have represented in their persons the public justice or the wisdom of government, and in this capacity have put to death wicked men; such persons have by no means violated the commandment, "Thou shalt not kill."[17]

According to Augustine's explanation, then, the command to enact the *herem* warfare against the Canaanites is interpreted, not as being a violation of the Decalogue, but as a kind of deputation of divine judgment to the people of Israel, who do not violate the commandment by taking the physical life of the Canaanites. Along similar lines, Thomas Aquinas would go on to argue that insofar as man has merited physical death through original sin, God cannot be charged with injustice when he takes the life of anyone, even those innocent of actual sin, such as children.[18] As Hannah says in the book of Samuel: "The LORD kills and brings to life" (1 Sam 2:6).

   4. *The Deuteronomic Concession Explanation*: Fourth and finally, in more recent times, scholars have emphasized that, from a salvation-historical point of view, the command to pursue *herem* warfare against the cities of Canaanites in the land is not part of the original Sinai covenant, but a concession to Israel's sinfulness and hard-heartedness:

The Israelites practiced *herem* warfare, in which whole cities and their inhabitants were devoted to destruction.... This holy war was a concession of the

---

[17] Augustine, *The City of God* 1.21, in *NPNF1* 2:15.
[18] See Thomas Aquinas, *Summa Theologica* I–II, q. 94, a. 5.

Deuteronomic covenant, announced after the Israelites had twice lapsed into idolatrous worship during the wilderness period; its stern provisions were necessary because God knew that otherwise his people were too weak to resist the attraction of Canaanite idolatry.[19]

This explanation pays close attention to the historical context of the commands to execute the *herem*, noting carefully that total warfare against the Canaanites is not part of God's original plan for Israel but, rather, the last in a series of concessions designed to keep Israel from falling prey to the idolatry of the Canaanite peoples. This progression can be summed up in chart form:

Historical Context	Command to Israelites
1. *Mount Sinai*:	Be a "kingdom of priests". (Ex 19:5–6)
2. *Post-Golden Calf*:	Destroy altars of Canaanites and make no covenant with them. (Ex 34:11–16)
3. *Post-Apostasy at Moab*:	Destroy altars and drive out the Canaanites from the land. (Num 33:50–56)
4. *Final Speech of Moses*:	Utterly destroy the Canaanites in the land, as well as any Israelite city that becomes idolatrous. (Deut 7:1–11; 12:29–31; 20:10–18; cf. Deut 13:12–18)

Notice here that there is nothing said about *herem* warfare in the early stages of the exodus, when the first generation arrives at Mount Sinai. To the contrary, God calls Israel to be a "kingdom of priests", who will lead by worshipping him. It is only *after* the worship of the Golden Calf (Ex 32) that Moses begins delivering commands about having to destroy the altars of Canaan when Israel enters the Promised Land, and only *after* the apostasy at Beth-peor on the plains of Moab (Num 25) that he adds to this the command to expel the Canaanites. And it is only at the very end of his life, when Israel's habitual tendency to commit idolatry has become abundantly clear, that Moses changes the instructions one final time, adding a command to carry out *herem* warfare against the Canaanite cities of the land.

In support of this salvation-historical explanation, scholars emphasize that the Old Testament itself describes the *herem* laws of Deuteronomy and various other concessions—such as the permission to divorce—as *"not good"*.[20]

> I [the LORD] gave them my statutes and showed them my ordinances, by whose observance man shall live [= the Ten Commandments]....
>
> Moreover *I gave them statutes that were not good* and ordinances by which they could not have life [= certain laws of Deuteronomy]. (Ezek 20:11, 25)

---

[19] Scott W. Hahn, *Kinship by Covenant: A Canonical Approach to the Fulfillment of God's Saving Promises*, Anchor Yale Bible Reference Library (New Haven, Conn.: Yale University Press, 2009), 946–47.

[20] See Scott W. Hahn and John S. Bergsma, "What Laws Were 'Not Good'? A Canonical Approach to the Theological Problem of Ezekiel 20:25–26", *Journal of Biblical Literature* 123.2 (2004): 201–18.

Jesus likewise speaks in the New Testament of the permission to divorce in Deuteronomy as something that Israel was "allowed" to do because of the hardness of their hearts:

> [The Pharisees] said to [Jesus]: "Why then did Moses command one to give a certificate of divorce, and to put her away?" He said to them, *"For your hardness of heart Moses allowed you to divorce your wives,* but from the beginning it was not so." (Mt 19:7–8)

Notice that this explanation emphasizes the canonical and historical *context* of the various commands given by God. It stresses the point that not all laws in the Old Testament are created equal, and any evaluation of their moral or theological character must be carried out with the utmost attention to when, where, why, and how the law is given. In the case of the divine command to carry out the *herem* against the Canaanites, it is clear that although Moses commands the second generation of Israelites to enact total warfare against the Canaanites, "from the beginning it was not so."

The "Dark Passages" in Scripture

In closing, however one answers the question of *herem*, it is important to stress that, while the Old Testament supplies rich meditations on the meaning of the death of the innocent (Wis 4:7–15), ultimately, the theological question of God's justice in permitting the death of persons innocent of actual sin among the Canaanites needs to be referred to the *Cross of Christ*, which is *the definitive hermeneutical principle for understanding both God's justice and his mercy* in salvation history.

The Cross reveals God the Son, who himself experienced an innocent death of the worst kind; God the Father, who willingly gave up an innocent son; and God the Spirit, who raised the innocent Son from the dead (Rom 8:11), thereby triumphing over death. Therefore, when God permits the death of the innocent, he does not ask of them anything God himself, in the person of the Son, has not experienced in his human nature. He himself understands their suffering and has demonstrated through the Cross that he can right the wrongs of this temporal life in the life to come. For this reason, Jesus teaches that *physical death* is not to be feared (Lk 12:4), because it is only temporal. God may take life because he first gave it as an unmerited gift, and he can restore it in the world to come. He is the Lord of life and death (Deut 32:39), and, as the entirety of Scripture attests, he is also a loving Father who will restore life to the innocent in the resurrection. In the words of Pope Benedict XVI:

> In discussing the relationship between the Old and the New Testaments, the Synod also considered *those passages in the Bible which, due to the violence and immorality they occasionally contain,* prove *obscure and difficult.* Here it must be remembered first and foremost that *biblical revelation is deeply rooted in history.* God's plan is manifested *progressively* and it is accomplished slowly, *in successive stages* and despite human resistance. God chose a people and patiently worked to guide and educate them. Revelation is suited to the cultural and moral level of distant times and thus describes facts and customs, such as cheating and trickery, and acts of violence and massacre, without explicitly denouncing the immorality of such things. This can

be explained by the historical context, yet it can cause the modern reader to be taken aback, especially if he or she fails to take account of the many "dark" deeds carried out down the centuries, and also in our own day. In the Old Testament, the preaching of the prophets vigorously challenged every kind of injustice and violence, whether collective or individual, and thus became God's way of training his people in preparation for the Gospel. So it would be a mistake to neglect those passages of Scripture that strike us as problematic. *Rather, we should be aware that the correct interpretation of these passages requires a degree of expertise, acquired through a training that interprets the texts in their historical-literary context and within the Christian perspective which has as its ultimate hermeneutical key "the Gospel and the new commandment of Jesus Christ brought about in the paschal mystery."* I encourage scholars and pastors to help all the faithful to approach these passages through an interpretation which enables their meaning to emerge in the light of the mystery of Christ.[21]

Joshua in the Living Tradition

Despite the historical and theological difficulties raised by the book of Joshua, it has played a surprisingly significant role in the living tradition of the Church, especially as a rich source of typology.

Joshua as a Prefiguration of Jesus

For example, in the early centuries of the Christian Church, the book of Joshua was frequently interpreted as containing important *types* of Christ. This typological reading was especially popular in Greek-speaking circles, facilitated by the fact that in the Greek Septuagint, the name of Joshua is "Jesus" (Greek *Iēsous*). For example, Saint John Chrysostom remarks:

> *The name of Joshua* [=JESUS] *was a type....* [T]his man was on this account so called in type; for he used to be called Hoshea. Therefore the name was changed: for it was a prediction and a prophecy. *He brought the people into the promised land, as JESUS [does] into heaven*; not the Law; since neither did Moses [bring them into the Promised Land] but remained without. The Law has not power to bring in, but grace.[22]

In other words, the Church Fathers saw great significance in the fact that for all Moses' greatness, he was not able to lead Israel into the Promised Land. His inadequacy was viewed as representative of the limitations of the Old Covenant itself, which does not have the power to lead mankind into the Promised Land of the vision of God. Beyond Moses, there is need of "salvation", a "Joshua" who can accomplish what Moses could not. Just as Joshua succeeds Moses, circumcises the people, gets them to obey as they had never done in the wilderness, and leads them to claim their rightful inheritance (Josh 2–5), so Jesus, the new "Joshua", succeeds Moses as the great prophet of God, circumcises the hearts of God's people through baptism and the gift of the Holy Spirit (Acts

---

[21] *VD* 42 (emphasis added).
[22] John Chrysostom, *Homilies on Hebrews* 27.6, in *NPNF1* 14:489.

2:37–38; Col 2:11–13), and enables an obedience never before possible through the power of the same Spirit (Rom 8:3–4), leading the people of God into the inheritance of the heavenly Promised Land (1 Pet 1:3–4).

Rahab as an Example of God's Mercy and a Type of the Church

Intriguingly, when it comes to the typological interpretation of the book of Joshua, the figure of Rahab the prostitute of Jericho is almost as prominent as Joshua himself. In the New Testament, she is brought forward alongside Abraham as an example of an Old Testament figure who demonstrated both faith and works (Jas 2:21–25). In ancient rabbinic tradition, it is held that Rahab married Joshua, was the ancestress of the prophet Jeremiah and the prophetess Huldah, and is regarded along with Sarah, Abigail, and Esther as one of the "four women of surpassing beauty in the world".[23]

In the early Church Fathers, two aspects of the figure of Rahab stand out as significant. First, she is regarded as an example of God's mercy toward those who have led morally depraved lives but who turn away from immorality to serve the living and true God. In his catechetical lectures to converts, Cyril of Jerusalem uses Rahab to exhort those becoming Christians that no matter what their past sins, they are not beyond the pale of God's mercy:

> But perhaps even among women some one will say, I have committed fornication, and adultery, I have defiled my body by excesses of all kinds: is there salvation for me? *Turn thine eyes, O woman, upon Rahab, and look thou also for salvation;* for if she who had been openly and publicly a harlot was saved by repentance, is not she who on some one occasion before receiving grace committed fornication to be saved by repentance and fasting?[24]

Along similar lines, Rahab was also held up by a number of early Fathers as a type of the Church, which would contain converts drawn from among the Gentile nations:

> This Rahab, although she is called a prostitute, nevertheless is a sign of the virgin church, considered as a foreshadow of the coming realities at the end of the age, where she alone is preserved to life among all who are perishing.... Just as the apostle says, "An unfaithful wife is sanctified through her faithful husband (1 Cor 7:14)", so also is the church, coming from the infidelity of the Gentiles and prostitution with idols, sanctified through the body of Christ, of which we are members.... Because the church, as I have often said, gathered from the multitude of Gentiles, was then called a prostitute, therefore the church is found in the figure of Rahab, the hostess of saints.[25]

---

[23] Babylonian Talmud, *Megillah* 14b–15a, in Isidore Epstein, ed., *The Babylonian Talmud*, 35 vols. (London: Soncino, 1935–1952).

[24] Cyril of Jerusalem, *Catechetical Lectures* 2.9, in *NPNF2* 7:10.

[25] Origen, *Tractates on the Books of Holy Scripture* 12, in John R. Franke, ed., *Joshua, Judges, Ruth, 1–2 Samuel*, Old Testament 4, Ancient Christian Commentary on Scripture, ed. Thomas C. Oden (Downers Grove, Ill.: InterVarsity Press, 2005), 9.

It is remarkable that, despite Rahab's identity as a pagan prostitute, ancient Christians did not hesitate to hold her up as a model of conversion from a sinful past and even as containing within herself an aspect of the mystery of the Church.

The Destruction of the Canaanites and Destruction of Sinful Attachments

As noted above, one of the most difficult aspects of the book of Joshua is its depiction of the Israelites carrying out *herem* warfare against the Canaanite inhabitants of the land. In the living tradition of the Church, this aspect of the book came to be interpreted as a figure for Christians who have been delivered from bondage to sin and death by baptism (as in the crossing of the Jordan) but who continue to consent to evil desires and sins. For example, in the mystical writings of Saint John of the Cross (sixteenth century A.D.), we find a lengthy reflection on the spiritual meaning of the *herem*:

> [God] has withdrawn them from the world, slain the giants which are their sins, and destroyed the multitude of their enemies (*the occasions of sin encountered in the world*) for the sole purpose of their entering with greater freedom into the promised land of divine union. Nevertheless, in spite of all this, they will fraternize and make pacts with the insignificant people [literally, "little folk"] of their imperfections by not mortifying them completely. And God in His anger allows them to go from bad to worse in their appetites.
>
> *We find another figure of this in the Book of Joshua.* There we read that *God commanded Joshua, when he was about to enter into possession of the promised land, to destroy everything in the city of Jericho* without leaving anything alive, neither men nor women, young nor old, nor any animals. And He ordered him not to covet or seize any of the booty [Josh 6:18, 19, 21]. The lesson here is that *all objects living in the soul*—whether they be many or few, large or small—*must die in order that the soul enter divine union*, and it must bear no desire for them but remain detached as though they were nonexistent to it, and it to them.[26]

Notice here how the entire spiritual exegesis of John of the Cross presupposes that the exodus from Egypt is a prefiguration of the spiritual life and the entry into the Promised Land a foreshadowing of entry into union with God. Like other Christians, he uses the passages on *herem* war, not to justify earthly warfare, but rather to explain the radical, all-or-nothing nature of spiritual warfare (cf. Eph 6) and the total mortification of desires for anything other than God.

The Defeat of Jericho as a Prefiguration of the End of the World

Finally, given the typological identification of Joshua with Jesus and of Rahab with the Church, it is perhaps unsurprising that the Church Fathers also saw the destruction of the city of Jericho by Joshua as a prefiguration of the judgment

---

[26] John of the Cross, *The Ascent of Mount Carmel* I.11.7–8, in *The Collected Works of St. John of the Cross*, trans. Kieran Kavanaugh, O.C.D., and Otilio Rodriguez, O.C.D. (Washington, D.C.: ICS Publications, Institute of Carmelite Studies, 1979), 98–99 (emphasis added).

of the world by Jesus at the end of time. From this point of view, the city of Jericho is a kind of *microcosm* ("little universe"); what happens to it locally at the time of Joshua will happen to the world at the final advent of Christ:

> How, therefore, is Jericho captured? The sword is not drawn against it; the battering ram is not arranged, nor is the spear hurled. The priestly trumpets alone are employed, and by these the walls of Jericho are overthrown.
>
> We frequently find Jericho to be placed in Scripture as a figure of this world.... In what way, therefore, will the consummation be given to it? By what instruments? By the sound, it says, of trumpets. Of what trumpets? Let Paul make known the mystery of this secret to you. Hear what he himself says: "The trumpet will sound," he says, "and the dead who are in Christ will rise incorruptible" [1 Cor 15:52], and "The Lord himself with a command, with the voice of the archangel and with the trumpet of God, will descend from heaven" [1 Thess 4:16]. At that time, therefore, Jesus our Lord conquers Jericho with trumpets and overthrows it, so that out of it, only the prostitute is saved and all her house.[27]

Notice that for Origen, the supernatural, non-military—one might say, liturgical—nature of Jericho's defeat is itself a sign of the fact that when Christ returns at the end of time, he will conquer the world, not by the sword, but by the sound of the trumpet and the power of his presence.

The Book of Joshua in the Lectionary

In Joshua, the conquest of Canaan begins with a liturgical procession across the Jordan, followed by the covenant-initiation rite of circumcision (Josh 5:1–9, a type of baptism), the celebration of the Passover (Josh 5:10–12, a type of the Eucharist), and the "liturgical conquest" of Jericho (Josh 5:13–6:27, a type of the ascetical struggle). The book ends with Joshua leading a covenant-renewal ceremony for all Israel (Josh 24:25).

Despite the liturgical character of the book, there are very few readings from Joshua in the modern celebration of the Liturgy of the Word. Most of them (three of five) are selected from Joshua's farewell speech, in which he calls Israel to "choose this day whom you will serve... as for me and my house, we will serve the LORD" (Josh 24:15). In this way, the Church remembers Joshua primarily as Moses' successor, who led the people in the land and forcefully called them to renew their covenantal commitment to the Lord (see tables on next page.)

Conclusion

The book of Joshua serves as an epilogue to the Pentateuch, in which the promise of the gift of the land to the descendants of the patriarchs is finally fulfilled (cf. Gen 12:7). The book is permeated with the memory of Moses and the language of Deuteronomy. Joshua is obedient to all that Moses commanded; he conquers the main centers of Canaanite power and establishes Israel permanently in the

---

[27] Origen, *Homilies on Joshua* 6.4, 71–72, in Franke, *Joshua, Judges*, 38–39.

Readings from Joshua for Sundays, Feast Days, Liturgical Seasons, and Other Occasions

MSO = Masses for Special Occasions; *OM* = Optional Memorial; *VM* = Votive Mass; *Rit* = Ritual

Passage	Description	Occasion	Explanation
5:9a, 10–12	Joshua celebrates the Passover with Israel in the land, and the manna ceases.	*4th Sun. of Lent (C)*	Lent of Year C includes a selection of highlights of salvation history in the first reading, in chronological order through Lent and oriented to sacramental catechesis. This reading marks a key stage in Israel's journey: celebrating Passover in the land. Soon the catechumens will celebrate the new Passover, the Eucharist, within the Church.
24:1–2a, 15–17, 18b	Joshua calls Israel to choose which god they will serve; the Israelites choose the Lord.	*21st Sun. in OT (B)*	This reading clearly complements the Gospel, John 6:60–69, the conclusion of the Bread of Life discourse, when many disciples turn away from Jesus, and he calls the Twelve to decision: "Do you also wish to go away?" Just as Israel responded to the call of the first Joshua by affirming its covenant with the Lord, so Peter on behalf of the Church responds to the call of the second Joshua by affirming: "You are the Holy One of God."

Reading of Joshua for Daily Mass: Ordinary Time, Year I: Week 19

Day	Passage Read	Description
Th	3:7–10a, 11, 13–17	The Jordan ceases its flow as the priests enter the water with the ark; Israel passes over on dry ground.
F	24:1–13	Joshua reviews salvation history from the time of Abraham through the conquest and settlement of the Promised Land.
Sa	24:14–29	Joshua calls the people of Israel to renew their commitment to the Lord and celebrates a covenant-renewal ceremony with them at Shechem.

land of Canaan. At the end of his life, he renews the Deuteronomic covenant with Israel (Josh 24:25), but not without warning Israel sternly about the implications of the covenant curses (Josh 24:19–22).

In spiritual interpretation, Joshua is a type of Christ, who leads Israel through prefigurements of the sacraments into the Promised Land, a foretaste of heaven, life in God's presence. The warfare against the Canaanites poses theological questions that can only be resolved in light of the Cross; but the spiritual sense of these texts powerfully reminds us of the necessity of unrelenting combat in the spiritual life and of the very real dangers posed by compromise with sin or the spiritual forces of evil (Eph 6:12).

For Further Reading

Commentaries and Studies of Joshua

Billings, Rachel M. *"Israel Served the Lord": The Book of Joshua as Paradoxical Portrait of Faithful Israel*. ND Reading the Scriptures. Notre Dame, Ind.: University of Notre Dame Press, 2013.

Boling, Robert G. *Joshua*. Anchor Bible 6. New York: Doubleday, 1982.

Bright, John. *A History of Israel*. 4th ed. Louisville, Ky.: Westminster John Knox Press, 2000.

Gottwald, Norman K. *The Tribes of Yahweh: A Sociology of the Religion of Liberated Israel, 1250–1050 B.C.E.* Maryknoll, N.Y.: Orbis, 1979.

Hamilton, Victor. *Handbook on the Historical Books*. Grand Rapids, Mich.: Baker Academic, 2001. (See pp. 15–95.)

Nelson, Richard D. *Joshua: A Commentary*. Old Testament Library. Louisville, Ky.: Westminster John Knox Press, 1997.

Noth, Martin. *A History of Israel*. Translated by Stanley Goodman. New York: Harper & Row, 1960.

Walton, John H., ed. *Joshua, Judges, Ruth, 1 & 2 Samuel*. Vol. 2 of *Zondervan Illustrated Bible Backgrounds Commentary*. Grand Rapids, Mich.: Zondervan, 2009. (See pp. 2–93.)

Historical Issues in Joshua

de Vaux, Roland. *The Early History of Israel*. Translated by David Smith. 2 vols. London: Darton, Longman, and Todd, 1978. (See pp. 473–680.)

Hoffmeier, James K. "The Structure of Joshua 1–11 and the Annals of Thutmose III". Pages 165–79 in *Faith, Tradition, and History: Old Testament Historiography in Its Near Eastern Context*. Edited by A. R. Millard, James Karl Hoffmeier, and David W. Baker. Winona Lake, Ind.: Eisenbrauns, 1994.

Kitchen, Kenneth A. *On the Reliability of the Old Testament*. Grand Rapids, Mich.: Eerdmans, 2006. (See pp. 159–99.)

Lohfink, Norbert. "Harem". In *Theological Dictionary of the Old Testament*. Edited by G. Johannes Botterweck et al. 15 vols. Grand Rapids, Mich.: Eerdmans, 1974–2006. (See vol. 5, pp. 180–99.)

Niditch, Susan. *War in the Hebrew Bible: A Study in the Ethics of Violence*. New York: Oxford University Press, 1993.

Wood, B. G. "Did the Israelites Conquer Jericho? A New Look at the Archaeological Evidence". *Biblical Archaeological Review* 16 (1990): 44–59.

Theological Issues in Joshua

Copan, Paul. *Is God a Moral Monster? Making Sense of the Old Testament God*. Grand Rapids, Mich.: Baker Books, 2011. (See pp. 158–97.)

Hahn, Scott W. *Kinship by Covenant*. Anchor Yale Bible Reference Library. New Haven, Conn.: Yale University Press, 2009.

———. "War and Warfare". *Catholic Bible Dictionary*. New York: Doubleday, 2009.

———, and John S. Bergsma. "What Laws Were 'Not Good'? A Canonical Approach to the Theological Problem of Ezekiel 20:25–26". *Journal of Biblical Literature* 123.2 (2004): 201–18.

Ramage, Matthew J. *Dark Passages of the Bible: Engaging Scripture with Benedict XVI and Thomas Aquinas.* Washington, D.C.: Catholic University of America Press, 2013.

Thomas, Heath A., Jeremy Evans, and Paul Copan. *Holy War in the Bible: Christian Morality and the Old Testament Problem.* Downers Grove, Ill.: IVP Academic, 2013.

Joshua in the Living Tradition

Benedict XVI, Pope. *Verbum Domini* (Post-Synodal Apostolic Exhortation, the Word of the Lord). Boston: Daughters of Saint Paul, 2010.

Daniélou, Jean, S.J. *From Shadows to Reality: Studies in the Biblical Typology of the Fathers.* Translated by Dom Wulstan Hibberd. Westminster, Md.: Newman Press, 1960.

Franke, John R. ed. *Joshua, Judges, Ruth, 1–2 Samuel.* Old Testament 4 of Ancient Christian Commentary on Scripture. Edited by Thomas C. Oden. Downers Grove, Ill.: InterVarsity Press, 2005. (See pp. 1–98.)

John of the Cross, Saint. *The Collected Works of St. John of the Cross.* Translated by Kieran Kavanaugh, O.C.D., and Otilio Rodriguez, O.C.D. Washington, D.C.: ICS Publications, Institute of Carmelite Studies, 1979. (See pp. 98–99.)

Origen. *Homilies on Joshua.* Translated by Barbara J. Bruce. The Fathers of the Church 105. Washington, D.C.: Catholic University of America Press, 2002.

12. JUDGES

Introduction

The book of Judges (Hebrew *sepher shophetim*) relates the history of Israel from the time of Joshua until the rise of the prophet Samuel. In contrast to the time under Moses and Joshua, the period of the judges was marked by religious, social, and political chaos, alleviated occasionally by the activities of charismatic leaders who delivered Israel from oppression by its enemies and who sometimes also served as religious and civil authorities. The book describes Israel's history in this time period as a repeating cycle of disobedience, punishment, repentance, and restoration. The people would *disobey* the Lord, usually by lapsing into Canaanite paganism; experience *punishment* from God in the form of defeat and subjugation by their enemies; cry out to the Lord in *repentance*; and be *restored* to peace through the ministry of a "judge" sent by God. After a time of peace and plenty, the people would forget God, fall back into disobedience, and repeat the cycle again.

The Place of Judges in the Canonical History

On the one hand, the book of Judges continues themes introduced in Deuteronomy that culminate in the Babylonian exile at the end of 2 Kings.[a] On the other hand, we should simultaneously take note of the uniqueness of this book and the "sea change" that takes place between Joshua and Judges. Moses is mentioned almost sixty times in Joshua but only five times in Judges, and his commandments only once (Judg 3:4). The book ends, not like Joshua did, with an appeal for fidelity to the Mosaic covenant, but with an implied hope for a coming king. The division between Joshua and Judges marks the point of the salvation-historical narrative at which anticipation of the coming Davidic covenant begins to overshadow retrospection on the Mosaic. For the rest of the Old Testament—including the historical books, the psalms, the wisdom literature, and the prophets—Israel's past will remain firmly rooted in Moses, but its future hopes will lie entirely with David.

[a] Martin Noth, *The Deuteronomistic History*, 2nd ed., JSOTSup 15 (Sheffield: JSOT Press 1991), 35–39, 71–80.

Although the ministry of some judges brought success and prosperity to Israel, on the whole the sacred author paints this era with some of the darkest colors in the entire Old Testament. By the end of the book, the reader has been prepared to understand the rationale for the institution of the monarchy, which—for all its faults—is preferable to the kind of moral and political anarchy that often prevailed in Israel during the times of the judges.

Literary Structure and Style of Judges

The book of Judges falls into three major parts: (1) a double introduction (Judg 1:1–3:6); (2) a central narrative (Judg 3:7–16:31); and (3) a double epilogue (Judg 17:1–21:25). The double introduction consists of two complementary descriptions of the situation of Israel in the generations immediately after the death of Joshua. The first introduction (Josh 1:1–2:5) is more material and specific; the second (Josh 2:6–3:6), more theological and general, including a programmatic description of the history to follow.

The central narrative consists of thirteen narrative units, each telling the story of one of twelve judges and one "anti-judge", the short-lived King Abimelech. These narrative units vary widely in length, from a single verse for the judge Shamgar (Judg 3:31) to four chapters devoted to Samson (Judg 13–16). It is typical to distinguish the "major" judges—those who are given extended narratives—from the "minor" judges, who are merely listed without any narrative detail:

	Text	Six "Major" Judges	Six "Minor" Judges	Home of Judge	Primary Enemy	Years
1	3:7–11	A. Othniel		Judah	Mesopotamians	40
2	3:12–30	B. Ehud		Benjamin	Moabites	80
3	3:31		a. Shamgar	Southern Dan?	Philistines	?
4	4:1—5:31	C. Deborah		Ephraim	Northern Canaanites	40
5	6:1—8:32	D. Gideon		Manasseh	Midianites	40
X	8:33—9:57	X. Abimelech		Shechem	Other Israelites	3
6	10:1–2		b. Tola	Issachar/Ephraim	?	23
7	10:3–5		c. Jair	Gilead (pr. Gad)	?	22
8	10:6—12:7	E. Jephthah		Gilead (pr. Gad)	Ammonites	6
9	12:8–10		d. Ibzan	Bethlehem (Judah)	?	7
10	12:11–12		e. Elon	Zebulun	?	10
11	12:13–15		f. Hillel	Ephraim	Amalekites?	8
12	13:11—16:31	F. Samson		Southern Dan	Philistines	20

By a close analysis of this chart, we can see the sacred author's literary artistry at work. There are six major and six minor judges described, with the reign of the "anti-judge" Abimelech placed roughly in the middle. The judges are widely distributed among the tribes and regions of Israel, and their opponents likewise are representative of their nearby traditional enemies. Intriguingly, some scholars

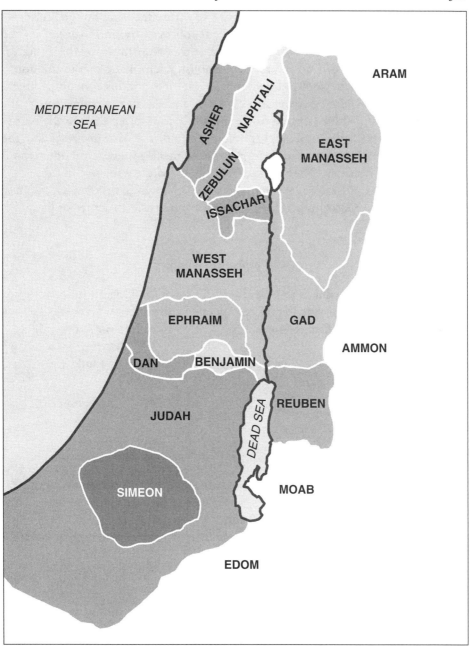

Israel Under the Judges

have also noted that the accounts of the major judges move in the geographical direction of south to north, linking the gradually increasing corruption with the movement from positive southern judges (such as Othniel and Ehud) to tragic and morally questionable northern judges (Samson and Jephthah).[1]

_____
[1] See Victor Hamilton, *Handbook on the Historical Books* (Grand Rapids, Mich.: Baker Academic, 2001), 103–5.

The double epilogue to the book consists of a story focusing on the liturgical/ cultic abuses of the period (Judg 17:1–18:31) followed by one focusing on the social abuses (Judg 19:1–21:25). In the first story, a Levite from Bethlehem is abducted by the tribe of Dan in order to establish a schismatic cult in the north. In the second, a Levite from Bethlehem is threatened, and his concubine killed, in Gibeah of Benjamin, resulting in a civil war and the near-annihilation of the tribe of Benjamin. These last two stories probably took place early in the period of the judges and have been dischronologized and intentionally placed at the end of the book by the sacred author, in order to make a theological point about this era in Israel's history. They are signaled by an *inclusio* remark: "In those days there was no king in Israel; every man did what was right in his own eyes" (Judg 17:6 and 21:25; see also Judg 18:1; 19:1). Thus, the basic structure of Judges is as follows:

Outline of the Book of Judges

I. Prologue: Failures of Israel in the Time of the Judges (Judg 1:1—3:6)
   A. Material, Specific, Retrospective Introduction (1:1—2:5)
   B. Theological, General, Prospective Introduction (2:6—3:6)

II. Central Narrative: Twelve Judges and an Anti-Judge (Judg 3:7—16:31)
   A. Othniel (3:7–11)
   B. Ehud (3:12–30)
   C. Shamgar (3:31)
   D. Deborah (4:1—5:31)
   E. Gideon (6:1—8:32)
   X. Abimelech (8:33—9:57)
   F. Tola (10:1–2)
   G. Jair (10:3–5)
   H. Jephthah (10:6—12:7)
   I. Ibzan (12:8–10)
   J. Elon (12:11–12)
   K. Hillel (12:13–15)
   L. Samson (13:11—16:31)

III. Epilogue: Abuses of the Time of the Judges (Judg 17–18)
   B'. Theological and Liturgical Abuse in this period (17:1—18:31)
   A'. Material, Social, Civil Abuse in this period (19:1—21:25)

Double inclusion of the prologue and epilogue

In the larger scheme of biblical history, the sacred author is preparing the reader to understand and accept the kingship, which will be established with Saul but will reach its high point under David.

In addition to its literary structure, Judges deserves some comment on its *literary style*. The book of Judges at times attains high literary art and includes some of the finest examples of storytelling in the Old Testament—in fact, in all of world literature. The narratives in Judges are colorful, dramatic, highly entertaining, and by turns comic and tragic. The sacred author has carefully selected which judges to describe in detail, and, despite the very great differences in character and social location of each of the major judges, a unifying theme through the accounts is *irony*—specifically, the ironic inversion of norms. With the exception of Othniel, the major judges and some minor ones are unexpected and unusual personages, not the ones who would naturally rise to the leadership of society: Ehud is left-handed, an ill omen for most cultures in antiquity. Shamgar, the mighty champion against the Philistines, wields as his heroic weapon an ox-goad, a farm implement consisting of a pointed stick for prodding oxen. Deborah and Jael are women, the latter of which delivers Israel by means of a bowl of warm milk, a hammer, and a tent peg. Gideon is the youngest son of an insignificant family and is a whining coward. Jephthah is the son of a prostitute. Samson is a Nazirite, a type of consecrated religious, who nonetheless has a fatal attraction to brawling and womanizing, defying the usual expectations for a consecrated person. All of these judges are ironic characters who invert the usual norms or expectations for social, prophetic, and spiritual leadership. The sacred author highlights them to emphasize the chaotic nature of the period, during which society was "turned upside down". There is a complete failure of leadership from the leadership classes: the priesthood (Levi) and the aristocracy of the larger tribes (Judah and Joseph). In this situation, God raises up the odd and unlikely to deliver his people.

Overview of Judges

The Time of the Judges and the Cycle of Sin (Judges 1:1–3:6)

The first introduction to Judges sounds very similar in style to the book of Joshua and is obviously intended as a segue from that book (Judg 1:1–2:5). Most of the information here was in fact already communicated in scattered places in the previous book (see Josh 13–17). The tribes of Judah, Simeon, and Ephraim have some initial successes after the death of Joshua, but for the most part the sacred author focuses on the failure of the tribes to drive out the Canaanites from a list of key locations throughout their territory. At the conclusion of the introduction, an angel brings a message from God to the people: they have been disobedient to the command to drive out the peoples of the land; therefore God will punish Israel by means of these peoples.

The second introduction complements and repeats elements of the first but provides a more theological perspective and a programmatic overview of the pattern of the book (Judg 2:6–3:6). Here we find out, for the first time, that after the death of Joshua the people abandon their exclusive devotion to the Lord and begin worshipping the gods of the Canaanites among whom they live. This religious infidelity is both a cause and an effect of their inability to drive the Canaanites from the land. The people then fall into the cyclical pattern of (1) sin ➜ (2) suffering ➜ (3) supplication ➜ (4) salvation ➜ (5) setback, or (1) rebellion ➜ (2) retribution ➜ (3) repentance ➜ (4) redemption ➜ (5) relapse, which is described here and repeated throughout the narrative of the book (Judg 2:11–23). The introduction closes with a brief summary of the people remaining in the land who will "test" the people of Israel (Judg 3:1–6). In this way, the second introduction looks ahead to the pattern and structure of Judges and essentially provides an "abstract" of the message of the book.

The Twelve Judges and the One "Anti-Judge" (Judges 3:6—16:31)

As mentioned above, although twelve judges of Israel are recounted, only six of these are "major" judges, about whom substantial information is given. This overview will focus on these more prominent figures, as well as the "anti-judge", King Abimelech.

1. *Othniel*: Othniel is the only major judge who comes from an important lineage in Israel—from the aristocracy of Judah, a nephew of the celebrated hero Caleb (Judg 3:7–11). Early in the Judges period, Othniel delivers Israel from a certain Cushan-rishathaim, a king of northwest Mesopotamia (Hebrew *aram-naharayim*, "Aram of the Two Rivers") who must have made an incursion into the Levant. Described in completely positive terms, Othniel brings "rest" to the land for the remarkably long time of forty years.

2. *Ehud*: The story of Ehud the Benjaminite is one of the most memorable and uncensored of all those in the book (Judg 3:12–30). He delivers Israel from oppression from the obese Eglon, king of Moab, whose name is remarkably close to the word "round" or "rotund" (Hebrew *'agol*). Ehud's left-handedness—usually considered something negative (cf. Eccles 10:2)—is an advantage in his covert operations. We should note that other members of the tribe of Benjamin are also identified elsewhere in Scripture for their ability to fight either right- or left-handed (see 1 Chron 12:2). Weapons were usually strapped on the left thigh to facilitate a quick draw with the right hand. Ehud's dagger on his right thigh slips past King Eglon's security guards, who would not have expected it. As becomes clear later in the narrative, Eglon apparently receives Ehud and his "message" while seated on his privy. Although this use of the commode as a place for a royal audience seems strange to modern sensibilities, it was an attested practice in the ancient Near East and elsewhere. The context is doubly emphasized when the narrative tells us that Ehud stabbed Eglon so deeply in the belly that "the dirt" (that is, feces) "came out" (Judg 3:22). Ehud dispatches the vulnerable Eglon and escapes to rally Israelite militia, while Eglon's servants wait for him to emerge from the chamber. The resulting military victory is decisive and brings eighty years of peace.

3. *Deborah*: Deborah truly fits the profile of a "judge". As a prophetess, she actually fills a civil and juridical role from her "seat" in the hill country of Ephraim (Judg 4:1—5:31). She is a civil, not military, official and calls on Barak the Naphtalite, a military commander, to launch an attack against Israel's northern oppressor, Jabin, king of Hazor, and his general, Sisera. Barak turns out to be pusillanimous, however, and requires Deborah to accompany him to shore up his morale. As a result, Deborah prophesies that the victory will go to the hand of a woman. Barak does rally the northern tribes at Mount Tabor (later identified as the traditional site of the Transfiguration) and defeats the forces of Sisera. Sisera himself flees and hides among the tents of his allies, the Kenites; but Jael, his hostess, impales his skull with a tent peg while he sleeps. The whole affair is

celebrated in an epic poem attributed to Deborah and Barak (Judg 5). This poem has been recognized by many scholars as genuinely archaic. Against skeptics who regard the Israelite national identity to be a "late" creation (late monarchic, exilic, or postexilic), it stands as an ancient witness to cooperation among at least ten of the twelve tribes (southern Judah and Simeon excepted) against a common enemy, united by in a national identity ("Israel") and deity (the Lord).

Thus, the Deborah narrative emphasizes God's ability to raise up the marginalized—in this case, two women—in order to lead his people and work his salvation.

4. *Gideon*: The account of Gideon (Judg 6:1—8:32) does the same, because Gideon is introduced as a weak coward (Judg 6:11–27). Due to her infidelity, the Lord has given Israel into the power of the Midianites, who ravage the landscape. When Israel repents, God chooses an unlikely savior: this Gideon of Manasseh, whom the angel of the Lord discovers cowering in a wine press, attempting to thresh grain out of sight of the Midianites. (Wine presses were placed in the center of vineyards, far back from the roads, while threshing floors were located in public places.)[2] Gideon protests his commission from the angel and requires multiple miraculous signs to bolster his courage. The Lord, however, is intent on gaining glory by defeating Midian with almost the weakest human instruments possible. Although thirty thousand soldiers gather for battle, God winnows the Israelite force down to three hundred men who exhibit uncouth drinking habits, lapping up water like dogs (Judg 7:5). These three hundred launch a surprise "attack" on the Midianites that is more psychological than military, more a prank than an assault: frightening them during the early morning hours with torches, trumpets, and shouting. This touches off a cascading panic among the Midianite forces, who are eventually routed with the help of militia from Ephraim. In this way, Gideon provides peace for Israel for forty years (Judg 8:28). However, though Gideon wins the war, he loses the peace by setting up an illicit shrine in his hometown of Ophrah, in the northern part of the western (Cisjordanian) territory of Manasseh.

5. *Abimelech*: The story of Abimelech could be regarded as a continuation of the story of Gideon, but we feel it should be understood as a narrative in its own right, the story of an "anti-judge" who sets himself up as king and oppresses Israel rather than its neighbors (Judg 8:33—9:57). Abimelech is a young son of Gideon by a concubine from Shechem in the tribal territory of Ephraim. He persuades the Shechemites—who formed a major city in Israel—to throw off the rule of Gideon's descendants and make Abimelech himself the sole king. This they do, slaughtering all Gideon's sons except the youngest, who throws a curse on Abimelech and escapes. Abimelech's rule is brief and ill-fated—soon a civil war flares up that takes the lives of both Abimelech and the treacherous leaders of Shechem.

6. *Jephthah*: After the "minor" judges Tola and Jair, the transjordanian Israelites in the territory claimed by the Ammonites (between the Arnon River on the south and the Jabbok on the north) faced a threat from a resurgent Ammonite kingdom. The elders of this territory, broadly known as Gilead and distributed among the tribes of Reuben and Gad, call on a certain Jephthah to be their

---

[2] See Daniel I. Block, "Judges", in *Joshua, Judges, Ruth, 1 & 2 Samuel*, vol. 2 of *Zondervan Illustrated Bible Backgrounds Commentary*, ed. John H. Walton (Grand Rapids, Mich.: Zondervan, 2009).

military leader (Judg 10:6—12:7). This Jephthah, the son of the Manassite chief
Gilead and a prostitute, gained his experience in battle as a bandit and outlaw—a
kind of Robin Hood without the gentility. He is an effective military leader
who faces down and defeats the Ammonite king. In the process, he rashly vows
to offer to the Lord whatever comes forth from his house to greet him when
he returns victorious. Tragically, this turns out to be his only daughter (Judg
11:29–40). It is debated what exactly he did to her—the simplest reading of the
text is that he offered her as a human sacrifice. However, human sacrifice was
strictly contrary to the law of Moses, and there are questions about how and
where such a sacrifice would have been carried out. Some scholars argue that he
consecrated her for service to the sanctuary in the manner of the "women who
served at the entrance to the tent of meeting" (1 Sam 2:22), because this was the
equivalent for human beings of being offered as a burnt offering (see Ex 13:1,
11–16).[3] Those who hold this position note that she departs for two months to
lament her *virginity*, not her *life* (Judg 11:37–40). Jephthah's "rule" over Israel is
short-lived (six years) and marked by civil war between the tribe of Ephraim and
the Transjordanian tribes under Jephthah's leadership (Judg 12:1–7).

7. *Samson*: The last judge, Samson from the tribe of Dan, receives the most
attention (Judg 13:11—16:31). He is never described as exercising civil or juridical leadership over Israel, but instead acts as a maverick champion blessed with
supernatural strength, vandalizing the territory of the oppressing Philistines and
defeating them in battle. He has a weakness for Philistine women, and his first
marriage (Judg 14–15) and his affair with the Philistine harlot Delilah (Judg 16)
provide occasion for conflict between himself and the Philistine community,
ultimately leading to his undoing.

One of the most common questions contemporary readers have about the
story of Samson is: What is the significance of Samson's hair? Is he some kind
of mythological superhero? Why does the cropping of his locks lead him to lose
all of his strength? In order to answer these questions, it is critical to read the
story of Samson in its overarching historical and canonical context. According
to Judges, Samson's birth is announced to his parents by an angel, who instructs
them to raise him as a Nazirite, a lay person specially consecrated to the Lord by
a vow—though Samson's case is unusual, because his vow is lifelong (cf. Num
6:1–21). The vow of a Nazarite consisted of three key elements, each of which
is broken by Samson in the course of the narrative, with the cutting of his hair
representing the climax:

Threefold Nazarite Vow	*Samson's Threefold Infidelity*
1. No contact with "a dead body" (Num 6:6–8)	1. Samson eats honey from the lion's corpse. (Judg 14:5–9)
2. No "wine or strong drink" (Num 6:3–4)	2. Samson hosts a great "feast". (Judg 14:10–20)
3. "No razor shall come upon his head" (Num 6:5)	3. Samson allows Delilah to cut off his hair. (Judg 16:13–22)

---

[3] See Howard F. Vos, *Nelson's New Illustrated Bible Manners & Customs* (Nashville: Thomas Nelson, 1999),
117.

Once this Nazarite background is taken into account, the otherwise-bizarre story of Samson suddenly becomes clear. Samson's tragic fall is the result of his threefold transgression of his lifelong Nazarite vows. Moreover, in the whole Delilah affair, Samson is marked by an almost supernatural foolishness in not recognizing that Delilah means him harm and intends to betray him to the Philistines. This remarkable foolishness is highlighted by the sacred author, who is trying to drive home the point to his Israelite readership that their mixed marriages with Gentiles are going to lead to the destruction of their civil and religious identity. Although he wins a great victory over the Philistines in his death (Judg 16:23–31), Samson is a tragic figure whose lack of self-control prevents him from achieving any lasting success as a leader of God's people.

The movement from Othniel to Samson in the central narrative of Judges is roughly but not exactly downhill. Othniel is the model judge—all others are marked by something unusual. The early judges Othniel, Deborah, and Gideon seem to supply civil leadership for the people. After the disastrous "reign" of Abimelech, the judgeships seem to become shorter. Jephthah's rule is marked by civil war. The minor judges after him have only brief careers. Samson is scarcely a "judge" at all but, rather, an independent champion and troublemaker. Israel is slowly disintegrating.

The Time of the Judges and the Age of Relativism (Judges 17–21)

Judges concludes with two narratives about events that may have occurred earlier in the era but have been moved to the end of the book to drive home the sacred author's main point.

Liturgical Abuses in the Time of the Judges

Unlike Joshua, Judges usually presents examples of liturgical abuse or violation rather than faithful worship. This is especially the case from Gideon forward. So we have:

- worship of pagan gods (Baal and Asherah) being forced on Israelites by other Israelites (Judg 6:25–32);
- Gideon setting up an illicit shrine (Judg 8:22–28);
- Jephthah's perhaps well-meant but nonetheless rash and tragic vow of sacrificial worship, leading to the illicit offering of his daughter (Judg 11:29–40; cf. Mt 5:34);
- Samson's multiple violations of his consecrated status (Judg 14:1–3, 5–9; 16:1, 4, 17–19);
- the illicit cult of Micah and the Danites (Judg 18:1–31);
- a religious festival at Shiloh (site of the Tabernacle) not mandated in the law of Moses (Judg 21:19–21) or at least involving practices (dancing of young women) never foreseen by the law.

In particular, the Micah-Dan account (Judg 18) reveals the cavalier attitude taken by the Israelites toward worship and the complete ignorance of the liturgical norms established by Moses that prevailed during this time. Sadly, it would not be the only era of salvation history marked by liturgical ignorance and abuse. Judges is largely a counterexample: how things ought not to be done. Unsurprisingly, the later Christian tradition found few if any sacramental types in the book.

1. *The First Epilogue: Micah, the Levite, and the Danites*: The first narrative concerns a certain Micah of the tribe of Ephraim, a wealthy man who sets up a private shrine in his home and eventually persuades a certain Levite from Bethlehem in Judah to serve him as his personal priest-chaplain (Judg 17:1–18:31). The tribe of Dan, however—unable to secure its assigned territory and wandering through the hill country of Ephraim in search of a permanent home—happens on Micah's shrine and decides to confiscate it as its own, along with its priest. The Danites move north, capture the city of Laish in Galilee, and settle there, with Micah's shrine as their permanent place of worship under the ministry of this Levite, a certain Jonathan descended from Moses. The whole narrative reveals the Israelite's *complete disregard for the Mosaic law*, which does not allow for personal or tribal shrines or for non-Aaronic Levites serving as priests. The sacred author's point is that liturgical chaos reigned during this period of Israel's history.

2. *The Second Epilogue: The Levite's Concubine and the Tribe of Benjamin*: Should there be any doubt about this downward spiral, the second epilogue makes the point even more shockingly by telling the tale of a Levite connected to Bethlehem in Judah. This Levite takes a concubine from among the girls of Bethlehem. While traveling from Bethlehem to his home in the hills of Ephraim, he stops in Gibeah, the main city of the Benjaminites. There, he gets treated as the angels were in Sodom and Gomorrah (Gen 19): he receives no hospitality from any townsperson, but instead they surround the home of his host at night demanding to have relations with him. Appallingly, the Levite hands his concubine over to the townsmen, who physically and sexually abuse her until she dies. When the Levite returns home, he divides up the body of his concubine and sends pieces to each of the other tribes along with an appeal for justice, in a gruesome act mimicking the customary dismemberment of an animal as a kind of "war-call" among the tribes (cf. 1 Sam 11:7). The other tribes are outraged and gather in assembly at Mizpah, where they decide to go to war against Benjamin. After initial defeats, the combined Israelite army sacks the Benjaminite capital of Gibeah in much the same fashion as Ai (cf. Josh 8:1–29). The men of Benjamin are almost completely wiped out. After the battle, however, the tribes grieve that one of their number (Benjamin) may be completely eliminated. They show mercy to the six hundred Benjaminite survivors and acquire wives for them by warfare (Judg 21:8–12) and abduction (Judg 21:16–24). So the sacred author closes the book with a story marked throughout with some of the most shocking depravity in the Old Testament. This is the kind of social and moral anarchy that took place when "there was no king in Israel; *every man did what was right in his own eyes*" (Judg 21:25). The horror of the book of Judges is the ugly face of rampant relativism.

Historical Issues in Judges

Joshua vs. Judges on the Conquest of the Land?

No historical issue in Judges looms larger than the question: Do the accounts of the settlement of the land in the books of Joshua and Judges contradict each other?

According to one point of view, Joshua represents a *"conquest" model* of Israel's entrance into the land, in which the Israelites cleanly defeat, exterminate, and replace the inhabitants of Canaan. Judges, on the other hand, is supposed to represent a *"settlement" model* of Israel's occupation, in which the people of Israel move in alongside existing Canaanites. A key text is from the opening chapter of Judges, which emphasizes the failure of the Israelites to drive out the peoples of the land:

> Manasseh did not drive out the inhabitants of Beth-shean and its villages, or Taanach and its villages, or the inhabitants of Dor and its villages, or the inhabitants of Ibleam and its villages, or the inhabitants of Megiddo and its villages, but the Canaanites persisted in dwelling in that land. *When Israel grew strong, they put the Canaanites to forced labor, but did not utterly drive them out.* (Judg 1:27–28)

For a number of contemporary biblical scholars, Joshua's account is usually judged to be idealized and contrary to archaeology, whereas the settlement model in Judges is more "realistic".[4] Although there are undoubtedly differences between the books of Joshua and Judges, as recent scholarship has shown, the contrast between them is overdrawn. The view that they are irreconcilably contradictory can only be sustained by failing to pay close attention to the actual *data* in both books and by ignoring important literary conventions of ancient Near Eastern historiography.[5]

For example, as we saw in the previous chapter, the accounts of the overthrow of the Canaanites in Joshua need to be understood in light of the use of hyperbole in ancient conquest literature. Although Joshua conquered and temporarily depopulated a number of cities, they were not immediately settled with an Israelite population. Instead, Joshua always returned with the Israelite army to Gilgal (for example, Josh 10:15, 43; 14:6). There are notices in Joshua itself of territories that remained to be conquered and subdued. Chief among these are God's words to Joshua at the end of his life:

> Now Joshua was old and advanced in years; and the LORD said to him, "You are old and advanced in years, and *there remains yet very much land to be possessed.* This is the land that yet remains...." (Josh 13:1–2)

The material in Judges that overlaps with Joshua is largely limited to the opening chapter, which includes a list of places *not* conquered by Israel (Judg 1:27–36). Some but not all of these failures were already noted in Joshua.

Moreover, it is important to emphasize that after the opening chapters, the bulk of Judges, with the exception of the account of the migration of the tribe of Dan (Judg 17–18), is not at all concerned with either conquest or settlement. Instead, the narratives presume that Israel is already in the land but is being attacked, oppressed, or subjugated by other peoples. In only one case does the threat arise primarily from the original inhabitants of the land: Deborah and Barak face the threat of a resurgent northern Canaanite force under

---

[4] See John J. Collins, *Introduction to the Hebrew Bible* (Minneapolis: Fortress Press, 2004), 186–91.

[5] Kenneth A. Kitchen, *On the Reliability of the Old Testament* (Grand Rapids, Mich.: Eerdmans, 2003), 159–240.

the leadership of Jabin and Sisera in the Galilee-Jezreel Valley region (Judg 5). *Otherwise, every other conflict described in Judges is with groups on the borders or periphery of Israelite territory*: Arameans, Moabites, Midianites, Ammonites, Philistines.

The book of Judges does not show Israel in conflict with the "seven nations" of Canaan that are the focus of Joshua's attacks. To the contrary, Israel seems to be getting along fine with the remaining Canaanite populations—from the vantage point of the sacred author, this is precisely the problem! The cultural assimilation with the Canaanites leads to adoption of the Canaanite cults and abandonment of fidelity to the Lord, resulting in a withdrawal of divine protection and punishment at the hand of *external* enemies (Judg 2:11–15). As the book progresses, the Philistines emerge as the most serious threat. The Philistines are *not* one of the indigenous "seven nations" of the land described by Moses—the infamous "Hittites, Girgashites, Amorites, Canaanites, Perizzites, Hivites, and Jebusites" (cf. Deut 7:1). Rather, the Philistines are a *European* seafaring people related to the Greeks who invaded and settled the southern seacoast of the Levant at about the same time Israel was invading from the east across the Jordan. As we will see in subsequent chapters in the books of Samuel, it is the Philistines, not indigenous peoples, who will constitute the threat to Israel's integrity that provokes the institution of the monarchy.

In sum, when we read closely and make careful distinctions between peoples and places, Joshua and Judges do not in fact present irreconcilable accounts of Israel's origins in the Promised Land. Both books acknowledge that many strategic locations were never fully secured when Israel entered the land. The narratives of Judges presume that the tribes are already settled—albeit often under duress—in the territories assigned to them in the book of Joshua. In the book of Joshua, the focus is on conflict with *internal* peoples of the land; in Judges, religious and cultural assimilation with these internal groups eventually leads to an inability to defend against *external* enemies.

When Was the Time Period of the Judges?

For scholars who take the historicity of the book of Judges seriously, another question arises over the historical time period being described by the author. Of course, for scholars who dismiss Judges as a combination of late, ideologically driven fiction and collections of folklore with only a kernel of historical recollection, this is not an issue. But for those who consider the book to be substantially historical in character, there are schools of thought that are divided over the date of the exodus and conquest, as discussed earlier.

On the one hand, scholars who opt for an early exodus (fifteenth century B.C.) would place the period of the judges roughly between 1380 and 1050 B.C. On the other hand, scholars who opt for a late exodus (thirteenth century B.C.) would squeeze the period of the judges into a shorter time frame, between roughly 1200 and 1050 B.C. The main difficulty for both these schema is that if we tabulate the "reigns" of each judge and the periods of "peace" that each one brought to Israel *sequentially*, we end up with a figure of around three hundred years. Moreover, from a sequential perspective, more time would have to be added in order to allow for "interregna", during which the people defected from the

Lord, and other unknown time periods, such as the judgeship of Shamgar (Judg 3:31) and the length of rule of the generation immediately after Joshua (Judg 2:7). In short, a sequential tabulation of length of time from the data in Judges cannot be fit into any reasonable chronological scheme; therefore it is universally acknowledged that many of the judgeships, though described in sequence, had to have been concurrent.

Rereading the book of Judges, the theory of concurrent judges appears quite reasonable. For one thing, many of the judges had only limited geographical influence. For example, Ehud was active in the *central* territory of Benjamin and Ephraim; Deborah among the *northern* ten tribes; Gideon in the Jezreel valley and surroundings; Abimelech in the area around Shechem; Jephthah in Gilead *east* of the Jordan; Samson in the *southwestern* territory bordering Philistia. Although there are some chronological indicators that certain judges follow others, the accounts of other judges are introduced abruptly, without a strong indication of temporal sequence (for example, Judges 3:7; 6:1; 10:6). More than one had to have been active simultaneously, within different regions of Israel, confronting different enemies (Canaanites in the north, Moabites/Midianites in the center, Ammonites in the east, Philistines to the southwest). The choice of twelve judges to narrate—six major and six minor—may be part of the literary art of the book as well. The sacred author may have been intentionally selective and passed over other contemporary leaders known from his sources, traditions, and memory. The twelve recounted may be intended to serve as a representative sample and a symbol for Israel.

There are close analogies for this type of historiography in Judges, in which concurrent rulers are described sequentially. Kenneth Kitchen points out that Egyptian king lists for the second intermediate period—a time of political turmoil between the Middle and New Kingdoms (ca. 1800–1550)—enumerate in succession the reigns of the pharaohs totaling more than five hundred years during an era that could only have lasted around two hundred and fifty years at the most.[6] A similar phenomenon can be found in Mesopotamian records from the Old Babylonian "second intermediate period" of the early second millennium.[7] In both the Egyptian and Mesopotamian intermediate periods, the reason for disparity between chronology and textual records is that concurrent rulers of different regions of the nation had overlapping reigns. Thus the situation in Judges is not unprecedented: the Judges era was a kind of "Israelite intermediate period" that posed a challenge to ancient historiographers, since there was no firm dynastic succession on which to base an exact chronology. The listed rulers *appear* to follow each other directly, although that is not always asserted in the text.

The Book of Judges and Archaeological Evidence

Although there is no explicit archaeological evidence for the Israelites leaders described in the book of Judges, certain pieces of extra-biblical evidence provide some support for the overall historical plausibility of the book.

---

[6] See discussion in Kenneth Kitchen, *On the Reliability of the Old Testament* (Grand Rapids, Mich.: Eerdmans, 2003), 203–9.

[7] Ibid., 203–4.

For example, recent archaeological excavations of Dan/Laish in northern Israel fit well with the account of its conquest and settlement by the tribe of Dan (Judg 18).[8] Moreover, the Midianite peoples, who oppress the Israelites during the time of Gideon, can be identified with the northwest Arabian culture centered on the site of Qurayya, which archaeological evidence suggests flourished in the thirteenth to eleventh centuries B.C. and then disappeared. Significantly, all biblical references to the Midianites as an active people are found in Exodus through Judges—the very books covering the time period of their culture (for example, Judg 6:1–8:28). Along similar lines, the picture of increasing threats from the Philistines presented in Judges agrees with the archaeological record of these people, who seem to have settled on the coast of the Mediterranean Sea in the land of Canaan in the late thirteenth century B.C., becoming increasingly powerful until the tenth century B.C., the time of the rise of the Israelite monarchy, after which they declined. Finally, archaeological surface surveys in central Canaan, in the hill country associated with Ephraim and Manasseh, appear to show an explosion of new, small settlements in the twelfth and eleventh centuries B.C., displaying what appears to be a pattern of progressive east-to-west development. Remains from these sites show only a basic material culture and a diet of sheep, goat, perhaps some deer, but *no pigs*—unlike contemporaneous sites across the Jordan (in Ammonite territory) or along the Philistine coast. This evidence coheres well with the biblical picture of Israelites entering the land from the east (across the Jordan) and first settling in the easily defensible and lightly inhabited hill country.

Before closing, it is worth noting here that the famous victory stele of Pharaoh Merneptah, known as the *Merneptah Stele* (ca. 1209 B.C.), seems clearly to indicate that "Israel" was an established people in the land of Canaan, significant enough that the pharaoh could boast of defeating them.[9] This stele, however, was inscribed prior to the bloom of settlements in the hill country found in the archaeological surveys, which do not seem to have begun until the twelfth century B.C. So we are left with a historical puzzle. The Merneptah Stele provides indisputable evidence of Israel's presence in the land before the archaeological record shows traces of them. As is so often the case, there is no perfect agreement between the archaeological and textual data, even with contemporaneous, nonbiblical texts. Perhaps our dating methods are inaccurate, or else Israel initially settled into Canaan in the tents they used in their wanderings and only slowly began to build permanent settlements and commit themselves to an agricultural life-style.

The Origin of the Book of Judges

The book of Judges is interesting among the books of the Old Testament: it is formally *anonymous*, and there is no strong Jewish or Christian tradition about its authorship. Opinions vary about the dating of the book. Even what one means by the "date" of a book is debatable: Should the "date" of the book be considered the last time an editorial hand touched it or the time the book acquired the basic form it still retains?

---

[8] See Block, "Judges", 95–241.
[9] See ibid., 143–45.

The latest editorial remark in Judges takes place when it says that "Jonathan the son of Gershom, son of Moses, and his sons were priests to the tribe of the Danites *until the day of the captivity of the land*" (Judg 18:30). If the "captivity of the land" here refers to the Babylonian exile, this is an editorial remark from the early to mid-sixth century (post 587 B.C.). If it refers to the Assyrian exile of the northern tribes (more likely in context), then this remark stems from after 722 B.C. However, it may also refer to the Philistine incursion that destroyed Shiloh (where the Tabernacle was located) and perhaps Dan as well (ca. 1060 B.C.; see Jer 7:12–14; 1 Sam 4:1–11). Archeologists have found a destruction layer at Dan from this time period, with evidence of rebuilding later.

The double conclusion of the book seems to have been intentionally composed by the one who gave the book its present shape, and it corresponds with the double introduction. Therefore, the intentions of the double epilogue also give a clue to the intentions of the book's composer/compiler. We note that the epilogues are "wrapped" by the *inclusio*, "In those days there was no king in Israel; every man did what was right in his own eyes" (Judg 17:6; 18:1; 19:1; 21:25). This is an apology for the kingship: although theocracy is the ideal, kingship appears to be a practical necessity to maintain social and religious order. Further, we note that the final narrative includes locations that will be significant in the story of David's rise to kingship over Saul in 1 Samuel: Bethlehem, Jerusalem, and Gibeah. The Levite "protagonist" of the final story is treated with great hospitality in Bethlehem of Judah, David's hometown (Judg 19:1–9). When he finally leaves, he cannot take refuge in Jerusalem, because no one has been able to conquer it. So he and his Bethlehemite concubine continue to Gibeah of Benjamin, Saul's hometown, where they are treated horrifically (Judg 19:22–30). Then, all Israel unites to oppose the Benjaminites of Gibeah (Judg 20). But they spare the survivors (Judg 21).

In sum, the book of Judges climaxes with Israel's need for a king (Judg 21:25). But where can they find one who will treat them well and not poorly? The narrative gives the reader hints: perhaps in Bethlehem, where people are treated well; but not Gibeah, where people are treated poorly. Recall that David the Judahite is from Bethlehem, while Saul the Benjaminite is from Gibeah. Judges also suggests the need for a king who can conquer the Jebusites in Jerusalem. Who can do that? As we will see, it is not Saul but David who conquers the Jebusites (see 2 Sam 5:6–10). Finally, the horrific story of the Levite's concubine and the civil war against the tribe of Benjamin (Judg 19–21), although probably occurring early in the Judges period, seems to have been intentionally dischronologized and placed at the end in order to give the book as a whole a pro-Bethlehem, anti-Gibeah outlook. This would fit well with a historical circumstance in which the Davidic monarchy (Bethlehem) still required bolstering against counterclaims from Benjaminite Gibeah. Gibeah, Benjamin, and the remnants of the Saulide dynasty ceased to be serious threats to the Davidic dynasty from the reign of Solomon forward; during the divided monarchy, rival claimants came from the tribe of Ephraim, not Benjamin. Perhaps, then, the pro-monarchic, pro-Davidic book of Judges was composed by an unknown author early in the Davidic monarchy, since David continued to face pro-Saulide opposition almost to the end of his life (2 Sam 16:1–14).

How Should We Interpret the Shocking Narratives in the Book of Judges?

Many readers are understandably disturbed by the narrative of Judges, especially readers who may have been raised on a selective exposure to Scripture that emphasized the biblical characters as moral examples to help guide Christian behavior. In Judges, however, there are very few characters who provide consistent moral example and many gut-wrenching examples of violence, cruelty, and liturgical and sexual abuse: Gideon's treatment of the men of Succoth and Peniel (Judg 8:13–17); Jephthah's slaughter of the sons of Gideon (Judg 9:5); Micah's extremely aberrant cult and its subsequent adoption by an entire tribe (Judg 18:1–31); and the horrific treatment of the Levite's concubine, followed by almost genocidal retribution against Benjamin. Although they are used to save Israel from its enemies, the behavior of several of the judges themselves (Gideon, Jepththah, Samson) is marked by gross moral failures.

It cannot be emphasized enough that the narratives of Judges are intended by the sacred author to be *descriptive*, not *prescriptive*. In other words, he describes how things actually were during the time of the judges, not how they ought to have been. A picture of how things "ought to be" is provided in the following book, Ruth. In Judges, however, the reader is meant to be repulsed by the narratives, shocked by how bad things get when "everyone does what is right in his own eyes" (Judg 21:25), an ancient description of moral *relativism* (disbelief in any absolute moral standards) and its close cousin *subjectivism* (each personal subject is his own final arbiter of truth). Inasmuch as moral relativism and subjectivism are once again rampant in world culture, we see contemporary manifestations of some of the same horrific behavior found in the book of Judges.

Judges in the Living Tradition

Like the book of Joshua that precedes it, Judges has played no little role in the history of Christian thought, despite the moral difficulties raised by its often tragic and gruesome depiction of the spiritual state of an Israel that lived during a time when there was no human king and acted as if there were no divine king. As with Joshua, the book was quite popular both for its memorable heroes and heroines and for its typological potential.

The Enemies in the Land and the Battle for Holiness

As we saw above, one of the main issues that dominates the book of Judges is the battle between the people of Israel and their many enemies, both within and on the borders of the Canaan. Given the emphasis in the preceding books of the Pentateuch on *arriving* in the Promised Land, one might be tempted to wonder: Why does God allow Israel to be afflicted by its enemies even after receiving the inheritance of the land? In a series of conferences on the spiritual and mystical life, Saint John Cassian (ca. A.D. 360–432) explains the spiritual reason:

> We read something like this as it appears *in mystical fashion* in the book of Judges with respect to the extermination of the spiritual nations that are opposed to Israel: "These are the nations that the Lord forsook, so that by them he might instruct Israel, so that they might grow accustomed to fighting with their enemies." And again, a little further on: "The Lord left them so that he might test Israel with them, whether or not they [the Israelites] would hear the commandments of the Lord...." God did not begrudge Israel their peace or look with malice upon them, but he planned this conflict in the knowledge that it would be beneficial.

Thus, constantly oppressed by the onslaught of the nations, they would never feel that they did not need the Lord's help.[10]

From John Cassian's point of view, then, God permitted the enemies of Israel to afflict them constantly in order to help them not to forget their need for his assistance. Indeed, it is a sobering moral insight that, according to the book of Judges, it was precisely during the times of peace and "rest"—economic, military, and national prosperity won by the judges—that the people of Israel were most inclined to forget about God and fall back into sin. After that, "whenever the judge died, they turned back and behaved worse than their fathers" (Judg 2:19). Judges makes clear that each generation must learn afresh the lesson of its dependence on God.

Deborah, Jael, and the Mystery of the Church

One of the most striking aspects of the book of Judges is the prominence of *female* deliverer figures and leaders—something modern readers might not expect to find in an ancient work such as this. How do we explain a woman such as Deborah functioning as a judge in an ancient warrior society? Or the figure of Jael, who, although a pagan, so gruesomely and completely overthrows Sisera, the enemy of Israel? In the Christian tradition, it has always been popular to interpret Deborah and Jael according to the allegorical sense of the text and to see in them, not only historical deliverers of God's people, but inspired *types* of the Church.

For example, at the turn of the third century, Origen of Alexandria interprets the book of Judges as a "mystical history" and sees in the figure of Jael a prefiguration of the Church, which defeats Satan and her spiritual enemies not through military means but by the wood of the Cross:

> What, therefore, does the web of all this *mystical history* show us? *The woman Jael,* that foreigner about whom Deborah's prophecy said that victory would be had "through the hand of a woman" (Judg 4:9), *symbolizes the church, which was assembled from foreign nations.* ... She killed him with a stake, then, which is to say that *she overthrew him by the power and cunning of the wood of the cross.*[11]

Along similar lines, in the fourth century, Saint Ambrose, bishop of Milan, used the images of Deborah and Jael to exhort the Christian women of his diocese to emulate such figures of virtue:

> So, then, Deborah foretold the event of the battle. Barak, as he was bidden, led forth the army; *Jael carried off the triumph ... who in a mystery revealed to us the rising of the Church from among the Gentiles,* for whom should be found a triumph over Sisera, that is, over the powers opposed to her.... And so according to this

---

[10] John Cassian, *Conference* 4.6.3–4, in John R. Franke, ed., *Joshua, Judges, Ruth, 1–2 Samuel,* Old Testament 4, Ancient Christian Commentary on Scripture, ed. Thomas C. Oden (Downers Grove, Ill.: InterVarsity Press, 2005), 109.

[11] Origen, *Homilies on Judges* 5.5, in Franke, *Joshua, Judges,* 117 (emphasis added).

history a woman, that the minds of women might be stirred up, became a judge, a woman set all in order, a woman prophesied, a woman triumphed, and joining in the battle array taught men to war under a woman's lead. But in a mystery it is the battle of faith and the victory of the Church.[12]

From this mystical point of view, the historical battles and bloodshed in Judges point to the deeper mystery of the spiritual warfare in which the Church plays the role of both mother (Deborah) and warrior (Jael).

The Silence of Scripture on the Problem of Jephthah's Daughter

In a somewhat less mystical mode, it is also worth noting that the moral difficulties presented by the book of Judges were not "discovered" by modern critics of Scripture but were long recognized by the Fathers of the Church. For example, in a series of answers to questions about the book of Judges, Saint Augustine stresses that although the book of Judges *records* the shocking account of the sacrifice of Jephthah's daughter, it does not approve of the act:

> The Scriptures do not seem to pass judgment on this vow and its fulfillment as it does quite clearly in the case of Abraham, when he was ordered to sacrifice his son and did so. *Rather, the Scriptures seem to have only recorded the matter and left it to the reader to evaluate....* The Scriptures never approve or disapprove of the act explicitly but let the matter stand, to be evaluated and contemplated after consulting the righteousness and law of God.[13]

Here we see Augustine laying out for his audience an important principle of correct biblical interpretation: the moral and theological implications of any given passages of Scripture, such as the sacrifice of Jephthah's daughter, need to be evaluated in the light of the *whole* of Sacred Scripture, in order to avoid misinterpreting the intent of the human and divine authors. In this instance, the silence of Scripture does not constitute an endorsement; indeed, as we saw above, the whole point of the book of Judges was to emphasize the moral relativism of the era before the rise of the Davidic monarchy.

The Passion of Samson and the Passion of Christ

Finally, in addition to the feminine types of the Church contained in Judges, there is also one male figure who was interpreted as a prefiguration of Christ in the patristic era: Samson. At first glance, Samson might not appear to be a likely candidate for such a typological interpretation: as we saw above, he broke his vows, and, perhaps even more distressingly, his death can be understood as one of the very few "suicides" recorded in Scripture (cf. 1 Sam 31:4). However, in the fifth century A.D., Caesarius, bishop of Arles (in southern France), saw

---

[12] Ambrose, *Concerning Widows* 8.47, 50, in *NPNF2* 10:399.
[13] Augustine, *Questions on Judges* 49.7, in Franke, *Joshua, Judges*, 138 (emphasis added).

in the spiritual sense of the suffering and death of Samson a prefiguration of the Passion and crucifixion of Christ:

> "Therefore [Samson's] enemies brought him to play the buffoon before them" (Judg 16:27). Notice here an image of the cross. *Samson extends his hands spread out to the two columns as to the two beams of the cross. Moreover, by his death he overcame his adversaries, because his sufferings became the death of his persecutors.* For this reason Scripture concludes as follows: "Those he killed at his death were more than those he had killed during his lifetime" (Judg 16:31). *This mystery was clearly ful-filled in our Lord Jesus Christ*, for at His death He completed our redemption which He had by no means published during His life.[14]

This is a stunning example of the ancient Christian use of typology to explain otherwise mysterious aspects of books of the Old Testament. Following the principle that the historical warfare waged by the judges against the enemies of Israel is a type of the spiritual warfare of the New Covenant, Caesarius here transforms the death of Samson from a quasi-suicide to one final act of battle. Samson defeats the enemies of Israel precisely by means of his death, just as Christ would go on to defeat far more of the forces of darkness through his cru-cifixion than he ever did through the exorcisms and healings performed during his public ministry. The parallel becomes even more striking when we recall that Samson's death takes place in the temple of the pagan god Dagon, whose pillars he pulls down around him (Judg 16:23).

The Book of Judges in the Lectionary

In the contemporary Lectionary, Judges, like Joshua, is utilized only sparingly. It is never read on a Sunday or feast day or for any ritual, votive, or special occa-sion Masses. Its liturgical proclamation is limited to four days of Week 20 in Ordinary Time and December nineteenth in the Season of Advent. Although the Lectionary often avoids morally difficult texts in Scripture, the story of the sacrifice of Jephthah's daughter is one of the few episodes from the book of Judges that is proclaimed in the liturgy (see next page).

Conclusion

The book of Judges recounts one of the darkest periods—morally, spiritually, politically, socially—in Israel's history. Abandonment of the worship of the Lord in favor of Canaanite paganism was rampant; and even efforts to worship the Lord were often carried out either in ignorance or in contempt of divine law. Although the sufferings of this era were periodically alleviated by the judges, who often displayed true heroism, fortitude, and religious zeal, nonetheless even many of these charismatic leaders were deeply flawed and thus unable to lead Israel to greater fidelity.

---

[14] Caesarius of Arles, *Sermon* 118.6, in St. Caesarius of Arles, *Sermons*, vol. 2, *81–186*, trans. Sr. Mary Magdeleine Mueller, O.S.F., The Fathers of the Church 47 (Washington, D.C.: Catholic University of America Press, 1964), 189.

Liturgical Readings of Judges		
Day	Passage Read	Description
Mon., Week 20 (I)	2:11–19	The "Deuteronomic abstract" of the book of Judges describes the cycle of disobedience–punishment–repentance–salvation by a judge–peace–reversion that characterizes the book.
Tues., Week 20 (I)	6:11–24a	This passage includes the appearance of the angel of the Lord to Gideon and his initial commissioning.
Wed., Week 20 (I)	9:6–15	Abimelech is made king; Jotham utters his parable-curse against him.
Thurs., Week 20 (I)	11:29–39a	Jephthah's rash vow and the offering of his daughter is remembered perhaps because the daughter's willing self-sacrifice, in a state of virginity, may be considered a type of the religious life, of the Blessed Virgin, or of Christ himself.
Dec. 19	13:2–7, 24–25a	The annunciation of the birth of Samson to his parent is paired with the Gospel reading of the birth of John the Baptist (Lk 1:5–25). Samson is a type of John the Baptist: both are Nazirites marked by great vigor, the power of the Holy Spirit, and fiery personalities.

Judges marks the point in the biblical narrative where it becomes apparent that the economy of the Mosaic covenant, even in its final Deuteronomic form, is inadequate for the flourishing of God's people. The sacred author begins to turn our attention forward, toward the anticipation of a king who will inaugurate a New Covenant (2 Sam 7:1–17; Ps 89:19–37) that will not replace but, rather, assimilate and even transform the Mosaic covenant.

For Further Reading

Commentaries and Studies of Judges

Ackerman, Susan. *Warrior, Dancer, Seductress, Queen: Women in Judges and Biblical Israel.* Anchor Bible Reference Library. New York: Doubleday, 1998.

Boling, Robert G. *Judges.* Anchor Bible 6. New York: Doubleday, 1975.

Hamilton, Victor. *Handbook on the Historical Books.* Grand Rapids, Mich.: Baker Academic, 2001. (See pp. 15–95.)

Soggin, J. Albert. *Judges: A Commentary.* Old Testament Library. Philadelphia: Westminster Press, 1981.

Vos, Howard Frederic. *Nelson's New Illustrated Bible Manners & Customs.* Nashville: Thomas Nelson, 1999. (See pp. 109–45.)

Historical Issues in Judges

Block, Daniel I. "Judges". Pages 94–241 in *Joshua, Judges, Ruth, 1 & 2 Samuel.* Vol. 2 of *Zondervan Illustrated Bible Backgrounds Commentary.* Edited by John H. Walton. Grand Rapids, Mich.: Zondervan, 2009.

Bright, John. *A History of Israel.* 4th ed. Louisville, Ky.: Westminster John Knox Press, 2000. (See pp. 133–37, 173–76.)

de Vaux, Roland. *The Early History of Israel.* Translated by David Smith. 2 vols. London: Darton, Longman, and Todd, 1978. (See pp. 683–94, 751–73.)

Kitchen, Kenneth A. *On the Reliability of the Old Testament.* Grand Rapids, Mich.: Eerdmans, 2006. (See pp. 199–239.)

Judges in the Living Tradition

Caesarius of Arles, Saint. *Sermons.* Vol. 2 *(81–186).* Translated by Mary Magdeleine Mueller, O.S.F. The Fathers of the Church 47. Washington, D.C.: Catholic University of America Press, 1964.

Franke, John R., ed. *Joshua, Judges, Ruth, 1–2 Samuel.* Old Testament 4 of Ancient Christian Commentary on Scripture. Edited by Thomas C. Oden. Downers Grove, Ill.: InterVarsity Press, 2005. (See pp. 99–180.)

Origen. *Homilies on Judges.* Translated by Elizabeth Ann Dively Lauro. The Fathers of the Church 119. Washington, D.C.: Catholic University of America Press, 2010.

Thompson, John Lee. *Writing the Wrongs: Women of the Old Testament among Biblical Commentators from Philo through the Reformation.* Oxford Studies in Historical Theology. Oxford: Oxford University Press, 2001. (See pp. 100–178.)

13. RUTH

Introduction

The book of Ruth is a perfectly written romantic narrative that provides an oasis of relief between the turmoil and horrors of the book of Judges and the trials and tribulations of the books of Samuel. From a literary point of view, Ruth is immediately appreciable as a simple yet elegant tale of courtship—a true literary masterpiece that has appealed to readers for centuries. Nevertheless, the sacred author has also woven serious theological motifs throughout the narrative by means of symbols and keywords recognizable to the careful reader. Although commonly neglected by theologians, biblical scholars, and even the contemporary Lectionary, the book of Ruth remains one of the most popular and appealing narratives in the Old Testament. Indeed, given her identification as the ancestress of King David (Ruth 4:18–22; cf. Mt 1:5), the book was read as having messianic and typological significance in both ancient Jewish and Christian tradition.

In the Christian canon, Ruth follows the book of Judges and precedes 1–2 Samuel. This ordering is particularly apt: the book situates the narrative within the time of the Judges (Ruth 1:1) and ends with the genealogy of David, the protagonist of the books of Samuel (Ruth 4:18–22).

The Book of Ruth in the Jewish Canon

In the contemporary Jewish canon of Scripture, the book of Ruth is not located between Judges and Samuel. Instead, Ruth is part of the third and final section of the Jewish Tanakh known as the "Writings" (Hebrew *Ketubim*). Within this section, Ruth is one of five books known in Jewish tradition as the *Megilloth* ("[festival] scrolls"). According to Jewish liturgical custom, each of these five short books is read at a particular liturgical festival:

The Megilloth

1. Ruth—read at Pentecost ("Weeks")
2. Song of Solomon—read at Passover
3. Ecclesiastes—read on Tabernacles
4. Lamentations—read on 9th of Ab (Temple Destruction)
5. Esther—read on feast of Purim ("Lots")

Intriguingly, Ruth typically follows Proverbs and precedes the Song of Solomon in Jewish Bibles, so the figure of Ruth has come in Jewish tradition to be associated with both the "woman of noble character" (Prov 31:10–31; see Ruth 3:11!) and the bride in the Song of Solomon.

In this way Ruth serves as an excellent segue between the period of the judges and the rise of the monarchy. Furthermore, by placing the story of Elimelech and Naomi—who are from Bethlehem (Ruth 1:2)—after Judges, the book of Ruth provides a third story of Bethlehemites after the two that conclude Judges in its double epilogue (Judg 17–18; 19–21). Even more clearly than Judges, the book of Ruth affirms that Bethlehem is a place of refuge for Israel—a city where (the ancestors of) a good king may be found.

Literary Structure of Ruth

The book of Ruth exhibits a very elegant chiastic structure centered around the dramatic nighttime encounter between Ruth and Boaz at the threshing floor:

Outline of the Book of Ruth

A. The Line of Elimelech ("God Is My King") (1:1–5)
  B. Naomi and Her Daughters-in-Law: Lacking Everything (1:6–22)
    C. The Courtship of Boaz and Ruth (2:1–23)
      D. Ruth and Boaz at the Threshing Floor (3:1–18)
    C'. The Marriage of Boaz and Ruth (4:1–12)
  B'. Naomi and Her Daughter-in-Law: Lacking Nothing (4:13–17)
A'. The Line of Boaz (to David, God's Chosen King) (4:18–22)

Notice how the book begins and ends with short passages focused on family *genealogies*, which in Scripture typically follow the families of either priestly and/or royal descent. The introduction describes the line of a certain Elimelech of Bethlehem, who has two sons, but the sons die without fathering any children, so the line disappears. The conclusion of the book is the family line of Boaz traced from his ancestor Perez to his great-grandson David. Thus we move from a Judean, Bethlehemite line that has apparently ended (Ruth 1:1–5) to one that continues and promises future (royal) succession (Ruth 4:18–22). In this way, the book of Ruth continues the Old Testament theme of endangered family lines—such as that of Abraham and Sarah (Gen 15:1–6)—that, through God's grace and providence, go on to bring forth a multitude of descendants and even royalty.

Overview of Ruth

Prologue: Elimelech's Family and the Sojourn in Moab (Ruth 1:1–5)

Although most of the story of Ruth is told from a female perspective, it is significant that the narrative begins with focus on a certain Bethlehemite named *Elimelech* (Hebrew for "My God Is King"). Although Elimelech himself is an Israelite of Judean heritage, he and his family are forced to leave the Promised Land and seek refuge in the pagan territory of Moab, west of the Jordan River, due to a famine. There, tragically, he and his two sons die, leaving three widows behind.

There is dark irony in this introduction: in Hebrew, the name *Bethlehem* means "House of Bread"—that is, a place of abundant food. Apparently, the town was so named because of its abundant agricultural fertility in antiquity.

Hence, it is truly ironic that the famine was so bad that it forced Bethlehemites such as Elimelech to emigrate to *Moab*, a hated enemy territory that, according to the Pentateuch, had its origins in the sinful act of Lot and his daughter (Gen 19:36–37) and frequently posed a threat to Israel (cf. Judg 3:12–30). Although God may be Elimelech's king, the narrative immediately raises the question of divine providence, and whether and how this God is providing for those who follow him and are (apparently) faithful to him.

Naomi and Her Daughters-in-Law: Lacking Everything (Ruth 1:6–22)

After the death of the men in the family, the three widows—Naomi, the mother-in-law, and her two Moabite daughters-in-law, Orpah and Ruth— decide to return to Naomi's hometown of Bethlehem. Naomi delivers a tearful speech imploring them to return to Moab, since she can provide them with no future in Bethlehem. Orpah turns back, but Ruth swears an oath never to abandon Naomi. The two travel on and arrive at Bethlehem at the beginning of the barley harvest.

The speeches of Naomi and Ruth in this passage have a high dramatic and literary quality. Special attention must be paid to Ruth's declamation, one of the most powerful in Scripture:

> And she [Naomi] said, "See, your sister-in-law has gone back to her people and to her gods; return after your sister-in-law." But Ruth said, "Entreat me not to leave you or to return from following you; *for where you go I will go, and where you lodge I will lodge; your people shall be my people, and your God my God*; where you die I will die, and there will I be buried. May the LORD do so to me and more also if even death parts me from you." (Ruth 1:15–17)

What a stunning confession of faith in the God of Israel and fidelity to family! And this, remember, on the lips of a *pagan* woman, whose family of origin was rooted in immorality, idolatry, and opposition to God. In context, Ruth's beautiful proclamation constitutes a covenant-oath by which she formally binds herself as kin to Naomi and her family and thereby breaks the kinship ties with her own people. Moreover, since the Israelites were the "people of the Lord", or the family of God, Ruth's covenant-oath also involves a change of religion—what we would call today a "conversion"—and a formal adherence to the God of Israel. Like Rahab before her in the book of Judges, Ruth throws in her lot with the people and God of Israel. Finally, her oath sets up the tension to be resolved in the rest of the book: Will the God of Elimelech and Naomi show faithfulness (Hebrew *hesed*) to this foreign woman who binds herself to him by covenant?

The Courtship of Boaz and Ruth (Ruth 2:1–23)

Once resettled in Bethlehem, Ruth goes out to glean grain to provide a subsistence for herself and Naomi. She happens into the fields belonging to Boaz, a wealthy relative. Boaz is very concerned for Ruth's welfare, providing her extra food and instructing his servants to treat her well and not to "molest" (Hebrew *naga'*) her (Ruth 1:8–9), a word that highlights her physical and social vulnerability as a poor widow (cf. Gen 32:26; 26:11; 20:6).

This chapter introduces Boaz, who will be the male protagonist of the story. In Hebrew, *bo'az* means "in him is strength", and he lives up to his name, ultimately using his "strength" to save Ruth, Naomi, and their nearly defunct family line. The sacred author highlights Boaz's piety: his first recorded words are "The LORD be with you!" (Ruth 2:4). In fact, throughout the book, the author shows Bethlehem to be a place of lived devotion to YHWH. This is particularly true of Boaz, who takes care to follow not only the letter but also the spirit of the Mosaic law, which mandated leaving grain behind for the poor to glean:

> When you reap your harvest in your field, and have forgotten a sheaf in the field, you shall not go back to get it; *it shall be for the sojourner, the fatherless, and the widow*; that the LORD your God may bless you in all the work of your hands. (Deut 24:19; cf. Lev 19:9–10)

Significantly, Ruth falls into all three categories of the vulnerable in society: the sojourner (she is a resident alien or immigrant), the fatherless (she has no family), and the widow (she has no husband). The question is pressed now even further: Will God bless the work of Boaz's generous hands, as it says in the law of Moses?

Notice here the striking contrast between Boaz's admirable concern for the dignity and welfare of a poor foreign woman and the way women were sacrificed, abused, murdered, dismembered, and abducted in the book of Judges. In this way, the canonical juxtaposition of the book of Ruth with the book of Judges makes clear that the treatment of women in Judges was non-normative and contrary to the spirit of the covenant; in Ruth, the sacred author clearly provides a model or *"prescriptive"* narrative for the relationship between the sexes. Indeed, Boaz goes further than merely protecting Ruth; he calls down divine blessing upon her for the covenant fidelity she has shown to Naomi:

> But Boaz answered her, "All that you have done for your mother-in-law since the death of your husband has been fully told me, and how you left your father and mother and your native land and came to a people that you did not know before. *The LORD recompense you for what you have done, and a full reward be given you by the LORD, the God of Israel, under whose wings you have come to take refuge!"* (Ruth 2:11–12)

Now the question is: Will Boaz's blessing be fulfilled, and will God show faithfulness to Ruth? As we will see, the image of protection "under the wing" will come into play significantly in the following chapter. For now, it suffices to note that although kindness toward the vulnerable is commanded by the Mosaic law, Boaz clearly goes above and beyond any legal or even moral imperative in his care for Ruth. This suggests that he is developing an affection for her personally.

The Dramatic Encounter at the Threshing Floor (Ruth 3:1–18)

At this point in the narrative, Naomi—likely recognizing Boaz's affection for Ruth—devises a plan to press the issue of marriage with Boaz in a rather forward way. She urges Ruth to beautify herself, go down to Boaz's harvest party, and offer herself to him when the party is over and he is in a good mood.

The dramatic climax of the book is reached during Ruth and Boaz's hushed and intense dialogue in the middle of the night on the threshing floor, after the harvest festival has ended. The scene has an undeniable erotic tension:

> And when Boaz had eaten and drunk, and his heart was merry, he went to lie down at the end of the heap of grain. Then she came softly, and uncovered his feet, and lay down. At midnight the man was startled, and turned over, and behold, a woman lay at his feet! He said, "Who are you?" And she answered, "I am Ruth, your maidservant; *spread your garment over your maidservant, for you are next of kin.*" (Ruth 3:7–9)

What are we to make of this mysterious exchange between a man and a woman in the middle of the night? The key to answering these questions lies in the words of Ruth, when she asks Boaz to "spread your garment over your maidservant"—in Hebrew, literally, "spread *your wing* [of your garment] over your maidservant." The "spreading of the wing" of the garment was a betrothal ritual in ancient Israel that carried connotations of marital intimacy (see Ezek 16:8). Had Boaz decided to consummate on the threshing floor, Ruth would have become his wife by that act (cf. Ex 22:16). However, such an action would have been lacking in propriety, a breach of social custom. Although clearly attracted to Ruth, Boaz refuses to pursue this attraction in a disordered way. He insists on following law and proper custom, which dictated, among other things, that a closer male relative have the first right to wed Ruth.

Ruth's request that Boaz "spread his wing" over her has a deeper meaning in the canonical context. Earlier, Boaz blessed her for seeking refuge under the "wings of the LORD". By repeating the key word "wing" (Hebrew *kanaph*), the sacred author shows that the "wing" (protective power) of the Lord will actually be manifested by Boaz's "wing". Boaz will be the one through whom God will grant protection to Ruth.

Along these lines, one final aspect of the mysterious nighttime conversation demands explanation: namely, Boaz's reference to a "near kinsmen" (Hebrew *go'el*) (Ruth 3:12). Unfortunately, some modern English translations of this Hebrew word (such as the RSV) obscure its literal meaning of "redeemer". The key passage in Boaz's dialogue with Ruth reads literally as follows:

> Now, I am in fact a redeemer (Hebrew *go'ēl*), but there is another redeemer closer than I. Stay where you are for tonight, and tomorrow, if he will act as redeemer for you, good. But if he will not, as the LORD lives, I will do it myself. Lie there until morning. (Ruth 3:12–13 [NABRE])

With these words, Boaz appears to be alluding to the Israelite custom known as *levirate* marriage (from the Latin, *levir*, "brother-in-law"), by which a brother-in-law (or the next nearest male relative) had the duty of raising up children with the widow of his deceased kinsman (see Gen 38; Deut 25:5–10). Here the concept seems to have been fused with that of the "kinsman-redeemer"

(Hebrew *go'el*), who had the duty of buying back family property sold because of economic hardship and family members who were forced to sell themselves as slaves (cf. Lev 25:25–30).[1] In this way, Boaz will function not only as Ruth's husband, but as her deliverer, her "redeemer".

The Marriage of Ruth and Boaz (Ruth 4:1–17)

Boaz wastes no time in resolving the situation. The law as practiced in those days tied the marriage of the widow to the redemption of her husband's property (Ruth 4:5). Boaz offers the redemption of Naomi's husband Elimelech's land to the nearest male relative. He declines, and Boaz is only too happy to redeem the land and wed Ruth himself.

Given the importance of genealogies manifested so far in the Pentateuch and historical books, as well as the criticisms of pagan peoples who do not worship the Lord, it is striking that the people of Bethlehem pronounce a blessing over Ruth—a Gentile woman!—that likens her to one of the mothers of Israel:

> Then all the people who were at the gate, and the elders, said, "We are witnesses. May the LORD make the woman, who is coming into your house, like Rachel and Leah, who together built up the house of Israel." (Ruth 4:11)

With this, we see the first great example of a Gentile woman becoming not just a part of Israel (as with Rahab) but a *matriarch* in Israel—a mother of future kings.

Naomi and Her Daughter-in-Law: Lacking Nothing (Ruth 4:13–17)

Should there be any doubt about the fidelity of the Lord to his promises, the narrative quickly moves on to document that the marriage of Boaz and Ruth produces a son, Obed, whom Naomi cares for as his nurse. In striking contrast to the famine and tragedy with which the book opens, Ruth and Naomi— the Israelite and the Gentile convert—are now both comfortably situated *in the Promised Land*, as part of the family and household of Boaz, the protector and redeemer, with the family lineage no longer in danger of demise. Indeed, the heir in question is none other than "the father of Jesse, the father of David"— the king who is to come (Ruth 4:17).

Epilogue: The Family Line of David (4:18–22)

Just as the book opened with the genealogy of Elimelech, so now it closes with an account of the descendants of Perez, the ancestor of Boaz himself, so as to trace the covenant family line down to the time of David. In this way, the story of Ruth is of salvation-historical significance: it is not just a romantic tale of a

---

[1] Dale W. Manor, "Ruth", in *Joshua, Judges, Ruth, 1 & 2 Samuel*, vol. 2 of *Zondervan Illustrated Bible Backgrounds Commentary*, ed. John H. Walton (Grand Rapids, Mich.: Zondervan, 2009), 257.

young woman who goes from tragedy to triumph, but, even more, it is the story of God's provident care for the ancestors of King David, who will stand at the very center of the books of Samuel.

Historical Issues in Ruth

Origins of the Book of Ruth

Unlike other books of the Old Testament (such as Jeremiah or Ezekiel), the book of Ruth is formally *anonymous*, and there is no strong Christian or Jewish tradition identifying its author. The date of the composition of the book continues to be debated, with scholars proposing dates anywhere from the early Davidic monarchy (tenth century B.C.) to sometime after the Babylonian exile (fourth century B.C.).

In terms of internal evidence, there are several clues worth highlighting. First, the book reflects the knowledge and practice of some laws found in the Pentateuch, especially the law regarding leaving some of the gleanings of the harvest for "the sojourner, the fatherless, and the widow" (Deut 24:17–19). Indeed, at one point Boaz's statement, "if he is not willing to do the part of next of kin" (Ruth 3:13), echoes the Pentateuchal law stating what to do "if the man does not wish to take his brother's wife" (Deut 25:7).[2]

On the other hand, the book also knows of customs unattested in the Pentateuch or elsewhere in Scripture, such as the taking off of a sandal in order to "confirm a transaction" (Ruth 4:7), as well as applications of Mosaic law not strictly required by its letter: such as the extension of the role of levirate marriage (Deut 25:5–10) beyond uterine brothers to further male relatives (Ruth 4:1–6), not to mention integration of levirate marriage with the redemption of the land of the deceased by the "redeemer" (Hebrew *go'el*) (cf. Lev 25:28–55; Num 36:5–12). Second, in terms of linguistic indications, although the book of Ruth is written in Hebrew, it also contains several *Aramaisms*—that is, borrowings from Aramaic, the ancient language spoken in Damascus and areas under its control. Third and finally, the latest historical person or event mentioned by the book is David, whose name is in fact the final word of the last verse (Ruth 4:21), thus explicitly anchoring the book in the post-Davidic period.

What scholars make of this internal evidence will depend in large part on other conclusions about the dating of the materials in the Pentateuch as well as the linguistic situation in the ancient Near East. In previous generations, the Aramaisms and knowledge of Pentateuchal laws were considered to be proof that Ruth was postexilic, since according to Julius Wellhausen the laws of the Pentateuch were historically late, and Aramaisms likewise were thought to be a sign of postexilic Hebrew. More recently, it has been recognized that Aramaisms penetrated Israelite Hebrew long before the exile, especially in the dialect of Hebrew spoken by the ten tribes to the north (closer to Damascus). Also, for scholars who see the Pentateuchal law as reflecting late second-millennium

---

[2] See Victor Hamilton, *Handbook on the Historical Books* (Grand Rapids, Mich.: Baker Academic, 2001), 199.

realities, the book's apparent familiarity with the Pentateuch is no impediment to a date during the time of the Davidic monarchy. As a result, a number of scholars hold that the book can be dated to sometime during the late tenth century B.C.[3]

The Book of Ruth and the Davidic Monarchy

Indeed, since Ruth is a Moabite, and the Moabites were ancestral enemies of Israel (Deut 23:3–6), it seems highly unlikely that someone later in Israelite history—especially the author of this book, who is clearly pro-Davidic—would have invented the idea that David was descended from a Gentile. Far more plausible is the conclusion that David's descent from Ruth and Ruth's Moabite ancestry are well-known facts, which the author of the book both explains and defends by means of this touching story of human virtue and divine providence. Moreover, it also seems unlikely that someone creating a story at a late date in Israel's history on the basis of the laws in the Pentateuch would compose the narrative of the wedding outlined herein, since the legal customs described do not strictly follow the letter of the Torah (see Ruth 4:1–7).

In sum, the book of Ruth is strongly pro-Davidic, emphasizing that David's ancestors were pious worshippers of the Lord, even his Moabite great-grandmother. There is evidence elsewhere in Scripture of David's Moabite heritage: he sends his family to Moab for safety when pursued by Saul (1 Sam 22:3–4). It may be that David's Moabite blood was seized upon by his critics to delegitimize his claim to the throne, and Ruth was written in part to defend David's heritage. If this suggestion is correct, then a date of composition sometime during the Davidic monarchy is historically plausible, although not demonstrable.

Ruth in the Living Tradition

When we turn from the historical background of the book to its history of interpretation, it must be admitted that Ruth has never been the center of much attention. This is somewhat understandable, given its size. Nevertheless, it is remarkable that in both Jewish and Christian tradition, the characters in this little book were viewed as prefigurations of the Messiah and Israel in Jewish tradition and types of Christ the Bridegroom and the Church his Bride in Christian tradition.

Ruth the Gentile Matriarch and the Church of the Gentiles

For example, in his fifth-century homilies on the Gospel of Matthew, Saint John Chrysostom, bishop of Constantinople, teaches that Ruth's identity as a former pagan and idolater turned believer in the God of Israel is a prefiguration of the Church, whose members are loved by Christ despite their idolatrous background and family origins:

---

[3] See Robert L. Hubbard Jr., *The Book of Ruth*, New International Commentary on the Old Testament 8 (Grand Rapids, Mich.: Eerdmans, 1988), 23–35.

See, for instance, what befell Ruth, how like it is to the things which belong to us. For she was both of a strange race, and reduced to the utmost poverty, yet Boaz when he saw her neither despised her poverty nor abhorred her mean birth, as Christ having received the Church, being both an alien and in much poverty, took her to be partaker of the great blessings. But even as Ruth, if she had not before left her father, and renounced household and race, country and kindred, would not have attained unto this alliance; so the Church too, having forsaken the customs which men had received from their fathers, then, and not before, became lovely to the Bridegroom.[4]

Along similar lines, in the early Middle Ages, Saint Isidore of Seville (ca. A.D. 560–636) developed this typological interpretation of Ruth, adding to it that Ruth's entry into the Promised Land and her confession of faith in the God of Israel were both prefigurations of the conversion of the nations:

Now let us look at Ruth, for she is a type of the church. First she is a type because she is a stranger from the Gentile people who renounced her native land and all things belonging to it. She made her way to the land of Israel. And when her mother-in-law forbade her from coming with her she persisted, saying, "Wherever you go, I shall go; your people shall be my people; and your God shall be my God. Whichever land receives you as you die, there I too shall die." This voice without doubt shows that she is a type of the church. *For the church was called to God from the Gentiles in just this way: leaving her native land (which is idolatry) and giving up all earthly associations, she confessed that he in whom the saints believed is the Lord God.*[5]

In other words: in the book of Ruth, we see clearly that the conversion of the Gentile nations is *not* an exclusively "New Testament" phenomenon. Over a millennium before the birth of the apostle Paul, the God of Israel was already drawing certain righteous Gentiles such as Ruth into the covenant family of the people of God, prefiguring what would happen in a widespread way with the inauguration of the New Covenant.

Boaz the Redeemer and Christ the Bridegroom

As soon as we see Ruth (the bride) as a type of the Church, it is easy to see why the Christian tradition has also recognized Boaz her bridegroom and "redeemer" as a prefiguration of Christ. According to Isidore of Seville, the unnamed relative of Ruth who refused to wed her is a type of John the Baptist, and Boaz a type of Christ:

It is thought that this passage prefigures John the Baptist who, when he himself was thought by the people of Israel to be Christ and was asked who he was, did not deny who he was but confessed it, saying he was not Christ.... He confessed the good news about the Lord, saying, "He who has the bride is the bridegroom."

---

[4] John Chrysostom, *Homilies on Matthew* 3.5, in *NPNF1* 10:17.

[5] Isidore of Seville, *On Ruth* 7, in Leslie Smith, *Medieval Exegesis in Translation: Commentaries on the Book of Ruth* (Kalamazoo, Mich.: Medieval Institute Publications, 1996), 7.

... Just as he [the unnamed relative who refused to marry Ruth] told her he was not her kinsman but then afterwards Ruth was united with Boaz, so Christ, who is the true bridegroom of the church, whom the sayings of all the prophets proclaim, was deemed worthy, from all Gentile nations, to claim the church, to present to God the Father unnumbered people throughout the whole orb of the world, because his kinsman took off the sandals.[6]

What a striking reading of the spiritual sense of the Scriptures! Isidore not only sees Christ as the fulfillment of Boaz the bridegroom; he also connects the book of Ruth's reference to the custom of taking off one's "sandal" to confirm the transfer of the bride (Ruth 4:7) to John the Baptist's famous statement about being unworthy to "untie" the "sandal" of the Messiah (Jn 1:27). Isidore is noticing a few of the many parallels between Christ and Boaz:

Boaz as a Type of Christ	
Boaz	Jesus
In the line of David (Ruth 4:21)	From the line of David (Mt 1:1)
Name means "in him is strength" (Ruth 2:1)	St. Paul says we find our strength in him (1 Tim 1:12; Eph 6:10; 2 Tim 4:17)
Is the kinsman of Naomi and Ruth (Ruth 2:20)	Is our kinsman by sharing our flesh (Heb 2:14)
Serves as "redeemer" of Naomi and Ruth (Ruth 3:13)	Christ "redeems" us from sin and death (Gal 3:13)
Took Ruth "under his wing" (Ruth 3:9)	Longs to take his people "under his wing" (Mt 23:37)
Feeds Ruth, his future bride, with the gift of finest grain (Ruth 2:14; 3:15)	Feeds the Church, his bride, with his own body in the form of bread (Mt 26:26)

In terms of the moral sense of the text, it is important to note that Boaz also sets a clear moral example for other men among the community of God's people: the ideal man of the Lord actively manifests the Lord's concern for the poor by concrete acts of mercy toward them and can expect a reward from the Lord for such upright behavior even in this life.

The Moabite Woman Becomes a Mother of the Messiah

Finally, it is important to note that the overall upshot of the book of Ruth is that a Gentile woman—indeed, a descendant of Moab!—because of her faith and her virtue, is rewarded by becoming a mother in Israel and ancestress of the Messiah himself. In the words of Saint Jerome:

[6] Ibid.

Yet when she [Naomi] was thus deprived of her natural protectors, Ruth, a stranger, never left her side. And see what a great thing it is to comfort a lonely woman! *Ruth, for her reward, is made an ancestress of Christ.*[7]

In the earliest Christian tradition, it is in this role above all—as "matriarch" of Israel and the Messiah—that Ruth remains most prominent. Indeed, she is mentioned as such on the very first page of the New Testament, when Matthew points out that Jesus of Nazareth belongs to the family of "Boaz the father of Obed *by Ruth*" (Mt 1:5).

The Book of Ruth in the Lectionary

Unfortunately, Ruth is read in the liturgy on only two days in Ordinary Time and otherwise never appears in the Lectionary or the Divine Office. Thus, the touching story and spiritual sweetness of the book are primarily the object of private meditation.

Liturgical Readings of Ruth		
Day	Passage Read	Description
Fri., Week 20 (I)	1:1, 3–6, 14b–16, 22	After the sojourn in Moab, Naomi and Ruth return to Bethlehem.
Sat., Week 20 (I)	2:1–3, 8–11; 4:13–17	Boaz and Ruth meet in the fields; Boaz marries Ruth.

Conclusion

In its Christian canonical order, Ruth provides a stark contrast to the book of Judges, demonstrating that during this anarchic period of Israel's history, there was one place where true piety toward the Lord continued to be practiced: Bethlehem. Out of this idyllic community, from a noble Israelite (Boaz) and a virtuous Gentile convert (Ruth), will arise David (Ruth 4:21), the good king so strongly desired at the end of the book of Judges (Judg 21:25). A short romance of great charm and elegance, the book of Ruth's spiritual sense speaks of the nuptial relationship of Christ with the Church and of the individual believer with Christ through the messianic wedding banquet of the Eucharist.

For Further Reading

Commentaries on and Studies of Ruth

Hamilton, Victor. *Handbook on the Historical Books.* Grand Rapids, Mich.: Baker Academic, 2001. (See pp. 187–209.)

Hubbard, Robert L., Jr. *The Book of Ruth.* New International Commentary on the Old Testament 8. Grand Rapids, Mich.: Eerdmans, 1988.

---

[7] Jerome, *Letter* 39.5, in *NPNF2* 6:53.

Linafelt, Tod, and Timothy K. Beale. *Ruth and Esther*. Berit Olam. Collegeville, Minn.: Liturgical Press, 1999. (See pp. 1–83.)

Manor, Dale W. "Ruth". Pages 242–65 in *Joshua, Judges, Ruth, 1 & 2 Samuel*. Vol. 2 of *Zondervan Illustrated Bible Backgrounds Commentary*. Edited by John H. Walton. Grand Rapids, Mich.: Zondervan, 2009

Ruth in the Living Tradition

Franke, John R., ed. *Joshua, Judges, Ruth, 1–2 Samuel*. Old Testament 4 of Ancient Christian Commentary on Scripture. Edited by Thomas C. Oden. Downers Grove, Ill.: InterVarsity Press, 2005. (See pp. 181–92.)

Neusner, Jacob. *The Mother of the Messiah in Judaism: The Book of Ruth*. Bible of Judaism Library. Harrisburg: Trinity Press International, 1993.

Smith, Lesley. *Medieval Exegesis in Translation: Commentaries on the Book of Ruth*. Kalamazoo, Mich.: Medieval Institute Publications, 1996.

14. THE BOOKS OF SAMUEL

Introduction

On the one hand, the two books of Samuel were originally one composition and show signs of being designed as a single literary unit. On the other hand, they are also clearly a part of a much larger composition, tracing the history of Israel from creation to the destruction of Jerusalem and the Babylonian exile (Genesis–2 Kings). At the turn of the third century A.D., Origen records that for the Jews, these two books were one book, "*Samouel*, that is, 'The called of God'".[1] Apparently it was the early Jewish translators of the Greek Septuagint (LXX) who divided the book in two, probably because of its length, which would have been difficult to contain on a single scroll. As with other books of Jewish Scripture, the Septuagint textual tradition also gave different names to the books of Samuel, referring to them as the first two of the four "books of Kingdoms", with 1–2 Samuel corresponding to 1–2 Kingdoms and, confusingly, 1–2 Kings corresponding to 3–4 Kingdoms. Most editions of the Latin Vulgate followed this Septuagintal practice of considering Samuel and Kings a set of four books, 1–4 Kings.

Although named after the prophet Samuel, the story of whose birth introduces the work, the main figure of these two books is without doubt David. He is the central figure who connects nearly every other major character in the narrative: Samuel is the prophet who anoints David; Saul is the royal predecessor and father-in-law of David; Jonathan is the beloved friend of David; Joab is the loyal general of David; and so forth. Although David has already been mentioned in Ruth, he is only truly introduced in this book (see 1 Sam 16). Thereafter he takes over from Moses as *the* dominant figure of the Old Testament: whereas Moses is mentioned 767 times in the Jewish Scriptures (Masoretic Text), David is mentioned 1075 times. The second half of 1 Samuel (16–30) and the entire book of 2 Samuel are dedicated to detailing David's life. Intriguingly, the Old Testament pays more *biographical* attention to David than to any other character—more so even than Moses, since only small portions of Exodus through Deuteronomy could be considered biography of Moses as an individual. Indeed, in the entire canon, the only figure to eclipse David in terms of biographical attention will be Jesus himself in the four Gospels.

The primary reason for David's significance within the Old Testament is his reception of an *everlasting covenant* from God (2 Sam 7:8–16; 2 Sam 23:5; Ps 89:20–37) that bestows upon himself and his heirs the status of *son of God* and universal high king (Ps 89:27). The sonship that was offered to Israel at Sinai, but

---

[1] Origen quoted by Eusebius of Caesarea, *Church History* 6.25.2, in *NPNF2* 1:272.

rejected in its subsequent history of idolatry, is granted now to the Davidic king. In this way, Israel experiences the blessings of divine filiation, at least indirectly. This Davidic covenant assimilates and integrates many of the promises and blessings of previous covenants and will become the focus of the eschatological hopes of Israel in the prophets. The books of Samuel recount the antecedent events to David's reception of this covenant and his lived response to it. Raymond Brown, the most influential Catholic Bible scholar of the twentieth century, captured the significance of the Davidic king and covenant when he wrote:

> The story of David brings out all the strengths and weaknesses of the beginnings of the religious institution of the kingdom for the people of God.... *The kingdom established by David ... is the closest Old Testament parallel to the New Testament church.*... To help Christians make up their mind on how the Bible speaks [to Church issues] it would help if they knew about David and his kingdom, *which was also God's kingdom* and whose kings, with all their imperfections, God promised to treat as "sons" (2 Sm 7:14).[2]

As we will see, the enduring theological importance of the books of Samuel, which tell the story of David, and also of the books of Kings, in which David's kingdom reaches its zenith (followed by a long demise), will indeed revolve around the kingdom established by David and the covenant sonship bestowed upon him.

Literary Structure and Characteristics of 1–2 Samuel

How Are the Books of Samuel Structured?

One of the clear signs that the books of Samuel are indeed a single literary unit broken up into two because of length is the *inclusio* formed by the Song of Hannah (1 Sam 2:1–10) near the beginning of the book and the Song of David near the end (2 Sam 22). These two compositions share a great number of themes and motifs, including but not limited to (1) God as rock (1 Sam 2:2; 2 Sam 22:2); (2) the providential reversal of fortune (1 Sam 2:4–8; 2 Sam 22:28); (3) the crushing of the enemies of the Lord (1 Sam 2:10a; 2 Sam 22:43); (4) the manifestation of the Lord through storm phenomena (1 Sam 2:10b; 2 Sam 22:8–15); (5) God's fidelity to his anointed (Hebrew *mashiah*, "messiah") (1 Sam 2:10c–e; 2 Sam 22:51).

Thus, at the beginning of Samuel, Hannah expresses faith in the Lord and his "anointed" (*mashiah*), but the anointed himself is not identified (1 Sam 2:10). By the end of the books of Samuel, the anointed is clearly identified as David, the one through whom God manifests his great ministry of humbling the proud and exalting the humble. In other words, the hopes and prayers of Israel voiced by Hannah find a fulfillment in David and his heirs.

Treating the books of Samuel as a single literary unit, the structure can be outlined in a broad sense as follows:

---

[2] Raymond E. Brown, S.S., "Communicating the Divine and Human in Scripture", *Origins* 22.1 (May 14, 1992): 5–6.

The Location of the Ark in the Books of Samuel

The Ark of the Covenant has an important role to play in the books of Samuel. The narrative opens with the Ark of the Covenant residing in a shrine in the city of Shiloh (1 Sam 1–2). A major transition takes place when King David brings the ark from Shiloh up to the city of Jerusalem, with a short stop at the house of Obed-edom (2 Sam 6). Finally, the book closes with David purchasing the threshing floor of Araunah, which Solomon will use as the site of the Temple, the final resting place of the ark (2 Sam 24). So in the books of Samuel we move from the ark in its temporary quarters at Shiloh to the acquisition of its permanent resting place at Jerusalem, on the site of the future Temple. These liturgically significant geographical markers help establish the literary unity of the books.

Outline of 1 Samuel

   I. From Eli to Samuel: Eli's Demise, Samuel's Rise (1 Sam 1–7)
      A. From Samuel's Birth to Eli's Death (1–4)
      B. The Sojourn of the Ark in Philistia (5–6)
      C. The Judgeship of Samuel (7)

  II. From Samuel to Saul: Samuel Fades, Saul Fails (1 Sam 8–15)
      A. Samuel Gives the People Saul as King (8–12)
      B. Saul's Kingship Unravels (13–15)

 III. From Saul to David: Saul's Demise, David's Rise (1 Sam 16–31)
      A. David's Anointing and Early Successes (16:1–18:9)
      B. David on the Run from Saul (18:10–30:31)
      C. The Death of Saul (31:1–13)

Outline of 2 Samuel

  IV. The House of David vs. the House of Saul (2 Sam 1–4)
      A. Eulogy for Saul and Jonathan (1)
      B. Rivalry between the House of David and the House of Saul (2–3)
      C. The Death of Ish-bosheth, Saul's Heir (4)

   V. The Triumphs of David (2 Sam 5–10)
      A. David Established as King of Israel in Jerusalem (5–6)
      B. David Receives a Covenant (7)
      C. David Reaches the Height of His Power (8–10)

  VI. The Tragedies of David (2 Sam 11–20)
      A. The Sin of David: The Bathsheba Affair (11–12)
      B. The Sins of David's Sons: The Usurpation by Absalom (13–20)

 VII. Epilogue: A Retrospect on David's Reign (2 Sam 21–24)
      A. Plague Ended by Atonement: The Gibeonites (21:1–14)
         B. The Exploits of David's Men: Giant Killing (21:15–22)
           C. Poem 1: David's Song of Praise (22)

C'. Poem 2: David's Last Words (23:1–7)
  B'. The Exploits of David's Men: The Mighty Men (23:8–39)
  A'. Plague Ended by Atonement: The Census and Threshing Floor (24)

In the books of Samuel, there is a steady dramatic build toward the high point of the narrative: David's rule over the united twelve tribes of Israel and his reception of an eternal covenant of kingship from God (2 Sam 5–10). His sin with Bathsheba (2 Sam 11) marks the beginning of a decline culminating in David's exile and near-death (2 Sam 17:1–4). However, David is restored to kingship, and the books end with a balanced assessment of David's reign that recalls both David's virtue and his vice, but highlights most of all God's *hesed* (covenant fidelity) toward him.

1–2 Samuel as a Literary Masterpiece

Although all the books of Scripture are divinely inspired, they do not all display the same level of literary artistry. From a literary perspective, the books of Samuel stand out as one of the great masterpieces of literature in the Old Testament and, indeed, in all the literature of the ancient Near East. In order to appreciate this human dimension of the text, it is helpful to highlight some of the distinctive literary features of 1–2 Samuel.

One of the literary techniques utilized by the sacred author is to allow two protagonists to carry the story line together for long sections: usually one who is an established authority but in decline and the other who is seeking to become established and is advancing. This is true of Eli and Samuel (1 Sam 1–3), Samuel and Saul (1 Sam 8–15), Saul and David (1 Sam 16–31), and David and Absalom (2 Sam 13–19). Nonetheless, the pattern is not rigid, and in each case there are variations. For example, in the cases of Eli vs. Samuel (1 Sam 1–7) and Saul vs. David (1 Sam 16—2 Sam 5), a sinful ruler is successfully replaced by a righteous one. However, in the cases of Samuel vs. Saul (1 Sam 8–15) and David vs. Absalom (2 Sam 13–19), both rulers are flawed, but the younger challenger is more so; therefore the transition is abortive and the older ruler (Samuel, David) retains power and eventually transfers it to a worthier recipient (Samuel → David in 1 Sam 16; David → Solomon in 1 Kings 1).

Another remarkable literary feature of the books of Samuel is the complex characterization of the major personalities of the story. There are very few one-dimensional or "flat" characters. The "heroes" of the history are flawed, and the "villains" have their virtues. For example, Eli ultimately fails to restrain his wicked sons, but he is kind to Hannah (1 Sam 1:17), his blessings are efficacious (1 Sam 1:17, 2:20–21), and he humbly accepts God's will (1 Sam 3:18). Along similar lines, Samuel is an enormously successful prophet and judge, but a poor father—his sons, too, turn out to be wicked men (2 Sam 8:1–3). Likewise, Saul degenerates into attempted murder, massacre (2 Sam 22:6–23), and witchcraft (1 Sam 28:3–25), but his heroism (1 Sam 11:1–11) and prophetic inspiration (1 Sam 10:9–13) are not forgotten; in death he is magnificently eulogized (2 Sam 1:19–27). David is, of course, the great king of Israel, the center of the book (2 Sam 5–10), but his sins—sloth, adultery, drunkenness, lying, and murder of the innocent—are revealed in agonizing detail (2 Sam 11–20, 24). Finally, Absalom, the son of David, is a wicked usurper and attempted patricide, yet we sympathize with his indignation over his sister's rape and the subsequent lack of justice, and his final epitaph is filled with tragic pathos (2 Sam 18:16–18).

Indeed, the nuanced and complex characterization in Samuel is also extended to the large number of supporting characters, many of whom are fleshed out well enough that their personalities emerge from the text. So, in addition to the four successive leaders of Israel described in these books (Eli, Samuel, Saul, and David), we also see vivid portraits of Hannah, Jonathan, Joab, and several others (Michal, Abigail, Abner, Uriah, and so on). These minor characters are typically complicated as well: only a few escape all criticism, and some of these "ideal" characters upset expectations by dying tragically (Jonathan, Uriah). The result is that the books of Samuel present a literary, historical, and theological masterpiece: a richly textured, realistic, and certainly not sanitized account of the workings of God with human beings, in which God's plans advance sometimes because of, but more often in spite of, the deeds and characters of those with whom God chooses to work.

Overview of 1–2 Samuel

The Birth of Samuel and the Demise of Eli the Priest (1 Samuel 1–7)

The opening chapters of 1 Samuel serve as an important transition between the time of the judges and the rise of the monarchy by focusing on the last of all the judges of Israel: the prophet Samuel. In telling the story of Samuel, three aspects of the narrative stand out as significant.

First, Samuel, like certain of the patriarchs before him, has his origins in *a miraculous birth*. His mother, Hannah (Hebrew *Ḥannah*, "grace" or "gracious one"), is one of the two wives of Elkanah, an Ephraimite. Hannah is a devout woman, who worships annually with her husband at the Tabernacle in Shiloh. However, she is also infertile and suffers a great deal from Peninnah, Elkanah's other wife (1 Sam 1). Significantly, the tragic story takes a turn at the Tabernacle at *Shiloh*, where Hannah prays fervently for the Lord to give her the gift of a son. As a result of her prayer and the blessing of the high priest Eli, Hannah conceives supernaturally and gives birth to Samuel (Hebrew *shemu'el*, "God hears" or "name of God"). Remarkably, Hannah does not respond to the gift of her only child by coddling him and keeping him to herself; instead, as soon as the child is weaned, she offers him back to the Lord by bringing him to the Tabernacle and dedicating him to the sanctuary by means of what appears to be a lifelong Nazirite vow, by which Samuel is effectively consecrated as a kind of acolyte or priest in the sanctuary (even though he is not a Levite). Equally significant is the fact that Hannah also responds to the gift of Samuel by singing a song of rejoicing—popularly known as "the Song of Hannah"—in which the central theme is the Lord's humbling of the exalted and exultation of the lowly, culminating in the exaltation of "the power of his anointed [Hebrew *mashiah*]" (1 Sam 2:1–10). This theme will dominate the narrative of Samuel, in which one character after another is exalted to power from a state of lowliness, only to become proud and then to experience God's humbling in turn. Hannah's son, Samuel, will be the pivotal figure in transitioning Israel from the rule of judges to the rule of kings. He will be the "kingmaker", the undisputed moral authority who will anoint Israel's first two kings.

Second, in stark contrast to the piety and sacrifice of Hannah, there stands the wickedness and selfishness of the priestly family of Eli, who are the official ministers of the Tabernacle at Shiloh. With them, we see vestiges of the liturgical and moral chaos of the time of the judges on full display. In particular, two sins of the priesthood of this time stand out: Eli's priestly sons commit both liturgical abuses, by stealing meat from the sacrifices dedicated to the Lord (1 Sam 2:12–17), and sexual transgressions, by having relations with "the women who served at the entrance to the tent of meeting" (1 Sam 2:22). Although at first glance the two sins might seem unrelated, in an ancient Israelite context, it is important to recall that the relationship between God and his people was viewed as a nuptial covenant and that acts of cultic infidelity were considered "spiritual adultery" (cf. Hos 2; Ezek 16). For this reason, throughout salvation history, cultic offenses against the Lord's covenant often coincide with offenses against the matrimonial covenant in the form of sexual immorality (cf. Ex 32:6; Num 25:1–9). In any case, it is abundantly clear that the priestly family of Eli has become completely corrupt. As a result, by means of an anonymous "man of God" and by speaking to the boy Samuel in a revelation by night, God declares to Eli that the priesthood will be taken away from his family and given to "a faithful priest" (1 Sam 2:35) who will replace him.

Third and finally, as a result of the corruption of Israel's leaders, the great sign of the covenant with God—the Ark of the Covenant—is captured by *the Philistines*, the enemies of Israel who will stand front and center throughout the entire biblical history of Samuel, Saul, and, above all, King David. Historically, the Philistines were a Gentile people who settled on the southwest coast of Canaan sometime in the late second millennium B.C.[3] Whatever their exact origins, they are mentioned frequently in ancient Near Eastern literature outside the Bible, and, in the books of Samuel in particular, they stand out as the quintessential enemy of the people of Israel.

Indeed, it is by means of a Philistine invasion that God removes the high priest Eli from leadership over Israel,

---

The History of the Ark (1 Samuel 4–6)

Scholars often suggest that 1 Samuel 4–6 is part of a unique ancient source that recorded the history of the Ark of the Covenant—its movements and events associated with it. This source is thought to continue in 2 Samuel 6.

Whether these chapters come from a separate source or not, the ark does play an important, if subtle, role in Samuel, together with related objects: the ephod, Urim, and Thummim, which were used to inquire of the Lord, ordinarily in the presence of the ark in the sanctuary. Since the exodus, God has been leading the Israelites toward "rest" in their land, where they will have freedom to worship. Together with Kings, 1–2 Samuel tells the story of God's liturgical presence finally coming to "rest" in the Temple. 1–2 Samuel begins with the ark in ill-fated Shiloh and ends with the purchase of the ark's final place of rest.

---

[3] See V. Philips Long, "1 Samuel", in *Joshua, Judges, Ruth, 1 & 2 Samuel*, vol. 2 of *Zondervan Illustrated Bible Backgrounds Commentary*, ed. John H. Walton (Grand Rapids, Mich.: Zondervan, 2009), 284.

due to his failure to restrain his sons (1 Sam 2–5). In the process, the Ark of the Covenant is stolen by the Philistines, although they ultimately return it under the pressure of an alarming series of divine acts of judgment, which appear to include some kind of double plague involving "mice" as well as "tumors" (RSVCE) or "hemorrhoids" (NAB) (1 Sam 6:4)! Wasting no time in their desire to end such terrible plagues, the Philistines return the Ark of the Covenant to the Israelites, and Samuel replaces Eli as judge over Israel and fulfills the role of the last of the judges: "Samuel judged Israel all the days of his life" (1 Sam 7:15).

The Rise and Fall of King Saul (1 Samuel 8–15)

Arguably, one of the most pivotal events in the books of Samuel is when the Israelites take the momentous step of requesting a "a king" from Samuel and from God (1 Sam 8:5). Up to this point, of course, God himself has ruled his people as king, leading them through the mediation of prophets (such as Moses) or judges (such as Samuel). Needless to say, Samuel—as a prophet and judge himself—is displeased by the request of the people and tries to dissuade them, but they persist. And in persisting, we catch an important glimpse into why their demand for a king is so problematic:

> But the people refused to listen to the voice of Samuel; and they said, "No! but we will have a king over us, *that we also may be like all the nations*, and that our king may govern us *and go out before us and fight our battles*." (1 Sam 8:19–20)

Notice two striking aspects of why the Israelites want a king (and not a judge or prophet). First and foremost, they want to have a king because they want to be "like the nations". This is a striking rejection of their call from God as "first-born son" (Ex 4:22). Instead of being a kingdom of priests called to lead the nations, Israel now wants to follow the pagans. Second, and even more telling, they want a king who will "fight their battles". In other words, they want the *military power* that comes with an earthly king, so that they can feel protected. In other words, God's protection is not enough for them. They no longer trust the Lord to fight their battles for them. They have given in to fear of their enemies in general and the Philistines in particular.

In response to Israel's desire to be like the Gentiles, the Lord both acqui-esces to the people's demand and, through Samuel, warns them of the kinds of abuses a king "like the nations" will inflict on them: military draft, slavery, and taxation—even up to 10 percent (1 Sam 8:10–18)!

And it is under the shadow of these ominous prophecies that Samuel, in cooperation with the Lord's guidance, chooses Saul of Benjamin to be the first king of Israel (1 Sam 9). Ominously, this choice of king seems contrary to the patriarch Jacob's declaration that "the scepter" and "the ruler's staff"—that is, the kingship—would belong to the tribe of *Judah*, not to the tribe of Benjamin (see Gen 49:10), which, as we saw in an earlier chapter, became the small-est of tribes, being decimated after adopting the practices of Sodom (see Judg 19–20). Indeed, this ambiguity of the figure of Saul is present from the very beginning of his selection by Samuel and exaltation to the kingship. On the one hand, Saul has suitable physical attributes for a king and political leader (height and good looks) (1 Sam 9), is a valiant and successful warrior against the Ammonites (1 Sam 11), and is even empowered by God's "spirit" so that he can, at least temporarily, be numbered among "the prophets" (1 Sam 10). On the other hand, Saul commits a series of questionable or even egregious acts, beginning with his hiding among "the baggage" at the very moment he is being selected as king (1 Sam 10:20–24); arrogating to himself the role of priest by offering unlawful sacrifice (1 Sam 13:8–9); uttering a rash oath-curse that mars an Israelite victory and comes to rest on Jonathan, his heir (1 Sam 14:24–46); and finally by disobeying Samuel's prophetic command to execute the *herem* against the Amalekites and then lying about it afterward (1 Sam 15:1–22). For assuming the rights of the priesthood, he loses his dynasty (1 Sam 13:14). For disobeying Samuel's prophetic command, he loses his personal claim to the kingdom, which is "torn" away from him and given "to a neighbor of yours, who is better than you" (1 Sam 15:28). Thus the tide of leadership turns in Israel: this time to the figure of David himself.

> ### The Theological Problem of Kingship
>
> The institution of kingship in Israel is awkward. Early Mosaic law does not foresee it, but ultimately Moses permits it (Deut 17:14–20). Judges argues for it (Judg 21:25), but when the people ask for it, it is a sin (1 Sam 12:17), yet God grants their request (1 Sam 8:22).
>
> In God's original plan for Israel, he himself was to be their one king; yet in another sense, every Israelite was to share in a kingly and priestly role: "You shall be to me a *kingdom of priests*" (Ex 19:6). The concentration of the kingship in one man seemed simultaneously to displace the Lord as king and to confiscate the general kingship from the people. Nonetheless, the experience of the judges showed that Israel was not able to live successfully under the direct rule of God and sharing the common sovereignty. God works with Israel's failings, however. While granting their request, he already prepares for a reconciliation in which his own desire to rule his people directly will coincide with the people's desire for a human king. This reconciliation takes place in the Davidic covenant, in which the monarch is both son of David and also son of God (2 Sam 7:14), but more perfectly in the New Covenant, in which the monarch is true God and true Man. The New Israel participates in the kingship of Christ and so regains the royal priesthood once lost (1 Pet 2:9).

The Anointing of David and the Demise of Saul (1 Samuel 16–31)

In the wake of Saul's rejection as king, the Lord directs the prophet Samuel to choose one of the sons of a certain Jesse of Bethlehem so that he might be the "anointed" one (Hebrew *mashiah*) (1 Sam 16:6). Samuel obeys and anoints the shepherd boy David, the eighth and youngest son of Jesse, a man of the tribe of Judah and the city of Bethlehem. Significantly, it is at this pivotal moment in Israel's history that we see a visible expression of what it means to be a "messiah of the LORD" (Hebrew *meshiah-YHWH*), an "anointed" king:

> Now he [David] was ruddy, and had beautiful eyes, and was handsome. And the LORD said, "Arise, anoint him [Hebrew *meshakhehu*]; for this is he." Then Samuel took the horn of oil, and anointed him in the midst of his brothers; and the Spirit of the LORD [Hebrew *ruah-YHWH*] came mightily upon David from that day forward. (1 Sam 16:12–13)

Notice here that the essence of being the "messiah" or anointed king of Israel consisted of being anointed with the Spirit of God. By means of the visible sign of the anointing with oil, the Spirit is bestowed on David in a permanent way. The very first manifestation of the Spirit's power in David takes place when he plays the lyre for Saul in order to drive away the "evil spirit" that torments him. This is the first display of "exorcistic" power in the Old Testament (1 Sam 16:14–23).

Much more famously, David also becomes Saul's armor-bearer (bodyguard) and distinguishes himself in combat, above all against the Philistine giant Goliath, whose recorded height and stature were truly extraordinary: "six cubits and a span" (=9 feet, 9 inches) (MT), or "four cubits and a span" (=6 feet, 9 inches) (LXX) (1 Sam 17:4). Unfortunately for David, his successes in battle have an adverse effect, so that his popular reputation begins to exceed even that of Saul himself, with the women of Israel singing: "Saul has slain his thousands, and David his ten thousands" (1 Sam 18:7). Unsurprisingly, Saul becomes envious of David's growing popularity and begins to view David as a threat to his throne. The relationship of Saul and David becomes strained, and Saul makes the first of what will be many attempts to kill David over the remainder of his life, none of which goes according to plan (1 Sam 18:10–30). Although Saul's relationship with David sours, David enjoys the friendship and confidence of Jonathan, Saul's son and heir, as well as of Michal, Saul's younger daughter. Despite the conflict with their father, David enters into a covenant relationship with both of them: with Michal by means of marriage (1 Sam 18:20–29) and with Jonathan by means of multiple oaths and a deep friendship: David "loved him as he loved his own soul" (1 Sam 20:17).

As one might expect, Jonathan attempts to reconcile Saul and David, but the reconciliation is only temporary (1 Sam 19:7–10). Eventually, it becomes clear that King Saul is bent on murdering David, and both Michal and Jonathan assist David in fleeing from Saul's court (1 Sam 19–20). David takes refuge from Saul with the aging Samuel (19:18–24), with the priests of the town of Nob (21:1–9), in Philistine Gath (21:10–15), and in various strongholds in the

---

Textual Issues in the Goliath Narrative

The Hebrew Masoretic Text (MT) of the Goliath narrative seems to have been disturbed at some point in the history of its transmission. The Greek Septuagint (LXX) text reads more straightforwardly, as it lacks the account of David's shuttling provisions back and forth to his brothers (1 Sam 17:12–31) and Saul's dialogue with Abner (1 Sam 17:55–58), both of which pose some chronological problems in their present context.

Goliath's height in the Masoretic Text is six cubits and a span, or about ten feet (1 Sam 17:4). The LXX and other ancient texts specify four cubits and a span, or about six feet nine inches: a more modest figure but still very much a giant among his contemporaries.

In 2 Samuel 21:19, Elhanan of Bethlehem also slays a "Goliath the Gittite". Many scholars suggest Elhanan's deed was later attributed to David, creating the story of 1 Samuel 17. Another explanation is that Goliath named a son after himself, whom Elhanan later slew.

The meaning of the name Goliath is unknown, but it is interesting to note that names with the same form are attested at Gath in the tenth–ninth centuries B.C.

wilderness of southern Judah (the Negev; 1 Sam 21–22). Saul slaughters the priests of Nob, whom he suspects of sympathizing with David (22:11–19), and chases David unsuccessfully in the Negev on more than one occasion (23:15–28). Significantly, David displays his virtue and reverence for the office of anointed king: although David has multiple opportunities to assassinate Saul—such as when Saul was relieving himself in the very cave in which David was hiding!—he will not lift his hand against "the LORD's anointed [Hebrew *meshiah-YHWH*]" (1 Sam 24:6).

It is during this time of flight and persecution that David gathers around him a band of outlaws and discontents and continues to show his prowess in warfare. He not only wins the hand of Abigail as wife (1 Sam 25), but makes various victorious raids against the Geshurites, Girzites, and Amalekites (1 Sam 27). Eventually, however, David is compelled to take refuge in Philistine territory to escape from Saul. The king of Gath grants him the city of Ziklag as a home for himself, his men, and their families.

A dramatic confrontation develops, however, as the Philistines gather for battle against Saul and David is expected to join them (1 Sam 29). Providentially, the other Philistine kings do not trust David in a battle against his own people and Saul. David is sent back to Ziklag, which he finds destroyed by the Amalekites. He pursues the attackers and recovers the entire population of the town, which had been taken captive (1 Sam 30). Meanwhile, Saul is left to face the combined Philistine attack. Receiving no supernatural direction through prophet, priest, dream, or other means, he panics and resorts to breaking the law of Moses by consulting a "medium" or "witch" in the town of Endor (cf. Lev 19:31; 20:27). This witch ostensibly practices necromancy by conjuring up the spirit of the deceased Samuel to inform Saul of his imminent defeat and death (1 Sam 28). The prophecy comes true; Saul and his three oldest sons—including Jonathan—are slain in battle with the Philistines on Mount Gilboa. Tragically, the once-glorious King Saul comes to a bitter

---

The "Faithfulness" (Hebrew Hesed) *of David*

The account of the rise of David and demise of Saul, the longest section of 1–2 Samuel (1 Sam 16–31), shifts focus between David and Saul, as we observe the growth of the one and the degeneration of the other. The sacred author contrasts David and Saul in their practice of *hesed*, an important biblical concept describing covenant fidelity: the loyalty, love, and mercy expected between covenant partners.

David is an admirable practitioner of *hesed*, showing mercy to Saul even when it was in his power to slay him. Saul, on the other hand, consistently violates *hesed* toward David through his many attempts on his life.

But Saul also violates *hesed*—covenant fidelity—toward the Lord by putting the priests of the Lord at Nob to the *herem*-ban and then descending to the witchcraft forbidden by Mosaic law. Saul's *herem*-slaughter of the priest of Nob is particularly ironic, since he refused to practice *herem* against the Amalekites (1 Sam 15). David's *hesed* toward Saul is also *hesed* toward the Lord, because Saul remains a sacral king—"the LORD's anointed". David's refusal to "lift his hand against the LORD's anointed" established a political precedent in Judah that helped foster a culture opposed to assassination and civil war. As a result, David's dynasty ruled for about 400 years: the longest-lived dynasty in the ancient Near East.

---

and pathetic end by falling on his own sword—the one major example of suicide in the entire Hebrew Bible (1 Sam 31).

The House of David vs. the House of Saul (2 Samuel 1–4)

David performs his last act of *hesed* for Saul by avenging his death against the Amalekite man who claimed to slay him (2 Sam 1:1–16) and magnificently eulogizing Saul and Jonathan in a poem that has never been forgotten (2 Sam 1:17–27). Saul's death, however, introduces a schism within Israel, as the southern tribe of Judah anoints David as its king (2 Sam 2), whereas Saul's general Abner places Saul's son Ish-bosheth on the throne of the northern tribes and moves the capital to Mahanaim in the Transjordan. As a result, there is military struggle between the two claimants to the throne, and David's men prove to be stronger. Indeed, this entire section can be summed up with the lines:

> There was a long war between the house of Saul and the house of David; and David grew stronger and stronger, while the house of Saul became weaker and weaker. (2 Sam 3:1)

Despite the initial schism between north and south, eventually there is a falling out between Abner and Ish-bosheth, and Abner attempts to defect to David, taking all Israel with him. This plan is short-circuited by David's ruthless general Joab, who assassinates Abner against David's will (2 Sam 3). The northern coalition comes completely unraveled when Ish-bosheth in turn is also assassinated by his own commanders. It falls to David, ironically, to avenge Ish-bosheth's death against his murderers and to bury him with Abner in his (David's) capital, Hebron of Judah (2 Sam 4).

> ### The Names of Saul's and Jonathan's Sons
>
> According to the Masoretic Text (the standard Hebrew text of the Bible in Judaism), Saul had a son Ish-bosheth, and Jonathan a son Mephibosheth. The word *bosheth* means "shame"; "Ish-bosheth" is literally "man of shame". This is certainly not the name Saul gave his son. It was actually Ish-baal, "man of the lord". In ancient Hebrew, the term *baal* meant "lord, boss, husband" and was roughly synonymous with *adonai*, "lord". In time, however, *baal* came to be used exclusively for the Canaanite god Baal, and *adonai* for the Lord God. By the early medieval period, Jewish scribes could not bring themselves to write the word *baal* as part of an Israelite's name. They replaced it with *bosheth*, "shame", to express their contempt for Baal and all pagan deities. Saul and Jonathan, however, did not intend any pagan connotation in their sons' names.

The Establishment of the Davidic Kingdom and Covenant (2 Samuel 5–10)

After the death of Ish-bosheth, David enters a golden age when all he does meets with success. Indeed, the books of Samuel reach a narrative high point when all twelve tribes of Israel come to him in Hebron and make a covenant with him to be their king:

> Then *all the tribes of Israel* came to David at Hebron, and said, "Behold, we are your bone and flesh. In times past, when Saul was king over us, it was you that led out and brought in Israel; and the LORD said to you, 'You shall be shepherd of my people Israel, and you shall be prince over Israel.'" So all the elders of Israel came to the king at Hebron; *and King David made a covenant with them at Hebron before the LORD, and they anointed David king over Israel.* David was thirty years old

when he began to reign, and he reigned forty years. At Hebron he reigned over Judah seven years and six months; and at Jerusalem he reigned over all Israel and Judah thirty-three years. (2 Sam 5:1–5)

Notice two key aspects of this climactic moment. First, there is a distinction between the time when David reigned over the southern tribe of Judah and when he reigned from Jerusalem over all twelve tribes. We will see this distinction between north and south play out in the books of Kings with tragic consequences. Second, David's kingdom becomes the only one in the Old Testament established on the basis of a covenant. Having been made king of all twelve tribes, David strategically captures Jerusalem and moves his capital there. With the help of the Phoenician king Hiram of Tyre, he begins monumental architecture in the city. The Philistines hear of the activities of their former vassal and attack, but David (unlike Saul) repulses them (2 Sam 5).

After having centralized his government in the city of Jerusalem (formerly known as Jebus), David's first move is to bring the Ark of the Covenant up into the city (2 Sam 6). Although some scholars are skeptical about David's motives here, seeing this as a purely political move or manipulation of religion to advance David's reign, the text gives no evidence for such cynicism. To the contrary, as we have already seen, David is a man of covenant fidelity (Hebrew *hesed*) toward the Lord and is expressing this through worship, sacrifice, and placing the Ark of the Covenant at the very center of his kingdom.

Unfortunately, however, David's first attempt to bring the ark to Jerusalem ends in the disastrous death of Uzzah, who is struck down by God for touching the ark. The logic of this tragedy has to do with the holiness of the ark and the law of Moses, which commanded that the ark be transported by the Levites and held on poles, not set atop an oxcart (2 Sam 6:3, 6), presumably in order to make it easier to carry up the slope to Jerusalem (2 Sam 6:3; cf. Ex 25:14; Deut 10:18). Indeed, according to the Torah, even the Levites "must

---

David and the City of Jerusalem

David captured Jerusalem and made it his capital (2 Sam 5:6–10), a brilliant, strategic move that changed salvation history forever.

Jerusalem, formerly known as Jebus, lay on the border of the tribal territory of Judah and Benjamin. Both tribes had attempted to take the city, but neither succeeded.

Jerusalem/Jebus was an easily defensible site and key to holding the central hill country of Judah, Benjamin, and Ephraim, the heart of the Israelite territory. Failure to take and hold Jerusalem had always weakened the tribal confederation and separated southern Judah from the northern tribes.

David finally removes this impediment to national unity by capturing the city decisively. Since it was previously unclaimed, he could make it his capital without prejudice to any tribe. On the border of Benjamin and Judah—the Israelite north-south cultural divide, or "Mason-Dixon" line—Jerusalem was an ideal symbol of national unity, analogous to Washington, D.C., or Ottawa, Canada.

Modern Christians and Jews cannot imagine their sacred history without Jerusalem as Israel's central city, yet Jerusalem had no significant role in Israel's history or the biblical text prior to David's conquest in 2 Samuel 5:6–9. Without David, there would be no Jerusalem. Jerusalem's identity will always be bound up with David, his heirs, and his covenant.

not touch the holy things, *lest they die*" (Num 4:15). This liturgical violation is corrected in the second attempt to bring up the ark (2 Sam 6:13), and David meets with success.

Once the ark is dwelling in Jerusalem, a significant turning point takes place in the life of David: the longtime warrior king experiences "rest from all his enemies round about" (2 Sam 7:1). Such "rest" is the condition stipulated in the law of Moses for the establishment of a central sanctuary (Deut 12:10–11). As should be clear by now, Israel had seldom experienced any such rest since the time of Joshua and had grown negligent and undisciplined with regard to cultic law. But with the arrival of a time of "rest", David turns his mind to the reform of national worship. While centralization did not require a permanent sanctuary *per se*, the building of a large, permanent, and impressive sanctuary for the worship of the Lord—overshadowing those at other holy sites—would assist in the socioreligious transition that centralization would require. So David expresses his intention implicitly to Nathan the court prophet: "I dwell in a house of cedar, but the ark of God dwells in a tent" (2 Sam 7:2).

In response to David's request to build a "house" (Hebrew *beth*) for God (= temple), God delivers through the prophet Nathan one of the most significant oracles in the entire Old Testament (2 Sam 7:4–17). Several aspects of this critical text stand out as important:

1. *God Will Build David a "House"*: Nathan's response involves a wordplay on "house" (Hebrew *beth*), meaning either dynasty (as in the expression "House of Windsor") or a temple (as in the expression "House of God"). David wishes to build God a "house" in the form of a temple; God replies that he will build David a "house" in the form of a dynasty and that David's heir will build a house (temple) for God. In this way, a reciprocal relationship is permanently established between the house of God and the house of David. The house of David (Davidic dynasty), manifested in the reigning heir, will be perpetually responsible for the building and maintenance of the house of God (temple); but God for his part will always maintain the house of David.

2. *The Davidic Heir as "Son" of God*: In addition to promising to give David a dynasty, God also declares something remarkable through Nathan: David's "offspring" or "seed" who will eventually build the temple of the Lord is referred to as God's son. "I will be his father, and he shall be my son" (2 Sam 7:14). This is the first time in the Old Testament that an individual person (as opposed to a group; cf. Gen 6:1–4; Ex 4:22) is referred to as the "son of God".

3. *The Davidic Kingdom Covenant*: Finally, it is important to note that although the word "covenant" is not used in Nathan's oracle to David, several aspects strongly suggest it is implied. For one thing, the father-and-son language (2 Sam 7:14) is covenantal insofar as it establishes a divine family. Moreover, God's promise to give David a "great name" (2 Sam 7:9) is a direct echo of the promise of a "great name" (= royalty) that was given to Abraham (Gen 12:2) and incorporated into the second stage of the Abrahamic covenant (see Gen 17:4–6). By means of this allusion, the sacred author shows that the promise to Abraham "kings shall come forth from you" will find its ultimate fulfillment in the kingdom promised to David and his heirs. Last, but not certainly not least, not

only do parallel texts in the Psalms make explicit that a covenant was formed with David by this oracle (Ps 89:19–37; 132:1–18), but the book of Samuel itself ends by interpreting this event as establishing a covenant: "The oracle of David, the son of Jesse ... the anointed of the God of Jacob, the sweet psalmist of Israel.... [D]oes not *my house* stand so with God? *For he has made with me an everlasting covenant*, ordered in all things and secure" (2 Sam 23:1, 5).

In support of this interpretation, the chapters following Nathan's oracle also show that Abraham's role as "father of a multitude of nations" is fulfilled in David, who emerges as high king (= emperor) over a small but nevertheless multi-national empire (2 Sam 8:11, 12; 10:19). By the end of this section, many of the promises given to Abraham have been fulfilled in David, and he has reached the height of his power, displaying both military might (2 Sam 10) and sovereign charity, as he continues to show *hesed* toward Mephibosheth, son of Jonathan, by giving him the privilege of eating at the king's table as if he were one of the king's sons (2 Sam 9).

The Transgressions and Tragedies of King David (2 Samuel 11–20)

Most previous covenants in salvation history were broken or impaired shortly after their initial establishment, often in a way that involved or suggested an offense against matrimony, such as the sin of Ham (Gen 9:23), Abram's taking of Hagar (Gen 16:3–4), and the Golden Calf (Ex 32:6; cf. Gen 3:7). The Davidic covenant is no exception. Only shortly after the grant of the divine covenant, David commits a series of sins that go from bad to worse: beginning with the sloth of failing to go out with his troops and, instead, lazing about on his couch in the afternoon, David falls prey to lust, employing his royal power to rape Bathsheba, the young wife of one of his loyal and high-ranking "mighty men", Uriah the Hittite (cf. 2 Sam 23:8, 39). Upon learning that Bathsheba has become pregnant, David adds murder to the sin of adultery, as he instructs his general Joab to put Uriah at the front lines and then fall back, so that the unsuspecting husband will be slain in battle (2 Sam 11:14–26). With this act, the ominous words of the sacred author sound: although David and Bathsheba are later wed and bear a son, "the thing that David had done displeased the LORD" (2 Sam 11:27).

Understanding the Bathsheba Narrative (2 Samuel 11)

The sacred author paints a stark contrast between David the sinner and his victims, Bathsheba and Uriah, by highlighting the piety of the married couple. Bathsheba is bathing to cleanse herself from ritual impurity due to her fertility cycle (2 Sam 11:4) according to the Mosaic law (Lev 15:19–24). The ritual bath usually fell just prior to the time of ovulation, during a woman's peak time of fertility; as a result, David's one illicit encounter with Bathsheba resulted in conception (2 Sam 11:5). Uriah is a Gentile convert to Israelite Yahwism. Although a Hittite, he observes the pious Yahwistic practice of continence during battle as a sign of solidarity with the forces of Israel (cf. 1 Sam 21:4–5). He maintains this piety even when inebriated, in stark contrast with the behavior of David, who as sacral king should be the model and enforcer of Mosaic law but, in this instance, is slothful, lustful, deceptive, and murderous.

In response to David's sin with Bathsheba, God once again sends the prophet Nathan to deliver a message to David—but this time, not one of hope. Instead, Nathan tells the parable of the rich man and the poor man's lamb (2 Sam 12: 1–6), which climaxes in David's self-incriminating recognition and Nathan's ominous prophecy of what will now happen to the "house" of David:

> Nathan said to David, "*You are the man*. Thus says the LORD, the God of Israel, 'I anointed you king over Israel, and I delivered you out of the hand of Saul; and I gave you your master's house, and your master's wives into your bosom, and gave you the house of Israel and of Judah; and if this were too little, I would add to you as much more. Why have you despised the word of the LORD, to do what is evil in his sight? You have struck down Uriah the Hittite with the sword, and have taken his wife to be your wife, and have slain him with the sword of the Ammonites. *Now therefore the sword shall never depart from your house, because you have despised me, and have taken the wife of Uriah the Hittite to be your wife.*' Thus says the LORD, 'Behold, I will raise up evil against you out of your own house; and I will take your wives before your eyes, and give them to your neighbor, and he shall lie with your wives in the sight of this sun. For you did it secretly; but I will do this thing before all Israel, and before the sun.'" David said to Nathan, "*I have sinned against the LORD*." (2 Sam 12:7–13)

Notice how the punishment of David fits the crime. By means of his sins, David chose violence (the sword) and adultery, therefore his once-blessed "house" will now be plagued by precisely those two sins: violence and sexual transgressions.

Indeed, from this point forward in the narrative, the stability of David's household begins to unravel quickly, as the sins he has committed are replicated in his family and wreak havoc among those most dear to him. For example, David's son, the crown prince Amnon, follows the example of his father by using his influence to rape his beautiful half sister Tamar (2 Sam 13:1–22), an offense punishable by death in the Mosaic law. David is enraged but does not punish Amnon (2 Sam 13:21), thus following in the footsteps of his predecessors Samuel and Eli in his failure to discipline his sons (cf. 1 Sam 2:22–25; 8:3). Absalom, Tamar's full brother, is understandably indignant and bides his time until the opportunity arises to assassinate his offending half brother (2 Sam 13:23–36). Fearful of retribution, he flees into exile, but over the years he employs sympathetic contacts within David's court to achieve reconciliation with his father (2 Sam 14:1–33). In the wake of this turmoil, David's son Absalom slowly builds political support among the populace and within the court to the point that he is able to expel his father from Jerusalem and take his place

---

The "Passion of David" in 2 Samuel

The account of David's expulsion from Jerusalem (2 Sam 15–17) is often called the "Passion of David" and includes several types or anticipations of the sufferings of Jesus, Son of David. Like Jesus, David is betrayed by one who shared bread at his table (Ps 41:9; Jn 13;18); he leaves Jerusalem in sorrow by way of the Mount of Olives (2 Sam 15:30; Mt 26:30–46); his enemies plot to strike him at night, kill him alone, and scatter his followers (2 Sam 17:1–4; Jn 18:1–14). Nonetheless, in both cases, the primary betrayers die by hanging themselves (2 Sam 17:23; 18:9; Mt 27:5). In this and other ways, David is perhaps the primary type of the suffering, persecuted Messiah in the Old Testament.

in Jerusalem (2 Sam 15–16). In this way, David's sins of deceit and betrayal of Uriah also spring back upon his head, as he learns what it is like to be betrayed by his own flesh and blood. Nevertheless, in spite of Absalom's acts of sedition, many of the priests, key advisors, the royal bodyguard, David's chief generals, and most of the army remain loyal to David. By intrigue, military strength, and courage, Absalom's coup is eventually defeated, with Absalom himself coming to a humiliating end by getting his head caught in the branches of a tree, where he is executed in cold blood by Joab's men (2 Sam 18). After a time of mourning for his son and a small secondary rebellion under a man named Sheba, David's reign is finally secure once more (2 Sam 18–20).

Retrospect on David's Reign (2 Samuel 21–24)

After the account of rebellions ends, the chronological record of David's reign is abandoned, and we encounter a carefully balanced epilogue to the book, consisting of two dischronologized accounts of plagues (2 Sam 21:1–14; 24:1–25), two records of the exploits of David's men (2 Sam 21:15–22; 23:8–39), and two poems or psalms of David (2 Sam 22:1–51; 23:1–7), as discussed above.

The narrative throughout Samuel has been unsparing in showing both David's virtues and his vices, and the epilogue is no different. The epilogue remembers David's righteousness (2 Sam 22:21–15) yet ends with another account of his sin (2 Sam 24:1). In keeping with Hannah's Song (1 Sam 2:3–8; cf. 2 Sam 22:28), God exalted David as long as he was humble; but when he showed pride (2 Sam 12:1–7; 24:10), God brought him low again. How can Israel find hope in this fallible man? Only by trusting in God's *hesed*, covenant fidelity. The moral of the entire tumultuous narrative of the books of Samuel is uttered by David near the end: "Let us fall into the hand of the LORD, for his mercy is great" (2 Sam 24:14). Likewise, the center of the chiastic structure of these chapters lies in the declaration that God "shows mercy [*hesed*] to his anointed, to David, and his descendants for ever" (2 Sam 22:51). It is God's covenant promises to David—not David's strength or character in itself—that give reason for hope. In this regard, it is significant that the last act of the book is the purchase of the future site of the Temple, the place where atoning sacrifices will be offered (2 Sam 24). Even David's life required atonement through sacrifice; the hope for Israel is to be found, not in individual or corporate righteousness, but in the mercy and faithfulness of God, who graciously provides a place of worship and means of atonement for his weak and wayward people.

Historical Issues in 1–2 Samuel

The Debate over the Historicity of King David

For much of the history of modern biblical scholarship, the basic historicity of the books of Samuel has not been seriously doubted. For example, even Julius Wellhausen assumed that Samuel was essentially historical and could be used to help reconstruct the history of Israelite religion. Historical confidence in the books reached a zenith in the middle of the twentieth century, under the influence of the "American School" of archaeology, led by scholars such as W. F. Albright, G. E. Wright, and John Bright.[4] It was also aided by the sensational discovery of massive fortifications at Megiddo and other sites in the land of Israel that were thought to date to the time of David and Solomon.[5]

This confidence was challenged by the rise of so-called "biblical minimalism", a loose movement involving American and European biblical scholars and some Israeli archaeologists. The biblical exegetes were mostly those associated with the "Copenhagen School", so named because one of the most influential members of the movement, Niels Peter Lemche, teaches at the University of Copenhagen and used his position to form doctoral students in the mindset of this school. Other scholars of the "Copenhagen School" include American Thomas L. Thompson, Canadian John Van Seters, and Philip Davies of the U.K. The Copenhagen School cast doubt on the Old Testament narrative generally—not just Samuel and Kings—by the application of a thoroughgoing skepticism and hermeneutic of suspicion applied to all its claims. They support their negative assessment of the historicity of Samuel and Kings by appeal to the work of Israeli archaeologist Israel Finkelstein and some of his collaborators. In the 1980s, Finkelstein began to argue, based on his interpretation of ceramic remains, that the consensus dating of archaeological strata in the land of Israel was too old by about a century, starting from about the beginning of the first millennium. Roughly speaking, Finkelstein argued that archaeological levels previously dated to the tenth century B.C. (that is, to the time of David and Solomon) were actually from the *ninth* century B.C., with appropriate adjustments to the chronology above and below. As a result, Finkelstein's so-called "low chronology" reinterpretation of the archaeological record left little or nothing that could be attributed to the era of David and Solomon. The scholars of the Copenhagen School seized on Finkelstein's hypothesis and the fact that neither David nor Solomon had been found mentioned in non-Israelite inscriptions or documents to argue that the biblical accounts of both kings were largely fictitious.

Why No Explicit Mention of David and Solomon in Extra-Biblical Records?

One of the primary arguments of the biblical minimalists is based on the *lack of explicit extra-biblical inscriptional evidence* referring to King David (or, for that matter, King Solomon). According to this point of view, if David were an actual historical figure, we would have found some inscriptional reference to him outside of the biblical records. Since to date archaeologists have not discovered such evidence, it seems best to conclude that David is a legendary figure, little different from "Robin Hood" of English legend.

Although at first glance this argument might seem forceful, a number of biblical scholars and archaeologists have objected to it by pointing out that the Assyrian and Egyptian empires at that time leave *no* information regarding the kings

---

[4] See John Bright, *A History of Israel*, 4th ed. (Louisville, Ky.: Westminster John Knox Press, 2004).

[5] See Amihai Mazar, *Archaeology of the Land of the Bible, 10,000–586 B.C.E.*, Anchor Bible Reference Library (New York: Doubleday, 1992).

of the Levant (southern Judah) because they were not making trade or military excursions into that area during that period.[6] Indeed, in the tenth century B.C., the great empires of Egypt and Mesopotamia (for example, Assyria, Babylon) were *in decline* and did not have the military strength to venture into Canaan. On the one hand, this political situation of imperial decline created a kind of "power vacuum" in Canaan in the tenth century B.C., which, as a result, made possible the rise and establishment of the Israelite Empire under David and Solomon. On the other hand, the same conditions that made the rise of the Israelite monarchy possible also provide a plausible explanation for why they are not mentioned in extant Egyptian and Mesopotamian sources. Both civilizations were in decline, concerned with their own internal affairs, and lacked the strength to interfere in Canaan. Moreover—and this is important—it is not just David and Solomon who go unmentioned in this time period: Egyptian and Mesopotamian records of the tenth century say *nothing* of the rulers of *Edom, Moab, Ammon, Aram (Damascus), Tyre, Sidon, or any other city-state of the Levant*. Even the biblical minimalists are not willing to argue that none of these people existed in the tenth century B.C. just because they are not referenced in our extant sources.

In short, the case against David given by the minimalist school is both an argument from silence and a classic case of a *non sequitur*: just because the records of Egypt and the Mesopotamian empires that have happened to survive do not mention him does not mean that he and his kingdom did not exist. Indeed, when it comes to the biblical books themselves, we have a mountain of *textual* evidence in the Old Testament itself claiming precisely that he did.

Inscriptional Evidence for the "House of David"

Moreover, although we do not possess explicit extra-biblical evidence referring to David or Solomon as individuals, recent archaeology has unearthed extra-biblical evidence for the house or family "of David" (Hebrew *dawid*) in what are regarded as some of the most sensational archaeological discoveries of modern times.

1. *The Tel Dan Inscription mentions "The House of David"*: In the mid-1990s an inscription was unearthed at the site of the ancient city of Dan north of Galilee, apparently originating with Hazael, king of Damascus (fl. 842–805 B.C.; 1 Kings 19:15). In the inscription, Hazael boasts of killing a king of the "House of David" (*byt-Dwd*)—probably a reference to Ahaz. This inscription, known as the Tel Dan Stele, provided extra-biblical evidence that already in the ninth century B.C. the kingdom of Judah was called by the name of the founder of its ruling dynasty, David. Significantly, the form of the inscription corresponds exactly to the Assyrian expression for the kingdom of Israel at that time: the "House of Omri" (*Byt-'mry*)—that is, the dynasty of a real individual man, Omri (cf. 1 Kings 16:16).[7] Although the biblical minimalists of the Copenhagen

---

[6] See Kenneth A. Kitchen, *On the Reliability of the Old Testament* (Grand Rapids, Mich.: Eerdmans, 2003), 88–90.

[7] Ibid., 92.

School initially disputed the reading of the stele, almost all scholars outside their ranks have accepted it as extra-biblical confirmation of the historical existence of David and his dynasty.[8]

2. *The Moabite Mesha Stele mentions "the House of David"*: Subsequent to the discovery of the Tel Dan Stele, noted epigrapher and Bible scholar André Lemaire reevaluated the famous Mesha Stele, also dated to the ninth century B.C., and argued that the phrase "House of David" (*bt-[d]wd*) could be found in that inscription as well. If correct, this would mean that we possess at least two extra-biblical references to the dynasty of David in Judah within a century or so after his death, giving further support to his basic historicity.[9]

In addition to these two famous inscriptions mentioning David's name, since the archaeologist Israel Finkelstein began arguing for his low chronology, several archaeological sites have been excavated to reveal monumental buildings datable to the reigns of David and Solomon (for example, Khirbet Qeiyafa). As a result of such excavations, Finkelstein has had to revise his "low chronology" gradually toward the traditional "high chronology", so that the difference between the two is now within the margin of error for radiometric and other forms of dating. In short, in the wake of a number of recent discoveries, the influence of the biblical minimalism movement has been challenged and in some circles has begun to wane in influence.

The Historical "Realism" of the Books of Samuel

When it comes to the question of the historicity of King David and the historical plausibility of the claims made about him in the books of Samuel, one final consideration is the fact that the career of David is not whitewashed by the biblical author. To the contrary, the accounts in 1–2 Samuel are far more detailed and specific than would be necessary for a writer of fiction, including a great deal of awkward or inconvenient material, such as the incident with Bathsheba and Uriah as well as David's defection to the Philistines. Such material is very difficult to reconcile with the hypothesis that the books of Samuel are later, idealized "legends" about David. Nor do they square easily with the idealized images of both David and Solomon that came to dominate Jewish memory already by the sixth century B.C. in the works of certain prophets (see, for example, Jer 30–31, Ezek 34–37). Furthermore, the entire account of Saul's reign is awkward for many reasons. In light of such considerations, a large number of scholars continue to accept the picture of Saul's reign as basically historical, because there would be little or no motivation for later biblical authors to invent someone other than David—especially a Benjaminite—as the first king of Israel, in apparent contradiction to the prophecy of the patriarch Jacob regarding the kingship of Judah (see Gen 49:10)

Although controversy will doubtless continue, the skepticism of biblical minimalism regarding 1–2 Samuel has reached its high-water mark and is abating.

---

[8] For image, see Long, "1 Samuel", 338; Kitchen, *Reliability of the Old Testament*, 615.

[9] For image, see ibid.

Most biblical scholars accept that David was a pivotal historical figure in Israel's history, even if some of them consider aspects of the account of his reign to be exaggerated.[10] Others would argue that the biblical accounts in Samuel, when carefully read, are not even exaggerated. The descriptions of the kingdoms of Saul and David, interpreted in the light of ancient Near Eastern literary style, are actually modest and fit quite squarely into the *realia* of the Levant in the tenth century B.C.[11]

Theological Issues in 1–2 Samuel

The Davidic Covenant

The books of Samuel introduce us to the *Davidic covenant* (2 Sam 7:4–17), the importance of which can hardly be exaggerated, as it is the final covenant described in the Old Testament and the one that will set up the template for the "new" and/or "everlasting" covenant of the future king of Israel in the prophetic literature (for example, Jer 30–33; Ezek 34–37). The highest glory of the Davidic covenant is not reached until the building of the Temple under Solomon (1 Kings 8), so we will reserve the fullest discussion of the economy of the Davidic covenant and its relationship to previous covenants for our treatment of Kings. Here we will focus on aspects of the Davidic covenant highlighted in the text of Samuel.

The primary effect of the Davidic covenant was to establish the Davidic king as "son of God" (2 Sam 7:14). This was the status enjoyed by Adam before the fall and offered to Israel at Sinai (cf. Gen 1:26–27; cf. 5:3). Although the Israelites rejected divine sonship at the Calf and afterward, God did not entirely rescind their status as children. Under the Deuteronomic covenant, which has the form of a vassal treaty, the Israelites were reduced almost to the status of servants of God, with most of the privileges of sonship suspended (cf. Gal 3:23–25). Under the Davidic covenant, the full privileges of sonship—including the exercise of royal priesthood—are restored to the king. Inasmuch as the rest of Israel will enjoy indirectly the benefits of the filial relationship between their king and God, this represents progress for the entire people of God.

The Davidic covenant did not dispense the Davidic king from following divine law. Rather, "When he commits iniquity, I will chasten him with the rod of men" (2 Sam 7:14). David and each one of his heirs are subject to chastisement for their own iniquity—David himself experiences it in 2 Samuel 12–20. Nonetheless, the covenant will not be withdrawn from David's line: "I will not take my merciful love from him, as I took it from Saul, whom I put away from before you. And your house and your kingdom shall be made sure for ever before me" (2 Sam 7:15–16). The dynasty will continue, even if individual heirs experience punishment.

---

[10] See Baruch Halpern, *David's Secret Demons: Messiah, Murderer, Traitor, King* (Grand Rapids, Mich.: Eerdmans, 2001).

[11] See Long, "1 Samuel", 267–411.

David as Melchizedekian Priest-King of Jeru-Salem

One of the primary theological problems in reading through the books of Samuel can be stated as follows: Why does Saul's act of offering sacrifice when he is not a priest lead to his downfall (1 Sam 13), whereas David's acts of dressing like a priest, offering sacrifice, and bringing up the Ark of the Covenant to Jerusalem bring no similar punishment (2 Sam 6)?

Although the text of Samuel does not give an explicit answer to this question, recent scholarship has highlighted two key facts. First, David, unlike Saul before him, is part of the royal line of the tribe of Judah, from which the patriarch Jacob had promised the "scepter" would never depart (see Gen 49:10). Second, and more importantly, by centralizing the authority of the kingdom of Israel around the Ark of the Covenant and the city of Jerusalem, a case can be made that David is not arrogating to himself the rights of the Levitical priesthood but, rather, attempting to restore the pre-Levitical Melchizedekian priesthood, which is linked elsewhere in Scripture to the city of Jerusalem:

> After his [Abram's] return from the defeat of Ched-or-laomer and the kings who were with him, the king of Sodom went out to meet him at the Valley of Shaveh (that is, the King's Valley). And *Melchizedek king of Salem brought out bread and wine*; he was *priest* of God Most High. (Gen 14:17–18)

> In Judah God is known,
>   his name is great in Israel.
> His abode has been established in *Salem*,
>   his dwelling place in *Zion*. (Ps 76:1)

Following the rules of Hebrew poetic parallelism, it seems clear that in certain texts, the ancient city of Salem over which Melchizedek reigned was identified with Jeru-salem, the city of David. If this identification is at work in the books of Samuel, it would provide an explanation for David's otherwise inexplicable priestly actions: like Melchizedek, king of Jerusalem before him, David is acting as both king and priest. This suggestion becomes all the more plausible when we recall that David accompanies his priestly act of offering sacrifice with a strikingly Melchizedek-like act of giving bread and wine to the people of Jerusalem:

> [David] distributed among the people, the whole multitude of Israel, both men and women, to each *a cake of bread, a portion of wine* (Hebrew *'eshpar*), and a cake of raisins. (2 Sam 6:19 [RSVCE, slightly adapted])

When we realize the obscure Hebrew word *'eshpar* probably refers to a portion of wine rather than of "meat" (as in the RSVCE), then a case can be made that David is restoring not just the kingship to the city of Jerusalem, but the primordial priesthood of Melchizedek as well.[12] As a famous psalm will later declare

---

[12] See Scott W. Hahn, *Kinship by Covenant: A Canonical Approach to the Fulfillment of God's Saving Promises*, Anchor Yale Bible Reference Library (New Haven, Conn.: Yale University Press, 2009), 431n20.

about the Davidic king: "You are a priest for ever, according to the order of Melchizedek" (Ps 110:4).

The Role of Liturgy in 1–2 Samuel

Proper worship of the Lord and the Lord's presence through the liturgical vessels such as the Ark of the Covenant, the ephod of the priest, and the Urim and Thummim form an important underlying theme throughout the books of Samuel. The composition begins with the ark and the Tabernacle of Moses residing in Shiloh, with the liturgy under the direction of the negligent Eli and his actively sacrilegious sons, who commit grave liturgical abuses. This continues the characterization of the period of the judges as one of disordered worship. More directly, it also results in a temporary loss of the ark to the Philistines. Even when the ark is returned, it remains separated from the Tabernacle and the Holy of Holies: this disorder remains throughout the books of Samuel. As we will see, it is only finally corrected when Solomon reunites the Tabernacle and ark, builds a new Holy of Holies, and brings the ark into it (1 Kings 8:4–6).

Likewise, under the prophet Samuel, worship in Israel appears to have been irregular, directed by Samuel personally by virtue of his prophetic authority (1 Sam 7:9–10). Saul's reign begins poorly by his unauthorized leadership of sacrificial liturgy (1 Sam 13:10–11); nonetheless, he does make an effort to follow Mosaic norms for the offering of sacrifice and consumption of meat (1 Sam 14:33–35; cf. Lev 3:17; 7:26–27; 17:1–14; Deut 12:23–27), to acquire guidance from the presence of the Lord (1 Sam 14:36–42) through the ministry of the priesthood, and to observe liturgical feasts with his court (Num 29:6; 1 Sam 20:5, 18, 24, 27) according to ritual requirements (1 Sam 20:26). Despite these gestures, as catalogued above, Saul's kingship is ultimately lost because he arrogates to himself the priestly act of offering sacrifice and fails to carry out the commandments of Moses for warfare (1 Sam 13, 15).

In stark contrast to Saul, David is *granted* the privileges of acting as both king and priest: he has the rare privilege of experience of the liturgical presence of the Lord through the consumption of the holy bread, the Bread of the Presence (1 Sam 21:1–9). After Saul's ritual slaughter of the priests, the heir apparent to the high priesthood (Abiathar) defects to David, enabling David to inquire of the Lord by priestly ritual, which results directly in David's salvation (1 Sam 22:6—23:14). The same privilege is denied to Saul (1 Sam 28:6), no doubt largely because of his grave offense against the priesthood. Indeed, David's first priority upon the assumption of the kingship of united Israel is the restoration of the ark to a position of prominence for himself and for the people (2 Sam 6:1–19). The liturgical worship of the people by sacrifice under the leadership of David as Melchizedekian priest at this great event constitutes a spiritual high point in the history of Israel. David's concern for the dignity of the place of God's worship (2 Sam 7:2) and the fulfillment of the Mosaic centralization of the liturgy (2 Sam 7:1; cf. Deut 12:10–11) prompts the grant of the Davidic covenant, the climax of his career, in which the destiny of David's dynasty becomes inextricably tied to the destiny of the Temple (2 Sam 7:8–16). David's subsequent sin, however, initiates a chain of events resulting in his expulsion from Jerusalem and estrangement from God's presence manifested by the ark:

> Then the king said to Zadok, "Carry the ark of God back into the city. If I find favor in the eyes of the LORD, he will bring me back and let me see both it and his habitation." (2 Sam 15:25)

The continued solicitude of the priesthood for David's welfare is a concrete manifestation of the Lord's favor for David, despite his sin (see 2 Sam 15:27–28; 17:15–22; 19:11–15). At length David is brought back to see the ark and its habitation, and, as noted above, David's final recorded acts include the purchase of the place for the permanent dwelling of the ark (2 Sam 24). So the plot of the books of Samuel has moved from corrupted worship at Shiloh under the incompetent Eli (1 Sam 2:12–17) to David (the Melchizedekian priest-king) offering efficacious sacrifice at the future site of the Temple (2 Sam 24:25).

1 and 2 Samuel in the Living Tradition

Given the length of the books of Samuel, the memorable and dramatic stories contained therein, and the centrality of the figure of King David, it is perhaps unsurprising that the sacred history narrated in these books has, over the course of Church history, generated a remarkable amount of reflection and interpretation in the living tradition. Although commentaries on the books of Samuel by no means abound, the stories and people found in the narratives are the frequent objects of theological reflection in Christian literature throughout the centuries. In what follows, we will take a few moments to highlight just a few examples.

Hannah, Mother of Samuel, and Mary, Mother of Jesus

Perhaps one of the most memorable passages from the books of Samuel is the song of Hannah, mother of Samuel (1 Sam 2:1–10).

Apart from its indisputable beauty and grandeur, the significance of this song was solidified in the living tradition first and foremost by the fact that several of its images and words are taken up by Mary, the mother of Jesus, in her own song of praise—known as the *Magnificat*—during the visitation to Elizabeth (see Lk 1:39–45).[13] Moreover, in the context of the narrative as a whole, there are several striking parallels between the story of Hannah and Samuel and that of Mary and Jesus:

Hannah, Mother of Samuel	*Mary, Mother of Jesus*
"Maidservant" who "finds favor" (1 Sam 1:18)	"Handmaid" who has "found favor" (Lk 1:30, 38)

---

[13] See Victor Hamilton, *Handbook on the Historical Books* (Grand Rapids, Mich.: Baker Academic, 2001), 218–19.

Woman of "misery" or "lowliness" who is "exalted" (1 Sam 1:11; 2:1, 7–8)	Woman of "low estate" who is "exalted" (Lk 1:48; 1:52)
"My heart exults in the LORD!" (1 Sam 2:1)	"My soul magnifies the Lord!" (Lk 1:46)
Samuel grew "in stature and in favor" with "the LORD and with men". (1 Sam 2:26)	Jesus "increased in wisdom and in stature, and in favor with God and men". (Lk 2:52)

As these parallels make clear (and more could be given), in Luke's narrative of the birth of Jesus, Mary herself functions as a kind of new Hannah, who is "full of grace" (Greek *kecharitomenē*). (Remember, Hannah's name means "grace" in Hebrew.) By means of a miracle, Mary, like Hannah before her, will conceive a son who will be both priest and prophet, not to mention king.

In addition to this use of Hannah's Song in the New Testament, it is significant to note that some early Church Fathers saw the song as prophetic in itself. As Augustine notes, there are aspects of Hannah's Song that seem to point beyond themselves to a future that is not fulfilled by the birth of Samuel alone:

> Do you say that these are the words of a single weak woman giving thanks for the birth of a son? *Can the mind of men be so much averse to the light of truth as not to perceive that the sayings this woman pours forth exceed her measure?* ... Unless perchance any one will say that this woman prophesied nothing, but only lauded God with exulting praise on account of the son whom she had obtained in answer to prayer. What then does she mean when she says, "... [T]he barren hath born seven, and she that hath many children is waxed feeble?" Had she herself born seven, although she had been barren? She had only one when she said that; neither did she bear seven afterwards, nor six.... And then, when as yet no one was king over that people, *whence, if she did not prophesy, did she say what she puts at the end, "He giveth strength to our kings, and shall exalt the horn of His Christ?"*[14]

Here we see Augustine making an important distinction between the literal sense of the Song of Hannah, which is fulfilled in a preliminary way in the birth of Samuel, and the spiritual sense, which finds its ultimate fulfillment only in the birth of the true "anointed one", Jesus the "Christ".

How Could God "Repent" of Making Saul King?

In addition to typological interpretation of the books of Samuel, there were also certain moral and theological questions raised by the text that had to be confronted by the living tradition of the Church. One of these questions revolved around the turning point in the narrative, when God says: "I repent that I have made Saul king" (1 Sam 15:10). How does one explain this text, in light of the

---

[14] Augustine, *The City of God* 17.4, in *NPNF1* 2:340.

clear teaching of the New Testament that God does not change and that in God "there is no variation or shadow due to change" (Jas 1:16)? In taking up this question, Augustine pointed out that the text of 1 Samuel itself gives us a clue as to how to interpret this:

> Just as certain praiseworthy human qualities are not rightly predicated of God, so also are certain contemptible human qualities properly said to be in God, not as they are found in people but only in a very different manner and for different reasons. For shortly after the Lord had said to Samuel, "I repent that I have made Saul king," Samuel himself said of God to Saul: "He is not like a man, that he should repent." *This clearly demonstrates that even though God said, "I repent," it is not to be taken according to the human sense.*[15]

In other words, the Scriptures here, as elsewhere, are using analogical language to describe the actions of God in ways that are both similar to human actions ("repentance" = visible change in effects) and dissimilar (repentance = change within the person making the decision). In order to interpret such statements about God correctly, both their immediate context and the analogical nature of all human language about God should be taken into account.

King David as a Type of Christ

At the very center of the books of Samuel, of course, stands the figure of King David. It almost goes without saying that in the living tradition of the Church, starting with the New Testament itself, David has always been viewed as perhaps the premier prefiguration of Christ, insofar as he is "Messiah" (Greek *Christos*), the anointed king of Israel. In terms of the narratives in the books of Samuel, however, we find a striking catalogue of the parallels between David and Jesus in the works of Saint Aphrahat (fourth century A.D.), the great Persian Church Father, who had this to say:

> Also David was persecuted, as Jesus was persecuted. David was anointed by Samuel to be king instead of Saul who had sinned; and Jesus was anointed by John to be High Priest instead of the priests, the ministers of the Law. David was persecuted after his anointing; and Jesus was persecuted after His anointing. David reigned first over one tribe only, and afterwards over all Israel; and Jesus reigned from the beginning over the few who believed on Him, and in the end He will reign over all the world. Samuel anointed David when he was thirty years old; and Jesus when about thirty years old received the imposition of the hand from John. David wedded two daughters of the king; and Jesus wedded two daughters of kings, the congregation of the People and the congregation of the Gentiles.... For David's sake, sins were forgiven to his posterity; and for Jesus' sake sins are forgiven to the nations.[16]

---

[15] Augustine, *On Various Questions to Simplician* 2.2.5, in John R. Franke, ed., *Joshua, Judges, Ruth, 1–2 Samuel*, Old Testament 4, Ancient Christian Commentary on Scripture, ed. Thomas C. Oden (Downers Grove, Ill.: InterVarsity Press, 2005), 255.

[16] Aphrahat, *Demonstrations* 21.13, in *NPNF2* 13:397–98.

This is a striking catalogue of parallels between David in 1–2 Samuel and Jesus in the Gospels. Clearly, Church Fathers like Aphrahat not only took the New Testament identification of Jesus and David to heart, but they saw in the life of King David a kind of "pre-enactment" of what would eventually happen in the life of the new David, Jesus Christ. As we will see when we get to the book of Psalms, this typological interpretation of David will play a key role in the Christological reading of the Psalms of David.

The Ark of the Covenant as a Type of the Virgin Mary

Last, but certainly not least, one of the most important moments in the books of Samuel—liturgically speaking—is David's bringing up the Ark of the Covenant from Shiloh to its resting place in Jerusalem (2 Sam 6). On the level of history, this represents the final arrival of the visible sign of God's presence in the chosen city of Zion and on the mountain of Jerusalem (cf. Ps 76:1–2). Strikingly, some Church Fathers also noticed certain parallels between the arrival of the ark in Jerusalem and the visitation of Mary to Elizabeth, so that they also saw in the coming of the ark a prefiguration of the Visitation. Consider the words of the fifth-century bishop of Turin, Maximus, in explaining why David "danced" before the ark:

> The prophet David danced, then. *But what would we say that the ark was if not holy Mary, since the ark carried within it the tables of the covenant, while Mary bore the master of the same covenant?* The one bore the law within itself and the other the gospel, but the ark gleamed within and without with the radiance of gold, while holy Mary shone within and without with the splendor of virginity; the one was adorned with earthly gold, the other with heavenly.[17]

As we will see when we turn to the pages of the Gospel of Luke, Maximus' recognition of the parallel between the Ark of the Covenant and the Virgin Mary will have its roots in Luke's own description of the Annunciation and Visitation (Lk 1–2). For now, it should suffice to emphasize that for the Church Fathers, not only persons and events but signs and symbols such as the ark could be interpreted as types of the New Covenant.

David Is Promised the Kingdom of Christ

Given the richly typological readings of 1–2 Samuel we have seen thus far, it should come as no surprise that the Church Fathers also saw the everlasting kingdom promised to David (2 Sam 7) as being truly fulfilled in the kingdom of God inaugurated by Jesus Christ. Consider, for example, the words of the second-century Latin writer Tertullian:

> The prophet Nathan, in the first [book] of Kings [Samuel], makes a promise to David for his seed.... Now, because Christ rather than any other was to build the

---

[17] Maximus of Turin, *Sermon* 42.5, in Franke, *Joshua, Judges*, 346.

temple of God, that is to say, a holy manhood, wherein God's Spirit might dwell as in a better temple, Christ rather than David's son Solomon was to be looked for as the Son of God. *Then, again, the throne for ever with the kingdom for ever is more suited to Christ than to Solomon, a mere temporal king.*[18]

Notice here how Tertullian highlights aspects of the oracle that were promised to David but that were not fulfilled in Solomon—whose throne and temple certainly did not last forever—and attributes their ultimate fulfillment to Christ. Along similar lines, other Church Fathers, such as Basil the Great, will recognize the fact that David's earthly kingdom did not last forever as a clue to the proper interpretation of the oracle, which will only be fulfilled in the everlasting kingdom of God.[19]

The Repentance of King David as a Model

Finally, the account of Nathan's parable of the rich man and the poor man's lamb and David's subsequent repentance has always figured prominently in the moral teaching of the Church as an example of the power and importance of prompt confession and heartfelt repentance. In a series of homilies on repentance, Saint John Chrysostom singled out this moment in the life of David as a model for all Christians who have sinned grievously:

> [Nathan said:] *"You are the man, my king."* What did the king say? *"I have sinned against the Lord."* He did not say, "Who are you that censures me? Who sent you to speak with such boldness? With what daring did you prevail?" He did not say anything of the sort; rather, he perceived the sin. And what did he say? *"I have sinned against the Lord."* Therefore, what did Nathan say to him? *"And the Lord remitted your sin."* You condemned yourself; I [God] remit your sentence. You confessed prudently; you annulled the sin…. Can you see that what is written in Scripture was fulfilled: *"Be the first one to tell of your transgressions so you may be justified"*?[20]

This is the key to the mystery of David's favor before God in the books of Samuel. On the one hand, David is a grievous sinner; on the other hand, as soon as he is aware of the gravity of his sin, in the face of what he has done, he immediately moves to heartfelt repentance and humble confession.

The Books of Samuel in the Lectionary

In the contemporary Lectionary, there are two main clusters of texts most valued because of their Christological typology: those concerning the birth and

---

[18] Tertullian, *Against Marcion* 3.20, in *Ante-Nicene Fathers*, ed. Alexander Roberts and James Donaldson, vol. 3 (1885; repr., Peabody, Mass.: Hendrickson, 1994), 339.

[19] See Basil the Great, *Letter* 236.

[20] John Chrysostom, *On Repentance and Almsgiving* 2.2.9, trans. Gus George Christo, The Fathers of the Church 96 (Washington, D.C.: Catholic University of America Press, 2005), 20–21.

childhood of Samuel (1 Sam 1–3) and those concerning the elevation of David to the kingship (1 Sam 16, 2 Sam 5, 7). The Church also recognizes Hannah and Samuel as types of Mary and Jesus, following the example of Saint Luke, who composed the infancy narratives of our Lord (Lk 1–2) in such a way that they echo and recapitulate the early life of Samuel. Hannah typifies Mary as the woman of grace who miraculously conceives a child destined to be prophet and savior of Israel, and rejoices in a song of thanksgiving for God's power displayed in his elevation of the humble. Samuel typifies Christ as the prophet marked from birth who responds with immediate docility to the call of God (1 Sam 3:1–10) and will deliver Israel from oppression by their enemies (1 Sam 7:10–14) due to the poor leadership of his people (1 Sam 2:12,22; cf. Jn 10:7–15) by establishing a permanent kingship (1 Sam 16:13).

The Lectionary also recognizes the salvation-historical significance of several texts related to David's kingship and covenant discussed above. Nathan's oracle granting the covenant to David (2 Sam 7:4–17) is the most prominent text from Samuel in the Church's cycle of readings during Advent, and in Masses for Saint Joseph and the Blessed Virgin Mary. These readings highlight the intimate connection between the Davidic and New Covenant economies:

Readings from Samuel for Sundays, Feast Days, Liturgical Seasons, and Other Occasions			
MSO = Masses for Special Occasions; *OM* = Optional Memorial; *VM* = Votive Mass; *Rit* = Ritual			
Passage	Description	Occasion	Explanation
1 Sam 1:20–22, 24–28	Hannah conceives and bears Samuel, brings him to the Tabernacle, and offers him permanently to the Lord.	*Sun., Octave of Christmas: Holy Family* (opt. C)	Paired with the finding of the boy Jesus in the Temple (Lk 2:41–52), this reading suggests a typological relationship between Samuel and Jesus as great prophets sent in answer to prayer to deliver their people. It also suggests why Jesus may have stayed behind at the Temple: perhaps he thought his parents had brought him to stay permanently, like Samuel.
1:24–28	Hannah brings Samuel to the Tabernacle and donates him to the Lord.	Dec. 22	Paired with the *Magnificat* (Lk 1:46–56) and Hannah's Song as the responsorial, this reading compares two women of "grace" (Hebrew *hēn*) and their miraculously conceived, prophetic sons. Jesus is viewed as prophet-deliverer.
2:1, 4–8	Hannah's Song	*Responsorial Psalm*: Dec. 22; Immaculate Heart of the BVM; Common of the BVM, opt. 1	See above. On the Feast of the Immaculate Heart, Hannah's Song as the responsorial suggests the *Magnificat*, while the Gospel (Lk 2:41–52) speaks of Mary keeping "all these things in her heart". Thus the readings present a spectrum of emotion in the heart of our Blessed Mother.

(*continued*)

Readings from Samuel for Sundays, Feast Days, Liturgical Seasons, and Other Occasions (*continued*)
MSO = Masses for Special Occasions; *OM* = Optional Memorial;
VM = Votive Mass; *Rit* = Ritual

Passage	Description	Occasion	Explanation
3:1–10	Samuel hears the voice of the Lord calling to him within the Tabernacle.	*Rit*: For the Consecration of Virgins or Religious Profession, opt. 2; *MSO*: For Vocations to Holy Orders or Religious Life	Samuel's immediate obedience to the call of God is seen as an image of the believer who responds to God's call to a special vocation within the Church.
3:3b–10, 19	Samuel hears the voice of the Lord calling to him within the Tabernacle.	*2nd Sun. in OT (B)*	Paired with the calling of the first disciples (Jn 1:35–42), this reading suggests that, in Jesus, the disciples are hearing the very voice of God, just as Samuel did in the Tabernacle.
16:1b, 6–7, 10–13a	Samuel anoints David in the midst of his brothers.	*4th Sun. of Lent (A)*; Common of Pastors, opt. 3	The Sundays of Lent present a review of salvation history; here, this reading evokes the entire significance of David as a milestone in that history. David's anointing is a type of baptism; the Gospel (Jn 9) is also a symbolic catechesis on baptism. The pastors of the Church share the anointing of holy orders, a form of authority organically related to David's royalty through Jesus, the royal Son of David. The Church's pastors are viceroys of the Son of David.
26:2, 7–9, 12–13, 22–23	David slips into Saul's camp but spares Saul because he will not strike the Lord's anointed.	*7th Sun. in OT (C)*; *MSO*: For our Oppressors	Paired with Jesus' teaching on the love for enemies (Lk 6:27–38), this reading shows that our Lord's ethics are rooted in the Old Testament and, especially, his own royal Davidic heritage. David spared his enemies and was exalted by God for it.
2 Sam 5:1–3	David is made king over all Israel by a covenant.	*34th Sun. in OT: Christ the King (C)*	The kingship of Jesus Christ is the fulfillment of David's covenantal kingship over the entire people of God. The Gospel (Lk 23:35–43) reminds us that Christ's kingship in this life is manifest by the suffering of the Cross.
7:1–5, 8b–12, 14a, 16	Nathan's oracle granting David the covenant of kingship	*4th Sun. of Advent (B)*; Morning Mass of Dec. 24; Solemnity of St. Joseph,	The coming of Christ and his establishment of the New Covenant constitutes the fulfillment of all the covenantal promises granted to David. The Annunciation (Lk 1:26–38; 4th Sun. of Adv. B; Com. of the BVM, opt. 4) draws heavily from 2 Samuel 7. Likewise,

(continued)

	Readings from Samuel for Sundays, Feast Days, Liturgical Seasons, and Other Occasions (*continued*) *MSO* = Masses for Special Occasions; *OM* = Optional Memorial; *VM* = Votive Mass; *Rit* = Ritual		
Passage	Description	Occasion	Explanation
		Spouse of the BVM (Mar. 19); Common of the BVM, opt. 3; *VM*: St. Joseph	the Benedictus (Lk 1:67–79; Dec. 24) refers to "the horn of salvation of the house of David". On Masses of St. Joseph, we are reminded that the foster-father of the Lord was himself the heir of David—through him our Lord gained his claim to the throne. The BVM, too, was of Davidic descent, according to tradition.
12:7–10, 13	Nathan rebukes David for adultery with Bathsheba and the murder of Uriah.	*11th Sun. in Ordinary Time* (C)	Paired with the forgiveness of the sinful woman (Lk 7:36–50), this reading highlights the continuity of God's mercy on repentant sinners in both the Old and the New Covenants and the hypocrisy of the Pharisees, who would not forgive sinners, although God forgave the great hero of their faith, David.

Because of the importance of Samuel and David as types of Christ, a rather substantial sequence of selections from 1–2 Samuel are read during the weekly Masses in Ordinary Time, Year II, weeks 1–4. The larger number of weekday Mass readings allows the inclusion of many other significant events in salvation history: the loss of the ark; the request for a king; Saul's abortive kingship; David's defeat of Goliath; David's *hesed* toward Saul and Jonathan; the ascension of the ark to Jerusalem; David's sins and their consequences:

Reading of Samuel for Daily Mass: Ordinary Time, Year II: Weeks 1–4			
Week	Day	Passage Read	Description
1	M	1 Sam 1:1–8	Hannah is barren, Elkanah tries to comfort her.
1	Tu	1:9–20; (Resp.: 2:1, 4–8)	Hannah prays for a son; Eli blesses her; she conceives and bears Samuel.
1	W	3:1–10, 19–20	Samuel hears the Lord calling in the Tabernacle; he is established as a prophet.
1	Th	4:1–11	Hophni and Phineas bring the ark to battle; Philistines defeat Israel, capture the ark.
1	F	8:4–7, 10–22a	Israel asks for a king; Samuel tries to dissuade. They persist; God grants the request.
1	Sa	9:1–4, 17–19; 10:1	Samuel anoints Saul king over Israel.

(*continued*)

			Reading of Samuel for Daily Mass: Ordinary Time, Year II: Weeks 1–4 (continued)
Week	Day	Passage Read	Description
2	M	15:16–23	God rejects Saul as king because of his disobedience in the Amalekite campaign.
2	Tu	16:1–13	Samuel anoints David as king; the Holy Spirit rushes upon him.
2	W	17:32–33, 37, 40–51	David defeats the Philistine champion Goliath.
2	Th	18:6–9; 19:1–7	Saul becomes envious of David; Jonathan intercedes to reconcile the two of them.
2	F	24:3–21	David spares Saul's life in the cave and swears not to cut off Saul's line forever.
2	Sa	2 Sam 1:1–27 (excerpts)	David, informed of Saul's death, eulogizes Saul and Jonathan.
3	M	5:1–7, 10	David is anointed king of Israel and captures Jerusalem to serve as his capital.
3	Tu	6:12b–15, 17–19	David brings the ark up into Jerusalem successfully.
3	W	7:4–17	Nathan's oracle granting a covenant to David
3	Th	7:18–19, 24–29	David's prayer of thanksgiving for the grant of the covenant
3	F	11:1–4a, 5–10a, 13–17	David commits adultery with Bathsheba and has Uriah killed in battle.
3	Sa	12:1–7a, 10–17	Nathan rebukes David for his sin, and David repents.
4	M	15:13–14, 30; 16:5–13	Afraid of Absalom, David flees Jerusalem with his court while Shimei abuses him.
4	Tu	18:9–19:3 (excerpts)	Absalom is caught and slain; David's troops are victorious, but David grieves for his son.
4	W	24:2, 9–17	David orders a census. The Lord sends a plague, but stops it at the threshing floor.

The Office of Readings for the Liturgy of the Hours likewise contains extensive selections from the books of Samuel. The more important passages are paired with patristic commentary that expounds on Christological types or moral themes (friendship, forgiveness, repentance) found in the narrative (see table on next page).

Conclusion

The books of Samuel comprise an exceptionally rich source for Christian theological reflection because they document the transition of the people of God

		The Books of Samuel in the Office of Readings for the Liturgy of the Hours, Ordinary Time Weeks 12–14	
Week	Day	Passage Read	Description
12	Su	1 Sam 16:1–13	The anointing of David.
12	M	17:1–10, 32, 38–51	David defeats Goliath.
12	Tu	17:57—18:9, 20–30	Saul grows increasingly envious of David.
12	W	18:8–10; 20:1–17	The covenant between David and Jonathan.
12	Th	21:2–10; 22:1–5	David receives the Holy Bread and other aid from the priests while fleeing Saul.
12	F	25:14–24, 28–29	The account of David, Nabal, and Abigail.
12	Sa	26:5–25	David spares Saul after infiltrating Saul's camp.
13	Su	28:3–25	Saul consults the witch of Endor concerning his fate.
13	M	31:1–4; 2 Sam 1:1–16	The death of Saul and Jonathan; David's avenges their death against the Amalekite.
13	Tu	2 Sam 2:1–11; 3:1–5	David established as king over Judah; the war between the two royal houses.
13	W	4:2–5:7	Ish-bosheth assassinated. David executes his murderers, is anointed king over Israel, captures Jerusalem as his capital.
13	Th	6:1–23	The two attempts to bring the ark to Jerusalem; the falling out of David and Michal.
13	F	7:1–25	Nathan's oracle granting the covenant to David and David's prayer of thanksgiving.
13	Sa	11:1–17, 26–27	David's sin against Bathsheba and Uriah.
14	Su	12:1–25	Nathan rebukes David, and David repents.
14	M	15:7–14, 24–30; 16:5–13	David flees Jerusalem before Absalom, while being cursed by Shimei.
14	Tu	18:6–17, 24; 19:5	Absalom defeated, slain; David grieves for the loss of his son.
14	W	24:1–4, 10–18; 24b–25	David's census, the plague, and his repentance; the purchase of the threshing floor.

from the rule of judges under the economy of the Mosaic covenant to the rule of hereditary kings under the economy of the Davidic covenant. Since the New Covenant in Christ fundamentally restores and transforms the Davidic covenant economy—that is, the Church truly is the kingdom of the Son of David—the account of the origins and shape of this kingdom in Samuel continues to inform our understanding of the nature, shape, and mission of the Church. The account is graced with some of the most important types of Christ (Samuel, David) and his blessed mother (Hannah) in all of Scripture.

For Further Reading

Commentaries on and Studies of 1–2 Samuel

Brown, Raymond E., S.S. "Communicating the Divine and Human in Scripture". *Origins* 22.1 (May 14, 1992): 5–6.

Hamilton, Victor. *Handbook on the Historical Books*. Grand Rapids, Mich.: Baker Academic, 2001. (See pp. 211–378.)

McCarter, P. Kyle. *I Samuel*. Anchor Bible 8. New York: Doubleday, 1980.

———. *II Samuel*. Anchor Bible 9. New York: Doubleday, 1984.

Morrison, Craig E., O. Carm. *2 Samuel*. Berit Olam. Collegeville, Minn.: Liturgical Press, 2013.

Tsumura, David Toshio. *The First Book of Samuel*. New International Commentary on the Old Testament 9. Grand Rapids, Mich.: Eerdmans, 2007.

Historical Issues in 1–2 Samuel

Halpern, Baruch. *David's Secret Demons: Messiah, Murderer, Traitor, King*. Grand Rapids, Mich.: Eerdmans, 2001.

Kitchen, Kenneth A. *On the Reliability of the Old Testament*. Grand Rapids, Mich.: Eerdmans, 2003. (See pp. 81–158.)

Knoppers, Gary N. "The Historical Study of the Monarchy: Developments and Detours". Pages 207–35 in *The Face of Old Testament Studies: A Survey of Contemporary Approaches*. Edited by David W. Baker and Bill T. Arnold. Grand Rapids, Mich.: Baker Books, 1999.

Long, V. Philips. "1 Samuel" and "2 Samuel". Pages 267–491 in *Joshua, Judges, Ruth, 1 & 2 Samuel*. Vol. 2 of *Zondervan Illustrated Bible Backgrounds Commentary*. Edited by John H. Walton. Grand Rapids, Mich.: Zondervan, 2009.

Vaughn, Andrew G., and Ann E. Killebrew, eds. *Jerusalem in Bible and Archaeology: The First Temple Period*. Atlanta: Society of Biblical Literature, 2003.

1–2 Samuel in the Living Tradition

Chrysostom, Saint John. *Homilies on Hannah, David, and Saul*. Vol. 1 of *Old Testament Homilies*. Translated by Robert Charles Hill. Brookline: Holy Cross Orthodox Press, 2003.

———. *On Repentance and Almsgiving*. Translated by Gus George Christo. The Fathers of the Church 96. Washington, D.C.: Catholic University of America Press, 2005.

Franke, John R., ed. *Joshua, Judges, Ruth, 1–2 Samuel*. Old Testament 4 of Ancient Christian Commentary on Scripture. Edited by Thomas C. Oden. Downers Grove, Ill.: InterVarsity Press, 2005. (See pp. 193–401.)

Maximus of Turin, Saint. *The Sermons of St. Maximus of Turin*. Translated by Boniface Ramsey. Ancient Christian Writers 50. New York: Newman Press, 1989.

Origen. *Homilies on Jeremiah, Homily on 1 Kings 28*. Translated by John Clark Smith. The Fathers of the Church 97. Washington, D.C.: Catholic University of America Press, 1998. (See pp. 319–36.)

15. THE BOOKS OF KINGS

Introduction

As with 1–2 Samuel, the books of Kings were originally one book, a sequel to Samuel detailing some four hundred years of Israelite history, from the time of David's successors (ca. 960 B.C.) until the collapse of his kingdom at the hand of the Babylonian Empire (ca. 587 B.C.). According to the report of Origen, the Jews in antiquity called this book by its first two words, "Now King David ..." (Hebrew *wehamelech dawid*; cf. 1 Kings 1:1). How then did we get the name "Kings"? Apparently, the translators of the Greek Septuagint split the book in two to make it more manageable in size and called the resulting volumes 3 and 4 "Kingdoms" (Greek *basileiōn*). (As we mentioned in the last chapter, 1 and 2 Kingdoms are the names for 1 and 2 Samuel in the Greek Septuagint.) The point of division chosen—partway through the reign of King Ahaziah (cf. 2 Kings 1:1–18)—is not a major literary break in the narrative. Nonetheless, in modern Jewish Bibles, the work is broken at the same point into two volumes, known as "Kings 1" (Hebrew *melachim a*) and "Kings 2" (Hebrew *melachim b*).

The central focus of Kings is *the rise and fall of the Davidic kingdom*, although there are many other important themes in this long and rich composition. The first several chapters recount the glorious reign of Solomon, under which the Davidic covenant reaches its greatest visible expression, and, indeed, all the divine covenants to this point in salvation history seem to have been fulfilled, if briefly. The theological high point of the narrative of Kings and of the whole Old Testament to this point is Solomon's act of building and dedicating the Temple in Jerusalem (1 Kings 8). After this point in Israel's history, there is a steady decline, both spiritually and materially, beginning in the latter years of Solomon's own reign and culminating in the destruction of the Temple and Jerusalem and the exile of the last reigning son of David, with which the books of Kings come to an end (2 Kings 25).

Literary Structure, Style, and Themes in 1–2 Kings

The basic structure of Kings is tripartite. The first and third sections focus on a single Israelite kingdom ruled by a son of David in Jerusalem, so they resemble each other:

> A. One Kingdom under the Son of David: Solomon (1 Kings 1–11)
> B. Two Kingdoms, Israel and Judah (1 Kings 12–2 Kings 17)
> A'. One Kingdom under the Son of David: Judah Alone (2 Kings 18–25)

Furthermore, the long central section of the book (1 Kings 12—2 Kings 17), which tells the story of the divided monarchy, is arranged chiastically around the ministry of the two great prophets Elijah and Elisha:

A. The Divided Monarchy before the Great Prophets (1 Kings 12–16)
    B. The Divided Monarchy during Elijah's Ministry (1 Kings 17—2 Kings 1)
        C. The Transition from Elijah to Elisha (2 Kings 2)
    B'. The Divided Monarchy during Elisha's Ministry (2 Kings 3–13)
A'. The Divided Monarchy after the Great Prophets (2 Kings 14–17)

Ironically, for a composition so focused on royal reigns, it is the ministries of the *prophets* Elijah and Elisha that provide hope during the otherwise dismal account of the decline of the kingdoms of Israel and Judah. This may be one reason the Jewish tradition places the books of Kings among the "Former Prophets". The structural center point of the whole narrative is the transition from Elijah to Elisha (2 Kings 2), a narrative that is not incorporated into the account of the reign of any king. In light of such considerations, the books of Kings can be outlined as follows:

Outline of the Books of Kings

I. The Rise and Fall of King Solomon (1 Kings 1–11)
    A. Solomon's Tumultuous Accession (1–2)
    B. Solomon's Wisdom and Glory (3–4)
    C. Solomon Builds the Temple and Palace (5–8)
    D. The Height of Solomon's Glory (9–10)
    E. The Fall of and Death of King Solomon (11)

II. The Two Kingdoms: Israel vs. Judah (1 Kings 12—2 Kings 14)
    A. King Rehoboam (South) vs. King Jeroboam (North) (12:1—16:28)
        1. The Sin of Jeroboam: The Two Golden Calves (12:1—14:20)
        2. Kings of Judah: Rehoboam, Abijam, Asa (14:21—15:24)
        3. Kings of Israel: Nadab, Baasha, Elah, Zimri, Omri (15:25—16:28)
    B. The Prophet Elijah (1 Kings 16:29—2 Kings 2)
        1. Ahab's Reign in Brief (16:29–34)
        2. Elijah, the Great Drought, and the Aftermath (17:1—19:21)
        3. Ahab's War with Syria (20:1–43)
        4. Elijah, Ahab, and Naboth's Vineyard (21:1–29)
        5. Ahab's War with Syria Continued (22:1–40)
        6. King of Judah: Jehoshaphat (22:41–50)
        7. King of Israel: Ahaziah (22:51–53)
        8. Elijah and Ahaziah's Fatal Illness (2 Kings 1:1–18)
        9. Elijah Is Taken Up into Heaven (2:1–25)
    C. The Prophet Elisha (2 Kings 3:1–13:25)
        1. King of Israel: Jehoram (3:1–3)
        2. Elisha and Jehoram's War with Moab (3:4–27)
        3. Elisha's Miracles for Various Individuals (4:1—6:7)

Literary Features of 1–2 Kings

From a literary point of view, the first eleven chapters of Kings, which recount the reign of Solomon, are somewhat different from the rest of the book. In style and structure, they flow naturally from the books of Samuel and continue patterns from those books. However, beginning with division of the kingdom under Rehoboam and Jeroboam (1 Kings 12–14), the sacred author shuttles back and forth between northern Israel and southern Judah, giving an account of each king according to a stylized pattern of the following elements:

1. Date of the king's accession according to the regnal years of the other kingdom
2. Total years of his reign

3. For kings of Judah (usually), his age at accession
4. For kings of Judah, the name of his mother; for kings of Israel, the name of his father
5. A moral evaluation of his reign based on his fidelity to YHWH and especially YHWH's sanctuary in Jerusalem, often including a comparison or contrast with David (a positive model) for Judean kings or Jeroboam (a negative model) for Israelite kings
6. A notice of the most significant events in his reign
7. Referral to another source where more can be learned about the king's reign, usually the "Book of the Chronicles of the Kings of Judah" or "of Israel"
8. A notice of the king's death, burial place, and successor

For many kings, such as Hezekiah, Josiah, and Manasseh, the sacred author has quite a bit of material, including lengthy narratives, that are incorporated into the "significant events" section; whereas for others he has but a verse or two of summary information. Nonetheless, the reference to a fuller source and the death notice reliably indicate the end of a literary section. This literary pattern, closely but not perfectly followed, gives the books of Kings their characteristic style: solemn and stately, official and authoritative, occasionally dry and annalistic.

The author almost always narrates the reign of each king sequentially, so that the account of one king's reign is completed before the account of another's begins. The one exception is during the long reign of Joram of Israel (2 Kings 3:1—9:26), which contains the ministry of Elisha (2 Kings 4:1—9:3) and the reign of Jehoram of Judah (2 Kings 8:16–24) and overlaps with the reigns of Ahaziah of Judah (2 Kings 8:25—9:29) and Jehu of Israel (2 Kings 9:1—10:36). The disruption of the usually neat literary structure at this point is due to the fact that all these kings as well as the prophet Elisha were *contemporaries* who had a great deal of interaction with one another. Elisha anoints Jehu, who in turn slays Joram of Israel and Ahaziah of Judah in order to gain the throne of Israel (2 Kings 9:1–29).

Royal, Prophetic, and Priestly Themes

The books of Kings simultaneously view the history of Israel and Judah through the lenses of the three anointed roles: king, prophet, and priest.

First, the *royal theme* is dominant and close to the surface of the text: it traces the downfall of the Davidic monarchy from the first son of David to sit on the throne (Solomon) to the last to do so (Zedekiah). The mercy shown to Jehoiachin in the final pericope of the book gives a small but significant glimmer of hope that God's covenant with David has not been extinguished, despite the infidelities of so many of David's sons.

Second, the *prophetic theme* becomes dominant in the center of the book, during the ministries of Elijah under Ahab and Elisha under Jehoram, when the prophets take center stage from the kings during the heyday of the northern kingdom. Indeed, the literary crux of the work is the ascension of Elijah and the succession of Elisha (2 Kings 2), which reminds the reader that God has other officers and ways of working with his people besides the kings and their royal administration. And Elijah and Elisha are not the only prophets of note in the narrative: Nathan, Ahijah, Isaiah, Micaiah ben Imlah, Huldah the prophetess, and numerous unnamed prophets also make key interventions in the history of God's people (see table). The unexpected and gratuitous rise of these prophets "like Moses" (cf. Deut 18:15) is another cause for hope in the otherwise dismal history: perhaps God may yet send another prophet like Moses to lead his people out of the Assyrian and Babylonian exiles.

The Prophecy-Fulfillment Motif in Kings			
In	Prophet	Predicts	Fulfilled in
1 Kings 11:29–39	Ahijah	The kingship of Jeroboam over the ten tribes	1 Kings 12:15
1 Kings 11:39	Ahijah	The house of David will not be afflicted forever	2 Kings 25:27–30?
1 Kings 13:1–3	Unnamed	Josiah's destruction of the illicit altar of Jeroboam	2 Kings 23:15–20
1 Kings 14:7–11	Ahijah	The demise of the house of Jeroboam	1 Kings 15:29
1 Kings 16:1–4	Jehu	The demise of the house of Baasha	1 Kings 16:12
1 Kings 21:20–24	Elijah	The demise of Jezebel and the house of Ahab	2 Kings 9:30—10:17
1 Kings 22:17	Micaiah	The defeat and death of Ahab	1 Kings 22:35–38
2 Kings 1:16	Elijah	The death of Ahaziah	2 Kings 1:17
2 Kings 19:20–34	Isaiah	The fall of Sennacherib, salvation of Jerusalem	2 Kings 19:35–37
2 Kings 20:17	Isaiah	The deportation of royal wealth to Babylon	2 Kings 24:13
2 Kings 21:10–15	Unnamed	The downfall of Judah due to Manasseh's sin	2 Kings 24:2
2 Kings 22:15–17	Huldah	The destruction of Jerusalem	2 Kings 24:20
2 Kings 22:18–20	Huldah	Josiah's death before seeing the destruction	2 Kings 23:30

Third, the *priestly theme* focuses on the Jerusalem Temple, the place of priestly ministry, and traces the story of God's sanctuary from its glorious construction and dedication under Solomon (1 Kings 5–8) to its destruction and dismantling by the Babylonians (2 Kings 25). The theme of the central sanctuary is prominent throughout: the northern kings, beginning with Jeroboam's construction of two—not one, but two!—golden calves (1 Kings 12), are always criticized for promoting the illicit sanctuaries. The southern kings likewise are judged based on their attitude toward the central sanctuary and their toleration or prohibition of illicit sanctuaries. Hence, as well as being a history of the kingship, the books of Kings constitute a history of Israel's cult. The best kings (Solomon in his youth, Hezekiah, Josiah) are temple (re)builders and liturgical reformers. In this vein, it is no surprise that 2 Kings ends with hope that God may yet restore the house of David and the Temple of Solomon.

Overview of 1–2 Kings

The Rise and Fall of King Solomon (1 Kings 1–11)

With the opening chapters of the first book of Kings, we turn to what might be called the "glory days" of the Davidic kingdom. Indeed, one of the reasons the story of King Solomon is so famous and memorable is because it recounts the only time in Israel's history when all twelve tribes are united under a single king, who marshals the resources of Israel (and the surrounding nations) in the building of the glorious dwelling place of God that will become the central symbol of God's love for his people from the early first millennium all the way down to the time of Jesus: the Temple in Jerusalem. Within these opening chapters, there are at least four key aspects of Solomon's kingdom that stand out as important.

First, with the rise of Solomon to the throne, we have the preliminary fulfillment of God's promise to David that his own "seed" or "offspring"—that is, *a son of David*—would be king over the twelve tribes of Israel. To be sure, Solomon does not come to the throne without difficulty, for the first book of Kings begins with conflict over the throne that ensues while David is still alive (1 Kings 1). On the one hand, David's eldest surviving son, Adonijah, thinks he has a claim to the throne and begins gathering his supporters to have himself installed as king. On the other hand, the prophet Nathan and Bathsheba, the mother of Solomon, conspire together to have Solomon, the younger son, anointed as king. In the end, it is Solomon who emerges victorious when David commands Zadok the priest and Nathan the prophet to have Solomon ride David's own royal mule down to the Gihon spring and there be anointed king of Israel (1 Kings 1:32–40).

Second, and even more important, once he is established as king, Solomon does something that will mark him out from all of his successors: when the Lord appears to him by night in "a dream" and offers him anything he wishes, Solomon asks the Lord for "an understanding mind" to govern the people of Israel, to be able to "discern between good and evil" (1 Kings 3:9). In response to this remarkable request, God declares that he will give Solomon not only wisdom but also riches and honor, so

---

King Solomon and the Prostitutes
(1 Kings 3:16–28)

Confronted by two prostitutes, both claiming to have mothered the same infant, Solomon pretends to threaten the child's life in order to determine which of the women will put the child's well-being above her own interests. The real mother steps forward in this case, but whichever of the women had pled for the child's life would have deserved custody of him, so Solomon could not have gone wrong. The people perceived his ingenuity and praised him for it.

In the New Testament, Jesus' wisdom, too, will be tested by at least one case involving a prostitute (Jn 8:2–11) in which he finds a way to show both justice and mercy to the woman.

that no other king will ever compare with his glory (1 Kings 3:10–14). This is the origin of the famous *wisdom of Solomon*, which is supernaturally given to him and which he immediately demonstrates publicly by his remarkable judgments at court in the famous case of the two harlots and the child (1 Kings 3:16–28).

Third, as a direct result of his wisdom, King Solomon begins to transform the nation of Israel into an *international kingdom* (or "empire"), which has its influence not only over the twelve tribes but over the surrounding Gentile nations. These "glory days" are succinctly described by the author of Kings as follows:

> *Judah and Israel were as many as the sand by the sea; they ate and drank and were happy.* Solomon ruled over all the kingdoms from the Euphrates to the land of the Philistines and to the border of Egypt; they brought tribute and served Solomon all the days of his life. (1 Kings 4:20–21)

In other words, Solomon ushers in what might be called a *pax Solomonica*: a time of peace, when all twelve tribes of Israel are united under "twelve officers" (1 Kings 4:1–19); when the surrounding nations bring tribute to the king of Israel; and when the king of Israel is known above all for his wisdom "beyond measure" and high culture, composing some 3,000 "proverbs" (Hebrew *meshalim*), 1,005 "songs", and demonstrating unparalleled knowledge of the natural world (what we today would call the "natural sciences") (1 Kings 4:29–33). As a result, instead of Israel being separated from the nations as before, now "men came from all peoples to hear the wisdom of Solomon" (1 Kings 4:34). For a fleeting moment, then, it appears that Israel is beginning to live out the call to be a kingdom of priests (Ex 19:5–6) and a light to the surrounding nations (Is 60:3).

Fourth and finally, nowhere is this glory more apparent than in the building of *the first Temple in Jerusalem* (1 Kings 6–8). Significantly, this massive project is not an Israelite-only undertaking; instead, Solomon solicits the Gentiles to aid him in building the sanctuary by forming a trade alliance with King Hiram of Tyre (1 Kings 5:1–18). Unlike the Tabernacle under the Mosaic covenant, the Temple in Jerusalem under the Davidic covenant will be built by both Israelites and Gentiles. The building of the Temple is described in great detail (see 1 Kings 6), and any reader familiar with the Pentateuch will immediately recognize that the Temple of Solomon is both *similar to* and *greater than* the Tabernacle of Moses.[1] These similarities and differences can be summed up in the form of a chart:

The Tabernacle of Moses	The Temple of Solomon
1. Tripartite structure: 　a. Outer court 　b. Holy place 　c. Holy of Holies	1. Tripartite structure: 　a. Vestibule (Hebrew *'ulam*) 　b. Nave (Hebrew *hekal*) 　c. Inner sanctuary (Hebrew *debir*)
2. Tent, made of goat's hair	2. Temple, overlaid in pure gold
3. Two small gold cherubim placed atop the ark	3. Two giant gold cherubim (ca. 20 feet!) placed in the inner sanctuary

---

[1] Victor Hamilton, *Handbook on the Historical Books* (Grand Rapids, Mich.: Baker Academic, 2001), 395–96.

4. Small golden menorah; placed in Holy Place	4. Ten giant gold menorahs; placed in nave
5. Small bronze laver of water; placed in outer court (Ex 25–27, 30)	5. Ten bronze lavers of water; placed in vestibule (1 Kings 6–8)

What is the significance of these differences? One can only speculate, but in this case the number ten seems to function as a symbol of perfection or completion: Solomon has perfected on a grand scale for Israel and the nations what Moses began on a small scale for Israel alone.

The Temple of Solomon as a Microcosmos

The chapters describing the construction of the Temple in Jerusalem by Solomon (1 Kings 6–8) are the zenith of the Old Testament narrative, in which themes and anticipations from as far back as Genesis find their fulfillment.

For example, the gold, jewels, flowering trees, cherubim, plentiful water, and other aspects of the decoration of the Temple call to mind the description of Eden—the Temple is a new Eden, a new place of worship and communion with God. The Eden connection is reinforced by the naming of the Jerusalem spring, which flowed from the Temple Mount, after one of the rivers of Eden (the Gihon; cf. 1 Kings 1:45; Gen 2:13). The building of the Temple takes seven years; it is dedicated in the seventh month, in a festival of seven days, climaxed by a prayer of seven petitions (see 1 Kings 8:31, 33, 35, 37, 41, 44, 46). All these sevens recall the creation of the cosmos (Gen 1): the Temple is a microcosm (micro-cosmos), and the cosmos is a macrotemple. The building of the Temple is a kind of re-creation, the introduction of a new epoch in salvation history, restoring to God's people an Eden-like place of communion unavailable since the Fall (Gen 3:24) and which was the goal of the Exodus (Ex 15:17).

Remarkably, like David, his father, before him, upon the completion and dedication of the Temple, Solomon acts as both king and *priest*: offering sacrifice, leading a long prayer of seven petitions, and blessing the people (1 Kings 8:22–66). The holy ark is brought into the Temple, and the glory of the Lord not seen since the exodus (Ex 40:34) inhabits the building (1 Kings 8:10). The whole ceremony culminates in a joyous week-long festival in which the entire empire eats at the king's expense (1 Kings 8:62–65).

The author of Kings goes on to describe the state visit from the Queen of Sheba (modern-day Yemen)—probably to discuss trade relations and political alliances, in addition to the queen's personal curiosity—that marks the political high point of Solomon's reign (1 Kings 10:1–13). And yet, now that the Temple has been dedicated and Solomon's external glory is growing (1 Kings 9:10—10:29), we find him (almost Samson-like) systematically breaking each one of the three laws Moses had established to limit the self-aggrandizement of kings (Deut 17:16–17). Consider the following chart:

The Law of Moses for Kings	*King Solomon's Actions*
1. He must not multiply horses (Deut 17:16)	1. 1,400 chariots, 12,000 horsemen (1 Kings 10:26–29)

| 2. He shall not multiply wives for himself (Deut 17:17) | 2. 700 wives, 300 concubines (1 Kings 11:3) |
| 3. Nor shall he greatly multiply for himself silver and gold (Deut 17:17) | 3. 666 gold talents annually (1 Kings 10:14) |

Almost in the fashion of a new Adam, who fell because the fruit of the Tree of Knowledge was "good for food" (pleasure), a "delight to the eyes" (possession), and "desirable to make one wise" (power/pride) (Gen 3:6), King Solomon gives his heart over to the desire for pleasure (wives), possessions (gold), and power (horses, weaponry), allowing his trust in God to disappear.

In the wake of this triple transgression, Solomon becomes more and more corrupt, so that eventually "when Solomon was old his wives turned away his heart after other gods" (1 Kings 11:1–4), and he does what David never did: fall into the sin of idolatry. Indeed, Solomon descends to such depths that he sets up temples to the goddess Ashtoreth and even builds altars for the Moabite deity Chemosh and the Ammonite deity Molech, both of whom are worshipped by means of *human sacrifice* (1 Kings 11:5–8). God responds by declaring that most of the kingdom will be torn from Solomon and that political enemies will rise up from within and without the empire to trouble him (1 Kings 11:9–43). Thus ends the richest, most glorious, and wisest king Israel ever possessed, and thus ends the period of the united monarchy.

The Two Kingdoms under Rehoboam and Jeroboam (1 Kings 12—16:28)

After the death of Solomon, the narrative in the books of Kings gets very complicated very quickly, as the twelve tribes of Israel split into two kingdoms: (1) the northern kingdom of "Israel", consisting of *ten tribes*, and (2) the southern kingdom of "Judah", consisting of *two tribes*. Because contemporary readers of the Bible often wrongly assume that "Israel" and "Judah" are simply two ways of saying the same thing, the geographical and tribal differences between the kingdom of Israel (ten tribes) and the kingdom of Judah (two tribes) cannot be overemphasized.

By way of analogy, one may think of the Union soldiers in the north and the Confederate soldiers in the south, both of whom would consider themselves "true Americans".

Jews, Israelites, and "Israelians"

All descendants of the twelve tribes, including the tribe of Judah, are "Israelites". The period of the divided monarchy presents terminological problems because we cannot accurately contrast "Israelites" with "Judeans": Judeans *are* Israelites. We adopt a term coined by other scholars to refer specifically to Israelites of the northern kingdom: "Israelian". By contrast, an *Israeli* is a citizen of the modern state of Israel. The term *Jew* (Hebrew *yehudi*) is first used in the books of Kings (2 Kings 16:6) and becomes common only after the exile to refer to descendants of Judah, citizens of the Judean state. It only became a primarily *religious* term in the pagan world of the Greco-Roman Empire and in response to the rise of Christianity.

With this in mind, we can turn to the narrative. After the death of Solomon, all Israel gathers at Shechem (a neutral site) to discuss the kingship with Rehoboam, the rightful son and heir of Solomon. The northern tribes of Israel plead with Rehoboam to decrease their taxes and forced labor—"lighten the hard service of your father and his heavy yoke upon us", they say (1 Kings 12:4). Rehoboam refuses, and the ten northern Israel tribes revolt against him and choose Jeroboam, Solomon's former officer of forced labor, as their new king (1 Kings 12:6–24). Because Rehoboam declines to start a civil war between the north and south, Jeroboam is now free to set up his

---

The Israelite Schism as a "Divorce"

The account of Israel's rejection of Rehoboam (12:1–15) has the force of a "divorce" between the bride Israel and the Davidic king, her husband. Recall that David assumed the kingship over northern Israel on the basis of a covenant that employed language of "bone and flesh", echoing the covenant between Adam and Eve (2 Sam 5:1–3; cf. Gen 2:23–25). Moreover, later in the narrative, "all the people" of Israel are compared to "a bride [who] comes home to her husband" in relation to the Davidic king (2 Sam 17:3). In keeping with this imagery of the bridegroom king and the bridal people, Rehoboam's adolescent advisors urge him to make a crudely chauvinistic boast: "My little finger is thicker than my father's loins" (1 Kings 12:10), an only lightly disguised sexual euphemism. Rehoboam appears in the posture of the swaggering, abusive husband-king; bride Israel departs to her own familial home (1 Kings 12:16).

---

kingdom in the northern territories (1 Kings 12:21–25). However, Jeroboam makes one fateful mistake: in order to keep the northern tribes from continuing to worship at the Temple of Solomon in Jerusalem, he erects not one but two golden calves: one in the shrine at Dan (on the northern border of the kingdom, cf. Judg 18) and one in the shrine at Bethel (on the southern border of the kingdom, cf. Gen 28:10–22):

> And [King Jeroboam] said to the people, "*You have gone up to Jerusalem long enough. Behold your gods, O Israel, who brought you up out of the land of Egypt.*" And he set one in Bethel, and the other he put in Dan. And *this thing became a sin*, for the people went to the one at Bethel and to the other as far as Dan. *He also made houses on high places, and appointed priests from among all the people, who were not of the Levites.* And Jeroboam appointed a feast on the fifteenth day of the eighth month like the feast that was in Judah, and *he offered sacrifices upon the altar;* so he did in Bethel, sacrificing to the calves that he had made. And he placed in Bethel the priests of the high places that he had made. He went up to the altar which he had made in Bethel on the fifteenth day in the eighth month, in *the month which he had devised of his own heart;* and he ordained a feast for the sons of Israel, and went up to the altar to burn incense. (1 Kings 12:28–33)

This is what the rest of the books of Kings will refer to as the "sin of Jeroboam", and it will have devastating effects on the history of God's people. Jeroboam is a kind of new Aaron, replicating and doubling the idolatry of the Golden Calf in the exodus, even using Aaron's own words (Ex 32:4)! To make matters worse, he also acts like a new Saul, offering sacrifice at the altar although he himself is a general, not a priest (cf. 1 Sam 13). Finally, he simply creates a fake "priesthood" without authorization and devises a liturgical feast, not as Moses did from divine revelation, but out of "his own heart". From this point forward, there will be not only political but *cultic* schism between the Judeans and the northern "Israelians" (see sidebar on p. 397).

Given everything we have seen so far about how God responds to idolatry and self-exaltation to the priesthood, it should come as no surprise that by means of this sin, Jeroboam seals his own fate and that of the northern kingdom of Israel. By means of an anonymous prophet who comes to the shrine at Bethel, the Lord predicts the coming of Josiah, the reforming king who will destroy Jeroboam's idolatrous shrines (1 Kings 13:1–10; cf. 2 Kings 15:20). Because of Jeroboam's evil, his heir, Abijah, falls ill and dies, and another prophet, Ahijah, curses his line, so that it will be wiped out and replaced by a different royal dynasty in northern Israel (1 Kings 14:1–20). Indeed, because the northern kingdom lacks a deep-seated loyalty to a single dynasty, its history is one long line of bloody coups. For example, Jeroboam's son Nadab and his entire house are assassinated by one Baasha of Issachar, who moves the capital from Shechem to Tirzah (1 Kings 15:27–32). Baasha's son Elah is in turn assassinated by one Zimri, a chariot commander, who wipes out Baasha's whole house, just as Baasha did to Jeroboam (1 Kings 16:1–7). But there is no public sympathy for Zimri, so the people acclaim Omri—a popular general who has not been involved in any intrigues—as king (1 Kings 16:15–24). Omri moves the capital from the city of Tirzah to Samaria, where it will stay for the rest of northern Israel's history. Omri is politically and militarily capable and establishes a dynasty that will last four generations, taking up about half the narrative of the books of Kings, during which almost the entire ministries of Elijah and Elisha take place. Omri's line will only end with the zealous Yahwistic revolution of King Jehu (2 Kings 9–10). Omri's influence is so great that ancient extra-biblical texts from this time period typically refer to northern Israel as the "House of Omri", whereas Judah is called the "House of David", each named after its dynastic founder. (See "Historical Issues in 1–2 Kings" below.) For all Omri's practical competence, the sacred author still passes a negative evaluation of his reign because he continues to support the idolatrous worship of the Lord at the calf shrines Jeroboam established, with their non-Levitical priests and aberrant liturgical calendar (1 Kings 16:25–28).

Unfortunately, during the same time period in the southern kingdom of Judah, things do not look much better. Rehoboam, the king Judah, continues the pagan practices of his elderly father, Solomon, and encourages the proliferation of illicit shrines to the Lord (as well as to other gods) and cultic prostitution (1 Kings 14:21–24). In the words of the sacred author:

> And Judah did what was evil in the sight of the LORD, and they provoked him to jealousy with their sins which they committed, more than all that their fathers had done. For they also built for themselves high places, and pillars, and Asherim on every high hill and under every green tree; and there were also male cult prostitutes in the land. They did according to all the abominations of the nations which the LORD drove out before the sons of Israel. (1 Kings 14:22–24)

It is hard to overemphasize this point: although the author of Kings is clearly writing from the perspective of the southern kingdom, he does not whitewash the sins of Judah. From the very beginning of the schism, idolatry is being committed by the two southern tribes of Judah as well as by the ten northern tribes of Israel. Indeed, Rehoboam's son Abijam continues his father's practice of idolatry and is constantly at war with northern Israel (1 Kings 15:1–8). His son Asa, however, is a reformer who abolishes cultic prostitution and the worship of Asherah, but does not challenge the shrines to the Lord outside of Jerusalem (the "high places"). He stabilizes the border between Israel and Judah through battle, diplomacy, and fortification (1 Kings 15:16–24). Cultic schism results, as it often does in history, in political division and warfare. Clearly, no deliverance is to be expected from kings such as Jeroboam and Rehoboam, so into the midst of this idolatry and bloodshed God does what he has done previously in such situations: he sends a prophet.

The Prophet Elijah (1 Kings 16:29—2 Kings 2)

In order to place the life of the prophet Elijah in its proper context, it is critical to emphasize that the vast bulk of his activity takes place during the reign of the northern King Ahab, who is remembered as a great evildoer: "Ahab the son of Omri did evil in the sight of the LORD more than all that were before him" (1 Kings 16:30). Ahab not only continues the schismatic and idolatrous cult introduced by Jeroboam; he marries a pagan (Phoenician/Tyrian) woman, *Jezebel*, and worships her god, Baal, as well as Baal's consort, Asherah (1 Kings 16:31–33). Over the course of his reign, and at the behest of his wife, Ahab is in constant conflict with Elijah (for example, 1 Kings 17–19). Like Saul before him, Ahab spares an enemy king (Ben-Hadad of Syria) and is condemned for it by a prophet (1 Kings 20). And like David, who coveted the wife of Uriah, Ahab covets the vineyard of Naboth the Jezreelite and ultimately commits murder in order to acquire what he cannot rightfully attain. The story unfolds as follows: Naboth refuses to sell his ancestral land, and Ahab pouts. Seeing this, Jezebel has Naboth falsely executed so that Ahab can have his piece of property (1 Kings 21; cf. Lev 25:10–55). Although Ahab repents in response to Elijah's rebuke (1 Kings 21:27–29), the king eventually meets a tragic end like his wicked predecessors: he bleeds to death from an arrow wound after a battle against the king of Syria. In this way, the ominous prophecy of Elijah is fulfilled: the dogs licked up his blood (1 Kings 21:17–19; 22:38).

Right into the heart of such corruption, wickedness, and idolatry, God sends the prophet Elijah (Hebrew *Eli-Yah*, "My God is YHWH"). He is introduced abruptly as a "Tishbite, of Tishbe in Gilead" (1 Kings 17:1). Tishbe is unknown, but Gilead is the Transjordan region, home of the tribes of Reuben, Gad, and Manasseh. Elijah was probably well-known to the ancient reader and thus required little introduction. Although much could be said about the important ministry of this figure, for our purposes here, four aspects of Elijah the prophet stand out.

First, Elijah is not just any kind of prophet, but a *miracle-worker*. His first narrated act is to control the weather for three years, so that "there shall be neither dew nor rain these years, except by my word" (1 Kings 17:1). While the land under King Ahab languishes in a severe drought, Elijah himself avoids Ahab's retaliation by fleeing into the desert, where he is fed by ravens every morning and evening and given water to drink by one of the only brooks that seem not to have dried up (1 Kings 17:4–5). During this time, Elijah befriends a widow in Zarephath and saves her from starvation by miraculously causing her bread and oil continuously to replenish themselves (1 Kings 17:8–16). When her son takes ill and dies, Elijah adds yet another miracle by performing the first act of raising the dead recorded in Jewish Scripture (1 Kings 17:8–24). The distinctive nature of Elijah's ability to perform miracles is important to stress because readers sometimes have the mistaken impression that all of God's emissaries in the Old Testament have such powers. They do not. Elijah is the kind of prophet Israel has not seen since the time of Moses and Joshua. Into the midst of darkness and suffering, God unleashes visible signs of his power and fidelity to Israel.

Second, Elijah is also a *cultic reformer*, whose task is to call Israel out of its idolatrous worship of false gods. This aspect of his identity can be seen above all in the unforgettable account of the "liturgical showdown" between Elijah and the 450 prophets of Baal at Mount Carmel (1 Kings 18). After three years, Elijah comes out of hiding and confronts Ahab, challenging him to send the prophets of the god Baal ("Master" or "Owner") to a showdown to be held at Mount Carmel. Note well that this is a battle between *two altars*: the altar of Baal, whose priests cry out and mutilate their bodies in order to try to manipulate him to accept their sacrifices; and the altar of YHWH, whose heavenly fire can consume the sacrifices even after Elijah has doused the altar with water four times (1 Kings 18:30–35)! The purpose of Elijah's challenge is not just to mock Baal—as when he suggests that Baal might not be responding because he has "gone aside" to relieve himself!—but to show that he is no true god (1 Kings 18:27). In the end, he does just that: both Elijah and the 450 prophets of Baal attempt to call down fire from heaven; the Baal prophets fail in humiliation, but Elijah succeeds spectacularly, provoking a popular (if fleeting) mass conversion to Yahwism. In the wake of his victory, Elijah metes out the punishment for idolatry by executing the prophets

The Worship of YHWH in the North

Worshipping the LORD acceptably in northern Israel posed challenges and anomalies, since the only legitimate sanctuary for the celebration of the Mosaic liturgy was located in Jerusalem, which was usually inaccessible due to the political situation. In this predicament, Israelians faithful to the LORD looked to the prophets to meet their cultic/liturgical needs. Certain passages (2 Kings 4:23; 4:42) indicate that they visited the prophet at times when sacrifice was to be offered and presented the offerings prescribed by the law to him rather than to the illicit priesthood.

Prophets in Israel apparently always enjoyed, by virtue of their office, the right to offer sacrifice, and they made use of the Mosaic law of altar-building (Ex 20:24–26; cf. 1 Kings 18:30–32). The remnant of the faithful in Israel (1 Kings 19:18) was sustained in part by groups known as "the sons of the prophets" (Hebrew *bene-hannevi'im*; 1 Kings 20:35; 2 Kings 2:3, 5, 7, 15; 4:1, 38; 5:22; 6:1; 9:1). These were not literal sons, but disciples. They lived in community under the guidance of the great prophets (2 Kings 6:1) and may be seen as a prototype of consecrated religious life. Some were married (2 Kings 4:1), whereas others may have been celibate like the prophets themselves: nothing is ever said of a wife or child of Elijah or Elisha.

of Baal; he then prays for an end to the drought and miraculously accompanies
Ahab back to the palace in Jezreel (1 Kings 18:40–46).

King Ahab's wife Jezebel, however, is not pleased with the slaughter of her
god's prophets, and Elijah is forced to flee for his life into the territory of Judah,
then farther south into the Sinai Peninsula, to Mount Horeb (= Sinai) (1 Kings
19). There, like Moses before him, he speaks with God and receives a commission to anoint a new generation of leadership for Israel and Syria. Shortly
thereafter, he selects Elisha as his disciple, who will ultimately be his prophetic
successor (1 Kings 20; cf. 2 Kings 2).

Third, when interpreted in light of the Pentateuch, Elijah is also a kind of
new Moses figure.[2] There are a number of parallels between the lives of these
two prophets:

The Prophet Moses	*The Prophet Elijah*
Pharaoh seeks to kill Moses. (Ex 2:15)	Jezebel seeks to kill Elijah. (1 Kings 19:2)
Moses flees for his life to Midian. (Ex 2:15)	Elijah flees for his life to Horeb. (1 Kings 9:3, 8)
Moses comes to a burning bush. (Ex 3:2)	Elijah comes to a broom tree. (1 Kings 19:4)
Moses goes up Mount Sinai for "forty days and forty nights". (Ex 24:18)	Elijah goes to Mount Horeb/Sinai for "forty days and forty nights". (1 Kings 19:8)
God's glory "passes by" Moses in the "cleft of the rock" of Horeb. (Ex 33:22; cf. 34:6)	God "passed by" Elijah in the "cave" on Mount Horeb. (1 Kings 19:11)

In light of such parallels, it seems clear that Elijah is, so to speak, recapitulating
the life and history of Moses in himself. Like Moses before him, God gives Elijah both great powers and great trials by which to test his faith. At the end of it
all, God is calling Elijah to recognize him not only in the mighty signs of wind,
earthquake, and fire, but in the mystical theophany of the "still small voice"
(1 Kings 19:12).

Fourth and finally, Elijah is unique among all the prophets of the Old Testament insofar as he is the only one said to have ended his prophetic career, not
by dying, but by *ascending into heaven*. This takes place shortly after the death of
King Ahaziah, whose reign is cut short by an illness that Elijah pronounces ter-
minal because of Ahaziah's paganism (2 Kings 1). Elijah then travels with Elisha
by a circuitous route to the Jordan, where he performs one final miracle: like
Joshua before him, he parts the waters of the Jordan River, but instead of going
into the earthly Promised Land, Elijah ascends into heaven: "And as they still
went on and talked, behold, a chariot of fire and horses of fire separated the two
of them. And Elijah went up by a whirlwind into heaven. And Elisha saw it and
he cried, 'My father, my father! the chariots of Israel and its horsemen!' And he
saw him no more" (2 Kings 2:11–12).

[2] See ibid., 433.

The Prophet Elisha (2 Kings 3–14)

The prophet Elisha (Hebrew *Elî-sha*, "My God saves!") continues the ministry of his spiritual father, Elijah, under the same social and cultural conditions. A few brief points help situate his ministry in its context:

First, whereas Elijah ministers during the reign of King Ahab, Elisha's ministry takes place during the reign of several Israelite kings: initially, there is King Jehoram, who becomes king over Israel in Samaria immediately after the death of Ahab (2 Kings 3–8). Although Jehoram is not as wicked as Ahab—he puts away the pillar of Baal, for example—he still "did what was evil in the sight of the LORD" (2 Kings 3:1–3). Next, there is the figure of King Jehu, who is not only anointed king over Israel by the express command of Elisha himself but is commissioned to blot out the whole house of Ahab, including the wicked Jezebel (2 Kings 9:1–10). Jehu goes much farther than simply following this commission, however. He proceeds systematically to execute (1) Jehoram, king of Israel; (2) Ahaziah, king of Judah, and all his relatives; (3) the seventy sons of King Ahab; and (4) all of the prophets of Baal (2 Kings 9–10). It is this situation of utter chaos and bloodshed that leads to the sole instance of a reigning queen in Judah. After the assassination of her son King Ahaziah, Athaliah, a daughter of the northern Israelite dynasty of Omri, takes the Judean throne and slaughters all the "seed royal". Ahaziah's sister Jehosheba, however, hides Ahaziah's young son Joash (short for "Jehoash", cf. 2 Kings 11:2 and 11:21) and raises the boy in secret. When the boy is seven, the high priest Jehoiada musters the palace guard and the whole priesthood to proclaim Jehoash king. Athaliah is executed, and the child Joash takes the throne (2 Kings 11). It is during this (potentially confusing) time when *Joash son of Ahaziah* is reigning over Jerusalem in the south (2 Kings 13:10) and *Jehoash son of Jehoahaz* (also called "Joash", cf. 2 Kings 13:14!) is reigning over Israel in the north (2 Kings 13:10) that Elisha dies (2 Kings 13:14–21). Jehoash, last king of the house of Omri, did not reign for a particularly long time (twelve years), but his tenure witnessed all the major events of Elisha's ministry.

With this context in mind, perhaps the most important aspect of Elisha's ministry that merits highlighting is his status as *the greatest miracle-worker* of all the Old Testament prophets. As the reader will recall, before Elijah ascended into heaven, Elisha, his disciple, begged him that he might "inherit a double share" of the "spirit" of Elijah (2 Kings 2:9). Contrary to the literal sense, this does not mean "twice as much" as Elijah himself but, rather, *twice as much as the other spiritual sons of Elijah*, in the manner of a firstborn son inheriting twice as much as his younger brothers (cf. Deut 21:17). In the wake of receiving this gift, Elisha performs some thirteen recorded (and often unprecedented) miracles:

The Miracles of Elisha (2 Kings 2–13)

1. Parts the Jordan River with Elijah's cloak (2:13–14)
2. Transforms bitter water into fresh by casting salt into it (2:19–22)
3. Fills a wadi in Edom with water to overthrow enemy kings (3:16–18)
4. Provides an unending supply of oil for a poor widow to save her children from being sold into slavery (4:1–7)

5. Prophesies the birth of a son to a barren woman (4:15–17)
6. Raises the son of the woman from the dead (4:18–37)
7. Transforms poisonous pottage into edible stew by casting meal into it (4:38–41)
8. Multiplies bread for hundreds of people (4:42–44)
9. Cleanses Naaman the leper in the waters of the Jordan (5:1–27)
10. Makes an iron axe head float (6:1–7)
11. Blinds the Syrian army and opens the servants' eyes to the heavenly horses and chariots of fire defending Elisha (6:8–23)
12. Brings an end to famine (7:1, 16)
13. Raises a Moabite from the dead through the power of his bones (13:20–21)

What are we to make of this striking series of miracles? On the one hand, they are different from the miracles of Moses, insofar as they are performed more for individuals than for the nation of Israel as a whole. On the other hand, they also show that Elisha himself is a kind of new Elijah, since several of them—the parting of the waters of the Jordan, the miraculous feeding of people, the raising of the dead, the ending of a famine—call to mind the miracles of Elijah himself (2 Kings 2:8, 14; 1 Kings 17:14–16; 2 Kings 4:1–7; 1 Kings 17:17–23; 2 Kings 4:18–36; 1 Kings 18:41–45; 2 Kings 7:1, 16).[3]

Unlike his predecessor, Elijah, however, Elisha's life comes to an end with ordinary death. King Jehoash is present at Elisha's passing and receives from the prophet a blessing of three victories against Syria. It could have been more had Jehoash demonstrated greater zeal (2 Kings 13:14–24). At this time, the southern king in Judah is Amaziah (796–767 B.C.), a devout ruler who also experienced military success against Edom but overreached in provoking open war with the north. In the ensuing battle, Jehoash becomes the only northern king to invade Judah and capture Jerusalem. Nonetheless, he refrains from deposing Amaziah and leaves after looting the Temple and the palace (2 Kings 14:11–14). Obviously, despite his miraculous powers, the influence of the prophet Elisha over the nation and its leaders has had only a mild effect. Amaziah reigns another fifteen years before becoming only the second Davidide (after his father) to be assassinated and replaced by his son. In the north, Jehoash is succeeded on the throne of Israel by Jeroboam II (793–753 B.C.), who defeats and recaptures the realm of Syria and Damascus and restores Israelite sovereignty over the Transjordan to the Dead Sea (2 Kings 14:23–29).

The Fall of Israel: The Assyrian Exile (2 Kings 15–17)

In the wake of the death of Elisha, the northern kingdom of Israel is plagued by a succession of one evil king after another. While in the south, King Azariah/

---

[3] Ibid., 444–45.

Uzziah succeeds his assassinated father on the throne of David and rules righteously for fifty years (792–740 B.C.); in the north, things go from bad to worse, with a string of short-lived and ineffectual rulers, mostly usurpers (1 Kings 15:1–26). Jeroboam's son Zechariah reigns six months before Shallum assassinates and replaces him for one month. Menahem executes Shallum in turn and reigns for ten years. Menahem's son Pekahiah succeeds his father for two years, until Pekah, Israel's top military commander, assassinates him and takes the throne for twenty years (1 Kings 15:27–28).

It is during the time of Pekah, around 722 B.C., that something dramatic happens that changes the face of Israelite history forever: the Assyrian exile. This deportation takes place in two key stages: an initial deportation at the time of Pekah beginning with "Galilee" and "all the land of Naphtali" (2 Kings 15:29) and then a second major deportation, carrying off the remainder of the tribes and scattering them in Gentile territories (2 Kings 17:6). Although the description of this is lengthy, it is worth quoting in full, for it shows that the deeper reason for the Assyrian exile was not just political, but liturgical:

> Then the king of Assyria invaded all the land and came to Samaria, and for three years he besieged it. *In the ninth year of Hoshea the king of Assyria captured Samaria, and he carried the Israelites away to Assyria,* and placed them in Halah, and on the Habor, the river of Gozan, and in the cities of the Medes.
>
> *And this was so, because the sons of Israel had sinned against the* LORD *their God, who had brought them up out of the land of Egypt from under the hand of Pharaoh king of Egypt, and had feared other gods* and walked in the customs of the nations whom the LORD drove out before the sons of Israel, and in the customs which the kings of Israel had introduced. And the sons of Israel did secretly against the LORD their God things that were not right. They built for themselves high places at all their towns, from watchtower to fortified city; they set up for themselves pillars and Asherim on every high hill and under every green tree; and there they burned incense on all the high places, as the nations did whom the LORD carried away before them. And they did wicked things, provoking the LORD to anger, and they served idols, of which the LORD had said to them, "You shall not do this." *Yet the* LORD *warned Israel and Judah by every prophet and every seer,* saying, "Turn from your evil ways and keep my commandments and my statutes, in accordance with all the law which I commanded your fathers, and which I sent to you by my servants the prophets." But they would not listen, but were stubborn, as their fathers had been, who did not believe in the LORD their God. They despised his statutes, and his covenant that he made with their fathers, and the warnings which he gave them. They went after false idols, and became false, and they followed the nations that were round about them, concerning whom the LORD had commanded them that they should not do like them. And they forsook all the commandments of the LORD their God, and *made for themselves molten images of two calves;* and they made an Asherah, and worshiped all the host of heaven, and served Baal. And they burned their sons and their daughters as offerings, and used divination and sorcery, and sold themselves to do evil in the sight of the LORD, provoking him to anger. *Therefore the* LORD *was very angry with Israel, and removed them out of his sight; none was left but the tribe of Judah only.* (2 Kings 17:5–18)

This is the climactic and tragic culmination of everything we have seen so far in the books of Kings: as a result of their persistent apostasy, idolatry, immorality, and even human sacrifice, ten of the twelve tribes are forcibly exiled from the Promised Land to which Moses and Joshua had so long ago led their people. Although the later Babylonian exile of Judah (which we will examine shortly) is the more famous of the two exiles because it was accompanied by the destruction of the Jerusalem Temple, the Assyrian exile of the northern tribes was in some respects more devastating, because it involved the *vast majority* of the tribes of Israel.

Did Any Israelians Remain in the Land?

When read in isolation, the books of Kings give the impression that the Assyrian exile left no Israelians behind and that the present population of the northern territory is wholly descended from the five Gentile nations imported by the Assyrian king (2 Kings 17:24–41). Other biblical texts, as well as archaeology, give a fuller picture. The archaeological remains suggest that many of the poorest of the Israelians—farm laborers—were left behind in the exile and that other elements of the population fled to the safety of Judah, swelling the population of Jerusalem under Hezekiah (696–642 B.C.) to unprecedented proportions. This necessitated a major expansion of the city's defensive walls. Hezekiah (2 Chron 30:10–12, 18) and possibly Josiah (2 Chron 35:18) made forays into the north in which they invited the Israelian population to join them in worship at Jerusalem. In the New Testament, we see one example of such an Israelian in the south in the figure of the prophetess Anna, who is said to be "of the tribe of Asher" (Lk 2:36).

Moreover, unlike the Babylonian exile, which eventually came to an end with the return of the Judeans, the king of Assyria who deported the Israelian population to dispersed locations in the far north of his empire (Sargon II, 722–705 B.C.) also resettled the land with five Gentile ethnic groups from Mesopotamia and the northwestern Levant (1 Kings 17:24–41).

These peoples brought their gods with them, but they also began to worship what they perceived to be the god of the land of Israel, the LORD. So they established a syncretistic religious pattern not much different from that practiced by the Israelians themselves. The population of the northern territory became known after the exile as *the Samaritans*—after the capital city of the north, Samaria. The Samaritans were ethnically mixed descendants of the remnant Israelian population and the Gentile immigrants imported by Sargon II of Assyria (722–705 B.C.). They attempted to assist the returned Judeans in the rebuilding of the Temple after the Babylonian exile (587–537 B.C.) but were rebuffed by the Judeans (Ezra 4:1–5). In response, they built their own, rival temple on Mount Gerizim in the ancient territory of Ephraim. By the time of the New Testament, they had abandoned any paganism and were devout in their worship of the Lord, but they rejected the Jerusalem Temple (cf. Jn 4:19–21). In light of such history, it is little wonder that there was such tension between the Jews ("Judeans") and Samaritans in later centuries, since the latter were a living reminder of the idolatry of the northern kingdom and the decimation of the once glorious kingdom of David and Solomon in the wake of Israel's sin.

The Fall of Judah: The Babylonian Exile (2 Kings 18–25)

With Israel now gone, Judah alone remains as the successor state of the Davidic empire. Unlike the description of Israel in the north, which never bears witness to a single righteous king, the remaining chapters of 2 Kings bear witness to the "struggle for the soul" of the southern kingdom of Judah in the form of both extremely righteous and extremely wicked rulers.

At the very forefront of this righteous cultic renewal stands the energetic *King Hezekiah* (ca. 729–686 B.C.), who leads the southern kingdom in a major moral and political resurgence (1 Kings 18). In contrast to his father, Ahaz, Hezekiah purges Judah of paganism and also finally removes the illicit shrines that have been tolerated since the latter days of Solomon. With no immediate military threat from the north (Israel and Syria having been decimated by Assyria) and with a southern population now swollen with Israelian refugees, Hezekiah feels strong enough to dominate the surrounding territories and challenge Assyria itself. This latter effort is only partially successful, however: it provokes a costly war that leaves Hezekiah's realm much weaker.

Sennacherib, king of Assyria, invades Judah in 701 B.C. Sennacherib's own perspective on the campaign is recorded on at least two extant clay prisms; the Judean perspective is recorded in Scripture. Piecing the two accounts together and allowing for the bias of the Assyrian scribes, it appears that Sennacherib conquered the entire countryside of Judah with the exception of Jerusalem itself. He then demanded more tribute of Hezekiah than Hezekiah was able to provide (even after stripping the gold off the Temple doors, 2 Kings 18:16), so he sent his army to Jerusalem, also (2 Kings 18:17–35). There he mocked Hezekiah publicly. Hezekiah did penance and appealed to a new prophet on the scene— the famous figure of *Isaiah*—for an oracle (2 Kings 19:1–7). Isaiah prophesied defeat for the Assyrians, and "that night the angel of the LORD went forth, and slew a hundred and eighty-five thousand in the camp of the Assyrians", likely a reference to a providentially sent plague or epidemic within the enemy army (2 Kings 19:35). Assyrian accounts are silent about the plague, but tacitly admit that Sennacherib withdrew without capturing Jerusalem.

After the account of the famous siege of Jerusalem by Sennacherib, the Bible records Hezekiah's interactions with Isaiah the prophet later in his reign, including a miraculous healing when the king is close to death (2 Kings 20:1–11); and, even more significantly, a prophecy of the future Babylonian exile, in which what happened to the northern tribes at the hands of Assyria will one day happen to the remaining southern tribes at the hands of Babylon (2 Kings 20:12–19).

Tragically, after the death of King Hezekiah, all of his religious reforms are undone by his wicked son Manasseh (ca. 696–642 B.C.), who is remembered as the most evil of all the kings of Judah. His fifty-five-year reign constitutes a moral disaster from which Judah never fully recovers (2 Kings 21). His son

Amon reigns after him (642–640 B.C.) and continues his same policies (2 Kings 21:19–26). The fact that Amon was named after the Egyptian sun-god and chief deity gives the reader some indication of his father's, Manasseh's, religious sympathies: according to the Bible, he worships "all the host of heaven" (2 Kings 21:3). Perhaps Amon's paganizing becomes too much even for his court to tolerate: he becomes the third sitting Davidide to be assassinated and replaced by his son.

Like Hezekiah before him, King Josiah's thirty-one-year reign (640–609 B.C.) marks a religious high point in the memory of Judah (2 Kings 22). He begins cultic reforms and a restoration of the Temple, during which a copy of the "Book of the Law" is found—often thought to be at least a copy of Deuteronomy, if not the entire Torah (2 Kings 22:3–13). The public reading of this book to the king and people prompts a national repentance, and Josiah intensifies the reforms that were already underway, destroying illicit and pagan shrines, cleansing the Temple of pagan elements introduced by Manasseh and Amon, and suppressing cultic prostitution and child sacrifice. Significantly, the list of King Josiah's reforms reveals that an appalling degree of syncretism and pure paganism has been tolerated or encouraged within Jerusalem and the Temple itself by previous administrations (2 Kings 23:4–20). Once again, the sin of idolatry and immorality is not unique to the north.

The high point of Josiah's reign is a national Passover celebration hosted by the king in Jerusalem, which—at first glance—seems to signal the liturgical restoration of the people of God (2 Kings 23:21–23). But Josiah's reforms are too little, too late. They cannot reverse the course of the nation, and Judah, too, will end up in exile. At the end of his reign, Josiah thinks himself strong enough to challenge the army of Pharaoh Neco on the plains of Megiddo in northern Israel. He is defeated and slain in battle (2 Kings 24:28–30). His body is brought back to Jerusalem, and he is succeeded by his son Jehoahaz (609 B.C.) for three months, until the pharaoh arrives at Jerusalem, takes Jehoahaz hostage, and places his brother Eliakim (renamed Jehoakim, 609–598 B.C.) on the throne (2 Kings 23:31–35). During Jehoakim's brief reign, Babylon defeats Egypt to become the regional power and forces Jehoakim into vassalage. Jehoakim rebels, but he dies before having to face the Babylonian army, which appears three months into the reign of his son Jehoiachin (598–597 B.C., 2 Kings 24). The Babylonians conquer Jerusalem, deport the middle and upper classes, and leave Zedekiah (597–586 B.C.), Jehoiachin's brother, as king of a vassal state, while Jehoiachin himself is taken in chains to Babylon. Not to be outdone, King Zedekiah himself rebels ten years later, prompting Nebuchadnezzar of Babylon to return and raze Jerusalem and its Temple to the ground, leaving a certain Gedaliah, a Judean aristocrat, as governor of a decimated territory. Gedaliah, in turn, is assassinated by a certain Ishmael, a military captain of royal blood. Most of the remaining population flees to Egypt to escape retaliation from the Babylonians (2 Kings 25). Despite the pathetic condition to which the people of Judah have been reduced, the books of Kings end with a hopeful reference to the fact that, after thirty-seven years of exile, Evil-merodach of Babylon releases Jehoiachin, king of Judah, from prison, allows him to eat at the royal table, and gives him a living allowance from the crown for the rest of his life.

Historical Issues in 1–2 Kings

The Origins of Kings and the Prophet Jeremiah

Like other of the historical books, the books of Kings are *anonymous*. Unlike the books of the Pentateuch and the prophets, there is no strong religious tradition about their authorship. One rabbinic tradition attributes Kings to Jeremiah.[4] While there are similarities in language and perspective between Kings and Jeremiah, most scholars conclude that the rabbinic attribution is unlikely. One exception is the American scholar Richard Elliott Friedman and his students, who have argued that evidence points to Jeremiah's scribe, Baruch, as the editor of the historical books of the Old Testament (cf. Jer 36:4).[5]

1–2 Kings and the Deuteronomistic History (DtrH)

During the zenith of source criticism of the Pentateuch in the late nineteenth and early twentieth centuries, attempts were made to trace the putative Pentateuchal sources all the way into Kings, but these efforts did not meet with great success. In the middle of the twentieth century, there was a sea change in the scholarly perspective on the books of Samuel and Kings due to the work of German scholar Martin Noth, who advanced the view that the books of Deuteronomy through 2 Kings were in fact one historical composition, put together by a single editor. This editor, referred to as *the Deuteronomist*, shaped and collected earlier materials to tell the history of Israel through the lens of the Mosaic covenant in its Deuteronomic form.

Noth's basic theory of *a Deuteronomistic History*—often abbreviated by scholars as DtrH—was widely accepted, although usually with variations. For example, Harvard scholar Frank Moore Cross revised Noth's view by suggesting there was not one, but two Deuteronomists: one who edited together an optimistic narrative from Deuteronomy through the reign of Josiah (2 Kings 22–23); and a second who later redacted the whole composition from a more pessimistic viewpoint, adding the last chapters after the defeat of Josiah and the exile of Judah (2 Kings 24–25). Cross' "double redaction" view is standard in North American scholarship. In European scholarship, it is more common to find variations on the views of Rudolf Smend, who argued for a triple redaction: a basic Deuteronomistic history from Deuteronomy through 2 Kings, known as DtrG in German (G = *Grundschrift*), subsequently edited by someone with a strong prophetic perspective (the "prophetic" redaction, DtrP) and finally by a scribe interested primarily in the law (the "nomistic" redaction, DtrN).

There are certainly common themes, language, and motifs that unite the books of Deuteronomy through 2 Kings. At the same time, we have seen that each book has unique characteristics and emphases: they are by no means homogeneous. Furthermore, there are also themes and motifs that connect the

---

[4] Babylonian Talmud, *Baba Bathra* 14b, in Isidore Epstein, ed., *The Babylonian Talmud*, 35 vols. (London: Soncino, 1935–1952).

[5] See Richard Elliott Friedman, *Who Wrote the Bible?* (San Francisco: HarperOne, 1997).

historical books with earlier books of the Pentateuch, especially Genesis and Exodus. The theories of composition of a "Deuteronomistic History" can be useful in highlighting the overarching unity of Deuteronomy through 2 Kings but should not obscure the individuality of each book or the equally important unity of the "Primary History", Genesis through 2 Kings.

The Chronology of the Kings of Israel and Judah

The sacred author of the books of Kings pays a great deal of attention to chronological matters and has taken pains carefully to note the date of accession and length of reign of each king of Israel and Judah. However, a simple tabulation of the resulting figures produces many puzzling discrepancies. These are due to co-regencies (periods of dual kingship of father and son) and differences in counting years between Israel and Judah. It seems likely that one of the kingdoms observed the new year in the spring (the month Nisan), and the other in the fall (month Tishri). The two kingdoms probably also differed in their calculation of the year of accession, one following Egyptian practice, in which the entire year in which the king rose to the throne was considered the first year of his reign, and the other following Mesopotamian practice, in which the king's first year did not begin until the new year festival following his coronation. Scholarly opinions vary as to which kingdom followed which calendrical practices. Edwin Thiele[6] and Gershon Galil[7] have both worked out plausible chronologies of the dual monarchies, based on slightly different assumptions. Thiele's chronology, followed in this book, is as follows:

HOUSE OF JUDAH (south)		HOUSE OF ISRAEL (north)	
Rehoboam	930–913 B.C.	Jeroboam I	930–910 B.C.
Abijam	913–911	Nadab	910–909
Asa	911–870	Baasha	909–886
Jehoshaphat	873–848	Elah	886–885
Jehoram	848–841	Zimri	885
Ahaziah	841	Omri	885–874
Athaliah	841–835	Ahab	874–853
Joash	835–796	Ahaziah	853–852
Amaziah	796–767	Jehoram	852–841
Azariah/Uzziah	792–740	Jehu	841–814
Jotham	750–731	Jehoahaz	814–798
Ahaz	735–715	Joash	798–782
Hezekiah	729–686	Jeroboam II	793–753
Manasseh	696–642	Zechariah	753
Amon	642–640	Shallum	752
Josiah	640–609	Menahem	752–742

[6] Edwin Richard Thiele, *The Mysterious Numbers of the Hebrew Kings*, new rev. ed. (Grand Rapids, Mich.: Zondervan, 1984).

[7] Gershon Galil, *The Chronology of the Kings of Israel and Judah*, Studies in the History and Culture of the Ancient Middle East 9 (Leiden: Brill Academic, 1996).

Jehoahaz	609	Pekahiah	742–740
Jehoiakim	609–598	Pekah	740–732
Jehoiachin	598–597	Hoshea	732–722
Zedekiah	597–586	*Fall of Samaria in 722 B.C.	

*Destruction of Jerusalem in 586 B.C.

The Historical Value of Kings and the Debate over King Solomon

The most controversial historical aspect of the book of Kings by far is the description of the reign of Solomon. The biblical account of Solomon's wealth and empire cannot be confirmed as yet by external sources or archaeology. Accordingly, as discussed in the previous chapter, the Copenhagen School and other biblical "minimalists" regard the reign of Solomon as fictitious. However, the following observations need to be taken into account when reckoning with the lack of explicit external evidence:

1. *Scanty Archaeological Evidence for Levantine Kingdoms of the Period:* It cannot be overstressed that it is not only the kingdom of Solomon in the region of Canaan for which we lack evidence. To the contrary, contemporary archaeology has unearthed precious little evidence for *any* of the kingdoms in the Levant during the tenth century B.C. (the era of David and Solomon) from Egyptian or Mesopotamian sources because these great powers were in eclipse and had little interaction with the region. (The Levant is the region of the Eastern Mediterranean that today comprises the nations of Lebanon, Israel, Jordan, Syria, and Palestine.) This both explains why the Davidic-Solomonic empire was able to flourish in this time period and also why it is not well-attested in the extant sources from these other countries.

2. *The Brevity of Solomon's Glory:* The wealth and power attributed to Solomon in Scripture probably reflect only a brief period at the height of his reign, so a span of well less than forty short years (1 Kings 11:42). Later in his tenure, the Bible itself notes a decline in his wealth and power. The figures given for his income are less than those recorded by some of the kings of the "great empires" (Egypt, Assyria, Babylon), and the dimensions and design of his Temple and various halls are typical of Phoenician-influenced monumental buildings in the ancient Near East built in this time period—smaller than those in Egypt, larger than those in lesser realms (cf. 1 Kings 7). In other words, the description of his realm is in keeping with the *realia* of the ancient Near East in the tenth century B.C.[8]

3. *The Problem of Archaeology in Jerusalem Proper:* The best places to look for archaeological remains of Solomon's reign—above, all Jerusalem—are often very difficult to excavate due to practical or political reasons. In any event, most of what remained of Solomon's works would have been destroyed in the numerous invasions and destructions that befell Judah and Jerusalem subsequent

---

[8] See esp. John Monson, "1 Kings", in *1 & 2 Kings, 1 & 2 Chronicles, Ezra, Nehemiah, Esther*, vol. 3 of *Zondervan Illustrated Bible Backgrounds Commentary*, ed. John H. Walton (Grand Rapids, Mich.: Zondervan, 2009), 27–40.

to his time period (think here of the destruction by Babylon in 587 B.C., narrated in 2 Kings 25). Nonetheless, the claim that there is no monumental architecture attesting his and David's reign (Megiddo, Hazor, Gezer, cf. 1 Kings 9:15) is based on the controversial low dating scheme of archaeologist Israel Finkelstein and others, which is already falling into disfavor with a majority of scholars.

4. *The Ambiguity of Solomon:* Biblical minimalists who argue that Solomon is a legendary ideal rather than an actual historical king fail to take seriously the fact that Solomon was an ambiguous figure in Israel's history, remembered as much for his grievous offenses against the Deuteronomic Law as for his glory (1 Kings 10:14—11:43; cf. Deut 17:16–17). In light of the dark and tragic end to Solomon's life, there need not have been any compelling theological reason for the sacred author to invent the glory of his reign if there had been no factual basis for it. He does not do so for many other kings, who are simply described as wicked. Instead, the sacred author is honest about the defects and humiliations even of righteous kings whom he strongly commends, such as Hezekiah and Josiah.

Explicit External Evidence for Israelite and Judean Kings

Although there is admittedly a lack of explicit evidence for Solomon, the situation changes dramatically when we turn to the later kings of Israel and Judah. After the reign of Solomon, the dual monarchies were frequently defeated by their neighbors and the "great empires" in Egypt and Mesopotamia. The positive result of these defeats from the perspective of historical research is several excellent attestations of Israelite or Judean monarchs and/or events in their reigns from external ancient Near Eastern records. Thus, there are many events in Kings that can be dated securely by external sources. Nine major ones are listed in the chart below:

Dated Events in Kings Established by External Witnesses			
Date	Event	Recorded on	Text
853 B.C.	Ahab fights in the Battle of Qarqar.	The "Kurkh Monolith", a stele erected by Shalmaneser III of Assyria	"2,000 chariots, and 10,000 soldiers belonging to Ahab, the Israelite"
841	Jehu pays tribute to Shalmaneser III of Assyria.	The "Black Obelisk" of Shalmaneser III of Assyria	"The tribute of Jehu, son of Omri, silver, gold, bowls of gold, chalices of gold, cups of gold, vases of gold, lead, a sceptre for the king, and spear-shafts, I have received."
796	Jehoash of Israel pays tribute to Adad-nirari III.	The Tel al-Rimah Stele of Adad-Nirari III	"I received the tribute of Jehoash the Samarian."

(continued)

Dated Events in Kings Established by External Witnesses (*continued*)			
Date	Event	Recorded on	Text
738	Menahem of Israel pays tribute to Tiglath-Pileser III of Assyria.	Annals of Tiglath-Pileser III	"Mi-ni-ḫi.-im-mi of the city of Sa-mi-ri-na-ai" [= Menahem of Samaria]"
733/32	Ahaz of Judah pays tribute to Tiglath-Pileser III of Assyria.	Building inscription in clay of Tiglath-Pileser III	"I receieved the tribute of … Jeho-ahaz [= Ahaz] of Judah."
731	Hoshea of Israel pays tribute to Tiglath-Pileser of Assyria.	Inscription of Tiglath-Pileser	"The House of Omri [*Bit-Humria*, = Israel] .. overthrew their king Pekah [Pa-qa-ha] and I placed Hoshea [A-ú –si'] as king over them. I received from them 10 talents of gold, [?]- talents of silver as their [tri]bute and brought them to Assyria."
722	Samari falls to Shalmaneser V; the people are exiled by Sargon II.	Sargon II's inscription on the walls of the royal palace at Dur-Sarraku (Khorsabad)	"In my first year of reign … the people of Samaria … to the number of 27,290 … I carried away."
609	Pharaoh Neco and Josiah clash at Megiddo.	Herodotus	"Necos … also engaged in a pitched battle at Magdolos [= Megiddo] with the Syrians [i.e., Israelites], and conquered them."
587/86	The fall of Jerusalem to Nebuchadnezzar	The Babylonian Chronicles	"In the seventh year in the month Chislev the king of Babylon assembled his army, and … he laid siege to the city of Judah. On the second day of the month of Adar he conquered the city and took the king [= Jeconiah] prisoner. He installed in his place a king of his own choice [= Zedekiah], and after he had received rich tribute, he sent forth to Babylon."

With the books of Kings, we come to some of the richest confirmations of contextual plausibility from archaeology that we possess.[9] Besides these externally attested synchronisms in the chart above, students of the Bible should be familiar with some of the more famous inscriptions or archaeological finds that correspond to data recorded in Kings:

1. *The Pharaoh Shoshenq Stele at Megiddo*: According to the books of Kings, "Shishak king of Egypt" invaded Judah in the fifth year of the reign of Rehoboam (1 Kings 14:25). This is almost certainly Pharaoh Shoshenq I, who recorded a

---

[9] See ibid., 2–109, and Ian Provan, "2 Kings", in *1 & 2 Kings*, 111–219.

military campaign into Canaan/Palestine on the walls of the Temple of Amun in Karnak, listing Israelite cities among those he conquered. Remains of a stele of his, probably set up to commemorate the campaign, have been found at Megiddo, a city in northern Israel and the site of some remarkable archaeological work.

2. *The Stele of King Mesha of Moab*: According to the books of Kings, King Mesha of Moab rebelled against Israel after the death of Omri (2 Kings 3). Remarkably, Mesha's own account of his rebellion is recorded in part on the famous Mesha Stele, the beginning of which reads:

Source: commons.wikimedia.org

Line Drawing of Mesha Stele

I am Mesha, son of Kemoshyath, the king of Moab, the Dibonite. My father was king of Moab thirty years, and I reigned after my father. And I built this high-place for Kemosh in QRH ("the citadel"), a high place of [sal-] vation because he saved me from all the kings, and because he let me be victorious over all my adversaries. *Omri was king of Israel and he oppressed Moab for many days because Kemosh was angry with his land.* And his son replaced him; and he also said, "I will oppress Moab". In my days he spoke thus. But I was victorious over him and his house. And Israel suffered everlasting destruction.[10]

The inscription goes on to record several battles against Israel and may mention Judah as well under the title "House of David" (*bit-dawid*).

3. *The Inscription of King Hazael of Aram-Damascus*: In 1993 an inscription apparently from Hazael, the king of Aram-Damascus (Syria), was discovered at Tel Dan (ancient Dan) in northern Israel, in which Hazael appears to claim credit for Jehu's assassination of Jehoram of Israel and Ahaziah of Judah. The pertinent lines of the text read as follows:

---

[10] Translated by Kent P. Jackson in J. Andrew Dearman, *Studies in the Mesha Inscription and Moab* (Atlanta: Scholars Press, 1989), 93–95.

And the king of I[s-]rael entered previously in my father's land. [And] Hadad made me king. And Hadad went in front of me, [and] I departed from [the] seven [...] of my kingdom, and I slew [seve]nty kin[gs], who harnessed thou[sands of cha-]riots and thousands of horsemen (or: horses). *[I killed Jeho] ram son of [Ahab] king of Israel, and I killed [Ahaz]iahu son of [Jehoram kin]g of the House of David.* And I set [their towns into ruins and turned] their land into [desolation].[11]

The Tel Dan Inscription with "David" highlighted

The text is the first indisputable mention of David ("house of David", *bit-dawid*) outside of Scripture. David is recognized as the founder of the dynasty of Judah.

4. *The Black Obelisk of King Shalmaneser III of Assyria*: Jehu is perhaps the only ancient Israelite monarch for whom we have a contemporary likeness. He is portrayed here bowing down in obeisance while bringing tribute to Shalmaneser III of Assyria on the famous "Black Obelisk":

The Black Obelisk: Jehu bowing to Shalmaneser III

Such external evidence corroborates what the books of Kings themselves presuppose: the kings of Israel and Judah are historical figures of flesh and blood, real men and not figments of postexilic Jewish imagination.

5. *The Tunnel of King Hezekiah and the Siloam Inscription*: According to the biblical history, Hezekiah cut a tunnel to convey the water of the spring Gihon inside the city walls (2 Kings 20:2). Previously it flowed outside, down to the Brook Kidron, and therefore was unavailable to the populace during times of siege. Astonishingly, this tunnel has been found; it remains intact and still flows

---

[11] A. Biran and J. Naveh, "The Tel Dan Inscription: A New Fragment", *Israel Exploration Journal* 45.1 (1995): 1–18.

with the water of the Gihon. In 1838, the so-called "Siloam Inscription" was discovered near the mouth of the lower entrance of the tunnel. Carved into the rock wall in archaic Hebrew, it commemorated the completion of the conduit:

> And this is the story of the tunnel while ... the axes were against each other and while three cubits were left to cut [?] ... the voice of a man called to his counterpart, there was [?] in the rock, on the right ... and on the day of the tunnel [completion] the stonecutters struck each man toward his counterpart, ax against ax. Then flowed water from the source to the pool for 1200 cubits.[12]

The Siloam Inscription: commemorating the completion of Hezekiah's water tunnel

6. King Sennacherib of Assyria's Depiction of the Capture of Lachish: Hezekiah was a vigorous military and political leader who built up Judah to the point that it was able to challenge Assyrian domination. Besides Jerusalem itself, the most heavily fortified city in Judah was Lachish. The capture of Lachish by Sennacherib of Assyria is mentioned in 2 Kings 18:13–14 and portrayed extensively in a relief that once adorned Sennacherib's palace in Assyria. From the hail of stones and torches being hurled down by the Judean defenders of Lachish, it appears that the Assyrians encountered stiff resistance and were proud enough of their hard-earned victory to commemorate it within the king's own palace.

Line drawing of the Assyrian Lachish Relief

7. King Sennacherib's Prisms: Sennacherib was not able to capture Jerusalem, however, even if he brought Hezekiah to the point of acknowledging

---

[12] James Pritchard, *Ancient Near Eastern Texts relating to the Old Testament with Supplement*, 3rd ed. (Princeton, N.J.: Princeton University Press, 1969), 321.

Taylor Prism (a.k.a. Sennacherib Prism)

his suzerainty. Sennacherib's own account of his campaign against Judah is found on an inscribed clay prism, called the Taylor Prism or the Sennacherib Prism. It reads as follows:

> *Because Hezekiah, king of Judah, would not submit to my yoke, I came up against him, and by force of arms and by the might of my power I took 46 of his strong fenced cities; and of the smaller towns which were scattered about, I took and plundered a countless number. From these places I took and carried off 200,156 persons, old and young, male and female, together with horses and mules, asses and camels, oxen and sheep, a countless multitude; and Hezekiah himself I shut up in Jerusalem, his capital city, like a bird in a cage, building towers round the city to hem him in, and raising banks of earth against the gates, so as to prevent escape.... Then upon Hezekiah there fell the fear of the power of my arms, and he sent out to me the chiefs and the elders of Jerusalem with 30 talents of gold and 800 talents of silver, and diverse treasures, a rich and immense booty.... All these things were brought to me at Nineveh, the seat of my government.*[13]

The biblical and Assyrian accounts indicate that Sennacherib did not succeed in taking Jerusalem, though he attempted to do so; and that Hezekiah paid tribute to Sennacherib at some point. Sennacherib could not be expected to record the plague on his troops described in 2 Kings 19:35, but he attributes the break in the siege to Hezekiah's submission. Both Assyrian and biblical records are agreed that he never campaigned against Judah again and that he died at the hand of one or more of his sons and was succeeded by his son Esarhaddon (2 Kings 19:37).

8. *The Lachish Ostraca*: Lachish again figures prominently in the invasion and capture of Judah by the Babylonians over a century later. In 1935 archaeologists at Lachish discovered the "Lachish Ostraca", clay shards inscribed with ink that, when pieced together, formed the remains of at least nine letters to a certain Joash, the military commander of Lachish, from a junior officer Hosaiah stationed in an outlying town. The letters reveal the tense military situation just prior to the Babylonian invasion. In one

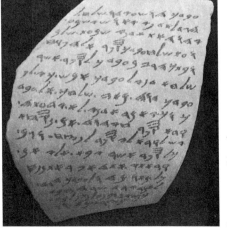

Lachish Ostacon 3

---

[13] Daniel David Luckenbill, *The Annals of Sennacherib* (Eugene, Ore.: Wipf & Stock, 2005), 32–33, 70–71.

letter Hosaiah complains that they can no longer see the military signal fires from Azekah, one of the major Judean fortress cities (Jer 34:7). The text of the third letter is the longest extant (the traditional transliteration of names in parentheses):

> *Your servant, Hoshayahu (Hoshaiah), sent to inform my lord, Yaush (Joash): May YHWH cause my lord to hear tidings of peace and tidings of good.* And now, open the ear of your servant concerning the letter which you sent to your servant last evening because the heart of your servant is ill since your sending it to your servant. And inasmuch as my lord said "Don't you know how to read a letter?" As YHWH lives if anyone has ever tried to read me a letter! And as for every letter that comes to me, if I read it. And furthermore, I will grant it as nothing. And to your servant it has been reported saying: The commander of the army Konyahu (Coniah) son of Elnatan (Elnathan), has gone down to go to Egypt and he sent to commandeer Hodawyahu (Hodaviah) son of Ahiyahu (Ahijah) and his men from here. And as for the letter of Tobiyahu (Tobiah or Tobijah), the servant of the king, which came to Sallum (Shallum), the son of Yaddua (Jaddua), from the prophet, saying, "Be on guard!" your ser[va]nt is sending it to my lord.[14]

9. *The Babylonian Prison Records of King Jehoaiachin*: The books of Kings conclude by mentioning the release of King Jehoiachin (Jeconiah) from prison and the provision of food and a living allowance for him (2 Kings 25:29–30). In the early 1900s, excavations of ancient Babylon unearthed ration tablets recording the provisions given to Jehoiachin and his five royal sons. One of the tablets reads:

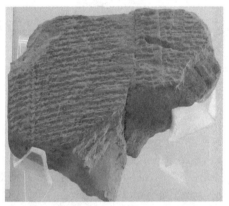

Source: en.wikipedia.org

10 [*sila* of oil] to *Ia-ku-u-ki-nu* (=Jehoiachin), the son of the king of *Ia-ku-du* (=Judah), 2 1/2 *sila* [of oil] for the five sons of the king of *Ia-ku-du* (=Judah).[15]

Jehoiachin Ration Tablet

In sum, the large number of external witnesses to persons, places, and events during the reign of the kings provide remarkable and unparalleled external support for the overall historicity of the narratives in 1–2 Kings and enable scholars to establish the basic chronology of this period with a fair degree of certainty.

Theological Issues in 1–2 Kings

Solomon and the Temple as Culmination of Salvation History

The account of the glory of Solomon's reign and the building of the Temple (1 Kings 3–8) represents the high point of the historical narrative of the Old

---

[14] Translation from Shmuel Aḥituv, *Echoes from the Past* (Jerusalem: CARTA Jerusalem, 2008), 63.
[15] James B. Pritchard, *The Ancient Near East: An Anthology of Texts and Pictures* (Princeton, N.J.: Princeton University Press, 2010), 205.

Testament from Genesis through Kings. Israel experiences a kind of preliminary fulfillment of the promises of all previous divine covenants.

The Adamic or Creation Covenant. In the overview above, we have already noted the details that serve to identify the Temple as a new Eden. Likewise Solomon is a new Adam figure, a priest-king who enjoys the status of a son of God (2 Sam 7:14; cf. Gen 1:27–28; 2:15). As a sacral king, he embodies the nation and, in a sense, lifts it up with him to experience the blessings of divine sonship.

The Noahic Covenant. The covenant with Noah was itself a partial restoration of the covenant with Adam, so all the motifs that serve to connect Solomon and the Temple to the Adamic/Creation Covenant also indirectly include ties to the Noahic economy, though these are somewhat less clear. Peculiar to the Noahic covenant is the construction of the ark, a "floating Eden" or zoological garden built with three levels (Gen 6:16). Scholars have noted a symbolic connection with the Temple, which likewise was built with three levels (1 Kings 6:6).

The Abrahamic Covenant. Solomon is the descendant of Abraham through whom the promise of kingship and suzerainty "of a multitude of nations" (Gen 17:5) is fulfilled. The three great promises given to Abraham: (1) great nationhood, (2) great name (= royalty), and (3) universal blessing all begin to be fulfilled under Solomon, who leads Israel to its greatest extent as a nation (1 Kings 4:20; cf. Gen 22:17;), manifests international suzerainty (1 Kings 4:21; cf. Gen 22:17b), and blesses all nations by bestowing on them the gift of his divine wisdom (1 Kings 4:29–34; cf. Gen 22:18). The Temple itself is built on Mount Moriah, the site of the sacrifice of Isaac (cf. Gen 22:2; cf. 2 Chron 3:1), a fact not lost on the rabbis, who thought of the Temple sacrifices as memorials of the *Aqedah* (see above on Gen 22).

The Mosaic Covenant. Solomon is a new Moses figure, who ascends a mountain (Zion, not Sinai) to receive divine instruction (wisdom, not law), which he conveys to his subjects (the nations, not just Israel). The key *foci* of the Mosaic liturgy, the ark, sacred vessels, and perhaps the Tabernacle itself (1 Kings 8:4), are brought into the Temple. This action along with the same decorative motifs and the glory cloud of YHWH (cf. Ex 40:34; 1 Kings 8:10) mark the Temple as the successor of the Tabernacle. It is the central sanctuary at the place "which the LORD your God will choose, to make his name dwell there", according to the prescriptions of Moses in Deuteronomy (Deut 12:11). During his dedicatory prayer over the Temple, Solomon states that all the blessings of the Mosaic covenant have been fulfilled at this moment (1 Kings 8:56).

The Davidic Covenant. The completion of the Temple under David's son Solomon fulfills one of the central elements of the Davidic covenant: the building of a "house" for YHWH (2 Sam 7:13). As Solomon stands to dedicate the Temple, every good thing promised to David seems to have been fulfilled (2 Sam 7:8–16). Subsequently, every good Davidic king is to be a Temple (re)builder and the cultic leader (or "first worshipper") of the kingdom. Thus we see that liturgical concerns are at the forefront of the sacred author's descriptions of the most commendable sons of David, such as Kings Joash, Hezekiah, and Josiah.

For a brief moment of Israel's history, then, after the dedication of the Temple, under the rule of Solomon, all the various covenant promises of the Old

Testament find a kind of temporal (and temporary) fulfillment. The Temple is central to this fulfillment: it is the new Eden, the new ark, the new Moriah, the new Tabernacle. It is the place of communion with God, where divine sonship, by means of covenant worship, may be experienced. One begins to understand, then, the importance of the Temple to salvation history, the utter catastrophe of its destruction at the end of the books of Kings (2 Kings 25:8–21), and the remarkable nature of Jesus' claim to be the New Temple (Jn 2:19–21).

The Relationship between Mosaic and Davidic Covenants in Kings

With this overarching salvation-historical framework in mind, it is also helpful to emphasize that there is a complex interplay between the Mosaic and Davidic covenants taking place in the books of Kings. Although contemporary readers can sometimes blur these differences by fusing the various covenants into one "Old Covenant", there are significant differences between the Mosaic and Davidic economies, some of which are summarized in the following table.

Notice here that, properly speaking, the Davidic covenant does not "replace" the Mosaic when its economy is established under David and Solomon. Instead, the Mosaic is *incorporated into* the Davidic covenant and *transformed* by the Davidic covenant.

	Mosaic	Davidic
Location	Mt. Sinai	Mt. Zion
Sanctuary	Tabernacle	Temple
Primary Sacrifice	Burnt Offering	Thank Offering
Form of Instruction	Law	Wisdom
Polity	National	International

The concrete relationship between the two covenants is illustrated by the cultic act of *bringing of the Tabernacle and other furnishings and vessels of the Mosaic liturgy into the Temple of the Son of David*:

> Then Solomon assembled the elders of Israel and all the heads of the tribes ... in Jerusalem.... And they brought up the ark of the LORD, the tent of meeting [= the Tabernacle of Moses], and all the holy vessels that were in the tent. (1 Kings 8:1, 4)

By means of such actions, the visible signs of the Mosaic covenant are assimilated or incorporated into the Davidic. The Mosaic covenant anticipated a "place which the LORD your God shall choose, to make his name dwell there" (Deut 12:11); and this place is permanently specified as Zion/Jerusalem by the Davidic covenant (Ps 132:1–18, esp. 13–14). The Mosaic anticipated Israel's domination of other nations (Deut 15:6), under a king who meditates on the law (Deut 17:18–20; cf. 1 Kings 2:1–4). At their best, David and Solomon fulfilled this vision. However, the Davidic covenant has a larger economy: it describes God's rule over the nations through his covenantal son, the Davidic king (Ps 2:1–12; 18:43; 89:20–27), whereas the Mosaic structured only God's direct rule over Israel. Under the Davidic covenant, Israel is still obliged to obey the Mosaic, and, indeed, the Davidic king is obliged to follow the law and ensure that the nation does likewise (1 Kings 2:1–4). The nations under vassalage to the Davidic king are not so obliged, however: for them, the Solomonic wisdom literature must suffice to light the path toward the Creator God (1 Kings 4:34), whom they are encouraged to worship in the Jerusalem Temple (1 Kings 8:41–43; Ps 47:1, 9; 86:9; 117:1).

Hence, the narrative of Kings may be described as a complex interplay between the Mosaic and Davidic covenants, in which the two covenants are complementary rather than contradictory. For example, during the reign of Solomon, Israel experiences the blessings of the Mosaic covenant (cf. Deut 28:1–14; 1 Kings 4:1–34); for most of the rest of Kings, it experiences the curses (Deut 28:15–54), culminating in exile. Throughout Kings, the curses for disobedience to the Mosaic covenant in Deuteronomy drive Israel and Judah toward judgment and destruction: this is the dominant theme, which Martin Noth and others acknowledge by describing it as the "Deuteronomistic History". At the same time, however, there is a motif of hope that does not dominate and yet is not overcome, and this hopeful motif derives from the irrevocable promises made in the covenant with David (1 Sam 7:14–16). This note is sounded several times throughout Kings (1 Kings 11:12–13, 32–36, 39; 15:5; 2 Kings 8:19; 19:34; 20:5; 21:7), and the final vignette of the entire narrative—when Evil-merodach frees Jehoiachin from prison—clearly portends hope for the people of Israel, since the Davidic line has not been cut off and God is still showing signs of mercy to the Davidic heir. In sum, then, the message of Kings is that Israel and Judah are condemned because of failure to keep the Mosaic covenant, but there remains a glimmer of hope for them through the line of David, to whom God has made irrevocable covenant promises.

As we will see later, when the Old Testament is read through the lens of the Mosaic covenant, especially by privileging the Pentateuch over the historical, prophetic, and poetic books, it creates difficulties in understanding the transition between the Old and the New Covenants. While it is true that Jesus Christ is a New Moses in many senses, nonetheless it is awkward at best to account for the forms and structures of the New Covenant solely as developments directly from those of the Mosaic economy. The Davidic covenant and its economy are the necessary middle term to understand the transition from Moses to Jesus.

The Liturgical Focus of 1–2 Kings

As was discussed above under literary structure, there is a clear priestly-liturgical theme throughout Kings that focuses on the proper place of worship, the Temple, as well as the proper celebration of worship at that place. In one sense, the history of Kings is the story of Israel's liturgy. The books begin with the construction and dedication of the Solomonic Temple and end with its destruction. Every king throughout is judged by a liturgical standard.

For example, every northern king of Israel ultimately "does evil in the eyes of the LORD", because he continues to support and promote the schismatic liturgy of Jeroboam, including (1) the illicit ordination of unauthorized persons to the priesthood (1 Kings 12:31b), (2) the incorporation of illicit images in worship (the Golden Calves; 1 Kings 12:28), (3) the sponsorship and proliferation of illicit sanctuaries (1 Kings 12:29–30a), and (4) the adoption of an idiosyncratic, "invented" liturgical calendar (1 Kings 12:32). These liturgical abuses recapitulated the catastrophic sin at the Golden Calf (Ex 32) and resulted in a northern cult that was *de facto* a different religion.

Meanwhile, in the southern kingdom, every king is judged by his relationship to the true cult: some support it, whereas others suppress it, corrupt it, or encourage rival cults of other gods. Even among the "good" kings who support the authentic liturgy in the Jerusalem Temple, most are judged for continuing to tolerate illicit sanctuaries throughout the land, the "high places" (see, for example, 2 Kings 24:18–20). Twice in Kings the son of David celebrates a liturgical feast at the proper sanctuary, the Temple in Jerusalem, and feeds the entire nation at his own expense: Solomon for the Temple dedication (1 Kings 8:65–66); and King Josiah at Passover (2 Kings 23:21–23). These joyous sacred feasts at the king's expense are climactic events signaling what true kingship should have as its goal.

In the theology of the books of Kings, then, the proper worship of God—meaning worship according to divinely revealed norms rather than according to political and cultural expediency—figures very prominently, even dominantly. Violations in this area are offenses against the first commands of the Ten Commandments and, therefore, fundamental breaches of the covenant between God and Israel. In this way, the books of Kings teach that the Assyrian exile of the ten northern tribes and the Babylonian exile of the two southern tribes, along with the devastating destruction of Jerusalem and its Temple, were ultimately due to false worship and the toleration of false worship.

1–2 Kings in the Living Tradition

Despite the understandable aversion of some readers to the multitude of monarchs and the swirl of historical events that populate the pages of 1–2 Kings, these books were extremely popular in the living tradition of the Church both for the moral lessons contained therein and, even more, for the spiritual sense of figures such as Solomon, Elijah, and Elisha and places such as the Jerusalem Temple. Because these books focus on the kingdom, they became a rich repository of Christian reflection and continue to find a place in the Lectionary.

The Anointing of Solomon and the Anointing of Christians

When we turn to the opening chapters of the books of Kings, we find several remarkable connections with the New Testament. For example, in the enthronement ritual for Solomon, he is taken to the Gihon (1 Kings 1:38, the spring that is Jerusalem's sole source of water) to be washed and anointed by the reigning prophet (Nathan) and priest (Zadok) (1 Kings 1:38). He then rides on a donkey up to the palace to the thunderous acclamation of the people (1 Kings 1:40–41). As New Testament scholars widely recognize, Jesus' triumphal entry into Jerusalem is a clear recapitulation of Solomon's "triumphal" ride to his anointing as king (see Mt 21:1–11 and parallels), thus fulfilling the prediction of Zechariah that the Messiah would enter Jerusalem in the same manner that Solomon had (Zech 9:9).

In the later tradition of the Church, this connection between the anointing of Solomon and the triumphal entry of Jesus was then picked up and applied to the sacramental anointing of Christians in the act of chrismation (what we today call "confirmation"):

> You must know that *this Chrism is prefigured in the Old Testament*.... The high priest, when installing Solomon as king, anointed him after he had bathed in Gihon. *But what was done to them in figure was done to you, not in figure but in truth*, because your salvation began from Him who was anointed by the Holy Spirit in truth.[16]

The Wisdom of Solomon and the Wisdom of Jesus

Along similar lines, the early Christian tradition, beginning with the New Testament, was also quick to pick up on other parallels between King Solomon (in his early years) and Jesus. For example, both Solomon and Jesus Christ are noted as ones blessed with divine wisdom (1 Kings 4:29; Mt 13:54; Lk 2:52; 11:31) who speak in "parables" (1 Kings 4:32 LXX) about trees, beasts, birds, fish, and other aspects of nature (1 Kings 4:33; cf. Mt 6:26; 8:20; 13:32; 13:47). As they sit in Jerusalem, their wisdom is tested by those who bring hard questions (1 Kings 3:16–28; 1 Kings 10:2–3; Mt 2:15–46).

Yet for all their similarities, it is clear that with Jesus of Nazareth, "something greater than Solomon is here" (Mt 12:42). In the words of Ephrem the Syrian, expounding the book of Kings in the fourth century A.D.:

> Since the narrative [of the book of Kings] is accurate in facts, nobody can have any doubt that Solomon received his noble sovereignty, his elevated thought and extraordinary power as a gift from God, thus it is evident that no one among those kings who were dead, nor among those who would succeed him, could be compared with him. *It is certain, nevertheless, that these qualities, and others, which are described in the psalms about Solomon, mostly are to be transferred to Christ*; otherwise the words ... would not be in absolute and complete agreement with their meaning and truth. Therefore Christ is that prince of peace whose wisdom and royal power were never preceded in time or overcome in greatness.[17]

The Twelve Officers of Solomon and the Twelve Apostles

It is not only major figures such as Solomon but even "minor" characters such as the twelve officers of Solomon over the kingdom (1 Kings 4:7) that drew the attention of ancient Christian commentators, seeing in them a prefiguration of the government of the kingdom of Jesus the Messiah, present on earth:

---

[16] Cyril of Jerusalem, *Mystagogical Lectures* 3.6, in *The Works of Saint Cyril of Jerusalem*, vol. 2, trans. Leo P. McCauley and Anthony A. Stephenson, The Fathers of the Church 64 (Washington, D.C.: Catholic University of America Press, 2000), 172–73.

[17] Ephrem the Syrian, *On the First Book of Kings* 3.12, in *1–2 Kings, 1–2 Chronicles, Ezra, Nehemiah, Esther*, ed. Marco Conti, Old Testament 5, Ancient Christian Commentary on Scripture, ed. Thomas C. Oden (Downers Grove, Ill.: InterVarsity Press, 2008), 14.

The officials elected by Solomon designate the order of the chosen ones whom Christ affirmed in his grace and appointed as rulers of his people. *Indeed, twelve prefects were selected to administer the incomes of this king and his house, because just as many apostles had to be distributed over the entire world and had to be appointed as treasures of the divine mysteries, so that they might nourish with living and immortal food the Israel of God....* Therefore, also the limits of each prefecture were clearly denoted, because, in a similar way, each apostle received a certain province: Simon preached in Rome, John in Ephesus, Matthew in Palestine and Thomas in the region of India.[18]

The Temple of Solomon and the International Church

Second Kings ends tragically, with the Temple destroyed and no possibility for the celebration of the liturgy. There is only a slight hope that the yawning chasm left by the destruction of the Temple may be adequately filled. The hopes of Israel were partially consoled by the construction of the Second Temple (in 516 B.C.) after the exile, but there was a strong sense that the Second Temple was inadequate. Ultimately, the hunger for the Temple and the restoration of a valid liturgy would only be met by the Christ. Thus, in the New Testament, the theme of Christ as New Temple (Jn 2:21)—and, by extension, the Church—is especially prominent in the Johannine literature (Jn 2:13–21; 4:19–24; 7:37–38; 19:34) and parts of the Pauline corpus (for example, Eph 2:19–21, and elsewhere).

As the tradition developed, this New Testament theme of the Church as New Temple led various ancient Christian writers to revisit the accounts of the building of Solomon's Temple in the books of Kings and to find in them prefigurations of what God would ultimately accomplish through the Church. Consider, for example, the Venerable Bede's explanation for why the Temple of Solomon—unlike the Tabernacle of Moses—was built by both Israelites and Gentiles:

For the servants of Hiram who cut down cedars from Lebanon for Solomon are the teachers chosen from among the gentiles.... Now with these servants were also the servants of Solomon and together they set about the work referred to because the first teachers from among the gentiles needed the apostles themselves, who had received training by being instructed in the word of faith.... What this symbolizes is plain, namely, that the apostles had a surer knowledge of how to preach to others the word of the Gospel which they were privileged to hear from the Lord, but the gentiles, converted from error and brought into conformity with the truth of the Gospel, had a better knowledge of the actual errors of the gentiles, and the surer their knowledge the more skilfully they learned to counteract and refute them. Paul indeed had a better knowledge of the mystery of the Gospel, which he had learned through revelation, but Dionysius was better able to refute the false teachings of Athens whose syllogisms as well as errors and all of whose arguments he knew since a boy.... For the Sidonians and Tyrians are rightly taken as a type of the gentiles because they were gentile peoples.[19]

---

[18] Ibid., 4.1, p. 22.

[19] Venerable Bede, *On the Temple* 1.2.4–5, trans. Seán Connolly, Translated Texts for Historians 21 (Liverpool: Liverpool University Press, 1995), 8–9.

Along similar lines, the Church Fathers were also quick to recognize the fact that Solomon's prayer of dedication of the Temple was not only focused on the twelve tribes of Israel, but included the Gentile nations, the "foreigners and strangers".[20] In this way, the preliminary ingathering of the nations that takes place under Solomon's empire in 1 Kings becomes a kind of foreshadowing of the universal ingathering of the nations that will take place during the era of the New Covenant.

The Prophets Elijah and Elisha as Typological Figures

As we saw above, on the one hand, the prophets Elijah and Elisha point back to the oracle of Moses that God would "raise up for you a prophet like me from among you, from your brethren" (Deut 18:15). On the other hand, when read through the lens of the New Testament and the living tradition, the lives of Elijah and Elisha also look *forward* to two greater prophets who are yet to come: (1) *John the Baptist* and (2) *Jesus of Nazareth*. Indeed, the four canonical Gospels will apply an Elijah-Elisha mold to the ministries of John and Jesus, although without perfect consistency.

Although at times Jesus himself will be cast in the role of Elijah, the dominant perspective is that John the Baptist is the Elijah who is to come (Mt 11:14, 17:12; Lk 1:17), wearing, for example, the same garb as this colorful prophet (2 Kings 2:8; cf. Mk 1:6). Although the contrast is by no means absolute, Elijah is a prophet of judgment and justice, while Elisha is a prophet of mercy. Thus, Elijah performs relatively few miracles of compassion (1 Kings 17:8–24) but is remembered for calling fire from heaven multiple times, killing the prophets of Baal, and delivering oracles of death and judgment against Ahab and Ahaziah (1 Kings 18). Elisha, on the other hand, has an extensive ministry of mercy, in

Miracles of Elijah/Elisha Recapitulated by Christ		
Miracle	Elijah/Elisha	Jesus
Multiplying food	Elijah: 1 Kings 17:13–16; Elisha: 2 Kings 4:1–7, 42–44; 2 Kings 7:1–16	Mt 14:19; 15:36; Mk 6:41, 8:6; Lk 9:16; Jn 2:7–8; 6:11
Raising the Dead	Elijah: 1 Kings 17:17–24 Elisha: 2 Kings 4:32–37	Mt 9:25; Mk 5:41; Lk 7:14; 8:54; Jn 11:43–44; cf. Jn 4:50
Curing leprosy	Elisha: 2 Kings 5:1–19	Mt 8:3; Mk 1:41; Lk 17:11–19
Giving sight to the blind	Elisha: 2 Kings 6:17, 20	Mt 9:29; 12:22; Mk 8:25; Lk 11:14; 18:42; Jn 9:7
Controlling the weather	Elijah: 1 Kings 17:1; 18:1–2, 41–46	Mt 8:26; Mk 4:39; Lk 8:24
"Go and tell John what you have seen and heard: the blind receive their sight, the lame walk, lepers are cleansed, and the deaf hear, the dead are raised up, the poor have good news preached to them." (Lk 7:22)		

[20] Ephrem the Syrian, *On the First Book of Kings* 8.21, in Conti, *1–2 Kings*, 60.

which he grants conception to the barren, healing to the sick, resurrection to the dead, food to the hungry, purity to the poisoned or defiled, and even forgiveness to enemies (2 Kings 6:21–23). The Gospel authors recognized this pattern and its applicability to the successive ministries of John the Baptist, prophet of judgment (Mt 3:7–12), and Jesus of Nazareth, prophet of mercy (Mt 11:28–30).

In particular, the ministry of Jesus in the Gospels is replete with specifically "Elishianic" miracles (Lk 7:22). Above all, the early Fathers saw Elisha's act of feeding the prophets with but a little bread (2 Kings 4:42–44) as a prefiguration of what Jesus would accomplish in his most widely recorded miracle: the feeding of the five thousand (Mt 14; Mk 6; Lk 9; Jn 6).[21]

The Ascension of Elijah and the Ascension of Jesus

Perhaps the most memorable scene in the entire books of Kings is the account of Elijah's ascension into heaven in the whirlwind and the chariots of fire (2 Kings 2). Given the singular nature of his fate in ascending into heaven, this marvel was widely regarded as a prefiguration of the Ascension of Jesus into heaven after his Resurrection from the dead. In one of his homilies on the Gospels, Venerable Bede writes:

> *The prophets proclaimed the mystery of the Lord's ascension not only by their words but also by their actions.* Both Enoch, the seventh ... from Adam, who was transported from the world (Gen 5:24), and Elijah, who was taken up into heaven, gave evidence that the Lord would ascend above all the heavens.... As they [Elijah and Elisha] went on conversing together, behold, Elijah was suddenly snatched away, and, as the Scripture says, "He ascended as if into heaven." *By this action of his soaring aloft it is meant that [Elijah] was not taken up into heaven itself, as was our Lord, but into the height of the air, from where he was borne invisibly to the joys of paradise.*[22]

This is a remarkable interpretation, for it answers the age-old Christian question: If heaven was not yet "opened" until Christ rose again, then to where did Elijah ascend? Moreover, Bede goes on to point out that the parallels do not stop with the ascension: just as Elisha received a double portion of the spirit of Elijah after his ascension, so, too, the disciples received the promised grace of the Holy Spirit after Jesus' Ascension at Pentecost.[23] In this way, the otherwise inexplicably singular privilege of Elijah's assumption into heaven becomes explicable as a unique prefiguration of the great mystery of Jesus' Ascension.

The Washing of Naaman and the Mystery of Baptism

In addition to typological prefigurations of the life and mysteries of Jesus, the living tradition also saw in the signs and wonders of Elijah and Elisha prefigurations

---

[21] See Ephrem the Syrian, *On the Second Book of Kings* 4.38, in Conti, *1–2 Kings*, 165.

[22] In Bede, *Homilies on the Gospels* 2.15, in bk. 2: *Lent to the Dedication of the Church*, trans. Lawrence T. Martin and David Hurst, O.S.B., Cistercian Studies 111 (Kalamazoo, Mich.: Cistercian Publications, 1991), 144–45.

[23] Ibid.

of the *sacraments* of the Church. Some of the more obvious of these can be summarized in the form of a chart. Several feeding miracles of these great prophets, as well as the two incidents in which Elijah himself was miraculously fed, were viewed as types of the Christian Eucharist.

Other miracles, such as the two resurrections of children and the healing of Naaman's leprosy, point to the regeneration of baptism. The bestowal of Elijah's spirit on Elisha, preparing him for his prophetic office, typifies the conferral of holy orders.

Sacramental Typology in the Elijah and Elisha Narratives	
Eucharistic Types	
1 Kings 17:1–7	Elijah miraculously fed in the wilderness
1 Kings 17:8–16	Provision of flour and oil for the widow of Zarephath
1 Kings 19:4–8	The angelic food for Elijah's journey to Sinia
2 Kings 4:42	Multiplication of food for one hundred men
Baptismal Types	
1 Kings 17:17–24	Resurrection of the widow of Zarephath's son
2 Kings 4:18–37	Resurrection of the Shunammite's son
2 Kings 5:1–19	Healing of Naaman's leprosy
Type of Holy Orders	
2 Kings 2:9–15	Bestowal of the Spirit on Elisha

To give just one example of this from the patristic era, Ephrem the Syrian, in his amazingly rich commentary on the books of Kings, sees a "mystery hidden in that unusual healing" of Naaman's leprosy by his dipping seven times in the waters of the Jordan river:

> Naaman was sent to the Jordan as to the remedy capable to heal a human being. Indeed, sin is the leprosy of the soul, which is not perceived by the senses, but intelligence has the proof of it, and human nature must be delivered from this disease by Christ's power which is hidden in baptism. It was necessary that Naaman, in order to be purified from two diseases, that of the soul and that of the body, might represent in his own person the purification of the nations through the bath of regeneration, whose beginning was in the river Jordan, the mother and originator of baptism.[24]

We have here a remarkable interpretation of this otherwise mysterious sign of Elisha. For Ephrem, then, the events and realities of the books of Kings point forward not only to the visible miracles that took place during the life of Jesus (such as his acts of healing lepers), but also to the invisible miracles that continue to take place in the sacraments of the New Covenant.

[24] Ephrem the Syrian, *On the Second Book of Kings* 5.10–11, in Conti, *1–2 Kings*, 167.

424

The Books of Kings in the Lectionary

When we turn to the contemporary Lectionary use of 1–2 Kings, we find that it makes some use of texts concerning Solomon, taken from the account of his prayer for wisdom (1 Kings 3) and his Temple dedication prayer (1 Kings 8). In these passages, the Church perceives Solomon as the model of the righteous ruler who seeks God's wisdom above all temporal goods and so typifies Christ himself as well as saints, religious, and lay faithful who have made sacrifices to acquire divine wisdom.

Otherwise, it is significant that almost all the texts from Kings are chosen from the Elijah or Elisha cycles, usually from accounts of their miracles, which anticipate similar miracles performed by Jesus in the Gospels and ultimately point toward the power of God bestowed in one or more of the sacraments. Here we see the contemporary Church very much in line with the patristic gravitation to the Elijah-Elisha sequences in Kings. The most extensively used portion of the entire book is the account of Elijah's flight from Jezebel, the angel's provision of food for his journey, his encounter with God at Sinai, and the commissioning of Elisha (1 Kings 19). The Church especially treasures the narrative of Elijah's angelic food for the journey (1 Kings 19:4–8), seeing in it a type of the Eucharist, our spiritual food for the journey of our exile here below, and especially of the viaticum, the last "meal" before our final journey to God's presence on the "holy mountain". The intimate conversation between Elijah and God at Sinai, where Elijah finds God, not in dramatic displays of power, but in God's "quiet whisper" or "still small voice" (1 Kings 19:11–15), is profoundly evocative of the experience of the devout believer who has long pursued the presence of God. Subsequently, Elisha's willingness to abandon all to follow this spiritual master who has spoken with God (1 Kings 19:19–21) sets a perennial example for all who would enter on the path of discipleship.

	Readings from Kings for Sundays, Feast Days, Liturgical Seasons, and Other Occasions		
	MSO= Masses for Special Occasions; *OM*= Optional Memorial; *VM*= Votive Mass; *Rit*= Ritual		
Passage	Description	Occasion	Explanation
1 Kings 3:5, 7–12	Solomon prays for and receives divine wisdom to rule the kingdom.	*17th Sun. in OT (A)*	Paired with the parables of the kingdom (Mt 13:44–52), this reading sets up a Solomon-Jesus typology: Solomon, the wise king who teaches in "parables" (1 Kings 4:32 LXX), typifies Jesus Christ, enthroned over the kingdom of heaven.
3:11–14	God grants Solomon wisdom, riches, honor, and	Common of Doctors of the Church, opt. 1;	Solomon typifies the Church's Doctors, who sought divine wisdom ahead of all temporal

(continued)

	Readings from Kings for Sundays, Feast Days, Liturgical Seasons, and Other Occasions (continued)		
	MSO = Masses for Special Occasions; OM = Optional Memorial; VM = Votive Mass; Rit = Ritual		
Passage	Description	Occasion	Explanation
	long life, provided he obeys the law.	MSO: For the Country or City, Civil Leaders, etc., opt. 5	goods. He also serves as model for civil leaders, whose temporal concerns would best be served by seeking transcendent wisdom.
8:41–43	Solomon's fifth petition of his Temple dedication prayer: for foreigners who pray at or toward the Temple	9th Sun. in OT (C)	This passage complements the Gospel (Lk 7:1–10), the healing of the Roman centurion's servant. Jesus' openness to Gentiles in his ministry and Church was anticipated already in the economy of the Davidic covenant and kingdom under Solomon.
8:55–61	At the Temple dedication, Solomon gives thanks for the fulfillment of Mosaic covenant promises and prays for the continued obedience of God's people.	MSO: In Thanksgiving to God, opt. 1	Solomon's prayer of thanksgiving provides words and a model for our own expressions of thanks to God for his blessings, especially for his fulfillment of covenant promises in Christ, the greater Son of David.
17:10–16	Elijah asks food of the widow of Zarephath and provides her with continual flour and oil for the duration of the famine.	32nd Sun. in OT (B)	This reading and the Gospel (Mk 12:38–44, "the widow's mite") show two examples, from the Old and New Covenants, of poor widows who offer their entire remaining wealth to God, in the presence of his prophet (Elijah/Jesus), serving as noteworthy examples of faith.
17:17–24	Elijah revives the dead son of the widow of Zarephath.	10th Sun. in OT (C)	This passage supports the Gospel (Lk 7:11–17, the raising of the son of the widow of Nain) by showing Jesus as a prophet, a New Elijah who can raise us from the dead.
19:1–8	Jezebel swears to kill Elijah; he journeys into the wilderness, sustained by bread and water from an angel.	Rit: Anointing of the Sick, opt. 1	The angelic bread given to Elijah to strengthen him on his journey to see God typifies the viaticum often given during the anointing of the sick.

(continued)

	Readings from Kings for Sundays, Feast Days, Liturgical Seasons, and Other Occasions (*continued*)		
	MSO=Masses for Special Occasions; *OM*=Optional Memorial; *VM*=Votive Mass; *Rit*=Ritual		
Passage	**Description**	**Occasion**	**Explanation**
19:4–8	Elijah falls asleep in sorrow while journeying in the wilderness, but an angel awakes him and provides him bread and water for his journey.	*19th Sun. in OT (B)*; *Rit*: Institution of Acolytes, opt. 5; Viaticum, opt. 1; *VM*: Most Holy Eucharist, opt. 6	Elijah's angelic bread is one of five Old Testament types of the Eucharist paired with the *ad seriatim* reading of John 6 in Ordinary Time of Year B, Sundays 17–21. The reading is also useful for other liturgical occasions with a Eucharistic focus.
19:4–9a, 11–15a	See above; then Elijah arrives at Sinai, complains to God; sees the wind, fire, and earthquake; and hears God's "still small voice".	Common of Holy Men and Women, opt. 5; *Rit*: Consecration of Virgins & Religious Profession, opt. 3; *MSO*: For Religious, opt. 1	Elijah typifies those with a religious vocation, who seek to serve God in ways beyond their own strength, but find themselves buoyed by the sacraments and learn to hear God's voice in quietness and peace, not in external spectacles.
19:9a, 11–13a	Elijah arrives at Sinai; sees the wind, fire, and earthquake; and hears God's "still small voice".	*19th Sun. in OT (A)*	This passage supports the Gospel (Mt 14:22–33, Jesus walks on the water and stills the storm) by showing that Jesus is the Lord, the same God who demonstrated his power over nature to the prophet Elijah.
19:16b, 19–21	Elijah commissions Elisha as his disciple and successor.	*13th Sun. in OT (C)*; Common of Holy Men and Women, opt. 6; *Rit*: Consecration of Virgins and Religious Profession, opt. 4; *MSO*: For Vocations to Holy Orders or Religious Life, opt. 4	Elisha abandons everything to follow Elijah, typifying the disciples of Christ, whom Jesus calls in the Gospel (Lk 9:51–62) to abandon all to follow him. The saints and religious of the Church hear and accept this call to discipleship in a radical and even literal way.
2 Kings 4:8–11, 14–16a	Elisha grants a son to the hospitable woman of Shunem.	*13th Sun. in OT (A)*	The Gospel (Mt 10:37–42) invokes a blessing and reward on those who "receive a prophet because he is a prophet"; the first reading provides an OT example of just such a blessing.
4:18b–21, 32–37	Elisha revives the Shunammite woman's dead son.	5th Week of Lent Optional Mass	Elisha typifies Jesus, who raises Lazarus from the dead in the Gospel (Jn 11:1–45), which in turn typifies baptism, for which Lent prepares.

(*continued*)

Readings from Kings for Sundays, Feast Days, Liturgical Seasons, and Other Occasions (*continued*)			
MSO = Masses for Special Occasions; OM = Optional Memorial; VM = Votive Mass; Rit = Ritual			
Passage	Description	Occasion	Explanation
4:42–44	Elisha feeds one hundred men with twenty loaves of barley and a sack of grain.	*17th Sun. in OT (B)*	Complementing John 6:1–15, Elisha's feeding miracle foreshadows and anticipates the feeding of the five thousand and ultimately the gift of the Eucharist.
5:1–15a	Elisha heals the Syrian general Naaman of his leprosy.	Mon., 3rd Week of Lent	Naaman's healing is one of several baptismal types explored by the Lenten weekday readings in preparation for Easter.
5:9–15a	See above.	Christian Initiation, opt. 6	
5:14–17	Naaman dips seven times in the Jordan and is healed.	*28th Sun. in OT (C)*	This healing anticipates the prophetic ministry of Jesus Christ, who will also heal foreigners of leprosy (Lk 7:11–19, the healing of the Samaritan leper), which is a type of baptism.
20:1–6	Through Isaiah, God heals Hezekiah and lengthens his life.	MSO: For the Sick, opt. 1	This passage encourages the sick person to have faith in God, who demonstrated supernatural power to heal the sick in both the Old and the New Covenants.

In addition to these Sunday readings, a relatively extensive selection of semi-continuous readings from 1–2 Kings is included in the biennial Lectionary for weekday Mass in weeks 4–5 and 10–12 of Year II. The readings are selected to familiarize the daily worshipper with the following: (1) the career of Solomon, including his virtues and vices; (2) the basic narrative arc of the northern kingdom, from Jeroboam to Hoshea; (3) many of the events in the career of the Elijah; (4) a few good kings of Judah, especially Hezekiah and Josiah; and (5) finally, the disastrous end of the Judean monarchy and Temple.

Reading of Kings for Daily Mass: Ordinary Time, Year II: Weeks 1–4			
Week	Day	Passage Read	Description
4	Th	1 Kings 2:1–4, 10–12	David charges Solomon to keep the law; David dies, succeeded by Solomon.
4	F	Sir 47:2–11	Sirach's eulogy on the greatness of David
4	Sa	1 Kings 3:4–13	Solomon prays for and receives divine wisdom to rule the kingdom.

(continued)

			Reading of Kings for Daily Mass: Ordinary Time, Year II: Weeks 1–4
			(continued)
Week	Day	Passage Read	Description
5	M	1 Kings 8:1–7, 9–13	The completion and dedication of the Temple
5	Tu	1 Kings 8:22–23, 27–30	The introduction of Solomon's dedicatory prayer for the Temple
5	W	1 Kings 10:1–10	The visit of the Queen of Sheba
5	Th	1 Kings 11:4–13	Solomon's heart is turned away by his wives; the Lord foretells his downfall.
5	F	1 Kings 11:29–32; 12:19	Ahijah anoints Jeroboam king over the ten northern tribes.
5	Sa	1 Kings 12:26–32; 13:33–34	Jeroboam establishes his schismatic, idolatrous cult, leading ultimately to northern Israel's downfall.
10	M	1 Kings 17:1–6	Elijah prophesies drought, flees to the wilderness, and is fed by ravens.
10	Tu	1 Kings 17:7–16	Elijah asks food of the widow of Zarephath and blesses her with flour and oil.
10	W	1 Kings 18:20–39	Elijah triumphs over the 450 prophets of Baal.
10	Th	1 Kings 18:41–46	Elijah prays to end the drought on Israel.
10	F	1 Kings 19:9a, 11–16	Elijah arrives at Sinai and hears the "still small voice" of God.
10	Sa	1 Kings 19:19–21	Elijah chooses Elisha as his successor.
11	M	1 Kings 21:1–16	The incident of Naboth's vineyard. Naboth is wrongly executed.
11	Tu	1 Kings 21:17–29	Elijah judges Ahab for Naboth's vineyard, and Ahab does penance.
11	W	2 Kings 2:1, 6–14	Elijah is taken up in the whirlwind; Elisha is left as his successor.
11	Th	Sir 48:1–14	Sirach's eulogy of Elijah
11	F	2 Kings 11:1–4, 9–18, 20	Athaliah's usurpation and the restoration Joash to the throne
11	Sa	2 Chron 24:17–25	Joash commits apostasy after the death of Jehoiada the high priest.
12	M	2 Kings 17:5–8, 13–15a	Hoshea, the last king of Israel, plus brief epilogue on the northern kingdom
12	Tu	2 Kings 19:9–36 (sel.)	Hezekiah cries to God under threat from the Assyrians, and God delivers him.
12	W	2 Kings 22:8–13; 23:1–3	Josiah finds the Book of the Law and initiates reforms.
12	Th	2 Kings 24:8–17	Jehoiachin's reign, defeat, deportation, and replacement by Zedekiah
12	F	2 Kings 25:1–12	Defeat of Zedekiah, capture of Jerusalem, destruction of Temple, exile to Babylon

Conclusion

The books of Kings tell the story of Israel from the accession of Solomon to the destruction of Jerusalem—that is, from the highest point in Israel's history (the dedication of the Temple under Solomon) to its lowest point (the destruction of the Temple and the Babylonian exile). Despite the constant ministry of God's prophets, the royal sponsorship of illegitimate worship leads first to the division and ultimately to the destruction of the kingdom of David. Neither the royal son of David, the Temple itself, nor even the ministry of the prophets is able to prevent the dissolution of the people of Israel. Nonetheless, this final chapter of the great "primary history" (Genesis–2 Kings) does not end without hope. The last reigning son of David, Jehoiachin, receives mercy at the end of his life, a sign that God has not forgotten his covenant with David and may yet send a royal son "greater than Solomon" (Mt 12:42) who will rebuild the Temple (Jn 2:19–21) and complete the prophetic ministry of Elijah and Elisha (Lk 7:16).

For Further Reading

Commentaries and Studies on 1–2 Kings

Cogan, Mordechai. *1 Kings*. Anchor Bible 10. New York: Doubleday, 2000.

———, and Hayim Tadmor. *2 Kings*. Anchor Bible 11. New York: Doubleday, 1988.

Cohn, Robert, and David W. Cotter, eds. *2 Kings*. Berit Olam. Collegeville, Minn.: Liturgical Press, 2000.

Gray, John. *1 and 2 Kings: A Commentary*. Old Testament Library. Philadelphia: Westminster Press, 1970.

Hamilton, Victor. *Handbook on the Historical Books*. Grand Rapids, Mich.: Baker Academic, 2001. (See pp. 379–475.)

Walsh, Jerome T. *1 Kings*. Berit Olam. Collegeville, Minn.: Liturgical Press, 1996.

Historical Issues in 1–2 Kings

Bright, John. *A History of Israel*. 4th ed. Louisville, Ky.: Westminster John Knox Press, 2000.

Friedman, Richard Elliott. *Who Wrote the Bible?* San Francisco: HarperOne, 1997.

Kitchen, Kenneth A. *On the Reliability of the Old Testament*. Grand Rapids, Mich.: Eerdmans, 2003. (See pp. 7–79, 107–58.)

Monson, John. "1 Kings". Pages 2–109 in *1 & 2 Kings, 1 & 2 Chronicles, Ezra, Nehemiah, Esther*. Vol. 3 of *Zondervan Illustrated Bible Backgrounds Commentary*. Edited by John H. Walton. Downers Grove, Ill.: InterVarsity Press, 2009.

———. "2 Kings". Pages 111–219 in *1 & 2 Kings, 1 & 2 Chronicles, Ezra, Nehemiah, Esther*. Vol. 3 of *Zondervan Illustrated Bible Backgrounds Commentary*. Edited by John H. Walton. Downers Grove, Ill.: InterVarsity Press, 2009.

Provan, Iain W., V. Philips Long, and Tremper Longman III. *A Biblical History of Israel*. Louisville, Ky.: Westminster John Knox Press, 2003. (See pp. 239–77.)

1–2 Kings in the Living Tradition

Ambrose. *De Helia et Ieiunio (On Elias [Elijah] and Fasting)*. Translated by Sister Mary Joseph A. Buck. Patristic Studies 19. Washington, D.C.: Catholic University of America Press, 1929.

————. *De Nabuthae* (Saint Ambrose on Naboth). Translated by Martin McGuire. Patristic Studies 15. Washington, D.C.: Catholic University of America Press, 1927.

Bede, Venerable. *Lent to the Dedication of the Church*. Vol. 2 of *Homilies on the Gospels*. Translated by Lawrence T. Martin and David Hurst, O.S.B. Cistercian Studies 111. Kalamazoo, Mich.: Cistercian Publications, 1991.

————. *On the Temple*. Translated by Seán Connolly. Translated Texts for Historians 21. Liverpool: Liverpool University Press, 1995.

Conti, Marco, ed. *1–2 Kings, 1–2 Chronicles, Ezra, Nehemiah, Esther*. Old Testament 5 of Ancient Christian Commentary on Scripture. Edited by Thomas C. Oden. Downers Grove, Ill.: InterVarsity Press, 2008. (See pp. 1–241.)

Cyril of Jerusalem. *The Works of Saint Cyril of Jerusalem*. Translated by Leo P. McCauley and Anthony A. Stephenson. The Fathers of the Church 64. Washington, D.C.: Catholic University of America Press, 2000.

16. THE BOOKS OF CHRONICLES

Introduction

In the Christian canon of Scripture, the books of Chronicles come after the end of what might be referred to as the "Primary History" (Genesis–2 Kings). With 1–2 Chronicles we come to something we have not yet encountered in the canon: a *retelling* of the history of God's people that begins with Adam and goes through to the time of the Babylonian exile. In contrast to the often dark and somewhat pessimistic Deuteronomic History, the books of Chronicles provide a different, somewhat more optimistic interpretation of salvation history. The author of Chronicles—referred to by modern scholars simply as "the Chronicler"—apparently intended to encourage the people of Judah in their task of rebuilding and restoring national life in the postexilic period.

The works of 1 and 2 Chronicles, like Samuel and Kings, were originally one book and were later divided by the translators of the Greek Septuagint. Eventually, this division was also accepted in the Jewish textual tradition. In the Jewish Bible, these books are titled "the Words (or Events) of the Days" (Hebrew *dibrê hayyamim*), meaning the "annals" or "historical records". Significantly, in the contemporary Jewish Bible, 1 and 2 Chronicles do not follow Kings, but are the *last books* in the third Jewish canonical division known as the Writings (Hebrew *ketuvim*). In this way, the retelling of the history of Israel in the books of Chronicles forms a canonical "last word" to followers of Judaism and thus brings the Jewish Bible to an end with the liturgical exhortation to "go up" to the city of Jerusalem and its Temple to worship the God of Israel:

> Thus says Cyrus king of Persia, "The LORD, the God of heaven, has given me all the kingdoms of the earth, and he has charged me to build him a house at Jerusalem, which is in Judah. *Whoever is among you of all his people, may the LORD his God be with him. Let him go up.*" (2 Chron 36:23)

In the Greek Septuagint (LXX), which has had far more influence on the Christian tradition, the books of Chronicles occupy a very different position. They were placed at the end of the historical books and given the title "Things Left Over" (Greek *Paraleipomenōn*), thereby implying a collection of miscellaneous matters not previously treated in the books of Kings. Needless to say, such a title has not made the books of Chronicles among the favorite or most read books of the Old Testament! The LXX canonical order and name were retained in the Latin Vulgate; they can still be seen today in older Catholic Bibles in English such as the Douay-Rheims, in which these books bear the Latin names *1 and 2 Paralipomenon*. In this position, the books of Chronicles come after the main historical narratives in the Old Testament and provide a reinterpretation of that narrative, which, although often overshadowed by the books of the "Primary History", provides an important work of *prophetic historiography* that begins to emphasize the typological nature of salvation history already in the Old Testament.[1]

Literary Structure of 1–2 Chronicles

One of the most significant and memorable aspects of the book of Chronicles is that they begin with *nine chapters of genealogies* (1 Chronicles 1–9)! What is the purpose of such a beginning? Although often baffling (and boring) to contemporary readers, the choice to begin the books in this way is deliberate: by means of these genealogies, the sacred author is summarizing all of salvation history from creation to his own generation (or close to it) in postexilic Judah (fifth or fourth century B.C.). After this initial section, there follows an account of the united kingdom of Israel under David and Solomon (1 Chron 10—2 Chron 9), and then of the kingdom of Judah from the division of the monarchy up to the return from Babylonian exile under King Cyrus of Persia (2 Chron 10–36). These, then, are the three major divisions of the books:

I. Genealogies from Adam to Postexilic Judah (1 Chron 1–9)
II. The United Kingdom of Israel and Judah (1 Chron 10—2 Chron 9)
III. The Kingdom of Judah, Its Fall and Return (2 Chron 10–36)

The initial genealogical section places special emphasis on the tribes of Judah, Levi, and Benjamin (1 Chron 1–9). These three tribes were of particular importance for postexilic Judah, since most of the Babylonian returnees came from one of them. Accordingly, Judah is placed first, with the royal line of David given special attention. Levi's genealogies are placed in the middle, and Benjamin's at the end. The other tribes are not forgotten, but their genealogies are placed before and behind Levi's. The central section, the history of the united kingdom, is divided into two unequal sections, the reign of David (1 Chron 10–29) and the reign of Solomon (2 Chron 1–9). For the Chronicler, David is the ideal king, and Solomon is almost an extension of David, who achieves the glories merited by his father. The third section, the account of the divided monarchy, follows the reigns of the kings of Judah from Rehoboam to Zedekiah. Northern kings are not of any interest; they are mentioned only if they had significant dealings with the king of Judah. The Chronicler's accounts of the Judean kings are longer than those in the books of Kings, frequently including more material about their positive political and religious accomplishments. The longest account is of the reign of righteous Hezekiah; but Rehoboam, Asa, Jehoshaphat, and Josiah also receive disproportionate treatment. A fuller outline of Chronicles is as follows:

---

[1] Scott W. Hahn, *The Kingdom of God as Liturgical Empire: A Theological Commentary on 1–2 Chronicles* (Grand Rapids, Mich.: Baker Academic, 2012).

Outline of the Books of Chronicles

I. Genealogies of Israel from Adam to the Return from Babylon (1 Chron 1–9)
 A. From Adam to Israel (1)
 B. Descendants of Judah (2:1—4:43)
  1. Descendants of Judah (2:1–55)
  2. Descendants of David (3:1–24)
  3. Descendants of Judah Again (4:1–23)
  4. Descendants of Simeon (Absorbed by Judah) (4:24–43)
 C. Descendants of the Transjordanian Tribes (5:1–26)
 D. Descendants of Levi (6:1–81)
 E. Cisjordanian Tribes (7:1–40)
  1. The Descendants of Benjamin (8:1—9:1)
  2. The Family Lines of the Postexilic Returnees in Jerusalem (9:2–34)
 F. The Genealogy of Saul (9:35–44)

II. The United Kingdom (1 Chron 10—2 Chron 9)
 A. The First Monarch: Saul, Prelude to David (1 Chron 10:1–14)
 B. The Reign of King David (11:1—29:30)
  1. The Coronation to the Resting of the Ark in Jerusalem (11:1—16:43)
  2. The Covenant with David (17:1–27)
  3. The Expansion of David's Realm (18:1—20:8)
  4. Site, Preparation, and Arrangements for the Temple and Liturgy (21:1—29:30)
 C. The Reign of King Solomon (2 Chron 1:1—9:31)
  1. Solomon's Wisdom and Wealth (1:1–17)
  2. Preparations, Building, Furnishing, Dedication of the Temple (2:1—7:22)
  3. Solomon's Wealth and Wisdom (8:1—9:12)

III. The Kingdom of Judah to the Return from Babylon (2 Chron 10:1—36:23)
 A. The Reign of Rehoboam (10:1—12:16)
 B. Abijam (13:1–22)
 C. Asa (14:1—16:14)
 D. Jehoshaphat (17:1—20:37)
 E. Jehoram (21:1–20)
 F. Ahaziah (22:1–9)
 G. Athaliah (22:10—23:15)
 H. Joash (23:16—24:27)
 I. Amaziah (25:1–28)
 J. Uzziah (26:1–23)
 K. Jotham (27:1–9)
 L. Ahaz (28:1–27)
 M. Hezekiah (29:1—32:33)
 N. Manasseh (33:1–20)

O. Amon (33:21–25)

P. Josiah (34:1—35:27)

Q. The End of Exile and Return of the Judeans (36)
  1. The Last Kings: Jehoahaz, Jehoiakim, Jehoiachin, Zedekiah (36:1–14)
  2. The Fall of Jerusalem (36:15–21)
  3. The Decree of Return under Cyrus (36:22–23)

Overview of 1–2 Chronicles

The Genealogy of Israel: From Adam to the Return (1 Chron 1–9)

By means of genealogies, the Chronicler summarizes the history of Israel from Adam to (presumably) his own postexilic generation (1 Chron 1–9). By means of these genealogies, the Chronicles are making at least two very important theological points. First, in contrast to some contemporary readings of the Old Testament, which would have the history of salvation begin with the call of Abraham (Gen 12:1–3), for the Chronicler, *salvation history*—that is, the history of God's covenant people—*begins with creation, with the figure of Adam* (1 Chron 1:1). Second, despite the recent destruction of the Temple and the exile of Judah to Babylon, *salvation history is not ended*. To the contrary, by tracing the genealogies from creation to the present, the Chronicler gives the important message to his readers that the contemporary generation, however troubled it may be, is still part of God's plan of salvation.

Within this postexilic context, for the Chronicler, the most important lineages are those of the majority of the returnees from Babylon: Judah, Levi, and Benjamin. For in the postexilic context, these tribes are the ones for whom God will continue to be active and present. Moreover, as we have already seen in our previous study of the Primary History (Genesis—2 Kings), the tribe of Judah is important because the *kingship* belonged to Judah, from which the royal line of David stems (1 Chron 3:1–24; cf. Gen 49:10). Likewise, the tribe of Levi is important because the *priesthood* belongs to Levi and to the lineages of the different clans within Levi (1 Chron 6:1–81; cf. Ex 32:29).

With that said, it is also important to stress that the Chronicler's collection of genealogies also pays generous attention to "cadet lines" in salvation history, such as Ishmael and Edom, as well as to the northern tribes. Also notable is the Chronicler's attention to the house of Saul, who stemmed from the tribe of Benjamin. He continues the generations of Saul through Jonathan, Meribaal (a.k.a. Mephibosheth), and Micah for several generations (cf. 2 Sam 9). By including these lines, the Chronicler's message to contemporary Benjaminites is clear: "Though Saul sinned, there is no permanent curse on his line or his tribe. God has a future for you." Even more, Saul's line is like a microcosm of all Israel: though they sinned, there is still hope for them because of their connection with David and the covenant God made with him (cf. 1 Sam 18, 21; 2 Sam 7). Hence, the Chronicler has an inclusive vision: all the tribes are important to God, even if two—Judah and Levi—are particularly special.

The United Kingdom (1 Chronicles 10—2 Chronicles 9)

With the genealogies completed, the Chronicler now turns to the formal retelling of the history of Israel. In this historical narrative, it is King David who receives by far the lion's share of attention. In this central section of the book, several aspects of the figure of David in Chronicles stand out as distinctive (in comparison with Samuel and Kings) and significant.

First, *there is almost no attention given to King Saul* in Chronicles. Unlike the books of Samuel, in which Saul is a dramatic figure about whom

> ### David as Liturgical Reformer
>
> One of the greatest contributions of Chronicles to biblical theology is the picture these books give us of David as a liturgical reformer who reinvigorates the liturgy of Israel by reassigning the Levites from duties related to the transportation and care of the Tabernacle to new responsibilities concerned with the maintenance of the Temple and assistance with worship (1 Chron 23:24–32). Particularly noteworthy is David's appointment of 4,000 Levitical singers and musicians to provide music of praise and thanks to accompany the offering of sacrifice. This represents a sea change in the character of Israel's liturgy, which up to that time appears to have taken place in silence, since Moses gave no instruction about music in the Tabernacle. The theological significance of the introduction of joyful music into worship and its connection with the thanksgiving, or *todah*, sacrifice will be discussed further in our treatment of Psalms.

we learn much, in Chronicles, Saul is dispatched within the space of a few short verses so that the author can get on to talking about David (1 Chron 10:1–14).

Second, *King David's role as liturgical reformer and cultic leader is greatly emphasized* in Chronicles. For example, the narrative of David's bringing of the Ark of the Covenant up to Jerusalem is greatly expanded, even including the psalms of "thanksgiving" that are sung on that occasion, which match the canonical Psalms 105 and 96 (see 1 Chron 11–16). In this vein, particular emphasis is placed on the fact that under King David, the privilege of carrying the Ark of the Covenant and ministering to the Lord is given to "the Levites", from whom David appoints "singers" for the sacred liturgy, "who should play loudly on musical instruments, on harps and lyres and cymbals, to raise sounds of joy" (1 Chron 15:16). Significantly, the Chronicler also informs us that King David appoints certain Levites, such as Asaph, Heman, and Jeduthun, "to invoke, to thank, and to praise the LORD" (1 Chron 16:4). These royally appointed cultic singers are significant, since their names will appear in the headings of many of the songs of praise contained in the Psalter (for example, Ps 39, 50, 73–83, 88). Indeed, after a moderate description of David's power and prestige (1 Chron 18:1—20:8), the rest of the account of his reign is taken up with events connected to the Temple: the choice of its site (1 Chron 21:1–22:1), the accumulation of building materials for it (1 Chron 22:2–19), David's extensive instructions for the Levites serving in it (1 Chron 23:1—26:32), David's instructions to Solomon about it (1 Chron 28:1–21), more accumulation of building materials (1 Chron 29:1–9), and, finally, David's passing of the responsibility for the Temple to Solomon (1 Chron 29:10–30). Significantly, it is the Chronicler alone who tells us that the instructions for the Temple given by David to Solomon were given to him directly by God, much like Moses' instructions for the Tabernacle:

All this he [David] made clear by *the writing from the hand of the* LORD *concerning it,* all the work to be done according to the plan. (1 Chron 28:19)

In this way, the Chronicler makes clear that the Temple, like the Tabernacle before it, is not just a human building, but a divinely instituted place of worship.

Third, *unlike David, the Chronicler has omitted almost all of the negative aspects of King Solomon's reign, focusing instead on his role as Temple builder.* For example, the sins of Solomon with his wives and the unedifying melodrama of the royal household in David's later years leading up to the accession of Solomon are notably absent (cf. 2 Sam 11–2 Kings 2). The account of Solomon's life is dominated by the description of the Temple building and dedication (2 Chron 2:1–7:22), which is taken almost verbatim from 1 Kings and bracketed with a few chapters about Solomon's wealth and wisdom (2 Chron 1:1–17; 8:1—9:31). Perhaps the most unique and significant aspect of the account of Solomon's Temple building lies in the explanation given by the Chronicler as to why Solomon—and not David—was permitted to build the Temple:

> Then he [David] called for Solomon his son, and charged him to build a house for the LORD, the God of Israel. David said to Solomon, "My son, I had it in my heart to build a house to the name of the LORD my God. But the word of the LORD came to me, saying, '*You have shed much blood and have waged great wars; you shall not build a house to my name, because you have shed so much blood before me upon the earth.* Behold, a son shall be born to you; he shall be a man of peace. I will give him peace from all his enemies round about; for his name shall be *Solomon,* and *I will give peace and quiet to Israel in his days.* He shall build a house for my name. He shall be my son, and I will be his father, and I will establish his royal throne in Israel for ever.'" (1 Chron 22:6–10)

Although there is debate among scholars over exactly which acts of bloodshed by David are meant here—his wars, his murder of Uriah, or the 70,000 who died because of his census? (cf. 1 Sam 22:22; 27:9; 2 Sam 11; 24)—one thing is clear: Solomon is chosen to build God's Temple because he is to be a man of peace, who finally brings "rest" to the land (1 Chron 28:2), in fulfillment of the prophecies of the Pentateuch (Deut 12:10).[2] Indeed, the very name "Solomon" (Hebrew *shelomoh*) is built from the Hebrew word for "peace" (Hebrew *shalom*).

The Kingdom of Judah: From the Divided Kingdom to the Return from Babylon (2 Chronicles 10–36)

After the death of Solomon, the Chronicler retells the history of the southern kingdom from King Rehoboam to King Zedekiah. Unlike the author of Kings, the Chronicler pays no attention to the northern kingdom: since it does not partake of the Davidic covenant, it is not theologically significant. Along similar lines, since the prophets Elijah and Elisha ministered in the north, the Chronicler scarcely mentions them. Instead, he lengthens the accounts of the reigns

---

[2] Ibid., 98–101.

of the Judean kings, often (but not always) with positive material about their military strength and religious reforms—material apparently omitted in Kings.

Since this history is well-known from the previous books, we will restrict ourselves to pointing out the significant differences in the Chronicler's account.

Whereas in the books of Kings, the southern kingdom of Judah appears to be perpetually weak, in Chronicles we learn that several Judean kings— Abijam, Asa, Jehoshaphat, Amaziah, Uzziah, Hezekiah—fielded impressive armies and enjoyed military success against the Philistines, northern Israel, Arabs, Edomites, Ammonites, and others. For example, in a lengthy account entirely unique to Chronicles, Jehoshaphat is described as defeating an impressive coalition of eastern nations (Edomites, Moabites, Ammonites) when he places at the front of his army the Levitical singers, whose praises prompt God to defeat the enemies of Israel even before the Israelite army arrives at the field of battle (2 Chron 20:1–30).

Moreover, whereas in Kings, the liturgical reforms and Temple cleansing of Josiah appears almost unprecedented (2 Kings 23:1–20), in the books of Chronicles we discover that several earlier kings—Asa, Jehoshaphat, Joash, Hezekiah, Manasseh—made efforts at reform, with varying degrees of success. In Kings, Josiah is the ultimate reformer king, and Hezekiah second to him; in Chronicles, this relationship is reversed. Hezekiah's reign and his reforms are the benchmark of the sons of David. Josiah comes in second.

Significantly, the inclusion of additional information about several particular kings changes their profile and significance to the history of the kingdom:

1. *King Joash*, who was evaluated positively in Kings (2 Kings 12:2), turns out to be a late-in-life apostate (2 Chron 24:17–22).

2. *King Uzziah's* leprosy, mentioned in Kings (2 Kings 15:5), turns out to be the result of his illicit usurpation of priestly duties in the Temple (2 Chron 26:16–21), despite the fact that he was otherwise a righteous king who enjoyed great power and long reign (2 Chron 26:1–15).

3. *King Hezekiah's* reforms, passed over briefly in Kings (2 Kings 18:1–8), are accorded far more attention (2 Chron 29–31!), and his great Passover celebration (2 Chron 30), wholly omitted in Kings, is truly the high point of post-Solomonic Judean history: at this event, all of Judah together with significant representation of the northern tribes join in Temple worship according to the Mosaic covenant under the righteous leadership of the Son of David.

4. Perhaps most surprising of all, *King Manasseh*, who is wholly vilified in Kings (2 Kings 21:1–9) and accounted as the primary cause of the Babylonian exile of Judah (2 Kings 23:26), is somewhat rehabilitated as a late-in-life penitent who reverses his moral direction after a punitive captivity in Babylon (2 Chron 33:10–13) and even initiates liturgical reforms (2 Chron 33:15–16)!

Chronicles' description of Josiah and the few last short-lived kings is taken virtually verbatim from the earlier history, with the one difference that the final account of the freeing of Jehoiachin from prison (2 Kings 25:27–29) is omitted and replaced by the even more hopeful account of Cyrus' decree of return

(2 Chron 26:22–23), giving the history a more clearly and robustly optimistic ending, which stands as the conclusion of the whole Bible in the Jewish tradition.

Historical Issues in 1–2 Chronicles

Chronicles is usually thought to have been written in the late fifth or fourth century B.C. (400s–300s B.C.) by an anonymous scribe, probably a Levite, since the author has extensive knowledge of and interest in Levitical affairs.

For most of the history of modern biblical studies, it has been assumed that Samuel and Kings were early and reliable historical sources, and any differences or additional information introduced by the Chronicler was of dubious historical value. However, the agreement between modern archaeological findings and some of the Chronicler's unique information—for example, his description of Pharaoh Shishak/Shoshenq I's campaign against Judah and Israel (2 Chron 12:1–12) and Hezekiah's redirection of the Gihon spring (2 Chron 32:17–30)—demonstrates that, at the very least, the Chronicler did have access to reliable historical sources aside from Samuel and Kings.[3] Therefore, even prescinding from faith in the inspiration and truth of Scripture, one would still need to evaluate each difference in the accounts of Kings and Chronicles on its own historical merits, rather than assuming that the Chronicles' unique material is always embellishment or exaggeration.

> ### Hezekiah in the Chronicler
>
> In Chronicles, Hezekiah appears as a much more powerful and energetic monarch than in Kings, where he is remembered almost exclusively for barely surviving a siege and a sickness. The Chronicler's more vigorous portrayal is probably closer to how Hezekiah was perceived by his contemporaries. The archaeological record of his reign shows impressive fortification projects and extensive stockpiles of supplies to withstand military invasion of Judah. He defied the greatest empire of his day, Assyria, and the Assyrians were unable finally to conquer his capital, Jerusalem. They were proud enough of their defeats of Hezekiah's outlying cities, however, to decorate the Assyrian royal palace with reliefs of those victories.

A notable incident in Chronicles that has not been verified by external sources is the account of Manasseh's exile to Babylon (2 Chron 33:10–11) and his subsequent repentance (2 Chron 33:12–17). These events are not recorded in 2 Kings or in the Babylonian annals; however, the Babylonian records *do* mention Manasseh as a vassal of the king of Babylon, a fact omitted in 2 Kings.[4]

The numbers given in Chronicles concerning the wealth, buildings, and military strength of the various kings often seem quite large and sometimes differ from those given in the Deuteronomistic History. In several instances, this may be attributed to textual corruption in the transmission of the Hebrew. In other cases, the large numbers may have the same explanation as those in the Pentateuchal censuses, discussed above. In still other cases, the Chronicler may have adjusted the received figures in order to convey their significance to his readership in contemporary values they would have understood.

---

[3] See Frederick J. Mabie, "2 Chronicles", in *1 & 2 Kings, 1 & 2 Chronicles, Ezra, Nehemiah, Esther*, vol. 3 of *Zondervan Illustrated Bible Backgrounds Commentary*, ed. John H. Walton (Grand Rapids, Mich.: Zondervan, 2009), 330–32, 359–63.

[4] See ibid., 364–66.

As a result of the inclusion of new and unique material, the Chronicler's accounts of the reigns of several kings—Rehoboam, Abijah, Jehoshaphat, Hezekiah, Manasseh—have a much different "spin" or "feel" than the shorter, more generalized accounts in Kings. One of the benefits of postmodern philosophy and literary studies has been the reawakening of the realization that all history writing is interpretive: there is no "value free", "neutral", or "purely objective" historical literature. All history is interpreted history, and there is more than one valid perspective on the meaning of human events.

In short, the books of Kings and Chronicles have a great deal in common: they both understand the demise of the kingdom of David to be the result of the defections of his sons and his subjects from the covenant law of God. Yet within that common perspective, the two sacred accounts have a number of differences in emphasis and detail, yielding complementary rather than competing visions of the history of Israel.

Theological Issues in 1–2 Chronicles

The books of Chronicles emphasize several key theological themes that are worth highlighting in order to grasp the significance of the work as a whole.

The Importance of the Twelve Tribes of Israel

Chronicles' perspective on the twelve-tribe confederation of Israel is ironically different from that of Kings. On the one hand, the narrative of the divided kingdom period in Kings is dominated by events in the north (1 Kings 12— 2 Kings 17). The northern kings are portrayed as more powerful than those of Judah, and most of the theological "action"—notably the ministries of Elijah and Elisha—takes place in the north. On the other hand, after the exile of Israel by the Assyrians, the author of Kings creates the impression that no survivors of the northern tribes are left. The population of northern Israel now consists entirely of the five Gentile nations brought in by the Assyrians (2 Kings 17). Apparently, the ten northern tribes have no more role in salvation history.

By contrast, the Chronicler has almost nothing to say about the northern kingdom and its kings—in his perspective, they were an uninteresting theological dead end from the beginning, because the "kingdom of the LORD" is "in the hand of the sons of David" by a "covenant of salt" (2 Chron 13:8, 5). On the other hand, the Chronicler is very much concerned with the *people* of the northern tribes. He takes care to record their genealogies at the beginning of his books (1 Chron 2). He details the pan-tribal, pan-Israelite support for the Davidic kingship (1 Chron 12:23–40), even including elements of the house of Saul (1 Chron 12:29). He clarifies that after the division of the kingdom, there were large immigrations of northerners into the territory of Judah at various times for religious or political reasons (2 Chron 11:13–17; 15:9–15; 31:6), implying that the tribe of Judah has assimilated descendants of many of the other tribes. Under Hezekiah and Josiah, the religious revival centered in Jerusalem reached the territories and peoples of the northern tribes (2 Chron 30:10–25; 34:6–7) who had been left behind from the exile. Furthermore, the Chronicler does not let us forget that "Judah" was never just one tribe but always included Levi, Benjamin, and Simeon (1 Chron 4:34–43). In the Chronicler's account, the people of Judah have assimilated persons from all the tribes and thus are the legitimate successor of the twelve tribes of Israel, all twelve of whom were party to the covenant with the Lord and, therefore, must be part of the anticipated restoration.

The Davidic Kingdom as the Liturgical Kingdom of God

Remarkably, the prominent New Testament expression "kingdom of God" (or "kingdom of heaven") *never occurs in the Old Testament*. However, its closest analogue, the Hebrew expression "the kingdom of the LORD", is twice used by the Chronicler to describe the kingdom of David:

> [David said:] And of all my sons (for the LORD has given me many sons) he has chosen Solomon my son to sit upon the throne of the *kingdom of the LORD* over Israel. (1 Chron 28:5)

> And now you think to withstand the *kingdom of the LORD* in the hand of the sons of David, because you are a great multitude and have with you the golden calves which Jeroboam made you for gods. (2 Chron 13:8)

Such statements drive home the important insight of Raymond Brown that we quoted in an earlier chapter: namely, that "[David's] kingdom ... was also God's kingdom", and "the kingdom established by David ... is the closest Old Testament parallel to the New Testament church".[5] If this was true in Samuel and Kings, it is even more so in Chronicles, in which the kingdom of YHWH is manifested on earth precisely through the kingdom of David, which is, in the words of biblical scholar Scott Hahn, a kind of *liturgical empire*.[6]

Indeed, the Chronicler places every bit as much if not more emphasis on the covenant with David,

> ### The "Qahal" in Chronicles
>
> One of the most important theological concepts in Chronicles is the *qahal*, the sacred "assembly" or "congregation" (2 Chron 1). The Hebrew noun *qahal* derives from a verbal root meaning "to gather or assemble" that occurs in both verbal and nominal forms about forty times in Chronicles. It almost always refers to a sacred assembly, a body of people representing the entire nation at worship in the Temple under the leadership of the king. In the LXX, the word *qahal* is translated as *ekklēsia*, which in turn is taken up in the New Testament as the descriptive term for the body of disciples who form around Jesus Christ, usually translated "church" in English (Mt 16:18; 18:17). The English word "church", however, is an etymological descendant of the Greek term *kyriakon dōma*, "the Lord's house".

which he reproduces from 2 Samuel 7 virtually verbatim in order to clarify that the sons of David ruled by divine right over Israel and the nations (1 Chron 17; cf. 2 Sam 7). If the Ark of the Covenant, the Temple, and the cultic liturgy were

---

[5] Raymond E. Brown, S.S., "Communicating the Divine and Human in Scripture", *Origins* 22.1 (May 14, 1992): 5–6.

[6] See Hahn, *Kingdom of God*, 13.

important in Samuel and Kings, they are *dominant* in Chronicles. The ideal king for the Chronicler is modeled on David, who is portrayed first of all as a liturgical reformer. David's military accomplishments are mentioned, but primarily as external signs of God's blessing and approval of his reign (1 Chron 18–19). Far more attention is given to his liturgical reforms of the Levites and his preparations for the building of the Temple. Likewise, the accounts of the reigns of his upright sons—Solomon, Jehoshaphat, (the young) Joash, Hezekiah, Josiah, (the elderly) Manasseh—are dominated by descriptions of their attentions to the Temple; the celebration of the liturgy; and the purification, reinvigoration, and reorganization of the priests, Levites, and Temple personnel. For the Chronicler, the kingdom of Israel is a liturgical empire, a political body whose main *raison d'être* is the celebration of the liturgy of the Lord in the Temple in Jerusalem. The high points of the narrative are, therefore, those occasions where the Davidic king rallies the priests and Levites and gathers "all Israel" to Jerusalem to celebrate a great liturgical feast: David's dedication of the ark (1 Chron 15–16), Solomon's dedication of the Temple (2 Chron 6–7), Asa's repair of the Temple and covenant renewal (2 Chron 15:8–15), Hezekiah's Passover (2 Chron 30), and Josiah's Passover (2 Chron 35:1–19). These events function as a kind of foretaste of the future restoration of the twelve tribes of Israel, for which the Chronicler himself is still waiting.

History Remembered and the Hope for the Restoration of Israel

Finally, we may observe that the Chronicler interprets the history of the Israelite monarchy in such a way as to encourage the efforts of his contemporaries to restore the kingdom and the Temple, which the books of Samuel and Kings did not do. Perhaps unintentionally, the author of Kings in particular composed a narrative that seems to imply that the righteous and devout cannot expect much material or temporal help from the Lord.

In Kings, the southern kingdom of Judah, despite having a licit cult and several righteous kings, often appears as militarily, politically, and economically inferior, even pathetic, compared to the dynamic northern kingdom, which appears to enjoy socioeconomic and military superiority despite being a kingdom of idolaters under wicked monarchs. Furthermore, in Kings, the accounts of the two most righteous sons of David, Hezekiah and Josiah, are dominated by their near- or actual deaths at the hands of foreign kings or illness. On the other hand, wicked men like Manasseh and Omri enjoy apparently long and prosperous reigns. The reader of Samuel and Kings, therefore, could get the impression that "good guys always finish last" and therefore there is little reason to expect that righteous behavior in the present will be blessed with any material or temporal benefit from God. This demoralizes and enervates efforts for reform and renewal.

The Chronicler, by contrast, rewrites the history of Israel to demonstrate that the reality was more complex than portrayed in Kings and that there was a correlation between the moral behavior of the monarchs and the success of their careers. This is usually called the Chronicler's emphasis on "immediate retribution"; that is, he shows that immorality brought quick temporal punishment in the lives of the Judean rulers, whereas righteousness led to economic and military strength and success. To take a couple of examples, in Chronicles we discover that several of the righteous kings of Judah enjoyed great military strength (2 Chron 17:12–19; 26:11–15). Abijah actually was more powerful than Jeroboam in his own lifetime because he placed trust in the Lord (2 Chron 13:3–22), whatever his other failings may have been. Likewise, in Chronicles Manasseh's long rule (fifty-five years) is not despite his great wickedness but is a result of his repentance and efforts at reform (2 Chron 33:10–17).

The way history is remembered always has an effect on the present. It can be healthy to meditate on the sins of the past; the author of Samuel and Kings does this excessively, not sparing even David and Solomon, and the Chronicler and his readers are only too aware of the narrative of Samuel-Kings. But too long a meditation on negative examples can be spiritually crippling. The Chronicler knows that for constructive action in the present, the people of God need to nurture their faith on examples of fidelity and divine deliverance in their history. Likewise, God's people need to be assured that there is a just God, who rewards the righteous in the end, and that even in the short term, efforts to restore the faith and institutions of the people of God are not doomed to arbitrary failure but can expect God's assistance.

1–2 Chronicles in the Living Tradition

Given the prominent tradition, going back to the Greek Septuagint, of referring to the books of Chronicles as some "Things Left Over", it is to be expected that their role in the living tradition is far outweighed by the more detailed books of Samuel and Kings. They were not, to say the least, the object of many commentaries. Nevertheless, as shown above, they play an essential role in rounding out the memory of the history of Israel, and certain distinctive aspects of their account have garnered the attention of writers through the ages.

The Threshing Floor of the Gentile Ornan as a Type of the Church

As we have seen on more than one occasion, ancient Christian writers were always on the lookout for aspects of Old Testament history that pointed forward to the remarkable conversion of the pagan nations to the worship of the one God of Israel. One example of this lay in the Church Fathers' interpretation of the threshing floor of the pagan Ornan as the chosen site for the Temple of the Israelites. Why would God choose a pagan site for his holy sanctuary? Venerable Bede answers this question by declaring that the threshing floor itself was prophetic:

> It is appropriate that this place [the Temple] should be on the threshing-floor of Ornan the Jebusite because the Church is customarily designated by the term threshing-floor as John [the Baptist] says ... *He will clear his threshing-floor* (Mt 3:12). Ornan, whose name means "enlightened" and who was a Jebusite by origin,

signifies the gentiles by his origin, and by *his name he indicates these same (gentiles) who were to be enlightened by the Lord and transformed into children of the Church.*[7]

King Solomon and the True Prince of Peace

Along similar lines, the Church Fathers did not fail to notice the typological significance of the important explanation in Chronicles for why King David was not allowed to build the Temple. On the one hand, they recognized that Solomon was the builder of the earthly Temple; on the other, they also noticed that Solomon failed to live up to the full meaning of his name and that the true peace would have to be brought by another descendant of King David:

> *Solomon means "peaceable"; as you can find in the Chronicles....* It is well known, however, that Solomon died without living long, and that his throne came to an end. He gives the name Solomon, therefore, to our peaceable Lord, of whom blessed Paul says, "For he is our peace, who has made the two one and has broken down the dividing wall" (Eph 2:14).... Now it was not Solomon who had dominion to the ends of the world but he who sprang from Solomon in his humanity, *Jesus Christ, and was called Solomon on account of his peaceable and gentle nature and his being the cause of peace.*[8]

Indeed, in the light of the New Covenant, it is the "Church"—the true "assembly" (Hebrew *qahal*; Greek *ekklēsia*)—gathered around the Eucharist under the Son of David and his royal princes in succession from the twelve apostles that is the liturgical empire for which the Chronicler longed. As the book of Hebrews tells us, it is to this "assembly [*ekklēsia*] of the first-born" (Heb 12:22–23) that the children of God do indeed "go up" in worship (cf. 2 Chron 36:23).

King Manasseh as a Model of Repentance from Terrible Sins

Finally, it is important to note that the Church Fathers read the books of Chronicles closely enough in comparison with Kings to notice the fact that in this work, although King Manasseh was a thoroughly wicked king, he also is recorded as having *repented* of his many sins. In the tender words of John Chrysostom:

> Manasses, having exceeded all in fury and tyranny, and having subverted the legal form of worship, and shut up the temple, and caused the deceit of idolatry to flourish and having become more ungodly than all before him, when he afterwards repented, was ranked amongst the friends of God. *Now, if looking to the magnitude of his own iniquities, he had despaired of restoration and repentance, he would have*

---

[7] Bede, *On the Temple* 1.5.4–5, trans. Seán Connolly, Translated Texts for Historians 21 (Liverpool: Liverpool University Press, 1995), 21.

[8] Theodoret of Cyrus, *Commentary on the Song of Songs* 3, trans. Robert C. Hill, Early Christian Studies 2 (Brisbane: Australian Catholic University, 2001), 73, as quoted in *1–2 Kings, 1–2 Chronicles, Ezra, Nehemiah, Esther*, ed. Marco Conti, Ancient Christian Commentary on Scripture, ed. Thomas C. Oden, Old Testament 5 (Downers Grove, Ill.: InterVarsity Press, 2008), 264.

missed all which he afterwards obtained; but as it was, looking to the boundlessness of God's tender mercy instead of the enormity of his transgressions, and having broken in sunder the bonds of the devil, he rose up and contended with him and finished the good course.[9]

In this way, King Manasseh in the books of Chronicles became an important model for Christians, giving hope to the hopeless and testifying to the fact that no sinner is so far gone that he cannot repent and receive mercy and forgiveness of the Lord.

The Books of Chronicles in the Lectionary

The books of Chronicles are accessible to believers almost exclusively through private reading, as the books are rarely used in the Lectionary and the Divine Office.

Among the few texts used, the most significant is the account of David's bringing of the ark up to Jerusalem (1 Chron 15:3—16:2), which is treated by the Church as a prefiguration of the Assumption of Mary and employed on the vigil of that feast and as a first-reading option in the Common of the Blessed Virgin Mary. Also significant is the account of King Joash's martyrdom of Zechariah son of Jehoiada (2 Chron 24:18–22), often considered the last of the Old Testament martyrs and apparently mentioned by Jesus in Luke 11:51: "the blood from Abel to *the blood of Zechariah*" will be "required of this generation". This passage is the first option for the Common of Martyrs, and the only passage from Chronicles read on a ferial day. Lastly, the final chapter of 2 Chronicles provides a useful theological summary of the decline, destruction, exile, and return of the people of Judah. Selections from it (2 Chron 36:14–16, 19–23) are employed to review this stage of salvation history during the Sundays of Lent in Year B.

Readings from Chronicles for Sundays, Feast Days, Liturgical Seasons, and Other Occasions			
MSO = Masses for Special Occasions; *OM* = Optional Memorial; *VM* = Votive Mass; *Rit* = Ritual			
Passage	Description	Occasion	Explanation
1 Chron 15:3–4, 15–16; 16:1–2	David brings the Ark of the Covenant into Jerusalem with the help of and musical accompaniment by the Levites.	*Vigil of the Assumption;* Common of the BVM, opt. 4	The Church perceives the Blessed Virgin as the new Ark of the Covenant, since she bore within herself the Word of God, the Bread from Heaven, and the great High Priest. The ascension of the ark to Jerusalem prefigures Mary's Assumption to heaven.

(continued)

---

[9] John Chrysostom, *Letter to the Fallen Theodore* 1.6, trans. W. R. W. Stephens, in *NPNF1* 9:95.

Readings from Chronicles for Sundays, Feast Days, Liturgical Seasons, and Other Occasions (continued)

MSO = Masses for Special Occasions; *OM* = Optional Memorial;
VM = Votive Mass; *Rit* = Ritual

Passage	Description	Occasion	Explanation
29:10, 11abc, 11d–12a, 12bcd	David's doxology at the end of his life, after commissioning Solomon to build the Temple	Responsorial Psalm for *MSO*: Dedication of a Church; In Thanksgiving to God	David's last doxology in his public farewell to Israel is the basis for the common doxology appended to the Lord's Prayer: "For Thine is the kingdom, the power, and the glory forever." The Church employs David's doxology on occasions of liturgical thanksgiving.
2 Chron 5:6–10, 13—6:2	Solomon has the ark brought into the Temple to the accompanying praise of the Levitical musicians and begins his prayer of dedication.	*MSO*: Anniversary of the Dedication of a Church, opt. 2	A church building, wherein the Eucharist is celebrated and reserved in the Tabernacle, is in some ways analogous to the Temple of old, which contained the bread from heaven, the manna, within the holy ark.
24:18–22	Joash martyrs Zechariah, son of Jehoiada.	Common of Martyrs, opt. 1	Jehoiada is often considered the last of the Old Testament martyrs because in the Jewish tradition 2 Chronicles is the last biblical book.
36:14–16, 19–23	Synopsis of the decline of Judah, the Babylonian exile, and Cyrus' decree of return	*4th Sun. of Lent (B)*	The Sundays of Lent present a brief summary of the major events of salvation history in the first readings. This reading covers the decline, exile, and return of Judah—a large swath of history in a few short verses.

Reading of Chronicles for Daily Mass: Ordinary Time, Year II: Week 11

Week	Day	Passage Read	Description
11	Sat	2 Chron 24:17–25	Joash martyrs Zechariah, the son of Jehoiada.

In the Liturgy of the Hours

14	Th	1 Chron 22:5–19	David's preparations for the building of the Temple, paired with St. Ambrose on Psalm 118, discussing the Christian as God's Temple
15	F	2 Chron 20:1–9, 13–24	Jehoshaphat's victory over the eastern hosts by means of the Levitical praise choirs
March 25, Annunciation		1 Chron 17:1–15	The Chronicler's version of the covenant with David, seen fulfilled in the words of Gabriel to Mary (Lk 1:30–33); also used in the Common of the BVM

Conclusion

The books of Chronicles retell the history of Israel in such a way as to assure the Jews living in Judah after the Babylonian exile that God's saving plan is still ongoing and they are part of it, that their national history provides reasons for pride and gratitude to God, and that they may expect God's support in their efforts to rebuild their national life around the worship of the Lord. Chronicles recasts the kingdom of David as a liturgical empire, a union of the twelve tribes of Israel and even other nations gathered around the Jerusalem Temple to celebrate the sacred liturgy revealed through Moses and reinvigorated by David. Chronicles' vision of the people of God as the "kingdom of the LORD" at worship under the leadership of the Son of David segues directly into Jesus' proclamation and establishment of the "kingdom of God", the *qahal* or *ekklēsia* of the New Covenant.

For Further Reading

Commentaries and Studies on 1–2 Chronicles

Hahn, Scott W. *The Kingdom of God as Liturgical Empire: A Theological Commentary on 1–2 Chronicles*. Grand Rapids, Mich.: Baker Academic, 2012.

Hamilton, Victor. *Handbook on the Historical Books*. Grand Rapids, Mich.: Baker Academic, 2001. (See pp. 477–501.)

Japhet, Sara. *I and II Chronicles: A Commentary*. Old Testament Library. Louisville, Ky.: Westminster John Knox Press, 1993.

Knoppers, Gary N. *1 Chronicles 1–9*. Anchor Yale Bible 12. New York: Doubleday, 2004.

———. 1 Chronicles 10-29. Anchor Yale Bible 12A. New York: Doubleday, 2007.

Myers, Jacob M. *2 Chronicles*. Anchor Bible 13. Garden City, N.Y.: Doubleday, 1965.

Historical Issues in 1–2 Chronicles

Bright, John. *A History of Israel*. 4th ed. Louisville, Ky.: Westminster John Knox Press, 2000.

Kitchen, Kenneth A. *On the Reliability of the Old Testament*. Grand Rapids, Mich.: Eerdmans, 2003. (See pp. 7–158.)

Mabie, Frederick James. "2 Chronicles". Pages 286–393 in *1 & 2 Kings, 1 & 2 Chronicles, Ezra, Nehemiah, Esther*. Vol. 3 of *Zondervan Illustrated Bible Backgrounds Commentary*. Edited by John H. Walton. Downers Grove, Ill.: InterVarsity Press, 2009.

Provan, Iain W., V. Philips Long, and Tremper Longman III. *A Biblical History of Israel*. Louisville, Ky.: Westminster John Knox Press, 2003.

Sherwin, Simon. "1 Chronicles". Pages 220–85 in *1 & 2 Kings, 1 & 2 Chronicles, Ezra, Nehemiah, Esther*. Vol. 3 of *Zondervan Illustrated Bible Backgrounds Commentary*. Edited by John H. Walton. Downers Grove, Ill.: InterVarsity Press, 2009.

1–2 Chronicles in the Living Tradition

Bede, Venerable. *On the Temple*. Translated by Seán Connolly. Translated Texts for Historians 21. Liverpool: Liverpool University Press, 1995.

Conti, Marco, ed. *1–2 Kings, 1–2 Chronicles, Ezra, Nehemiah, Esther*. Old Testament 5 of Ancient Christian Commentary on Scripture. Edited by Thomas C. Oden. Downers Grove, Ill.: InterVarsity Press, 2008. (See pp. 242–302.)

Theodoret of Cyrus. *Commentary on the Song of Songs*. Translated by Robert C. Hill. Early Christian Studies 2. Brisbane: Australian Catholic University, 2001.

17. EZRA AND NEHEMIAH

Introduction

Like Samuel, Kings, and Chronicles, the books of Ezra and Nehemiah seem to be one composition broken into two volumes during the history of the transmission of the biblical text. And, like the other historical books, there is considerable diversity in the tradition concerning the naming and delineation of Ezra and Nehemiah. In this case, however, the canonical books and other closely related non-canonical compositions have been counted among the books of "Esdras", the Greek form of the name Ezra (see chart).

	Masoretic Text (Hebrew)	Vulgate (Latin)	Septuagint (Greek)	Most English Versions	Alternate English Names
			Naming Traditions for the Books of Ezra		
1	Ezra	1 Esdras	Esdras B', or 2 Esdras	Ezra	Ezra-Nehemiah
2	Nehemiah	2 Esdras		Nehemiah	
3	*Absent*	3 Esdras	Esdras A', or 1 Esdras	1 Esdras	3 Ezra, or Greek Ezra
4		4 Esdras	*Absent*	2 Esdras	4 Ezra, or Latin Esdras

As the chart makes clear, in the Hebrew Masoretic Text, the two books are divided under the names Ezra and Nehemiah, but the glosses in the margins and other later rabbinic textual notes (known as the apparatus) treat them as one book. For example, the Jewish Masoretic scribes identified Nehemiah 3:32 as the midpoint of the composition. Moreover, no word count is given for Ezra alone, but total word count of Ezra-Nehemiah is given at the end of Nehemiah, showing that the Masoretes counted it as one book.

In contrast, the Septuagint book known as *1 Esdras* (Greek *Esdras A'*) is actually a combination of the last two chapters of Chronicles and the canonical book of Ezra, with one significant narrative expansion (1 Esdras 2:30—5:6) and a few verses of Nehemiah added on the end (Neh 7:73—8:12 = 1 Esdras 9:37-55). The canonical Ezra-Nehemiah in Greek translation is *2 Esdras* (Greek *Esdras B'*). This Septuagintal tradition differs significantly from the Latin Vulgate, in which Ezra and Nehemiah are called "1 Esdras" and "2 Esdras" respectively, as they appear in the Douay-Rheims.

Finally, the non-canonical document usually known today as *4 Ezra* (Vulgate *4 Esdras*) is an entirely unrelated work, a piece of apocalyptic literature similar in genre to the book of Revelation, relating visions supposedly seen by Ezra.

Although not Sacred Scripture, it has the unique position of being traditionally placed in an appendix to the Vulgate.

With this basic background in mind, following contemporary scholarship, we will refer to Ezra-Nehemiah as one book. This work segues smoothly from the end of Chronicles, recounting the fate of the Judeans who returned from Babylon following the Decree of Cyrus (ca. 537 B.C.) and paying particular attention to the rebuilding of the Temple and city walls, the renewal of the Mosaic covenant, and the separation of the Jews from the Gentile inhabitants of the land. In this way, it constitutes a small but significant testament to the return from exile and the rebuilding of Judean hopes and dreams for the land in the city of Jerusalem.

Literary Structure of Ezra and Nehemiah

The structure of Ezra-Nehemiah can be difficult to discern, in part because the book consists of a collection of documents of many different literary genres: third-person historical narration, first-person memoirs, genealogies, census reports, official letters, covenant documents, lists of many sorts, and other genres.

Nonetheless, it is possible to identify five major sections. The first six chapters (Ezra 1–6) describe the ups and downs of efforts to rebuild the Temple in Jerusalem from the initial Decree of Cyrus until its completion (ca. 537–516 B.C.). A period of more than fifty years is passed over in silence before the start of the next section (Ezra 7–10), which describes the priest-scribe Ezra's mission to Jerusalem around 458 B.C. to restore observance of the Mosaic law among the Judean returnees.

In the third section, Nehemiah records his mission to Jerusalem to rebuild the city walls around 444 B.C. (Neh 1–7), followed by what appears to be a lengthy description of a covenant-renewal ceremony under the leadership of both Ezra and Nehemiah that took place after the completion of the walls (roughly Neh 8–12). The fifth and final section is a somewhat melancholy epilogue written by Nehemiah about his return to Jerusalem many years later (ca. 427 B.C.?), only to discover religious laxity and social injustices that had grown up in his absence (Neh 13).

The following is a more detailed outline of the book:

Outline of Ezra and Nehemiah

I. From Cyrus' Decree to the Completion of the Temple, ca. 537–516 B.C. (Ezra 1–6)
   A. The Decree of Cyrus Permitting Return (1:1–6)
   B. The Return of the Temple Vessels (1:7–10)
   C. Census of the Returnees (2:1–70)
   D. Restoration of the Sacrificial Liturgy (3:1–7)
   E. Foundation of the Temple Relaid (3:8–13)
   F. The Building Slowed and Halted by Opposition (4:1—5:17)
   G. The Decree of Darius Permitting Temple Reconstruction (6:1–12)
   H. Completion of the Temple and Celebration of Passover (6:13–22)

II. Ezra's Mission of Reform and Renewal, ca. 458 B.C. (Ezra 7–10)
   A. Ezra Arrives in Jerusalem with a Letter of Commission (7:1–28)
   B. The Persons, Materials, and Manner of the Ezra's Return (8:1–36)
   C. Ezra's Prayer of Repentance upon His Arrival (9:1–15)
   D. People's Response to Ezra's Prayer: Separation from the Gentiles (10:1–43)

III. Nehemiah Rebuilds the Walls of Jerusalem, ca. 444 B.C. (Neh 1–7)
   A. The Prelude to the Rebuilding of the Walls (1–2)
      1. Nehemiah's Prayer (chap. 1)
      2. Nehemiah's Request (2:1–8)
      3. Nehemiah's Commission (2:9–10)
      4. Nehemiah's Inspection of the Walls (2:11–20)
   B. The Wall Is Built: List of the Builders (3:1–32)
   C. Hostile Plots Are Frustrated (4:1–23)
   D. Nehemiah's Efforts for Social Justice (5:1–19)
   E. More Hostile Plots Frustrated (6:1–14)
   F. The Wall Is Completed: List of Returnees (6:15—7:73)

IV. The Great Covenant Renewal, ca. 444 B.C. (Neh 8:1—13:3)
   A. Ezra and the Feast of Tabernacles (8–10)
      1. Reading of the Law (8:1–12)
      2. Celebration of Tabernacles (8:13–18)
      3. Public Confession of Sin (9:1–5)
      4. The Solemnization of the Covenant-Renewal Document (9:38—10:39)
   B. Census of the Returned Exiles (11—12:26)
      1. In Jerusalem (11:1–24)
      2. In the Suburbs (11:25–36)
      3. Priests and Levites (12:1–26)
   C. Nehemiah and the Dedication of the Wall (12:27—13:3)
      1. Wall Dedication Ceremony (12:27–43)
      2. Temple Officials (12:44–47)
      3. The Reading of the Law and Separation from the Gentiles (13:1–3)

V. Epilogue: Nehemiah's Disappointing Return After Several Years (Neh 13)
   A. Temple Reforms (13:4–14)
   B. Sabbath Reform (13:15–22)
   C. Marriage Reform (13:23–30)

Overview of Ezra and Nehemiah

The Decree of King Cyrus and the Rebuilding of the Temple (Ezra 1–6)

Ezra opens with an expanded repetition of the last two verses of 2 Chronicles (2 Chron 36:22–23; Ezra 1:1–4), forging a literary link between the two works and revealing the hand of providence in the return from exile:

> In the first year of Cyrus king of Persia, *that the word of the LORD by the mouth of Jeremiah might be accomplished,* the LORD stirred up the spirit of Cyrus king of Persia so that he made a proclamation throughout all his kingdom and also put it in writing:
> "Thus says Cyrus king of Persia: The LORD, the God of heaven, has given me all the kingdoms of the earth, and *he has charged me to build him a house at Jerusalem, which is in Judah.*" (Ezra 1:1–2)

Notice here that the role previously assigned to David and Solomon—that of building the "house" for YHWH—has now been taken over by a Gentile king. All this the sacred author sees as the hand of divine providence and the fulfillment of prophecy. As a result, Cyrus' decree provokes a large number of leading Jewish citizens to embark on a return migration to their homeland. The Temple vessels captured by Nebuchadnezzar are returned into the custody of a certain Sheshbazzar, a prince of Judah, and the restoration of the cult in Jerusalem begins.

Although the initial return to Jerusalem and Judah is led by Zerubbabel of the house of David, Jeshua the high priest, and other leading citizens (Ezra 2:1–2), the sacred author makes a point of showing that a remarkable number of Judeans participated in the return, providing a rough census of the returnees by family and clan (Ezra 2:2–70). The first order of business upon arrival in Jerusalem is to reestablish the altar of the Lord and restart the cycle of the sacrificial liturgy (Ezra 3:1–7). Next, the returnees lay the foundation for a new Temple and hold a celebration when the foundation is complete (Ezra 3:8–13):

> And all the people shouted with a great shout, when they praised the LORD, because the foundation of the house of the LORD was laid. *But many of the priests and Levites and heads of fathers' houses, old men who had seen the first house, wept with a loud voice when they saw the foundation of this house being laid,* though many shouted aloud for joy; so that the people could not distinguish the sound of the joyful shout from the sound of the people's weeping, for the people shouted with a great shout, and the sound was heard afar. (Ezra 3:11–13)

After word gets out about the rebuilding of the Temple, the so-called "people of the land" (Hebrew *'am ha'aretz*)—descendants of the peoples brought in by the Assyrians to repopulate northern Israel (2 Kings 17:24–41) and ancestors of the Samaritans—offer to help in the reconstruction of the Temple. However, the Jewish returnees rebuff them (Ezra 4:1–5). In response, the offended "people of the land" persuade the Persian authorities to put a stop to Jewish efforts at rebuilding the Temple (Ezra 4:6–24). Thus, the work of restoration ceases for many years, until around 520 B.C., when the prophets Haggai and Zechariah rise up and goad the populace into renewing their reconstruction efforts (Ezra 5). Their appeal to the newly ascended Persian King Darius to uphold the policy of his predecessor, Cyrus, concerning the rebuilding of the Jerusalem Temple meets with success. Darius encourages their efforts, and the "Second Temple" is completed to much celebration around 516 B.C. (Ezra 6:13–18). Then, for the first time in a very long time, there is a national celebration of the Feast of Passover in Jerusalem (Ezra 6:19–22). Thus the festival that had once functioned as a celebration of *entry* into the Promised Land under Joshua now functions as the celebration of the *return* to the land under Jeshua and Zerubbabel (see Josh 5).

The Mission of Ezra the Priest (Ezra 7–10)

Over half a century passes in silence. The narrative resumes in the seventh year of Artaxerxes, king of Persia (ca. 458 B.C.), who authorizes a certain Ezra, a priest and scribe of impeccable pedigree, to return to Jerusalem, revitalize the Temple cult, and impose Judean traditional law—that is, the law of Moses—on all the inhabitants of the Persian province of Trans-Euphrates (Ezra 7:1–28). Ezra returns with a large entourage of leading Jewish residents of Mesopotamia, many of them descendants of priestly or Levitical ancestors. Upon his arrival in Jerusalem, Ezra discovers that the upper classes of Judean society, including priests and Levites, have been intermarrying with the pagan peoples of the land, putting the covenant in grave danger:

> The sons of Israel and the priests and the Levites *have not separated themselves from the peoples of the lands with their abominations*, from the Canaanites, the Hittites, the Perizzites, the Jebusites, the Ammonites, the Moabites, the Egyptians, and the Amorites. For they have taken some of their daughters to be wives for themselves and for their sons; so that the holy race has mixed itself with the peoples of the lands. And in this *faithlessness* the hand of the officials and chief men has been foremost. (Ezra 9:1–2)

Notice here that the issue is not "interracial" marriage as modern people might construe it, but *intercultic* marriage with pagan peoples of the land—a problem seen before in Scripture, whether it was the Sethites and Cainites (Gen 6:1–4), the Israelites and Moabites (Num 25), or many other examples. In response to this crisis of intermarriage, Ezra calls for national reform and repentance. The leading citizens, priests, and Levites heed his call and separate from their Gentile wives and children (Ezra 10:1–44).

The Mission of Nehemiah and the Building of the Walls (Nehemiah 1–7)

Another sixteen years or so is passed over in silence before the narrative resumes in the first person by a certain Nehemiah son of Hacaliah (Neh 1:1). Unlike Ezra, who was an Aaronic priest, Nehemiah is a layman, and, as such, his lineage is not known, though he may have been a Judean aristocrat, perhaps even of the house of David.

This Nehemiah was "cupbearer" to King Artaxerxes, a position that amounted to a highly trusted royal advisor (Neh 1:11). Nehemiah both prays fervently to God and employs his influence with the king to obtain a royal commission to return to Jerusalem and fortify the city (Neh 1–2). Notwithstanding the efficacious character of Nehemiah's prayers, the fortification of a Jerusalem loyal to Persia may have served Persian imperial interests at this time, since the empire was threatened in the west by a resurgent Egyptian monarchy.[1]

---

[1] Kenneth A. Kitchen, *On the Reliability of the Old Testament* (Grand Rapids, Mich.: Eerdmans, 2003), 77–78.

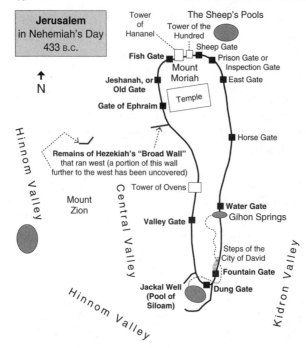

Jerusalem under Nehemiah

After being granted permission, Nehemiah returns to Jerusalem with a military force and letters from the king. After surveying the pathetic defenses of the city, he organizes the citizens into a construction force. The very real fear of attack by non-Jewish residents of the land forces the Jews to live in a state of constant military readiness (Neh 4–5). Even those engaged in constructing the walls have to be armed at all times (Neh 4:18, 23)! Nonetheless, despite the threats and interference, the Jerusalemites succeed in rebuilding the city walls in less than two months.

The Celebration of Tabernacles and the Completion of the Walls (Nehemiah 8–12)

With the wall complete, in the seventh month of the same year, Ezra and Nehemiah lead the people of Judah and Jerusalem in celebrating the Feast of Tabernacles (Neh 8). The description of this ceremony is remarkable, for it is the most ancient description we possess of a liturgical ceremony in the Old Testament in which the reading of the law of Moses—which was required for the Feast of Tabernacles (Deut 31:10–13)—is coupled with an *explanation* of the meaning of the text by ordained men: "And they [the Levites] read from the book, from the law of God, clearly; and *they gave the sense, so that the people understood the reading*" (Neh 8:8). The reason this explanation is necessary is that after living in Babylon for so long, the common people no longer spoke or understood classical Hebrew, but had adopted *Aramaic*, a northwest Semitic language similar to Hebrew that served as the international tongue of the Assyrian, Babylonian, and Persian empires successively.[2]

> *One Celebration or Two?*
>
> Nehemiah 8:1–10:39 describes a celebration of the Feast of Tabernacles (Booths) under the leadership of Ezra and Nehemiah that culminated in a formal renewal of the Mosaic covenant (Neh 9:38—10:39). Nehemiah 12:27—13:3 describes a very similar celebration occurring at the dedication of the city walls. The two descriptions may be complementary accounts of the same event: a celebration of the completion of the walls during the Feast of Tabernacles.

[2] See Edwin M. Yamauchi, "Ezra and Nehemiah", in *1 & 2 Kings, 1 & 2 Chronicles, Ezra, Nehemiah, Esther*, vol. 3 of *Zondervan Illustrated Bible Backgrounds Commentary*, ed. John H. Walton (Grand Rapids, Mich.: Zondervan, 2009), 398.

The reading of the law provokes spontaneous expressions of sorrow for sin among the people, but the leaders encourage the populace to be joyful at this time of covenant renewal, famously declaring: "the joy of the LORD is your strength" (Neh 8:10). Ezra's long prayer of repentance calls to mind themes from Solomon's prayer at the dedication of the Temple (Neh 9:6–37) and probably represents the theological heart and literary high point of Ezra-Nehemiah. In the aftermath of Ezra's reading and prayer, the leaders of the people formally ratify a covenant-renewal document, committing themselves to follow all the law of Moses, with special emphasis on four elements of pressing concern: (1) refraining from intermarriage; (2) observance of the Sabbath, both weekly and yearly; (3) observance of Mosaic laws of debt forgiveness; and (4) generous fulfillment of the laws of tithes and sacrifices for the support of the Temple cult and personnel (Neh 10).

The covenant document is followed by a rough census of the population of Jerusalem, Judah, and the Temple personnel around the time of the covenant renewal (Neh 11:1—12:26). It also records what appears to be Nehemiah's account of the dedication of the city wall (Neh 12:27—13:3), which may have been concurrent with Ezra's celebration of the Feast of Tabernacles. The walls of the city of Jerusalem are "dedicated" (Hebrew *channukah*), a term previously limited to the inauguration of the altar (Num 7:8–11; 2 Chron 7:9) and the Temple (Ezra 6:16–17), thereby, in a certain sense, extending the holiness of the sanctuary outward to the city.

Nehemiah's Return and the Crisis of Intermarriage (Nehemiah 13:4–30)

Nehemiah governs the province of Judah for twelve years before returning to the service of King Artaxerxes. After an undisclosed amount of time, he obtains permission from the king to return to Jerusalem to check on conditions there. He finds things in disarray, with foreigners having taken up residence in the Temple, the tithes and offerings unpaid, many of the Temple personnel having fled back to their homes, the Sabbath violated, and intermarriage with Gentiles resumed. Although Nehemiah takes strenuous measures to counteract these offenses, the book ends on a note of melancholy, as it becomes apparent that apart from the vigorous leadership of individuals like Nehemiah, the people of Judea are still incapable of observing the laws of the covenant. In addition to the partial nature of the restoration of the Temple, the moral restoration of the people is likewise incomplete and will need much more than just an excellent leader to come to fruition.

Historical Questions about Ezra and Nehemiah

The Origins of Ezra-Nehemiah

Ancient Jewish tradition attributes the authorship of Ezra-Nehemiah to Ezra himself.[3] While this is not impossible, it seems more likely that Ezra-Nehemiah

---

[3] See Babylonian Talmud, *Baba Bathra* 14b, in Isidore Epstein, ed., *The Babylonian Talmud*, 35 vols. (London: Soncino, 1935–1952).

Intermarriage in Ezra-Nehemiah

The intermarriage of Jewish men with foreign women arises as a major concern in Ezra-Nehemiah. Both reformers are forced to confront the issue (Ezra 9–10; Neh 13:3, 23–30).

It was primarily the upper classes of Judean society—"officials", "chief men", priests, and Levites (Ezra 9:1–2)—who were intermarrying with non-Jewish inhabitants. In a society where social influence, political power, property rights, and wealth were largely determined by heredity and therefore by marriage, the social and religious consequences of cultic exogamy were dire for the entire community. If unchecked, this practice would result in a new generation of the Judean leadership caste that did not share the culture, religion, or sympathies of the common Jews over whom they ruled and whose public resources they largely controlled (Neh 13:24). Furthermore, the choice of the leading male citizens to marry non-Jewish wives left devout Jewish women without eligible spouses, facing a painful choice between a life of practical widowhood or marriage to a foreigner and the resulting loss of religion, culture, and family identity. High-born men were placing their own personal interests above that of their community and especially of its women.

It is a naïve imposition of modern categories to think the marriages of the Jewish leaders with foreign women was the result of romantic attachment. Instead, such marriages were contracted for political, social, and economic reasons, most likely to ally upper-class Jews with the leadership classes of surrounding peoples, creating an intermingled, elite ruling caste for the entire region. The losers in this arrangement would be the common Jews (cf. Neh 5:1–13) and those who took seriously the worship of the Lord according to the Mosaic covenant.

Ezra and Nehemiah's efforts to dissolve these interreligious and interethnic marriages are very offensive to the modern ethic of inclusion, and most modern commentators are highly critical of the two reformers. Modern sensibilities regard marriage purely as a private affair based on affection. In traditional societies, however, marriage is a public institution with important social-justice consequences for the entire community.

was compiled by an unknown author who used material from Ezra and Nehemiah's own memoirs as well as many other kinds of documents at some time in the late fifth century (ca. 400s B.C.).

Through the mid-twentieth century there was a widespread scholarly consensus that 1–2 Chronicles and Ezra-Nehemiah were written by the same author, the primary evidence being the repetition of the end of Chronicles in the opening lines of Ezra-Nehemiah (see Ezra 1:1–4). The two works also share a clear concern for the Temple, liturgy, priests, Levites, and obedience to the covenant.

Since the mid-twentieth century, however, the consensus of common authorship has disintegrated and even reversed. Now the two works are generally considered independent, as scholars place more emphasis on their differences. For example, Chronicles places enormous emphasis on the Davidic covenant, whereas Ezra-Nehemiah says very little about it. Likewise, as we saw in the last chapter, Chronicles is more open to the inhabitants of northern Israel and even Gentile adherents to the religion of Israel (cf. 2 Chron 30, 35), whereas Ezra-Nehemiah is highly suspicious of them (Ezra 4, 13; Neh 13).

In the end, there is no way to prove or disprove common authorship of Chronicles and Ezra-Nehemiah, and the interpretation of the books does not greatly hinge on the question.

Was Ezra's Mission before or after Nehemiah?

The major historical controversy in Ezra-Nehemiah is the dating of Ezra's mission to the "seventh year of Artaxerxes the king" (Ezra 7:7). Several kings bore this name: if Ezra refers to Artaxerxes I, then his mission took place around 458 B.C.; but if he is referring to Artaxerxes II, then his mission would have taken place around 397 B.C., *after* that of Nehemiah (ca. 444 B.C.). Confusingly, this would mean that the historical order of Ezra and Nehemiah's missions would be the opposite of the canonical order of the books!

A minority of scholars argues for a late mission in the reign of Artaxerxes II, which would explain why Nehemiah never mentions Ezra in any of his first-person accounts.[4] A majority of scholars, however, deem it unlikely that the author and his community had such a poor memory of major events as to invert the chronological sequence of Ezra and Nehemiah, for the book in its received form clearly presents Ezra as prior to Nehemiah and the two of them cooperating in the days of Nehemiah's governorship (Neh 8:9). This would require Ezra's Artaxerxes to be the first king of that name, the same as Nehemiah's monarch (Neh 2:1; 13:6).

The Value of Ezra-Nehemiah as History

Significantly, the Persian kings mentioned in Ezra-Nehemiah are almost the only characters in the book who are attested in extra-biblical literature. The biblical book itself together with a few anecdotes in the minor prophets constitute almost our only written sources for the history of Judah in the Persian period. One of the few exceptions is the *Letter to Bagoas*, an Aramaic document written on papyrus from a Jewish colony in Elephantine, Egypt, to the leadership of Jerusalem, dated to the seventeenth year of King Darius II of Persia.[5] This letter mentions a certain *Bagohi* (=Bigvai, Neh 7:19; 10:16) as governor of Jerusalem, *Sanballat* as governor of Samaria (Neh 13:28), and *Jehohanan* as high priest (=Johanan, Neh 12:22–23), thus providing support for the historicity of these leaders in the time immediately after the career of Nehemiah.

There has been much debate over the authenticity of the passages of Ezra-Nehemiah that purport to be official letters (Ezra 4:6–16; 4:17–23; 5:7–17; 6:6–12; 7:11–26) or first-person memoirs of the two titular reformers. On purely historical grounds, the question cannot be finally decided. It is possible that the embedded documents were written by some later unknown author. However, it is also plausible that we have in the book edited versions of official correspondence and excerpts from longer memoirs written by Ezra and Nehemiah themselves. As Kenneth Kitchen concludes in his massive study of the reliability of the Old Testament: "There is no good reason to deny the authenticity of the biblical Aramaic correspondence and other usages that we find in the biblical books relating to this [postexilic] period."[6] Indeed, given the fact that Ezra was

---

[4] See Victor Hamilton, *Handbook on the Historical Books* (Grand Rapids, Mich.: Baker Academic, 2001), 504–6.

[5] Cf. Yamauchi, "Ezra and Nehemiah", 411.

[6] Kitchen, *Reliability of the Old Testament*, 78.

a "scribe" and Nehemiah a high-ranking royal official, there is every reason to believe that both men were highly literate and would have left a literary corpus at their deaths.

Theological Issues in Ezra and Nehemiah

Partial Fulfillment of the Prophecies of Restoration

The book of Ezra-Nehemiah brings salvation history—stopped at the exile in Kings and Chronicles—into the postexilic or Persian period. The dominant theme is *the partial fulfillment of prophecies of restoration*. Notably, Jeremiah delivered two oracles that suggested the exile would be about seventy years in length (Jer 25:11–12; 29:10), to which the author of Ezra-Nehemiah refers in the opening verse (Ezra 1:1). There are important elements of restoration, tangible signs of God's mercy, manifest in the era of Ezra and Nehemiah, that should not be minimized: (1) the return of a large number of Judeans to their homeland, (2) the freedom and even encouragement to live by and enforce the law of the Mosaic covenant, and (3) the rebuilding of the Temple and restoration of the liturgy.

On the other hand, equally significant elements of restoration, clearly predicted by the prophets, were *not* experienced during the Persian era: (1) the restoration of the house of David and the Davidic covenant (Jer 33:15–17); (2) the implementation of the "new covenant" with its promise of interior transformation (Jer 31:31–34); (3) the restoration of the twelve tribes in a new exodus (Is 11:11–16); and (4) the arrival of God's special servant, the "anointed one", or Messiah (Is 61:1).

As hopeful as the liturgical festival of covenant renewal at the Feast of Tabernacles/wall dedication was (Neh 8–12), the moral and social decay Nehemiah discovers after his extended absence make it painfully obvious that the glorious promises of Jeremiah's New Covenant have not been realized (Neh 13). Therefore, the mournful ending of Ezra-Nehemiah can be understood, in light of the whole canon, as the recognition of the need for a new intervention by God in the life of his people, beyond what was possible merely by renewing commitment to the Mosaic covenant (as in Neh 10:1–39). Moreover, the danger of loss of faith and identity posed by intermarriage in the postexilic period indicates that the promise of universal blessing to the nations (Gen 12:3; 22:18; and so on) through the seed of Abraham has not materialized; rather, the people of God are still in a defensive mode, needing isolation from the nations to preserve their own covenant relationship with God, rather than being empowered for an offensive advance in mission to the Gentiles.

The lack of fulfillment of many of the prophetic promises in the partial restoration under Persian patronage and the leadership of Ezra and Nehemiah led many Jews to the realization that the exile had not truly ended, even if many of them resided once more in their traditional homeland. This sense of continuing exile is reflected in the theology of the Dead Sea Scrolls and other non-canonical Jewish writings of the Second Temple period (ca. 537 B.C.–A.D. 70).

The Importance of the Liturgy in Ezra and Nehemiah

The vision of Israel (developed in Chronicles) as a kingdom focused on the liturgy is continued in Ezra-Nehemiah. However, the kingdom aspect is understandably muted due to the political impossibility of the restoration of the Davidic monarchy. Zerubbabel, one of the early governors, was a Davidide. Possibly Nehemiah was too. Messianic hopes swirled around Zerubbabel but were not realized in his person. In the absence of a visible son of David, the role of the priesthood and the Levites became all the more important, and Judah developed into a kind of Temple-state, a situation that remained more or less in place into the period of the New Testament. During much of this period, the high priest was *de facto* ruler of the populace, though a vassal under whatever foreign monarch held military control over the land of Israel.

As in Kings and Chronicles, liturgical celebrations manifesting the unity of God's people and celebrating his mercy form the high points of the narrative of Ezra-Nehemiah: the dedication of the Temple and celebration of Passover (Ezra 6:13–22), the Feast of Tabernacles, and the dedication of the city walls (Neh 8–12). The people of God find their identity in worship. In the absence of political power or economic prosperity, they find hope, joy, and peace in celebrating liturgy, which recalls God's saving acts in the

---

The Feasts in Ezra-Nehemiah

Ezra-Nehemiah records the celebration of two liturgical festivals, Passover and Tabernacles, both associated with the dedication (*chanukkah*) of some aspect of the Temple-city, either the Temple itself (Ezra 6) or the city walls (Neh 12).

The Feast of Passover is familiar, but Tabernacles less so. Tabernacles, also known as "Booths", recalled the events of the exodus, when the Israelites dwelt in temporary shelters ("tabernacles") as they journeyed in the wilderness. In time, the feast also came to be associated with God's wilderness dwelling among the people of Israel in the Tabernacle—his temporary shelter, or "booth"—and finally with the expectation of an eschatological dwelling place of God, the New Temple. Thus, the celebration of Tabernacles in Nehemiah 8:1—13:3 is fraught with expectations about the dwelling of God with his people.

---

past and anticipates the ultimate salvation of God in the future. In many ways, this paradigm remains in place for the people of the New Covenant.

Ezra and Nehemiah in the Living Tradition

When we turn to the interpretation of Ezra and Nehemiah in the ancient Christian Church, the results are both disappointing and exhilarating. On the one hand, these books are almost never discussed in any of the extant patristic literature, with one scholar only being able to locate four passages in the first several centuries of the Church.[7] On the other hand, in the late seventh century A.D., Bede the Venerable composed a full-length commentary on Ezra and Nehemiah that is a truly stunning example of early medieval literal and spiritual exegesis.[8]

---

[7] Marco Conti, ed., *1–2 Kings, 1–2 Chronicles, Ezra, Nehemiah, Esther*, Old Testament 5, Ancient Christian Commentary on Scripture, ed. Thomas C. Oden (Downers Grove, Ill.: InterVarsity Press, 2008), xxviii.

[8] Bede, *On Ezra and Nehemiah*, trans. Scott DeGregorio, Translated Texts for Historians 47 (Liverpool: Liverpool University Press, 2006).

In this work, Bede interprets the returning exiles of Judah and their leaders as prefigurations of Christ and the Church in ways that, though unexpected, are truly remarkable. What follows are but a few examples.

The Passion of Ezra the Priest and the Passion of Christ

Although the figure of Ezra may not loom large in the imagination of contemporary Christians—indeed, many Christians probably do not even know who Ezra was—this was not the case in the thought of Bede the Venerable. In his commentary on Ezra and Nehemiah, he finds in the suffering, the intercession, and the deliverance wrought by Ezra several striking prefigurations of Jesus.

For example, Bede interprets Ezra's climactic act of tearing his garments, falling on his knees, spreading out his hands, and begging God to forgive the sins of the Jews who had mixed with pagan women as a prefiguration of Christ's intercession for the human race:

> Typologically... in the fact that with [Ezra's] garment torn he falls on his knees, spreads out his hands to God and turns the mind of very many to repentance by pouring out prayers and tears ... he represents the Lord Saviour, who deigned to pray for our sins both before and at the very time of his passion and who allowed his hands to be stretched out on the cross and the garment of his own flesh to be torn with wounds and mortified at the appointed time on behalf of our restoration.... *This was aptly done at the time of the evening sacrifice* ... because the Lord at the end of the age offered the sacrifice of his own flesh and blood to the Father and ordered that it should be offered by us in bread and wine.[9]

In other words, by doing penance on behalf of a sinful people and by acting as a priestly intercessor, Ezra foreshadows the willingly accepted affliction of Christ the High Priest, who will stretch out his arms on the gibbet of the Cross to intercede for the salvation of the whole world. And just as Ezra the Priest interceded "at the time of the evening sacrifice" (Neh 9:4)—that is, around 3 P.M.—so, too, Jesus the High Priest intercedes for mankind and offers the sacrifice of himself at "the ninth hour" (= 3 P.M.)—also the time of the evening sacrifice (see Mk 15:33–34).

The Return from Captivity and the Return to the Heavenly Promised Land

Perhaps even more striking, Bede sees in the entire narrative of the deliverance wrought by Ezra—release from captivity, return to the Promised Land, and rebuilding of the city of Jerusalem—a prefiguration of redemption wrought by Jesus the High Priest:

> Now *Ezra himself was clearly a type of the Lord Saviour too*, inasmuch as he restored sacred Scripture, recalled the people out from captivity to Jerusalem, enriched the Lord's house with greater gifts, appointed leaders and guardians beyond the River Euphrates who were familiar with God's Law, and purified descendants of the exiles

---

[9] Ibid., 2.12, pp. 141–42.

from their foreign wives.... *He led the people out from captivity in Babylonia and brought them now liberated to Jerusalem and the Promised Land, not only because by suffering on that one occasion on the cross he redeemed the world through his own blood, and descending in to Hell he rescued all true Israelites [i.e., the elect] he found there and, leading them to the walls of the heavenly city, granted them the joys of inheritance they had once been promised; but also because daily gathering the faithful from the turmoil of this world, he calls them together to the fellowship of the Holy Church and the eternal kingdom....* He appointed leaders and guardians for all the people beyond the river who knew and taught God's Law because in the Holy Church, which not only has been cleansed in the river of sacred baptism but also by the sincerity of its faith has transcended the Babylonian river (that is, the turmoil of this changing world), he placed apostles, evangelists, pastors, and teachers. He purified the descendants of the exiles from their foreign wives because he forbade that those who by professing the faith had renounced the world should be enslaved any more to the enticements of the world.[10]

With these words, Bede picks up on the partial nature of the fulfillment achieved under Ezra and Nehemiah and sees in it, not a failure of God's promises, but a prefiguration of the greater return from captivity that will take place in the paschal mystery of Christ's death, descent, Resurrection, and Ascension into the heavenly Promised Land.

The Jews' Reading of the Law and the Liturgy of the Word

One of the things that strikes any attentive reader of Ezra and Nehemiah is the extraordinary amount of time dedicated to the public reading and hearing of the law of Moses, whether "from early morning until midday" (Neh 8:3) or "for a fourth of the day" and "for another fourth of it" (Neh 9:3), before Ezra's great confession of sin. In these acts of liturgical proclamation, Bede sees the biblical roots of the Christian daily reading of Scripture as he experienced it in the seventh century A.D.:

"And they rose up to stand, and they read from the Book of the Law of the Lord their God, four times a day, and four times at night they confessed and prayed to the Lord their God" (Neh 9:3). For who would not be amazed that such a great people had such extraordinary concern for devotion that four times a day—that is, at the first hour of the morning, the third, the sixth, and the ninth, when time was to be made for prayer and psalmody—they gave themselves over to listening to the divine law in order to renew their mind in God and come back purer and more devout.... *From this example, I think, a most beautiful custom has developed in the Church, namely that through each hour of daily psalmody a passage from Old or New Testament is recited by heart for all to hear,* and thus strengthened by the words of the apostles or prophets, they bend their knees to perseverance in prayer.[11]

Here we see one of the key contributions of Ezra-Nehemiah: a developing centrality of the liturgical proclamation of the inspired law of God. In the wake of the Babylonian exile, the priests and people retrieve the need for all God's people, and not only the priests, to hear the word of God proclaimed.

[10] Ibid., 2.14, pp. 151–52.
[11] Ibid., 3.28; pp. 200–201.

The Books of Ezra and Nehemiah in the Lectionary

The Church seldom reads from Ezra-Nehemiah in the Eucharistic liturgy or the Liturgy of the Hours. The most frequently-used passage is the description of Ezra's reading of the law of Moses in the hearing of the people during the Feast of Tabernacles (Neh 8). This great liturgical act of covenant renewal, focused on the proclamation of God's word, is understood as a foreshadowing of the Liturgy of the Word and of the feast of the Eucharist.

Readings from Ezra-Nehemiah for Sundays, Feast Days, Liturgical Seasons, and Other Occasions			
MSO = Masses for Special Occasions; *OM* = Optional Memorial; *VM* = Votive Mass; *Rit* = Ritual			
Passage	Description	Occasion	Explanation
Neh 8:2–4a, 5–6, 8–10	Ezra reads the law during the great covenant renewal at the Feast of Tabernacles after the completion of the walls.	*3rd Sun. in OT (C)*; *MSO*: Institution of Readers, opt. 3; Dedication of Altar or Church, opt. 1	Ezra, through the proclamation of the word of God, leads the people in covenant renewal after the exile. We know that his renewal was only partially successful. In the Gospel (Lk 4:14–21), Jesus proclaims God's word in the synagogue, following practices that may have originated with Ezra. Jesus will lead God's people into a definitive covenant renewal.

Readings of Ezra-Nehemiah for Daily Mass				
Yr	Week	Day	Passage Read	Description
I	26	W	Neh 2:1–8	Nehemiah asks King Artaxerxes for leave to return to Jerusalem and build its walls.
I	26	Th	Neh 8:1–4a, 5–6, 7b–12	Ezra reads the law during the great covenant renewal at the Feast of Tabernacles.
I	25	M	Ezra 1:1–6	Cyrus' decree and the initial return of the exiles to Judea
I	25	Tu	Ezra 6:7–8, 12b, 14–20	Darius' decree, the completion of the Temple, the celebration of Passover
I	25	W	Ezra 9:5–9	Ezra's prayer of repentance

Conclusion

The book of Ezra-Nehemiah extends the sacred history of Israel, which ended at the exile in Kings and Chronicles, down into the postexilic or Persian period. Three major events dominate the book: the initial return of the exiles under Zerubbabel and their ultimately successful efforts to rebuild the Temple (Ezra 1–6), the mission of Ezra to restore observance of the Mosaic law (Ezra 7–10), and the successful mission of Nehemiah to rebuild the walls of Jerusalem (Neh 1:1—13:3).

Ezra-Nehemiah is a book of partial fulfillments, which implies partial unful-fillments as well. By the end of the book, the people of Judah are blessed by living in their land once more, with freedom to practice their religion, a rebuilt Temple, and a restored Jerusalem. However, it is quite clear that the promised New Covenant has not arrived, the twelve tribes have not been restored, and the son of David has not returned to the throne in accordance with the Davidic covenant. The book ends on a melancholy note, looking forward in muted hope for the intervention of God.

Following a trajectory already present in their earlier history, in Ezra-Nehemiah the people of Judah learn ever more that their identity as a people is to be found in their worship of God at his Temple and obedience to his cov-enant law. They become a Temple-state, which, after the death of Nehemiah, will be increasingly ruled by the priesthood and especially the high priest.

For Further Reading

Commentaries and Studies on Ezra and Nehemiah

Blenkinsopp, Joseph. *Ezra-Nehemiah: A Commentary*. Old Testament Library. Philadel-phia: Westminster Press, 1988.

Fensham, F. Charles. *The Books of Ezra and Nehemiah*. New International Commentary on the Old Testament 10. Grand Rapids, Mich.: Eerdmans, 1982.

Hamilton, Victor. *Handbook on the Historical Books*. Grand Rapids, Mich.: Baker Aca-demic, 2001. (See pp. 503–28.)

Myers, Jacob M. *Ezra, Nehemiah*. Anchor Bible 14. Garden City, N.Y.: Doubleday, 1965.

Historical Issues in Ezra and Nehemiah

Berquist, Jon L. *Judaism in Persia's Shadow: A Social and Historical Approach*. Minneapolis: Fortress Press, 1995.

Kitchen, Kenneth A. *On the Reliability of the Old Testament*. Grand Rapids, Mich.: Eerd-mans, 2003. (See pp. 70–79.)

Stern, Ephraim. *The Assyrian, Babylonian, and Persian Periods (732–332 B.C.E.)*. Vol. 2 of *Archaeology of the Land of the Bible*. Anchor Bible Reference Library. New York: Doubleday, 2001.

Yamauchi, Edwin M. "Ezra and Nehemiah". Pages 395–467 in *1 & 2 Kings, 1 & 2 Chronicles, Ezra, Nehemiah, Esther*. Vol. 3 of *Zondervan Illustrated Bible Backgrounds Commentary*. Edited by John H. Walton. Downers Grove, Ill.: InterVarsity Press, 2009.

———. *Persia and the Bible*. Grand Rapids, Mich.: Baker Book House, 1994.

Ezra and Nehemiah in the Living Tradition

Bede, Venerable. *On Ezra and Nehemiah*. Translated by Scott DeGregorio. Translated Texts for Historians 47. Liverpool: Liverpool University Press, 2006.

Conti, Marco, ed. *1–2 Kings, 1–2 Chronicles, Ezra, Nehemiah, Esther*. Old Testament 5 of Ancient Christian Commentary on Scripture. Edited by Thomas C. Oden. Downers Grove, Ill.: InterVarsity Press, 2008. (See pp. 242–302.)

18. TOBIT

Introduction

In contrast to the books of Chronicles, which focus almost entirely on the fate of the southern tribes of Judah through the Babylonian exile and return of the Jews, the book of Tobit focuses its attention on one northern family from a clan of Naphtali and their experience of the earlier Assyrian exile. In this way, Tobit complements the books of Chronicles and Ezra-Nehemiah by providing the canonical perspective of northern Israelites on the experience of judgment and exile.

The original name of the book is unknown, but it was probably derived from the book's narrator, Tobit (Hebrew *tobîth*, "goodness"), or the protagonist: his son, Tobias (Hebrew *tob-yah*, "The LORD is good", or *tobî-yah*, "The LORD is my good"). In the Latin and Greek traditions, one or both of these characters give the book its name, under a wide variety of spellings (Greek *Tobit, Tobeit, Tobeith*; Latin *Tobias, Tobiae*). In the Vulgate and at least one other version, both father *and* son are called "Tobias".

The original language of the book of Tobit was most likely Aramaic.[1] This conclusion is grounded in the remarkable fact that in the mid-twentieth century, when the Dead Sea Scrolls were discovered at Qumran, among the many hundreds of scrolls were four fragments of the book of Tobit in Aramaic and two in Hebrew.[2] Although we cannot be certain, this may provide evidence that the book of Tobit was considered to be Scripture by the Jewish residents at Qumran, since the total number of manuscripts found (six) compares well with the number of copies found for undisputed scriptural books.

Tobit did not ultimately attain canonical status within later rabbinic Judaism and is not part of the contemporary Jewish Bible. However, it apparently was known, studied, and copied as an *aggadic midrash* (narrative explanatory expansion) of earlier Scripture. The canonical status of Tobit within the ancient Christian Church was affirmed by the majority but questioned by a few.[3] For example, Tobit is quoted as Scripture by Eastern Church Fathers such as Polycarp of Smyrna, Clement of Alexandria, Origen of Alexandria, Ephrem the Syrian, and John Chrysostom; it is also quoted by Western Church Fathers such as Clement of Rome, Hippolytus of Rome, Cyprian of Carthage, Ambrose of Milan, Augustine of Hippo, Hilary of Poitiers, and so on. Significantly, it is also identified as Scripture in the patristic councils of Rome (A.D. 382), Hippo (A.D. 393), and Carthage (A.D. 397).

---

[1] See Carey A. Moore, *Tobit*, Anchor Bible 40A (New York: Doubleday, 1996), 33–39.

[2] See Martin G. Abegg Jr., Peter Flint, and Eugene Ulrich, *The Dead Sea Scrolls Bible: The Oldest Known Bible Translated for the First Time into English* (San Francisco: HarperOne, 1999), 636–46.

[3] See Moore, *Tobit*, 52–53.

One significant voice to the contrary is that of Jerome. On the one hand, Jerome recognizes that the fifth-century Jews do not accept Tobit as Scripture in his preface to the Vulgate translation. On the other hand, he nevertheless translates it from Aramaic into Latin in obedience to the Catholic bishops, doing so in the course of a single day! As Jerome himself writes:

> I do not cease to marvel at the perseverance of your request. For you [bishops Cromatius and Heliodorus] require that I translate a book written in the Chaldean speech [i.e. Aramaic] into the Latin style, in particular the book of Tobias, which the Hebrews, cutting it from the catalogue of Holy Scriptures, have consigned to these writings which they call Hagiographa. I have done enough to accommodate your desire, not, however, enough to appease my own zeal. For they [i.e., the Hebrews] insist and accuse us of translating those studies of the Hebrews for Latin ears against their own canon. *But judging that it is better to displease the judgment of the Pharisees and to obey the commands of bishops, I have pressed on as I was able to do so,* since the language of the Chaldeans is close to Hebrew speech. Procuring a very experienced speaker of each language, I have appropriated the labor of one day; and whatever the one [who could read Aramaic] expressed in Hebrew words, this I had a stenographer take down in Latin.[4]

This passage gives us a remarkable insight into the canonical status of Tobit among Jews and Christians in the ancient Church as well as into the process of translation that led to the Latin Vulgate form of the book, which is regarded as less valuable today because of the hasty manner in which it was prepared.

The ancient manuscripts of Tobit present a remarkable number of text-critical challenges: they are much more fluid and diverse than those for most biblical books. On the one hand, this makes establishing a hypothetical original extremely difficult, if not impossible in some cases. On the other hand, the multiplicity of textual versions is a testament to just how *popular* the book of Tobit was among Jews and Christians in antiquity. The book comes down to us primarily in Greek and Latin translations, but there are multiple recensions (literary editions) of the book in both language traditions, some longer and some shorter. The Aramaic and Hebrew fragments from Qumran show agreement but also variation from the known Greek and Latin versions. As a result, there is considerable variation in the wording of many verses and in specific details of the text. Therefore it is wise, when interpreting Tobit, not to place too much weight on specific details or wording, which often differ in the manuscript tradition, but rather on the main points and narrative arc of the story.

Literary Structure of Tobit

The structure of the book of Tobit follows a narrative rather than logical development: introduction of the setting and characters, increasing complication of the central conflict(s), introduction of a hero, gradual resolution of the conflict(s), and denouement. The first three chapters introduce two main characters, Tobit (Tob 1:1—3:6) and Sarah (Tob 3:7–15), and bring them both to a point of

---

[4] Jerome, *Preface to Tobit*, in ibid., 62.

crisis at which they pray for death (Tob 3:1–6, 10–15). The turning point of the narrative comes immediately thereafter, as Raphael, the angelic hero of the story, is introduced (Tob 3:16–17). The body of the narrative recounts how Raphael guides Tobit's son, Tobias, on a journey that culminates in the resolution of the two main crises: Tobit's blindness and Sarah's lack of a husband (Tob 4–12). The last two chapters are a kind of epilogue consisting of Tobit's psalm of thanksgiving (Tob 13) and deathbed testament (Tob 14). The narrative can be outlined as follows:

Outline of the Book of Tobit

I. Introduction of Tobit and Sarah and Their Crises (Tob 1:1—3:15)
  A. Tobit's Piety Leads to Blindness, Poverty, and Contempt (1:1—3:6)
  B. Sarah's Piety No Protection against Contempt and Solitude (3:7–15)

II. Introduction of the Hero: The Angel Raphael (Tob 3:16–17)
  A. God Hears the Prayer of Tobit and Sarah (3:16)
  B. God Answers by Sending the Angel Raphael to Heal (3:17)

III. The Long Journey of Resolution and Healing (Tob 4–12)
  A. Tobit's Instructions to Tobias (4)
  B. Raphael Introduced as Tobias' Guide (5)
  C. The Miraculous Catch of the Great Fish (6:1–8)
  D. The Wedding of Tobias and Sarah and the Binding of Asmodeus (6:9—8:21)
  E. Raphael's Journey to Retrieve the Money (9)
  F. Tobias Returns and Heals Tobit, with Help of the Fish (10–11)
  G. Raphael Reveals His Identity and Departs (12)

IV. Epilogue (Tob 13–14)
  A. Tobit's "Prayer of Rejoicing" and Prophecy of the New Jerusalem (13)
  B. Tobit's Final Testament (14)

Overview of Tobit

The Blindness of Tobit and the Oppression of Sarah (Tobit 1:1—3:15)

The composition is introduced as "the book of the acts of Tobit" (Tob 1:1). The literal Greek expression here is "book of the words (Greek *logōn*) of Tobit", probably a reference to the fact that the first portion of the story is narrated in the first person by the figure of Tobit himself.

Significantly, this Tobit is *not* (strictly speaking) a "Jew"—that is, a southerner from the tribe of Judah. Rather, he is a northerner, an Israelite descended from the tribe of Naphtali, which was captured and exiled to Nineveh under the Assyrians several years prior to the definitive capture of Samaria and exile of the northern tribes in ca. 722 B.C. (see 2 Kings 15:29). Despite not being from the south himself, prior to the Assyrian exile of the ten northern tribes, Tobit is

---

God's Providential Care for the "Lost" Ten Tribes

Tobit is often said by scholars to represent "Second Temple Judaism", but the characters of the book are not Jews; they are *Israelites* of the tribe of Naphtali. Almost alone of biblical books, Tobit describes the plight and fortunes of the exiles of the northern tribes who maintained fidelity to the Lord. Like Chronicles and all the major prophets, the author of Tobit holds out hope for these northern tribes and anticipates that they will participate in the eschatological restoration. God still has a plan and future for all the tribes of Israel. Although they are not able to participate in the Temple liturgy in their places of exile, God will accept their practices of piety in lieu of the sacrifices prescribed by the Mosaic covenant.

---

one of the Israelites who does not participate in the schism of Rehoboam that leads to the divided kingdom (see 1 Kings 11), but, rather, he remains faithful to the Davidic covenant and the law of Moses by journeying to the Jerusalem Temple to worship there.

After his deportation to Nineveh, he rises to the rank of purchasing agent for the crown and accumulates some wealth. His life-style is marked by acts of charity toward his fellow Israelite exiles: feeding the hungry, clothing the naked, burying the dead (Tob 1:10–21). Despite the fact that the Gentile Ninevites ridicule his compassion, Tobit remains faithful to the law of God and is an ideal example of what a faithful Israelite should look like.

One of the first of many ironies in the book is that it is precisely Tobit's fidelity to the law of Moses that leads him straight into tragedy and despair. One year, on the Feast of Pentecost, Tobit interrupts his festive meal to bury a murdered countryman. Here Tobit's action appears to be one of the first examples of later Jewish tradition, which regarded the burial of the dead as an act of charity taking precedence over study of the law, the circumcision of one's son, or even sacrificing the Passover lamb![5]

Redemptive Suffering in Tobit

Tobit recognizes that the righteous suffer. In fact, their very righteous deeds are often the proximate cause of their suffering or persecution. Tobit, for example, provokes abuse from his Gentile neighbors by burying the dead. Furthermore, sleeping outside his house, in observance of the laws of corpse defilement, leads, not to blessing, but to his blindness and undoing. Even within families, the attempt to live by God's law does not always bring peace; it sometimes brings discord and conflict (Tob 2:11–14). While aware that many faithful die in sorrow (Tob 2:3), the book of Tobit is not fatalistic. It remains confident in the ultimate goodness of the Lord ("Tobias" = "the Lord is good") and holds out hope that God will yet reward the righteous, even in this life. The righteous suffering of Tobit and Sarah is not without purpose—it strengthens their prayers and moves God to send Raphael to heal and deliver them. In this way we see the beginnings of a theology of redemptive suffering. The humble acceptance of adversity, even adversity provoked by good deeds, has merit in God's eyes and prepares the way for ultimate salvation.

Of course, in the Torah, contact with a corpse makes a person unclean, and so Tobit refuses to defile his home but chooses instead to sleep outside (cf. Num 19:14–16). In a twist of tragic irony, Tobit's reward for caring for the dead and

---

[5] See Babylonian Talmud, *Megillah* 3b, in Isidore Epstein, ed., *The Babylonian Talmud*, 35 vols. (London: Soncino, 1935–1952).

fidelity to the law is blindness: he awakes to discover bird droppings on his eyes, which lead to infection and the loss of his sight. As a result, he also loses his ability to work, and his wife, Anna (Hebrew for "grace"), becomes the bread-winner of the family, but the stress of this arrangement causes the breakdown of their marital relationship (Tob 2:1–14). Blind, poor, and spurned by his wife, Tobit prays for death (Tob 3:1–6).

At this point, the sacred author introduces the second major character and crisis: the virgin Sarah (who shares a name with the matriarch of Israel) and her oppression by the demon Asmodeus, whose name either means "Destroyer" (Hebrew) or is a Persian form of *Aeshma Daeva*, the demon of lust.[6] On the same day Tobit prays for death, his younger kinswoman Sarah in far-off Media is mocked and reviled by her own maidservants, because seven husbands of hers have died on the wedding night without consummating marriage with her (Tob 7:9). Apparently, the reward for her virginity has been to be repeatedly assaulted by a demon, reviled by her servants, and a source of shame for her parents. Led to despair by such a situation, Sarah, too, contemplates suicide, but, thinking better about it, instead prays for death (Tob 3:10–15).

The Mission of the Angel Raphael (Tobit 3:16–17)

In one of the most remarkable descriptions of providence in the entire Old Testament, the book of Tobit then recounts how the prayers of Tobit and Sarah are simultaneously "heard in the presence of the glory of the great God" (Tob 3:16). God's response is striking: he does not "intervene directly", as later theologians might put it, but sends the angel Raphael (Hebrew for "God-has-healed") to bring *healing* to both Tobit and Sarah by taking away the film from Tobit's eyes and giving Sarah to Tobias, the son of Tobit, in marriage.

This turning point is remarkable for at least two reasons. First, it is one of the very few times in all of the Old Testament that one of the spiritual messengers from God known as "angels" is identified by a personal name. The only other two angels who are named in the Old Testament are Michael (Dan 12:1) and Gabriel (Dan 9:21). In later tradition, it is of course these three named angels—Michael, Gabriel, and Raphael—who will be identified as the "archangels". Second, this passage is also one of the earliest examples of the Jewish belief that angels not only bring messages from God to human beings; they also bring prayers *from human beings to God*. As Raphael will later reveal to Tobit:

> [W]hen you and your daughter-in-law Sarah prayed, *I brought a reminder of your prayer before the Holy One*; and when you buried the dead, I was likewise present with you.... So now God sent me to heal you and your daughter-in-law Sarah. I am Raphael, one of the seven holy angels *who present the prayers of the saints* and enter into the presence of the glory of the Lord. (Tob 12:12, 14–15)

Although it will take the rest of the narrative for Raphael's identity and mission to become clear to the humans involved, we can already see that God's provi-dence is being carried out through mediators rather than apart from them.

---

[6] Moore, *Tobit*, 25.

The Quest of Tobias and the Healing of Sarah and Tobit (Tobit 4–12)

Tobit, unaware that salvation is on the way, calls his son, Tobias, in order to send him to retrieve the family fortune kept with a cousin in Media before Tobit's imminent death (Tob 4). In a key section of the book, Tobit gives (what he thinks to be) a kind of "last testament", charging his son to avoid sin and to follow the commandments of God by keeping a series of key ethical exhortations:

1. Bury the dead (4:3, 4).
2. Honor your mother (4:4).
3. Give alms (4:7–11, 16–16).
4. Avoid sexual transgression (4:12–13).
5. Pay just wages (4:14).
6. Abstain from drunkenness (4:15).
7. Pursue wisdom (4:18).
8. Pray constantly (4:19).

By far the most attention is given to almsgiving, which is described as having the power (in some way) to atone for sin—"charity delivers from death"—and as a kind of sacrificial "offering" to God (Tob 4:10–11). Perhaps even more significant, in the very midst of this series of exhortations, Tobit delivers what may be the earliest extant Jewish "version" of the so-called "Golden Rule" when he tells Tobias: *And what you hate, do not do to anyone* (Tob 4:15).

Prayer, Fasting, and Almsgiving in Tobit

One of the most important contributions of the book of Tobit is its description of the lifestyle of those who worship the God of Israel. In Tobit, we see developing the traditional categories of what would later be known as the "corporal works of mercy". Tobit places prominent emphasis on feeding the hungry, clothing the naked, and burying the dead. Traditional Lenten disciplines of prayer, fasting, and almsgiving also appear as a triad for the first time in Scripture (Tob 12:8). These charitable acts, especially almsgiving, are an "offering" to the Lord (Tob 4:11)—in other words, they compensate for the inability to offer liturgical sacrifice—and they "store up treasure" in heaven; that is, they accumulate merit with God. They are also said to "deliver from death" and "purge sin", additional effects once attributed to the offering of sacrifice. This *liturgical* view of what modern scholars would describe as *ethical* actions represents a remarkable development in biblical teaching on the moral life. Indeed, insofar as Tobit is addressed primarily to those who find themselves physically unable to participate in the liturgy, it recommends the corporal works of mercy and the traditional practices of piety as ways of sharing in the ordinary effects of the cult in the absence of external worship.

Tobias accepts his father's commission and charge and departs to find a guide to accompany him on the journey to Media. Providentially, he happens upon Raphael, who poses as a kinsman named Azarias (Hebrew for "the LORD has helped") to gain the trust of son and father (Tob 5:1–15). Once again, we find fresh insights into early Jewish beliefs about angels when Tobit prays that God's "angel" might "attend" to Tobias while he is journeying with Azarias, in a manner akin to what later Christian tradition would refer to as a "guardian angel", whose role is to protect in special times of danger and risk (as journeys very much were in ancient times) (Tob 5:16–21).

Tobias and Raphael start on their journey. In a somewhat bizarre turn of events, while crossing the Tigris, Tobias encounters an unusual fish that leaps out of the river in order to devour him! Raphael instructs Tobias to catch and dissect the fish and obtain its heart, liver, and gall for their power to heal both spiritual and physical ailments (Tob 6:1–8). Proceeding on their journey, Raphael and Tobias come near to Ecbatana, the city of Sarah and her parents, Raguel and Edna. Raphael explains to Tobias that Sarah is God's intended bride for him; her previous suitors were slain by a demon who is obsessed with her. The heart and liver of the fish have exorcistic properties when burned; they will protect Tobias and Sarah on their wedding night (Tob 6:9–11).

When the two travelers enter Ecbatana, they find hospitality at the home of Raguel and Edna, and Tobias immediately requests the hand of Sarah in marriage, since he is her nearest kinsman-redeemer (Tob 7:10; cf. Ruth 4:4–10). Raguel consents, although he warns Tobias of his fears that he, too, will be slain like the other suitors. Nonetheless, Tobias takes Sarah as his wife by means of a binding agreement, in what is the earliest detailed description of an ancient Israelite marriage ceremony that we possess (Tob 7:11–15). After the wedding supper, Tobias and Sarah proceed to the bedroom in which the marriage is to be consummated. However, instead of moving immediately into nuptial relations, Tobias performs what amounts to an *exorcism* on his wedding night by taking the heart and liver of the fish upon the embers and using the smoke to drive away the demon (Tob 8:1–3)! After the demon is driven away, they pray together to God—invoking the primordial marriage of "Adam and ... Eve his wife"—before going to sleep for the night (Tob 8:6). Apparently, they delay the consummation of the marriage for a later night. (In the Latin Vulgate version, they explicitly abstain from marital relations for three nights.) Comically, at the very moment that they are driving out the demon, Raguel is outside preparing a grave for his new son-in-law (Tob 8:9–12)! When no death occurs and all is well, Raguel is overjoyed and throws a lavish fourteen-day wedding feast for his new son-in-law and daughter (Tob 9). Raphael leaves with a servant to collect the fortune that was the object of the journey in the first place and then returns to the feast.

Meanwhile, Tobit and Anna are greatly distressed that Tobias has delayed so long on his journey and fear the worst (Tob 10). Anticipating their fears, Tobias parts from his father-in-law, Raguel, and returns with Raphael and his new bride, Sarah, to Nineveh, where he is greeted with great relief by his parents (Tob 11). Tobias uses the gall of the fish to restore his father's sight. Overwhelmed with joy at Tobias' marriage and Tobit's healing, the family celebrates with a seven-day feast. At the end of the feast, when Tobit and Tobias summon Raphael to pay him generously for his services, the angel reveals his true identity, charges the two men to praise God in word and deed, and returns to heaven (Tob 12).

Tobias' Prophecy of a New Jerusalem and Final Testament (Tobit 13–14)

In the final section of the book, the focus once again shifts away from Tobias the son and back to Tobit the father, by recounting the words of his "prayer of rejoicing"—a psalm of praise in the style of the Davidic psalms, full of hope for the eschatological restoration of the twelve tribes of Israel, the coming of a new Jerusalem, and the restoration of the Temple to a state far more glorious than that of the Second Temple (Tob 13). Years later, Tobit also gathers his sons and grandsons to his deathbed and charges them, on the basis of the prophecy of Jonah, to leave the doomed city of Nineveh for the relative safety of Media and to keep the same laws and practices he commended to Tobias so long before. Tobit, and later Tobias, both die at an old age and receive magnificent funerals (Tob 14).

Historical Questions about Tobit

Origin, Genre, and Historicity of the Book of Tobit

Like many other of the historical books, the authorship of the book of Tobit is unknown, as we lack any data to assess it. Scholarly debate over the date of the book is likewise wide-ranging: in the modern period, scholars have suggested dates anywhere from the seventh century B.C. to the late second century A.D., with most scholars today settling on the second or third century B.C.[7] When it comes to the genre of the book and the question of its historical character, recent centuries have seen a massive shift in attitude.

On the one hand, there are a number of features in the book of Tobit that led to its being regarded by the Church's tradition as representing real persons and events. For example, in the earliest copies of the Greek Septuagint as we possess them, the book of Tobit is grouped with other historical books, such as Joshua, Judges, 1–2 Samuel, 1–2 Kings, 1–2 Chronicles, and so on. The obvious implication of this grouping is that the book was viewed as sharing the similar genre of history as these other texts. Moreover, the book opens with specific genealogical, chronological, and geographical details that give it the appearance of having historical intentions rather than the stuff of pure fiction (for example, Tob 1:1–15). The book presents itself as a narrative of events in history by references to datable reigns of international rulers (Shalmaneser, Sennacherib) and well-known geographical locations (Nineveh, Ecbatana, Rages). Although the presence of the angel, the miraculous catch of the fish, and the quasi-exorcism of the demon plaguing Sarah may strike the modern reader as too extraordinary to be true, there is no evidence that ancient readers regarded them as any more unbelievable than the angelic activity and miracles recorded elsewhere in the historical books of the Old Testament (for example, the miracles of Elijah and Elisha).

On the other hand, especially since the twentieth century, many scholars have concluded that the genre of Tobit is somewhere between a historical novella and a fictional "romance" or folktale intended both to entertain and to teach important moral lessons (such as almsgiving and burying the dead).[8] Such scholars regard Tobit as largely unhistorical in character primarily because of its

---

[7] Ibid., 40–41.
[8] Ibid., 17–21.

supernatural elements, such as a woman whose seven husbands were killed on their wedding night, angels that appear to be human, and a fish with curative organs. In addition, the book contains parallels with motifs in ancient folklore in which a righteous man pays respect to the dead and is rewarded for it as well as the idea of a dangerous bride (see the story of Ahiqar). Finally, these scholars point to historical difficulties in Tobit, such as attributing the capture of Nineveh to "Nebuchadnezzar and Ahasuerus", when other sources tell us it was captured by Nabopolassar with the help of Cyaxares of Media.

Theological Issues in Tobit

Tobias and Sarah as a New Adam and New Eve

One of the most fascinating theological aspects of the book of Tobit is the way in which certain characters and events echo or allude to earlier periods in salvation history or passages in Jewish Scripture. As Carey Moore puts it: the "most striking scenes and colors" in the book of Tobit are "decidedly *biblical* and Jewish. As one reads the book of Tobit, one can 'see' the patriarchs (especially Isaac, Jacob, and Joseph) and the suffering Job"—especially in relation to the betrothal scenes of Isaac and Jacob—and "one can 'hear' the demands of the Torah and the messages of Moses and Deuteronomy, of Proverbs and Deutero-Isaiah."[9] In other words, the story of Tobit and Tobias is recapitulating the lives of figures such as Isaac, Jacob, and Job.

In this vein, it is striking to note that a case can be made that Tobias is not just a "new Isaac" or "new Jacob", but a *new Adam*, who, as a bridegroom figure, succeeds in protecting his bride from danger where Adam failed. Compare the following charts:

Adam	*Tobias*
1. Fails to protect his bride from the serpent	1. Protects Sarah from the demon Asmodeus
2. Says and does nothing in the face of serpent's attack	2. Cries out to God in prayer and offers sacrifice in obedience
3. Evil spirit triumphs	3. Evil spirit is bound
4. He and his bride sin and suffer spiritual death (Gen 2–3)	4. He and Sarah pray and are saved from death (Tob 7–8)

Along similar lines, a number of striking intertextual parallels suggest that Sarah is a kind of *new Eve* figure who is both like and unlike her primordial mother:

Eve	*Sarah*
1. Attacked by the serpent after her "wedding" to Adam	1. Attacked by a demon on her wedding night

---

[9] Ibid., 18, 20.

2. Speaks with the demon; entices her husband to sin	2. Remains silent in the face of demon; follows her husband's lead in prayer: her only words: "Amen"
3. Sins and dies physically	3. Prays and is delivered from social "death"
4. Covers herself in shame at her nakedness	4. Taken in chaste love by her bridegroom; sleeps peacefully with him
5. Wedding turned into a funeral	5. Funeral turned into a wedding feast

It is unlikely that these numerous parallels are coincidental. Moreover, should there be any doubt about them, they find confirmation in the prayer of Tobias and Sarah, which explicitly *mentions* Adam and Eve as the prototype of married love:

> And they began to say ...
> "You made Adam and gave him Eve his wife as a helper and support.
>   From them the race of mankind has sprung.
> You said, 'It is not good that the man should be alone;
>   let us make a helper for him like himself.'" (Tob 8:5, 6)

When these parallels are combined with the explicit quotation of the book of Genesis, it seems clear that the author of Tobit sees in Tobias and Sarah a kind of "recapitulation" of the primordial trial of Adam and Eve, though in this case, the new Adam and new Eve together vanquish the demon and transform death into life.

Sexuality, Lust, and Marriage in Tobit

Consistent with other Old Testament texts, Tobit strongly discourages "sexual immorality" (Greek *porneia*)—understood as non-marital sexual activity—for both men and women (for example, Tob 4:12). The book has a high view of marriage. There is also an acute awareness of the social-justice aspects of marriage and the importance of the institution for the health of the believing community. Men who choose foreign wives in preference to the daughters of their own people show "pride" and "disdain" for the community (Tob 4:13), implying that none of the young women of their own people are "good enough" for them. Behind this sentiment lies the reality that exogamy (marriage outside the covenant community) left Israelite women without prospective husbands from their own people, facing the unhappy choice between being alienated from their community by accepting a foreign spouse themselves or else living a life of practical widowhood. In Tobit, choosing a wife from among one's own people is thus seen as an act of charity toward the whole community.

The author of Tobit also shows a prescient awareness of the corrupting influence of sexual lust, even within the marriage bond itself. Lust—that is, the kind of physical desire that objectifies the other person as a means to obtain pleasure for oneself—is not a legitimate grounds for marriage. Thus, Sarah's seven suitors were slain for their lust, even though their attempts to sleep with her were licit within the bonds of matrimony. Tobias, however, radically subjugates physical desire as a motivation for his marriage to Sarah: "I am not taking this sister of mine because of lust (Greek *porneia*), but with sincerity" (Greek *aletheia*, "truth") (Tob 8:7). In fact, in the Latin Vulgate textual tradition, the young couple remains continent for three days after their wedding night. In place of lust, the virtues of companionship, mutual support, and familial affection come to the forefront of Tobit's vision of the marital relationship (Tob 8:6–8). It is not that Tobit considers the body or physical pleasure evil *per se*: Sarah is noted as being "very beautiful" (Tob 6:12), and Tobias "yearned deeply" for her (Tob 6:17). But the book has a realistic awareness of the degree to which a self-centered sexual desire (lust) can mar and degrade the marriage relationship, especially by objectifying and depersonalizing the wife or even both spouses. Tobit's view of marriage, which emphasizes the personhood and equality of the wife, gentle affection and mutual support among the spouses, and openness to the gift of children, has profoundly shaped the later Christian understanding of matrimony.

Tobit in the Living Tradition

Although the book of Tobit has always been one of the most popular stories in the Old Testament, it has not garnered a great deal of theological attention. As with Ezra and Nehemiah, we must wait until the time of Bede the Venerable for a full-scale exposition of the book in its literal and spiritual dimensions. Nevertheless, once accessed in this way, the book of Tobit yields a remarkably rich harvest of spiritual meaning for the living tradition, despite being such a small book.

Tobias the Bridegroom and Christ the Bridegroom

First and foremost, as with other protagonists in the Old Testament, the Christian tradition picked up on the parallels between the victory of Tobias the bridegroom over the devil and Christ's victory over Satan:

> Sarah, Raguel's daughter, in a city of the Medes, who had been given to seven husbands whom a demon killed as soon as they went in to her, figuratively denotes the mass of the Gentiles.... [T]hey were all carried off by the devil inasmuch as they were given over to idolatry until the true bridegroom, our Lord, came. He overcame the enemy and through faith united them (i.e., the Gentiles) to himself, as Tobias took Sarah to wife after tying up the devil on the instructions and with the aid of the archangel.[10]

[10] Bede, *On Tobit* 3.7–8, in Seán Connolly, *Bede: On Tobit and On the Canticle of Habbakkuk* (Dublin: Four Courts Press, 1997), 43.

Here we see Jesus' exorcistic ministry being clearly interpreted as a kind of fulfillment of Tobias' overthrow of the demon—which is, admittedly, the most explicit case of exorcism in the Old Testament.

The Devouring Fish and the Devouring Devil

Along these lines, it is also intriguing that the Christian tradition as reflected by Bede seems to have seen in the strange event of the devouring fish from the river Tigris a figure of the devil:

> Here again the mystery of the Lord's passion is quite obviously signified. For the huge fish, which, since it wanted to devour him, was killed by Tobias on the angel's instructions, represents the ancient devourer of the human race, that is, the devil. When the latter desired the death of humanity in our Redeemer, he was caught by the power of the divinity.... In [the river Tigris] lurked a huge fish, inasmuch as the invisible seducer of the human race had the power of death.[11]

Such an interpretation, it must be noted, stands in continuity with the biblical imagery of Leviathan, a sea creature that is a threat to human beings and often depicted as opposed to God (for example, Job 41:1–34).

Sarah as a Prefiguration of the Church

If Tobias was seen as a prefiguration of Christ the Bridegroom and deliverer, it is easy to understand how Sarah also came to be viewed as a prefiguration of the Bride of Christ, the Church:

> *Raguel stands for the people of the Gentiles whom the Lord deigned to visit through his preachers in order to take himself a bride from their stock, that is, make of the Gentiles a church for himself.* Also Sarah's name befits the Church because of Sarah, the patriarch Abraham's wife, who bore Isaac the son of the promise, that is, the free people of the Church.[12]

Notice here the continued theme of mothers of Israel who are either taken from women of Gentile descent (as with Rahab or Bathsheba) or taken from among Gentile nations (as with Naomi). In this way, Sarah continues the trend of pointing beyond herself to a Church who will be mother to and taken from the nations.

Tobias and Sarah and Love "Strong as Death"

Finally, in much more recent times, it is remarkable to note that Pope John Paul II dedicated a number of general audiences to the book of Tobit in his series that

---

[11] Ibid., 6.1–2, pp. 46–47.
[12] Ibid., 6.6, p. 50.

Readings from Tobit for Occasional Masses

MSO = Masses for Special Occasions; *OM* = Optional Memorial;
VM = Votive Mass; *Rit* = Ritual

Passage	Description	Occasion	Explanation
7:6–14	Raguel blesses the marriage of Tobias and Sarah and writes up the marriage contract.	*Rit*: Sacrament of Matrimony, opt. 4	The marriage of Tobias and Sarah represents an ideal for all Christian marriages. The binding nature of the sacrament is anticipated already under the Old Covenant.
8:4b–8	Tobias and Sarah pray on their wedding night, expressing the wish to grow old together.	*Rit*: Sacrament of Matrimony, opt. 5	Tobias' prayer, emphasizing companionship and mutual support over physical lust, informs the Catholic understanding of matrimony.
8:5–7	See above.	Common of Holy Men and Women, opt. 7	This reading is especially appropriate for canonized married couples.
12:6–13	Raphael reveals that Tobit's corporal works of mercy caused his prayers to be heard in heaven.	Common of Holy Men and Women, opt. 8; proper for Feast of St. Jerome Emiliani, Priest	Many holy men and women, especially St. Jerome Emiliani, followed Tobit's example by feeding the hungry, clothing the naked, burying the dead, and giving alms.
13:1–2, 3–4, 6c, 6d, 6e	Tobit utters a prayer of praise to God, expressing thanks for God's deliverance while he was in exile.	*MSO*: For Refugees and Exiles, resp. psalm	Tobit serves as a model for the believer who cries to God and is heard while exiled far from his native land.

Reading of Tobit for Daily Mass: Ordinary Time, Year I: Week 9

Day	Passage Read	Description
M	1:3; 2:1a–8	Tobit interrupts his festive meal to bury the dead and is ridiculed for his efforts.
Tu	2:9–14	Birds blind Tobit; Anna becomes breadwinner, but the two fall to arguing.
W	3:1–11a, 16–17a	Tobit and Sarah pray in sorrow; God hears their prayers and sends Raphael.
Th	6:10–11; 7:1, 9–17; 8:4–9a	Tobias arrives in Ecbatana, weds Sarah, and prays with her in the nuptial chamber.
F	11:5–17	Tobias is reunited with his parents; he cures Tobit's blindness; all rejoice.
Sa	13:2, 6, 7, 10 [Vulg.]	Tobit gives thanks to God for all his mercy and faithfulness.

would later be collected under the title, "Theology of the Body".[13] In one of these reflections, the pope pointed to the love of Tobias and Sarah as a powerful image of sacrificial love:

> *Thus, from the very first moment, Tobias' love had to face the test of life-or-death.* The words about love, "strong as death", spoken by the spouses in the Song of Songs in the transport of their hearts, here takes on the character of *a real test.* If love proves to be strong as death, this happens above all in the sense that Tobias (and Sarah with him) go without hesitating toward this test. *They are later verified, because in this test of life-or-death, life has the victory, that is, during the test of the wedding night, love is revealed as stronger than death.* This happens on account of the prayer.[14]

These reflections may well be the most attention the book of Tobit has ever received from a pope in the history of the Christian Church.

The Book of Tobit in the Lectionary

Despite the rich moral and theological content of the book of Tobit, it is seldom read in the ordinary Eucharistic liturgy. However, the prayer of Tobias, which summarizes the book's theology of matrimony (see above), is extremely popular as a first reading in nuptial Masses. In this way, it is to the mystery of matrimony that this book makes its most significant liturgical contribution.

Conclusion

Written to readers living in exile, the book of Tobit aims to encourage those who maintain fidelity to the Lord and his covenants by assuring them of God's continued solicitude for their welfare and his ability to reward their faithfulness even with blessings in this life. For those unable for various reasons to participate in the Temple cult, Tobit recommends a life-style marked by what have become known as the corporal works of mercy and traditional practices of piety, which will be acceptable to God in lieu of cultic sacrifice. Tobit's remarkable view of matrimony—in which the overtly sexual is sublimated to primary concerns of affection, companionship, family, and the perpetuation of the community of faith—shaped and anticipated the teaching of Christ and his Church on this sacrament.

For Further Reading

Commentaries and Studies on Tobit

Abegg, Martin G., Jr., Peter W. Flint, and Eugene Ulrich. *The Dead Sea Scrolls Bible: The Oldest Known Bible.* Repr., San Francisco: HarperOne, 2002.

DeSilva, David Arthur. *Introducing the Apocrypha: Message, Context, and Significance.* Grand Rapids, Mich.: Baker Academic, 2002. (See pp. 63–84.)

---

[13] See John Paul II, *Man and Woman He Created Them: A Theology of the Body,* trans. Michael Waldstein (Boston: Pauline Books and Media, 2006), pp. 592–612.

[14] Ibid., 596 (emphasis added).

Fitzmyer, Joseph A. *Tobit*. Commentaries on Early Jewish Literature. Berlin and New York: Walter de Gruyter, 2002.

Moore, Carey A. *Tobit*. Anchor Bible 40A. New York: Doubleday, 1996.

Otzen, Benedikt. *Tobit and Judith*. Guides to the Apocrypha and Pseudepigrapha. London: T&T Clark, 2002.

Tobit in the Living Tradition

Connolly, Seán. *Bede: On Tobit and On the Canticle of Habakkuk*. Dublin, Ireland, and Portland, Ore.: Four Courts Press, 1997.

John Paul II, Pope. *Man and Woman He Created Them: A Theology of the Body*. Translated by Michael Waldstein. Boston: Pauline Books and Media, 2006. (See pp. 592–612.)

Voicu, Sever J. *Apocrypha*. Old Testament 15 of Ancient Christian Commentary on Scripture. Edited by Thomas C. Oden. Downers Grove: InterVarsity Press, 2010. (See pp. 1–33.)

19. JUDITH

Introduction

The book of Judith tells the story of a Jewish heroine in the period after the Babylonian exile who saved her city by assassinating the general of the besieging Gentile army. The book is not considered canonical in the Jewish tradition, although the figure of Judith is known and various traditions about her are recorded in rabbinic literature, some agreeing and some disagreeing with details in the canonical book.

Probably first composed in Hebrew, the book of Judith is fully extant only in Greek and Latin versions (*Ioudith* in the LXX; *Liber Iudith* in the Vulgate). The book is named after the heroine Judith, whose name (Hebrew *Yehudith*) literally means "Jewish woman" or "Jewess". The manuscript tradition for Judith shows a great deal of variation, with longer and shorter editions extant in Greek and Latin. As with the book of Tobit, the instability of the manuscript tradition for Judith cautions against placing too much interpretive weight on textual details.

Since the very first centuries of the Church, Judith has been considered Christian Scripture and was quoted as such by Church Fathers such as Clement of Rome, Clement of Alexandria, Basil the Great, Gregory the Theologian, Ambrose of Milan, John Chrysostom, Jerome, and Augustine of Hippo. The titular heroine, noted for her beauty, courage, wisdom, and chastity, has generally been understood as a type of the Virgin Mary and model of virtue (although, as we will see, there are some moral difficulties raised by the story of her deception).

Literary Structure of Judith

The book of Judith divides easily into two roughly equal halves. The first half of the book describes the growing threat to Judah, and especially to the city of Bethulia, due to King Nebuchadnezzar's aggression against the provinces in the western reaches of his empire (Jud 1–7). The heroine Judith is first introduced midway through the book, at the turning point of the narrative: "At that time Judith heard about these things" (Jud 8:1). The second half of the book describes the unfolding of Judith's plan for the salvation of her city, ending in the beheading of the Assyrian general Holofernes and the triumph of the Jews over the Assyrians (Jud 8–16). The two halves of the book give some evidence of being arranged in a balanced pattern and exhibit some smaller-scale internal chiasms, but there is not space here to analyze these more detailed structures.

477

Outline of the Book of Judith

I. Nebuchadnezzar Invades the West (Jud 1–7)
  A. The Western Peoples Ignore Nebuchadnezzar's Campaign against the Medes (1)
  B. General Holofernes Leads out the Army in Retaliation against the West (2)
  C. The Gentiles of the West Capitulate to Holofernes (3)
  D. Judea Prepares and Prays for Defense against Holofernes (4)
  E. Holofernes Holds a Council of War (5)
  F. The Ammonite Achior, Sympathetic to the Jews, Is Handed over to the Israelites (6)
  G. Holofernes Besieges the Jewish City of Bethulia (7)

II. Judith Beheads Holofernes, and the Jews Defeat the Gentile Army (Jud 8–16)
  A. Judith Introduced; Rebukes the Jewish Elders (8)
  B. Judith Prays a Great Prayer of Repentance (9)
  C. Judith Goes Out to the Assyrian Camp and Is Captured (10:1–19)
  D. Judith and Holofernes Engage in Dialogue and Dine with Each Other (10:20—12:9)
  E. Holofernes Hosts a Banquet at Which Judith Beheads Him (12:10—13:11)
  F. Judith Returns to Bethulia (13:12–20)
  G. The Ammonite Achior Hears Her Report and Converts (14:1–10)
  H. The Assyrians Flee and the Israelites Celebrate (14:11—15:12)
  I. The Great Song of Judith (16:1–20)
  J. Epilogue: The Celebration in Jerusalem and the Renown of Judith (16:21–25)

Overview of Judith

King Nebuchadnezzar and Assyria's War against the Jews (Judith 1–7)

The story begins in the twelfth year of Nebuchadnezzar, the king of Assyria, who desires to make war against Arphaxad, king of the Medes in Ecbatana. (The historical difficulties posed by these statements will be treated below.) According to the narrative of Judith, Nebuchadnezzar calls on all his vassals in the western part of his empire to join with him in his fight with the eastern Medes, but his western subjects ignore or rebuff him (Jud 1). Enraged, he vows revenge, but first must defeat the Median threat posed by Arphaxad. This he does without great difficulty, and then he turns his attention to punishing his insubordinate vassals (Jud 2). He dispatches his chief general, Holofernes, with the royal army to exact revenge. Holofernes rampages through the western territories of the empire, until all provinces except Judah have been crushed or have made submission out of fear (Jud 3).

Judah alone stands opposed to Nebuchadnezzar, even though the nation is weak, only recently having been restored from the Babylonian exile (Jud

4:1–3). Under the leadership of the high priest Joakim and the "council" (Greek *gerousia*) in Jerusalem—a kind of precursor to the later Sanhedrin—the people of Judah make aggressive preparations for the defense of their land, then join in prayer and acts of mortification to implore God for mercy (Jud 4:9–15).

Holofernes calls a council of his advisors and allies to plot the best strategy for proceeding against Judah. A certain Achior, leader of the Ammonites, advises Holofernes that the Judeans cannot be defeated unless they sin against their God. In a remarkable overview of salvation history (Jud 5:5–21), the Gentile Achior articulates the theological principle that is at the heart of the book:

> Now therefore, my master and lord, if there is any unwitting error in this people and they sin against their God and we find out their offense, then we will go up and defeat them. *But if there is no transgression in their nation, then let my lord pass them by; for their Lord will defend them, and their God will protect them, and we shall be put to shame before the whole world.* (Jud 5:20–21)

As might be expected, his sentiment provokes ridicule from General Holofernes and his entourage. In contempt, they hand Achior over to the besieged Judeans in the city of Bethulia, presumably to be killed along with them in the siege. Despite his being an Ammonite, the Bethulians have compassion on Achior and grant him sanctuary.

Because Bethulia controls some of the passes through the hills into Judah, Holofernes begins his invasion of the province by moving against this city (Jud 6). Rather than risk the loss of his troops in a direct assault, Holofernes seizes the city's water supply with the intention of thirsting them into submission. When the water is almost gone, Uzziah, leader of the Bethulians, urges the city's inhabitants to hold out and pray for God's deliverance for an additional five more days before giving up in surrender (Jud 7).

Judith and the Beheading of Holofernes (Judith 8–16)

Judith is now introduced for the first time as a beautiful, wealthy, virtuous, and prudent widow of the tribe of Simeon (Jud 8:1–8). Judith arises in public and re-bukes the leadership of the city of Bethulia for their lack of faith in God. She

---

Consecrated Widowhood and the Figure of Judith

After her husband, Manasseh, dies unexpectedly, Judith does not seek remarriage but begins to live her widowhood in a life completely consecrated to prayer, fasting, and acts of penance, such as wearing coarse sackcloth for undergarments (Jud 8:4–8). Although such acts of penance are known elsewhere in the Old Testament during times of mourning, Judith goes beyond the minimal requirements of the Old Covenant law to practice what amounts to a lifelong *asceticism*: long fasts, physical mortification, and chaste widowhood, though remarriage was licit for her. She also gave away all her wealth before her death, thus demonstrating exemplary almsgiving. Judith's example shows that mere literal compliance with the Old Covenant, though good, was not a sufficient life-style of gratitude to the God of Israel. More was necessary. Her chaste asceticism continues to serve as a model for Christian piety, especially for widows who choose not to remarry as well as for those called to religious life.

announces that she has a secret plan for the deliverance of the city and then prays a magnificent prayer of repentance and entreaty to the God of Israel (Jud 9), comparable to other great prayers of biblical figures like Solomon, Ezra, and Daniel (1 Kings 8; Ezra 9; Dan 9).

Judith then beautifies herself and goes out of the city accompanied only by her maid (Jud 10). They are soon captured and taken before Holofernes by officers of the Assyrian army, the whole of which is enraptured by her beauty.

Judith promises to reveal to Holofernes a stratagem by which to defeat the Bethulians (Jud 11). He and the widow engage in a dialogue together, express-ing mutual admiration, and share a meal in his lavish tent—although Judith eats kosher food she brought along (Jud 12).

Holofernes becomes entranced with Judith's beauty and wants to possess her. After giving her freedom in his camp for three days, he hosts a banquet on the fourth to which only his servants and Judith are invited. After the eating and drinking is over, the servants leave Holofernes and Judith alone in his tent. The widow would have been at the mercy of the rapacious tyrant, but he falls asleep in a drunken stupor. Praying for strength, Judith hacks off Holofernes head with two strokes of his own sword, places the head in the food bag of her maid, and slips away to Bethulia with her faithful servant (Jud 13). Once she arrives at the city gates, she reveals her grisly trophy, to the great rejoicing of the Jewish inhabitants. She advises them to hang the head from the city walls and

> ### Salvation Lies in Fidelity to the Covenant
>
> An important theme in Judith is that salvation lies in fidelity to the covenant. Ironically, this is first articulated in the book by the Gentile Achior the Ammo-nite, who warns Holofernes that the Judeans cannot be destroyed unless they sin against their God—that is, break their covenant with him (Jud 5:5–21). In the context of Judith, with the Mosaic cov-enant still in force, covenant fidelity was expressed by conscientious observance of ceremonial laws, especially those con-cerning food. For example, when Judith goes into the camp of Holofernes, she insists on bringing and eating her own food, in order to avoid being defiled by partaking of the unclean food of the Gen-tiles (Jud 12:1–4). From such passages, it is possible to hypothesize that the Jews to whom the book was addressed were tempted to dispense with the Mosaic lim-itations on their diet.

to arm themselves to pursue the Assyrian army. She also summons Achior the Ammonite, who confirms her story by recognizing Holofernes' face. Dumb-founded by the power of the God of Israel, the Ammonite converts to Judaism and receives circumcision on the spot (Jud 14).

When Holofernes' death is discovered, the Assyrian army begins to dissolve in disarray, and the forces of Judah pursue them and obtain a great victory (Jud 15:1–7). Judith leads the Bethulians in a song of praise and thanksgiving, and they plunder the Assyrian camp for a month, then make a pilgrimage to Jerusalem, where they offer sacrifice, feast, and rejoice for three months (Jud 15:8–16:20). Significantly, like many biblical books, Judith ends with the joyous celebration of the *liturgy* in the sanctuary—the Second Jerusalem Temple, in this case. The deliverance of God's people has its *telos* in the celebration of worship in God's presence.

After these things, Judith continues to live on her husband's estate, with much honor and fame, to a great old age, refusing the many offers of marriage

---

Judith as a Model of Faith

Judith is a great hero of faith, which she expressed in acts of courage against a foe who threatened her life and the life of her people. Her faith and courage are reminiscent of several other biblical heroes and heroines: David, who slew an invincible foe by cutting off his head; Esther, who saved her people by cunning dialogue at a royal banquet; and Gideon, who delivered Israel despite overwhelming odds. Above all, however, Judith resembles Jael, that unlikely woman warrior who slew the enemy general by striking his head while he slept in the tent (Judg 5). Like all her biblical predecessors, Judith is inspired and fortified by her faith and confidence in the God of Israel, who honors those who honor him and exalts the humble while humbling the proud. Even under the Old Covenant, faith was active and was necessary to live a life pleasing to God.

---

made to her. She dies with great honor, after freeing her slaves and distributing her property to her kinfolk in a final act of charity toward others (Jud 16:23–25).

Historical Questions about Judith

The author of Judith is unknown, although certainly he or she was a Jew, probably writing in the second century B.C., especially if the book is a cryptic description of events taking place during the Maccabean revolt against Antiochus IV Epiphanes (ca. 175–164 B.C.) (see below).

Judith contains a large number of apparent historical anachronisms, the most obvious of which is setting the action in the reign of "Nebuchadnezzar, who ruled over the Assyrians in the great city of Nineveh" (Jud 1:1). This appears to refer to the biblical Nebuchadnezzar (2 Kings 24:1 and so on)—historically Nebuchadnezzar II of Babylon (ca. 605–562 B.C.)—who was king of the *Babylonians*, not the Assyrians. However, it is true that after Nebuchadnezzar II's father, Nabopolassar (ca. 625–605 B.C.), defeated the Assyrians at Nineveh around 612 B.C., the kings of Babylon did adopt the royal styles and titles of Assyria along with those of Babylonia.

A more serious historical problem, however, is that Judith's "Nebuchadnezzar" is clearly reigning during the postexilic or Persian period (ca. 537–333 B.C.). As the other historical books of the Old Testament make clear, Nebuchadnezzar II ruled during the last days of the Judean monarchy (ca. 605–562 B.C.) and himself put an end to it and the Jerusalem Temple in 587 B.C. (see 2 Kings 24–25). However, on two occasions, the book of Judith explicitly situates its events after the exile of the Judeans and the overthrow and rebuilding of the Jerusalem Temple (see Jud 4:1–3; 5:18–19). This cannot be prior to ca. 516 B.C., more than seventy years after Nebuchadnezzar's death. For this reason, it is extremely difficult to place the story of Judith in a coherent historical time period based on a literal reading of the text as we have it.

There are other historical difficulties. No Arphaxad, king of the Medes (Jud 1:1), is known to history. Moreover, Holofernes (Jud 2:4) and Bogoas (Jud 12:11) are names of generals who served Artaxerxes III of Persia (425 B.C.–338 B.C.), not Nebuchadnezzar. Bethulia, the principal Judean city of the story, cannot be clearly identified with any historical city. Likewise, most of the other characters of the book cannot be identified with persons known from biblical or secular history.

In light of such difficulties, it is unlikely that the book of Judith as we have it intends to be a strictly historical book. Two alternatives for the book's literary genre are either *cryptic history* or *historical fiction*.

If Judith is *cryptic history*, the names and characters of the book are ciphers for historical personages whom, for whatever reason, the author does not wish openly to identify, probably because the political situation at the time of writing was still too volatile.

"Bethulia"

Judith's home city, "Bethulia", cannot be located historically and geographically. Some have suggested that the name is a corruption of "Bethel", a well-known Judean city, or else a cryptic reference to Jerusalem itself. The Hebrew word *bethûlah* means "virgin"; "Bethulia" may be a geographical form of this root (like "Virginia") meaning "Virgin of YHWH". If this is correct, then Bethulia may represent an ideal Judean city, a "virgin daughter of Zion", whose virginity represents purity in her devotion to the Lord.

The most popular proposals for the cryptic identity of "Nebuchadnezzar king of Assyria" is either (1) Artaxerxes III of Persia (425 B.C.–338 B.C.), who did campaign against rebels in the western reaches of his empire and did have generals of the name Holofernes and Bogoas; or (2) Antiochus IV Epiphanes, the Seleucid Greek ruler of Damascus who invaded Judah and attempted to suppress Judaism, as recorded in the books of Maccabees.

The other possibility is that Judith is intentional *historical fiction*—or "historical romance". From this point of view, the historical difficulties are intended, and the biblically literate reader is expected to recognize from the anachronistic introduction of Nebuchadnezzar as the "king of Assyria" that the book is not set in actual history. The author may have included some real persons or events in an embellished framework, presumably known to the original readership, but it is difficult now to distinguish a historical core from the narrative. Against this theory, however, is the fact that the most ancient readers of the text that we possess—the early Church Fathers—all seem to have regarded the book of Judith as a historical narrative and Judith as an actual historical figure.

Judith in the Living Tradition

Although the climactic act of Judith—the beheading of the general Holofernes while he slept—is a popular and well-known story, the book as a whole is one of the more neglected texts of the Old Testament in the Christian tradition of theological reflection. However, a few aspects of the book stand out in the history of Christian thought: first, the heroism of Judith as a woman of grace; second, the moral question of whether Judith was right in deliberately deceiving Holofernes; and third, the interpretation of Judith's victory over Holofernes as a type of the Virgin Mary's victory over the devil.

Judith as an Example of a Heroic Woman of Grace

Although the book of Judith is never cited in the New Testament itself, the figure of Judith is referred to in one of the earliest extra-biblical Christian writings we possess: the first letter of Clement, bishop of Rome, to the Corinthians. In his epistle, Clement cites Judith along with Esther as examples of women used by God to deliver his people:

> Many women also, being strengthened by the grace of God, have performed numerous manly exploits. The blessed Judith, when her city was besieged, asked of the elders permission to go forth into the camp of the strangers; and, exposing herself to danger, she went out for the love which she bare to her country and people then besieged; and the Lord delivered Holofernes into the hands of a woman.[1]

Notice here that Clement is not simply referring to the historical figure of Judith, but appears to be alluding to the book itself, in which Judith is called "blessed" above all women of Israel (Jud 13:18).

Was Judith's Deception a Sin?

The fact that Judith intentionally deceives Holofernes and seems to be praised for it presents a moral problem. How can Judith be so commended and praised for her virtue, when her assassination of Holofernes was predicated on a premeditated and deliberate act of deception? Does this not suggest that in some cases it is not a sin to lie, as long as the "ends" justify the "means"?

For example, Saint Thomas Aquinas takes up this question, noting that someone might argue that "Judith is commended (Judith 15:10, 11) although she lied to Holofernes; therefore [it would seem] not every lie is a sin."[2] However, Thomas replies to the contrary:

> *Some, however, are commended in the Scriptures, not on account of perfect virtue, but for a certain virtuous disposition, seeing that it was owing to some praiseworthy sentiment that they were moved to do certain undue things. It is thus that Judith is praised, not for lying to Holofernes, but for her desire to save the people, to which end she exposed herself to danger. And yet one might also say that her words contain truth in some mystical sense.*[3]

This is a remarkably nuanced position. On the one hand, for Thomas, the praise of Judith given at the end of the book (for example, Jud 13, 15, 16) is not for her act of lying, but for the virtue and courage she displayed in placing herself in danger in the self-defense of her people. On the other hand, because of the inspired nature of Scripture, Aquinas admits that there may also be some spiritual meaning to her words that transcends the literal meaning of the text. In any case, he maintains that it remains a sin to lie.

Judith as a Type of the People of God and of Mary

Judith, whose name simply means "Jewess", truly symbolizes and embodies all that is best of the faithful of Judah. She represents the "Judah of God"—that is,

---

[1] *1 Clement* 55:3–4, in *Ante-Nicene Fathers*, ed. Alexander Roberts and James Donaldson, vol. 1 (1885; repr., Peabody, Mass.: Hendrickson, 1994), 20.

[2] Thomas Aquinas, *Summa Theologica* II–II, q. 110, a. 3, obj. 3, in *Summa Theologica*, trans. the Fathers of the English Dominican Province (1948; Allen, Tex.: Christian Classics, 1981), 1661.

[3] Ibid., a. 3 ad. 3.

the ideal Jewish nation, the vision of what the Jews were called to be. Though beautiful, wealthy, and wise, she makes use of none of her attributes to pursue her own pleasure, but goes beyond the requirements of the law in order to live a life pleasing to God. By doing so, she wins salvation for her own people.

As a beautiful and chaste widow, Judith is a manifestation of the "virgin daughter of Zion" (Is 37:22) who serves as an ideal type of Judah and even all Israel in the prophets, especially Isaiah. Her widowhood represents the state of her people. Judah (and all Israel) lost her bridegroom king, the son of David, at the exile, and he has not returned. Judith's refusal to remarry is a model for all Judah, which should refuse alliances with Gentile rulers and entanglements with Gentile gods until her true husband, the Messiah, shall return. Judith represents the faithful remnant of Judah that lives in a state of ascetic purity until the arrival of the messianic Son of David.

In light of the New Covenant, Judith is a type of the chaste Bride of Christ, the Church, the personal archetype of which is the Virgin Mary. Just as Judith, the chaste wife, defeats Israel's foe by her wisdom and strikes off his head, so the Virgin Mary, the new Eve, crushes the head of the ancient foe, Satan, through the offering of her Son (Gen 3:15; Rev 12:9).

The Book of Judith in the Lectionary

Judith may be the most neglected book of the Old Testament in the current Lectionary. Uzziah's hymn of praise to Judith is the second option for the responsorial psalm in the Common of the Blessed Virgin Mary and the proper responsorial on the Feasts of Our Lady of Lourdes, Our Lady of Guadalupe, and the Basilica of Saint Mary Major (Jud 13:18–19). The description of Judith's virtue, prayer, and fasting during the years of her widowhood is the eighth option for the first reading in the Common of Holy Men and Women, being particularly appropriate for memorials of canonized widows (Jud 8:2–8). Otherwise, the book is never read in public worship in the Roman Rite. Thus, the book is remembered in the Church primarily for the character of Judith herself, who typifies the Virgin Mary and serves as a model of saintly widowhood.

Conclusion

The book of Judith tells the story of a heroic Jewish widow who saved the people of her city and nation by her courage and cunning. The characters and events of the book are not easy to place in history, but the purpose of the book is clear: to encourage the community of God's people to maintain conscientious observance of their covenantal commitments to God and faith that God is able to deliver them despite the apparently limitless strength of their persecutors. The person of Judith herself has been received in the Christian tradition as an important prefiguration of the Virgin Mary, the chaste widow and prudent woman who brought salvation for her people, although without the deception committed by Judith.

For Further Reading

Commentaries on Judith

DeSilva, David Arthur. *Introducing the Apocrypha: Message, Context, and Significance.* Grand Rapids, Mich.: Baker Academic, 2002. (See pp. 85–109.)

Gera, Deborah Levine. *Judith.* Commentaries on Early Jewish Literature. Berlin: Walter de Gruyter, 2013.

Otzen, Benedikt. *Tobit and Judith.* Guides to the Apocrypha and Pseudepigrapha. London: T&T Clark, 2002.

VanderKam, James C. *"No One Spoke Ill of Her": Essays on Judith.* Society of Biblical Literature Early Jewish Literature 2. Atlanta: Scholars Press, 1992.

Wills, Lawrence M. "The Book of Judith". *New Interpreter's Bible* 3. Nashville: Abingdon Press, 1999.

Judith in the Living Tradition

Aquinas, Saint Thomas. *Summa Theologica.* 5 vols. Translated by the Fathers of the English Dominican Province. 1948; Westminster, Md.: Christian Classics, 1981. (See II–II, q. 110, a. 3, ad. 3.)

20. ESTHER

Introduction

The book of Esther recounts the heroism of a Jewish orphan girl who rises to queenship during the reign of the Persian emperor Xerxes I (519–465 B.C.) and, together with her uncle Mordecai, exerts influence on the monarch to save and protect the Jewish people scattered throughout the Persian Empire.

Although there was some dispute in the early centuries A.D. about whether the book of Esther was inspired, it was ultimately accepted as canonical by all Jewish and Christian traditions. In the Jewish tradition, the work is simply known as "Esther" (Hebrew *'esther*). In the Jewish Tanakh, Esther is placed in the third canonical division, the Writings (Hebrew *kethuvim*). In Jewish tradition, the book of Esther is also one of the "Five Scrolls" (Hebrew *megilloth*), a set of five short canonical books—(1) Ruth, (2) Esther, (3) Lamentations, (4) Song of Songs, and (5) Ecclesiastes—read in their entirety during certain annual Jewish feasts. Esther is read during the Feast of *Purim* (Hebrew for "lots"), the origins of which the book describes. Surprisingly, the Hebrew text of Esther never once mentions God, though his presence and activity are constantly implied (see below).

Esther is extant in two remarkably different versions: the Hebrew version and the Greek version. The Greek version of Esther (Greek *esthēr*), which was contained in the Septuagint and accepted as canonical by the early Church, contains six chapters and 107 verses that are not present in the Hebrew version of Esther preserved in the Jewish tradition, which is only ten chapters long. The additional material preserved in Greek does not significantly change the plot, but consists mostly of prayers and letters inserted at appropriate places in the narrative, plus accounts of a prophetic dream of Mordecai placed at the beginning and end of the book to form an *inclusio*. These additions mention God constantly and stress the piety of Esther and Mordecai.

When translating the Latin Vulgate, Saint Jerome rendered the shorter Hebrew text available to him directly into Latin to produce his *Liber Esther*. He also translated the additional material from the longer Greek text, but rather than placing the long material in the appropriate places in the narrative, Jerome appended it as six extra chapters at the *end* of his translation of the Hebrew. As a result, the text and chapter numbers of Esther remain in a confusing state in Catholic Bibles to this day. The traditional chapter numbers follow the Vulgate, but if read in this order, all of the passages from the longer Greek version are encountered dischronologized at the end of the book. English translators of the Bible have handled this problem in different ways. The Douay-Rheims follows the Vulgate, with the chapter numbers in traditional order. The RSVCE follows the order of the Septuagint, with the result that the narrative flows properly but the chapter numbers are confusing. (For example, the RSVCE book of Esther *begins* with chapter 11!) Other versions, such as the NAB and NABRE, assign letters (A–F) to the "extra" chapters rather than their Vulgate numbers (11–16) and place them in their narrative order so that the book reads easily in order.

Unlike the Jewish Bible, in the Greek and Latin traditions Esther is placed at or near the end of *the historical books*, reflecting the Jewish and Christian belief that the book records historical events during the Persian period (ca. 537–333 B.C.).

Literary Structure of Esther

The plot of the book of Esther is rather straightforward, and the Catholic edition of the book in its canonical form can be outlined as follows (with the Greek material italicized as in the RSVCE):

Outline of the Book of Esther

I. The Exaltation of Esther as Queen
  A. *Mordecai's Dream (11:2–12)*
  B. *Two Eunuchs Plot against King Ahasuerus (12:1–6)*
  C. King Ahasuerus Deposes Queen Vashti (1:1–22)
  D. The Jewess Esther Becomes Queen (2:1–18)
  E. Mordecai Discovers the Plot against Ahasuerus (2:19–23)

II. Haman's Plot to Destroy the Jews
  A. Haman's Plan to Destroy the Jews (3:1–13)
  B. *A Copy of King Ahasuerus' Letter against the Jews (13:1–7)*
  C. The Promulgation of the King's Letter (3:14–15)

III. Esther Saves the Jewish People
  A. Esther Agrees to Help the Jews (4:1–17)
  B. *Mordecai's Prayer (13:8–18)*
  C. *Esther's Prayer (14:1–19)*
  D. Esther Appears before Ahasuerus Unsummoned (5:1–2)
  E. *Esther Is Received by the King (15:1–16)*
  F. Queen Esther's Plot and Haman's Plot (5:3–14)
  G. Ahasuerus Remembers and Honors Mordecai (6:1–13)
  H. The Unmasking and Execution of Haman (6:14—7:10)
  I. Esther Saves the Jewish People (8:1–12)

IV. The Deliverance of the Jews and the Feast of Purim
  A. *The Decree of Ahasuerus Delivering the Jews (16:1–24)*
  B. The Promulgation of the Decree (8:13–17)
  C. The Victory of the Jewish People over Their Enemies (9:1–19)
  D. The Institution of the Jewish Feast of Purim (9:20–32)
  E. The Reign of Ahasuerus and the Exaltation of Mordecai (10:1–3)
  F. *Mordecai's Dream Fulfilled (10:4–13)*
  G. *Postscript regarding the Letter of Purim (11:1)*

In addition to this plot-based outline of the book in its final form, it is remarkable to note that in both its Hebrew and Greek versions, the book of Esther reveals a deliberate and balanced literary structure.

For example, in the Hebrew version, the book begins with brief notices about the glory of Ahasuerus and his nobles (Esther 1:1–3; 10:1–3). Thereafter, the plot is structured around balanced pairs of banquets and edicts. The main opening and closing narratives concern banquets that result in, or result from, edicts. King Xerxes holds a festive banquet resulting in an edict deposing Vashti and ordering wives to obey their husbands (Esther 1). The book closes with the festive banquet of Purim, held in obedience to the edict of the king's *wife*, Esther (Esther 9:16–32)! Thus the opening and closing also illustrate the motif of irony that runs throughout the book.

The account of Esther's rise to queenship (Esther 2:1–18) has no later mirror parallel, but the remaining narrative is bracketed by accounts of a Jew (Mordecai) saving the king from his enemies, who are slain (Esther 2:19–23); and the king saving the Jews from their enemies, who are slain (Esther 9:1–15). An inner bracket again recounts two edicts obtained from King Xerxes: an edict of destruction of the Jews obtained by Haman (Esther 3) and one for the salvation of the Jews obtained by the queen (Esther 8).

Mordecai's efforts to persuade Esther to act for the benefit of her people (Esther 4) have no parallel, but the central narrative hinges on a neat chiasm. Two banquets Esther gives for the king and Haman (Esther 5:1–8; 7:1–10) surround accounts of Haman's efforts to "lift up" Mordecai on a stake (Esther 5:9–14) and his unwilling efforts to "lift up" Mordecai with royal honor throughout Susa (Esther 6).

The Literary Structure of Hebrew Esther

A. Prologue: The Greatness of Xerxes and Nobles (1:1–3)
  B. An Exuberant Feast of the King Results in an Edict Deposing Vashti (1:4–22)
    C. How Esther Rose to the Queenship (2:1–18)
      D. The King Saved by a Jew, Enemies Slain: Mordecai Saves Xerxes (2:19–23)
        E. Haman Obtains an Edict against the Jews (chap. 3)
          F. Mordecai Persuades Esther to Help (chap. 4)
            G. Esther Hosts the King at Her First Banquet, Haman Honored (5:1–8)
              H. Haman Prepares to "Lift Up" Mordecai on a Pole (5:9–14)
              H'. Haman Forced to "Lift Up" Mordecai in Honor (chap. 6)
            G'. Esther Hosts the King at Her Second Banquet, Haman Executed (chap. 7)
          E'. Esther Obtains an Edict from the King on Behalf of the Jews (chap. 8)

> D'. The King Saves the Jews, Enemies Slain: Jews Authorized
> to Fight Back (9:1–17)
> B'. An Exuberant Feast of the Jews Results from the Queen Esther's
> Edict (9:18–32)
> A'. Epilogue: The Greatness of Xerxes and Mordecai (10:1–3)

The structure of the longer Greek version of Esther is largely the same. The whole composition is now marked with an *inclusio* recounting Mordecai's dream (Esther 11) and its fulfillment (Esther 10). The author also inserts the texts of Ahasuerus' two decrees concerning the Jews at their proper place in the narrative (Esther 13, 16), and two extensive prayers—one of Mordecai, the other of Esther (Esther 13:8–18, 14:1–19)—are supplied after the description of Haman's plot to kill the Jews (Esther 4), just prior to the climactic action of the book focused around Esther's two banquets for the king.

The Literary Structure of Greek Esther

A. Mordecai's Dream (chap. 11)
> [D'. The King Saved by a Jew, Enemies Slain: Mordecai Discovers
> a Plot (chap. 12)]
> B. A Feast Resulting in the King's Edict: The King Deposes the Queen
> (chap. 1)
> > C. The King Chooses Esther as Queen (2:1–18)
> > > D. A Jew Saves the King, Enemies Slain: Mordecai Discovers a
> > > Plot (2:19–23)
> > > > E. Haman Obtains an Edict against All Jews (chap. 3) + Text of
> > > > Edict (chap. 13)
> > > > > F. Esther and Mordecai Prepare to Help the Jews
> > > > > > 1. Mordecai and Esther Fast (chap. 4)
> > > > > > 2. Mordecai and Esther Pray (13:8–18 and 14:1–19)
> > > > > > > G. Esther Invites the King to the 1st Banquet, Haman
> > > > > > > Honored (15:1–16; 5:3–8)
> > > > > > > > H. Haman Plans to "Raise Up" Mordecai (5:9–14)
> > > > > > > > H'. Haman Forced to "Raise Up" Mordecai (chap. 6)
> > > > > > > G'. Esther Invites the King to the 2nd Banquet, Haman
> > > > > > > Hanged (chap. 7)
> > > > > E'. Esther Obtains an Edict on Behalf of All Jews (chap. 8) +
> > > > > Text of Edict (chap. 16)
> > > > D'. The King Saves the Jews, Enemies Slain (9:1–15)
> > B'. An Exuberant Feast Results from the Queen's Edict (9:16–32)
> A'. Epilogue: Mordecai's Dream Fulfilled (chap. 10)
Postscript: The Translation of the Greek Version (chap. 11)

In sum, the book of Esther, especially in the Hebrew text, is a literary masterpiece employing a wide range of literary and rhetorical devices, including humor, foreshadowing, repetition, chiasm, dramatic inversion, and irony.

Overview of Esther

In this overview, we will look first at the Hebrew version of the book and then comment briefly on the material extant only in the Greek and Latin editions.

The Exaltation of Esther as Queen (Esther 1–2)

The author announces the events described in the book as taking place "in the days of Ahasuerus, the Ahasuerus who reigned from India to Ethiopia over one hundred twenty-seven provinces" (Esther 1:1). The name Ahasuerus (Hebrew *Ăhashwērôsh*) is a transliteration of the Persian *Xšayaršā*, who is known in the West by his Greek name: Xerxes. King Xerxes I, also known as Xerxes "the Great" (519–465 B.C.), was the much-feared enemy of the Greeks in the ancient histories of Herodotus and Thucydides.

In the book of Esther, King Ahasuerus (Xerxes) sets in motion the events that lead to the exaltation of Esther by hosting a lavish banquet for his high officials in Susa, one of the capitals of the Persian Empire (Esther 1). Near the end of the banquet, when he is in high spirits, he commands his queen, Vashti, to appear before his male guests, to be admired for her beauty. In later rabbinic tradition, the king orders her to appear unclad except for her crown, but this is not at all clear from the text.[1] It is certainly the case, however, that the king's command is contrary to court etiquette, which dictated that the royal women, especially the queen, be sequestered from public view. That is probably the grounds for Vashti's refusal to appear: she prefers to risk the king's wrath than to be publicly humiliated in front of his male guests.

Ahasuerus is befuddled and angered by the queen's non-compliance and consults with his advisors, who recommend that he depose the queen and issue an edict to that effect, lest word of Vashti's action lead to domestic turmoil throughout the empire:

> Not only to the king has Queen Vashti done wrong, but also to all the princes and all the peoples who are in all the provinces of King Ahasuerus. For this deed of the queen will be made known to all women, causing them to look with contempt upon their husbands, since they will say, "King Ahasuerus commanded Queen Vashti to be brought before him, and she did not come." ... So when the decree made by the king is proclaimed throughout all his kingdom, vast as it is, all women will give honor to their husbands, high and low. (Esther 1:16–17, 20)

The irony of this rationale is, of course, that it is ultimately Esther who will be honored by the king himself, by means of another decree!

Later, on the advice of his courtiers, the king inaugurates a "beauty contest" to select a new queen (Esther 2). Beautiful virgins from throughout his realm are chosen to undergo extensive cosmetic treatments—"six months with oil of

---

[1] See *Targum Esther* 1:11; cf., however, Josephus, *Antiquities* 11.191, in Carey A. Moore, *Esther*, Anchor Bible 7B (New York: Doubleday, 1971), 13.

The Names of Esther and Mordecai

Esther has both a Hebrew name, *Hadassah* (meaning "myrtle"; cf. Is 51:19; 55:13), and a Babylonian name, *'Estēr*, probably a variant of the name of the goddess Ishtar (a.k.a. Ashtarte or Asherah). The name Mordecai is a Hebrew transliteration of the Babylonian name *mardukka* or *mardukku*, from the god Marduk, patron of Babylon. Mordecai probably had another, Hebrew, name by which he was known in the Jewish community.

The fact that both Esther and Mordecai have names derived from Mesopotamian gods shows the level of cultural assimilation the Jews underwent during the time of the exile. Other Jews in exile also took, or were given, Babylonian names based on pagan deities: for example, Daniel and his three companions (Dan 1:7).

---

myrrh and six months with spices and ointments for women" (Esther 2:12)!— and then allowed to spend one night with the king. The one most pleasing to the King would be selected to replace Vashti.

A certain maiden named Esther, an orphan of the tribe of Benjamin being raised by her uncle Mordecai, a royal official, enters this "beauty contest", wins, and is named queen at a great banquet in her honor.

Mordecai's Age in Esther

At first glance, the book seems to indicate that Mordecai was taken into exile with Jehoiachin ca. 597 B.C. (Esther 2:5–6). In this case, Mordecai would have been improbably old (>100 years) during the reign of Xerxes I. However, these verses may simply mean that Kish, Mordecai's great-grandfather, or else his family generally, was exiled in 597 B.C.

Meanwhile, Mordecai, in the course of his official duties, overhears two palace eunuchs plotting to assasinate King Ahasuerus. He informs the king, who has the eunuchs executed and records Mordecai's meritorious intervention. But Mordecai receives no reward.

Haman's Plot to Destroy the Jews (Esther 3)

At this time, a certain Haman, an Amalekite descended from the wicked King Agag (1 Sam 15:8–33), is promoted in the king's service above all the other courtiers (Esther 3). Mordecai refuses to bow to this Haman when he enters and leaves the royal palace, which infuriates the Agagite. Not content to have Mordecai alone executed, Haman decides to wipe out his entire race, the Jews. He and his associates cast a *pur* (Hebrew for "lot" or "die", loanword from Persian) to choose the day on which the Jewish nation would be destroyed, and the *pur* gives the thirteenth day of the twelfth month, Adar (Esther 2:7). Haman bribes the king for an edict of extermination against all descendants of Judah, scheduled for the thirteenth of Adar, and a public proclamation to that effect is made throughout the empire.

Mordecai and Haman and Salvation History

Significantly, the conflict between Mordecai and Haman that drives much of the plot is deeply rooted in the history of Israel. Mordecai is a Benjaminite, a "son of Kish" (Esther 2:5) like King Saul of old (1 Sam 10:11, 21). Haman is an Agagite—that is, a descendant of Agag, king of Amalek (1 Sam 15:8–9). The conflict between the two is thus a replay of the conflict between Saul and Agag in Israel's early history. The informed reader remembers that Saul failed to annihilate the Amalekites as he was ordered (1 Sam 15:9). If he had, the wicked Haman would not be present to threaten the Jews.

Thus, even in exile the Jews continue to reap the consequences of the infidelities in their earlier history. Haman the Agagite attempts to complete the annihilation of Israel intended by his ancient ancestors (Deut 25:17), but Mordecai, a kind of new Saul, arises to save Israel from his hand. Part of Saul's downfall consisted in laying his hands on the plunder of the Amalekites (1 Sam 15:9,15); therefore, when the Jews vindicate themselves against their enemies on the thirteenth of Adar, they will refrain from touching the plunder (Esther 9:16). Thus, although little is said explicitly of the covenant history of Israel in Esther, the biblically literate reader can recognize that themes from Israel's history continue to play out even in the Persian exile.

Queen Esther Saves the Jewish People (Esther 4–8)

In great distress over the edict against the Jewish people, Mordecai mourns publicly in sackcloth and ashes and sends word to Esther, asking her to intervene with the king (Esther 4).[2] Esther sends word back, explaining that, despite her status as queen, she is not free to initiate contact with the king and can do so only at the risk of her life. Mordecai insists that she must take that chance and, in doing so, lays bare the understanding of divine providence that is at the very heart of the book:

> Then Mordecai told them to return answer to Esther, "Think not that in the king's palace you will escape any more than all the other Jews. For if you keep silence at such a time as this, relief and deliverance will rise for the Jews from another quarter.... *And who knows whether you have not come to the kingdom for such a time as this?*" (Esther 4:13–14)

In the face of these words, Esther concedes, but she requests that all the Jews in Susa fast for her for three days—an important testament to the Jewish belief in the power of intercessory fasting (Esther 2:16)—before she attempts to intercede with the king.

After three days of fasting, Esther beautifies herself and makes bold to enter the king's throne room unbidden (Esther 5). Fortunately, the king is pleased with her and extends his scepter, the sign of welcome. Touching the scepter, Esther delivers her invitation for the king and his vizier, Haman, to attend a private banquet she will host that very evening. The king and Haman accept the invitation; at the banquet, the king asks Esther what her real petition is. Perhaps

---

[2] See image of a mourning woman putting dust on her head in Anthony Tomasino, "Esther", in *1 & 2 Kings, 1 & 2 Chronicles, Ezra, Nehemiah, Esther*, vol. 3 of *Zondervan Illustrated Bible Backgrounds Commentary*, ed. John H. Walton (Grand Rapids, Mich.: Zondervan, 2009), 490.

from failure of nerve or sensing that the moment is not yet right, Esther delays, asking the king to come to dine with her again the following evening, when she will make her request known.

Between the two banquets transpires an ironic and darkly humorous incident between Mordecai and Haman (Esther 6). Haman leaves the palace after Esther's banquet and encounters Mordecai, who still refuses to bow to him. Indignant, Haman returns home and orders an enormously high pole—about seventy-five feet (= "fifty cubits") high (Esther 7:9)—on which to impale Mordecai.

> *Means of Execution in Esther*
>
> Most English versions speak of Haman constructing a "gallows" on which to hang Mordecai. The Hebrew speaks simply of a "tree" or "wooden thing" (Hebrew *ʿēts*) being built from which to "hang" (Hebrew *talah*) Mordecai. This is more likely a huge pole or pike on the top of which the victim was impaled. Persians practiced impalement rather than hanging with a noose in Western fashion.

Meanwhile, King Ahasuerus is unable to sleep and calls for someone to read to him from the royal chronicles to calm his insomnia. Providentially, the record of Mordecai's intervention to save the life of the king is read, and the king asks whether Mordecai was ever rewarded. Informed that he was not, the king resolves to rectify this injustice. At this very moment, Haman enters the palace to request permission for Mordecai's execution. The king calls Haman into the inner chambers and asks him how he should honor a very faithful servant. Haman, thinking that the king wishes to honor *him*, suggests an elaborate parade in the royal chariot, garbed in royal robes. The king is pleased and orders Haman to carry out precisely that suggestion for Mordecai the Jew! With no choice but to obey, Haman carries out the king's command and parades Mordecai around the capital city of Susa, then rushes home to his family in shame.

Scarcely has he arrived home when servants come to escort him to Esther's second banquet (Esther 7). This time, when the king asks for Esther's petition as they relax over wine after the meal, she reveals her true concerns. She pleads for the king to act to save her and her fellow Jews from the edict of extermination Haman has obtained. Indignant at Haman for manipulating him into authorizing the extermination of the nation of his own queen, the king storms out into the garden. Haman throws himself on Esther's couch to plead for his life. When the king reenters the room, he mistakes Haman's posture as an attempt to violate Esther and orders Haman to be hanged on the very gibbet that he had built for Mordecai.

The Deliverance of the Jews and the Feast of Purim (Esther 9–10)

But this is not the end of the story. Reversing the king's previous edict of extermination is difficult, since the laws of the Medes and Persians cannot be repealed or revoked (Esther 8:8; cf. Dan 6:8,15). Esther suggests to the king a solution: promulgate a *second* edict, permitting the Jews to arm themselves and fight back against their enemies on the thirteenth of Adar. The king consents and promulgates another decree. When the appointed day arrives, the Jews prevail against their enemies in a great victory. Together with Mordecai, whom the king installs in Haman's former position, Esther promulgates an edict to her own Jewish people, commanding them to commemorate the thirteenth of Adar as a festive holiday annually in perpetuity (Esther 10). This becomes known as the Feast of *Purim* or "Lots", from the Akkadian (Babylonian) word *pur*, meaning lot.

The Greek Chapters of Esther

The plot of Greek Esther is the same as that of Hebrew Esther, with several pieces of extra material. The book now opens by introducing Mordecai, providing his genealogy, and recounting an apocalyptic dream he has had of two dragons in combat, whose fight is resolved by a tiny spring that grows into a great river and puts an end to hostilities (Esther 11). This is followed by a somewhat more detailed duplicate account of Mordecai's intervention against the king's traitorous eunuchs (Esther 12; cf. 2:19–23). The rest of the plot unfolds unchanged, except that the Greek version gives the text of the king's two edicts (Esther 13, 16) and records lengthy prayers from Mordecai and Esther while they are in distress over the edict of extermination (Esther 13:8—14:19). The two prayers are particularly important and have a strong influence on the way the book is read in Greek, because they provide a window into the piety and inner experience of Mordecai and Esther through this period of trial. The author of the Hebrew edition of Esther is very laconic and gives us little or no view into the inner life of the hero or heroine. From Greek Esther, however, we learn that Esther is in fact a pious Jew, and her close association with a Gentile king and his court is a source of constant pain to her (Esther 14:15–19).

Greek Esther closes with Mordecai explaining his dream: he and Haman are the two dragons in conflict, and Esther the little spring of water that grew into a river of salvation. The explanation of the dream provides closure to the Greek version of the story. A postscript (Esther 11:1) details some information about when and by whom the Greek translation was made, in a manner similar to that found in the prologue to the Greek edition of the book of Sirach.

Historical Issues in Esther

The Origins of Hebrew and Greek Esther

The book of Esther in both its Hebrew and Greek editions is an anonymous work, although rabbinic Jewish tradition attributes it to the early postexilic "Men of the Great Assembly".[3] As with the other historical books, however, there is little to no data upon which to base any solid conclusions about authorship.

When it comes to questions of dating, distinctions must be made between the origins of the Hebrew and Greek editions. With reference to Hebrew Esther, estimates of the date of the book vary from shortly after the events recorded would have occurred (mid-fifth century B.C.) to the Maccabean period (mid- to late second century B.C.), during which we get our earliest reference to the events in Esther with a fleeting reference to the Feast of Purim as "Mordecai's

---

[3] Babylonian Talmud, *Baba Bathra* 14b, in Isidore Epstein, ed., *The Babylonian Talmud*, 35 vols. (London: Soncino, 1935–1952).

day" (2 Mac 15:36). The complete absence of any Greek loanwords, clear signs of acquaintance with Greek culture, or hints of awareness of the Seleucid persecution and Maccabean revolt suggests that Hebrew Esther was composed during the Persian period—that is, prior to 333 B.C. Most commentators agree that the author was familiar with Persian culture generally and specifically with court etiquette and the capital at Susa. Accordingly, the book may have been written in or near that city in the mid- to late fifth century (400s B.C.).[4]

Significantly, the Greek version of the book explicitly informs its readers as to when it was translated, when the postscript declares:

> *In the fourth year of the reign of Ptolemy and Cleopatra*, Dositheus, who said he was a priest and a Levite, and Ptolemy his son brought to Egypt the preceding Letter of Purim, which they said was genuine and had been translated by Lysimachus the son of Ptolemy, one of the residents of Jerusalem. (Greek Esther 11:1)

On the one hand, this postscript gives us positive evidence that at least one portion of the Greek version—the letter regarding Purim (Esther 10:4–12, 11:1)—was translated into Greek in Jerusalem and then brought to the Greek-speaking community in Egypt as its audience. On the other hand, it is hard to pin down exactly when the "fourth year" of the reign of Ptolemy and Cleopatra was, since there were several Hellenistic Egyptian royal couples who adopted the names Ptolemy and Cleopatra.[5] The evidence slightly favors the period of joint rule of King Ptolemy VIII and his bride, Cleopatra, placing the publication of the Greek version of the book in Alexandria around 114 B.C.[6] Whatever may be the case, we know that the longer Greek version of Esther was in circulation by the first century A.D., since both the Jewish historian Josephus and the apostolic Church Father Clement of Rome allude to parts of Esther that are found only in the Greek version, such as Esther's prayer[7] and the contents of Ahasuerus' edict against the Jews.[8] In other words, the earliest external witnesses we possess to the book know the longer Greek version that would eventually be canonized by the early Church.

The Debate over the Historicity of Esther

The historicity of Esther is widely disputed. Most contemporary scholars regard the book as fiction or a kind of historical "novella", but a minority of scholars concur with the traditional Jewish and Christian tradition that it is historical.

On the one hand, several arguments can be levied *against* the substantial historicity of the book.[9] (1) First, there is no extra-biblical confirmation of

---

[4] Edwin M. Yamauchi, *Persia and the Bible* (Grand Rapids, Mich.: Baker, 2010), 226–28.

[5] David A. DeSilva, *Introducing the Apocrypha: Message, Context, and Significance* (Grand Rapids, Mich.: Baker Academic, 2002), 117.

[6] Carey A. Moore, *Daniel, Esther, and Jeremiah: The Additions*, Anchor Bible 44 (New York: Doubleday, 1977), 252.

[7] *1 Clement* 55; cf. Esther 14–15.

[8] Josephus, *Antiquities* 11.215–16; cf. Esther 13. See DeSilva, *Introducing the Apocrypha*, 125.

[9] See Moore, *Esther*, xlv–lxvi.

the events recorded in it. In particular, we lack any extra-biblical evidence for either Queen Vashti or Esther in ancient Greek accounts of the reign of King Xerxes of Persia. (2) Second, and perhaps even more important, many of the events described in the book are regarded as intrinsically *improbable* or *inaccurate*, such as the number of provinces being listed as 127 (Esther 1:1); Ahasuerus' feast lasting for six months (Esther 1:4); the selection of a "queen" from among women outside the seven noble families of Persia;[10] the age of Mordecai being somewhere around 130 years (cf. Esther 2:6–7; 11:4); the king's permission for an entire race of people to be destroyed and plundered in his empire (Esther 3:12–15); the timing of Haman's return to the palace (Esther 6:4); or the edict permitting Jews to defend themselves with arms (Esther 8:11–12). (3) Finally, from this point of view, the book of Esther belongs to the ancient Jewish genre of the "novel" or "court tale", which was understood to be largely fictional.[11] This explains the hyperbolic character of the story and the "stock characters" of the gullible king and the wicked vizier.[12] Others see the book as a legend concocted in order to explain the origins of the Jewish festival of Purim, which may have originated as a pagan festival in honor of the Persian gods Ishtar and Marduk.

On the other hand, there are a number of arguments that can be mounted in favor of the historicity of Esther. (1) First and foremost, in terms of literary genre, the book of Esther itself suggests that it was intended to be interpreted as history, and the most ancient Jewish interpretations of the book that we possess clearly regarded it as such. For example, not only does the Hebrew version of Esther invite the reader to consult "the Chronicles of the kings of Media and Persia" (Esther 10:2), but the royal edicts present in Greek Esther are clearly meant to signal to the reader that the book belongs to the genre of historiography and "to lend greater credibility to the historicity of the story".[13] In addition, the book often records the year, month, or day on which certain events were purported to have happened (Esther 1:3; 2:1, 6; 3:7, 13; 8:12; 9:1), giving the appearance of historiography. Significantly, the first-century Jewish historian Josephus incorporates the book of Esther into his history of the Jewish people, clearly interpreting it as a chronicle of events that took place during the Persian period.[14] In other words, if we are to believe that Esther was originally published as an ancient Jewish romance or work of fiction, we also have to believe that none of the ancient inter- preters of which we know understood the genre, so that the book was mis- interpreted as history until the modern period. (2) Second, and even more striking, the author manifests an authentic knowledge of the Persian history, culture, and language:[15]

---

[10] Cf. Herodotus, *History* 3.84.

[11] L. M. Wills, *The Jewish Novel in the Ancient World* (Ithaca, N.Y.: Cornell University Press, 1995).

[12] John J. Collins, *Introduction to the Hebrew Bible* (Minneapolis: Fortress Press, 2004), 540.

[13] Moore, *Esther*, 383.

[14] See *Jewish Antiquities* 11.184–296; DeSilva, *Introducing the Apocrypha*, 125.

[15] Moore, *Esther*, xli; Edwin M. Yamauchi, *Persia and the Bible* (Grand Rapids, Mich.: Baker, 1996), 237–39.

1. Extension of Xerxes' empire from India to Ethiopia (Esther 1:1)
2. Palace of Xerxes at the city of Susa (Esther 1:2)
3. Tendency of Xerxes to caprice and anger (Esther 1:12; 7:7–8; cf. Herodotus, *History* 7.24, 35, 37–39; 9.108)
4. Persian practice of hanging or suspension as a form of capital punishment (Esther 2:23; 5:14; 7:10)[16]
5. Observance of "lucky days" where lots are cast (Esther 3:7)
6. Persian loanwords, such as "nobles" (*partemim*); "turban" (*keter*); "pavilion" (*bitan*); "satrapies" (*'ahashdarpenim*); "royal horses" (*'ahashteranim*); and so on (Esther 1:3, 5, 11; 3:12; 8:10)

(3) Third, although the events in the book of Esther are clearly extraordinary, there is nothing (strictly speaking) beyond the realm of possibility; indeed, nothing supernatural or miraculous is even claimed to have taken place! Moreover, we know from other sources that ancient Near Eastern kings did in fact take foreign women to wife, such as the Assyrian king Sennacherib, who was married to (among others) the Palestinian woman Zakutu-Naqiya.[17] (4) Fourth, the author includes details—such as the pagan names of Esther (from the goddess Ishtar) and Mordecai (from the god Marduk)—not particularly flattering to Jewish sensibilities and therefore unlikely to have been invented. (5) Fifth, there is no positive evidence for any alternate account of the origin of the Feast of Purim, which has been observed since antiquity (2 Mac 15:36).[18]

In addition to these positive arguments for historicity, it is important to point out that the arguments against historicity need to be weighed carefully. For example, while it is true that most of the events of the book are not independently confirmed, at the same time, our information about the reign of Xerxes is extremely limited. Indeed, the primary source for what we know about Xerxes is the *Greek* historian Herodotus, but Herodotus was almost solely concerned with Xerxes' campaign against the Greek city-states allied with Sparta and Athens in the years around 480 B.C. He has little to say about the rest of Xerxes' reign, and what he does say about it is sometimes dubious or apparently legendary. Besides Herodotus, other historical sources provide little assistance. Xerxes' own inscriptions tend to be stylized copies of those of his royal predecessors and have little historical value. Many economic documents from the Persian Empire have been discovered, but they shed no light on the history of the royal court. Therefore, much of the reign of Xerxes I is shrouded in historical silence, making arguments from silence even more tenuous than usual. Moreover, there is an unexplained chronological gap in the book between the third year of Xerxes (Esther 1:3) and the seventh (Esther 2:16), when Esther is selected as queen. This otherwise unaccountable gap seems to correspond to the four years Xerxes I was gone from Susa campaigning against the Greeks—the years recorded most heavily by Herodotus. Significantly, the name Mordecai,

---

[16] Cf. Tomasino, "Esther", 486.
[17] Moore, *Esther*, 20.
[18] Josephus, *Antiquities* 11:295.

at one time considered unattested extra-biblically, is now recognized as the Hebrew form of the Babylonian name *Mardukka* or *Mardukku*, and excavated Persian records mention as many as four or five different individuals with that name who served in various government capacities during the reign of Xerxes.[19] Accordingly, one of them may be the biblical Mordecai.[20]

The most serious historical problem in Esther is the lack of attestation of Vashti and Esther in extra-biblical records. The ancient Greek historian Herodotus does mention an "Amestris" who was married to Xerxes, whom some biblical scholars have tried to identify with Vashti,[21] but the argument is tenuous, based on the unverifiable claim that the name underwent a series of phonetic transformations. However, it should be noted that almost our sole source for the datum that Xerxes' wife was named "Amestris" is Herodotus, and the information Herodotus provides is contradictory. For example, he records that "every Persian has many lawful wives and keeps still more concubines", yet he names only one wife of Xerxes, "Amestris", and never calls her "queen". Seven of the nine times he mentions her are all in a single lurid legend concerning her supposed grisly revenge on a rival,[22] which may not be historical. In one of the other two occurrences of her name, Herodotus identifies her as the *grandmother* of Xerxes' wife.[23] Therefore, it may be doubted that Herodotus had access to extensive and accurate information about Xerxes' marital history.

Along similar lines, the figure of 127 provinces for the Persian Empire is typically claimed to be unhistorical (Esther 1:1) because the Persian Empire in fact was divided into approximately twenty *satrapies*, each under a *satrap*, a Persian viceroy.[24] However, the Hebrew text does not say "satrapies", but "provinces" (Hebrew *medinôt*), and it is well-known that each satrapy included numerous semi-autonomous provinces. For example, the Persian satrapy of "Beyond the River", or Trans-Euphrates, included Judea, Samaria, Ammon, Aram (Syria), and almost certainly other provinces, and this reality is reflected in the Aramaic correspondence recovered from the Jewish colony in Elephantine, Egypt, dating to the late 400s B.C. Indeed, history demonstrates that in any given nation, the exact number of territory divisions is something that is often in flux, but 127 is not an unreasonable figure for the distinct nationalities and city-states incorporated into the Persian Empire.

In the final analysis, in the absence of further external evidence, it is difficult to treat the arguments either for or against historicity as conclusive. One may well concede that a number of events in Esther are improbable, especially in their timing. However, if the events surrounding Esther and Mordecai had all been probable and predictable, the narrative of their lives would not have been remembered as a particular example of God's extraordinary *providence*. As it is, the Jewish community remembered this narrative because the unlikely

---

[19] Tomasino, "Esther", 481 and 505.
[20] Yamauchi, *Persia and the Bible*, 234–36.
[21] Ibid., 230–32.
[22] Herodotus, *Histories* 9.109–13.
[23] Ibid., 7.61 and 114.
[24] Collins, *Introduction to the Hebrew Bible*, 539.

but fortuitous—yes, *providential*—sequence of events gave evidence to them of God's sovereign guidance of history.

The Greek Sections of Esther

The sections of Esther preserved in Greek do appear to have been composed after the main body of the book and present a few notable difficulties. Ahasuerus/Xerxes is called "Artaxerxes" in the Greek sections, which is simply a translation error in the textual transmission, probably arising from the difficulty of matching the Hebrew name 'ahashwerosh with the Greek names of the Persian monarchs, which are often much farther removed from the Persian phonetics than is the Hebrew. Also, the date of Purim is given as the fourteenth rather than the thirteenth of Adar in one section (Esther 13:6).

Theological Issues in Esther

Why Is God's Name Never Mentioned in Hebrew Esther?

The most important theological theme in the book of Esther is God's providential guidance of history, even when his name is not explicitly invoked and no obvious divine intervention (such as through miracles) can be seen.

In the Hebrew text of Esther, *God's name is never mentioned*, a fact that gave some later rabbis reason to dispute the canonicity of the book. In rabbinic language, a biblical book that was inspired was described as "making the hands unclean"—meaning communicating holiness by means of touch—whereas a book that was not inspired was described as "not making the hands unclean". Regarding Esther, in the Babylonian Talmud, we read:

> Rab Judah said in the name of Samuel: [The scroll] of *Esther does not make the hands unclean.* Are we to infer from this that Samuel was of the opinion that Esther was not composed under the inspiration of the holy spirit? How can this be, seeing that Samuel has said that Esther was composed under the inspiration of the holy spirit? It was composed to be recited [by heart], but not to be written.[25]

Notice here that well into the third century A.D.; there was debate among Jewish rabbis over whether or not Esther was inspired. Although they do not say why, the most obvious explanation for this is because the book never mentions God.

But why not? Although some scholars have proposed that Esther adopts an essentially secular view of history, this is demonstrably not the case. Rather, the failure to mention God explicitly is part of the author's literary art, yet another form of irony, one of his favorite literary devices. Mordecai and Esther are not irreligious persons: at the crisis point in the narrative, when Haman's edict has been promulgated and the fate of the Jews and Esther herself is uncertain, the

---

[25] Babylonian Talmud, *Megillah* 7a, in Epstein, *Babylonian Talmud.*

queen calls for a three-day *fast* of all the Jews in Susa the capital (Esther 4). Fasting is a distinctly religious act, a solemn form of prayer. There is no "secular" fasting. The implication of the plot is that the fortuitous chain of events that transpires after this are the result of the Jews' solemn petition of God.

Moreover, although God's name is not mentioned, the astute reader will see his hand everywhere, in a whole series of "coincidences": the deposition of Vashti, the rise of Esther, Mordecai's "chancing" upon the treasonous eunuchs, the king's insomnia, Haman's fortuitous arrival at court, and many other instances. The plot of the book reaches its climax with the origin of the Feast of "Purim"—that is, the lots or dice that Haman threw to determine the thirteenth of Adar. Lots are a symbol of random chance, and the plot depends on a number of events that happen apparently by chance, but the final message of the book is that nothing takes place by chance: the hand of God guides all affairs toward the salvation of his people.

The Explicit Religiosity of Greek Esther

The larger Greek Esther makes explicit what was implicit in the earlier Hebrew. The *inclusio* of Mordecai's dream (Esther 11, 10) emphasizes that all these events transpired in fulfillment of a divine plan, revealed to Mordecai in cryptic form before it occurred. Above all, the long prayers of Mordecai and Esther reveal the piety of the two protagonists, only implied in the Hebrew narrative (Esther 13:8–18; 14:1–19). In their prayers, Mordecai and Esther defend themselves from suspicions or accusations that may have occurred to early readers of the book: for example, that Mordecai's refusal to bow to Haman was rash arrogance that endangered his people (Esther 13:13); or that Esther was "living it up" in royal style with the Gentile king while her people suffered deprivations (Esther 14:16–18). In the end, Greek Esther is less subtle as a piece of literature than Hebrew Esther but is perhaps more useful as a sacred text for public proclamation, because the piety and motivation of the protagonists are brought to the forefront. The book of Esther emphasizes God's concern for the people of Israel, even though they may be scattered far and wide in foreign lands, in danger, by turns, of assimilation and annihilation.

Esther in the Living Tradition

As with the other shorter historical books, such as Tobit and Judith, in the history of Christianity, the book of Esther has not garnered the same kind of exegetical and theological attention as books such as Genesis, the Psalms, or the prophets. Esther is never cited in the New Testament and rarely referenced by the Church Fathers. As far as we know, there was no Christian commentary written on the book until the ninth-century work of the Frankish monk and theologian Rabanus Maurus (ca. 836 A.D.).[26]

Nevertheless, when Esther is discussed, the unforgettable figures of Mordecai, Queen Esther, and Haman and the events described in the book are often

---

[26] Moore, *Esther*, xxxi.

interpreted as prefigurations of Christ, the Church, and her enemies by the living tradition of the Church.

Queen Esther's Wedding Feast and the Eucharistic Wedding Feast

One of the consistent themes that we find in the writings of the Fathers is the idea that Esther—like Ruth, Judith, and other heroines of salvation history—is a type of the Church. One particularly striking example of this comes from Rabanus' interpretation of the section that describes how King Ahasuerus "gave a great banquet" for the occasion of his wedding: "it was Esther's banquet" (Esther 2:18):

> It is evident that the magnificent banquet for Esther's wedding, prepared for both the princes and the people, represents the greatest bliss that is enjoyed by the entire human race, both great and small, *for the spiritual union of Christ with the church.* In this banquet, in fact, no carnal foods are consumed by those who are worthy to participate in it. Instead they consume a spiritual diet of wisdom and virtue. In this banquet, all the faithful receive the holy mysteries of the body and blood of the Lord as a remedy for their salvation. Here the meal of eternal life resides.[27]

From this point of view, the glorious exaltation of the Jewess Esther at the royal wedding feast of the king of Persia is a kind of foretaste of the exaltation of the Church as at the royal wedding supper of Christ, the true King of the Universe.

Haman and the Antichrist

In a similar vein, it is no great leap to see in the wickedness of Haman the Agagite a negative prefiguration of the powerful persecutors who would wage sometimes seemingly irrational (but always bloodthirsty) war against the people of God in this world. Again, in the words of Rabanus:

> Nothing else is symbolized by the arrogant Haman than the opulence of the powerful of this world who take advantage of the benefits conceded to them by divine mercy.... *They are guilty of striving to transfer to themselves the honor and reverence that are rightly due to God alone. And so they pursue with hatred all those who do not want to act according to such behavior or comply with it.* They persecute them with afflictions and endeavor to put them to death.[28]

This is a fascinating explanation of the otherwise seemingly irrational hatred of the many powerful people in this world who have risen up to persecute both the Jewish people and the Church. Like Haman before them, this hatred is ultimately driven by a kind of spiritual envy, which covets the worship and honor

---

[27] Rabanus Maurus, *Explanation of the Book of Esther* 4, in *1–2 Kings, 1–2 Chronicles, Ezra, Nehemiah, Esther,* ed. Marco Conti, Old Testament 5, Ancient Christian Commentary on Scripture, ed. Thomas C. Oden (Downers Grove, Ill.: InterVarsity Press, 2008), 379.

[28] Ibid., 6, p. 382.

that are due to God alone, in the spirit of the Antichrist figure that the apostle Paul will refer to as "the son of perdition", who opposes the worship of anything but himself (2 Thess 2:3–4). Indeed, later on in his commentary, Rabanus explicitly describes the edict to slaughter the Jews during the twelfth month of Adar as a prefiguration of the fierce persecution that the Church will face during "the last days".[29]

The Persecution of Mordecai and the Persecution of Christ

Although King Ahasuerus was viewed as a type of Christ in his glory, Mordecai the Jew was viewed as a type of the suffering Messiah. For example, the third- to fourth-century Syriac Church Father known as Aphrahat makes the following striking comparison between the two figures:

> Mordecai also was persecuted as Jesus was persecuted. Mordecai was persecuted by the wicked Haman; and Jesus was persecuted by the rebellious People. Mordecai by his prayer delivered his people from the hands of Haman; and Jesus by His prayer delivered His people from the hands of Satan.... Because of Mordecai, Esther was well pleasing to the king, and went in and sat instead of Vashti, who did not do his will; and because of Jesus, the Church is well pleasing to God, and has gone in to the king, instead of the congregation which did not His Will.... Mordecai trod upon the neck of Haman, his persecutor; and as for Jesus, His enemies shall be put under His feet.[30]

Notice here once again the equation of the enemies of God's people (such as Mordecai) with Satan and the demonic forces who levy their powers against Christ and the Church.

The Intercession of Queen Esther and the Role of the Virgin Mary

In addition to viewing Esther as a type of the Church, more recent expressions of the Church's tradition have also recognized in Esther's act of intercession a prefiguration of the Virgin Mary. In the words of Pope John Paul II:

> Esther [unlike Judith] did not kill the enemy but, by playing the role of mediator, interceded for those who were threatened with destruction.... The Old Testament tradition frequently emphasizes the decisive action of women in the salvation of Israel, especially in the writings closest to the coming of Christ. In this way the Holy Spirit, through the events connected with Old Testament women, sketches with ever greater precision the characteristics of Mary's mission in the work of salvation for the entire human race.[31]

---

[29] Ibid.

[30] Aphrahat, *Demonstrations* 21.20, in *NPNF2* 13:400.

[31] John Paul II, "Women's Indispensable Role in Salvation History", General Audience of March 27, 1996, in Pope John Paul II, *Theotókos: Woman, Mother, Disciple. A Catechesis on Mary, Mother of God* (Boston: Pauline Books and Media, 2000), 74–75.

In other words, just as Esther's primary role was mediator and intercessor on behalf of the Jewish people, so Mary acts as intercessor on behalf of the entire world.

The Feast of Purim and the Feast of Easter

In keeping with the principle we have noted elsewhere in the tradition, in which the annual feasts of the Old Covenant are viewed as fulfilled in Christ and the Church, it is remarkable that even the Feast of Purim, which is not rooted in the law of Moses, was viewed by some Christians as having been fulfilled in the Feast of Easter. In his festal letter to the Church at Alexandria, Athanasius exhorts Christians to celebrate Easter with the same kind of joy and piety that Esther and the Jewish people celebrated the Feast of Purim:

> Let us keep the feast in that way that he has established for our salvation—the holy day of Easter.... Remember that ... in the time of Esther the people kept a feast to the Lord because they had been delivered from a deadly decree. They called a feast, thanking and praising the Lord because he had changed the situation for them. Therefore, let us keep our promises to the Lord, confess our sins, and keep the feast to him—in behavior, moral conduct, and way of life.[32]

The Book of Esther in the Lectionary

Despite its appeal throughout history as a memorable narrative, in the contemporary Lectionary, the book of Esther is not read on any Sundays or feast days. However, the Lectionary does occasionally utilize the prayers of Greek Esther, which show Esther and Mordecai in the posture of supplicants, faithful worshippers reduced to powerlessness and desperation, threatened with death by the highest authorities in a world-encompassing empire, who turn to God in their time of deepest need.

For example, on the Thursday of the First Week of Lent, portions of Esther's prayer (Esther 14:1, 3–5, 12–14 = C:12, 14–16, 23–25) are read together with Jesus' teaching on prayer in the Sermon on the Mount (Mt 7:7–12): "Ask, and it will be given you; seek, and you will find; knock, and it will be opened to you." In this way, Esther is remembered as a woman of prayer, and the dramatic answers to her prayer in the book of Esther serve to illustrate the truth of Jesus' teaching. Likewise, an excerpt of Mordecai's prayer (Esther 13:8–14, 17 = C:1–7, 10) is the tenth option for the first reading in the Common of Holy Men and Women and is particularly appropriate for the memorials of saints who resisted arrogant or tyrannical governments or rulers. Excerpts from both Mordecai and Esther's prayers (Esther 13:9–14, 18; 14:1–4 = C:2–7, 11–15) are also the first option for Masses for persecuted Christians, for threatening weather or "any need", and the sixth option for Masses for various civil concerns or civil

---

[32] Athanasius, *Festal Letters* 8, in Athanasius, *The Resurrection Letters*, trans. Jack N. Sparks (Nashville: Thomas Nelson, 1979), quoted in Conti, *1–2 Kings*, 397.

officials. On these special occasions, Mordecai and Esther are recalled as godly individuals who cried out to God in a dire situation of mortal crisis and whose prayers were heard and answered affirmatively.

In addition, selected excerpts of Esther are read in the Liturgy of the Hours from Sunday through Thursday of the Twenty-Ninth Week in Ordinary Time. The selections provide enough of the narrative to convey the basic plot of the book.

Conclusion

The book of Esther records how an attempt to exterminate the Jewish people from the Persian Empire was foiled and reversed through the efforts of two Jews, Mordecai and his niece Esther, who rose to positions of prominence within the Persian court and used their influence to better the fortunes of their people. The book has been handed down in two literary forms: an elegant and subtle Hebrew edition and a longer, more theologically explicit Greek edition. The book emphasizes the providence of God in history, even through seemingly "chance" encounters or events. The Church treasures the prayers of Mordecai and Esther from the longer Greek version, in which these two Old Testament saints provide a model of supplication in a time of great crisis.

For Further Reading

Commentaries and Studies on Esther

Crawford, Sidnie White. "The Book of Esther". Pages 853–972 in vol. 3 of *New Interpreter's Bible*. Nashville: Abingdon Press, 1999.

DeSilva, David Arthur. *Introducing the Apocrypha: Message, Context, and Significance.* Grand Rapids, Mich.: Baker Academic, 2002. (See pp. 110–26.)

Levenson, Jon D. *Esther: A Commentary.* Old Testament Library. Louisville, Ky.: Westminster John Knox Press, 1997.

Moore, Carey A. *Daniel, Esther, and Jeremiah: The Additions.* Anchor Bible 44. New York: Doubleday, 1977.

———. *Esther.* Anchor Bible 7B. New York: Doubleday, 1971.

Historical Issues in Esther

Briant, Pierre. *From Cyrus to Alexander: A History of the Persian Empire.* Winona Lake, Ind.: Eisenbrauns, 2002.

Collins, John J. *Introduction to the Hebrew Bible.* Minneapolis: Fortress Press, 2004. (See pp. 539–42.)

Tomasino, Anthony. "Esther". Pages 469–505 in *1 & 2 Kings, 1 & 2 Chronicles, Ezra, Nehemiah, Esther.* Vol. 3 of *Zondervan Illustrated Bible Backgrounds Commentary.* Edited by John H. Walton. Downers Grove, Ill.: InterVarsity Press, 2009.

Wills, Lawrence M. *The Jewish Novel in the Ancient World.* Ithaca, N.Y.: Cornell University Press, 1995.

Yamauchi, Edwin M. *Persia and the Bible.* Grand Rapids, Mich.: Baker Book House, 1990.

Esther in the Living Tradition

Athanasius, Saint. *The Resurrection Letters.* Translated by Jack N. Sparks. Nashville: Thomas Nelson, 1979.

Conti, Marco, ed. *1–2 Kings, 1–2 Chronicles, Ezra, Nehemiah, Esther.* Old Testament 5 of Ancient Christian Commentary on Scripture. Edited by Thomas C. Oden. Downers Grove, Ill.: InterVarsity Press, 2008. (See pp. 374–99.)

John Paul II, Pope. *Theotókos: Woman, Mother, Disciple: A Catechesis on Mary, Mother of God.* Boston: Pauline Books, 2000. (See pp. 73–75.)

21. THE BOOKS OF MACCABEES

Introduction

The main body of the historical and prophetic books of the Old Testament ends with the era of the return from Babylonian exile in the fifth century B.C., whereas the New Testament begins with the appearance of Jesus of Nazareth in the first century A.D. However, the books of Maccabees are significant because they provide a partial history of the *second century* B.C., during an era that is sometimes referred to as the "Intertestamental Period" (roughly, the fourth–first centuries B.C.). From a Catholic perspective, such language is inaccurate, because the books of Maccabees are not "between" Testaments; they are *part of* the Old Testament. Nevertheless, by giving us a window into the late Second Temple period, they do serve as a kind of historical "bridge" between the two major divisions of the canon.

Like certain other historical books of the Old Testament, the books of Maccabees are anonymous, and their authors remain completely unknown.[1] The title "Maccabees" is taken from the name of the family of Levites who are the heroes of both books (see 1 Mac 1–3). The Greek word *maccabaeus* seems to come from an Aramaic word meaning "hammer". At first, this was only an epithet (nickname) for Judas, the son of Matthias, the most famous military hero of the family, who recaptured Jerusalem from enemy hands and rededicated the Temple in 165 B.C., and who was "called Maccabeus" (1 Mac 2:4). In time, however, Judas' nickname became used as a surname for his whole family, although they are more accurately called the "Hasmoneans" after their ancestor Asamoneus.

The two books of Maccabees are not a two-volume work in sequence, like 1–2 Samuel, but, rather, two very different but complementary accounts of roughly the same events: the Jewish struggles for independence, under the leadership of the Maccabees, against the Seleucid emperor Antiochus IV Epiphanes (176–166 B.C.) as well as his successors. The first book of Maccabees presents a soberly historical account of these events from about 175–134 B.C., whereas 2 Maccabees presents a heavily dramatic, passionate, and theologically interpreted account of a shorter but overlapping time period (180–161 B.C.).

Although they now form a complementary pair in the Catholic canon of Scripture, the two works have very different literary histories. According to most scholars, 1 Maccabees was originally written in Hebrew, as indicated by the presence of a number of Semitisms (for example, 1 Mac 1:13, 36; 2:47–48), but remains extant only in Greek copies of the Septuagint. On the other hand,

---

[1] David A. DeSilva, *Introducing the Apocrypha: Message, Context, and Significance* (Grand Rapids, Mich.: Baker Academic, 2002), 247–48, 268–69.

2 Maccabees seems to have been composed in Greek from the first and employs the literary conventions of that language, such as Greek alliteration (for example, 2 Mac 4:18; 12:22; 15:37). Despite being composed in Hebrew and being the primary historical witness to the origins of the Jewish Feast of Dedication—that is, Hanukkah—1 Maccabees was not ultimately accepted by rabbinic Judaism as part of their Scriptures. The book's positive view of the Romans may have doomed its chances of acceptance (cf. 1 Mac 8), especially since the Jewish canon was not finalized until after the Roman destruction of the Temple (A.D. 70). In the same way, 2 Maccabees was rejected, although its narratives are much beloved in Jewish religious culture, especially the account of the martyrdom of the mother and her seven sons. In Jewish tradition, the binding of Isaac (Gen 22) and the martyrdom of the mother and her sons (2 Mac 7) are often seen in light of each other. In fact, the Maccabean mother is seen as surpassing Abraham in faith, since she gave seven sons and herself to death, whereas Abraham offered but one son and received him back alive. In this way, the Maccabean mother is a prototype and model for all subsequent Jews martyred for their fidelity to the law of Moses.

Within the Christian tradition, although the books of Maccabees were somewhat less discussed than other canonical books by the early Fathers, we do find them used by Hippolytus, Origen, Cyprian of Carthage, Hilary of Poitiers, Gregory the Theologian, Basil, Ambrose, Jerome, Augustine, and John Chrysostom. Significantly, Origen, Cyprian, Hilary, and Augustine explicitly identify one or both books as Scripture. Starting with the Council of Rome (A.D. 382), 1–2 Maccabees were explicitly included in the canonical lists of the Church and remained so through the ecumenical councils of Florence (A.D. 1441) and Trent (A.D. 1563). Although eventually removed from the Old Testament canon by the Protestant reformers, they remain an essential part of the Catholic and Orthodox canons of Scripture.

In ancient manuscripts and lists of the Old Testament by the Church Fathers, 1–2 Maccabees appear in various places in the canonical order.[2] For example, Augustine lists them with the other historical books, whereas the Council of Carthage places them at the end of the Old Testament. The Septuagint tradition eventually settled on placing them after Esther (as the end of the historical books) and preceding Job (the start of the poetical books). The New American Bible, used by most English-speaking Catholics in the United States, follows this order. The Latin Vulgate tradition, however, settled on 1–2 Maccabees as the conclusion of the Old Testament. The Revised Standard Version, Catholic Edition, follows this order.

Literary Style and Structure of 1–2 Maccabees

Written originally in Hebrew, 1 Maccabees consciously continues the biblical tradition of military historiography, frequently evoking parallels between the battles of the Maccabees and the exploits of ancient Israel military heroes such as Joshua, the judges, and David. Hebrew prose does not lend itself to excessive

---

[2] See Lee Martin McDonald, *The Biblical Canon: Its Origin, Transmission, and Authority* (Grand Rapids, Mich.: Baker Academic, 2007), 439–44.

ornamentation or complexity, so the narrative unfolds in a plain but noble style
with frequent use of biblical idioms. By contrast, 2 Maccabees, while thoroughly Hebrew and Jewish in heart, employs a heavily ornamented, "baroque"
Greek literary style much admired in the Hellenistic period, especially among
Greek speakers in Asia.

The structure of 1 Maccabees is straightforward and easy to recognize. After
an introduction that describes the religious persecution of the Jews under Antiochus IV Epiphanes in 175–165 B.C. (1 Mac 1), the sacred author describes the
successive careers of Mattathias, the patriarch of the Hasmonean (or Maccabean)
clan (1 Mac 2), and his sons Judas Maccabeus (1 Mac 3:1–9:19), Jonathan
(1 Mac 9:20–12:53), and Simon (1 Mac 13:1–16:24). Apparently it was the
author's intention only to record the careers of the first generation of Maccabees (the sons of Mattathias), because the history ends abruptly with Mattathias'
grandson John Hyrcanus, son of Simon, as high priest and ruler of Judah, but
says almost nothing of his reign (1 Mac 16:23–24). In this way, the first book of
Maccabees can be outlined as follows:

Outline of 1 Maccabees

I. Background of the Revolt: The Persecution under Antiochus IV (1 Mac 1)
    A. The Life and Death of Alexander the Great (1:1–7)
    B. The Rise of Antiochus Epiphanes (1:8–10)
    C. The Persecution of the Jews and Jerusalem by Antiochus (1:1–64)

II. The Revolt of the Sons of Mattathias (1 Mac 2–16)
    A. The Career of Mattathias (2)
    B. The Career of Judas Maccabeus (3:1—9:19)
    C. The Career of Jonathan (9:20—12:53)
    D. The Career of Simon (chaps. 13–16)

The structure of 2 Maccabees is somewhat more complex. The editor of
the book states that his intention is to give "the story of the campaigns against
Antiochus Epiphanes and his sons Eupator", and that is indeed the basic twofold
structure of the core of the book: (1) campaigns against Antiochus Epiphanes
(2 Mac 4:7—10:9); and (2) campaigns against Antiochus Eupator (2 Mac 10:10—
13:26). However, the campaigns against Epiphanes required some historical
background to be properly understood, and the struggle against Eupator did not
result in peace until the forces of his usurper, Demetrius, were defeated, so the
editor composed a prologue and epilogue to the core of the narrative. Hence, a
fuller outline of the book can be given:

Outline of 2 Maccabees

I. Editorial Introduction: Letters to Diaspora Jews about Hanukkah (2 Mac 1)
    A. Cover Letter 1: Keep the Feast of Dedication (124 B.C.) (1:1–10)
    B. Cover Letter 2: Keep the Feast of Dedication (164 B.C.) (1:11—2:18)
    C. End of Historical Preface: Epitome of Jason of Cyrenes' Work (2:19–32)

II. Historical Prologue: Troubles under Seleucus IV Philopator (2 Mac 3:1—4:6)

III. Campaigns against the Greek Kings (2 Mac 4:7—13:26)
   A. Campaigns against Antiochus Epiphanes (4:7—10:9)
   B. Campaigns against Antiochus Eupator (10:10—13:26)

IV. Historical Epilogue: Troubles under Demetrius I Soter (2 Mac 14:1—15:36)

V. Editorial Conclusion: "Apologies if I Have Not Pleased" (2 Mac 15:37–39)

Interestingly, there is a basic chiastic structure to the book, in which the center is the account of the cleansing of the Temple and founding of the Feast of Dedication by Judas Maccabeus (2 Mac 10:1–9). Moreover, we note that both of the two major cycles of narrative (3:1—10:9 and 10:10—15:36) end with

1. the death of one who attacked the Temple (2 Mac 9:28–29; 15:28–33);
2. the purification or preservation of the Temple (2 Mac 10:1–7; 15:34–35); and
3. a public vote to observe a holy day to commemorate the event in perpetuity (2 Mac 10:8; 15:36).

Thus, the structure of the book highlights its intention to encourage the continued liturgical celebrations of God's presence in his Temple.

Overview of 1 Maccabees

The Persecution of the Jews by Antiochus Epiphanes (1 Maccabees 1)

The book of 1 Maccabees begins with a brief description of the career of Alexander the Great, his death in 323 B.C., and the division of his kingdom among his generals (the *diadochoi*, "successors") (1 Mac 1:1–9). It then skips forward to 175 B.C. and the accession to the throne of Antiochus IV Epiphanes, the seventh successor of Seleucus I Nicator, Alexander's general and successor. (Seleucus I had gained control of the Asian portion of Alexander's realm, which, as a result, came to be known in modern scholarship as the *Seleucid* Empire.)

Antiochus Epiphanes' rule was disastrous for Jewish culture, religion, and national identity. He encouraged and supported groups of Jews who wished to Hellenize by adopting Greek culture and abandoning the "holy covenant", even going so far as to "remove the marks of circumcision"—a procedure known as *epispasm*, about which very few details are known (1 Mac 1:11–15). Even more devastating, Antiochus pillaged the Temple on his return from an Egyptian campaign, sent one of his commanders to plunder and burn Jerusalem, and decreed the abolition of Judaism and all its practices (1 Mac 1:15–64). Finally, and most egregious of all, he turned the Temple into a pagan shrine and tortured and executed Jews found practicing their ancestral religion. In the otherwise sober book of 1 Maccabees, we find this graphic description of Antiochus' desecration of the Temple and persecution of the Jews:

Now on the fifteenth day of Chislev, in the one hundred and forty-fifth year, they erected a desolating sacrilege upon the altar of burnt offering. They also built altars in the surrounding cities of Judah, and burned incense at the doors of the houses and in the streets. The books of the law which they found they tore to pieces and burned with fire. *Where the book of the covenant was found in the possession of any one, or if any one adhered to the law, the decree of the king condemned him to death.* They kept using violence against Israel, against those found month after month in the cities. And on the twenty-fifth day of the month they offered sacrifice on the altar which was upon the altar of burnt offering. *According to the decree, they put to death the women who had their children circumcised, and their families and those who circumcised them; and they hung the infants from their mothers' necks.*

But many in Israel stood firm and were resolved in their hearts not to eat unclean food. They chose to die rather than to be defiled by food or to profane the holy covenant; and they did die. (1 Mac 1:54–63)

It is in the midst of such atrocities that one priestly family—the family of Mattathias—rises up in revolt.

The Career of Mattathias (1 Maccabees 2)

During this time, a certain Mattathias of the priestly order of Joarib leaves Jerusalem and settles in the Judean town of Modein with his five sons, John, Simon, Judas, Eleazar, and Jonathan (1 Mac 2:1–5). When royal officials arrive in Modein to force the populace to embrace pagan sacrifice, Mattathias revolts and leads a guerrilla force into the Judean mountains. About this time, a large number of pious Jews hiding in the wilderness of Judah are massacred by royal forces because they will not fight back on the Sabbath (1 Mac 2:29–38). This debacle persuades Mattathias to adopt a policy of fighting even on the seventh day, and his guerrilla force grows rapidly as like-minded Jews join his band. Based in the wilderness, Mattathias begins to raid the populated areas of Judah, defending pious Jews, terrorizing Gentiles and apostate Jews, and enforcing the observance of Jewish law. But Mattathias passes away only a few years into the revolt (166 B.C.), leaving leadership of the movement to Judas Maccabeus, the ablest warrior among his five sons.

Judas Maccabeus and the Feast of Hanukkah (1 Maccabees 3:1—9:19)

Thus, Judas Maccabeus, third son of Mattathias, is acclaimed successor of his father and military commander of the Jewish rebel force. His initial defeat of Seleucid commanders sent against him, Appolonius and Seron, persuades Antiochus Epiphanes that a larger army has to be raised (1 Mac 3:10–31). He departs to his capital, Antioch, to raise money for an army by imposing tribute on his eastern provinces, leaving one Lysias, the king's friend, in charge of the western empire. Lysias sends the general Gorgias with a force of about fifty thousand men to eliminate Judas. Despite seemingly overwhelming odds, Judas and his outnumbered force rout the Greek army with courage, innovation, and prayer reminiscent of Gideon, Samuel, and David. Lysias himself invades again with a larger force the following year, only to be routed once more. By this time

Judas has grown strong enough to recapture Jerusalem itself; after doing so, he rebuilds the city and purifies and rededicates the Temple (1 Mac 4:36–61). It is this rededication that leads to the establishment of a new annual Jewish feast: the Feast of "Dedication", more commonly known today as *Hanukkah*, to be celebrated in the month of Chislev (= December):

> Early in the morning on the twenty-fifth day of the ninth month, which is the month of Chislev, in the one hundred and forty-eighth year, they rose and offered sacrifice, as the law directs, on the new altar of burnt offering which they had built. At the very season and on the very day that the Gentiles had profaned it, it was dedicated with songs and harps and lutes and cymbals. All the people fell on their faces and worshiped and blessed Heaven, who had prospered them. So they celebrated the dedication of the altar for eight days, and offered burnt offerings with gladness; they offered a sacrifice of deliverance and praise. They decorated the front of the temple with golden crowns and small shields; they restored the gates and the chambers for the priests, and furnished them with doors. There was very great gladness among the people, and the reproach of the Gentiles was removed.
>
> *Then Judas and his brothers and all the assembly of Israel determined that every year at that season the days of dedication of the altar should be observed with gladness and joy for eight days, beginning with the twenty-fifth day of the month of Chislev.* (1 Mac 4:52–59)

It is an interesting twist of history that, although Hanukkah is still celebrated within contemporary Judaism, the account of the origin of the feast is canonical for Catholics but apocryphal for Jews.

In any case, at this point, Judas' career enters a new phase. The royal armies of Antiochus having been defeated, the threat to the Judeans now becomes the non-Jewish ethnic groups living in and around Judea, who fear and resent the resurgence of Judean power. Judas enjoys initial victories over the Edomites, Baeanites, and Ammonites (1 Mac 5:1–8), but it soon becomes necessary for him and his brothers to lead a two-pronged campaign into the northern territories of Galilee (west of the Jordan) and Gilead (east of the Jordan) to rescue large Jewish populations there from their hostile neighbors. They defeat the Gentile forces and escort the Jewish inhabitants down to Judea to relocate in regions under Jewish military control.

During these events, Antiochus Epiphanes has been attempting to raise funds in the east through the imposition of tribute and the robbing of temples. His efforts, however, provoke rebellion among local inhabitants, and his plans fail. Forced to withdraw to Babylon, an imperial stronghold, the king becomes deathly ill upon hearing the news of the defeat of his forces in Judea. He dies, believing himself accursed because of his abuses of Jerusalem and its inhabitants

---

Eupator and Demetrius

Seleucus IV Philopator (187–175 B.C.) had a son, Demetrius, who was taken as a hostage to Rome. His brother Antiochus (IV Epiphanes, 175–164 B.C.) replaced Seleucus IV on the throne and was succeeded in turn by his own son Antiochus V Eupator (164–161 B.C.). In 161 B.C., Demetrius escaped from Rome and made his way back to Antioch, where he easily overthrew the unpopular Eupator and replaced him, taking the name Demetrius I Soter (161–150 B.C.).

(1 Mac 6:8–16). Philip, his most trusted advisor, is left in command with a commission to establish Antiochus' son as king.

Meanwhile, word reaches Lysias in Antioch that Epiphanes has died, so he places his son Antiochus V on the throne, giving him the epithet Eupator ("of a good father"). Eupator immediately raises an army twice the size of Lysias' earlier force and invades Judea to put down the Maccabean revolt. The size of the king's force, which includes fearsome war elephants, overawes Judas' army, leaving the king in control of most of Judea and Jerusalem (1 Mac 6:32–54). The king's victory is short-lived, however, because word soon arrives that Philip is approaching Antioch with the intention of usurping the throne. Realizing he cannot fight Philip and put down the Jewish revolt simultaneously, Eupator makes peace with Judas and withdraws to reclaim his throne (1 Mac 6:55–63).

Eupator's reign is cut short, however, when his cousin Demetrius, the rightful heir to the throne, suddenly returns from Roman exile and takes back the crown in a brief and effective coup (1 Mac 7:1–32). Unfortunately, Demetrius has no love for Judaism, either. A party of Jewish Hellenists led by a certain Levite, Alcimus, immediately persuade Demetrius to intervene in Judea, so he sends a powerful army under his advisor Bacchides to drive Judas out of Jerusalem and install Alcimus as high priest and *de facto* leader of the nation. This invasion succeeds in its objectives, but after Bacchides withdraws to return to Antioch, Alcimus cannot maintain his power and appeals for another intervention. Demetrius sends another force under a General Nicanor to eliminate Judas' guerrilla army, but Judas lies waiting until the time and location are favorable to him and then strikes and defeats the Seleucid force, killing and beheading Nicanor on the "thirteenth of Adar" (=March 27, 160 B.C.) (1 Mac 7:33–50). This date was observed as a holiday for a few generations thereafter.

Nonetheless, Judas, knowing that he cannot hold out against the Seleucid monarchy forever without assistance, seeks the help of Rome, a rapidly growing world power. He sends envoys who successfully negotiate a peace treaty of mutual assistance with the Romans (1 Mac 8:1–32). The Roman alliance, however, is not sufficient to save Judas from the immediate Seleucid threat. Demetrius again sends Bacchides and Alcimus, the Hellenized high priest, to invade Judah with a large army. This time Judas, despite his valor, is overwhelmed by the force, killed in combat, and eventually buried in "the tomb of their fathers at Modein" (1 Mac 9:1–22).

The Career of Jonathan (1 Maccabees 9:20—12:53)

After the death of Judas Maccabeus, Bacchides appoints Hellenized Jews in positions of power in Judea, and persecution now breaks out against any who had previously been allied with the Maccabees (1 Mac 9:23–27). The remaining supporters of the Maccabees urge Jonathan to take over the leadership of the movement, and Jonathan accepts. Jonathan and his forces live and fight as renegades for some years, hiding in the marshes of the Jordan, as Bacchides and the Seleucid puppet Alcimus rule the country. After the death of Alcimus, however, Bacchides makes a concerted effort to eliminate Jonathan, but fails in his attempt to capture Jonathan's stronghold, Bethbasi (near Bethlehem). Disillusioned with the Judean campaigns, Bacchides arranges a peace with Jonathan and withdraws his forces to Antioch, leaving Jonathan in control of a small territory around Michmash in southern Samaria, north of Jerusalem (1 Mac 9:28–73).

After five years, rivalries within the Seleucid royal house begin to play to Jonathan's favor. In 152 B.C., Alexander Epiphanes, (supposedly) the son of Antiochus IV, arrives in Syria and begins an attempt to overthrow Demetrius II. Both Demetrius and Alexander need peace with Jonathan in order to consolidate their claims to the throne, so a "bidding war" ensues, with each rival offering greater and greater concessions to Jonathan in order to win his support (1 Mac 10:1–45). Jonathan sides with Alexander Epiphanes, who already has the support of the Romans and has not yet done any harm to the Jews (1 Mac 10:46–47). Jonathan makes a wise choice, because Alexander's forces rout Demetrius and slay him in battle, securing Alexander's place on the throne (1 Mac 10:48–50). Alexander then enters into a marriage alliance with Ptolemy VI Philometor of Egypt (181–145 B.C.), and Jonathan enjoys the patronage of both kings, enhancing his wealth, power, and prestige (1 Mac 10:51–66). About three years later (ca. 147 B.C.), Jonathan has the opportunity to prove the value of his friendship, when Alexander's reign is threatened by the arrival of Demetrius II Nicator, son of Alexander's vanquished rival. Jonathan defeats the forces Demetrius sends against Palestine under his general Appolonius, and Alexander shows gratitude by bestowing even greater honors on Jonathan (1 Mac 10:67–89).

Alexander Epiphanes' reign will be short-lived, however. His father in-law, Ptolemy VI, conspires with Demetrius II, and—through a combination of intrigue and force—defeats him and takes his throne. Ironically, Ptolemy VI dies himself only a few days after deposing Alexander Epiphanes, thus leaving the Seleucid Empire under the power of Demetrius II (1 Mac 11:1–22).

Demetrius is initially hostile to Jonathan, but after being placated with gifts, he confirms Jonathan's position as ruler of the traditional territory of Israel as a kind of viceroy within the Seleucid Empire (1 Mac 11:23–40). The alliance is in Demetrius' best interests—in fact, he is forced to rely on a bodyguard of Jewish soldiers provided by Jonathan to save his life during a revolt of his own troops (1 Mac 11:41–53). Demetrius' reign is brief, however, as Alexander Epiphanes' son Antiochus VI Dionysus suddenly appears on the international scene from his hiding place in Arabia. Antiochus' forces drive Demetrius out of Antioch, and Antiochus wins Jonathan's assistance as an ally by confirming him as de facto king of Jerusalem. In response, Jonathan rallies his own troops and the Seleucid forces in Palestine to the cause of Antiochus VI and repulses the troops sent by Demetrius to overthrow him (1 Mac 11:54–74).

Jonathan begins to seek some external support so as not always to be suffering from the intrigues and infighting of the Seleucid dynasty. He sends envoys to Rome and Sparta, who successfully reaffirm treaties of mutual support made with those nations in previous years (1 Mac 12:1–23). Together with his brother Simon, he campaigns through Palestine and north toward Damascus, repulsing the forces of Demetrius and reinforcing his own military garrisons. In 140 B.C., however, Jonathan's fortunes suffer a reverse when Antiochus VI's general, Trypho (=Diodotus Tryphon), betrays the king and marches against Jonathan.

Unable to defeat Jonathan in combat, Trypho feigns friendship until Jonathan dismisses his troops, and then has the Maccabean leader taken hostage (1 Mac 12:39–53).

The Career of Simon (1 Maccabees 13–16)

Jonathan's capture leaves Simon, his brother, in charge of Judea and the Maccabean forces. Trypho invades Judea, taking Jonathan along as a hostage, but after failing to achieve a military advantage over the Jewish forces led by Simon, he withdraws from Judea toward the north and puts Jonathan to death (1 Mac 13:1–24). Simon recovers Jonathan's bones and buries him in honor, along with the rest of the family, in Modein, the ancestral town of the Hasmoneans (1 Mac 13:25–30).

Trypho returns to Antioch, where he assassinates Antiochus VI Dionysus and assumes the throne himself as Diodotus Tryphon. Simon revolts against his rule and allies himself with his erstwhile enemy Demetrius II in order to defeat Trypho. Demetrius grants Simon and Judea virtual economic and political autonomy, so the people begin to reckon the date by Simon's accession to the high priesthood (1 Mac 13:31–42). The new political situation enables Simon finally to capture and pacify the Seleucid fortresses in Gazara and in Jerusalem (the hated "Citadel"), which had been thorns in the side of the Maccabees since the beginning of the oppression under Antiochus Epiphanes (1 Mac 13:43–53). Simon makes his son, John Hyrcanus, chief commander of the forces loyal to the Maccabees.

Around 140 B.C., Demetrius II marches into the eastern provinces of the Seleucid Empire to gather tribute to fund his war against Trypho. There he is captured by the Persians, and Demetrius' departure to the east ushers in a period of peace and prosperity for Simon and Judea (1 Mac 14:1–45). Without the interference of Trypho or Demetrius, Simon is able to expand his realm, reinforce cities, and renew alliances with the Romans and Spartans. The grateful populace of Judah eventually confirms Simon in the offices of "high priest", "commander and ethnarch of the Jews and priests", and "protector of them all" (1 Mac 14:47).

In 138 B.C., Antiochus VII Sidetes, younger brother of the captured Demetrius II, comes from Rhodes and invades Syria with an enormous mercenary force, with the intent to remove Trypho and obtain the throne. At first, Antiochus VII speaks favorably to Simon and confirms all the concessions that the Maccabean rulers were granted by previous Seleucids. At the same time, the Romans are making good on their alliance with the Jews by sending letters to all the kings of the eastern Mediterranean, warning them of the protected status the Jews enjoy by virtue of their treaty with Rome (1 Mac 15:15–24). Nonetheless, when Antiochus realizes he will prevail over Trypho, he turns on Simon and begins to view him as a threat (1 Mac 15:25–41). He sends a certain Cendebeus with a large force to make an incursion into Judea to defeat Simon or at least compel him to give up tribute and territory. Though outnumbered, Simon's sons Judas and John repulse these Seleucid troops as the previous generation of Maccabees did (1 Mac 16:1–10).

So Judea has peace for a few years, until 134 B.C., when the Maccabean-appointed governor of Jericho, Ptolemy son of Abubus, becomes a traitor and has Simon and his sons Mattathias and Judas executed while they are enjoying a banquet in Jericho (1 Mac 16:11–17). This leaves Simon's son John Hyrcanus to take his father's place as high priest and governor of Judea (1 Mac 16:18–22). Having recounted the careers of the first generation of Maccabees, the narrative stops abruptly with a brief summary of Hyrcanus' successful reign (1 Mac 16:23–24).

Overview of 2 Maccabees

Prologue: Two Letters and an Introduction (2 Maccabees 1:1—2:32)

The received form of 2 Maccabees begins with two cover letters from the Jewish leadership of Jerusalem addressed to the Jewish leadership of Egypt in the city of Alexandria. The first, a brief missal dated to ca. 124 B.C., mentions the troubles experienced during the revolt of a certain Jason (ca. 143 B.C.) and concludes with an exhortation for the Egyptian Jews to observe the Feast of Dedication (Hanukkah) (2 Mac 1:1–10). The second, much longer epistle is dated forty years earlier (ca. 164 B.C.), within a year of the Temple cleansing that gave rise to the observance of Hanukkah (2 Mac 1:11—2:18). It includes accounts of the manner of death of Antiochus IV Epiphanes (2 Mac 1:11–17); the transmission of fire from the altar of the First Temple to the altar of the Second, through the mysterious liquid *naphtha* discovered by Nehemiah (2 Mac 1:18–36); and (3) the hiding of the Ark of the Covenant on Mount Nebo by Jeremiah (2 Mac 2:1–8). Like the previous letter, the purpose of this one is to exhort the Jews of Egypt to celebrate the Feast of Dedication (or Purification) concurrently with the Jews of Jerusalem (2 Mac 2:16–18). We note that the sacred author's intention is only to include the content of these letters, not necessarily to endorse the historicity of the accounts contained within them.

> ### The Feast of Booths and the Feast of Dedication
>
> The Mosaic cycle of feasts (Lev 23) included a celebration of the sanctuary: the Feast of Booths (or "Feast of Tabernacles"). In later Judaism, the Feast of Booths became the great liturgical celebration of the Temple. When the Feast of Dedication (Hanukkah) was instituted to commemorate the purification and rededication of the Temple under Judas Maccabeus, it was regarded as a smaller version or "reprise" of the Feast of Booths. Thus, 2 Maccabees 1:9 calls it "the feast of booths in the month of Chislev", as opposed to the Mosaic Feast of Booths, which takes place on the 15th of Tishrei (usually falling from late September to late October). In the Gospel of John, the account of Jesus' ministry during the Feast of Tabernacles (Jn 7:1—10:21) is followed immediately by his teaching during the Feast of Dedication (10:22–39). John groups them together because of the similarity in theme of the two feasts.

Immediately after the two cover letters are concluded, 2 Maccabees begins the body of the book proper with something almost entirely unique among Old Testament books: the author speaks to the readers directly and explains how and why he went about compiling the book in question (2 Mac 2:19–32). The author—or better, the "editor"—of 2 Maccabees explains that his composition is an abridgement of a five-volume history of the Maccabean period written by a certain Jason of Cyrene (2 Mac 2:23). Significantly, unlike Jason, our editor expressly states that he is trying to compose, not a work of rigorous historiography focused on "exact details", but an accessible, memorable, popular account to inform a wide audience concerning the central events of this time period and their religious significance (2 Mac 2:24–32).

The Troubles under Seleucus IV Philopator (2 Maccabees 3:1—4:6)

Before relating the dramatic persecutions and insurrections under Antiochus IV Epiphanes, the editor provides the historical lead-up to the great struggle.

The story opens in the early 170s B.C., when Judea is at peace under the leadership of the high priest Onias III (196–175 B.C.), son of Simeon II, and relations with the Seleucid emperor Seleucus IV Philopator are cordial (2 Mac 3:1–3; cf. Sir 50:1–24). This era of peace and prosperity is not to last, however, because of the ambitions of a certain Simon of the priestly clan of Bilgah. Simon has a falling out with Onias concerning the management of the city market, so in retaliation he informs the Seleucid administration that the Temple treasury contains enormous wealth ripe for the taking. The emperor Seleucus sends his prime minister, Heliodorus, to Jerusalem on a covert mission to rob the Temple. The populace soon gets wind of the plot, and there is an uproar of protest and lamentation about the imminent defiling of the Temple. When Heliodorus enters the Temple courts, however, he finds himself being flogged almost to death by angelic warriors (2 Mac 3:22–30)! He would have died had not Onias made intercession for him and offered sacrifice. As it is, he returns to Seleucus and gives testimony to the divine power active in the Jerusalem Temple.

This is not to be the end of troubles, however, because now the previously mentioned Simon spreads false charges against Onias, accusing him of instigating the whole debacle with Heliodorus. The civil strife becomes so bad that Onias himself undertakes a journey to speak to Seleucus about the situation.

The Struggle against Antiochus IV Epiphanes (2 Maccabees 4:7—10:9)

Unfortunately, King Seleucus dies before Onias III can obtain the king's assistance with the civil discord in Judea. Seleucus is replaced, not by his son Demetrius (who is being held hostage), but by his younger brother Antiochus, who takes the cognomen *Epiphanes* (manifestation of God). The troubles under Antiochus begin, at first, not with the king himself, but with the intrigues and politicking of rival candidates for the Jerusalem high priesthood (2 Mac 4:7–50).

At this time, Onias is replaced in the high priesthood by his brother Jason, who bribes Antiochus for the position. Jason launches a campaign of aggressive Hellenization in Jerusalem and Judea, so that the traditional religion and culture of Judaism are neglected even by the priestly caste. After three years, however, Jason himself is deposed in favor of his assistant Menelaus, who outbids Jason for the office while on a diplomatic mission to see Antiochus. This Menelaus permits and commits various sacrileges, including theft from the Temple treasury. When the deposed Onias III publicly protests these abuses, Menelaus connives to have him assassinated, which takes place around 171 B.C. (2 Mac 4:30–38). The Judean senate (the Sanhedrin) brings charges to Antiochus against Menelaus, but Menelaus bribes a high-ranking courtier to sway the king, and Antiochus acquits Menelaus and executes his innocent accusers instead.

As one might expect, conditions in Jerusalem and Judea deteriorate rapidly when Jason, the previously deposed high priest, starts a civil war and attacks Jerusalem in an attempt to depose Menelaus and regain the priesthood for himself (2 Mac 5:1–27). Unable to take Jerusalem, however, he ends up withdrawing and later dies while on his way to seek asylum in Sparta. Antiochus, however, hears the reports of the civil war while he is campaigning against the Ptolemies in Egypt. Withdrawing from Egypt and heading north through Israel, he attacks Jerusalem, thinking that the city is in revolt against him. He massacres thousands of Jews and sacks the Temple, assisted by the obsequious compliance of Menelaus. He harasses the populace, slaughters many people, and leaves Seleucid commanders in charge of the country. At this time, Judas Maccabeus leaves Jerusalem and begins to live in the wilderness with a small band of men.

After this, Antiochus decides to outlaw the practice of Judaism in Israel and seeks to force all Jews to observe Greek religion (2 Mac 6:1—7:42). The Temple is defiled and converted to a sanctuary of Zeus Olympus. The Seleucid authorities torture and execute anyone caught practicing traditional Jewish religion— for example, by reading the Scriptures, observing the Sabbaths and other Feasts, or circumcising their children. At this point in the narrative—which overlaps significantly with the opening of the first book of Maccabees (cf. 1 Mac 1–3)— the author provides in great detail two particular accounts of martyrdom under Antiochus that are not contained in the earlier book: (1) the execution of a very elderly scribe, Eleazar, who chooses to be put to death rather than even pretend to eat pork (2 Mac 6:18–31); and (2) the martyrdom of an unknown Jewish mother and her seven sons (2 Mac 7:1–42). After watching all seven of her sons be tortured to death for refusing pork, the mother herself is executed. In one of the most unforgettable sections in the book, throughout these tortures, the sons and the mother speak movingly and courageously about their faith in the God of Israel, the justice of the final judgment, and the hope of the resurrection. Particularly moving is the mother's final speech to her last son:

> [L]eaning close to him, she [the mother] spoke in their native tongue as follows, deriding the cruel tyrant: "My son, have pity on me. I carried you nine months in my womb, and nursed you for three years, and have reared you and brought you up to this point in your life, and have taken care of you. *I beg you, my child, to look at the heaven and the earth and see everything that is in them, and recognize that God did not make them out of things that existed.* Thus also mankind comes into being. Do not fear this butcher, but prove worthy of your brothers. *Accept death, so that in God's mercy I may get you back again with your brothers.*"
>
> While she was still speaking, the young man said, "What are you waiting for? I will not obey the king's command, but I obey the command of the law that was given to our fathers through Moses.". . .
>
> The king fell into a rage, and handled him worse than the others, being exasperated at his scorn. So he died in his integrity, putting his whole trust in the Lord.
>
> Last of all, the mother died, after her sons. (2 Mac 7:27–30, 39–41)

It is during this period of unprecedented persecution that Judas Maccabeus gathers together a force of about six thousand Jewish men and engages in guerilla warfare against the Seleucid occupiers (2 Mac 8:1–36). Judas is a keen military strategist, relying on surprise attacks, often at night, to overcome the superior forces of his enemies. He encourages traditional Jewish piety, including prayer and the recitation of Scripture, among his men and is generous in distributing wealth captured in battle among the survivors and victims of the religious persecution. Hearing of Judas' success, the Seleucid governor sends a very large force of infantry and cavalry under the leadership of a certain nobleman, Nicanor, and a General Gorgias to annihilate the Jewish resistance. Far outnumbered, Judas rallies his six thousand men, appealing to their faith in the God of their fathers and the great victories of Israel in biblical history. To the surprise of all, he routs the Seleucid army, forcing Nicanor and Gorgias to flee back to the capital of Antioch.

Antiochus himself hears the news of the defeat of Nicanor (and the other expeditions sent against Judas) while he is retreating from a disastrously unsuccessful attempt to rob the temple treasury of Persepolis in Persia, the far eastern region of his empire (2 Mac 9:1–29). Enraged against the Jews, Antiochus at first intends to march his own army to Jerusalem to destroy Judas and his forces, but he is struck with illness, compounded by injuries sustained from being thrown from his chariot. Humbled by God, he writes letters appointing his son Antiochus Eupator as king and then dies in much suffering, far from his capital.

At about the time of Antiochus Epiphanes' death, Judas Maccabeus gains control of Jerusalem and the Temple Mount (2 Mac 10:1–9). He and his followers cleanse the Temple of any sign or remnant of paganism, build a new altar, and restart the sacrificial liturgy on the twenty-fifth of Chislev, three years to the day after the Temple was defiled. The Jewish population celebrates the rededication of the Temple after the manner of the Feast of Booths and by popular vote establish this date as an annual liturgical festival (the Feast of Dedication, *Hanukkah*). This account of the rededication of the Temple forms the center and focal point of the structure of the book (2 Mac 10:1–9).

The Struggle against Antiochus V Eupator (2 Maccabees 10:10—13:26)

The second half of the book details the struggle against Antiochus V Eupator and its aftermath: the conflict with Demetrius II and his general, Nicanor.

Upon the death of Antiochus IV Epiphanes, his son Antiochus V Eupator assumes the throne with a high-ranking royal official, Lysias, acting as advisor and regent (2 Mac 10:10–38). Eupator begins his reign by maintaining his father's hostile policies toward Judaism. However, Judas Maccabeus is now in control of Jerusalem, and his battle-tested troops comprise the most effective military force in the region. Judas takes advantage of his new-found strength to pacify the neighboring Idumeans and hunt down Timothy, the military leader of anti-Maccabean forces in the Transjordan (Ammon and Gilead). These military efforts against local peoples anger Lysias, the king's regent, and he invades Judea with a large force of mercenaries. Unable to defeat Maccabeus, however, he is forced to negotiate a peace between Eupator and the Jews loyal to the

THE BOOKS OF MACCABEES

Maccabeans that allows them to maintain their religion, law, and customs, and a number of official letters are written to this effect (2 Mac 11:1–38).

Having established peace with the imperial government, Judas sets about removing threats to Jewish safety posed by various hostile cities and local governors in the region (2 Mac 12:1–38). He attacks and conquers the Gentile cities of Joppa, Jamnia, Caspin, Charax, Karnion, Scythopolis, and the local governors Timothy (north Transjordan) and Gorgias (Idumea). While attacking the city of Adullam in Judah, some of Maccabeus' men fall in battle. In a significant episode, these men are later discovered to have pagan talismans on their bodies, so Judas raises money to have expiatory sacrifices made on their behalf at the Temple (2 Mac 12:39–45). This is the earliest clear indication of a Jewish belief in the efficacy of prayers for the dead.

Judas' military exploits in the region again anger Lysias, who launches a second, larger invasion of Judea in order to eliminate the Maccabean threat (2 Mac 13:1–26). The two armies join battle at the Maccabean hometown of Modein. Judas is able to inflict losses but has to withdraw in the face of Lysias' overwhelming numbers. Lysias moves on and attempts to capture the Maccabean stronghold of Beth-zur but is rebuffed. About this time, he receives word that Philip, a high-ranking nobleman left in charge in Antioch, has seized the government. Being forced to return to the capital to regain and consolidate his power, Lysias strikes a hasty peace with Judas and withdraws, leaving Judea in Maccabean control.

The Struggle against Demetrius I and Nicanor (2 Maccabees 14–15)

Peace with the Seleucids is short-lived, however, as Demetrius, son of Seleucus IV (older brother and predecessor of Antiochus Epiphanes), suddenly lands with an army on the coast of Syria and quickly deposes and kills both Eupator and Lysias. Alcimus, a disgruntled candidate for the high priesthood, makes his way to Antioch to denounce Judas Maccabeus to the new king. Demetrius, convinced Judas is a threat to the peace of his empire, dispatches a certain Nicanor with a large army and orders him to capture Jerusalem, kill Judas, and place Alcimus in the high priesthood (2 Mac 14:1–17).

Upon arriving at Jerusalem, however, Nicanor decides he does not want to face Judas in open battle on the latter's home territory (2 Mac 14:18–46). He turns to diplomacy and manages to develop a friendship with Judas. Alcimus is incensed at Nicanor's sudden amity with the Maccabees and writes to Demetrius in protest. The king sends letters disavowing the treaties Nicanor has made with Judas. Nicanor does not act immediately, but Judas notices a change in his disposition and—suspecting something is amiss—withdraws from Jerusalem with his forces to the north, the region of Samaria.

Nicanor now decides to pursue Judas and engage him in open battle (2 Mac 15:1–11). Outnumbered as usual, Judas encourages his troops by appeal to the traditional faith and Scriptures of Israel and also relates to them a personal dream in which he has seen Onias III and the prophet Jeremiah come to him to confirm his future victory:

What he saw was this: *Onias, who had been high priest, a noble and good man*, of modest bearing and gentle manner, one who spoke fittingly and had been trained from childhood in all that belongs to excellence, *was praying with outstretched hands for the whole body of the Jews.* Then likewise a man appeared, distinguished by his gray hair and dignity, and of marvelous majesty and authority. And Onias spoke, saying, "*This is a man who loves the brethren and prays much for the people and the holy city, Jeremiah, the prophet of God.*" (2 Mac 15:12–14)

With these words, 2 Maccabees not only provides us with some of the earliest biblical evidence of the Jewish practice of *prayers for the dead* (2 Mac 12:39–45); it also provides us with ancient testimony to the Jewish belief in the *prayers of the dead*: that is, that the souls of the righteous dead continue to intercede for the living on earth. With the high morale that such a vision gives to the men, Judas and his men attack Nicanor's army on the plains of Samaria and rout them all. Nicanor himself dies in the conflict, and Judas takes his head and right arm back to Jerusalem to hang on the wall near the Temple. The populace agrees by consensus to declare the day of victory, the thirteenth of Adar (the eve of Purim), as a public holiday in perpetuity (2 Mac 15:15–36). Thus ends the body of the work.

Epilogue: "The Best That I Could Do" (2 Maccabees 15:37–38)

The editor ends his narrative with Judas in control of the holy city, expresses the wish that his story has been pleasing, and, in another unique passage in all of Scripture, apologizes to the reader, stating with all humility: "If it is well told and to the point, that is what I myself desired; if it is poorly done and mediocre, that was the best I could do" (2 Mac 15:38).

Historical Questions about 1–2 Maccabees

First Maccabees is our best source for the history of Judah during the time period it describes, beginning with the accession of Antiochus IV Epiphanes as Seleucid emperor in 175 B.C. and ending with the start of the reign of John Hyrcanus as high priest in Jerusalem in 134 B.C. In this way, 1 Maccabees presents a tremendous amount of very specific data on the developments of these forty years, and historians of the time period have spilled a great deal of ink trying to reconstruct the exact sequence, absolute dating, and geographical location of the events described as well as the precise motivations of the different Seleucid kings, Maccabean commanders, and other prominent figures who guided the course of events. While scholars debate the precise dating and interpretation of hundreds of individual events recounted in 1 Maccabees, the general consensus is that the author was a good historian who intended to write accurate history and was largely successful.[3]

On the other hand, the author of 2 Maccabees makes it clear that his intentions, and his chosen *genre*, are not purely historical. Indeed, more than any

---

[3] See DeSilva, *Introducing the Apocrypha*, 250–53.

other biblical author, he repeatedly emphasizes that his primary goal is not exactitude but, rather, brevity, drama, and the rhetorical delight of the reader:

> For considering the flood of numbers involved and the difficulty there is for those who wish to enter upon the narratives of history because of the mass of material, *we have aimed to please those who wish to read,* to make it easy for those who are inclined to memorize, and to profit all readers. (2 Mac 2:24–25)

> For us who have undertaken the toil of abbreviating ... *leaving the responsibility for exact details to the compiler,* while devoting our effort to arriving at the outlines of the condensation. (2 Mac 2:26, 28)

> It is the duty of the original historian to occupy the ground and to discuss matters from every side and *to take trouble with details,* but the one who recasts the narrative should be allowed to strive for brevity of expression and to forego exhaustive treatment. (2 Mac 2:30–31)

In other words, the author of this work is an unashamed popularizer, not an academic historian, though that does not mean he intends to misrepresent what actually happened. His intention is to compose a popular, memorable account of the origin of two liturgical feasts: the twenty-fifth of Kislev (Feast of Dedication/Hanukkah, 2 Mac 10:5–8) and the thirteenth of Adar (Eve of Mordecai's Day, 2 Mac 15:36).

In older scholarship, there was a tendency to understand any difference in presentation, interpretation, or content between 1 and 2 Maccabees as due to the literary license of the latter author. In more recent times, however, there is greater recognition of the fact that, while taking the differences in genre into consideration, 2 Maccabees can be a source of genuine historical information that complements the accounts of the earlier book.[4] Nonetheless, there is also a consensus that the editor of 2 Maccabees was less concerned than his counterpart about precision in dating events and that he sometimes presents episodes out of chronological order for the purpose of streamlining his narrative or highlighting certain themes.

Theological Issues in 1–2 Maccabees

The reign and activity of the Maccabees were highly controversial theologically, both for their contemporaries and for subsequent generations. On the one hand, there could be no doubt about the sincerity of their zeal for the Jewish law, culture, and national independence, at least for Mattathias and his sons. Moreover, their remarkable victories over truly overwhelming odds did give sufficient testimony to divine activity. However, not all other Jews agreed with their decisions to fight on the Sabbath (1 Mac 2:39–41), much less with their decision to execute Jews who disagreed with their implementation of the law (1 Mac 2:44). Furthermore, the decision of the Maccabees to take the office of high priest (1 Mac 10:20), combined with the vestments and symbols of royalty

---

4 Ibid., 273–76.

(1 Mac 10:20, 62, 64), disturbed pious Jews who were well aware that the high priesthood belonged to the line of Aaron through Zadok and the kingship to the sons of David. The Maccabees were of neither line.

Therefore, the rule of the Maccabees was theologically ambivalent. The author of 1 Maccabees recognizes that God worked through the Maccabees, and he does compare them implicitly to great military heroes of Israel's history, especially the judges and the young David, who like the Maccabees were renegade heroes with unclear status and authority. He exercises restraint in his historiography, presenting the facts as they were, and refrains from invoking blanket divine authorization for the Maccabean dynasty beyond saying they were "the family of those men through whom deliverance was given to Israel" (1 Mac 5:62).

The author of 2 Maccabees is less restrained in his theological interpretation. He does highlight the divine purpose in the career of Judas Maccabeus, but that purpose is not the glorification or establishment of the Maccabean dynasty: it is the honor and glory of God's dwelling place, the holy Temple. It is not for the Maccabees' own sake, but for the sake of his House that the Lord God of Israel raises up the family of Judas to strike down those who impugned the dignity of the living God and his Sanctuary. Temple and liturgy form the center of 2 Maccabees, because in the author's view the center of human existence—especially for the people of God—is the celebration of God's presence, in the place and manner specified by the covenant.

Theology of Persecution, Martyrdom, and Bodily Resurrection

For the first time in its history, the Jewish nation in the period of the Maccabees faced persecution and death, not for political or ethnic reasons, but for their religion *per se*. Rabbinic Judaism continues to see in the Maccabean martyrs the beginning of the Jewish theology of martyrdom. In particular, the Jewish tradition correlates Abraham and Isaac's ordeal at the *Aqedah* (Gen 22:1–18) with the suffering of the Maccabean mother and her sons in 2 Maccabees 7. The mother's suffering was a participation in the suffering of Abraham, only her merits were greater, because the lives of her *seven* sons were not spared at the brink of death, and she herself followed them into the netherworld. In fact, 2 Maccabees presents one of the clearest and most explicit expressions of hope in the bodily resurrection, based on God the Creator of all *ex nihilo* (2 Mac 7:11, 20–23; 12:43–45). Moreover, the account of Judas Maccabeus' offering of sacrifices (ritual prayers) for those slain in battle is one of the earliest testimonies to the faith of God's people not only in the possibility of resurrection but also in purification of the soul after death—a purification that will later come to be known as "purgatory" (2 Mac 12:39–45).

1–2 Maccabees in the Living Tradition

Although 1 and 2 Maccabees are not quoted as often by the early Church Fathers as other historical books of the Old Testament, there are several key ways in which these two books have made significant contributions to the living tradition of Christian faith and theology.

The Theology of Martyrdom and Creatio ex Nihilo

Although many Christians may take for granted the idea that God created the world "out of nothing" (Latin *creatio ex nihilo*), it is a fact of history that the opening lines of the book of Genesis did not lead all its readers to that conclusion (cf. Gen 1:1–3). In addition to Genesis' own testimony, the famous speech of the Jewish mother to her sons before being martyred (2 Mac 7) continues to be cited as explicit biblical support for creation out of nothing, which was defined as an article of faith at the ecumenical Fourth Lateran Council (A.D. 1215). In modern times, the *Catechism of the Catholic Church* quotes the Jewish mother's speech at length as biblical testimony to this article of faith:

> We believe that God needs no pre-existent thing or any help in order to create, nor is creation any sort of necessary emanation from the divine substance. God creates freely "out of nothing"....
>
> *Scripture bears witness to faith in creation "out of nothing" as a truth full of promise and hope.* Thus the mother of seven sons encourages them for martyrdom: "... Look at the heaven and the earth and see everything that is in them, and recognize that God did not make them out of things that existed. Thus also mankind comes into being." (*CCC* 296–97, citing 2 Mac 7:22–23, 28)

This is an excellent example of the fact that, despite the connotations of the term "deuterocanonical", these books of the Old Testament are not theologically secondary. Instead, in certain key cases, they play important roles in shaping the practice and belief of the Christian faith.

Prayers for the Dead and the Doctrine of Purgatory

Lest there be any doubt about this, we need only turn to a second major theological and liturgical contribution of 2 Maccabees: its famous endorsement of the pious practice of prayers for the dead (2 Mac 12:45). This practice of praying for the dead is well documented in the first centuries of the Church; consider, for example, the words of Saint Augustine, which contain echoes of the story of Judas Maccabeus and his deceased troops:

> During the time, moreover, which intervenes between a man's death and the final resurrection, the soul dwells in a hidden retreat, where it enjoys rest or suffers affliction just in proportion to the merit it has earned by the life which it led on earth.
>
> Nor can it be denied that the souls of the dead are benefited by the piety of their living friends, who offer the sacrifice of the Mediator, or give alms in the church on their behalf [cf. 2 Mac 12:43–45]. But these services are of advantage only to those who during their lives have earned such merit that services of this kind can help them. For there is a manner of life which is neither so good as not to require these services after death, nor so bad that such services are of no avail after death.[5]

---

[5] Augustine, *The Enchiridion, Addressesd to Laurentius; Being a Treatise on Faith, Hope, and Love*, 109–10, in *NPNF1* 3:272.

Now, since prayers can help neither those in hell (who are beyond help) nor those in heaven (who have no need of help), the practice of prayer for the dead implies a third place or state in the afterlife where the intercessions of those on earth can be of help. The Church calls this third place or state purgatory. The ultimate salvation of those in purgatory is assured, but they require purification before entrance to heaven. In this process of purification, the prayers of others can be of assistance. This teaching was stated authoritatively by the Second Vatican Council in 1963, which actually quotes 2 Maccabees in support of the practice:

> In full consciousness of this communion of the whole Mystical Body of Jesus Christ, the Church in its pilgrim members, from the very earliest days of the Christian religion, has honored with great respect the memory of the dead; and *"because it is a holy and a wholesome thought to pray for the dead that they may be loosed from their sins"* (2 Mac 12:45) *she offers her suffrages for them.*[6]

This point is significant to stress both because the reality of the final purification after death is not only denied by most Protestant Christians (with the exception of some high-church Anglicans and Lutherans), but also because many Christians today continue mistakenly to believe that the Roman Catholic Church expressly added 2 Maccabees and the rest of the deuterocanonical books to the canon of Scripture at Trent in order to gain biblical support for the doctrine of purgatory and the practice of prayers for the dead. As we saw in chapter 1, this is historically incorrect, since the present canon of Scripture, including 2 Maccabees, can be found stated already by the Council of Rome (A.D. 382), the Council of Hippo (393), the Council of Carthage (397), Saint Augustine (397), Saint Thomas Aquinas (1256), and the Council of Florence (1441). The Council of Trent, responding to the Reformation, simply reaffirmed the canon of Scripture established in the Western Church since the late fourth century.

The Books of Maccabees in the Lectionary

The contemporary Roman Lectionary, when it reads from the books of Maccabees, prefers the accounts of heroic martyrdom from 2 Maccabees and employs them on liturgical occasions marked by the themes of persecution, martyrdom, or hope in the resurrection.

Significantly, the account of the martyrdom of the Jewish mother and her seven sons (2 Mac 7:1–2, 9–14) is proclaimed on Sunday in the Thirty-Second Week in Ordinary Time C. Typically this would be the second Sunday of November, during which the Church turns to the Last Things in preparation for the Solemnity of Christ the King. The reading from 2 Maccabees, an excerpt from the martyrdom of the seven brothers, has profound correlations with the Gospel (Lk 20:27–38), in which Jesus is challenged by the Sadducees over the issue of the resurrection of the dead. In both readings we have seven

---

[6] Second Vatican Council, *Lumen Gentium* (November 21, 1964), 50.

brothers who die without issue. In both, the hope of the resurrection dominates the narrative. We see Jesus as the one who definitely teaches and proves that the Lord is the God of the Living, the God in whom the Maccabean martyrs put their hope for resurrection.

The weekday Lectionary reserves readings from Maccabees for the Thirty-Third Week in Ordinary Time (I), again during the final four weeks of the Church year. Similarly, the Liturgy of the Hours reads a selection from the two books during the Thirty-First Week in Ordinary Time. In both cases, the accounts of the persecutions and martyrdoms are employed during the end of the Church year as types and images of the final tribulation and judgment (Mt 24:9–29), to help inspire the resolve of Christians to remain faithful through the trials to come.

Readings from the books of Maccabees are also offered as optional first readings in the Common of Martyrs, Masses for the Dead, and in special Masses for persecuted Christians.

Readings from Maccabees in the Lectionary and Liturgy of the Hours on Sundays, Feast Days, Liturgical Seasons, and Other Occasions			
MSO = Masses for Special Occasions; *OM* = Optional Memorial; *VM* = Votive Mass; *Rit* = Ritual; *LH* = Liturgy of the Hours			
Passage	Description	Occasion	Explanation
1 Mac 2:49–52, 57–64	Mattathias urges his sons to give their lives for the covenant, reminding them of the example of David, Elijah, Daniel, and others.	*MSO*: For Persecuted Christians, opt. 2	Mattathias' exhortation to offer one's life for the covenant serves to steel the resolve of Christians facing persecution and offers the consolation of the great saints of Scripture who faced persecution throughout salvation history.
1 Mac 4:52–59	The Jews rededicate the altar of the Temple and celebrate the first Hanukkah.	*Rit*: Dedication of an Altar, opt. 3	The altar dedicated in a Christian church is in continuity with the altar of God through salvation history. On the Christian altar, the sacrifice of the Eucharist will be offered, which fulfills the meaning of the sacrifices on the altar of Jerusalem.
2 Mac 6:18, 21, 24–31	Eleazar, the aged patriarch, dies under torture at age ninety, unwilling to recant and thus leave a bad example to the young.	Common of Martyrs, opt. 2	Eleazar's martyrdom is particularly appropriate for persons martyred in old age. Eleazar is their model, showing that the experience of the saints in Scripture is replicated by the saints of the age of the Church.

(continued)

Readings from Maccabees in the Lectionary and Liturgy of the Hours on Sundays, Feast Days, Liturgical Seasons, and Other Occasions (*continued*)

MSO = Masses for Special Occasions; *OM* = Optional Memorial;
VM = Votive Mass; *Rit* = Ritual; *LH* = Liturgy of the Hours

Passage	Description	Occasion	Explanation
2 Mac 7:1–2, 9–14	The first four sons of the Maccabean mother die under torture, while professing their faith in God and fidelity to his law.	*32nd Sun. in OT*; St. Charles Lwanga, Martyr (June 3); Common of Martyrs, opt. 3	The last four Sundays of the liturgical calendar (31st–34th) are concerned with the Last Things: final tribulation, return of Christ, judgment, resurrection. The Gospel reading (Lk 20:27–38) also concerns the themes of seven brothers who die and the question of the resurrection. The Maccabean sons die professing faith in the resurrection, and Jesus affirms the reality of it in the Gospel, over against Sadducee skeptics (Lk 20:27–38).
2 Mac 7:1, 20–23, 27b–29	The Maccabean mother encourages her final son to accept death in hope of the God who can raise the dead.	Common of Martyrs, opt. 4	The Church is reminded, through the mouth of the Maccabean mother, that hope in the resurrection is natural and rational if we believe God created the world from nothing.
2 Mac 12:43–46	Judas Maccabeus raises money to offer sacrifices for deceased soldiers, to assist them in attaining the resurrection.	Masses for the Dead, opt. 1	This key biblical text encourages believers to offer prayer and sacrifices for the faithful departed, so that they may be cleansed and forgiven of their sins and attain heaven. It is one of the main biblical evidences for the doctrine of purgatory.

Conclusion

Taken together, the books of Maccabees form a narrative bridge by giving an account of the history of the people of Israel during the period between the end of the ministry of the classical prophets and the dawning of the era of the New Covenant. In Maccabees, we witness the development of the theology of righteous martyrdom, a theology that will find its culmination in Jesus' death on the Cross, and its continuation in the suffering perseverance of the Church through history. In the living tradition of the Church, the sufferings of Judah under Antiochus IV Epiphanes have also functioned as an important type of the sufferings of Christians during the final tribulation before the Second Coming. To be sure, the Maccabees themselves remain ambivalent heroes, clearly used

Reading of Maccabees for Daily Mass: Ordinary Time, Year I: Week 33			
Week	Day	Passage Read	Description
33	M	1 Mac 1:10–15, 41–43, 54–57, 62–63	Antiochus Epiphanes encourages his people to give up their local religions. Traitorous Jews start a Hellenic movement in Judah and Jerusalem. Judaism is outlawed, and observant Jews are martyred, notably Eleazar, the aged patriarch.
33	Tu	2 Mac 6:18–31	The martyrdom of Eleazar. He prefers to die rather than give scandalous example to the young, especially since he has but a few more years to live in any event.
33	W	2 Mac 7:1, 20–31	The Maccabean mother encourages her seventh and last son to accept martyrdom, reasoning from *creatio ex nihilo* to God's power to grant resurrection. The son accepts her counsel and dies under torture.
33	Th	1 Mac 2:15–29	When imperial troops come to Modein to impose pagan worship, Mattathias rebels and leads a guerilla force of observant Jews into the hills.
33	F	1 Mac 4:36–37, 52–59	Judas and his brothers regain control of Jerusalem and rededicate the altar of the Temple—the origin of Hanukkah.
33	Sa	1 Mac 6:1–13	Antiochus Epiphanes recognizes his evildoing as he lies dying in a foreign land after an unsuccessful military campaign.

The Books of Maccabees in the Office of Readings for the Liturgy of the Hours, Ordinary Time, Week 31			
Week	Day	Passage Read	Description
31	Su	1 Mac 1:1–24	Alexander acquires an international empire, but dies, leaving it to his generals. In time, Antiochus Epiphanes becomes king in Asia. He encourages Hellenizers among the Jews and sacks the city and Temple while returning from his campaign against Egypt.
31	M	1 Mac 1:43–63	Antiochus Epiphanes decrees the suppression of Judaism, forcing Jews to offer sacrifice to pagan gods. Many Jews defect to paganism; those who do not are tortured and executed. The Temple is defiled with a "horrible abomination" on the 15th of Chislev.
31	Tu	1 Mac 2:1, 15–28, 42–50, 65–70	Mattathias leaves Jerusalem for Modein. When pressured to offer pagan sacrifice, he kills the king's agents and leads a band of renegades out into the hill country. His band of zealots terrorizes the royal forces and Jewish collaborators. Mattathias dies, leaving his sons Simon and Judas in charge.
31	W	1 Mac 3:1–26	Judas proves to be a brave warrior and brilliant strategist. He defeats the early armies sent against him, and his renown spreads throughout the nations.

(continued)

			The Books of Maccabees in the Office of Readings for the Liturgy of the Hours, Ordinary Time, Week 31 (*continued*)
Week	Day	Passage Read	Description
31	Th	1 Mac 4:36–59	The origin of Hanukkah: Judas finds himself in control of Judea, so his forces take over Jerusalem, purifying and rededicating the Temple on the 15th of Chislev, proclaiming a liturgical feast to commemorate it in perpetuity.
31	F	2 Mac 12:32–46	Judas collects money to offer expiatory sacrifices for those slain in battle, showing his faith in the resurrection and the reality of a state in the afterlife where the prayers of the living are efficacious for the dead.
31	Sa	1 Mac 9:1–22	Judas dies valiantly in battle, and his brothers bury him in Modein. His brave deeds and battles were many and glorious.

by God, but just as clearly not the fulfillment of the covenant promises to the houses of Levi and David (cf. Jer 33:14–26). Their aggressive, political, military form of reign thus serves as a foil for the peaceful, apolitical, spiritual, but no less historical kingdom of God established by Jesus the Christ, Son of David.

For Further Reading

Commentaries and Studies on 1–2 Maccabees

DeSilva, David Arthur. *Introducing the Apocrypha*. Grand Rapids, Mich.: Baker Academic, 2002. (See pp. 244–79.)

Doran, Robert. "The First Book of Maccabees". Pages 1–178 in vol. 4 of *The New Interpreter's Bible*. Nashville: Abingdon Press, 1996.

———. "The Second Book of Maccabees". Pages 179–299 of *The New Interpreter's Bible*. Nashville: Abingdon Press, 1996.

Goldstein, Jonathan A. *1 Maccabees*. Anchor Bible 41. New York: Doubleday, 1976.

———. *2 Maccabees*. Anchor Bible 41A. New York: Doubleday, 1983.

Historical Issues in 1–2 Maccabees

Cohen, Shaye J. D. *From the Maccabees to the Mishnah*. 2nd ed. Louisville, Ky.: Westminster John Knox Press, 2006.

Grabbe, Lester L. *Judaism from Cyrus to Hadrian*. 2 vols. Minneapolis: Fortress Press, 1992.

Harrington, Daniel J. *The Maccabean Revolt: Anatomy of a Biblical Revolution*. Wilmington, Del.: Michael Glazier, 1988.

1–2 Maccabees in the Living Tradition

Augustine, Saint. *The City of God*. Translated by Marcus Dods. In *Nicene and Post-Nicene Fathers*, 1st series, vol. 2. 1887. Repr., Peabody, Mass.: Hendrickson, 1994. (See no. 18.36.)

Cyprian of Carthage, Saint. "On the Exhortation to Martyrdom Addressed to Fortunatus". Pages 496–507 in vol. 5 of *Ante-Nicene Fathers*. Edited by Alexander Roberts and James Donaldson. 1886. Repr., Peabody, Mass.: Hendrickson, 1994.

Origen. *An Exhortation to Martyrdom, Prayer, and Other Selected Works*. Translated by Rowan A. Greer. Mahwah, N.J.: Paulist Press, 1988. (See nos. 22–27.)

The Wisdom Literature

22. THE PLACE OF THE WISDOM LITERATURE IN THE CANON

Following the historical books of Genesis through Esther, the second major genre division in the Catholic Old Testament is the poetic books, also known as the wisdom literature: Job through Sirach. The exact classification of these books of Scripture is somewhat varied: they can be referred to as the *sapiential* books, with reference to their didactic aim in imparting wisdom; or as the *moral* books, with reference to the abundance of instructions they possess regarding how one should live justly; or as the *poetic* books, with reference to their poetical form—this latter being one of the primary reasons they have been by far the most popular portion of the Christian Old Testament throughout the centuries.

The rationale for the sequence of these books is a certain canonical-historical sensibility. For example, the account of Job is set in the period of the patriarchs, so his book is placed first, functioning as a kind of transition from the historical books to the poetical books. The Psalms are associated with David and fall next. Then follow all the books associated with Solomon, David's son; first the three texts preserved in Hebrew (Proverbs, Ecclesiastes, Song of Solomon); and then the book preserved in Greek (Wisdom of Solomon). Last of all comes Sirach (traditionally known as "Ecclesiasticus"), a large work that is identified with the late postexilic period and that successfully summarizes and assimilates a great deal of God's revelation to Israel with an eye toward its practical application in daily life.

As with the historical books, the tradition of the Church groups these books together because of their similarity of *literary genre*. All of the books in this collection are "poetic" in the sense that they employ an artistic rather than prosaic use of language. Historical narrative is rare in these books; the concern is to convey, not information about past events, but guidance for wise living. This is true even of the books of Job, Psalms, and Song of Solomon, which differ generically in important ways from other more typical "books of wisdom". Despite their difference in genre, there are good reasons to consider these three books also to be wisdom books, and thus, in the broadest definition, there is a complete overlap of the "poetical books" and the "wisdom literature" of the Old Testament.

The relationship between the poetic books and the rest of the Old Testament canon has sometimes been considered a theological problem. At first glance, the covenant-historical theme so prominent in the historical books and the prophets is not readily apparent in all of the poetic books. Therefore, some scholars have proposed that the poetic (or wisdom) books present a *different theology* from the rest of the Old Testament, a distinct approach or perspective on how to be God's people and live in relationship with him.

While the poetic books certainly do bring a unique and valuable perspective to the question of how to live as God's people, this perspective is *complementary* to, not *competitive* with, the covenant-historical motif in the other Old Testament books. In fact, all the poetic books are grounded in some way in the canonical presentation of the sequence of divine covenants with mankind.

Job and the Adamic Covenant

For example, Job presents events taking place in very ancient times, and Job himself develops into a *new Adam*, or "alternate Adam", figure. Like Adam, Job is a royal and priestly father who enjoys an intimate relationship with God yet undergoes a serious, potentially lethal test by Satan that tries his faith in God's goodness and love toward him. Unlike Adam, Job ultimately prevails in this test of faith, and the covenant relationship between Job and God stands. As we will see, in the living tradition of the Church, Job's trials will become a type and anticipation of the Passion of Jesus, the definitive New Adam.

Job thus explores the potential relationship with God available to a righteous Gentile who falls only under the Adamic or creation covenant, which in the biblical story line was renewed with Noah. Job teaches that the Adamic distrust of God's fatherly intent is not obligatory for all human beings, but some can choose, like Job, to maintain faith in God even in the most rigorous trials of the present life.

The Psalms and the Davidic Covenant

The Psalms, as we shall see, are deeply rooted in the Davidic covenant. This is especially true in light of David's filial relationship with God and his exuberant expressions of *todah* ("thanks" or "praise") to God for God's *hesed* ("covenant faithfulness"). The flow of the psalms in some ways follows the fortunes of David's kingdom, and key royal psalms occur at strategic locations in the literary structure of the Psalter. In this way, the Psalter presents a spirituality of prayer and praise that is grounded on the promises of the Davidic covenant and radically open to the fulfillment of those promises in the New Covenant (see especially Ps 89). The theme of the Psalter can be summarized by the well-known refrain, "Give thanks to the LORD, for he is good; his *mercy* [Hebrew *hesed*] endures forever." Once it is understood that *hesed* refers specifically to *covenant fidelity*, it becomes apparent that the Psalms as a book constitute one act of praise to God for his faithfulness to his covenant promises.

The Wisdom Books and the Universal Wisdom of Solomon

The next four poetic books are specifically associated with Solomon in the Jewish and Christian tradition. As such, they represent the divine wisdom given to the son of David by which he ruled his multi-ethnic empire. These wisdom books serve the same function in the Davidic covenant as the legal collections in Exodus–Deuteronomy serve in the Mosaic covenant. Just as Moses gives the Torah as the divine instruction for the people of *Israel*, so Solomon gives Wisdom as the form of instruction for *all the nations* incorporated into the Davidic empire. That is why much of the moral instruction of the wisdom books is very general in nature and does not mandate the specific ceremonial or ritual observances obligatory only for the people of Israel. Using the language of later theological discourse, the wisdom books are in this way virtually an exposition of the natural law, which can be put into practice regardless of the nationality or geographical location of the reader.

The Song of Solomon is certainly not written in a typical wisdom genre. Does this carefully arranged set of love poems of Solomon and his ideal bride belong among the other wisdom books? Indeed it does; for if the fear of the Lord is wisdom's beginning, the love of the Lord is wisdom's end (Deut 6:5). For this reason, the motif of nuptial love for the wisdom of the Lord is particularly strong in certain wisdom books (Prov 8:1–9:11; 31:10–31; Wis 7–9). The association of the Song with these books invites the reader to interpret the Song as a development of this nuptial theme and to perceive the beautiful bride as the personification of divine wisdom, whom one should embrace.

Sirach as a Summary of Salvation History

Fittingly, Sirach is the last of the poetic books, since it is a massive work of integration and distillation of the entire Old Testament revelation. The sacred author of Sirach has meditated on all the Scriptures of Israel in order to summarize their moral message. If earlier wisdom books did not draw explicit lines of connection between wisdom and themes so important to the rest of the Old Testament—namely, the law (Torah), the liturgy, and covenant history—Sirach synthesizes them completely. Here there is a comprehensive integration of natural law, revealed law, sacred worship, and salvation history: the author of Sirach finds the highest expression of God's universal wisdom manifested in the law, liturgy, and history of the people of Israel. With good reason this book is also called *Ecclesiasticus*—that is, the "little book of the Church"—because it was so widely used in fundamental catechesis in the early centuries.

An Invitation to the Poetic Books

The poetic books of the Old Testament constitute arguably the Church's most treasured collection within the Scriptures of Israel. They include (1) the book most often read, sung, and prayed in the Church's rhythm of liturgical prayer: *the Psalms*; (2) the book most widely used for training pagan nations in Judeo-Christian morality: *Sirach*; and (3) the book used most extensively (in antiquity) for sacramental mystagogy: *the Song of Solomon*. In a very real way, in the history of the Church, it was these books to which Christians turned for *spiritual reading* in the form of prayer, praise, and meditation. It is somewhat unfortunate that in the modern period, this aspect of the wisdom literature has been eclipsed by the spiritual writings of more recent mystics, such as John of the Cross, Teresa of Avila, and others. Yet these later mystics themselves constantly cite the wisdom books! These inspired books, which nourished the saints, continue to lay before the reader an invitation to the feast of divine wisdom:

> Wisdom has built her house,
>   she has set up her seven pillars.
> She has slaughtered her beasts, she has mixed her wine,
>   she has also set her table.
> She has sent out her maids to call
>   from the highest places in the town,
> "Whoever is simple, let him turn in here!"
>   To him who is without sense she says,
> "Come, eat of my bread
>   and drink of the wine I have mixed.
> Leave simpleness, and live,
>   and walk in the way of insight." (Prov 9:1–6)

23. JOB

Introduction

In dramatic format, the book of Job recounts the life and sufferings of a righteous Gentile of ancient times as he undergoes prosperity, disaster, depression, and—finally—restoration during a period of painful testing by YHWH. The book is a masterpiece of world literature and the Old Testament's most direct treatment of the problem of evil and *theodicy*—that is, the justice of God.

Unlike some of the poetical books, Job is considered canonical in all traditions. Indeed, from ancient times right up to today, it remains one of the most popular and widely read books in the Old Testament. It takes its name from the main character: "Job" (Hebrew *'iyyob*; Greek *Iōb*; Latin *Liber Iob*). The meaning of Job's name is uncertain but may be derived from a Semitic root meaning "enmity" or "adversity".

The text of the book is relatively stable, and most ancient versions read similarly to the Hebrew. The exception is the original Septuagint, which preserved a somewhat shorter form of the book apparently condensed from the longer Hebrew. Origen replaced the verses missing from the Septuagint with verses from another Greek translation (Theodotion) to produce the form of the text widely used in the early Church.

In the Jewish tradition, Job falls in the third canonical division, the "Writings" (Hebrew *ketuvim*), and is usually placed immediately after the Psalms. In the Christian tradition, Job ordinarily appears as the first of the poetic books, or wisdom literature. The reason for this appears to be based on the traditional identification of Job with "Jobab, the son of Zerah", one of the ancient kings of Edom (Gen 36:33), a land that, though Gentile, was known for its wisdom (Obad 8–9). From this point of view, Job would be set either in the patriarchal or pre-patriarchal age and, thus, in an earlier time period than that presumed by any of the other books of poetry, which are largely associated with the Davidic and Solomonic eras. It may also be the case that the prose prologue and epilogue of the book (Job 1–2; 42:7–16) function as a kind of generic bridge between the historical books and the wisdom literature.

Literary Structure of Job

The book of Job is structured like a drama or play—in fact, it can and has been dramatized on the stage. The literary structure is extremely clear: a "narrator" delivers a prose prologue (Job 1–2) and epilogue (Job 42:7–16) that surround the "action" (Job 3:1—42:6), which consists of spoken parts for six characters:

Job; his three friends Eliphaz, Bildad, and Zophar; a young man named Elihu; and God himself.

The character Job has an opening soliloquy, which is followed by three cycles of dialogue (Job 4–27). Each cycle follows the same clear structure: the three friends speak to Job in order of age and dignity: Eliphaz (Job 4; 15; 22), then Bildad (Job 8; 18; 25), then Zophar (Job 11, 20, 27?). After each speech, Job gives a response (Job 6–7; 9–10; 12–14; 16–17; 19; 21; 23–24; 26–27[?]). In general, each friend encourages Job to confess that his hidden sins have led to his present sufferings, and Job refuses to do so in his replies. The third cycle (Job 22–27) appears disturbed, because Zophar has no third speech. Some think that Job 27 was originally the third speech of Zophar and has been misattributed to Job in the textual transmission. Others think Zophar's "missing" speech is intentional: as the dialogue progresses, the three friends grow increasingly frustrated and increasingly blunt with Job (cf. Bildad's last speech, Job 25). Finally, in chapter 27, Zophar, the least patient of the three, has no more to say!

In any event, after Bildad's third speech (Job 25), the three friends fall silent, and Job delivers a series of soliloquies, including a response to Bildad (Job 26); a parody of the three friends' theology (Job 27); a poem on wisdom (Job 28); a lengthy lament (Job 29–30); and a dramatic courtroom oath (Job 31)—the longest oath in ancient literature—in which he asserts his innocence and calls on God to acquit him. After Job and his three friends have ceased speaking, the young man Elihu comes forward and rebukes all four at great length (Job 34–37), although it is not clear that he has any new material to contribute to the discussion. Finally, God appears in a whirlwind and speaks to Job in two speeches (Job 38:1—40:2; 40:6—41:34), each followed by a brief reply from Job (Job 40:4–5; 42:1–6). The narrator's prose epilogue (Job 42:7–17) concludes the book. Thus, the book can be outlined as follows:

Outline of the Book of Job

I. Prologue (Job 1–2)
   A. The Greatness of Job (1:1–5)
   B. The Testing of Job (1:6—2:10)
      1. The First Test: Job's Possessions (1:6–22)
      2. The Second Test: Job's Person (2:1–10)
   C. The Three Friends of Job (2:11–13)

II. The Dialogues of Job and His Friends (Job 3—42:6)
   A. Job's Opening Soliloquy (3)
   B. The First Cycle (4–14)
      1. Eliphaz's First Speech (4–5) and Job's Reply (6–7)
      2. Bildad's First Speech (8) and Job's Reply (9–10)
      3. Zophar's First Speech (11) and Job's Reply (12–14)
   C. The Second Cycle (15–21)
      1. Eiphaz's Second Speech (15) and Job's Reply (16–17)
      2. Bildad's Second Speech (18) and Job's Reply (19)
      3. Zophar's Second Speech (20) and Job's Reply (21)

Overview of Job

Prologue: Job's Greatness in the Face of Tragedy (Job 1–2)

The sacred author introduces Job as a man from Uz, a desert region to the east of Israel associated with Edom (Lam 4:21), whose inhabitants were considered relatives of the Arameans (Gen 22:21). This geographical context is extremely significant, for it signals to the reader that Job is *not an Israelite*. Nevertheless, he is "blameless and upright" (Job 1:1). Indeed, he is "the greatest of all the people of the east", who were renowned for their wisdom (Job 1:3; cf. 1 Kings 4:31). He is not only extremely wealthy and blessed with numerous children; he is also so pious that during times of feasting, he rises "early in the morning" to offer atoning sacrifices on behalf of his sons, just in case they have sinned against God (Job 1:5). In this way, Job mirrors other figures from the patriarchal period, such as Abraham, Isaac, and Jacob, who—long before the institution of the Levitical priesthood (cf. Ex 32)—act as both fathers and priests by building altars and offering sacrifices (for example, Gen 31). Prior to the Mosaic covenant, it appears that each father served as priest on behalf of his own family.

First Test: Job Loses His Children and Possessions (Job 1:6–22)

With the blamelessness and righteousness of Job clearly established, the scene switches from earth to the heavenly court of YHWH and the "sons of God" (Hebrew *beney' ha'elohim*)—that is, angels who populate the heavenly realm (Job 1:6). Among these beings one is singled out: "Satan", whose name literally means "the Adversary" (Hebrew *hashatan*) and who is described as coming *from* earth *to* heaven after "going back and forth on the earth, and from walking up and down on it"—apparently in search of human beings to accuse or afflict in some way (Job 1:7). Significantly, *it is not Satan who brings Job to God's attention, but God who invites Satan to "consider" Job*, pointing out that Job's righteousness is unique on the earth (Job 1:8). Thus the stage is set for one of the great questions in the book of Job: namely, the extent to which God, in his divine providence, not only permits but causes otherwise righteous persons to experience suffering. In response, Satan proposes that Job is only righteous because of his many material blessings. If God were to take these temporal goods away from him, he would immediately "curse" God to "his face", and his righteousness would be no more (Job 1:11). In the face of this challenge, the Lord consents to let Satan deprive Job of his many earthly blessings, which Satan proceeds to do. In the course of a single day, Satan not only wipes out all of Job's possessions; he even causes the tragic death of all of Job's sons and daughters. Stunningly, after losing everything dear to him, Job's response is not only mourning, but worship:

> Then Job arose, and tore his robe, and shaved his head, and fell upon the ground, and worshiped. And he said, "Naked I came from my mother's womb, and naked shall I return; *the LORD gave, and the LORD has taken away; blessed be the name of the LORD.*"
> In all this Job did not sin or charge God with wrong. (Job 1:20–22)

Here we see in Job not only a model of piety, but an almost unparalleled example of complete surrender to divine providence, which will constitute one of the central themes of the book.

Second Test: Job Is Afflicted with Sickness (Job 2:1–10)

Again Satan appears before the Lord, who points out that Job has maintained his righteousness. Satan insists that this is merely because God has not yet afflicted "his bone and his flesh"—in other words, Job's own person (Job 2:4–5). Satan charges that if God allows Job to suffer *sickness*, his righteousness will evaporate, and he will curse God (Job 2:6). The Lord consents to let Satan afflict Job's body—but not to kill him—and Job is struck with a skin disease. At this point, even Job's wife upbraids him, declaring that he should simply go ahead and "curse God, and die", either through suicide or divine stroke (Job 2:9). But

---

"Curse" God and Die!

Much of the drama in the opening chapters of Job revolves around whether or not, in the face of unspeakable tragedy and suffering, Job will "sin" by cursing God. Intriguingly, in each of these instances, although the English translation says "curse", the actual Hebrew expression is "bless" (Hebrew *barak*). For example, Job's wife literally says to him: "Bless [*barek*] God and die!" (Job 2:9). How do we explain this? In this case, it appears that the Hebrew word for "bless" is being used euphemistically to mean "curse"—that is, to "bless" God in an unholy or unrighteous manner.

Job refuses to do so, declaring once again his total abandonment to divine providence: "Shall we receive good [Hebrew *tôb*] at the hand of God, and shall we not receive evil [Hebrew *ra'*]?" (Job 2:10).

Can "Evil" Come from a Good God?

One of the striking features of the book of Job for any contemporary reader is the direct and immediate way in which Job attributes "evil" to God (e.g., Job 2:10). Most readers of the Bible bring to it the theological conviction that God is *omnibenevolent*—that is, "all-good". Indeed, according to Church teaching, "God is infinitely good and all his works are good" (see *CCC* 385). Nevertheless, Job declares that we must accept "evil" when it comes from God. How can these two be reconciled?

One key factor in answering this question is to realize that Hebrew does not always distinguish between *moral evil* (which God cannot commit) and *suffering* (which God can and does permit). In Hebrew, one word sometimes covers both: "evil" (Hebrew *ra'*). Hence, a literal translation of Job's predicament would read: "No one spoke a word to him, for they saw that his evil [Hebrew *ra'*] was great" (Job 2:13). Clearly, this cannot mean Job's *moral* evil, since the text is emphatic that Job "did not sin [Hebrew *hata'*]"—that is, commit an act of moral evil against God (Job 1:22; 2:10). Only context can make clear in any given case whether the evil in question is a *moral* evil or what Christian tradition will refer to as *physical* evil (see *CCC* 310–11).

Job's Three Wise Friends (Job 2:11–13)

Hearing of his disasters and misery, three friends of Job arrive to commiserate with him: (1) Eliphaz the Temanite, (2) Bildad the Shuhite, and (3) Zophar the Na'amathite. The friends, like Job, are non-Israelite easterners. Significantly, their names also help to situate the context of the book of Job in the patriarchal period: Eliphaz was a traditional Edomite name (Gen 36:15), and Teman was the son of Esau who gave his name to a region of Edom renowned for its "wisdom" (Jer 49:7). Shuah was a son of Abraham by his concubine Keturah (Gen 25:2) and the ancestor of an Arabian tribe. Na'amah, from which Zophar came, was a city in or near Edom that only later became associated with the tribe of Judah (Josh 15:21, 41). Each of these wise friends of Job condoles with him in ancient Near Eastern fashion, sitting in silence for an extended period until the suffering one is willing to speak.

Job's Opening Lament: Death Alone Brings "Rest" (Job 3)

Like a tragic hero in a play of Shakespeare, the ash-covered and sore-ridden Job rises to deliver a great and moving soliloquy cursing the day of his birth. In this speech, Job uses the language of creation from Genesis—such as "day", "light", "darkness", "days", "months", and, above all, "rest"—in an inverted fashion (see Job 3:3–13). In Genesis "rest" comes at the completion of creation, whereas for Job, only death will bring the "rest" he desires.[1] In the face of tremendous suffering, Job desires and describes the "un-creation" of his personal universe, beginning with the day of his birth. In the process, he makes significant mention of the "rousing up" of Leviathan (Job 3:8), the primordial chaos serpent who embodied evil and will reappear in the final divine speech (Job 41). The

---

[1] Daniel J. Estes, *Handbook on the Wisdom Books and Psalms* (Grand Rapids, Mich.: Baker Academic, 2005), 38.

mention of Leviathan here and in the final divine speech form an *inclusio* around the central narrative of the book, which concerns man's struggle against the forces of evil, of which Leviathan is the iconic symbol. They also lend credence from an intertextual perspective to the view that Job is a kind of *Adamic* figure, who undergoes a trial involving a malevolent serpent (here, Leviathan) who seeks his suffering and death (compare Gen 3). Indeed, it may well be that the links between Adam and the serpent in Genesis and Job—Leviathan, and Satan in the book of Job—foreshadow the explicit identification of "that ancient Serpent" with "Satan" in the New Testament (Rev 12:7–9).

Job and His Three Friends: Dialogues on Sin and Suffering (4–27)

After Job's soliloquy lament, Eliphaz starts off the three cycles of dialogues between Job and his friends, in which each friend in turn will make an intervention and receive a reply from Job.

The three friends adhere to a traditional principle of *retributive suffering*—that suffering is the result of sin. The principle is true enough, in many instances; but the three friends over-generalize to the point that *all* suffering is the result *only* of one's personal sin. Witnessing Job's sufferings, they conclude that he must have sinned, and through the three cycles of dialogue, they keep insisting with increasing vehemence that Job should confess his hidden iniquity and admit that God was just in judging him and punishing him in this way. Job, on the other hand, continues to maintain his innocence. He criticizes his friends' advice as the empty mouthing of platitudes he already knows and could produce himself. Contrary to their claims, he insists that the righteous do not always prosper nor are the wicked always punished, as one can plainly see by observing human society.

In general, the dialogues become increasingly blunt and antagonistic as the cycles progress. As an illustration, we may take the three speeches of Eliphaz. In the first speech, Eliphaz strikes a gentle tone (Job 4). He asks if he can interject a comment (Job 4:1) and acknowledges that Job has been a great counselor himself in the past (Job 4:4). He points out that no one, not even the angels, is righteous before God; therefore Job should not be embarrassed to confess his sin (Job 4:17–19). He tells Job what he (Eliphaz) himself would do in Job's situation and encourages Job to regard his sufferings as God's discipline, meant for his own good, and to seek the restoration of peace and safety by reconciling with God (Job 4:8–26).

In Eliphaz's second speech (Job 15), the gentle tone is abandoned. He dismisses Job's talk as a lot of hot air that undermines true religion and accuses Job of being arrogant in his stubbornness, even though he is no older or wiser than his friends (Job 15:2–11). In fact, Job has given himself to blasphemy, even though no one is righteous before God, not even the angels (Job 15:12–15). Finally, Eliphaz describes the terrible fate of a wicked man that Eliphaz himself has witnessed. The wicked man's fate sounds strikingly like Job's condition, with the obvious implication that Job should simply own up to whatever sin he has committed that brought such tragedy down upon his head.

In Eliphaz's final speech, all subtlety is gone (Job 22). Eliphaz directly accuses Job of almost unthinkable wickedness: the usury of his own relatives, stripping

---

Job's Hope for a "Redeemer"

Three times in his book, Job mentions the possibility of a mediator or intermediary between himself and God. In one of his speeches, he despairs that there is no "umpire" between himself and God, though he wishes there were (Job 9:33). More hopefully, he expresses confidence that he has a "witness" on his behalf in heaven (Job 16:19). Most famously, he is emphatic: "For I know that my Redeemer [Hebrew *go'el*] lives, and at last he will stand upon the earth; and after my skin has been thus destroyed, then from my flesh I shall see God" (Job 19:25). These passages of hope are difficult to translate and to understand within the context of Job, since they do not accord with Job's apparent hopelessness in his other speeches. In the canonical form of the book, Job vacillates between hope and despair in his suffering. In light of the entire canon, we recognize that Job's desire for, and sometimes confidence in, a "redeemer" or mediator between himself and God will be fully realized in Jesus Christ, the Redeemer who mediates between God and man.

---

clothes off the backs of the poor, and sadistically withholding food, drink, and other assistance from the hungry, thirsty, widows, and orphans (Job 22:5–9)! Therefore God's judgment is amply justified, and Job should repent (Job 22:10–11, 21–30).

Job's general response, not only to Eliphaz but to all his friends, is well summed up when he declares: "Far be it from me to say that you are right; till I die I will not put away my integrity from me. *I hold fast my righteousness, and will not let it go; my heart does not reproach me for any of my days*" (Job 27:5–6). Thus, we see here not only the "patience" of Job—which his friends take for unbelievable stubbornness—but the innocence of Job, upon which he insists.

Job's Final Soliloquies and His Plea for Divine Justice (Job 26–31)

After Bildad's final, brief intervention (Job 25), Job's friends despair of changing Job's mind and fall silent. Job fills the silence with a series of soliloquies, first responding to Bildad (Job 26), then asserting his own innocence (Job 27:1–6), and then delivering a short oration mimicking the style of his accusers, perhaps

---

Job's Oath and Old Testament Morality

The self-maledictory oath that Job utters is remarkable in all the Old Testament for the height and refinement of its moral sensibility (Job 31). Job recognizes as sin even the most subtle actions, or failures to act, typically overlooked by religious persons in Job's day and in our own. Job recognizes that the sin of adultery can be committed by a glance (Job 31:1) or in the heart (Job 31:9). He recognizes the full human dignity and rights even of his male and female slaves (Job 31:13–15). He recognizes many sins of omission, such as failure to provide for the poor, the widow, and the orphan. Even interior matters of the heart, involving no exterior action, do not escape his notice, such as trusting in wealth, taking pride in riches, or experiencing joy over the downfall of enemies (Job 31:24, 25, 29). Job's moral inventory goes far beyond the requirements of the Mosaic law and will not be matched again in the canon until Jesus' exposition of the New Law in the Sermon on the Mount (Mt 5–7). Indeed, many of Jesus' moral teachings in the Sermon parallel Job's examination of conscience: e.g., avoiding adultery of the heart (cf. Job 31:1, 9a; Mt 5:27–28), love for enemies (cf. Job 31:29; Mt 5:43–48), and not trusting in temporal wealth (cf. Job 31:24–25; Mt 6:19–21).

---

to show he knows their craft well enough to perform it himself (Job 27:7–25). Changing tone, he delivers a beautiful poem on the "home" of wisdom, concluding that only God knows where it resides (Job 28). He laments the loss of his former honor, dignity, and prosperity (Job 29) and contrasts it with his present humiliation and degradation (Job 30). Finally, using the legal language of the courtroom, he utters a lengthy oath swearing his innocence of even the most subtle sins (Job 31)—like prurient glances at young women (Job 31:1), privately gloating over the downfall of personal enemies (Job 31:29), or failure to confess sin out of fear of public embarrassment (Job 31:33–34)—and makes a formal plea, in the form of a dramatic oath, for God the Judge to hear his case and acquit him (Job 31:35). This oath sets up a narrative tension: Will God, who has been totally silent thus far, heed the summons and appear to answer Job?

Elihu's Speeches and the Mysteries of God (Job 32–37)

The sacred author allows the narrative tension of Job's oath to hang in the air while a certain young man named Elihu—unnoticed and unmentioned up to this point—interjects with a lengthy monologue. Elihu is a "Buzite" (Job 32:2), an ethnic group related to the Arameans (that is, Syrians) and distant relatives of the people of Israel (Gen 22:21). Elihu explains that up until now, he has remained silent to allow the older men to speak. Now, however, he is frustrated both with Job and with his three friends: with Job, because of his apparent arrogance in presuming to stand in judgment on God's actions; with his three friends, for being unable to refute Job's arguments effectively.

Despite his pretensions to wisdom, however, Elihu does not contribute much that is truly new during his lengthy intervention. If there is anything different in Elihu's speeches, it is probably a matter of emphasis. Whereas Job's three friends expended their energies in an effort to convince Job to repent of the *personal sins* that had resulted in his sufferings, Elihu attempts to persuade Job that *God's ways and wisdom* are far beyond human comprehension and, therefore, it is not possible for Job to pass judgment on God's justice. The implication seems to be: in order adequately to evaluate the justice of God, one would have to have knowledge of the workings of the universe that is far beyond human cognitive capacities. Human beings can never competently judge God, because they will never have a knowledge base large enough to do so. Since this principle also functions prominently in the divine speeches (Job 38–42), Elihu's intervention forms an appropriate segue to them, when God finally breaks the divine silence.

The Divine Speeches: God Breaks His Silence (Job 38–42)

At last God responds to the challenge issued by Job in his great oath delivered prior to Elihu's monologue (Job 31). Appearing in a whirlwind, the Lord does not answer Job's questions directly, as one might expect, but instead poses questions to Job. In his first speech (Job 38:1—40:2), God challenges Job to answer a series of queries concerning the creation and governance of the natural world, with the intention of demonstrating that Job has neither the (1) wisdom nor the (2) power to create and govern the cosmos as God does. The relevance of this divine speech to Job's challenges to the justice of God throughout the book is not immediately clear to all readers. Nonetheless, the divine reply *is* relevant: God's point is that Job neither is the sort of being nor has the necessary knowledge to judge adequately the justice (or injustice) of God's providence. To use philosophical language, Job has neither the ontological nor the epistemological standing to assess the morality of God's action. At the end of the divine speech, Job acknowledges the point (Job 40:3–5).

In the second divine speech, God puts a finer edge on his previous argument. God asks Job whether he can control the malevolent beasts—Behemoth and Leviathan—as God does. These two animals appear to be a land dragon and sea dragon, respectively, and were identified—especially Leviathan—as embodiments of the forces of evil. The point of God's question to Job is: Can you control the forces of chaos and evil as I can? In response, Job acknowledges that he is not up to the task and had been presuming to judge God when he had neither the wisdom nor power to do so: "Therefore I have uttered what I did not understand, things too wonderful for me, which I did not know" (Job 42:3).

Epilogue: The Restoration of Job and His Happy Death (Job 42:7–17)

The ending of Job is very surprising. Although Job twice admits he was foolish for questioning God's justice, in the end God passes judgment on Job's *friends* and vindicates Job himself! The three friends "have not spoken of me what is right, as my servant Job has" (Job 42:7). Divine forgiveness of the three friends is made contingent on Job's intercessory prayer for them. But finally all are forgiven and reconciled to Job, God, and each other. God then restores Job's material prosperity to twice what it was before, blessing him with wealth, children, long life, and peace. So "Job died, an old man, and full of days" (Job 42:17).

Historical Issues in Job

The Origins of the Book of Job

Unlike certain other books of the Bible, about whose authorship there is little or no debate in the tradition, since ancient times readers have disagreed about when and how this book originated. For example, some ancient Jewish rabbis saw the book of Job as having been written by Moses,[2] whereas others attributed the book to one of the prophets or to Job himself—writing in the third person.[3] (By contrast, most modern scholars have taken an agnostic position, recognizing that there is no clear way to identify the author based on the evidence we possess. From this perspective, the book should be regarded as anonymous.)[4]

Given the problems with assigning the book an author, it is unsurprising that the date of the composition is widely disputed, with scholars proposing dates that range from the time of the patriarchs (ca. eighteenth century B.C.) all the

---

[2] Babylonian Talmud, *Baba Bathra* 14b, in Isidore Epstein, ed., *The Babylonian Talmud*, 35 vols. (London: Soncino, 1935–1952).

[3] Gregory the Great, *Moralia in Job* 1.1–2.

[4] Estes, *Handbook*, 11–14.

way to the late postexilic period (fourth century B.C.).[5] Whatever the exact time of composition, however, it is important to note that the events described by the book of Job are clearly set in the patriarchal period—that is, the second millennium B.C.[6] For example, Job is described as living the life of a tribal chieftain similar to Abraham, Isaac, and Jacob, whose wealth consists of cattle and servants (Job 1:3; 42:12; cf. Gen 12:16; 32:5); there is no special Levitical priesthood or centralized sanctuary cult, but Job himself acts as priest, offering sacrifice for his family (Job 1:5; 42:8); and Job's life-span of 140 years parallels the longevity of the patriarchs like Abraham, who lives 175 years (Job 42:16; cf. Gen 25:7).

In terms of literary unity, most scholars divide the work into two major parts: (1) the prose story of Job in the prologue and epilogue (Job 1–2; 42:7–17) and (2) the poetic speeches that constitute the body of the book (Job 3:1—42:6). These two compositions are often thought to have different dates. A very commonly expressed opinion is that the prose narrative is old (that is, preexilic), but the poems were composed in the Judean exile or later (post-587 B.C.) by an author struggling with the justice of God in light of the suffering of the Jews. While this is possible, the case for interpreting Job as a postexilic meditation on the suffering of Judah's exile is weak, for at least several reasons:

1. Job's situation and suffering are not really analogous to that of Judah: Job is sinless and is not part of the Mosaic covenant people of God; Judah was in a clearly defined covenant relationship, against which it continually offended by its habitual falls into idolatry (for example, Is 1, Jer 3).

2. The author of the book never attempts to connect the figure of Job with the distinctive issues of Israel and Judah's sufferings and historical situations. Not only are Israel and Judah never mentioned, but Job and his three friends are all non-Israelites: Edomites, Aramaens (Syrians), or Arabs. Thus, the book examines the relationship of man to God apart from the particular history of Israel.

3. In light of the despicable behavior of the Edomites toward the Judeans during the fall of Jerusalem and the Davidic monarchy (cf. Jer 49; Ezek 25:12–14; 35:15; 36:5; Joel 3:19; Amos 1:6, 9, 11; Obad; Mal 1:4), it would be highly unlikely—indeed, almost unthinkable—for a postexilic Jewish author or editor to choose an Edomite as the righteous suffering hero of his book and hold him up as a model of righteousness for the Jewish people![7]

4. In any event, there is no reference to anything identifiable with the Babylonian exile of Judah in the book. It is naïve to think that the sacred writers of Israel never struggled with theodicy or the problem of evil until the Babylonian exile and that any exploration of suffering must be related to the sufferings of Judah in the sixth century B.C. In fact, as recent scholarship has demonstrated, the most striking literary parallels to Job's image of a *righteous sufferer* come from ancient Near Eastern texts dating well back to the second millennium B.C.[8] Some examples of these are the following:

---

[5] Ibid., 13.

[6] Marvin H. Pope, *Job*, Anchor Bible 15 (New York: Doubleday, 1973), xxxi.

[7] Ibid., xxxiv.

[8] Izak Cornelius, "Job", in *The Minor Prophets: Job, Psalms, Proverbs, Ecclesiastes, Song of Songs*, vol. 5 of *Zondervan Illustrated Bible Backgrounds Commentary*, ed. John H. Walton (Grand Rapids, Mich.: Zondervan, 2009), 248–49.

Ancient Near Eastern Parallels to Job

Several very ancient wisdom texts from Mesopotamia also explore the issue of the suffering of the righteous and the justice of divinity. This example is from the second millennium B.C.:

> You have doled out to me suffering ever anew,
> I entered the house, heavy is the spirit,
> I, the young man, went out to the street, oppressed is the heart,
> With me, the valiant, my righteous shepherd has become angry, has looked upon me inimically,
> My herdsman has sought out evil forces against me who am not (his) enemy,
> My companion says not a true word to me, . . .
> (And) you, my god, do not thwart him,
> You carry off my understanding,
> The wicked has conspired against me
> Angered you, stormed about, planned evil.
> I, the wise, why am I bound to the ignorant youths?
> I, the discerning, why am I counted among the ignorant?
> Food is all about, (yet) my food is hunger,
> On the day shares were allotted to all, my allotted share was suffering.

—Sumerian wisdom text, *A Man and His God*, in James B. Pritchard, ed.
Ancient Near Eastern Texts, 3rd ed. (Princeton, N.J.: Princeton
University Press, 1969), 590, lines 30–45.

---

1. *Dialogue of a Man with His Soul* (Egyptian, ca. 2000–1600 B.C.)
2. *A Man and His God* (Sumerian, ca. 2000–1800 B.C.)
3. *Ludlul bel Nemeqi* (Akkadian, ca. 1700–1300 B.C.)
4. *Babylonian Theodicy* (Babylonian, ca. 1000 B.C.)

Whatever the date of its final composition, in terms of its literary genre, the closest parallels to the book of Job are from the ancient Near Eastern world of the second millennium B.C., not the postexilic (Second Temple) period.

The Hebrew Poetry of the Book of Job

The Hebrew of the poetic core of the book of Job is very difficult, some of the most difficult in the Bible. Some attribute this to the antiquity of the language, others to the use of a different dialect of Hebrew, still others simply to the peculiar diction of the author. The Hebrew of the prose portions, however, is clear, standard Biblical Hebrew. In light of these differences, it is possible, then, that the poetic and prose sections of the book were composed at different times and brought together to form the book as we know it. However, this is not certain, and the relative dating of the prose and poetic sections cannot be clearly determined. In the book as it stands, the prose and poetic sections presume one another and contribute to the dynamic quality and interest of the book. For example, without the prologue, we would not know that Job was actually righteous and would read the dialogues assuming that his friends were correct and that Job was a pompous, self-righteous "windbag". On the other hand, without the dialogues, the prose narrative would be a trite moral fable about bearing suffering in silence until God restores one's fortunes. In the final analysis, it is the tension between the prose and poetic sections of Job that gives the book its peculiar power as a profound theological exploration of the question of evil and the meaning of suffering.

Is Job a Historical Figure?

The book of Job is written, not in a historical genre, but as poetic drama investigating one of the central philosophical and theological questions of human life: the question of suffering. In light of this, the theological message of the book does not hinge on the historicity of the events described.

Nonetheless, it is important to note that the Jewish and Christian tradition has always assumed that Job was a real person, the broad outlines of whose life have been dramatized in the book. For example, the figure of Job is referred to in both the Old and New Testaments, with specific reference to the virtues that he manifests in both the prologue and body of the book:

> The word of the LORD came to me.... "Even if these three men, Noah, Daniel, and Job, were in it [the land of Judah], they would deliver but their own lives by their *righteousness*, says the Lord GOD." (Ezek 14:12, 14)

> You have heard of *the steadfastness of Job*, and you have seen the purpose of the Lord, how the Lord is compassionate and merciful. (Jas 5:11)

Significantly, such testimony did not lead to any agreement in the rabbinic tradition about exactly when the figure of Job lived. For example, some ancient Jewish rabbis regarded Job as having lived at the time of the patriarchs,[9] often identifying him with "Jobab" the king of Edom, grandson of Esau and great-great-grandson of Abraham himself (Gen 36:33).[10] However, other ancient rabbis believed that Job lived at the time of Moses,[11] while still others believed him to be one of the people who returned to the land of Israel after the Babylonian exile.[12]

Given everything we have seen so far, there is no reason in principle to deny that a certain man named Job lived in antiquity whose righteousness and sufferings were legendary and became the basis for the powerful poetic drama contained in the book. If this is the case, it would not be unlike the way in which the English poet Shakespeare adopted the lives of historical figures such as Julius Caesar, Anthony and Cleopatra, and various English kings as the basis for his plays.

Theological Issues in Job

Job as a New Adam

In the canonical chronology of human history, Job appears to be a contemporary of the patriarchs, who (unlike them) is not the recipient of the Abrahamic

---

[9] Babylonian Talmud, *Baba Bathra* 15b.
[10] Cf. Pope, *Job*, xxx.
[11] Babylonian Talmud, *Sanhedrin* 106a, *Sotah* 11a.
[12] Babylonian Talmud, *Baba Bathra* 15a.

covenant but operates only under the covenant with Adam that was renewed after the Flood, in damaged form, with Noah and encompasses all Noah's descendants (cf. Gen 8–9). From this point of view, Job is, in a sense, a kind of new Adam, whose life experience recapitulates that of the first man:

Adam	*Job*
1. "Be fruitful and multiply" (Gen 1:28)	1. Seven sons and three daughters (Job 1:2–3, 10)
2. Both priest and king; has "dominion" and works in the Garden of Eden (Gen 1:27–28; Gen 2:15)	2. Both priest and king; offers sacrifice for others; rules over whole region (Job 1:5; 29:25)
3. Tested by the serpent to call into question God's goodness (Gen 3:4–7)	3. Tested by the Satan to call into question God's goodness (Job 1:6—2:10)
4. Tempted by the voice of his wife to disobey God and "die" (Gen 3:12)	4. Tempted by the voice of his wife to "curse God, and die" (Job 2:9–10)

By depicting Job as a new Adam, the sacred author suggests that even after the Fall, not everyone is condemned to repeat Adam's fateful decision to rupture his relationship with God when faced with evil and suffering. There is a path of fidelity, blazed by Job, that accepts the testing of Satanic forces in the world while maintaining communion with God, even while protesting injustice and holding out hope for ultimate vindication.

The Satanic Test of Job

In order to understand the theological drama of Job, it is necessary to ponder what is at stake in Satan's accusations to God and testing of Job. Satan's central accusation is, "Does Job fear God for nothing?" (Job 1:9). In other words, Satan claims Job does not love God for God's own sake, but that Job loves God *instrumentally*, in order to derive temporal goods and material benefits from him. Job's apparent love of God is actually just a form of self-interest or self-love in disguise.

While this accusation obviously impugns Job and his motivation in serving God, it also is an implicit detraction of God. God, apparently, is not lovable in himself. Satan implies that if God did not "buy off" his friends through temporal blessings, he would not have any friends at all.

In this way, the Satanic accusation is actually a cynical critique of the entire relationship between God and human beings (Job 1:9–12). While to all appearances it is a relationship of mutual fidelity and generosity, where Job eagerly serves God and God generously blesses Job, from the perspective of "the Accuser" (Hebrew *hashatan*), in reality, it is nothing but a sham. Job serves God only to get material gain, and God is so pathetically unlovable that he would have no friends if he did not win them through material goods, as he has "bought" Job.

Therefore, the central theological question raised by the opening chapters of Job concerns the integrity of the relationship between God and man. Is it possible for man to serve God disinterestedly, purely for God's sake and not for the sake of temporal gain? And reciprocally, is God worthy of service in himself, for his innate goodness and not merely for the blessings he bestows? Thus the reputation of *both* Job *and* God is at stake in the drama that follows. In the end, Satan is proven wrong: Job remains faithful to God despite being bereft of benefits, demonstrating the integrity of the relationship between God and his creature, one that it is not based merely on cynical self-interest.

Four Answers to the Problem of Evil

The problem of evil is obviously a central issue in the book of Job. One way to state the problem is this: If God is both all-good and all-powerful, why do bad things happen to good people? Significantly, the book provides, not just one answer to the problem, but several. In particular, four stand out.[13]

1. First and foremost, the book of Job clearly teaches that *not all suffering is the direct punishment of personal sin*. In making this point, Job clearly rejects the answer to the problem of evil mouthed by his three friends, who continue to insist that his sufferings do, in fact, follow a strict view of "retribution theology". In other words, they deny that bad things ever happen to good people. Job and the sacred author of the book both realize that this simplistic answer is inadequate and does not correspond to the reality of human experience, in which the innocent often not only suffer, but suffer such horror and tragedy as to call into question the justice of God.

2. Second, and equally important, the book of Job insists that *in some cases, suffering and death are caused by the malevolent actions of evil spirits like Satan*. In stark contrast to a modern secular world view, in which invisible spiritual forces either do not exist or have no real power over human beings, the book of Job insists that there are other personal agents in reality besides God and human beings, some of whom are evil. In other words, bad things happen to good people, not because God directly wills it as a punishment for their sins, but because of the activity of these evil agents, especially Satan.

Of course, as soon as we say this, it must be conceded that this explanation is not completely adequate: it shifts the framing of the question of evil, but it does not provide a final answer. It allows us to say that evil is not *directly willed* by God; nonetheless, in the book of Job, he does *permit* it. Indeed, as we saw above, God even seems to invite it by calling Satan to "consider" Job and his righteousness (Job 1:8). Hence, later theology will go on to make a distinction between God's *active* and *permissive* will. Indeed, the book of Job itself is emphatic that evil takes place only by God's permission (Job 1:12; 2:6); thus, Job regards his sufferings as being the responsibility of God (Job 2:10), and God, in fact, accepts ultimate responsibility (Job 2:3). Nonetheless, the fact that God permits evil remains a problem.

3. Third, the book of Job insists that *God uses suffering to test the faith of human beings, strengthen their holiness, and lead them to a love that is selfless*. In this way,

---

[13] Cf. Estes, *Handbook*, 26–28.

evil itself can become the means of testing the integrity of a human being's relationship to God. The implication is: without righteous suffering, it would never be proven that an individual's love for God was genuine rather than mere self-interest. This explanation for evil is never withdrawn in the course of the book. The sacred author regards it as a valid, if not exhaustive, answer for the problem of innocent human suffering.

Of course, to say that evil or suffering is a divine test does not resolve all issues. Other questions remain. Any individual sufferer may rightly ask, "Why me and not some other person? Why am *I* chosen as a test case for mankind?" Moreover, one can question the degree and severity of the suffering: "In order to prove my fidelity, is it really necessary that I suffer *so much?*" Or again: "Since God knows my heart by his omniscience and knows the outcome in advance, why does he submit me or anyone else to the test of suffering?"

4. Fourth, the book of Job ends by asserting that, in the final analysis, *mere human beings lack the capacity to evaluate divine justice.* This is the answer provided by Elihu near the end of his intervention and in the divine speeches that bring the book to its climax (Job 39–42). As noted in the above, God's challenges to Job (concerning Job's lack of knowledge or control over all the aspects of the universe for which God is responsible) appear on initial reading to be a "shock and awe" strategy on God's part, to overpower Job rather than actually to address his questions. However, on further reflection, God's challenges to Job *do* constitute an answer to Job's questioning of the justice of God: God is pointing out that, in order adequately to assess whether God is justified in his providential guidance of any particular event, Job would have to be a much different being—a being like God himself, able to comprehend (and guide) all the factors that interact and must be taken into account as cosmic history moves forward. While not addressing Job's particular case, God is implying that there are factors beyond Job's comprehension that provide the rationale for innocent suffering. Whether the reader is satisfied with this response depends on whether the reader trusts or distrusts God to be speaking truthfully on this subject. Job, for his part, adopts the posture of trust and is shown to have been right in the epilogue that follows (Job 42:10–17).

Redemption, Afterlife, and the Vision of God

An important factor within the discussion of the problem of evil and theodicy is the reality of life after death. If this present life is not all that there is, perhaps some of the evils suffered in this life are justified because they are linked to some benefit in the next.

The reality of the resurrection and life everlasting is only slowly revealed in the Old Testament, coming into clearer focus in the chronologically later books. Job typically reflects a pessimistic view about the afterlife but also contains a theme of hope for a future resurrection and vision of God that will satisfy the heart wounded by the evils of this world.

In keeping with the passionate and poetic nature of the monologues and dialogues, Job is not consistent about his stance toward the afterlife. In one breath, he describes it as a place of rest preferable to suffering on earth (Job 3:13), in another, as a place of gloomy non-existence from which there is no return (Job 7:7–10; 10:21–22; 14: 11:11–12; 16:22). Yet at another time, he expresses the hope that his stay in Sheol will be temporary, until he is called forth again (Job 14:13–17); and in a famous and controversial passage, he expresses confidence that in the future he will somehow see God directly in his present body:

> For I know that my Redeemer lives,
>   and at last he will stand upon the earth;
> and after my skin has been thus destroyed,
>   *then from my flesh I shall see God,*
> whom I shall see on my side,
>   *and my eyes shall behold, and not another.* (Job 19:25–27)

This expectation of Job is actually fulfilled, of course, when God appears to him in a theophany toward the close of the book (Job 38:1—42:6). Thus the vision of God is a profound theme in Job: in the midst of his suffering, Job expresses the wish to see God (Job 19:25–27)—that is, to be restored to communion with him; and Job is finally satisfied and drops his case when he gains the sight of God:

> I had heard of you by the hearing of the ear,
>   *but now my eye sees you.*
> therefore I despise myself,
>   and repent in dust and ashes. (Job 42:5)

It is extremely significant that Job drops his "court case" against God at the *vision of God*, and *not only after his temporal goods are restored* (cf. Job 42:10–17). This reveals that the central struggle for Job during his period of suffering is not the loss of his children and property—horrible and tragic as those are—but the experience of alienation from God. In the final analysis, it is this experience of being abandoned by God that draws out of Job his deepest longing—for the vision of God and the communion that vision makes possible. Job expresses the same longing as Moses on Mount Sinai, when he cries: "I beg you, show me your glory!" (Ex 33:18), and as King David in the Psalms, when he sings: "When shall I come and behold the face of God?" (Ps 42:2).

Job in the Living Tradition

Given the universal experience of human suffering and the universal human love for drama, it is not surprising that Job has been, and continues to be, one of the most widely read books in the Old Testament. Given its theological and philo-sophical character, it has merited the attention of many writers, saints, and theo-logians in the living tradition who see in it the beginnings of an answer to the problem of evil that will only ultimately be answered through the suffering, death, and Resurrection of Christ.

The Passion of Job and the Passion of Christ

Above all, the story of Job's *innocent* suffering at the hands of Satan and by divine permission has been viewed in the living tradition of the Church as a kind of prefiguration of the sufferings of the perfectly innocent one— Jesus Christ.

For example, in the fourth-century A.D. writings of Zeno, bishop of Verona, we find this striking comparison between the passion of Job and the Passion of Jesus:

> *Is Job a type of Christ?* If I am right, he is, and the comparison will reveal the truth of my claim. . . . We may compare Job and Christ in many ways. *As Job was tempted by the devil three times, so too Christ was tempted three times.* The Lord set aside his riches out of love for us and chose poverty so that we might become rich, while Job lost all that he possessed. A violent wind killed Job's sons, while the sons of God, the prophets, were killed by the fury of the Pharisees. *Job became ulcerated and disfigured, while the Lord, by becoming man, took on the defilement of the sins committed by all mankind.* The wife of Job tempted him to sin, much as the synagogue tried to force the Lord to yield to corrupt leadership. Thus he was insulted by the priests, the servants of his altar, as Job was insulted by his friends. And as Job sat on a dunghill of worms, so all the evil of the world is really a dunghill which became the Lord's dwelling place, while men that abound in every sort of crime and base desire are really worms.
>
> *The restoration of health and riches to Job prefigures the resurrection, which gives health and eternal life to those who believe in Christ.* Regaining lordship over all the world, Christ says: "All things have been given to me by my Father." And just as Job fathered sons, so too did Christ, for the apostles, the sons of the Lord, succeeded the prophets. Job died happily and in peace, but there is no death for the Lord. He is praised forever, just as he was before time began, and as he always will be as time continues and moves into eternity.[14]

In this striking exposition of the life of Job, Zeno considers Job's sufferings a virtual death, a descent into Hades and Sheol, from which he is "resurrected" when he sees God (Job 38:1–42:6), is vindicated, and his fortunes restored (Job 42:7–12).

According to this typological interpretation of the book, we see that the ultimate answer to the problem of evil posed by Job will only be given when the innocent Christ takes the sufferings of the whole world upon himself on Calvary in order both to deliver mankind from suffering and death and to lead them to the resurrection of the dead and the vision of God, for which righteous Job longs in his plea for divine justice. Such typology drives home the point that there is no simple one-to-one correspondence between the gravity of our sins and the apparent gravity of the temporal suffering that we receive here on earth. For no one has ever suffered like Jesus Christ suffered, and yet he is the most innocent of all. Indeed, seeing Jesus as a new Job reveals exactly why God may

---

[14] Zeno of Verona, *Tractate* 15.2, in J. P. Migne, *Patrologia Latina* 11.441–43, from the Office of Readings for the Eighth Week in Ordinary Time, *The Liturgy of the Hours* (New York: Catholic Book Publishing, 1975), 3:285–86.

permit certain evils or forms of suffering, because from them he draws out and makes possible a greater good.

On the other hand, there are significant elements of discontinuity between Job and Jesus. Job does not know why he is suffering and undergoes the experience unwillingly; whereas Jesus knows precisely why he must suffer and enters "willingly into his Passion".[15] In Job, the redemptive value of suffering is not yet clear, and the resurrection is only dimly anticipated; whereas in Christ these realities are crystal clear and radically transform the experience of suffering for the believer. Finally, whereas Job's sufferings leave him feeling alienated from God, the sufferings of the disciple of Jesus bond him more closely in communion with Christ crucified. Thus, the Cross is a major advance in dealing with the problem of evil and theodicy, permitting some of the questions left open in Job to be resolved and providing greater spiritual resources for coping with the experience of evil than were available to Job and others living prior to the New Covenant.

Behemoth, Leviathan, and the Figure of Satan

One of the most mysterious aspects of the book of Job is its unforgettable and lengthy description of the two creatures—"Behemoth" (Job 40:15–24) and "Leviathan" (Job 41:1–34)—that constitute the climax of a litany of beasts and birds that are beyond Job's ability to explain (see Job 38:4—40:15). Contemporary scholarship continues to debate whether Behemoth and Leviathan are intended to represent actual animals or whether they are mythological creatures symbolizing evil.[16] Intriguingly, a similar debate seems to have taken place in the early Church on through the early Middle Ages, as reflected in the writings of Eastern Fathers such as Ephrem the Syrian (fourth century A.D.) and Isho'dad of Merv (ninth century A.D.):

> The Behemoth is a dragon, that is, a land animal, just as the Leviathan is an aquatic sea animal.[17]

> The Behemoth is a dragon without equal. The Interpreter [= Theodore of Mopsuestia] calls it "an imaginary dragon" that the author [of Job] has poetically invented by himself.... In the whole creation, he says, there is no animal that is unique and not male or female, because all animals have been created in pairs. On the other hand, those who assert that this book was written by the divine Moses maintain the reality of the Behemoth. *It is a figure of Satan, they say, and as this animal destroys everything it sees, so Satan does the same thing secretly....* Both in its name and in its action it is the figure of Satan, because, according to the sense of the word, Behemoth means "through it death", that is, death has entered among people through it. But the Jews assert that it is an ox, and, some day they will eat it and the Leviathan as well when they come back.[18]

---

[15] Eucharistic Prayer II, from *Daily Roman Missal*, ed. James Socias, 3rd ed. (Woodridge, Ill.: Midwest Theological Forum, 2010), xx.

[16] Pope, *Job*, 270–79.

[17] Ephrem the Syrian, *Commentary on Job* 40.15, in *Job*, ed. Manlio Simonetti and Marco Conti, Old Testament 6, Ancient Christian Commentary on Scripture, ed. Thomas C. Oden (Downers Grove, Ill.: IVP Academic, 2006), 209.

[18] Isho'dad of Merv, *Commentary on Job* 40.10 (15), in Simonetti and Conti, *Job*, 209.

Such comments provide us an important window into the patristic and medieval hermeneutic of letter and spirit, whereby virtually every aspect of the Old Testament was viewed as having both a literal signification and a typological or spiritual meaning.

The Book of Job and the Doctrine of Providence

In addition to the typological value of the figure of Job, the book was also cherished for the significant contribution it makes to the doctrine of providence—that is, the way in which we understand God's sovereignty over creation and history and how he guides all things to a good end: namely, himself. For example, in the Middle Ages, Saint Thomas Aquinas chose the book of Job as the object of one of his most detailed scriptural commentaries and has this to say about its role in the canon:

> This opinion [that all things are governed by chance] ... is found to be especially harmful to the human race, for *if divine providence is taken away, no reverence for or fear of God based on truth will remain among men.* Anyone can discern easily enough how great an apathy toward virtue and a proneness to vice follow from this condition.... For this reason, the first and most important concern of those who pursued wisdom in a divine spirit for the instruction of others was to remove this belief from the hearts of men. Therefore, after the giving of the Law and the Prophets, the Book of Job is placed first in the number of the Hagiographa, that is, the books written wisely through the Spirit of God for the instruction of men, the whole intention of which turns on showing through plausible arguments that human affairs are ruled by divine providence.[19]

This is a remarkable insight into the canonical function of Job. Aquinas rightly recognizes that before people can be led to the praise of God and the pursuit of wisdom found in the Psalter and Solomonic literature, one must first deal with the question of why there is suffering and whether a God who permits such suffering is indeed just and worthy of praise. In modern times, in which the doctrine of providence has been very much eclipsed by a secular world view that attributes all things to chance, the book of Job continues to have a key role to play in the living tradition.

Job as a "Righteous Gentile" and the Noahic Covenant

Intriguingly, the recent *Catechism of the Catholic Church* singles out the figure of Job as an example of certain Gentiles in the Old Testament who demonstrate the righteousness and holiness that can be attained by non-Israelites who live according to the universal covenant made by God with mankind at the time of Noah:

> The Bible venerates several great figures among the Gentiles: Abel the just, the king-priest, Melchizedek—a figure of Christ—and the upright "Noah, Daniel,

---

[19] Thomas Aquinas, *The Literal Exposition on Job: A Scriptural Commentary concerning Divine Providence*, trans. Anthony Damico and Martin D. Yaffe, Classics in Religious Studies 7 (Atlanta: Scholars Press, 1989), 68.

and Job" [Ezek 14:14]. Scripture thus expresses *the heights of sanctity that can be reached by those who live according to the covenant of Noah*, waiting for Christ to "gather into one the children of God who are scattered abroad." (*CCC* 58 [emphasis added])

This is a fascinating exposition of Job's significance within the broader history of salvation: he represents those "righteous Gentiles" who demonstrate that, though God has bound salvation to the covenant with Abraham, the previous covenant with Noah remains in force among all peoples of the world, calling them to righteousness, holiness, and the fear of the Lord demonstrated by Job the Edomite.

Is Suffering Always the Result of Personal Sin?

Last, but certainly not least, there is the question of how suffering relates to sin. Indeed, one of the most pressing and universal issues that arises in the course of human life is the question: "Why am I suffering so much? Is God punishing me for my sins?"

In his teaching on the Christian meaning of human suffering, Pope Saint John Paul II used the book of Job as an inspired example of the fact that not all suffering is the direct result of a person's sins. Like Job before them, the innocent can and do experience suffering:

> A judgement that views suffering exclusively as a punishment for sin runs counter to love for man. This had appeared already in the case of Job's "comforters" who accuse him with arguments based on a conception of justice devoid of any opening to love (cf. Job 4ff.). One sees it still better in the case of the man born blind: "Who sinned, this man or his parents, that he was born blind?" (Jn 9:2). It is like pointing the finger against someone. It is a judgement which passes from suffering seen as a physical torment, to that understood as a punishment for sin: someone must have sinned, either the man in question or his parents. It is a moral imputation: he suffers, therefore he must be guilty.
>
> To put an end to this petty and unjust way of thinking, it was necessary to reveal in its essential profundity the mystery of the suffering of the Innocent One, the Holy One, the "Man of Sorrows!" Ever since Christ chose the Cross and died on Golgotha, all who suffer, especially those who suffer without fault, can come face to face with the "Holy One who suffers", and find in his passion *the complete truth about suffering*, its full meaning and its importance.
>
> In the light of this truth, all those who suffer can feel called to share in the work of Redemption accomplished by means of the Cross.[20]

Perhaps more than any other aspect of Job, it is the insistent message of the book that sin and suffering do not always have a direct causal relationship that has the power to speak to every human being that has ever experienced the feeling of being abandoned or punished by God in the midst of suffering.

---

[20]John Paul II, "The Meaning of Suffering in the Light of Christ's Passion", nos. 6–7, General Audience of November 9, 1988; in *L'Osservatore Romano*, November 14, 1988, p. 23.

The Book of Job in the Lectionary

In the Church's liturgy, Job is primarily remembered as a model of the righteous person near to death. Several texts from Job are offered for use during the sacrament of the anointing of the sick to express the anguish that the suffering person experiences as death approaches. The most-used text for Church rites associated with death, however, is Job's expression of confidence in the existence of a Redeemer and the prospect of seeing God in his (apparently resurrected) flesh (Job 19:23–27). Thus, the hope of Job lives on in the heart of the Church. He is one of the first of God's faithful in history to anticipate the resurrection and the beatific vision of God.

Readings from Job for Sundays, Feast Days, Liturgical Seasons, and Other Occasions *MSO* = Masses for Special Occasions; *OM* = Optional Memorial; *VM* = Votive Mass; *Rit* = Ritual			
Passage	Description	Occasion	Explanation
3:1–3	Job curses the day of his birth.	*Rit*: Anointing of the Sick, opt. 2	Job's bitterness provides words to express the agony of the dying believer.
7:1–4, 6–7	Job bemoans the suffering and transience of his life.	*5th Sun. in OT (B)*	Job's words describe the physical suffering so characteristic of human life; the Gospel (Mk 1:29–39) describes Jesus' healing ministry, in which he alleviates many forms of the suffering Job bemoans. Jesus is the answer to the problem of human suffering.
7:1–4, 6–11	See above. Plus, Job complains in bitterness of soul.	*Rit*: Anointing of the Sick, opt. 3	Job provides words to express the suffering of the dying believer.
7:12–21	Job complains bitterly of God's afflictions on him, and asks for pardon of sins.	*Rit*: Anointing of the Sick, opt. 4	See above.
19:23–27a	Job expresses confidence in his Redeemer and in the hope of seeing God in his flesh.	*Rit*: Anointing of the Sick, opt. 5; Viaticum, opt. 2; Mass for the Dead, opt. 2	Job's famous expression of confidence in a redeemer and the beatific vision articulate the hope of the Christian who dies in the arms of the Church.
31:16–20, 24–25, 31–32	Job curses himself if he has not carried out works of mercy, such as clothing the naked and feeding the hungry.	*MSO*: For the Country, City, Public Officers, etc., opt. 7; For Famine, opt. 2	Job enumerates the works of social justice, reminding public leaders of their responsibilities toward the weak and vulnerable of society.

(continued)

Readings from Job for Sundays, Feast Days, Liturgical Seasons, and Other Occasions (*continued*)			
MSO = Masses for Special Occasions; *OM* = Optional Memorial; *VM* = Votive Mass; *Rit* = Ritual			
Passage	Description	Occasion	Explanation
38:1, 8–11	God challenges Job, whether he can control the sea as God does.	*12th Sun. in OT (B)*	The reading from Job emphasizes that none but God can control the sea; in the Gospel (Mk 4:35–41), Jesus calms the storm on the Sea of Galilee, demonstrating his divinity.

In the celebration of the daily Eucharist, the Twenty-Sixth Week in Ordinary Time is dedicated to meditating on Job in the first readings. The readings selected suffice to convey some of the narrative arc of the book: the Satanic test, Job's lament, his famous expression of hope (Job 19:21–27), his final encounter with God, and the restoration of his fortunes. The three friends and their speeches, however, never appear in the readings selected for Mass:

Reading of Job for Daily Mass: Ordinary Time, Year II: Week 26		
Day	Passage Read	Description
M	Job 1:6–22	The first test of Job; Job does not "sin or charge God with wrong".
Tu	Job 3:1–3, 11–17, 20–23	Job curses the day of his birth and wishes for death.
W	Job 9:1–12, 14–16	Job feels like God is against him and is too exalted and powerful to pay attention to Job's grievances.
Th	Job 19:21–27	Job expresses confidence that he has a redeemer and will one day see God face to face.
F	Job 38:1, 12–21; 40:3–5	God points out the limitations of Job's knowledge, and Job acknowledges his ignorance.
Sa	Job 42:1–3, 5–6, 12–17	God restores Job's fortunes, and he dies "an old man, and full of days".

Extensive selections from Job are read in the Office of Readings during the Eighth and Ninth Weeks of Ordinary Time. These scriptural readings are carefully paired with appropriate complementary passages from the Fathers, especially Saint Gregory the Great's *Moral Commentary on Job* (the *Moralia*) and Saint Augustine's *Confessions*. Augustine's *Confessions* are typically paired with those passages of Job in which the holy patriarch speaks in the first person, lamenting and pouring out his soul to God, and Saint Gregory's *Moralia* complement the less introspective passages.

Conclusion

The book of Job is a drama based on the life of a holy man in antiquity whose righteous sufferings became legendary. The central issues of the book are the problem of evil and theodicy (the justice of God). The book rejects the view that all suffering and evil are the direct result of personal sin, proposing instead that one reason for the presence evil is to test the integrity of the relationship between God and man. Beyond that, the book ultimately asserts that human beings are not in a position to judge God's justice or reasons for permitting evil, since to be adequate, such a calculus would have to include a comprehensive evaluation of the governance of the cosmos, including all its interacting elements, which is beyond the cognitive capacity of mankind. Therefore a posture of humble trust in the midst of suffering, modeled by Job in his replies to the divine speeches, is the best approach to the reality of evil in the world.

Job represents the best treatment of the problem of evil possible prior to the revelation of Jesus Christ. Obviously, the Passion, death, and Resurrection of Christ mark the definitive advance in our ability to understand the role of suffering and evil within the plan of salvation. Certain passages in Job reflect a hope or anticipation of a Redeemer, a resurrection, an afterlife, and a final vision of God. Dimly seen in Job, these realities are fully revealed only in the New Testament.

For Further Reading

Commentaries and Studies on Job

Estes, Daniel J. *Handbook on the Wisdom Books and Psalms.* Grand Rapids, Mich.: Baker Academic, 2005. (See pp. 11–139.)

Fyall, Robert S. *Now My Eyes Have Seen You: Images of Creation and Evil in the Book of Job.* New Studies in Biblical Theology 12. Downers Grove, Ill.: InterVarsity Press, 2002.

Murphy, Roland E. *The Book of Job: A Short Reading.* New York: Paulist Press, 1999.

———. *The Tree of Life: An Exploration of the Biblical Wisdom Literature.* 3rd ed. Grand Rapids, Mich.: Eerdmans, 2002. (See pp. 33–48.)

Newsom, Carol A. "The Book of Job". Pages 319–637 in vol. 4 of *New Interpreter's Bible.* Nashville: Abingdon Press, 1996.

Perdue, Leo G., and W. Clark Gilpin, eds. *The Voice from the Whirlwind: Interpreting the Book of Job.* Nashville: Abingdon Press, 1992.

Pope, Marvin H. *Job.* Anchor Bible 15. New York: Doubleday, 1973.

Historical Questions and the Book of Job

Cornelius, Izak. "Job". Pages 246–315 in *The Minor Prophets, Job, Psalms, Proverbs, Ecclesiastes, Song of Songs.* Vol. 5 of *Zondervan Illustrated Bible Backgrounds Commentary.* Edited by John H. Walton. Grand Rapids, Mich.: Zondervan, 2009.

Job in the Living Tradition

Aquinas, Saint Thomas. *The Literal Exposition on Job: A Scriptural Commentary concerning Divine Providence.* Translated by Anthony Damico and Martin D. Yaffe. Classics in Religious Studies 7. Atlanta: Scholars Press, 1989.

Gregory the Great, Saint. *Moralia in Job: Or Morals on the Book of Job.* 3 vols. Ex Fontibus, 2012.

Simonetti, Manlio, and Marco Conti. *Job.* Old Testament 6 of Ancient Christian Commentary on Scripture. Edited by Thomas C. Oden. Downers Grove, Ill.: IVP Academic, 2006.

24. PSALMS

Introduction

The book of Psalms, often called the Psalter, is a book unlike any other. A collection of 150 sacred prayers and songs, the Psalter is longer, more frequently quoted in the New Testament, and more extensively read in the Lectionary than any other Old Testament book. Since the time of the Church Fathers, if not before, it has been considered a summary of the teaching of the entire Old Testament, or even all of divine revelation, together with a comprehensive description of all the states of the soul in the presence of God. Forming the basis of the Liturgy of the Hours and used extensively in the Eucharistic liturgy as well the rites of other sacraments, the Psalms continue to be the living heartbeat of the Church's prayer to the present day. Indeed, for those Christians who pray the Liturgy of the Hours, an understanding of the Psalms is essential (cf. *CCC* 1176).

The title "Psalms" comes from the Greek word for a "song" (Greek *psalmos*) often used to translate the Hebrew "song, melody" (Hebrew *mizmor*). This Hebrew word is derived from the verbal root *zamar*, meaning "to make music", almost always in the context of worship. Significantly, in one ancient manuscript of the Greek Septuagint (Alexandrinus), the title of the book is the "Psalter", taken from the word for a "stringed instrument" (Greek *psalterion*), which is sometimes used to translate the Hebrew word "lyre" (Hebrew *kinnor*). This title emphasizes that the sacred songs contained in the Psalter were, by and large, intended to be sung with the accompaniment of the kind of stringed instruments that were used in the Temple. In other copies of the Septuagint, the book was entitled simply *Psalmoi*, "Psalms", and in the Latin Vulgate, as the *Liber Psalmorum* ("Book of Psalms"). By contrast, in the Jewish tradition, the book is known simply as the "Praises" (Hebrew *tehillim*), ultimately from the verbal root "to praise" (Hebrew *halal*), which focuses less on the instrumental nature of the songs than on their role in the liturgical worship of God. Indeed, the book ends in a climactic expression of praise to God (Ps 145–50).

The book of Psalms is held as canonical in all Jewish and Christian traditions, although in the first century, the Sadducees and the Samaritans apparently did not accept it as inspired. The high regard in which the Psalms were held by most Jewish contemporaries of Jesus is indicated by the extensive quotation of the Psalter in the New Testament, usually in a prophetic or messianic sense.

Literary Characteristics of the Psalms

The Techniques of Hebrew Poetry

All of the psalms are Hebrew poetry, not prose. In contrast to classical English poetry, Hebrew poetry does not rhyme. As for rhythm, it is likely that it did have some metrical pattern in antiquity, but there is no modern scholarly consensus on how to scan the meter of the psalms.

More than rhyme or rhythm, the essential characteristic of Hebrew poetry is *parallelism of thought* between two or three poetic lines. These lines are known as *cola* (singular *colon*). The typical base unit of a Hebrew poem is a *bicola*, a pair of lines exhibiting some form of parallelism. Of the various forms of parallelism utilized in the Psalter, the following are the most significant for its proper interpretation:

1. *Synonymous Parallelism*: this occurs when the lines of a bicola express the same or a similar meaning in two different forms, such as in Psalm 2:

> Why do the nations conspire
>   and the peoples plot in vain? (Ps 2:1)

2. *Antithetical Parallelism*: this takes place when the idea or meaning expressed in the first line is contrasted or inverted in the second, such as the following:

> For the LORD knows the way of the righteous,
>   but the way of the wicked will perish. (Ps 1:6)

3. *Synthetic Parallelism*: this is said to occur whenever the second line completes, expands, or further illuminates in various ways the meaning expressed in the first line. Within this broad category, scholars have proposed various more precise subcategories, such as *complementary parallelism*, when the second line completes the thought of the first, such as the following:

> I have set my king
>   on Zion, my holy mountain. (Ps 2:6)

There is also *staircase parallelism*, when the following line builds on or augments the idea of the first, such as here:

> Ascribe to the LORD, O sons of God,
>   ascribe to the LORD glory and strength.
> Ascribe to the LORD the glory of his name. (Ps 29:1–2)

In addition, there is *emblematic parallelism*, when one line states an idea plainly, and the other conveys the same via a symbol, image, simile, or metaphor:

> As a father pities his children,
>   so the LORD pities those who fear him. (Ps 103:13)

While the *bicola* dominates Hebrew poetry, occasionally a single line will stand alone (*monocolon*), or the author will employ a three-line *tricola*. A tricola slows the rhythm of the poem and gives it a solemn feel. Psalm 1 begins with a monocolon followed by a stately tricola:

Blessed is the man
who walks not in the counsel of the wicked,
nor stands in the way of sinners,
nor sits in the seat of scoffers. (Ps 1:1)

This tricola displays synonymous parallelism, although there is a progression of meaning: the sequence "walk"—"stand"—"sit" shows increasing comfort in the company of evildoers.

Hebrew poetry also displays a wide variety of literary devices and structures beyond these basic ones; the interested reader will find suggestions for further study of the subject at the end of this chapter.

The Literary Genres of the Psalms

The psalms display great diversity of subject matter and style. Many scholars have expended a great deal of effort in developing systems of categorizing the psalms on the basis of formal characteristics as well as content. Many of these systems of classification are too precise and technical to be helpful for most students. Here we will present only the more basic genres:

1. *Lament Psalms*: The most common genre of psalm is the lament. The lament is a cry or petition to God to come to the aid of the psalmist, who is suffering some form of distress. The most common forms of distress are physical illness, false accusation, and persecution from enemies, and not infrequently all three (for example, Ps 22, 38). The lament may include the following elements:

1. A description of the distress the psalmist experiences
2. A cry/petition to God for deliverance
3. Either an assertion of innocence or a confession of sin
4. An appeal for judgment on the evildoer(s)/persecutor(s)
5. A vow or promise to give thanks and/or offer sacrifice after deliverance
6. An expression of confidence that God has heard or will hear the psalmist's plea

Scholars distinguish individual laments from community laments. The largest concentration of individual laments are to be found in book 1 of the Psalter (Ps 1–41), and almost all are attributed to David, who seems to be especially associated with this genre. Communal laments are much less common in the Psalter; book 3 (Ps 73–89) contains the largest concentration of them.

2. *Thanksgiving or "Todah" Psalms*: Thanksgiving psalms, also called "*todah* psalms" (from the Hebrew word *todah* meaning "praise" or "thanksgiving") are the positive complement to the laments. If laments were prayed when in distress, prior to God's act of deliverance, *todah* psalms were performed afterward in gratitude to God. A *todah* psalm may include the following elements:

1. Expression(s) of praise/thanks to God
2. A recitation of the distress from which God delivered the psalmist

3. Affirmation(s) of the virtues (mercy, forgiveness, fidelity, and so on) of the Lord

4. Resolution(s) to perform the sacrifices vowed when in distress

5. Exhortation(s) for others to join in the psalmist's praise

Like laments, *todah* psalms may be in the voice of an individual (for example, Ps 66, 116, 118) or of the whole community (Ps 107). Significantly, some psalms combine both a lament with its corresponding *todah*, so that the psalm makes a complete cycle from lament to praise (for example, Ps 22, 28, 31, 56, 69, 71). We would classify these "complete" psalms as examples of the *todah* genre— see the discussion below under "Historical Issues in the Psalms." More rarely, a psalm will begin in thanksgiving but end as a lament (for example, Ps 9, 40). Such psalms correspond to an occasion in which the psalmist experiences salvation from one crisis but still faces other threats.

3. *Hymns*: Hymns are similar to thanksgiving psalms but may be distinguished by their more general or comprehensive nature. Whereas a thanksgiving/*todah* psalm typically thanks God for a specific act of deliverance, hymns praise God in a more general way, either for his innate attributes or his goodness displayed in creation or his fidelity to Israel throughout the history of salvation. Hymns vacillate between recounting the various praiseworthy perfections or virtues of the Lord in the *indicative* and issuing exhortations to praise the Lord in the *imperative*. Some hymns lay the stress either on the *indicative* (for example, Ps 65, 103) or on the *imperative* (for example, Ps 150), but most include both. Scholars have noted that the laments far outnumber the *todah* psalms within the Psalter, even though these two genres are clearly complementary. It may be, however, that the general nature of the hymns allowed them to be pressed into service as substitutes for the *todah*, so that the ancient worshipper, who had taken upon his lips one or more of the laments when in distress, may have employed one or more of the hymns in lieu of a formal *todah* to express gratitude when the time of salvation arrived (for example, Ps 111–113). The hymns tend to be concentrated in books 4 and 5 of the Psalter (Ps 90–150). Five hymns conclude the entire collection (Ps 146–150), thereby clearly shaping the message of the Psalter as a whole and providing the foundation for the traditional Jewish description of the Psalms as *tehillim*, "praises".

4. *Royal Psalms*: These psalms are distinguished, not by formal characteristics, but by subject matter. They focus on the person of the king, the son of David, offering praise to God for God's power/fidelity shown through the king or else offering petition on his behalf. Several of these stand out as most important for both the Jewish and Christian traditions (for example, Ps 2, 45, 72, 89, 110, and 132). Royal psalms frequently occupy strategic positions in the structure of the Psalter: for example, at the introduction of the whole collection (Ps 2), at the end of book 2 (Ps 72), and at the end of book 3 (Ps 89). The strategic placement of the royal psalms suggests that the Psalter is, in its final form, an overwhelmingly *Davidic* book: it is very much a book about the royal son of David. Indeed, as recent scholarship has demonstrated, in Second Temple Judaism (both Greek and Hebrew speaking), early Christianity, and rabbinic Judaism, the royal psalms were consistently interpreted in a messianic

or eschatological sense, going all the way back to the earliest titles of the psalms in the Greek Septuagint.[1] While these royal psalms certainly describe the historical kingship of David and his heirs, they also point beyond themselves to an age of salvation that remains in the future and, therefore, to a fulfillment by the definitive Son of David who is to come. (On the importance of David and the Davidic covenant to the theology of the psalms, see the discussion below, "Theological Issues in the Psalms".)

5. *Mount Zion Psalms*: These psalms, which are closely related to the royal psalms, focus on the attributes and glories of the holy city Jerusalem, the seat of the Davidic kingdom and site of the holy Temple (for example, Ps 46, 48, 68, 84, 87, 99(?), 122, 125, 132, 137). Some Zion psalms overlap with other categories: for example, Psalm 132 is both a royal and a Zion psalm, Psalm 137 is a lament concerning Zion, and Psalms 46 and 48 could be considered hymns about Zion. Although contemporary readers sometimes overlook the point, Mount Zion was the place of the revelation of the Davidic covenant, even as Mount Sinai was for the Mosaic covenant. As such, it is, so to speak, the geographical apex of the various mountains of salvation history, which move in the following progression:

1. Mount Eden (Adam)
2. Mount Ararat (Noah)
3. Mount Moriah (Abraham)
4. Mount Sinai (Moses)
5. Mounts Gerizim and Ebal (Joshua)
6. Mount Zion (David)

By focusing their hopes on Mount Zion, the Psalms clearly reflect a reorientation of Israel's faith and worship from the Mosaic economy instituted at Sinai to the Davidic economy associated with Zion (see Ps 68:7–18). As the locus of the liturgy, Zion becomes much more than a mere geographical place; it becomes a kind of "sacrament" or embodiment of the Lord with his people through the cult and the sanctuary authorized by the covenant. Loyalty to Zion is an expression of loyalty to YHWH himself and to his covenant son, the heir of David, who reigns in Zion.

6. *Wisdom or "Torah" Psalms*: Wisdom psalms share themes and motifs with the biblical wisdom literature, including an emphasis on wise or righteous behavior in everyday life and the exultation of God's "law" or "instruction" (Hebrew *torah*). The most important and obvious wisdom psalms are Psalms 1, 19, 37, and 119. Wisdom themes can also be found in several other psalms of different genres (for example, Ps 112). It is possible that Psalms 1 and 119 once formed an *inclusio* around a shorter psalter, before Psalms 120–150 were added, in order to frame the Psalms as a book of wisdom—that is, God's instruction in how to live. Some scholars also argue that Psalm 19 occupies a pivotal position in book 1 of the Psalter (Ps 1–41). The effort to place these wisdom psalms

---

[1] David C. Mitchell, *The Message of the Psalter: An Eschatological Programme in the Book of Psalms, Journal for the Study of the Old Testament* Supplement Series 252 (Sheffield: Sheffield Academic Press, 1997), 15–40.

in key locations reveals an intention on the part of the sacred editors to connect
the book of Psalms with the other wisdom literature. Since "the fear of the
LORD is the beginning of wisdom", the wise life ought to be ordered around
prayer and worship of the Lord. The Psalter presents us with the vicarious experience of just such a life and provides us with words and texts to "perform" such
a life ourselves.

7. *Other Kinds of Psalms.* Despite the importance of grasping the above categories, it is also important to remember that not all psalms fit into the above
genres. Moreover, the above categories can be further subdivided by other
formal and material considerations. Scholars suggest additional smaller genre
categories, such as *acrostic psalms*, in which every line or verse begins with the
next letter of the Hebrew alphabet (Ps 9–10, 25, 34, 37, 111–12, 119, 145);
psalms of confidence, expressing trust in the Lord in a general way without reference to a specific crisis experienced by the psalmist (Ps 11, 16, 23, 62–63); the
infamous *imprecatory psalms*, which include curses against enemies or evildoers
(Ps 69 and 109, also Ps 5–6, 11–12, 35, 37, 40, 52, 54, 56, 58, 69, 79, 83, 137,
139, and 143); *didactic psalms* of a primarily instructional nature, closely related
to, or overlapping with, Wisdom-Torah psalms (Ps 15, 37, 49, 52, 127); *psalms
of ascent* sung by pilgrims ascending to Jerusalem in antiquity (Ps 120–134);
and *messianic psalms* prophesying or foreshadowing the coming Christ (virtually all royal psalms, plus Ps 22, 31, 41 and others). Some psalms are of
mixed genre, and still other psalms are virtually *sui generis*—that is, unique in
style and/or content (for example, Ps 50, 81). In the end, focus on the actual
text of the psalm takes precedence in interpretation over finding the exact
generic classification.

The Literary Structure of the Psalter

The book of Psalms is obviously not tightly organized. Just as in a modern
hymnal, songs of quite different styles, composition dates, and even content
are placed side by side. Nonetheless, in recent years the study of the overall
structure of the Psalter has yielded fruit, revealing that there is, indeed, a
very rough "narrative flow" through the Psalter, accomplished primarily
through the strategic placement of royal psalms and the grouping of certain
genres of psalms into certain books.[2] The book of Psalms can thus be outlined
as follows:

Outline of the Book of Psalms

   I. Book 1: Introduction and Laments of David (Ps 1–41)
      A. Introduction (1–2)
         1. The Way of Blessing (1)
         2. Royal Messianic Introduction (2)
      B. The Laments of King David (3–41)

---

[2] For example, Mitchell, *Message of the Psalter.*

II. Book 2: The Rise of the Davidic Kingdom (Ps 42–72)
   A. Psalms of the Sons of Korah (42–49)
   B. Psalm of Asaph (50)
   C. Psalms of David (51–72)

III. Book 3: Fall of the Davidic Kingdom (Ps 73–89)
   A. Psalms of Asaph (73–83)
   B. Psalms of the Sons of Korah (84–89)

Asaph Psalms

Korah Psalms

IV. Book 4: Reflections on the Fall of the Kingdom and Exile (Ps 90–106)
   A. Moses' Plea for Mercy on God's People (90)
   B. Psalms of God's Universal Sovereignty (91–104)
   C. Concluding Reflection on Israel's History (105–6)
      1. God's Faithfulness to Israel through History (105)
      2. Israel's Unfaithfulness to God through History (106)

V. Book 5: Rejoicing and Restoration of the Temple (Ps 107–150)
   A. Introductory *Todah* for Return from Exile (107)
   B. Cycle 1 from Lament to Praise (108–18)
      1. Davidic Psalms of Petition (108–9)
      2. Praise of the Davidic Priest King (110)
      3. *Todah* Psalms (111–18)
      4. Interlude: Praise of God's Law (119; onetime conclusion)
   C. Cycle 2 from Lament to Praise (120–36)
      1. The Psalms of Ascent to the Jerusalem Temple (120–34)
      2. Hymns of Praise (135–36)
   D. Cycle 3 from Lament to Praise (137–50)
      1. Lament over Exile (137)
      2. Collection of Davidic Laments (138–44)
      3. Davidic Praise of God's Kingdom (145)
      4. Concluding Hymns of Praise (146–50)

As this outline makes clear, the five books of the Psalter provide us with an overarching framework and thus an important key for interpreting the book in its final, canonical form.

Overview of the Book of Psalms

The fundamental structure of the Psalter is its division into five books: book 1 (Ps 1–41); book 2 (Ps 42–72); book 3 (Ps 73–89); book 4 (Ps 90–106); and book 5 (Ps 107–50). When read as a whole, each book is quite distinct in character and "mood".

Book 1: Introduction and Laments of David (Psalms 1–41)

1. *Introduction: Psalms 1–2:* Although formally Psalms 1 and 2 belong to book 1 of the Psalter, they are unlike most of the other psalms in book 1 and have certainly been placed intentionally at the beginning of the Psalter to serve as an

introduction, not just to book 1, but to the entire collection. These two psalms are united by the theme of "blessing" or, more literally, "happiness" (Hebrew *'asher*) (Ps 1:1; 2:12d). They present two alternate ways to achieve true happiness, either through meditating on God's law (Ps 1:2) or by taking refuge in the Lord and his "anointed one" (Hebrew *mashiah*) (Ps 2:12d).

In this way, Psalm 1 functions as a kind of "wisdom" introduction, suggesting that the Psalter is a book of wisdom along with Proverbs, Ecclesiastes, and so on. In other words, in addition to being a songbook of praise, the Psalter is also a guide for right living.[3] The Psalter therefore reveals "the way of the righteous", and David, the quintessential psalmist, is the man who "delights in the law of the LORD" and meditates on it "day and night" (Ps 1:2). By contrast, Psalm 2 is a royal psalm—indeed, a messianic psalm—that extols the royal son of David who is installed in Zion as a "son" of God and suzerain of the whole earth (Ps 2:7–12). Following Hermann Gunkel, whose early form-critical work on the Psalms remains influential,[4] contemporary scholars believe that Psalm 2 was a coronation hymn used at the installation of a new king. By implication, the rest of the Psalter will tell us more about this great son, including how we may "take refuge in him" (Ps 2:12d). Taken together, then, Psalms 1 and 2 suggest there are two ways to

---

Psalm 2 in Hebrew

Few translations render the ending of Psalm 2 literally according to the Hebrew, but here is strict translation of the traditional Hebrew (Masoretic) text:

> Serve the LORD with fear, and rejoice
>   with trembling,
> Kiss the son, lest he be angry, and you
>   perish on the way, for his wrath
>   flares up in a moment.
> Blessed are all who take refuge in him.
> (Ps 2:11–12)

Thus, in the Hebrew text, it is the "son" (that is, the Davidic king) whose anger should be feared and in whom one should seek refuge.

The word "son", however, is in Aramaic (*bar*) not Hebrew (*ben*), which gives translators pause and reason to suspect a textual error. However, Aramaic borrowings into Hebrew were not unusual throughout Israel's history.

---

blessing: following the law of the Lord (Ps 1:2) and taking refuge in the Messiah (Ps 2:12d; see inset), and the psalms will teach us to do both.

2. *The Laments of David (3–41):* The remainder of book 1 contains, with a few exceptions, lament psalms attributed to David without a clear internal structure. In the thirty-nine psalms of this section, David expresses a wide range of emotions, and his fortunes vis-à-vis the Lord and his enemies rise and fall. Although there are hymns and thanksgivings (Ps 8, 18, 28, 31), the mood of this book is controlled by the preponderance of laments, especially at the beginning (Ps 3–7) and end (Ps 38–41). In the final psalm of the book, David is abandoned by friends and surrounded by enemies as he lays ill because of his sins (Ps 41:4–10). He expresses confidence in YHWH (Ps 41:1–3, 11–12), but it is not clear that he has experienced salvation, and there is as yet no flourish of praise. (Psalm 41:13 is the formal conclusion of book 1, not properly part of Psalm 41.) For

---

[3] Gordon Wenham, *The Psalms as Torah: Reading Biblical Song Ethically* (Grand Rapids, Mich.: Baker Academic, 2012).

[4] Hermann Gunkel, *An Introduction to the Psalms: The Genres of the Religious Lyric of Israel*, completed by Joachim Begrich, trans. J.D. Nogalski (Macon, Ga.: Mercer University Press, 1998).

the most part, book 1 presents *the sufferings and trials of David* at the hands of his enemies, confident of salvation but still being persecuted and not yet delivered by the hand of God.

Book 2: The Triumphs of David (Psalms 42–72)

Books 2 and 3 of the Psalter are joined by a chiastic literary pattern based on attributed authorship. The pattern begins and ends with Psalms of the Sons of Korah (Ps 42–49; 84–88; Ps 86, an exception), then Psalms of Asaph (Ps 50; 73–83). These groups bracket a Davidic collection (Ps 51–72), culminating in a psalm about Solomon (Ps 72) that without doubt forms the emotional high point of the first three books of the Psalter. The stress points of the structure—the middle (Ps 72) and the end (Ps 89)—are both marked by royal psalms associated with men of great wisdom, such as Solomon and Ethan (cf. 1 Kings 4:31). These psalms are key to understanding the flow of books 2–3, as we will see below.

Book 2 of the Psalms exhibits many differences from book 1. Significantly, for the first time, non-Davidic psalms are introduced: Psalms 42–50 are attributed to the *Levitical singers* David appointed for the Jerusalem sanctuary after he had consolidated his royal power (1 Chron 9:19; 16:5). For the first time we find Mount Zion psalms exalting the greatness of the city of David and its sanctuary (Ps 46, 48, 68). In this book also we find two exuberant royal psalms (Ps 45, 72), the like of which has not been seen since Psalm 2. Finally, a study of the ending of the psalms shows that in book 2, compared to book 1, far fewer psalms end with a plea for assistance, and far more end on a note of praise (see chart).

Analysis of the Conclusions of the Psalms: Book 1 vs. Book 2		
Psalms that end in …	Book 1 (3–41)	Book 2 (42–72)
Sorrowful plea	12, 39, 40 [total 3]	70 [total 1]
Plea	3, 9, 14, 20, 25, 33, 35, 36, 38, 39 [10]	44 [1]
Confident plea	5, 10, 17, 19, 26, 27, 28 [7]	51, 53, 55, 60 [4]
Expression of confidence	4, 6,1 1, 16, 21, 23, 31, 34, 27, 41 [10]	42, 43, 46, 48, 49, 58, 62 [7]
Explicit praise	7, 8, 13, 18, 22, 24, 29, 30, 32 [9]	45, 47, 52, 54, 56, 57, 59, 61, 63–69, 71–72 [17]
In book 2 of the Psalms, there is greater optimism and emphasis on praise.		

A study of the end of book 2 is instructive. Psalm 71 (whose Davidic attribution seems carried over from the previous psalm (Ps 70) to which it once may have been joined) appears to reflect David near the end of his life:

> Do not cast me off *in the time of my old age*;
> forsake me not when my strength is spent....
> So even to *old age and gray hairs*,
> O God, do not forsake me. (Ps 71:9, 18)

Near death, he expresses hope for resurrection:

> You who have made me see many sore troubles
> will revive me again;
> *from the depths of the earth*
> *you will bring me up again.* (Ps 71:20)

The following psalm is preceded by the heading "A Psalm of Solomon" (Hebrew *li-shlōmōh*). It may be understood as a prayer Solomon composed for himself, but the subscription—"The prayers of David, the son of Jesse, are ended" (Ps 72:20)—suggests rather that Psalm 72 is to be understood as a prayer of David. From this point of view, the Hebrew superscription should be understood as "about Solomon" rather than "by Solomon". Therefore, Psalms 71–72 seem to present David in his old age (Ps 71), his final act being to invoke the blessing of a glorious reign upon his son and heir, Solomon (Ps 72). Indeed, according to the canonical history, this prayer of David is heard, and under Solomon Israel briefly experiences the blessings described in Psalm 72, when the kingdom begins to expand and include the Gentile nations (see 1 Kings 4).

The overall movement of book 2 progresses, therefore, from the laments of Psalms 42–44 (similar in feel to those of book 1) through psalms that explore the glory of Mount Zion and the rule of the Davidic king (Ps 45–48), followed by many psalms that end in praise as God delivers David from sins, sickness, and enemies (Ps 51–69). These culminate in David in old age (Ps 71, or better, 70–71 understood as one) and a description of the reign of Solomon (Ps 72). If book 1 portrayed David predominantly in the posture of crying out to God in distress, book 2 places greater emphasis on the glories of David's rule, his capital in Zion, his triumph over every threat by God's mercy and power, and the transfer of the kingdom to Solomon, his glorious successor (Ps 72).

Book 3: Collapse of the Davidic Kingdom and Covenant (Psalms 73–89)

Book 3 of the Psalter exhibits yet a different character from the two preceding books. Book 1 was dominated by Davidic psalms, and book 2 ended with a significant collection of his "prayers" (Ps 51–72). In book 3, however, there is only one Davidic psalm (Ps 86). In this way, we may speak of the "disappearance" of David in this book. Instead, in this shorter collection (only seventeen psalms), the *Levitical singers* dominate the attribution of authorship: *Asaph* is credited with the first twelve (Ps 73–84), and the *Sons of Korah* with most of the rest (Ps 84–85, 87–88). In this way, book 3 may be the most important reminder of the fact that while the entire Psalter was often attributed to David in later centuries, the final form of the Psalter itself makes extremely clear that there are many psalms not attributed to David.

With this in mind, it is intriguing to note that the mood of book 3 is by far the darkest of the five books of the Psalter. The first psalm of the book recounts how the psalmist almost lost his faith when he saw the wicked prosper at the expense of the upright (Ps 73). The body of the book contains the highest concentration of community lament psalms to be found anywhere in the Psalter

(Ps 74, 79–80, 83, 85). All of these reflect dire distress and crisis for the whole kingdom of David, and at least two of which (Ps 74, 79, 80[?]) refer specifically and shockingly to the sacking and/or destruction of the Temple and Jerusalem, either in 587 B.C. or else on some earlier occasion (see 1 Kings 14:25–26; 2 Kings 14:13–15). One psalm consists of a recitation of sacred history, with a heavy-handed emphasis on all of Israel's infidelities (Ps 78), and another is a *sui generis* petition from *God* to *Israel* to repent of its stubbornness (Ps 81)—the only such "reverse petition" in the Psalter!

Book 3 ends with two of the most despondent psalms in the Psalter. Psalm 88 is entirely unique, the only lament psalm to conclude with neither praise nor expression of confidence nor even a plaintive appeal, but instead an assertion of hopelessness: "You have caused loved one and friend to shun me; my companions are in darkness" (Ps 88:18). Psalm 89, on the other hand, is for two-thirds of its length a hymn of praise to God for his power displayed in creation and in his covenant with David; but then it changes abruptly into a pathetic lament as the psalmist recounts the apparent abrogation of all God's trustworthy promises and covenant with his anointed king (the son of David) (Ps 89:38), whose sufferings and humiliations are shared and borne also by the psalmist himself (Ps 89:50–51). The mood of the Psalter has reached its lowest point.

The relatively few optimistic psalms of praise in book 3, the preponderance of communal laments reflecting national crisis, the several psalms of rebuke toward the nation of Israel, and the hopelessness of the endings of Psalms 88 and 89 amply justify the conclusion that this book represents a reaction to the shock of the decline and collapse of the kingdom of David. Indeed, it may even reflect the mood and sentiments of the Temple personnel not long after the destruction of the Temple in 587 B.C. Whereas book 2 ended with a blessing invoked over the glorious reign of Solomon (Ps 72), book 3 ends with the heir of David dethroned, shamed, and humiliated (Ps 89), and the "covenant" with David—such an important theme since Psalm 2—appears to have been "renounced" and terminated, his "crown" being "defiled in the dust" (Ps 89:39).

Book 4: Meditations from the Perspective of the Exile (Psalms 90–106)

Book 4 has been referred to as the editorial "heart" of the Psalter, and it is true that there is a greater continuity of themes among these seventeen psalms than is typically found in other books of the collection.

Book 4 opens with Psalm 90, the only psalm attributed to Moses in the Psalter. In fact, seven of the eight times Moses is mentioned in the Psalms occur in book 4. David and his covenant have dominated the Psalter up to this point, but in Psalm 89 the Davidic monarchy and covenant seem to have come to an end as the people enter into exile. In the "absence" of David, the people of Israel turn to earlier covenant mediators for guidance. For this reason, *Moses and Abraham* appear in book 4 though they have been largely absent beforehand (for Moses, see Ps 90; 99:6; 103:7; 105:26; 106:16, 23, 32; for Abraham, see Ps 105:6, 9, 42; earlier, cf. only Ps 47:9, 77:20).

Although Psalm 90 is in the mouth of Moses, it works well as a psalm of lament for Israel in exile. It begins, "LORD, you have been our dwelling place in all generations." This emphasis on God as "dwelling place", "refuge", "rock", and so on, will run throughout book 4 (Ps 90:1; 91:2, 4, 9; 92:15; 94:22; 95:1). Since the people of Israel have lost their land, capital, and Temple, they now have to turn to God alone as their "dwelling place" in the exile. Along similar lines, although Psalm 90 has elements of consolation, it is for the most part a lament appropriate for the exile:

> For we are consumed by your anger;
>> by your wrath we are overwhelmed.
> You have set our iniquities before you,
>> our secret sins in the light of your countenance....
> Return, O LORD! How long?
>> Have pity on your servants!...
> Make us glad as many days as you have afflicted us,
>> and as many years as we have seen evil. (Ps 90:7, 13, 15)

Psalm 90 is followed by ten psalms (Ps 91–100) that share a number of distinct themes appropriate for Israel in exile: (1) God as "rock" and "refuge", since Israel now lacks any physical dwelling place or protection (Ps 90:1; 91:2, 4, 9; 92:15; 94:22; 95:1); (2) the "reign of God", who is still enthroned even if the human king, the son of David, has been dethroned (Ps 93:1; 94:2; 96:10, 13; 97:1; 97:8; 98:9; 99:1; cf. 102:12; 103:19; 105:5, 7); (3) God's glory displayed in *creation*, still visible even if God's king is no longer ruling in Zion and the stone Temple no longer stands (Ps 93:1b–4; 95:4–5; 96:11–12; 97:1–6; 98:7–8; cf. 104:1–32); (4) praise of God by *singing*, especially "a new song" (Ps 96:1; 98:1), as a way of moving beyond the sadness of Israel's history and cultivating the virtue of hope in the future (Ps 92:1; 92:4; 95:1–2; 96:1–2, 4, 12; 98:1, 4 –5, 8; 100:2, 4; cf. 101:1; 104:33; 105:2; 106:1, 47). After these ten psalms mostly of praise (Ps 91–100), the book's only two Davidic psalms (Ps 101, 103) bracket a lament calling for God to restore Jerusalem from exile:

> But you, O LORD, are enthroned for ever,
>> your name endures to all generations.
> You will arise and have pity on Zion;
>> it is the time to favor her;
>> the appointed time has come.
> For your servants hold her stones dear,
>> and have pity on her dust. (Ps 102:12–14)

It is clear from this passage that no significant restoration of Jerusalem and its people has taken place yet, so most likely this psalm was composed prior to the work of Ezra and Nehemiah and most likely prior to Cyrus' decree of return.

The last three psalms of book 4 show a remarkable degree of continuity, as they recount in succession God's mighty deeds in creation (Ps 104), in the period from Abraham to the exodus (Ps 105), and in the period from the exodus up through the exile (Ps 106). Thus, these three psalms give a more or less complete recounting of *salvation history*, and at every turn God's faithfulness is contrasted with Israel's unfaithfulness. In particular, Psalm 105 highlights God's covenant faithfulness, and Psalm 106 places a contrasting emphasis on Israel's *unfaithfulness*. Psalm 106 then ends the entire book with a plea for deliverance from the exile:

> Save us, O LORD our God,
> *and gather us from among the nations,*
> that we may give thanks to your holy name
> and glory in your praise. (Ps 106:47)

Thus, there is reason to see in book 4 a reflection on the reality of the apparent failure of the Davidic kingdom and covenant as well as the exile. Living in a literal or metaphorical exile, the psalmist acknowledges Israel's sin, pleads for restoration, and reorients his theological framework—at least for the time being—to the earlier covenants with Moses and Abraham.

Book 5: The Restoration of the Temple (Psalm 107–150)

The abrupt mood shift between the end of book 4 and the beginning of book 5 is indicative of the overall contrast between the two books. Book 4 ends with a plea for restoration from exile (Ps 106), whereas book 5 begins with a thanksgiving (Hebrew *todah*) psalm praising God for restoring his people from exile:

> O give thanks to the LORD, for he is good;
> for his mercy endures for ever!
> Let the redeemed of the LORD say so,
> whom he has redeemed from trouble
> *and gathered in from the lands,*
> from the east and from the west,
> from the north and from the south. (Ps 107:1–3)

The dominant mood throughout book 5 will be one of praise, and certain psalms will specifically reflect the joy of the worshipper going up to the rebuilt Temple (for example, Ps 122).

Book 5 is the longest and structurally most complex of the books of the Psalter, perhaps because during the development of the Psalter additional materials kept being added to the final book. There is reason to suspect that at one time the Psalter ended with Psalm 119, later with Psalm 136, and finally achieved its canonical form with the addition of Psalms 137–50. In any event, one way to analyze the structure of book 5 is as three cycles that move from lament to praise (Ps 107–19; 120–36; 137–50). The last Davidic psalm in each cycle marks a transition, after which lament ceases and unqualified praise takes over.

The Structure of Book 5

I. Cycle One from Lament to Praise (107–19)
   A. Thanksgiving Introduction to Book 5 (107)
   B. Laments of David (108–9)

1. *The First Cycle (Psalm 107–19)*: The first cycle begins with a *todah* (Psalm 107) that forecasts the shift of mood and perspective between books 4 and 5. Immediately following are two Davidic laments in which David cries to the Lord for deliverance from his foes. The final Davidic psalm in this cycle is Psalm 110, a coronation hymn (like Ps 2) that invokes blessing on the Davidic priest-king and promises him universal dominion as the son of God. The remaining psalms in this cycle are all hymns and thanksgivings (Ps 111–19). The collection of Psalms 113–18 are known as the *Hallel* ("Praise!") psalms and were later recited in Jewish tradition in the course of the Passover liturgy. They conclude with two of the most theologically significant thanksgiving/*todah* psalms in the Psalter: Psalms 116 and 118. In these psalms, the suffering servant of the Lord is delivered from death and exalted so that he is able to offer sacrifice in the Temple:

> The LORD preserves the simple;
>   when I was brought low, he saved me....
> For you have delivered my soul from death,
>   my eyes from tears,
>   my feet from stumbling;...
> What shall I render to the LORD
>   for all his bounty to me?
> *I will lift up the chalice of salvation*
>   *and call on the name of the LORD.* (Ps 116:6, 8, 12–13)

> I was pushed hard, so that I was falling,
>   but the LORD helped me....
> The LORD has chastened me sorely,
>   but he has not given me over to death.
> *Open to me the gates of righteousness,*
>   *that I may enter through them*
>   *and give thanks to the LORD.* (Ps 118:13, 18–19)

Notice here how the *todah* psalms culminate in sacrificial libation of wine by the servant (the "chalice of salvation") as well as thanksgiving in the Temple.

Psalm 119 ends this cycle. A psalm of praise of the law of God, it may well have once formed an *inclusio* with Psalm 1 around an original, shorter Psalter, framed in such a way as to present the entire collection as a meditation on God's law. The longest psalm and chapter in the Bible, Psalm 119 is an acrostic poem consisting of twenty-two stanzas of eight lines each. Every line of each stanza begins with the same Hebrew letter, with one stanza for each letter of the Hebrew alphabet in succession. The intention of this literary structure is to present praise of God's law "from A to Z" (or Hebrew, from *'aleph* to *taw*!): that is, absolutely comprehensively.

What Does the "Steadfast Love" of God Mean?

The most characteristic refrain in the Psalter is the following: "O give thanks to the LORD, for he is good, for his mercy [Hebrew *hesed*] endures for ever" (Ps 136:1, etc.).

This and similar verses can be found in many psalms. Arguably this couplet expresses the theme of the entire Psalter: give thanks to God for his goodness and his everlasting mercy.

The concept of "mercy", also frequently translated "steadfast love", needs to be unpacked. The English "mercy" follows the tradition of the LXX, which employed the Greek *eleos* to render the Hebrew word *hesed*, whose meaning is actually much more specific: "covenant fidelity". It is frequently remarked that the Hebrew term for "covenant", *berith*, is uncommon in the Psalms (only twenty-one occurrences, albeit in strategic locations), and therefore scholars question whether the psalms share the covenantal perspective on God's relationship to his people to the same degree as the historical and prophetic books. But to limit the covenant theme in the psalms to the occurrences of *berith* is greatly to misunderstand the Psalter. The term *hesed* is dominant throughout the book of Psalms (130 occurrences), and it is a clearly covenantal term, expressing the loyalty appropriate to a covenant relationship. Its close relationship to covenant (*berith*) can be seen in this famous verse of Isaiah: "Incline your ear, and come to me; hear, that your soul may live; and I will make with you an everlasting covenant [*berith*], my steadfast love [*hesed*] of David" (Is 55:3). In the this bicola, "covenant" and "steadfast love" are placed in synonymous parallelism because they refer to the same reality, the Davidic covenant. And so we give God thanks for his "mercy"—that is, his *hesed*, covenant faithfulness—using the words of David and the other sacred authors of the psalms in our own worship.

---

2. *The Second Cycle (Psalms 120–36)*: Following Psalm 119, the sacred editors added the fifteen "psalms of ascent"—that is, pilgrimage songs sung by worshippers journeying up to the Temple Mount in Jerusalem (Ps 120–34). There is a progression—albeit uneven—in the psalms of ascent from alienation to intimacy with God in the Temple. The psalmist begins far from the Temple, exiled in "Meshech" and "Kedar" (Ps 120), but then "lifts up" his "eyes" to "the hills" of Judah where the Temple lies (Ps 121:1). In Psalm 122, he arrives at the holy city: "Our feet have been standing within your gates, O Jerusalem!", and the following psalms meditate on the city of Zion and the sometimes turbulent relationship between God and Israel that Zion represents (Ps 122:2).

Psalm 132 marks a decisive turning point: a psalm about the Davidic covenant and God's combined choice of David as king and Zion as dwelling place, it is followed only by psalms of praise. The psalmist now seems to enter the Temple courts where he beholds the anointing of the high priest (Ps 133:2) and then remains in the Temple into the night, enjoying peaceful communion with the Lord in the intimacy of quiet darkness, singing praises to the Lord together with the priests who stand on duty through the night watches (Ps 134:1–3). Thus, from Psalm 120 to 134 there is a progression from distance to intimacy with God's presence in the Temple.

This psalm cycle then ends with two exuberant psalms doubtless composed to be chanted in the Temple courts: a hymn of praise calling on priests and people to extol the Lord (Ps 135) and a comprehensive thanksgiving/*todah* litany based on the classic two-part refrain:

> [A] O give thanks to the Lord, for he is good,
> [B] for his mercy endures for ever. (Ps 136:1)

The latter psalm is significant, because it reveals to us how variations on the first line were chanted by a priest or worship leader, with the congregation responding with the second.

3. *The Third Cycle (Psalms 137–50).* Psalms 135 and 136 would constitute an appropriate ending to the book of Psalms, but our canonical Psalter does not stop here. Psalm 137 plunges us from the heights of thanksgiving in 136 back into the depths of despair, with the most explicit description of the Babylonian exile in the Psalter:

> By the waters of Babylon, there we sat down and wept,
>   when we remembered Zion....
> How shall we sing the Lord's song
>   in a foreign land?
> If I forget you, O Jerusalem,
>   let my right hand wither! (Ps 137:1, 4–5)

With these words, book 3 begins a new cycle moving from lament to praise. What follows is the longest collection of Davidic psalms (Ps 138–45) we have seen since book 1, in which—mixed with praise and expressions of confidence—David cries out for deliverance from sickness, sin, and especially his enemies. The last Davidic psalm in the entire Psalter again marks a transition: David unreservedly extols the glories of the kingdom of God:

> All your works shall give thanks to you, O Lord,
>   and all your saints shall bless you!
> They shall speak of *the glory of your kingdom*,
>   and tell of your power,
> to make known to the sons of men your mighty deeds,
>   and the glorious splendor of *your kingdom*.

> *Your kingdom is an everlasting kingdom,*
> and your dominion endures throughout all generations.
> The LORD is faithful in all his words,
> and gracious in all his deeds. (Ps 145:10–13)

With these words, we see the Psalter drawing to its close with an eschatological theme that will become increasingly important in the life of ancient Israel and early Christianity: the hope for the glorious "kingdom" (Hebrew *malkût*) of God. After lifting up this hymn in praise of God's kingdom, the following five psalms represent a symphonic finale of exuberant praise (Ps 146–50), the literary equivalent of the last movement of Beethoven's Ninth Symphony. There is an obvious intention to be comprehensive: these last five psalms encourage the praise of God for every blessing (Ps 146–47) by everyone (Ps 148) with every thing (Ps 150).

Historical Issues in the Psalms

The Origin of the Book of Psalms

One of the most hotly debated topics in the history of Psalms scholarship is the question of *authorship*, which is deeply bound up with how one should understand the *superscriptions* (or "headings") that are prefixed to many of the psalms. Many superscriptions attribute the psalm to some historical figure, such as Moses, David, the Sons of Korah, or Asaph. Although there is some variation in these superscriptions among the various ancient manuscripts of the Psalter, it is significant to note that they are present both in the ancient Greek translation of the Psalter in the Septuagint as well as in the Dead Sea Scrolls, which include the most ancient extant Hebrew copies of the Psalms that we possess.[5] In the Masoretic Text (MT) of the Hebrew Psalter, the attributions of various psalms can be summarized as follows:

1. *Moses*	1 psalm (90)
2. *David*	73 psalms (for example, 3, 7, 18, 34, 51–52, 54, 56–57, 59, 60, 63, 142, and so on)
3. *Solomon*	2 psalms (72, 127) .
4. *Asaph*	12 psalms (50, 73–83)
5. *Sons of Korah*	11 psalms (42, 44–49, 84–85, 87–88)
6. *Ethan the Ezrahite*	1 psalm (88)
7. *Heman the Ezrahite*	1 psalm (89)
8. *Jeduthun* (with David?)	3 psalms (39, 62, 77)

Significantly, an additional thirteen psalms are ascribed to David in the Greek Septuagint superscriptions (Ps 32, 42, 70, 90, 92–98, 103, 136, following the LXX numbering), making a total of 86 Davidic psalms in the Greek Psalter.

---

[5] Martin G. Abegg Jr., Peter Flint, and Eugene Ulrich, *The Dead Sea Scrolls Bible: The Oldest Known Bible Translated for the First Time into English* (San Francisco: HarperOne, 1999), 505–89.

Presuming that the Hebrew version reflects an earlier tradition, this would seem to reflect a tendency within ancient Jewish tradition to expand David's influence within the Psalter as the centuries passed. This is but one of the reasons contemporary scholars have approached these attributions with caution and even skepticism when it comes to attempting to draw historical conclusions about their origins and authorship.

With that said, there is still the question of exactly what these superscriptions mean. The form they often take—"of David" (Hebrew *le-dawid*) (Ps 3)—is somewhat ambiguous. On the one hand, the Hebrew prefix *le-* may be translated as "of" or "by"—that is, as an indication of authorship. This is clear from the thirteen cases in which the ascription *le-dawid* is supplemented by the description of an occasion in the life of the historical figure of David that prompted the composition of the poem (see Ps 3, 7, 18, 34, 51–52, 54, 56–57, 59–60, 63, 142). The most famous of these is the superscription for Psalm 51, the famous psalm of repentance, which reads:

> To the choirmaster. A Psalm of David, *when Nathan the prophet came to him, after he had gone in to Bathsheba.* (Ps 51, superscription)

Along similar lines, there can be no doubt that some of the most ancient interpreters of the Psalms we possess interpreted such titles as attributions of authorship.[6] For example, the books of Chronicles depicts at least portions of the Psalter as stemming from David:

> And Hezekiah the king and the princes commanded the Levites to sing praises to the LORD with *the words of David and of Asaph the seer.* (2 Chron 29:30)

Along similar lines, in the New Testament, the Davidic authorship of the psalms is assumed even for some psalms that have no Davidic superscription (Mt 22:41–46; Mk 12:35–37; Lk 20:42–44; Acts 1:16; 2:25–34; 4:25–26; Rom 4:6–8; 11:9; Heb 4:7). For example, in the Gospels, Jesus responds to a question about the Messiah with the following:

> "*How is it then that David, inspired by the Spirit, calls him Lord*, saying, 'The Lord said to my Lord,
> Sit at my right hand,
> till I put your enemies under your feet' [= Ps 110:1]
> If David thus calls him Lord, how is he his son?" (Mt 22:43–45)

Clearly, in antiquity, not only were the superscriptions in the Psalter known, but at least some of them were commonly understood as attributions of authorship. This is especially the case when we recall that Asaph, Heman, and Ethan were persons of little consequence in the history of Israel and Judah, so it is highly unlikely that the psalms would be ascribed to them unless it was believed that in some way those psalms had had their origin with those persons.

---

[6] Artur Weiser, *The Psalms: A Commentary*, Old Testament Library (Louisville, Ky.: Westminster John Knox Press, 1962), 94.

On the other hand, the Hebrew prefix *le-* can also mean "about", in this way indicating the subject rather than the author of the psalm. For example, Psalm 72, referred to as "of Solomon" (Hebrew *li-shlōmōh*), appears to be a prayer *for* rather than *by* Solomon. This is especially so when we notice that the subscription implies it was considered one of the "prayers of David" (Ps 72:20). Thus, a commonsense approach to the superscriptions would be to regard them as intended to convey authorship in most but not every case, and each example should be judged on the basis of the content and context of the individual psalm.

What Role Did David Play in the Origin of the Davidic Psalms?

With that said, the putative author about which there is the most debate is not Solomon, Moses, Asaph, or the Sons of Korah, but David.[7]

On the one hand, many contemporary scholars generally dismiss the possibility of Davidic authorship except in the case of a few psalms that display undeniable archaic influences (such as parallels with thirteenth-century B.C. Canaanite literature) and whose content would be hard to place in the mouth of anyone but David or some newly established chieftain-king similar to him (for example, Ps 18). Biblical minimalists of the Copenhagen school deny that David existed or that there was literacy within Israel in his time. Less radical scholars dismiss Davidic authorship of many psalms based on a number of considerations, such as

1. the presence of *Aramaisms* (borrowings from Aramaic) pointing to a date later than the time of David (ca. 1000 B.C.);
2. third-person *descriptions of David* within the psalms, including those attributed to David himself (for example, Ps 18:50; 20:9; 21:1, 7; 122:5; 144:10);
3. anachronistic references to *the Jerusalem Temple*, which was not built until *after* David's death, during the reign of Solomon (Ps 5:7; 11:4; 23:6; 27:4; 29:9; 36:8; and so on);
4. the tendency to *expand Davidic attributions*, such as in the Greek Septuagint and in the Dead Sea Scrolls.

In light of such considerations, many contemporary scholars are either extremely cautious about attributing any historical value to the superscriptions in the Psalter or dismiss their value altogether.

On the other hand, the force of these arguments against Davidic origins of some psalms can be subjected to critical scrutiny. First, advances in historical linguistics have revealed Aramaisms in almost *all* stages of the Hebrew language, rendering them tenuous evidence for the date of any given composition. Second, and even more important, royal figures in both antiquity and modernity have not hesitated to refer to themselves in the third person. For example, King Hammurabi mixes first- and third-person language concerning himself in the epilogue to his famous Code, which dates to at least seven hundred years

---

[7] Daniel J. Estes, *Handbook on the Wisdom Books and Psalms* (Grand Rapids, Mich.: Baker Academic, 2005), 141–44.

before David's lifetime. There is, therefore, no a priori reason for concluding that King David could not have mixed first- and third-person self-references in some cases. Third—and this is critical—although the Jerusalem Temple was not built until after David's death, there was of course a central *sanctuary* during his lifetime, such as the sacred *tent* David pitched for the ark (2 Sam 6:17) or the Mosaic Tabernacle, which is sometimes referred to as "the house of the LORD" (Josh 6:24) or the "temple of the LORD" (1 Sam 1:9). In Psalm 27, for example, God's dwelling is described as a "house" (v. 4), a "temple" (v. 4), and a "tent" (vv. 5, 6), all within the space of three verses! Furthermore, many references to the Lord's Temple in the psalms do not appear to be references to any physical structure but refer, rather, to God's heavenly temple (Ps 11:4; 18:6; 23:6; 27:4; 36:8). Hence, although it is possible for references to the "temple" in the Psalter to refer to the post-Davidic Jerusalem Temple, not all uses of such language necessarily refer to that house of worship; as always, each usage must be judged on a case-by-case basis.

Moreover, there are a couple of positive considerations that favor the historical credibility of at least some of the Davidic attributions found in the Hebrew Psalter.[8]

1. *David as Royal Musician and Cultic Founder*: First and foremost, it is critical to recall that in the ancient Near East, it was typical for royal figures such as Pharaoh Akhenaten (Egypt), Princess En-hedu-anna (Ur), and, later on, King Intef II (Thebes) to function as the patron of the national cult(s) and to compose hymns of praise, often to gods or goddesses. As Kenneth Kitchen writes: "Thus David would be no oddity in being a royal author of religious poetry, after his shepherd days were long past."[9] In such a milieu, there would be ample political and social motivation for David to present himself in this fashion as one who composed (or commissioned) sacred song. This is, of course, exactly how the historical books depict David, as skilled at both poetry and music and as the founder of the sacred music sung in the Jerusalem sanctuary:

> Moreover *he* [king David] *appointed certain of the Levites as ministers before the ark of the LORD, to invoke, to thank, and to praise the LORD*, the God of Israel. *Asaph was the chief*, and second to him were Zechariah, Jeiel, Shemiramoth, Jehiel, Mattithiah, Eliab, Benaiah, Obed-edom, and Jeiel, who were to play harps and lyres; Asaph was to sound the cymbals.... So David left Asaph and his brethren there before the ark of the covenant of the LORD.... With them were Heman and Jeduthun, and the rest of those chosen and expressly named to give thanks to the LORD, for his mercy endures for ever. *Heman and Jeduthun had trumpets and cymbals for the music and instruments for sacred song*. (1 Chron 16:4–5, 37, 41–42)

Note here the multiple testimonies across the genres of the psalms, the historical books, and even one of the prophets, all witnessing to the historical memory of

---

[8] See Kenneth A. Kitchen, *On the Reliability of the Old Testament* (Grand Rapids, Mich.: Eerdmans, 2003), 104–7.

[9] Ibid., 105.

David as songwriter and patron of the liturgy: 1 Samuel 16:17; 18:10; 2 Samuel 1:17; 3:33; 6:5, 15; 22:1; 23:1; 1 Chronicles 16:4–6; 2 Chronicles 29:30; Amos 6:5. Given the fact that there were attractive alternative candidates for such a role—why not the prophet Samuel, or Solomon, since he built the Temple?—it is reasonable to conclude that one plausible explanation for these testimonies is that David was, in fact, a musician and cult founder.

2. *The Obscurity of the Musical Superscriptions*: Second, and equally important, scholars who argue for the historical credibility of some of the superscriptions also point out that the obscurity of many of them points toward their antiquity and preexilic origins:

> It should be noted that these psalm headings are obscure simply because they are *ancient*—being no longer fully understood when the Psalms were translated into Greek (for the Septuagint Old Testament) in the third or second century B.C. Full liturgical usages of Solomon's temple fell out of use for over half a century while it lay in ruins (586–538 and following); not all of that ceremonial would be restored at the opening of the Second Temple in 515; it would probably be in a simpler form. So ancient headings passed out of active use, and thus out of currency.[10]

Thus, it appears that many superscriptions of the psalms were already in place during the monarchic period and were no longer understood properly in the Second Temple era.

When Were the Individual Psalms Written?

Given the multiplicity of attributions within the Psalter itself and the debate over authorship and origins, it is to be expected that the dates proposed for individual psalms vary quite widely.[11]

On the early end of the spectrum, almost half the psalms are attributed to David (tenth century B.C.) and one to Moses (fifteenth or thirteenth century B.C.). As just noted above, while there is scholarly debate about how to understand the attributions of authorship, there is no reason to doubt that many of the psalms are preexilic. Several psalms reflect the optimism of the early years of the Davidic kingdom (for example, Ps 2, 18, 68, 72, 89:1–37, 110). The unabashed confidence of these psalms would have been ironic and unlikely to have been composed later in Judah's history, when the monarchy was in chaos or ruins. Moreover, as the work of Mitchell Dahood has shown,[12] there are extensive connections between the Psalms and Ugaritic (Canaanite) poetry from the thirteenth century B.C., even if Dahood has a tendency to exaggerate the significance of the parallels in his exuberance for the then-newly discovered texts from Ras Shamra (Ugarit). Finally, new support for the antiquity of the

---

[10] Ibid., 106–7.

[11] See John W. Hilber, "Psalms", in *The Minor Prophets: Job, Psalms, Proverbs, Ecclesiastes, Song of Songs*, vol. 5 of *Zondervan Illustrated Bible Backgrounds Commentary*, ed. John H. Walton (Grand Rapids, Mich.: Zondervan, 2009), 317–19.

[12] Mitchell Dahood, *Psalms*, 3 vols., Anchor Bible 16–17A (New York: Doubleday, 1965–1970).

psalms in book I in particular has now arisen from studies of the development of the Hebrew alphabet. Abecedaries (alphabet lists) found in the land of Israel dating to the twelfth through tenth centuries B.C. demonstrate that in this time period, the alphabetic order differed slightly, with *peh* (= P) preceding *ayin* (= O). There are good reasons to believe that the four alphabetic acrostic psalms in book I (Ps 9–10, 25, 34, 37) originally followed this antique order rather than the *ayin-peh* (O–P) order that eventually prevailed after the Babylonian exile.

On the late end of the chronological spectrum, there are psalms that obviously reflect the experience of the Babylonian exile (for example, Ps 137). Others seem to describe the destruction of the Temple and Jerusalem in 587 B.C. (for example, Ps 74, 79, 89:38–51), although one cannot be absolutely sure that the disaster being described is not some earlier defeat and ransacking of the city, of which there were several. Psalm 126 clearly reflects some aspect of the postexilic restoration, perhaps Cyrus' decree of return, the rebuilding of the Temple, the rebuilding of the walls under Nehemiah, or all of the above. In light of such evidence, the Psalter clearly achieved its present form only in the postexilic period, and it is not unlikely that various psalms in book 5 in particular were composed for the liturgy of the Second Temple and incorporated into the Psalter during its final editorial stages.

The "Life-Setting" (Sitz-im-Leben) of the Todah Psalms

When it comes to many portions of the Old Testament, it is often not possible to reconstruct with any confidence the way a particular unit functioned in the daily life of ancient Israel—that is, its social-historical context, known by the German phrase *Sitz-im-Leben* ("life-setting"). As Hermann Gunkel and the early form-critics convincingly argued at the beginning of the twentieth century, this is not the case with the psalms. The sacred poems themselves, as well as the historical books, provide ample evidence that many of them were sung, chanted, or recited in the context of worship in the Jerusalem sanctuary—at first at the Davidic tent (2 Sam 6) and then at the Solomonic Temple (1 Kings 8).

In particular, it seems clear that many of the psalms (including all the laments, thanksgivings, and perhaps some hymns) fit into what may be called a "psalm cycle" or even the "*todah* cycle": a sequence of experiences in the life of the ancient Israelite worshipper in which the singing of a psalm (or series of psalms) concluded with the joyful offering of some form of sacrifice—usually the *todah*, or "sacrifice of thanksgiving"—in the sanctuary.[13] To clarify the significance of this suggestion, it is necessary to understand something about the law and practice of the *todah*, or thanksgiving sacrifice.

1. *The* Todah, *or Thanksgiving Sacrifice.* The basic legislation for the *todah* sacrifice is laid out in the book of Leviticus:

---

[13] See C. Hassell Bullock, *Encountering the Book of Psalms: A Literary and Theological Introduction* (Grand Rapids, Mich.: Baker Academic, 2001), 151–64.

And this is the law of the sacrifice of peace offerings which one may offer to the LORD. If he offers it *for a thanksgiving*, then he shall offer with *the thank offering* unleavened cakes mixed with oil, unleavened wafers spread with oil, and cakes of fine flour well mixed with oil. With the sacrifice of his peace offerings *for thanksgiving* he shall bring his offering with cakes of leavened bread. And of such he shall offer one cake from each offering, as an offering to the LORD; it shall belong to the priest who throws the blood of the peace offerings. And the flesh of the sacrifice of his peace offerings *for thanksgiving* shall be eaten on the day of his offering; he shall not leave any of it until the morning. (Lev 7:11–15)

Several unique features of the *todah* sacrifice should be noted. First, unlike the *burnt*, *sin*, or *guilt* offerings, the *todah* was never offered because of sin and was never obligatory on the offerer. It did not express notions of atonement, reparation, mortification, or penitence for the sin or unworthiness of the worshipper. Instead, it expressed pure gratitude and joy for a gratuitous act of deliverance bestowed on the worshipper by YHWH. Second, large amounts of choice bread, including leavened bread, were offered together with the *todah*, whereas bread was not offered with most other forms of sacrifice, and leavened bread never. Third and finally, the entire sacrificial animal was consumed by the worshipper and his entourage before the following sunrise; whereas in other forms of sacrifice, the animal was wholly burned (as with the burnt or whole offerings) or consumed by the priests (as with the sin and guilt offerings).

2. *The Superiority of the* Todah *Sacrifice:* It follows that the *todah* sacrifice was a joyous event and the occasion for a feast. Since the ritual required the consumption of the entire sacrificial animal within a limited time, the worshipper brought family and friends with him for the celebration, and these appear to be the addressees for the testimonial portions of the *todah* psalms. The poor, too, may have been invited to help consume the feast (Ps 34:2; 22:26). The mood and spirituality of the *todah* were thus quite distinct from other liturgical rituals, and some psalms, in fact, assert the superiority of worshipping God through the *todah*:

> Hear, O my people, and I will speak,
>   O Israel, I will testify against you.
> I am God, your God.
> I do not reprove you for your sacrifices;
>   your burnt offerings are continually before me....
> For every beast of the forest is mine,
>   the cattle on a thousand hills.
> I know all the birds of the air,
>   and all that moves in the field is mine.
>
> If I were hungry, I would not tell you;
>   for the world and all that is in it is mine.
> Do I eat the flesh of bulls,
>   or drink the blood of goats?

Offer to God a sacrifice of thanksgiving,
    and pay your vows to the Most High;
    and call upon me in the day of trouble;
    I will deliver you, and you shall glorify me.
                (Ps 50:7–8, 10–15)

In this famous passage, the psalmist contrasts a spirituality based on the *burnt offering*—which was entirely consumed in smoke as an offering to God and lent itself to being understood as "food" or "payment" to God—with a spirituality based on *todah* sacrifice, in which the Israelite learned to live according to a pattern of dependence on God and exuberant expression of gratitude for his salvation. The command "offer to God a sacrifice of thanksgiving [Hebrew *zebah tōdah*]" (Ps 50:14) does *not* refer to the substitution of songs or verbal expressions of praise and thanksgiving for a liturgical animal sacrifice but, rather, refers to the *todah*, in which an animal was ritually slaughtered but then consumed in celebration by the worshippers. Thus Psalm 50 asserts the superiority of the *todah* to other forms of sacrifice.

3. *The* Todah *Cycle as a* Sitz-im-Leben *for Some Psalms:* Although there are a wide variety of genres in the psalms, serving various didactic, devotional, and liturgical purposes, there are good reasons to suggest that most of the laments and thanksgivings were composed for what might be called the *todah* cycle. This cycle is a sequence of human experiences that culminated in the joyful offering of the *todah* in the sanctuary precincts (and sometimes other sacrifices, as in Ps 66:13, 15). The fundamental shape of this cycle exhibits a movement from *lament* to *praise*, and can be outlined as follows:

The Psalm or Todah *Cycle, with References to Psalm 22*

Lament Sub-cycle
1. Description of crisis (sickness, enemy threat, false accusation) (22:6–8, 12–18)
2. Cry to the Lord for deliverance (22:1–2, 19–21)
3. Confession of sin or affirmation of righteousness (22:8, 10)
4. Appeal for judgment on the evildoer(s) (22:19–21; cf. 28:4-5)
5. Vow to offer sacrifice and give thanks after the Lord grants salvation (22:22, 25)
6. Expression of confidence in the Lord (22:3–5, 9–11)
7. [Act of salvation by God—often not identified in the psalm]

Praise Sub-cycle
8. Performance of the vowed sacrifice in the Temple (22:25)
9. Celebration of the sacrificial meal, including feeding the "poor" (22:26)
10. Public testimony of thanks in the presence of the "congregation", the worshippers assembled in the Temple. May include recitation of the distress from which the psalmist was delivered. (22:22–24, 27–31)

Some psalms, like Psalm 22 used as the example above, reflect the entire cycle from lament to praise, all narrated as if in the present. However, in lived experience, there would obviously be a temporal hiatus between the time of suffering and the time during which the Lord performed the undescribed act of deliverance that brought salvation to the psalmist (cf. Ps 22:21–23). Other psalms narrate the whole cycle in the present tense (Ps 28, 31, 52, 54, 56–57, 69, 71) or have abbreviated praise cycles (Ps 59, 61, 109). Significantly, several psalms are *todah* psalms proper, in which elements of the lament sub-cycle are narrated retrospectively, from the viewpoint of the psalmist who has already been saved and is now celebrating the praise sub-cycle (Ps 18, 21, 30, 32, 34, 66, 68, 107, 111, 116, 118, 138). Still other psalms display abbreviated, generalized, or otherwise adapted forms of the *todah* (for example, Ps 75, 92, 100, 105–6, 135–36, 145). Finally, it will be noticed that most of the psalms classified as *laments* fit naturally into the first part of the *todah* cycle (for example, Ps 25, 38, 39, 40:11–17, 44, 51, 55, 60, 70, 74, 80, 85, 88, 141, 143). Indeed, many of the lament psalms include expressions of confidence or hope that anticipate the time when the psalmist will enter into the second part, the thanksgiving sub-cycle (Ps 3–7, 10, 12–13, 16–17, 26–27, 31, 35–36, 41–43, 59, 61, 64, 77, 79, 86, 102, 109, 140, 142, 144).

In sum, the movement from lament to thanksgiving for deliverance is typical of a great many psalms. In fact, generally speaking, the Psalter itself moves from a concentration of lament psalms in book 1 to a concentration of thanksgivings and hymns in book 5. Thus we can say that many individual psalms, and the Psalter as a whole, display a "*todah* shape".

Theological Issues in the Psalms

Following the direction given by the sacred editor of the canonical psalms, who provided a wisdom introduction (Ps 1) and a Davidic-messianic introduction (Psalm 2) to the Psalter as a whole, we will consider the theology of the psalms under the categories of *wisdom* and *messianism*.

The Psalms as a Book of Wisdom

Wisdom in ancient Israel was never purely theoretical or abstract; rather, it was intensely practical and moral. "Wisdom" (Hebrew *hokhmah*) referred not so much to immense intellectual knowledge (although it could include that), but most of all to the ability to make sound judgments about how to live life in a way that led to human flourishing for the individual, the family, and the community. Indeed, recent scholarship has emphasized the fact that the Psalms themselves may be regarded as *torah*—meaning "instruction"—for how ancient Israelites were to live their lives and walk with God (what we would call today "ethics").[14]

All of the biblical wisdom literature aims to communicate this *hokhmah*, the prudence necessary to live life well. Psalm 1 and several others—notably Psalm 119—suggest that the book of Psalms, despite its quite different genre vis-à-vis the other books of wisdom, does communicate *hokhmah*. Meditating on the psalms is, indeed, a way to "meditate" on the "law [*torah*] of the LORD" (Ps 1:2)

---

[14] See Gordon Wenham, *The Psalms as Torah: Reading Biblical Song Ethically* (Grand Rapids, Mich.: Baker Academic, 2012).

that will enable one to become "like a tree planted by streams of water, that yields its fruit in its season, and its leaf does not wither" (Ps 1:3).

How do the psalms communicate *hokhmah* and teach the *torah* or instruction of YHWH? Some psalms do so in a straightforward manner. Didactic in form, they enumerate moral laws and truths about "the way things are" (Ps 15, 24). Others draw instructive lessons for how to act (and not act) by reviewing the history of Israel (Ps 78, 95, 105–6). But most psalms are not overtly didactic. Rather, they teach *hokhmah* in an indirect form. Through the psalms, the reader is invited to share the inner spiritual life of the psalmist—in particular, David— and, by sharing this experience, gradually become accustomed to the habits of mind and heart involved in living all of life in direct relationship to God and in constant dialogue with him.

The Psalms as a Book of Davidic Messianism

The Psalms reflect a shift in the spirituality and liturgy of the people of Israel from the Mosaic covenant economy to the Davidic covenant economy. Although Christian readers can sometimes overlook the fact by referring to both of them under the rubric of the "Old Covenant", the Mosaic and Davidic covenants differed significantly, as is illustrated by the chart below.

The Mosaic covenant is associated with Mount Sinai and the Tabernacle sanctuary. God's instructions came in the form of *law* (Hebrew *torah*) intended for the people of Israel alone, because the presumed polity (form of governance) was nationalistic. No instruction for music or song in the liturgy is provided in the Mosaic

	Mosaic	Davidic
Location	Sinai	Zion
Sanctuary	Tabernacle	Temple
Form of Instruction	Torah	Wisdom
Polity	National	International
Style of Liturgy	Silent	Musical
Preferred Sacrifice	Burnt Offering	Todah

law, with the exception of the blowing of trumpets on certain occasions. The preferred form of sacrifice, given pride of place among the listings of offerings (Lev 1), was the solemn *whole* or *burnt* offering (Hebrew *'olah*), in which the entire animal was consumed in flame to God, with neither priest nor people participating in the meal.

The Davidic covenant, on the other hand, was associated with Mount Zion and the Temple built by David's heir, Solomon. King Solomon also instructed the nations in the will of God through the wisdom literature, which for the most part consisted in an explication of the natural law, free from Israelite ceremonial obligations, and thus able to be practiced among all the nations that were incorporated into the Davidic-Solomonic empire. David himself was a liturgical reformer who introduced joyful music and song into the liturgy, and liturgical practice—if the psalms are any indication—came to be dominated by the offering of the *todah*, as was seen in Psalm 50 above.

Thus the psalms truly represent a reconfiguration of the spirituality and liturgy of Israel around the Davidic covenant rather than the Mosaic. Of course, the Mosaic law continued to be obligatory and honored among the pious of

Israel, as Psalms 1, 19, 119, and others attest. Yet the hopes of God's people now extended *beyond* the horizon of the Mosaic covenant to the sweeping and universal promises associated with David, his kingdom, and his heirs.

Not only does David figure prominently in the Psalms as the ideal psalmist, but royal psalms are placed in strategic locations in the Psalter: as part of the two-fold introduction (Ps 2), marking the emotional climax and finale of book 2 (Ps 72), and marking the emotional low point of the entire Psalter and conclusion of book 3 (Ps 89). Then, as we noticed, significant royal/Davidic psalms mark the transition from lament to praise in the three cycles of book 5 (Ps 110, 132, 145).

If the Psalms in their final form are read as the "story" of the Davidic king, he is introduced in Psalm 2, reaches the height of glory in Psalm 72, and experiences exile and rejection in Psalm 89. After Psalm 89, there is no clear answer to the problem of the rejection of the Davidic covenant brought up at the end of this psalm. Although certain psalms do reflect resolution (at least partial) to the problem of the exile (Ps 107:3; 126) and the destruction of the Temple (Ps 122), no psalm reflects the restoration of the son of David to the throne, because there was, of course, no such restoration in history. But the fact that important Davidic psalms appear late in the Psalter among psalms that reflect a postexilic context reflects a conviction that the promises of God to David have not been, and cannot be, finally rejected; rather, they are yet to be fulfilled (Ps 110, 132). In other words, the Psalter is a book of hope for the future restoration of Israel under the figure of an "anointed one" (Hebrew *mashiah*), who is also a son of David. The figure of the Davidic king destined to rule the nations will return.[15]

The Davidic "Constellation" of Motifs in the Psalms

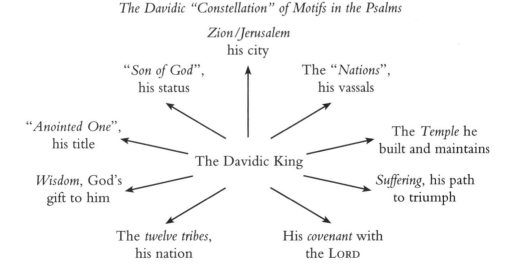

In other words, long before the birth of Jesus, the Psalms were read by the people of Israel as *messianic*, in at least two ways: the Psalms were understood as eschatological prophecies and descriptions *about* the Messiah and as the first-person speech *of* the Messiah, the future Son of David.

---

[15] Mitchell, *Message of the Psalter*.

The Psalms in the Living Tradition

A very strong case can be made that, after the four Gospels, there is no book of Scripture that has been more foundational, more central, or more widely cited, memorized, and meditated upon than the book of Psalms. For example, in the New Testament, the Psalms are by far the most frequently quoted book of the Old Testament. In the age of the early Church Fathers, commentaries and homilies on the Psalms are written by a stunning array of figures: Hippolytus of Rome, Origen of Alexandria, Jerome of Bethlehem, Eusebius of Caesarea, Athanasius of Alexandria, Basil of Caesarea, Gregory of Nyssa, Didymus the Blind, Evagrius of Pontus, John Chrysostom of Constantinople, Theodore of Mopsuestia, Theodoret of Cyrus, Cyril of Alexandria, Hesychius of Jerusalem, Hilary of Poitiers, Ambrose of Milan, Augustine of Hippo, and Cassiodorus of Calabria, just to name the major figures. And that is to say nothing of the commentaries written in later centuries by figures such as Thomas Aquinas, Peter Canisius, Cornelius Lapide, and countless others!

In short, a case can be made that the Psalter is by far the most popular and commented-upon book of the Old Testament in the history of the Church. In the Ancient Christian Commentary on Scripture series, the two volumes on the Psalms total one thousand pages of double-columned text, and that is just a "sampling" of the patristic material.[16] In light of this situation, it should go without saying that all we can do here is give a few examples of key ways in which the Psalter was read by Christians in the living tradition of the Church.

Jesus Prayed the Psalms during His Earthly Life

Before doing so, however, it may be helpful to point out first that, given the fact that Jesus of Nazareth was a first-century Jew, we can be quite certain that Jesus prayed these particular prayers during his earthly life. In laying the foundations for the Christological reading of the Psalms so characteristic of the living tradition, the *Catechism of the Catholic Church* rightly highlights several points, which can be summarized as follows:

1. The book of Psalms was *the prayer book of the Jewish people*.
2. The Psalms *commemorate* past acts of salvation and *anticipate* future redemption.
3. *The Psalms were "prayed by Christ"* during his earthly life as a devout Jew.
4. *Jesus fulfilled the Psalms* through his Passion, death, and Resurrection.
5. For these reasons, the Psalms remain "essential" to the prayer of the Church. (Cf. *CCC* 2586)

The historical fact that the Psalms were prayed by Jesus is essential to understanding how it is that the Church, from the beginning, saw these prayers attributed

---

[16] See Craig A. Blaising and Carmen S. Hardin, *Psalms 1–50*, Old Testament 7, Ancient Christian Commentary on Scripture, ed. Thomas C. Oden (Downers Grove, Ill.: InterVarsity Press, 2008), and Quentin F. Wesselschmidt, *Psalms 51–150*, Old Testament 8, Ancient Christian Commentary on Scripture, ed. Thomas C. Oden (Downers Grove, Ill.: InterVarsity Press, 2007).

to David, Asaph, and others as being fulfilled in Christ. On the level of history, this process of identifying Jesus with the voice of the psalmist began *with Jesus himself*, as he, as a first-century Jew, took the words of the psalms upon his lips in personal and communal prayer and made them his own. These prayers, above all others, remain "essential" to the worship of the Church because they are the only prayers we possess that are both inspired by the Holy Spirit and prayed by Jesus himself during his earthly life.

In the language of later Trinitarian theology, one could sum it up this way: the Psalms were (1) inspired by the Holy Spirit, the Third Person of the Trinity, (2) prayed by Jesus Christ, the Second Person of the Trinity, and (3) offered to the Father, the First Person of the Trinity. In this way, Jesus' praying of the Psalms consecrates them as a special entry into the life of the Trinity (cf. *CCC* 260).

The Messianic Psalms and the Life of Christ

Indeed, in one sense, it is the historical fact of Jesus himself having prayed the Psalms that lays the foundation for the messianic interpretation of the Psalms that is so prevalent in the teachings of Jesus himself and the writings of the New Testament. And, over and over again, the preeminent interpretation of the Psalms is a *messianic* or *Christological* interpretation, in which Jesus himself (or one of the New Testament writers) places a psalm on the lips of Jesus or interprets the psalm as having been fulfilled in the life, death, Resurrection, and Ascension of Jesus.

For example, in the Gospel of Matthew, Jesus himself interprets certain psalms with reference to himself, thus either implying or stating outright that he is the messianic fulfillment of these psalms:

The Life of Jesus	The Book of Psalms
The triumphal entry into Jerusalem (Mt 21:14–17)	"Blessed is he who enters" (Ps 118)
	"By the mouth of babies" (Ps 8)
The rejection of Jesus by the elders (Mt 21:42)	"The stone which the builders rejected" (Ps 118)
Jesus' question about the Messiah (Mt 22:41–46)	"The Lord said to my Lord" (Ps 110)
The death of Jesus on the Cross (Mt 27:45–50)	"My God, my God, why have you forsaken me?" (Ps 22)

Significantly, this messianic or Christological interpretation of the book of Psalms with reference to Jesus continues in the rest of the New Testament. For example, in his very first sermon, the apostle Peter at Pentecost declares that two of the psalms of David were only partially applicable to David himself and have now been fulfilled in the death, Resurrection, and Ascension of Jesus of Nazareth:

The Life of Jesus	*The Book of Psalms*
Death, burial, and failure of his body to corrupt in the grave (Acts 2:29–33)	"You do not give me up to Sheol, or let your godly one see the Pit." (Ps 16)
The Resurrection and Ascension of Jesus into heaven (Acts 2:34–36)	"The Lord says to my lord: 'Sit at my right hand.'" (Ps 110)

Notice here how Peter highlights those aspects of the Psalms which are *discontinuous* with the life of the original psalmist (who in this case he takes to be David) and uses these aspects in particular to show that the Psalms were awaiting a greater fulfillment than their initial application to the life of the psalmist—such as David dying and being buried and experiencing bodily corruption, as well as never ascending to the right hand of God (Acts 4:29, 34)—and then showing how these elements *have been* fulfilled in the life of Jesus.

Psalm 22 and the Passion of the Messiah

Above all, one may contend that it is this kind of Christological interpretation of the Psalms that will go on to dominate the way in which they are interpreted in the living tradition of the Church. Not only are there many other examples of such interpretation in the New Testament (for example, Acts 4:23–31; Heb 1–13), but the early Church Fathers and later Christian commentators universally agreed that the ultimate fulfillment of the Psalms took place in the life, death, and Resurrection of Jesus himself.

Although many examples of this could be given, perhaps the most famous is Psalm 22, which is identified as a "Psalm of David" but contains descriptions of sufferings—such as the psalmist's "hands and feet" being "pierced" and the casting of "lots" for his "garments" (Ps 22:16–18)—which David himself never literally experienced. Perhaps more than in any other psalm, the Church Fathers saw in this a prophecy of the Passion and death of Jesus. For example, in his famous work *Proof of the Gospel*, in which he makes the case for the truth of Christianity from Old Testament history and prophecy, Eusebius of Caesarea writes of this psalm:

> The Psalm refers to Christ and no one else, for its contents harmonize with none other but him.... But if any one would apply them to some other person, whether king, prophet or other godly man among the Jews, let him prove if he can how what is written is in harmony with him.... What gathering of evil people pierced his feet as well as his hands, stripped him of his raiment, divided some of it among themselves and cast lots for the remainder?... Who are the brothers, and what church is it of which this suffering one says, "In the midst of the church I will hymn you" [Ps 22:25 LXX], adding, not the one Jewish nation but "all the earth shall understand, and turn to the Lord, and all the kindreds of the nations shall worship before him" [Ps 22:27 LXX]? It is for you yourself to test every expression in the psalm and see if it is possible to apply them to any chance character. You will find them only applicable to our Savior, who is most true and most to

be trusted and who applied the words of the psalm to himself, as the Evangelists bear witness.[17]

In other words, for Eusebius, although Psalm 22 begins with a cry of dereliction—"My God, my God, why have you forsaken me?"—it ends with the praise of God being sung by the suffering righteous one in the "assembly" or "church" (Greek *ekklēsia*; Hebrew *qahal*) and the conversion of the Gentile nations to the one true God. This historical fact—the conversion of countless numbers of pagan Gentiles to the worship of the God of Israel, was seen as one of the greatest proofs for the fulfillment of the Psalms in the death and Resurrection of Jesus of Nazareth, the Messiah.

The Psalms and the Life of the Individual Christian

As we saw above, as the liturgical prayer book of the people of Israel, the Psalms were not only attributed to great figures such as King David, King Solomon, Moses, the Levitical singers Asaph, the Sons of Korah, or the wise men Ethan and Heman. They were also prayed and sung by *the people of Israel*, who took the words of the Psalter and made them their own, especially during the annual religious festivals in Jerusalem and while offering sacrifices in the Temple. Because of this, the Psalms have a double function: they are both *"personal"* prayers and *"communal"* prayers (see *CCC* 2586). Along similar lines, in the living tradition of the Church, the Psalms were viewed as being fulfilled not only in the life of Jesus, but in the lives of his disciples as well. Indeed, since Christians are incorporated into Christ, the Psalms may be read with profit as words *about*, and words *of*, the Christian believer.

In the early centuries of the Church, perhaps no Christian author expressed this better or more succinctly than Saint Athanasius of Alexandria, who wrote a famous letter to a friend of his in which he showed how the entire Psalter contained inspired prayers for any possible occasion in the life of a Christian.

Among all the books, the Psalter has certainly a very special grace, a choiceness of quality well worthy to be pondered; for, besides the characteristics which it shares with the other [books of Scripture], it has this peculiar marvel of its own, that within it are represented and portrayed in all their great variety the movements of the human soul. *It is like a picture, in which you see yourself portrayed and, seeing, may understand consequently how to form yourself upon the pattern given.* Elsewhere in the Bible you read only that the Law commands this or that to be done, you listen to the Prophets to learn about the Saviour's coming, or you turn to the historical books to learn the doings of the kings and holy men; but in the Psalter, besides these things, your learn about *yourself.* You find depicted in it all the movements of your soul, all its changes, its ups and downs, its failures and recoveries. *Moreover, whatever your particular need or trouble, from this same book you can select a form of words to fit it,* so that you do not merely hear and then pass on, but learn the way to remedy your ill. . . .

[17] Eusebius of Caesarea, *Proof of the Gospel* 10.8.491–92, trans. W.J. Ferrar (1920; repr., Eugene, Ore.: Wipf & Stock, 2001), as quoted in Blaising and Hardin, *Psalms 1–50*, 168–69.

Briefly, then, if indeed any more is needed to drive home the point, the whole divine Scripture is the teacher of virtue and true faith, but the Psalter gives a picture of the spiritual life....

It is possible for us, therefore, to find in the Psalter not only the reflection of our own soul's state, together with precept and example for all possible conditions, but also a fit form of words wherewith to please the Lord on each of life's occasions.[18]

For Athanasius, then, the Psalms are not only fulfilled in the life of Jesus; they are also, in a sense, fulfilled in the lives of every individual disciple who takes the inspired words of this book of prayer and makes it his own.

The "Table" of Psalm 23 and the Feast of the Eucharist

In order to illustrate this ancient Christian interpretation of the Psalms with reference to the lives of believers, we give here one example from one of the most beloved of all psalms: "The LORD is my shepherd" (Ps 23).

In the literal sense of the text, the psalm refers to David being shepherded, protected, and provided for by the Lord. In the living tradition of the Church, the images of God's providing a feast for David were seen as fulfilled in the lives of believers, not only in a general way, but in particular through the sacraments. As Saint Ambrose declares: "How often have you heard Psalm 23 and not understood it! See how it is applicable to the heavenly sacraments."[19] In the same vein, Eusebius of Caesarea writes:

> In place of the ancient sacrifices and whole burnt-offerings the incarnate presence of Christ ... was offered. And this very thing He proclaims to his Church as a great mystery expressed with prophetic voice. As we have received a memorial of this offering which we celebrate on a table by means of symbols of His Body and saving Blood according to the laws of the new covenant, we are taught again by the prophet David to say, "Thou hast prepared a table before me ..." [Ps 23:5]. Here it is plainly the mystic Chrism and the holy Sacrifices of Christ's Table that are meant.[20]

In other words, for Eusebius and other early Christians, not only do the messianic and moral aspects of the Psalter find fulfillment in Christ and the Church, but also the *liturgical* realities described by the Psalter are ultimately fulfilled in the sacrificial banquet of the Eucharist.

The Book of Psalms as the Summary of All Scripture

Given the universal application of the Psalms to the life of Jesus, of each individual disciple, and indeed of all human beings, the Psalter eventually came

---

[18] Athanasius, "Letter to Marcellinus on the Interpretation of the Psalms", in *On the Incarnation*, trans. by a Religious of C.S.M.V. (Crestwood, N.Y.: St. Vladimir's Seminary Press, 1993), 103–4.

[19] Ambrose, "On the Sacraments" 5.3.13, in *Theological and Dogmatic Works*, trans. Roy J. Deferrari, The Fathers of the Church 44 (Washington, D.C.: Catholic University of America Press, 1963), 312.

[20] Eusebius of Caesarea, *Proof of the Gospel* 1.10.39, pp. 60–61.

to be regarded as in a certain sense the *summa* of all inspired Scripture. In the thirteenth century, Thomas Aquinas produced a commentary on the Psalms in which he argued that everything that is taught elsewhere in the Bible is contained in some way in the Psalter:

> The material [in the Psalter] is universal, for while the particular books of the Canon of Scripture contain special materials, this book [of Psalms] has *the general material of Theology as a whole*. . . . Now the work of God is fourfold; namely, that of creation . . . , governance . . . , reparation . . . , glorification. . . . There is a complete treatment of all these things in this doctrine. First, of the work of creation, Psalm 8 ("I will see your heavens, the work of your fingers"). Second, of the work of governance, because in this book all the stories of the Old Testament are touched upon: Psalm 77 ("I will open my mouth in parables . . ."). Third, of reparation, with respect to the head, namely Christ, and with respect to all the effects of grace, Psalm 3 ("I lay down, and sleep comes to me . . ."). *All the things that concern faith in the incarnation are so clearly set forth in this work that it almost seems like Gospel, and not prophecy.* Fourth, there is the work of glorification: Psalm 149 ("The saints will exult in his glory . . ."). *And this will be the reason why the Psalter is read more often in the Church, because it contains the whole of Scripture.*[21]

Surely it is remarkable that Thomas Aquinas, whose most famous work is the "Summary of All Theology" (Latin *Summa Theologica*) should describe the book of Psalms as itself the *Summa Scriptura*: the summary of all Scripture!

The Book of Psalms in the Lectionary

Obviously, the Psalms are the most liturgical book of the Old Testament. In our own day and time, both in the Lectionary for Mass and in the Liturgy of the Hours, the Psalter is without contest the most frequently read book, exceeding even any one of the four Gospels. In this way, the Psalms are the beating heart of the Church's life of prayer. In fact, the use of the Psalms in the liturgy is so extensive that it is not possible here to offer the tables and analyses of the use of the Psalms in the Lectionary as we have with other books, for such a task would require a separate volume! Indeed, the Psalter is the one book that the Church as a whole, when the Lectionary and the Liturgy of the Hours are combined, prays *every single day* of the year, without ceasing. In this way, the Psalms are truly both "the masterwork of prayer in the Old Testament" and "essential to the prayer of the Church" in the New Covenant (*CCC* 2585, 2586).

Conclusion

The Psalms are a collection of sacred songs of widely different genres and dates of composition spanning over half a millennium of Israel's history. They

---

[21] Thomas Aquinas, *Exposition on the Psalms of David*, introduction, trans., and ed. J. Kenney, O.P., available at http://dhspriory.org/thomas/.

are arranged in five books, whose dominant moods and perspectives roughly follow the fortunes of the kingdom of David, from David's sufferings (book 1) through his triumphs (book 2), to the decline of his kingdom (book 3) and the exile (book 4), culminating in the partial restoration of the postexilic period and the hope for a future eschatological restoration (book 5). Many of the psalms are attributed to David and were written for recitation while offering sacrifice in the Temple, in particular the thanksgiving or *todah* sacrifice and the cycle of human experiences that culminated in offering that sacrifice. The person of David and the constellation of elements that surrounded the Davidic monarchy—the covenant, Zion, the Temple, the "nations", and others—are constant features of the Psalms. In the postexilic period, the Psalms began to be understood as sacred speech about—and by—the royal Son of David who was to come, the "anointed one", or Messiah. Thus were they understood by Jesus, the New Testament authors, and the Church, even to this day. As the sacred songs of the Davidic liturgy, the recitation of the Psalms continues as an essential element in the celebration of the thanksgiving sacrifice of the New Covenant, the Eucharist, and in its extension, the Liturgy of the Hours. In the Church's liturgy, she employs the Psalms in order constantly to offer thanks to God for his *hesed*, his covenant fidelity in taking up and fulfilling the Davidic covenant and its promises in the New Covenant offered through Jesus Christ.

For Further Reading

Commentaries and Studies on the Psalms

Attridge, Harold W., and Margot Elsbeth Fassler, eds. *Psalms in Community: Jewish and Christian Textual, Liturgical, and Artistic Traditions*. Atlanta: Society of Biblical Literature, 2003.

Bullock, C. Hassell. *Encountering the Book of Psalms: A Literary and Theological Introduction*. Grand Rapids, Mich.: Baker Academic, 2001.

Dahood, Mitchell J. *Psalms*. 3 vols. Anchor Bible 16–17A. Garden City, N.Y.: Doubleday, 1966–1970.

Estes, Daniel J. *Handbook on the Wisdom Books and Psalms*. Grand Rapids, Mich.: Baker Academic, 2005. (See pp. 141–211.)

Goldingay, John. *Psalms*. 3 vols. Baker Commentary on the Old Testament Wisdom and Psalms. Grand Rapids, Mich.: Baker Academic, 2006–2008.

Gunkel, Hermann. *Introduction to Psalms: The Genres of the Religious Lyric of Israel*. Completed by Joachim Begrich. Translated by James D. Nogalski. Macon, Ga.: Mercer University Press, 1998.

Mitchell, David C. *The Message of the Psalter: An Eschatological Programme in the Books of Psalms. Journal for the Study of the Old Testament*, Supplement Series 252. Sheffield: Sheffield Academic Press, 1997.

Mowinckel, Sigmund. *The Psalms in Israel's Worship*. Translated by D. R. Ap-Thomas. 2 vols. New York: Abingdon Press, 1962.

Schaefer, Konrad. *Psalms*. Berit Olam. Collegeville, Minn.: Liturgical Press, 2001.

Wenham, Gordon J. *Psalms as Torah: Reading Biblical Song Ethically*. Grand Rapids, Mich.: Baker Academic, 2012.

Wright, N.T. *The Case for the Psalms: Why They Are Essential.* San Francisco: Harper-One, 2013.

Historical Questions and the Psalms

Abegg, Martin, Jr., Peter Flint, and Eugene Ulrich. *The Dead Sea Scrolls Bible: The Oldest Known Bible Translated for the First Time into English.* San Francisco: HarperOne, 1999. (See pp. 505–89.)

Braun, J. *Music in Ancient Israel/Palestine: Archaeological, Written, and Comparative Sources.* Translated by Douglas W. Scott. Grand Rapids, Mich.: Eerdmans, 2002.

Hilber, John W. "Psalms". Pages 316–463 of *The Minor Prophets, Job, Psalms, Proverbs, Ecclesiastes, Song of Songs.* Vol. 5 of *Zondervan Illustrated Bible Backgrounds Commentary.* Edited by John H. Walton. Grand Rapids, Mich.: Zondervan, 2009.

Keel, Othmar. *The Symbolism of the Biblical World: Ancient Near Eastern Iconography and the Book of Psalms.* Translated by Timothy J. Hallett. New York: Seabury Press, 1978.

The Psalms in the Living Tradition

Ambrose, Saint. "On the Sacraments". In *Theological and Dogmatic Works.* Translated by Roy J. Deferrari. The Fathers of the Church 44. Washington, D.C.: Catholic University of America Press, 1963.

Aquinas, Saint Thomas. *Exposition on the Psalms of David.* Translated and edited by J. Kenney, O.P. Available at http://dhspriory.org/thomas/.

Athanasius. "Letter to Marcellinus on the Interpretation of the Psalms". In *On the Incarnation: The Treatise De incarnatione Verbi Dei.* Translated by a religious of C.S.M.V. Crestwood, N.Y.: Saint Vladimir's Seminary Press, 1993. (See pp. 97–119.)

Augustine, Saint. *Expositions of the Psalms.* Translated by Maria Boulding. New York: New City Press, 2000–2003.

Basil the Great, Saint. "Homilies on the Psalms". Pages 151–359 in *Exegetic Homilies.* Translated by Agnes Clare Way. The Fathers of the Church 46. Washington, D.C.: Catholic University of America Press, 1963.

Benedict XVI, Pope. *A School of Prayer: The Saints Show Us How to Pray.* San Francisco: Ignatius Press, 2012. (See pp. 67–115.)

Blaising, Craig A., and Carmen S. Hardin. *Psalms 1–50.* Old Testament 7 of Ancient Christian Commentary on Scripture. Edited by Thomas C. Oden. Downers Grove, Ill.: InterVarsity Press, 2008.

Cassiodorus. *Explanation of the Psalms.* Translated by P.G. Walsh. Ancient Christian Writers 51–53. Mahwah, N.J.: Paulist Press, 1990–1991.

Chrysostom, Saint John. *Commentary on the Psalms.* Translated by Robert Charles Hill. 2 vols. Brookline, Mass.: Holy Cross Orthodox Press, 1998–1999.

Daley, Brian E., S.J., and Paul R. Kolbet. *The Harp of Prophecy: Early Christian Interpretation of the Psalms.* Notre Dame, Ind.: University of Notre Dame Press, 2015.

Eusebius of Caesarea. *Proof of the Gospel.* Translated by William John Ferrar. 1920, Eugene, Ore.: Wipf & Stock, 2001.

John Paul II, Pope. *Psalms and Canticles: Meditations and Catechesis on the Psalms and Canticles of Morning Prayer.* Collegeville, Minn.: Liturgy Training Publications, 2007.

——— and Benedict XVI. *Psalms and Canticles: Meditations and Catechesis on the Psalms and Canticles of Evening Prayer.* London: Catholic Truth Society, 2006.

Kriegshauser, Laurence, O.S.B. *Praying the Psalms in Christ*. ND Reading the Scriptures. Notre Dame, Ind.: University of Notre Dame Press, 2009.

Theodoret of Cyrus. *Commentary on the Psalms: Psalms 1–72*. Translated by Robert C. Hill. The Fathers of the Church 101. Washington, D.C.: Catholic University of America Press, 2000.

Wesselschmidt, Quentin F. *Psalms 51–150*. Old Testament 8 of Ancient Christian Commentary on Scripture. Edited by Thomas C. Oden. Downers Grove, Ill.: InterVarsity Press, 2007.

25. PROVERBS

The book of Proverbs is a collection of short sayings expressing the basic principles for leading a prudent and virtuous life. It is the foundational book of the wisdom literature collection: it lays out the fundamental principles of "wisdom" (Hebrew *hokhmah*), or prudence for living, and all other wisdom books may be viewed as building on it, either by dealing with apparent exceptions to the principles it lays out (such as Job and Ecclesiastes) or by further development of the principles themselves (for example, Wisdom of Solomon and Sirach).

In the Jewish tradition, the title of Proverbs is taken from the opening line of the book: "The proverbs of Solomon" (Hebrew *mishlēy Shelōmōh*). In the Jewish Bible, the book as a whole is situated in the third canonical division, the Writings (Hebrew *kethuvim*), after Psalms and Job and before Ruth and the Song of Solomon. In this way, the song of the virtuous woman with which the book ends (Prov 31:10–31) goes on to be exemplified by the heroines Ruth and the bride of the Song. In the Greek Septuagint, the book is titled "proverbs/sayings of Solomon" (Greek *paroimiai Solomōntos*) and is always the first of the Solomonic "trilogy": (1) Proverbs; (2) Ecclesiastes; (3) Song of Solomon. In the Latin Vulgate tradition, the book has several names, from which we get the English title "Proverbs" (Latin *Liber Proverbiorum Solomonis* or *Liber Proverbiorum* or simply *Proverbia*). Here, it is the first of the "Solomonic" Pentalogy: (1) Proverbs; (2) Ecclesiastes; (3) Song of Solomon; (4) Wisdom of Solomon; (5) Sirach. Of course, no one ever held that the last of these works was authored by Solomon, but, as we will see below, even wisdom writings explicitly not attributed to Solomon were often incorporated into the Solomonic wisdom literature and thus considered extensions of his tradition.

Before diving into the contents of the book proper, it is important to point out that a "proverb" (Hebrew *mashal*; Greek *parabolē* or *paroimia*) in biblical literature is any compressed, instructive statement employing artistic—rather than ordinary—use of language. Although usually a pithy, two-line sentence, the category of *meshalim* (Hebrew) or *parabolai* (Greek) was broad enough to include longer discourses like oracles, riddles, and the instructive "parables" told by Jesus in the Gospels (Mt 13:34–35). Indeed, Jesus is known for teaching in "figures" (Greek *paroimiais*) to his disciples (Jn 16:25–29). Such teachings were considered the very foundation of education in ancient Israel and the preferred method of instruction by many teachers and prophets.

Literary Structure of Proverbs

There are different ways to analyze the structure of the book of Proverbs. If we follow the explicit introductions found in the traditional Hebrew text (that is, the Masoretic Text), one derives the following sevenfold structure:

I. Proverbs of Solomon 1: Ten Discourses to His "Son" (Prov 1–9)
II. Proverbs of Solomon 2: Couplets (Prov 10:1—22:16)
III. Words of the Wise 1: Counsel and Knowledge (Prov 22:17—24:22)
IV. Words of the Wise 2: Judging Rightly (Prov 24:23–34)
V. The Proverbs of Solomon 3: More Couplets (Prov 25–29)
VI. The Words of Agur (Prov 30)
VII. The Words of Lemuel (Prov 31)

Although neither has an explicit introductory statement in the traditional Hebrew text, there is evidence that the collection of Numerical Proverbs (Prov 30:15–33) and the Song of the Noble Woman (Prov 31:10–31) are distinct units, because the Septuagint order of the text in Proverbs 25–31 differs in the following way:

Masoretic Text (MT)	Septuagint (LXX)
24:23–34 "Further Words of the Wise"	30:1–14 "Words of Agur"
25:1–29:27 "Proverbs of Solomon copied by the men of Hezekiah"	24:23–34 "Further Words of the Wise"
30:1–14 "Words of Agur"	30:15–33 Numerical Proverbs
30:15–33 Numerical Proverbs	31:1–9 "Words of Lemuel"
31:1–9 "Words of Lemuel"	25:1–29:27 "Proverbs of Solomon copied by the men of Hezekiah"
31:10–31 Song of the Noble Woman	31:10–31 Song of the Noble Woman

If one regards Proverbs 30:15–33 and 31:10–31 as separate units, the following structural analysis becomes possible:

Outline of the Book of Proverbs

Prologue: Solomon's Discourses to His Son (Prov 1–9)
I. Proverbs of Solomon 1 (Prov 10:1—22:16)
II. Words of the Wise 1 (Prov 22:17—24:22)
III. Words of the Wise 2 (Prov 24:23–34)
IV. Proverbs of Solomon 2 (Prov 25–29)
V. Words of Agur (Prov 30:1–14)
VI. Numerical Proverbs (Prov 30:15-33)
VII. Words of Lemuel (Prov 31:1–9)
Epilogue: The Song of the Noble Woman (Prov 31:10–31)

In this pattern, there is a strong connection between the prologue and the epilogue. These are the two places in the book where spousal imagery dominates. In the prologue, "Solomon" constantly exhorts his "son" to marital fidelity and the rejection of promiscuity, while personifying Wisdom and Folly as a desirable wife and a loose woman, respectively (Prov 1–9). The interweaving of the themes of wisdom and nuptiality is not prominent again in the book until the finale, the Song of the Noble Woman (31:10–31), in which the message of the whole book is concretized in the person of the ideal wife, who perfectly exemplifies all the virtues of wisdom and is, in fact, the embodiment of Lady Wisdom from the prologue. If this structural analysis is correct, it would have in its favor that there seems to be a reference within the book of Proverbs to its sevenfold structure, near the end of the prologue:

> Wisdom has built her house,
>> she has set up her *seven pillars*. (Prov 9:1)

It is possible that the "seven pillars" are, in one sense, the sevenfold division of the book, whether analyzed in the first or second way above. There are also smaller textual divisions within the text, especially within the prologue, that will be discussed below.

Overview of Proverbs

Prologue: Solomon's Discourses to His Son (Proverbs 1–9)

The introduction to the book of Proverbs identifies the author of the initial section, the purpose of the book, and its central teaching:

> The proverbs of Solomon, son of David, king of Israel:
>
> That men may know *wisdom* and *instruction*,
>> understand *words of insight*,
> receive instruction in wise dealing,
>> righteousness, justice, and equity;
> that prudence may be given to the simple,
>> knowledge and discretion to the youth—
> the wise man also may hear and increase in learning,
>> and the man of understanding acquire skill,
> *to understand a proverb and a figure,*
>> *the words of the wise and their riddles.*
>
> The fear of the LORD is the beginning of knowledge;
>> fools despise wisdom and instruction. (Prov 1:1–7)

Notice here the reference to the various forms of instruction that the book will contain: "wisdom" (Hebrew *hokhmah*), "instruction" or "discipline" (Hebrew *mūsar*), "words of insight" or "understanding" (Hebrew *biynah*), the understanding of a "proverb" or "parable" (*mashal*), a "figure" or "enigma" (Hebrew *melitzah*).

Even apart from any knowledge of Hebrew, this variety of terms should cue us in to the fact that there are a diversity of teaching forms adopted in the book. Equally significant, notice that the *goal* of the instruction imparted by the book is not specialized knowledge or professional advancement, much less

---

What Is "The Fear of the LORD"?

Contemporary readers are sometimes put off by the central teaching of Proverbs, that "the fear of the LORD" is the "beginning of wisdom" (Prov 1:7). What does this expression mean?

On the one hand, it is important to stress that "fear" (Hebrew *yir'ah*) does not mean "terror" so much as "reverence" or "awe". On the other hand, as Proverbs itself makes clear later, "fear of the LORD" is not just an uncontrollable emotional response to God's power and majesty; instead, it is something a person *chooses* when he does not despise the truth: "They hated knowledge and did not choose the fear of the LORD" (Prov 1:29). In this context, the "fear of the LORD" clearly refers to a recognition of, or submission to, "God's moral authority" over creation and our action.[a] Seen in this light, "the fear of the LORD" can also be defined as *humility*. Indeed, according to the literary feature of synonymous parallelism, it is significant that on occasion in Proverbs the "fear of the LORD" is coupled with "humility" (Hebrew *'anawah*) (Prov 15:33; 22:4).[b]

Once this meaning is clear, it becomes obvious why the fear of the Lord is the "beginning of wisdom". Apart from the humble submission to God's truth and moral authority, there can be no growth in wisdom, which has as its end righteousness and virtue. The truth about reality is that God is God, and human beings are not.

[a] Ellen F. Davis, *Proverbs, Ecclesiastes, and the Song of Songs*, Westminster Bible Companion (Louisville, Ky.: Westminster John Knox Press, 2000), 29.
[b] Ibid., 98–100.

---

a modern-day "degree", but rather a *virtuous life*: "righteousness" (Hebrew *tzedeq*), "justice" (Hebrew *mishpat*), "equity" or "integrity" (Hebrew *mesharim*), "prudence" or "cleverness" (Hebrew *'armah*), and so on.

After this initial description of the overarching purpose of the book, the rest of the lengthy prologue of Proverbs consists in eleven exhortations from Solomon to his "son" (Prov 1:8–19; 2:1–22; 3:1–10, 11–20, 21–35; 4:1–9, 10–27; 5:1–23; 6:1–19, 20–35; 7:1–27). In the midst of these are interspersed three discourses in which "Wisdom" (Hebrew *hokhmah*) personified—often called "Lady Wisdom"—speaks (Prov 1:20–33; 8:1–36; 9:1–18). These speeches of Lady Wisdom form an asymmetric frame or *inclusio* around the main body of King Solomon's exhortations (Prov 2–7), capped by a conclusion in which the "foolish woman" or "woman of stupidity" (Hebrew *'eshet kesilūth*)—often called "Lady Folly"—speaks as an inverted caricature of Lady Wisdom, leading her "disciples" to "the depths of Sheol", the realm of the dead (Prov 9:13–18).

The eleven exhortations of the prologue generally have a tripartite structure: an exordium (an admonition to learn wisdom), a lesson, and a conclusion. A large number of traditional *bicola* or couplet proverbs are incorporated into the exhortations, addressing a wide variety of virtues and vices such as lying, laziness, violence, humility, self-discipline, piety, docility, and others. The prologue stresses the relationship between wisdom and creation (Prov 3:19–20). In particular, Lady Wisdom's discourse regarding her role in creation identifies her as the ordering and guiding principle behind the formation of the entire cosmos (Prov 8:1–36); she herself was "acquired" or "created" (Hebrew *qanah* can mean either) before all other things (Prov 8:22).

Most of all, the prologue is remarkable for its *nuptial* portrayal of the pursuit of wisdom, in which heavy and repeated exhortations to marital fidelity and abstinence from promiscuity (Prov 2:16–19; 5:1–23; 6:23–35; 7:1–27) are mixed with personifications of Lady Wisdom as an *ideal wife* (Prov 1:20–33; 3:13–18; 4:6–13; 8:1–21; 9:1–12) and Lady Folly—who is also the "strange woman" (Hebrew *zarah*)—as a loose woman and an adulteress (Prov 9:13–18; cf. 2:16–19; 5:1–14; 7:10–23). By means of these contrasting images, Proverbs describes nuptial *fidelity* as the quintessential virtue of wisdom and *adultery* as the quintessential act of foolishness. The ideal reader of the prologue is clearly a young man beginning his adult life, for whom matters of sexual purity and marital fidelity are of paramount concern. However, the meaning of this complex portrayal of wisdom-as-ideal-bride transcends mere physical chastity and fidelity. It will recur in the epilogue (Prov 31:10–31) and is extremely important for the theological message of the book as a whole (see below).

Proverbs of Solomon 1 (Proverbs 10:1—22:16)

The first and largest collection of proverbs in the book is attributed to Solomon and consists of hundreds of *bicola* (two-line verses) usually exhibiting antithetical parallelism (that is, a contrast), well-illustrated by the first in the collection:

> A wise son makes a glad father,
> but a foolish son is a sorrow to his mother. (Prov 10:1)

Most proverbs are phrased in the indicative and contain an observation about life that has an implication for one's behavior:

> A man of quick temper acts foolishly,
> but a man of discretion is patient. (Prov 14:17)
> [*Therefore, one ought to be patient.*]

More rarely, the proverb is phrased in the imperative:

> Commit your work to the LORD,
> and your plans will be established. (Prov 16:3)

For the most part, the proverbs appear to be arranged randomly, although here and there scholars have identified small collections consisting of three or more proverbs in succession united by a common theme. It is impossible to summarize the topics addressed by the proverbs, as they cover virtually all vices and virtues and elements of daily living (see below, "Theological Issues in Proverbs"). They tend to be practical in outlook, and while piety toward the Lord is encouraged, almost nothing is said about cultic matters or the liturgy. The emphasis is on living daily life with prudence—that is, in a way that leads to righteousness, virtue, and human flourishing.

Words of the Wise 1 (Proverbs 22:17—24:22)

This collection of "the words of the wise" (Prov 22:17) also addresses a wide variety of life situations but is much shorter than the first Solomonic collection and exhibits greater literary variety. The antithetical *bicola* can scarcely be found. Instead, there are many synonymous or synthetic *bicola*, such as the one focused on the sanctity of one's land:

> Remove not the ancient landmark
>> which your fathers have set. (Prov 22:28)

There are also many *quatracola*, or pairs of *bicola* joined as a set, such as one teaching on the relationship between wisdom, righteousness, and what we would refer to today as "psychological health":

> My son, if your heart is wise,
>> my heart, too, will be glad.
> My soul will rejoice
>> when your lips speak what is right. (Prov 23:15–16)

Units of three lines (Prov 22:29) or many more lines (Prov 23:6–8; 23:29–35) can also be found in this small collection of teachings.

Parallels between Proverbs 22:1—24:22 and the Instruction of Amenemope (ca. 1200 B.C.)	
Amenemope	Proverbs
"Beware of robbing the poor, and oppressing the afflicted." (chap. 2)	"Do not rob the poor, because he is poor, or crush the afflicted at the gate." (Prov 22:22)
"Associate not with a passionate man, Nor approach him for conversation; Leap not to cleave to such an one; That terror carry thee not away." (chap. 10)	"Make no friendship with a man given to anger, nor go with a wrathful man, lest you learn his ways and entangle yourself in a snare." (Prov 22:24–5)
"Eat not bread in the presence of a ruler, And lunge not forward with your mouth before a governor. When you are replenished with that to which you have no right, It is only a delight to thy spittle. Look upon the dish that is before thee, And let that (alone) supply thy need." (chap. 23)	"When you sit down to eat with a ruler, observe carefully what is before you; and put a knife to your throat if you are a man given to appetite. Do not desire his delicacies, for they are deceptive food." (Prov 23:1–3)

Much has been written about a possible connection between this section of Proverbs and an Egyptian wisdom composition from ca. 1200 B.C. known as the *Instruction of Amenemope*. Both appear to be collections of thirty wisdom sayings (cf. 22:20 RSVCE, NAB). About half a dozen of the sayings are similar enough that one suspects a common source or some form of literary dependence. However, the large differences between the two compositions in wording and in order argue against direct literary dependence in either direction. Probably both are drawing on traditional wisdom literature forms and topics common throughout the ancient Near East.

The collection may have originally been intended to train young men in the virtues necessary to serve in court (such as civil servants) and includes advice on situations they were likely to encounter, such as etiquette at royal banquets (Prov 23:1–8).

Words of the Wise 2 (Proverbs 24:23–34)

A small collection of six proverbs of various lengths and literary forms follows, on the topics of justice, diligence, honesty, vengeance, and sloth (Prov 24:23b, 24–25, 26, 27, 28–29, 30–34). In this section of the book, we encounter one of the most striking features of the book of Proverbs: its absolute intolerance of *laziness*, which the later tradition would identify as the "deadly sin" of sloth:

> I passed by the field of a sluggard,
> > by the vineyard of a man without sense;
> and behold, it was all overgrown with thorns. . . .
> Then I saw and considered it;
> > I looked and received instruction.
> A little sleep, a little slumber,
> > a little folding of the hands to rest,
> and poverty will come upon you like a robber,
> > and want like an armed man. (Prov 24:30–34)

Notice here how the wisdom in question is not the fruit of direct divine *revelation*, but of *observation*, which any person using reason should be able to obtain.

Proverbs of Solomon 2 (Proverbs 25–29)

According to the superscription, this collection of proverbs of Solomon was written down by the "men of Hezekiah king of Judah", who reigned in the late eighth to seventh centuries (715–686 B.C.). The typical Solomonic antithetical *bicola* returns, although slightly different forms, including quatrains, are sprinkled in. Unlike the first collection, there is more evidence here of an attempt to group some proverbs by theme, such as those regarding "the fool" (Prov 26:3–12). Here we continue to see the scorn that is heaped both on the fool and on the lazy person:

> Like a dog that returns to his vomit,
> > is a fool who repeats his folly. (Prov 26:11)

> As a door turns on its hinges,
> > so does the sluggard in his bed.
> The sluggard buries his hand in the dish;
> > it wears him out to bring it back to his mouth. (Prov 26:14–15)

Words of Agur (Proverbs 30:1–14) and Numerical Proverbs (30:15–33)

Proverbs 30:1–14 is attributed to Agur, son of Jakeh of Massa. Massa was, apparently, a location in northern Arabia or southern Aram (Syria) (cf. Gen 25:14; 1 Chron 1:30). This section exhibits Aramaisms and unfamiliar diction that may indicate a different Semitic dialect from standard Biblical Hebrew. Agur reflects on the mystery of God, the truth of God's words, the virtues of moderation, the evils of slander, and the characteristics of the oppressive elite (Prov 30:2–14).

Numerical structures dominate the following collection of proverbs. Four of them share the structure "Three things are (*description*) ... and four are (*further description*)" (Prov 30:15b–16, 18–19, 21–23, 29–31). The most famous of these is the description of the diligence and order of the animal kingdom:

> Four things on earth are small,
> but they are exceedingly wise:
> *the ants* are a people not strong,
> yet they provide their food in the summer;
> *the badgers* are a people not mighty,
> yet they make their homes in the rocks;
> *the locusts* have no king,
> yet all of them march in rank;
> *the lizard* you can take in your hands,
> yet it is in kings' palaces.
> (Prov 30:24–28)

This is a classic example of what the later tradition would go on to refer to as "reading the book of creation". In Proverbs, even the visible world reveals invisible mysteries about how the virtuous human life should be lived.

Words of Lemuel, King of Massa (Proverbs 31:1–9)

This short section is actually a collection of advice that King Lemuel of Massa (a Syro-Arabic kingdom to the east of Israel) received from his mother concerning principles of wise rule. She counseled her son to avoid indulgence in sex and alcohol (Prov 31:3–5) but, rather, to provide mercy and justice for the poor, dying, and distressed (Prov 31:6–9). This is what "social justice" doctrine looks like in the Old Testament.

Epilogue: the Valiant Woman (Proverbs 31:10–31)

Finally, perhaps the most famous literary unit in Proverbs is the description of the "valiant woman" with which the book closes. This chapter has come to be known as "the Proverbs 31 woman". Intriguingly, the poem is an acrostic, with each of the twenty-two lines beginning with the next letter of the Hebrew alphabet. The intent is to portray comprehensiveness, praise of a great woman "from A to Z".

The phrase "noble woman" (Prov 31:10) is variously translated: "good wife" (RSVCE) or "woman of worth" (NAB). The Hebrew, however, is a more vigorous expression: literally, it reads "a woman of force" or "woman of valor" or "woman of strength" (Hebrew *eshet hayîl*). The basic meaning of the adjective *hayîl* is "force", and its primary context in the Hebrew Scriptures is military, used to describe an army (2 Sam 24:4) or to characterize commandos, such as the "mighty men of valor" (Hebrew *gibborê hayîl*; see Josh 10:7). So the phrase in Proverbs has the sense "woman of valor" or "valiant woman".

The poem begins by stating the "woman of valor" is "far more precious than jewels". This statement was also made about wisdom herself, not once but twice in the prologue:

> She is *more precious than jewels*,
> and nothing you desire can compare with her. (Prov 3:15)

> [F]or wisdom is *better than jewels*,
> and all that you may desire cannot compare with her. (Prov 8:11)

This obvious literary connection with the prologue's description of Lady Wisdom alerts us to the fact that the poem operates on two levels of meaning. On the one hand, it is describing an ideal wife in ancient Israelite culture. On the other hand, it is an allegorical description of Lady Wisdom herself, similar to the songs of Wisdom from the prologue (Prov 1:20–33; 8:1–36; 9:1–12), as the following table shows:

Parallels between Lady Wisdom and the Valiant Woman		
Characteristic	Lady Wisdom	The Valiant Woman
More precious than jewels	"She is more precious than jewels." (Prov 3:15; 8:11)	"She is far more precious than jewels." (Prov 31:10)
Provides food and direction for her household	"She has slaughtered her beasts, she has mixed her wine, she has also set her table. She has sent out her maids to call." (Prov 9:2–3)	"She brings her food from afar. She rises while it is yet night and provides food for her household and tasks for her maidens." (Prov 31:14b–15)
Repays her lover with prosperity	"I love those who love me.... Riches and honor are with me, enduring wealth and prosperity.... [I] endow ... with wealth those who love me." (Prov 8:17–18, 21)	"The heart of her husband trusts in her, and he will have no lack of gain. She does him good, not harm, all the days of her life." (Prov 31:11–12)
Sound instruction comes from her mouth	"Hear, for I will speak noble things, and from my lips will come what is right, for my mouth will utter truth;... all the words of my mouth are righteous." (Prov 8:6–8)	"She opens her mouth with wisdom, and the teaching of kindness is on her tongue." (Prov 31:26)

(continued)

Parallels between Lady Wisdom and the Valiant Woman (*continued*)		
Characteristic	Lady Wisdom	The Valiant Woman
Incomparable to others	"Nothing you desire can compare with her." (Prov 3:15, cf. 8:11)	"Many women have done excellently, but you surpass them all." (Prov 31:29)
Contrasted with merely physical attraction	"Do not desire her [the loose woman's] beauty in your heart, and do not let her capture you with her eyelashes." (Prov 6:25)	"Charm is deceitful, and beauty is vain." (Prov 31:30a)
Associated with fear of the Lord	"The fear of the LORD is the beginning of wisdom." (Prov 9:10)	"A woman who fears the LORD is to be praised." (Prov 31:30b)

Far from being a mere afterthought or appendix, the poem about the valiant woman is the climactic summation of the entire book. The sacred author is not content to give us mere precepts and instructions on wisdom, but wishes to show us wisdom in action in daily life, wisdom embodied in a living person. So, in this poem, wisdom has become incarnate in the woman of valor, who exhibits all the virtues of wisdom—prudence, justice, fortitude, temperance—from "A to Z", comprehensively.

It is striking that, of all the characters the sacred author could have chosen to embody wisdom in the poetic finale of his work, he does not choose a king, priest, prophet, or sage ... but a wife and mother!—thus defying the modern caricature that considers the sacred authors as misogynistic and unable to recognize the value of women or their contribution to society. The wide range of activities in which the valiant woman is involved—the preparation of food (vv. 14–15), governance of a bustling estate (15b, 27), real estate transactions (16a), agriculture (16b), textile production (13, 24), social justice and works of mercy (20), education (26), retail (18a), wholesale (24b), and child-rearing (28a)—also contradicts the stereotype that women's roles within society were constrained and/or unrecognized in Old Testament times. Nonetheless, most of the valiant woman's activities are in the private sphere, outside of the direct public eye, because the wise woman does not feel the need to aggrandize herself. It is her family that gives her public praise (vv. 28–29), since it is written, "Let another praise you, and not your own mouth" (Prov 27:2).

Historical Issues in Proverbs

The Origins of the Book of Proverbs

Unlike other books of the Bible about which scholars must postulate hypothetical sources and attribute them to different authors (such as Isaiah), the book of Proverbs explicitly describes itself as a composite work that was gathered together over time. As we saw above, the body of the work attributes certain portions to Solomon himself (Prov 10:1; 25:1), other parts to anonymous sages known as "the wise" (Prov 22:17; 24:23), and the final two sections to two otherwise-unknown Gentiles: Agur (Prov 30:1–14) and King Lemuel (Prov 31:1–9). Certain scribes working for King Hezekiah gain credit for compiling five chapters in the middle of the book (Prov 25–29; cf. 25:1). In light of all these explicit internal indications, it seems clear that the opening line—"the proverbs of Solomon, son of David, king of Israel" (Prov 1:1)—cannot be interpreted as attributing authorship of the entire book to him, but rather it serves "the function of noting Solomon's foundational importance to the collection".[1]

With that said, there is still the question of whether the portions of the book ascribed to Solomon may be regarded as having originated with him. On the one hand, most twentieth-century scholars dismissed the Solomonic authorship of any part of Proverbs for a variety of reasons.[2] First and foremost, there is the widespread skepticism about the historicity of Solomon and his reign, due to the rise of biblical minimalism, which we discussed above (see chapter 15 on 1–2 Kings). Obviously, if the picture of Solomon in 1–2 Kings as a great king, builder, and wise man is itself unhistorical, then there is no reason to take seriously the attributions of wisdom sayings to him in the book of Proverbs. Second, doubts about the Solomonic origin of Proverbs are also raised because of other works in the wisdom literature that scholars agree were written long after Solomon's time and yet attributed to him, such as the Wisdom of Solomon or the *Psalms of Solomon*, both of which are usually dated to the first centuries B.C. or A.D. In light of such works, scholars argue that similar attributions in the Hebrew book of Proverbs cannot be taken as conclusive evidence for Solomonic origins or authorship.[3]

On the other hand, more recent scholarship has levied several arguments in favor of the book having its "inception", if not its "final editing", with Solomon and his times.[4] Scholars in favor of this view marshal three major arguments in support of the Solomonic origins of parts of the book:

1. *King Solomon and the Wisdom of the East:* First and foremost, although it might seem obvious, it should be stressed that the contents of the book of Proverbs cohere with the historical evidence we possess about Solomon's contact with the wisdom of the ancient Near East as well as with the literary activity in which he was believed to have engaged. According to the books of Kings, Solomon reigned during a period in which international trade made Israel and its capital, Jerusalem, a cosmopolitan society (tenth century B.C.), and he himself produced a remarkable output of literary activity:

Solomon's wisdom surpassed the wisdom of all the people of the east, and all the wisdom of Egypt. For he was wiser than all other men, wiser than Ethan the

---

[1] Tremper Longman III, *Proverbs*, Baker Commentary on the Old Testament Wisdom and Psalms (Grand Rapids, Mich.: Baker Academic, 2006), 25.

[2] John J. Collins, *Introduction to the Hebrew Bible* (Minneapolis: Fortress Press, 2004), 487–88.

[3] R. B. Y. Scott, *Proverbs, Ecclesiastes*, Anchor Bible 18 (New York: Doubleday, 1965), 10.

[4] Daniel J. Estes, *Handbook on the Wisdom Books and Psalms* (Grand Rapids, Mich.: Baker Academic, 2005), 217; Andrew E. Steinmann, "Proverbs 1–9 as a Solomonic Composition", *Journal of the Evangelical Theological Society* 43 (2000): 659–74.

Ezrahite, and Heman, Calcol, and Darda, the sons of Mahol; and his fame was in all the nations round about. He also uttered three thousand proverbs; and his songs were a thousand and five.... And men came from all peoples to hear the wisdom of Solomon, and from all the kings of the earth, who had heard of his wisdom. (1 Kings 4:30–32, 34)

At the very least, this evidence shows that Solomon is depicted in the most ancient histories we possess as having been the royal patron of wisdom for the people of Israel and the surrounding peoples. As Daniel Estes points out: "Unless those records are discounted as totally fictional, their existence suggests that Solomon was renowned for his wisdom."[5] One plausible historical explanation for this renown was that Solomon actually engaged in such literary wisdom activity.

2. *Parallels with Ancient Near Eastern Wisdom Literature from the Time of Solomon*: Second, as recent scholarship has demonstrated, when it comes to the contents and genre of the book of Proverbs, we possess a wealth of ancient Near Eastern parallels with which to compare the book. On the basis of such a comparison, scholars have shown that the book of Proverbs has the strongest connections in content and form with ancient Near Eastern wisdom literature from the turn of the *second and first millennia* B.C.—especially the Egyptian work known as the *Instruction of Amenemope* (usually dated to the twelfth century B.C.). Indeed, the contents of the book fit much better in the context of the preexilic Israelite monarchy than in postexilic Judaism.[6] Kenneth Kitchen writes:

> We have, in fact, some forty works of instructional "wisdom"—to which class the four books in Proverbs belong—from the ancient Near East, half of these deriving from Egypt, and all closely dated from the third to first millennia. These enable us to establish an outline history of this entire genre of writings, and to eliminate most of the guesswork where Proverbs is concerned.... Parallelism is the dominant poetical form (especially in couplets) during the third and second millennia, but much less so in this class of texts in the first millennium, when one-line epigrams and miniature essays increasingly replace parallelism....
>
> Where does this fixed framework leave Solomon? Solomon I [Prov. 1–24] ... is clearly transitional, as it has a traditional exhortative prologue (as in third- and second-millennium texts), which is relatively long (as in first-millennium texts). He uses parallelism (especially two-line couplets) mainly throughout, which is again traditional for the third, second, and early first millennia. Hence, for these and other such reasons, he belongs squarely at the hinge between the third/second millennia and the first at about 1000, which is close to Solomon's historical date in any case.... As for Solomon II (Prov. 25–29), Hezekiah's time (late eighth/ early seventh century) is late enough. By the sixth century use of parallelism is beginning to wane, and drastically so, later, in instructional wisdom works. So the headings at Prov. 1:1 and 25:1 must be taken seriously for strictly factual reasons.[7]

[5] Estes, *Handbook*, 215.

[6] See Tremper Longman III, "Proverbs", *The Minor Prophets: Job, Psalms, Proverbs, Ecclesiastes, Song of Songs*, vol. 5 of *Zondervan Illustrated Bible Backgrounds Commentary*, ed. John H. Walton (Grand Rapids, Mich.: Zondervan, 2009), 465–70.

[7] Kenneth A. Kitchen, *On the Reliability of the Old Testament* (Grand Rapids, Mich.: Eerdmans, 2003), 135–36.

Notice here that Kitchen is saying not only that the prologue and parallelism of the book of Proverbs matches the time of Solomon, but that it does *not* match the wisdom literature produced long after his day. In terms of basic historiographical method, this is a reasonable argument in favor of the Solomonic origins of the Solomonic portions of the book (especially Prov 1–24).

3. *The Multiple Superscriptions and the Antiquity of the Solomonic Portions:* Third and finally, the very fact that there are multiple superscriptions in Proverbs— some of them to Gentile wise men such as Agur and Lemuel who are almost completely unknown to us—argues *for*, not against, the antiquity of the superscriptions. If there were absolutely no controls on the origins of the material in the book, one would simply expect the entire book to be attributed to King Solomon and the other superscriptions either never to have existed or to have been eliminated. Moreover, the superscription of Proverbs 25:1 indicates further editorial work done on the book during the reign of Hezekiah (late eighth to early seventh century B.C.). Although we do not know when the book reached its final form, the reign of Hezekiah is an attractive option, since the early part of his reign seemed to witness an economic and cultural renaissance of Judean society and a spirit of optimism about the future, at least until the Assyrian campaign devastated the land. Features of Proverbs would fit this period: it exhibits an optimistic tone, seems to assume a righteous king is reigning, and reflects nothing yet of the trauma of the exile.

Theological Issues in Proverbs

The Book of Proverbs as a "Handbook" of the Moral Life

Although the book of Proverbs is widely neglected in contemporary Christianity, it was in fact designed as a kind of "handbook" to the virtuous life. Indeed, if there is any book of the Bible that was explicitly designed to function as a guidebook meant to be memorized and put into action, it is this one. In this way, Proverbs anticipates what will eventually come to be known as *moral theology*: that is, teachings meant to guide one in living life rightly, in accordance with the will of God, so as to choose good and avoid evil, to root out vice and build up virtue. In order to see this clearly, it is helpful to list here the number of sayings in the book that give instruction on common virtues and vices:

The Seven Deadly Sins and Seven Opposing Virtues in Proverbs

1. Pride (Prov 21:24; 29:23)	*1. Humility* (Prov 1:7; 3:5, 7; 15:33)
2. Anger (Prov 15:18; 19:19; 27:4)	*2. Gentleness/Patience* (Prov 12:16; 16:32; 19:11; 29:8, 11)
3. Envy (Prov 24:19–20; 27:4)	*3. Joy in the Good of Others* (Prov 24:17–18)
4. Greed (Prov 11:1; 15:27; 20:10, 23; 17:8, 23; 19:6; 25:14; 28:21)	*4. Generosity* (Prov 18:16; 19:17; 21:14; 28:27)

5. Lust (Prov 6:24–29)	*5. Chastity* (Prov 5:15–20)
6. Gluttony/Drunkenness (Prov 20:1; 21:17; 23:19–21, 29–35)	*6. Temperance* (Prov 23:1–3, 6–8)
7. Sloth (Prov 6:9–11; 10:4; 13:4; 24:30–34; 26:13–16)	*7. Diligence* (Prov 6:6–8; 10:5; 13:5; 28:19; 31:27)

This is by no means an exhaustive list of moral topics addressed by Proverbs.[8] Nevertheless, it shows the extent to which the book of Proverbs was intended to function as a kind of "guidebook" to a life of righteousness and virtue.

The Book of Proverbs and Salvation History

Proverbs and other wisdom books pose something of a problem for biblical theologians because the covenant-historical perspective that dominates the Pentateuch, the historical books, and the prophetic literature seems absent. In Proverbs, for example, almost nothing explicit is said about covenant, law, salvation history, Mount Sinai, the cult, and so on. For this reason some scholars have despaired of integrating the wisdom literature with the rest of the Old Testament and simply concede that it presents an alternative theology to the other books.

Such a radical disjunction between the supposedly "secular" wisdom of Proverbs and other books is not necessary. The key to understanding the role of the wisdom literature, and Proverbs in particular, is the *Solomonic* character of the book. By leading with the Solomonic superscription, the book of Proverbs anchors the wisdom literature to the covenant history of Israel, linking it to the Davidic covenant as the form of instruction suitable for his empire. Just as Moses provided Israel with the law, which was particular, nationalistic, and cultic, appropriate to its role as a separate and priestly people, so Solomon later provided his international empire with Wisdom, which was universal, international, and "secular" in the sense of focused on "this-world" (Latin *saecula*; 1 Kings 4:21, 34). Although Proverbs firmly insists that reverence for the Lord, the God of Israel, is the foundation for accumulating wisdom, nonetheless, the proverbs themselves are largely observations and exhortations of the natural law with regard to daily living. In stark contrast to the Pentateuch, *one need not be an Israelite or reside close enough to the Temple to make regular pilgrimages in order to put the exhortations of Proverbs into practice.* As we will see, when we come to the New Covenant, through which the empire of David and Solomon will be restored and transformed in the Church, the universality of the wisdom literature will prove central to moral catechesis within the Church.

The Book of Proverbs and the Liturgy of the Temple

With that said, it must be stressed that the book of Proverbs is not purely "secular" wisdom, in the contemporary sense of secularism. Indeed, although

---

[8] For such a list, see Longman, *Proverbs* (Baker), 549–78.

Proverbs emphasizes the practice of virtue in daily life in an international context with less focus on the liturgy than in some other books, there are a couple of references to the Israelite liturgy that are important to highlight and that make clear that the book reflects a thoroughly theological world view.

First and foremost, Proverbs identifies "the fear of the LORD" as the beginning of wisdom (Prov 1:7). As already noted above, the term "fear" conveys an attitude of reverence, which is broader than, but would include, formal acts of worship. Far from being secular, wisdom in Proverbs flows out of a fundamental attitude and lifestyle characterized by religious reverence of the God of Israel.

Second, Proverbs also encourages faithful and diligent participation in the sacrificial cult, when it teaches:

> Honor the LORD with your substance
>   and with the first fruits of all your produce;
> then your barns will be filled with plenty,
>   and your vats will be bursting with wine. (Prov 3:9–10)

Notice here that this is not an exhortation to participate in just *any* cult by offering the sacrifice of first fruits, but in the cult of "the Lord" (Hebrew *YHWH*), the one God of Israel.

Third and finally, it is intriguing that in the prologue, both Lady Wisdom and Lady Folly are characterized as calling out to men from "the heights" and "high places" of the city (cf. Prov 8:2–4, 9:13–14). The heights of any ancient city, including Jerusalem, were the sacred precincts, where the temple or temples were located. Thus, Lady Wisdom and Lady Folly are portrayed as competing forms of worship. Lady Wisdom represents the cult of the Lord, characterized by marriage and covenant fidelity; whereas Lady Folly represents foreign cults, characterized by fertility rituals and promiscuity:

> Wisdom has built her *house*,
>   she has set up her seven pillars.
> *She has slaughtered her beasts, she has mixed her wine,*
>   *she has also set her table.*
> She has sent out her maids to call
>   from the highest places in the town,
> "Whoever is simple, let him turn in here!"
>   To him who is without sense she says,
> *"Come, eat of my bread*
>   *and drink of the wine I have mixed.*
> Leave simpleness, and live,
>   and walk in the way of insight." (Prov 9:1–6)

Wisdom's "house" with "seven pillars" is a Temple image; the banquet with slaughtered beasts and mixed wine is a sacred or sacrificial meal. Indeed, in the ancient Israelite cult, the feast of bread and wine seems to have been associated specifically with the "Bread of the Presence", which was placed with libations of wine on the Golden Table in the Holy Place of the Tabernacle of Moses and the Temple of Solomon (see Ex 25; Lev 24:1–8; 1 Kings 7:48). With this background in mind, Wisdom is depicted as a feast to be consumed, like the sacrificial offerings of bread and wine in the Tabernacle and the Temple.

The Covenantal and Spousal Nature of Wisdom

The word "covenant" (Hebrew *berith*) occurs only once in Proverbs, and with reference to a marital covenant (Prov 2:17), not to one of the great covenants of salvation history. Nonetheless, Proverbs does have important covenantal themes.

First, there is theological significance to the fact that the reader is addressed throughout the prologue as "son". Solomon is the presumed speaker (Prov 1:1); therefore, in his address of the reader as "son", he invites the reader into a covenant relationship with himself. "Son" is a covenant category, and Solomon himself enjoyed divine sonship by virtue of his being heir of the Davidic covenant (1 Sam 7:14; Ps 89:26–27). Solomon offers to extend that blessing to his readers. If the reader accepts his invitation to sonship, then through him the reader will indirectly experience the blessings of divine sonship. In this way, in Proverbs, every reader is, in a sense, invited into the blessings of the Davidic covenant by entering into a relationship with David's heir through the embrace of the gift of divine wisdom that Solomon himself received from God and offers in turn to the reader.

Second, the covenantal significance of the nuptial presentation of Lady Wisdom needs to be explained. We have already noted in the overview how strong the nuptial theme is in the prologue and epilogue (Prov 1–9, 31:10–31). The sacred author frequently uses spousal language to describe Lady Wisdom:

> Happy is the man who finds wisdom,
>   and the man who gets understanding,
> for the gain from it is better than gain from silver
>   and its profit better than gold.
> She is more precious than jewels,
>   and nothing you desire can compare with her.
> Long life is in her right hand;
>   in her left hand are riches and honor.
> Her ways are ways of pleasantness,
>   and all her paths are peace.
> She is a tree of life to those who lay hold of her;
>   those who hold her fast are called happy. (Prov 3:13–18)

> Keep hold of instruction, do not let go;
>   guard her, for she is your life. (Prov 4:13)

> Say to wisdom, "You are my sister,"
>   and call insight your intimate friend;
> to preserve you from the loose woman,
>   from the adventuress with her smooth words. (Prov 7:4–5)

On the other hand, descriptions of wisdom are applied to the ideal wife in the epilogue, as seen above. So there is a fluidity in Proverbs between the image of the virtuous wife and the image of Lady Wisdom: the two are mutually illuminative.

In this way, the young man or "son" who is the implied reader of the book is exhorted on two levels. On a natural level, he is encouraged to remain faithful to the "wife of [his] youth" (Prov 5:18) or, if not yet married, to seek a wise woman as the ideal partner, rather than one who is merely alluring. On a theological level, Wisdom herself is presented to the young man as *the ideal spouse*. In both cases, the "son" who is the reader is exhorted to enter into, or embrace more fully, a covenant relationship: the covenant with his wife and a covenantal relationship with Lady Wisdom. In fact, all readers of the book are implicitly encouraged to enter into a spousal relationship with the Wisdom of the Lord.[9]

Proverbs in the Living Tradition

For whatever reason, "the book of Proverbs is not high on the reading list of many modern Christians."[10] However, as even a cursory glance at the writings of the Church Fathers shows, the same was not true of ancient Christianity, which saw in this book the very foundations of moral instruction and an indispensable source of practical wisdom for avoiding vice and cultivating virtue.

Christ the "Righteous" and "Wise" Man:

"The LORD ... blesses the abode of the righteous." (3:33)
"But the path of the righteous is like the light of dawn." (4:18)
"The LORD does not let the righteous go hungry." (10:3)
"Blessings are on the head of the righteous." (10:6)
"The memory of the righteous is a blessing." (10:7)
"The mouth of the righteous is a fountain of life." (10:11)
"The lips of the righteous feed many." (10:21)
"The desire of the righteous will be granted." (10:24)
"The righteous is established for ever." (10:25)
"The righteous is delivered from trouble." (11:8)
"The desire of the righteous ends only in good." (11:23)
"The fruit of the righteous is a tree of life." (11:30)
"The tongue of the wise brings healing." (12:18)
"The teaching of the wise is a fountain of life." (13:14)
"The wise man's path leads upward to life, that he may avoid Sheol beneath." (15:24)

Proverbs as One of the First Books Christians Should Read

For example, in his letter to a Christian mother named Laeta regarding how to instruct her daughter in Scripture, Jerome listed the book of Proverbs, after the Psalter, as one of the first books to be learned:

---

[9] Ibid., 216–17.
[10] Ellen F. Davis, *Proverbs, Ecclesiastes, and the Song of Songs*, Wesminster Bible Companion (Louisville, Ky.: Westminster John Knox Press, 2000), 11.

Every day she should give you a definite account of her Bible-reading.... For her the Bible must take the place of silks and jewels.... Let her learn the Psalter first, and find her recreation in its songs; *let her learn from Solomon's Proverbs the way of life*, from Ecclesiastes how to trample on the world. In Job she will find an example of patient virtue. Thence let her pass to the Gospels; they should always be in her hands. She should steep herself in the Acts and the Epistles. And when she has enriched her soul with these treasures she should commit to memory the Prophets, the Heptateuch, Kings and Chronicles, Esdras and Esther: then she can learn the Canticle of Canticles without any fear.[11]

Notice here that the reason Jerome puts Proverbs in such a prominent place is because of its value as a handbook of "moral theology": those who read it learn "the way of life".

Two Kinds of "Fear of the Lord"

As we saw above, one of the foundational principles of the book of Proverbs—and, indeed, much of the wisdom literature—is that the "fear of the LORD" is the beginning of knowledge (Prov 1:7). Not only modern commentators but ancient readers recognized that there are different kinds of "fear" and that the kind being inculcated by Proverbs needs to be rightly understood. In the words of Venerable Bede:

Two things constitute the fear of the Lord: first, the servanthood which is called the beginning of knowledge or wisdom and, second, the friendship which accompanies the perfection of wisdom. *Servile fear* is the *beginning* of wisdom because whoever begins to taste it after the error of sins is corrected by this first divine fear, lest he be led into torments. *But perfect love casts this fear out. Holy fear* of the Lord then follows, remaining forever, and is augmented by charity, not removed by it. *This is the fear with which the good son is afraid, lest he offend the eyes of his most loving father in the least degree.*[12]

With these remarkable words, Bede solves a problem for many readers of the Bible: If the "fear" of the Lord is the beginning of wisdom, then how does "perfect love" cast out "fear" (1 Jn 4:18)? Because the two fears are very different: servile fear is the beginning of the spiritual life, but holy fear, animated by charity, is the perfection of the spiritual life.

The Pursuit of Wisdom and the Pursuit of Money

Along similar lines, one of the most striking teachings in the book of Wisdom is the exhortation to pursue wisdom zealously, to "cry out" for her and "seek it" as if it were "silver", a precious commodity that in antiquity was difficult and dangerous to obtain (Prov 2:1–5). In one of his sermons, Augustine uses this image to call people to love God as much as they love money:

---

[11]Jerome, *Letter to Laeta* 107, 9, 12; cited in Benedict XV, Encyclical on St. Jerome *Spiritus Paraclitus* (September 15, 1920), no. 41.

[12]Bede, *Commentary on Proverbs* 1.1.7, in J. Robert Wright, *Proverbs, Ecclesiastes, and the Song of Solomon*, Old Testament 9, Ancient Christian Commentary on Scripture, ed. Thomas C. Oden (Downers Grove, Ill.: InterVarsity Press, 2005), 7.

It's unfitting, it's insulting, that wisdom should be compared with money, but love is being compared to love. What I see here, after all, is that you all love money in such a way that when love of money gives the order, you undertake hard labor, you put up with starving, you cross the sea, you commit yourselves to wind and wave. I have something to pick on in the matter of what you love, but I have nothing to add to the love with which you love. "Love like that, and I don't want to be loved any more than that," says God. "I'm talking to the riffraff, I'm speaking to the greedy: You love money; love me just as much. Of course, I am incomparably better; but I don't want more ample love from you; love me just as much as you love money."[13]

If one ponders the lengths to which human beings go to obtain money and the extent to which human society is animated and driven by the pursuit of money, one realizes the radical and challenging nature of Proverbs' exhortation to pursue *wisdom* like silver.

The "Creation" of Wisdom, the Incarnation, and the Council of Nicaea

Although Proverbs consists of a wealth of worldly wisdom, one of the most explicitly theological portions of the book is the hymn about the "creation" of wisdom at "the beginning" of God's work, "the first of his acts of old" (Prov 8:22–36). In the early Church, it was universally held that Proverbs 8 described the Second Person of the Trinity, whom the New Testament describes as "Christ the power of God and *the wisdom of God*" (1 Cor 1:24).

Because of this, a great deal of controversy was generated in the early Church over how to interpret the verses in which Wisdom states that "The LORD acquired me" or "The LORD created me at the beginning of his work" (Prov 8:22). The Hebrew verb *qanah* can mean either "acquire" or "create". In the lead-up to the Council of Nicaea, the priest Arius and his followers argued that *qanah* means "created" and thus the Son should be viewed as a creature and, hence, a lesser being than God the Father. Against the Arians, the Catholics argued either that *qanah* means "acquired", upholding the uncreated equality of the Son with the Father, or that the word "created" refers to the mystery of the Incarnation and not to the eternal procession of the Son from the Father, the Son being "begotten, not made". Consider, for example, the words of Athanasius, whose entire life was spent warring against the Arians:

> "We have read," they will say, "in the Proverbs, 'The Lord created me a beginning of His ways unto His works'" [Prov 8:22]; this Eusebius and his fellows used to insist on, . . . saying that the Son was one of the creatures, and reckoning Him with things originated. But they seem to me to have a wrong understanding of this passage. . . . If then son, therefore not creature; if creature, not son; for great is the difference between them, and son and creature cannot be the same, unless His essence be considered to be at once from God, and external to God.[14]

[13] Augustine, *Sermon* 399.11, in Wright, *Proverbs*, 17.
[14] Athanasius, *Defense of the Nicene Definition* 3.13, in *NPNF2* 4:158.

Along similar lines, Hilary of Poitiers, who was known as "the Athanasius of the West", recognizes that this doctrinal issue is very much a question of exegesis:

> Ignorance of prophetic diction and unskilfulness in interpreting Scripture has led them [the Arians] into a perversion of the point and meaning of the passage, *The Lord created me for a beginning of His ways for His works* [Prov 8:22]. They labour to establish from it that Christ is created, rather than born, as God, and hence partakes the nature of created beings, though He excel them in the manner of His creation and has no glory of Divine birth but only the powers of a transcendent creature. We in reply ... will make this very passage of Wisdom display its own true meaning and object. We will show that the fact that He was created for the beginning of the ways of God and for His works, cannot be twisted into evidence concerning the Divine and eternal birth, because creation for these purposes and birth from everlasting are two entirely different things.... There is a Wisdom born before all things, and again there is a wisdom created for particular purposes; the Wisdom which is from everlasting is one, the wisdom which has come into existence during the lapse of time is another.[15]

As these quotations should make clear—and many more could be given[16]—in stark contrast to the oblivion into which the book of Proverbs has fallen in modern times, in the early Church, it contained what may well be one of the most consequential theological passages in the entire Old Testament. To a large extent, the Arian crisis revolved around how one interpreted this single chapter from the book of Proverbs.

The Bread and Wine of Wisdom's Feast and the Banquet of the Eucharist

As we noted above, one of the central moments in the book is when Lady Wisdom declares that her "table" has been set and her "wine" has been mixed and invites all who hear to come and eat of her "bread" (Prov 9:1–6). In the living tradition, this picture of "Wisdom's Banquet" was seen as being fulfilled in the sacrificial feast of the Eucharist. In the words of Cyprian of Carthage:

> The Holy Spirit through Solomon shows forth the type of sacrifice of the Lord, making mention of the immolated victim and of the bread and wine and also of the altar and of the apostles. "Wisdom," he says, "has built a house and she has set up seven columns. She has slain her victims, mixed her wine in a chalice, and has spread her table." *He declares the wine is mixed, that is, he announces in a prophetic voice that the chalice of the Lord is mixed with water and wine.*[17]

Along similar lines, Pope Gregory the Great identified the "seven pillars" of Lady Wisdom (Prov 9:1) with "the very sacraments themselves".[18]

---

[15] Hilary of Poitiers, *On the Trinity* 1.35, in *NPNF2* 9:50.

[16] See Wright, *Proverbs*, 60–67.

[17] Cyprian of Carthage, *Letter* 63.5, in *Letters 1–81*, trans. Sr. Rose Bernard Donna, The Fathers of the Church 51 (Washington, D.C.: Catholic University of America Press, 1965), 205, as quoted in Wright, *Proverbs*, 73.

[18] Gregory the Great, *Morals on the Book of Job* 4.17.43, in Wright, *Proverbs*, 73–74.

The Virtuous Wife, the Bride of Christ, and the Virgin Mary

In the Church's tradition, the woman of Proverbs 31 has frequently been seen as the model for Christian women as well as believers generally, a type of the Church, and even as a type of the Virgin Mary. In this way, we see Christians drawing out the moral as well as typological senses of the text.

For example, in terms of the moral sense, Saint Gregory of Nazianzus saw in his sister, Saint Gorgonia, an image of the virtuous woman:

> The divinely inspired Solomon in his instructive wisdom, I mean in his Proverbs, praises the woman who keeps her house and loves her husband.... He praises her who is engaged honorably at home, who performs her womanly duties with fearless courage ... and who exhibits all other qualities for which he extols in song the modest and industrious woman. If I were to praise my sister on such counts, it would be like praising a statue for its shadow.[19]

According to the spiritual sense, Saint Caesarius of Arles applies these virtues to the Bride of Christ, the Church:

> The catholic church was not only preached after the coming of our Lord and Savior ... but from the beginning of the world, it was designated by many figures and rather hidden mysteries. Indeed, in holy Abel the catholic church existed, in Noah, in Abraham, in Isaac, in Jacob, and in the other saintly people before the advent of our Lord and Savior. Truly, Solomon says of her, "Who shall find a worthy wife?" [Prov 31:10]. What does he mean, "Who shall find"? Here, we should understand the difficulty, not impossibility, of finding her. That valiant woman is the church.[20]

Finally, the Church recognizes in certain descriptions of the valiant woman striking anticipations of the characteristics of the Mother of God, whom Christians since ancient times have invoked as the Seat of Wisdom:

The Valiant Woman (Proverbs 31) and the Blessed Virgin	
"She opens her mouth with wisdom, and the teaching of kindness is on her tongue." (Prov 31:26)	"Let it be to me according to your word." (Lk 1:38) "Do whatever he tells you." (Jn 2:5)
"Her children rise up and call her blessed." (Prov 31:28)	"All generations will call me blessed." (Lk 1:48)
"Many women have done excellently, but you surpass them all." (Prov 31:29)	"More blessed are you than all women." (Lk 1:42 [author's trans.] The Greek phrase "Blessed are you among women" (Lk 1:42) is a Hebraism meaning "More blessed are you than all other women.")

[19] Gregory of Nazianzus, *Funeral Oration on His Sister, Saint Gorgonia,* 8.9, in Gregory of Nazianzus and Ambrose, *Funeral Orations,* trans. Leo P. McCauley, The Fathers of the Church 22 (Washington, D.C.: Catholic University of America Press, 1953), 106, as quoted in Wright, *Proverbs,* 186.

[20] Caesarius of Arles, *Sermon* 139.1, in Caesarius, *Sermons,* vol. 2, *81–186,* trans. Sr. Mary Magdeleine Mueller, O.S.F., The Fathers of the Church 47 (Washington, D.C.: Catholic University of America Press, 1964), 276, as quoted in Wright, *Proverbs,* 186.

The Book of Proverbs in the Liturgy

The three most significant passages of Proverbs used in the Lectionary are three of the poems in which Wisdom is personified as a woman (Prov 8, 9, and 31). The significance of the poem of Wisdom at work in creation (Prov 8:22–31) to early Church development of the doctrine of the Trinity is reflected in the choice of this text for Trinity Sunday in Year C. Significantly, the invitation to the banquet set by Wisdom on the heights of the city (Prov 9:1–6) is clearly revealed as a type of the Eucharist by its association with John 6:51–58, during the reading of the entirety of the Bread of Life discourse in John 6 during Ordinary Time of Year B (Weeks 17–21). Finally, the Lectionary holds up the poem of the virtuous woman of Proverbs 31 as an example of diligence in Christian discipleship, in combination with the parable of the talents (Thirty-Third Sunday in Ordinary Time, Year A) or else on the feast days of saints, especially married women who attained sanctity. Thus, in the Church's memory, perpetuated in the liturgy, Proverbs is treasured for its presentation of Wisdom as a person, which the Church sees fulfilled in Christ and those who conform themselves to him:

Readings from Proverbs for Sundays, Feast Days, Liturgical Seasons, and Other Occasions *MSO* = Masses for Special Occasions; *OM* = Optional Memorial; *VM* = Votive Mass; *Rit* = Ritual			
Passage	Description	Occasion	Explanation
2:1–9	The one who seeks wisdom diligently will ultimately find it.	Proper of St. Benedict; *Rit*: Blessing of Abbots/ Abbesses, opt. 1	St. Benedict exemplified the diligent search for wisdom; abbots and abbesses likewise need to set an example in this regard.
4:7–13	Above all, one should acquire wisdom and treasure her carefully, and she will bestow long life and honor.	*Rit*: Blessing of Abbots/Abbesses, opt. 2	Wisdom is a necessary attribute for the leader of a monastic community.
8:22–31	God acquired wisdom before all creatures, and wisdom assisted as a workman in the process of creation.	*Holy Trinity Sunday (C)*; Common of the BVM, opt. 5	Wisdom active in creation is the Second Person of the Trinity, now fully revealed in Jesus Christ. Mary, who bore the Son of God, is likewise associated as the Seat of Wisdom.
9:1–6	Wisdom builds her house, sets her table, and invites all the simple to a rich feast.	*20th Sun. in OT (B)*; *Rit*: Installation of Acolytes; *VM*: Most Holy Eucharist	Read with John 6:51–58, Wisdom's invitation to a feast appears as a clear type of the Eucharistic banquet, where Christ, who is God's wisdom, offers himself as food. Acolytes are like the "maidservants" of Wisdom who help set the table and invite the guests.

(continued)

Readings from Proverbs for Sundays, Feast Days, Liturgical Seasons, and Other Occasions (*continued*)			
MSO = Masses for Special Occasions; *OM* = Optional Memorial; *VM* = Votive Mass; *Rit* = Ritual			
Passage	Description	Occasion	Explanation
31:10–13, 19–20, 30–31	The virtuous woman is of great value; she does good all her days and receives praise at the city gates.	*33rd Sun. in OT (A)*; Common of Holy Men and Women, opt. 11; Proper of St. Frances of Rome & St. Jane Frances de Chantal; *Rit*: Conferral of Marriage, opt. 6	Read with the parable of the three servants and the talents (Mt 25:14–30), the noble wife of Proverbs 31 becomes the image and example of the faithful servant of Christ who works diligently to bring good to her Divine Bridegroom in his absence. This eulogy of the excellent wife is particularly appropriate for canonized married women and for the conferral of the sacrament of marriage.

Reading of Proverbs for Daily Mass: Ordinary Time, Year II: Week 25		
Day	Passage Read	Description
M	3:27–34	A collection of aphorisms about living in peace with one's neighbors
Tu	21:1–6	Another collection of proverbs, concerned mostly with the proper dispositions of the "heart" or center of a man's existence
W	30:5–9	These proverbs urge reverence for the word of God and moderation of life-style.

Conclusion

The book of Proverbs is a collection of practical advice for daily living, including observations and exhortations in support of practicing the natural virtues and the natural law. Its relationship with the larger structure of biblical theology is secured by its association with Solomon. From a canonical perspective, it represents the international form of divine instruction Solomon provided for the international empire he ruled by virtue of the Davidic covenant. The book is remarkable for its personification of God's attribute of Wisdom as a woman—indeed, the ideal wife. The Church has seen in this personification an anticipation of the Incarnation of the Second Person of the Trinity and of the role of Mary, Seat of Wisdom.

For Further Reading

Commentaries and Studies on Proverbs

Davis, Ellen F. *Proverbs, Ecclesiastes, and the Song of Songs*. Westminster Bible Companion. Louisville, Ky.: Westminster John Knox Press, 2000.

Estes, Daniel J. *Handbook on the Wisdom Books and Psalms*. Grand Rapids, Mich.: Baker Academic, 2005. (See pp. 213–69.)

Fox, Michael V. *Proverbs 1–9*. Anchor Bible 18a. New York: Doubleday, 2000.

Longman, Tremper, III. *Proverbs*. Baker Commentary on the Old Testament Wisdom and Psalms. Grand Rapids, Mich.: Baker Academic, 2006.

Murphy, Roland E., O.Carm. *Proverbs*. Word Biblical Commentary 20. Nashville: Thomas Nelson, 1998.

Waltke, Bruce K. *The Book of Proverbs*. 2 vols. New International Commentary on the Old Testament 13–14. Grand Rapids, Mich.: Eerdmans, 2004–2005.

Historical Questions and the Book of Proverbs

Collins, John J. *Introduction to the Hebrew Bible*. Minneapolis: Fortress Press, 2004. (See pp. 488–89.)

Kitchen, Kenneth A. *On the Reliability of the Old Testament*. Grand Rapids, Mich.: Eerdmans, 2003. (See pp. 134–36.)

Longman, Tremper III. "Proverbs". Pages 463–503 in *The Minor Prophets, Job, Psalms, Proverbs, Ecclesiastes, Song of Songs*. Vol. 5 of *Zondervan Illustrated Bible Backgrounds Commentary*. Edited by John H. Walton. Grand Rapids, Mich.: Zondervan, 2009.

Scott, R.B.Y. *Proverbs, Ecclesiastes*. Anchor Bible 18. New York: Doubleday, 1965.

Steinmann, Andrew E. "Proverbs 1–9 as a Solomonic Composition". *Journal of the Evangelical Theological Society* 43 (2000): 659–74.

Proverbs in the Living Tradition

Caesarius, Saint. *Sermons*. Vol. 2 *(81–186)*. Translated by Sr. Mary Magdeleine Mueller, O.S.F. The Fathers of the Church 47. Washington, D.C.: Catholic University of America Press, 1964.

Cyprian, Saint. *Letters 1–81*. Translated by Sr. Rose Bernard Donna. The Fathers of the Church 51. Washington, D.C.: Catholic University of America Press, 1965.

Gregory of Nazianzus, Saint, and Saint Ambrose. *Funeral Orations*. Translated by Leo P. McCauley. The Fathers of the Church 22. Washington, D.C.: Catholic University of America Press, 1953.

Wright, J. Robert. "Proverbs". Pages 1–189 in *Proverbs, Ecclesiastes, Song of Solomon*. Edited by J. Robert Wright. Old Testament 9 of Ancient Christian Commentary on Scripture. Edited by Thomas C. Oden. Downers Grove, Ill.: InterVarsity Press, 2005.

26. ECCLESIASTES

Introduction

Ecclesiastes is one of the most atypical books of the Old Testament, a composition virtually unique both in its genre and in the manner in which it voices opinions seemingly contrary to the mainstream of biblical teaching. In it, a *persona* who seems to identify himself as King Solomon engages in a philosophical thought-experiment about the meaning of life that leads him to the brink of despondency. Despite the darkness of the book, however, believers through the ages have found solace and catharsis in its pages, and spiritual writers have continued to recommend meditation on it as an aid to detachment from the temporal world and its fleeting pleasures.

In the Jewish tradition, Ecclesiastes is known by the Hebrew title of the primary voice of the book: *Qoheleth*. The Hebrew word *Qoheleth*, usually translated as "the Preacher" (RSVCE), is a rare and unusual word. It literally means "one who calls an assembly" and is a feminine active participle based on the word for "an assembly, a congregation" (Hebrew *qahal*). The Greek Septuagint translated the Hebrew *Qoheleth* literally, building a participle from the well-known Greek word "assembly" or "congregation" (Greek *ekklēsia*); from this we get the title *Ekklēsiastēs*, which is transliterated in the Latin Vulgate as *Ecclesiastes*, thus the English title of the book. Many modern English translations render *qoheleth* as "the Preacher", trying to convey the sense of "congregational leader".

In the Jewish tradition, the Book of Qoheleth is part of the "Writings" (Hebrew *ketuvim*), specifically one of the "five scrolls" (Hebrew *megillot*) read at the great liturgical feasts. To this day, Qoheleth is read during the celebration of the Feast of Tabernacles (Hebrew *Sukkoth*) in the autumn. At first glance, the reading of such a dour book seems ill-suited for the festive occasion of Tabernacles; nonetheless, there are two possible explanations. First, Tabernacles is a harvest festival that has an element similar to the American Thanksgiving. Ecclesiastes teaches a balanced view of feasting: affirming its legitimate enjoyment when it declares: "Go, eat your bread with enjoyment, and drink your wine with a merry heart" (Eccles 9:7). Nevertheless, at the same time, the book urges temperance and the recognition of coming death and judgment: "But know that for all these things God will bring you into judgment" (Eccles 11:9). Second, and even more important, as we will see, in the books of Kings, Solomon is reported as having "assembled" (Hebrew *qahal*) the people of Israel to himself for the dedication of the Temple during the seventh month at the time of the Feast of Tabernacles (1 Kings 8:1–2, 5, 55–61). Presumably, this text was connected in Jewish tradition with the proclamation of the book of the "One Who Assembles" (Hebrew *qoheleth*)—namely, Solomon.

In the Greek Septuagint and the Latin Vulgate, Ecclesiastes found a settled place after Proverbs and before Song of Solomon, which three books were not only associated with King Solomon but also came to be understood in the Christian spiritual tradition as representing the three ages of the interior life: the (1) purgative, (2) illuminative, and (3) unitive ways to God, respectively.

Literary Genre and Structure of Ecclesiastes

The genre of Ecclesiastes is unique in the canon of Scripture. Like Job and the Song of Solomon, the book has multiple voices and could in theory be performed as a drama. However, in Ecclesiastes, the number of voices is minimal: there is only a narrator (Eccles 1:1, or 1:1–11; and 12:9–14) and "Qoheleth" (Eccles 1:12–12:8). The first-person speech of Qoheleth dominates the book; therefore, the genre of Ecclesiastes may helpfully be compared to a one-man, one-act play, introduced and concluded by a narrator. After a brief introduction, a speaker calling himself "Qoheleth" strides onto the stage to deliver a series of powerful and poetic soliloquies, at the conclusion of which the curtain falls and the narrator's voice summarizes the message of the dramatic monologue for the audience. That is not to suggest that Qoheleth was composed for performance; it is a "literary drama", so to speak, written to be read and pondered rather than performed, like certain existentialist plays in modern times (such as Beckett's *Waiting for Godot*).

The structure of Ecclesiastes is intentionally loose and rambling. Qoheleth often engages in asides or digressions. Nonetheless, careful study does reveal a basic pattern and progression in the work. After an opening soliloquy (Eccles 1:2–11) and an introduction (Eccles 1:12–18), Qoheleth delivers six reflections on the theme of "vanity" (Hebrew *hevel*; Eccles 2:1–6:9). Afterward, there is a transition and introduction to the second half of the book, where the motif of "vanity" (*hevel*) is less prominent and the idea of ignorance or incomprehensibility comes to the fore (Eccles 6:10–12). Thus Qoheleth delivers four meditations on the theme "one can't find out" (Eccles 7:1–8:17) and another four on "one doesn't know" (Eccles 9:1–11:6). Qoheleth's dramatic meditation reaches its finale with the recitation of a masterful poem on youth, aging, and death (Eccles 11:7–12:8). After the "curtain drop", the voice of the narrator focuses the message of the drama for the audience, lest Qoheleth's provocative speeches be misunderstood or misapplied (Eccles 12:9–14).

Outline of the Book of Ecclesiastes

I. Prologue (Eccles 1:1–11): "All Is Vanity!"

II. Vanity (Eccles 1:12–18; 2:1—6:9)
    A. Introduction (1:12–18): "I Applied My Mind to Seek ... Wisdom"
    B. Six Units on the Theme "Vanity" (2:1—6:9)
        1. Vanity of Pleasure (2:1–11)
        2. Vanity of Wisdom, Madness, Folly (2:12–17)
        3. Vanity of Labor (2:18–26)

Overview of Ecclesiastes

Introduction: All Things Are "Vanity"! (Ecclesiastes 1)

The voice of the narrator introduces the book, announcing that what follows are "The words of the Preacher [*Qoheleth*], the Son of David, king in Jerusalem" (Eccles 1:1). This description immediately suggests Solomon, since Solomon was not only the royal son of David and king in Jerusalem but also the one who is reported in the first book of Kings as having gathered the people of Israel in a liturgical "assembly" (Hebrew *qahal*) when he dedicated the newly built Temple:

> Then Solomon assembled [Hebrew *yaqhel*] the elders of Israel and all the heads of the tribes, the leaders of the fathers' houses of the sons of Israel, before King Solomon in Jerusalem, to bring up the ark of the covenant of the LORD out of the city of David, which is Zion. And all the men of Israel assembled [Hebrew *yiqahalū*] to King Solomon at the feast in the month Ethanim, which is the seventh month. (1 Kings 8:1–2; cf. 8:5, 55–61)

Later statements by Qoheleth himself will confirm this Solomonic identification (for example, Eccles 12:9).

As anyone familiar with this book knows, the most famous and most mysterious lines of the book are stated at the outset: "Vanity of vanities", says Qoheleth, "vanity of vanities! All is vanity" (Eccles 1:2). Unfortunately, the traditional use of the English word "vanity" can be very misleading, since we tend to associate this word with "disordered self-love" or "overattention to one's appearance". The Hebrew word translated as "vanity" is *hebel*, which literally means "vapor, mist, breath". As Ellen Davis points out, the chief meaning of this word is to "connote *ephemerality*",[1] as in the following parallels:

> I loathe my life; *I would not live for ever.*
>   Let me alone, for *my days are a breath* [Hebrew *hebel*]. (Job 7:16)

> Men of low estate are *but a breath* [Hebrew *hebel*],
>   men of high estate are a delusion. (Ps 62:9)

In this way, Ecclesiastes is emphasizing the fleetingness and, therefore, emptiness of all of the things of this world (see also Ps 39:4–6). Intriguingly, this Hebrew word is also the name of Adam and Eve's firstborn: "Abel" (Hebrew *habel*), whose life was fleeting because taken by Cain (Gen 4:2). The word *hebel* is also commonly used as a synonym for "false idol" (for example, Deut 32:21). Thus, the term is difficult to translate and has a wide range of meanings that must be determined to some extent by context.

With this in mind, the prologue announces many of the main themes of the book (Eccles 1:2–11):

1. the fleetingness of all things;
2. the lack of any true profit from human labor;
3. the cyclical monotony of time;
4. the transience of human memory.

In the introduction, Qoheleth now speaks in his own voice, introducing himself as one who was "king over Israel in Jerusalem" (Eccles 1:12). On the one hand, the audience is intended to recognize him as Solomon, for his wisdom was "surpassing all who were over Jerusalem before me", and he reigned over "Israel" from Jerusalem (Eccles 1:16, 12). No other son of David except Solomon surpassed all his predecessors in wisdom and ruled over *Israel* (rather than Judah alone) from Jerusalem. On the other hand, the use of the past tense ("was king") is somewhat odd and difficult to square with Solomon's life (see discussion below, "Historical Issues in Ecclesiastes"). At this point, Qoheleth (Solomon) announces that he made it a life quest to acquire wisdom about life, but that, in the end, he was frustrated, finding it all to be vain (Eccles 1:14, 17b).

Examples of How Virtually Everything Is "Vanity" (Ecclesiastes 2:1—6:9)

The structure of this next part of the book is loose, repetitive, and difficult to delimit. However, one attractive solution is to recognize the repeated phrase, "This also is a vanity and a striving after the wind", as marking the end of six

---

[1] Ellen F. Davis, *Proverbs, Ecclesiastes, and the Song of Songs*, Wesminster Bible Companion (Louisville, Ky.: Westminster John Knox Press, 2000), 167.

rambling but distinct units that provide examples of the fleetingness of human life and experience (see Eccles 2:11, 17, 26; 4:4, 16; 6:9).

In this case, Solomon sets out to pursue three common human goals, three pursuits to which many men devote their entire lives:

1. "Pleasure" or "Joy" (Hebrew *simha*) (Eccles 2:1–11)
2. "Wisdom" (Hebrew *hokhmah*) (Eccles 2:12–17)
3. "Toil" or "Labor" (Hebrew *'amal*) for Possessions (Eccles 2:18–26)

Notice the universal nature of the judgment rendered here: these pursuits represent the goals of the hedonist, the philosopher, and the ordinary laborer together. No one escapes this critique: Solomon finds all three approaches to life to be *hebel*, or meaningless, because all men die, and whatever temporal goods they gained—whether pleasures, knowledge, or accomplishments—is ultimately for naught, for it all passes away. Notice also how the three principal pursuits listed here correspond remarkably to the three reasons for the Fall given in the book of Genesis:

Fall of Adam and Eve	*Three Pursuits of Humans*
1. Good for Food (= Pleasure)	1. Pleasure
2. Delight to the Eyes (= Possessions)	2. Possessions
3. Desirable to Make One Wise (= Pride)	3. Wisdom

In light of these and other connections, some scholars have even suggested that Ecclesiastes is a meditation on the human condition after the Fall as described in Genesis 3.[2]

In the next section, Solomon turns his mind to two frustrating aspects of reality that he encountered during his threefold pursuit of meaning in life: the cyclical monotony of time (Eccles 3:1–15) and the scandal of injustice (Eccles 3:16—4:4). In his famous poem "For everything there is a season"—which was popularized in American culture by The Byrds' 1964 hit, "Turn! Turn! Turn!"—combined with the following meditation, Qoheleth stresses that no true progress is made in human affairs: instead, the same things simply repeat themselves (Eccles 3:1–15). Even more insidiously, wickedness has corrupted human activity, even on the highest levels of society where righteousness and justice should be exercised. Moreover, since death comes to both the righteous and the wicked, it is not clear that wickedness is sanctioned and righteousness rewarded "under the sun"—that is, in this world.

Solomon next turns his attention to the themes of loneliness and companionship. Loneliness is indeed very vain (Eccles 4:7–11), but friendship is not (Eccles 4:9–12). Significantly, *friendship* is one of the few aspects of human life that Ecclesiastes does *not* dismiss as *hebel*. Nonetheless, the meditation closes on a dour note, as Solomon cryptically reflects on an "old and foolish king" who

---

[2] See Duane A. Garrett, *Proverbs, Ecclesiastes, Song of Solomon*, New American Commentary 14 (Nashville: Broadman, 1993).

has isolated himself from friendship and "will no longer take advice". Some interpret this as a cryptic self-reference, in which the young man who will replace the old and foolish king is none other than Jeroboam vis-à-vis Solomon (see 1 Kings 11:26—12:20). In any event, even the grandiose succession of kings, about which so much is made, "also is vanity and a striving after wind" (Eccles 4:16).

In what may be the most rambling section of the entire book, Solomon offers a good deal of practical advice in the form of proverbs (Eccles 5:1–12) followed by reflections on the evils of life, such as sudden loss of fortune (Eccles 5:13–17) and the inability to enjoy one's accomplishments in life (Eccles 6:1–6). The best one can do in life is to enjoy as much as possible the simple pleasures of day-to-day living and avoid thinking about the future, because the inevitability of death means there is no advantage of the wise man over the fool: "this also is vanity and a striving after wind" (Eccles 5:18, 20; 6:8).

On Human Ignorance (Ecclesiastes 6:10—11:6)

In the middle of Ecclesiastes 6, the author now shifts focus and transitions from the vanity or ephemerality of human life to the ignorance of human beings: what later philosophy would refer to as the limits of human reason (Eccles 6:10–12).

In doing so, the book first highlights four areas where human ignorance is on full display. First, he utters a series of inverted proverbs, in which he reverses all the usual judgments about *what is better or worse*—for example, "the day of death, than the day of birth" (Eccles 7:1)—because the sorrows and tribulations of this world help human beings to realize that "the end of all men" is "the house of mourning" (Eccles 7:1–14). Second, Qoheleth urges his readers to *moderation* in all things, including the pursuit of wisdom and curiosity:

> All this I have tested by wisdom; I said, "I will be wise"; but it was far from me.
> That which is, is far off, and deep, very deep; who can find it out? (Eccles 7:23–24)

Third, Qoheleth warns the reader (in very politically incorrect fashion!) of the difficulty of finding a *righteous woman*: "One man among a thousand I found, but a woman among all these I have not found" (Eccles 7:28). One cannot help but wonder if there is an allusion here to Solomon's many idolatrous wives (1 Kings 11)! Fourth, he laments the seeming impossibility of understanding the apparent *injustice* in the world: for kings can do as they wish without accountability (Eccles 8:14); likewise the wicked do evil and seem to get away with it (Eccles 8:9–15).

Along similar lines, the next section (Eccles 9:1–11:6) gives various examples of how little men really know—a section that is almost completely antithetical to the modern-day mantra that "we know so much more" than people used to know. Qoheleth highlights the fact that one fate, death, comes to all people, the good and the bad, the wise and the foolish (Eccles 9:1–6). He recommends taking pleasure in life, love, and work as much as possible, because it is the best that can be done in one's short and meaningless life (Eccles 9:7–10). Above all, human ignorance is on display when it comes to the hour of death:

For man does not know his time. Like fish which are taken in an evil net, and like birds which are caught in a snare, so the sons of men are snared at an evil time, when it suddenly falls upon them. (Eccles 9:12)

In the face of such limitations, Qoheleth points out the ways in which wisdom itself—although better than foolishness—is ultimately vain, since even the wise man is forgotten (Eccles 9:13—10:15). In particular, the gains of wisdom can all be undone by a foolish king, who can ruin a kingdom (Eccles 10:6—11:2).

In his final meditation on human ignorance, Qoheleth turns to *the mysteries of creation*, some of which not only remain mysterious, but grow more mysterious, the more we learn. Qoheleth here uses the mystery of the most common of occurrences—human conception—as an example of how little we know about the mystery of all that is:

As you do not know how the spirit comes to the bones in the womb of a woman with child, so you do not know the work of God who makes everything. (Eccles 11:5)

Because complete knowledge of the courses of nature are beyond human grasp, a certain level of ignorance of God's providence must simply be accepted (Eccles 11:5). Notice here that Ecclesiastes is teaching *realism* rather than a *cynicism* that would lead to despair: rather than being paralyzed into inaction with fear of outcomes beyond one's control, one should work industriously on multiple plans of action simultaneously, because "you do not know which will prosper, this or that, or whether both alike will be good" (Eccles 11:6).

On Youth and Old Age (Ecclesiastes 11:7–12:7)

Perhaps one of the most poignant, memorable, and universally applicable portions of Ecclesiastes is the final poem on youth and old age (Eccles 11:7—12:1). In this section, Qoheleth returns to the theme of the end of life and addresses himself to the young, exhorting them to live in such a way that that they do not forget either their *origin* (as created by God) or their *end* (as mortal beings who will one day die). In some of the most famous words of the book:

Remember also your Creator in the days of your youth, before the evil days come, and the years draw nigh, when you will say, "I have no pleasure in them." (Eccles 12:1)

What follows this exhortation is a stunning poem that uses various metaphors to describe the deterioration of the human body and the eventual failure of all the faculties by which human beings take pleasure in the things of this world.[3]

From the perspective of Ecclesiastes, then, either human beings will learn not to give their hearts to the pleasures of this world by heeding the words of wisdom in their youth, or the Creator himself will teach them how fleeting such pleasures are by experience, as they all fade away, one by one, with the slow breakdown of the body over time as it makes its way toward the day of death.

[3] Davis, *Proverbs*, 223–25.

The Metaphors of Aging in the Final Poem (11:7—12:7)	
Metaphor	Symptom of Aging
"The sun and the light and the moon and the stars are darkened."	Eyesight fails
"The keepers of the house tremble."	Hands begin to shake
"The strong men are bent."	Legs are weak and bowed
"The grinders cease because they are few."	Teeth fall out
"Those that look through the windows are dimmed."	Eyesight fails
"The doors on the street are shut."	Mouth is closed, remains silent
"When the sound of the grinding is low."	Hearing fails
"One rises up at the voice of a bird."	Light and restless sleep in old age
"They are afraid also of what is high, and terrors are in the way."	Loss of physical courage due to increased frailty
"The almond tree blossoms."	Hair turns white
"The grasshopper drags itself along and desire fails."	Sexual desire fails
"The silver cord is snapped", etc.	Death arrives

Epilogue: Qoheleth and the Divine Judgment (Ecclesiastes 12:8–14)

The narrator's voice takes over once more, as he quotes Qoheleth in a virtual repetition of the opening lines, forming an *inclusio* around the book as a whole: "Vanity of vanities, says the Preacher, all is vanity" (Eccles 12:8; cf. 1:2).

Despite all the provocative and potentially scandalous things Qoheleth has said in the course of the book, the narrator commends him as a wise man who taught the people knowledge by studying and arranging "proverbs" (Hebrew *meshalim*) with great care (Eccles 12:9). Again, this suggests an identification of Qoheleth with Solomon (cf. 1 Kings 4). The narrator asserts that the "sayings of the wise are like goads" (Eccles 12:11)—this metaphor seems a fitting description of the provocative effect of Ecclesiastes on its readers. He suggests the provocation is intentional: the reader is being prodded outside his comfort zone. Indeed, this is the moral of the book:

> The end of the matter; all has been heard. Fear God, and keep his commandments; for this is the whole duty of man. *For God will bring every deed into judgment, with every secret thing, whether good or evil.* (Eccles 12:13–14)

From one angle, this is a somewhat surprising conclusion. On the one hand, a case could be made from certain sayings in Ecclesiastes that human beings should simply do as they wish without regard to God and his commandments, since death comes to all anyway and there is no meaningful afterlife. On the other hand, some of Qoheleth's last exhortations are to remember the Creator and the coming judgment while one is yet young (Eccles 11:9; 12:1); so the conclusion here is not completely unanticipated in Qoheleth's own statements. In any case, in its final form, the conclusion functions to place the rest of the teachings of the book in the context of the individual's final or ultimate judgment before God, which somehow goes beyond the good and evil things of this life and this world. This is a remarkable and distinctive contribution of Ecclesiastes and will set the stage for the later articulations of the doctrine of individual judgment (what would later be known as "the particular judgment").

Historical Issues in Ecclesiastes

The Origins of the Book of Ecclesiastes

Who wrote the book of Ecclesiastes? And when was it written?

On the one hand, as with Proverbs before it, the book of Ecclesiastes has always been associated in both ancient Jewish and ancient Christian tradition with King Solomon. This association is based on several factors. Above all, the opening line of the book identifies the mysterious figure of *Qoheleth* with "the son of David, king in Jerusalem" (Eccles 1:1). Given the fact that this same Qoheleth is described as a "sage" or "wise man" (Hebrew *hakam*) who taught "knowledge" to the people in the form of "proverbs" (Hebrew *meshalim*) (Eccles 12:9), there is really only one king who fits the profile: Solomon, who was known for both his wisdom and his proverbs (1 Kings 4) and who is even said to have called an "assembly" (Hebrew *qahal*) of the people of Israel at the dedication of the Temple (1 Kings 8:1, 2, 5, 55–61).

With that said, it is interesting that in both ancient Jewish and Christian traditions, there were certain currents of thought that recognized the possibility that someone other than Solomon himself may have been involved in the production of the book of Ecclesiastes as we have it. For example, in rabbinic Jewish literature, there was a tradition that the book was either edited or published later than Solomon's own lifetime, around the time of King Hezekiah:

> Hezekiah and his colleagues wrote [that is, edited/published] Isaiah, Proverbs, the Song of Songs *and Ecclesiastes*.[4]

Along similar lines, the fourth-century Church Father known as Didymus the Blind of Alexandria also posited that someone else may have written in the persona of Solomon. In his question-and-answer formatted commentary on Ecclesiastes, Didymus writes:

> *Question:* [Are the] words of Ecclesiastes said by the author personally? *Answer:* ... Either the real author is Solomon, or some [other] wise men have written it. Maybe we should opt for the latter so that nobody may say that the speaker talks about himself.[5]

---

[4] Babylonian Talmud, *Baba Bathra* 14b, in I. Epstein, ed., *The Babylonian Talmud*, 35 vols. (London: Soncino, 1935–52).

[5] Didymus the Blind, *Commentary on Ecclesiastes* 7.9, in J. Robert Wright, *Proverbs, Ecclesiastes, and the Song of Solomon*, Old Testament 9, Ancient Christian Commentary on Scripture 9, ed. Thomas C. Oden (Downers Grove, Ill.: InterVarsity Press, 2005), 192.

To be sure, even with such ancient examples of openness to the possibility of later editorial activity, it remains the case that the book was attributed to Solomon himself by the majority of ancient writers, both Christian and non-Christian.

On the other hand, in modern times, the majority of scholars have abandoned Solmonic authorship, for several reasons. (1) First and foremost, as we pointed out about, the introduction and epilogue to Ecclesiastes speak of Qoheleth (= Solomon) in the *third person*, as if he were a figure from the past: "I, Qoheleth, was king of Israel, in Jerusalem" (Eccles 1:12 [author's trans.]). From this point of view, the text itself is suggesting that time has elapsed between the life of Solomon and the publication of the book. (2) Second, many of the sayings and teachings in the book appear to represent the viewpoint of a subject in a kingdom, not the king himself. For example, he complains about injustice (Eccles 3:16) as well as the tyrannical rule of those with power (Eccles 5:8), warning in particular about the danger of a young king— like Solomon himself (Eccles 10:16–18)! (3) Third, there is an argument from the Hebrew *language*. According to some scholars, the Hebrew language found in Ecclesiastes appears more similar to what is known as "Late Biblical Hebrew"—that is, the kind of Hebrew found in Esther, Daniel, 1–2 Chronicles, Ezra-Nehemiah—than the older form of Hebrew, known as "Classical Biblical Hebrew", that would have been spoken and written in Solomon's day (ca. tenth century B.C.). (4) Fourth and finally, as with the book of Proverbs, the Solomonic origin of Ecclesiastes is also rejected because of other works in the wisdom literature that scholars agree were written long after Solomon's time and yet attributed to him, such as the Wisdom of Solomon or the *Psalms of Solomon*. In light of these literary parallels, scholars argue that similar attributions in Ecclesiastes cannot be taken as evidence for the origins of the book. In light of such arguments—especially the linguistic one—many scholars today would not only deny Solomonic origins of the book but would date it to the Persian period (ca. sixth–fourth centuries B.C.) or even the Hellenistic period (ca. fourth–second centuries B.C.).[6]

With that said, it is worth noting here that in recent times, a significant minority of contemporary scholars have argued for the Solomonic or at least preexilic origin of Ecclesiastes. For one thing, in terms of language, some experts in the Hebrew language reject the linguistic arguments for a late date, making the case that the language of Ecclesiastes is in fact preexilic.[7] Moreover, in terms of content, many of the skeptical or pessimistic views expressed in Ecclesiastes can be closely paralleled in nonbiblical ancient Near Eastern literature extending back to the second millennium B.C.[8] In light of such parallels, it is possible that Solomon wrote a work providing the basis for some or all of Ecclesiastes, which was then later recast in its present, younger form of Hebrew in the postexilic (Persian) period (ca. 530–330 B.C.). From this point of view, the general

---

[6] See Choon-Leong Seow, *Ecclesiastes*, Anchor Bible 18C (New York: Doubleday, 1997), 11–21.

[7] D. C. Fredericks, *Qoheleth's Language: Reevaluating Its Nature and Date* (Lewiston, N.Y.: E. Mellen Press, 1988).

[8] Duane Garret, "Ecclesiastes", in *The Minor Prophets: Job, Psalms, Proverbs, Ecclesiastes, Song of Songs*, vol. 4 of *Zondervan Illustrated Bible Backgrounds Commentary*, ed. John H. Walton (Grand Rapids, Mich.: Zondervan, 2009).

reflections on mortality by no means demand familiarity with Hellenistic philosophy: "There is no compelling reason to believe that Ecclesiastes is influenced by Greek literature."[9]

Most contemporary scholars, however, adopt the simpler solution that Ecclesiastes was composed in the Persian period by an author who adopted the persona of Solomon as the primary "voice" of his composition. What is not disputed is that the sacred author wished Qoheleth to be understood as Solomon, because the wealth, wisdom, and sovereignty attributed to Qoheleth would only truly be characteristic of David's first heir. Just as the words of Hamlet need to be understood according to the prince of Denmark's personality and history within the play written by Shakespeare, so also the words of Qoheleth need to be understood according to Solomon's personality and history within the canonical "drama" of the Old Testament. This was certainly the intention of the sacred author. Within the drama of the Old Testament, Qoheleth's words are those of an elderly Solomon, disillusioned with his great successes and frustrated with life. The Old Testament portrays the end of Solomon's reign as a time when he lost exclusive faith in the Lord (1 Kings 11:4). Therefore, the reader has canonical reason to read Qoheleth's words critically, recognizing that Solomon was wise, but not impeccable.

Theological Issues in Ecclesiastes

The major theological issue with the book of Ecclesiastes is how to reconcile its skeptical and pessimistic world view with the faith-filled perspective more typical of biblical literature. In order to explain this tension, it is important first to gain a coherent picture of Qoheleth's world view.

Qoheleth's "Wisdom" and the Visible World

Qoheleth attempts to find the meaning of life by applying *wisdom*—in this case, roughly synonymous with *reason*—to all that exists "under the sun", a phrase repeated twenty-eight times in the course of the book (Eccles 1:3, 9, 14; 2:11, 17–20, 22; 3:16; 4:1, 3, 7, 15; 5:13, 18; 6:1, 12; 8:9, 15 [2x], 17; 9:3, 6, 9 [2x], 11, 13; 10:5)! This phrase refers to what one would call, in philosophical terms, the "empirical, phenomenal" world: that is, the world of appearances and experience, but not ultimate realities. "Beyond the sun" would be the abode of the Divine, and Qoheleth does not, or cannot, extend his thoughts that far; his perspective is strictly limited to what is "under the sun".

When he applies his reason to the visible world, Qoheleth's attempt to discover meaning is frustrated by five realities:

1. *The Cyclical Monotony of Time*: Human events seem to repeat themselves in patterns without substantive progress.
2. *The Unsatisfying Nature of All Pleasure*: Pleasures are momentary and bring no lasting happiness.

---

[9] Ibid., 509.

3. *Social Injustice*: Violations of the moral order are absurd and apparently without just retribution.

4. *The Incomprehensibility of Life*: Life does not yield its meaning easily to pure reason.

5. *Death*: All of the goods of this life, including life itself, ultimately come to an end.

These five realities are all interrelated, and the greatest of them is death. Death puts an end to personal progress and restarts the cyclical monotony; it puts an end to pleasures, strikes down both good and bad without regard to justice, and so renders life meaningless. Thus Qoheleth returns constantly to the problem of death and ends his meditations with the beautiful, if somewhat morbid, poem on aging and the end of life (Eccles 11:7—12:7).

The Question of Death and the Afterlife

Admittedly, death was a theological problem in the Old Testament, because the nature of the afterlife was not clearly and completely revealed prior to the death, Resurrection, and Ascension of Jesus.

Other sacred writers, such as Job, David, and some other psalmists, also expressed despondence over the prospect of dying (Job 7:9; 10:21–22; Ps 6:5; 88:12–19; 89:48; and so on). However, these same Old Testament persons made courageous leaps of faith to believe that, in some mysterious way, their relationship to God and their own existence would continue beyond death (see Job 19:25–27; Ps 16:10; 21:4; 23:6; 30:3, 12; 37:28; 41:12; 49:15; 61:4; 86:13; 139:8). In later Old Testament literature, this step of faith is answered by God with clearer revelation concerning the hope of life after death in the forms of the bodily resurrection of the dead (see Ezek 37:1–14; Dan 12:1–3; Wis 2). Qoheleth never takes this step, but insistently remains with only those data his wisdom can perceive "under the sun", which lead him—despite what some commentators claim—not to a categorical denial, but to an agnosticism about immortality and life after death (Eccles 3:18–22).

Ecclesiastes and the Limits of Human Reason

One way in which the perspective of Ecclesiastes can be incorporated into the fuller perspective revealed by the Scriptures as a whole is to consider the book a kind of philosophical "thought-experiment".

From this point of view, Ecclesiastes is an attempt to find out what results from limiting one's perspective only to temporal, material, empirical reality (things "under the sun") and unaided human reason. The results are meager. It leads, not to happiness, but to despondency. Significantly, Qoheleth's thought does *not* degenerate into atheism or even agnosticism, since God's existence is a fact accessible to reason from the existence and design of the cosmos and the things in it, and the author is unequivocal about the fact that creation is "the work of God who makes everything" (Eccles 11:5). Nevertheless, he cannot reason to God's goodness, the immortality of the soul, or to an ultimate meaning in life.

In this way, Ecclesiastes represents a useful intellectual exercise for believers to engage in. Since the temptation to abandon the perspective of faith is always present for believers—especially in the face of social injustice, the ephemerality of life, and the mystery of suffering and death—it is helpful to discover where such a faithless perspective, consistently applied, eventually leads. There is no hope or joy down this intellectual path, and the discovery of this fact leads to a certain "openness" or "waiting" for more to be said about how God will eventually "bring every deed into judgment, with every secret thing, whether good or evil" (Eccles 12:14).

Ecclesiastes in the Living Tradition

Given the universal experience of suffering and the transience of earthly pleasures, as one might expect, Ecclesiastes has attracted a good deal of attention throughout Church history. Indeed, according to one scholar's estimate, we possess "some fifty commentaries" on the book from the era of the early Church Fathers, ranging from full-length expositions by figures like John Chrysostom and the Venerable Bede to passing comments and discussions in various formats.[10] What follows are but a few examples of how this book has been read and utilized in the living tradition of the Church.

The Renunciation of the World and Growth in Virtue

The Christian tradition has often contextualized the perspective of Ecclesiastes according to its canonical order after Proverbs and before the Song of Solomon. Proverbs represents the purgative way to God, the approach to God through growth in moral knowledge, in which one learns to reject evil and sin. Ecclesiastes represents the illuminative path to God, in which the intellect is illuminated in order to realize the transient and unsatisfying nature of created things. The Song of Solomon represents the unitive path, the way of love and communion with the only truly desirable thing: God himself.

Indeed, the reader of Ecclesiastes will find Qoheleth's meditations on the vanity of all created things—pleasure, wealth, and power—an effective testimony to the power of detachment from the things of this world. In the words of the fourth-century Father John Cassian:

> In Ecclesiastes the divine wisdom has indicated that there is an appropriate time for everything—that is, for all things, whether they be fortunate or be considered unfortunate and sad. As it says, "There is a time for all things, and a time for everything under heaven...." It has therefore been determined that none of these things is a permanent good, except when it is carried out in the right time and in correct fashion. Thus the very things that turn out well now, since they were done at the right time, are found to be disadvantageous and harmful if they are tried at an inopportune or inappropriate moment. The only exception to this is those things that are essentially and of themselves either good or bad and that can never be turned to their contraries, such as justice, prudence, fortitude,

---

[10] See Wright, *Proverbs*, xxi–xxii.

temperance, and the other virtues, and, on the other hand, the vices, which can never be understood differently.[11]

In other words, the spiritual journey inevitably involves self-denial, mortification, and ascesis. Because of this, there is always the temptation to abandon the path and seek consolation in temporal pleasures and achievements: sexual pleasure, food, wealth, fame, power. Ecclesiastes, by contrast, teaches the paradox of choosing to value the things of God over the passing things of the world: it is precisely by means of detachment from the temporal goods of this world that one is enabled not only to avoid evil (as in Proverbs) but to grow in virtue.

Ecclesiastes Written to Make Its Readers Yearn for Eternal Life

Indeed, Augustine argued that the very purpose of Ecclesiastes was to inculcate in the reader a longing for eternal life:

> This wisest man devoted this whole book to a full exposure of this vanity, evidently with no other object than that we might long for that life in which there is no vanity under the sun, but verity under Him who made the sun.[12]

If Augustine is correct, then, in a certain sense, *every human person must go through the experience of Ecclesiastes either personally or vicariously in order to grasp the significance of the good news of eternal life.* Persons who remain convinced that their happiness will be attained with wealth, pleasure, or power will never see the need for a salvation and a good that goes beyond the good things that exist "under the sun". One needs first to despair of finding lasting happiness in temporal affairs before a life focused on eternal goods begins to make sense.

Continuing reflection along the lines laid out by Saint Augustine, we may regard Ecclesiastes as the one Old Testament book that most poignantly articulates the question whose answer is Jesus of Nazareth. Qoheleth continually asks rhetorical questions expressing the plight of the human experience: Is there anything new under the sun (Eccles 1:10a)? Who knows if the spirit of a man goes upward (Eccles 3:21)? Who can show a man what will be after him (Eccles 6:12)? Who can tell him how it will be (Eccles 8:7)? The answer to all these questions is the God-Man, Jesus Christ (see table on p. 635). Ecclesiastes is unflinching in expressing the agnosticism and fatalism that would suffocate human happiness if the Incarnation, Passion, and Resurrection of Jesus Christ had never taken place. In light of the whole canon, Ecclesiastes describes the hungers of the human heart that find satisfaction in Jesus.

Does Ecclesiastes Deny the Reality of Life after Death?

With that said, Ecclesiastes may also be regarded as the one Old Testament book that most poignantly poses the question of whether there *is* any life after

---

[11]John Cassian, *Conference* 21.12.3–4, in John Cassian, *Conferences*, trans. Boniface Ramsey, Ancient Christian Writers 57 (Mahwah, N.J.: Paulist, 1997), 728–29.

[12]Augustine, *City of God* 20.3.1, in *NPNF1* 2:423.

Questions of Qoheleth Whose Answer Is Christ	
Ecclesiastes	New Testament
"What does man gain for all the toil?" (1:3; 2:22; 3:9)	"Labor … for the food which endures to eternal life." (Jn 6:27)
"Is there a thing of which it is said, 'See, this is new'?" (1:10)	"This chalice … is the new covenant in my blood." (Lk 22:20)
"Who knows whether the spirit of man goes upward?" (3:21)	"He [who] ascended on high". (Eph 4:8–10)
"Who can bring [a man] to see what will be after him?" (3:22; 6:12; 8:7; 10:14)	"I am the first and the last … now write what you see … what is to take place hereafter." (Rev 1:17, 19)
"That which is, is far off, and deep, very deep; who can find it out?" (7:24)	"[Christ] also descended into the lower parts of the earth.… He who descended is he who also ascended far above all the heavens." (Eph 4:9–10)
"Who knows what is good for man?" (6:12)	"I am the good shepherd; I know my own and my own know me, … and I lay down my life for the sheep." (Jn 10:14–15)

death. In the living tradition, rhetorical questions mentioned above (Eccles 1:10; 3:21; 6:12; 8:7) were viewed, not as a *rejection* of the truth about life after death, but rather as *questions* waiting for an answer whose fullness would only come through the light of the New Covenant. For example, when it came to Ecclesiastes teaching that human beings and animals have "the same" fate (Eccles 3:19), Didymus the Blind writes:

> When [Ecclesiastes] says that "the fate of humans and the fate of animals is the same" [Eccles 3:19], he does not mean what happens to reason but what happens to the outward body.… If one investigates the nature of death, then the death of animals is not like the death of humans. Human death divides the soul from the body, and after the division the soul remains. *But the death of animals destroys soul and body, since they have been created simultaneously.*[13]

This is an excellent example of how the living tradition of the Church reads Old Testament texts through the lens of the analogy of faith: given what we know from the faith about the differences between human beings (which possess a spiritual and immortal soul) and animals (which do not), the words of Ecclesiastes regarding human death can be interpreted rightly when proper distinctions are made. Indeed, one could argue that Qoheleth captures the fatalism and despondency of even the best philosophies that operate apart from the light of the fullness of revelation of the Resurrection. It can in a sense be likened to the "bad news" ("there is no hope beyond death") necessary for full appreciation of the "good news" of the offer of eternal life.

[13] Didymus the Blind, *Commentary on Ecclesiastes* 99.1, in Wright, *Proverbs*, 232.

"Toiling" for the Bread of This World and the Bread of Eternal Life

One very particular way in which Ecclesiastes was read in the light of the Gospel is the sacramental interpretation that was often drawn out of its many sayings on the pleasures of food and drink. In the face of the futility of earthly pleasures, Qoheleth exhorts his readers to enjoy the food and drink of this world in moderation (Eccles 9:7). In this reference to food and drink, Saint Gregory of Agrigentum sees a foretaste (pun intended) of the Eucharistic banquet:

> *Come, eat your bread in gladness and drink your wine with a cheerful heart* ... [Eccles 9:7]. If we would interpret this text in its obvious and ordinary sense, it would be correct to call it a righteous exhortation ... to embrace a simple way of life and to be led by doctrines which involve a genuine faith in God....
>
> But a spiritual interpretation of the text leads us to a loftier meaning and teaches us to take this as the heavenly and mystical bread, which has come down from heaven, bringing life to the world [Jn 6:33], and to drink a spiritual wine with a cheerful heart, that wine which flowed from the side of the true vine at the moment of his saving passion.... For whoever eats this bread and drinks this mystical wine enjoys true happiness and rejoices, exclaiming, *You have put gladness into my heart.*
>
> Indeed, I think this is the bread and this is the wine that is referred to in the book of Proverbs by God's subsistent Wisdom, Christ our Savior, saying: *Come, eat my bread and drink the wine I have mixed for you* [Prov 9:5], hereby referring to our mystical sharing in the Word.[14]

Notice here the distinction Gregory makes between the literal and spiritual senses of the text. For him and for other Fathers, the earthly good of food and drink and the natural life they give, in the final analysis, are shadows of the supernatural good of wisdom that is received in the bread and wine of the Eucharist. Moreover, this new eating and drinking enables a reorientation of our life, so that our "toil" now becomes meaningful. In the words of Jesus: "Do not labor for the food which perishes, but for the food which endures to eternal life, which the Son of man will give to you" (Jn 6:27). This meaningful "toil" is a work of faith, the very virtue Solomon chose not to exercise. In the Eucharist, one finds the satisfaction, joy, and meaning that eluded Israel's wisest man.

The Book of Ecclesiastes in the Lectionary

Perhaps because of the provocative nature of its contents, Ecclesiastes is seldom read in the Lectionary. Its sole use on a Sunday or feast day is on the Eighteenth Sunday in Ordinary Time, Year C, where its teaching on the "vanity" of the things for which men labor (Eccles 1:2, 2:21–23) is paired with the Gospel parable about the rich fool and Jesus' teaching on not being anxious about worldly possessions (Lk 12:13–21). In this way, the readings complement one another to drive home the point that "a man's life does not consist in the abundance

---

[14] Gregory of Agrigentum, *Commentary on Ecclesiastes*, in *The Liturgy of the Hours*, vol. 3, Office of Readings, Friday, Seventh Week in Ordinary Time (New York: Catholic Book Publishing Co., 1975), 251–52.

of his possessions" (Lk 12:15); therefore it is dangerous to "lay up treasure for [oneself]" (Lk 12:21) instead of being "rich toward God" (Lk 12:21).

In the Twenty-Fifth Week in Ordinary Time, Year II, the Lectionary for daily Mass also utilizes Ecclesiastes, reading the book's three literary masterpieces: the opening prologue on the theme "There is nothing new under the sun" (cf. Eccles 1:2–11); the poem on time, "For everything there is a season" (cf. Eccles 3:1–11); and the concluding poem on aging, "Remember your Creator in the days of your youth" (cf. Eccles 11:9—12:8). In this way, participants in the daily Eucharist can taste some of the richest meditations in the book:

Reading of Ecclesiastes for Daily Mass: Ordinary Time, Year II: Week 25		
Day	Passage Read	Description
Th	1:2–11	The opening prologue, in which Qoheleth sets the tone for the book: all things are vanity, time is a cyclical monotony, there is nothing new "under the sun".
F	3:1–11	The famous poem "For everything there is a season, and a time for every matter under heaven" concludes with the reflection: "[God] has made everything beautiful in its time; also he has put eternity into man's mind, yet so that he cannot find out what God has done." (v. 11)
Sa	11:9—12:8	The concluding poem on youth, aging, and death: "Remember also your Creator in the days of your youth, before the evil days come … and the spirit returns to God who gave it. Vanity of vanities … all is vanity."

In contrast to the Lectionary, the Liturgy of the Hours includes very generous portions of Ecclesiastes in the Office of Readings for the Seventh Week in Ordinary Time, skillfully paired with passages from the Fathers and Doctors that highlight the spiritual senses of Qoheleth's words: (1) detachment from worldly things and dying to self; (2) the inadequacy of reason and the necessity of faith, hope, and love to arrive at true wisdom; (3) Christ as our spiritual food and drink, especially in the Eucharist; (4) Christ as the source of the eternal light and life for which Qoheleth longed:

Ecclesiastes in the Office of Readings for the Liturgy of the Hours, Ordinary Time, Week 7			
Day	First Reading	Second Reading	Comment
Su	1:1–18	On Charity by St. Maximus the Confessor	All things are vanity, and there is nothing new under the sun. Qoheleth introduces himself and describes his quest for wisdom and his ultimate frustration. St. Maximus stresses that love for God means detachment from the world: "If a man possesses any strong attachment to the things of this earth, he cannot possess true charity."

(continued)

			Ecclesiastes in the Office of Readings for the Liturgy of the Hours, Ordinary Time, Week 7 (*continued*)
Day	First Reading	Second Reading	Comment
M	2:1–3, 12b–26	A Homily on Ecclesiastes by St. Gregory of Nyssa	Qoheleth describes his pursuits of pleasure, wealth, and accomplishments, and the emptiness he found in it all. St. Gregory holds up St. Paul as an example of one who "kept his eyes on Christ" and, through persecution, deprivation, and suffering, learned detachment from all temporal goods.
Tu	3:1–12	See above.	Qoheleth says there is time for everything and bemoans the cyclical monotony. He also decries injustice and expresses agnosticism about life after death. St. Gregory explores the spiritual sense of "a time to be born, and a time to die". The Christian is born by receiving God into us, becoming a child of God. Afterward, he is called to die to self daily, like St. Paul.
W	5:9—6:8	Commentary on Ecclesiastes by St. Jerome	Qoheleth bemoans the transience of wealth. It provokes worry, is lost easily, is taken by another, or brings no pleasure to its owner. St. Jerome applies Qoheleth's advice to "eat, drink, and take pleasure in one's toil" to spiritual food and drink, which is prayer and contemplation of Scripture. Christ brings the satisfaction men cannot find in the things of this world.
Th	6:12—7:28	An Instruction from St. Columban, abbot	Qoheleth shares a string of proverbs to help in coping with the troubles of life, but ultimately concludes that wisdom "was beyond me ... it is deep, very deep." St. Columban applies this to the mystery of God's nature, the Holy Trinity. Insight into the mystery of God is not gained by Qoheleth's reasoning but by perfection of life, simplicity of heart, and faith.
F	8:5—9:10	Commentary on Ecclesiastes by St. Gregory of Agrigentum, bishop	Qoheleth meditates on the fact that the same fate, death, comes to all, rendering wisdom and folly, righteousness and wickedness, all meaninglessness. He commends the enjoyment of the simple pleasures of life: "Eat your bread with joy and drink your wine with a merry heart." St. Gregory accepts the literal sense of these words as commendation of a life-style of contentment, gratitude, and joy, but sees their spiritual sense as applicable to the Eucharist, the meal of true happiness.
Sa	11:7—12:14	See above.	Qoheleth commends light and life and the enjoyment of both before the onset of aging. St. Gregory explores the spiritual sense of Qoheleth's words, "Light is sweet!" Christ is the light of the believer. In gazing upon him with the eyes of faith, the Christian discovers the joy and lasting happiness that eluded Qoheleth.

Conclusion

In Ecclesiastes, the sacred author takes an unflinching look at temporal, physical reality—life "under the sun"—to determine whether meaning or purpose can be found in it. Applying reason to human experience, he concludes that life and all its pursuits are ephemeral, futile, and "vain" (Hebrew *hebel*), because the same fate (death) comes to all people and wipes away all human pursuits and activities. Ecclesiastes' reasoning is correct, though based on a limited perspective, without benefit of faith and the revelation of eternal life and bodily resurrection through Christ. Nonetheless, contextualized within the fullness of truth presented in the entire canon, Ecclesiastes presents a provocative and invigorating exhortation to abandon attempts to find human happiness by the pursuit of temporal goods. It is ultimately in Christ that one finds the solution to the problems of death and meaninglessness so poignantly described by Qoheleth in Ecclesiastes.

For Further Reading

Commentaries and Studies on Ecclesiastes

Davis, Ellen F. *Proverbs, Ecclesiastes, and the Song of Songs*. Westminster Bible Companion. Louisville, Ky.: Westminster John Knox Press, 2000. (See pp. 159–228.)

Estes, Daniel J. *Handbook on the Wisdom Books and Psalms*. Grand Rapids, Mich.: Baker Academic, 2005. (See pp. 271–392.)

Garrett, Duane A. *Proverbs, Ecclesiastes, Song of Songs*. New American Commentary 14. Nashville, Tenn.: Broadman Press, 1993.

Murphy, Roland E., O. Carm. *Ecclesiastes*. Word Biblical Commentary 23A. Dallas, Tex.: Word Books, 1992.

Seow, Choon-Leong. *Ecclesiastes*. Anchor Bible 18C. New York: Doubleday, 1997.

Historical Questions and Ecclesiastes

Fredericks, Daniel C. *Qoheleth's Language: Reevaluating Its Nature and Date*. Lewiston, N.Y.: Mellen Press, 1988.

Garrett, Duane. "Ecclesiastes". Pages 504–17 in *The Minor Prophets, Job, Psalms, Ecclesiastes, Song of Songs*. Vol. 5 of *Zondervan Illustrated Bible Backgrounds Commentary*. Edited by John H. Walton. Grand Rapids, Mich.: Zondervan, 2009.

Ecclesiastes in the Living Tradition

Bonaventure, Saint. *Commentary on Ecclesiastes*. Works of Saint Bonaventure 7. Translated by Robert J. Karris and Campion Murray. New York: Franciscan Institute Publications, 2005.

Cassian, John, Saint. *Conferences*. Translated by Boniface Ramsey. Ancient Christian Writers 57. Mahwah, N.J.: Paulist Press, 1997.

Hall, Stuart G., ed. *Gregory of Nyssa Homilies on Ecclesiastes: An English Version with Supporting Studies*. Berlin: Walter de Gruyter, 1993.

International Commission on English in the Liturgy. *The Liturgy of the Hours*. Vol. 3. *Ordinary Time: Weeks 1–17*. New York: Catholic Book Publishing, 1975.

Jerome, Saint. *Commentary on Ecclesiastes*. Translated and edited by Richard J. Goodrich and David J. D. Miller. Ancient Christian Writers 66. Westminster, Md.: Newman Press, 2012.

Wright, J. Robert. "Ecclesiastes". Pages 190–285 in *Proverbs, Ecclesiastes, Song of Solomon*. Old Testament 9 of Ancient Christian Commentary on Scripture 9. Edited by Thomas C. Oden. Downers Grove, Ill.: InterVarsity Press, 2005.

27. THE SONG OF SOLOMON

Introduction

The Song of Solomon is a collection of love songs or poems with a loose narrative structure. On the surface of the text, the Song describes the joy, the longing, and the love between King Solomon the bridegroom (Song 3:7–11) and his bride, apparently identified as the "Shulammite" woman (Song 6:13). Over the course of its long history, however, the Song has been variously interpreted as an allegory of the divine love between YHWH and the people of Israel, between Christ the Bridegroom and the Church as his Bride, and between God and the soul.

Unlike most books of the Bible, this one has an explicit title in the Hebrew text: "The Song of Songs, which is Solomon's" (Hebrew *shîr hashîrîm asher lishlōmōh*) (Song 1:1), from which we get both the Greek "Song of Songs" (Greek *'asma asmatōn*) as well as the Vulgate's "Canticle of Canticles" (Latin *canticum canticorum*). In every case, the title reflects the Hebrew superlative: just as the Hebrew expression "Holy of Holies" means the *most holy place* (Ex 26:33) or "heaven of heavens" means *the highest heaven* (Deut 10:14), so too "Song of Songs" means *the greatest of all songs*. That is what the Song of Solomon is: the greatest song ever written. Indeed, according to Rabbi Akiba, a famous Jewish sage who lived in the early second century A.D., the Song of Solomon was the holiest book in all of Jewish Scripture:

> No man in Israel ever disputed about the Song of Songs that it does not render the hands unclean, for all the ages are not worth the day on which the Song of Songs was given to Israel; for *all the Writings are holy, but the Song of Songs is the Holy of Holies.*[1]

Notice two things about Rabbi Akiba's statements. First, he is asserting that no one ever disputed that the Song of Solomon was inspired Scripture. (Although it is counterintuitive, rabbinic Judaism taught that inspired books "rendered the hands unclean". Thus, to say a text "rendered the hands unclean" was to declare it to be Scripture.)

Second, he is making clear that the Song of Songs was classified among the third part of Jewish Scripture, known as the Writings (Hebrew *ketubim*). Indeed, in later Jewish tradition, the Song was one of the *Megilloth* ("Five Scrolls")—Ruth, Esther, Ecclesiastes, Lamentations, Song of Solomon—read during annual Jewish festivals. Intriguingly, the Song of Solomon is read *during the Feast of Passover*, probably because of the biblical evidence in the prophets identifying the

---

[1] Mishnah, *Yadayim* 3.5, in Herbert Danby, *The Mishnah* (Oxford: Oxford University Press, 1933), 782.

events of the exodus and Mount Sinai as an act of betrothal between YHWH and Israel (for example, Hos 2; Ezek 16). Significantly, fragments of four copies of the Song were found among the Dead Sea Scrolls, indicating reverence for the text even within the rigorous, celibate sect of the Essenes.[2]

The Greek Septuagint and Latin Vulgate traditions place the Song of Solomon among the wisdom books as the last of the Solomonic trilogy: (1) Proverbs; (2) Ecclesiastes; (3) Song of Solomon. As we will see, this led to understanding these works as descriptions of the three ages of the spiritual life: (1) the purgative; (2) the illuminative; and (3) the unitive ways. Despite its erotic character, the Song appears in the earliest lists of canonical books and was never seriously contested. The Greek and Latin translations follow the Hebrew text without significant deviation, indicating that the transmission of the text of the Song has been relatively stable. In English-speaking Catholicism, the Song is often called the "Canticle" or "Canticles" under the influence of the Latin title of the book.

The Interpretation of the Song of Solomon

At this point we would ordinarily proceed into a discussion of the literary structure and genre of the book we are studying. However, in the case of the Song of Solomon, opinions over exactly how the book as a whole should be interpreted have been so diverse that it will be helpful to take a few moments to introduce the major interpretive options that have been proposed over the centuries. Perhaps more than any other book, when it comes to the Song, there are as many interpretations as there are interpreters. Nevertheless, five major approaches to the book stand out in the history of interpretation.

1. The Erotic Love Interpretation

According to this interpretation, the bridegroom in the Song should be understood as a man (usually Solomon himself), and the bride is a woman and lover (usually the Shulammite woman), and the central theme of the book is the celebration of *erotic love* within the context of marriage. This erotic interpretation is quite ancient, going back at least as far as the time of Theodore of Mopsuestia, who wrote:

> [Solomon] took Pharaoh's daughter as his wife. But she was dark, as all the Egyptian and Ethiopian women are.... The Hebrews and their beautiful wives, and the other princesses as well, ridiculed her on account of her unseemliness, her small height and her dark complexion. To avoid any irritation on her part and so that no hostility would result between him and the Pharaoh, Solomon exclusively built for her a house of valuable stones [and decorated it] with gold and silver. During the meals he chanted [the Song of Solomon] in her presence in order to honor her, and he made known with it that she was dark yet beautiful and loved by him.[3]

---

[2] See Martin G. Abegg Jr., Peter Flint, and Eugene Ulrich, *The Dead Sea Scrolls Bible: The Oldest Known Bible Translated for the First Time into English* (San Francisco: HarperOne, 1999), 611–18.

[3] Theodore of Mopsuestia, *Paraphrase of the Commentary*, in Dimitri Z. Zaharopoulos, *Theodore of Mopsuestia on the Bible: A Study of His Old Testament Exegesis* (New York: Paulist Press, 1989), 50.

In modern times, this erotic interpretation has also prevailed as the dominant interpretation of the Song, and is well represented by the comments of the French Catholic exegete Émile Osty, who writes:

> *The Song celebrates love, human love, and only human love.* . . . The tons of comments poured over this booklet did not succeed in hiding the truth which is so clear to the eyes of the unprepared reader: *in its literal, first and direct meaning, the Song deals with human love* uniting man and woman in marriage.[4]

Notice here that for Osty, this is an *exclusively* erotic interpretation: the Song of Solomon is about erotic human love and no other kind. All allegorical or spiritual interpretations are rejected.

2. The Divine Love Interpretation

According to this interpretation, the bridegroom in the Song represents YHWH, the God of Israel, who is sometimes identified as a "bridegroom" in Jewish Scripture (Is 62), and the bride is Israel (or Jerusalem), the people of God (Is 54), and the central theme of the book is the divine love of YHWH for his people, as revealed in salvation history (for example, Ezek 16; Hos 2; Is 52, 62, and so on).

As far as we know, this is the most ancient Jewish interpretation of the Song, going back at least as far as the first century A.D., when Josephus grouped the Song among the books containing "hymns to God",[5] when the extra-biblical Jewish writing known as *4 Ezra* took images from the Song to describe the relationship between God and Jerusalem (*4 Ezra* 5:23–28), and when Rabbi Akiba denounced any erotic or literalistic interpretation when he declared:

> He who sings the Song of Songs in a banquet hall and makes it into a kind of ditty has no place in the world to come.[6]

A similar interpretation is found in the Christian Church Father Origen of Alexandria, who was apparently influenced by the Jewish rabbis of his day in taking a similar view of the Song:

> Located in the middle of the Bible, the Song lifts to its height *the great fundamental image*, going from the first chapters of Genesis to the last chapter of Revelation: *mankind has become the bride of God*.[7]

This divine love interpretation is usually referred to as the *allegorical* interpretation of the Song, since it treats the literal figures of Solomon (the bridegroom) and the Shulammite woman (the bride) as allegories for God and Israel.

---

[4] Émile Osty, quoted in Blaise Arminjon, *The Cantata of Love: A Verse by Verse Reading of the Song of Songs*, trans. Nelly Marans (San Francisco: Ignatius Press, 1988), 34.

[5] Josephus, *Against Apion* 1.40.

[6] Tosefta, *Sanhedrin* 12.10, in *The Tosefta*, trans. Jacob Neusner (Peabody, Mass.: Hendrickson, 2002), 2:1187.

[7] Origen, in Arminjon, *Cantata of Love*, 41.

3. The Messianic Interpretation

The third view, the messianic interpretation, also sees the Song as an allegory. However, it differs in that it identifies the bridegroom as the Messiah—the future anointed king of Israel (for example, Is 11; Jer 30–33; and so on)— whereas the bride is the people of the Messiah, whether Jerusalem (from the Jewish perspective) or the Church (from the Christian perspective). Examples of this interpretation can be found in the Ancient Jewish Targums—Aramaic translations of the Song of Solomon—as well as the early Church Fathers, especially St. Augustine.

> "My beloved, I have laid [it] up for you" (Song 7:14)....When it shall be the good pleasure of the Lord to redeem his people from exile, *He will say to the King Messiah....* "Arise now, and receive the kingdom I have stored up for you."[8]

> But now the Song of Songs is a certain spiritual pleasure of holy minds, in *the marriage of that King and Queen-city, that is, Christ and the Church*. But this pleasure is wrapped up in allegorical veils, that the Bridegroom may be more ardently desired, and more joyfully unveiled.[9]

For the messianic (or Christological) interpretation, the joy of the marital union described by the Song is either a figure of Israel's longing for the messianic age of salvation (from the Jewish perspective) or a celebration of the union that has already been inaugurated in Christ's love for the Church.

4. The Mystical Interpretation

The fourth view, which may be (loosely) referred to as the mystical interpretation, also interprets the bridegroom in the Song as God. However, this view identifies the bride more with the soul of an individual person rather than with the collectivity of Israel or the Church. Consider, for example, the comments of Saint Thérèse of Lisieux and Pope Saint John Paul II writing to consecrated women:

> If I had time, I would like to comment on the Song of Songs. I have discovered in this book such profound things about the union of the soul with her beloved.[10]

> Your personal journey must be like an original new edition of the famous poem in the Song of Songs.[11]

Although in the early centuries the more corporate messianic interpretation prevailed, in the Christian tradition, especially since the Middle Ages, the mystical

---

[8] *Targum of Canticles* 7.14, in Philip S. Alexander, *The Targum of Canticles*, Aramaic Bible 17A (Collegeville, Minn.: Liturgical Press, 2003), 188.

[9] Augustine, *City of God* 17.20.2, in NPNF1 2:358.

[10] Thérèse of Lisieux, quoted in Arminjon, *Cantata of Love*, 39.

[11] John Paul II, Address to French Women Religious, May 30, 1980, quoted in Arminjon, *Cantata of Love*, 41.

interpretation has had far and away the largest number of supporters, in figures such as Saint Bernard, Saint Bonaventure, Saint Thomas Aquinas, Saint Teresa of Avila, Saint John of the Cross, and many others.

5. The Liturgical Interpretation

Finally, and most recently, there is a view that might be called the liturgical interpretation. Like the divine love interpretation, this view identifies the bridegroom as YHWH, the God of Israel. However, unlike some of the other views propounded so far, this view identifies the bride not only with the people of Israel, but with a number of referents, all tied to the worship of YHWH: the Tabernacle of Moses, the Temple of Solomon, the city of Jerusalem, and the people of Israel as a whole. From this point of view, the love being described in the Song of Solomon is primarily manifested in *sacrificial worship*. In the words of Old Testament scholar Ellen Davis, who proposes this particular view:

> The image of the bride [in the Song of Solomon] ... is like one of those pictures whose content shifts before your eyes.... Looking closely, we see at one moment a human love scene.... Then we blink, and now we see the special intimacy between God and Israel, which reaches its high point in Temple worship.[12]

It is crucial to emphasize that for this liturgical interpretation, the literal meaning of the Song is itself figurative: the Hebrew author is deliberately using images of the Temple, the Tabernacle, Jerusalem, and the land when describing the bride in the Song in order to signal to the reader that the Song is more than just a story of Solomon and his bride but is really about YHWH and Israel.[13] One of the reasons so many later readers miss this is because they are not reading the text in its original Hebrew, in which the parallels with other parts of the Hebrew Bible are so explicit.

In what follows, we will focus first on what the human author of the Song is trying to communicate in the literal sense of the text before turning to how it has been interpreted in the living tradition.

The Literary Genre and Structure of the Song

There is no consensus on the literary genre of the Song. The biggest point of debate concerns the overall unity of the book. Some scholars emphasize the disunity of the book, seeing the Song as a kind of *anthology* of love poems only loosely related to one another, if at all. Other commentators who emphasize the unity of the book have gone so far as to argue that the Song is a kind of poetic *drama* with a plot, which could be acted out like a lyric opera. Indeed, as early as the late second century A.D., Origen of Alexandria suggested that the

---

[12] Ellen F. Davis, *Proverbs, Ecclesiastes, and the Song of Songs*, Wesminster Bible Companion (Louisville, Ky.: Westminster John Knox Press, 2000), 269.

[13] See ibid., 231.

Song was "written in dramatic form and, like a story that is acted on the stage, with dialogue between the characters".[14] The truth probably lies somewhere in between, for the final form of the book is both difficult to outline and, at the same time, appears to have a series of movements that, when taken together, form a coherent whole. However one interprets the overall structure, what is clear is that there are three predominant "voices" in the songs: (1) the man/bridegroom; (2) the woman/bride, and (3) the "daughters of Jerusalem", a chorus of women who are the bride's companions.

With that said, opinions concerning the literary structure of the Song are extremely diverse, with no two commentators providing exactly the same outline. On our reading, there are seven major divisions of the Song, arranged chiastically:

Outline of the Song of Solomon

   1. (A) Opening Colloquy of the Bride, the Groom, and the Chorus
     (1:1—2:7)
     2. (B) Bridegroom's Invitation to Elope (2:8–17)
       3. (C) First Dream Sequence: The Bride Seeks the Groom at Night
         (3:1–5)
         4. (D) Solomon and His Bride Ride into Jerusalem (Song
           3:6—5:1)
       5. (C') Second Dream Sequence: The Bride Seeks the Groom at
         Night (5:2—6:10)
     6. (B') Daydream Sequence: The Bride and Groom Ride Together
       (6:11—8:4)
   7. (A') Final Colloquy of the Bride, Groom, and Chorus (8:5–14)

The justification for this outline will be provided in the overview below. For now, one will notice the prevalence of *dreams* as an organizational principle in the Song of Solomon: there are two actual dreams (Song 3:1–5; 5:2—6:10) and one daydream (Song 6:11—8:4). In addition, the dreamy nature of the Song is reinforced by the repeated refrain, "stir not up nor *awaken* love until it please." The word "love" in this phrase has a double meaning: it can also mean "the loved one", a reference to the bride herself, who is called simply "Love" (Hebrew *'ahaba*; Song 7:6). One is justified, therefore, in viewing most of the "events" in the Song as dreams, daydreams, or poetic "virtual reality".

Another justification for adopting this perspective is that the plot of the Song does not make sense if the events described in the various scenes literally take place. For example, the Song closes with the bride and groom still unmarried, with the bride boasting of her virginity (Song 8:10), the groom's party approaching to escort the bride to the wedding (Song 8:13), and the bride calling out for them to make haste (Song 8:14). Yet earlier in the book, the bride and groom seem to be already wed and approach each other for

[14] Origen, *Commentary on the Song of Songs*, prologue, 2, in Origen, *The Song of Songs, Commentary and Homilies*, trans. R. P. Lawson, Ancient Christian Writers 26 (Westminster: Newman, 1957), 23.

consummation (Song 3:6—5:1). The earlier dream sequences, therefore, are almost certainly anticipatory—a wedding day dreamed of but not yet experienced. Similar surreal or virtual scenes are not uncommon in love songs or romantic tales even today.

Overview of the Song of Solomon

The Groom, the Bride, and the Chorus Sing (Song 1:1—2:7)

One of the first and most difficult aspects of interpreting the Song of Solomon is figuring out, at any given point, *who exactly is speaking*. Some modern translations actually add identifications to the text to make it more readable (see NAB). In this opening scene, all three voices—the bridegroom, the bride, and the chorus of the "daughters of Jerusalem"—have speaking parts. Consider, for example, the following verses, to which we have added the (implied) speakers:

> *Bride*: "O that you would kiss me with the kisses of your mouth!" (cf. Song 1:1–4).
> *Chorus*: "We will exult and rejoice in you ..." (Song 1:4).
> *Bride*: "I am very dark but comely, O daughters of Jerusalem ..." (cf. Song 1:5–7).
> *Groom*: "If you do not know, O fairest among women ..." (cf. Song 1:8–10).
> *Chorus*: "We will make you ornaments of gold ..." (Song 1:11).
> *Bride*: "While the king was on his couch ..." (cf. Song 1:12–14).
> *Groom*: "Behold, you are beautiful, my love ..." (cf. Song 1:15–17).
> *Bride*: "I am a rose of Sharon, a lily of the valleys" (Song 2:1).
> *Groom*: "As a lily among brambles, so is my love among maidens" (Song 2:2).
> *Bride*: "As an apple tree ... so is my beloved among young men ..." (cf. Song 2:3–7).

Significantly, because the original Hebrew text has gendered *endings* on pronouns, it is relatively easy to distinguish when the bride is speaking to the groom (in which case "you" is masculine) or the groom is speaking to the bride (in which case "you" is feminine). Even clearer is the chorus of the daughters of Jerusalem, since they can be distinguished by occurrences of the first-person plural "we" (Song 1:4, 11).

With this in mind, the Song opens with a flurry of activity, as the bride declares her desire for the affection of the groom: "Oh, that you would kiss me ...!" (Song 1:2), while hastening to the king's chambers, perhaps together with her companions, "the daughters of Jerusalem" (Song 1:1–4; cf. Ps 45:13–14). The chorus praises the love of the royal groom (Song 1:4b), and the bride then addresses the chorus of "daughters", explaining why she is dark: her brothers made her work outside in the sun (Song 1:5–7). She then turns to the groom, addressing him as if he were a shepherd, to ask where he pastures his flock (Song 1:7). The groom responds cryptically, then launches into a praise of the bride's attractions and beauty (Song 1:8–9). The chorus promises to make jewelry for the bride, and for the next several verses a dialogue between bride and groom ensues in which they praise each other's beauty with vivid metaphors of food, spices, flora, and fauna (Song 1:9–17).

Suddenly, however, the pleasant dialogue of bride and groom is brought to an abrupt halt by the bride crying out:

> O that his left hand were under my head,
>   and that his right hand embraced me!
> I adjure you, O daughters of Jerusalem,
>   by the gazelles or the deer of the field,
> that you stir not up nor awaken love
>   until it [literally "she"] please.
>
> (Song 2:6–7)

This is unexpected. Is the groom not present? Has he not been pleasantly conversing with the bride? This sudden cry of the bride suggests that things are not as they seem—perhaps what has transpired so far (Song 1:1—2:5) was a vision or a dream. This is reinforced by the bride's adjuration of the daughters not to "stir up nor awaken love until she please". On one level, she is exhorting them not to arouse love at an inappropriate time—that is, when no consummation is possible or appropriate. On the other hand, it can be understood as a self-reference to the bride—she does not wish to be awakened because she is dreaming pleasantly of her groom (in Song 1:1—2:5). Either way, the emphasis falls on the *unfulfilled* desire of the bride for her bridegroom.

The Bridegroom Invites the Bride to Come Away (Song 2:8–17)

A new unit appears when the bride cries out: "The voice of my beloved! Behold, he comes" (Song 2:8). This is definitely a transition from what has happened thus far, where the beloved *seemed* to be present but we found out it was all a dream (cf. Song 2:6–7). Now, the beloved appears to be approaching, bounding down from the hills until he stands outside the garden where the bride bides her time with her companions (Song 2:8–9). Then he appeals to her in an exquisite poem to run away with him into the hills, to enjoy the beauties of nature in the spring (Song 2:10–15). The bride then speaks and seems to indicate that her beloved is now embracing her: "My beloved is mine and I am his, he pastures his flock among the lilies" (Song 2:16). However, she immediately takes it back once again when she emphasizes the *unfulfilled* nature of their union, when she calls upon him to make haste and "be like a gazelle, or a young stag upon rugged mountains" (Song 2:17).

The Bride Goes Seeking the Bridegroom in a Dream (Song 3:1–5)

Once again, the scene abruptly shifts. The bride is now in her bedchamber: "Upon my bed by night, I sought him whom my soul loves" (Song 3:1). She rises and searches through the city till she finds her beloved and brings him back to her home. The scene ends with the refrain seen before: "I adjure you, O daughters of Jerusalem ... stir not up nor awaken love until it please" (Song 3:5).

Although this description of the bride seeking her groom is not explicitly identified as a dream, a number of features suggest that the events being described are not "actually" taking place. For one thing, they are fantastic: no young woman would wander alone in the city at night, nor would her beloved be simply wandering the streets to be found (Song 3:1–4). Much more likely, the poem is describing the kind of unfulfilled searches that are a common part of human dreaming. Moreover, the repeated adjuration—"I adjure you, daughters of Jerusalem ... that you stir not up nor awaken love *until she please*" (Song 3:5)—strongly suggests the bride is asleep and does not wish to be awakened (because she is having pleasant dreams of being with her beloved). Finally, as we will see momentarily, the same basic narrative will recur in a later sequence in the book, in which it will be explicitly marked as a dream (Song 5:2—6:10).

King Solomon and His Bride Ride into Jerusalem (Song 3:6—5:1)

Again the scene changes abruptly. An unmarked voice—a narrator?—describes the vision of Solomon being carried into Jerusalem from the eastern wilderness (the Jordan valley), exuding fine perfumes and surrounded by bodyguards (Song 3:6–10). The voice exhorts the chorus, the "daughters of Zion", to go forth and see the sight: glorious Solomon wearing the nuptial crown marking "the day of his wedding" (Song 3:11).

Although it is this passage above all that led interpreters over the centuries to identify the bridegroom in the Song with Solomon, the relationship between the description of entering Jerusalem (Song 3:6–11) and the following dialogue between the groom and the bride is admittedly not clear (Song 4:1—5:1). However, from the fact that Solomon is wearing a nuptial crown (Song 3:6–11) and that the male voice describes his beloved explicitly as his "bride" who is anointed with fabulously expensive perfumes available only to royalty (Song 4:1–15), it seems reasonable to conclude that the dialogue is that of the newly wedded royal couple (Song 4:1—5:1). From this point of view, the triumphant scene describing the wedding procession of Solomon and his bride (Song 3:6ff.) segues into a more intimate scene, in which the reader is taken inside the royal nuptial litter to hear the romantic intimacies of the king and his new queen (Song 4:1—5:1).

If this is correct, then Solomon the groom praises the beauty of the bride, giving metaphorical descriptions of each part of her body:

> Behold, you are beautiful, my love,
> behold, you are beautiful!
> Your eyes are doves
> behind your veil.
> Your hair is like a flock of goats,
> moving down the slopes of Gilead.
> Your teeth are like a flock of shorn ewes
> that have come up from the washing,
> all of which bear twins,
> and not one among them is bereaved.

> Your lips are like a scarlet thread,
>   and your mouth is lovely.
> Your cheeks are like halves of a pomegranate
>   behind your veil.
> Your neck is like the tower of David,
>   built for an arsenal,
> whereon hang a thousand bucklers,
>   all of them shields of warriors.
> Your two breasts are like two fawns,
>   twins of a gazelle,
>   that feed among the lilies. (Song 4:1–5)

It is at this point in the reading of the Song that readers are often puzzled. What kind of description of a woman is this? On the one hand, some of the images used by the bridegroom are poetic and beautiful, such as "scarlet" or "doves". Others are clearly figurative, such as when he praises her virginity: "A garden locked is my sister, my bride, a garden locked, a fountain sealed" (Song 4:12). Her virginal integrity indicates that her love for him is exclusive, given to no one else. On the other hand, some of the comparisons seem downright bizarre: Who would ever compare a woman's neck to a tower, or her hair to goats, or her breasts to gazelles?

One could always chalk this up to primitive imagery and poor taste. However, as mentioned above, there may be more going on here. The Hebrew imagery used to describe the bride occurs elsewhere in the Bible applied to the city of Jerusalem and the Temple[15] (see below, "Theological Issues in the Song of Solomon").

For now, suffice it to say that the bride responds to this strange praise, inviting her royal spouse to embrace her: "Let my beloved come to his garden, and eat its choicest fruits" (Song 4:16). The groom advances to embrace his beloved: "I come to my garden, my sister, my bride, I gather my myrrh with my spice" (Song 5:1). As the royal couple moves toward the marital embrace, the "curtain falls" on the scene, so to speak, and the chorus blesses the royal union using the metaphor of food and drink: "Eat, O friends, and drink: drink deeply, O lovers!" (Song 5:1). Once again, it is critical to note that the consummation of the marriage, though implied, is never described.

The Bride Dreams of Her Wedding Night (Song 5:1—6:10)

The scene shifts yet again. The bride is asleep, but her "heart was awake" (Song 5:2). In Jewish Scripture, the "heart" (Hebrew *leb*) was the seat of thought as well as emotion, so that, in more contemporary language, the phrase means: "I was asleep, but my mind was racing." In other words, the bride experiences vivid dreaming.[16]

---

[15] See Brant Pitre, *Jesus the Bridegroom: The Greatest Love Story Ever Told* (New York: Image, 2014), 24–25.

[16] Roland E. Murphy, O. Carm., *The Song of Songs*, Hermeneia (Minneapolis: Fortress Press, 1990), 170.

The plot of this dream sequence is very similar to the earlier reverie: the bride imagines herself awake and cannot find her beloved, so she wanders about the city at night in search of him until she finds him (Song 5:2—6:10; cf. 3:1–5). However, in this case, the bride dreams that the bridegroom is knocking on her chamber door, but because she has already disrobed and prepared for bed, she does not open for him until she hears his hand at the door latch and her "heart is thrilled" (literally, her "guts churn") within her (Song 5:2–5).[17] Rushing to the door, however, she finds her beloved has gone, so she ventures out into the night once again to find him (Song 5:6). The city watchmen find her and beat her for violating the "curfew" customs of ancient urban life (Song 5:7). So she cries to the chorus, the daughters of Jerusalem, to help her find the bridegroom (Song 5:8).

The chorus asks what is so special about the beloved, that it should make the effort to help in finding him (Song 5:9). This introduces the only visual description of the groom by the bride to be found in the book:

> My beloved is all radiant and ruddy,
>   distinguished among ten thousand.
> His head is the finest gold;
>   his locks are wavy,
>   black as a raven.
> His eyes are like doves
>   beside springs of water,
> bathed in milk,
>   fitly set.
> His cheeks are like beds of spices,
>   yielding fragrance.
> His lips are lilies,
>   distilling liquid myrrh.
> His arms are rounded gold,
>   set with jewels.
> His body is ivory work,
>   encrusted with sapphires.
> His legs are alabaster columns,
>   set upon bases of gold.
> His appearance is like Lebanon,
>   choice as the cedars.
> His speech is most sweet,
>   and he is altogether desirable.
> This is my beloved and this is my friend,
>   O daughters of Jerusalem. (Song 5:10–16)

Notice here how the description is not only difficult to visualize but utilizes images elsewhere associated with the Temple, such as the "cedars" of "Lebanon" (Song 5:15). What are we to make of this? Once again, it may be the case that the otherwise-bizarre imagery being utilized to describe the bridegroom is

---

[17] Davis, *Proverbs*, 277.

meant to signal to the reader that he represents the Divine Bridegroom, YHWH (see below, "Theological Issues in the Song of Solomon").[18]

In any case, after such a rousing description, the daughters of Jerusalem now express interest in helping with the search (Song 6:2–3). After an ambiguous description of what appears to be a nuptial embrace, the bridegroom proceeds to reciprocate the loving visual description given him first by the bride by lavishly describing her own body in terms very similar to those he has used before (Song 6:4–7; cf. 4:1–5). He concludes by praising her beauty above that of all the other royal women; in fact, the other royal women recognize her superiority (Song 6:8–10).

The Bride Dreams of Riding in the Prince's Chariot (Song 6:11—8:4)

Once again, the scene changes: now the bride is awake; she walks down to the orchard and begins to fantasize: "Before I was aware, my fancy set me in a chariot beside my prince" (Song 6:12). As the couple rides away, the chorus cries out, "Return, return, O Shulammite ... that we may look upon you" (Song 6:13). But the prince rebuffs them: "Why should you look upon the Shulammite ...?" (Song 6:13). He then gives the most complete visual description of his beloved in the book, from her feet to her hair, culminating in an expression of his desire for her, couched in metaphors of fine food and flora (Song 7:1–9). The bride responds by affirming her affection for her prince and—as he once did for her—invites him to go forth with her into the springtime countryside, where she can express her affection to him (Song 7:11–13). She says she wishes he were her brother—then she could always express her affection publicly without offense (Song 8:1–2). Suddenly, however, the bride once more cries out with the refrain:

> O that his left hand were under my head,
>   and that his right hand embraced me!
> I adjure you, O daughters of Jerusalem,
>   that you stir not up nor awaken love
>   until it please. (Song 8:3)

As before, this refrain is surprising. Has the bridegroom not been embracing her this whole time? Has she not been in his company as he praises her beauty (Song 7:1–9)? But then, we recall, it was her "fancy" that set her in the chariot beside her prince (Song 6:12). Once again, the entire sequence in which the bridegroom and bride have finally come together is but a daydream, a flight of fancy.

The Bride, the Bridegroom, and the Chorus Sing (Song 8:5–14)

In the final section of the poem, a voice—probably the same that announced the coming of Solomon from the wilderness (cf. Song 3:6)—announces that the bride is now "coming up from the wilderness, leaning on her beloved" (Song 8:5). Although the Song has been "dreamy" to this point, everyone now seems

---

[18] See Pitre, *Jesus the Bridegroom*, 22–23.

awake, for the bride describes awakening her beloved under the apple tree (Song 8:5). Then she declares her desire to be united to her beloved, uttering the most famous lines in the book:

> Set me as a seal upon your heart,
>> as a seal upon your arm;
> for love is strong as death,
>> jealousy is cruel as the grave.
> Its flashes are flashes of fire,
>> a most vehement flame.
> Many waters cannot quench love,
>> neither can floods drown it.
> If a man offered for love
>> all the wealth of his house,
>> it would be utterly scorned. (Song 8:6–7)

In the very midst of this climactic declaration about the power of love over death, the chorus interrupts the voice of the bride and shifts attention to an as-yet-unintroduced "little sister", who has not yet reached the age of physical maturity: "We have a little sister, and she has no breasts" (Song 8:8). Apparently, this young girl is the bride, who dreams of her wedding day but is not yet ready to be wed. Indeed, the chorus has anxiety over the coming betrothal of this bride-to-be, when they say: "What shall we do for our sister, on the day when she is spoken for?"—that is, betrothed (Song 8:8). Then, if she is found to be a "wall"—that is, a virgin—they will "build upon her a battlement of silver": that is, heap jewelry on her in celebration of her betrothal (Song 8:9). But if she is a "door"—in other words, not a virgin—they will "enclose her with boards of cedar"—that is, lock her in an inner room under close watch (Song 8:9). The bride now boasts of her eligibility for marriage. She is virginal, ready for marriage, and attractive to her beloved: "I am a wall, and my breasts are like towers; then I was in his eyes as one who brings peace" (Song 8:10, author's translation).

The final verses of the Song are difficult to interpret. They speak of a vineyard of Solomon let out to caretakers and of the bride's own vineyard, whose profit she hands over to Solomon (one thousand pieces of silver) and the "keepers" (two hundred pieces of silver) (Song 8:11–12). The vineyard may be a metaphor for the body of the bride, and the pieces of silver a reference to a dowry or bride-price given by, or returned to, Solomon, with gifts given to wedding attendants or family members (the "keepers of the fruit"). For our purposes here, what matters most is this: *despite the bride's many dreams about the night of consummation, the Song as a whole in its final form ends with the wedding not yet consummated.* Indeed, it ends with the refrain of the bride calling out for the bridegroom to come and take her away to the wedding:

> Make haste, my beloved,
>> and be like a gazelle,
> or a young stag
>> upon the mountains of spices. (Song 8:14)

Thus, once again, the note of expectation is sounded, and the marriage, by implication, not yet celebrated.

Historical Issues in the Song of Solomon

Is the Song of Songs a Unified Text?

On an initial reading, the Song seems very disjointed, a montage of poems and images without a coherent plot. With more study, however, one begins to recognize repeated refrains, phrases, images, and motifs that link the different sections of the Song to one another:

1. The Bridegroom (Song 1:3; 3:7, 11; 8:11)
2. The Bride (Song 1:5; 2:15–16; 3:4; 6:2, 8; 7:10; 8:2, 8, 12, 13)
3. Daughters of Jerusalem (Song 1:4; 2:7; 3:5; 5:8, 16; 8:4)
4. Young Stag (Song 2:8, 17; 8:14)
5. Feeding the Flock among the Lilies (Song 2:16; 4:5; 6:2)
6. Fairest among Women (Song 1:7; 5:9, 17)

Because such images and characteristic expressions run throughout the various chapters of the poem, it is reasonable to conclude that, while some of the individual poems of the Song may have originally been composed as independent love songs (for example, Song 2:8–15), a strong editorial hand must have knit the Song into a final unified composition.

The Origin of the Song of Solomon

As with several other books of the Old Testament we have surveyed so far, when it comes to the Song of Solomon, the vast majority of ancient interpreters followed the lead of the superscription of the book—"The Song of Songs, which is Solomon's" (Song 1:1)—as well as other references to Solomon in the book (Song 3:7–11; 8:11–12), in ascribing it to the tenth-century king of Israel, Solomon the son of David. The only datable references in the book are those to Solomon, but, of course, this only establishes a *terminus a quo*—that is, an earliest possible date.

Modern scholars who have favored this ancient view—though they are few in number—offer several considerations in support of identifying the author with Solomon.[19]

First, Solomon is described in the book of Kings as having composed more than a thousand "songs" (*shirō*) (1 Kings 4:32), so that the existence of a song attributed to him, as opposed to some other king of Israel, fits the historical record. In the words of the second-century book of Sirach:

> Your name [Solomon] reached to far-off islands,
> and you were loved for your peace.

[19] See Marvin Pope, *Song of Songs*, Anchor Bible 7C (New York: Doubleday, 1977), 2–33.

For your songs and proverbs and parables,
and for your interpretations, the countries marveled at you.
(Sir 47:16–17)

Some might dismiss these comments as legendary, but it should be remembered that royalty in antiquity were some of the few in society who did have the leisure and wealth to engage in literary pursuits, and, furthermore, it was politically expedient to portray themselves as patrons of the arts. History knows many kings and emperors—from Julius Caesar to Mao Zedong—who themselves produced works of art or literature, and many more who had such commissioned under their name.

Second, scholars have also suggested that the abundant imagery of fauna and flora in the Song coheres with the description of King Solomon as both a poet and an expert in the natural world of "trees ... beasts ... birds, and of reptiles, and of fish" (1 Kings 4:33).

Third, certain considerations may not support Solomonic authorship directly but do suggest the origin of the Song during or near the time of his reign. For example, M. H. Segal argues that a host of elements described in the Song—such as "the tents of Kedar", the "thousand shields" of David's tower, the frequent mentions of "cedar" wood and "ivory" and many other items (Song 1:17; 3:9; 4:4; 5:14–15; and so on)—correspond exactly to the large influx of wealth into Jerusalem during the Solomonic period, when the first Temple and many other buildings were constructed out of the surplus of Solomon's wealth (cf. 1 Kings 6–8, 9–10). From this point of view, the Song seems to arise out of the circles of the royal court at this time period or shortly thereafter.

Fourth, and perhaps more significantly, in one of the later poems in the Song, the bridegroom says of the bride:

You are beautiful as *Tirzah*, my love,
comely as *Jerusalem*. (Song 6:4)

In this verse, Jerusalem, the capital of the southern kingdom under David, is used as a parallel with Tirzah, which became the capital of the northern kingdom of Israel under King Jeroboam I and his successors up to Omri (ca. 930–880 B.C.; 1 Kings 14:17; 16:23). Thus, the parallelism of this verse reflects the social and political situation in the late tenth–early ninth century B.C., when Tirzah and Jerusalem were cities of comparable size and glory, so that Tirzah was the logical choice for a rival capital when the kingdom split. Song of Solomon 6:4 is unlikely to have been composed after King Omri shifted the northern capital to Samaria (ca. 880 B.C.; 1 Kings 16:23) and Tirzah rapidly declined in wealth and influence. Moreover, since there is no hint yet in Song 6:4 of bitter rivalry between the two cities, the evidence may tilt in favor of the composition of this couplet during the late united monarchy.

Intriguingly, only during the reign of David and Solomon did the Jerusalem monarchy rule over the northern Israelite territories mentioned in the book (Tirzah, Hermon, Senir, Lebanon, Heshbon), even to Damascus, so that a royal prince or princess could be expected to have seen the towers of that city (Song

7:4). Not long after Solomon's reign, the territory ruled by Jerusalem became quite constrained, and many of the geographical images in the book would have lost their significance to a Jerusalemite audience. The references to extremely rare and expensive spices and other luxury items and to a wide range of exotic geographical locations within the Levant from Jerusalem to Damascus indicate that the author and his intended readership were persons of sufficient wealth to have experienced these luxuries and traveled to these locations. This would be supporting evidence for the origin of the Song during the reign of Solomon, if his reign was at all like its biblical description in 1 Kings 1–11.

On the other side of the historical ledger, ever since antiquity, there have been readers of the Song who think that it was composed *about* Solomon (rather than by him), at a time long after he was gone. For one thing, the title, "The Song of Songs, which is of [or to] Solomon", like similar superscriptions in the Psalms, could indicate authorship or subject: that is, the Song could be "by" Solomon or "about" Solomon. The third-person references to Solomon in the book tend to lend weight to interpreting the title as indicating subject: "about Solomon".

Moreover, already in rabbinic Judaism, some of the sages held that the work as we have it was not authored by Solomon but written in the person of Solomon:

> Who wrote the Scriptures?... Hezekiah and his colleagues wrote Isaiah, Proverbs, *the Song of Songs* and Ecclesiastes.[20]

With that said, once the book is detached from the figure of King Solomon, it becomes very difficult to pinpoint its date of origin, since there are no other historical persons mentioned in the book, and scholars are forced to hypothesize on the basis of other internal clues, such as language.

For example, some argue from the presence of two loanwords from Persian and Greek—"paradise" (Hebrew *pardēs*, Song 4:13) and "palanquin" (*'appiryôn*, Song 3:9)—that the book had to have been composed in the postexilic Persian period (ca. 537–333 B.C.).[21] Other scholars hold that the entire book cannot be dated by these two words—which could be unusual early borrowings during the "cosmopolitan" reign of Solomon, or a late insertion—and argue instead that the book could be dated on linguistic grounds as early as 900 B.C.[22] Indeed, in the twentieth century, the number of dates proposed for the Song are almost as diverse as the scholars who propose them, ranging anywhere from the tenth century B.C. (whether or not Solomon was directly involved) all the way down to the fourth century B.C. In the words of Marvin Pope: "The dating game as played with ... the Song of Songs ... remains imprecise and the score is difficult to compute. There are grounds for both the oldest and the youngest estimates."[23]

---

[20] Babylonian Tamlud, *Baba Bathra* 14b, in I. Epstein, *The Babylonian Talmud*, 35 vols. (London: Soncino, 1935–52).

[21] John J. Collins, *Introduction to the Hebrew Bible* (Minneapolis: Fortress Press, 2004), 481.

[22] Scott B. Noegel and Gary A. Rendsburg, *Solomon's Vineyard: Literary and Linguistic Studies in the Song of Songs* (Atlanta: Society of Biblical Literature, 2009).

[23] Cited in Murphy, *Song of Songs*, 3.

Theological Issues in the Song of Solomon

Does the Song of Solomon Condone Extramarital Sex?

In the modern period, one of the biggest controversies over the Song of Solomon is whether it portrays premarital sexual intercourse favorably or not. How one answers this question is based very much on various theories about the source-critical background of the poem as well as on one's overall interpretation of the poem in its final form.

For example, those scholars who reject the literary unity of the Song argue that individual sections must be interpreted independently of the rest of the Song and taken as accounts, not of dreams, but of actual behavior. When this is done, then it is possible to read the poems as describing premarital sex in positive terms. In the words of John Collins:

> In view of the changing voices and perspectives, it is difficult to defend the structural unity of the poem.... The most striking aspect of the Song, however, is its uninhibited celebration of sexual love. Just how uninhibited it is, is a matter of interpretation.... There is little to indicate that the lovers are married. The poem in 3:6–11 may celebrate a wedding procession, but in most of the poems the lovers evidently do not live together.... It is clear then that the love envisioned is not protected by the institution of marriage. There is no indication that it is adulterous (that either party is married to anyone else.) Most probably, the lovers are young and unmarried.[24]

There are several major problems with this position:

First and foremost, notice that in order to maintain the "non-marital" interpretation of the love of the bridegroom and bride, Collins is forced to take the various texts *out of context*, by positing that they were "originally" in a non-nuptial context, whereas the poem itself speaks of "the day of his wedding" (Song 3:11)! Indeed, as we saw above, the central scene of the Song is clearly a description of Solomon on a wedding day (Song 3:6–11) followed by a dialogue between Solomon and his bride (Song 4:1–5:1) in which "Solomon" repeatedly calls his beloved "my sister"—a term of *spousal* endearment—and "my bride".

Second, the premarital sex interpretation also is forced to ignore the explicit references to the fact that the bride is *dreaming* when she imagines encounters with the bridegroom, upon her "bed", "by night", while she "slept" (Song 3:1–2; 5:2–3). To be sure, some of the activity described indirectly or metaphorically in the dreams or daydreams of the Song would, if actually lived out, have put the romantic couple in compromising situations or would have led to premature consummation of their relationship. But these dreams and daydreams are not reportage of actual events. They are expressions of the desire of the bride who anticipates her upcoming union, from which she awakes and cries out in frustration: "Oh, that his left hand were [actually] under my head and his right hand embraced me!" At the end of the book, the couple is still apart, but the wedding party has arrived to take the bride away (Song 8:13–14).

---

[24] Collins, *Introduction*, 482–83.

Third, and perhaps most important of all, this interpretation cannot do justice to the fact that the bridegroom praises the bride precisely for her *virginal integrity*: "A garden locked is my sister, my bride, a garden locked, a fountain sealed" (Song 4:12). At the end of the Song, it places a high value on maintaining sexual integrity prior to marriage: "If she is a wall, we will build upon her a battlement of silver" (Song 8:9). In this context, the bride boasts about her virginity: "I am a wall!" (Song 8:10, cf. NABRE). Taken together, all this data makes clear that, contrary to what some scholars want to claim (for whatever reason), the singers of the Song are not endorsing sexual promiscuity before marriage. To the contrary, in the actual form that we have it, the Song strongly praises both marital love *and* premarital abstinence.

Of course, this is exactly what one would expect when one reads the Song in light of Jewish Scripture as a whole, since the Pentateuch makes clear that premarital sexual relations are against the law:

> If there is a betrothed virgin, and a man meets her in the city and lies with her, then you shall bring them both out to the gate of that city, and you shall stone them to death with stones.... If a man meets a virgin who is not betrothed, and seizes her and lies with her, and they are found, then the man who lay with her shall give to the father of the young woman fifty shekels of silver, and she shall be his wife, because he has violated her; he may not put her away all his days. (Deut 22:23–24, 28–29)

In short, when the individual sections of the Song are read in the light of the final form of the book as we have it and within the context of the entire Old Testament canon, there is no way to maintain from a literary or historical perspective that the Song endorses (much less celebrates) extramarital sexual contact for women or for men. To the contrary, if it celebrates anything, it is the created goodness of sexuality within the marital covenant bond.

The Song as a Hebrew Allegory of YHWH's Love for Israel

What, then, are we to make of the love described in the Song of Solomon? Is there any theological significance to what is being described here, or is it simply a poetic celebration of the joy of married love, with Solomon and his bride as the example par excellence?

As mentioned above, when the original Hebrew expressions utilized in the Song are read carefully, a strong case can be made that the author of the Song is not only telling a poetic drama of Solomon's wedding day but also deliberately intending to invoke the nuptial relationship between YHWH as Bridegroom and the people of Israel as the bride.[25]

For example, when we compare the (otherwise-bizarre) images used to describe the beauty of the bride with parallel passages from elsewhere in Jewish Scripture, we discover something remarkable: the bride in the Song looks strikingly like the city of Jerusalem!

---

[25] See Davis, *Proverbs*, 238–302.

The Temple in Jerusalem	The Bride in the Song of Solomon
And [Solomon] made the [curtain in the Temple] of blue and purple and crimson fabrics and fine linen. (2 Chron 3:14)	I am very dark, but comely, O daughters of Jerusalem, like the tents of Kedar, like the curtains of Solomon. (Song 1:5)
[Solomon] built the house of the Forest of Lebanon;...upon three rows of cedar pillars, with cedar beams. (1 Kings 7:2)	The scent of your garments is like the scent of Lebanon. (Song 4:11)
In front of the house [Solomon] made ... a hundred pomegranates and put them on chains. (2 Chron 3:15–16)	Your shoots are an orchard of pomegranates with all choices fruits. (Song 4:13)
On that day there shall be a fountain opened for ... inhabitants of Jerusalem.... On that day living waters shall flow out from Jerusalem. (Zech 13:1, 14:8)	A garden locked is my sister, my bride,... a garden fountain, a well of living water. (Song 4:12, 15)

Along similar lines, when we compare the strange things said about the bridegroom in the Song with descriptions of YHWH, the God of Israel, elsewhere in Jewish Scripture, we discover something equally remarkable: the bridegroom looks very much like God!

YHWH, the God of Israel	The Bridegroom in the Song
You shall love the LORD your God with all your heart, with all your soul. (Deut 6:4–5)	[Him] whom my soul loves. (Song 1:7, 3:1, 2, 3, 4)
This is the day which the LORD has made; let us rejoice and be glad in it. (Ps 118:24)	The king has brought me into his chambers. We will exult and rejoice in you. (Song 1:4)
The LORD is my shepherd, I shall not want; he makes me lie down in green pastures. (Ps 23:1–2)	Tell me ... where you pasture your flock, where you make it lie down. (Song 1:7)
More to be desired are they [the ordinances of the LORD] than gold;... sweeter also than honey. (Ps 19:9–10)	His speech is most sweet, and he is altogether desirable. (Song 5:16)

In light of such linguistic parallels, Old Testament scholar Ellen Davis has made a very strong case that the Hebrew author of the Song intends for the reader to see in the figure of the bride the Temple in Jerusalem and in the figure of the bridegroom an image of YHWH, the Maker and Husband of the people of Israel (cf. Is 54). In support of this, it is critical to note that such a nuptial view of the covenant between God and Israel is abundantly attested in Jewish Scripture, especially the prophetic corpus (see Is 1:21; 3:16—4:6; 5:1–7; 54:4–8; 62:1–5; 66:7–13; Jer 2–3; Ezek 16, 20; Hos 1–3).

From this point of view, the Song of Solomon would function as a poetic contribution to the biblical portrait of YHWH as Bridegroom and Israel as the bride. Indeed, given the dream character of the book and the fact that it ends with the marriage not yet consummated, the Song would also take on a potentially "eschatological" outlook, insofar as it ends with Jerusalem still awaiting the coming of and union with the Divine Bridegroom.

The Song of Solomon in the Living Tradition

If the Song of Songs had been understood in antiquity only to affirm the goodness of marital love, it would never have been canonized. Instead, the most ancient Jewish and Christian interpretations of the Song we possess, beginning already in other Old and New Testament books (for example, the Wisdom of Solomon and the Gospel of John), viewed the book in a symbolic or spiritual sense. When various individuals did rise up and insist that the Song should be understood according to its literal-physical sense alone, their views were largely rejected.

For example, in the fourth century A.D., Theodore of Mopsuestia, bishop and member of the Antioch school of exegesis that emphasized the literal sense, insisted that that the Song of Solomon was simply a hymn written by King Solomon to appease the daughter of the pharaoh, whom he had taken to wife but who was rejected by his other wives because of her dark skin.[26] For this and other literalistic interpretations of biblical texts, Theodore's exegesis was roundly condemned in A.D. 553 by the Council of Constantinople II: "If anyone defends the impious Theodore of Mopsuestia ... and if he does not condemn him and his impious writings and those as well who ... [say] that his positions are orthodox ... let him be anathema."[27] In this case, Theodore's exegesis is the exception that proves the rule: the Song was interpreted virtually universally as an allegory of divine love and mystical contemplation.

The Books of Solomon and the Three Stages of the Spiritual Life

One of the most ancient and enduring views of the Song that we possess was the view that it represented the mystical climax of the three books of Solomon dealing with the spiritual life. From this point of view—which was above all popularized by Origen's famous and influential *Commentary on the Song of Songs*—the books of (1) Proverbs, (2) Ecclesiastes, and (3) the Song of Solomon correspond to the first, second, and third stages of the spiritual life, usually described as the (1) purgative, (2) illuminative, and (3) unitive ways (as in the writings of Dionysius the Areopagite).

For example, in his preface to his commentary, Origen provides an explanation for why the Song comes last in the three books of "philosophy" given by

---

[26] See J. Robert Wright, *Proverbs, Ecclesiastes, and the Song of Solomon*, Old Testament 9, Ancient Christian Commentary on Scripture, ed. Thomas C. Oden (Downers Grove, Ill.: InterVarsity Press, 2005), 299–300.

[27] Second Council of Constantinople, canon 12, in Henrich Denzinger, *Compendium of Creeds, Definitions, and Declarations on Matters of Faith and Morals*, ed. Peter Hünermann, Robert Fastiggi, and Anne Englund Nash, 43rd ed. (San Francisco: Ignatius Press, 2012), nos. 434–35, p. 151.

Solomon. Although the quote is lengthy, Origen's view is so influential, it is worth quoting in full:

> This, then, was the reason why the master [Solomon], who was the first to teach men divine philosophy, put at the beginning of his work *the Book of Proverbs*, in which, as we said, the moral science is propounded—so *that when a person has progressed in discernment and behaviour he may pass on thence* to train his natural intelligence and, by distinguishing the causes and natures of things, may recognize the vanity of vanities that he must forsake, and the lasting and eternal things he ought to pursue. And so from Proverbs he goes on to *Ecclesiastes*, who teaches, as we said, that all visible and corporeal things are fleeting and brittle ... and he is bound to spurn and despise them, renouncing the world bag and baggage....
>
> *This book [the Song of Solomon] comes last* that a man may come to it when his manner of life has been purified, and he has learnt to know the difference between things corruptible and things incorruptible; so that nothing in the metaphors used to describe and represent the love of the Bride for her celestial Bridegroom—that is, of the perfect soul for the Word of God—may cause him to stumble. For when the soul has completed these studies, ... it is competent to proceed to *dogmatic and mystical matters*, and in this way advances to *the contemplation of the Godhead with pure and spiritual love.*[28]

Notice here that Origen does not think that the Song is for just anyone to pick up and read. Instead, in order to interpret it correctly and not in a strictly literalistic sense (which may cause the reader to "stumble" with lustful thoughts), the reader must first have both studied and passed through the stages of spiritual growth embodied in the Solomonic books of Proverbs and Ecclesiastes. In the living tradition of the Church, this will become a standard view, with other Church Fathers likewise asserting that the three books of Solomon constitute "a kind of ladder with three steps—moral, physical, and mystical."[29]

The Disrobing of the Bride and the Disrobing of the Baptized

Although many readers are familiar with the fact that the Song was interpreted as an allegory of the mystical life of the soul, far fewer are aware that the Song also played a key role in the ancient Christian teaching on the mysteries of the sacraments. Indeed, if one peruses the mystagogical homilies for catechumens and converts to Christianity written by figures such as Saint Cyril of Jerusalem and Saint Ambrose of Milan, one finds that the nuptial imagery utilized in the Song was interpreted as being fulfilled in the celebration of the sacraments of initiation—especially baptism and the Eucharist.

For example, in his catechesis, the fourth-century bishop Cyril of Jerusalem interprets the disrobing of the bride (Song 5:3) as being fulfilled in the early Christian practice of disrobing for baptism:

> Immediately, then, upon entering [the waters of baptism], you removed your tunics. This was a figure of the "stripping off of the old man with his deeds" [Col

---

[28] Origen, *Song of Songs*, prologue, 3, pp. 43–44.
[29] Theodoret of Cyrus, *Commentary on the Song of Songs*, preface, in Wright, *Proverbs*, 288.

3:9]. Having stripped, you were naked, in this also imitating Christ, who as naked on the cross.... May the soul that has once put off that old self never again put it on, but say with the Bride of Christ in the Canticle of Canticles: "I have put off my garment: how shall I put it on?" [Song 5:3].[30]

Notice here that for the Fathers, baptism is much more than just the forgiveness of original sin or the incorporation of the baptized into the Christian community. For Cyril, baptism is both a mystical participation in the Cross of Christ, who was stripped of his garments before being crucified, and a mystical marriage, in which the disrobing of the baptized signifies both the "putting off" of the old and nuptial union with Christ the Bridegroom as members of the Church, his Bride.

The Kiss of the Bridegroom and the Eucharist of Christ

Along similar lines, the celebration of the Eucharist was also described to catechumens in nuptial terms. For example, in his lectures on the sacraments to catechumens in the fourth century A.D., Saint Ambrose of Milan interprets the very first line of the Song—"O that you would kiss me with the kisses of your mouth!" (Song 1:2)—as being fulfilled in their first Holy Communion:

> You have come to the altar, the Lord Jesus calls you, for the text speaks of you or of the Church, and he says to you: "Let him kiss me with kiss of his mouth" [Song 1:2].... You see that you are pure from all sin, since your faults have been blotted out [in baptism]. This is why He judges you to be worthy of heavenly sacraments and invites you to the heavenly banquet: "May He kiss me with the kiss of His mouth" [Song 1:2].... Seeing yourself pure from all sins and worthy to come to the altar of Christ, ... *you see the wonderful sacraments, and you say: "May He kiss me with the kiss of His mouth", that is, may Christ give me a kiss.*[31]

It should go without saying that this is not the way the Eucharist is explained to most Christians, not to mention new converts! And yet, we find that in many of the Church Fathers, the Song of Solomon played an essential role in what we might call "nuptial catechesis"—that is, a mystagogical approach to the sacraments that was focused on the invisible reality of Christ's love being poured out on Christians through these nuptial mysteries.[32]

The Bride in the Song and Jesus' Appearance to Mary Magdalene

Before bringing this section to a close, it is worth noting that the identification of the Bridegroom of the Song with Christ was seen by the Church Fathers as beginning in the New Testament itself, with the account of Jesus' appearance

---

[30] Cyril of Jerusalem, *Mystagogical Catechesis* 2.2, in *The Works of Saint Cyril of Jerusalem*, trans. Leo P. McCauley, S.J., and Anthony A. Stephenson, vol. 2, The Fathers of the Church 64 (Washington, D.C.: Catholic University of America Press, 1970), 161–62.

[31] Ambrose, *On the Sacraments* 5.5–7, in Jean Daniélou, S.J., *The Bible and the Liturgy* (Notre Dame, Ind.: University of Notre Dame, 1956), 204–5.

[32] See Daniélou, *Bible and the Liturgy*, 191–207.

to Mary Magdalene immediately after the Resurrection (Jn 20:1–18). At least since the fourth century A.D., Fathers such as Saint Cyril of Jerusalem recognized these striking parallels between the account of Mary's encounter with Christ and the sequence of events in the bride's first dream (Song 3:1–5). In his teaching on the mystery of Easter Sunday, Cyril writes:

> But before He entered through the closed doors, the Bridegroom and Suitor of souls was sought by those noble and brave women. They came, those blessed ones, to the sepulchre, and sought Him Who had been raised.... Mary came seeking Him, according to the Gospel, and found Him not: and presently she heard from the Angels, and afterwards saw the Christ. Are then these things also written? He says in the Song of Songs, *On my bed I sought Him whom my soul loved* [Song 3:1]. At what season? *By night on my bed I sought Him Whom my soul loved* [Song 3:1]: *Mary, it says, came while it was yet dark. On my bed I sought Him by night, I sought Him, and I found Him not* [Song 3:1]. And in the Gospels Mary says, *"They have taken away my Lord, and I know not where they have laid Him"* [Jn 20:13]. But the Angels being then present cure their want of knowledge; for they said, *Why seek ye the living among the dead* [Lk 24:5]?... But she knew not, and in her person the Song of Songs said to the Angels, *"Saw ye him whom my soul loved? It was but a little that I passed from them* (that is, from the two Angels), *until I found Him Whom my soul loved. I held Him, and would not let Him go"* (Song 3:3–4).[33]

With these words, Cyril provides us with a remarkable background to the mysterious scene in which the risen Christ commands Mary: "Do not hold me" (Jn 20:17). Although Mary is of course not his ordinary bride—after all, she calls him Teacher! (Jn 20:16)—she does in some way represent the Church, the Bride of Christ, who seeks him and awaits his return from his Father's house (Jn 14:3).

We should note that recent scholarship on the Gospel of John has confirmed the insight of Cyril and other Fathers that this Gospel intentionally uses imagery from the Song of Solomon applied to Jesus.[34] So, for example, in addition to the allusions to Song 3:1–5 in John 20:1, 11–17, the account of the anointing of Jesus at Bethany with "pure nard" intentionally alludes to Song 1:12 (nard, after all, in the whole Old Testament, is mentioned only in the Song of Solomon). Thus, the Gospel of John demonstrates that from the very beginning of Christian history, the Song of Solomon was already interpreted messianically in light of Jesus of Nazareth.

The Song of Solomon and the Assumption of Mary

No overview of the role of the Song in the living tradition of the Church would be complete without mentioning the Mariological interpretation of the bride that eventually arose in the history of the Church. Indeed, in 1950, when Pope

---

[33] Cyril of Jerusalem, *Catechetical Lectures* 14.12–13, in NPNF2 7:97.

[34] Ann Roberts Winsor, *A King Is Bound in the Tresses: Allusions to the Song of Songs in the Fourth Gospel*, Studies in Biblical Literature 6 (New York: Peter Lang, 1999).

Pius XII defined the dogma of the bodily Assumption of Mary into heaven, he referenced the fact that many Catholic writers had applied the "coming up" of the bride from the desert (Song 3:6), along with other biblical texts, to Mary's Assumption into heaven:

> Often there are theologians and preachers who, following in the footsteps of the holy Fathers, have been rather free in their use of events and expressions taken from Sacred Scripture to explain their belief in the Assumption.... Likewise they mention the Spouse of the Canticles "that goes up by the desert, as a pillar of smoke of aromatical spices, of myrrh and frankincense" to be crowned (Song 3:6; cf. 4:8; 6:9). *These are proposed as depicting that heavenly Queen and heavenly Spouse who has been lifted up to the courts of heaven with the divine Bridegroom.*[35]

Notice here that Pius XII recognizes that the Mariological interpretation is according to what we would call the "spiritual sense" of the text, and nevertheless he draws upon this mystical interpretation as one of the factors involved in defining the dogma of the bodily Assumption of Mary as belonging to the Catholic faith.

The Song of Solomon in Church History and the Catechism

Although much much more could be said about the role of the Song of Solomon in the living tradition of the Church, these examples should suffice to give the reader a sense of how rich and widespread was its interpretation in the early centuries of Christianity. In the Middle Ages, the Song continued to be read as an allegory of the relationship of Christ and the Church, especially as this general relationship was expressed in the specific relationship of each believer with Christ. Most famous of all such readings is Bernard of Clairvaux's collection of sermons on the Song, which extends to four volumes. Marian readings of the Song of Solomon have also developed, especially in the modern period, based on the fact that Mary is the model for all believers as well as the archetype of the Church: virgin bride and fruitful mother.[36] Most recently, it played an important role in the development of Saint John Paul II's series of general audiences that have come to be known as the *Theology of the Body*, although, intriguingly, the sections written on the Song of Solomon were never publicly delivered and were only later published posthumously, in which the pope explores the vision of human love depicted in the Song.[37]

Indeed, it is significant to note that when one comes to the most recent expression of the Church's teaching Magisterium—the 1992 *Catechism of the Catholic Church*—the Song of Solomon is cited *both* for its vision of the goodness of "human love" as a reflection of God's love (*CCC* 1611) *and* for the image of "contemplative prayer", the mystical union of Christ and believer:

---

[35] Pope Pius XII, Apostolic Constitution *Munificentissimus Deus*, Defining the Dogma of the Assumption, 26 (emphasis added).

[36] For example, Pope, *Song of Songs*, 188–91.

[37] See John Paul II, *Man and Woman He Created Them: A Theology of the Body*, trans. Michael Waldstein (Boston: Pauline Books and Media, 2006).

What is contemplative prayer?... *Contemplative prayer seeks him "whom my soul loves"* [Song 1:7; cf. 3:1–4]. (*CCC* 2709 [emphasis added])

The Song of Solomon in the Lectionary

Along with Exodus 12 and Psalm 23, the Song of Solomon was the most heavily used text of the Old Testament for sacramental instruction in the early Church.[38] Sadly, however, the book is neglected in the contemporary Lectionary. It is never read on a Sunday or major feast day and is omitted even from the cycle of weekly readings during Ordinary Time. The only significant readings of the Song in Mass are on December 21, on which the springtime invitation to elope with the Bridegroom (Song 2:8–17) is read as an anticipation of the liturgical "arrival" of Christ on Christmas, understood as the coming of the Bridegroom. Significantly, the first account of the bride's dream (Song 3:1–5) is an optional first reading on the Feast of Saint Mary Magdalene, on which it is paired with John 20:1–18, the Gospel text that draws so heavily from its imagery. Finally, selections from the description of love strong as death (Song 2, 8) are also options for wedding Masses and the consecration of women religious, since both these liturgical occasions have strong nuptial themes.

Readings from the Song of Solomon for Sundays, Feast Days, Liturgical Seasons, and Other Occasions *MSO* = Masses for Special Occasions; *OM* = Optional Memorial; *VM* = Votive Mass; *Rit* = Ritual			
Passage	Description	Occasion	Explanation
2:8–14	The invitation of the groom to the bride to "come away" with him into the spring countryside	Dec. 21; *Rit*: For the Consecration of Virgins or Religious Profession, opt. 5	On Dec. 21, the Church perceives the birth of Christ as the arrival of her Bridegroom and the end of the winter of her exile in sin. Virgins and Religious are the model "bride" who hears the voice of the Groom calling one away to a life devoted to him.
2:8–10, 14, 16a; 8:6–7a	Selections from the groom's invitation to elope (2:8–16) are combined with the poetic meditation on "love as strong as death" in 8:6–7.	*Rit*: Conferral of Matrimony, opt. 7	In the liturgical celebration of matrimony, the intense love of the groom and bride of the Song is taken as a model for the mutual affection of the Christian spouses.
3:1–4b	The bride's first dream sequence (3:1–5)	Feast of St. Mary Magdalene	On this feast, Song 3:1–5 is paired with John 20:1–2, 11–18, in order to highlight the similarities of the passage, which shows Mary Magdalene at the Resurrection to be a model of the believer who has become "bride" to Jesus the "Bridegroom".

(*continued*)

---

[38] See Daniélou, *Bible and the Liturgy*, 162.

Readings from the Song of Solomon for Sundays, Feast Days, Liturgical Seasons, and Other Occasions (*continued*)			
MSO = Masses for Special Occasions; *OM* = Optional Memorial; *VM* = Votive Mass; *Rit* = Ritual			
Passage	Description	Occasion	Explanation
8:6–7	The poem on love noted for its line "Love is as strong as death."	Common of Virgins; *Rit*: For Consecration of Virgins or Religious Profession, opt. 6; *MSO*: For Religious, opt. 2	This text reflects the powerful and personal bond between Christ and the believer who enters consecrated or religious life.

Conclusion

The Song of Solomon is a collection of poems that have been carefully edited into one long composition with a loose but real unity. In its canonical form, the Song constitutes a series of dreams and anticipatory visions of the upcoming wedding of a young woman to her beloved, Solomon himself. While the Song uses images of the created goodness of physical beauty and the marital embrace, it has been preserved and treasured by Jews and Christians primarily for its spiritual meaning, which describes the nuptial relationship between YHWH and Israel, between Christ and the Church, or between God and the individual soul. Within the Church, the Song was widely used by the Fathers for sacramental catechesis and was a favorite text for *lectio divina* and spiritual commentary in the medieval period. Somewhat neglected in the modern Lectionary, the Song nonetheless remains an excellent sacred text for private devotion and meditation.

For Further Reading

Commentaries and Studies on the Song of Solomon

Alexander, Philip S. *The Targum of Canticles.* Collegeville, Minn.: Liturgical Press, 2003.

Collins, John J. *Introduction to the Hebrew Bible.* Minneapolis: Fortress Press, 1998. (See pp. 480–84.)

Davis, Ellen F. *Proverbs, Ecclesiastes, and the Song of Songs.* Westminster Bible Companion. Louisville, Ky.: Westminster John Knox Press, 2000. (See pp. 231–302.)

Estes, Daniel J. *Handbook on the Wisdom Books and Psalms.* Grand Rapids, Mich.: Baker Academic, 2005. (See pp. 393–444.)

Longman, Tremper, III. *Song of Songs.* New International Commentary on the Old Testament 16. Grand Rapids, Mich.: Eerdmans, 2001.

Murphy, Roland E., O. Carm. *The Song of Songs.* Hermeneia. Minneapolis: Fortress Press, 1990.

Pope, Marvin. *Song of Songs.* Anchor Bible 7C. New York: Doubleday, 1977.

Historical Questions and the Song of Solomon

Abegg, Martin, Jr., Peter Flint, and Eugene Ulrich. *The Dead Sea Scrolls Bible: The Oldest Known Bible Translated for the First Time into English*. San Francisco: HarperOne, 1999. (See pp. 611–18.)

Garrett, Duane. "Song of Songs". Pages 519–31 in *The Minor Prophets, Job, Psalms, Proverbs, Ecclesiastes, Song of Songs*. Vol. 5 of *Zondervan Illustrated Bible Backgrounds Commentary*. Edited by John H. Walton. Grand Rapids, Mich.: Zondervan, 2009.

Keel, Othmar. *Song of Songs: A Continental Commentary*. Translated by Frederick J. Gaiser. Continental Commentary 22. Minneapolis: Fortress Press, 1994.

Noegel, Scott B., and Gary A. Rendsburg. *Solomon's Vineyard: Literary and Linguistic Studies in the Song of Songs*. Atlanta: Society of Biblical Literature, 2009.

Segal, M. H. "The Song of Songs". *Vetus Testamentum* 12 (1962): 470–90.

Songs of Solomon in the Living Tradition

Arminjon, Blaise. *The Cantata of Love: A Verse by Verse Reading of the Song of Songs*. Translated by Nelly Marans. San Francisco: Ignatius Press, 1988.

Cyril of Jerusalem, Saint. *The Works of Saint Cyril of Jerusalem*. Translated by Leo P. McCauley, S.J., and Anthony A. Stephenson. 2 vols. The Fathers of the Church 61, 64. Washington, D.C.: Catholic University of America Press, 1969–1970.

Daniélou, Jean, S.J. "The Canticle of Canticles". Pages 191–207 in *The Bible and the Liturgy*. Notre Dame, Ind.: University of Notre Dame, 1956.

Gregory of Nyssa, Saint. *Commentary on the Song of Songs*. Translated by Casimir McCambley. Brookline, Mass.: Hellenic College Press, 1987.

Gregory the Great, Saint. *On the Song of Songs*. Translated by Mark DelCogliano. Collegeville, Minn.: Liturgical Press, 2012.

John Paul II, Pope. *Man and Woman He Created Them: A Theology of the Body*. Translated by Michael Waldstein. Boston: Pauline Books and Media, 2006.

Norris, Richard A., Jr. *The Song of Songs: Interpreted by Early Christian and Medieval Commentators*. The Church's Bible 1. Grand Rapids, Mich.: Eerdmans, 2003.

Origen. *The Song of Songs, Commentary and Homilies*. Translated by R. P. Lawson. Ancient Christian Writers 26. Westminster, Md.: Newman Press, 1957.

Pitre, Brant. *Jesus the Bridegroom: The Greatest Love Story Ever Told*. New York: Image, 2014. (See pp. 20–27.)

Theodoret of Cyrus. *Commentary on the Song of Songs*. Translated by Robert C. Hill. Early Christian Studies 2. Brisbane: Australian Catholic University, 2001.

Winsor, Ann Roberts. *A King Is Bound in the Tresses: Allusions to the Song of Songs in the Fourth Gospel*. Studies in Biblical Literature 6. New York: Peter Lang, 1999.

Wright, J. Robert. "Song of Solomon". Pages 286–368 in *Proverbs, Ecclesiastes, Song of Solomon*. Edited by J. Robert Wright. Old Testament 9 of Ancient Christian Commentary on Scripture. Edited by Thomas C. Oden. Downers Grove, Ill.: InterVarsity Press, 2005.

Zaharopoulos, Dimitri Z. *Theodore of Mopsuestia on the Bible: A Study of His Old Testament Exegesis*. New York: Paulist Press, 1989.

28. THE WISDOM OF SOLOMON

Introduction

The next book in the corpus of Old Testament wisdom literature goes by various names: either "the Wisdom of Solomon" (Greek *Sophia Salōmōnos*), as in the tradition of the Greek Septuagint, or "the Book of Wisdom" (Latin *Liber Sapientiae*), as in the Latin Vulgate tradition. As far as the poetic books of the Old Testament go, the Wisdom of Solomon is theologically quite significant, since it provides perhaps the most thorough treatment of such matters as the origins of sin and death, the immortality of the soul, the final judgment, and the resurrection of the dead of any book prior to the New Testament writings. For this reason, some see Wisdom as a kind of canonical "answer" to the questions raised by Ecclesiastes: if in Ecclesiastes the canonical Solomon expressed skepticism about the life to come and despondency over the prospect of death, in Wisdom he has found that death is not the final answer and that righteousness finds its reward in the life to come.

In contrast to the other poetic books examined so far, the Wisdom of Solomon was not accepted as inspired by rabbinic Judaism, which canonized only Proverbs, Ecclesiastes, and the Song of Solomon. Indeed, perhaps under the influence of his Jewish contemporaries, Saint Jerome himself expressed doubts about its status as canonical Scripture, viewing it as a "false writing" (Greek *pseudepigraphon*; Jerome, Preface to the Solomonic Writings). On the other hand, the book of Wisdom appears to have been accepted by at least some ancient Greek-speaking Jews, as it is extant in every copy of the Greek Septuagint that we possess. More importantly, it was extremely popular among the majority of early Church Fathers, being treated as Scripture from the time of the apostolic Fathers onward[1] and quoted by Saint Augustine of Hippo some eight hundred times![2]

Perhaps most significant of all, the Wisdom of Solomon was declared to be inspired Scripture by the Councils of Hippo and Carthage (A.D. 393 and 397), which spoke of it as one of the "five books of Solomon", thus grouping it together with Proverbs, Ecclesiastes, Song of Solomon, and Sirach (see below, "Historical Issues in the Wisdom of Solomon"). From this point of view, the books of Proverbs through Wisdom can be viewed as a kind of theological odyssey of the "canonical Solomon": (1) in Proverbs, he attains the wisdom that leads to temporal success; (2) in Ecclesiastes, he despairs of temporal success

---

[1] See, for example, *1 Clement* 27, citing Wisdom 11:21; 12:12; Irenaeus, *Against Heresies* 4.38.3, alluding to Wisdom 6:18; Clement of Alexandria, *Stromateis* 5.108.2.

[2] David Winston, *The Wisdom of Solomon*, Anchor Bible 43 (New York: Doubleday, 1979), 67.

because death renders it vain; (3) in the Song, he discovers that love is stronger than death (Song 8:6); (4) in Wisdom, he falls in love with Lady Wisdom and so attains immortality.

Literary Structure of the Wisdom of Solomon

The Wisdom of Solomon falls naturally into two main parts. In the first part, Solomon exhorts the "rulers of the earth" to love righteousness (Wis 1:1), which will enable them to become wise and reign forever, following Solomon's own example (Wis 1–9). In the second part, the sacred author seeks to demonstrate his thesis about the connection of righteousness, wisdom, and immortal reign by tracing and justifying wisdom's actions through the sacred history of Israel, from creation to the exodus (Wis 10–18).

The first part can also be broken down into two main sections: First, Solomon focuses on the relationship between righteousness, wisdom, and immortality, especially highlighting the eternal life of the righteous with God and the judgment that will face the unrighteous after death (Wis 1–6). Second, Solomon teaches the "rulers of the earth" how he himself attained wisdom—namely, by seeking her in humble prayer from God and then living in spousal communion with her thereafter (Wis 7–9).

Outline of the Book of Wisdom

I. Wisdom Leads to Eternal Kingship (Wis 1–9)
  A. The Love of Righteousness and the Gift of Immortality (1—6:20)
    1. Exhortation to Righteousness, the Key to Life (1:1–15)
    2. The World View of the Unrighteous (1:16—2:24)
    3. The Fate of the Righteous vs. the Unrighteous (3:1—5:23)
    4. Exhortation to Rulers to Seek Wisdom (6:1–20)
  B. King Solomon's Love for Lady Wisdom (6:21—9:18)
    1. The Lord Gave Solomon Wisdom in Answer to Prayer (6:21—7:22)
    2. Solomon Describes Wisdom as a Beautiful Bride (7:22—8:1)
    3. Solomon's Romance with Wisdom (8:2–21)
    4. Solomon's Prayer for Wisdom (9:1–18)

II. Wisdom in Salvation History (Wis 10–19)
  A. Wisdom's Actions from Creation to the Exodus (10:1–21)
  B. Wisdom's Actions in the Exodus (11–19)
    1. First Example: Water Punishes Egyptians and Benefits Israelites (11:6–14)
    2. Second Example: Animals Punish the Egyptians and Benefit the Israelites (11:15–26)
    3. Third Example: Punishment of the Canaanites by *Herem* (12:1–27)
      a. Excursus on Idolatrous Worship (13:1—15:17)
    4. Fourth Example: Rain of Hail vs. Rain of Manna (15:18—16:15)
    5. Fifth Example: Darkness for Egyptians vs. Light for Israel (17:1—18:4)

6. Sixth Example: Death of Firstborn vs. Deliverance of Israel (18:5–19)
7. Seventh Example: Crossing of the Red Sea and Providence (18:20—19:22)

As this outline makes clear, the second part of the book has a much different feel from the first, as Solomon traces the activities of wisdom through salvation history. One chapter covers wisdom's work from creation up to the exodus (Wis 10), whereas eight chapters are devoted to wisdom in the exodus itself (Wis 11–19).

Overview of the Wisdom of Solomon

Righteousness, Wickedness, and the Suffering Son of God (Wisdom 1–6)

This first section of the Wisdom of Solomon begins and ends with exhortations to the rulers of the earth, emphasizing that "wisdom" (Greek *Sophia*) is only obtained through "righteousness" or "justice" (Greek *dikaiosynē*) (Wis 1:1–15 and 6:1–20). The thrust of these opening sections is that God calls all men—but especially kings and all leaders in authority—to account for their righteousness or face the consequences for unrighteousness. It is in the context of such exhortations that the Wisdom of Solomon provides us with what is easily the most detailed discussion of *life after death* in the Old Testament and the contrasting eternal fates of the righteous and the wicked. Within this section, the author makes several key points about the question of immortality:

First, after the opening exhortation for rulers to love righteousness and declaring that "righteousness is immortal" or "deathless" (Greek *athanatos*) (Wis 1:1–15), the sacred author goes on to give a remarkable description of how the unrighteous—the "ungodly" or "impious"—see the world (Wis 1:16—2:24). According to the Wisdom of Solomon, the wicked of this world are what we would call today atheists and materialists, whose only goal in life is to maximize their temporal pleasure at the expense of others and to persecute the righteous who dare to rebuke them by word or example. Indeed, notice the strikingly "modern"-sounding perspective of the unrighteous, whose world view anticipates a number of developments and movements in modern philosophy and culture, including the following:

The World View of the Wicked in the Wisdom of Solomon

1. *Atheistic Evolutionism*: The view that chance and necessity alone, without the guidance of any agent (such as God), have led to human life. The impious say: "We were born by mere chance" (Wis 2:2).

2. *Epiphenomenalism*: The belief that the mind is an illusion arising as a by-product of biological, material processes. The impious say: "Reason is a spark kindled by the beating of our hearts" (Wis 2:2).

3. *Materialism*: The belief that matter is all that exists and the denial of any meaningful spiritual reality, including the human soul. The impious say: "When it [reason] is extinguished, the body will turn to ashes, and the spirit will dissolve like empty air" (Wis 2:3).

4. *Hedonism*: The belief that physical and temporal pleasure is the goal of life. The impious say: "Let us take our fill of costly wine and perfumes, and let no flower of spring pass by us" (Wis 2:7).

5. *Relativism*: The belief that there is no objective moral order and that power alone establishes right and wrong (thus Nietzsche). The impious say: "Let our might be our law of right, for what is weak proves itself to be useless" (Wis 2:11).

Of course, all of these "-isms" are mutually interrelated. They lead one to another and inform one another.

Second, and even more intriguing, in the Wisdom of Solomon, the impious are not simply content to revel in their wickedness; they are also driven to persecute those who do seek righteousness and who stand as a sign of contradiction against their impious world view (Wis 2:10–11). Indeed, at this point the Wisdom of Solomon provides us with a mysterious description of the persecution and death of the righteous man:

> Let us lie in wait for the righteous man,
> because he is inconvenient to us and opposes our actions;
> he reproaches us for sins against the law,
> and accuses us of sins against our training.
> He professes to have knowledge of God,
> and calls himself a child of the Lord.
> He became to us a reproof of our thoughts;
> the very sight of him is a burden to us,
> because his manner of life is unlike that of others,
> and his ways are strange.
> We are considered by him as something base,
> and he avoids our ways as unclean;
> he calls the last end of the righteous happy,

The Wisdom of Solomon and "Purgatory"

It is sometimes charged that certain passages of Wisdom directly contradict other key passages in Scripture or Catholic teachings. For example, some readers contend that Wisdom contradicts the existence of purgatory when it states: "But the souls of the righteous are in the hand of God, and no torment will ever touch them" (Wis 3:1). However, a close reading of this passage shows that "the righteous" who are with God are precisely those who have *already suffered on earth* before their deaths, as in the persecutions described earlier (cf. Wis 2:12–24). Although they looked like they were being "punished", they were in fact being "tested" and "tried" and "disciplined" like "gold in the furnace" (Wis 3:4–6). In other words, "the righteous" under discussion are clearly those persecuted and martyred for their holiness, so that there is no longer any need for further purification. The book of Wisdom does not directly address the fate of those who die in God's friendship *without* undergoing such purification or without attaining holiness or detachment from all sin. Indeed, the book elsewhere suggests that such purification is necessary, since, with reference to living with wisdom, "nothing defiled gains entrance into her" (Wis 7:25).

and boasts that God is his father.
Let us see if his words are true,
and let us test what will happen at the end of his life;
for if the righteous man is God's son, he will help him,
and will deliver him from the hand of his adversaries.
Let us test him with insult and torture,
that we may find out how gentle he is,
and make trial of his forbearance.
Let us condemn him to a shameful death,
for, according to what he says, he will be protected.

(Wis 2:12–20)

As any reader familiar with the New Testament will recognize, after the descriptions of the Suffering Servant in Isaiah 52–53 and Psalm 22, this passage is perhaps the most striking parallel with the Gospel accounts of Jesus' Passion in all of the Old Testament. In it, we see the rejection, persecution, and execution of a righteous man who calls God his "father" (Greek *pater*) and refers to himself as the "son of God" (Greek *huios theou*) (Wis 2:16–17).

As we will see below, the parallels were not lost on the living tradition of the Church. For now, however, we need only note that the Wisdom of Solomon is highlighting that the rejection of righteousness by the wicked of this world is not simply a "private" misfortune for the individuals who choose to walk the path of impiety. Rather, it inevitably leads to persecution, suffering, and death for those who insist on living lives according to righteousness: above all, for the mysterious righteous man who is also the "son of God".

Third and finally, after the implicit persecution and execution of the righteous man, the Wisdom of Solomon launches into an extended discourse on the fact that the lives of the righteous end, not with their death, but with "immortality" (Greek *athanasia*; cf. Wis 3:1–9). Here we find the answer to the question of life after death that was raised in the book of Ecclesiastes: in truth, the righteous only *appear* to have died; in reality, they are alive with God, who has accepted them as a kind of sacrificial offering after the purifications of their suffering (Wis 3:5–6; 5:15–20). They will reign with God in the life to come. In this way, the reality of eternal life with God turns all the usual measures of success in life— wealth, old age, numerous children, even persecution and execution by the wicked!—upside down. It is better to be righteous and barren, a eunuch, or die in youth than a wicked person who begets many children and lives to long old age, because the reward of righteousness is eternal life (Wis 4:1–9). Indeed, as the sacred author goes on to insist—in a clearer and more direct way than anywhere else in the Old Testament—a day of judgment will come when the righteous will be vindicated in the presence of God and the wicked who taunted and persecuted the righteous man will realize and acknowledge their error (Wis 5:1–14). In this day of judgment, the creation itself will join God in fighting against the wicked, and justice will be done on behalf of those who chose righteousness rather than wickedness in this life (Wis 5:15–23).

Fourth and finally, this grand opening section concludes with another exhortation to the rulers of the earth to take to heart what he has said so that they may learn to rule wisely and avoid the judgment of God (Wis 6:1–21). The close relationship between righteousness, wisdom, immortality, and rulership is nicely summarized in the *sorites*—a poem in the form "if A, then B; if B, then C; and so on"—that ties together all the themes of the first section of the book:

> The beginning of wisdom is the most sincere desire for instruction,
> and concern for instruction is love of her,
> and love of her is the keeping of her laws,
> and giving heed to her laws is assurance of immortality,
> and immortality brings one near to God;
> *so the desire for wisdom leads to a kingdom.*
> Therefore, if you delight in thrones and scepters, O monarchs over
>   the peoples, honor wisdom, that you may reign for ever.
>
> (Wis 6:17–21)

Thus, wisdom, righteousness, immortality, and kingly rule are all related in such a way that the acquisition of wisdom results in an eternal reign: "[W]isdom leads to a kingdom" (Wis 6:20). Significantly, the kingdom mentioned here by the Wisdom of Solomon—as the book will make clear a few chapters later—is none other than "the kingdom of God" (Greek *basileia theou*) (Wis 10:10)—the first extant reference in the Old Testament to the expression that will stand at the very center of the teaching of Jesus of Nazareth (Mk 1:14).

King Solomon and Lady Wisdom as Spouses (Wisdom 6:21—9:18)

Having made his case that wisdom is a necessary prerequisite for the just governing of human affairs, Solomon now begins a discourse to the "rulers of the earth" on the nature and acquisition of wisdom itself:

> I will tell you what wisdom is and how she came to be....
> Therefore be instructed by my words,
> and you will profit.
>
> (Wis 6:22, 25)

Solomon was born in ordinary fashion with no supernatural origin, but he achieves supernatural wisdom by praying to God for it (Wis 7:1–22). God bestowed the "spirit of wisdom" (Greek *pneuma sophias*) upon him (Wis 7:7), a spirit that Solomon describes in stunning words:

> [W]*isdom, the fashioner of all things*, taught me.
> For in her there is a spirit that is intelligent, holy,
> unique, manifold, subtle,
> mobile, clear, unpolluted,
> distinct, invulnerable, loving the good, keen,
> irresistible, beneficent, humane,
> steadfast, sure, free from anxiety,
> *all-powerful, overseeing all....*

For wisdom is more mobile than any motion;
because of her pureness *she pervades and penetrates all things.*
For she is *a breath of the power of God,*
and a pure emanation of the glory of the Almighty;
therefore nothing defiled gains entrance into her.
For she is *a reflection of eternal light,*
a spotless mirror of the working of God,
and an image of his goodness.
Though she is but one, she can do all things,
and while remaining in herself, she renews all things;
in every generation she passes into holy souls
and makes them friends of God, and prophets;
for God loves nothing so much as the man who lives with wisdom.
For she is more beautiful than the sun,
and excels every constellation of the stars.
Compared with the light she is found to be superior,
for it is succeeded by the night,
but against wisdom evil does not prevail.
She reaches mightily from one end of the earth to the other,
and *she orders all things well.*

(Wis 7:22—8:1)

Note in the italicized phrases that Lady Wisdom shares all the major divine attributes—omnipotence, omniscience, omnipresence, omnibenificence. She is in every sense divine. This makes even more striking the fact that Solomon—combining the nuptial imagery of Lady Wisdom in Proverbs and the bride of the Song of Solomon—then describes wisdom as *the ideal bride*, with whom he fell in love in his youth and whom he desires both to marry and to live with (Wis 8:2–21). Therefore he prays to God to give her to him as his spouse, a prayer that brings this section to its climax and conclusion (Wis 9:1–18).

Wisdom's Actions from Creation to the Exodus (Wisdom 10)

With the prayer of Solomon for Lady Wisdom concluded, the second part of the book of Wisdom shifts into a very different manner of exposition (Wis 10–19). In this part of the book, the sacred author recounts wisdom's activity throughout *all of salvation history*, from the creation of Adam to the conquest of the Promised Land under Joshua. However, this account itself can be divided up into two parts: one chapter covers wisdom's activities from Adam up to the exodus (Wis 10), and then *eight chapters* cover the events of the exodus, especially the plagues (Wis 11–18).

Three aspects of the initial section stand out as significant: First, in contrast to some contemporary renditions of salvation history, which speak of it as beginning with the call of Abraham, for the Wisdom of Solomon, "wisdom" (Greek *sophia*) is active in the world *from the very beginning* of human history, when she protects Adam, "the first-formed father of the world, when he alone had been created" (Wis 10:1), and then throughout the book of

Genesis, with the figures of Noah, Lot, Jacob, and Joseph (Wis 10:1–14). Second, in the course of this catalogue of holy ones, we find the first occurrence of the expression "kingdom of God", with Lady Wisdom being the one who "shows" the heavenly kingdom to Jacob with the mysterious vision of "Jacob's Ladder", the gate between heaven and earth (Wis 10:10). Third and finally, it is significant that the sacred author sees wisdom as the agent of the deliverance in the exodus from Egypt: it is she who both dwells in the soul of Moses and appears to them as the "starry flame through the night" in the form of the pillar of fire (cf. Wis 10:15–21). In short, the author sees wisdom, not as simply the personified object sought by the few who are wise, but as the primary divine agent of salvation present and acting in the history of God's people from creation through the exodus.

Wisdom's Actions in the Exodus from Egypt (Wisdom 11–19)

With that said, of all the saving events that stand out as significant for the author of Wisdom, the exodus from Egypt stands out as the example *par excellence*. Indeed, the entire rest of the book is devoted to the role of wisdom in the exodus (Wis 11–19), though these events are not always narrated in chronological order (for example, the conquest of the land is narrated in Wisdom 12 whereas the crossing of the Red Sea is in Wisdom 19).

Beginning with the call of Moses, "a holy prophet" (Wis 11:1), the sacred author ranges over the events from the plagues to the conquest of the land. He contrasts the slaking of the Israelites' thirst in the desert with the punishment

> **Idolatry as the Source of All Other Evils**
>
> In the midst of his study of wisdom's actions in the sacred history of Israel, the sacred author devotes two chapters to an analysis of the phenomenon of idolatry (Wis 11–12). Significantly, the author traces nearly all personal and societal evil to this fundamentally cultic error: "The worship of idols not to be named is *the beginning and cause and end of every evil*" (Wis 14:27). In this way, the book of Wisdom paints a picture of man as *homo religiosus* or *homo liturgicus*: human beings are by nature oriented to prayer and worship. Indeed, mankind *will* worship, all else notwithstanding. The only real difference in this regard between the people of God and their enemies is their object of worship: either the Creator or creatures.

of the Egyptians through thirst in the plague of the Nile-to-blood (Wis 11:1–14) and points out the poetic justice of punishing the Egyptians through the very swarms of irrational creatures that they worshipped, as in the plagues of frogs and insects (Wis 11:15–12:2).

Significantly—as we noted above in our discussion of *herem* war in the book of Joshua—the book of Wisdom defends God's justice in the way the Canaanites were driven out of the land of Israel (Wis 12:3–22). At this point, the author returns to the theme of the Egyptians being punished by the very creatures they worshipped (Wis 12:23–27). He devotes great detail to the foolishness of idolatry—the worship of lifeless objects made by human hands as if they were powerful gods—highlighting over and over again that the Egyptians were punished through the animals they worshipped (Wis 13:1—16:1). In contrast, God sent various animals to his people the Israelites: quail to feed them (Wis 16:2–4), the burning serpents to "warn" them (Wis 16:5–19), followed by the miraculous

---

Does Wisdom Contradict "Creation out of Nothing"?

Some readers argue that when the book of Wisdom contradicts the doctrine of "creation out of nothing" (Latin *creation ex nihilo*) when it states that God "created the world out of formless matter" (Wis 11:17). However, the verse does not say that "formless matter" is itself eternal and uncreated. Indeed, we find a similar expression in the book of Genesis, which speaks of God creating "the heavens and the earth" and then says that the earth was "without form and void" (Hebrew *tohu wabohu*) (Gen 1:2). As we saw above, the literal sense of Genesis is that God called the cosmos into existence (Gen 1:1), but that it lacked form initially (Gen 1:2). Thereafter, in the first three days, God provided its form (Gen 1:3–19). The Wisdom of Solomon thus reflects such a reading of Genesis, in which God first called formless matter into being and then formed it.

---

manna from heaven (Wis 16:20–29), which illustrated the principle that the cosmos aligns itself with the righteous (Wis 16:24).

Returning to the plague narrative, the sacred author also sees poetic justice in the fact that the Egyptians were punished by the darkness that heretofore they had loved as a cover for their wickedness (Wis 17:1–21), whereas the Israelites enjoyed light (Wis 18:1–4). God's justice was also at work in the plague of the death of the firstborn, since the Egyptians themselves had long before been "resolved to kill the infants of your holy ones"—that is, the children born to the Israelites (Wis 18:5). Strikingly, it is at this point that we see not only the personification of divine "wisdom" (Greek *sophia*), the agent of God's salvation, but the personification of the heavenly "word" (Greek *logos*), who "comes down from heaven" as the agent of God's punishment on the night of the Passover:

> For while gentle silence enveloped all things,
> and night in its swift course was now half gone,
> *your all-powerful word* [Greek *logos*] *leaped from heaven, from the royal*
> *throne,*
> *into the midst of the land that was doomed,*
> a stern warrior carrying the sharp sword of your authentic command,
> and stood and filled all things with death,
> and touched heaven while standing on the earth.
>
> (Wis 18:14–16)

To be sure, when the Israelites sinned, they, too, faced plagues of death in the wilderness, but they were protected by righteous, priestly intercession (Wis 18:20–25). By contrast, the self-destructive wickedness of the Egyptians reached its ultimate finale in the annihilation of the pharaoh's pursuing armies at the Red Sea (Wis 19:1–5), while the people of Israel, crossing the Red Sea, experienced a virtually new creation, as they found nature assisting them in their journey toward the Promised Land (Wis 19:6–12).

In sum, when recounting the events of the plagues and the exodus, the sacred author is concerned to show that God was just, not cruel, in his punishments of the Egyptians. In order to do so, he highlights three principles: (1) God uses the same reality or aspect of the cosmos to inflict punishment on the wicked and blessing on the righteous (Wis 11:5; 18:8); (2) the wicked are punished through the very things by which they sin (Wis 11:16; 16:1); and (3) nature allies itself with God and the righteous but against the wicked (Wis 16:24; 19:18–21). This doctrine of *divine providence* is the overarching thrust of the second half of the book: "For in everything, O Lord, you have exalted and glorified your people; and you have not neglected to help them at all times and in all places" (Wis 19:22).

Historical Issues in the Wisdom of Solomon

The Origins of the Wisdom of Solomon

As with all of the other wisdom books we have examined so far, since ancient times, readers have debated whether and to what extent the book of Wisdom as we have it originated with the historical figure to which it was attached. However, unlike certain of the other books, when it comes to the Wisdom of Solomon, there is virtual unanimity among scholars that the book was written first in Greek and may even have been the last book of the Old Testament to be written and, thus, cannot possibly have been authored in its present form by the historical figure of Solomon.

To be sure, since the first centuries of the Church (we have no ancient Jewish opinions on the matter), there were those who took the passages in which the first-person narrator is clearly speaking in the person of King Solomon (see Wis 7:1–5; 8:13–14; 9:7–12) as evidence of Solomonic authorship.[3] Indeed, some Church Fathers even posited that the book was first written in Hebrew.[4] In modern times, a few scholars have attempted to make the case for a Hebrew original based on the use of poetic parallelism, Semitic-type conjunctions, and a remarkable number of Hebraisms—such as the expression "sons of men" (Wis 9:6) strewn throughout the work.[5]

However, by far the dominant position, from ancient times until today, has been that the Wisdom of Solomon was written *in honor of Solomon*, but was not authored by Solomon himself (as with certain sections of Proverbs). For example, already in the second century A.D., the ancient list of inspired Scriptures known as the *Muratorian Canon* not only ascribes the book to "friends of Solomon" but places it among the writings of the New Testament!

> Further an epistle of Jude and two with the title John are accepted in the catholic Church, and *the Wisdom written by friends of Solomon in his honour.*[6]

Along similar lines, Saint Augustine of Hippo, who clearly regarded the book as inspired Scripture, writes:

---

[3] See, for example, Clement of Alexandria, *Stromateis* 6.93.2.

[4] See, for example, Cyprian, *On Mortality* 23; Lactantius, *Divine Institutions* 4.16.

[5] Winston, *Wisdom of Solomon*, 15–17.

[6] *Muratorian Canon* 68–70, in E. Hennecke and W. Schneemelcher, *New Testament Apocrypha*, vol. 1, trans. Robert M. Wilson (Philadelphia: Westminster Press, 1963), 44–45.

Next are the ... three books of Solomon, viz., Proverbs, Song of Songs, and Ecclesiastes. For two books, *one called Wisdom and the other Ecclesiasticus, are ascribed to Solomon from a certain resemblance of style, but the most likely opinion is that they were written by Jesus the son of Sirach.* Still they are to be reckoned among the prophetical books, since they have attained recognition as being authoritative.[7]

Although Augustine was not committed to the view that the same person authored the books of Wisdom and Sirach (he later retracted it), the quotation here is still significant. It demonstrates that for the early Church Fathers, the inspired character of a given book of Scripture was not tied absolutely to whether or not it originated historically with the person with whom it was associated. In this instance, Augustine, like the Muratorian Canon, clearly sees the sections in which Solomon speaks in the book of Wisdom as a literary device and not a claim of actual Solomonic authorship.

In this way, Augustine anticipated the virtual consensus of modern scholarship on Wisdom, which holds that the book was written in Greek sometime in the late Second Temple period (between the third century B.C. and the first century A.D.). The major arguments for this conclusion are several.

1. First and foremost, scholars point to *linguistic features* that strongly suggest the text as we have it was *composed in Greek* rather than translated from Hebrew. For example, there are multiple examples of Greek alliteration—the deliberate repetition of the first consonants in a series of words—such as "they will be made holy who observe holy things in holiness" (Greek *hosiōs ... hosia hosiōthēsontai*) (Wis 6:10; see also 2:10, 14; 3:8, 16; 4:5; 5:12, 18; 15:15; 17:20). There is also the repeated use of Greek assonance—the deliberate repetition of vowel and consonant sounds (for example, Wis 1:10; 2:23; 5:14, 17; 7:13; 12:25–26), as well Greek puns (known as "paranomasia") (for example, Wis 4:3; 5:10, 22; 14:5; 17:12–13; and so on).[8]

2. Second, and equally important, is the evidence that the book of Wisdom *uses the Greek Septuagint* translation of Jewish Scripture, which was not produced until around 200 B.C. or so. For example, Wisdom appears to quote the Septuagint version of Isaiah 3:10 and 44:20 as well as Job 9:12, 19 (see Wis 2:12; 12:12; 15:10), in which the Greek differs very much from the Hebrew.[9] Such usage would place the production of the Greek book as we have it sometime during the late Second Temple period.

3. Third and finally, we may cite the presence of *technical Greek philosophical terms*, some of which do not appear in Greek literature outside the Bible before the first century A.D.[10] Consider, for example, the following terms, many of which appear in the writings of Epicurean philosophy as well as Plato and Aristotle:

[7] Augustine, *On Christian Doctrine* 2.13, in *NPNF1* 2:539.
[8] Winston, *Wisdom of Solomon*, 16–17.
[9] Ibid., 17–18.
[10] Ibid., 1–23.

Greek Philosophical Terms Found in the Wisdom of Solomon

1. Incorruption (Greek *aphtharsia*) (2:23)
2. Immortality (Greek *athanasia*) (4:1)
3. Providence (Greek *pronoia*) (14:3; 17:2)
4. Analogy (Greek *analogōs*) (13:5)
5. Irrational Creatures (Greek *alogōn zōon*) (11:15)
6. Formless Matter (Greek *hylē amorphos*) (11:17)
7. Virtues (Greek *aretai*) (8:7)
   a. Temperance (Greek *sōphrosynēn*)
   b. Prudence (Greek *phronēsin*)
   c. Justice (Greek *dikaiosynēn*)
   d. Fortitude (Greek *andreian*)

In light of these and other aspects of the book, the modern scholarly consensus is that the Wisdom of Solomon is heavily influenced by Greek philosophy and rhetoric. It gives every evidence of having been composed originally in Greek; and a variety of factors, including the dominating concern with Egyptian matters (such as idolatry) in the second half of the book, lead many commentators to suggest that it may have been composed for the large Jewish community in Alexandria, Egypt, some time between the third century B.C. and the first century A.D.[11]

Theological Issues in the Wisdom of Solomon

Immortality, Final Judgment, and Resurrection

The primary contribution of the book of Wisdom to biblical theology is its robust teaching on the immortality of the soul, final judgment, and resurrection. These teachings, in a sense, solve the central problem of the book of Ecclesiastes, in which Solomon was unable to make moral sense out of this present life ("under the sun") because of the way that death seemed to come randomly to both the righteous and the wicked.

In Wisdom, however, "Solomon" realizes that the inequities of *this life* will in fact be rectified in *the next life*. He teaches clearly that the souls of the righteous find a home with God, where they experience peace and blessing (Wis 3:1–13). Extended passages in the first half of the book seem to entail both a future resurrection of some sort (though its bodily nature is not clearly defined) and a general judgment vindicating the righteous and punishing the wicked (Wis 3:7–8 and 4:20—5:23). This eternal or transcendent perspective enables the author to judge as ultimately blessed those persons who in this life suffer many apparent misfortunes: persecution, barrenness, poverty, and even persecution and death.

---

[11] See David A. DeSilva, *Introducing the Apocrypha: Message, Context, and Significance* (Grand Rapids, Mich.: Baker Academic, 2002), 131–34.

The Wisdom of Solomon and the Holy Spirit

Another major contribution of the book of Wisdom is to the developing theology of the Holy Spirit in the Old Testament. The book not only describes divine "wisdom" (Greek *sophia*) in *personal terms*, but virtually identifies her with the spirit of God: that is, the Holy Spirit:

The Holy Spirit in the Wisdom of Solomon

For wisdom is a kindly *spirit*. (Wis 1:6)

In her there is a *spirit* that is intelligent, *holy*, unique ... all-powerful, overseeing all. (Wis 7:22–23)

She is a *breath* of the power of God, and a pure emanation of the glory of the Almighty. (Wis 7:25)

Perhaps most significant of all, by means of poetic parallelism, the figure of "Wisdom" (Greek *Sophia*) is identified with the figure of the "Holy Spirit" (Greek *hagios pneuma*):

Who has learned your counsel, unless you have given *wisdom*, and sent your *holy Spirit* from on high? (Wis 9:17)

Notice here the significant progress being made in the book of Wisdom, in which we see articulated a reality hinted at previously in the Pentateuch, when God says "Let us make man in our image" (Gen 1:26)—namely, that there are multiple persons in God and that God's Spirit is in fact a person.

The Wisdom of Solomon in the Living Tradition

In stark contrast to the relative neglect of the Wisdom of Solomon in the modern period—especially since the time of the Protestant Reformation, when the inspired nature of the book was rejected by many Christians—in the patristic era, the book of Wisdom was extremely popular and cited by such giants as Augustine of Hippo hundreds of times in their writings. This influence is no doubt due in part to the theological richness of the book, which, as we have already seen, takes up issues such as the immortality of the righteous, the final judgment, and the origins of sin and death and which contains remarkably rich texts on the "holy spirit" of God and the "word" of God, all of which function as precursors to New Testament Christology and pneumatology. Indeed, as even a few examples should suffice to show, the Wisdom of Solomon played a key role in the living tradition of the Church, functioning almost as a kind of "bridge" between the Old and New Testaments.

The Suffering Son of God and the Passion of Christ

Wisdom was appreciated for its philosophical and theological teachings but was also viewed as prophecy. This is above all the case with the striking depiction of the persecution, suffering, and death of the "righteous man" who is also the "son of God" (Wis 2:10–24). It is little wonder that the early Church Fathers saw in this text a prophecy of the persecution, suffering, and death of the one true righteous man, Jesus Christ. Indeed, Hilary of Poitiers listed it as one of the key prophecies of the Passion in his "cascade" of texts:

> After the preaching of the prophets came the judgments of God, as though echoing back to the voice that had predicted their coming. The voice of one cascade was, "Let us plot against the righteous one, because he is an embarrassment to us and opposes himself to our actions, calling himself a child of the Lord" (Wis Sol 2:13). Another sound of the cascade is, "He was like a lamb led to the slaughter, as a sheep mute before his shearers, and he did not open his mouth" (Is 53:7). There is another voice, also: "They have pierced my hands and my feet, I can count all my bones" (Psalm 22:1).... *What need is there now to recall all the voices of the cascades, since the prophetic books are full of the insults directed at the Lord and of his passion?*[12]

Notice here that there is no sense for Hilary in which the Wisdom of Solomon is "deuterocanonical". To the contrary, it is listed first in a catena (or "cascade") of the most powerful and striking prophecies of the Passion of Jesus in the inspired Scriptures of the Old Testament.

The Wisdom of Solomon, the "Analogy" of Being, and Natural Philosophy

For example, it is the book of Wisdom that gives to theology the extremely important principle that theologians would later come to term "the analogy of being". Based on Wisdom's teaching that "a corresponding perception [Greek *analogias*]" of the Creator can be seen in creatures (Wis 13:5), theologians have concluded that human beings, even apart from supernatural divine revelation, can reason by analogy from the existence and attributes of creatures to a firm knowledge of the existence and attributes of God. Consider, for example, the striking teachings of two fourth-century Church Fathers:

> *If it is not possible to see the divine nature with the eyes of flesh, it is possible to gain an image of the divine power of the Creator from his works.* Solomon says this: "In fact, one knows the author by analogy from the greatness and beauty of creatures" (Wis Sol 13:5). *He does not say simply that one knows the author from creatures but adds "by analogy."* The more we consider his creatures in a contemplative way, in fact, the more God will show himself to be great.[13]

> *God has a face that shows itself through his creatures.* It is said, in fact, "one knows the author by analogy from the greatness and beauty of creatures" (Wis Sol 13:5). *One knows him by the analogy of faith....* Faced with the fact that the world moves in an orderly way and with the beauty of nature, we derive an image of the beauty

---

[12] Hilary of Poitiers, *Homilies on the Psalms* 41.12, in Sever J. Voicu, "Wisdom of Solomon", in *Apocrypha, Old Testament 15*, Ancient Christian Commentary on Scripture, ed. Thomas C. Oden (Downers Grove, Ill.: InterVarsity Press, 2010), 50.

[13] Cyril of Jerusalem, *Catechetical Lectures* 9.2, in Voicu, "Wisdom of Solomon", 148.

and greatness of God. If present things are great, how much greater will the one who made them be. Thus, if one gains an image of God from the world, from the order and arrangements of providence, then the hidden side of his face is no longer hidden. *The Greek philosophers also reasoned in this way, deducing an image of God from creatures and their beauty.*[14]

Although a case could be made that other passages in the Old Testament presupposed what might be called a kind of "philosophy of nature" or "natural philosophy", only here in the book of Wisdom do we see the principle of analogical reasoning fully and explicitly articulated. In a way, this will anticipate the arguments for the existence of God by later theologians (like Thomas Aquinas), who will appeal to the order and beauty of the created world as a reason for believing in the unseen Creator (for example, Thomas' "Fifth Way").

Wisdom, "Light from Light", and the Nicene Creed

Perhaps the most significant and widespread theological impact of the Wisdom of Solomon may come from a place many would not expect: the Christological profession of the Nicene Creed (also known as the Nicene-Constantinopolitan Creed). In this creed, which was formulated at the Councils of Nicaea (A.D. 325) and Constantinople (A.D. 381) and continues to be professed by "the great Churches both East and West to this day" (*CCC* 195), the faithful proclaim:

> We believe in one Lord, Jesus Christ,
> the only begotten Son of God,
> born of the Father before all ages,
> God from God, *Light from Light*,
> true God from true God.

Like other expressions in the Creed that are drawn from Scripture such as "only-begotten" (Jn 3:16), the mysterious image of "light from light" is taken from the Wisdom of Solomon, which describes "wisdom" as *"a reflection of eternal light"* (Wis 7:26). For example, in his famous work on the Trinity, Augustine of Hippo appealed to this passage as a foundation for the equality of the Son with the Father:

> What wonder, therefore, if He is sent, not because He is unequal with the Father, but because He is "a pure emanation (*manatio*) issuing from the glory of the Almighty God?" [Wis 7:25 Latin Vulgate] For there, that which issues, and that from which it issues, is of one and the same substance. For it does not issue as water issues from an aperture of earth or of stone, but as light issues from light. *For the words, "For she is the brightness of the everlasting light"* [Wis 7:26], *what else are they than, she is light of everlasting light?* ... "It is the brightness of that light," namely, of eternal light, and so shows it to be equal. For if it were less, then it would be its darkness, not its brightness; but if it were greater, then it could not issue from

---

[14] Didymus the Blind, *On the Psalms* 30.21, in Voicu, "Wisdom of Solomon", 148.

it, for it could not surpass that from which it is educed. Therefore, because it issues from it, it is not greater than it is; and because it is not its darkness, but its brightness, it is not less than it is: therefore it is equal.[15]

Writing in defense of the Council of Nicaea, Gregory of Elvira explicitly tied the profession of faith to the book of Wisdom: "If you were to say 'light from light' [as in the Creed] and had to explain it in detail, I would ask how you conceive of this 'light from light'.... In fact, of this the prophet said, 'In you is the source of life, and in your light we see light' (Ps 36:10). Or Solomon, when he says, 'She is a reflection of eternal light' ..." (Wis 7:26).[16]

Given the monumental status of the Nicene Creed, there are few Old Testament texts (apart from Genesis 1) that can lay claim to the kind of influence that Wisdom's depiction of the "eternal light" of wisdom has had on Christian theology.

Wisdom and the Origins of Death in the Catechism

Finally, one of the great questions asked by men of all times and places is: "Where did death come from?" The opening chapters of the Wisdom of Solomon are significant in that they contain the most explicit and extended meditation on the origin of death, when they declare that "God did not make death, and he does not delight in the death of the living.... [T]hrough the devil's envy death entered the world" (Wis 1:13, 2:24).

Significantly, these lines are cited twice by the *Catechism of the Catholic Church*. First, the Catechism appeals to Wisdom 1:13 and 2:24 in summarizing its teachings on the creation of man in Paradise, in the state of original holiness before the Fall (see *CCC* 413, summarizing *CCC* 355–90). Second, it appeals to them again when formulating its teaching on the origins of bodily death:

> *Death is a consequence of sin.* The Church's Magisterium, as authentic interpreter of the affirmations of Scripture and Tradition, teaches that death entered the world on account of man's sin [cf. Gen 2:17, 3:3; 3:19; Wis 1:13; Rom 5:12; 6:23]. Even though man's nature is mortal, God had destined him not to die. *Death was therefore contrary to the plans of God the Creator and entered the world as a consequence of sin* [cf. Wis 2:23–24]. "Bodily death, from which man would have been immune had he not sinned" is thus "the last enemy" of man left to be conquered. (*CCC* 1008, citing Vatican II, *Gaudium et Spes* 18.2 [emphasis added])

This is a parade example of the theological impact that the Wisdom of Solomon has had and continues to have on the living tradition up to this very day. Against those who might be inclined to assert that death was part of God's plan from the beginning or to doubt that it entered the world because of sin, the Church

---

[15] Augustine, *On the Trinity* 4.20.27, in *NPNF1* 3:83.

[16] Gregory of Elvira, *On the Faith*, 5, in Voicu, "Wisdom of Solomon", 100.

asserts—in part because of the testimony of the Wisdom of Solomon—that bodily death is in fact a consequence of human sin, undoing the state of immortality in which God created man and woman before the Fall.

The Wisdom of Solomon in the Lectionary

In contrast to some of the other poetic books, the Wisdom of Solomon, for its size, is one of the most-read Old Testament books in the modern Lectionary and Liturgy of the Hours. No doubt this is because of its vigorous affirmations of eternal life and vindication at the last judgment for those who suffer for the sake of righteousness. In these passages, which are particularly concentrated in the first chapters of the book, the Church finds great consolation. They are frequently read in the Lectionary or the Liturgy of the Hours when either the Gospel or the liturgical occasion suggests themes of suffering, martyrdom, death, judgment, and/or eternal life. Selections from the later chapters, where Solomon prays for wisdom and describes wisdom's attributes (Wis 6–9), are often paired with Gospel texts where either the *person* of Christ or his *teaching* is shown to be the embodiment and summation of the divine wisdom, as well as on the feast days of Doctors of the Church, who through prayer and humility were blessed with the divine wisdom Solomon once enjoyed. Finally, passages from the description of wisdom's role in salvation history that emphasize God's just and merciful providence over the realm of nature and human affairs (Wis 11–18) are read on occasions when the Gospel or liturgical celebration lends itself to meditation on God's providence.

Readings from Wisdom in the Lectionary and Liturgy of the Hours on Sundays, Feast Days, Liturgical Seasons, and Other Occasions			
MSO = Masses for Special Occasions; *OM* = Optional Memorial; *VM* = Votive Mass; *Rit* = Ritual; *LH* = Liturgy of the Hours			
Passage	Description	Occasion	Explanation
1:13–15, 2:23–24	God did not create death: the natural order is wholesome. God created man for immortality, but the devil brought death into the world.	*13th Sun. in OT (B)*	Combined with the Gospel (Mk 5:21–43) of the healing of the dead girl and sick woman, Jesus is revealed as restoring creation to its original justice and undoing the curse of death introduced through the deceit of the devil.
2:1a, 12–22	The wicked plot to persecute the righteous man who offends them, who boasts he is a son of God.	Fri., 4th Week of Lent; *VM*: The Holy Cross	This reading from Wisdom influenced the evangelists' accounts of the Passion. It is read with Gospels that describe the Passion or the events leading up to it, showing Jesus to be the ultimate righteous man who provokes the envy and hatred of the wicked.

(continued)

Readings from Wisdom in the Lectionary and Liturgy of the Hours on Sundays, Feast Days, Liturgical Seasons, and Other Occasions (*continued*)

MSO = Masses for Special Occasions; *OM* = Optional Memorial;
VM = Votive Mass; *Rit* = Ritual; *LH* = Liturgy of the Hours

Passage	Description	Occasion	Explanation
2:12, 17–20	The wicked resolve to torture and kill the righteous man, to see if God will really protect him.	*25th Sun. in OT (B)*	Jesus predicts his Passion, death, and Resurrection in the Gospel reading (Mk 9:30–37), which we recognize as long anticipated in the Scriptures of Israel.
3:1–6	The righteous seem dead but are at peace, immortal, accepted by God as a worthy sacrifice.	*LH*: Common of Martyrs, Canticle I for Vigils	The author of Wisdom encourages us to take an eternal and spiritual perspective on the unjust death of the faithful.
3:1–9	All the above; also, the righteous shall rule in glory in the world to come, and those who trust in God in this life may find comfort in his care for his faithful ones.	*All Souls*, opt. 1; Masses for the Dead, opt. 3; Common of Martyrs, opt. 5; Proper: St. Sixtus II; St. Maximillian Kolbe; St. Andrew Kim Taegon, St. Paul Chong Hasang, & companions; Sts. Cosmos & Damian	This passage offers great consolation on the occasion of the death of righteous men and women and so is frequently read at Masses for such occasions.
3:1–15	All the above; also, the wicked will be judged even in this life, and righteous virgins and eunuchs will receive favor at the final judgment.	*LH*: Office of Readings, Common of Several Martyrs in Lent	Wisdom 3:1–15 provides an extensive theology of death and dying from an eternal and supernatural perspective. What counts as a "success" in this life is radically redefined in light of eternal beatitude or judgment in the life to come.
3:7–9	The righteous shall share God's rule over the cosmos in the world to come; even now, the faithful may take comfort in this truth.	*LH*: Common of Apostles and of Martyrs, Canticle II for Vigils	See above.
4:7–15	The death of the righteous at a young age should not be understood as an evil; God has brought them quickly to blessedness.	*All Souls*, opt. 2; Masses for the Dead, opt. 4	This reading is particularly apt for a holy person who dies in youth; the sacred author reminds us that untimely death is not the evil we perceive it to be from our temporal perspective.

(*continued*)

Readings from Wisdom in the Lectionary and Liturgy of the Hours on Sundays, Feast Days, Liturgical Seasons, and Other Occasions (*continued*)

MSO = Masses for Special Occasions; *OM* = Optional Memorial;
VM = Votive Mass; *Rit* = Ritual; *LH* = Liturgy of the Hours

Passage	Description	Occasion	Explanation
5:1–15	At the final judgment, the righteous shall stand forth boldly, while their persecutors repent in shame for all the evil done against them.	*LH*: Office of Readings, Common of Holy Men in Lent, Advent, Christmas	On the memorials of various saints, this reading reminds us of the glorious reward they have attained and that also awaits us if we persevere in holiness.
6:12–16	Wisdom is close and easily found by those who look for it; it waits at their gates and seeks them out.	*32nd Sun. in OT (A)*	Combined with the Gospel parable of the wise and foolish virgins (Mt 25:1–13), the wise virgins appear as embodiments of divine wisdom and models for the Christian, who should eagerly seek out the Bridegroom, Jesus Christ.
7:7–11	Solomon prayed, and the Spirit of Wisdom came on him; he treasured it above power, wealth, health, beauty, and light itself, because it brought him every good thing.	*28th Sun. in OT (B)*	Combined with the Gospel account of the rich young man, the difficulty of the rich entering the kingdom, and the temporal and eternal rewards of those who abandon all for Christ (Mk 10:17–30), we see Solomon as the model of the Christian disciple, who should abandon temporal riches to obtain the eternal riches of divine wisdom.
7:7–10, 15–16	See above; also Solomon prays that his words (i.e., teaching) will be guided by God, the source of all wisdom.	Common of Doctors, opt. 2; Proper: St. Thomas Aquinas; St. Robert Bellarmine	In the Doctors of the Church, we see realized the model of Solomon, the ideal wise man who attained his great wisdom, not in himself, but by seeking it in humility from God.
7:7–16, 22b–30	Solomon prayed, and wisdom was given him; he describes the beauties, virtues, and effects of wisdom, which is virtually identified with God's Spirit.	*LH*: Common of Doctors, Office of Readings in Lent, Advent, Christmas	In the second reading, William of Thierry emphasizes that the Christian should approach the mysteries of faith with prayer for the Holy Spirit, who can grant insight where human reason fails. The Doctors of the Church practiced this pious means to penetrate the divine mysteries.
9:1–6, 9–11	Solomon humbles himself, confesses his weaknesses, and pleads for God to	*LH*: Canticle for Morning Prayer, Sat., Week III	Solomon models a certain posture in our relationship with God, to which the believer must return again and again.

(*continued*)

Readings from Wisdom in the Lectionary and Liturgy of the Hours on Sundays, Feast Days, Liturgical Seasons, and Other Occasions (*continued*)			
MSO = Masses for Special Occasions; *OM* = Optional Memorial; *VM* = Votive Mass; *Rit* = Ritual; *LH* = Liturgy of the Hours			
Passage	Description	Occasion	Explanation
	send him wisdom from above, who can share with him divine knowledge.		
9:9–11, 13–18	Wisdom is with God and sent from God; without the gift of wisdom, man is feeble in his reasoning, because burdened with physical frailty.	*Rit*: Anointing of the Sick, opt. 6	At the point of death or in a period of grave illness, these words of Wisdom remind us of the frailty and perishability of the body, the unimaginable goodness of the heavens, and the salvific power of divine wisdom and the Holy Spirit.
9:13–18b	Unaided reason cannot understand the things of God; even earthly things are hard to discern. True wisdom is a gift of God along with the Holy Spirit.	*23rd Sun. in OT (C)*	Combined with the Lord's call to count the cost of discipleship (Lk 14:25–33), the reading from Wisdom urges us to abandon earthly calculations and scheming in favor of total commitment to the transcendent "logic" of discipleship to Christ.
10:17–21	Wisdom "gave holy men the reward of their labors", delivering Israel through the sea and judging Egypt, so prompting songs of praise.	*LH*: Common of Apostles and of Martyrs, Canticle III for Vigils	This passage articulates our dispositions of joy on the feasts of the saints, who have attained the reward described in Wisdom.
11:22—12:2	Creation is as a speck before God, but he loves each and every thing he has made, which leads him to be gentle with the wicked, leading them to repentance.	*31st Sun. in OT (C)*	In the Gospel, the account of the repentance of Zacchaeus (Lk 19:1–10), we see Jesus as embodying the love of the Creator, who cares for every small thing (Zacchaeus was very short) and is patient with the wicked (Zacchaeus the corrupt tax collector) to lead them to salvation.
12:13, 16–19	Though God is all-powerful and answerable to no one, nonetheless he governs the world with mercy and kindness, teaching men that they, too, must be kind.	*16th Sun. in OT (A)*	Combined with the parable of the weeds and the wheat (Mt 13:24–43), we understand that God's refusal to root up the weeds (sinners) from within the Church is not a failure of his justice but an expression of his mercy, desiring that all may come to salvation.

(*continued*)

	Readings from Wisdom in the Lectionary and Liturgy of the Hours on Sundays, Feast Days, Liturgical Seasons, and Other Occasions (*continued*)		
	MSO= Masses for Special Occasions; *OM*= Optional Memorial; *VM*= Votive Mass; *Rit*= Ritual; *LH*= Liturgy of the Hours		
Passage	Description	Occasion	Explanation
16:20–21, 26; 17:1a	God fed Israel with the "food of angels" (manna), which adapted to every palate, teaching Israel that not farming but God's word was the source of sustenance.	*LH*: Canticle III for the Vigil of Corpus Christi	On the vigil of Corpus Christi, Wisdom 16 reminds us of one of the most important types of the Eucharist in the Old Testament, the heavenly manna, which is a sign of God's merciful governance of the world and generous provision for his people.
18:6–9	The people of Israel were warned of the coming Passover; they were prepared, escaped the angel of death, and offered righteous sacrifices in peace.	*19th Sun. in OT (C)*	The Gospel (Lk 12:32–48) warns Christians to be ready for the Second Coming, like servants waiting for their master's return to the house. We should be like the Israelites, who were not taken by surprise on the night of the Passover, but were saved because they had been warned.

Significantly, generous selections from Wisdom are read in sequence on ferial days of Week Thirty-Two of Year I in Ordinary Time and yearly in the Liturgy of the Hours, Office of Readings, in Week Thirty in Ordinary Time. The readings in the Liturgy of the Hours are skillfully matched with selections from Saint Clement of Rome and other saints who expound further the same passage of Wisdom read in the first reading, or at least themes from it. Readings from Wisdom are appropriate in these late weeks of the liturgical year, when the Church turns her attention to the Last Things, about which Wisdom has a great deal to say.

		Reading of Wisdom for Daily Mass: Ordinary Time, Year I: Week 32
Day	Passage Read	Description
M	1:1–7	Solomon exhorts the rulers of the world to seek divine wisdom, but to do so in sincerity, since wisdom will not inhabit a deceitful, sinful soul.
Tu	2:23—3:9	God created man for immortality; death comes through the devil. Nonetheless, God grants immortality to the righteous. They only seem to have died; they will reign in glory in the age to come.
W	6:1–11	Solomon sternly warns world rulers that their authority is given by God, and he will hold them strictly to account on the day of judgment for any injustice they commit.

(*continued*)

		Reading of Wisdom for Daily Mass: Ordinary Time, Year I: Week 32 *(continued)*	
Day	Passage Read	Description	
Th	7:22b—8:1	Solomon describes the perfections of wisdom: it is a breath, an emanation of God, pure, pervasive, irresistible, more precious than any created good.	
F	13:1–9	Men have been led astray by the beauty of created things to deify elements of creation rather than to worship the one true God who made all things. This error is both intellectual and moral.	
Sa	18:14–16; 19:6–9	God sent his word as a warrior to judge Egypt; the creation was "fashioned anew" during the exodus, the "dry land" coming up out of the water, that the people of Israel could pass over in safety.	

			Wisdom in the Office of Readings for the Liturgy of the Hours: Ordinary Time, Week 30
Day	First Reading	Second Reading	Comment
Su	1:1–15	*1st Clement*	Rulers should seek wisdom so they may rule well; wisdom is a kindly spirit that comes to pure souls; God has made the world good, and righteousness is undying. Clement's epistle likewise picks up and expands on the theme of God's loving and wise providence over all creation.
M	1:16—2:1a, 10–24	*1st Clement*	The wicked summon and are in league with death. They persecute the godly man because he is an offense and rebuke to them. They think to kill him, but they reason unsoundly, not understanding the immortality of wisdom and righteousness. Thus it becomes clear that God knows the inmost thoughts of the wicked. In *1st Clement*, the early pope exhorts the young Roman Church to a life of holiness in thought and in deed, because God knows our inmost thoughts. Since nothing is hidden from him, our life-style must be one of humility, chastity, and love.
Tu	3:1–19	*1st Clement*	The souls of the just only seem to have died; they are at peace with God, having been accepted as sacrificial offerings. They will rule in the age to come, whereas the wicked will be punished. Virgins and eunuchs will have an eternal reward, whereas the many progeny of the wicked will come to no good. Clement, too, focuses on the theme of resurrection, pointing to signs of resurrection in the natural world and urging us to holiness that we may share in the resurrection.
W	6:1–25	*1st Clement*	Rulers especially should seek out wisdom that they may rule justly, for God will judge rulers severely, and it is only through wisdom that they can rule in righteousness.

(continued)

Wisdom in the Office of Readings for the Liturgy of the Hours: Ordinary Time, Week 30 (*continued*)			
Day	First Reading	Second Reading	Comment
			For his part, Clement urges believers also to keep in mind the coming judgment and to "follow the way of truth, casting away all that is unholy" in order to share God's eternal reward.
Th	7:15–30	St. Athanasius, *Against the Arians*	Wisdom taught Solomon all things, even the workings of the natural order. It is a supernatural spirit, the breath and emanation of God, more valuable than any created thing. St. Athanasius stresses a distinction between uncreated wisdom, which is with God and is God (i.e., the Second Person), and created wisdom, which is the sign or evidence of wisdom impressed, as it were, on every creature, giving testimony to the creative act of divine and uncreated wisdom.
F	8:1–21b	Baldwin of Canterbury	Solomon sought wisdom as his bride, knowing that it is more valuable than all things and that all riches, honor, and authority would come to him through it. Baldwin of Canterbury reflects on Christ, the "word, power, and wisdom of God", who is more "powerful and piercing than any two-edged sword", who brings life and wisdom to all who receive him.
Sa	11:20b–12:2, 11b–19	St. Catherine of Siena, *Dialogue on Divine Providence*	Creation is as a speck before God, but he loves each and every thing he has made, which leads him to be gentle with the wicked, leading them to repentance. God the Father speaks likewise to St. Catherine, explaining to her his love and providence for man, mankind's twisting of God's good gifts, and the gift of Christ to make satisfaction for the wicked and lead them to repentance.

Conclusion

In the Wisdom of Solomon, the sacred author expounds on the eternal fates of the righteous and unrighteous and demonstrates that wisdom, righteousness, immortality, and kingly rule are all ultimately interrelated. Wisdom appears fully characterized as a person, as the "breath" or "Spirit" of God, who has been active throughout the sacred history of Israel. The book of Wisdom presents the most fully formed eschatology to be found in the Old Testament, and many themes and theological truths in the book are taken up also in the teachings of the New Testament. The Church treasures this book in the Lectionary and the Liturgy of the Hours as a source of inspiration and consolation on liturgical occasions that call to mind themes of death, martyrdom, eternal life, final judgment, and the acquisition of divine wisdom.

For Further Reading

Commentaries and Studies on the Wisdom of Solomon

Collins, John J. *Jewish Wisdom in the Hellenistic Age.* Louisville, Ky.: Westminster John Knox Press, 1997.

DeSilva, David Arthur. *Introducing the Apocrypha: Message, Context, and Significance.* Grand Rapids, Mich.: Baker Academic, 2002. (See pp. 127–52.)

Kolarcik, Michael, S.J. "The Book of Wisdom". *New Interpreter's Bible,* vol. 5. Nashville: Abingdon Press, 1997.

Murphy, Roland E., O. Carm. *The Tree of Life: An Exploration of Biblical Wisdom Literature.* 3rd ed. Grand Rapids, Mich.: Eerdmans, 2002.

Winston, David. *The Wisdom of Solomon.* Anchor Bible 43. New York: Doubleday, 1979.

The Wisdom of Solomon in the Living Tradition

Hennecke, Edgar, and Wilhelm Schneemelcher. *New Testament Apocrypha.* Vol. 1. Translated by Robert McLachlan Wilson. Philadelphia: Westminster John Knox Press, 1963. (See pp. 44–45.)

Voicu, Sever J. "Wisdom of Solomon". Pages 34–175 in *Apocrypha.* Old Testament 15 of Ancient Christian Commentary on Scripture. Edited by Thomas C. Oden. Downers Grove, Ill.: InterVarsity Press, 2010.

29. SIRACH

Introduction

Sirach is the last of the wisdom books in the Catholic canon of the Old Testament. As such, it may be regarded as a massive summation of the Israelite wisdom tradition—a meditation on the entirety of Israel's Scriptures from the perspective of "wisdom" (Hebrew *hokhmah*), the practical knowledge of righteous living. Because Sirach provides such a useful digest of the moral teachings of the Jewish Scriptures, the early Church used it extensively in catechesis and moral instruction, so much so that it came to be known as "Ecclesiasticus"—that is, "the Church's little book".

Sirach is known by more names than any other biblical book. The full title of the book in antiquity, in Greek and probably Hebrew as well, was "The Wisdom of Jesus the Son of Sirach" (Greek *Sophia 'Iēsou huiou Seirach*) (cf. Sir 50:27). A plethora of shortened titles in Hebrew, Greek, and Latin can be found in the Fathers and the rabbis of antiquity, including "Wisdom", "Wisdom of Jesus", "Book of Wisdom", "Wisdom of Sirach", "Proverbs of Jesus of Sirach", and others. The brief title "Son of Sirach" (Hebrew *ben Sira*) eventually prevailed in the Jewish circles, and this name is often used in scholarly writing today, for the book and for its author. As mentioned, the Latin tradition eventually bestowed on it the name Ecclesiasticus, although Saint Jerome's title in the Vulgate was "The Book of Jesus Son of Sirach" (Latin *Liber Iesu Filii Sirach*). As one might expect, all of this has led to quite a bit of confusion among some first-time readers of the Old Testament. Since any title including "Wisdom" is easily confused with the Wisdom of Solomon, and "Ecclesiasticus" with Ecclesiastes, the name "Sirach" has now become common in modern editions of the Bible (for example, RSVCE and NAB), and this is the title we will use below.

In terms of its canonical status, Sirach has a very interesting history.[1] Modern Judaism and Protestantism classify Sirach among the "apocrypha". This view of Sirach can be traced back to ancient times—for example, in the third century A.D. collection of rabbinic traditions known as the Tosefta, which explicitly states that Sirach is not inspired:

> [T]he books of Ben-Sira and all books written after the prophetic period do not defile the hands [that is, are not inspired Scripture].[2]

On the other hand, there is abundant evidence that many ancient Jews *did* accept Sirach as inspired Scripture. In the last hundred years or so, ancient Hebrew

---

[1] Patrick W. Skehan and Alexander A. Di Lella, *The Wisdom of Ben Sira*, Anchor Bible 39 (New York: Doubleday, 1987), 18–20.

[2] Tosefta, *Yadayim* 2.13, in ibid., 20.

copies of Sirach were discovered at Masada, among the Dead Sea Scrolls, and in an important collection of ancient Jewish writings from Egypt known as the "Cairo Geniza". Taken together, these manuscripts demonstrate not only that Sirach was originally composed in Hebrew, but that it was treated as a sacred text by a remarkable number of Jews in the Second Temple period. Moreover, Greek editions of Sirach are also present in every ancient copy of the Septuagint we possess, suggesting that the book was also revered by ancient Greek-speaking Jews and translated along with other books considered to be inspired Scripture. Finally, it is striking that in later rabbinic traditions preserved in the Babylonian Talmud (ca. fifth century A.D.), some rabbis continue to quote the book of Sirach as if it were Scripture. For example, according to the Talmud, in the fourth century, Rabbi Ben Mari not only quotes Sirach as Scripture but indicates that he considers it part of the third section of the Jewish Bible, known as the "Writings":

> Raba said to Rabbah b. Mari.... This matter was written in the Pentateuch, repeated in the Prophets, mentioned a third time in the Writings.... *[It is] mentioned a third time in the Writings, as written:* "Every fowl dwells near its kind and man near his equal" [Sir 13:15].[3]

In other words, despite the eventual rejection of Sirach by medieval Judaism and later by Protestantism, it was, in fact, regarded as Scripture by a substantial number of Jews during the Second Temple period and beyond. It was this latter view that the early Church inherited; not only was Sirach viewed as inspired by the majority of Church Fathers, but it was (as stated above) one of the most popular books in the Old Testament, generating a remarkable amount of commentary.

Based on the manuscript evidence, it seems clear that Sirach was originally written in Hebrew and circulated in at least two editions: a shorter and a longer. The first Greek translation was made by the author's grandson, as the prologue to the book attests, and also circulated in a shorter and longer edition in that language. The longer Greek edition was anonymously translated into Latin at some point, and Saint Jerome incorporated this "Old Latin" translation virtually unchanged in the Vulgate. Other translations of the four Hebrew and Greek editions were made into other ancient languages (Syriac, Ethiopic, and so on). As a result, the textual tradition of Sirach is confusing and displays a wide range of variation, though without changing the teaching of the book substantively. The (reconstructed) shorter Greek version of the author's grandson is treated as the "standard text" of Sirach in most modern English translations, and will be treated as such below.

Literary Structure of Sirach

Sirach is a self-consciously *literary* work, one that intentionally employs a wide variety of rhetorical and literary devices. The author was a professional scribe,

---

[3] Babylonian Talmud, *Baba Kamma* 92b, in Isidore Epstein, ed., *The Babylonian Talmud*, 35 vols. (London: Soncino, 1935–1952).

a literary expert of his day. As in earlier wisdom literature, especially Proverbs, the two-line *bicola* prevails. But Jesus ben Sira also employs a wide variety of other literary forms, including hymns, acrostic poems, encomia, and at least one *todah* psalm.

Many authors are inspired by previous works: for Sirach, the book of Proverbs was the literary model. Like Proverbs, Sirach mixes long poems in praise of wisdom (as in Prov 1, 8, 9, and so on) with loosely organized collections of proverbs. Unlike Proverbs, however, Sirach shows greater thematic unity and an effort to group proverbs by topic.

The basic macrostructure of Sirach consists of poems in praise of wisdom that join together blocks of proverbial instruction. There are three major divisions of the book: a first collection of instruction (Sir 1–23), a second collection of instruction (Sir 24–43), and a review of sacred history (Sir 44–50). The joints between these three major divisions are marked by great poems praising wisdom evident in creation: (Sir 1:1–20; 24:1–34; and 42:15—43:33). Within the first two large blocks of instruction, less conspicuous poems—either praises of wisdom or prayers—mark the transitions between smaller units of instruction (Sir 4:11–19; 6:18–31; 14:20—15:8; 16:24—17:24; 22:27—23:6; 33:16–18; 36:1–17; 39:12–35). Often it is hard to determine if these poetic units are meant to introduce or conclude sections. Perhaps they do both, and it is best to think of them as *links* joining the various units of teaching material.

The book in its present form begins with a prologue written by the grandson who translated it into Greek and concludes with a double epilogue consisting of a *todah* psalm (Sir 51:1–11) and an acrostic poem (Sir 51:13–30)—very much like the ending of Proverbs (cf. Prov 31:10–31[!])—about the author's successful search for wisdom. The complete structure of the book would then be as follows:

Outline of the Book of Sirach

Prologue to the Greek Version by the Author's Grandson

I. All Wisdom Comes from the Lord (Sir 1–23)
    A. Guidance for the Young Man (1:1—4:10)
        1. Introductory Poem: All Wisdom Comes from the Lord (1:1–20)
        2. Instruction: Guidance for a Young Man (1:21—4:10)
    B. On Speech and Friendship (4:11—6:17)
        1. Introductory Poem: Wisdom Breathes Life into Her Sons (4:11–19)
        2. Instruction: On Speech (4:20—6:4) and Friendship (6:5–17)
    C. On Dealing with Persons from All Walks of Life (6:18—14:19)
        1. Introductory Poem: From Your Youth, Choose Instruction (6:18–31)
        2. Instruction: How to Deal with Persons from All Walks of Life (6:31—14:19)
    D. On Refraining from Sin (14:20—16:23)
        1. Introductory Poem: Blessed the Man Who Meditates on Wisdom (14:20—15:8)
        2. Instruction: Refraining from Sin and Ungodliness (15:9—16:23)

Overview of Sirach

Prologue to the Greek Translation by the Grandson of Jesus ben Sira

The edition of Sirach present in most English Bibles is unique among the books of the Old Testament insofar as it contains a prologue telling exactly who the author was, when and why it was written, and (in this case) why it has been translated.

As the prologue states, the grandson of Jesus ben Sira ("Jesus" is the Greek version of the Hebrew name "Joshua") translated his grandfather's book of wisdom from Hebrew into Greek in the "thirty-eighth year of Euergetes"— that is, King Ptolemy VII Euergetes II of Egypt, whose thirty-eighth year would be approximately 132 B.C. Given this date of the Greek translation, Jesus ben Sira himself probably wrote the original Hebrew edition around 200 B.C., near the end of the reign of the high priest Simon II the Just (219–199 B.C.), since the Hebrew fragments of Sirach 50 speak of Simon as though he were still living at the time of composition.

Interestingly, the grandson-translator apologizes for errors of translation that might remain despite his diligence, since, as he rightly points out, converting Hebrew to Greek is not an easy task. The purpose of the work is that "those who love learning should make even greater progress in living according to the law." Even more specifically, the Greek translation is intended for "those living abroad who wished to gain learning, being prepared in character to live according to the law" (Sirach, prologue). In other words, he is translating it for Greek-speaking Jews in the *diaspora* ("abroad") who want to maintain their cultural and religious heritage and live lives of righteousness.

Guidance for the Young Man (Sirach 1:1—4:10)

Although without complete consistency, the opening chapters of Sirach are generally aimed toward the young man, as made clear in the repeated address "My son" (some thirteen times in the first part of the book). Like the book of Proverbs, then, the book intends, first and foremost, to instruct young men about how to live righteously in the world.

A poem on wisdom strongly reminiscent of Proverbs 8 begins the first section and the book as a whole (Sir 1:1–20). The message of the poem is typical of the wisdom literature: "Wisdom" (Hebrew *hokhmah*; Greek *Sophia*) is "from the Lord" (Sir 1:1). She was created before all other things and was involved in the process of creating the rest of the cosmos. "To fear the Lord is the beginning of wisdom" (Sir 1:14), and wisdom will bestow every good thing on the one who attains her.

The following body of instruction seems aimed at the young man who is *beginning* to seek out wisdom. The programmatic verse states: "My son, if you come forward to serve the Lord, remain in justice and in fear, and prepare yourself for temptation" (Sir 2:1). The young man is warned that the path of wisdom—which is synonymous with seeking out the Lord—will be difficult and involve trials requiring perseverance (Sir 2:2–18). The honoring of both father and mother is fundamental to the wise and righteous life (Sir 3:1–16). The humility and docility shown toward parents should develop into virtues characteristic of one's whole life (Sir 3:17–31). In addition to social duties toward one's parents, one has obligations of social justice toward the poor, needy, and disadvantaged (Sir 4:1–10).

Speech and Friendship (Sirach 4:11—6:17)

Another poem on wisdom marks a transition to a new unit of instruction to the young man (Sir 4:11–19). Wisdom "breathes life into her sons". She bestows on them glory like that of priests—who "minister to the Holy One"—(Sir 4:14) and kings—who "judge the nations" (Sir 4:15). However, apprenticeship to wisdom involves trials and tests before it yields reward (Sir 4:17–18).

What follows is a series of instructions mostly concerned with control of one's mouth (Sir 4:20–6:4), but since "a pleasant voice multiplies friends" (Sir 6:5), the sage transitions into a discussion of friendship—a widely discussed topic in ancient philosophy—including important advice on how to distinguish between true and false friends and other related issues (Sir 6:5–17).

On Dealing with Persons from All Walks of Life (Sirach 6:18—14:19)

Another poem on wisdom marks the transition to a new unit (Sir 6:18–31). In this poem, the sage praises Lady Wisdom. Although at the beginning she may seem harsh (Sir 6:20), at last she yields rest and joy (Sir 6:28). By means of a striking image, Ben Sira urges the young man to become a *slave of wisdom*: he is to put his feet into her "chains" and his neck into her "collar", until he finds that the "chains" become a strong protection and the "collar" a "glorious robe" (Sir 6:29).

With wisdom as guide, the sage now turns to one of the most practical and wide-ranging sections in the entire book: how to relate with people from all walks of life and in all sorts of social situations. In this section, Ben Sira explains how to deal with a stunning array of different kinds of people: the wise man, the king, the judge, God himself, the mourner, one's brother, a friend, one's wife, one's servant, children, daughters, parents, priests, the poor, the dead, the sick, the powerful, the rich, the ill-bred, the repentant, the elderly, sages, sinners, the insolent, the fool, the wrathful, loose women, female singers, virgins, harlots, beautiful women, the wives of other men, murderers, and neighbors (Sir 7–9)! He continues with more advice on dealing with magistrates, kings, rich and poor men, the wise and the foolish, friends and enemies (Sir 10:1–13:26), and even how to deal with oneself (Sir 14:1–19).

On Refraining from Sin (Sirach 14:20—16:23)

The next section is introduced by a poem strongly influenced by the Psalms, the Song of Solomon, and Proverbs. Alluding to Psalm 1:1, the sage declares: "Blessed is the man who meditates on wisdom" (Sir 14:20). He then proceeds to describe the blessed man in images taken from the bridegroom's invitation to the bride to elope (Sir 14:23–25; cf. Song 2:8–17). The man who pursues wisdom in this way will win her as his wife (Sir 15:1–2), and she will bring him every blessing bestowed by an ideal wife (Sir 15:3–8; cf. Prov 31:10–31). Once again, we encounter in the wisdom literature the striking image of the wise man's *nuptial* relationship with Lady Wisdom, implying that her pursuit is a total and lifelong commitment, not a "hobby" or side-interest or even a "profession".

What follows is a loosely organized exhortation against offending the Lord through sin, which is probably best expressed when the sage declares:

The eyes of the Lord are on those who fear him,
   and he knows every deed of man.
He has not commanded any one to be ungodly,
   and he has not given anyone permission to sin. (Sir 15:19–20)

In other words, the wise man should not presume on God's mercy or think he will overlook sin.

On Self-Control (Sirach 16:24—22:26)

A long and somewhat rambling poem on creation introduces the next section (Sir 16:24—18:14). First, the sage describes God's creation of the material universe (Sir 16:24–30) before describing the creation of man in original justice and mankind's subsequent sin (Sir 17:1–20). This section is significant because, among other things, it explicitly speaks about a primordial *covenant* between God and the first human beings:

The Lord created man out of earth,
   and made him into his own image;
he turned him back into earth again,
   but clothed him in strength like his own....
He created in them the knowledge of the spirit;
   he filled their hearts with understanding,
   and showed them good and evil....
He established with them an eternal covenant,
   and showed them his justice and his judgments.
Their eyes saw his glorious majesty,
   and their ears heard the glory of his voice.
                                    (Sir 17:1–2, 7, 12–13)

After this description of creation, Ben Sira then discourses in a loosely organized way about the relationship between divine creation, justice and mercy, and human sin and repentance (Sir 17:22—18:14), ultimately concluding with an exhortation to repent and seek mercy from God, the loving Creator (Sir 18:9–14).

What follows is a block of instruction largely on the theme of *self-control*, or self-restraint, the overriding concept being articulated when the sage teaches: "A wise man is cautious in everything, and in days of sin he guards against wrongdoing" (Sir 18:27). So the sage exhorts the young man to exercise restraint over his judgments, vows, appetites, speech, friendships, and behavior (Sir 18:15—19:30). Since the tongue is so powerful, the sage includes another large section on control of it (Sir 20:1–31). But control of the tongue is not enough; one must also discipline one's thoughts, from which come disciplined external behavior and the discipline of one's children (Sir 21:1—22:26). The unit of instruction concludes with a prayer for self-control (Sir 22:27—23:6), which can be summed up in the words: "O that a guard were set over my mouth, and a seal of prudence upon my lips.... O that whips were set over my thoughts, and the discipline of wisdom over my mind!" (Sir 22:27; 23:2).

On Control of Speech, Especially Oaths and Vows (Sirach 22:27—23:27)

The prayer for self-control simultaneously concludes the previous section of instruction and introduces the following one, which focuses once again on control of the tongue: "Listen, my children, to instruction concerning speech" (Sir 23:7). The sage warns strenuously against the (apparently perennial) problem of the casual and habitual use of oaths (Sir 23:7–11) and lewd or rude speech (Sir 23:12–15). Marriage is established by the swearing of oaths, so the sage transitions to a discussion of fidelity to one's marital vows and abstinence from sexual sin (Sir 23:16–27). Apparently, for Sirach, the ability to control one's tongue is related directly to the ability to control other parts of the body.

Guidance for the Older Man (Sirach 24:1—33:18)

The second major part of Sirach begins with an aesthetically and theologically well-developed first-person poem reminiscent in theme and style to Proverbs 8 (Sir 24:1–34). Significantly, as in Proverbs, wisdom reiterates her precedence before all other creatures and her role in creation (Sir 24:3–6). In a new twist, however, she identifies Israel and Israel's Temple as her particular dwelling place (Sir 24:8–12). She describes her development into attractive womanhood in language strongly reminiscent of the Song of Solomon (Sir 24:13–22). Strikingly, at this point, the sage interrupts wisdom's discourse to identify her with the Torah of Moses (Sir 24:23–29). He then speaks in the first person, expressing his resolve to "again make instruction shine forth like the dawn" (Sir 24:32)—that is, to renew his educational project begun in the first half of the book (Sir 1–23).

In this second half of the book, there is a general, if inconsistent, shift in focus toward the older man who has reached the height of his influence in society.

This is signaled early on in the sage's instruction:

> You have gathered nothing in your youth;
> how then can you find anything in your old age?
> What an attractive thing is judgment in gray-haired men,
> and for the aged to possess good counsel!
> How attractive is wisdom in the aged,
> and understanding and counsel in honorable men! (Sir 25:3–5)

So, while it includes much wisdom that is generally applicable to persons in all states of life, the second part of Sirach seems intended as remedial wisdom for the older man. The topics addressed presume that the reader is married (Sir 25:7—26:18); has money to lend and the means to be surety for others (Sir 29:1–20); has sons (Sir 30:1–13) and daughters (Sir 26:10–12); and be prone to ill health (Sir 30:14–17), poor sleep (Sir 31:1–7), overeating (Sir 31:12–22), and, being a respected member of society, being invited to banquets (Sir 31:25—32:13). In

---

He Who Loves His Son Will Whip Him Often (Sirach 30:1)

Ben Sira writes at a time when corporal punishment was unexceptional and commonly meted out by the courts for criminal offenses.

A father was responsible to enforce law in his household and, thus, to punish both sons and servants (cf. Sir 33:26). Cultural views of corporal punishment change with time and place. Ben Sira's point remains that sons must be disciplined effectively, whatever form that may take.

In the *Catechism of the Catholic Church*, Sirach's teaching that "he who loves his son will not spare the rod" (Sir 30:1; Latin) is cited in the section on the human family and the responsibility that parents have to "guide and correct" their children, where it is balanced with the New Testament teaching that fathers should not "provoke [their] children to anger, but bring them up in the discipline and instruction of the Lord" (Eph 6:4, quoted in *CCC* 2223).

---

all these situations, as in many others, the mature man can proceed successfully only if he proceeds with caution, following the Torah of the Lord and the principles that can be derived from it:

> Guard yourself in every act,
>   for this is the keeping of the commandments.
> He who believes the law gives heed to the commandments,
>   and he who trusts the Lord will not suffer loss. (Sir 32:23–24)

The first unit of the second part ends with a retrospective comment by the author, Jesus ben Sira, about his place in the tradition of Israel's Scriptures:

> I was the last on watch;
>   I was like one who gleans after the grape-gatherers;
> by the blessing of the Lord I excelled,
>   and like a grape-gatherer I filled my wine press.
> Consider that I have not labored for myself alone,
>   but for all who seek instruction.
> Hear me, you who are great among the people,
>   and you leaders of the congregation, listen. (Sir 33:16–18)

Death Is Better Than a Miserable Life (Sirach 30:17)

Ben Sira aims to give some perspective on death: it is not always an unmitigated evil and can bring peace to those who are suffering. Nonetheless, Sirach never advocates suicide: life and death are in the hand of the Lord, not human beings.

This is a fascinating self-conscious reflection on his own vocation as a wisdom teacher. By means of it, Ben Sira concludes the first unit of the second part (Sir 24:1—33:18) and also introduces the second unit (Sir 33:19—36:17). We again note that it is the "great" and the "leaders" that the sage addresses in this second part—that is, men who have reached social standing.

More Advice for the Older Man (Sirach 33:19—36:17)

Ben Sira continues with more advice on matters of concern for the man of standing: caution about distributing one's estate too early in life (Sir 33:19–23), guidance for the training of servants (Sir 33:24–31), the interpretation of dreams (Sir 34:1–8), and the complementarity between liturgical worship and social justice (Sir 34:18—35:20). On this last subject, the sage ultimately exhorts his reader to acts of mercy toward the poor and oppressed, in imitation of God, who is merciful. This leads him into a strikingly eschatological concluding prayer, in which he pleads that God will have mercy on Israel, judge its enemies, restore its tribes, and renew blessing upon Jerusalem, and its Temple and priesthood (Sir 36:1–17).

On Relating to Others (Sirach 36:18—39:11)

After the prayer for mercy, Jesus ben Sira renews his instructional discourse, this time focusing mainly, though not exclusively, on how to relate properly with other persons, including women (Sir 36:21–26), true and false friends and confidants (Sir 37:1–26), and various tradesmen, craftsmen, and professionals (Sir 38:1—39:11).

This section on the trades and professions is a very clear literary subunit, as the sacred author describes the value and esteem due to different vocations and those who practice them: physicians (Sir 38:1–15), farmers (Sir 38:25–26), craftsmen (Sir 38:27), smiths (Sir 38:28), and potters (Sir 38:29). In a remarkable anticipation of what has come to be referred to as the "universal call to holiness", Sirach insists not only that even the most common of laborers plays an essential role in society, but that labor itself is a form of prayer:

> All these rely upon their hands,
>   and each is skilful in his own work....
> But they keep stable the fabric of the world,
>   and their prayer is in the practice of their trade. (Sir 38:31, 34)

In short, all human workers are valuable to society (Sir 38:31–34), though the scholar who devotes himself to the study of God's law has a more noble calling (Sir 39:1–11).

In a concluding poem of praise that could equally well be considered an introduction to the following block of teaching, the sage praises God for the goodness of all his works (Sir 39:12–35). The argument of the poem is that, although certain aspects of creation seem unpleasant or bad, when viewed in the entire economy of the universe, they are seen to have a good purpose; therefore, when viewed in the widest possible context, all the works of the Lord are good:

> The works of the Lord are all good,
>   and he will supply every need in its hour.
> And no one can say, "This is worse than that,"
>   for all things will prove good in their season.
> So now sing praise with all your heart and voice,
>   and bless the name of the Lord. (Sir 39:33–35)

Coping with the Troubles of Life (Sirach 40–43)

The poem in praise of God's world and works (Sir 39:12–35) forms an excellent segue into the following block of instruction, which largely concerns how to cope with those aspects of reality which—despite their ultimate good purpose within God's plan—still seem bad (Sir 40:1—42:14). In this section, which may be a continuation of the poem, Jesus ben Sira reflects on all the trials, troubles, and sufferings of life. For the sage, such things are not proof of the evil intent or incompetence of the Creator, because they are ultimately the result of Adam's sin: "Much labor was created for every man, and a heavy yoke is upon the sons of Adam" (Sir 40:1). Indeed, every person now experiences such burdens. Despite the universal experience of suffering, however, the wise man retains faith that, in the end, the wickedness of the wicked will be punished and the kindness of the righteous will be rewarded (Sir 40:12–17).

The sage then delivers a series of poetic comparisons of the goods of life, with an aim to distinguishing those which are best—that is, those things which one should seek to mitigate the sufferings of life. For Ben Sira, the very best things are an excellent wife (Sir 40:19, 23), the love of wisdom (Sir 40:20), the voice of friendship (Sir 40:21), fertile fields (Sir 40:22), almsgiving (Sir 40:24), good counsel (Sir 40:25), and, above all, the fear of the Lord (Sir 40:26–27). Strikingly, Sirach declares that even if these goods cannot be attained or do not suffice to protect one from catastrophic misfortune, one should not descend to the level of begging (Sir 40:28–30). To this, death is preferable (Sir 40:28).

Speaking of death, the sacred author finds it opportune, as he nears the conclusion of his instructions for the mature man, to meditate on the reality of *death* and offer advice on how to deal with it. For Ben Sira, death is not an absolute evil. Though the thought of it troubles those who are enjoying this world's pleasures, it is sweet release for those who are suffering (Sir 41:1–2). One should not fear death, because it is the inevitable and irresistible decree of God (Sir 41:3–4). One should take care, however, not to leave behind a brood of ungodly children (Sir 41:5–10) or a bad reputation, for one's reputation will outlive one's physical life (Sir 41:11–13).

Speaking of reputation, Ben Sira then shifts into a discussion of things that enhance it by bringing honor and things that decrease it by bringing shame. Society's definitions of honor and shame, however, are not to be accepted without critique. Instead, Sirach lists those things which ought to be regarded as shameful—such as sexual immorality, lying, false witness, unjust economic practices, theft, gluttony, selfishness, rudeness, lustful and adulterous looks, abusive words, gossip—whether society sees them as such or not (Sir 41:17–23). He also catalogues a list of those things which are honorable—such as obedience to the law, mercy in judgment, generosity, just economic transactions, profit, the disciplining of one's children, record taking, and so on—despite what anyone may think (Sir 41:1–8). Men are particularly vulnerable to fall into dishonor in matters that involve women. Therefore, the sacred author concludes with strong exhortations to take precautions with a daughter who lacks natural modesty (the "headstrong" daughter of Sir 42:9–11) and to avoid all lustful looks and inappropriate relationships with women (Sir 42:12–14).

At this point in the book, all direct instruction is now complete. Ben Sira concludes with yet another poem praising God for his wisdom manifested in creation (Sir 42:15–33). After recounting the glory and wonder of the heavenly bodies (Sir 43:1–10), the skies (Sir 43:11–22), and the sea (Sir 43:23–26), the sacred author concludes that it is not possible to praise God enough, because not even the greatness of his works can be fully recounted, and he is still greater than his works (Sir 43:27–33).

The Glory of the "Famous Men" and "Fathers" of History (Sirach 44–51)

After praising God for his good works in the order of creation, Sirach now turns to praise God for his good works in the order of redemption: that is, in all of salvation history.

In this section, Ben Sira proceeds to eulogize all the major heroes of Israel's sacred history, in what amounts to a truly stunning overview of the saints of the Old Testament: Enoch, Noah, Abraham, Isaac, Jacob, Moses, Aaron, Phinehas, Joshua, Caleb, the judges, Samuel, Nathan, David, Solomon, Elijah, Elisha, Hezekiah, Isaiah, Josiah, Jeremiah, Ezekiel, the twelve minor prophets, Zerubbabel, Jeshua ben Jozadak, and Nehemiah (Sir 44:16—49:13). A final colophon honors some characters omitted at the beginning: Joseph, Shem, Seth, and Adam (Sir 49:14–16).

At the end of these "praises of the Fathers", Ben Sira appends an encomium to "Simon the high priest, son of Onias" (= Simon II the Just), who appears to have been the currently reigning high priest in Jerusalem when the book was written (ca. 219–199 B.C.; Sir 50). This dramatic description of the liturgical role of the high priest is not only one of the most detailed descriptions of cultic worship that we possess from this period but also implies that the glories of Israel's saints and sacred history reach their expression and culmination in *the liturgy of the Temple*. As descendant of Aaron and Phinehas,

> #### The Book of Sirach and the Centrality of the Covenant
>
> In its final overview of God's works in salvation history (Sir 44–49), the book of Sirach quite intentionally highlights those figures with whom or through whom a divine covenant was formed: Noah, the three patriarchs (Abraham, Isaac, and Jacob), Moses, Aaron, Phinehas, and David. Indeed, Sirach makes this explicit when he states that the "righteous deeds of the fathers" will not be forgotten and that "their descendants stand by the *covenants*" (Sir 44:12). Significantly, this inspired summary of salvation history provides a canonical precedent for a covenant-focused approach to salvation history, such as employed in this textbook and in the *Catechism of the Catholic Church* (see CCC 54–64, 68–73).

the high priest is in a sense the personal embodiment of Israel's religious heritage, who brings the glory of the past fathers of salvation history into the present by renewing the covenants and imparting his priestly "blessing" (Sir 50:20–21).

With this glorious song of praise completed, Jesus ben Sira concludes his work with a doxology and prayer for mercy (Sir 50:22–24), a complaint about the traditional enemies of Israel (Sir 50:25–26), and an epilogue in which he identifies himself as the author and invokes a blessing on the reader who puts his words into practice (Sir 50:27–29). At this point, two poetic compositions are appended to the end of the book: the first is a psalm of thanksgiving or *todah* psalm in classic Davidic style (Sir 51:1–11). Written in the first person and immediately following Ben Sira's epilogue, the psalm presents itself as a composition of the author himself. He describes a general situation of persecution and proximity to death, his remembrance of the Lord and prayer for deliverance, and finally his thanksgiving for God's salvation (Sir 51:3–12).

The second appendix is an acrostic poem in which Ben Sira describes his lifelong quest to attain wisdom (Sir 51:13–30). The poem consciously evokes the Song of the Valiant Woman (Prov 31:10–31), which is also an acrostic. Both poems envisage wisdom as a beautiful and desirable woman, but Proverbs praises Lady Wisdom from a third-person perspective, whereas Sirach relates the sage's first-person account of his courtship of her. Significantly, he began his quest for her with prayer and sought her at the Temple, thus linking wisdom to the liturgy and law of Israel (Sir 51:13). He employs some of the romantic imagery of the Song of Solomon to describe the development of his love for her (Sir 51:15). With struggle, he attained wisdom and began to enjoy her fruits (Sir 51:16–22). In a passage reminiscent of Proverbs' description of the "call" of Lady Wisdom (Prov 9:1–12), Ben Sira brings his book to its ultimate conclusion with a call for the "untaught" to lodge at his "school"—that is, to read and meditate on his book (Sir 51:23–30).

Historical Issues in Sirach

The Origins of the Book of Sirach

Unlike almost every other book of the Old Testament we have discussed so far, there is very little debate over the authorship and date of the book of Sirach. As noted above, this is primarily because the prologue to the Greek version of the book tells us quite explicitly when, where, why, and by whom it was written, and most scholars see no reason to doubt the information given to us by the prologue.[4] According to this data, Sirach was written in Jerusalem by one "Jesus the son of Sirach [Hebrew *ben Sira'*], son of Eleazar, of Jerusalem" (Sir 50:27), in the lifetime of Simon II the Just (Sir 50:1), who acted as high priest between 219–196 B.C. According to the prologue, the grandson of Jesus ben Sira translated it into Greek in Alexandria in the thirty-eighth year of the reign of King Ptolemy Euergetes in Egypt (ca. 132 B.C.). It is worth noting that this was a time of immense cultural and political change for the Jewish people, both inside and outside the land, so that Ben Sira's emphasis on fidelity to the Scriptures of Israel and the covenants of God may be seen as a response to the question of how to live faithfully in the context of the emerging Hellenistic world.

Theological Issues in Sirach

Does Sirach Teach the Hatred of Women (Misogyny)?

Some of the most striking and potentially difficult aspects of Sirach immediately faced by any modern-day reader of the text are his startlingly and oftentimes

---

[4] See David A. DeSilva, *Introducing the Apocrypha: Message, Context, and Significance* (Grand Rapids, Mich.: Baker Academic, 2002), 157–61.

extremely negative statements about women, wives, and even daughters. Consider, for example, the following statements:

> The birth of a daughter is a loss. (Sir 22:3)

> I would rather dwell with a lion and a dragon,
>   than dwell with an evil wife. (Sir 25:16)

> Better is the wickedness of a man than a woman who does good. (Sir 42:14)

What are we to make of such passages? Are they evidence, as many scholars have suggested, of biblical "misogyny" (= hatred of women)? Or is there some other way to explain them? In attempting to interpret these texts correctly, several considerations must be taken into account.

1. First and foremost, in each case, *these texts must not be taken out of context*. Instead, they should be read according to the literary conventions being employed by Sirach and in the light of what the entire book of Sirach has to say about women (see below). For example, when Sirach states that he would "rather dwell with a lion and a dragon than dwell with an evil wife" (Sir 25:16) and that "any iniquity is insignificant compared to a wife's iniquity" (Sir 25:19), it is critical to realize that he is using a common literary device known as *hyperbole*—that is, exaggerating a point for the sake of emphasis. He is not speaking literally or objectively, but subjectively and hyperbolically. Of course there are worse iniquities among mankind than those of a wife (Ben Sira himself lists them elsewhere!), but Sirach's point is that none of these other evils affect a *husband's* life more profoundly, which is of course quite true.

Along similar lines, when Ben Sira says that "the wickedness of a man" is "better" than "a woman who does good" (Sir 42:14), his statements must be interpreted in their immediate *context*. When this is done, it is clear that Ben Sira is saying that one would be better off *socializing* with a wicked man than with a good woman. Indeed, the surrounding verses are a warning against womanizing: "Do not sit in the midst of women" (Sir 42:12). Remember that Ben Sira is writing primarily to married men. For them, socializing with women was potentially dangerous, putting them in the near occasion of the sin of adultery, whether of the heart or even of the flesh. That is what Sirach means when he says "it is a woman who brings shame and disgrace" (Sir 42:14b). In other words, with reference to the married men for whom he is writing, they would be better off trying their chances with disreputable men, rather than risk forming an attachment with a woman other than one's wife. Indeed, Ben Sira discourages any interaction between men and women that could threaten the exclusive bond of love between husband and wife (cf. Sir 9:3–9).

Finally, when Sirach states that "the birth of a daughter is a loss" (Sir 22:3), his words must be interpreted in the context of the Hebrew poetic device known as *synonymous parallelism*, in which parallel lines mutually illuminate the meaning of other lines (see above in chapter on the Psalms). When the line is read in its poetic context, it becomes very clear that Sirach is not referring to the birth of any daughter, but the birth of a *shameful* daughter, since in the very next verse he praises a *sensible* daughter:

It is a disgrace to be the father of an *undisciplined son,*
  and the birth of *a[n undisciplined] daughter* is a loss.
A *sensible daughter* obtains her husband,
  but *one who acts shamefully* brings grief to her father. (Sir 22:3–4)

Taken as a whole, then, the passage seems to be contrasting unsensible daughters with sensible ones—not declaring that *all* daughters are worthless.

2. Moreover, the negative statements about women in Sirach must also be interpreted *in the light of the entire book of Sirach,* which as a whole contains many passages that display a great esteem for women. Consider, for example, some of the following:

Whoever *glorifies his mother* is like one who lays up a treasure. (Sir 3:4)

Be like a father to orphans,
  and in the place of a husband *to their mothers.* (Sir 4:10 [author's trans.])

Do not deprive yourself of a wise and good wife,
  for her charm is worth *more than gold.* (Sir 7:19)

A modest wife adds charm to charm,
  and *no balance can weigh the value of a chaste soul.* (Sir 26:15)

Children and the building of a city establish a man's name,
  but *a blameless wife is* accounted *better than both.* (Sir 40:19)

Notice here the indisputably positive and exalted view of women being affirmed by Ben Sira: a mother should be honored equally with her husband by her children; vulnerable women (such as widows) not only are not to be abused, but are to be cared and provided for; a virtuous wife is greater than all possible possessions, even friends, children, wealth, or fame! At one point, Sirach compares the holy beauty of a good wife to the beauty of the Jerusalem Temple and the Golden Lampstand of the Holy Place (Sir 26:16–18)! This is a far cry from the supposed "hatred of women" of which Sirach is so frequently accused. Indeed, in statements in stark contrast to other ancient (and modern) views, Sirach insists that women should *never* be treated as objects of sexual pleasure, going so far as to condemn not only all extramarital relations but even lustful looks and taking advantage of "maidservants" (Sir 9:3–9; 41:20–22; 42:12). To be sure, the reasons against this are often pragmatic, with the temporal and social (rather than spiritual) consequences being emphasized; nevertheless, they are a far cry from the widespread ancient view that held that men could act as they pleased toward women, especially the vulnerable or socially disadvantaged. And of course, wisdom itself is continually personified as a woman, a wife and mother, something no true misogynist would ever have done.

3. Third and finally, it must be admitted that while Sirach is unequalled in his praise of virtuous women, he is equally unsparing in his criticism of evil

women. He points out the havoc wrought by a wicked wife in the strongest terms (Sir 25:16–26), describing her sin as the very worst (Sir 25:19). Yet for all that, Ben Sira never condones physical force against a woman; at the very worst, a husband may be forced to separate from such a wife (Sir 25:26). Indeed, a case could be made that Ben Sira, unlike many other ancient people, displays a *healthy realism* about the magnitude of a woman's influence—for good or for ill—on her husband, her home, her family, and human society.

In sum, when the entirety of Sirach's teaching on a man's relationship to women is taken together, one may say that the sacred author has great respect for the capacity of women both for good and for ill. The virtuous woman is refulgent with the divine glory of the Temple (Sir 26:16–18); no higher praise can be given short of divinizing her. Thus, if some passages are strident in their description of a wicked woman, it is because of the ancient principle *corruptio optimi pessima*, "the corruption of the very best is the very worst."

The Role of Wisdom in Law, Liturgy, and Salvation History

The canonical placement of the book of Sirach already suggests that it functioned in antiquity as a kind of climax to the wisdom literature tradition. Indeed, in terms of its contents, Sirach both summarizes and expands the teaching found in earlier wisdom books and integrates into the wisdom perspective three important themes or elements of Israel's tradition that the earlier books did not treat extensively: the law, the liturgy, and salvation history.

1. *Wisdom and the Law:* Earlier wisdom literature did not explore the relationship between the Mosaic "law" (Hebrew *torah*) and the teachings of "wisdom" (Hebrew *hokhmah*). In fact, there was an implicit sense that the two had different audiences: the law was for Israel, and wisdom for all people. Significantly, in the book of Sirach, however, the sacred author shows that ultimately law and wisdom are united. For example, after a long description of Lady Wisdom as active in creation and finding a resting place in Israel (Sir 24:1–22), Ben Sira says concerning her:

> Come to me [wisdom], you who desire me,
>   and eat your fill of my produce....
> Whoever obeys me will not be put to shame,
>   and those who work with my help will not sin.

> All this is *the book of the covenant* of the Most High God,
>   *the law* which Moses commanded us
>   as an inheritance for the congregations of Jacob.
> *It fills men with wisdom*, like the Pishon,
>   and like the Tigris at the time of the first fruits. (Sir 24:19, 22–25)

This is a striking assertion: for Sirach, ultimately, the law of Moses and divine wisdom coalesce. Although they are two different expressions of the divine will, they are ultimately compatible, since both are given by the same Author.

2. *Wisdom and Liturgy*: As we saw above, earlier wisdom literature, particularly Proverbs, paid relatively little attention to liturgical worship and the sacrificial cult at the Jerusalem Temple. In Sirach, however, Lady Wisdom is said to have taken up her abode in Israel's sanctuary: first in the Tabernacle, then in the Temple (Sir 24). Moreover, the encomia of Israel's great heroes of faith (Sir 44–49) conclude with the grand description of high priest Simon II celebrating the sacrificial ritual of the Day of Atonement in all his vested glory (Sir 51), suggesting that the wisdom evident in the lives of all Israel's "famous men" truly finds its embodiment and climactic expression in the ministry of the high priest in the Temple.

Sirach's insistence on the close relationship of wisdom to the liturgy may seem counterintuitive at first, but it is in fact a natural outworking of the fundamental insight from early wisdom literature that "to fear the LORD is the beginning of wisdom" (Sir 1:14). As we have seen elsewhere, "fear of the LORD" is an idiom expressing religious reverence, which is broader than, but certainly includes, liturgical worship. In worship, human beings acknowledge and orient themselves toward their true end, or *telos*, which is God himself. The God-ward orientation that liturgy effects in human beings is essential for wisdom, because without proper orientation to their true end, they cannot make adequate judgments about the value of the temporal things of this world. Liturgy informs the intellect and shapes the world view necessary to gain insight into the true nature of things and moral quality of actions.

3. *Wisdom and Salvation History*: One searches the poetical books of Job, Proverbs, and Ecclesiastes in vain for any explicit discussion of the relationship between God's wisdom and salvation history. The book of Sirach, however, forges just such a connection by concluding its teaching with an extensive review of the progress of sacred history based on the succession of "famous" or righteous heroes of Israel, from Adam to Nehemiah (Sir 44–49). In this way, for Sirach, the entire history of Israel becomes a source of wisdom: the righteous actions of the heroes of faith, and also (at times) their sins, become examples of how to live (or how not to live) one's life in a manner pleasing to God and in conformity with the order also manifested in the fabric of creation.

Thus, while the relationship between wisdom and the law of Moses, the Temple liturgy, and the sacred history of Israel was left unexplored in earlier wisdom books, in Sirach the sacred author shows the inherent inner connections between these three realities and divine wisdom. In this way, the book builds a bridge to the New Testament, in which wisdom, Torah, Temple, and liturgy will coalesce in the person of Jesus Christ, divine Wisdom incarnate.

Sirach in the Living Tradition

As might be expected, given the traditional name "Ecclesiasticus" (the church's book), the book of Sirach has played an extremely prominent role in the living tradition of the Church, especially with regard to her moral instruction. For example, in the *Ancient Christian Commentary on Scripture*, most of the volume (more than two hundred pages) on the so-called Old Testament

"Apocrypha" is dedicated to patristic excerpts and comments on the book of Sirach. What follows are a few of the more prominent examples of Sirach's enduring influence.

The Teachings of Jesus Son of Sirach and Jesus of Nazareth

Despite the eventual rejection of Sirach as inspired Scripture by both medieval Judaism and Protestantism, contemporary scholarship is recognizing the fact that this widely read Hebrew book has left its imprint on the pages of the New Testament itself, including the Gospels. Although the book of Sirach is never directly quoted by the New Testament writings, the verbal and conceptual parallels between it and several New Testament writings are so many and so consistent that Protestant and Catholic scholars alike agree that Sirach directly influenced the authors of the New Testament. Consider, for example, some of the following parallels:

The Teachings of Sirach	*The New Testament*
Give to one who asks. (Sir 4:4)	Give to one who asks. (Mt 5:42)
Generosity makes one a child of God. (Sir 4:10)	Forgiveness marks one as a child of God. (Mt 5:45)
Against vain repetition in prayer. (Sir 23:1, 4)	Against vain repetition in prayer. (Mt 6:9; cf. Jas 3:9)
Addresses God as "Father" in prayer. (Sir 23:1, 4)	Address God as "Father" in prayer. (Mt 6:9; cf. Jas 3:9)
Those who hold grudges will face the punishment of God. (Sir 28:1–5)	Those who hold grudges will face the punishment of God. (Mt 6:12, 14–15)

Perhaps the most striking of these parallels is Sirach's teaching on the connection between almsgiving and "laying up treasure" for oneself that is not of this world:

> Lose your silver for the sake of a brother or a friend,
>   *and do not let it rust* under a stone and be lost.
> *Lay up your treasure according to the commandments of the Most High,*
>   and it will profit you more than gold.
> *Store up almsgiving in your treasury,*
>   and it will rescue you from all affliction. (Sir 29:10–12)

But when you give alms, do not let your left hand know what your right hand is doing, so that your alms may be in secret; and your Father who sees in secret will reward you....
Do not lay up for yourselves treasures on earth, where moth and *rust* consume and where thieves break in and steal, *but lay up for yourselves treasures in heaven,* where neither moth nor rust consumes and where thieves do not break in and steal. For where your treasure is, there will your heart be also. (Mt 6:3–4, 19–21)

Once again, although Jesus in the Gospels is not quoting Sirach, in light of these (and many other) striking verbal and conceptual parallels, Protestant scholar David DeSilva writes:

> The parallels between Ben Sira and the sayings of Jesus preserved in Matthew and Luke are so striking and numerous as to render it certain that *Jesus Ben Joseph knew and valued some of the sayings of Jesus Ben Sira.*[5]

Indeed, as DeSilva and others have shown, these parallels are not only contained in the Gospels but are present elsewhere in the New Testament, in the epistles of James (cf. Sir 15:11–20; Jas 1:13–14), John (cf. Sir 14:2; 1 Jn 3:21–22), Romans (cf. Sir 33:12–13; Rom 9:20–21), and elsewhere. In short, unlike certain other books of the Old Testament we have studied so far (including some undisputed books), the book of Sirach's role in the living tradition was vibrant and widespread from the very inception of the Church.

Charity toward the Poor and the Atoning Power of Almsgiving

One of most important "social teachings" of Sirach is its insistence on the necessity of caring for the vulnerable in society such as the poor, widows, and orphans (Sir 3:30—4:10). In the context of such exhortations, however, Sirach provides a fascinating theological insight into almsgiving, when it teaches that just as "water extinguishes a blazing fire: so almsgiving atones for sin" (Sir 3:30). On the basis of such passages, the early Church Fathers developed a robust theology of almsgiving, such as when the fifth-century figure of John Cassian writes:

> The burden of our sins is also overwhelmed by the affection of love, for "love covers a multitude of sins" (1 Pet 4:8). In the same way, by the fruits of almsgiving a remedy is also provided for our wounds because "as water extinguishes fire, so does almsgiving extinguish sins" (Sir 3:30; Latin Vulgate 3:33).... "Seek judgment, relieve the oppressed, judge the orphan, defend the widow. And come, reason with me, says the Lord, and though your sins were as scarlet, yet they shall be as white as snow."[6]

Indeed, as one scholar has shown in his recent study of charity, the Jewish and Christian belief that almsgiving atoned for sins led to a kind of mystagogy of charity, by which the poor and vulnerable were understood as "living altars", and the alms given to them as sacrifices and loans to God that he would eventually pay back.[7]

---

[5] Ibid., 193 (emphasis added).

[6] John Cassian, *Conferences* 3.20.8, in Sever J. Voicu, "Ecclesiasticus, or the Wisdom of Jesus the Son of Sirach", in *Apocrypha*, Old Testament 15, Ancient Christian Commentary on Scripture, ed. Thomas C. Oden (Downers Grove, Ill.: InterVarsity Press, 2010), 199.

[7] See Gary A. Anderson, *Charity: The Place of the Poor in the Biblical Tradition* (New Haven, Conn.: Yale University Press, 2013).

The Book of Sirach and the Doctrine of Human Free Will

As anyone familiar with the history of the Church knows, one of the perennial debates within Christianity at least since the time of Pelagius has been the question: Are human beings really free? Do we have the power to choose good and avoid evil?

In this regard, the book of Sirach played a key role in the living tradition by providing explicit scriptural testimony to the reality of human free will when it stated that God "created man in the beginning, and he left him in the power of his own inclination. If you will, you can keep the commandments" (Sir 15:14–15). On the basis of this text, one fourth-century Church Father wrote:

> As Scripture attests, God formed human beings, making them in his own image and likeness, and left the faculty of decision in their hands. "He put before them fire and water, saying, 'Reach out your hand to what you will'" (Sir 15:17 Latin Vulgate). God "put before the man," it said, "water and fire," that is, rest and punishment, forgiveness and torment, life and death.[8]

In magisterial teaching on human free will, Sirach 15:14 continues to be *the* foundational text for the Church's unhesitating affirmation of the truth that man is "created with free will" and with "the dignity of a person who can initiate and control his own actions" (*CCC* 1730, citing *Gaudium et Spes* 17). Given the role that debates over fate and free will continue to play in philosophy and theology, it is of no little significance that Sirach provides the explicit biblical foundation for the Church's doctrine of human free will.

The Latin Sirach and Augustine's Theory of a One-Day Creation

As we saw in our discussion above of Genesis, one of the debated points among the Church Fathers was whether or not the six "days" of creation in Genesis 1 (known as the *Hexaemeron*) should be taken as six literal/historical days or a merely symbolic description of how the world was made. Although it is widely known that Augustine of Hippo took the minority position in arguing that the six days should be interpreted symbolically, what is less often discussed is the fact that Augustine's theory of an instantaneous (rather than six-day) creation was based directly on his interpretation of the description of creation in the Latin version of Sirach.

Although the Septuagint of Sirach 18:1 states that "he who lives for ever created the whole universe" (Greek *ta panta koinē*), the Latin version used by Augustine read that "he created everything at the same time (Latin *creavit omnia simul*)." Significantly, this (mis-)translation had a dramatic effect on Augustine's reading of the six days of Genesis:

> The creator, after all, about whom scripture told this story of how he completed and finished his works in six days, is the same as the one about whom it is written elsewhere, and assuredly without there being any contradiction, that *"he created all things simultaneously together"* (Sir 18:1 [Latin Vulgate]). And, consequently, the

---

[8] Gaudentius of Brescia, *Sermons* 13.16–18, in Voicu, "Ecclesiasticus", 252.

one who made all things simultaneously together also made simultaneously these six or seven days, or rather this one day six or seven times repeated. So, then, what need was there for the six days to be recounted so distinctly and methodically? *It was for the sake of those who cannot arrive at an understanding of the text, "he created all things together simultaneously"* [Sir 18:1] unless scripture accompanies them more slowly, step by step, to the goal to which it is leading them.[9]

This is an excellent example both of how influential the book of Sirach was for the Church's theology of creation and how Augustine arrived at the novel position that the world was not created in six days but in "one day". Starting from the position that all Scripture is true and cannot contradict itself, Augustine was led to embrace his minority view on the creation of the world by following the Latin edition of Sirach.

The Book of Sirach in the Lectionary

The contemporary Lectionary is generous in its use of readings from Sirach, employing a wide variety of readings from all sections of the book for different occasions. In particular, the Lectionary takes advantage of the similarities between the moral instructions in Jesus son of Sirach and the moral instruction of Jesus son of Joseph in the Gospels and couples them together. In this way, the Lectionary highlights that Jesus' moral doctrine was not entirely a *novum* or innovation; rather, it had strong precedent already in Judaism and canonical Scripture before his coming. Although Jesus *does* introduce new teaching, the true novelty of the Gospel concerns more his *person* than his *ethics*.

The Church also finds Sirach's various encomia to scholars, virtuous persons, and wives as edifying reading for the feast days or memorials of several saints who fall into those categories.

In the readings for daily Mass, two weeks are devoted to a representative sampling of Ben Sira's teaching early in Year I of Ordinary Time (weeks 7–8). In addition, Sirach's encomia of David and Elijah are employed to conclude the semi-continuous reading of the narratives of those two great heroes out of the books of Samuel and Kings in Year II, weeks 4 and 11.

Conclusion

The book of Sirach is a kind of *summa sophia*: a summary of the entire tradition of Israelite wisdom. In this book, important constitutive elements from Israel's other Scriptures—namely, law, liturgy, and sacred covenantal history—are finally integrated into a holistic "wisdom" perspective on all of life. Remarkably, the teachings of Jesus ben Sira often anticipate the moral instruction of Jesus of Nazareth. Because of its practicality, comprehensive scope, and affinity to the teachings of the Gospels, the early Church used Sirach extensively for catechesis on the building of virtue and the avoidance of vice, and the modern Lectionary continues to draw on its riches frequently.

[9] Augustine, *On the Literal Meaning of Genesis* 4.33.52, in Saint Augustine, *On Genesis*, trans. Edmund Hill et al. (Hyde Park, N.Y.: New City Press, 2002), 273.

Passage	Description	Occasion	Explanation
2:7–11	An exhortation for those who "fear the LORD" to hope for good things, everlasting joy, and mercy	Common of Holy Men and Women, opt. 12	The saints were those who feared the Lord, died in the hope of "good things", and experienced the fulfillment of that hope for joy and mercy.
2:7–13	See above, with an additional rebuke of the timid and double-minded	Memorial of St. Cajetan	St. Cajetan set an example in fear of the Lord, hope in God's mercy, and unflinching proclamation of the truth of the Gospel.
3:3–7, 14–17a	Honoring one's parents leads to long life, forgiveness of sins, and treasure in heaven.	*Holy Family Sunday*	This passage helps us to understand Jesus' willingness to submit himself to his parents, despite his divinity, throughout his childhood.
3:17–24	An exhortation to meekness; humility, including intellectual humility, should increase with greatness.	Common of Holy Men and Women, opt. 13	Particularly appropriate for memorials of holy men and women who, despite great gifts of intellect and leadership, displayed admirable humility.
3:17–18, 20, 28–29	The truly great must humble themselves; but the proud are wicked.	*22nd Sun. in OT (C)*	This passage complements the Gospel, in which Jesus uses the occasion of a feast at the house of a Pharisee to teach about humility at social occasions and in general.
15:1–6	Those who love wisdom will find it to be a mystical wife who cares for them in every way.	Common of Doctors, opt. 3; St. Bernard, St. Albert the Great	Certain Doctors of the Church exemplified the search for wisdom; St. Bernard in particular found a spousal or nuptial relationship with God's wisdom in his spiritual journey.
15:16–21	"Before a man are life and death, whatever he chooses will be given him."	*6th Sun. in OT (A)*	Sirach 15:16–21 emphasizes man's free will and the choice between life and death. When this passage is joined to the Sermon on the Mount (Mt 5:17–37), we recognize that Jesus is offering life through his moral teaching, and we must choose it.
24:1–4, 12–16	Wisdom came forth from the Lord, took root in Israel, and grew into a tree of great beauty, like the Tree of Life.	*2nd Sun. after Christmas (ABC)*	When this passage is paired with the prologue of John (Jn 1:1–18) at Christmastide, we recognize Jesus Christ as God's wisdom who has taken flesh and taken root within Israel, growing up into a Tree of Life for all the nations.

(continued)

Readings from Sirach in the Lectionary and Liturgy of the Hours on Sundays, Feast Days, Liturgical Seasons, and Other Occasions (*continued*)

MSO = Masses for Special Occasions; *OM* = Optional Memorial; *VM* = Votive Mass; *Rit* = Ritual; *LH* = Liturgy of the Hours

Passage	Description	Occasion	Explanation
24:1, 3–4, 8–12, 19–21	Wisdom came forth from the Lord, and inhabited the Tabernacle and Temple; it invites all to eat its sweet produce.	Common of the BVM, opt. 6	On feasts of the BVM, we recognize her as a type of the Tabernacle or Temple—that is, a dwelling place of God and of his wisdom. Also, the "produce" of the Virgin is Christ, sweet to our taste in the Eucharist.
26:1–4, 13–16	A good wife is the greatest blessing to the man who fears the Lord; her glory is like that of the Temple.	Common of Holy Men and Women, opt. 14; St. Monica, St. Hedwig; *Rit*: Conferral of Marriage, opt. 8	This eulogy of the excellent wife is particularly apt for memorials of holy married women.
27:5–8	"The fruit discloses the cultivation of a tree; so the expression of a thought discloses the cultivation of a man's mind."	*8th Sun. in OT (C)*	This passage complements the Gospel (Lk 6:39–45), in which Jesus teaches that "no good tree bears bad fruit ... each tree is known by its own fruit." Sirach helps us interpret Christ's words: the "fruit ... of a tree" are the words of a man.
27:30—28:7	Anger, vengeance, and unforgiveness are abominations of the wicked. The righteous man shows mercy to his neighbor.	*24th Sun. in OT (A)*	Jesus ben Sira and Jesus of Nazareth stress the same truth: in the Gospel (Mt 18:21–35), Jesus tells the parable of the unforgiving servant, expressing in story what Sirach explains didactically.
35:12–14, 16–18	The Lord is a righteous judge who grants justice to the poor, fatherless, and widow but who judges the unmerciful, arrogant, and wicked.	*30th Sun. in OT (C)*	Jesus tells the parable of the Pharisee and sinner at prayer (Lk 18:9–14), illustrating the principle articulated by Sirach that "the prayer of the humble pierces the clouds" but God resists the "insolent".
39:6–10	The one who devotes himself to the study of God's law will pour out instruction and receive praise and eternal memory among the nations.	Common of Doctors, opt. 4; Pope St. Leo the Great	The Doctors of the Church are models of the scribe who studies God's law, so highly praised by Jesus ben Sira.

(*continued*)

| Readings from Sirach in the Lectionary and Liturgy of the Hours on Sundays, Feast Days, Liturgical Seasons, and Other Occasions (*continued*) |||| |
| MSO = Masses for Special Occasions; OM = Optional Memorial; VM = Votive Mass; Rit = Ritual; LH = Liturgy of the Hours |||| |
Passage	Description	Occasion	Explanation
44:1, 10–15	Let us praise famous men, who were merciful and righteous; their descendants keep the covenant, and their memory never fades.	Sts. Joachim and Anne	Sts. Joachim and Anne are like grandparents of the whole Church. Through Mary we feel ourselves to be their spiritual descendants, who continue to keep the covenant and cultivate the memory of our spiritual ancestors.
48:1–4, 9–11	Elijah was taken up in a whirlwind of fire and will return to bring about repentance at the end time.	Sat., 2nd Week of Advent	This reading falls in the middle of weeks 2–3 of Advent, which are devoted to pondering the forerunner, John the Baptist, and his significance as a new Elijah.
50:22–24	May God be blessed, who is merciful to us. May he give us joy, peace, and mercy all our days.	MSO: In Thanksgiving to God, opt. 2	This passage expresses in inspired words the sentiments of Thanksgiving that motivate the offering of this Mass.
51:1–8	Ben Sira's *todah* or psalm of thanksgiving: he gives thanks to God for deliverance from death and the power of the wicked.	Common of Martyrs, opt. 6	Although the martyrs appear to have failed and been killed, nonetheless with the eyes of faith we know they have been delivered from true death and from the power of the wicked.
51:8–12	See above; Ben Sira concludes with thanks and resolves to "bless the name of the Lord."	Most Holy Name of Jesus, opt. 2	The sanctity of the "name of the Lord" in the Old Testament now accrues to the Most Holy Name of Jesus in the New Covenant economy.

| Reading of Sirach for Daily Mass: Ordinary Time, Year I: Weeks 7–8 ||||| |
Yr	Week	Day	Passage Read	Description
I	7	M	1:1–10	All wisdom comes from the Lord. Wisdom is as unfathomable as creation itself, and only God truly possesses it.
I	7	Tu	2:1–11	He who seeks to serve the Lord will experience suffering and testing. Yet the one who trusts and endures will find everlasting joy and mercy.

(continued)

			Passage Read	Description
Yr	**Week**	**Day**		
I	7	W	4:11–19	Those who seek wisdom will find life, joy, glory, love, kingship, and blessing, but they will be tested before attaining all this.
I	7	Th	5:1–8	Do not presume on your wealth, strength, or God's mercy.
I	7	F	6:5–17	Be careful whom you embrace as a close friend; nevertheless, when you find a worthy friend, it is a great blessing.
I	7	Sa	17:1–15	God created mankind, blessed them with many dignities, and commanded them to be righteous.
I	8	M	17:20–24	The Lord shows mercy toward the almsgiver, the kindly, and the repentant.
I	8	Tu	35:1–12	The practice of God's law is as important as sacrificial worship; nonetheless, sacrificial worship is to be practiced, since God commanded it and blesses the sincere worshipper.
I	8	W	36:1, 4–5a, 10–17	A prayer for mercy on Israel, its Temple, and its holy city, and for vengeance on its enemies.
I	8	Th	42:15–25	The works of the Lord are glorious and beyond comprehension; yet he himself is all-knowing. All he has made is good.
I	8	F	44:1, 9–13	Let us now praise famous men, renowned for their mercy and righteousness. Their descendants keep the covenants, and their glory does not pass away.
I	8	Sa	51:12cd–20	Ben Sira's concluding poem on his search for wisdom. He sought it from his youth with prayer and discipline; his prayer was heard, and he obtained wisdom.
II	4	F	47:2–11	Ben Sira's eulogy for David recounts his glory in battle, love for the Lord, skill in songwriting, and liturgical reforms. This passage concludes the reading of the David narratives from 1–2 Samuel and 1 Kings in Year II.
II	11	Th	48:1–14	This is Ben Sira's eulogy for Elijah and Elisha. Elijah was taken up in a whirlwind and will return to preach repentance. Elisha worked wonders in life and even in death. This passage concludes the reading of the Elijah narrative from 1–2 Kings in Year II.

Reading of Sirach for Daily Mass: Ordinary Time, Year I: Weeks 7–8 (*continued*)

For Further Reading

Commentaries and Studies on Sirach

Coggins, Richard. *Sirach*. Guides to the Apocrypha and Pseudepigrapha. Sheffield: Sheffield Academic Press, 1998.

Collins, John J. *Jewish Wisdom in the Hellenistic Age*. Louisville, Ky.: Westminster John Knox Press, 1997.

Crenshaw, J. L. "Sirach". Pages 601–867 in vol. 5 of *New Interpreter's Bible*. Nashville: Abingdon Press, 1997.

DeSilva, David A. *Introducing the Apocrypha: Message, Context, and Significance*. Grand Rapids, Mich.: Baker Academic, 2002. (See pp. 153–97.)

Murphy, Roland, O.Carm. *The Tree of Life: An Exploration of the Biblical Wisdom Literature*. 3rd ed. Grand Rapids, Mich.: Eerdmans, 2002. (See pp. 65–82.)

Reardon, Patrick Henry. *Wise Lives: Orthodox Christian Reflections on the Wisdom of Sirach*. Ben Lomond, Calif.: Conciliar Press, 2009.

Skehan, Patrick W., and Alexander A. Di Lella. *The Wisdom of Ben Sira*. Anchor Bible 39. New York: Doubleday, 1987.

Sirach in the Living Tradition

Anderson, Gary A. *Charity: The Place of the Poor in the Biblical Tradition*. New Haven, Conn.: Yale University Press, 2013. (See pp. 56–60.)

Augustine, Saint. *On Genesis*. Translated by Edmund Hill et al. Hyde Park, N.Y.: New City Press, 2002. (See p. 273.)

Voicu, Sever J. "Ecclesiasticus, or the Wisdom of Jesus the Son of Sirach". Pages 176–415 in *Apocrypha*. Old Testament 15 of Ancient Christian Commentary on Scripture. Edited by Thomas C. Oden. Downers Grove, Ill.: InterVarsity Press, 2010.

The Prophetic Literature

30. ISAIAH

Introduction

The book of Isaiah is *the* great prophetic book of the Old Testament and is rivaled only by the Psalms in its influence over subsequent Jewish and Christian practice and belief. Although not a "systematic theologian" in the later sense, to a certain extent Isaiah is to the Old Testament what the apostle Paul is to the New: the great, comprehensive theological mind who provides an overarching framework into which the insights and contributions of the other inspired authors can be fit.

With the sole exception of the Samaritans and the Sadducees (who accepted only the books of the Pentateuch as inspired), the book of Isaiah held unquestioned authority and was extremely influential in both Semitic- and Greek-speaking Judaism as well as in the early Church. The book itself is usually called simply by the name of its prophetic author: "Isaiah" (Hebrew *yeshîyahu*), meaning "The LORD saves" (Is 1:1; cf. Greek *Ēsaias*; Latin *Isaias*). Within the Jewish tradition, Isaiah was eventually chosen as the first book of what are known as the "latter prophets" (Hebrew *nevi'im 'aharim*), preceding the books of Jeremiah and Ezekiel as well as the Book of the Twelve (Hosea–Malachi). In the Greek Septuagint tradition (later preserved by early Christians), the canonical order is somewhat diverse. In some ancient manuscripts, the wisdom books are followed by the Book of the Twelve (Hosea–Malachi), which precede Isaiah and the other major prophets. In other ancient manuscripts of the Septuagint, however, the wisdom literature is followed by the book of Isaiah as the first of what came to be known as the "major prophets"—Isaiah, Jeremiah, Ezekiel, Daniel (in chronological order)—with "minor prophets" afterward. Saint Jerome, when translating the Latin Vulgate, followed the latter order, and Isaiah's position at the head of the major prophets became the canonical order now familiar to most Christians in the West.

Significantly, when the Dead Sea Scrolls were discovered in the mid-twentieth century, scholars learned that the book of Isaiah was one of the three most popular books in the collection. With fragments of twenty-one different copies discovered at Qumran, Isaiah was second only to the Psalms (thirty-six copies) and the book of Deuteronomy (thirty copies).[1] Indeed, the only complete, intact copy of a biblical book to be recovered among the Dead Sea Scrolls was a manuscript of Isaiah, the Great Isaiah Scroll (known by scholars as *1QIsaiah^a*).

---

[1] See Martin G. Abegg Jr., Peter Flint, and Eugene Ulrich, *The Dead Sea Scrolls Bible: The Oldest Known Bible Translated for the First Time into English* (San Francisco: HarperOne, 1999), 267.

Furthermore, Isaiah is the *most-quoted biblical book* in the nonbiblical Dead Sea Scrolls, and no less than six commentaries (*pesharim*) on the book were also found. This important historical fact shows not only that Isaiah was popular among the early Christians, but that first-century Jews themselves saw it as a prophecy of major importance.

The influence of Isaiah among the Dead Sea Scrolls is paralleled in the New Testament. Isaiah is second only to the Psalms as the *most-quoted biblical book* by the New Testament authors; furthermore, the quotations are often not merely important but *fundamental* for the Gospel message (for example, Is 40:3 in Mk 1:2–3; Is 42:1–4 in Mt 12:18–21; Is 6:9–10 in Mt 13:14–15). Thus, in the early Church, the book of Isaiah was often considered "the fifth Gospel". In the words of Saint Jerome:

> [Isaiah] *should be called an evangelist rather than a prophet*, because he describes all the mysteries of Christ and the church so clearly that one would think he is composing a history of what has already happened rather than prophesying what is to come.[2]

In short, it is virtually impossible to overestimate the significance of the book of Isaiah for Christian theology, especially when it comes to prophecy and fulfillment.

When we turn to the liturgical traditions of both Judaism and Christianity, Isaiah also plays a dominant role. In the synagogue, Isaiah is the prophet of choice read for the "second reading", known as the *haftarah*, a selection from the prophets read to accompany the Sabbath unit from the law (the *sederah*). In the Catholic liturgical tradition, the frequency with which Isaiah is read is second only to that of the Psalms among Old Testament books. In fact, in the contemporary Lectionary of the Roman rite, the book of Isaiah is actually read in the Lectionary more frequently than the Gospel of Mark! Following an ancient tradition, the Liturgy of the Hours reads the majority of Isaiah semicontinuously throughout Advent, where it is understood as a prophecy of both the First and Second Coming of the Messiah.

In short, although (as we will see) the interpretation and origins of the book of Isaiah are much disputed, no one disputes its power, influence, and enduring significance for both Judaism and Christianity ancient and modern.

Literary Structure of Isaiah

The book of Isaiah divides into two major parts: (1) Isaiah 1–39 and (2) Isaiah 40–66. Generally speaking, the first part of the book (Isaiah 1–39) seems addressed to Jerusalem and Judah in the second half of the eighth century B.C., when Assyria was the great oppressor and threat to its national existence. The second part of the book (Is 40–66) seems to be addressed to Jerusalem and Judah during or after the exile to Babylon (ca. 587–537 B.C.). Oracles of judgment

---

[2] Jerome, *Preface to Isaiah*, in Steven A. McKinion, *Isaiah 1–39*, Old Testament 10, Ancient Christian Commentary on Scripture, ed. Thomas C. Oden (Downers Grove, Ill.: InterVarsity Press, 2004), 3.

predominate in the first part, but oracles of consolation in the second. The two parts are intentionally joined by a section of sustained historical narrative regarding the prophet Isaiah and the reign of King Hezekiah (Is 36–39). After closing off the first part of the book by describing Hezekiah's triumphant resistance against Assyria (Is 36–38), the narrative then shifts focus to Hezekiah's ill-omened dealings with Babylon (Is 39), which foreshadow the focus on exile in Babylon in the second half of the book (Is 40–66). Keeping this in mind, a basic outline of the major components of Isaiah would look something like the following:

Outline of the Book of Isaiah

I. Zion Chastised but Victorious over Assyria (Is 1–39)
   A. Synopsis of the Ministry of Isaiah (1–12)
      1. Introduction: Judgment yet Hope for Jerusalem (1)
      2. Further Development of the Themes of Judgment and Hope (2–5)
      3. Isaiah's Call Vision and the Divine Purpose of His Ministry (6)
      4. Children Who Are "Signs" Pointing to a Coming Savior-King (7–11)
      5. Doxology to God for His Saving Power (12).
   B. God's Judgment of the Whole Earth (13–27)
      1. Oracles against Individual Gentile Nations (13–23)
      2. The Final Judgment of the Whole Earth: The "Apocalypse of Isaiah" (24–27)
   C. Oracles of Judgment and Consolation toward Israel under Assyrian Threat (28–35)
   D. Hezekiah: Type of the Coming King (36–39)
      1. Hezekiah and Assyria (36–38)
      2. Hezekiah and Babylon (39)

II. Zion Chastised yet Victorious over Babylon (Is 40–66)
   A. Redemption for Zion (40–55)
   B. Retribution and Restoration for Zion and the Nations (56–66)

The second part of Isaiah is less easy to subdivide. It is common to recognize a division between Isaiah 40–55 and Isaiah 56–66, because Isaiah 40–55 is almost exclusively comprised of oracles of consolation that seem to presume a Judean readership that is just about to return to their land after exile in Babylon, whereas Isaiah 56–66 at times seems addressed to a Judean community that has returned to Jerusalem but is already defecting from fidelity to the Lord. However, the evidence used to argue for a shift in perspective between Isaiah 55 and 56 is not very compelling, and there are many similarities in language, theology, and motifs that bind Isaiah 40–66 together.

Without being dogmatic, we will adopt the typical bipartite division of Isaiah 40–55 and 56–66, understanding the first unit to be predominantly focused on the redemption of Zion and the second to reflect an expanded focus on retribution and restoration for Zion and the nations. This is by no means an absolute distinction, because there are indications of salvation for the nations already in Isaiah 40–55 (for example, Is 42:1, 6; 49:6; 55:5). Nonetheless, the literary structure of the two sections show a different emphasis. For example, Isaiah 40–55 begins with a voice calling for the preparation of a highway for the new exodus, a return of God's people to their homeland that God himself will lead (Is 40:1–11), and ends with a vision of the people being led forth by God "in joy" and "peace" (Is 55:12–13). Isaiah 56–66, however, begins with a promise of the inclusion of *foreigners* into the covenant community of Israel (Is 56:1–8) and ends with a glorious vision of the homecoming of Israel *and the nations* (Is 66:18–23). Thus, in the shift between Isaiah 40–55 and 56–66, there appears to be a greater stress on the inclusion of the Gentiles in the eschatological community of God.

Overview of Isaiah

Isaiah and His Prophecies about Jerusalem (Isaiah 1–5)

The opening chapters of the book begin by introducing us to the prophetic figure to whom its oracles are attributed. The opening line not only gives the name and identity of the prophet, but also the time span of his ministry and the subjects of his vision:

> The vision of *Isaiah the son of Amoz*, which he saw concerning Judah and Jerusalem in the days of Uzziah, Jotham, Ahaz, and Hezekiah, kings of Judah. (Is 1:1)

With these words, we meet the mysterious figure of Isaiah, who, as far as we can tell, appears to have been a member of a leading family in Jerusalem (cf. Is 3:1–17, 24; 4:1; 8:2). According to this superscription, Isaiah apparently began his prophetic ministry when he was called by God around 742 B.C., in the year of Uzziah's death (Is 6:1–8), and continued prophesying for an extraordinarily long period of time, during the reigns of multiple kings in Jerusalem:

1. King Uzziah (ca. 783–742 B.C.)
2. King Jotham (ca. 742–735 B.C.)
3. King Ahaz (ca. 735–715 B.C.)
4. King Hezekiah (ca. 715–687 B.C.)

Although the last clearly datable oracles in the book take place around the time of the siege of Jerusalem by Sennacherib in the reign of Hezekiah (ca. 701 B.C.), the most ancient Jewish tradition we possess holds that, as a very old man, Isaiah was executed by Hezekiah's son, the wicked King Manasseh (ca. 668 B.C.):

> Isaiah, from Jerusalem, died under Manasseh by *being sawn in two*, and was buried underneath the Oak of Rogel.[3]

---

[3] *Lives of the Prophets*, in D.R. Hare, "Lives of the Prophets", *The Old Testament Pseudepigrapha*, vol. 2, ed. James H. Charlesworth, Anchor Bible Reference Library (New York: Doubleday, 1985), 385.

If this tradition is based on history, then Isaiah's prophetic ministry may have spanned over half a century.

In any case, according to the book of Isaiah, the subjects of Isaiah's prophetic "vision" are "Judah and Jerusalem" (Is 1:1). An analysis of the book reveals it is especially the latter, *the city of Jerusalem*—frequently referred to by the Davidic name of "Zion"—that dominates Isaiah's oracles. "Zion shall be redeemed by justice, and those in her who repent, by righteousness", says the prophet (Is 1:27). In this and many other places, "Zion" in Isaiah has an almost transcendent role. Zion is the city that embodies and symbolizes the entire kingdom of Judah and, at times, the entire twelve-tribe people of Israel. It is the type, symbol, and icon of the people of God, and the entire book in all its parts reflects a Zion-centric perspective.

The opening chapter of Isaiah is an oracle of judgment and consolation to Jerusalem (as representative of the whole kingdom) during a time of siege, perhaps during the Syro-Ephraimite War (ca. 735 B.C.) or the invasion by Sennacherib (701 B.C.). In this opening chapter, the prophet articulates many themes that will recur again and again throughout the book, even in the second part (Is 40–66):

Does Isaiah Condemn All Sacrificial Worship?

All throughout the book, Isaiah criticizes not only the worship of idols but also the vain worship of the Lord according to the rubrics of the Mosaic law (e.g., Is 1). Sometimes such oracles have been interpreted by Christians as a critique of the Old Covenant liturgy *per se*, or even as a critique of all liturgical worship. Such views fail to recognize that the basic reason for Isaiah's critique of the Mosaic cult as practiced by his contemporaries was the sin of *hypocrisy*.

Although they observed the external requirements of liturgical worship, the interior dispositions of the Israelites (their "hearts"; Is 29:13) did not correspond to the meaning of the rites, and they did not complement their liturgical acts with the practice of justice and mercy (that is, charity) toward their neighbors (Is 1:15–20). Thus, while not a critique of all liturgical worship, Isaiah's strident rebuke of the practice of the cult does expose the weakness of worship under the Old Covenant—namely, that the rites did not have the power to absolve or sanctify the worshippers (cf. Heb 10:1–11). While Isaiah does not describe how the cult will be transformed in the coming eschatological era, the prophet's criticisms of present liturgical practice (e.g., Is 66:1–4) do lead the reader to expect that some fundamental reform of the liturgy will accompany the establishment of the economy of the New Covenant, one that will actually transform the worshippers by the forgiveness of sin and the outpouring of God's own spirit.

---

1. *Judgment of Jerusalem*: Jerusalem and its kingdom are experiencing disaster as punishment for grave covenant infidelity (Is 1:2–11).

2. *The Problem of Hypocritical Worship*: The liturgical worship in Jerusalem has no efficacy, because the people disregard the moral law and commit great injustice (Is 1:12–17).

3. *Repentance, Restoration, and the Forgiveness of Sins*: Turning away from sin is still possible and will lead to forgiveness and restoration, so that Jerusalem's sins, "like scarlet", will become "white as snow" (Is 1:18–20).

4. *Zion as the Bride of YHWH*: The city of Jerusalem (Zion) is depicted as the bride of the Lord who has become a harlot because of her spiritual infidelities toward God. Nevertheless, in the future, she will be restored to bridal purity again (Is 1:21–26).

5. *Judgment of the Wicked*: Unlike those who repent, the wicked among the people will be destroyed in the imminent judgment, but a righteous, repentant remnant will be saved to experience a glorious restoration (Is 1:28–31).

> ### *The Word of the Lord in Isaiah 2:1–5*
>
> Isaiah 2:1–5 is an extremely influential oracle in salvation history and in the development of Judaism and Christianity. It is repeated virtually verbatim in Micah 4:1–3. A key phrase in this oracle states that "the word of the LORD [shall go forth] from Jerusalem. He shall judge between the nations" (Is 2:3b–4). The Hebrew grammar is ambiguous: the "he" that shall judge between the nations could be the Lord or, on the other hand, the word of the Lord that has gone forth from Jerusalem. This is an important text for the gradual revelation of the personhood of the word of God, and the development of Trinitarian doctrine.

In the course of these oracles regarding Jerusalem and the coming judgment and saving acts of God, Isaiah delivers two extremely significant oracles. First, he speaks of a future time when the city of Jerusalem will be restored, a New Law will come, and even the Gentile "nations" (Hebrew *goyim*) will be converted to the worship of the one true God of Israel:

> The word which Isaiah the son of Amoz
>   saw concerning Judah and Jerusalem.
> It shall come to pass in the latter days
>   that the mountain of the house of the LORD
> shall be established as the highest of the mountains,
>   and shall be raised above the hills;
> and all the nations shall flow to it,
>   and many peoples shall come, and say:
> "Come, let us go up to the mountain of the Lord,
>   to the house of the God of Jacob;
> that he may teach us his ways
>   and that we may walk in his paths."
> For out of Zion shall go forth the law,
>   and the word of the Lord from Jerusalem. (Is 2:1–3)

As anyone who has been to Jerusalem knows, it is hardly "the highest of the mountains of the earth." Instead, Isaiah is delivering what we might call an *eschatological* prophecy—a prophecy about the "latter" or "end" days—when Jerusalem will be not only restored but exalted to such glory as it has never known before. Second, and equally important—in the meantime, however, the prophet focuses on the sins of the people of God. He does so above all through the "Song" of YHWH's "Vineyard" (Is 5:1–7). In this prophetic "parable", Isaiah uses imagery strikingly similar to what the Song of Songs uses to depict YHWH's relationship with Jerusalem, Judah, and Israel as that of a husbandman to a vineyard. The "vineyard" of the Lord has borne no fruit, so he will remove its wall and let it return to a wild state.

In light of such a damning parable, it is perhaps no wonder that the subsequent oracles are focused on judgment for sin, in the form of six woes: against those who (1) "join house to house"—that is, wealthy landowners (Is 5:8–10); (2) those who rise early to get drunk—that is, party animals (Is 5:11–17); (3) those who practice falsehood—that is, liars (Is 5:18–19); (4) those who "call evil good and good evil"—that is, the corrupt and duplicitous (Is 5:20); (5) those who "are wise in their own eyes"—that is, the arrogant (Is 5:21); and (6) those who are bribable drunkards (Is 5:22–23). If these are the kinds of oracles Isaiah of Jerusalem was known for delivering, it is small wonder that he faced opposition and persecution from corrupt leaders!

Isaiah's Vision of the Seraphim and His Prophetic Call (Isaiah 6)

Although Isaiah's vision of the heavenly temple clearly seems to have been, chronologically speaking, the first divine revelation Isaiah received, which provided the impetus for the beginning of his prophetic ministry, nonetheless it is not placed first in the book. Isaiah is caught up to the heavenly temple in the year of King Uzziah's death, where he beholds God's glory and the ministry of the six-winged *seraphim*. He bemoans his sinfulness or "unclean lips", but a *seraph* purifies his lips with a coal from the heavenly altar. The prophet then volunteers to answer the divine call for a messenger: "Here am I! Send me!" His commission to preach is phrased as follows:

> And he said, "Go, and say to this people:
>   'Hear and hear, but do not understand;
> see and see, but do not perceive.'
> Make the heart of this people fat,
>   and their ears heavy,
>   and shut their eyes;
> lest they see with their eyes,
>   and hear with their ears,
> and understand with their hearts,
>   and turn and be healed." (Is 6:9–10)

This introduces the theme of Israel as blind and deaf, which will recur throughout the book, often in the second half (Is 40–66). But here the blindness and deafness are spiritual rather than physical. Isaiah's message will "fall on deaf ears". Nonetheless, he is commanded to continue to prophesy until the land is laid waste and abandoned, the population exiled, and only a decimated remnant left.

Children Who Are Signs of Future Salvation (Isaiah 7–12)

After Isaiah's call vision, the next several chapters are loosely united around the theme of God's gift of a child who is a sign of coming salvation. Given the fact that the first of these children is called Immanuel, this collection of oracles is sometimes referred to by scholars as "the book of Immanuel" (Is 7–12).

In the first oracle, the prophet offers the sign of the child "Immanuel" to the house of David (the royal family) and the people of Judah (Is 7:1–25). YHWH commands the prophet Isaiah to go to King Ahaz of Judah (who reigned ca. 735–715 B.C.) to reassure the king in his military struggle with Syria and the northern kingdom of Israel (here referred to as "Ephraim"). Isaiah asks Ahaz to choose a sign from the Lord; out of false humility, King Ahaz refuses, so Isaiah proposes a sign:

> And he said, "Hear then, O house of David! Is it too little for you to weary men, that you weary my God also? Therefore the Lord himself will give you a sign. Behold, a virgin [Hebrew *ha 'almah*] shall conceive and bear a son, and shall call his name Immanuel." (Is 7:13–14)

As we will see below, there has been a centuries-long debate over the exact identity of the mother of Immanuel and over whether or not the Hebrew term should be translated as "the virgin" (NAB) or "a young woman" (RSV) or "the young woman" (NABRE) (see below, "Theological Issues in Isaiah"). For now, what is abundantly clear is that Isaiah goes on to declare that before the child reaches the age of discretion, the Lord will bring the threat of Syria and Ephraim to an end through the intervention of the king of Assyria (Is 7:15–20). The northern kingdom of Israel will be depopulated, but the survivors will live in peace (Is 7:21–25).

In the second oracle, Isaiah describes another child who is a sign, this time his own son (Is 8:1–22). In this case, Isaiah himself goes to "the prophetess", who is apparently his wife, and she conceives and bears a son whom they name *Maher-shalal-hash-baz* (Hebrew for "The spoil speeds, the prey hastes") (Is 8:2–3). The symbolic meaning of his son's name also refers to the imminent plundering and spoilage of the northern kingdom of Israel and to the overthrow of the northern city of Samaria at the hands of the Assyrians. The oracle concludes with Isaiah commanding his disciples to preserve his testimony and teaching (Is 8:16) and to recognize that he (Isaiah) and his children are living "signs and portents" of God's imminent judgment on his people (Is 8:16–22).

In a third oracle, Isaiah delivers yet another forecast about a royal child who will be a sign of salvation for the entire nation (Is 9:1–8). In this instance, the child in question is explicitly identified as coming in "the latter time" and as an heir to the Davidic kingdom:

> *For to us a child is born,*
> > *to us a son is given;*
> *and the government will be upon his shoulder,*
> > *and his name will be called*
> *"Wonderful Counselor, Mighty God,*
> > *Everlasting Father, Prince of Peace."*
> Of the increase of his government and of peace
> > there will be no end,
> *upon the throne of David, and over his kingdom,*
> > to establish it, and to uphold it
> with justice and with righteousness
> > from this time forth and for evermore. (Is 9:6–7)

Anyone familiar with Handel's famous *Messiah* will recognize that we have here one of the best-known messianic prophecies in the entire Old Testament. According to Isaiah, this child who will be Davidic king in the "latter time" (Is 9:1) will bring happiness to all Israel by *reversing* the effects of the Assyrian exile mentioned earlier. Starting with the northern region near Galilee, the tribal territory of Zebulun and Naphtali (Is 9:1–2)—the first region devastated by the Assyrian onslaught (ca. 732–22 B.C.; cf. 2 Kings 15)—the future royal child will usher in a time of peace (Is 9:2–5). Perhaps most striking of all, the future child-king will be referred to by divine titles: "Wonderful Counselor, *Mighty God*, Everlasting Father, Prince of Peace" (Is 9:6). Although some English translations obscure the point (such as the NAB's infelicitous "God-hero"), the literal Hebrew expression is indeed "Mighty God" (Hebrew *'el gibbor*) (Is 9:6). Moreover, the title "Prince of Peace" identifies this child as a new Solomon (Hebrew *Shlomo*, "Peaceful One"), the first "Prince of Peace" of the Davidic kingdom. Finally, notice that—in stark contrast to the northern kingdom about to be decimated—the kingdom of this future Davidide will have no end but, rather, will be established "forever".

The fourth and final oracle of a child also predicts the coming of a royal son, who will arise from the fallen family of King David, whose father was "Jesse":

> There shall come forth a shoot from the stump of Jesse,
>   and a branch shall grow out of his roots.
> *And the Spirit of the* LORD *shall rest upon him*,
>   the spirit of wisdom and understanding,
>   the spirit of counsel and might,
>   the spirit of knowledge and the fear of the LORD. (Is 11:1–2)

Notice here that the future royal child will also display Solomonic characteristics such as wisdom (Is 11:2–3) and supernatural power (Is 11:4), yet he will be a child who rules in peace over all the earth (Is 11:6–16, esp. 11:10). Together these two oracles of the future Davidic child (Is 9:1–7 and 11:1–16) form bookends (an *inclusio*) around oracles of judgment against Israel, Judah, and Assyria (Is 9:8—10:34). God will use Assyria to punish northern Israel for its warmongering and social injustice (Is 9:8–21; 10:1–4), and Judah likewise (10:12), before turning on Assyria itself to judge its sins (10:5–11, 13–19). Nevertheless, out of all this catastrophe a small remnant of Israel will survive to experience God's compassion and restoration (Is 10:20–34).

The oracle of the "shoot" from "the stump of Jesse" (Is 11:1–16) is the longest and most detailed prophecy of the coming royal son and in many ways is *the* messianic prophecy *par excellence* in the book of Isaiah. It draws together eschatological motifs that will recur throughout the rest of the book, including the second half (Is 40–66). These may be neatly divided into three future hopes:

1. *New King and Kingdom* (Is 11:1–5): The prophet foresees a new son from the royal line who, like David (1 Sam 16), will be anointed with the Holy Spirit (Is 11:2), giving him the divine wisdom once possessed by Solomon (11:2–3; cf. Prov. 1:1–7).

2. *New Creation* (Is 11:6–9): The prophet foresees a restoration of creation. The "holy mountain" of God—that is, Mount Zion or Jerusalem—is described as a new Eden, with a return to the vegetarian peace that once reigned before the Fall (cf. Gen 1:29–30; Gen 9:3). The "little child" that shall "lead them" (Is 11:6b) may be the "shoot of Jesse" himself (11:1) and the "child"/"son" promised earlier (Is 9:6).

3. *New Exodus* (Is 11:10–16): The prophet predicts a recapitulation of the exodus from Egypt, with differences. This new exodus will be led, not by Moses, but by the "root of Jesse"—that is, the future Davidic king (Is 11:10). The old exodus brought Israel out from Egypt, but the new exodus will bring the Israelites back from all the places they have been dispersed throughout the world, especially by Assyria (Is 11:16). The old exodus had no role for the Gentile "nations" (Hebrew *goyim*), but in the new exodus, the "nations" (Gentiles) will be gathered to the Lord and the root of Jesse together with Israel (Is 11:10).

The tripartite eschatology of new kingdom, new creation, new exodus is a useful summary of the prophetic hopes for the "latter days" found throughout the book of Isaiah, and these themes will be developed even further in subsequent parts of the book, especially in the second half.

Therefore, Isaiah 11 can be understood as a *précis*, or summary, of Isaiah's positive vision for the end times, while Isaiah 12 forms a conclusion of the introductory unit of Isaiah. Read synthetically, the message of this introduction is that Jerusalem, Judah, and all Israel are facing God's judgment for covenant violations, primarily by means of the Assyrians. While the devastation will be severe, a righteous remnant of the nation will survive to see an heir of the house of David arise to help usher in a new era of peace and restoration for Israel and the nations, centered on Jerusalem/Mount Zion. In response to this ultimately positive vision of future salvation, the prophet composes a pair of *todah* psalms, calling on the inhabitants of Zion and of the whole earth to join together in praise of God (Is 12:1–2; 12:4–6).

God's Judgment of the Whole Earth (Isaiah 13–27)

In the next major section of Isaiah, the prophet shifts his attention away from the various oracles about the future child-king and toward a series of oracles focused on the coming judgment of (1) the Gentile nations (Is 13–23) and (2) the entire earth (Is 24–27).

First, in striking contrast to the Jerusalem and Judah-centered opening oracles of the book, in the first of these, Isaiah proceeds to deliver a series of oracles of judgment against all the major Gentile nations of the ancient Near East, denouncing the following peoples:

1. Babylon (Is 13:1—14:23)
2. Assyria (Is 14:24–27)
3. Philistia (Is 14:28–32)
4. Moab (Is 15:1—16:14)

5. Damascus (Is 17:1–14),
6. Ethiopia (Is 18:1–7; 20:1–6)
7. Egypt (Is 19:1—20:6)
8. Babylon again (21:1–10)
9. Edom (Is 21:11–12)
10. Arabia (Is 21:13–17)
11. The "Valley of Vision" and Jerusalem (Is 22:1–25)
12. Tyre (Is 23:1–18).

Notice here that the oracles against the nations *begin with Babylon*, which actually receives two oracles (Is 13, 21). This undermines the impression sometimes given that the first half of the book is focused *only* on Assyria (Is 1–39), while the second half is focused *only* on Babylon (Is 40–66). The reality is that Babylon is an important adversary throughout the book of Isaiah (for example, Is 13, 21, 38–39, 40–41, and so on). It is also important to note that interspersed among the prophecies of punishment against the nations are short oracles of hope for an eventual restoration of Zion and Israel.

Second, after this wide-ranging condemnation of so many of Israel's neighbors and enemies, the prophet then delivers a lengthy oracle in which YHWH is spoken of as laying waste to "the earth" (Is 24:1) in general and the mysterious "city of chaos" in particular (Is 24:10). The apparently cosmic scope of this judgment has led some contemporary scholars (somewhat anachronistically) to refer to this entire section as "the Isaiah Apocalypse" (Is 24–27). Although the exact object of the judgment here is unclear, what is very clear is that this time of judgment will result in punishment of the nations and exultation of Mount Zion and Jerusalem. Indeed, the prophet delivers a remarkable vision of an *eschatological banquet* set for all nations on Mount Zion, associated with removal of death from the natural order and the forgiveness of sins (Is 25:6–12). The prophet responds to this vision of justice and mercy of God with psalms of thanksgiving that praise God as if this divine intervention had already taken place (Is 25:1–5; 26:1–21). Finally, the entire unit concludes with an oracle (Is 27:2–13) that picks up the motif of Israel-as-vineyard last seen in Isaiah 5. But whereas the earlier oracle foresaw only judgment on the vineyard (Is 5:1–7), now the Lord promises it will flourish and "fill the whole world with fruit" (Is 27:6). Though Jerusalem and all Israel have been punished by many nations and by exile, yet in the days to come God will regather them from the Gentile nations among whom they have been scattered so that all will come to worship the Lord on his "holy mountain".

The Assyrian Crisis and Future Judgment and Salvation (Isaiah 28–35)

After the rather comprehensive description of God's judgment of the whole earth and the final consummation (Is 13–27), the book of Isaiah now returns to oracles that are focused much more on the immediate situation of Israel and Judah in the late eighth century B.C. (Is 28–35). These oracles describe a time when Israel is under threat of destruction from the Assyrian Empire, as in the opening chapters of the book (cf. Is 1–5).

At the heart of these oracles stands Isaiah's rebuke of the leaders of the northern kingdom "Ephraim" (Is 28:1–13) and also those of Jerusalem (Is 28:14–29) for the self-indulgent life-styles of prince, priest, and prophet, by which they leave the common people without moral or civil guidance. As a result of these sins, a siege of Jerusalem, the "city where David encamped", is coming, which will bring shame and disgrace to the leaders of the people, in particular the false prophets (Is 29:1–16). Nevertheless, in the wake of judgment, a time of hope and restoration will also come, when "the deaf shall hear" and the "blind shall see", when the meek and poor shall rejoice (Is 29:18–19), when the evildoers shall be cut off, and when Jacob shall suddenly discover he has many children (Is 29:18–23).

Once again, in these oracles, the political situation of the eighth century is front and center: the prophet delivers lengthy oracles that have as their primary thrust a warning to the people of Jerusalem that they must rely on the Lord rather than on the power of Egypt to defend them against the onslaught of the Assyrian Empire (Is 30:1–33; 31:1–9). In the midst of these oracles of judgment, Isaiah also speaks words of promise, such as the oracle about the coming of the "Teacher" (Hebrew *mōreh*) who, although presently hidden, will one day reveal himself:

> Yes, O people in Zion who dwell at Jerusalem; you shall weep no more. He will surely be gracious to you at the sound of your cry; when he hears it, he will answer you. And though the Lord give you the bread of adversity and the water of affliction, yet your Teacher will not hide himself any more, but your eyes shall see your Teacher. (Is 30:19–20)

In the wake of the coming of this mysterious Teacher, idolatry will be abandoned and even nature itself will be renewed (Is 30:22–26). Indeed, God's victory will be followed by the restoration of a righteous king and royal administration for Jerusalem (Is 32:1–8), in contrast to the wicked leadership denounced earlier (Is 28). In the meantime, however, the "wealthy lady" of the capital city should be warned, because judgment on Judah will fall within a year (Is 32:9–15), leading to a desolation that will last until the outpouring of God's Spirit ushers in an age of peace and tranquility (Is 32:15–20).

The last three chapters of this section are given over to a series of oracles about the restoration and glory of Zion in the eschatological age (Is 33–35). Significantly, these visions contain both forecasts of the divine judgment of wicked nations (such as Edom) and prophecies of restoration that utilize the imagery of the future *exodus* and the renewal of *creation* that will take place when God himself finally comes:

> "Behold, your God
>   will come with vengeance,
> with the recompense of God.
>   He will come and save you."
> Then the eyes of the blind shall be opened,
>   and the ears of the deaf unstopped;

then shall the lame man leap like a deer,
> and the tongue of the mute sing for joy.
For waters shall break forth in the wilderness,
> and streams in the desert;
the burning sand shall become a pool,
> and the thirsty ground springs of water;
the haunt of jackals shall become a swamp,
> the grass shall become reeds and rushes.

And a highway shall be there,
> and it shall be called the Holy Way. (Is 35:4–8)

Once again, the book of Isaiah moves readily from the particular (the Assyrian crisis) to the universal (the final restoration of the people of God and the cosmos) in what appear to be eschatological visions of the future age of salvation.

The Reign of Hezekiah and the Coming Exile in Babylon (Isaiah 36–39)

The first half of Isaiah concludes with historical accounts about King Hezekiah for the following reasons: (1) Hezekiah may have been seen as the immediate historical fulfillment of the prophecies of a righteous son of David from earlier in the book (cf. Is 7:14–16; 9:1–7; 11:1–5; 16:5; 32:1). (2) During Hezekiah's reign, Assyria was beaten back and never again posed a threat to Judah, in fulfillment of various earlier oracles (Is 10:5–19; 30:27–33). (3) Hezekiah's reign also marked the transition from *Assyria* to *Babylon* as the major world power and threat against the kingdom of Judah, forming a segue between the Assyrian focus of the first half of Isaiah and the Babylonian focus of the second half of the book.

Source: commons.wikimedia.org

The Sennacherib Prism gives the Assyrian account of the events of Isaiah 36–37 and is kept in the Museum of the Oriental Institute of the University of Chicago

In this portion of Isaiah, there are three narratives concerning Hezekiah's reign: (1) the account of his successful resistance to the invasion of Sennacherib, king of Assyria (Is 36–37); (2) Hezekiah's recovery from a life-threatening illness (Is 38); and (3) his ill-considered revelation of his royal wealth to the envoys of Babylon, which eventually leads to the invasion of Judah by Babylon (Is 39). In each of these narratives, the prophet Isaiah plays a major role by delivering an oracle that is fulfilled, resolving the narrative tension. Two aspects of this series of narratives stand out as particularly significant.

First, in this section (Is 36–37), we find virtually the same account as in the historical books concerning the invasion of Judah by Sennacherib, king of Assyria (see 2 Kings 18:13—19:37 and 2 Chron

---

Sennacherib's Siege of Jerusalem

There is some controversy over the actual course of historical events during Sennacherib's siege of Jerusalem in 701 B.C. Some conclude that the account of Hezekiah's submission in 2 Kings 18:13–16 contradicts the account of Hezekiah's resistance in 2 Kings 18:17–37 and its parallels in Isaiah and Chronicles. Sennacherib's own account of his Judean campaign is extant: he claims to have shut up Hezekiah in Jerusalem like a bird in a cage and to have exacted a tribute much larger than the one listed in Scripture (see 2 Kings 18:14). Equally significant, he does not mention the mass death of his soldiers recorded in the Old Testament (Is 37:36 and parallels).

When allowance is made for exaggeration and bias in Sennacherib's records, a coherent account of the sequence of events can be reconstructed from the biblical and extra-biblical data. After the costly defeat of Lachish, Hezekiah offered to pay tribute to Sennacherib in return for his withdrawal. We may surmise from Hezekiah's subsequent desperation—he even had the gold stripped off the doors of the Temple—that Sennacherib demanded a greater tribute than Hezekiah could provide. Dissatisfied with the sum Hezekiah came up with, Sennacherib sent his army to Jerusalem to demand total surrender of the Judean capital. Hezekiah then made his famous prayer and penance, Isaiah delivered an oracle of salvation, and a plague—probably some form of epidemic—struck the Assyrian army, leading to its withdrawal and return to Assyria.

32:1–26). After the epic siege of Lachish, the most heavily fortified city of the kingdom, the Assyrian king sends his high military command to Jerusalem to demand the surrender of Hezekiah and his capital. Speaking in the language of the common people, the Assyrian general (the *rabshakeh*) mocks the God of Judah, intimidating and demoralizing the populace (Is 36:1–22). Hezekiah, hearing the report, responds with heartfelt prayer, fasting, and penance (Is 37:1–20). The prophet Isaiah delivers an oracle of salvation, that Zion shall not be conquered, a remnant of Israel shall emerge from the city, and the king of Assyria shall return to his own land (Is 37:21–35). And so it happens: an angel of the Lord strikes the army of Assyria with a plague, and the king and his surviving soldiers break the siege and return to Nineveh, where the king is assassinated (Is 37:36; cf. 10:16).

Second, the sacred author recounts that, after Hezekiah's brush with death, miraculous recovery from illness, and his striking *todah* psalm of thanksgiving (Is 38:1–22), envoys from Babylon arrive, and Hezekiah—perhaps carried away with pride—shows them the full extent of his power and wealth (Is 39:1–5). In response to this foolish act, Isaiah the eighth-century prophet declares that all the wealth Hezekiah displayed, and his own heirs and descendants, will one day be carried off to Babylon (Is 39:5–7). Thus ends the first part of the book of Isaiah on the ominous note of an oracle no longer focused on the Assyrian threat of the eighth century B.C. but, rather, on the eventual overthrow of Judah by *Babylon*—something that would take place some 150 years later, in the sixth century B.C.—thus forming a perfect transition into the focus of the next chapters of the book.

The One God, the New Exodus, and the Suffering Servant (Isaiah 40–55)

In the first half of Isaiah, oracles of judgment predominate, although the mood is periodically lifted by glimpses of what was to come "in the latter days" (Is 2:2) when Mount Zion would be exalted (Is 2:1–5) and a righteous son of David would reign once more (Is 9:1–7; 11:1–16). In the second half of the book (Is 40–66), oracles of hope and consolation predominate. Since antiquity, this portion of Isaiah seems to have been interpreted as one long description of the glorious age to come—the age when God will do "new things" for Zion (Is 42:9; 43:19; 48:6)—and of "what is to come hereafter" (Is 41:23). Because these chapters of Isaiah demonstrate perhaps a greater continuity of theme and literary idiom than any other major section of the book, its contents can be analyzed according to three major recurrent themes: (1) the one God and the futility of idol worship; (2) the hope for the new exodus; and (3) the songs of the "Suffering Servant" of the Lord.

1. *Monotheism and the Sin of Idolatry*: Perhaps more than any other portion of the Old Testament, the second half of the book of Isaiah proclaims not only *monolatry* (the worship of one God) but also a triumphant *monotheism* (the existence of only one true God). For example, the book emphasizes the utter incomparability of YHWH, who has made the world and who is taught by no one (Is 40:12—41:7). For this reason, he gives strength to those who trust in him and who refuse to worship idols—which practice is absurd, since they are "all a delusion", mere "molten images" that are "empty wind" (Is 41:29). Indeed, God's ability and power to bring about all these good promises is proven by the fact that he long ago foretold events presently being fulfilled, something the idols of the nations cannot and have not done, as is made clear in what is perhaps the most explicitly monotheistic text in the Hebrew Scriptures:

> Thus says the LORD, the King of Israel
> and his Redeemer, the LORD of hosts:
> *"I am the first and I am the last;*
> *besides me there is no god.*
> Who is like me? Let him proclaim it,
> let him declare and set it forth before me.
> *Who has announced from of old the things to come?*
> Let them tell us what is yet to be.
> Fear not, nor be afraid;
> have I not told you from of old and declared it?
> And you are my witnesses!
> *Is there a God besides me?*
> *There is no Rock; I know not any."* (Is 44:6–8)

Indeed, in contrast to the glory of God, who predicted the things now being fulfilled, the idols of the nations are nothing but worthless artifacts made by a craftsman, blind and deaf, and those who worship them become like them (Is 44:9–20). In light of the emptiness and futility of idol worship, the Lord calls all the idolaters of the nations to abandon their worthless gods that cannot save and acknowledge himself as the one true God who can predict the future before it happens (Is 45:20–25). In particular, the idols of Babylon cannot save them (Is 46:1–3), and the remnant of Israel should recognize the fact and return to their

God from any idolatry into which they may have fallen, now that the Lord has
acted to fulfill his word spoken long ago (Is 46:3–13).

2. *The New Exodus and Good News for Zion*: The second major theme for
this part of the book of Isaiah is the repeatedly stated hope for a new exodus,
which will consist of the ingathering of the scattered exiles of Israel and the
renewal of the nuptial covenant between YHWH the Bridegroom and Zion
the Bride—a covenant that had been forged during the first exodus (cf. Hos
1–2). For example, the second part of Isaiah begins with a proclamation of
"comfort" to "Jerusalem" because its sins are forgiven (Is 40:1–2). In this
opening oracle, an unidentified voice cries out to prepare the "highway" in
the wilderness, for God will gather his people to the land, thus echoing the
exodus from Egypt (Is 40:3–11). Along similar lines, the prophet elsewhere
promises "water" to the thirsty, drawing on imagery of the journey to Mount
Sinai, when water was provided in the desert for Israel (Is 41:17–20; cf. Ex
17; Num 21). In one of the longest and most developed descriptions of the
new exodus in the book (Is 42:21—43:28), the prophet declares that God will
gather his scattered children and will recapitulate some of the miracles of the
first exodus: creating dry ground through the waters (Is 43:16), overwhelming
the armies of the foes (Is 43:17), and providing water in the desert (Is 43:20).
In this case, however, the exodus will be, not from Egypt to the Promised
Land, but from Babylon to Mount Zion, as the prophet makes clear when
he states:

> Go forth from Babylon, flee from Chaldea,
>   declare this with a shout of joy, proclaim it,
> send it forth to the end of the earth;
>   say, "The LORD has redeemed his servant Jacob!"
> They thirsted not when he led them through the deserts;
>   he made water flow for them from the rock;
>   he cleft the rock and the water gushed out. (Is 48:20–21)

These are the "new things" that God is declaring through the prophet (Is 48:6): a
new exodus from death to life, in which God's children not only will be set free
from captivity in Babylon but will journey in hope to a restored city of "Zion",
who—though she appears to have been "divorced" or "put away" by YHWH
her Bridegroom (Is 49:14—50:3)—will in fact be "comforted" and renewed like
the garden of "Eden" when she hears the "good news" of "the return of the
LORD to Zion" (Is 51:1—52:12). As in the days of the exodus, the Lord will bind
himself to his people by means of a marriage covenant, so that Jerusalem will
realize that her "Maker" is her "husband" (Is 54:1–17) and that this God, the
one God, will make with her "an everlasting covenant", rooted in his "steadfast,
merciful love for David" (Is 55:1–13). In stark contrast to these powerful visions
of hope for Zion, the "virgin daughter of Babylon" is the one who will now
experience desolation (Is 47:1–15).

3. *The Servant Songs*: The third and final aspect of this portion of Isaiah that
ties the unit together is perhaps the most famous (and controversial) aspect of
the book as a whole: the various oracles about the mysterious figure of the

"servant" (Hebrew *'ebed*) of the Lord. In 1892, the German scholar Bernard Duhm provided the classic analysis of these so-called "Servant Songs" in his Isaiah commentary, in which he counted just four songs: Isaiah 42:1–4; 49:1–6; 50:4–9; and 52:13—53:12. Since Duhm, there has been scholarly discussion about the parameters of the Servant Songs (where they begin and end) and whether other similar passages in the second half of Isaiah ought also to be considered "Servant Songs", especially Isaiah 61:1–3, but sometimes others as well. In our analysis, three other passages (Is 41:8–16; 44:1–5; and 44:21–28) have so many literary features in common with the traditional four Servant Songs that there are good reasons to speak of a total of seven "Servant Songs" in the book, whose contents can be summarized as follows:

The "Servant Songs" in Isaiah 40–55

1. *Israel as God's Servant (Is 41:8–16)*: In this song, Israel, also called Jacob, is identified as God's servant. Although Israel is oppressed by Gentile nations at the present, God promises to vindicate his servant against his enemies in the future.

2. *A Covenant to the People and a Light to the Nations (Is 42:1–9)*: In this second song, the "servant" is not just a personification but an individual who has a mission to "the people" (that is, the nation of Israel) and the Gentile nations. The servant is anointed with the Spirit of God as a royal figure, establishes a "law" (Hebrew *torah*), and shows mercy to the poor and vulnerable. Remarkably, the servant himself is described as "a covenant" to both Israel and the Gentiles "to open the eyes that are blind, to bring out the prisoners" (Is 42:6). The language of being "given as a covenant to the people" is unusual, difficult to translate and to understand: How can a person *become* a covenant?

3. *The Outpouring of God's Spirit (Is 44:1–5)*: In the third servant song, the Lord once again identifies the servant as "Israel" and "Jacob" and promises to pour out "water on the thirsty land"—an image for pouring out "my Spirit upon your descendants, and my blessing on your offspring".

4. *Cyrus Sent to Restore God's Servant Israel (Is 44:21–28)*: In the fourth servant song, the "servant", who is identified as "Israel", is assured of forgiveness of sins, redemption from exile, and the restoration of the city of "Jerusalem" and even its "temple". Strikingly, this fulfillment will be brought about by "Cyrus", the king of Persia, whom the Lord identifies as his "shepherd" (Is 44:28).

5. *The Mission of the Servant to Israel and the Nations (Is 49:1–13)*: In the fifth servant song, for the first time, the "servant" himself speaks, declaring that his mission is to "gather Israel to him" and to spread salvation to all the "nations", the "end of the earth" (Is 49:5–6). Although "deeply despised, abhorred by the nations", the servant will ultimately receive the homage of the kings of the earth, becoming a "covenant to the people" by leading them in a new exodus (Is 49:7–8).

6. *The Persecution and Vindication of the Servant (Is 50:4–11)*: In the sixth servant song, the servant again speaks in the first person, declaring that he has been docile to the Lord's commission, even though it involved giving his "back" to those who "struck" him and his "cheeks" to those who "pulled out the beard", not hiding his face from "shame and spitting" (Is 50:6). Yet the servant has not been

overcome by his persecutors, because the Lord stands near to vindicate him, and ultimately he will prevail over his adversaries.

7. *The Suffering and Death of the Servant for Many (Is 52:13—53:12)*: The seventh servant song is the longest and most enigmatic of them all. It describes the rejection of the servant as without physical beauty, sorrowful, despised by others, and regarded as one punished by God (Is 53:1–4). It also makes clear that the servant is an individual as distinct from the nation, since he is wounded for their "transgressions" and the "iniquity" of the people is laid upon him, while they have gone astray "like sheep" (Is 53:6). Indeed, like a "lamb that is led to the slaughter", the servant is killed and laid in the grave with the wicked (Is 53:7–9). All this is the will of God. Nevertheless, after the servant's self-offering, the Lord will restore his prosperity, and his death will cause "many" to become righteous, because he bore their iniquity (Is 53:10–12).

We will take up the debate over the precise identity of the servant below (see "Theological Issues in Isaiah"); for now, the main point is that in this second part of the book (Is 40–55), God's plan of redemption for Israel and Zion will be carried out in a particular way by the servant of the Lord, who embodies Israel yet has a mission to restore Israel and call the nations to the Lord as well.

The New Temple, the New Jerusalem, and a New Creation (Isaiah 56–66)

While the second half of Isaiah exhibits a large amount of literary and thematic unity, there are some differences between Isaiah 40–55 and Isaiah 56–66. For example, whereas in Isaiah 40–55 the message of comfort and redemption for Zion is more or less unqualified, in Isaiah 56–66 it becomes clear that not all of God's people will share in the promised redemption. The people of God, represented by Zion, will experience a sifting: out of them will be separated a group called "my servants", who have been faithful to the Lord and will experience his salvation. The rest will experience judgment along with the Gentiles who have rejected God. On the other hand, there will be a division among the Gentiles as well, and those who seek the Lord and keep his covenant will experience his blessing along with the faithful of his people, his "servants". With such distinctions in mind, the final oracles in the book of Isaiah can also be analyzed according to three basic themes: (1) the new Temple, (2) the new Jerusalem, and (3) the hope for a new creation.

1. *The New Temple*: Given the central significance of the Temple for ancient Israelite practice and belief, it is perhaps unsurprising that the book of Isaiah climaxes with a glorious vision of the restoration of the Temple. What is surprising, however, is the fact that the prophet envisions the coming of a future Temple in which even "foreigners" (= Gentiles) and "eunuchs" (that is, childless men who are ritually unable to act as priests; cf. Deut 23:1–2) will be able not only to enter the covenant if they are willing to keep its conditions, but even to "minister" to him by performing priestly or quasi-priestly services in the sanctuary (Is 56:1–8). Indeed, the theme of Gentiles coming to worship at the holy mountain of God will recur at the very end of the book, which

contains the stunning vision of a kind of "new priesthood", in which "some" of the Gentiles will even be taken by God "for priests and for Levites" (Is 66:21)! Such striking forecasts of the future sanctuary go hand in hand with the fact that in this portion of Isaiah, the prophet enacts a comprehensive indictment of the sins of the people, both the corrupt leaders and the populace, who do not observe the Sabbath and who practice idolatry (Is 56:9—59:21). Indeed, later on in this section, in the tradition of the psalms, the prophet takes up a lengthy lament over the sinfulness of the people and over God's apparent powerlessness to act as he did in the past, at the time of Moses and the exodus from Egypt (Is 63–64), to which the Lord responds by declaring that much of Israel has rejected him, though a small remnant of his "servants" will be saved (Is 65:1–16).

2. *The New Jerusalem*: Even more central to the final chapters of the book is the hope not only for a new Temple but for a new Jerusalem: the glorious restoration of the city of Zion. In this section, Zion is once again described as the place to which both Israel and the Gentiles will be gathered, offering sacrifice together on God's "altar" (Is 60:1–22). Significantly, we discover at this point what might be called "the Eighth Servant Song"—an oracle in which an individual speaks who is "anointed" (Hebrew *mashah*) with "the Spirit of the LORD" in order to preach "good tidings" (or "good news") to the captives and commissioned to proclaim "the year of the LORD's favor"—that is, the Jubilee Year, involving the release of prisoners and comfort to those who mourn in Zion (Is 61:1–4; cf. Lev 25:8–10). The servant reiterates and augments earlier promises to Zion: it shall be rebuilt, foreigners shall voluntarily serve it, its citizens will eat the wealth of the nations and enjoy a priestly status, and the voice of Zion responds: "I will greatly rejoice in the LORD, my soul shall exult in my God", it says, because the Lord has clothed it in nuptial garments of salvation and righteousness (Is 61:10–11). What we see here, once again, is the image of the *nuptial restoration* of Zion—that is, the renewal of the everlasting marriage covenant between God and his people. This bridal restoration is powerfully depicted in the fact that Zion is personified once more as a young woman and bride, a bride newly taken by her husband, the Lord, and given a "new name":

> For Zion's sake I will not be silent,
>   for Jerusalem's sake I will not keep still,
> Until her vindication shines forth like the dawn
>   and her salvation like a burning torch.
> Nations shall behold your vindication,
>   and all kings your glory;
> You shall be called by a new name
>   bestowed by the mouth of the LORD.
> You shall be a glorious crown in the hand of the LORD,
>   a royal diadem in the hand of your God.
> *No more shall you be called "Forsaken,"*
>   *nor your land called "Desolate,"*
> *But you shall be called "My Delight is in her,"*
>   *and your land "Espoused."*

> For the LORD delights in you,
>   and your land shall be espoused.
> *For as a young man marries a virgin,*
>   *your Builder shall marry you;*
> And as *a bridegroom* rejoices in his bride
>   so shall *your God* rejoice in you. (Is 62:1–5 NABRE)

This is a striking vision of the age of salvation. Notice here that the city being described truly is a "new" Jerusalem, since it is given a new name: it will now be known as "Married" (Hebrew *Beulah*) land, the place of the nuptial covenant between God and his people. In fact, in a vision very similar to that quoted above, the prophet once more foresees Zion suddenly discovering its numerous sons, born almost in a moment: at that time, all who love it shall rejoice, nursing at its "breasts", while the prosperity and wealth of the nations flows to it (Is 66:7–13).

3. *The New Creation*: Last, but certainly not least, are the prophet's oracles of a new creation. These oracles constitute the climactic ending of the book of Isaiah, showing once more that its vision of salvation is not merely national, but universal and even cosmic. In these final oracles, the Lord announces the creation of "new heavens and new earth", especially a re-created Jerusalem, in which the curses of the Fall described in Genesis are undone and creation restored to what looks very much like a new Eden (Is 65:17–25). To be sure, there will be false worshippers upon whom judgment shall fall (Is 66:1–6), but the bulk of what the prophet depicts are oracles of salvation, announcing the final coming of the Lord to Zion, the ingathering of both Israel and the Gentiles to the renewed city, and the creation of "the new heavens and the new earth" (Is 66:6–24). Within this influx of the nations to the Lord on his holy mountain will be found survivors of the people of Israel. From among them, or perhaps from among the nations as well, the Lord will select new priests and Levites. In the new heavens and new earth that the Lord shall create, all flesh shall worship before him, while those who rebel against him will be consigned to eternal fire, where, in what is perhaps the starkest vision in the Old Testament of what would later be called "hell", the prophet ends by pronouncing that "their worm shall not die, their fire shall not be quenched" (Is 66:24).

Historical Issues in Isaiah

Aside from issues raised by the various historical narratives (for example, Is 7–8 and 36–39), most questions of a historical nature concerning the book of Isaiah hang on the issue of the date and authorship of the book or its various sections. Indeed, the amount of scholarly discussion devoted to the question of the origins of the book in the last two centuries is truly remarkable and is surpassed only by the attention paid to the origins of the Pentateuch.[4] In what follows, we will give a brief historical overview of the development of views about the origin of the book of Isaiah and its various parts.

---

[4] See Jacob Stromberg, *An Introduction to the Study of Isaiah* (London: T&T Clark, 2011).

The Origins of Isaiah in Scripture and Tradition

The most ancient testimony we have regarding the origins of the book of Isaiah comes to us from the Second Temple period, in the books of Chronicles and Sirach. In the books of Chronicles, the author tells that that "the rest of the acts of Hezekiah, and his good deeds, behold, they are written in *the vision of Isaiah the prophet the son of Amoz*, in the Book of the Kings of Judah and Israel" (2 Chron 32:32; cf. Is 1:1). The former statement seems to be a clear reference to the historical narratives about Hezekiah (Is 36–39), giving us evidence that the first part of the book existed and was attributed to the prophet Isaiah by at least the time of the Chronicler (ca. 400 B.C.). Perhaps even more significantly, in the book of Sirach, toward the end of the book in the catalogue of "famous men" of salvation history, Ben Sira has this to say about Isaiah the prophet:

> For Hezekiah did what was pleasing to the Lord,
>   and he held strongly to the ways of David his father,
> which *Isaiah the prophet* commanded,
>   who was great and faithful in his vision.
> In his days the sun went backward,
>   and he lengthened the life of the king.
> *By the spirit of might he saw the last things,*
>   *and comforted those who mourned in Zion.*
> *He revealed what was to occur to the end of time,*
>   *and the hidden things before they came to pass.* (Sir 48:22–25)

The reason this passage from Sirach is significant is because he clearly attributes both the first part of the book of Isaiah and the second part of the book to the prophet who lived at the time of Hezekiah (compare Is 38–39). When he says, for example, that Isaiah "comforted those who mourned in Zion" (Sir 48:24), this is clearly a reference to Isaiah 40 ("Comfort, comfort, my people"). Likewise, when he says that Isaiah revealed what would happen at "the end of time" (Sir 48:25), this is an obvious reference to Isaiah 64–66 and the coming of the new heavens and new earth and the final judgment. Indeed, Sirach even seems to recognize that Isaiah is remarkable in that he prophesies *far into the future* about "hidden things before they came to pass" (Sir 48:25, quoting Is 42:9). Hence, our most ancient scriptural testimony not only mentions the prophet Isaiah but attributes all three parts of the book to the eighth-century prophet.

Along similar lines, the text of the New Testament attributes all of the various portions of the book indiscriminately to the prophet Isaiah. Consider, for example, the following list of citations from the various parts of Isaiah:

Isaiah 1–39
    Is 6:10   attributed to Isaiah by Jesus (Mt 13:14–15)
                attributed to Isaiah by John (Jn 12:39–41)

Isaiah 40–54
    Is 40:3   attributed to Isaiah by Matthew (Mt 3:3)
                attributed to Isaiah by John (Jn 1:23)

Is 42:1   attributed to Isaiah by Matthew (Mt 12:17)
Is 53:1   attributed to Isaiah by Paul (Rom 10:16)
             attributed to Isaiah by John (Jn 12:38)
Is 53:4   attributed to Isaiah by Matthew (Mt 8:17)
Is 53:7–8   attributed to Isaiah by Luke (Acts 8:28)

Isaiah 55–66
Is 61:1   attributed to Isaiah by Luke (Lk 4:17; indirect)
Is 65:1–2   attributed to Isaiah by Paul (Rom 10:20–21)

More examples could be given; but these should suffice to demonstrate that in the New Testament as in the Old, the entirety of the book of Isaiah is attributed to the prophet Isaiah.

After the biblical period, this same trend continues in the ancient Jewish and Christian tradition. Particularly noteworthy in this regard is the evidence from Josephus, the first-century Jewish historian, who not only recognizes that the second part of Isaiah contains references to events that transpired more than a century after his lifetime, but actually posits that the reason King Cyrus of Persia allowed the Jews to return from exile was his reading of the oracles of Isaiah. In the words of Josephus:

> Thus says King Cyrus: "Since the Most High God has appointed me king of the habitable world, I am persuaded that He is the god whom the Israelite nation worships, for He foretold my name through the prophets and that I should build His temple in Jerusalem in the land of Judaea." *These things Cyrus knew from reading the book of prophecy which Isaiah had left behind two hundred and ten years earlier.* For this prophet had said that God told him in secret, "It is my will that Cyrus, whom I shall have appointed king of many great nations, shall send my people to their own land and build my temple." Isaiah prophesied these things one hundred and forty years before the temple was demolished. *And so, when Cyrus read them, he wondered at the divine power and was seized by a strong desire and ambition to do what had been written.*[5]

The historical significance of Josephus' witness is hard to overestimate, for it shows that the question of how Isaiah the son of Amos (eighth century B.C.) could refer to King Cyrus of Persia (sixth century B.C.) *by name* centuries before his time was not something "discovered" by modern exegetes but was well known by the ancients themselves. Moreover, it provides an explanation for why the Persian king would not only release the Jews from exile but provide funds for the rebuilding of their capital and their temple: he was moved to do so not only by some interior inspiration, but by the oracles of Isaiah himself. As Josephus makes clear, despite the enormous time-gap between Isaiah and Cyrus, for most of Jewish and Christian history, the view that prevailed was that the book was a unified composition, the composition of Isaiah, the son of Amoz, who had visions of events that would only take place far into the future.

---

[5] Josephus, *Antiquities* 11.3–6; in Josephus, *Jewish Antiquities: Books 9–11*, vol. 4, trans. Ralph Marcus, Loeb Classical Library 326 (Cambridge, Mass.: Harvard University Press, 1937), 315–16.

Modern Arguments for Multiple Authorship: First, Second, Third Isaiah

In the modern period, however, scholars began to question the traditional view of Isaianic authorship and origins of the book in all its parts. Since the German biblical scholar Bernhard Duhm published his influential commentary on Isaiah in 1892, contemporary scholarship has widely come to accept the theory (in various forms) of *multiple authorship* of the book of Isaiah.

According to this point of view, there is a major shift in perspective from the first part of the book, which scholars came to refer to as "First Isaiah" (Is 1–39), and the second part of the book, which came to be known as "Second Isaiah" (Is 40–66). Whereas most of First Isaiah presumes the Judeans are *still in their land*, being pressured by the Assyrian threat (for example, Is 7), Second Isaiah seems to presume that the Judeans are *already in exile* in Babylon, but presently being released by Cyrus to return to their homeland (for example, Is 44–45). Therefore, while "First Isaiah", or at least much of it, could be linked with Isaiah of Jerusalem (the eighth-century prophet), "Second Isaiah" must have been written by an unknown but later prophet figure (end of the sixth century B.C.).

After this distinction became popular in scholarship, a further distinction was hypothesized within "Second Isaiah" itself. Scholars theorized that the perspective of the book shifted yet again, with Isaiah 40–55 seeming to reflect the *optimism of the initial return to Jerusalem* under Cyrus (late sixth century B.C.), whereas Isaiah 56–66 seemed to reflect the *trials and difficulties* that developed in postexilic Judah (late sixth to early fifth century B.C.). As a result, scholars began to speak of a further distinction between "Second Isaiah" (or "Deutero-Isaiah"; chaps. 40–55) and "Third Isaiah" (or "Trito-Isaiah"; chaps. 56–66). Hence, the results of the theory of multiple-Isaianic authorship can be summarized as follows:

1. *First Isaiah* (Is 1–39): Isaiah the eighth-century prophet (preexilic period)
2. *Second Isaiah* (Is 40–55): anonymous prophet (exilic period)
3. *Third Isaiah* (Is 56–66): anonymous prophet (postexilic period)

In support of this basic theory of multiple authors for First, Second, and Third Isaiah, scholars have marshaled several major arguments that have convinced the majority of contemporary scholars:

First, as noted above, there is a shift in emphasis from the threat of the Assyrian Empire in First Isaiah (for example, Is 7–11) to the evils of Babylon in Second Isaiah (for example, Is 40–41, 47). Indeed, this part contains oracles in which the exile of the Judeans to Babylon is described as something *already having taken place* and now coming to an end:

> *Go forth from Babylon, flee from Chaldea,*
>   declare this with a shout of joy, proclaim it,
>   send it forth to the end of the earth;
>   say, "The LORD has redeemed his servant Jacob!" (Is 48:20)

Second, scholars note a shift in tone from the focus on judgment in First Isaiah (for example, Is 1–2) to a focus on restoration and return in Second and Third

Isaiah (Is 40–41, 64–66). Third, the second part of Isaiah contains *an explicit reference* to King Cyrus of Persia (reigned 559–530 B.C.):

> ["The LORD] says of Cyrus, 'He is my shepherd,
>   and he shall fulfil all my purpose';
> saying of Jerusalem, 'She shall be built,'
>   and of the temple, 'Your foundation shall be laid.' "

> Thus says the LORD to his anointed, to Cyrus,
>   whose right hand I have grasped,
> to subdue nations before him. (Is 44:28—45:1)

Since contemporary scholars typically do not believe in the possibility of divine revelation or prophetic foreknowledge, these verses are for them incontrovertible evidence that the oracles in the second half of Isaiah stem, not from the time of Isaiah himself (late eighth century B.C.), but from events taking place almost 150 years after his death (ca. sixth century B.C.). As John Collins writes: "With the rise of critical scholarship in the late eighteenth century, scholars were unwilling to believe that a prophet who lived in the eighth century would have prophesied so specifically about the sixth."[6] Indeed, to this day, the tripartite origin of Isaiah continues to be the dominant view among scholars, with most major commentaries being published according to these divisions.[7]

Difficulties with the Theory of Multiple Authorship

However, apart from the question of ancient external testimony, there are several major difficulties with the modern theory of multiple authors of Isaiah that are worth noting.[8]

First, it is important to recognize that references to the Babylonian exile are not restricted to the second half of the book (Is 40–66). To the contrary, on several occasions, First Isaiah speaks about the Babylonian exile and the destruction of the Temple. For example, the very first oracle against the Gentile nations is "The oracle concerning Babylon which Isaiah the son of Amoz saw" (Is 13:1). Moreover, First Isaiah also contains forecasts of the return of the exiles and the overthrow of "the king of Babylon" (Is 14:1–22). Perhaps most important of all, First Isaiah ends with a narrative that claims that in the eighth century B.C. (at the time of Hezekiah), Isaiah prophesied that Babylon—not Assyria—would one day come and bring the Judeans into exile:

> Then Isaiah said to Hezekiah, "Hear the word of the LORD of hosts: Behold, the days are coming, when all that is in your house, and that which your fathers have stored up till this day, shall be carried to Babylon; nothing shall be left, says the LORD. And some of your own sons, who are born to you, shall be taken away; and they shall be eunuchs in the palace of the king of Babylon." (Is 39:5–7)

---

[6] John J. Collins, *Introduction to the Hebrew Bible* (Minneapolis: Fortress Press, 2004), 307.

[7] For example, Joseph Blenkinsopp, *Isaiah*, 3 vols., Anchor Yale Bible 19–19b (New Haven, Conn.: Yale University Press, 2000—2003).

[8] See John N. Oswalt, *The Book of Isaiah*, vol. 2 (Grand Rapids, Mich.: Eerdmans, 1998), 3–6; Robert B. Chisholm Jr., *Handbook on the Prophets* (Grand Rapids, Mich.: Baker Academic, 2002), 13–14.

In short: one does not have to look to Second Isaiah (Is 40–66) to find oracles about the Babylonian exile: they are already present throughout First Isaiah (Is 13–14, 21, 38–39). Of course, scholars who support multiple authors of Isaiah are aware of this and hypothesize that all such passages are later interpolations. In the words of John Collins: "Not everything in chapters 1–39 can be attributed to the eighth-century prophet [Isaiah], however.... The oracles against Babylon in chapters 13–14 are most naturally dated to a time after Babylon had replaced Assyria as the dominant power."[9] Of course, such hypotheses necessarily weaken the overall argument, since the existence of First Isaiah is predicated upon the theory that the first part of the book is focused on the Assyrian period (eighth century B.C.) and does not look forward to the Babylonian period (sixth century B.C.). By having to admit that there are parts of "Second Isaiah" in "First Isaiah", the arguments for the existence of a "First Isaiah" lose force.

Second, as a number of recent studies have shown, there are a remarkable number of similarities of diction and theme that run through the first, second, and third portions of Isaiah, so that one can speak about a real unity to the final form of the book.[10] In the words of Walter Brueggemann: "II Isaiah theologically is seen to be organically derived from I Isaiah."[11] Consider, for example, the following distinctively "Isaianic" themes:

Some Unified Themes across the Book of Isaiah

First Isaiah (1–39)	Second and Third Isaiah (40–66)
Jerusalem as "Daughter of Zion" and Bride of the Lord (Is 1:1–31)	Jerusalem as "Daughter of Zion" and Bride of the Lord (Is 52:1; 62:1–11; 66:8)
Future "Law" (*torah*) goes forth from Zion to Gentiles (Is 2:3)	Future "Law" (*torah*) goes forth from Zion to Gentiles (Is 42:3–4; 51:2–4)
Gathering of Israel and Gentiles to God's "mountain" (Is 2:2–3; 11:8–9)	Gathering of Israel and Gentiles to God's holy "mountain" (Is 56:7–8; 65:25; 66:20)
"Wolf" and "Lamb" lie together No suffering on "holy mountain" (Is 11:6–9)	"Wolf" and "Lamb" lie together No suffering on "holy mountain" (Is 64:18–25)
God pours out his "Spirit" on future king and people (Is 11:1–4; 32:22)	God pours out his "Spirit" on his servant and his people (Is 61:1–2)
Oracles against "Babylon" (Is 13:1–19; 14:4–22; 21:9; 39:1–7)	Oracles against "Babylon" (Is 43:14; 47:1; 48:14–20)
The "arm" of the Lord brings judgment and salvation (Is 30:30; 33:2)	The "arm of the Lord" brings judgment and salvation (Is 40:10–11; 48:14; 51:5–9; 62:8)

---

[9] Collins, *Introduction to the Hebrew Bible*, 308.

[10] For example, R. Margalioth, *The Indivisible Isaiah: Evidence for Single Authorship of the Prophetic Book* (New York: Yeshiva University, 1964).

[11] W. Brueggemann, "Unity and Dynamic in the Isaiah Tradition", *Journal for the Study of the Old Testament* 29 (1984): 89–107, here 96.

In light of these and other parallels across the book of Isaiah, scholars such as John Oswalt conclude: "From ch. 1 to ch. 66, the various parts of the present book all reflect the other parts."[12] Of course, it is possible to explain such parallels as the result of Second Isaiah knowing of, and consciously imitating, First Isaiah, but such admissions once again have the effect of weakening the argument to multiple authors based on the differences between the parts of the book.

Third and finally, while it is truly remarkable that Isaiah mentions Cyrus by name as the one who will release the exiles and rebuild the Temple, from a Christian perspective, there is nothing at all theologically problematic or philosophically impossible about a prediction. It should go without saying that God, who is omniscient, could reveal detailed information to one of his prophets. However, the problem with arguing on *literary* grounds that Second Isaiah must come from the exilic period (for example, in the manner of some of the later psalms) is that Second Isaiah itself insists that one of the reasons his message should be listened to is because—unlike the false gods of the nations—YHWH is able to *foretell events long before they happen*. Indeed, the omniscience and foreknowledge of God are a major hallmark of Second Isaiah:

> I am the LORD, that is my name;
> my glory I give to no other,
> nor my praise to graven images.
> Behold, the former things have come to pass,
> and new things I now declare;
> *before they spring forth*
> *I tell you of them.* (Is 42:8–9)

> Remember this and consider,
> recall it to mind, you transgressors,
> remember the former things of old;
> for I am God, and there is no other;
> *I am God, and there is none like me,*
> *declaring the end from the beginning*
> *and from ancient times things not yet done.* (Is 46:8–10)

> *The former things I declared of old,*
> they went forth from my mouth and I made them known;
> then suddenly I did them *and they came to pass....*
> You have heard; now see all this;
> and will you not declare it?
> *From this time forth I make you hear new things,*
> *hidden things which you have not known.* (Is 48:3, 6)

As John Oswalt has noted, these passages pose a major problem for the theory of multiple authorship because they involve the prophetic author of "Second

12 Oswalt, *Book of Isaiah* 2:4.

Isaiah" in a substantial self-contradiction: "His God Yahweh cannot tell the future any more than the gods can, but he wishes his hearers to believe that Yahweh can. In order to prove this point, the prophet tries to get his readers to believe that it was really Isaiah of Jerusalem who said these things, all the while knowing this was not true. He even goes so far as to alter some of the earlier writings (e.g., ch. 13 with its reference to Babylon), or to insert some of his own (chs. 34–35) in order to make those writings correspond more closely to his own work."[13] In other words, the question of the exilic dating of Isaiah 40–66 is different from, say, Psalm 137, because we are dealing with a different *literary genre*: unlike with the Psalms, in the book of Isaiah the genre is prophetic literature that explicitly claims to be uniquely *predictive* in character.

In short, the origins of the book of Isaiah remain a profound enigma for scholarship. Some scholars see, not just the traditional three, but evidence of numerous authors throughout the work, while others are convinced that large sections are so unified as to come from one hand. There are undeniable continuities and discontinuities in different sections and chapters. The continuities could be explained by the historical continuity of a "school" of Isaiah, but how such a school could have survived intact through the historical tumult between the mid-eighth and the mid-fifth centuries B.C. is difficult to explain. The apparently "late" parts of the book are usually attributed to a single late sixth-century B.C. literary genius, but it does seem remarkable that the name and identity of this profound theologian were completely forgotten by Jewish tradition and left no trace in the historical record. The oracles of Third Isaiah are often taken as indicative of societal conflict in postexilic Jerusalem; however, the abuses highlighted by the prophetic author are so similar to those excoriated earlier in the book (for example, Is 1–12) that some have suggested that parts of Third Isaiah are not in fact younger but, rather, older oracles that have been displaced to the end of the composition.

Thus, it is helpful to bear in mind that, whatever various scholars conclude about the origins of the book of Isaiah, it is, of course, the final canonized form of the book that is theologically normative, and not various hypothetical earlier stages of composition.

With this in mind, we can now turn to a couple of key theological issues in the final form of the text.

Theological Issues in Isaiah

Is Immanuel Conceived of a "Virgin" or a "Young Woman"?

As is well known, this famous oracle is taken as a prophecy of the virginal conception of Christ in the New Testament (Mt 1:23). For centuries, however, there has been a debate over the original meaning of Isaiah's oracle.

On the one hand, most modern interpreters contend that Isaiah is *not* referring to a virginal conception, since the Hebrew word used by Isaiah is *'almah*, which many feel is best translated as "young woman". Those who favor this

---

[13] Ibid., 5–6.

position point out that the ordinary Hebrew word for "virgin" (*bethulah*) is not used in Isaiah 7:14. From this point of view, then, the "sign" given to King Ahaz is the birth of his son Hezekiah, who, by the time he reaches the age of reason, will witness the overthrow of the northern kingdom. Indeed, there are aspects of the oracle that seem indisputably to envision an immediate fulfillment in the ending of the Syro-Ephraimite crisis (Is 7:14–17), events that took place in the lifetime of King Hezekiah, son of Ahaz (ca. 732 B.C.).

On the other hand, other interpreters contend that Isaiah is referring to a miraculous conception and birth. We determine the meaning of the Hebrew word *'almah* ultimately by analyzing the way it is used in the Hebrew text of the Bible: it occurs seven times, and in those cases it is never applied to a married woman: Genesis 24:43; Exodus 2:8; Isaiah 7:14; Psalm 68:26 MT; Proverbs 30:19; Song of Solomon 1:3; 6:8. Indeed, in some cases *'almah* is used as a synonym for "virgin" (*bethulah*), as when Rebekah is referred to both as a "maiden/young woman" (*'almah*) *and* a "virgin (*bethulah*) whom no man had known" (Gen 24:16, 43). Again, in Song of Solomon 6:8, the category *'almah* is distinguished from the categories "queen" and "concubine"— that is, from those who have already had relations with the king. Perhaps, then, the Hebrew word *'almah* does not *denote* virginity, but does *connote* it, like the English word "maiden".

> **How Do Scholars Determine the Meaning of Biblical Words?**
>
> When dealing with the meaning of Hebrew words, we must remember that there is no dictionary or lexicon from ancient times that tells us definitively the meaning of a Hebrew term in antiquity. We moderns must derive or work out the meaning of the Hebrew terms based, in most cases, almost exclusively on the way the Hebrew word is used in the biblical text itself, since there is not very much nonbiblical literature extant in classical Hebrew. Studies of ancient translations give us an idea of what scholars in antiquity thought the Hebrew meant, and research in cognate languages (Ugaritic, Aramaic, Akkadian, Arabic, etc.) can be helpful, but there is always an element of guesswork in biblical lexicology.

Intriguingly, the Jewish translators of the Greek Septuagint usually translated *'almah* with the non-specific expression "young woman" (Greek *neanis*), except in two cases, where the context seems to have implied virginity: the story of Rebekah the virgin (Gen 24:43) and the oracle of the "virgin" (Greek *parthenos*) who conceives Immanuel (Is 7:14). In this view, the "sign" (Hebrew *'oth*)— which Isaiah uses elsewhere to refer to a miracle of nature (Is 37:30; 38:7)—is the miraculous conception of the child by a virgin. Again, it is important to remember that the decision to render *'almah* with the Greek *parthenos*, "virgin", was made by Jewish translators themselves about two hundred years prior to the dawn of the Christian era (see Is 7:14 LXX).

When evaluating this issue, it is also critical to remember that biblical prophecy can have more than one horizon of fulfillment. In other words, the same prophecy may have both *preliminary* as well as *ultimate* fulfillments. In the case of Isaiah 7:14, the preliminary fulfillment of the "Immanuel" child may well have been Hezekiah son of Ahaz, and the *'almah* may have been Abijah, a young bride of Ahaz (2 Chron 29:1), who was probably not yet intimate with the king. Before Hezekiah was a young man, the Syro-Ephraimite threat had evaporated. Yet Hezekiah himself is an important *type* of the Messiah in the book of

Isaiah. For example, in the pivotal historical chapters about the end of Isaiah's life (Is 36–39), Hezekiah is the righteous yet suffering savior-king, reminiscent of David and anticipating the future Messiah. Indeed, Hezekiah may even have been the immediate referent of the other prophecies of a royal child (Is 9:1–7 and 11:1–5). However, to the extent that these oracles point not only to a new king but to a new kingdom, a new exodus, and a new creation, *the birth and life of Hezekiah by no means fulfill them* (cf. Is 7:14–16; 9:1–7; 11:1–5). Instead, Hezekiah's life leaves these oracles as *prophetic words "waiting" for ultimate fulfillment.* Hezekiah was born of a "maiden" (*'almah*) in the usual manner, but later one would be born of a mother who remained a maiden before, during, and after his birth. Hezekiah was "Immanuel" ("God with us") in a mediated sense: his righteous reign was a sign of God's closeness to his people. But later one would be born who was truly "God with us" in a literal sense. Applied to Hezekiah, the poetry and language of these oracles is hyperbolic: complete fulfillment awaits another.

The Eschatology of Isaiah

As we saw above, the book of Isaiah begins with and contains numerous oracles about "the latter days"—that is, the future age of salvation when God would fulfill his promises and send the long-awaited Davidic king, restore the tribes of Israel, and exalt the city of Zion (for example, Is 2, 9, 11, 40–41, 61–66). In other words, Isaiah is a richly *eschatological* book. Indeed, many of the eschatological expectations associated with God's inbreaking into history at the end of time may be organized around the three themes of the pivotal oracle about the "shoot" from the "stump of Jesse": (1) new kingdom (Is 11:1–5), (2) new creation (Is 11:6–9), (3) new exodus (Is 11:10–16). To this we might also add a fourth, implicit teaching: (4) new covenant.

1. *The Expectation of a New Kingdom*: The first half of Isaiah contains two important oracles of a coming ideal king (Is 9:1–7 and Is 11:1–16). Historically, the ideal son of David described by these passages has been identified with the mysterious figure described in the Servant Songs of the second half of the book (Is 42:1–9; 49:1–13; 50:4–9; 52:13—53:12; 61:1–3). Although modern critical scholarship would resist identifying the Davidic son (Is 9:1–7 and 11:1–5) with the servant of Second Isaiah, for the ancient reader, who read the book as a unity, this identification was easy to make, because the servant is clearly a royal figure who establishes "justice" for all the earth (cf. Is 42:1–4; cf. 11:4). The establishment of justice was the responsibility of a king, not a prophet or priest. Moreover, he is described with epithets elsewhere applied to David: "servant", "chosen one", "anointed one" with the "Spirit" (cf. Is 42:1; 61:1; Ps 89:19–20; 1 Sam 16:13). There are also close similarities in description between the royal son and the servant, such as "the Spirit of the Lord shall rest upon him" (Is 11:2), "I have put my Spirit upon him" (Is 42:1), "The Spirit of the Lord God is upon me" (Is 61:1), the expression "he shall strike the earth with the rod of his mouth" (Is 11:4), and "He made my mouth like a sharp sword" (Is 49:2). When taken together, these parallels indicate that the final version of the book

intends an identification of the figures. Reading the oracles of the royal son (Is 9:1–7; 11:1–5, 10) together with the Servant Songs gives us a composite picture of a coming Spirit-anointed (Is 11:2, 49:1; 61:1), divinely wise (Is 11:2) savior figure from the house and line of David (Is 9:7; 11:1, 10) with a mission to Israel and the nations (Is 11:10; 42:6; 49:6), who possesses divine qualities (Is 9:6); preaches good news to the poor (Is 61:1); leads the blind out of darkness (Is 42:7); becomes a "covenant" to the people (Is 42:6; 49:6); suffers rejection, persecution, disfigurement, shame, abuse, and ultimately death (Is 49:4,7; 50:5–6; 52:13—53:9) during a priestly act of self-sacrifice (Is 53:7–10), which results in forgiveness of sins and sanctification for many (Is 53:11–12); gathers Israel and the nations to himself (Is 11:10); and rules forever (Is 9:7).

2. *The Expectation of a New Exodus*: The new exodus theme in Isaiah is widely recognized and studied. It appears in a remarkable number of passages in all the various parts of the book (Is 11:11–16; 35:1–10; 40:9–11; 41:17–20; 42:14–17; 43:2–8; 44:3–4; 48:20–21; 49:9–12; 50:2; 51:9–11; 52:3–12; 55:12–13; 63:10–14). On the one hand, this new exodus will resemble the old: the Lord will extend his hand, dry up bodies of water for his people to cross, and provide abundant water for them during their journey through the desert. On the other hand, this new exodus will be different: in Moses' place leading the people will be the Lord's servant, the "root of Jesse" (Is 11:10). The place of departure will not be Egypt but Assyria and all the lands—north, west, south, and east—to which the Lord has scattered his people. The destination will be Mount Zion, not Mount Sinai (cf. Ex 19–20). And instead of trackless paths in the wilderness, this time there will be a "way" or "highway" for safe and easy travel (Is 35, 40).

3. *The Expectation of a New Creation*: In the eschatological "chronology" of the book of Isaiah, the "new exodus" logically precedes and leads to the "new creation", which is closely associated with, and may be identical to, the renewed Zion that forms the destination of the new exodus, even though in some passages the *description* of the new creation actually precedes that of the new exodus (for example, Is 11:6–16). The key "new creation" passages are also abundant (for example, Is 11:6–9; 30:23–26; 51:3–6; 65:17–25; 66:22–23). In order to understand the shape of this Isaianic hope, it is theologically crucial to recognize the close connection between the new creation and the Temple-city on Mount Zion, Jerusalem. Note, for example, that the description of the kingdom of peace is situated on "my holy mountain" (Is 11:6–9), a designation of the Temple Mount and, more broadly, Jerusalem. In another oracle, it is Zion that experiences the new creation: "For the LORD will comfort Zion ... and will make her wilderness like Eden, her desert like the garden of the LORD" (Is 51:3). Another oracle states: "I create new heavens and a new earth, and the former things shall not be remembered", but the next verse specifies, "Behold, I create *Jerusalem* a rejoicing, and her people a joy" (Is 65:17–18). The subsequent description does not, in fact, concern the whole cosmos, but just the city of Jerusalem, concluding, "They shall not hurt or destroy *in all my holy mountain*" (Is 65:25). Indeed, the final important reference to the new creation mentions the "new heavens and the new earth" in the midst of passages describing the

eschatological pilgrimage of the nations and the remnant of Israel to "my holy mountain Jerusalem" and a climactic promise that "from new moon to new moon ... all flesh shall come to *worship* before me" (Is 66:22–23). The reason for this close connection between the concept of a new creation and the site of the Temple is because, in ancient Israelite thinking, the Temple was a small representation of the universe (*microcosm*), whereas the universe itself was one great sanctuary (*macrotemple*) (cf. Is 66:1). Hence, the implication of all this new-creation imagery employed in the book of Isaiah is that it may refer either to a literal renewal of the physical cosmos or else to the construction of a new Temple that cultically renews the world.[14]

4. *The Expectation of a New Covenant*: Although Jeremiah is the only prophetic book to speak explicitly of the hope for a "new covenant" (Jer 31:31), the book of Isaiah shares the hope for the establishment of a future "covenant" that will both fulfill the promises made to David and transcend them at the same time. The hope of a coming New Covenant in Isaiah is expressed especially in passages that speak of the servant of the Lord actually *becoming* a "covenant" to "the people" (Is 42:6, 49:8) or that promise to Zion in the latter days a "covenant of peace" (Is 54:10). Above all, there is the Lord's declaration that he will make (future tense) an everlasting covenant with his people:

> For I the LORD love justice,
>   I hate robbery and wrong;
> I will faithfully give them their recompense,
>   and *I will make an everlasting covenant with them.*
> Their descendants shall be known among the nations,
>   and their offspring in the midst of the peoples. (Is 61:8–9)

Indeed, early in the book, the prophet declares that a meal offered for free to the poor and thirsty will be the means by which they will enter into "an everlasting covenant", which is identified with the covenant bond (Hebrew *hesed*) that God had for David—that is, the Davidic covenant (Is 55:1–3). This new covenant relationship is also identified with a special outpouring of God's Spirit on those who repent and their offspring (Is 59:20–21).

In sum, the fact that the "latter days" (the coming eschatological era) in Isaiah are characterized both by a New Covenant and by the themes of new kingdom, new exodus, and new creation implies, on the one hand, that the economy of this New Covenant will involve a *recapitulation* of elements of the Davidic covenant associated with kingship, the Mosaic covenant associated with the exodus, and the Adamic covenant associated with creation. On the other hand, careful examination of the economies of these previous covenants with the description of the eschatological era in Isaiah also makes it clear that the New Covenant that Isaiah describes is not a simple restoration of any or all of the previous covenants of salvation history, but a *transformation* of them as well. Indeed, important

---

[14] See G. K. Beale, *The Temple and the Church's Mission: A Biblical Theology of the Dwelling Place of God*, New Studies in Biblical Theology 17 (Downers Grove, Ill.: InterVarsity Press, 2004).

passages of Isaiah make it clear, for example, that elements of the Mosaic covenant will be revised or even *abrogated* in the coming age and that therefore the covenant to come is truly a *novum*.

For example, when it comes to the Mosaic covenant, Isaiah makes clear that in the coming age, foreigners and eunuchs, who were excluded from the worshipping assembly of Israel (Hebrew *qahal*, Greek *ekklēsia*) by the final form of the Mosaic covenant (Deut 23:1, 3–7), will be able to enter the worshipping assembly, offer sacrifice, and perhaps even perform priestly "ministry" (Hebrew *sharet*; Is 56:1–8). Again, Isaiah also suggests that the status of priesthood in the coming era will no longer be limited to the tribe of Levi and the sons of Aaron but will be opened at least to all Israelites and perhaps also to Gentiles who draw near to the Lord in the latter days (Is 61:6 and 66:21). Finally, the strident critique of the Mosaic sacrifices and even of the physical Temple at the beginning and end of the book (Is 1:10–14; 66:3–4) suggests that there is something fundamentally inadequate about the Mosaic liturgy (namely, it is impotent truly to absolve and sanctify the worshippers) and opens the possibility that a fundamentally new liturgy will characterize the age to come.

Is the Suffering Servant in Isaiah an Individual or a Group?

Since the ancient parting of Judaism and Christianity, there has been a longstanding debate over the interpretation of the servant passages in the book of Isaiah (Is 42, 49, 50, 52–53, cf. 61). The debate can be framed in terms of two major questions: (1) Who exactly is the servant? And (2) is the servant an individual figure or a group? To these questions, scholars have given a wide array of answers, with the following proposals being among the most famous:

Who Is the Servant in Isaiah?

1. The Messiah (an individual)
2. Israel (a collective)
3. Isaiah (referring to himself in the third person)
4. Jeremiah (who suffered persecution and rejection)
5. Moses
6. Otherwise unknown figure in the sixth century B.C.

For our purposes here, it is important to note, as we saw above, that there are good reasons to conclude that the servant in Isaiah is *both* an individual figure who is in distinct contrast with the people of God as a whole, since he is righteous and bears their sins; and a *collective* figure, who is identified explicitly as "Israel".

On the one hand, the servant in Isaiah is clearly an *individual* figure, who is in contrast with the people of God as a whole. Not only is this individual called by God "from the womb" of his mother (Is 42:1, 49:1), but he cannot be completely identified with the people, since his righteousness is contrasted with their sinfulness and he suffers for *their* sins:

All we like sheep have gone astray;
   we have turned every one to his own way;
and the Lord has laid on him
   the iniquity of us all ...
   he shall see the fruit of the travail of his soul and be satisfied;
by his knowledge shall *the righteous one, my servant,*
   make many to be accounted righteous;
   and he shall bear their iniquities. (Is 53:6, 11)

On the other hand, the image of the servant is also undeniably used with reference to the people of Israel as a whole, as in one of the earlier oracles:

And he said to me, *"You are my servant,*
   Israel, in whom I will be glorified." (Is 49:3)

What are we to make of this evidence? How can the servant in Isaiah be both an individual deliverer and a collective figure for Israel?

It is critical to recall that in ancient Israelite society, the idea that the king could act as a representative or embodiment of the people as a whole was commonplace; and certain texts identify the servant as a royal figure. Indeed, as we will see elsewhere, this is precisely how the various "beasts" in the book of Daniel will function: they represent both the "kings" of the Gentile nations and their "kingdoms" (see Dan 7:1–25). If the Isaianic servant is king of Israel, that would explain why, in one sense, he is distinct from the people but, in another sense, is the embodiment or representative of the nation as a whole.

Also helpful is the fact that the book of Isaiah refers not only to "the servant of the Lord" (singular), but to the "servants of the Lord" (see Is 63:17; 65:8–9, 13–14). According to such passages, there will be a division with the people of the Lord: the majority who forsake the Lord will perish in the coming judgment, but a remnant of faithful will survive to experience the promised blessing and restoration in the future. The fullest, most explicit development of the remnant theme comes in one of the final oracles in the book, which emphasizes a very dramatic dichotomy within the people of God between the majority and a faithful remnant referred to as "my servants" (Is 65:1–16). The majority will experience eschatological curses, while the "servants" will receive the eschatological blessings and ultimately be called by a "new name". In other words, what happens to the individual servant of the Lord will also happen to the "servants of the Lord" collectively. Just as the individual servant suffered rejection, persecution, and death, followed by vindication, so too the servants of the Lord will go through tribulation and persecution but will ultimately be vindicated by God in the new heavens and the new earth.

Isaiah in the Living Tradition

While the composition history and final-form interpretation of Isaiah remain an enigma from the perspective of modern scholarship, the Church has always been convinced, from the very beginning of the Gospel proclamation, that in the life and ministry of Jesus of Nazareth and the growth of the Church, one finds the hermeneutical key for unlocking the meaning of the book of Isaiah.

The Book of Isaiah in the New Testament

The influence of Isaiah on the New Testament is profound, and quotations from Isaiah are used to *identify* and *define* the ministries of both John the Baptist (Mk 1:1–3 and parallels) and Jesus Christ (Mt 1:23; 2:6; 4:12–16; 13:14–15; Lk 4:16–21). Perhaps most notable is that, in his inaugural sermon at Nazareth, Jesus himself claims to be the mysterious figure who is "anointed" by the "Spirit of the LORD" in the second part of the book:

> And he came to Nazareth, where he had been brought up; and he went to the synagogue, as was his custom, on the sabbath day. And he stood up to read; and there was given to him *the book of the prophet Isaiah*. He opened the book and found the place where it was written,
>
> > "*The Spirit of the Lord is upon me,*
> > *because he has anointed me to preach good news to the poor.*
> > He has sent me to proclaim release to the captives
> > and recovering of sight to the blind,
> > to set at liberty those who are oppressed,
> > to proclaim the acceptable year of the Lord.*"
>
> And he closed the book, and gave it back to the attendant, and sat down; and the eyes of all in the synagogue were fixed on him. And he began to say to them, "*Today this Scripture has been fulfilled in your hearing.*" (Lk 4:16–21)

The significance of this point should not be underestimated: according to Luke's account, Jesus *begins* his public ministry in his hometown by declaring that Isaiah's oracle of the messianic servant has been finally fulfilled. In light of these and many other texts, it should come as no surprise that the book of Isaiah has continued to have a profound influence upon the living tradition of the Church.

Isaiah Must Be Understood Historically and Spiritually

From the very earliest days of Christianity, it was recognized not only that the book of Isaiah spoke of future realities that would ultimately be fulfilled in Christ, but that the book should also be interpreted in its historical context, as contemporary scholarship in particular strives to do. For example, in the late fourth to early fifth century A.D., Saint Cyril of Alexandria gave this advice to interpreters of Isaiah:

> The word of the holy prophets is always difficult to surmise. It is filled with hidden meanings and is pregnant with announcements of divine mysteries.... Those who want to expound these subtle matters must be diligent, I believe, to work in a logical way to thoroughly examine all of the symbols in the text to gain spiritual insight. *First, the interpreter must determine the historical meaning and then interpret the*

spiritual meaning, in order for readers to derive benefit from every part of the text. The exposition must be clearly seen to be complete in every way.[15]

This is salutary advice for modern as well as ancient readers: in order to derive the full benefit from the oracles of Isaiah, it is important first try to ascertain their meaning in their original historical context before moving too quickly to their spiritual fulfillments. In this way, the "spirit" of the text builds on (rather than abandons) the "letter".

Conceived of a "Virgin" or a "Young Woman"?

Contrary to what some contemporary readers of the Bible assume, the debate over whether Isaiah's prophecy of the "sign" of the child (Is 7:14) should be translated as a "virgin" or a "young woman" is not a modern innovation but an ancient debate between Jewish and Christian readers of Isaiah during the early centuries of the Church. In such debates, the Church Fathers insisted, contrary to their Jewish opponents, that Isaiah was in fact speaking of a miraculous virginal conception:

> Isaiah tells of the mystery of our faith and hope: "Behold a virgin shall conceive, and bear a son, and shall call his name Emmanuel." I know that the Jews are accustomed to meet us with the objection that in Hebrew the word *Almah* does not mean a virgin, but *a young woman*. And, to speak truth, a virgin is properly called *Bethulah*, but a young woman, or a girl, is not *Almah*, but *Naarah!* What then is the meaning of *Almah?* A hidden virgin, that is, not merely virgin, but a virgin and something more, because not every virgin is hidden, shut off from the occasional sight of men.[16]

Along similar lines, in the fifth century, Saint John Chrysostom pointed out that the letter of Isaiah's prophecy does not make sense unless the "sign" is a miraculous conception:

> And what goes before also establishes this interpretation. For he doth not merely say, "Behold, the Virgin shall be with child," but having first said, "Behold, the Lord Himself shall give you a sign," then he subjoins, "Behold, the Virgin shall be with child." *Whereas, if she that was to give birth was not a virgin, but this happened in the way of marriage, what sort of sign would the event be?* For that which is a sign must of course be beyond the course of common events, it must be strange and extraordinary; else how could it be a sign?[17]

This is a significant exegetical observation in favor of the conclusion that the "sign" promised to Ahaz will only ultimately be fulfilled in the virginal conception of Jesus Christ. Indeed, the *Catechism of the Catholic Church* will go on to

---

[15] Cyril of Alexandria, *Commentary on Isaiah, Introduction*, in McKinion, *Isaiah 1–39*, 2.

[16] Jerome, *Against Jovinianus* 1.32, in *NPNF2* 6:370.

[17] John Chrysostom, *Homilies on the Gospel of Matthew* 5.4, in *Nicene and Post-Nicene Fathers*, 1st series, ed. Philip Schaff, vol. 10 (1888; repr., Peabody, Mass.: Hendrickson, 1994), 33.

teach that the Church sees in the "virginal conception" of Jesus a divine work
that constitutes the "fulfillment" of the divine promise that was given in the
oracle of Isaiah 7:14 (see *CCC* 497).

The Shoulders of Immanuel and the Wood of the Cross

As we saw above, one of the most remarkable series of oracles in Isaiah is the
series of "Emmanuel" prophecies, which speak of the birth of a child upon
whose shoulders the government shall rest (Is 9:6). Intriguingly, the early
Church Fathers saw in this image a prefiguration of the fact that Christ would
reign through the wood of the Cross, which he carried upon his shoulders
to Calvary:

> When Isaac himself carried the wood for the sacrifice of himself, in this, too, he
> prefigured Christ our Lord, who carried his own cross to the place of his passion.
> *Of this mystery much had already been foretold by the prophets: "And his government
> shall be upon his shoulders"* [Is 9:6]. Christ, then, had the government upon his
> shoulders when he carried his cross with wonderful humility. Not unfittingly
> does Christ's cross signify government: by it the devil is conquered and the whole
> world recalled to the knowledge and grace of Christ.[18]

Emmanuel, "Mighty God", and the Divinity of Christ

Along similar lines, the fact that Isaiah not only refers to the future Davidic king
as Immanuel ("God with us") but even lists one of his names as "Mighty God"
(Is 9:6) was not lost on the Church Fathers, who argued from these texts that
God was revealing through Isaiah the *divinity* of Jesus:

> Furthermore, we must prove that Jesus was beforehand promised from ancient
> times in the Prophets and was called the Son of God.... And Isaiah said, *Unto us a
> child is born ... and his Name shall be called Wonderful, and Counsellor, and mighty God
> of the ages, and Prince of peace* [Is 9:6]. Therefore tell me, O wise doctor of Israel,
> who is He that was born and whose name was called *Child* and *Son* and *Wonderful*
> and *Counsellor*, the *mighty God of the ages*, and *Prince of peace, to the increase of* whose
> government and to whose *peace* (he said), *there is no end*? For if we call Christ the
> Son of God, David taught us (this); and that we call Him God, this we learned
> from Isaiah.[19]

This is a stunning testimony to the role that Isaiah played in forming the faith of
the early Christians in the divine identity of Christ. Above all, it was the prophet
Isaiah who taught them to refer to Jesus the Messiah not only as Son of God,
but as "God" himself.

---

[18] Caesarius of Arles, *Sermon* 84.3, in Caesarius, *Sermons*, vol. 2 (*81–186*), trans. Sr. Mary Magdeleine
Mueller, O.S.F., The Fathers of the Church 47 (Washington, D.C.: Catholic University of America Press,
1964), 17.
[19] Aphrahat, *Demonstration* 17.9, in *NPNF2* 13:390.

The Spirit of the Messiah and the Seven Gifts of the Holy Spirit

Another text that was richly mined by the living tradition is Isaiah's description of the "Spirit of wisdom" coming upon the future Davidic king (Is 11:2–3). It is directly from this text that the Church developed the "seven gifts" of the Holy Spirit, as in the words of Ambrose of Milan:

> [B]y the sanctification of these seven gifts of the Spirit, as Isaiah said, is signified the fulness of all virtue; the Spirit of wisdom and understanding, the Spirit of counsel and strength, the Spirit of knowledge and godliness, and the Spirit of the fear of God. One, then, is the River, but many the channels of the gifts of the Spirit.[20]

Here we see that Isaiah was central not only for the development of early Christian *Christology* (theology of Christ) but also for early Christian *pneumatology* (theology of the Holy Spirit). We should note that the enumeration of seven gifts of the Spirit is based on the Greek version of the text (LXX), which differs just slightly from the traditional Hebrew (MT).

The New Jerusalem and the Virgin Birth

One of the most remarkable patristic interpretations of the second half of Isaiah revolves around the singular role that Isaiah's visions of the new Jerusalem—the bride of YHWH (for example, Is 54, 62, 65–66)—played in the development of the early Christian belief that the mother of Jesus not only conceived him as a virgin but gave birth as a virgin, in a miraculous childbirth that was free from labor pains (cf. Gen 3:16). In Isaiah 66, the prophet utters the following mysterious oracle about the new Jerusalem:

> Before she was in labor
>   she gave birth;
> before her pain came upon her
>   she was delivered of a son.
> Who has heard such a thing?
> Who has seen such things? (Is 66:7–8)

It was precisely this Isaianic oracle that was interpreted by a number of ancient Christian writers as having been fulfilled in the virginal and miraculous birth of Jesus. Consider, for example, the words of the fourth-century writer Gregory of Nyssa:

> In fact, his [Jesus'] birth alone occurred without labor pains, and he alone began to exist without sexual relations.... *Even the prophet Isaiah affirms that her giving birth was without pain, when he says: "Before the pangs of birth arrived, a male child came forth*

---

[20] Ambrose, *On the Holy Spirit* 1.16.179, in *NPNF2* 10:113–14.

and was born" (Is 66:7). Therefore, he was chosen to introduce a twofold innovation into the order of nature, since he did not begin to exist because of sin, nor
was he born in pain.[21]

Similar interpretations of Isaiah 66 as being fulfilled by the virginal and miraculous birth of Jesus can also be found in the writings of Methodius of Olympus
and John Damascene,[22] showing the direct impact the book of Isaiah had on
early Christian debates over the exact interpretation of the article from the
Apostles' Creed: "born of the Virgin Mary".

The Book of Isaiah in the Lectionary

Isaiah is second only to the Psalms in its influence over the Jewish and Christian
liturgy. In synagogue worship, Isaiah is read to complement the reading of the
Torah (the *haftarah* portion) more often, and on more significant occasions, than
any other book of the Hebrew Bible. Likewise in Catholic worship, Isaiah is
read more frequently than any other Old Testament book but the Psalms and
earns its moniker as "the fifth Gospel" by rivaling the four Gospels in its frequency. In fact, in the contemporary Roman Lectionary, readings from Isaiah
(forty-four times) in the Lectionary for Sundays and major feasts exceed those
from the Gospel of Mark (thirty-six times) and are just shy of those from the
Gospel of Matthew (forty-eight times)!

The Christian liturgy understands the book of Isaiah to be a prophecy of the
"coming of the LORD", both his first coming in the Incarnation of Jesus Christ
and his Second Coming at the end of time. For this reading, ancient liturgical
tradition incorporated the reading of all—or nearly all—of the book of Isaiah
during the season of Advent. This tradition has been recovered in the current
Liturgy of the Hours and, less comprehensively, also in the Lectionary for Mass
on Sundays and ferial days. Important readings from Isaiah are also included in
the Lectionary during Lent, and especially during Holy Week, when all the
main "Servant Songs" are read in succession from Holy Monday through Good
Friday (Is 42:1–7; 49:1–6; 50:4–9; 61:1–3; 52:13—53:12). Moreover, important
covenantal and Eucharistic passages, such as the resumption of the nuptial relationship between the Lord and his people (Is 54:5–14) and the invitation to the
poor to eat the free meal of the Davidic covenant (Is 55:1–11), are incorporated
into the readings for the Easter Vigil.

With such an "embarrassment of riches", it is not possible to discuss the significance of all the passages employed in the liturgy, but we will limit ourselves
here just to those used at the most prominent solemnities of the liturgical year:

1. *The Feast of Christmas*: Isaiah 9:1–6, the promise of a "child" and "son"
from the line of David who will be "Wonderful Counselor, Mighty God, Everlasting Father, Prince of Peace", is read for Midnight Mass at Christmas, the

---

[21] Gregory of Nyssa, *Commentary on the Song of Songs* 13, in Luigi Gambero, *Mary and the Fathers of the Church*, trans. Thomas Buffer (San Francisco: Ignatius Press, 1999), 158–59.

[22] See Methodius of Olympus, *Oration concerning Simeon and Anna* 3; John Damascene, *On the Orthodox Faith*, 4.14.

liturgy traditionally associated with the very moment of the birth of Christ, when a child with divine attributes was given to Joseph and Mary and through them to all mankind. The beautiful poem about the joyful resumption of matrimony between God and Zion in Isaiah 62:1–5 also appears at the Christmas Vigil. In one sense, Christ our Bridegroom has now arrived in the Incarnation to expose mankind to himself as his bridal people. In another sense, the Feast of the Incarnation marks the "wedding" of divine nature with human nature, two natures "married" in one person. God demonstrates his nuptial intentions toward mankind by joining human flesh to himself, resulting in salvation.

2. *Holy Thursday Chrism Mass*: The first-person servant song of Isaiah 61:1–3, beginning "The Spirit of the LORD is upon me, because he has anointed me to preach good news to the poor", is read for the Chrism Mass on Holy Thursday. In the context of the liturgy, the speaker of this Song is understood to be Christ himself. His anointing to "preach good news", "proclaim the year of the LORD's favor", "release for prisoners", and so on, is shared by all who are joined to him by the sacraments, and the holy chrism consecrated at this Mass symbolizes the anointing of the Holy Spirit that grants the Church her sacramental powers.

3. *Passion Sunday and Good Friday*: The shorter "Suffering Servant Song" (Is 50:4–7) appears at Palm (Passion) Sunday, to complement the Gospel reading in which Christ quite literally suffers the abuse described by Isaiah. The longer or "Great Suffering Servant Song" (Is 52:13—53:12) is read in its entirety on Good Friday, when the Passion account is proclaimed once more as the Gospel reading. In this way the Christian faithful recognize that the sufferings of the Christ were neither arbitrary nor unanticipated but, rather, took place according to prophecy and thus the express will and foresight of God.

4. *The Easter Vigil Readings*: Two passages from the second half of Isaiah with important sacramental implications occur as part of the seven Old Testament readings of the Easter Vigil. Isaiah 54:5–11, the fourth reading of the vigil, promises the resumption of the joyful marriage between the Lord and his people, the restoration of a "covenant of peace" as at the time of Noah, and the rebuilding of Zion as a Temple-city. Likewise, Isaiah 55:1–11, the fifth reading of the vigil, given its emphasis on eating and drinking at the Davidic covenant banquet, is particularly appropriate as mystagogy during the Easter Vigil for catechumens preparing to receive the Eucharist for the very first time.

5. *The Feast of Epiphany*: The famous passage "Arise, shine; for your light has come" (Is 60:1–6) introduces the Scripture readings for Epiphany, emphasizing the themes of revelatory light, the incoming of the kings of the nations to Zion, and the bringing of sacred gifts of "gold and frankincense" from the East. This bears obvious affinity with the visitation of the Magi (Mt 2:1–12) read as the Gospel for this feast.

6. *The Feast of the Baptism of the Lord*: What we have called the second servant song, Isaiah 42:1–4, 6–7, is employed at the Feast of the Baptism, because the divine voice at the Jordan partially echoes Isaiah: "Behold my servant, whom I uphold, my chosen, in whom my soul delights" (Is 42:1). Moreover, the promise "I have put my Spirit upon him" (Is 42:1) is visibly manifested in the descent of the Spirit as a dove over the baptized Lord.

In this short review only of those readings from Isaiah for the most prominent solemnities, we recognize that the Church understands Isaiah to be a book about the Messiah, and all the key moments of his life and ministry are understood as the fulfillment of the oracles delivered by this great prophet. The basis for the Church's liturgical deployment of Isaiah was articulated already by John the Evangelist: "Isaiah said this because he saw his glory and spoke of him" (Jn 12:41).

Readings from Isaiah in the Lectionary and Liturgy of the Hours on Sundays, Feast Days, Liturgical Seasons, and Other Occasions *MSO* = Masses for Special Occasions; *OM* = Optional Memorial; *VM* = Votive Mass; *Rit* = Ritual; *LH* = Liturgy of the Hours			
Passage	Description	Occasion	Explanation
1:10, 16–20	God strongly rebukes the leaders of Jerusalem for violations of justice; he promises forgiveness for repentance by a sword for intransigence.	Tues., 2nd Week of Lent	In the Gospel (Mt 23:1–12), the Lord rebukes the Pharisees for their oppressive spiritual governance over the Jews of his day; so a parallelism is set up between the corrupt Israelite leadership rebuked by Isaiah and that rebuked by Jesus. Jesus is the great successor of the prophets.
2:1–5	In the latter days, the nations shall stream to Zion, from which the word of the Lord will go forth to judge the nations in peace.	*1st Sun. of Advent (A)*; Mon., 1st Week of Advent (BC); *MSO*: For the Evangelization of Peoples, opt. 1	The eschatological vision of Isaiah, in which the nations stream to the Lord at Zion and he judges the nations in justice, is understood with reference to the Second Coming and final judgment, but also as spiritually fulfilled in the missionary work and spread of the Church throughout the world.
4:2–6	"In that day" the "branch of the LORD" will flourish, and all those left in Zion will be purified and protected by God.	Mon., 1st Week of Advent (A)	Isaiah's beautiful image of Zion restored and protected by the Lord is understood as a picture of the heavenly banquet in the kingdom of God at the end of time, described by the Lord in the Gospel (Mk 8:1–11, esp. 11).
5:1–7	The song of the vineyard: God cultivated his vineyard (Israel), but it bore no good fruit (righteousness); so it will be trampled (judged).	*27th Sun. in OT (A)*	Isaiah's song of the vineyard helps us to understand the parable of the tenants (Mt 21:33–43). The "vineyard" is a long-standing symbol for the people of Israel in the biblical tradition. Moreover, we recognize Jesus as a great prophet in the mold of Isaiah of old.

(continued)

Readings from Isaiah in the Lectionary and Liturgy of the Hours on Sundays,
Feast Days, Liturgical Seasons, and Other Occasions (*continued*)

MSO = Masses for Special Occasions; *OM* = Optional Memorial;
VM = Votive Mass; *Rit* = Ritual; *LH* = Liturgy of the Hours

Passage	Description	Occasion	Explanation
6:1–8	Isaiah's call vision: In the year that Uzziah died, Isaiah sees the seraphim of God's throne room; his lips are purified, and he volunteers for God's mission.	St. Nicholas; Common of Pastors, opt. 4	The purification of Isaiah's lips and his willingness to volunteer for the mission of proclaiming God's word make him a prototype of the holy pastor, especially St. Nicholas.
6:1, 6–8	See above.	*MSO*: For Vocations to Holy Orders or Religious Life, opt. 5	Like Isaiah, the one who enters religious life has heard a special call from God to a life consecrated to divine service and the proclamation of the divine word.
6:1–2a, 3–8	See above.	*5th Sun. in OT (C)*	The Gospel recounts the call of the disciples (Lk 5:1–11) on the occasion when Jesus preached from Peter's boat. Both Peter and Isaiah are taken aback by their "uncleanness" or "sinfulness". Both Isaiah and the disciples accept God's commission to preach. The prophetic ministry of the OT is continued in that of the apostles.
7:10–14	God provides King Ahaz with a sign: "a virgin shall conceive and bear a son, and shall call his name Immanuel."	*4th Sun. of Advent (A)*; Annunciation of the Lord (Mar. 25); Advent, Dec. 20; Common of BVM, opt. 7	Isaiah may have been prophesying the more immediate birth of Hezekiah; but Hezekiah was a type of Christ, whose birth more perfectly fulfills the language of Isaiah's oracle. The Church deploys this text on liturgical occasions thematically related to the conception or birth of our Lord, and especially the BVM's role in these events.
8:23b— 9:3	The people of Galilee, who walked in darkness, shall see a great light and increase their joy.	*3rd Sun. in OT (A)*	The Gospel (Mt 4:12–23) records the fulfillment of this prophecy, as Jesus begins his ministry in Galilee, the tribal territory of Zebulun and Naphtali. The territory of Israel first destroyed and exiled (by Assyria) is the first to witness the spiritual restoration of Israel through Jesus Christ.
9:1–6	See above, plus the promise of a "child", a "son" who will be "Wonderful	*Christmas at Midnight (ABC)*; Common of BVM, opt. 8	Isaiah's text speaks of a child with divine attributes: "Mighty God", "Everlasting Father". Because it anticipates the Incarnation and hypostatic union, it is

(*continued*)

Readings from Isaiah in the Lectionary and Liturgy of the Hours on Sundays, Feast Days, Liturgical Seasons, and Other Occasions (*continued*)

MSO = Masses for Special Occasions; *OM* = Optional Memorial;
VM = Votive Mass; *Rit* = Ritual; *LH* = Liturgy of the Hours

Passage	Description	Occasion	Explanation
	Counselor, Mighty God, Everlasting Father, Prince of Peace"		proclaimed at the primary Mass of the Feast of the Incarnation.
9:1–3, 5–6	See above, abbreviated.	*MSO*: For Peace and Justice, opt. 1	This reading focuses attention on Jesus' role as "Prince of Peace"—that is, one who brings both spiritual and social peace to mankind.
11:1–4	A "shoot" from Jesse shall come forth, anointed with divine wisdom, to judge with equity the poor and the wicked.	*Rit*: Confirmation, opt. 1	The first option for the celebration of confirmation, this text is the basis for the traditional "seven gifts of the Holy Spirit" understood to be bestowed through this sacrament.
11:1–10	See above; plus, the "wolf shall dwell with the lamb" on the holy mountain, and the "root of Jesse" shall gather the nations.	*2nd Sun. of Advent (A)*; Tues., 1st Week of Advent	This passage presents a fairly broad description of the coming messianic king and his role: dispensing divine wisdom, judging the wicked and righteous, bringing peace, gathering the nations. Read early in Advent, it presents a synopsis of the purpose of Christ's "coming".
12:2–3, 4bcd, 5–6	A song of triumph: God has become the prophet's "strength", "song", and "salvation". He draws water from the wells of salvation, giving thanks to God, shouting in praise and joy.	*Responsorial: 3rd Sun. of Advent (C); Baptism of the Lord (B); Easter Vigil (5th Resp.);* Sacred Heart Friday (B); Visitation of BVM	This doxological conclusion to the first unit of Isaiah (Is 1–12) expresses joy in response to the revelation of God's plan of salvation. The image of drawing water "with joy . . . from the wells of salvation" is an important baptismal type, appropriate for liturgies with baptismal themes.
22:19–23	God replaces Shebna with Eliakim in the role of royal steward; he is a "father" to Jerusalem who wears the key of the house of David to "open" and "shut" with authority.	*21st Sun. in OT (A)*	This important text about the replacement of one Davidic royal steward (Shebna) with another (Eliakim) is crucial for understanding the Gospel (Mt 16:13–20), in which Jesus bestows on Peter the "keys of the kingdom", which were the badge of office for the ancient role of royal steward, the officer second only to the king in Israel.

(*continued*)

Readings from Isaiah in the Lectionary and Liturgy of the Hours on Sundays,
Feast Days, Liturgical Seasons, and Other Occasions (*continued*)

MSO = Masses for Special Occasions; *OM* = Optional Memorial;
VM = Votive Mass; *Rit* = Ritual; *LH* = Liturgy of the Hours

Passage	Description	Occasion	Explanation
25:6a, 7–8b	The Lord will swallow up death forever in the last days.	Funerals for Unbaptized Children, opt. 1	The promise of God's final victory over death provides hope during liturgical rites during a time of grief.
25:6a, 7–9	See above, plus a concluding doxology: "Let us be glad and rejoice in his salvation."	Mass for the Dead, opt. 1; Funerals for Baptized Children, opt. 1	The concluding celebratory doxology is included at Masses for baptized persons, since the gift of the sacrament provides greater confidence in the ultimate beatitude of the deceased.
25:6–9	See above, only including the description of the eschatological banquet (v. 6)	*All Souls (opt. 3)*	See above.
25:6–10a	See above.	*28th Sun. in OT (A)*; Wed., 1st Week of Advent; *MSO*: For the Grace of a Happy Death	Jesus tells the parable of the wedding feast (Mt 22:1–14), which incorporates themes of the eschatological banquet God will provide on Zion when he abolishes death. Isaiah 25:6–10a helps reveal the eschatological meaning of Jesus' parable.
26:1–6	"In that day" the people will praise God for the "strong city" of salvation that he sets up for them, for the Lord God is an "everlasting rock".	Thurs., 1st Week of Advent	Through Isaiah 26:1–6, we recognize that when Jesus speaks of those who build "upon the rock" rather than "on sand" at the conclusion of the Sermon on the Mount (Mt 7:21, 24–27), he identifies himself as the Lord, our "everlasting rock".
29:17–24	"In that day" the deaf, blind, meek, and poor will be healed and the wicked be cut off. Jacob will no longer be ashamed.	Fri., 1st Week of Advent	Paired with the Gospel account of the healing of two blind men (Mt 9:27–31), this text reminds us that Jesus' earthly ministry fulfilled prophecies about the coming "day of the Lord".
30:19–21, 23–26	"In that day" Zion shall weep no more. They shall see their Teacher, who will instruct and bless their land with every blessing.	Sat., 1st Week of Advent	Jesus shows himself to be the promised "Teacher" who goes about Israel bringing blessing and healing (Mt 9:35—10:1, 5, 6–8).

(*continued*)

Readings from Isaiah in the Lectionary and Liturgy of the Hours on Sundays, Feast Days, Liturgical Seasons, and Other Occasions (*continued*) *MSO* = Masses for Special Occasions; *OM* = Optional Memorial; *VM* = Votive Mass; *Rit* = Ritual; *LH* = Liturgy of the Hours			
Passage	Description	Occasion	Explanation
32:15–18	The Spirit will be poured out on high, blessing the land. "My people will abide in a peaceful habitation . . . quiet resting places."	*MSO*: For the Country, City, Public Officials, or Progress of Peoples, opt. 8; For Peace and Justice, opt. 2	In Mass for peace, justice, and good government, Isaiah 32:15–18 reminds us of the ideal of justice and righteousness for human society that God intends and will one day establish in the eschaton.
35:1–6a, 10	The desert shall blossom; the blind, deaf, lame, and dumb will be healed; the ransomed of the Lord will return with singing to Zion.	*3rd Sun. of Advent (A)*	In the Gospel (Mt 11:2–11), Jesus quotes extensively from this verse, telling John's disciples that the prophecies are being fulfilled before their eyes, indicating that the kingdom of God has arrived.
35:1–10	See above; plus, the desert shall become a wetland, and a highway shall be there for the redeemed.	Mon., 2nd Week of Advent; *Rit*: Anointing, opt. 7	This passage is part of the semi-continuous reading of Isaiah during Advent, but it also complements the Gospel (Lk 5:17–26), in which Jesus heals a lame man let down through the roof of his house.
35:4–7a	God will come to save; the blind, deaf, lame, and dumb will be healed; the parched ground will become a pool.	*23rd Sun. in OT (B)*	In fulfillment of this passage, Jesus cures a deaf and dumb man in the Gospel reading (Mk 7:31–37).
40:1–11	Comfort my people. A voice cries in the wilderness, "Prepare the way of the LORD." Every valley shall be exalted; the glory of the Lord shall be revealed. A herald brings good tidings to Zion; the Lord comes as a shepherd.	Tues., 2nd Week of Advent	The last verse of the passage (Is 40:11) develops the image of the Lord as kindly shepherd of his sheep Israel, and in the Gospel, Jesus tells the parable of the shepherd (Mt 18:12–14) who is unwilling that any should perish.

(*continued*)

Readings from Isaiah in the Lectionary and Liturgy of the Hours on Sundays, Feast Days, Liturgical Seasons, and Other Occasions (*continued*)

MSO = Masses for Special Occasions; *OM* = Optional Memorial;
VM = Votive Mass; *Rit* = Ritual; *LH* = Liturgy of the Hours

Passage	Description	Occasion	Explanation
40:1–5, 9–11	See above.	*2nd Sun. of Advent (B); Baptism of the Lord* (opt. C)	This passage is read early in Advent with the description of the ministry of John the Baptist (Mk 1:1–8), whom the Church acknowledges as the fulfillment of this prophecy. It is also paired with John's baptism of Jesus (Lk 3:15–16, 21–22) since it speaks both of a herald (John) and of the coming of the Lord (Jesus) to shepherd his people.
40:25–31	Who is like God, who brings out the stars and knows them by name? God does not grow weary, but "they who wait for the LORD shall renew their strength, . . . mount up with wings like eagles, . . . walk and not faint."	Wed., 2nd Week of Advent	This passage complements Jesus' words "Come to me, all who labor and are heavy laden" (Mt 11:28–30), showing that the attributes of the Lord in the OT prophets are manifested through Jesus of Nazareth.
41:13–20	"Fear not, you worm Jacob, . . . I [the LORD] will make of you a threshing sledge. . . . I will open rivers on the bare heights . . . [and] set in the desert the cypress, . . . that men may see and know that the hand of the LORD has done this."	Thurs., 2nd Week of Advent	The Gospel speaks of "men of violence" who take the kingdom "by force" (Mt 11:11–15). This may be a positive image of the spiritually aggressive who permit nothing to impede them from entering the kingdom of heaven (cf. Lk 14:26) and fits the militant imagery of Isaiah 41:13–20 (a "threshing sledge").
42:1–3	"Behold my servant. . . . I have put my Spirit upon him. . . . He will faithfully bring forth judgment."	*Rit*: Confirmation, opt. 2	In the context of confirmation, Isaiah 42:1–3 suggests the confirmand is an *alter Christus*, another Christ, who shares his anointing and mission.
42:1–4, 6–7	See above; plus, the servant shall judge the earth. God	*Baptism of the Lord (ABC)*	In the account of the Baptism (Mt 3:13–17), the divine commendation of Jesus ("in whom I am well pleased")

(*continued*)

Readings from Isaiah in the Lectionary and Liturgy of the Hours on Sundays, Feast Days, Liturgical Seasons, and Other Occasions (*continued*)

MSO = Masses for Special Occasions; *OM* = Optional Memorial;
VM = Votive Mass; *Rit* = Ritual; *LH* = Liturgy of the Hours

Passage	Description	Occasion	Explanation
	will give him as a "covenant to the people ... a light to the nations", to cure the blind and free the prisoner.		reprises Isaiah 42:1, and the whole passage (42:1–7) may be taken as a description of the ministry of Jesus: establishing justice, becoming a covenant, enlightening nations, freeing prisoners.
42:1–7	See above.	Mon. of Holy Week	During Holy Week, most of the Servant Songs are read in order to review the prophetic description of the role of the Christ.
43:16–21	As God once parted the Red Sea, now he will make a "way" and "rivers" in the wilderness for the sake of his people.	*5th Sun. of Lent (C)*	This passage functions as part of a review of salvation history in the first readings during Lent. It represents the hopes of the Israelites for restoration while they suffer the hardship of the exile.
43:18–19, 21–22, 24b–25	As above; yet Israel does not return to God; rather, it wearies him with its iniquities. Nonetheless, he will "blot out" their "transgressions" for his own sake.	*7th Sun. in OT (B)*	The Gospel reading revolves around the power of Jesus to forgive sin (Mk 2:1–12, the paralytic lowered by his friends). This is a power proper to the Lord God in the Old Testament, now exercised by Jesus of Nazareth.
44:1–3	"Fear not, O Jacob. ... I will pour water on the thirsty land, ... my Spirit upon your descendants."	*Rit*: Christian Initiation, opt. 7	The baptismal typology present in this text, with its association of water sprinkling and the gift of the Spirit, is fully deployed in the Rite of Christian Initiation.
44:1–5	As above; plus, "They shall spring up like grass.... One will say, I am the LORD's ... and surname himself by the name of Israel."	*Rit*: Consecration of Virgins & Religious Profession, opt. 7	Isaiah's vision of new "children" of Israel, born by the outpouring of the Spirit, who eagerly call themselves by the name of the Lord, is fulfilled in religious who embrace a total identification with the Lord and his ministry.
45:1, 4–6	The Lord has anointed Cyrus as his servant, even if Cyrus is unwitting that it is the Lord's doing.	*29th Sun. in OT (A)*	Isaiah 45:1–6 asserts God's dominion over the earth and the subsidiary role of King Cyrus. In the Gospel (Mt 22:15–21), Jesus teaches: "Render ... to Caesar the things that are Caesar's, and to God the things that are God's", stressing the distinction between the sacred and the political.

(continued)

Readings from Isaiah in the Lectionary and Liturgy of the Hours on Sundays, Feast Days, Liturgical Seasons, and Other Occasions (*continued*)

MSO = Masses for Special Occasions; *OM* = Optional Memorial;
VM = Votive Mass; *Rit* = Ritual; *LH* = Liturgy of the Hours

Passage	Description	Occasion	Explanation
45:6c–8, 18, 21c–25	There is no God but the Lord; he alone creates all things, knows all things. Unto him every knee shall bow and tongue swear. All flesh should come to him for salvation.	Wed., 3rd Week of Advent	This oracle follows the pattern of semi-continuous reading of Isaiah in the weekday Masses of Advent. The Gospel (Lk 7:18–23) has a loose connection, as Jesus' miracle and healings reported to John the Baptist are a kind of realization of the promise of salvation to the earth in Isaiah 45:22.
48:17–19	If the Israelites had listened to the Lord, they would have had peace like a river and become numerous like grains of sand.	Fri., 2nd Week of Advent	Jesus' rejection by his contemporaries ("this generation") in the Gospel (Mt 11:16–19) is parallel to the rejection of the Lord by Israel and the consequent failure to experience blessing.
49:1–6	The servant of the Lord speaks: "The LORD called me from the womb … to bring Jacob back to him." The Lord will also "give [him] as a light to the nations."	Nativity of the Baptist (June 24); Tues. of Holy Week	The role of the servant of the Lord to call Israel to repentance is primarily manifested in Jesus Christ, but secondarily in John the Baptist. During Holy Week, this great servant song is read as part of the prophetic description of the role of the Messiah in preparation for the observance of the Triduum.
49:3, 5–6	See above.	*2nd Sun. in OT (A)*	This passage is read with John's account of the Baptism of the Lord (Jn 1:29–34), because the servant's role as a "light to the nations" is understood as manifest at the Baptism as one of the three "epiphany" events: the Magi, the Baptism, the wedding at Cana.
49:8–15	The Lord has given the servant "as a covenant to the people", to restore them and their land, to lead a new exodus back to Zion, which the Lord cannot forget.	Wed., 4th Week of Lent	This passage reminds the faithful of the prophetic profile of the servant of the Lord, soon to be fully manifested in the experience of Christ during Holy Week.
49:13–15	Even if a woman could forget her sucking child, yet the Lord would not forget Zion.	*VM*: Sacred Heart, opt. 4	This dramatic image, in which the heart of God is compared to that of the mother of a nursling, serves to drive home the profound love of the Sacred Heart.

(*continued*)

Readings from Isaiah in the Lectionary and Liturgy of the Hours on Sundays, Feast Days, Liturgical Seasons, and Other Occasions (*continued*)

MSO = Masses for Special Occasions; *OM* = Optional Memorial;
VM = Votive Mass; *Rit* = Ritual; *LH* = Liturgy of the Hours

Passage	Description	Occasion	Explanation
49:14–15	See above.	*8th Sun. in OT (A)*	This passage is paired with Jesus' teaching on providence in the Sermon on the Mount (Mt 6:24–34). God is concerned even about sparrows; how much more his children? Both readings stress God's solicitude for the believer.
50:4–7	The Servant says, "I gave my back to those who struck me, ... I hid not my face from shame and spitting", yet "the Lord God helps me; ... I know that I shall not be put to shame."	*Palm Sunday*	This passage clarifies that the sufferings of the Christ, which are read in full on Palm/Passion Sunday, were not arbitrary or accidental but, rather, foreseen in the providence of God, the outworking of his will.
50:4–9a	See above. Plus, the servant declares his innocence.	*24th Sun. in OT (B)*; Wed. of Holy Week; *MSO*: For Our Oppressors, opt. 2; *VM*: Holy Cross, opt. 3	This passage complements Jesus' predictions of his Passion and his call to "take up [your] cross and follow me" (Mk 8:27–35). All who would follow Christ will share in his sufferings.
52:7–10	"How beautiful upon the mountains are the feet of him who brings good tidings.... The Lord has comforted his people, he has redeemed Jerusalem."	*Christmas Day*; St. Anthony Mary Claret; St. Columban; Common of Pastors, opt. 5	This unrestrained peal of joy by the prophet gives words to the Church's emotions at the celebration of the Incarnation of Christ, through whom God has definitively comforted and redeemed his people.
52:13– 53:12	The song of the Suffering Servant: "Surely he has borne our griefs ... with his stripes we are healed.... Like a lamb that is led to the slaughter ... he bore the sin of many, and made intercession for the transgressors."	*Good Friday*; *Rit*: Anointing, opt. 8; *VM*: Holy Cross, opt. 4; Jesus Christ Eternal High Priest, opt. 1	This longest and most famous of the passages describing the sufferings of the servant is reserved for Good Friday, when the Passion account is read again. The reading assures the faithful that the abuses suffered by Jesus were not accidents of history but expressions of the will of God revealed long before. The reading is redolent with priestly imagery, as the servant makes a sacrificial offering of his own body.

(*continued*)

Readings from Isaiah in the Lectionary and Liturgy of the Hours on Sundays, Feast Days, Liturgical Seasons, and Other Occasions (*continued*)

MSO = Masses for Special Occasions; *OM* = Optional Memorial;
VM = Votive Mass; *Rit* = Ritual; *LH* = Liturgy of the Hours

Passage	Description	Occasion	Explanation
53:1–5, 10–11	Excerpts from the above. "Upon him was the chastisement that made us whole, and with his stripes we are healed."	*MSO*: For the Sick, opt. 2	When praying for the sick, this reading teaches us that Christ expressed solidarity with our sickness by suffering bodily infirmity himself and that his sufferings merit for us the grace of healing.
53:10–11	The Lord's will is for the servant to make himself an offering for sin, that many may be accounted righteous.	29th Sun. in OT (B)	This passage clarifies the salvation-historical significance of Jesus' saying, "The Son of man ... came ... to give his life as a ransom for many", which concludes the Gospel reading (Mk 10:35–45), the pericope of James and John asking for the best seats in the kingdom.
54:1–10	The Lord will resume his covenant love for Zion; he will take it back like a wife only briefly forsaken.	Thurs., 3rd Week of Advent	This passage is part of the semi-continuous reading of Isaiah during the season of Advent.
54:5–14	See above. Plus, the Lord will rebuild Zion with precious stones and grant it righteousness and prosperity.	*Easter Vigil (4th Reading)*	This passage helps shape the vision of the Church as both Bride and Temple, a dual reality applied to the individual believer through the sacrament of baptism.
55:1–3	Let all the poor come and eat of a meal that will initiate them into the everlasting Davidic covenant.	*18th Sun. in OT (A)*	This passage is associated with the Gospel account of the feeding of the 5,000 (Mt 14:13–21) in order to draw out the Eucharistic typology of Jesus' miracle.
55:1–3, 6–9	See above. Plus, the Lord's thoughts and ways are higher than mankind's.	*MSO*: For Reconciliation, opt. 1	In the context of reconciliation, this reading characterizes the Eucharist as a meal of mercy for those who are poor in spirit, i.e., repentant.
55:1–11	See above. Plus, the word of the Lord will not return empty without accomplishing God's purpose.	*Baptism of the Lord (opt. B); Easter Vigil (5th reading)*	The strong Eucharistic overtones of this passage are particularly appropriate at the Easter Vigil, as many prepare to receive the sacrament for the first time. In the context of the Baptism, the "voice" of Isaiah 55:1–11 is understood as that of the baptized, the anointed Christ himself.

(*continued*)

Readings from Isaiah in the Lectionary and Liturgy of the Hours on Sundays, Feast Days, Liturgical Seasons, and Other Occasions (*continued*)

MSO = Masses for Special Occasions; *OM* = Optional Memorial;
VM = Votive Mass; *Rit* = Ritual; *LH* = Liturgy of the Hours

Passage	Description	Occasion	Explanation
55:6–9	"Seek the LORD while he may be found ...; let the wicked forsake his way.... My ways [are] higher than your ways and my thoughts than your thoughts."	*25th Sun. in OT (A)*; *MSO*: For Remission of Sins, opt. 1	This passage, with its obvious themes of repentance, complements the parable of the laborers in the vineyard (Mt 20:1–16a). God's mercy in this parable seems to defy the human sense of justice: "my thoughts [are higher] than your thoughts."
55:6–11	See above. Plus, the word of the LORD is like the rain that renders the fields fertile: it will not return empty without accomplishing God's purpose.	*MSO*: For Famine, opt. 3	This passage implies that the rain is a gift from God, analogous to his word and effective in the natural order, to "bring forth ... bread to the eater", a paramount concern in time of famine.
55:6–13	See above. Plus, "You shall go out in joy, and be led forth in peace ... all the trees of the field shall clap their hands."	*MSO*: For Productive Land, opt. 2.	The description of fertile fields blessed with rain as a sign of the efficacy of the word of God fits the attitude of thankfulness for the gift of productive land.
55:10–11	Like the rain that fertilizes seed, the word of the Lord will not return empty, without accomplishing his purpose.	*15th Sun. in OT (A)*; Tues., 1st Week of Lent; *Rit*: Institution of Readers, opt. 4	This passage complements Jesus' parable of the sower (Mt 13:1–23), which shares the same parallelism of seed and word. It is deployed also for those who serve by proclaiming the fertile word.
56:1, 6–7	The foreigners who join themselves to the Lord shall worship in the Temple, God's "house of prayer for all peoples".	*20th Sun. in OT (A)*; *MSO*: For the Church, opt. 1; For the Evangelization of Peoples, opt. 2	This passage provides prophetic context for the pericope of the Canaanite woman (Mt 15:21–28) and the inclusion of all the peoples of the earth within the Temple of Jesus' Body, which is the Church.
56:1–3a, 6–8	See above, preceded by an exhortation to do justice and concluded with a promise of the ingathering of Israel.	Fri., 3rd Week of Advent	The last of the semi-continuous readings from Isaiah during the weekdays of Advent, this reading again helps paint the picture of the economy of the New Covenant to be inaugurated by the servant of the Lord.

(*continued*)

Readings from Isaiah in the Lectionary and Liturgy of the Hours on Sundays, Feast Days, Liturgical Seasons, and Other Occasions (*continued*)
MSO = Masses for Special Occasions; *OM* = Optional Memorial; *VM* = Votive Mass; *Rit* = Ritual; *LH* = Liturgy of the Hours

Passage	Description	Occasion	Explanation
57:15–19	The Lord dwells in a high and holy place, but also with one of a "contrite and humble spirit".	*MSO*: For Peace and Justice, opt. 3	This passage comforts the faithful who are downtrodden by violence and injustice and who come to the Lord in a spirit of contrition and humility to seek redress of wrongs.
58:1–9a	Israel complains that God does not heed their fasting; God rebukes them for abusing their poor on their fast days; doing justice is a true "fast".	Fri. after Ash Wed.	These early readings in Lent serve to instruct the faithful in what constitutes fasting pleasing to God.
58:6–11	To care for the poor and oppressed is a pleasing "fast" to the Lord; he will bless those who do such things with every good thing.	St. Louis of France; St. Margaret of Scotland; Common of Holy Men/ Women, opt. 15; *MSO*: For the Country, City, Public Officials, Progress of Peoples, opt. 9	This passage is used on the memorials of saints who put into practice the Lord's commands about service to the poor and oppressed and in Masses where prayer is offered for public officials to follow their example.
58:7–10	"If you pour yourself out for the hungry and satisfy the desire of the afflicted, then shall your light rise in the darkness and your gloom be as the noonday."	*5th Sun. in OT (A)*	The Gospel (Mt 5:13–16) teaches that the disciples of Christ are salt and light: "Let your light so shine before men, that they may see your good works and give glory to your Father." Through Isaiah, "light" is defined as acts of justice and mercy to the needy.
58:9b–14	Those are blessed who care for the poor, oppressed, and hungry and observe the Sabbath day.	Sat. after Ash Wed.	This passage continues the catechesis on the proper form of fasting that runs through the first readings of the early days of Lent.
60:1–6	"Arise, shine; for your light has come." Nations	*Epiphany*; MSO. For the Church, opt. 2; For the	"Epiphany", the "shining forth" of Christ, is the proper context for this prophecy of the gathering of the nations

(*continued*)

Readings from Isaiah in the Lectionary and Liturgy of the Hours on Sundays, Feast Days, Liturgical Seasons, and Other Occasions (*continued*)
MSO = Masses for Special Occasions; *OM* = Optional Memorial; *VM* = Votive Mass; *Rit* = Ritual; *LH* = Liturgy of the Hours

Passage	Description	Occasion	Explanation
	and kings shall come to your light, caravans of camels bearing gold and frankincense from the East.	Evangelization of Peoples, opt. 3	to the light of God. The light of Christ continues to shine through the Church, as she evangelizes the nations.
61:1–2a, 10–11	"The Spirit of the Lord GOD is upon me, ... [he] has anointed me to bring good tidings to the afflicted.... The LORD ... has clothed me with the garments of salvation" and will cause righteousness among the nations.	*3rd Sun. of Advent (B)*	In this liturgical context, the words of Isaiah are applied to the forerunner, John the Baptist, who himself was "anointed" to preach "good news" to the people.
61:1–3a	"The Spirit of the Lord GOD is upon me, ... [he] has anointed me to bring good tidings to the afflicted, ... proclaim liberty to the captives ... [and] the year of the LORD's favor", to grant gladness to those who mourn in Zion.	St. Anthony of Padua; St. Martin of Tours; Common of Pastors, opt. 6; *Rit*: Holy Orders, opt. 3; *MSO*: For the Election of the Pope or a Bishop; For Priests, opt. 1	Saintly preachers and those called to a preaching vocation within the Church are conformed in a special way to Christ in his role as the anointed preacher to the poor of the earth.
61:1–3a, 6a, 8b–9	See above. Plus, "you shall be called priests of the LORD", and God will make an everlasting covenant with his people.	*Chrism Mass*; *Rit*: Confirmation, opt. 3	The theme of anointing conforms to the chrism and confirmation Masses, both directly tied to the conferral of the anointing of the Spirit for the common and/or ministerial priesthood.
61:9–11	"I will greatly rejoice in the LORD ... [who] has clothed me with the garments of salvation ... as a bride adorns herself	Immaculate Heart; Common of BVM, opt. 9; *Rit*: Consecration of Virgins & Religious	The feminine persona of this joyful voice of thanks is easily applied to the Blessed Mother and to the women religious who follow in her footsteps, seeking a nuptial relationship with God.

(*continued*)

Readings from Isaiah in the Lectionary and Liturgy of the Hours on Sundays,
Feast Days, Liturgical Seasons, and Other Occasions (*continued*)

MSO = Masses for Special Occasions; *OM* = Optional Memorial;
VM = Votive Mass; *Rit* = Ritual; *LH* = Liturgy of the Hours

Passage	Description	Occasion	Explanation
	with her jewels.... The Lord GOD will cause righteousness and praise to spring forth before all the nations."	Profession, opt. 8; *MSO*: For Religious, opt. 3	
62:1–5	Zion shall be vindicated and called "Married", because its sons shall marry it and God will rejoice over it like a bride.	*Christmas Vigil; 2nd Sun. in OT (C)*	The Incarnation represents the "marriage" of divine and human natures. This passage is employed also with the reading of the wedding at Cana (Jn 1:1–11), showing the larger salvation-historical overtones of this event in Jesus' life.
62:11–12	"Say to the daughter of Zion, 'Behold, your salvation comes ... his reward is with him....' They shall be called ... 'The redeemed of the LORD ... a city not forsaken.'"	*Christmas at Dawn*	This passage expresses the joy of the bridal people of God at the arrival of Christ our Bridegroom.
63:7–9	The prophet (or the servant) recounts the "steadfast love" (covenant fidelity) of God toward Israel.	*MSO*: In Thanksgiving to God, opt. 3	This passage articulates the sentiment of thanks for covenant faithfulness to God appropriate for liturgical observances of thanksgiving.
63:16b– 17, 19b; 64:2–7	A cry to God to have mercy on his people, for they have all become unclean and faded away because of their iniquities.	*1st Sun. of Advent (B)*	This passage prompts a posture of penitence among the faithful at the start of Advent, focused on the Second Coming (Mk 13:33–37) and the repentance necessary to prepare for it.
65:17–21	The Lord will restore Jerusalem and bless it abundantly: "No more shall there be in it an infant that lives but a few days."	Mon., 4th Week of Lent	This passage accompanies the account of the healing of the official's servant (Jn 4:43–54), showing Jesus' healing ministry to be an expression of the prophecies of the restoration of Israel.

(*continued*)

	Readings from Isaiah in the Lectionary and Liturgy of the Hours on Sundays, Feast Days, Liturgical Seasons, and Other Occasions (*continued*)		
	MSO = Masses for Special Occasions; *OM* = Optional Memorial; *VM* = Votive Mass; *Rit* = Ritual; *LH* = Liturgy of the Hours		
Passage	Description	Occasion	Explanation
66:10–14c	"Rejoice with Jerusalem ... that you may ... be satisfied with her consoling breasts", for the Lord will extend peace and prosperity to her "like a river".	*14th Sun. in OT (C)*; Common of BVM; Our Lady of Lourdes; St. Thérèse of Lisieux	This passage is paired with the mission of the seventy-two (Lk 10:1–20) to reveal the healing and preaching mission of the disciples as the "river of peace and prosperity" to Israel promised by the prophet. In other contexts, the BVM or other female saints are seen as realizations of the image of the "virgin mother Zion".
66:18–21	"I am coming to gather all nations and tongues; and they shall come and shall see my glory": an eschatological vision of the incoming of the nations.	*21st Sun. in OT (C)*	Jesus warns the disciples to enter the kingdom by the narrow door: "There you will weep ... when you see Abraham and ... all the prophets in the kingdom of God and you yourselves thrust out. And men will come from east and west, and from north and south, and sit at table in the kingdom of God" (Lk 13:28–29).

The readings from Isaiah in daily Mass focus on historical narratives embedded in the book that provide some information about the eighth-century B.C. ministry of the prophet Isaiah.

Reading of Isaiah for Daily Mass: Ordinary Time, Year II: Weeks 14–15			
Week	Day	Passage Read	Description
14	Sa	6:1–8	Isaiah's call vision: He sees the heavenly throne room of God, the six-winged seraphim calling "Holy, holy, holy", and receives his commission as a prophet.
15	M	1:10–17	God calls Jerusalem "Sodom" and "Gomorrah" and rebukes the leaders for hypocritical worship. He urges them to repent and do justice.
15	Tu	7:1–9	Isaiah goes to meet Ahaz and tells him the Syrians and Ephraimites will soon be vanquished.
15	W	10:5–7, 13b–16	Assyria is arrogant, not realizing that it is just an axe in the hands of the Lord that will soon be judged itself.
15	Th	26:7–9, 12, 16–19	The prophet utters a psalm of lament on behalf of Jerusalem and Judah, but ends in praise: "The dead shall live, their bodies shall rise!"
15	F	38:1–6, 21–22, 7–8	Hezekiah falls sick, but he repents and weeps bitterly; God adds fifteen years to his life.

The Liturgy of the Hours employs more Canticles from Isaiah than from any other biblical book outside the Psalms themselves:

Canticles of Isaiah in the Office of Readings for the Liturgy of the Hours	
Passage	Occasion
2:2–3	Common of the Dedication of a Church, Vigil Canticle II
2:2–5	Monday, Week III, Morning Prayer, Canticle
12:1–6	Thursday, Week II, Morning Prayer, Canticle; Vigil for Christ the King, Canticle
26:1–4, 7–9, 12	Tuesday, Week III, Morning Prayer, Canticle
33:2–10	Vigil for Sundays of Ordinary Time, Canticle I
33:13–16	Wednesday, Week III, Morning Prayer, Canticle; Vigil for Sundays of Ordinary Time, Canticle II
38:10–14, 17–20	Tuesday, Week II, Morning Prayer, Canticle; also for Morning Prayer of the Office of the Dead
40:10–17	Thursday, Week III, Morning Prayer, Canticle
42:10–16	Monday, Week IV, Morning Prayer, Canticle
45:15–25	Friday Week I, Morning Prayer, Canticle
61:6–9	Vigil of an Apostle, Canticle I
61:10—62:3	Vigil of the BVM, Canticle I
61:10—62:5	Wednesday, Week IV, Morning Prayer, Canticle; Vigil of Christ the King, Canticle III (34th Sun. in OT)
62:4–7	Common of the BVM, Vigil, Canticle II
66:10–14a	Thursday, Week IV, Morning Prayer, Canticle

Isaiah in the Office of Readings for the Liturgy of the Hours for Advent, Christmas, and Epiphany (Dischronologized readings are in bold.)			
Passage	Occasion	Passage	Occasion
1:1–18	Sun., 1st Week of Advent	21:6–12	Sat., 1st Week
1:21–27; 2:1–5	Mon., 1st Week	22:8b–23	Sun., 2nd Week of Advent
2:6–22; 4:2–6	Tues., 1st Week	24:1–18	Mon., 2nd Week
5:1–7	Wed., 1st Week	24:19—25:5	Tues., 2nd Week
11:1–10	*See Christmas.*	25:6—26:6	Wed., 2nd Week
16:1–5; 17:4–8	Thurs., 1st Week	26:7–21	Thurs., 2nd Week
19:16–25	Fri., 1st Week	27:1–13	Fri., 2nd Week

(continued)

Isaiah in the Office of Readings for the Liturgy of the Hours for Advent, Christmas, and Epiphany (*continued*) (Dischronologized readings are in bold.)			
Passage	Occasion	Passage	Occasion
29:1–8	Sat., 2nd Week	46:1–13	Dec. 18
29:13–24	Sun., 3rd Week of Advent	47:1, 3b–15	Dec. 19
30:18–26	Mon., 3rd Week	48:1–11	Dec. 20
30:27–33; 31:4–9	Tues., 3rd Week	48:12–21	Dec. 21a
31:1–3; 32:1–8	Wed., 3rd Week	49:1–9	*See Baptism.*
32:15—33:6	Thurs., 3rd Week	49:9b–13	Dec. 21b
33:7–24	Fri., 3rd Week	49:14—50:1	Dec. 22
42:1–8	*See Fri. after Jan 2.*	51:1–11	Dec. 23
42:1–9	*See Baptism.*	51:17—52:2, 7–10	Dec. 24
45:1–13	Dec. 17	**11:1–10**	Christmas

The Liturgy of the Hours also follows ancient Church tradition by reading the book of Isaiah (semi-)continuously during Advent up to Christmas and then again from Epiphany to the Baptism. Particular emphasis is placed on four passages that are not read in sequence but reserved for the highest feast days: Isaiah 11:1–10, read at Christmas; Isaiah 42:1–9 and 49:1–9, read at the Baptism; and Isaiah 60:1–22, read at Epiphany.

Another, quite different, selection of readings from Isaiah occurs in the Twentieth Week in Ordinary Time. Like the selections from Isaiah in the first readings for daily Mass in Ordinary Time, this sequence focuses on the historical ministry of the prophet in the context of eighth-century B.C. Jerusalem.

Isaiah in the Office of Readings for the Liturgy of the Hours, Season of Epiphany	
42:1–8	Fri. between Jan 2 and Epiphany
61:1–11	Sat. between Jan 2 and Epiphany
60:1–22	Epiphany
61:1–11	Mon. after Epiphany
62:1–12	Tues. after Epiphany
63:7–19	Wed. after Epiphany
63:19b—64:11	Thurs. after Epiphany
65:13–25	Fri. after Epiphany
66:10–14; 18–23	Sat. after Epiphany
42:1–9; 49:1–9	Baptism of the Lord

Conclusion

Isaiah is the first and greatest of the prophetic books in the Church's canon, unrivaled in its theological and liturgical influence except by the Psalms and Gospels. The prophet condemned his contemporaries for their violations of God's covenant given through Moses but is best remembered for his lyrical descriptions of the coming "anointed one", or Messiah, and the era of peace he will inaugurate

Passage	Day	Description
		**Isaiah in the Office of Readings for the Liturgy of the Hours, Ordinary Time, Week 20**
6:1–13	Su	Isaiah's call vision, when he sees the heavenly throne room of God, the six-winged seraphim calling "Holy, holy, holy", and receives his commission as a prophet. The people will not listen to his message until they are driven into exile and only a remnant remains.
3:1–15	M	The Lord will bring siege on Jerusalem and Judah until they are reduced to a tiny remnant, barely subsisting, due to their sins.
7:1–17	Tu	In the midst of the Syro-Ephraimite War, Isaiah utters the "Immanuel" prophecy to Ahaz.
9:7—10:4	W	The prophecy of the Davidic "Son" who will be "Wonderful Counselor, Mighty God" and rule in peace; followed by an oracle of judgment against Ephraim and Judah.
11:1–16	Th	Prophecy of a "shoot" from Jesse, anointed by the Spirit to rule in peace and justice. Creation will be renewed, and a new exodus will follow.
30:1–18	F	Isaiah warns Israel not to trust in Egypt for salvation but to trust in the Lord.
37:21–35	Sa	Isaiah's oracle against Sennacherib, predicting his defeat and departure after the siege of Jerusalem.

(Is 9, 11, 35, 40–66). Isaiah's "Servant Songs", his celebrated poetic descriptions of an eschatological savior figure, constitute a sort of "proto-Christology"; his prophetic descriptions of restored Zion, inhabited by the redeemed "remnant" of Israel and the nations, constitutes a "proto-ecclesiology"; and his visions of a messianic feast and the outpouring of God's Spirit like water constitute a "proto-pneumatology". Thus the early Church was convinced that in this prophetic book, the sum of her faith could be found in types and figures.

For Further Reading

Commentaries and Studies on Isaiah

Blenkinsopp, Joseph. *Isaiah*. 3 vols. Anchor Yale Bible 19–19b. New York: Doubleday, 2000–2003.

Childs, Brevard S. *Isaiah*. Old Testament Library. Louisville, Ky.: Westminster John Knox Press, 2000.

Chisholm, Robert B., Jr. *Handbook on the Prophets*. Grand Rapids, Mich.: Baker Academic, 2002. (See pp. 13–152.)

Kaiser, Otto. *Isaiah*. 2 vols. Old Testament Library. Louisville, Ky.: Westminster John Knox Press, 1996.

Oswalt, John N. *The Book of Isaiah*. 2 vols. Grand Rapids, Mich.: Eerdmans, 1986–1998.

Wildberger, Hans. *Isaiah: A Continental Commentary*. 3 vols. Translated by Thomas H. Trapp. Continental Commentary 23a–c. Minneapolis: Fortress Press, 1991–2002.

Historical Issues in Isaiah

Baker, David W. "Isaiah". Pages 3–277 in *Isaiah, Jeremiah, Lamentations, Ezekiel, Daniel.* Vol. 4 of *Zondervan Bible Backgrounds Commentary.* Edited by John Walton. Grand Rapids, Mich.: Zondervan, 2009.

Collins, John J. *Introduction to the Hebrew Bible.* Minneapolis: Fortress Press, 1998. (See pp. 307–308.)

Doorly, William J. *Isaiah of Jerusalem: An Introduction.* New York: Paulist Press, 1992.

Josephus. *Jewish Antiquities: Books 9–11.* Vol. 4. Translated by Ralph Marcus. Loeb Classical Library 326. Cambridge, Mass.: Harvard University Press, 1937.

Margalioth, Rachel. *The Indivisible Isaiah: Evidence for the Single Authorship of the Prophetic Book.* New York: Yeshiva University, 1964.

Stromberg, Jacob. *An Introduction to the Study of Isaiah.* London and New York: T&T Clark, 2011.

Isaiah in the Living Tradition

Childs, Brevard S. *The Struggle to Understand Isaiah as Christian Scripture.* Grand Rapids, Mich.: Eerdmans, 2004.

Cyril of Alexandria, Saint. *Commentary on Isaiah.* 3 vols. Translated by Robert Charles Hill. Brookline: Holy Cross Orthodox Press, 2008–2009.

———. "Commentary on Isaiah". In *Saint Cyril of Alexandria: Interpreter of the Old Testament.* Edited by Alexander Kerrigan. Analecta Biblica 2. Rome: Pontifical Biblical Institute, 1952.

Elliott, Mark W. *Isaiah 40–66.* Old Testament 11 of Ancient Christian Commentary on Scripture. Edited by Thomas C. Oden. Downers Grove, Ill.: InterVarsity Press, 2007.

Ephrem the Syrian, Saint. "Commentary on Isaiah". In *Saint Cyril of Alexandria: Interpreter of the Old Testament.* Edited by Alexander Kerrigan. Analecta Biblica 2. Rome: Pontifical Biblical Institute, 1952.

Eusebius of Caesarea. "Commentary on Isaiah". In *Saint Cyril of Alexandria: Interpreter of the Old Testament.* Edited by Alexander Kerrigan. Analecta Biblica 2. Rome: Pontifical Biblical Institute, 1952.

———. *Proof of the Gospel.* 2 vols. Translated by William John Ferrar. 1920. Repr., Eugene, Ore.: Wipf & Stock, 2001.

Gambero, Luigi. *Mary and the Fathers of the Church.* Translated by Thomas Buffer. San Francisco: Ignatius Press, 1999.

Manley, Johanna. *Isaiah through the Ages.* Menlo Park, Calif.: Monastery Books, 1997.

McKinion, Steven A. *Isaiah 1–39.* Old Testament 10 of Ancient Christian Commentary on Scripture. Edited by Thomas C. Oden. Downers Grove, Ill.: InterVarsity Press, 2004.

Sawyer, John F. A. *The Fifth Gospel: Isaiah in the History of Christianity.* New York: Cambridge University Press, 1996.

Theophylact. *The Explanation of Blessed Theophylact of the Holy Gospel according to St. Matthew.* Introduction by Christopher Stade. House Springs, Mo.: Chrysostom Press, 1992.

Wilken, Robert Louis. *Isaiah: Interpreted by Early Christian and Medieval Commentators.* The Church's Bible. Grand Rapids, Mich.: Eerdmans, 2007.

31. JEREMIAH

Introduction

The book of Jeremiah is the longest book of the prophets in the traditional Hebrew (Masoretic Text). Nonetheless, the book is clearly second to Isaiah in its theological and liturgical influence. Although there are several thematic, literary, and theological similarities between Isaiah and Jeremiah, one significant difference is that in Jeremiah, the biography of the prophet himself takes on a much more prominent role. Moreover, a significant body of literature also came to be associated with Jeremiah: in addition to the book of Jeremiah itself, (1) the book of Lamentations and (2) the book of Baruch, the scribe of Jeremiah, also came to be considered part of the composition "Jeremiah" in certain documents and canon lists of the early Church and the Church Fathers (for more on Lamentations and Baruch, see chapters 32–33).

The Textual History of the Book of Jeremiah

The book of Jeremiah is considered canonical by rabbinic Judaism and all branches of Christianity. However, in antiquity the book circulated in at least two distinct literary forms: (1) a *shorter* version of Jeremiah, preserved by the Greek Septuagint (LXX); and (2) a *longer* version of the book preserved in the Masoretic Text (MT). In fact, the Greek LXX version of Jeremiah is about one-eighth shorter than the Hebrew MT version (that is, around 2,700 words less). Another major difference between the two versions (LXX and MT) concerns the order of the chapters. In the MT, the book of Jeremiah ends with the so-called "oracles against the nations" (Jer 46–51), whereas in the LXX, these oracles are all located within chapter 25 (according to the English chapter divisions). Needless to say, as a result of such differences, scholars have debated whether the shorter or longer edition was more original and whether the changes were due to the freedom of the Greek translators or to variations among Hebrew editions of the book.

Our knowledge of the textual history of the book of Jeremiah changed dramatically with the discovery of the Dead Sea Scrolls in the late 1940s. Among the Qumran scrolls, scholars found fragments of Hebrew manuscripts of Jeremiah following *both* the shorter LXX edition and the longer MT.[1] Thus it became apparent that two different *Hebrew* editions were in circulation prior to the translation of the Septuagint. In fact, the additions to the text of Jeremiah in the MT seem to be the result of a conscious process of editing of the

---

[1] Martin G. Abegg Jr., Peter Flint, and Eugene Ulrich, *The Dead Sea Scrolls Bible: The Oldest Known Bible Translated for the First Time into English* (San Francisco: HarperOne, 1999), 382–83.

earlier text form reflected in the LXX. The additions were added to clarify, specify, amplify, and generally elucidate the oracles of the prophet. For example, the MT provides headings and historical/biographical information, absent in the LXX, about the circumstances under which certain prophetic oracles were delivered. As a result, Jeremiah MT is longer but easier for later generations of readers to understand. Indeed, around the turn of the fifth century A.D., Saint Jerome translated a Hebrew version of Jeremiah similar in form to the Masoretic Text for the Vulgate, and so the longer version of Jeremiah has become the standard text in the Catholic tradition.

The Life and Times of the Prophet Jeremiah

Since the book of Jeremiah contains a large number of historical narratives as well as sermons and oracles with precise dates and historical circumstances, it is useful briefly to review the history of Judah during the lifetime of Jeremiah so as to read the book with greater understanding.

We have more detail about the life of Jeremiah than that of any other prophet in the Old Testament. Jeremiah—whose name, tellingly, means "The LORD will restore" (Hebrew *Yirmeyahu*; Greek *'Ieremias*)—was born during the reign of King Josiah of Judah (ca. 640–609 B.C.). He was the son of an unnamed priest from the town of Anathoth (following the RSV), one of the cities of the Levites (Jer 1:1; cf. Josh 21:8). He served as a priest and prophet during the tumultuous and dark years leading up to the dominant event in his lifetime: the invasion of Judah by the Babylonian Empire and the destruction of Jerusalem and its Temple in the year 587 B.C. (cf. 2 Kings 25). Despite years of persecution (and even attempts at execution), Jeremiah survived the siege and destruction of Jerusalem and is recorded as still prophesying to the Jews in Egypt as late as 585 B.C. (Jer 40–43). According to later Jewish tradition, it was Jeremiah who actually removed the Ark of the Covenant from the Temple in Jerusalem and hid it in a cave on Mount Nebo, east of the Jordan River (2 Mac 2:4–8), before the Babylonians came and destroyed the Temple.

The life and ministry of Jeremiah spanned the reigns of several consequential (and tragic) kings in the southern kingdom of Judah. He was born during the reign of King Josiah, who led a political and religious revival of the Judean state in the late seventh century (640–609 B.C.). This "Josianic reform", as scholars refer to it, involved a return to careful observance of the Mosaic covenant, prompted by the famous "finding of the law" in the Temple around 622 B.C. (2 Kings 22:3—23:27). After Pharaoh Neco II slew Josiah in the battle on the plains of Megiddo (2 Kings 23:28–30), he was succeeded briefly by his son Jehoahaz (609 B.C., also called "Shallum"; cf. Jer 22:11–12). Within three months, however, Pharaoh Neco's troops arrived and deposed Jehoahaz, replacing him with his brother Eliakim, to whom the pharaoh gave the throne name Jehoiakim (2 Kings 23:31–35). Jehoiakim reigned for eleven years (609–598 B.C.), during which time Judah's previous good fortunes were eclipsed. In the fourth year of Jehoiakim's reign, the Babylonians once again attacked the Assyrian capital of Carchemish and soundly defeated the combined Assyrian and Egyptian forces (605 B.C.).

With this defeat, Assyria ceased to exist, Pharaoh Neco II withdrew the remains of his army within the borders of Egypt, and the territory of the Levant was exposed to being seized by the Babylonians—thus paving the way for the eventual overthrow of the kingdom of Judah. In this same year (605 B.C.), King Jehoiakim became a vassal of Nebuchadnezzar II of Babylon (605–582 B.C.), and Nebuchadnezzar deported some members of the royal house and aristocracy to serve as hostages guaranteeing Jehoiakim's political compliance. This was the first and smallest of the waves of exiles to Babylon and included the prophet Daniel and his companions (cf. Dan 1:3–7). Contrary to the messages of Jeremiah, King Jehoiakim rashly rebelled against Nebuchadnezzar around 598 B.C., thinking that the support of Egypt would enable him to withstand the Babylonian king. But the Egyptian assistance did not materialize. Jehoiakim himself, however, died while the Babylonians were en route to besiege Jerusalem and never experienced the disaster that resulted from his policies. That sorry fate awaited his hapless son King Jehoiachin, who reigned for three months before giving himself up to Nebuchadnezzar and the besieging Babylonian forces (ca. 597 B.C.), who promptly deported him and all the upper and middle classes of Jerusalem and Judah—royalty, aristocracy, priests, scribes, craftsmen, soldiers—to captivity in Babylon (2 Kings 24:10–17). This was the second and largest wave of exiles to Babylon, from whom the majority of the postexilic Judean community would ultimately arise. The poor people of the land were left behind, ruled by a skeleton administration under Jehoiachin's uncle Mattaniah, the son of Josiah and younger brother of Jehoiakim and Jehoahaz. Mattaniah took the throne name Zedekiah (2 Kings 24:18–20).

King Zedekiah ruled eleven years in Jerusalem, but ultimately followed the same pro-Egyptian, anti-Babylonian policy as his brother Jehoiakim and experienced a similar fate (597–587 B.C.). Eventually, the Babylonians placed Jerusalem under siege, and the city fell in 587 B.C., at which time Nebuchadnezzar captured Zedekiah, executed his sons in front of his face, gouged out his eyes, and deported him in chains to Babylon (2 Kings 25:7). All the remaining middle and upper classes of Judah and Jerusalem were deported in this third wave of exiles to Babylon (587 B.C.; 2 Kings 25:11). Although this wave of exiles was much smaller than the second, the event was more traumatic because it coincided with the destruction of the Temple and city by fire and the end of the rule of Davidic kings. In the wake of the destruction of Jerusalem, King Nebuchadnezzar of Babylon appointed a certain aristocrat, Gedaliah, as governor of Judah (Jer 40:5), but Gedaliah was assassinated within a year or two (Jer 41:1). Many of the few remaining Jews in Judah fled to Egypt for refuge from Babylonian reprisal, taking Jeremiah and his scribe, Baruch, along with them (Jer 42:1—43:13). Jeremiah is last recorded prophesying judgment against the idolatrous Jews in Egyptian exile around 585 B.C. (Jer 44:1–30).

Although the book itself does not tell us how his life ended, according to one extra-biblical first-century Jewish writing, "he [Jeremiah] died in Taphnai of Egypt, having been stoned by his people."[2]

---

[2] *Lives of the Prophets* 2.1, in D.R. Hare, "Lives of the Prophets", in *The Old Testament Pseudepigrapha*, vol. 2, ed. James H. Charlesworth, Anchor Bible Reference Library (New York: Doubleday, 1985), 386–88.

Literary Structure of Jeremiah

The organizational structure of the book of Jeremiah is not always easy to discern and continues to be a subject of debate among biblical scholars. Nonetheless, there is widespread agreement that the first and last chapters form a prologue and epilogue to the work, both expressing a dominant theme of judgment on Judah and a minor theme of hope for a future restoration (Jer 1 and 52). There is also widespread agreement that the book divides roughly into two major halves: (1) Jeremiah 1–25 and (2) Jeremiah 26–51. Although there is much in common between the two parts, there are also some clear literary differences: the first half is loosely organized, seldom dated or provenanced, and largely poetic. The second half, however, is better organized, with date, provenance, and circumstances provided for almost every oracle or incident recounted, and consists largely of prose, with the exception of the "Oracles against the Nations" with which the book ends (Jer 46–51). If Jeremiah 2–6 is recognized as a kind of general summation of the prophet's message, we arrive at the following basic outline:

Outline of the Book of Jeremiah

I. Prologue: Jeremiah's Call and Commission: Judgment and Hope (Jer 1:1–19)
 A. Historical Context (1:1–3)
 B. Jeremiah's Call (1:4–11)
 C. Jeremiah's First Programmatic Vision (1:11–12)
 D. Jeremiah's Second Programmatic Vision (1:13–19)

II. Summary of Jeremiah's Prophetic Message (Jer 2:1—6:30)
 A. Israel Is an Unfaithful Bride, Part 1 (2:1—3:5)
 B. Israel Is an Unfaithful Bride, Part 2 (3:6—4:4)
 C. The Lord Brings Evil from the North (4:5—6:30)

Book 1 of Jeremiah (7–25)

III. Judgment from the Temple to the Nations (Jer 7–25)
 A. Sermons and Signs from Jeremiah's Ministry (7:1—17:18)
  1. The "Temple Sermon" and Ensuing Lament (7:1—9:26)
  2. The Dialogue on Idolatry and Judgment (10:1–25)
  3. The "Covenant Sermon" and Ensuing Dialogue of Complaint (11:1—12:17)
  4. Two Prophetic Signs and an Oracle about Harlotry (13:1–27)
  5. The Oracle of the Great Drought and Ensuing Dialogue (14:1—15:21)
  6. The Sign of Celibacy and Related Oracles (16:1—17:18)
 B. Persecution: The Benjamin Gate–Potter's House Incidents (17:19—20:18)
  1. The "Sabbath Sermon" at the Benjamin Gate (17:19–27)
  2. The Lesson at the Potter's House (18:1–23)

What we have called part 1 and part 2 of Jeremiah both show a similarity of structure: each part begins with a sermon of judgment that Jeremiah delivers at the Temple (cf. Jer 7 and 26), then recounts oracles and incidents from the prophet's life that bring him into conflict with kings, priests, prophets, and people (cf. Jer 8–24 and 27–44), and finally concludes with oracles of judgment against the whole earth (cf. Jer 25 and 46–51). Since the Temple was viewed as the mystical center of the cosmos, the movement from judgment on the Temple to universal judgment is particularly appropriate.

Key Dates in the Book of Jeremiah

When reading the book of Jeremiah, it is important to keep in mind that the oracles and incidents are not evenly distributed throughout the reigns of the kings under whom he ministered but, rather, are clustered around dates of crisis:

1. 609 B.C.: the year of Josiah's death, Jehoahaz/Shallum's deposition, and Jehoiakim's first regnal year (Jer 22:11–23; 26:1–24);
2. 605 B.C.: the fourth year of Jehoiakim, the year of the Battle of Carchemish, the imposition of Babylonian suzerainty, and the initial (small) exile of upper-class hostages (Jer 25:1–38; 36:1–32; 45:1–5; 46:1–28);
3. 597 B.C.: the year of Jehoiachin/Jeconiah's surrender of Jerusalem, the second and largest wave of exiles to Babylon, and the accession of Zedekiah (Jer 24:1–10; 27:1—29:32);

4. 587 B.C.: the year of the destruction of the Temple and Jerusalem, the end of Davidic rule, and the third and last wave of exiles to Babylon. All the words and deeds of Jeremiah in 21:1–10; 32:1—34:22; 37:1—44:30; and 52:1–30 occur within a year or two before or after this date.

By keeping these key dates in mind while reading, one can "anchor" the various prophetic oracles of Jeremiah to the times, places, and political situations he is addressing.

Literary Sub-Genres in Jeremiah

The book of Jeremiah displays a wider range of distinct genres than most of the other prophets, and the diversity gives the book a certain literary dynamism. Among the different genres we may distinguish the following:

1. *Sermons*: messages from the Lord rendered in prose, portrayed as delivered orally to a public audience on a specific occasion, and later recorded (for example, Jer 7:1—8:3).
2. *Oracles*: messages from the Lord rendered in poetry, delivered orally or in written form or both (for example, Jer 2:1—3:5).
3. *Confessions*: deeply personal speeches of the prophet directed to God, typically marked by lament or complaint (for example, Jer 11:18–20; 12:1–4).
4. *Dialogues*: in which the prophet will speak to the Lord, often expressing a complaint or posing a question, followed by the Lord's response, sometimes through several iterations (for example, Jer 10:1–25; 11:1—12:17; 14:1—15:21).
5. *Prophetic Signs*: records of a public demonstration with a moral or theological message, often using a specific person, place, or thing as a visible object lesson. Significantly, these signs are not mere symbols; they effect what they signify, setting the symbolized events in motion (for example, Jer 13:1–11).
6. *Letters*: between a prophet and certain addressees, communicating a message from the Lord (for example, Jer 29:1–28).
7. *Historical Narratives*: of events in the prophet's life, often similar in style to the narratives constituting the Deuteronomistic History, especially the books of Kings (for example, Jer 37–44).

By keeping these various literary genres in mind while reading, one can more easily navigate the vast array of material in this extremely long and complex compilation.

Overview of Jeremiah

The Call of Jeremiah the Prophet (Jeremiah 1)

The prologue of Jeremiah consists of four sections: the historical context of his ministry (Jer 1:1–3), his initial call experience and commissioning (Jer 1:4–10), and two visions—that of the rod of almond and that of the boiling pot—whose content characterizes his entire ministry (Jer 1:11–19). In this opening section of the book, we learn several important facts about Jeremiah:

First, his prophetic ministry begins during the reign of King Josiah of Judah and continues all the way through the tumultuous years leading up to "the captivity of Jerusalem" under Babylon in 587 B.C. (Jer 1:1–3).

Second, given the description of the call vision, Jeremiah was a youth when he was divinely summoned to the prophetic ministry. The Lord commissions him in these famous words:

> "Before I formed you in the womb I knew you,
> and before you were born I consecrated you;
> I appointed you a prophet to the nations."
> Then I said, "Ah, Lord GOD! Behold, I do not know how to speak,
>   for I am only a youth." But the LORD said to me,
> "Do not say, 'I am only a youth';
> for to all to whom I send you you shall go,
> and whatever I command you you shall speak....
> "Behold, I have put my words in your mouth.
> See, I have set you this day over nations and over kingdoms,
> to pluck up and to break down,
> to destroy and to overthrow,
> to build and to plant."
>
> (Jer 1:5–7, 9–10)

Notice here that Jeremiah's career is described with six verbs: the first four describe judgment ("pluck up", "break down", "destroy", "overthrow"), and the last two describe restoration ("build" and "plant"). These verses, which contain both judgment and hope but put the greater emphasis on judgment, are an apt characterization of the kind of prophetic ministry Jeremiah is going to carry out and, indeed, of the character of the book of Jeremiah as a whole. Most of the book of Jeremiah is judgment; the few oracles of hope, although significant, are largely limited to a single section (Jer 29–33).

Third, in addition to this programmatic description of his prophetic call, Jeremiah also describes two prophetic visions, one of a "rod of almond" (Jer 1:11–12) and the other of a "boiling pot" pouring out from the north (Jer 1:13–19). The meaning of the almond-branch vision depends on a wordplay between "almond" (Hebrew *shaqed*) and "watching" (Hebrew *shoqed*). The Lord asserts, "I am watching over my word to perform it" (Jer 1:12). Likewise, the boiling pot in the north represents Babylon and all its allies, who will be "poured out" over Judah in a southward sweep. Strictly speaking, Babylon was far to the east of Judah, but the transportation routes of the Fertile Crescent channeled the Babylonian armies northwest up the Euphrates and then southward down to Judah through Lebanon (or Syria), Galilee, and Samaria. Indeed, these two visions set the stage for the rest of the book of Jeremiah: God's vigilance to fulfill the prophetic word, however ominous, and the coming of destruction from the north (Babylon) will constitute much of the focus of this prophet's life and career.

Spiritual Adultery and the New Exodus (Jeremiah 2–6)

After the prologue's introduction to the life of Jeremiah and certain central messages in the book, the next major section also contains oracles that are unified by another critical theme in the work of this prophet: the image of the sinful city of Jerusalem as a wayward "bride" of YHWH the divine "Bridegroom".

In a series of oracles, Jeremiah describes the chosen city, Jerusalem, the heart of all Israel, as a wife once in love with the Lord who has succumbed to lust for other lovers, committed spiritual adultery, and has now been divorced as a result (Jer 2:2–3, 23–25; 3:1–10, 20). Consider, for example, the following striking description of how both Israel (the northern tribes) and Judah (the southern tribes) played the "harlot" through acts of idolatry on the pagan hilltop sanctuaries:

> The LORD said to me in the days of King Josiah: "Have you seen what she did, that faithless one, Israel, *how she went up on every high hill and under every green tree, and there played the harlot?* And I thought, 'After she has done all this she will return to me'; but she did not return, and her false sister Judah saw it. She saw that for all the adulteries of that faithless one, Israel, I had sent her away with a decree of divorce; yet her false sister Judah did not fear, but *she too went and played the harlot.* Because harlotry was so light to her, she polluted the land, *committing adultery with stone and tree.*" (Jer 3:6–9)

Marriage is a covenant relationship between spouses. Therefore, just as marriage demands the exclusive devotion of the partners, so the covenant with the Lord demanded Judah's exclusive worship and obedience. The imagery of spiritual "harlotry" or "adultery" is also appropriate given the likelihood that the ancient pagan idolatry into which the people of Judah were falling involved acts of cultic prostitution (cf. Is 57:7–8).[3] The sins of the people of Judah are *not just the breaking of a "rule", but are the betrayal of a relationship* with a personal God.

In light of such acts of spiritual adultery, it is no wonder that Jeremiah goes on to deliver several vivid, dramatic descriptions of the disaster that awaits Judah and Jerusalem at the hands of the foe from the north (Jer 4:6; 6:1, 22). Nevertheless, in the midst of these oracles of judgment, he also speaks of the coming "new exodus", in which the scattered people of God will be gathered to Jerusalem, which shall be called "the throne of the LORD". This "new exodus" will be so momentous that "the ark of the covenant of the LORD"—the sign of the first exodus and first covenant—"shall not ... be remembered, or missed" (Jer 3:16–17). Significantly, this "new exodus" will entail, not just the return of the southern tribes of Judah from exile, but the restoration of all twelve tribes: the joining of "the house of Judah" (two southern tribes) and "the house of Israel" (ten northern tribes) in a return from "the land of the north" to which they have been exiled (Jer 3:18).

Book 1: Judgment from the Temple to the Nations (Jeremiah 7–25)

As we saw above in our discussion of the structure of Jeremiah, the next major section can be described as "book 1" of Jeremiah's prophecies of judgment,

---

[3] Raymond C. Ortlund, *God's Unfaithful Wife: A Biblical Theology of Spiritual Adultery* (Downers Grove, Ill.: InterVarsity Press, 1996), 83.

Did God Intend for Israel to Offer Animal Sacrifices?

Jeremiah 7:22–23 contains a puzzling statement: "For in the day that I brought them out of the land of Egypt, I *did not speak to your fathers or command them concerning burnt offering and sacrifices*. But this command I gave them: 'Obey my voice.'"

Is Jeremiah denying that instructions for animal sacrifice were given at Sinai (e.g., Lev 1–7)? Certainly not. This oracle in Jeremiah 7 is an instance of hyperbole, a shocking *overstatement* for the sake of *emphasis*, like Jesus' later teachings about "hating" one's family (Lk 14:26). Expressed literally, Jeremiah's point is this: The intention of the Lord in revealing himself to Israel after the exodus was not to acquire slaughtered animals but to gain its obedience in a covenant relationship (cf. Ps 50:7–13).

The literary structure of the Pentateuch shows that "burnt offerings and sacrifices" are not at the heart of God's law or the Sinai covenant. The heart of the covenant law is the Ten Commandments, which, interestingly enough, do not prescribe animal sacrifice (Ex 20:1–17). Furthermore, when the covenant is first established (Ex 19–24), the commands concerning animal sacrifice are few and vague: the only obligatory sacrifice is that of the firstlings (Ex 22:30). The vast majority of sacrificial laws are added into the covenant legislation only *after* Israel sins with the Golden Calf (Ex 32; see Lev 1–7).

---

prophecies that begin with the Temple in Jerusalem and end with the Gentile nations (Jer 7–25). Although there are many ways we could cover this substantial amount of material, perhaps the most helpful way to analyze it is to divide it up into two kinds of material: (1) accounts of the *actions* of Jeremiah, in the form of prophetic signs; and (2) accounts of the *words* of Jeremiah, in the form of prophetic oracles and sermons.

With reference to the actions of Jeremiah, one of the most memorable and remarkable aspects of this portion of the book is the fact that it contains so many striking prophetic signs. These signs—symbolic actions intended to effect what they signify—can be listed as follows:

1. *The Sign of the Dirty Loincloth*: Perhaps the most bizarre prophetic sign in the entire Old Testament is what may be referred to as the sign of the "dirty underwear" (Jer 13:1–27). With this sign, God commands Jeremiah to go the Euphrates River and hide his loincloth in the cleft of a rock, return later, and then use the "clingy", soiled loincloth as a visible sign of how Israel and Judah, though currently unfaithful, will eventually "cling" to the Lord (Jer 13:1–11)!

2. *The Sign of Wine Jars*: This act is a kind of "virtual" prophetic sign, involving a public proverb and mental image more than a physical deed (Jer 13:12–27). God commands Jeremiah to proclaim that "Every jar shall be filled with wine" (Jer 13:12), an ancient slogan of prosperity. However, Jeremiah is to inform the populace that the "wine" filling the jars will be the vintage of God's wrath against Israel, because of its spiritual "harlotry", a likely a reference both to sexual promiscuity (often linked to fertility deities) and to the worship of false gods through idolatry (Jer 13:25–27).

3. *The Sign of Jeremiah's Celibacy*: A third truly unique sign of the prophet Jeremiah is God's command to him to remain celibate (Jer 16:1–13). According to this sign, Jeremiah is not to "take a wife" or have children as a warning to his generation that anyone born in his day will suffer death, disease, and disaster

(Jer 16:1–4). Moreover, Jeremiah is not to participate in any public mourning (for example, at funerals) or celebration (for example, at weddings) as a sign that soon all celebrations will cease and the dead will be so numerous that they will remain unmourned and unburied (Jer 16:5–9), all as a result of Israel's idolatry (Jer 16:10–13).

4. *The Sign of the Broken Potter's Vessel*: Yet another of Jeremiah's famous signs revolves around the act of going down to "the potter's house" and taking a potter's earthen flask, which the prophet is commanded to break at the Potsherd Gate near the valley of Hinnom (Jer 18:1—19:15). Unlike the sign of the dirty loincloth, the meaning of this act is simple to grasp: just as the potter's vessel is broken, so will "this people and this city" be broken in the overthrow of Jerusalem (Jer 19:11). Once again, the cause is their idolatry and detestable worship of Baal and other foreign gods, which included human sacrifice (Jer 19:1–9).

The people did not respond well to such signs of judgment, and, in response to the final sign, they begin to make plots against Jeremiah (Jer 18:18). Eventually, Jeremiah is arrested, beaten, and placed in stocks near the Benjamin Gate by Pashhur, the chief priest (Jer 20:1–2). This causes the prophet to curse the day he was born in one of his most poignant laments (Jer 20:7–18).

In addition to the acts of Jeremiah, this portion of the book also contains some of the most significant *words* of Jeremiah, in the form of sermons and oracles. By isolating these various "sermons", we can also highlight some of the key themes in the book as a whole:

1. *The Sermon on the Destruction of the Temple*: One of the most important oracles delivered by the prophet takes place when he stands "in the gate of the LORD's house" (Jer 7:1) and declares that the city and its sanctuary will eventually be destroyed, like the sanctuary at Shiloh before it (Jer 7:1—9:26; cf. 1 Sam 4–5). Indeed, he warns the people that the liturgy of the Temple will not save them, if in the meantime they abuse the poor and vulnerable of society, violate the Ten Commandments, and worship other gods, such as Baal and Asherah, the "queen of heaven"—even engaging in child sacrifice (Jer 7:5–44). At the prospect of this coming destruction, the prophet launches into one of his characteristic lament-and-dialogue oracles, in which personal expressions of Jeremiah's grief are mixed with expressions of the Lord's own sorrow for being compelled to punish his people (Jer 8:18—9:3).

2. *The Oracle against Idolatry*: A second major sermon is Jeremiah's oracle against the absolute foolishness and wickedness of idol worship (Jer 10:1–25). In a style strikingly reminiscent of the book of Isaiah, Jeremiah affirms the doctrine of YHWH as Creator of all things and idols as powerless, false images, "a work of delusion", worshipped by those who are "stupid" (Jer 10:14–15).

3. *The Sermon on the Covenant*: In yet another sermon, the Lord commands Jeremiah to go to the cities of Judah and Jerusalem to call the Judeans back to obedience to "this covenant"—probably a reference to the Mosaic covenant as summarized in Deuteronomy (Jer 11:1—12:17). Yet because they are stubborn and will not obey "this covenant", the Lord will bring upon them "all the words of this covenant", meaning the covenant curses of desolation and exile (see Deut

27–32). Nonetheless, in the end the Lord will have compassion on Judah and even on the Gentiles who acknowledge the Lord (Jer 12:14–17).

4. *The Oracle of the Great Drought*: The combined format of oracle of judgment plus prophetic dialogue is also present in Jeremiah's oracle of the coming drought (Jer 14:1—15:21). The Lord answers Jeremiah's charge of being unmerciful by declaring that it is the people who have been unfaithful. Strikingly, the Lord declares that not even the intercessions of Moses and Samuel could save Judah, because the abominations of King Manasseh were so great (Jer 15:1–9; cf. Ex 32:11–34; 33:12–17; 1 Sam 12:19–25; 2 Kings 21:1–18).

5. *Oracles of the New Exodus*: In addition to the above oracles of judgment, Jeremiah also delivers oracles in which he promises that God will save his people one day in a new exodus that will eclipse the ancient exodus from Egypt in memory and magnitude (Jer 16:14–15). Before that, however, the Lord will thoroughly punish the sons of Israel for their idolatry, sending foes to hunt them down wherever they may hide (Jer 16:16–21). Instead of the law of the Lord, it is their own sins that are indelibly engraved on the hearts of the Judeans (Jer 17:1–23); nevertheless, if they repent, the scattered children of God will one day be restored to the Promised Land (Jer 17:24–27).

6. *Oracles of Judgment on Kings, Prophets, People, and Nations*: By far the most extensive collection of oracles are the prophecies of judgment that bring book 1 of Jeremiah to a close (Jer 21:1—25:38). In this section, Jeremiah delivers a host of scathing denunciations against the king (Jer 21:1—23:7); the (false) prophets (Jer 23:9–40); the people as a whole (Jer 24:1—25:14)—both those who were not exiled (Jer 24:1–10) and those who were (Jer 25:1–14)—and finally all the Gentile nations (Jer 25:15–38). Although these oracles are full of woe and judgment, none of them entails a rejection of God's covenant with David. On the contrary, the section includes a rare prophecy of hope: at some future, unspecified time ("the days are coming ...") the Lord will raise up a righteous branch for David, a king who will reign in righteousness (Jer 23:5–6) and lead a new exodus for Israel (Jer 25:7–8).

Indeed, as the final oracle makes clear, the divine punishment that took the form of the Babylonian captivity will not last forever, but for "seventy years" (Jer 25:11). Not only Israel and Judah, but all the nations of the earth will drink the "cup of the wine of wrath" (Jer 25:15): Egypt, Philistia, Edom, Moab, Ammon, Tyre, Sidon, the Mediterranean islanders and the desert tribes, Arabia, Zimri, Elam (Persia), Media, and finally Babylon itself. All must be punished, since if the Lord is punishing his own people, justice demands he also judge the Gentile idolaters (Jer 25:15–38).

Book 2: Judgment from the Temple to the Nations (Jeremiah 26–51)

As we saw above, the second half of the book of Jeremiah moves in roughly the same order as the first, starting with the judgment of the Jerusalem Temple and then moving outward to the judgment of the whole world (Jer 26–51). This enormous body of prophetic material consists of a number of major sections, which can be outlined as follows:

1. *The Temple Sermon in the First Year (?) of Jehoiakim (Jer 26:1–24)*: Significantly, book 2 of Jeremiah begins, like book 1, with an account of Jeremiah's "second Temple sermon" (Jer 26; cf. Jer 7:1–11). This oracle is dated to "the beginning of the reign of King Jehoiakim" (609 B.C., the first regnal year?; Jer 26:1). The common theme in Jeremiah's sermon in both chapters is the comparison of Jerusalem with Shiloh, the previous site of the sanctuary, which was destroyed by the Philistines in the days of Samuel (1 Sam 5). Although the book does not recount any particular reaction to Jeremiah's first sermon in the Temple, the response to his "second" Temple sermon is violent and negative:

> And when Jeremiah had finished speaking all that the LORD had commanded him to speak to all the people, then the priests and the prophets and all the people laid hold of him, saying, "You shall die! Why have you prophesied in the name of the LORD, saying, 'This house shall be like Shiloh, and this city shall be desolate, without inhabitant'?" And all the people gathered about Jeremiah in the house of the LORD. (Jer 26:8–9)

However, when Jeremiah defends himself by claiming the authority of revelation from the Lord, a dispute arises between the princes and the people and the prophets and priests over whether to put him to death or spare him and heed his words, as they had with previous prophets (such as Micah). Ultimately, Ahikam son of Shaphan, a high-ranking member of the royal court, exercises his influence to ensure that Jeremiah is spared (Jer 26:24).

2. *The Sign of the Yoke and Ensuing Controversy (Jer 27:1—28:17)*: In the fourth year of the reign of Zedekiah (ca. 593 B.C.), Jeremiah performs another prophetic sign-act. He makes a yoke and wears it, and then he publicly prophesies to Judah and the surrounding nations that the Lord is placing all nations under the yoke of Nebuchadnezzar, king of Babylon, and any who do not submit will be destroyed (Jer 27:1–15). Moreover, those exiled to Babylon with King Jehoiachin (ca. 597 B.C.) would not be returning soon (Jer 27:16–22). It is easy to imagine that such an oracle would not go over well! In fact, the false prophet Hananiah opposes Jeremiah to his face, seizing his yoke and breaking it, as a sign of a counter-prophecy that Nebuchadnezzar's power would soon be broken (Jer 28:1–11). But Hananiah's words are proven to be a lie, and within a year he dies for his opposition to the Lord (Jer 28:12–17).

3. *Letter to Those Exiled with Jehoiachin: Restoration after Seventy Years (Jer 29:1–32)*: Soon after the exile of 597 B.C., when Jehoiachin is deported and King Zedekiah appointed, Jeremiah sends a letter to the exiles in Babylon, urging them to settle down and make permanent homes, since the exile will last a generation ("seventy years"). Then God will visit them, and they will be restored to their land and to right relationship with YHWH. As for those who were not exiled, they are like "vile figs", and will experience the wrath of the Lord because they do not heed his word. The prophets who have arisen in Babylon, preaching a short exile and speedy return, are liars and pretenders: Jeremiah denounces them by name (Jer 29:21–32).

4. *The New Exodus and the New Covenant (Jer 30:1—31:40)*: At the very center of the book of Jeremiah stands what scholars have referred to as "the Book of

Comfort" (Jer 30–33) because, in the midst of so many oracles of judgment, these chapters contain oracles of the restoration of Israel and the inauguration of a "new covenant" associated with a "new exodus" and the return of the Davidic king (who in later Jewish writings would be referred to as "the messiah"; Jer 30–33). The significance of this section is highlighted by the fact that, while most of book 2 is prose narration (Jer 26–45), these chapters are mostly set as poetry (Jer 30–33). Jeremiah 31:31 contains the only use of the phrase "new covenant" in the Old Testament. (On the significance of this, see below, "Theological Issues in Jeremiah".)

5. *The Sign-Act of the Redemption of the Field (Jer 32:1–44)*: In the tenth year of Zedekiah (ca. 588 B.C.), during the Babylonian siege of Jerusalem, Jeremiah redeems the field of his cousin Hanamel in his hometown, Anathoth, a Levitical city located in the tribal territory of Benjamin. The laws of redemption of ancestral property are found in the Pentateuchal legislation concerning the Jubilee Year (Lev 25:8–55), but it is not clear how the transaction described in Jeremiah falls under these laws. In any event, Jeremiah's purchase of ancestral land at a time when it seemed that all Judah was about to be dispossessed and deported is a public act of faith in the future of the nation. Indeed, God responds to Jeremiah's lament by assuring him that he will eventually restore his people in a New Covenant involving a new exodus and a new heart of obedience (Jer 32:36–44).

6. *Restoration and Covenant Fidelity to Levi and David (Jer 33:1–26)*: While Jeremiah is imprisoned during the final siege of Jerusalem (ca. 588–87 B.C.), he receives yet another oracle of hope. After the Lord has cleansed Judah and Jerusalem by means of the Chaldean invasion and exile, he will restore the fortunes of Judah and the fortunes of Israel and rebuild them "as they were at first". Significantly, this restoration will include the forgiveness of sin (Jer 33:8), the restoration of nuptial joy (Jer 33:11), and the offering of the *todah,* or sacrifice of thanksgiving (Jer 33:11). The peace of Judah shall return, so that flocks will quietly graze under the watch of their shepherds throughout the region.

Perhaps most significant of all, in the time of restoration, the Lord will show his faithfulness to the house of David and the house of Levi, two houses of Israel with whom he made covenants. Despite the eventual demise of the Davidic kingdom and destruction of the Jerusalem Temple, one day, both kingship and priesthood will be restored: a "righteous Branch" shall arise to rule from the throne of David (Jer 33:15), and Levi will "never lack a man ... to make sacrifices for ever" (Jer 33:18). In fact, the Lord's covenant faithfulness to Levi and David is as unshakable as his commitment to the covenant of creation and his providence over the cycles of nature (Jer 33:19–26).

7. *The Doom of Zedekiah and Judgment for Breaking the Covenant of Liberation (Jer 34:1–22)*: These hopeful visions of the future quickly dissipate as the narrative of the book turns back to the painful reality of the present, which is characterized by covenant infidelity on the part of Judah and Jerusalem. King Zedekiah will be defeated and exiled by Nebuchadnezzar, though the Lord will show mercy by allowing him to die in peace (Jer 34:1–7). An example of the iniquity for which Zedekiah was judged follows: during the siege of Jerusalem (ca. 589 B.C.?), the king and the aristocracy made a covenant with the populace to

observe once again the laws of social justice—in particular, the manumission of slaves—found in the Mosaic law (cf. Ex 21:1–6; Lev 25:8–55; Deut 15:12–18). This was to gain the support of the slave populace during the siege. When the siege was temporarily lifted, however, the upper classes quickly reenslaved their fellow Jews. Therefore, on behalf of the Lord, Jeremiah proclaims that the curses for covenant violation will soon fall on all the leading citizens of Jerusalem.

8. *The Fidelity of the Rechabites (Jer 35:1–19)*: In this narrative, Jeremiah contrasts the infidelity of the leaders of Judah and Jerusalem with the fidelity of the tribe of the Rechabites to the word of their ancestor, Jonadab son of Rechab, who commanded them never to drink alcohol and always to maintain a nomadic life-style. The Rechabites, now dwelling within Jerusalem during the Babylonian siege, are a living and visible sign against the corrupt and the wicked, and a challenge to the rest of the Jewish people.

9. *Jehoiakim Burns Jeremiah's Scroll (Jer 36:1–32)*: The first large unit of book 2 of Jeremiah ends with a paradigmatic scene of covenant rejection: the burning of the prophetic scroll by the king. In the fourth year of Jehoiakim (ca. 605 B.C.), the Lord commands Jeremiah to write "all the words that I have spoken to you" on a scroll (Jer 36:2), to be read publicly to the people during a day of fasting at the Temple, in the hopes that the people of Judah will repent. Jeremiah complies, composing the scroll with the help of his scribe, Baruch. The following year, Jeremiah sends Baruch to the Temple to read the scroll in the hearing of the people. The reading causes a sensation, and the princes of the people summon Baruch to read the scroll to them. After hearing it, they advise Baruch and Jeremiah to hide. Word gets to the king, Jehoiakim, who commands one of his scribes to procure the scroll and read it to him (Jer 36:20–22). As each column is read aloud in the king's winter palace, he cuts it off and burns it in his brazier, dramatizing his absolute contempt for the word of God (Jer 36:23–26). In response, the Lord commissions Jeremiah to rewrite the scroll in its entirety (Jer 36:27–32) with amplification: "many similar words were added to them" (Jer 36:32).

10. *The "Passion of Jeremiah" (Jer 37:1—45:5)*: This historical narrative of Jeremiah's experience during the last years of Jerusalem begins with Nebuchadnezzar's final siege of Jerusalem already underway in the last years of Zedekiah (589–587 B.C.). At this time, the king implores Jeremiah to intercede with the Lord, but the prophet informs the royal court clearly that the Babylonian armies will prevail and that destruction and exile are inevitable (Jer 37:1–10). During a break in the siege, Jeremiah attempts to go to Anathoth to visit his ancestral property, but he is accused of desertion to the enemy and imprisoned in the court of the guard (Jer 37:11–21). The princes of Judah are not satisfied with this punishment, so they have him thrown into a cistern to die. An Ethiopian royal servant, Ebed-melech the eunuch, succeeds in gaining the king's permission to rescue Jeremiah from slow and certain death in the cistern and place him back in custody in the court of the guard (Jer 38:7–13). The king arranges to meet privately with Jeremiah to inquire about his fate at the hand of the Babylonians, but, though warned, the king does not heed or act on the warnings from the prophet (Jer 38:14–28). As a result, the inevitable comes: the Babylonian army breaches the wall of Jerusalem and captures the city (Jer 39:1–3).

Zedekiah and his bodyguard flee toward the Jordan but are caught at Jericho (Jer 39:4–5). Nebuchadnezzar slays the king's sons before his eyes, blinds him, and deports him to Babylon along with the remaining inhabitants of the city (Jer 39:6–10). The Babylonians entrust Jeremiah to the care of Gedaliah, the aristocrat they appoint as governor over the remnant of poor people left in the land to till the fields (Jer 36:11—40:6). After the Chaldeans leave, those Judeans who have taken refuge in the nearby countries of Edom, Moab, and Ammon return to Israel and seek protection under Gedaliah, who rules from Mizpah in Benjamin (Jer 40:7–12). A brief period of peace and plenty ensues, but it is short-lived: a conspiracy by one Ishmael the son of Nethaniah, a member of the royal house who has the backing of the king of Ammon, succeeds in assassinating Gedaliah (Jer 40:13—41:3). Military commanders loyal to Gedaliah defeat Ishmael, rescue the hostages he has taken from Mizpah, and force him to flee (Jer 41:4–18). The remaining Judean populace, now led by Johanan son of Kareah, a Judean military commander, fear reprisals by the Babylonian authorities for Gedaliah's murder and seek Jeremiah's advice about what to do (Jer 42:1–6). Jeremiah advises them not to flee to Egypt, but to seek the favor of the Babylonian authorities, since they were not complicit in the assassination of Gedaliah, whom the Babylonians had appointed (Jer 42:7–22). The populace, however, rejects Jeremiah's advice, accusing him of being a tool of his scribe, Baruch (Jer 43:1–3). They flee to Egypt against the prophet's warning and force the prophet and Baruch to accompany them (Jer 43:4–7). In this way, the last recorded words of the prophet (apparently) are a series of oracular denunciations of the pharaoh, the Egyptians, and the idolatrous Jewish refugees who have fled to Egypt seeking safety (Jer 43:8—44:30). The sad narrative of Jeremiah's final days concludes with an epilogue, a dischronologized account of an oracle of comfort given specifically to Baruch son of Nereiah, Jeremiah's long-suffering scribe (Jer 45:15). The placement of this oracle at the end of the account of the last years of the prophet's life suggests to some that Baruch was the one who recorded these events.

11. *The Oracles against the Nations (Jeremiah 46–51)*: The last major subsection of the book of Jeremiah consists of a series of oracles against the nations, composed, for the most part, in classical Hebrew poetic style. Since Egypt was the focus of the preceding historical narratives (Jer 43–45), the oracles begin with the land of the pharaoh (Jer 46:1–28) and proceed to Philistia (Jer 47), Moab (Jer 48), Ammon (Jer 49:1–6), Edom (Jer 49:7–22), Damascus (Jer 49:23–27), Kedar and Hazor (Jer 49:28–33), Elam (Jer 49:34–39), and finally Babylon, to whom the most space is devoted (Jer 50:1—51:64). These oracles are rich in literary style and poetic imagery but thin in terms of theological content. The message remains the same throughout: the Lord is coming to judge the nations for their iniquities, their worship of false gods, and their abuse of the Lord's people Israel. While these prophecies are largely negative in tone, it should be remembered that judgment on Israel's enemies implies vindication and restoration for the people of God. Therefore, the oracles against the nations are, in a sense, the photographic negative of the oracles of restoration and consolation given earlier in the "Book of Comfort" (Jer 30–33). This is their positive function in the overall structure of the book of Jeremiah. Furthermore, even the nations are not

without hope for some good thing from the Lord; certain passages indicate that, like Isaiah before him, Jeremiah also sees a future that involves hope and restoration for the nations (Jer 48:47; 49:6, 39).

Epilogue: The Fates of Zedekiah and Jehoiachin (Jeremiah 52)

The epilogue to the book of Jeremiah consists of historical narratives about the fall of Jerusalem, the fate of Zedekiah, and the fate of Jehoiachin, all of which represent fulfillments of prominent predictions made by Jeremiah in the course of the book: the capture and destruction of Jerusalem and the Temple in 587 B.C., the deportation of the people, and the miserable fate of Zedekiah, all of which the prophet had foretold (Jer 4:5–6:30; 21:1–10; 24:1–10; and so on). But the final brief report is one of hope: Jehoiachin is released from prison and granted a living allowance from the royal court for the remainder of his life (Jer 52:31–34). This act of kindness and compassion on the last legitimate ruling king recalls Jeremiah's prophecy that Jehoiachin and the exiles that went with him in 597 B.C. were the "good figs" that would one day be built up and planted (Jer 24:4–7)—that is, form the foundation for the restoration of the nation after the exile.

Historical Issues in Jeremiah

The Origins of the Book of Jeremiah

Who wrote the book of Jeremiah? And when was it written? Given the fact that the book contains a wide variety of literary genres, including sermons, oracles, and historical narratives about Jeremiah, it should go without saying that scholars have proposed an equally wide variety of hypotheses about how each of the various portions of the book originated and eventually came to be collected into what we know today as "the book of Jeremiah". Indeed, as Jack Lundbom points out, like the Old Testament itself, the book of Jeremiah can aptly be described as "really a 'book of books'—that is a collection of several different 'scrolls' from various time periods and contexts".[4] Hence, any attempt to speak about the date and authorship of Jeremiah would need to take into account its extremely complex and diverse components as well as the role of such figures as Baruch, the scribe of Jeremiah (for example, Jer 36).

With these qualifications in mind, there are a few basic points that should be made in support of the conclusion that the book of Jeremiah originated with the prophet of the same name. First and foremost, the book itself explicitly states that the prophet Jeremiah dictated portions of its contents to his scribe, Baruch, to be written in a "scroll" and then read publicly:

> In the fourth year of Jehoiakim the son of Josiah, king of Judah, this word came to Jeremiah from the LORD: "*Take a scroll and write on it all the words that I have spoken to you* against Israel and Judah and all the nations, from the day I spoke to

---

[4] Jack R. Lundbom, *Jeremiah*, vol. 1, Anchor Yale Bible 21A (New York: Doubleday, 1999), 100.

you, from the days of Josiah until today. It may be that the house of Judah will hear all the evil which I intend to do to them, so that every one may turn from his evil way, and that I may forgive their iniquity and their sin."

Then Jeremiah called Baruch the son of Neriah, and Baruch wrote upon a scroll at the dictation of Jeremiah all the words of the LORD which he had spoken to him. (Jer 36:1–4)

Without speculating about the exact contents of this scroll, there is good reason for concluding that the portions of the book of Jeremiah that are explicitly attributed to him may have come about as a result of the same kind of activity: prophetic revelation followed by scribal inscription. Indeed, the fact that Jeremiah has the scroll rewritten and expanded(!) after its being burnt by the king also provides remarkable evidence for the fact that prophetic oracles could and did develop over time by means of alterations and expansions at the hands of their own authors.

On the other hand, it also seems clear that certain portions of the book fall into other categories that may have had different origins from that of a scroll dictated by Jeremiah to his scribe for public reading. In his famous and influential commentary on Jeremiah, John Bright proposes three major categories of material in this regard:

1. *"Confessions/Laments" of Jeremiah*: These first-person prayers and laments that express the feelings of the prophet may have never been spoken publicly but transmitted in some other fashion (Jer 11:18—12:6; 15:1–21; 17:14–17; 18:18–23; 20:7–18).

2. *"Biography" of Jeremiah*: These biographical narratives about Jeremiah seem to have been written by someone else—Baruch is the likely candidate (for example, Jer 26–29, 34–45).

3. *Prose Discourses*: This material is very diverse in kind and is scattered throughout the book (for example, Jer 7:2–15; 11:1–17; 26:2–6; and so on). It is very difficult to postulate exactly how this material originated or was preserved.

However one explains the complex process of development that led to the final version—and this will always be a matter of speculation—it seems reasonable, given the evidence, to conclude that the contents of the book of Jeremiah ultimately go back to the time of the prophet himself.[5]

In support of this basic position, it is worth noting that (1) no positive evidence (archaeological or textual) has been found contradicting the historical claims of the book; (2) the book of Jeremiah shows sustained and detailed interest in persons and events that are mentioned nowhere else in Scripture, were only of significance in Jerusalem during the lifetime of the prophet, and were quickly forgotten thereafter; and (3) little if anything in the book reflects any awareness of the actual course of events by which Jerusalem and Judea were resettled and rebuilt during the Persian period.[6] Since the subject matter and tenor of the prophecies largely fit the historical milieu they claim

---

[5] See John Bright, *Jeremiah*, Anchor Bible 21 (New York: Doubleday, 1965), lv–lxxxv.

[6] See Steven Voth, "Jeremiah", in *Isaiah, Jeremiah, Lamentations, Ezekiel, Daniel*, vol. 4 of *Zondervan Illustrated Bible Backgrounds Commentary*, ed. John H. Walton (Grand Rapids, Mich.: Zondervan, 2009), 229–371.

for themselves, there is no compelling reason to doubt the substantial accuracy of the book's self-presentation as the compilation of the oracles of Jeremiah with the help of his scribe, Baruch son of Neraiah.

The Difference between the LXX and the MT Versions of Jeremiah

As noted above, it now seems clear from the evidence of Qumran that the Masoretic Text (MT) of Jeremiah represents an editorial reworking of the Hebrew version behind the Septuagint (LXX), aimed at amplifying and clarifying the prophet's work for subsequent generations. Who was responsible for this editorial work? Since little if anything in the MT additions demands a date after the exile, proposals for the date and identity of the MT editor range from Baruch himself in the mid-exilic period to some unknown second-century scribe.[7] Since the MT reworking does not substantially change the message or theology of the prophet, but merely improves the literary shaping of his work, this is a question that may safely remain open.

A Sample Comparison of the LXX and the MT: Jeremiah 25, the "Seventy Years" of Exile	
Septuagint (LXX)	Masoretic Text (MT)
[1]The Word that came to Jeremias concerning all the people of Juda in the fourth year of Joakim, son of Josias, king of Juda; [2]which he spoke to all the people of Juda, and to the inhabitants of Jerusalem, saying, [3]In the thirteenth year of Josias, son of Amos, king of Juda, even until this day for three and twenty years, I have both spoken to you, rising early and speaking, [4]and I sent to you my servants the prophets, sending them early; (but ye hearkened not, and listened not with your ears;) saying, [5]Turn ye every one from his evil way, and from your evil practices, and ye shall dwell in the land which I gave to you and your fathers, of old and for ever. [6]Go ye not after strange gods, to serve them, and to worship them, that ye provoke me not by the works of your hands, to do you hurt. [7]But ye hearkened not to me.	[1]The word that came to Jeremiah concerning all the people of Judah, in the fourth year of Jehoiakim the son of Josiah, king of Judah (that was the first year of Nebuchadnezzar king of Babylon), [2]which Jeremiah the prophet spoke to all the people of Judah and all the inhabitants of Jerusalem: [3]"For twenty-three years, from the thirteenth year of Josiah the son of Amon, king of Judah, to this day, the word of the LORD has come to me, and I have spoken persistently to you, but you have not listened. [4]You have neither listened nor inclined your ears to hear, although the LORD persistently sent to you all his servants the prophets, [5]saying, 'Turn now, every one of you, from his evil way and wrong doings, and dwell upon the land which the LORD has given to you and your fathers from of old and for ever; [6]do not go after other gods to serve and worship them, or provoke me to anger with the work of your hands. Then I will do you no harm.' [7]Yet you have not listened to me, says the LORD, that you might provoke me to anger with the work of your hands to your own harm.

(continued)

---

[7] See Lundbom, *Jeremiah*, 57–62.

A Sample Comparison of the LXX and the MT: Jeremiah 25, the "Seventy Years" of Exile (*continued*)

Septuagint (LXX)	Masoretic Text (MT)
[8]Therefore thus saith the Lord; Since ye believed not my words, [9]behold, I *will* send and take a family from the north, and will bring them against this land, and against the inhabitants of it, and against all the nations round about it, and I will make them utterly waste, and make them a desolation, and a hissing, and an everlasting reproach. [10]And I will destroy from *among* them the voice of joy, and the voice of gladness, the voice of the bridegroom, and the voice of the bride, the scent of ointment, and the light of a candle. [11]And all the land shall be a desolation; and they shall serve among the Gentiles seventy years. [12]And when the seventy years are fulfilled, I will take vengeance on that nation, and will make them a perpetual desolation. [13]And I will bring upon that land all my words which I have spoken against it, *even* all things that are written in this book.[a]	[8]"Therefore thus says the LORD of hosts: Because you have not obeyed my words, [9]behold, I will send for all the tribes of the north, says the LORD, and for Nebuchadnezzar the king of Babylon, my servant, and I will bring them against this land and its inhabitants, and against all these nations round about; I will utterly destroy them, and make them a horror, a hissing, and an everlasting reproach. [10]Moreover, I will banish from them the voice of mirth and the voice of gladness, the voice of the bridegroom and the voice of the bride, the grinding of the millstones and the light of the lamp. [11]This whole land shall become a ruin and a waste, and these nations shall serve the king of Babylon seventy years. [12]Then after seventy years are completed, I will punish the king of Babylon and that nation, the land of the Chaldeans, for their iniquity, says the LORD, making the land an everlasting waste. [13]I will bring upon that land all the words which I have uttered against it, everything written in this book, which Jeremiah prophesied against all the nations. [14]For many nations and great kings shall make slaves even of them; and I will recompense them according to their deeds and the work of their hands." (RSVCE)

Analysis: The Masoretic Text appears amplified and specified. Less specific prophecies in the LXX ("a family from the north", v. 9) are more clearly identified ("all the tribes of the north ... and Nebuchadnezzar the king of Babylon", v. 9), perhaps with the intention of making it clear to subsequent generations how Jeremiah's oracles were historically fulfilled.

[a] Translated by C. L. Brenton, *The Septuagint with Apocrypha: Greek and English* (repr., Peabody, Mass.: Hendrickson, 1998), 933.

Theological Issues in Jeremiah

The "New Covenant" in the Book of Jeremiah

Jeremiah is unique among the books of the Old Testament in that it explicitly foretells the coming of a "new covenant" (Jer 31:31). Moreover, upon closer examination, it becomes clear that it is a kind of "covenant logic" that undergirds Jeremiah's condemnation of his contemporaries as well as his vision of hope for the future. Indeed, the theological message of the book of Jeremiah may be summarized in two statements: (1) Israel stands condemned before God for violations of the Mosaic covenant, but (2) there is hope for the future in the

New Covenant the Lord will establish. Let us explicate these two movements of Jeremiah's message with reference to specific texts.

1. *Condemnation on the Basis of the Mosaic Covenant*: One of the most striking aspects of the book of Jeremiah is just how *negative* it is. Indeed, the book is so full of oracles of tribulation and woe, death and destruction, that in the English language, the word "Jeremiad" was at one time a common way of referring to a long list of woes or complaints. Why is this prophet so dour? The answer is simple: Jeremiah bases his condemnation of his Israelite contemporaries on the stipulations of the Mosaic covenant. For example, in his Temple sermon, he charges the people of Jerusalem and Judah with violations of the Ten Commandments (Jer 7:9; cf. Deut 5:7–21). Israel has worshipped foreign gods (Deut 5:7; Jer 7:6, 9) through idolatry (Deut 5:8–9; Jer 10:2–5), trivialized the name of the Lord through false prophecy (Deut 5:11; Jer 5:12–13), and violated the Sabbath (Deut 5:12–15; Jer 17:21–27). Indeed, as scholars have long noted, Jeremiah's whole book so particularly reflects the language and laws of the book of Deuteronomy that various proposals for common authorship of the two works have been made in the history of biblical criticism. In Jeremiah one finds reflections of Moses' command to circumcise the heart (cf. Deut 10:6; Jer 4:4), to refrain from idolatry "on every hill and under every green tree" (cf. Deut 12:2; Jer 2:20; 3:6, 13; 17:2), and to practice the manumission of Hebrew slaves (cf. Deut 15:12–18; Jer 34:8–22).

Thus there is a strong relationship between Moses and Jeremiah. Jeremiah may be viewed as the "executor" who comes to implement Moses' "last will and testament", the book of Deuteronomy. Deuteronomy is the final form of the Mosaic covenant. Israel has violated its stipulations, thus triggering the covenant curses, the greatest of which, as it turns out, was exile from the land (Deut 27–32). As a prophet, Jeremiah comes to enforce the Mosaic covenant; when his appeals to Israel to repent and return to covenant fidelity fall on deaf ears, he announces the implementation of the curses. The prophet may be regarded as bringing a covenant-lawsuit (in Hebrew, a *rib*) on behalf of the Lord against Israel (cf. Jer 2:9).

2. *Hope for a New Covenant to Come*: While the present is characterized by the curses of the Mosaic covenant, Jeremiah holds out firm hope for covenant renewal in the future. This hope is expressed by the repetition of the *covenant formula*, the expression, "I will be your God, and you shall be my people." This phrase and its many variations express the heart of the covenant relationship and recur throughout as a future hope (see Jer 7:23; 11:4; 24:7; 30:22; 31:1, 33; 32:38).

But "in that day" when once more Israel will be the Lord's people, and the Lord their God, what shape shall the covenant take? Will it be a simple renewal under the terms of the Mosaic law or some other arrangement? Jeremiah addresses this question directly in the most pivotal oracle of his entire book, which is worth quoting and analyzing in full:

Behold, the days are coming, says the LORD, when I will make a new covenant with the house of Israel and the house of Judah, not like the covenant which I made with their fathers when I took them by the hand to bring them out of the land of Egypt, my covenant which they broke, though I was their husband, says the LORD. But this is the covenant which I will make with the house of Israel after those days, says the LORD: I will put my law within them, and I will write it upon their hearts; and I will be their God, and they shall be my people. And no longer shall each man teach his neighbor and each his brother, saying, "Know the LORD," for they shall all know me, from the least of them to the greatest, says the LORD; for I will forgive their iniquity, and I will remember their sin no more. (Jer 31:31–34 RSVCE1)

Notice that this New Covenant is made with *all twelve tribes*: both the ten northern tribes (the "house of Israel") and the two southern tribes (the "house of Judah"). This means that the New Covenant will not be exhausted simply by the return of the southern tribes from exile in Babylon but will demand an even greater act of restoration that will bring back all of the descendants of the northern tribes from the Gentile nations among whom they have been scattered (cf. Is 66).

Second, notice also that the New Covenant is depicted in some way as a *nuptial relationship*. Indeed, Jeremiah describes the first covenant as "my covenant which they broke, *though I was their husband*" (Jer 31:32). In all likelihood, the italicized phrase is a *double entendre*. It may equally well be translated "and I showed myself [to be] their Master" (RSVCE2). It seems quite possible that Jeremiah intended both senses of this phrase. "My covenant which they broke, *though I was their husband*" reflects a view common in the prophets that the covenant formed at Sinai established a marriage-like bond between the Lord and Israel (cf. Jer 2:1—4:4). On the other hand, "my covenant which they broke, *and I showed myself [to be] their Master*" would refer to the increasingly tense relationship between the Lord and Israel evident in the Pentateuchal narrative from Sinai to Deuteronomy (Ex 19–24). As we pointed out above in our treatment of the Pentateuch, the covenant relationship between the Lord and Israel undergoes three stages, progressing from a *kinship-type* covenant at Sinai before the Calf, characterized by reciprocity, mutuality, and familial affection; to a *vassal-type* covenant in Deuteronomy, characterized by a vassal-suzerain or master-servant relationship enforced by fearsome curses (Deut 27–32). Thus, in the course of the Pentateuch itself, God was compelled to "show himself to be their Master" and was so again more recently in his implementation of the Deuteronomic curses on Jeremiah's contemporaries.

Third, notice also that the New Covenant is clearly *distinct* from the Mosaic covenant formed at the time of the departure from Egypt. Jeremiah proceeds to list the three characteristics that will distinguish the "new covenant" from the "old covenant": (1) "I will write my law in their hearts." This means that the law will be internalized, not merely external. (2) "They shall all know me." This means that there will be an infused, experiential knowledge of God (Hebrew *yada'*, "to know", can refer to intimate familiarity; cf. Gen 4:25). (3) "I will forgive their iniquity." This means that the New Covenant will come about at the same time that God brings about the forgiveness of sins. These three characteristics contrast with the Mosaic covenant, in which (1) the law was written on tablets of stone, (2) knowledge of God was didactic and cognitive, and (3) the sacrificial cultus neither effected the forgiveness of sins nor transformed the worshipper (see Jer 6:20; 7:21–22).

Of course, Jeremiah's description of the "new covenant" does not exhaust his vision of the new age God will inaugurate at the time this covenant is formed. The prophet mentions several other events or characteristics of the "latter days"—that is, the eschatological era. The prophecies of a new exodus and of the restoration of the Davidic monarchy are particularly important. Jeremiah's teaching on the new exodus in the latter days is very similar to Isaiah—in fact, there is no substantial difference between the prophets on this point: in the future, God will lead his people back to their home by an easy and gentle way from all the places to which they have been scattered (Jer 23:7–8). As in Isaiah, Jeremiah associates this new exodus with the appearance of a Davidic heir, the "Branch" of David (Jer 23:5–6; cf. 30:9; 33:15). In fact, Jeremiah is emphatic that the covenant with David will never be revoked (Jer 33:15–26). It follows, therefore, that the promised New Covenant (Jer 31:31) will, in some way, involve a restoration and renewal of the Davidic covenant. This perspective is also similar to that of Isaiah, who speaks of an "everlasting covenant" (Is 61:8) identified with the servant of the Lord (Is 42:6; 49:8) and the covenant fidelity offered to David (Is 55:3) involving the gift of the Holy Spirit (Is 59:21). Thus, there is a large degree of overlap between the eschatological vision of Isaiah and that of Jeremiah.

> ### Jeremiah's "New Covenant," the Last Supper, and the Gift of the Holy Spirit
>
> When at the Last Supper Jesus says, "This chalice which is poured out for you is the *new covenant* in my blood" (Lk 22:20), he clearly indicates that his actions with the apostles in the cenacle constitute the fulfillment of Jeremiah's prophecy in Jeremiah 31:31, the only passage in the Hebrew Scriptures to employ the phrase "new covenant". The New Covenant Christ established in the Upper Room was formed first of all between himself and the Twelve, who were the mystical representation and sacramental nucleus of all twelve tribes of the New Israel, for the New Covenant was to be with "the house of Israel and the house of Judah". The New Covenant involves primarily the bestowal of the Holy Spirit through the sacraments, which is evident in the same Upper Room on the evening of the first Easter, when the Lord met the Twelve and "breathed on them, and said to them, 'Receive the Holy Spirit. If you forgive the sins of any, they are forgiven; if you retain the sins of any, they are retained'" (Jn 20:22–23). Jeremiah prophesied the New Covenant would be written on the heart, communicate knowledge of God, and forgive sins (Jer 31:33–34). The gift of the Holy Spirit (1) engraves the law of God in the heart of the believer (Rom 5:5; cf. Rom 13:8–10) and (2) infuses in him experiential knowledge of God, so that he knows God for who he is, "Abba! Father!" (Rom 8:16–17) and is (3) cleansed of his sins by the activity of that same Spirit (Rom 8:2).

The Thanksgiving Sacrifice, the Liturgy, and the Coming of the Messiah

Like many of the prophets, Jeremiah may be understood as a book about the proper liturgy or about a conflict between true and false liturgies. In one sense, Jeremiah's complaint against the people of Israel concerns their liturgical celebration.

On the one hand, they perform the sacrificial rituals in the Temple according to the Mosaic law (Jer 6:20; 7:21). On the other hand, they do not confirm the meaning of this sacrificial liturgy by observing the moral law (7:5–11), and this hypocrisy eviscerates the Temple cult of any meaning or merit (6:20). Moreover, the Israelites disregard the exclusive nature of the cult of the Lord and combine it syncretistically with pagan idolatry (Jer 1:16; 2:23–28; 7:9, 18, 30–31; 11:12–17; 17:2; 18:15; 19:4, 13; 32:29; 44:1–25), including not merely illicit but morally abhorrent rituals like child sacrifice (Jer 7:31; 19:5; 32:35). In sum, Israel celebrates the Lord's liturgy hypocritically, while simultaneously participating in the false worship of the pagan deities.

Despite Jeremiah's fame (or infamy) as the prophet who spoke against the Temple, he is not against liturgy, sacrifice, or the sanctuary in itself. In fact, Jeremiah envisions the Temple and its liturgy functioning again in the age to come at the time of the messianic king, the new David (Jer 33:11). He desires, not the abolition of sacrificial liturgy, but the purification of its practice (cf. Jer 17:24–26). Jeremiah most clearly expresses his expectations for the renewal of the liturgy in the age to come in one of the oracles about the time of the future king:

> Thus says the LORD: In this place of which you say, 'It is a waste without man or beast,' in the cities of Judah and the streets of Jerusalem that are desolate, without man or inhabitant or beast, there shall be heard again the voice of mirth and the voice of gladness, the voice of the bridegroom and the voice of the bride, the voices of those who sing, *as they bring thank offerings to the house of the LORD*:
>
> > "Give thanks to the LORD of hosts,
> > for the LORD is good,
> > for his mercy endures for ever!"
>
> For I will restore the fortunes of the land as at first, says the LORD. (Jer 33:10–11)

Notice here once again the *nuptial* dimension of the age of salvation: it will include the restoration of the "voice of the bridegroom and the voice of the bride"—that is, the renewal of marital joy with the Temple-city. This may, in fact, be a reference to the singing of the Song of Solomon or similar compositions at the celebration of marriages. Moreover, the restoration of nuptial joy is closely associated with the voices of those who sing as they bring "thank offerings" (Hebrew *todah*) to the Temple. In these lines, Jeremiah quotes the typical refrain of some of the best-known *todah* psalms: "Give thanks to the LORD, for he is good; for his mercy [steadfast love (Hebrew *hesed*)] endures for ever" (Ps 106:1; 118:1, 29; cf. 136:1–26). Considering the eschatological significance of the thank offering, or *todah*, as explored above in our treatment of the Psalms, it is striking that Jeremiah singles out *this* form of sacrifice as particularly expressing the character of worship in the age to come, at the time of the messianic "Branch" of David (Jer 33:14–16). Indeed, this verse lays the foundation for the later rabbinic saying: "In the time to come all sacrifices will cease, but the sacrifice of thanksgiving [Hebrew *todah*] will not cease."[8]

---

[8] *Leviticus Rabbah* 9.7; cited in Jack R. Lundbom, *Jeremiah*, vol. 2, Anchor Yale Bible 21B (New York: Doubleday, 2004), 536.

Jeremiah in the Living Tradition

When compared with the book of Isaiah, the book of Jeremiah has received relatively less attention in the living tradition of the Church.[9] Nevertheless, this does not mean *no* attention. In fact, one of the longer collections of patristic homilies that we possess is Origen of Alexandria's twenty homilies on the book of Jeremiah, which by themselves consist of hundreds of pages.[10] Moreover, in the contemporary Roman Lectionary, the book of Jeremiah figures quite prominently. In what follows, we will provide a few highlights of how the book has continued to be interpreted in the living tradition of the Church.

Jeremiah's Call from the Womb and the Killing of the Unborn

One of the more unexpected areas in which the book of Jeremiah contributed to the theological anthropology of Christianity lies in his opening account of his call, when he speaks about how God knew and consecrated him from the time he was in his mother's womb (Jer 1:5). Remarkably, this text became the foundation for the argument of a number of early Church Fathers that unborn children are in fact human beings and that, as a result, abortion is immoral.[11] Consider, for example, the words of the second-century Latin apologist Tertullian:

> The embryo therefore becomes a human being in the womb from the moment that its form is completed. The law of Moses, indeed, punishes with due penalties the man who shall cause abortion [cf. Ex 21:22–25], inasmuch as there exists already the rudiment of a human being, which has imputed to it even now the condition of life and death, since it is already liable to the issues of both, although, by living still in the mother, it for the most part shares its own state with the mother.[12]

To be sure, Tertullian does not manifest the precision of later Church teaching. Nevertheless, he stands at the origins of the living tradition of the Church, which finds its most recent expression in the *Catechism of the Catholic Church*, which uses God's declaration to Jeremiah that he "knew" him before he was formed "in the womb" and before he was "born" (Jer 1:5) as a biblical foundation for its teaching that human life must be respected and protected from "the moment of conception" and that the unborn must be recognized as having "the rights of a person" (*CCC* 2270, citing Jer 1:5). This is a premier example of what we might refer to as the "moral sense" of an Old Testament text that has implications that go far beyond its original meaning.

---

[9] See Dean O. Wenthe, *Jeremiah, Lamentations*, Old Testament 12, Ancient Christian Commentary on Scripture, ed. Thomas C. Oden (Downers Grove, Ill.: InterVarsity Press, 2009), xxiii–xxv.

[10] See Origen, *Homilies on Jeremiah, Homily on 1 Kings 28*, trans. John Clark Smith, The Fathers of the Church 97 (Washington, D.C.: Catholic University of America Press, 1998).

[11] See Michael J. Gorman, *Abortion in the Early Church* (Eugene, Ore.: Wipf & Stock, 1998), 56–57.

[12] Tertullian, *A Treatise on the Soul* 37, in *Ante-Nicene Fathers*, ed. Alexander Roberts and James Donaldson, vol. 3 (1885; repr., Peabody, Mass.: Hendrickson, 1994), 217–18.

The Life of Jeremiah and the Life of Jesus

Besides his theology of the New Covenant, Jeremiah's other major contribution to salvation history and Christian theology is the way in which his own life points forward to the suffering, rejection, and execution of Jesus, more so than any other prophet. Biography plays only a small role in Isaiah but a large role in Jeremiah. In many ways, the person of the prophet becomes absorbed into his prophetic ministry, so that his own experiences as much as his words become transformed into "prophecy". The Church has long recognized the striking correlation between the character and travails of Jeremiah and those of Jesus, beginning already in the lifetime of Jesus, in which some people apparently answered the question: "Who do men say that the Son of man is?" by responding: "Jeremiah" (Mt 16:14). Consider the following similarities between the life of Jeremiah and the life of Jesus:

	The Life of Jeremiah	The Life of Jesus
1. Chosen from the womb by God	Jer 1:5	Lk 1:31
2. Destined for rejection and conflict with his people	Jer 1:18–19	Lk 2:34–35
3. Called to prophetic celibacy	Jer 16:1–4	Mt 19:10–12
4. Likened to a sacrificial lamb	Jer 11:19	Jn 1:29, 36
5. Betrayed by those closest to him	Jer 12:6	Jn 13:18, 38
6. Preached against Temple and predicted destruction of Jerusalem	Jer 26:2–6	Mk 11:15–19; 13:1–2, and parr.
7. Opposed and persecuted by chief priests and elders	Jer 20:1–3; 26:7–9	Mk 11:18
8. Condemned to death for speaking against the Temple	Jer 26:8–9	Mk 14:57–58
9. Tried by partly sympathetic but weak-willed magistrate	Jer 37:16—38:28	Jn 18:28—19:16
10. Cast into a pit and raised up from it again	Jer 37:6–13	Jn 19:40—20:18

In light of such a remarkably extensive list of parallels, it is no wonder that the Church's tradition holds up Jeremiah as a prototype or prefiguration of the suffering prophet that will be fully realized in Jesus of Nazareth. Indeed, a remarkable number of Church Fathers saw in Jeremiah's description of himself as a "gentle lamb led to the slaughter" (Jer 11:19) a prophetic word pointing forward to the Passion of Christ.[13] Consider, for example, the words of the fourth-century Christian apologist Lactantius:

[13] See Wenthe, *Jeremiah*, 98–100.

Jeremiah, too, said, "... I was carried as a meek lamb to be the victim. They devised counsels against me, saying, 'Let us put wood on his bread and cut him off from the land of the living ...'" (Jer 11:18–19 LXX). *Now the wood signifies the cross and the bread His body, because He is Himself the food and life of all who believe in the flesh that He put on and by which He hung on the cross.*[14]

The Todah Sacrifices Fulfilled in the Liturgy of the Church

As we saw above, one of the most remarkable theological and liturgical contributions of Jeremiah is his vision of the sacrifices of "thanksgiving" that will be offered in the era of the New Covenant at the time of the coming of the Messiah (Jer 31, 33). Given the centrality of the Eucharist (Greek for "thanksgiving") for the early Church, it is unsurprising that Church Fathers such as Jerome saw this oracle of Jeremiah as fulfilled in the liturgy of the Church:

> A type of these events previously occurred in Zerubbabel and Ezra, when the people returned and the city was begun to be built on its heights and religion observed in the temple, all of which is contained in Ezra's own book. But this was more fully and more perfectly completed in the Lord and Savior and his apostles, when the city was built on its heights—about which it is written, "A city set on a hill cannot be hidden" (Mt 5:14)—and the temple was founded in accordance with order and ceremony, so that whatever was done carnally by the people in the past would be completed spiritually in the church. Then praise went forth—or thanksgiving, for this is what *thoda* means (Jer 30:19)—so that all of the apostles would be able to say "grace and peace to you" (1 Cor 1:3).[15]

Notice that Jerome not only equates the celebration of the Jeremianic sacrifices of thanksgiving with the Christian Eucharist; he also sees the temporal and partial restoration of Israel that took place after the Babylonian exile as a type of the ultimate ingathering of Israel and the nations that takes place in the going forth of the gospel to the ends of the earth and the gathering of God's people to offer the Eucharist.

One God Gave the Old and New Testaments

From the very beginnings of the Church, one of the first questions faced by Christians was: Is the God of the Christians the same as the God of Israel? If so, then why are there two testaments? This was, of course, the challenge of Marcionism, which held that the God of the Old Testament was a different deity from that of the New.

---

[14] Lactantius, *Divine Institutes* 4.14, in Wenthe, *Jeremiah*, 99–100.
[15] Jerome, *Six Books on Jeremiah* 6.9.3–5, in Wenthe, *Jeremiah*, 204.

The book of Jeremiah played a key role in answering this question, since it provided explicit Old Testament evidence for a *"new* covenant" (Jer 31:31–33). Because of this, figures like the great Eastern Father John Chrysostom used this pivotal text to refute the idea that there were two different gods:

> [W]e say, that there is but one and the same Legislator of either covenant, who dispensed all meetly, and adapted to the difference of the times the difference between the two systems of law. Therefore neither are the first commandments cruel, nor the second hard and grievous, but all of one and the same providential care.
>
> For that He Himself gave the old covenant also, hear the affirmation of the prophet, or rather (so we must speak), of Him who is both the one and the other: "I will make a covenant with you, not according to the covenant which I made with your fathers" [Jer 31:31].[16]

Chrysostom is following the theological trajectory of the New Testament documents themselves, especially the letter to the Hebrews, which quotes Jeremiah 31:31–34 in Hebrews 8:8–12 (the longest single quote of the Old Testament in the New) to show that the message of a "new covenant" preached by the Church was not some Christian "innovation" or novelty, but a central hope of Jewish Scripture itself. Jeremiah, of all the prophets, is the most explicit in his anticipation of a New Covenant, and so his book serves in a special way to establish a "hermeneutic of continuity" between the Old and New Testaments.

What about the Promise of an Everlasting Levitical Priesthood?

In addition to Jeremiah's oracle about a New Covenant, he also prophesies that David will never lack a king to sit on his "throne" (Jer 33:15–17) and that "the Levitical priests" will never lack a man to offer sacrifices in the "presence" of the Lord (Jer 33:18–19). As is well known, the Davidic monarchy collapsed after the Babylonian destruction of Jerusalem in 587 B.C., and the Levitical priesthood was decimated by the destruction of the Second Temple in A.D. 70, never to be restored again. What, then, do we make of these oracles of Jeremiah?

Remarkably, the early Church Fathers not only saw that the "thanksgiving sacrifices" (Jer 30:19) were fulfilled in the Eucharist, but they also saw the promise of the perpetual throne of David and the perpetual priesthood fulfilled in Christ the King and the New Covenant priesthood. In the words of Theodoret of Cyrus:

> We see the fulfillment of this prophecy [Jer 33:18–25] as well. When the new covenant was given, in keeping with the divine promise, the priesthood was also given according to the order of Melchizedek, and those to whom it was promised offer the spiritual sacrifice to God continually. Then he says, as it is impossible for

---

[16]John Chrysostom, *Homilies on the Gospel of Matthew* 16.8, in *NPNF1* 10:109–10.

day to become night, so it is impossible for the Davidic monarchy to be destroyed. The fulfillment of this prophecy is also clear: Christ, who is of David according to the flesh, does not occupy the throne here below. He does, however, govern all things as he sits next to the Father. This is precisely what he also says about the priests and the Levites, noting that their line will be compared with the host of heaven and the sand of the sea. The facts confirm what is said: the whole land and sea are full of high priests and the deacons performing the liturgy of the Levites.[17]

The early Church took the prophecies of the Old Testament seriously but, at the same time, saw them fulfilled both *Christologically* and *sacramentally*. It is no earthly throne or earthly priesthood that will constitute worship in the age of the Messiah, but the heavenly throne of Christ the King and the heavenly worship, in which the priests and deacons on earth participate whenever and wherever the Eucharist is celebrated. In other words, the temporal and earthly Levitical priesthood does not truly pass away with the coming of Christ; rather, it is perfected and fulfilled in the eternal and heavenly Melchizedekian priesthood of Christ in the new and everlasting covenant.

Fidelity to the Covenant of Levi (*Jer 33:17–22*)

Another approach to understanding God's fidelity to the covenant with Levi can be found in the theology of St. Luke. A key text is Acts 6:7, which records an important stage in the growth of the early Church:

> "And the word of God increased; and the number of the disciples multiplied greatly in Jerusalem, *and a great many of the priests were obedient to the faith.*"

This text witnesses to the fact that a large number of the heirs of the Levitical covenant did, in fact, enter into the New Covenant. Did they then lose their priestly status? No, for Peter testifies:

> "You are a chosen race, a *royal priesthood*, a holy nation" (1 Pet 2:9).

In the Church, every believer becomes a priest in Christ (*CCC* 901–3). The priesthood is not confiscated from the descendants of Levi, but shared with the whole community. Therefore, the large number of Levitical priests who joined the New Covenant community in Acts 6:7 did not lose their priestly status, and in them and their descendants Jeremiah's words are fulfilled: "The Levitical priests shall never lack a man in my presence" (Jer 33:18).

The Book of Jeremiah in the Lectionary

We have seen how "liturgical" the book of Jeremiah is: both major parts of the book begin from the Temple and move out to the world, based on the concept that the Temple is microcosm and the world is macrotemple. Jeremiah criticizes the people for their hypocritical celebration of the liturgy of YHWH and their illicit participation in the false liturgies of pagan gods. He envisions the final restoration of a new Temple and a new liturgy characterized by the joyful

---

[17] Theodoret of Cyrus, *On Jeremiah* 7.33.18, in Wenthe, *Jeremiah*, 228.

celebration of the *todah*-thanksgiving sacrifice. Therefore, it is very fitting that his prophecies continue to be proclaimed during the "thanksgiving sacrifice" of God's people today.

In the contemporary Roman Lectionary, several of Jeremiah's laments and/ or descriptions of persecution are read during the Sundays of Ordinary Time and in the season of Lent, paired with Gospel pericopes in which Jesus Christ faces similar suffering or persecution. We have observed the strong typological parallels between the biographies of Jeremiah and Jesus above. Thus, the dominant use of the book in the Lectionary is to provide a prophetic background and typological model for understanding the sufferings of the Messiah.

In addition, a couple of the messianic oracles of Jeremiah (Jer 23:5–8; 33:14–16) are read during Advent to build liturgical anticipation for the coming of Jesus Christ as Davidic King. The famous "new covenant" passage (Jer 31:31–34) is read triennially near the end of Lent as preparation for understanding the institution of the Eucharist and the Lord's Passion as covenant-establishing events. The same passage is also an option for use at ritual Masses celebrating a covenant-forming sacrament (baptism, matrimony) or sacramental (consecration or religious profession).

Finally, Jeremiah's call and commissioning (Jer 1:4–19) provide reading options for several Masses that view Jeremiah as a type of Jesus Christ (Fourth Sunday in Ordinary Time, Year C), John the Baptist (Vigil of Nativity and Martyrdom of the Baptist), or those called to the "prophetic" (preaching) ministry of the Church.

	Readings from Jeremiah in the Lectionary and Liturgy of the Hours on Sundays, Feast Days, Liturgical Seasons, and Other Occasions		
	MSO=Masses for Special Occasions; *OM*=Optional Memorial; *VM*=Votive Mass; *Rit*=Ritual; *LH*=Liturgy of the Hours		
Passage	Description	Occasion	Explanation
1:4–5, 17–19	The Lord has called the prophet from the womb and strengthened him like a "fortified city" against the whole land.	*4th Sun. in OT* (C)	Paired with the Lord's first sermon in Nazareth (Lk 4:21–30), where the townspeople attempt to kill him, the first reading sets up a typological relationship between Jeremiah and Jesus, so that we see the prophetic pattern recapitulated in the ministry of the Lord.
1:4–9	The Lord has chosen the prophet from the womb; though he is youthful, the Lord will strengthen him and place words in his mouth.	Common of Pastors, opt. 7; Conferral of Orders, opt. 4; Candidacy for Orders, opt. 4; *MSO*: For Priests, opt. 2; For Vocations, opt. 6	This passage has special application to those who take on a prophetic role in the Christian community (holy orders), to assure them of God's calling (vocation) and his strength and guidance for their ministry.

(*continued*)

	Readings from Jeremiah in the Lectionary and Liturgy of the Hours on Sundays, Feast Days, Liturgical Seasons, and Other Occasions (*continued*)		
	MSO = Masses for Special Occasions; *OM* = Optional Memorial; *VM* = Votive Mass; *Rit* = Ritual; *LH* = Liturgy of the Hours		
Passage	**Description**	**Occasion**	**Explanation**
1:4–10	See above, plus the commission "to pluck up and to break down ... to build and to plant"	Vigil for the Nativity of the Baptist (June 23)	The Church understands the Baptist as a second Jeremiah, chosen from the womb (Lk 1:15, 44) with a dual commission of judgment and consolation (cf. Lk 3:16–17).
1:17–19	The Lord commands the prophet not to be dismayed; the people will oppose him but will not prevail.	Martyrdom of the Baptist (August 29)	Herod's opposition to John, leading to John's beheading, is seen as typical of the pattern of the true prophet, who always finds persecution. Nonetheless, the Lord's word will always prevail.
7:2–7	Jeremiah's "Temple sermon": Jerusalem is reminded that the Temple building does not guarantee blessing, but God's presence is contingent on the practice of justice and mercy according to the law.	*LH*: Canticle III Vigil for the Dedication of a Church	At the dedication of a Church, the Christian people are reminded not to attach superstitious confidence to a building, to the neglect of the practice of virtue and the truths of the faith.
7:23–28	Jeremiah is to rebuke the Israelites, yet they will not listen to him, for they are more rebellious than their fathers. They are a nation that does not obey or accept discipline.	Thurs., 3rd Week of Lent	Paired with the accusation that Jesus casts out demons by Beelzebul (Lk 11:14–23), we see a parallel between Israel in Jeremiah's day and the Jewish leaders of Jesus' day. Neither is docile to the word of the true prophet.
11:18–20	Jeremiah feels like a lamb led to the slaughter among those who persecute him, but he commits his cause to the Lord.	Sat., 4th Week of Lent	When this passage is paired with the account of the controversy over Jesus during the Feast of Tabernacles (Jn 7:40–53), when the chief priests and Pharisees condemn him over Nicodemus' protests, Jeremiah appears as the type and prefiguration of Jesus, the true Lamb of God who will be slaughtered.
14:17–21	Jeremiah laments the destruction of his people and pleads with the Lord to have mercy for the sake of his covenant.	*LH*: Canticle for Morn. Prayer, Fri, Week III	Friday is a traditional day of penitence in the Church's prayer, and Jeremiah's prayer in 14:17–21 poignantly articulates the posture of the penitent believer.

(*continued*)

	Readings from Jeremiah in the Lectionary and Liturgy of the Hours on Sundays, Feast Days, Liturgical Seasons, and Other Occasions (*continued*)		
	MSO = Masses for Special Occasions; *OM* = Optional Memorial; *VM* = Votive Mass; *Rit* = Ritual; *LH* = Liturgy of the Hours		
Passage	Description	Occasion	Explanation
17:5–8	Jeremiah's rendition of Psalm 1: The man who trusts in man is a desert shrub; he who trusts in the Lord is a tree planted by water.	*6th Sun. in OT (C)*	This reading complements the blessings and woes of the Sermon on the Plain (Lk 6:17, 20–26), enabling us to see Jesus' definitions of what it is to "trust in man" or "trust in the LORD".
17:5–10	See above, plus "the heart is deceitful above all things.... I the LORD ... test the heart, to give to every man according to his ways."	Thurs., 2nd Week of Lent	In light of the Gospel (Lk 16:19–31), Dives and Lazarus, we see that sometimes those who trust in the Lord (Lazarus) experience the associated blessings only in the life to come, but the Lord's recompense to the evil and to the righteous will inevitably come.
17:7–8	Jeremiah's rendition of Psalm 1: Blessed is the man who trusts the Lord; he is like a tree planted beside waters.	*LH:* Canticle I, Vigil for Holy Men and Women	Jeremiah's version of the first psalm is generally applicable to the saints, who stand as spiritual examples of the "tree planted by [streams of] water".
18:18–20	Jeremiah's colleagues plot against him, and the prophet cries to the Lord for vindication and deliverance.	Wed., 2nd Week of Lent	During the season of Lent, Jeremiah's persecutions and rejections by his contemporaries serve as a type and model for understanding the rejection and abuse heaped on Jesus during the Passion.
20:7–9	Jeremiah feels deceived and misused by the Lord, yet he cannot be silent, because the divine word is like a fire in his bones.	*22nd Sun. in OT (A)*; Common of Holy Men and Women, opt. 16; *MSO:* For Vocations, opt. 7	Jeremiah again appears as the prototype of the suffering prophet, persecuted by those to whom he preaches, the model of the ministry of Christ. The saints also experienced many similar sufferings; yet the Church needs those for whom the fire of God's word overpowers the fear of persecution.
20:10–13	Following the form of a lament psalm, Jeremiah describes betrayal by his close friends yet expresses confidence in God and offers thanks in advance for deliverance.	*12th Sun. in OT (A)*; Fri., 5th Week of Lent	In the Gospel (Mt 10:26–33), Jesus comforts the disciples: though they will suffer rejection, their heavenly Father knows every hair of their head, and they are worth more than sparrows. Together, these readings encourage the suffering believer with confidence in God and hope for eternal reward.

(*continued*)

Readings from Jeremiah in the Lectionary and Liturgy of the Hours on Sundays, Feast Days, Liturgical Seasons, and Other Occasions (continued)

MSO = Masses for Special Occasions; *OM* = Optional Memorial;
VM = Votive Mass; *Rit* = Ritual; *LH* = Liturgy of the Hours

Passage	Description	Occasion	Explanation
23:1–6	Woe to the shepherds who destroy God's flock! Yet in the future, he will gather his flock and appoint them good shepherds. He will raise up for David a righteous Branch.	*16th Sun. in OT (B)*	Jesus is the Good Shepherd, who has compassion on the Jews, who are "like sheep without a shepherd" (Mk 6:30–34). This reading prepares us to understand the feeding of the 5,000 as an act of the "shepherd" feeding his "flock". Jesus is the promised Branch of David, the definitive Shepherd.
23:5–8	See above, plus a promise of a new exodus for Israel in the latter days	Advent, Dec. 18	Paired with the account of the betrothal of Joseph and Mary (Mt 1:18–24), the Jeremian passage appears as a key Christological prophecy, reminding us of the roles the Lord Jesus was sent to fulfill.
31:7–9	Let Jacob rejoice: the Lord will gather his people with gentleness to Zion; among them will be the blind, lame, and vulnerable.	*30th Sun. in OT (B)*	This passage is paired with the healing of blind Bartimaeus (Mk 10:46–52) to help the believer recognize that the healing ministry of Christ was part of his leadership of a "new exodus" out of bondage to sin into the freedom of the sons of God in the "heavenly Zion".
31:10–12ab[cd], 13	The Lord will gather his people to Zion and bless them there with Edenic abundance and great joy.	Sat., 5th Week of Lent (resp.); *LH*: Canticle for Morning Prayer, Thurs., Week I (31:10–14)	This Jeremian passage (31:10–13) is a popular responsorial canticle, expressing joy for the restoration of "Israel" and "Zion" that the Church believes has been accomplished in Christ.
31:31–34	The promise of a New Covenant, not like the old, in which the law will be written on the heart, all will know God, and sins will be .	*5th Sun. of Lent (B)*; *Rit.*: Christian Initiation, opt. 8; Conferral of Marriage, opt. 9; *VM*: Sacred Heart, opt. 5	This passage is read near the end of Lent, in preparation for understanding the Eucharist as the "New Covenant in my blood" established on Holy Thursday. It is also appropriate for baptism, the entrance into the New Covenant, and Matrimony, which mirrors the New Covenant in the covenantal bond of the spouses.
31:31–37	See above, plus a promise that Israel's descendants will never be cast off	*Rit*: Consecration of Virgins and Religious Profession	Those entering the religious life seek a profound experience of the New Covenant, in which their lives become personal realizations of the nuptial, covenantal relationship between God and his people.

(continued)

| Readings from Jeremiah in the Lectionary and Liturgy of the Hours on Sundays, Feast Days, Liturgical Seasons, and Other Occasions (*continued*) ||||
| *MSO* = Masses for Special Occasions; *OM* = Optional Memorial; *VM* = Votive Mass; *Rit* = Ritual; *LH* = Liturgy of the Hours ||||
Passage	Description	Occasion	Explanation
33:14–16	The promise of a "righteous Branch" that will "spring forth for David" to execute "justice and righteousness"	*1st Sun. of Advent (C)*	This promise of a son of David coming in future days opens the readings for Advent, immediately calling attention to Jesus' coming as a fulfillment of God's promises of covenant fidelity to David and his house.
38:4–6, 8–10	Jeremiah is cast into a cistern by the royal princes, but saved through the intercession of Ebed-melech the Ethiopian.	*20th Sun. in OT (C)*	The conflict that Jeremiah provokes within his own household and his own ministers illustrates Jesus' teaching in the Gospel (Lk 12:49–53) that he came not "to give peace on earth" but "division" and that households will be divided against each other. This is the effect of a true prophet, who presents the unpopular truth of God.

Jeremiah is read semi-continuously in the weekday Lectionary in Year II, Weeks 16–18. The selected passages aim to give the Christian faithful a representative exposure to the life and message of the prophet, highlighting some of the more significant events, sermons, and oracles, while avoiding some passages that the faithful will have already heard in the Sunday Lectionary. In the weekday

| Reading of Jeremiah for Daily Mass: Ordinary Time, Year II: Weeks 16–18 ||||
Week	Day	Passage Read	Description
16	W	1:1, 4–10	The call and commission of the prophet
16	Th	2:1–3, 7–8, 12–13	Israel has abandoned God like an unfaithful bride, forsaking him for the Baals (pagan gods) who cannot help it.
16	F	3:14–17	The Lord will bring a remnant back to Zion and appoint them good shepherds. The ark will no longer be missed, and all nations will gather in Jerusalem.
16	Sa	7:1–11	The Temple sermon: Israel must not place confidence in the Temple to the neglect of the Ten Commandments and the laws of justice and charity. They have made the Temple "a den of robbers".
17	M	13:1–11	The sign-act of the linen waistcloth: Israel has become worthless, like a rotted waistcloth buried in the ground.

(continued)

Reading of Jeremiah for Daily Mass: Ordinary Time, Year II: Weeks 16–18 (*continued*)			
Week	Day	Passage Read	Description
17	Tu	14:17–22	A lament psalm of Jeremiah: The prophet's people are destroyed all around him. Has God rejected Judah completely? Will he really break his covenant? Hope is only in the Lord; the idols are worthless.
17	W	15:10, 16–21	A complaint of Jeremiah that his prophetic role is too much for him; followed by an oracle of encouragement from the Lord
17	Th	18:1–6	The potter's house lesson: The potter reworks and recasts a marred pot; can the Lord not do the same with Israel?
17	F	26:1–9	The Temple sermon repeated: Jeremiah predicts Jerusalem will become like Shiloh; the people and princes try to put him to death.
17	Sa	26:11–16, 24	The priests and prophets try to execute Jeremiah. He speaks in his own defense, but to no avail. Ahikam son of Shaphan intervenes to spare his life.
18	M	28:1–17	Hananiah the false prophet opposes Jeremiah and his teaching on the "yoke of the king of Babylon", but dies an untimely death under the curse of the Lord.
18	Tu	30:1–2, 12–15, 18–22	The beginning of the "Book of Comfort". After Judah's sorrow, it and Jerusalem will have restoration of honor, numbers, joy, and peace. The covenant will be renewed.
18	W	31:1–7	God will renew his "everlasting love" to Israel, who will be like a joyful virgin bride once more. Peace, prosperity, and praise will fill Zion and all Israel.
18	W	31:10, 11–12ab, 13 (resp.); also Yr I, OT, Week 25 Sa (resp.); Yr II, OT Week 16 F (resp.)	The Lord will lead a new exodus back to Zion, where Israel will experience Eden-like peace and prosperity. Nuptial joy will again adorn the city.
18	Th	31:31–34	The New Covenant passage: In the future the Lord will grant a New Covenant unlike the Mosaic, which will involve the writing of the law on their hearts, infused knowledge of God, and forgiveness of sins.

cycle, nothing is read after chapter 31, thus omitting Jeremiah's "Passion" (Jer 37–45) and the "Oracles against the Nations" (Jer 46–51).

The semi-continuous readings from Jeremiah in the Liturgy of the Hours, weeks 21–23, are similar in structure and intent to the daily Mass readings. The readings are longer, and a few additional ones are added, including two

Jeremiah in the Office of Reading for the Liturgy of the Hours, Ordinary Time: Weeks 21–23			
Week	Day	Passage Read	Description
21	Tu	1:1–19	The historical context of Jeremiah's ministry, his call and commission, and two initial visions: the almond branch and boiling pot in the north
21	W	2:1–13, 20–25	Israel is an unfaithful bride who forgets her first love and goes lusting after foreign gods she had not known before.
21	Th	3:1–5, 19—4:4	Israel is a bride who has turned to harlotry, who cannot expect to return to her husband. It worships pagan idols and practices injustice, but God calls it to circumcise the foreskin of its heart.
21	F	4:5–8, 13–28	The Lord brings a destroying army from the north that will make Judah a wasteland.
21	Sa	7:1–20	Jeremiah's Temple sermon: Judah must not put false confidence in the Temple, thinking it will protect it despite its evil behavior. Shiloh was the site of the Tabernacle, yet it was not spared. God commands Jeremiah not to intercede for this rebellious people.
22	Su	11:18–20; 12:1–13	Jeremiah complains to the Lord: Why do the wicked prosper? Why are God's people abandoned? The Lord has given his heritage over to their enemies.
22	M	19:1–5, 10—20:6	Jeremiah breaks an earthen pot at the Potsherd Gate as a sign of judgment on Judah; Pashhur the chief priest imprisons Jeremiah at the Benjamin Gate but receives an oracle of judgment.
22	Tu	20:7–18	Jeremiah's complaint: Preaching God's word brings him persecution and contempt, yet he cannot restrain the word within him. He cries out for vindication, yet curses the day of his birth.
22	W	26:1–15	The second account of Jeremiah's Temple sermon: Jeremiah prophesies that Jerusalem will become like Shiloh. The people and princes think to put him to death, but Jeremiah defends himself as the messenger of the Lord.
22	Th	29:1–14	Jeremiah's letter to the exiles: put down roots, the exile will be long; nonetheless, the Lord has plans "to give you a future and a hope" after seventy years are completed for Babylon.
22	F	30:18—31:9	The Lord will restore Zion like a virgin daughter; he will gather the survivors from the north in a new exodus, with tenderness and compassion. He will restore Israel to divine sonship.
22	Sa	31:15–22, 27–34	Though the Israelites mourn in distress now, the days are coming when the Lord will "build" and "plant" them and make with them a New Covenant better than the Old.
23	Su	37:21; 38:14–28	Zedekiah imprisons Jeremiah in the court of the guard, yet he comes to consult with him in secret. Jeremiah urges him to surrender to the Chaldeans, but the king rejects his advice out of fear.
23	M	42:1–16; 43:4–7	The surviving Judeans under Johanan son of Kareah seek Jeremiah's advice. He urges them to stay and obey the Babylonians, but they reject his word and flee to Egypt.

selections from the biographical "Passion" section (Jer 37–45) that provide a glimpse of the end of the prophet's life.

Conclusion

Jeremiah is the longest prophetic book in the Hebrew Bible by word count but stands second to Isaiah in stature and influence because it has somewhat less to say about the age to come. Jeremiah's fundamental contribution to the Church's faith is his prophecy and theology of the "new covenant" (Jer 31:31–34) and his description of the sacrificial worship of that covenant in the surrounding chapters (Jer 30–33). These passages profoundly shape the theological perspective of the New Testament authors and their understanding of Jesus Christ, who himself claimed to fulfill Jeremiah's prophecies through the blood of the "new covenant" (Lk 22:19–22; 1 Cor 11:23–25). Jeremiah is also remembered for typifying and foreshadowing the sufferings of Christ through his own personal experiences.

For Further Reading

Commentaries and Studies on Jeremiah

Bright, John. *Jeremiah*. Anchor Bible 21. Garden City, N.Y.: Doubleday, 1965.

Chisholm, Robert B., Jr. *Handbook on the Prophets*. Grand Rapids, Mich.: Baker Academic, 2002. (See pp. 153–215.)

Day, John. *King and Messiah in Israel and the Ancient Near East*. Library of Biblical Studies 270. London: T&T Clark, 2013.

Holladay, William Lee. *Jeremiah*. 2 vols. Hermeneia. Philadelphia: Fortress Press, 1986–1989.

Lundbom, Jack R. *Jeremiah*. 3 vols. Anchor Yale Bible 21A, 21B, and 21 C. New York: Doubleday, 1999–2004.

Ortlund, Raymond C., Jr. *Whoredom: God's Unfaithful Wife in Biblical Theology*. Grand Rapids, Mich.: Eerdmans, 1996.

Historical Questions and Jeremiah

Abegg, Martin, Jr., Peter Flint, and Eugene Ulrich. *The Dead Sea Scrolls Bible: The Oldest Known Bible Translated for the First Time into English*. San Francisco: HarperOne, 1999. (See pp. 382–406.)

Hare, D. R. "Lives of the Prophets". Pages 386–88 in vol. 2 of *The Old Testament Pseudepigrapha*. Edited by James H. Charlesworth. Anchor Bible Reference Library. New York: Doubleday, 1985.

Oates, Joan. *Babylon*. Rev. ed. London: Thames & Hudson, 1986.

Stern, Ephraim. *Archaeology of the Land of the Bible*. Vol. 2, *The Assyrian, Babylonian, and Persian Periods (732–332 B.C.E.)*. Anchor Bible Reference Library. New York: Doubleday, 2001.

Voth, Steven M. "Jeremiah". Pages 229–371 in *Isaiah, Jeremiah, Lamentations, Ezekiel, Daniel*. Vol. 4 of *Zondervan Illustrated Bible Backgrounds Commentary*. Edited by John H. Walton. Grand Rapids, Mich.: Zondervan, 2009.

Jeremiah in the Living Tradition

Gorman, Michael J. *Abortion in the Early Church*. Eugene, Ore.: Wipf & Stock, 1998.

Origen. *Homilies on Jeremiah, Homily on 1 Kings 28*. Translated by John Clark Smith. The Fathers of the Church 97. Washington, D.C.: Catholic University of America Press, 1998. (See pp. 3–273.)

Wenthe, Dean O. *Jeremiah, Lamentations*. Old Testament 12 of Ancient Christian Commentary on Scripture. Edited by Thomas C. Oden. Downers Grove, Ill.: Inter-Varsity Press, 2009. (See pp. 1–271.)

32. LAMENTATIONS

Introduction

The book of Lamentations consists of five laments over the destruction of Jerusalem, the first four composed as acrostic poems following the twenty-two letters of the Hebrew alphabet. The book is traditionally ascribed to the prophet Jeremiah, and it gives every indication of having been composed by a great Hebrew literary artist soon after the events it bemoans, expressed in language and images very similar to those found in Jeremiah.

In the Jewish tradition represented by the Masoretic Text, the book of Lamentations is called by its first Hebrew word, *'Eykah* ("How!" or "Oh how!"), or else by the Hebrew term *Qinnot*, meaning "Lamentations" or "Dirges". The book is placed in the third Jewish canonical category, the "Writings" (Hebrew *ketuvim*), where—along with Ruth, Ecclesiastes, the Song of Solomon, and Esther—it comprises one of the "Five Scrolls" (Hebrew *megillot*) read on particular holy days. In the case of Lamentations, it is read on the *Ninth of Av* (Hebrew *Tisha B'Av*)—which usually falls sometime in July-August—the traditional day of the year on which both the First and Second Temples were destroyed, though there are some discrepancies about the exact timing (cf. 2 Kings 25:8–9; Jer 52:12).

In the Christian tradition, the canonical placement of the book of Lamentations was heavily influenced by the Greek Septuagint tradition, which was followed by the Latin Vulgate. In the Septuagint, Lamentations was considered, along with Baruch, to be a part of the book of Jeremiah. As a result, it is omitted as a separate book in some canonical lists, even though its canonical status was never in doubt. In the Vulgate, Jerome appends "The Dirges, that is, the Lamentations of Jeremiah the Prophet" (*Threni, id est Lamentationes Jeremiae Prophetae*) directly to the end of Jeremiah 52:34 and does not mark the end of the book of Jeremiah (*explicit liber hieremiae prophetae*) until after Lamentations 5:22. The Septuagint tradition, however, eventually came to place Baruch directly after Jeremiah, and "Lamentations" (Greek *thrēnoi*) after Baruch. Significantly, in the Christian tradition, Lamentations was often read, recited, or meditated upon during Passion Week, especially on Good Friday, the commemoration of the destruction of the body of Christ, which is the New Temple (cf. Jn 2:21).

Literary Structure of Lamentations

Lamentations is a self-consciously literary work and displays clear, intentional structure. The book consists of five poetic laments, which happily coincide with the chapter divisions. The first four of these are *acrostic* poems: that is, each of the verses or strophes begins with one of the twenty-two letters of the

Hebrew alphabet in order (Lam 1, 2, 3, and 4). The intention of the acrostic genre is to express a sense of completion and comprehensiveness. In other words, the book offers a lament for Jerusalem "from A to Z"—that is, as completely as possible.

The third of the five laments (Lam 3) is the longest and grandest, whereas the other four are all twenty-two verses long. Therefore, there is a rough chiastic or concentric pattern: the third, central lament is bracketed by Laments 1–2 and 4–5:

Outline of the Book of Lamentations

A. A Prayer of Jerusalem: "How Lonely Is Zion!" (chap. 1)
  B. Acrostic Lament 1: "How Angry Is the LORD toward Zion" (chap. 2)
    C. The Prophet's Complaint: "I Have Seen Affliction" (chap. 3)
  B'. Acrostic Lament 2: "How the Gold Has Grown Dim!" (chap. 4)
A'. A Prayer of Jerusalemites: "Remember What Has Befallen Us!" (chap. 5)

As mentioned, the first four laments are acrostic poems. Laments 1, 2, and 4 are simple acrostics, in which each verse starts with each successive letter of the Hebrew alphabet. Lament 3 is somewhat more complex, as it allots three verses to each Hebrew letter. Lament 5 departs from the acrostic pattern, but it still consists of twenty-two verses. In this way, the Hebrew poet retains the literary balance with the entire composition even while breaking free of the constraints of the strict acrostic form in order more directly to express his emotions to God.

Overview of Lamentations

The Destruction of Jerusalem, Daughter of Zion (Lamentations 1)

The first lamentation is marked by a sustained personification of Jerusalem, described at first in the third person as a woman weeping bitterly in her disgrace and shame (Lam 1:1–11). About halfway through the poem, Jerusalem herself begins to speak in the first person, in a striking lament regarding what the Lord has done to her because of her sins. Speaking to those who pass by, gawking at her desolation, she cries:

> Is it nothing to you, all you who pass by?
>   *Look and see*
> *if there is any sorrow like my sorrow*
>   which was brought upon me,
> which the LORD inflicted
>   on the day of his fierce anger.
> (Lam 1:12)

Speaking almost in the figure of the unfaithful bride we have seen elsewhere in the prophets, Jerusalem goes on to lament that her "lovers" have deceived her; and now, having abandoned the Lord, she has no one to comfort her

(Lam 1:18–21). She concludes with a prayer for deliverance and the punishment of those who did evil against her (Lam 1:21–22).

It Is YHWH Who Brought Jerusalem to an End (Lamentations 2)

The second poem in the book places the bulk of its emphasis on the fact that it is YHWH himself, "the LORD", who has wrought the destruction of "the daughter of Zion" (Lam 2:1–2). In essence, this acrostic is a series of poetic descriptions of how God, in his wrath and indignation at the sins of Jerusalem, "has become like an enemy" to his people (Lam 2:5), delivering them into the hands of their foes, so that the "sanctuary" of the Temple and the "wall" of the city of Zion have been ruined (Lam 2:7–8).

Like the earlier lament, this one switches between third-person description and first-person complaints, culminating in a passionate exhortation to Jerusalem to pray and a graphic prayer for the Lord to deliver his people:

> Arise, cry out in the night,
>   at the beginning of the watches!
> Pour out your heart like water
>   before the presence of the Lord!
> Lift your hands to him
>   for the lives of your children,
> who faint for hunger
>   at the head of every street.
>
> (Lam 2:19)

With these words, we see that, from the perspective of the author, the suffering endured by the people of Jerusalem should not drive them to *stop* praying—as suffering can so easily do—but rather to *intensify* their prayer, so that they pour out their hearts "like water" before the Lord—an image taken directly from the sacrifices of blood, which would be poured out "like water" on the altar of the now-decimated sanctuary (cf. Deut 12:16, 24).[1]

The Lament of the Man Who Has Seen Affliction (Lamentations 3)

The grand center of the book, with its triple-line acrostic structure, is not actually a lament over Jerusalem, but a classic *confession* of an individual—traditionally identified with Jeremiah the prophet—"the man who has seen affliction" (Lam 3:1). In this poem, the author complains of mistreatment by both God and men (Lam 3:1–21) and cries out for deliverance and justice (Lam 3:55–66).

Two aspects of this, the centerpiece of the book, stand out as noteworthy. First, despite the raw emotion with which the author describes how he is afflicted, abandoned, and even persecuted by God (cf. Lam 3:10–15), nevertheless, in the very midst of the poem, the poet does not give up hope:

---

[1] Delbert R. Hillers, *Lamentations*, Anchor Bible 7A (New York: Doubleday, 1976), 40.

> Remember my affliction and my bitterness,
>   the wormwood and the gall!
> My soul continually thinks of it
>   and is bowed down within me.
> *But this I call to mind,*
>   *and therefore I have hope:*
>
> *The steadfast love of the LORD never ceases,*
>   *his mercies never come to an end;*
> *they are new every morning;*
>   great is your faithfulness.
> "The LORD is my portion," says my soul,
>   "therefore I will hope in him."
>
> (Lam 3:19–24)

This is a startling expression of hope for one who has just confessed that it is this same God, the Lord, who has preyed on him "like a bear" or "like a lion", who "bent his bow" and shot his heart full of the arrows of suffering (Lam 3:10–12). But it lays forth the great paradox of this book: Lamentations is not a work of cynicism but, in the final analysis, a plea for deliverance and an assertion of hope that—despite all appearances to the contrary—"the LORD *is good* to those who wait for him" (Lam 3:25).

Poem about the Fall of Jerusalem (Lamentations 4)

The fourth acrostic in the series consists primarily (though not exclusively) of a third-person poetic description of the fall of the city of Jerusalem. The description of the sufferings contained herein is extremely graphic, culminating with a "beatitude" for those who had the good fortune of being killed by the sword:

> Happier were the victims of the sword
>   than the victims of hunger,
> who pined away, stricken
>   by want of the fruits of the field.
>
> *The hands of compassionate women*
>   *have boiled their own children;*
> *they became their food*
>   *in the destruction of the daughter of my people.*
>
> (Lam 4:9–10)

With this imagery, we see the fulfillment of the oracles from the book of Deuteronomy, in which one of the climactic covenant curses would be siege, starvation, and the cannibalizing of children by their own mothers (cf. Deut 28:56–57).

The Prayer of the Jerusalemites (Lamentations 5)

The opening lament and prayer of the personified city of Jerusalem (Lamentations 1) are balanced by the concluding lament and prayer of a body of *Jerusalemites*, speaking in the first person plural.

Like the opening chapter, which speaks about the fallen "princess" who has become "like a widow" (Lam 1:1), so too the final poem declares that the "crown" has "fallen from our head", so that Mount Zion lies desolate (Lam 5:16). It then goes on to describe all the sufferings and persecutions of the siege survivors—once again, in graphic detail (Lam 5:1–18)—before praying to God for restoration (Lam 5:19–21) and ending with the query asked by many who have suffered sickness, death, and destruction: "[H]ave you utterly rejected us? Are you exceedingly angry with us?" (Lam 5:22).

Thus, the book of Lamentations begins and ends with Jerusalem lamenting and crying out for deliverance, but at the heart of the book is the suffering experienced by the "man who has seen affliction" (Lam 3:1), who received abuse at God's hand and yet trusts and serves him and, likewise, shares his people's suffering even though he is in conflict with them.

Lamentations and the Hebrew Alphabet

The first four chapters of Lamentations are acrostic poems. Scholars of previous generations, however, were puzzled by the fact that in each of them, the Hebrew letter *peh* (= "P") preceded the Hebrew letter *ayin* (= "O"). The modern order of Hebrew letters is *ayin-peh*.

Studies of ancient Hebrew inscriptions, however, have now made it clear that the preexilic Hebrew alphabet placed *peh* before *ayin*, and the modern *ayin-peh* order was adopted only in postexilic times. The fact that the acrostics of Lamentations follow the preexilic Hebrew order of the alphabet constitutes strong evidence for the position that they are not postexilic compositions. The poems of Lamentations appear to have been composed shortly after the events described.

Interestingly, it appears the acrostic psalms in books 1–3 of the Psalter originally followed the more ancient order of the alphabet also, although well-meaning scribes have "corrected" the order in some of them.

Historical Issues in Lamentations

The Origins of the Book of Lamentations

The date of Lamentations can be fixed with relative certainty within a narrow time frame. The book must have been composed after the destruction of Jerusalem and the Temple in 587 B.C., yet the utter lack of any awareness of concrete signs of hope for restoration may indicate a completion date prior to 562 B.C., when Jehoiachin was released from prison, giving hope for continuation of the Davidic line (Jer 52:31–34). The detailed descriptions of the horrors immediately before and after the invasion of the city by the Babylonian forces—with bodies still scattered in the streets (Lam 4:8), people resorting to cannibalism (Lam 2:20; 4:10), and random acts of rape and terrorism at the hand of the occupying forces (Lam 5:11–12)—strongly argue for composition by an eyewitness within a few years of the event. This author-eyewitness must have been well educated and possessed of considerable literary skill. He was not among those deported to Babylon after the siege, since everything in the book still reflects a Judean geographical perspective (cf. Lam 1:5).

Who then was the author (or authors) of these five poems? As is so often the case with Old Testament books, scholars are divided.

On the one hand, the traditional view of both Judaism and Christianity attributes the book to the prophet Jeremiah, and a number of reasons can be forwarded in favor of this view. First, the books of Chronicles speak of the prophet Jeremiah composing a "lament" for the funeral of King Josiah that was recorded in the book of "laments"—giving some credence to the fact that these are the kinds of poems for which Jeremiah was known (2 Chron 35:25).[2] More directly, despite the later separation of Lamentations from Jeremiah in the medieval Jewish Tanakh, the most ancient Jewish evidence we possess attributes it to the prophet Jeremiah. For example, the Greek Septuagint contains the following preface to Lamentations:

> And it happened that, after Israel was taken captive, and Jerusalem was made desolate, Jeremiah sat weeping and lamented this lament over Jerusalem and said. (LXX Preface to Lamentations [author's trans.])

In addition to this external evidence, in terms of internal indicators, there are a number of close, even striking parallels of theme and language between the book of Jeremiah and the book of Lamentations. Consider, for example, the following:

	The Book of Lamentations	The Book of Jeremiah
No comfort in her lovers	Lam 1:2	Jer 2:33
Uncleanness in her skirts	Lam 1:9	Jer 2:34; cf. 13:22–24
Fire in my bones	Lam 1:13	Jer 20:7–9
Eyes flowing with tears	Lam 1:16; 2:9, 11, 18; 3:48–49	Jer 9:1, 18; 13:17; 14:17
Yoke of Jerusalem	Lam 1:14; 5:5	Jer 27
Law and prophet perish—that is, false prophets and sinful priests	Lam 2:9; cf. 2:14; 4:13	Jer 18:18; cf. 2:8; 5:31; 14:13
Women eating their children	Lam 2:20; 4:10	Jer 19:9
Wormwood and gall	Lam 3:15, 19	Jer 9:15; 23:15
Zion like Sodom and Gomorrah	Lam 4:6	Jer 23:14
Drinking cup of judgment	Lam 4:21	Jer 25:15; 49:12

Perhaps the most striking of all the parallels between Lamentations and Jeremiah, however, is when the author of the third poem declares that "those who

---

[2] Cf. Josephus, *Antiquities* 10.78–79, who apparently thinks this refers to the book of Lamentations.

were my enemies without cause ... flung me alive into the pit" (Lam 3:52–54), in a precise parallel with what happened to Jeremiah at the hands of his persecutors (Jer 38:1–28). Indeed, it is difficult to imagine there was in Judah yet another individual besides Jeremiah who could have penned the third poem (Lam 3:1–66), who shared with the prophet the same sense of a unique vocation to a life of suffering and the same complex love-hate relationship with the Lord and the people of Judah reflected in this poem. In light of these and other parallels, many commentators throughout history have been inclined to ascribe the book to the prophet.

On the other hand, scholars who oppose attributing the book of Lamentations to Jeremiah make the following observations.[3] First, they hold that the Septuagintal attribution to Jeremiah, which would have been made at the earliest in the third century B.C., is too far removed from the sixth-century prophet to be of any value. Second, they point out that certain assertions contained in the poem appear to contradict what we find in the book of Jeremiah. For example, the book of Lamentations bewails how the people "watched for a nation which could not save" (Lam 4:17), whereas Jeremiah was hostile toward reliance on other Gentile nations for protection and did not wait for help from Egypt (Jer 37:5–10). Likewise, the description of "the LORD's anointed"—presumably, the contemporary Davidic king, Zedekiah—as one under whom the people would take refuge in the midst of the nations (Lam 4:20) is difficult to square with Jeremiah's oracle against Zedekiah that he would be given into the hand of Babylon (Jer 37:17), although it agrees with Jeremiah's confidence in the Davidic covenant (Jer 23:5, 30:9; and so on). Finally, according to Lamentations, the prophets of Jerusalem have "no vision" from the Lord which scholars consider very odd for Jeremiah, himself a prophet, to say (Lam 2:9), although he does express similar sentiments in Jeremiah 2:8, 26, 30; 4:9; 5:13, 31; 13:13; 14:13–15; 23:9–31; 26:1–16, and other places. In light of such observations, many scholars today do not attribute the book of Lamentations to Jeremiah himself.[4] Instead, they attribute the book to a contemporary, yet unknown author of similar education, social standing, literary skill, geographical and temporal location, theological perspective, and personal experience.

Theological Issues in Lamentations

The Theology of Divine Providence and the Function of Laments

The main contribution of Lamentations is not to systematic or even biblical theology, but to what one might call practical theology, spirituality, or the theology of prayer. Lamentations has been treasured by readers because of its brutal honesty before God in the face of crisis, disaster, and horrific human suffering. As such, it has provided a language for the expression of the emotions of believers

---

[3] See Hillers, *Lamentations*, xix–xxiii.

[4] Robert B. Chisholm, *Handbook on the Prophets* (Grand Rapids, Mich.: Baker Academic, 2002), 216–17.

in similar situations down through the ages. Lamentations provides a canonical form for the expression of spiritual grief in the face of disaster that seems to call into question the love and faithfulness of God.

Ironically, in the very midst of its lament, it also embraces an extremely strong theology of divine providence, holding that all things come from God and that no one should complain about punishments for sins:

> Who has commanded and it came to pass,
>   unless the Lord has ordained it?
> Is it not from the mouth of the Most High
>   that good and evil come?
> Why should a living man complain,
>   a man, about the punishment of his sins?
>   (Lam 3:37–39)

To be sure, in the later poem, it becomes clear that it is "our fathers" who have sinned and the children who "bear their iniquities" (Lam 5:7). Nevertheless, although explicit expressions of faith and confidence are rare in Lamentations (see 3:21–36), an implicit act of trust in divine providence runs throughout, for if it were really the case that God did not hear or act on the pleas of his people, the prophetic author would not even bother to compose these laments. In this way, and somewhat ironically, the lament was and is an act of fortitude and faith: " 'The LORD is my portion,' says my soul, 'therefore I will hope in him' " (Lam 3:24).

The Destruction of the Temple and the People-as-Sanctuary

At the heart of the grief expressed in Lamentations is the loss of the Temple, the place of worship and communion with God, the sanctuary that bestowed on Jerusalem/Zion its special status among the cities of the world (Lam 2:7). Certain texts in Lamentations suggest that there is a mystical union of fates between the sanctuary and the people. For example, in one verse, the author sets up an equivalence between the "precious sons of Zion" and the "holy stones" of the Temple (Lam 4:1–2). Such texts are moving toward a theology of the people-as-sanctuary that will become more explicit in later Jewish and Christian tradition, observable in the Dead Sea Scrolls (for example, *1QSRule of the Community*) and the New Testament (for example, Ephesians).

Lamentations in the Living Tradition

Given the fact that Lamentations was widely regarded as the final chapter of the book of Jeremiah in ancient and medieval times, it has tended to be treated as part of that work and, as would be expected, not given the same attention as the longer books of the prophets. Nevertheless, at least two aspects of the text have stood out as theologically significant in the living tradition: the redemptive power and purpose of temporal suffering and the brief reference to "the LORD's anointed [Hebrew *mashiah*]" (Lam 4:20) as a prophecy of the Passion of Christ.

God's "Wrath" Is Not Vengeance but Meant to Lead Us to Repentance

One obvious question raised by any reader of Lamentations is: Why does God allow suffering? Or, to put it more pointedly: How can a supposedly "good" God (Lam 3:25) punish his people in this way?

This question was taken up in the fourth century by Saint Ambrose in a treatise on repentance. In this reflection, Ambrose argued that the "wrath" or "anger" of God in Scripture is always directed toward the spiritual repentance and salvation of the people who undergo it:

> Is it not evident that the Lord Jesus is angry with us when we sin in order that He may convert us through fear of His indignation? His indignation, then, is not the carrying out of vengeance, but rather the working out of forgiveness, for these are His words: "If thou shalt turn and lament, thou shalt be saved." *He waits for our lamentations here, that is, in time, that He may spare us those which shall be eternal.* He waits for our tears, that He may pour forth His goodness.... Jeremiah, too, may certainly teach when he says: "For the Lord will not cast off for ever; for after He has humbled, He will have compassion according to the multitude of His mercies ..." [Lam 3:31]. This passage we certainly find in the Lamentations of Jeremiah, and from it, and from what follows, we note that the Lord humbles all the prisoners of the earth under His feet, in order that we may escape His judgment.[5]

This is certainly a very different way of looking at divinely allowed (or bestowed) temporal punishments. For Ambrose, in every case, the unleashing of God's temporal "wrath" is always meant to aid human beings in escaping eternal punishment.

The "Taking" of the Messiah and the Death of Christ

By far the most popular passage from Lamentations in the living tradition is the fleeting reference to the "taking" of "the LORD's anointed" (Hebrew *mashiah*; Greek *christos*) (Lam 4:20). Although in its historical context, this appears to be a reference to the exile of King Zedekiah, the early Church Fathers overwhelmingly saw in it a prophecy of the Passion and death of Christ. For example, Rufinus of Aquilea writes:

> [T]hey who boast themselves of their knowledge of the Law will, perhaps, say to us, "You blaspheme in saying that the Lord was subjected to the corruption of death and to the suffering of the Cross." Read, therefore, what you find written in the Lamentations of Jeremiah: "The Spirit of our countenance, Christ the Lord, was taken in our corruptions, of whom we said, we shall live under His

---

[5] Ambrose, *Concerning Repentance* 1.5.22–23, in *NPNF2* 10:333.

shadow among the nations" [Lam 4:20 LXX]. Thou hearest how the Prophet says that Christ the Lord was taken, and for us, that is, for our sins, delivered to corruption.[6]

As should be immediately evident, there are differences here between the Greek version of Lamentations and the Hebrew. Nevertheless, explicit reference to the death of "the Messiah of the Lord" (Greek *christos kyriou*; Lam 4:20 LXX) was seen as a biblical prophecy of the atoning death of Christ.

The Book of Lamentations in the Lectionary

Lamentations grieves the loss of the Temple, which was the place of worship and communion with God, and the sanctuary that bestowed on Jerusalem/ Zion its special status among the cities of the world. Lamentations also focuses, in the third chapter, on the sufferings and persecution of God's special prophet. This central poem can be understood as a Christological text. Jesus Christ is the ultimate suffering prophet, who experienced (in a certain sense) the wrath of God (Lam 3:1–20), wept for God's people (3:48–49), descended into the pit (3:52–57), and experienced God's vindication (3:58–60) over against his persecutors (3:61–66). Furthermore, in Christ, the true Temple is united with the person of the true prophet (Jn 2:21). So, the persecution of the prophet and the destruction of the Temple become one act. For this reason, there is an ancient tradition within the Church of meditation on Lamentations during Passion Week and especially Good Friday, the day when the New Temple, Christ's Body, was destroyed.

Unfortunately, the current Roman Lectionary for Mass largely neglects the book of Lamentations. It is never read on Sundays or feast days. In the weekday cycle, a single reading is proclaimed on Saturday of the Twelfth Week in Ordinary Time (Lam 2:2, 10–14, 18–19). In this case, the emphasis is on the historical context of Lamentations, since the reading takes place the day after the semi-continuous readings from Kings conclude with the destruction of the Temple (2 Kings 25:1–12). In addition, the sole passage of hope and confidence in the book provides reading options for Masses "In Time of Earthquake, or For Rain, or For Good Weather, or To Avert Storms, or For Any Need" (Lam 3:17–26, opt. 2); for the Dead (Lam 3:17–26, opt. 6); and for funerals for children (Lam 3:22–26, opt. 2).

The Liturgy of the Hours includes a short span of readings from Lamentations in the Office of Readings on Thursday through Saturday of the Twenty-Third Week in Ordinary Time (Lam 1:1–12, 18–20; 3:1–33; 5:1–22). These readings fall after Jeremiah and before Ezekiel in the cycle of semi-continuous readings from the prophets. The accompanying second readings from the Fathers suggest spiritual interpretations in which the holy city now destroyed is a type of the suffering believer or the crucified body of Christ.

---

[6] Rufinus of Aquilea, *A Commentary on the Apostles' Creed* 19, in *NPNF2* 3:551.

Conclusion

The short book of Lamentations, consisting of four laments over the destruction of Jerusalem (chaps. 1–2, 4–5) surrounding what appears to be a very long individual lament strikingly similar to the life of Jeremiah, is treated by the Church as an extension of the book of Jeremiah. Although in antiquity Lamentations was an object of meditation for Holy Week, the current Lectionary neglects the book, perhaps because its tone of grief is difficult to reconcile with the joy that should characterize the celebration of the New Covenant. Nonetheless, the lived experience of the disciple of Christ even today—or especially today—does often meet with suffering, persecution, disasters, and destruction that cannot be reconciled in any obvious way with the loving providence of God. Therefore, until the end of the age, there will still be some place for a theology of lament and the need for inspired and canonical articulations of the grief of God's suffering people.

For Further Reading

Commentaries and Studies on Lamentations

Berlin, Adele. *Lamentations: A Commentary*. Old Testament Library. Louisville, Ky.: Westminster John Knox Press, 2002.

Chisholm, Robert B., Jr. *Handbook on the Prophets*. Grand Rapids, Mich.: Baker Academic, 2002. (See pp. 216–23.)

Ferris, Paul W., Jr. "Lamentations". Pages 373–99 in *Isaiah, Jeremiah, Lamentations, Ezekiel, Daniel*. Vol. 4 of *Zondervan Illustrated Bible Backgrounds Commentary*. Edited by John H. Walton. Grand Rapids, Mich.: Zondervan, 2009.

Hillers, Delbert R. *Lamentations*. Anchor Bible 7A. New York: Doubleday, 1976.

Theological Issues in Lamentations

Kaiser, Walter C., Jr. *A Biblical Approach to Personal Suffering*. Repr., Eugene, Ore.: Wipf & Stock, 2003.

Parry, Robin A. *Lamentations*. Two Horizons Old Testament Commentary. Grand Rapids, Mich.: Eerdmans, 2010.

Lamentations in the Living Tradition

Wenthe, Dean O. *Jeremiah, Lamentations*. Old Testament 12 of Ancient Christian Commentary on Scripture. Edited by Thomas C. Oden. Downers Grove, Ill.: InterVarsity Press, 2009. (See pp. 273–304.)

33. BARUCH

Introduction

The short book of Baruch is a collection of four compositions—historical, poetic, prophetic, and epistolary—associated with the literary legacy of the sixth-century prophet Jeremiah. While the character of the different compositions is diverse, they each advance the general unifying theme that Israel should avoid idolatry and covenant infidelity while patiently waiting for the fulfillment of God's good promises after the Babylonian exile.

Baruch is not considered inspired Scripture in rabbinic Judaism and is not extant in Hebrew, although it now seems clear to many scholars that the entire book, including the Letter of Jeremiah (Baruch 6), was originally composed in that language. Baruch is included in our oldest and best manuscripts of the Septuagint (for example, Vaticanus, Alexandrinus), and the Septuagint Greek became the basis of virtually all other ancient versions (with the possible exception of the Syriac Peshitta).

Long considered a part of the book of Jeremiah by the early Church Fathers, the attestation of the inspired status of Baruch is among the best of any of the disputed books of the Old Testament. In the Greek Septuagint tradition, we find the order Jeremiah–Baruch–Lamentations. The antiquity of this order is supported by the fact that the Septuagint translator of the last portion of the book of Jeremiah (see Jer 26–52) also seems to have translated the first sections of the book of Baruch (see Bar 1:1–3:8). In the Latin Vulgate, however, Lamentations is appended without break at the end of Jeremiah, followed by Baruch as a separate book (that is, Jeremiah–Lamentations–Baruch). In compiling the Vulgate, Jerome did not retranslate Baruch but simply incorporated the Old Latin translation (made from the Greek of the Septuagint). The final chapter of the book is in reality an independent composition known as "The Letter of Jeremiah" (Bar 6). This document has its own textual history and is found separate from Baruch in some of the ancient codices of the Septuagint.

In much the same way that the book of Sirach functions as a kind of summary of the wisdom literature and overview of salvation history, so too the book of Baruch is replete with major themes found throughout both the Pentateuch (especially Deut 28–30) and the Prophets as a whole, so that it functions as a kind of brief "summa" of prophetic exhortations to the people of God and their hopes for the future.

Literary Structure and Overview of Baruch

Given the brevity and obviously composite character of the book of Baruch, we can treat both its literary structure and the overview of its contents simultaneously in this section. In terms of basic structure, the book as a whole can be outlined in terms of four compositions:

Outline of the Book of Baruch

I. Narrative: Baruch and the Repentance of the Babylonian Exiles (Bar 1:1—3:8)
   A. Baruch Reads a Book that Leads the Exiles to Repent (1:1–9)
   B. The Letter the Exiles Send to the Survivors in Jerusalem
      1. Instructions for Public Worship and Prayer (1:10–14)
      2. A Communal Prayer of Confession of Sins (1:15—2:10)
      3. A Prayer for Forgiveness and Deliverance (2:11—3:8)

II. A Poem in Praise of Wisdom (Bar 3:9—4:4)
   A. Exhortation to "Learn Wisdom" (3:9–14)
   B. The Quest for Wisdom (3:15–31)
   C. The Coming of Wisdom in "the Book of the Commandments" (3:16—4:4)

III. Oracle of Hope: "Take Courage, My Children!" (Bar 4:5—5:9)
   A. The Exile Was Not for Destruction but for Discipline (4:5–20)
   B. God Will Soon Deliver You from the Hand of the Enemy (4:21–26)
   C. God Who Brought Calamities Will Bring Salvation (4:27–29)
   D. Arise, Jerusalem, and Behold Your Children Coming to You (4:30—5:9)

IV. The Letter of Jeremiah to the Exiles regarding Idolatry (Bar 6:1–73)
   A. Introduction and Message to the Exiles (6:1–7)
   B. Diatribe against the Foolishness of Idolatry (6:8–73)

As the above outline makes clear, the first section of the book consists of a narrative account of the public repentance of Judean exiles in the land of Babylon instigated by the public reading of a book by Baruch, Jeremiah's scribe (Bar 1:1–9). This brief narrative is followed somewhat abruptly by a copy of a long letter these repentant exiles sent to the Judeans still living in the ruins of Jerusalem, consisting of instructions for offering sacrifice (Bar 1:10–14) and a long accompanying prayer composed of a communal confession of sin (Bar 1:15—2:10) followed by a plea for deliverance (Bar 2:11—3:8). As various scholars have noted, this opening narrative, like the book of Jeremiah before it, is strikingly similar to the confessional prayer of the prophet Daniel on behalf of his people (see Dan 9:4–19).[1] In both cases, the prayer admits that Israel's sin is the cause of her current suffering in exile and begs God to forgive her sin and restore the people from exile.

---

[1] See David A. DeSilva, *Introducing the Apocrypha: Message, Context, and Significance* (Grand Rapids, Mich.: Baker Academic, 2002), 207–8.

The second part of Baruch shifts (again, very abruptly) into a remarkable poem in praise of "wisdom" (Greek *phronēsis*; Bar 3:9—4:4). This poem strongly resembles other such poems in the Hebrew wisdom tradition (cf. Sir 24), with which it shares the same basic theme: out of all the places on earth, wisdom makes her home specifically in Israel (cf. Sir 24). However, the book of Baruch is distinguished by the fact that it not only *personifies* wisdom but speaks of it coming to dwell on earth with human beings in the Book of the Law:

> He [God] found the whole way to knowledge,
> and gave her to Jacob his servant
> and to Israel whom he loved.
> *Afterward she appeared upon earth and lived among men.*
>
> *She is the book of the commandments of God,*
> *and the law that endures for ever.*
> All who hold her fast will live,
> and those who forsake her will die.
> Turn, O Jacob, and take her;
> walk toward the shining of her light.
> (Bar 3:36—4:2)

In the context of the book as a whole, this quasi-"incarnational" description of wisdom functions as a central part of the exhortation to the exiles to return to God by returning to the Scriptures—especially the law—in which they will discover the "light" of Lady Wisdom.

The third section in the book consists of a prophetic oracle of encouragement to Jerusalem (Bar 4:5—5:9). This oracle may be entitled "Take courage, my children, and cry to God!" from the refrain that recurs, with variation, four times, thereby dividing the oracle into four units (Bar 4:5–20; 4:21–26; 4:27–29; 4:30—5:9). Just as the opening narrative and confession were very similar to those in the book of Daniel, so too this prophetic oracle contains strong parallels with many passages in the second half of Isaiah (for example, Is 40:1–11; 49:1–26; 60:1—62:12; 66:5–21). The sacred author personifies Jerusalem as a mother who grieves for the loss of her children to exile but who will soon rejoice to see her enemies defeated and her children returning to her from the places where they were scattered (Bar 4:36—5:7). Here we see a powerful articulation of the central hope of the prophetic literature for the *ingathering of the exiles to mother Jerusalem*, not just from Babylon, but from "west and east"— that is, from throughout the world (Bar 5:5).

The fourth and final section consists of the "Letter of Jeremiah", a discourse that presents itself as a letter that Jeremiah sent to the Babylonian exiles (Bar 6). This epistle is comprised of two sections. The first is a brief synopsis of the message of Jeremiah's letter to the exiles (cf. Jer 29:4–23), the message of which can be summed up as follows: "Settle down in Babylon, because the exile will last a long time" (cf. Bar 6:1–7). The second section is a relentless diatribe against the utter foolishness of idol worship (Bar 6:8–73; cf. Jer 10:1–16). The purpose of this diatribe is to prevent the exiles from falling into the worship of Babylonian idols by pointing out just how ridiculous it is to worship statues that cannot make themselves, protect themselves, clean themselves, move themselves, save themselves (or anyone else, for that matter), speak for themselves, and so on. Significantly, it is in the course of this epistle that we find explicit evidence that one reason such idol worship constituted a temptation for Israel was that the worship of these "gods" involved sexual relations with temple prostitutes:

> Why then must any one think that they are gods, or call them gods?
> Besides, even the Chaldeans [=Babylonians] themselves dishonor them.... [T]he women, with cords about them, sit along the passageways, burning bran for incense; and when one of them is led off by one of the passersby and is lain with, she derides the woman next to her, because she was not as attractive as herself and her cord was not broken. Whatever is done for them is false. (Bar 6:40, 43–44)

For Baruch, then, the very presence of the cult prostitutes is testimony to the fact that these are not gods at all, but utter folly.

Historical Issues in Baruch

The Origins of the Book of Baruch

Who wrote the book of Baruch? And when was it written? Given archaeological discoveries of two ancient seals (known as *bullae*) stamped with the name of "Baruch", we know he was a real historical figure. But did he have anything to do with the composition of the Old Testament book that is ascribed to him?

As we have already seen, the book of Baruch is quite clearly a composite of four very different documents juxtaposed with one another. To be sure, the introduction presents the first part of the book as "the words ... which Baruch the son of Neraiah

Two *bullae* (seals) stamped with Baruch's name have been found in Jerusalem.

... wrote in Babylon, in the fifth year, on the seventh day of the month, at the time when the Chaldeans took Jerusalem and burned it with fire" (Bar 1:1). It then reports that Baruch read "the words of this book in the hearing of Jeconiah [Jehoiachin] the son of Jehoiakim ... and in the hearing of all the people" (Bar 1:3). However, the claim for Baruch's authorship probably was only intended to extend as far as the end of the "book" that the exiles sent to Jerusalem to be recited at the altar in the razed Temple (Bar 3:8). In this regard, the contents of this "book", the prayer of confession and deliverance (Bar 1:15—3:8), seem to have been written in a Hebrew heavily influenced by the language of Jeremiah and Deuteronomy.[2] No mention is made in the letter and prayer

---

[2] Cf. Carey A. Moore, *Daniel, Esther, and Jeremiah: The Additions*, Anchor Bible 44 (New York: Doubleday, 1977).

of confession (Bar 1:15—3:8) of any of the historical developments in the later exilic or postexilic periods, and the submissive posture toward Babylon is radically different from the attitude of gloating toward this city that prevailed after its fall in 537 B.C. (Bar 2:21). Accordingly, the opening letter and confession (Bar 1:15—3:8) *could* have been written by Baruch son of Neraiah. On the other hand, as the attachment of the "Letter of Jeremiah" (Bar 6) makes clear, the collection of these various compositions does not imply that Baruch was the author of all of them. As a result, the poem in praise of wisdom (Bar 3:9—4:4) and the oracle of exhortation to the exiles (Bar 4:5—5:9) may or may not have been attributed to Baruch by the final editor of the work.

Indeed, most contemporary scholars reject the origin of any of the component parts with Baruch, the scribe of Jeremiah, for the following reasons.[3] First, the date formula that begins the book seems to indicate the "fifth year" after the destruction of Jerusalem, thus placing Baruch in Babylon with the exiles around 582 B.C. However, according to the book of Jeremiah, Baruch was taken with the Jewish exiles to Egypt around 585 B.C. (Jer 43:6). Most scholars accept the claim that Baruch remained in Egypt with Jeremiah and did not return to Babylon so soon afterward. Along similar lines, Baruch is said to have read the words of his book in the presence of King "Jeconiah" [=Jehoiachin] (Bar 1:3). Jehoiachin was not released from prison until 562 B.C., at the death of Nebuchadnezzar and the ascension of Evil-merodach (Amel-Marduk), his successor. Jehoiachin would have still been incarcerated at the date given in Baruch (that is, 582 B.C.). Second, the book of Baruch describes the "silver vessels" from the Temple that Nebuchadnezzar had taken from Jerusalem as being returned to the city so that sacrifices could be offered "upon the altar" (Bar 1:9–10). It is very difficult to explain how these vessels could have been obtained and returned so soon after the destruction of Jerusalem by Nebuchadnezzar or exactly what "altar" is being referred to as functioning such a short time after the overthrow of the city. Of course, several texts indicate that Jeremiah, and presumably his scribe, Baruch, as well, were considered public allies of the Babylonians (Jer 40:1–6; 43:3). Therefore, Baruch may have had some influence with the Chaldean authorities to obtain these items of lesser value. Moreover, the book of Jeremiah itself provides evidence that sacrifices were being offered in some manner at the site of the decimated Temple (Jer 41:5), so the book of Baruch may well be referring to this practice.

Perhaps most significant of all, the book of Baruch seems to be literarily dependent on the second part of Isaiah and the book of Daniel, which scholars widely view as exilic (Second Isaiah) and postexilic (Daniel). For example, the oracle of encouragement for Jerusalem (Bar 4:5—5:9) echoes the language, motifs, and concepts from the second half of Isaiah (Is 40–66). Along similar lines, Baruch identifies Nebuchadnezzar as the "son" of "Belshazzar" (Bar 1:11, 12; cf. Dan 5:2, 11, 13, 18, 22) and draws on the prayer of Daniel on behalf of his people (Bar 1:15—3:8; cf. Dan 9:4–19). As most scholars point out, however, Belshazzar did not assume power as co-regent of Babylon with his father Nabonidus until 553 B.C., some decades later. Taken together, this evidence

---

[3] See DeSilva, *Introducing the Apocrypha*, 202–5.

leads most scholars to date the book of Baruch to sometime in the second century B.C., after the widely held date for the book of Daniel.[4]

Theological Issues in Baruch

Three of the four sections of the book of Baruch—the poem on wisdom, the oracle of encouragement to Jerusalem, and the Letter of Jeremiah—are beautiful texts suitable for liturgical recitation but do not make a significant theological contribution beyond the older and similar biblical texts on which they are based. However, the first section—Baruch's ministry and prayer (Bar 1:1–3:8)—does include at least three advances in biblical theology.

The Prophecy of Moses and the "New Covenant"

The opening section of Baruch is an excellent and relatively succinct summary of the "Deuteronomistic" perspective on the history of Israel—that is, the perspective of the historical books Deuteronomy through 2 Kings (Baruch 1:1—3:8). The hallmarks of this perspective are as follows: (1) Israel received the land of Canaan on condition of its fidelity to the Mosaic covenant, as articulated in Deuteronomy; (2) Israel throughout its history repeatedly violated that covenant, despite the constant ministry of the prophets; (3) Israel ultimately received the curses of the covenant (Deut 27–32), culminating in expulsion from its land and scattering in exile; (4) if Israel repents in exile, the Lord will renew his covenant with it and bring it back into the land. This entire historical perspective is found already in the Pentateuch (Deut 30:1–10). Baruch paraphrases Deuteronomy (Bar 2:27–35; cf. Deut 30:1–10), with this important variation: Moses is said to have spoken on behalf of God as follows: "I will make an *everlasting covenant* with them to be their God and they shall be my people" (Bar 2:35). Nowhere in Deuteronomy 30, however, does Moses use the word "covenant". Moses does, however, famously assert that at some time after the exile of Israel, "the LORD your God will circumcise your heart and the heart of your offspring" (Deut 30:6). Knowing that circumcision was a covenant-making ritual (Gen 17:10), Baruch connects Moses' prophecy of the "circumcision of the heart" (Deut 30:6) with Jeremiah's promise of a "new covenant" (Jer 31:31) and provides a dynamic equivalent paraphrase of Deuteronomy 30 by having Moses himself speak directly of an "everlasting covenant" (Bar 2:28–35). And indeed, Baruch's paraphrase of Moses is true to the intention of the Deuteronomic prophecy. Thus, Baruch's prayer is a helpful piece of biblical intertextuality that serves theologically to link more clearly the covenant and prophecies of Moses to the time of their fulfillment in the ministry of Jeremiah, the destruction of Jerusalem, the exile, and subsequent restoration. This is, on the whole, a major contribution to the synthesis of various Old Testament covenant texts.

----

[4] Ibid., 205.

The "Prayer of the Dead" on Behalf of Israel

The second advance concerns the explicit appeal in Baruch for the Lord to hear "the prayer of the dead of Israel", which takes place at the end of the "letter" of public confession:

> O Lord Almighty, God of Israel, *hear now the prayer of the dead of Israel* and of the sons of those who sinned before you, who did not heed the voice of the Lord their God, so that calamities have clung to us. (Bar 3:4)

Depending on how one dates this portion of the text, this may well be the earliest and most explicit evidence we possess for the ancient Israelite belief that the dead, in the intermediate state before the final resurrection, could in fact offer "prayers" (Greek *proseuchēs*) to God on behalf of the living. To be sure, the view of the afterlife in the Old Testament is often murky, and not all Old Testament texts share a consistent perspective. Yet the biblical view is never annihilationist: even in the most pessimistic scenario, the souls of the dead go down to Sheol, where they exist in a liminal state. In this passage, Baruch indicates that the souls of the dead of Israel can pray to God from their liminal state of existence.

The Quasi-Incarnation of Wisdom and the Loss of the Liturgy

The third advance relates to the theology of the incarnation. In the poem on wisdom (Bar 3:9–4:4), the sacred author says of divine wisdom that "afterward she appeared upon earth and lived among men" (Bar 3:37). While the ancient author seems to have intended by these words a figurative description of divine wisdom's "appearance" in written form, as the Scriptures of Israel (cf. Bar 4:1), nonetheless the literal sense of his words are a significant development in the personification of wisdom.

Notice here that this development regarding wisdom seems to be directly tied to the *liturgical crisis* of the destruction of the Temple depicted in the book. Though all the Jews have left with which to offer worship is a lonely altar in the midst of a destroyed shell of a building in Jerusalem, nonetheless the message of Baruch is that a repentant remnant were able to express their faith in God's promise of covenant renewal by perpetuating the liturgy during the absolute nadir of their national hopes and fortunes (Bar 1:1–3:8; cf. 2:37). Indeed, the other sections of the book—the poem, the oracle, and the letter—may be understood as encouragements to continue the expression of faith through worship in the middle of exile. Above all, the poem on wisdom reminds Israel that divine wisdom finds its highest expression in the "book of the commandments of God" (Bar 4:1)—that is, the Pentateuch, at the heart of which are the rubrics for the sacrificial liturgy (Ex 25–Lev 7). Along similar lines, the oracle encourages Israel with the hope that the Temple-city Jerusalem will be restored (Bar 4:5—5:9). Finally, the letter confirms faithful Israelites in their exclusive worship of the Lord by revealing the irrationality of competing forms of worship (Bar 6).

Baruch in the Living Tradition

Like Lamentations before it, Baruch is generally treated in the living tradition as a part of the book of Jeremiah and, as such, has not played a very prominent role. However, despite its brevity, it takes a significant role in several key places in the contemporary Lectionary as one of the few readings selected for the Easter Vigil, and as one of the prophecies "bridging" the Old and New Testaments during the eschatologically-charged season of Advent.

The Coming of Wisdom and the Mystery of the Incarnation

As mentioned above, probably the most theologically significant and influential passage from Baruch in the living tradition is the description of "wisdom" as "appearing upon earth" and dwelling "among men" (Bar 3:37). For a number of early Church Fathers, this text was interpreted as one of the most important prophecies of the actual appearance of the eternal Word of the Father among men in the mystery of the Incarnation. Consider, for example, the words of Saint Hilary of Poitiers:

> [L]isten now to Jeremiah ...: *This is our God.... Afterward did He shew Himself upon earth and dwelt among men* [Bar 3:37]. For previously he had said, *And He is Man, and Who shall know Him?* [Jer 17:9 LXX]. Thus you have God seen on earth and dwelling among men.... Who then is This who was seen and dwelt among men? He must be our God, for He is God visible in human form, Whom men can handle.[5]

Notice here how Hilary treats the book we refer to as "Baruch" as simply one of the oracles of the prophet Jeremiah. Similar statements are made by other Church Fathers, who seem to have regarded portions of Baruch as stemming from "Jeremiah the prophet".[6]

The Book of Baruch in the Lectionary

Baruch is employed only twice in the contemporary Roman Lectionary for Sundays and holy days, but in prominent locations. Most notably, the poem regarding the quest for Wisdom and her coming to live among human beings occupies the position of sixth reading in the Easter Vigil (Bar 3:9–15, 32—4:4). In its penultimate position in the sequence of seven readings from the Scriptures of Israel, this passage from Baruch serves as an exhortation to the faithful, and especially those about to be baptized, to recognize that God's own wisdom, the very path to life, is contained in the Scriptures of Israel, which alone are salvific, in contrast to the writings, religions, and philosophies of the Gentiles. Furthermore, the assertion that Wisdom "has appeared on earth, and lived among men"

---

[5] Hilary of Poitiers, *On the Trinity* 4.42, in *NPNF2* 9:84.
[6] For example, Irenaeus, *Against Heresies* 5.35.1–2.

is understood as an anticipatory statement concerning Jesus Christ, who is divine Wisdom incarnate, the very "book of the precepts of God" become flesh and dwelling among us (cf. Jn 1:14).

In addition, the conclusion of the oracle of encouragement to Jerusalem (Bar 5:1–9)—which is strongly influenced by passages of the second half of Isaiah (for example, Is 40:3–5; 60:1–7)—is read on the Second Sunday of Advent in Year C. In this way, it marks the transition from the First Week of Advent, with its focus on the Second Coming, to the Second Week of Advent, focused on the forerunner of the Messiah, John the Baptist. In this way, Baruch 5:1–9 is, essentially, a prophecy of the new exodus that virtually quotes Isaiah 40:3–4 (cf. Bar 5:7), a passage that John the Baptist applies to himself. Read in conjunction with Luke's description of the beginning of the ministry of the Baptist (Lk 3:1–6), this oracle from Baruch places the Baptist's mission in the larger context of the prophetic hope for a new exodus of Israel to God from the places of its exile (Bar 5:1–9). We see that the exodus and its "highway" are not so much geographical as spiritual realities. Israel's true exile is spiritual and not merely physical. The Baptist's way of repentance is the true "highway" by which Israel will begin to travel back to the New Temple, which is Christ himself.

Finally, two readings from Baruch (Bar 1:15–22 and 4:5–12, 27–29) are also read at daily Mass, Friday and Saturday of the Twenty-Sixth Week in Ordinary Time, during a stretch of the Lectionary cycle (Year 1, Weeks 25–27) in which the Church exposes the faithful to representative readings from the histories (Ezra-Nehemiah) and minor prophets of the postexilic period.

The Liturgy of the Hours reads most of the first two sections of Baruch (Baruch's prayer, 1:15—2:5, 3:1–8; the poem on wisdom, 3:9–15, 24—4:4) on Friday and Saturday of the Twenty-Ninth Week in Ordinary Time, as part of a larger survey of late (postexilic) Old Testament books that extends from the Twenty-Eighth Week through the Thirty-Fourth Week. Baruch's prayer is coordinated with a reading on the subject of repentance from Augustine. The poem on wisdom, with its line "she has appeared on earth, and moved among people" (Bar 4:1), is paired with a sermon on the Incarnation by Peter Chrysologus.

Conclusion

The book of Baruch is a composite work consisting of four documents: a communal prayer of repentance and deliverance attributed to Baruch (Bar 1:1—3:8), a poem on wisdom (Bar 3:9—4:4), an oracle of encouragement to Jerusalem after the exile (Bar 4:5—5:9), and the letter of Jeremiah to the exiles (Bar 6:1–73) warning them against idolatry. The different documents each have a different tone and composition history. In their present canonical form, one may say that the book functions to encourage the people of Israel, living in some form of exile, to repent of sin, maintain hope in God's good promises, and stay faithful in their worship of the God of their ancestors, rather than of the idols of the nations.

For Further Reading

Commentaries and Studies on Baruch

DeSilva, David A. *Introducing the Apocrypha: Message, Context, and Significance.* Grand Rapids, Mich.: Baker Academic, 2002. (See pp. 198–213.)

Moore, Carey A. *Daniel, Esther, and Jeremiah: The Additions.* Anchor Bible 44. New York: Doubleday, 1977. (See pp. 255–358.)

Saldarini, Anthony J. "Baruch and the Letter of Jeremiah". *New Interpreter's Bible*, vol. 6. Nashville: Abingdon Press, 2001.

Baruch in the Living Tradition

Voicu, Sever J. *Apocrypha.* Old Testament 15 of Ancient Christian Commentary on Scripture. Edited by Thomas C. Oden. Downers Grove: InterVarsity Press, 2010. (See pp. 416–42.)

34. EZEKIEL

Introduction

Ezekiel—whose name means "God makes strong" (Hebrew *yehezqe'l*)—is the third of the great prophets in the Jewish and Christian traditions. In Judaism, he is also the last great prophet, while Christian tradition counts Daniel as a fourth. Although Ezekiel is typically overshadowed by Isaiah and Jeremiah in the history of theology and biblical study, he stands out as unique among the major prophets for several reasons: (1) the prominence of priestly language and concerns in his book, (2) his careful literary organization and coherence, (3) the vivid, surreal, and sometimes shocking character of his visions and extended allegories, and (4) the strange, even bizarre public behavior the prophet employed in conveying his messages. Ezekiel has been a challenging book to interpret and understand for both Jews and Christians, but nonetheless it has made a substantial contribution to the Christian faith, especially through its heavy influence on the New Testament book of Revelation.

In terms of its status as inspired Scripture, Ezekiel was clearly viewed as authoritative in ancient Judaism. For example, Jesus ben Sira mentions the prophet among the heroes of Jewish tradition (Sir 49:8–9), and several documents among the Dead Sea Scrolls are heavily influenced by his thought and language (for example, the *Damascus Document* and the *Temple Scroll*). Perhaps most significantly, the book of Ezekiel was translated into Greek as part of the Septuagint for Hellenistic Jews in the diaspora. However, despite this widespread influence of Ezekiel in the Second Temple period, there was some resistance within early rabbinic Judaism to receiving Ezekiel as inspired Scripture for three reasons: (1) the discrepancy between the laws and ritual regulations of Ezekiel's vision of the future Temple (see Ezek 40–48) and those of the Pentateuch; (2) the danger that reading the surreal heavenly visions of the divine "chariot" (Hebrew *merkavah*, Ezek 1–3, 10) posed for the spiritually immature; and (3) the shockingly graphic language of the allegories of Jerusalem-as-harlot (Ezek 16, 23). Therefore, Jewish tradition took measures to control the reading of the book. According to the collection of rabbinic traditions known as the Mishnah (ca. A.D. 200), there were severe restrictions on reading Ezekiel's opening vision of the chariot-throne:

> They may not use the chapter of the Chariot [Ezekiel 1] as a reading from the Prophets; but Rabbi Judah permits it.[1]

---

[1] Mishnah, *Megillah* 4:10, in Herbert Danby, *The Mishnah* (Oxford: Oxford University Press, 1933), 207.

The Chariot [may not be expounded] before one alone, unless he is a Sage that understands his own knowledge.[2]

As a result of such difficulties, the rabbis debated Ezekiel's status as Scripture well into the fifth century A.D., but they finally established a consensus in its favor, provided certain restrictions were placed on how (and by whom) the book was read.

By contrast, the canonicity of Ezekiel was never seriously disputed in the early Church, which always placed the book among the prophets after Isaiah and Jeremiah.

Much like Jeremiah, the book of Ezekiel circulated in at least two Hebrew literary editions in antiquity, a shorter and a longer version. The shorter edition is represented by the Septuagint translation. The Hebrew text that was translated by Jerome for the Vulgate is 4 to 5 percent longer. The additional material consists largely of amplifications and clarifications, similar to those of the MT of Jeremiah, but much less extensive. While the shorter edition looks original, the longer edition may also be very old.

Literary Structure of Ezekiel

The book of Ezekiel is better (or at least, more obviously) structured than most prophetic compositions, perhaps because Ezekiel, as a member of a high-ranking priestly family, would have received the best literary education available within Judean society. The prophet is careful to note the year, month, and day on which significant revelations came to him, so that a chain of date notations runs as a thread of continuity through the book (Ezek 1:1; 8:1; 20:1; 24:1; 26:1; 29:1, 17; 30:20; 31:1; 32:1, 17; 33:21; 40:1). With only one or two exceptions, the dates follow in chronological order, so that the book progresses from older revelations to more recent. With this in mind, the book as a whole can be divided into four major sections.

Dates of Ezekiel's Prophecies

With few exceptions, Ezekiel dates his prophecies from the beginning of the exile of King Jehoiachin (ca. 597 B.C.). Thus the dates of his revelations in contemporary notation are roughly as follows:

Ezek 1:1	593 B.C.	Ezek 29:1	587 B.C.	Ezek 32:17	586–85 B.C.
Ezek 8:1	592 B.C.	Ezek 29:17	571 B.C.	Ezek 33:21	585 B.C.
Ezek 20:1	591 B.C.	Ezek 30:20	587 B.C.	Ezek 40:1	573 B.C.
Ezek 24:1	588 B.C.	Ezek 31:1	587 B.C.		
Ezek 26:1	587–86 B.C.	Ezek 32:1	585 B.C.		

Thus, there is a general chronological flow from earlier to later prophecies, the only exception of more than a few months being Ezekiel 29:17—21.

---

[2] Mishnah, *Hagigah* 2:1, in Danby, *Mishnah*, 213.

Part 1 recounts the ministry and messages of Ezekiel prior to the destruction of Jerusalem (Ezek 1–24). This unit divides into four parts, marked by date formulas (Ezek 1:1; 8:1; 20:1; 24:1): (1) In the "fifth year of the exile" (Ezek 1:2), the prophet receives a long vision of God seated on his movable throne or "chariot" (Ezek 1:1–3:15), followed by several prophetic sign-acts (Ezek 3:16—5:17) and oracles of judgment (Ezek 6–7). (2) A year later, in the "sixth year" of the exile (Ezek 8:1), he introduces a second long vision, this time of the Temple (Ezek 8–11), followed by sign-acts (Ezek 12:1–20) and oracles of judgment (Ezek 12:21—19:14). (3) In the "seventh year" of the exile (Ezek 20:1), there are more oracles of judgment on Jerusalem, Judah, and Israel. (4) Finally, there is an oracle dated to the beginning of the Babylonian siege of Jerusalem (the "ninth year" of exile), the beginning of the end (Ezek 24:1). The death of Ezekiel's wife at the end of the chapter prefigures the destruction of God's "bride", Jerusalem, and brings the first major unit of the book to a close.

Part 2 contains "oracles against the nations" (Ezek 25–32). This section can be compared to similar oracles of judgment against the Gentiles in other books of the major prophets (for example, Jer 46–51 or Is 13–30). Ezekiel's collection begins with the smaller nations of Ammon, Moab, Edom, Philistia (Ezek 25), followed by longer treatments of the world powers Tyre (Ezek 26–28) and Egypt (Ezek 29–32).

Part 3 consists of prophecies of restoration for Jerusalem, Judah, and Israel after the exile (Ezek 33–39). It begins with an introduction stressing Ezekiel's duty as a watchman for Israel, followed by a longer subunit of oracles of consolation and restoration to Israel (Ezek 33–37), similar in theme, mood, and sometimes diction to Jeremiah's "Book of Comfort" (Jer 30–33). The flip side of consolation and restoration for Israel is judgment on its enemies, so the unit concludes with an extended vision of the fall of Israel's enemy, cryptically named "Gog" (Ezek 38–39).

Part 4 is the extensive and unforgettable vision of a new Temple and liturgy, situated in a newly restored, reallocated, and resettled land of Israel (Ezek 40–48). This tightly integrated section proceeds in several stages, including a detailed description of the dimensions of the Temple proper (Ezek 40–42), the return of God's presence to the Temple (Ezek 43), a set of new laws governing the liturgy (Ezek 44–46), a vision of the river of life flowing from the Temple (Ezek 47), and the boundaries of the eschatological Promised Land (Ezek 48).

According to these four major sections, the book can be outlined as follows:

Outline of the Book of Ezekiel

I. Ezekiel's Message and Ministry before the Fall of Jerusalem (Ezek 1–24)
   A. In the Fifth Year of the Exile (1–7)
      1. Ezekiel's Vision, Call, and Commission (1–3)
      2. Sign-Acts: Brick-Siege of Jerusalem and the Sharp Sword of Judgment (4–5)
      3. Oracles of Judgment on Israel (6–7)

C. Ezekiel's "Book of Comfort" (34–37)
    1. New Shepherds for Israel: God and David (34)
    2. Judgment on Israel's Enemy, Edom (35)
    3. A New Heart and Spirit for Israel (36)
    4. Israel's "Dry Bones" Resurrected (37:1–14)
    5. Israel's "Two Sticks" Rejoined (37:15–28)
D. Prophecy against Israel's Enemy, "Gog" (38–39)

IV. Ezekiel's Temple Vision (Ezek 40–48)
  A. The Dimensions of the Temple (40–42)
  B. The Return of God's Presence to the Temple (43)
  C. New Laws for the Liturgy (44–46)
  D. The River of Life from the Temple (47)
  E. The Boundaries of the Holy Land (48)

Thus, the macrostructure of Ezekiel resembles that of the other major prophets in that it includes a section dedicated to the ministry and message of the prophet during his own lifetime (Ezek 1–24; cf. Is 1–12 or Jer 1–25); a set of "oracles against the nations" (Ezek 25–32; cf. Jer 46–51; Is 13–30); and a section of eschatological prophecies of restoration (Ezek 33–48; cf. Is 40–66; Jer 30–33).

Overview of Ezekiel

Vision of the Chariot-Throne and Prophetic Commission (Ezekiel 1–3)

The book of Ezekiel opens with the prophet living "among the exiles" near the river Chebar somewhere in Chaldea (= Babylonia) (Ezek 1:1). In these opening lines, Ezekiel reports that his visions came to him in his "thirtieth year", the age at which normally he would begin his priestly service (Ezek 1:1; cf. Num 4:30). Five years earlier, Ezekiel had been deported from Israel in the second and largest of the three major exiles from Jerusalem, in which King Jehoiachin was taken (597 B.C.; cf. Ezek 1:2; 2 Kings 24:10–17).

Ezekiel then relates the fantastic and surreal vision he saw, by which he was called and commissioned by God to serve as a prophet. He describes in detail the heavenly "chariot" (Hebrew *merkavah*) of God—a kind of mobile throne—that appears in a storm at a great distance moving toward him. The throne is composed of "four living creatures", angelic beings with multiple wings and eyes and four faces: that of a human, an eagle, an ox, and a lion (Ezek 1:5). Under each creature is a "wheel within a wheel" surrounded by eyes. When the throne draws near, Ezekiel sees above it "the likeness of the glory [Hebrew *chabod*] of the LORD" (Ezek 1:28) himself, enthroned in a human form, who speaks to him, calling him to a prophetic ministry to the hard-hearted people of Israel (Ezek 1:26—3:7). As a sign of this ministry, the Lord causes Ezekiel to eat a scroll, inscribed on front and back with "words of lamentation and mourning and woe", representing the prophetic word that enters into him (Ezek 2:9–10). Then the vision of the cherubim-throne departs. Seven days later, the word of the Lord returns to Ezekiel, commissioning him to be a "watchman" for the house of Israel, to warn the Israelites to turn from their sin lest they experience the judgment of God (Ezek 3:4–27). The vision of God's glory returns, and the Lord informs Ezekiel of a certain supernatural dumbness that will afflict him, which the Lord will lift only when he wishes Ezekiel to speak his word to the people of Israel.

What are we to make of this mysterious vision? How are we to explain what is going on here? The first thing that needs to be stressed is that Ezekiel's call and commissioning vision—like the works of other exilic prophets, such as Jeremiah—is filled with imagery from the Pentateuch, specifically from Exodus and the theophany to Moses on Mount Sinai. For example, just as at Sinai, God appears to Ezekiel in the midst of a storm (Ezek 1:4; cf. Ex 19:16–18). Likewise, the angelic beings that Ezekiel sees are strikingly similar to the cherubim atop the Ark of the Covenant (Ex 25:18–20), which seem to function as a throne or footstool for the divine presence. In this way, the "chariot" throne of angels in Ezekiel's vision is in some sense the heavenly reality of God's enthroned presence that was symbolized by the Ark of the Covenant. The wings and wheels of the throne emphasize its mobility: the presence of God is not limited to a certain location. The number of cherubim (four) may be related to the fact that four cherubim were depicted inside the Holy of Holies in Solomon's Temple: two on the ark (Ex 25:18) and two overshadowing the ark (1 Kings 6:23). God speaks to Ezekiel from his position seated above the cherubim (Ezek 1:28), a privilege otherwise shared only by Moses himself (Ex 25:22). Like Moses, Ezekiel receives a divine document inscribed on the front and back (Ezek 2:10; cf. Ex 32:15). Like Moses, he suffers a speech impediment (Ezek 3:26; cf. Ex 4:10), although Ezekiel's is divinely caused. All these parallels serve to invest Ezekiel with the authority of a prophet who stands as Moses' worthy successor, as Moses himself had promised: "The LORD your God will raise up for you a prophet like me" (Deut 18:15).

Of course, there are also differences between Ezekiel and Moses. Moses was sent to speak to the pharaoh, who refused to listen because he was "hard of heart" (Ex 4:21; 7:13–14). But in Ezekiel's day, it is not the pharaoh but the people of Israel themselves who are "of a hard forehead and of a stubborn heart" (Ezek 3:7). Israel has become as resistant to God's word as the pharaoh was of old and, as a result, will suffer a similar fate.

Prophetic Signs and Oracles against the City of Jerusalem (Ezekiel 4–7)

Ezekiel's public ministry begins with two striking prophetic "signs": symbolic actions meant to effect what they signify by unleashing the power given by God to the prophet.

In the first sign-act, God commands Ezekiel to build a scale model of Jerusalem in a public place and use the model to act out the siege of the city (Ezek 4). He is to lay on his left and right sides for 390 and 40 days respectively, to symbolize the "years of punishment" that Israel and Judah will undergo. As part of the sign, Ezekiel is instructed to perform an act that both reveals how such prophet signs function and indicates one of the more shocking symbols Ezekiel in particular would be called upon to perform:

"And you, take wheat and barley, beans and lentils, millet and spelt, and put them into a single vessel, and make bread of them. During the number of days that you lie upon your side, three hundred and ninety days, you shall eat it.... And you shall eat it as a barley cake, baking it in their sight on human dung." And the LORD said, "Thus shall the people of Israel eat their bread unclean, among the nations where I will drive them." (Ezek 4:9, 12–13)

Understandably, Ezekiel begs the Lord to reconsider such a defiling (and disgusting) sign, pointing out that he has never eaten anything unclean. As a result, the Lord relents and allows him to bake the bread over cow dung instead of human dung! Clearly, as a prophet of woe, Ezekiel is going to be called to enter into the very depths of misery in order to symbolize to his people the desperation to which the exiles will be reduced because of their sinfulness.

In the second sign, God commands Ezekiel to shave his head and save the hair (Ezek 5:1–17). He then divides the hair into unequal portions to be burned, struck with sword, scattered to the wind, or bound in the prophet's robe. Once again, the sign signifies the various fates to befall the inhabitants of Jerusalem: to fall to the sword, to be burned with their city, to be "scattered to the wind" in the coming exile, or (for a few) to be saved.

Other prophets, most notably Jeremiah, also employed sign-acts to instruct the people of Israel. Ezekiel is not unique in this practice. Nonetheless, his sign-acts are more numerous and seem more provocative (or even outrageous), causing some interpreters to call into question the prophet's psychological balance and sanity.[3] However, it is critical to remember that in ancient Israel, the role of the prophet often involved ecstatic or eccentric behavior inappropriate for other persons (cf. 1 Sam 19:24). The hyperbolic character of Ezekiel's actions should be interpreted as attempts to break through the hardness of heart among his fellow Israelites. The prophet has been called to become *in his very person* a "sign" or "portent" (Hebrew *môphēt*) of the message he is delivering (Ezek 12:6, 11; 24:24, 27).[4]

The revelations to Ezekiel from the fifth year of exile (593 B.C.) come to a close with written accounts of two oracles of judgment against Israel, each beginning with "The word of the LORD came to me." The first is a prophecy "against the mountains of Israel": the Lord will soon bring the sword against them and fill their valleys with the slain (Ezek 6:1–14). The "mountains of Israel" refer to the high places (hilltops) that the Israelites employed for pagan worship and/or illicit worship of the Lord (cf. Ezek 6:13). The second prophecy is a vivid poetic montage on the theme "the end has come!" (Ezek 7:1–27). The prophet employs words to paint scene after scene of the doom that is about to fall upon Jerusalem and Judah because of their iniquities.

The Sins in the Temple and the Destruction of Jerusalem (Ezekiel 8–11)

One of the questions that may arise in the minds of readers of the tragic history of Jerusalem is: How bad really were the sins of the people? How corrupt had

---

[3] See Daniel I. Block, *The Book of Ezekiel*, vol. 1, New International Commentary on the Old Testament 20 (Grand Rapids, Mich.: Eerdmans, 1997), 9–12.

[4] See ibid., 11.

Jerusalem really become, for it to suffer such a horrific end at the hands of the Babylonians?

These questions find an extended answer in the next section of Ezekiel's visions, which are dated to a new year, "the sixth year" of the exile (592 B.C.; Ezek 8:1). In the middle of this year, while sitting with certain elders of the people in exile in Babylon, Ezekiel is caught up in a vision and taken to the Temple in Jerusalem, where a man with supernatural appearance takes him on a tour of the inner courts of the sanctuary, to see what is *really* going on there. And what does he see? (1) Seventy elders of Israel worshipping images of "beasts" and "creeping things" in the Temple (Ezek 8:7–13); (2) women in the north gate of the Temple weeping for "Tammuz", the pagan goddess (Ezek 8:14–15); (3) and twenty-five men with their backs to the Temple "worshiping the sun" toward the east (Ezek 8:16–18). In other words, Ezekiel discovers that the corruption of the leaders and people has made its way into the very heart of the Holy Place itself.

In response to this total defilement of the Temple, the Lord sends out six "men" (who appear to be angels) to execute the idolaters among the people of Jerusalem. However, before doing so, he also sends a messenger to "put a mark [Hebrew *taw*]"—the letter "T", which in ancient Hebrew script was a cross— "upon the foreheads of the men who sigh and groan over all the abominations that are committed" in the city (Ezek 9:4). After the slaughter of the idolaters, the glory-throne of the Lord rises with the cherubim and departs toward the east. Significantly, the glory of the Lord pauses at the east gate of the Temple, where the Lord entrusts Ezekiel with two oracles: one of judgment against the wicked counselors of Jerusalem (Ezek 11:1–13) and one of consolation, which promises the gift of "one heart", "a new spirit", and "a heart of flesh" for the people of Israel at some unspecified time in the future when God will renew his covenant with them (Ezek 11:19–20). After these oracles have been entrusted to Ezekiel, the Lord enthroned on the cherubim departs the Temple and the city, and is last seen standing above the mountain that is "on the east side"—that is, the Mount of Olives (Ezek 11:23).

The theological message of this vision is simple but profound: despite God's promises to Jerusalem, his glorious presence is not inseparably tied to that place, even to the Temple. In effect, the abominations being practiced by the elders and inhabitants of Jerusalem and Judah have driven out the glory of the Lord, who has headed east to be a "sanctuary" for the exiles in Babylon. Nonetheless, for all the imminent destruction, there remains hope for covenant renewal and the return of God's presence in the future.

Signs, Oracles, and Allegories of Israel (Ezekiel 12–19)

The next section of the book consists of a series of prophetic signs, oracles, and extended allegories of judgment against Jerusalem and the people of Israel.

The section begins with a sign: at some unspecified time in the sixth year of exile, God commands Ezekiel to dress, pack, and act like an exile by leaving his home for some distant place (Ezek 12:1–16). This would probably involve

Ezekiel stripping naked, since captives generally were forced to march into exile unclothed (cf. Is 20:1–6). In fact, the Hebrew verb meaning "to go into exile" is formed from a root meaning "to be naked". As expected, Ezekiel's activities attract attention, which provides him the opportunity to deliver his prophecy: the prince of Israel and those remaining in Jerusalem will be forced into exile in the manner he is depicting. In addition to his public portrayal of the exile, Ezekiel is also to eat and drink while "quaking" and "trembling", to dramatize the fear that will fall on the inhabitants of Jerusalem (Ezek 12:17). Though Ezekiel's contemporaries think his message will not be fulfilled or only at a much later time, the Lord will quickly bring all his words to fruition.

These signs of Jerusalem's exile are followed by a series of oracles and extended allegories condemning Israel, Judah, and Jerusalem for their sins. Like similar prophecies in Jeremiah, Ezekiel condemns the false prophets of Israel for their made-up visions and concocted oracles (Ezek 13). Strikingly, Ezekiel declares that the idolatry of the "house of Israel" has become so bad that not even the intercessions of "Noah, Daniel, and Job" would suffice to avert God's wrath (Ezek 14:1–23). In particular, the city of Jerusalem has become to God like "the wood of the vine"—that is, not useful for making anything, but only for being burned in the fire (Ezek 15).

Perhaps the most beautiful—and simultaneously disturbing—of Ezekiel's prophetic oracles is the extended allegory (the longest in the book) describing the relationship between the Lord and Jerusalem as that of *a bridegroom* and *an adulterous bride* (Ezek 16:1–63). In this oracle, Ezekiel retells the story of the exodus as a love story: he likens Jerusalem to an orphan girl adopted by the Lord, who raised her, doted on her, and, when she had "reached the age for love", "pledged" himself to her by means of a "covenant" so that she became his bride (Ezek 16:1–14). After all this, Jerusalem abandoned her divine spouse and used all the wealth he bestowed on her to buy sex favors from foreigners, even going so far as to slaughter the children she bore to the Lord in the pursuit of her lovers (Ezek 16:15–34). As a result, the Lord will hand her over to the power of her lovers, who care nothing for her and will abuse her and destroy her (Ezek 16:35–58). Yet for all this, the Lord will remember his love for Jerusalem in her youth, and restore to her an "everlasting covenant"—that is, a renewed marriage relationship that will be established when God forgives the sins of his people (Ezek 16:59–63).

In yet another allegory, Ezekiel compares Babylon and Egypt to two eagles who struggle for control of a cedar branch representing the royal house of Judah (Ezek 17). Right now, the transplanted branch is withering in the conflict of shifting alliances, but in the future God himself will plant the branch—which represents the people of Jerusalem—"on the mountain height of Israel", so that it will become "a noble cedar" where all "birds" and "beasts"—which represent the Gentile nations—will seek refuge (Ezek 17:23). Thus, Ezekiel anticipates not only the restoration of Israel, but the conversion of the Gentile nations to the recognition of the one true God.

The penultimate prophecy of Ezekiel's "sixth year" is an extended sermon on individual culpability for sin: though the Israelites believe they are suffering for

---

Does Ezekiel Condone the Abuse of Women?

The graphic imagery of the allegories in which Jerusalem is portrayed as an adulterous and murderous wife whom the Lord eventually hands over to her lovers for punishment (Ezek 16 and 23) has aroused protest in modern times from critics who suggest these passages condone the abuse of women in society. Since contemporary secular society no longer considers adultery a crime but, in fact, glamorizes it in literature and cinema and also approves of maternal infanticide under the guise of abortion, it is somewhat unsurprising that the figure of adulterous, child-murdering Jerusalem should attract more sympathy among contemporary commentators than it did among Jews and Christians in antiquity. Nonetheless, before the sacred author is accused of misogyny, a few factors need to be kept in mind:

1. Ezekiel 16 and 23 are parables employing the rhetorical device of *hyperbole* in order to shock its readers to attention and in order to communicate. Such use of hyperbole is still practiced to this day, especially in dire or serious circumstances.

2. Furthermore, it is *not* the Lord in these parables who abuses wife-Jerusalem but the pagan Gentile lovers she chose in preference to her Lord-husband. The Lord's only act is (metaphorically) to "strip her bare" and give her over to her lovers by allowing the Temple sanctuary to be laid bare (Ezek 16:35–37). Yet Jerusalem has *already* stripped herself for her lovers and chosen them over the Lord (Ezek 16:23–28). So the Lord's "punishment" is simply an affirmation of Jerusalem's free will. The abuse Jerusalem receives is actually at the hands of the "lovers" she pursued by her own choice.

3. It is a misuse of the prophetic genre to treat these oracles as if Ezekiel intended to lay out guidelines for male-female interaction in society. To read him that way is to read him against authorial intent and take his words out of context.

4. There is no actual evidence that either of these chapters has been used in Jewish or Christian tradition as justification for the abuse of women.

5. For all Jerusalem's crimes as bride, the Lord promises ultimately to *take her back* and *restore his love, affection, and covenant* with her (Ezek 16:59–63). This speaks to matrimonial permanence and fidelity in the face of staggering infidelity.

---

the sins of their fathers and, indeed, embrace this concept of trans-generational punishment, God insists that each person shall die for his own sin:

> The soul that sins shall die. The son shall not suffer for the iniquity of the father, nor the father suffer for the iniquity of the son; the righteousness of the righteous shall be upon himself, and the wickedness of the wicked shall be upon himself. (Ezek 18:20)

The prophet then goes on proclaim the justice of God and the importance of the state in which one ends one's life: namely, that the sinner who repents will be ultimately saved and the righteous man who backslides will be ultimately lost. In short, the Lord will return to each according to his ways. This is divine justice, even if the people of Israel resist it. Indeed, the Lord defends himself against any accusation of injustice when he highlights that Israel is not fit to pass judgment on anyone, much less God: "O house of Israel, are my ways not just? Is it not *your* ways that are not just?" (Ezek 18:29).

The oracles of the sixth year conclude with a lament for the princes of Israel, containing two shorter analogies in which their mother (Jerusalem) is likened first to a lioness whose cubs have been caught and caged (Ezek 19:1–9) and, then, to a vine once verdant but now consumed and withered (Ezek 19:10–14).

Salvation History and the Spiritual Adultery of Jerusalem (Ezekiel 20–23)

The material gathered under the "seventh year" of the exile (Ezek 20:1) comprises four extensive, self-contained compositions, which take up the question of salvation history and how it is that Jerusalem has gotten herself into the situation of exile through her sinfulness.

First and foremost, in what may well be one of the most significant intra-canonical interpretations of the Pentateuch in the Old Testament, Ezekiel retells the history of salvation from the time of Moses to the destruction of Jerusalem (Ezek 20). He begins with Israel in Egypt (Ezek 20:1–9) and proceeds through the exodus (Ezek 20:10), the law-giving at Sinai (Ezek 20:11–12), the various rebellions in the wilderness (Ezek 20:13–14), the oath condemning the first generation to die in the wilderness (Ezek 20:15; cf. Num 14:20–22), the rise of the second generation in the wilderness (Ezek 20:18–20), the rebellion of the second generation (Ezek 20:21–22; cf. Num 25:1–15), the oath to scatter Israel in the exile (Ezek 20:23–24; cf. Deut 4:26–28), the giving of the "no-good laws" (that is, certain laws of Deuteronomy) to the second generation (Ezek 20:25–26; cf. Deut 12–26), and the entrance and settlement of the land and subsequent idolatry (Ezek 20:27–29). The upshot of this concentrated overview is simple: throughout all Israel's history, it has tried to rebel against the Lord and be like the pagan nations, but it shall never succeed (Ezek 20:32). Instead, the

---

What Are the "No-Good Laws"
of Ezekiel 20:25–26?

In his retelling of the history of Israel, the prophet speaks of "statutes that were not good" (literally, "no-good laws") that the Lord gave Israel, so that he "defiled them through their very gifts in making them offer by fire all their first-born" (Ezek 20:26). The usual explanation is that this refers to the sacrifice of firstborn sons by burning them on the altars to the god Molech (cf. Lev 18:21; 20:2–5; 2 Kings 23:10; Jer 32:35). By some mental gymnastics, Ezekiel is supposed to have attributed this practice to the will or law of the Lord.

However, this explanation will not work. First of all, despite the fact that English translations add the words "by fire", they are not in the actual Hebrew text of Ezekiel 20:26. Instead, these words are added by translators to accommodate the text to the Molech-sacrifice interpretation (e.g., RSV, NAB). Furthermore, Molech did not demand the offering of the firstborn; he accepted the sacrifice of any and all children. There is no evidence in Scripture or the history of Israel of a practice of offering firstborn children.

The key to understanding these verses is to recognize that the law-giving spoken of here occurs in the narrative of Ezekiel 20 as the giving of the law to the *second generation* in the wilderness, which would correspond to Deuteronomy in the Pentateuch (cf. Deut 1). It is well known that Deuteronomy changed the laws governing the sacrifice of *firstborn animals* and made other alterations to the cultic and ethical statutes of Israel that would have been forbidden under the more rigorous legislation given in Leviticus and Numbers (the "Priestly" and "Holiness" Codes).[a] Thus, Ezekiel's "no-good laws" are certain laws of Deuteronomy, which was a second covenant, "besides the covenant" made at Sinai (Deut 29:1). Deuteronomy permitted practices that were far from the divine ideal (cf. Mt 19:8; and further below, "Theological Issues in Ezekiel").

[a] See Scott W. Hahn and John S. Bergsma, "What Laws Were Not Good? A Canonical Approach to the Theological Problem of Ezekiel 20:25–26", *Journal of Biblical Literature* 123 (2004): 201–18.

Lord will bring about a *new exodus*, in which he will gather Israel from all the places of its exile out into the wilderness, where the Lord will confront Israel, purify the nation, and impress upon it his great holiness and the gravity of its sins. Then he will bring the Israelites into their land, where they will worship him "on my holy mountain, the mountain height of Israel" (that is, the Temple Mount) (Ezek 20:40). They shall know that God is the Lord and shall "loathe" themselves for all their iniquities.

This review of sacred history is followed by a series of oracles that continue to heap condemnation on Jerusalem. First, there is the "oracle of the unsheathed sword", in which God declares that he has "unsheathed the sword" against Jerusalem because it did not respond to "the rod" or anything of wood (Ezek 21:1–27). In other words, partial discipline has not caused repentance, so now deadly judgment will fall on the city. The Ammonites, too, will share the judgment that falls on Jerusalem (Ezek 21:28–32). In the following oracle, Ezekiel systematically condemns the secular and sacred leadership of the people: the princes (Ezek 21:1–25), the priests (Ezek 21:26–27), and the prophets (Ezek 21:28–31). All are guilty of extensive violations of the law of Moses, violations that Ezekiel carefully enumerates: murder, contempt for parents, abuse of orphans and widows, contempt for sacred objects and Sabbath rest, slander, lewdness, incest, adultery, extortion—in a word, the people have "forgotten" the Lord and act as if he did not exist (Ezek 22:6–12).

The prophecies of the seventh year conclude with another extended allegory in which Jerusalem and Samaria—the former capital of the northern kingdom—are compared to harlots (Ezek 23). The two cities, says Ezekiel, are like two sisters named *Oholah* (= Samaria) and *Oholibah* (= Jerusalem), who grew up in promiscuity in Egypt, but nonetheless were espoused to the Lord and bore him children. Then the sisters—whose names are somehow related to the word "tent" (Hebrew *'ohel*)—engaged in wanton adultery: Oholah (Samaria) with the men of Assyria, Oholibah with the men of Babylonia (cf. 2 Sam 16:22 for the image of the nuptial "tent"). As a result, the Lord will turn them over to their lovers, who will mistreat them and abuse them. Thus their crimes of infidelity will come back on their own heads, and, as is so often the case in the Old Testament, they will be punished by the very things by which they sinned.

The Boiling Pot and the Death of Ezekiel's Wife (Ezekiel 24)

The "ninth year" of exile saw the beginning of the final Babylonian siege of Jerusalem, which would ultimately lead to the destruction of the city and Temple and deportation of all remaining inhabitants (ca. 587 B.C.). Ezekiel dates two prophecies to this terrible year. First, he records the allegory of "the boiling pot", in which the prophet likens Jerusalem to an old rusted pot in which flesh is boiled until it is dried and charred and then the pot melted in the flames as well (Ezek 24:1–14). This may have been a prophetic sign-act, too, but it is unclear whether Ezekiel was to act out the words of the allegory publicly. The second was another prophetic sign, one that demonstrated perhaps more than any other that the prophet was called to become the personal embodiment of the word of God to his people:

Also the word of the LORD came to me: "Son of man, behold, I am about to take *the delight of your eyes* away from you at a stroke; yet you shall not mourn or weep nor shall your tears run down. Sigh, but not aloud; make no mourning for the dead. Bind on your turban, and put your shoes on your feet; do not cover your lips, nor eat the bread of mourners." *So I spoke to the people in the morning, and at evening my wife died.* And on the next morning I did as I was commanded.

And the people said to me, "Will you not tell us what these things mean for us, that you are acting thus?" Then I said to them, "The word of the LORD came to me: 'Say to the house of Israel, Thus says the Lord GOD: *Behold, I will profane my sanctuary*, the pride of your power, *the delight of your eyes*, and the desire of your soul; and your sons and your daughters whom you left behind shall fall by the sword. And you shall do as I have done; you shall not cover your lips, nor eat the bread of mourners.'" (Ezek 24:15–22)

Notice the striking analogy here between Ezekiel and his bride (the "delight of his eyes") and YHWH and the Jerusalem Temple. By means of this analogy, the death of Ezekiel's wife becomes a prophetic sign of the passing away of God's spouse, Jerusalem, and the fact that Jerusalem will depart without being mourned, since the would-be mourners will be struggling merely to survive.

Oracles against the Nations (Ezekiel 25–32)

In the next major section of the book of Ezekiel, the prophet launches into a string of prophetic oracles against the Gentile nations (Ezek 25–32). He begins with the oracles against the surrounding smaller nations—Ammon (Ezek 25:1–7), Moab (Ezek 25:8–11), Edom (Ezek 25:12–14), and Philistia (Ezek 25:15–17)—declaring that they will all be punished because they gloated over Jerusalem's destruction and took advantage of the decimation of Judah to pillage and abuse the survivors.

After these oracles against smaller nations come two large complexes of oracles against two major powers that bordered Israel: Tyre (Ezek 26:1—28:19) and Egypt (Ezek 29–32). Ezekiel treats both these major powers in a similar pattern: first, there is an oracle of condemnation, followed by a lament, for the nation as a whole (Ezek 26–27, 29—30:9); second, there is an oracle of condemnation, followed by a lament, for the nation's king (Ezek 28:1–19; Ezek 30:20—32:32). Since the small nation of Sidon was always closely associated with Tyre, the short oracle against Tyre is tacked on after the extensive treatment of Sidon, followed by a short oracle of blessing

> **The King of Tyre and the Fall of the Angels**
>
> In Ezekiel 28:1–19, the king of Tyre is described as if he were the most glorious cherub in the Garden of Eden, who rebels against God and is cast out due to his excessive pride. Of course, this cannot have been literally true of the king of Tyre. In some way, Ezekiel seems to be applying to the king of Tyre an ancient tradition of angelic rebellion in the heavenly court (cf. Job 1–2; 1 Enoch 1–5). Although Ezekiel did not intend to address demonology specifically, it seems that his "king of Tyre" recapitulated on a human level a more original and archetypical fall from grace and rebellion against God, that of the Satan himself, along with the wicked angels (Lk 10:18; 2 Cor 11:14; Rev 12:9). Indeed, we find similar ideas about holy and wicked angels in the book of Daniel, in which such beings act at the heads of the nation of Israel and its enemies (see Dan 7–8; 12:1–4).

to Israel marking the transition between the prophecies about Tyre and those about Egypt (Ezek 28:20–26).

Perhaps the most striking aspect of these oracles against Tyre and Egypt is the way in which Ezekiel treats both of the kings as quasi-angelic beings, whose enmity against Israel is as much (if not more) a *spiritual* reality as it is a political reality. Both of these rulers are condemned because their great power and beauty led them to elevate themselves in the presence of God. For example, the king of Tyre is described as having claimed divinity for himself, saying, "I am a god" (Ezek 28:2). He is compared to the most glorious cherub "in Eden, the garden of God", who, because of his sin, is "cast" down from "the mountain of God" (Ezek 28:11–19). Likewise, the pharaoh is compared to both the "dragon" of the Nile and to the most glorious tree in that divine garden (Ezek 31:1–18). In other words, the sin of these rulers is an implicitly satanic arrogance resulting in self-worship and rivalry with God himself. By giving themselves over to such demonic aspirations, the kings of Tyre and Egypt have retraced the steps of the first being to rebel against God and, like him, will be punished by being thrown down from their exalted status.

The New Exodus and the New Creation (Ezekiel 33–39)

The next section of Ezekiel consists of prophecies to Israel *after* the fall of Jerusalem and the last deportation to Babylon in 587 B.C. These oracles are given by the prophet in the "twelfth year" of exile, after a survivor from Jerusalem arrives in Ezekiel's village to inform him that "the city has fallen" (Ezek 33:21). After an initial section reprising Ezekiel's prophetic role as a watchman (Ezek 33:1–20), the subsequent oracles show a marked change in tone from the earlier sections of the book. Like the prophecies of salvation in other books (for example, Is 40 and Jer 30), Ezekiel turns from predominant condemnation to prevailing consolation. In the course of these oracles, several key hopes stand out as significant.

1. *The New Exodus and the New Heart*: After rebuking the corrupt "shepherds" (leaders) who are abusing the "sheep" (the scattered people of Israel), Ezekiel declares that a day is coming when the Lord himself will be shepherd and seek out the lost, bring back the strayed, bind up the crippled, and strengthen the weak, by bringing the scattered children of God back to the Promised Land. Although the explicit language of "exodus" does not appear here, what is being foretold can very much be described as a new exodus: just as God had shepherded his people from exile to the Promised Land at the time of the exodus from Egypt, so too will he bring them home to the Promised Land in a new "return from exile" (cf. Ezek 20:33–38). Indeed, after an oracle against Edom (Ezek 35:1–15), the prophet goes on to describe this new exodus as involving a new act of cleansing with water:

> And I will vindicate the holiness of my great name, which has been profaned among the nations, and which you have profaned among them; and the nations will know that I am the LORD, says the Lord GOD, when through you I vindicate my holiness before their eyes. For I will take you from the nations, and gather

you from all the countries, and bring you into your own land. *I will sprinkle clean water upon you,* and you shall be clean from all your uncleannesses, and from all your idols I will cleanse you. A new heart I will give you, and *a new spirit I will put within you*; and I will take out of your flesh the heart of stone and give you a heart of flesh. *And I will put my spirit within you,* and cause you to walk in my statutes and be careful to observe my ordinances. You shall dwell in the land which I gave to your fathers; and you shall be my people, and I will be your God. (Ezek 36:23–28)

In other words, just as the first Israelites had prepared to meet God on Mount Sinai by washing with water to receive the law on tablets of stone (Ex 19:10–15; 32:15–16), so now in the new exodus, God will prepare his people by cleansing them from sin with water—but this time, so they can receive his law and his spirt "within" them in their "heart". Strikingly, this new exodus will also surpass the old exodus in that it will (in some way) involve a new creation as well, since the Promised Land itself will become "like the garden of Eden" (Ezek 36:35).

2. *The New Creation and the New Kingdom*: In the face of such a glorious oracle of hope for the future, one might be tempted to ask: "What about those Israelites who die before the new exodus takes place?" In response to such a question, Ezekiel gives another vision for the future, in which he shows how those Israelites who die before it is realized should not despair, because God is

> *Does the Vision of Dry Bones Actually Prophesy the Bodily Resurrection of the Righteous?*
>
> Many commentators correctly point out that Ezekiel 37:1–14 is an image of the national restoration of the people of Israel from exile. While this is true, the vision also has implications for the bodily resurrection of the individual Israelites. In other words, the historical return of Israelites to the land does not solve the problem of the continuing exile of those who die outside the Promised Land. Indeed, what good is an earthly return to the land for some if many more will die in exile long before the promises are realized? Against these counsels of despair, the prophet, inspired by God, asserts that, if necessary, God will raise his faithful ones out of their graves and forcibly incorporate them into the national restoration, so that the nations might know that he is the Lord. Thus, *the restoration of Israel* in a new exodus and *the resurrection of the dead* are complementary, not contradictory, concepts. When the vision of the dry bones is interpreted in its broader context in Ezekiel, it is directly linked to the broader hopes for a new exodus, New Covenant, and even a new creation, in which the land will be made "like the garden of Eden" (Ezek 34, 36).

able to raise them from their graves in order to experience the eschatological blessings of this "new creation". That is the point of the famous "vision of the valley of dry bones" (Ezek 37:1–14). Taken up by the Spirit, Ezekiel sees a valley filled with dry bones. Prompted by the Lord, he "prophesies to the Spirit", and the bones assemble themselves into skeletons, clothe themselves with flesh, and finally present themselves as a great, living army. This vision represents the whole house of Israel, who will "know that I am the LORD, when I open your graves, and raise you from your graves, O my people" (Ezek 37:12–13).

In order to understand Ezekiel's oracle properly, it is critical to note that he is tying this future resurrection to the restoration of *the kingdom of David* to *all twelve tribes of Israel*. He symbolizes this in yet another prophetic sign, in which God instructs Ezekiel to take two sticks and unite them into one:

1. First Stick: "For Joseph" (= ten northern tribes of Israel)
2. Second Stick: "For Judah" (= two southern tribes of Judah)
3. United Stick: The Kingdom of David (= all twelve tribes together)

Although the word "messiah" does not occur here, Ezekiel is telling us that the new exodus, the new creation, and the new kingdom will all come when the future Davidic king finally arrives:

> *My servant David shall be king over them; and they shall all have one shepherd....* I will make a covenant of peace with them; it shall be an everlasting covenant with them; and I will bless them and multiply them, and will set my sanctuary in the midst of them for evermore. My dwelling place shall be with them; and I will be their God, and they shall be my people. Then the nations will know that I the LORD sanctify Israel, when my sanctuary is in the midst of them for evermore. (Ezek 37:24, 26–28)

Notice here how all of the themes of Ezekiel's prophecies are coming together: there will be a new exodus, with a new kingdom, a New Covenant, and even a new Temple! In other words, all of the tragedies of the Assyrian and Babylonian exiles will not only be undone but will be surpassed by the coming of a Shepherd-King and a New Temple that will never be destroyed but will last "for evermore".

Of course, salvation for the faithful is always accompanied by judgment for the unfaithful. In this case, the flip side of the restoration of Israel is judgment on its enemies: hence, Ezekiel pronounces the doom of "*Gog*" and "*Magog*", probably ciphers for the king and people of Babylon, the enemies of God's people (Ezek 38–39). "Gog" will lead his people against Israel, but the Lord will overthrow them and prove his power (Ezek 38:1—39:20). Afterward, Israel will dwell secure, having been gathered from every place to which they were exiled in the new exodus, and God will pour out his Spirit on them (Ezek 39:21–29).

The New Temple (Ezekiel 40–48)

The fourth and last unit of the book of Ezekiel is a lengthy, well-integrated vision of a new Temple situated in a restored Land of Israel in the end time (Ezek 40–48). Ezekiel sees the vision of the new Temple in the "twenty-fifth year of our exile" (Ezek 40:1)—around 573 B.C., counting twenty-five years from 597 B.C.—and thus, some time after the tragic reality of the loss of Jerusalem and its Temple has set in.

And yet, there is hope for the future, for in his vision, a "man" escorts Ezekiel through a *future* Temple, measuring and providing the dimensions of the stairs, courts, antechambers, buildings, walls, and other features of the sanctuary (Ezek 40–42). The Temple thus measured is very large—much bigger than the Solomonic Temple and, in fact, too big even to fit on the Temple Mount in Jerusalem (Ezek 40:5–19)!

In any case, after the "man" measures the Temple, Ezekiel once again beholds the chariot cherubim-throne of God returning to enter the Temple by means of the east gate, the same entrance by which he left (cf. Ezek 11:22–25). The Lord speaks to Ezekiel from his throne and commands him to relate to Israel the dimensions of the new Temple and the new "ordinances and laws" that will govern the sacrificial liturgy celebrated within it. These new ordinances and laws take up a large part of the vision (Ezek 43:13—46:24) and cover such matters as the dimensions of the altar (Ezek 43:13–17), the ritual for consecrating the Temple (Ezek 43:18–27), the blocking up of the east gate (Ezek 44:1–3), the regulations for admitting worshippers (Ezek 44:4–14), the regulations for legitimate priests and priestly conduct (Ezek 44:15–31), the dimensions of the sacred precinct (Ezek 45:1–9), the size and weight of specific offerings (Ezek 45:10–17), the annual feasts (Ezek 45:18–25), and the unique role of the "prince"—who appears to be the Davidic king—in public worship (Ezek 46:1–18).

At this point, Ezekiel describes perhaps the most famous aspect of this mysterious new Temple: the river flowing out of the "right side of the threshold of the temple" (Ezek 47:1). This river—which is clearly miraculous—gets deeper and deeper as it travels east and south, toward the Dead Sea, though no tributaries flow into it. It brings life and health wherever it goes, even healing the Dead Sea so that its waters are fresh and life-giving and full of "very many kinds" of fish, "like the fish of the Great Sea" (Ezek 47:10). Once again, we see here imagery of a *new creation*, in which all that is dead will be brought to life, even the infamous "Dead Sea".

This vision of the Temple is central to the book's understanding of liturgy. In these chapters, Ezekiel envisions a new society for Israel, completely organized around the celebration of the liturgy. The Temple is the center of the capital, which is the center of the sacred precinct, which is the center of the Levitical/priestly territory, which is at the center of the nation. The whole nation is a kind of Temple-state, a society whose purpose is the perpetuation of the true cult. The Temple is the center of this society, because the sacrificial liturgy celebrated within it perpetuates communion with God within the parameters of a covenantal relationship. Thus, there is in this society a *centripetal motion* from its farthest boundaries toward the Temple—all members of society make pilgrimage to the Temple for worship. On the other hand, there is also a *centrifugal motion* from the Temple outward, expressed in the image of the river of life flowing from the Temple to the neediest part of the land, the Dead Sea, where it brings life, health, and fertility. The message of this vision is that the Temple, the place of liturgical communion, is the center and source of divine blessing for the life of the nation.

Last of all, Ezekiel sees the new dimensions of the Promised Land, including the outer borders (Ezek 47:13–23), the areas allotted for each tribe (Ezek 48:1–7; 23–29), the Temple-city and its precinct (Ezek 48:8–20), and the prince and his family (Ezek 48:21–22). He sees the twelve gates of the city, one for each tribe, and the name of the city is "The LORD is there" (Ezek 48:35). With this, Ezekiel's prophecies come to a striking conclusion: a new exodus, a New Covenant, a new creation, a new Temple, and a new Promised Land. Despite being in the "Old" Testament, Ezekiel is truly the prophet of the God who will make "all things new" (cf. Rev 21:5).

Historical Issues in Ezekiel

The Origins of the Book of Ezekiel

In striking contrast to the other major prophets, both ancient and contemporary commentators are largely agreed upon the fact that the book of Ezekiel is what it presents itself to be: the work of the prophet and priest Ezekiel, whose public ministry took place at the time of the Babylonian exile. Indeed, in the case of Ezekiel, the ordinary situation is reversed: while ancient rabbinic tradition held that "the men of the Great Synagogue wrote Ezekiel",[5] many modern scholars think the book was (for the most part) actually composed by the prophet himself!

To be sure, in the early twentieth century, when it was extremely popular in scholarly circles to question the authorship of most ancient works, there were several scholars who argued for radically late datings of Ezekiel, some even going so far as to date the book to the third century B.C. due to alleged references to inter-Jewish conflicts in Hellenistic Palestine.[6] By the mid-twentieth century, scholars had mounted a number of arguments favoring the conclusion that the book was substantially the work of the prophet himself or, at least, his close disciples,[7] for several reasons:

1. Throughout the book of Ezekiel, the distinct and unusual literary style and theological perspective of the author remain constant. As a result, there is little reason to hypothesize significant contributions by anyone other than the prophet himself or to engage in the dismemberment and stratification carried out on such apparently composite works as Isaiah and Jeremiah. Instead, many scholars hold that the book is substantially the work of a single author, a truly "literary" prophet.

2. The language of the book reflects the transition from classical to postclassical Hebrew prose that took place during the exile—something that would cohere perfectly with the text actually being written by a prophet who experienced the Babylonian exile.

3. The historical references and dates in the book align well with external historical sources from the time period.

4. Nothing in the book of Ezekiel reflects any awareness of the events that transpired during the late exilic period or the early postexilic period.

5. Along these lines, Ezekiel's vision of the restoration of Israel (Ezek 34–37, 40–48) does not align at all with actual events of the postexilic restoration of Judah and Jerusalem in the early Persian period. For that reason, many scholars

---

[5] Babylonian Talmud, *Baba Bathra* 14b, in Isidore Epstein, ed., *The Babylonian Talmud*, 35 vols. (London: Soncino, 1935–1952).

[6] For example, Charles Cutler Torrey, *Pseudo-Ezekiel and the Original Prophecy* (New Haven, Conn.: Yale University Press, 1930), 99.

[7] For example, Walter Zimmerli, *Ezekiel*, trans. Ronald E. Clements and James D. Martin, 2 vols., Hermeneia (Philadelphia: Fortress, 1979–1983).

do not hold that Ezekiel's prophecy of the new Temple (Ezek 40–48), which appears to be the last section of the book composed,[8] was written after the exile and attributed to Ezekiel. Why retroject an apparently unfulfilled prophecy into the mouth of a controversial prophet?

In light of such considerations, several English-speaking studies since the late twentieth century have presumed substantial authorship by the prophet Ezekiel (or those very close to him) and concentrate on the final form of the book.[9]

Did Ezekiel Copy the Priestly Source (P)?

Another historical issue in Ezekiel concerns the relationship of his book to the sources of the Pentateuch. It has long been recognized that the language of Ezekiel has extensive parallels with passages from the Pentateuch, especially the so-called "Priestly source" and the section of Leviticus known as the "Holiness Code". This poses a problem for traditional formulations of the Documentary Hypothesis, since Julius Wellhausen and others proposed that the Priestly and Holiness materials were not in written form until the postexilic period. Wellhausen proposed that the parallels between Ezekiel and the Priestly/Holiness materials were due to the Priestly authors *using Ezekiel*. However, meticulous studies of these parallels since the end of the late twentieth century have shown that Ezekiel, writing in the early exilic period, is *using the Priestly/Holiness materials*, which were already in written form. Thus, what Wellhausen and others called the "Priestly source" of the Pentateuch is probably preexilic. (For more on this issue, see *Excursus*.)

Excursus: The Relationship of Ezekiel to the Pentateuchal Sources

It has long been recognized that the language of Ezekiel is frequently very close to that of the so-called "Priestly source" (P) of the Pentateuch, especially the so-called "Holiness Code" (Lev 17–26). Less frequently, Ezekiel reflects knowledge of language and concepts from Deuteronomy (D).

On the face of it, this apparent literary relationship between Ezekiel and the Pentateuch poses a challenge to the classic Graf-Wellhausen Documentary Hypothesis, according to which the Priestly source was the *last* of the Pentateuchal literary strata, added only in the *postexilic* period (post-539 B.C.). As we saw in chapter 2, according to the standard version of the Documentary Hypothesis, the postexilic Jerusalem priesthood, under the influence of guilt from the sins that led to the exile and succumbing to a legalistic understanding of their relationship with God, contrived the extensive cultic regulations that characterize the parts of the Pentateuch labeled "P". The obvious problem this raises can be formulated as a question: *If the Priestly source is a postexilic composition, how can the prophet Ezekiel—who lived and wrote during the exile—be familiar with it?*

---

[8] Ibid., 2:327–28.

[9] Daniel I. Block, *The Book of Ezekiel*, 2 vols., New International Commentary on the Old Testament 20–21 (Grand Rapids, Mich.: Eerdmans, 1997–1998); Moshe Greenburg, *Ezekiel 1–20*, Anchor Bible 22 (New York: Doubleday, 1983).

Wellhausen's explanation was that Ezekiel was the forerunner of the Priestly source, and thus the parallels in language and concept could be explained as the dependence of the Priestly materials on Ezekiel. This remained the standard explanation for more than a century, as the scholarly guild assumed that Wellhausen's views were the result of careful study of the similar passages in Ezekiel and the Pentateuch. At the end of the twentieth century, however, studies appeared demonstrating that Wellhausen had never engaged in a careful study of the book of Ezekiel and its relationship to the Pentateuchal sources, and his views on the subject amounted to casual observations and conjecture in harmony with his grand hypothesis about the development of Israelite religion.[10] Close examination of the parallels between Ezekiel and Leviticus render implausible the position that Leviticus depends on Ezekiel.[11] Without becoming too technical, the issue can be summed up as follows: the language of Ezekiel reflects a later form of Hebrew than that used by Leviticus and includes terms borrowed from foreign languages (as a result of the exile) that do not appear in Leviticus.[12] Moreover, when a parallel occurs between Ezekiel and Leviticus, examination of the context of the parallel in both books generally makes it easy to discern Ezekiel's theological purpose in quoting Leviticus, but it seldom if ever elucidates why Leviticus is quoting Ezekiel.[13]

For example, the prophet Ezekiel specifies that in the future, if the Davidic king gives a gift of land to one of his servants, it will revert to the crown in the "year of liberty" (Ezek 46:17). The "year of liberty" (Hebrew *derôr*) is clearly the Jubilee Year (Lev 25:8–55), the only sacred year in the Israelite tradition that involved the reversion of land to its owner. On the Jubilee Year, the Israelites were "to proclaim liberty (Hebrew *derôr*)" throughout the land. Thus, most scholars agree there is some relationship between Ezekiel 46 and Leviticus 25. But which text is older and serves as a source for the other?

If Leviticus is older, the situation makes good sense. The Mosaic law gave a provision for the reversion of land in the Jubilee, the "year of liberty". But the Mosaic law was given, according to the biblical claim, long before the rise of the monarchy in Israel, and none of the Pentateuchal laws reflect the presence of a monarchy in Israelite society.[14] There is only the permission for the establishment of a king at some point in the future (Deut 17:14–20). Ezekiel, however, lives *after* the establishment of the covenant of kingship with David and intends to make amendments to the sacred law of Israel to govern the conduct of the monarchy. Thus, he amends the Jubilee legislation in Leviticus by the addition

[10] Michael A. Lyons, *From Law to Prophecy: Ezekiel's Use of the Holiness Code*, Library of Hebrew Bible/Old Testament Studies 507 (London: T&T Clark, 2009).

[11] Risa Levitt Kohn, *A New Heart and a New Soul: Ezekiel, the Exile, and the Torah*, Journal for the Study of the Old Testament, Supplement Series 358 (Sheffield: Sheffield Academic, 2002), 77–78; John Sietze Bergsma, *The Jubilee from Leviticus to Qumran: A History of Interpretation*, Vetus Testamentum Supplements 115 (Leiden: Brill, 2007); Lyons, *From Law to Prophecy*.

[12] Avigdor Hurvitz, *A Linguistic Study of the Relationship between the Priestly Source and the Book of Ezekiel: A New Approach to an Old Problem*, Cahiers de la Revue biblique 20 (Paris: Gabalda, 1982).

[13] Levitt Kohn, *A New Heart*; Lyons, *From Law to Prophecy*.

[14] Jeffrey H. Tigay, *Deuteronomy*, JPS Torah Commentary, vol. 5 (Philadelphia: Jewish Publication Society, 1996), xix–xxiv.

of a clause regulating its application to the crown. He evidently assumes that Leviticus 25, or some other text like it, is already in existence, because he mentions the "year of liberty" as a known entity whose general operation he does not need to explain (Ezek 46:17).

Now let us imagine the reverse scenario. Could Leviticus 25 be dependent on Ezekiel 46? Perusal of the texts shows that this scenario does not make sense. Leviticus does not incorporate or presume any of the specifics of Ezekiel's oracle. Although Leviticus mentions how the Jubilee law should apply in many different situations, application to the king is not mentioned at all. So one would have to presume that the author of Leviticus was in some way influenced by Ezekiel's passing reference to the "year of liberty", but then refused to incorporate any of the specifics of Ezekiel's law into his comprehensive description of the operation of the Jubilee Year (Lev 25:8–55). This seems unlikely.

The situation is similar when careful examination is made of other parallels between Ezekiel and the "Priestly source" or any other Pentateuchal text. Ezekiel reflects heavily the language and concepts of the "Priestly" legislation of the Pentateuch (Lev 12–26, including the "Holiness Source"), as we would expect from a high-ranking member of the priesthood of Jerusalem. However, Ezekiel also incorporates language and concepts from Deuteronomy and from the historical books (a.k.a. the Deuteronomistic history). For example, Ezekiel reuses Deuteronomy's phrase "upon the hills and under every green tree" (Deut 12:2; cf. Ezek 6:13). Perhaps even more important, Ezekiel embraces the *Davidic* covenant, which is a central theme in the historical books (Judges— 2 Kings) but appears *nowhere* in the Pentateuch. Indeed, the Priestly legal materials of the Pentateuch (roughly Ex 24–Num 36) show no influence of Deuteronomy and know nothing of David, Jerusalem, Zion, or any other aspect of the Davidic covenant. This only makes sense, because according to the biblical presentation, the Priestly law of the Pentateuch was given to Israel *before* Deuteronomy and *before* the rise of the Davidic monarchy. Ezekiel, on the other hand, writes *after* the giving of Deuteronomy and *after* the establishment of the Davidic covenant and monarchy, and so his language and theology reflect Priestly, Deuteronomic, and Davidic language and concepts. If the Priestly materials of the Pentateuch were in fact composed in the postexilic period and were dependent on Ezekiel, why do they not reflect any of the Deuteronomic or Davidic aspects of Ezekiel's thought or the late elements in his Hebrew diction?

In light of this, it seems reasonable to conclude that, because Ezekiel already shows familiarity with the Priestly materials of the Pentateuch in the early exile, then the Priestly materials are truly at least preexilic if not older. This agrees with other indications of the antiquity of the Priestly and Holiness materials in the Pentateuch already pointed out by a number of scholars.[15] In this way, the prophetic book of Ezekiel plays a critical (if surprising) role in the historical question of the origins of the Pentateuchal literature.

[15] Jacob Milgrom, *Numbers*, JPS Torah Commentary 4 (New York: Jewish Publication Society, 1989), xxxii–xxxv.

Theological Issues in Ezekiel

How Do We Explain the Unfulfilled Prophecies in Ezekiel?

One last aspect of Ezekiel presents a unique problem when raising the question of its historical origins: namely, the apparently unfulfilled prophecies present in the book.

For example, in one oracle, Ezekiel prophesies that Nebuchadnezzar, king of Babylon, will conquer the city of Tyre and scrape it clean like a bare rock (Ezek 26:1–14; Tyre was built on an island off the coast of Lebanon). Extra-biblical sources indicate that Nebuchadnezzar besieged the city for thirteen years, and eventually the Tyrians submitted to him and became his vassals. Tyre was not captured and destroyed, however. In fact, later on in the book, the prophet Ezekiel himself recognizes this and promises that Nebuchadnezzar will receive from Egypt the booty to reward his army that he should have gained from Tyre (Ezek 29:17–20).

On the one hand, scholars admit that these oracles likely do go back to Ezekiel himself. After all, who would later retroject into Ezekiel's mouth oracles that did not seem to come true? On the other hand, these texts raise a theological problem: If Ezekiel is a prophet of God, how can it be that his words (apparently) did not come true (cf. Deut 18:22)?

The answer is probably to be found in the concept of the *conditional* nature of certain prophecies. From this perspective, God remains sovereign and able to mitigate his punishments based on the behavior of human beings, even if the phrasing of certain prophetic oracles does not explicitly make an appeal for repentance. For example, in the book of Jonah, the prophet's message to Nineveh sounds absolute: "Forty days, and Nineveh shall be overthrown!" (Jon 3:4). Nonetheless, the king and people of Nineveh repent (Jon 3:5–9), and the Lord shows mercy by sparing the city, though it means not "fulfilling" the prophetic word (cf. Jon 4:11). Along similar lines, the prophet Isaiah delivers a seemingly unconditional oracle to King Hezekiah: "Set your house in order; for you shall die, you shall not recover" (Is 38:1). Nonetheless, Hezekiah repents with weeping (Is 38:3), and the Lord responds in mercy, adding fifteen years to his life (Is 38:5). Finally, in the book of Jeremiah, submission to the king of Babylon, God's servant to execute judgment, is explicitly offered as a *condition* for Judah to avoid destruction: "Thus says the LORD, the God of hosts, the God of Israel, *If* you will surrender to the princes of the king of Babylon, *then* your life shall be spared, and this city shall not be burned with fire, and you and your house shall live. But *if* you do not surrender to the princes of the king of Babylon, *then* this city shall be given into the hand of the Chaldeans, and they shall burn it with fire" (Jer 38:17–18).

When we take such parallels into account, we can reasonably suggest that the prediction of destruction of Tyre implicitly assumes Tyre's continued antagonism toward the Babylonian power (Ezek 26:1–14). As the above examples demonstrate, the conditional nature of prophecy is not always explicit. When, after thirteen years of siege, the Tyrians made their submission to Nebuchadnezzar, God apparently had mercy on that city, in a way similar to Nineveh in the book of Jonah. In short, in the Old Testament, when oracles of future judgment are involved, a change in the disposition of the subject of the oracle can in fact prompt a merciful response from God.

Ezekiel on the Imperfect Nature of the Mosaic Covenant

Although Ezekiel has many unique emphases and perspectives, his overarching message remains very close to that of Isaiah and Jeremiah: Israel is condemned for failure to keep the Mosaic covenant, but in the future God will form with them a New Covenant. This twofold movement is important to emphasize, for it shows that already in the Old Testament period the prophets were recognizing the temporary nature of the Mosaic covenant and looking forward to an eschatological covenant that would be truly "new". In order to see this movement, we will take a moment to examine how Ezekiel deals with these respective covenants.

1. *Ezekiel and the Mosaic Covenant*: When threatening judgment on Jerusalem and Judah, Ezekiel is more specific about the offenses for which they are being judged than some of the other prophets. In fact, he lists the people's iniquities in such a way that it is often possible to identify specific commandments of the Pentateuchal law that he has in view (see table):

Ezekiel 22:6–12 with Pentateuchal Source Texts	
Ezek 22:6: " Behold, the princes of Israel in you, every one according to his power, have been bent on shedding blood."	Gen 9:6: "Whoever sheds the blood of man, by man shall his blood be shed; for God made man in his own image" (cf. Ex 20:13; Deut 5:17).
Ezek 22:7: "*Father and mother* are treated with contempt in you;	Ex 20:12: "Honor your *father and your mother*, that your days may be long in the land which the LORD your God gives you" (cf. Deut 5:16).
the *sojourner* suffers extortion in your midst; the *fatherless and the widow* are wronged in you."	Deut 24:17: "You shall not pervert the justice due to the *sojourner* or to the *fatherless*, or take a *widow's* garment in pledge."
Ezek 22:8: "You have despised my *holy things,*	Lev 22:15: "The priests shall not profane the *holy things* of the sons of Israel."
and *profaned* my *sabbaths*."	Ex 31:14: "You shall keep the *sabbath,* because it is holy for you; every one who *profanes* it shall be put to death."
Ezek 22:9: "There are men in you who *slander* to shed blood,	Ex 20:16: "You shall not *bear false witness* against your neighbor" (cf. Deut. 5:20).
and men in you who eat upon the *mountains*;	Deut 12:2: "You shall surely destroy all the places where the nations ... served their gods, upon the high *mountains* and upon the hills."

(continued)

Ezekiel 22:6–12 with Pentateuchal Source Texts (*continued*)	
men commit *lewdness* in your midst."	Lev 18:17: "You shall not uncover the naked-ness of a woman and of her daughter,... they are your near kinswomen; it is *wickedness*."
Ezek 22:10: "In you men uncover their fathers' nakedness;	Lev 18:8: "You shall not uncover the naked-ness of your father's wife; it is your father's nakedness" (cf. 20:11).
in you they humble women who are *unclean* in their *impurity*."	Lev 15:19: " When a woman has a discharge of blood ... she shall be in her *impurity* for seven days.... [24] And if any man lies with her ... he shall be *unclean*."
Ezek 22:11: "One commits abomination with his *neighbor's wife*;	Lev 18:20: "And you shall not lie carnally with your *neighbor's wife*" (cf. Ex 20:17; Deut 5:21; 22:24).
another lewdly defiles his daughter-in-law;	Lev 18:15: "You shall not uncover the naked-ness of your daughter-in-law."
another in you defiles his *sister*, his *father's daughter*."	Lev 18:9: "You shall not uncover the naked-ness of your *sister*, the *daughter of your father*."
Ezek 22:12 "In you men *take bribes* to shed blood;	Ex 23:8: "And you shall *take* no *bribe*" (cf. Deut 16:19; 27:25).
you take *interest* and *increase*	Lev 25:36: "Take no *interest* from [your brother] or *increase*" (cf. Ex. 22:25; Deut 23:19).
and make gain of your neighbors by *extortion*;	Lev 19:13: "You shall not *oppress* your neigh-bor or rob him" (cf. Lev 6:2,4; Deut 24:14).
and you have *forgotten* me, says the Lord God."	Deut 8:18: "You shall *remember* the LORD your God."

Ironically, although Ezekiel shows the greatest familiarity of any of the prophets with the texts of the Mosaic law, he also makes the most explicit acknowledgment of the limitations of the Mosaic covenant. Most notably, in his classic recitation of salvation history, at the point in the recitation when the Deuteronomic covenant is being described (Ezek 20), the prophet refers to the Deuteronomic law in the following way:

> Moreover I gave them statutes that were not good and ordinances by which they could not have life; and I defiled them through their very gifts in making them offer by fire all their first-born, that I might horrify them [literally, "render them desolate"]. (Ezek 20:25–26)

As we saw above, many attempts have been made to identify these "no-good laws" with the regulations of Molech child-sacrifice, as if Ezekiel were attributing pagan child-sacrifice to the Lord! However, the key to understanding the passage is to see that it refers to *the Deuteronomic law*, whose cultic and ethical standards were less rigorous than the laws previously given in the Pentateuch. Ezekiel makes specific reference to the laws governing the consecration of the firstborn or "firstlings". A basic principle of the Old Testament cult, established at the first Passover, was that the firstborn of every man and animal was dedicated to God. Animals were sacrificed, and human beings redeemed. Pentateuchal law prior to Deuteronomy strictly forbade the substitution of other animals to be sacrificed in place of the firstborn (Lev 27:10, 33)—the firstborn itself had to be sacrificed (Lev 27:26). Yet Deuteronomy *permitted* the sale of the firstborn animals and the purchase of substitutes at the site of the sanctuary (Deut 14:23–26!), a clear relaxation of a higher standard of worship demanded in Leviticus. In Ezekiel 20:25–26, then, the prophet uses hyperbolic language to describe how God allowed the law to be "dumbed down" for the second generation of Israel in the wilderness.

The Deuteronomic law also introduced other practices that were far from an ethical ideal: *herem* war against the Canaanites (Deut 20:16–18), captive wives (Deut 21:10–14), and permission to divorce (Deut 24:1–4). From the perspective of the so-called "Priestly" or "Holiness" legislation (that is, the laws of Leviticus and Numbers), Deuteronomy, the laws given to the second generation in the wilderness, comprised statutes that were "not good" from both a cultic and ethical standpoint. Thus, although Ezekiel stands in the tradition of the "prophet like Moses", he is aware that there are limitations to the covenant Moses mediated. It is not surprising, then, that in his vision of the new Temple (Ezek 40–48), not a single law that Ezekiel proposes for the eschatological age is identical to the analogous statute found in the Pentateuch. This disparity between the laws of Ezekiel's eschatological age and those of Moses almost prevented the book from being received as canonical by the rabbis. In more recent times, the disparity has been explained by hypothesizing that Ezekiel is an early form of the Priestly law of the Pentateuch. That explanation, however, is unlikely for reasons mentioned above. A better reason for the disparity is that Ezekiel is conscious of the fact that the Mosaic law is imperfect and knows that its specifics must be altered in the age to come.

2. *Ezekiel and the New Covenant*: Indeed, the limitations of the Old Covenant make necessary an eventual intervention by God to establish a New Covenant without the impediments of the old. For Ezekiel, the future age of salvation will be marked by the establishment of a "covenant of peace" or "everlasting covenant" between Israel and the Lord (cf. Ezek 34–37). Drawing together the implications of several of the prophet's individual oracles, we can create a synthetic picture of his view of this coming epoch:

1. *New Priesthood*: The corrupt leadership ("shepherds") of God's people will be replaced by God himself as Shepherd of Israel (Ezek 34:15) together with the Davidic king (Ezek 34:23); yet, curiously, there will be only one shepherd (Ezek 34:23).

2. *New Creation*: There will be a restoration of the conditions of the initial creation, as blessing, rain, fruitfulness, peace between man and animals, and Edenic conditions in general will prevail around God's "hill" (Ezek 34:26–28; 36:11, 30, 35; and so on). Even those who die before these blessings are attained will be resurrected so that they may share in the eschatological blessings of the Lord (Ezek 37:1–14).

3. *New Exodus*: God's people will be regathered from their places of exile and brought to the Promised Land in a new exodus (Ezek 34:11; 36:24).

4. *New Spirit*: Adapting the Mosaic prophecy of the "circumcision of the heart" after the exile (Deut 30:6; circumcision is a covenant ritual), there will be a sprinkling of "clean water" (Ezek 36:25) associated with the forgiveness of sins (Ezek 36:25, 29) and the gift of a "new heart" and a "new spirit" (Ezek 36:26)—namely, God's own Spirit, which will enable obedience to the will of God (Ezek 35:27) and a reestablishment of covenant communion ("You shall be my people, and I will be your God" [Ezek 36:28]).

5. *New Covenant*: The twelve tribes of Israel will be restored under the leadership of the Davidic king, who will facilitate a "covenant of peace", an "everlasting covenant" involving the restoration of the blessing of the new creation (cf. Ezek 37:15–28).

6. *New Temple*: God's Temple and presence will be restored in the midst of the people on a scale far beyond anything previously experienced, where they will serve as the center of life and blessing for all (Ezek 40–48).

Clearly, the idea of both continuity and discontinuity between the Old and New Covenants is *not* something that was only created during the New Covenant period; it was something spoken of by the prophets centuries before Christianity ever came on the scene.

The Liturgical Hope of Ezekiel and the Future Temple

Especially in North American Christianity, a pressing question remains: Is Ezekiel's Temple vision intended to be a literal description? Should believers expect a restored Israelite state in the end times, divided into tribal territories, with a rebuilt stone Temple in Jerusalem according to the prophet's dimensions? Political attitudes toward the modern state of Israel are often linked to this theological question.

Although many readers of the text have (understandably) interpreted Ezekiel's prophecy with reference to an earthly temple and a geographical and political restoration, certain factors suggest that Ezekiel's Temple vision was never intended to be realized literally. For example:

1. *The Symbolic Size of the New Temple*: For one thing, the dimensions of the Temple make it too large to fit on the site of the Temple Mount in Jerusalem. Moreover, not only are the dimensions of the Temple overly large, but they also may be stylized. The modern commentator Walther Zimmerli has noted that the macrodimensions of the Temple and its precincts were all *multiples of fifty*, a number that in Israelite tradition signified the Jubilee Year and the restoration of

peace and freedom with God and man (Lev 25:8–55). He suggests the Temple was an architectural sign of freedom, a kind of "architectural Jubilee", implying that the freedom and restoration of the people in the future would be found through worship in God's presence.[16] Furthermore, although the prophet provides a fairly comprehensive floor plan for the Temple precincts, he specifies very few vertical dimensions of the Temple or associated buildings. Thus, the plan provided was not intended to be complete and comprehensive; any actual construction would involve a great deal of guesswork.

2. *The Symbolic Location of the New Temple*: Intriguingly, the site of the new Temple is in the geographic center of the land of Israel (Ezek 48:1–29), which would place it closer to Samaria and the tribe of Ephraim, not near Jerusalem, which is far to the south. Yet there are no signs that Ezekiel wishes to abandon Jerusalem: in the rest of the book he speaks of its restoration. One may conclude, then, that in the Temple vision of chapters 40–48, the prophet is foreseeing something more supernatural than merely the restoration of the earthly city of Jerusalem.

3. *The Miraculous Nature of the New Temple*: Perhaps most significant of all, there are supernatural features of the Temple that point far beyond the ordinary rebuilding of the earthly Temple. For example, the river of life that flows from the Temple grows continuously deeper, although no tributaries flow into it (Ezek 47:1–16). It supernaturally causes salt water to become fresh (Ezek 47:8–10), except when salt water is useful to the local human population, in which case it is left alone (Ezek 47:11). The geology and hydrology of the Holy Land could never permit a natural river to gush from the top of the Temple Mount and flow into the Dead Sea.

Together, these factors suggest that Ezekiel's Temple is intended to represent a miraculous and *eschatological* reality, not merely a natural stone building.[17] However, in Ezekiel's day, it was by no means clear how this eschatological hope would be actualized in history. What was clear was that the liturgy of this new Temple would be truly new, without the limitations of the old.

Ezekiel in the Living Tradition

Like the other major prophets—Isaiah, Jeremiah, and Daniel—the book of Ezekiel has received a substantial amount of attention in the living tradition of the Church. From the very beginning of Christianity, its many symbolic visions— the four angelic creatures of the chariot-throne of God, the description of the "fall" of the Satanic prince of Tyre, the mysterious "east gate" of the Temple that remained closed, the river of miraculous water flowing from the side of the new Temple—all of these were interpreted as prophecies of realities that came to pass in the New Covenant. In stark contrast to contemporary preaching—which largely neglects the book of Ezekiel, despite its substantial

---

[16] Bergsma, *Jubilee from Leviticus*, 189–90.

[17] G. K. Beale, *The Temple and the Church's Mission: A Biblical Theology of the Dwelling Place of God*, New Studies in Biblical Theology 17 (Downers Grove, Ill.: InterVarsity Press, 2004), 335–64.

influence on the contemporary Lectionary—this prophet garnered a great deal of attention in antiquity from such figures as Origen of Alexandria, Pope Gregory the Great, and Theodoret of Cyrus, all of whom composed lengthy series of homilies entirely focused on the book of Ezekiel.[18] In what follows, we will take a few moments to highlight some of the more significant portions of Ezekiel and how they influenced Christian worship and theology.

The Influence of Ezekiel in the New Testament

More than all of the rest of the New Testament combined, the Gospel of John and the book of Revelation are both heavily influenced by the book of Ezekiel. For example, in the Gospel of John, in the very midst of the Feast of Tabernacles, which involved rituals anticipating the eschatological Temple as the source of water for all Israel, Jesus identifies *himself* as the source of eschatological water by paraphrasing Ezekiel 47 and declaring: "Out of his heart shall flow rivers of living water" (Jn 7:37–38). The Fourth Evangelist clearly sees a sign of the river of water flowing from the new Temple when he interrupts the Gospel to describe the flow of water and blood from the side of Christ on the Cross (Jn 19:34). Along similar lines, the book of Revelation, like Ezekiel before it, ends with a vision of an angel measuring the new Jerusalem and the new "Temple" (Rev 21–22). At the very climax of this vision, John describes a river of "the water of life" flowing from the "throne of God and the Lamb" in the heavenly city of Jerusalem, which is also the bride of Christ (Rev 21:1–2; 22:1).

As these interpretations of Ezekiel make clear, the Church does not anticipate an eschatological rebuilding of a stone Temple in Jerusalem, complete with reimplementation of the Mosaic animal sacrifices. God gave Ezekiel and his contemporaries visions of a future Temple and liturgy employing architectural, ritual, and geographical language they could understand. However, the disparity between the specifics of Ezekiel's vision and its realization in Christ and the Church is due to the fact, not that the realization *fails to fulfill*, but rather that it *over-fulfills* the vision; that is, it *exceeds all older categories in surpassing expectations*. The sanctuary of the Body of Christ is so much larger, more accessible, more "central" to the people of God; the sacrifice of the Body and Blood of the new Davidic King is so far superior to animal offerings; the river of living water, which is the Holy Spirit conveyed through the sacraments, is so far superior to a geographical river flowing into the Dead Sea, that the new economy God inaugurates exceeds the promises made to the prophet.

The Four Creatures of the Chariot-Throne and the Four Evangelists

Perhaps the most "visible" sign of Ezekiel's role in the living tradition can be found in the spiritual interpretation given by the early Church Fathers to the

---

[18] See Origen. *Homilies 1–14 on Ezekiel*, trans. Thomas P. Scheck, Ancient Christian Writers 62 (Mahwah, N.J.: Paulist Press, 2010); Gregory the Great, *Homilies of St. Gregory the Great on the Book of the Prophet Ezekiel*, trans. Theodosia Gray (Etna, Calif.: Center for Traditionalist Orthodox Studies, 1990); Theodoret of Cyrus, *Commentary on the Prophet Ezekiel*, vol. 2 of *Commentary on the Prophets*, trans. Robert C. Hill (Brookline, Mass.: Holy Cross Orthodox Press, 2007).

vision of the "chariot-throne" (Ezek 1). In the tradition of the Church, it was extremely popular to interpret the four creatures associated with the throne— the man, the lion, the ox, and the eagle—with the four evangelists. Although there was some debate about exactly which creature was to be assigned to which Gospel, it was Pope Gregory the Great's identification from his series of homilies on Ezekiel that became the standard interpretation in the West:

> The preface of each Gospel avers that these four winged creatures denote the four holy Evangelists. Because he began from the generations of humankind, *Matthew* is justly represented by a *man*; because of the crying in the wilderness, *Mark* is rightly indicated by a *lion*; because he started from sacrifice, *Luke* is well described as an *ox*; and because he begins with the Divinity of the Word, *John* is worthily signified by an *eagle*, he who says, "In the beginning was the Word ..." (John 1:1) while he stretched toward the very substance of divinity, he fixed his eye on the sun as if in the fashion of an eagle.[19]

Although many Christians today would easily be able to identify the four beasts with each of the evangelists, it seems less likely that most are aware that these identifications are rooted in this spiritual interpretation of the chariot vision in Ezekiel or in the similar vision of John in the Apocalypse (see Rev 4:6–7).

The Prince of Tyre and the Fall of Satan

A second area in which Ezekiel profoundly influenced the living tradition of the Church was in its angelology, with specific reference to doctrines about the creation and fall of Satan. A remarkable number of early Church Fathers interpreted the oracle against the prince of Tyre (Ezek 28), not merely as a figurative comparison between the Gentile king and the devil, but also as a source of information about the fall of Satan. Consider, for example, the catechetical lectures of Cyril of Jerusalem:

> The devil then is the first author of sin, and the father of the wicked.... [H]aving been created good, he has of his own free will become a devil, and received that name from his action. For being an Archangel he was afterwards called a devil from his slandering: from being a good servant of God he has become rightly named Satan; for "Satan" is interpreted *the adversary*. And this is not my teaching, but that of the inspired prophet Ezekiel: for he takes up a lamentation over him and says, *Thou wast a seal of likeness, and a crown of beauty; in the Paradise of God wast thou born*: and soon after, *Thou wast born blameless in thy days, from the day in which thou wast created, until thine iniquities were found in thee* [Ezek 28:12–13].[20]

Notice here how Cyril derives not only an account of Satan's fall from the book of Ezekiel, but also the teaching that he was created good as an "archangel" but freely chose evil. In other words, Satan is a corrupted creature, not some kind of

---

[19] Gregory the Great, *Homilies on Ezekiel* 1.4.1, pp. 40–41.
[20] Cyril of Jerusalem, *Catechetical Lectures* 2.4, in *NPNF2* 7:9.

"evil principle" eternally opposed to the "good principle", as in certain dualistic world views. Other Church Fathers used Ezekiel in similar ways when defending these teachings about the origin and fall of Satan.[21]

The Closed Gate of the Temple and the Virgin Birth of Christ

After the image of the four beasts of the chariot, perhaps the most popular use of Ezekiel in the living tradition is the interpretation of his vision of the east "gate" of the new Temple that shall "remain shut" (Ezek 44:1–3) as a prophecy of the virginal conception and birth of Jesus. Although modern readers may find such an interpretation extremely puzzling, it was *the* standard interpretation of Ezekiel's vision, in both Eastern and Western Church Fathers. Consider the following:

> Some people nobly understand the Virgin Mary as the door that is closed, who before and after birth remained a virgin, through which only the Lord God of Israel enters.[22]

> It is very likely that these words [in Ezek 44:1–3] refer to the womb of the Virgin, through which no one enters and from which no one departs other than the only one who is the Lord.[23]

Indeed, the fourth-century writer Rufinus of Aquileia goes a bit farther and uses the prophecy to defend the *perpetual* virginity of Mary—before, during, and forever after the birth of Christ:

> What could be said with such evident reference to the inviolate preservation of the Virgin's condition? That Gate of Virginity was closed; through it the Lord God of Israel entered; through it He came forth from the Virgin's womb into this world; and the Virgin-state being preserved inviolate, *the gate of the Virgin remained closed for ever.*[24]

What are we to make of these examples of patristic exegesis? Above all, it is critical to note that the Church Fathers are *assuming* that their readers understand that the new Jerusalem spoken of by the prophets—the miraculous "bride" and "mother", the "daughter of Zion" (the Temple-city) who gives birth without pangs in Isaiah 65–66, for example—is a type of the Virgin Mary, miraculous mother of the Messiah. Once this identification is granted, then and only then can we understand how it is that they saw in the various figures and symbols— such as the closed east gate of the New Temple—prophecies that were fulfilled in Christ and his mother. In other words, in this instance, the Mariology of the

---

[21] For example, Tertullian, *Against Marcion* 2.10; Augustine, *City of God* 11.15.

[22] Jerome, *Commentary on Ezekiel* 13.44.1–3, in Kenneth Stevenson and Michael Glerup, *Ezekiel, Daniel*, Old Testament 13, Ancient Christian Commentary on Scripture, ed. Thomas C. Oden (Downers Grove, Ill.: InterVarsity Press, 2008), 40.

[23] Theodoret of Cyrus, *Commentary on Ezekiel* 16.44, in Stevenson and Glerup, *Ezekiel, Daniel*, 40.

[24] Rufinus of Aquileia, *A Commentary on the Apostles' Creed* 9, in NPNF2 3:547.

Fathers ("daughter Zion" = Mary) "precedes" and explains their Christology (closed gate = Virgin Birth).

The Book of Ezekiel in the Lectionary

Ezekiel is a priest, and from beginning to end his prophecy is liturgical and Temple-centered. The first part of the book may be understood as an explanation for why the presence of the Lord abandoned the Jerusalem Temple (Ezek 1–11), and the final part of the book as an account of the conditions that will prevail when the new Temple arrives and the presence of the Lord returns (Ezek 40–48). In a way, the book of Ezekiel follows the general flow of the book of Exodus: both begin with the call of a great prophet (Ex 1–3; Ezek 1–3), recount his tumultuous ministry to stiff-necked Israel (Ex 4–34; Ezek 4–39), and end with the establishment of a new sanctuary and the inauguration of a new liturgy (Ex 35–40; Ezek 40–48).

Recognizing the inherently liturgical focus of Ezekiel, the current Roman Lectionary is generous in its use of Ezekiel in the Liturgy of the Word, selecting texts for the first reading of Sundays and holy days that either (1) display clear typological parallels between the person, mission, and message of Ezekiel and those of Jesus Christ as presented in the Gospel reading or (2) provide a foundation for understanding the salvation-historical roots of some aspect of the New Covenant economy.

The most heavily used text of Ezekiel in the liturgy is the prophecy of the "sprinkling with clean water" that will effect a "new heart" and a "new spirit" (Ezek 36:16–28, esp. vv. 24–28). The Church understands this passage, the functional equivalent of Jeremiah's promise of the New Covenant (Jer 31:31–34), as a prophecy of the reality of baptism, which initiates the disciple of Christ into the New Covenant by the bestowal of the Holy Spirit. Accordingly, this text is the final and climactic reading from the Old Testament during *the Easter Vigil*, as it prepares the gathered baptizands and worshippers to understand the roots of baptism already in the Old Testament.

Next in prominence is the vision of dry bones (Ezek 37:1–14), which is read (in part or in whole) at Pentecost and on the Fifth Sunday of Lent (with the raising of Lazarus, Jn 11:1–45). As we saw above, one sense of the vision of dry bones is a foreshadowing of the restoration of Israel. The event of Pentecost (Acts 2:1–11) is the restoration of Israel in principle: the twelve apostles are the twelve new patriarchs, around whom the gathered exiles of Israel reform the nucleus of a new, spiritual Israel, now empowered by the outpouring of the Spirit promised by the prophets (see Acts 2:5–11). Another sense of the vision of dry bones is bodily resurrection of the dead: this meaning is highlighted when the passage is paired with the raising of Lazarus (Jn 11:1–45).

Also prominent is Ezekiel's prophecy of God as Shepherd of Israel (Ezek 34:11–16), proclaimed on the Feast of Christ the King, the climax of the liturgical calendar, where it complements the parable of the sheep and the goats (Mt 25:31–46). In this way, the Lectionary declares Christ to be divine, the Lord, the Shepherd-King and judge of Israel and the nations. The same text is available as an option on numerous other liturgical occasions that focus on the gift of pastors (literally "shepherds") to the Church or the tender love of God for his people, his "flock".

Finally, we may mention the vision of the river of life proclaimed on the Feast of the Lateran Basilica (November 9) and for the dedication of a church or for infant baptism (Ezek 47:1–12). Although church buildings are not the new "Temple of God" *per se*, they may be understood as sanctuaries from which flow the river of the sacraments, which is also the flow of the Holy Spirit to the people of God (cf. Jn 7:38–39). Since the Lateran Basilica is the home church of the bishop of Rome, as successor of Peter, it is a fitting symbol of how in the Church universal, manifested visibly through her places of worship, Ezekiel's vision finds its fulfillment.

Readings from Ezekiel in the Lectionary and Liturgy of the Hours on Sundays, Feast Days, Liturgical Seasons, and Other Occasions			
MSO= Masses for Special Occasions; *OM*= Optional Memorial; *VM*=Votive Mass; *Rit*=Ritual; *LH*=Liturgy of the Hours			
Passage	Description	Occasion	Explanation
2:2–5	Ezekiel is commissioned to preach to "a nation of rebels" who are "impudent and stubborn".	*14th Sun. in OT (B)*	This passage is paired with Mark 6:1–6, Jesus' rejection in his "own country" (i.e., Nazareth), setting up a typological relationship between Ezekiel and Jesus, both priest-prophets called "Son of Man".
3:16–21	God makes Ezekiel a "watchman" for Israel. If he does not warn them of their sins, he will be responsible for their demise.	*MSO*: For City, Country, Public Officials, Progress of Peoples, opt. 10	By implication, public officials have a "watchman's" role for the public; they must exercise moral judgment and warn the populace of social evil that will result in God's punishment.
3:17–21	See above.	*OM*: St. John Vianney; Common of Pastors, opt. 8	This passage is suited to liturgical memorials of pastors who spoke clearly of their flocks' sins and motivated them to repentance.
17:22–24	The Lord will plant a sprig on the mountain of Israel that will become a great tree where will dwell all beasts and birds.	*11th Sun. in OT (B)*	The oracle of Ezekiel speaks figuratively of the kingdom of David and the reestablishment of the Davidic king, shedding light on Jesus' parable of the mustard seed (Mk 4:26–34). In the New Covenant, the kingdom of David and the kingdom of God are one.
18:21–28	The Lord takes no pleasure in the death of the wicked. If the wicked repents, he will be saved; if the righteous sins, he will die.	Fri., 1st Week of Lent	This passage serves as an exhortation to repent at the beginning of Lent, and as an encouragement that mercy is possible even for the previously hardened sinner.

(continued)

Readings from Ezekiel in the Lectionary and Liturgy of the Hours on Sundays, Feast Days, Liturgical Seasons, and Other Occasions (*continued*)

MSO = Masses for Special Occasions; *OM* = Optional Memorial;
VM = Votive Mass; *Rit* = Ritual; *LH* = Liturgy of the Hours

Passage	Description	Occasion	Explanation
18:21–23, 30–32	See above, plus concluding exhortation to "repent and turn from all your transgressions … turn, and live!"	*MSO*: For Remission of Sins, opt. 2	This passage emphasizes the mercy of God and the urgency of repentance in the liturgical context focused on the remission of sins.
18:25–28	God will punish or reward each man for his deeds, whether he repents or backslides, yet Israel regards this as unfair.	*26th Sun. in OT (A)*	Jesus teaches that repentant tax collectors and prostitutes will enter the kingdom before hypocritical scribes and Pharisees, which seems wrong to Jesus' contemporaries. So we see a continuity in God's justice and Israel's recalcitrance across the testaments.
33:7–9	God makes Ezekiel the watchman for Israel. He must warn the wicked man or else be responsible for his demise.	*23rd Sun. in OT (A)*	Paired with Jesus' instructions on dealing with the offending brother (Mt 18:15–20), this reading emphasizes frank correction among members of the household of faith.
34:11–12, 15–17	The Lord himself promises to search out his sheep and be their shepherd. He will judge between sheep, rams, and he-goats.	*34th Sun. in OT: Christ the King (A)*	This passage complements the parable of the sheep and the goats (Mt 25:31–46), highlighting Jesus' identity as the Lord, universal King, and final judge.
34:11–16	The Lord himself will shepherd the Israelites. He will gather them from the nations, feed them on the mountains of Israel. He will seek the lost, bind up the crippled, strengthen the weak, curb the strong.	Fri. after 2nd Sun. after Pentecost: Sacred Heart-C; *OM*: St. Norbert; St. Sylvester I; Common of Pastors, opt. 9; *MSO*: For the Church; *VM*: Sacred Heart	On the Feast of the Sacred Heart, this passage emphasizes the tender love of God toward his people. In saintly pastors of the Church (e.g., Norbert and Sylvester), we see manifestations of God the Good Shepherd.
36:16–17a, 18–28	The Lord will gather the Israelites from exile, sprinkle clean water on	*Easter Vigil (7th Reading)*	The Church sees Ezekiel's oracle as a prophecy of baptism, the "sprinkling of clean water" that cleanses Israel and the nations from their sin, conveying

(*continued*)

Readings from Ezekiel in the Lectionary and Liturgy of the Hours on Sundays, Feast Days, Liturgical Seasons, and Other Occasions (*continued*)			
MSO = Masses for Special Occasions; *OM* = Optional Memorial; *VM* = Votive Mass; *Rit* = Ritual; *LH* = Liturgy of the Hours			
Passage	**Description**	**Occasion**	**Explanation**
	them, and grant them a new heart and a new spirit, so they will observe his law.		the Holy Spirit, which renews the heart and enables fulfillment of the law of love.
36:16–28	See above.	*LH*: 2nd reading, Easter Sunday	See above.
36:24–28	See above.	*Rit*: Christian Initiation, opt. 9; Infant Baptism, opt. 2; Confirmation, opt. 4; *MSO*: For the Laity, opt. 1; For Christian Unity, opt. 2; *LH*: Sat., Week VI, Morn. Prayer, Canticle; Canticle II for Vigils in Lent	In addition to an application to baptism, the language of "putting my spirit within you" is also applicable to confirmation. The new heart, new spirit, and covenant relationship are privileges common to all the laity. The gathering "from all the countries" bespeaks the unity of the people of God.
37:1–14	Ezekiel sees the resurrection of the valley of dry bones. God will raise the Israelites from their graves and put his Spirit within them.	*Pentecost Sunday: Vigil Mass (Opt. 3)*	The assembly of the twelve apostles, who are the twelve patriarchs of the reconstituted tribes of Israel, receive the Holy Spirit at Pentecost and preach to the crowds of Jews gathered from every part of the diaspora. In light of Ezekiel, we recognize Pentecost as the "resurrection" of Israel.
37:12–14	God will raise the Israelites from their graves and put his Spirit within them. They will know that "I AM the LORD" when "I raise you from your graves."	*5th Sun. of Lent (A)*	Complements the raising of Lazarus (Jn 11:1–45), the penultimate "sign" in John's Gospel before the Passion and Resurrection. In light of Ezekiel, the raising of Lazarus proves that Jesus is the LORD, since he can raise Israelites from their graves.
37:15–19, 21b–22, 26–28	Ezekiel joins the two "sticks" of the houses of Israel and	*MSO*: For Christian Unity, opt. 3	The split between Israel and Judah under the Old Covenant is a type of the divisions within Christianity,

(*continued*)

Readings from Ezekiel in the Lectionary and Liturgy of the Hours on Sundays, Feast Days, Liturgical Seasons, and Other Occasions (*continued*) *MSO* = Masses for Special Occasions; *OM* = Optional Memorial; *VM* = Votive Mass; *Rit* = Ritual; *LH* = Liturgy of the Hours			
Passage	Description	Occasion	Explanation
	Judah as a sign of the reunification of God's people.		which God promises one day to overcome.
37:21–28	The Lord will gather the Israelites from all the nations of their exile, bring them to their own land, unify them, grant them a covenant of peace, and dwell in their midst forever.	Sat., 5th Week of Lent	Near the end of Lent, this important prophecy helps us to understand what has been fulfilled in the New Covenant. It corresponds to the Gospel (Jn 11:45–56), where Caiaphas unwittingly prophesies that Jesus "should die for the nation, and not for the nation only, but to gather into one the children of God who are scattered abroad".
43:1–2, 4–7a	Ezekiel sees the presence of the Lord return to the Temple and take up permanent abode there.	Common of the Dedication of a Church, opt. 4	The physical church building, as the perpetual repository of the reserved Body of Christ, is a "home" or "dwelling place" of God's presence in perpetuity.
47:1–2, 8–9, 12	Ezekiel sees the river of life flowing from the Temple threshold, bestowing life wherever it reaches.	Lateran Basilica (Nov. 9); Common of the Dedication of a Church, opt. 5	In the Gospel (Jn 2:13–22), Jesus' body is identified as the New Temple, from which the river of the Holy Spirit flows (Jn 7:37–38; 19:34). Nonetheless, the physical church building, as the location of the celebration of the sacraments, is by analogy a "Temple" from which flows the "rivers of living waters" (the Holy Spirit in the sacraments).
47:1–9, 12	See above. The river gets continually deeper. On its banks grow trees for food and healing.	Tues., 4th Week of Lent; *Rit*: Infant Baptism, opt. 3	The Church understands the "rivers of living waters" as a baptismal type. Combined with the healing at Bethesda (Jn 5:1–3, 5–16), another baptismal type, it serves to catechize baptizands during Lent.

The Church reads Ezekiel semi-continuously at weekday Mass (Year II, Weeks 19–20) and in the Liturgy of the Hours (Ordinary Time, Weeks 24–26). With one exception (Ezek 28:1–10), every passage read in Mass is read also in the Liturgy of the Hours, which invariably employs longer readings including more of the context for each passage. The selections are meant to provide the faithful with a representative exposure to the prophet and his life, ministry, and message.

			Reading of Ezekiel for Daily Mass: Ordinary Time, Year II: Weeks 19–20
Week	Day	Passage Read	Description
19	M	1:2–5, 24–28c	Ezekiel sees the appearance of the glory of the Lord riding upon the cherubim-throne.
19	Tu	2:8—3:4	Ezekiel is commissioned to speak by eating the divine scroll written on front and back.
19	W	9:1–7; 10:18–22	A vision: Jerusalem's faithful are marked with an X; the rest are slain, starting from the Temple. The cherubim-throne of God's presence leaves the Temple for good.
19	Th	12:1–12	God commands Ezekiel to exit the city dressed like, and in the manner of, an exile, as a sign of Jerusalem's impending exile.
19	F	16:1–15, 59–63	Israel was a young maiden who grew up poor but was betrothed and indulged by God. Then she played the harlot and was cast away, but God will renew his covenant with her once more.
19	Sa	18:1–10, 13b, 30–32	"The soul that sins shall die": each one will receive from God as his actions merit. Repent, for God takes no pleasure in the death of the wicked.
20	M	24:15–23	Ezekiel witnesses his wife die without mourning; likewise will Israel watch the destruction of the Temple yet not be able to mourn.
20	Tu	28:1–10	The Lord pronounces judgment on the king of Tyre.
20	W	34:1–11	The Lord judges the wicked shepherds of Israel and will himself come to shepherd his flock.
20	Th	36:23–28	The Lord will gather Israel from the nations, sprinkle clean water on them, and give them a new heart and a new spirit to obey him.
20	F	37:1–14	Ezekiel sees the valley of dry bones brought to life; these are those from the house of Israel raised from their graves.
20	Sa	43:1–7ab	Ezekiel sees the glory of the Lord return to the Temple.

			Ezekiel in the Office of Readings for the Liturgy of the Hours, Ordinary Time, Weeks 24–25
Week	Day	Passage Read	Description
24	Su	1:3–13, 22–28	Ezekiel beholds the cherubim bearing the throne of the Lord.
24	M	2:8—3:11, 17–21	Ezekiel eats the divine scroll and receives his prophetic commission from God to be a "watchman" for the house of Israel.
24	Tu	8:1–6, 16—9:11	In a vision, Ezekiel is taken to the Temple and witnesses the abominations practiced there. The innocent are marked with an X, but the violators are slain by angels of judgment.
24	W	10:18–22; 11:14–25	In a vision, Ezekiel sees the throne of God's presence, borne by cherubim, arise and depart from Jerusalem.

(continued)

		Passage	
Week	Day	Read	Description
24	Th	12:1–16	As a public sign, Ezekiel dresses for exile, digs through the city wall, and departs as if into exile. This will be the fate of all in Jerusalem.
24	F	16:3–63 (selections)	Jerusalem is a young woman who grew up to be betrothed by the Lord, only to turn to harlotry. The Lord will punish her, but finally take her back and renew his covenant with her.
24	Sa	18:1–13, 20–32	No longer shall anyone die for his father's sin, but each one will receive the reward or punishment his deeds deserve.
25	Su	24:15–27	Ezekiel's wife dies; he does not mourn. It is a sign: so the Judeans will not mourn when Jerusalem is destroyed before their eyes.
25	M	34:1–6, 11–16, 23–31	The Lord rebukes the evil shepherds of Israel and promises that he himself, and David his servant, shall shepherd his sheep in days to come.
25	Tu	36:16–36	The Lord will sprinkle clean water on Israel and grant them a new heart and new spirit so they will obey his statutes.
25	W	37:1–14	Ezekiel sees a valley of dry bones restored to life, a symbol of Israel.
25	Th	37:15–28	Prophecy of the re-union of the "two sticks", the house of Israel and the house of Judah, under "my servant David"
25	F	40:1–4; 43:1–12; 44:6–9	Ezekiel sees a vision of the new Temple. God's glory returns to it from the east. No longer will it be defiled by the kings and by foreigners.
25	Sa	47:1–12	Ezekiel sees the river of life flowing out from the Temple, bringing life and healing everywhere it flows.

Ezekiel in the Office of Readings for the Liturgy of the Hours, Ordinary Time, Weeks 24–25 (continued)

Conclusion

Ezekiel is often overshadowed by his fellow prophets Isaiah and Jeremiah. Nevertheless, this "major prophet" makes major contributions to the progress of salvation history toward the New Covenant. The historical and literary detail of his book provide a helpful snapshot of the development of Israelite theology and literature at the end of the First Temple period and the beginning of the exile. Moreover, Ezekiel's vision of the eschatological age of covenant renewal reaffirms and develops the eschatological and messianic hopes found in the other prophets—the new exodus, the new creation, the new Temple, and the New Covenant—while incorporating a strong emphasis on renewal of the sanctuary and liturgy that the New Testament understands as fulfilled in Christ and the Church.

For Further Reading

Commentaries and Studies on Ezekiel

Block, Daniel Isaac. *The Book of Ezekiel.* 2 vols. New International Commentary on the Old Testament 20–21. Grand Rapids, Mich.: Eerdmans, 1997–1998.

Boadt, Lawrence. *Ezekiel's Oracles against Egypt: A Literary and Philological Study of Ezekiel 29–32*. Biblia et orientalia 37. Rome: Pontifical Biblical Institute, 1980.

Chisholm, Robert B. *Handbook on the Prophets*. Grand Rapids, Mich.: Baker Academic, 2002. (See pp. 231–90.)

Greenberg, Moshe. *Ezekiel 1–20*. Anchor Bible 22. New York: Doubleday, 1983.

Zimmerli, Walther. *Ezekiel: A Commentary on the Book of the Prophet Ezekiel*. 2 vols. Translated by Ronald E. Clements and James D. Martin. Hermeneia. Philadelphia: Fortress Press, 1979–1983.

Historical Issues in Ezekiel

Bergsma, John Sietze. *The Jubilee from Leviticus to Qumran: A History of Interpretation*. Supplements to *Vetus Testamentum* 115. Leiden and Boston: Brill, 2007. (See pp. 177–90.)

Hurvitz, Avi. *A Linguistic Study of the Relationship between the Priestly Source and the Book of Ezekiel: A New Approach to an Old Problem*. Cahiers de la Revue biblique 20. Paris: Gabalda, 1982.

Levitt Kohn, Risa. *A New Heart and a New Soul: Ezekiel, the Exile and the Torah*. Journal for the Study of the Old Testament, Supplement Series 358. Sheffield: Sheffield Academic, 2002.

Lyons, Michael A. *From Law to Prophecy: Ezekiel's Use of the Holiness Code*. Library of Hebrew Bible/Old Testament Studies 507. London: T&T Clark, 2009.

Tigay, Jeffrey H. *JPS Torah Commentary: Deuteronomy*. Vol 5. Philadelphia: Jewish Publication Society, 1996.

Theological Issues in Ezekiel

Beale, G.K. *The Temple and the Church's Mission: A Biblical Theology of the Dwelling Place of God*. New Studies in Biblical Theology 17. Downers Grove, Ill.: Apollos: Inter-Varsity Press, 2004.

Hahn, Scott W., and John S. Bergsma. "What Laws Were Not Good? A Canonical Approach to the Theological Problem of Ezekiel 20:25–26". *Journal of Biblical Literature* 123 (2004): 201–18.

Joyce, Paul M. "King and Messiah in Ezekiel". Pages 323–37 in *King and Messiah in Israel and the Ancient Near East*. Edited by John Day. *Journal for the Study of the Old Testament*, Supplement Series 270. Sheffield: Sheffield Academic Press, 1998.

Ezekiel in the Living Tradition

Gregory the Great, Saint. *Homilies of Saint Gregory the Great on the Book of the Prophet Ezekiel*. Translated by Theodosia Gray. Etna, Calif.: Center for Traditionalist Orthodox Studies, 1990.

Origen. *Homilies 1–14 on Ezekiel*. Translated by Thomas P. Scheck. Ancient Christian Writers 62. Mahwah, N.J.: Paulist Press, 2010.

Stevenson, Kenneth, and Michael Glerup. *Ezekiel, Daniel*. Old Testament 13 of Ancient Christian Commentary on Scripture. Edited by Thomas C. Oden. Downers Grove, Ill.: InterVarsity Press, 2008. (See pp. 1–147.)

Theodoret of Cyrus. *Commentary on the Prophet Ezekiel*. Vol. 2 of *Commentary on the Prophets*. Translated by Robert C. Hill. Brookline: Holy Cross Orthodox Press, 2007.

35. DANIEL

Introduction

The book of Daniel is one of the most influential—and controversial—of the Old Testament prophetic writings. The book's literary form, canonical location, genre, date of composition, textual history, and interpretation have been—and continue to be—matters of sometimes heated dispute. Nonetheless, the influence of Daniel on the New Testament, the early Church, and Christian theology and especially eschatology is undeniable. From the time of Jesus himself, whose two most characteristic teachings—the coming of "the kingdom of God" and the "the Son of man"—are both strongly *Danielic* (see Dan 2:44–45; 7:13–14), the book of Daniel has exerted powerful influence on the shape of the Christian faith.

In the Jewish tradition, the book of Daniel—whose name means "God is my judge" (Hebrew *dāniyē'l*)—is placed in the third part of the Scriptures, the Writings (Hebrew *ketuvim*), and not in the second part, the Prophets (Hebrew *nevi'im*). Some speculate that this classification is due to the late origins of the book; perhaps the prophetic canon was considered closed by the time Daniel was written or accepted as a sacred writing. Others suggest it is merely a genre distinction: the miracle stories and apocalyptic visions of Daniel were considered atypical of a "prophetic" book. Still others propose that it is a *linguistic* difference: unlike every other book of the Hebrew Bible, which is composed primarily in Hebrew, the majority of the book of Daniel is preserved in Aramaic, a closely related language spoken by Jews in and after the Babylonian exile (see Dan 2:4—7:28). Nevertheless, by the first century A.D., Daniel was clearly considered authoritative by the authors of the Dead Sea Scrolls, Josephus, and the writers of the New Testament. Centuries later, by the time of the standardization of the Masoretic Text (A.D. 700–1000), Daniel assumed a place near the end of the Writings, after Esther but before Ezra-Nehemiah. This arrangement promotes the interpretation of the book as a "biography" among a series of "biographies" of late biblical heroes or heroines such as Esther, Mordecai, Ezra, and Nehemiah.

In Christian tradition, the book is also typically known simply as "Daniel" (Greek *Daniēl*) or "the Book of the Prophet Daniel" (Latin *Liber Danihelis Prophetae*). Significantly, unlike in the rabbinic tradition, Daniel is classified as the fourth and last of the four "Major Prophets": Isaiah, Jeremiah, Ezekiel, and Daniel. In fact, in many early canonical lists and ancient Greek manuscripts of the Septuagint, the Book of the Twelve (minor prophets) precedes the four major prophets, thereby situating Daniel as the last prophet—and the last Old Testament book.[1] This canonical arrangement emphasizes Daniel's role as the

---

[1] See, for example, the list of Athanasius and Codex Vaticanus in Lee Martin McDonald, *The Biblical Canon: Its Origin, Transmission, and Authority* (Grand Rapids, Mich.: Baker Academic, 2007), 439–44.

prophetic bridge between the Old and New Testaments: he is the one who prophesied the coming and death of "a messiah" (Dan 9:25 [author's trans.]), the destruction of Jerusalem (Dan 9:26; 12:11), and the resurrection of the dead (Dan 12:1–3). In the Latin West, however, there was an increasing tendency to place the four major prophets before the twelve minor prophets and to employ the books of Maccabees as the last books of the Old Testament, a *historical* bridge between the Old and New Testament periods. In this order, Daniel is far less conspicuous, sandwiched between Ezekiel and Hosea. This canonical order became crystalized at the Councils of Florence (A.D. 1442) and Trent (A.D. 1546) and is the order found in Catholic and Protestant Bibles today.

As is the case with other Old Testament books—such as Jeremiah, Ezekiel, and Esther—the book of Daniel circulated in more than one literary edition in antiquity: a shorter version, and one or more longer versions. The traditional Hebrew version (the Masoretic Text) preserved the *shorter* form of Daniel, while the Greek versions preserved a longer form including the three following sections:

1. The Prayer of Azariah and the Song of the Three Young Men (Dan 3:24–90)
2. The Story of Susanna (Dan 13)
3. Bel and the Dragon (Dan 14)

The weight of evidence indicates these "additions" were originally composed in Hebrew or Aramaic and then later translated into Greek.[2] However, the original Septuagint translation (also called the "Old Greek") was so idiosyncratic that it was almost entirely replaced in Christian codices of the Old Testament with a more accurate translation attributed to Theodotion, the Greek-speaking convert to Judaism who produced a thorough revision of the Septuagint (ca. A.D. 150). For example, the Hebrew text from which Jerome translated the Vulgate reflected the shorter rather than longer version of the book, so he marked these "additions" with an obelus (÷) and translated them into Latin from the Greek of Theodotion. Although Theodotion's version placed the story of Susanna at the beginning of the book of Daniel (because the events take place in Daniel's youth) and Bel and the Dragon at the end, Jerome placed both additional stories at the end of the book, producing the arrangement familiar to Catholics ever since. In what follows, we will analyze the book of Daniel in this, its final canonical form, while recognizing that the complex textual history of this biblical book requires it to be studied in three languages: Hebrew, Aramaic, and Greek.

Literary Structure of Daniel

The shorter form of Daniel in the Masoretic Text is composed in two languages: Hebrew and Aramaic. Based on language alone, one would divide Daniel into three sections: a Hebrew introduction (Dan 1—2:3) and conclusion (Dan 8–12)

---

[2] See Carey A. Moore, *Daniel, Esther, and Jeremiah: The Additions*, Anchor Bible 44 (New York: Doubleday, 1977), 25.

surrounding an Aramaic core (Dan 2:4—7:28). Why the shift from one language to another? Although we can only speculate, William Dumbrell has suggested that the middle chapters are in Aramaic[3]—the international language of Daniel's day—because they are concerned with the flow of international events, especially the sequence of world empires (Dan 2 and 7). On the other hand, the opening and closing chapters are in Hebrew, the national language of Israel, because they are concerned with how world history affects God's chosen nation (Dan 1 and 8–12).

Analyzed by genre, however, the book breaks into two sections: the "court tales" of Daniel and his companions in the service of the Babylonian and Persian royalty (Dan 1–6) and the prophetic dream visions of Daniel himself (Dan 7–12). Furthermore, scholars have noted the presence of a *chiasm* in the structure of Daniel: two strikingly similar visions of a sequence of four world kingdoms followed by a fifth supernatural one (Dan 2 and 7); two tales of persecution—the three young men in the fiery furnace and Daniel in the lions' den (Dan 3 and 6); and two remarkably parallel interpretations by Daniel of a disturbing dream or vision of a Persian king concerning his imminent downfall (Dan 4 and 5).

As noted above, the Prayer of Azariah and the Song of the Three Young Men, along with the accounts of Susanna and Bel and the Dragon, were probably independent narratives about Daniel and his companions that were incorporated into the central narrative of the book. Accordingly, the canonical form of the book of Daniel may be outlined as follows (the Greek portions are in italics and the chiastic structure indicated by the letters to the right):

Outline of the Book of Daniel

1. Daniel and Companions Prevail through Exile and Testing (Dan 1)
2. Four Kingdoms and a Fifth: The Metallic Image (Dan 2) — A
3. The Three Young Men in the Fiery Furnace (Dan 3) — B
   a. *The Prayer of Azariah (Dan 3:1–22)*
   b. *The Song of the Three Young Men (Dan 3:23–68)*
4. Nebuchadnezzar's Vision, Madness, Restoration (Dan 4) — C
5. Belshazzar Sees the Handwriting on the Wall (Dan 5) — C'
6. Daniel Survives the Lions' Den (Dan 6) — B'
7. Four Kingdoms and a Fifth: the Beasts and the Son of Man (Dan 7) — A'
8. Vision of the Ram and Goat: Persia Succeeded by Greece (Dan 8)
9. Seventy Weeks of Years: the Chronology until the Messiah (Dan 9)
10. Kings of North and South: The Struggle over the Holy Land (Dan 10–11)

---

[3] William Dumbrell, *The Faith of Israel: A Theological Survey of the Old Testament* (Grand Rapids: Baker, 2002), 304.

Overview of the Book of Daniel

Daniel and His Companions in Babylon (Daniel 1)

The book of Daniel begins in "the third year of Jehoiakim" (ca. 605 B.C.), the year Nebuchadnezzar established hegemony over the Levant and subjected the king of Judah to vassalage, taking hostages from the aristocracy and royal house to ensure his obedience. Daniel and his three companions are among those taken hostage, but the sacred author also notes that Nebuchadnezzar took liturgical "vessels" from the house of God in Jerusalem and deposited them in the temples of his idols

---

The Meaning of Names in Daniel

Almost all personal names in Daniel are *theophoric*—that is, embedded with the name of a god—based on either Israelite or Babylonian religion:

> Daniel: "God is my judge"
> Belteshazzar: "O Bel, protect the king!"
> Nebuchadnezzar: *nabûkudurri-uṣur*, "O god Nabu, save my firstborn son!"
> Hananiah: "The LORD is gracious"
> Misha'el: "Who is what God is?" i.e., "Who is like God?"
> Azariah: "The LORD is my help"
> Shadrach: *shudur-aku*, "Command of (the moon god) Aku"
> Meshach: *mî-sha-aku*, "Who is like (the moon god) Aku?"
> Abednego: *ebed-nebo*, "Servant of Nabu," or *ebed-nergal*, "Servant of Nergal"
> Belshazzar: "O Bel, protect the king!"
> Gabriel: "God is my champion"

There is no "secular" space in ancient society—culture, politics, and religion are inseparable. The struggle in the book of Daniel is the struggle of God with the gods, his kingdom against theirs.

---

in Babylon (Dan 1:2). The author intends a parallelism between the young men and these liturgical objects: both are sacred vessels, consecrated to God's service but now brought into a profane and profaning environment. The holy vessels will reappear at Belshazzar's fateful last banquet (see Dan 6). Meanwhile, the young men will be tested, to see if they maintain their holiness and devotion to the one true God in the midst of impure surroundings.

After introducing the issue of conflict between rival cults symbolized by the deposition of YHWH's vessels in Marduk's temple, the author then introduces the protagonists (Dan 1:3–4): young Israelite men from "the royal family"—meaning, of course, the family of King David—whose freedom from any "blemish" (Hebrew *me'um*) (Dan 1:4) calls to mind the standards for both sacrifices and priests in the cult of YHWH (cf. Lev 21:17–23; 22:22–25; Num 19:2;

Deut 15:21; 17:1) and whose three-year training recalls the ideal age of sacrificial animals in some texts (cf. Gen 15:9; 1 Sam 1:24).

Although the young men have no opportunity for participation in the liturgy of the Jerusalem Temple while they are in exile, they are concerned to retain the cultic purity that would enable them to worship. Accordingly, they avoid "defiling" themselves with the king's "rich food" (Dan 1:8), consisting of (unclean) meat and wine. The issue here may not be the violation of Mosaic food laws alone, but also the fact that the food of the king would have been ritually offered to his deities prior to his consumption of it, with a portion of the meat sacrificed on the pagan altars and a portion of the wine poured out in libation. The rejection of even the king's wine may well indicate that it was a desire to *abstain from participation in the Babylonian cult* that motivated Daniel and the young men not to "defile" themselves. They request water and vegetables that were not part of the "king's rich food" and therefore would not have been ritually offered to the king's deities (cf. Dan 1:15). Thus, the book opens with a liturgical focus: describing how Daniel and his companions maintain the cultic-ritual purity necessary for proper worship of the Lord even in a defiling, profaning environment.

The Four Pagan Kingdoms and the Kingdom of God (Daniel 2)

The next episode is the unforgettable account of Nebuchadnezzar's dream about the metallic "image" and Daniel's miraculous interpretation thereof (Dan 2). After having a disturbing dream, King Nebuchadnezzar of Babylon summons all his advisors—the "magicians, the enchanters, the sorcerers, and the Chaldeans" (Dan 2:2)—and makes a stunning demand: he insists that they tell him not only the interpretation of his dream, but also the contents of the dream itself! His advisors offer to interpret the dream if the king will recount it to them, but Nebuchadnezzar demands they prove the supernatural nature of their interpretation by showing that they can interpret his dream without his even telling them of its contents. Understandably, the wise men demur, and the enraged king plans to execute them all, including Daniel and his companions. Daniel, however, intercedes with the captain of the guard to stay the executions until he has had time to pray and seek the revelation of the king's dream and its interpretation from the Lord (Dan 2:17–24).

The prayers of Daniel and his three companions are answered, and Daniel goes before the king to recount his dream to him: Nebuchadnezzar saw a man's image with a head of gold, chest of silver, midsection of bronze, and legs of iron. Then a stone "cut out by no human hand" struck the image, destroying it, and grew to become a mountain filling the world (Dan 2:31–35).

The Dream of Nebuchadnezzar (Daniel 2)		
1. Head:	Gold	= First Kingdom
2. Chest and Arms:	Silver	= Second Kingdom
3. Belly and Thighs:	Bronze	= Third Kingdom
4. Legs and Feet:	Iron and Clay	= Fourth Kingdom
5. Stone "Cut by No Human Hand":	Breaks Image	= Fifth Kingdom

After recounting the dream, Daniel also provides an interpretation: the four metallic sections of the image are a sequence of world empires ("kingdoms"), each of lesser excellence than the former. Most significant of all, the stone that grows to be a mountain that spreads throughout the earth is nothing less than *the kingdom of God* that will be established and put an end to these empires:

> And in the days of those kings *the God of heaven will set up a kingdom which shall never be destroyed*, nor shall its sovereignty be left to another people. *It shall break in pieces all these kingdoms and bring them to an end, and it shall stand for ever;* just as you saw that *a stone was cut from a mountain by no human hand*, and that it broke in pieces the iron, the bronze, the clay, the silver, and the gold. A great God has made known to the king what shall be hereafter. The dream is certain, and its interpretation sure. (Dan 2:44–45)

In the face of Daniel's revelation, Nebuchadnezzar is understandably awed by the prophet's access to supernatural knowledge and promotes him and his companions within the imperial administration.

What, then, is the meaning of the metallic image seen by Nebuchadnezzar and its destruction by the "stone" cut by no human hand? The metallic image is an idol, representing the false systems of pagan worship promoted by the various world empires in succession. The stone "cut out by no human hand" is clearly a sacred stone suitable for an altar or temple (see Ex 20:25; 1 Kings 6:7). It was common in the ancient Near East to view temples as mystical representations of the cosmic or primordial mountain of God ("Eden" in the Hebrew tradition). Therefore, the growth of the sacred stone into a "great mountain" that fills "the whole earth" (Dan 2:35) certainly refers to the building of a universal temple. But this universal temple is simultaneously the kingdom of God, as Daniel's explanation of the dream makes clear (Dan 2:44). The metallic idol

---

The Four Kingdoms of Nebuchadnezzar's Dream

Since the time of the Second Temple period (e.g., *4 Ezra, 2 Baruch*), the four kingdoms symbolized by the metallic image in Daniel 2 have been interpreted as four consecutive empires:

1. Babylon
2. Medo-Persia
3. Greece
4. Rome

In modern times, however, many scholars have proposed the alternative sequence:

1. Babylon
2. Media
3. Persia
4. Greece

The problem with the latter proposal is that the book of Daniel itself makes clear that *it regards the Medes and Persians as one empire, not two*, as when it says that the empire is given to "the Medes and Persians" (Dan 5:28; cf. 6:8, 12, 15; 8:20). Combined with the identification of the stone "not cut out by human hand" with the kingdom of God (Dan 2:44–45), the more ancient interpretation gave rise to the expectation that the kingdom of God would come during the time of the Roman Empire—that is, the reign of the fourth kingdom. For this and other reasons, there was great eschatological expectation among Jews during Jesus' earthly ministry.

represents, then, the kingdom of man and its false worship, contrasted with the temple-mountain kingdom of God and its true worship, and the fact that one day, true worship will prevail over the pagan kingdoms of the world.

The Three Young Men in the Fiery Furnace (Daniel 3 MT and LXX)

The next episode shifts the focus back to the fate of Daniel's three companions: Shadrach, Meshach, and Abednego (Dan 3). In this account, Nebuchadnezzar sets up a golden idol of preposterous size in the plain of Dura near Babylon and compels all his royal officials to worship it on pain of death. Daniel's three companions refuse, because to do so would violate their exclusive commitment to the one true God. The enraged king throws them into a furnace to be incinerated, but the Lord sends an angel to preserve them in the midst of the flame.

In the Greek version of Daniel, one of the three young men, Azariah—whose name fittingly means "YHWH is my help"—prays a prayer of repentance and plea for deliverance while walking in the fire (Dan 3:1–22 LXX), a prayer that bears some strong similarities to Daniel's own prayer for repentance and deliverance later in the book (cf. Dan 9:3–19 MT). Seeing that the Lord is preserving them from the flame, the three young men also sing a splendid litany of praise in which they call upon every facet of creation, both visible and invisible, from the cherubim in the heavenly temple to the beasts and cattle and to the spirits and souls of the righteous who have died, to "bless the Lord" and praise and exalt him forever (Dan 3:28–68 LXX). Remarkably, when taken together, the Prayer of Azariah and the Song of the Three Young Men form a complete *todah*, or thanksgiving sacrifice cycle, as discussed above in our treatment of the Psalms.

Eventually, in both the Hebrew and Greek versions, Nebuchadnezzar realizes the furnace is ineffective when he sees "four men" walking about in the furnace unhurt, and "the appearance of the fourth is like a son of the gods" (Dan 3:25 MT)—a point of correspondence with the Greek version, which explicitly states that "the angel of the Lord" comes into the furnace to protect the three men (Dan 3:26 LXX). In utter amazement, Nebuchadnezzar summons the trio to come out. He issues a decree protecting the God of Israel from defamation and promotes the young men in the royal service. Here again, we witness a conflict between systems of worship. The three young men will not participate in the pagan cult of Babylon. Instead, they are willing to offer their own bodies to the Lord as a sacrifice to him. The Prayer of Azariah states this sacrificial theology most poignantly:

> And at this time there is no prince, or prophet, or leader,
>> no burnt offering, or sacrifice, or oblation, or incense,
>> no place to make an offering before you or to find mercy.
> Yet with a contrite heart and a humble spirit may we be accepted,
>> as though it were with burnt offerings of rams and bulls,
>> and with tens of thousands of fat lambs;
>> such may our sacrifice be in your sight this day,
>> and may we wholly follow you,
>> for there will be no shame for those who trust in you.
>
> (Dan 3:15–17)

Denied access to the true liturgy and compelled to participate in a false one, the three young men refuse to comply and, instead, become willing human sacrifices to their own God. But happily God shows his sovereignty by sparing them this fate and vindicating his worshippers.

The Great Tree Cut Down and the Kingdom of God (Daniel 4)

The next section begins with a letter from Nebuchadnezzar, writing in the first person, to his subjects, describing his personal experiences in recent years. At the height of his reign, Nebuchadnezzar has another dream—this time of a tree that grows to tower above the earth, becoming a home and haven for all birds and beasts. In his dream, an angel from heaven descends and decrees that the tree be hewn down and only a stump of it left in the field (Dan 4:1–18). The king summons Daniel, and the Israelite seer (reluctantly) informs him that the dream refers to the king himself, who will lose his mind and be driven out into the wilderness to live like an animal.

After the passage of a year, the prophetic dream becomes a reality. While walking on the roof of his palace and praising himself for his greatness, Nebuchadnezzar is struck by God with madness (Dan 4:28–37). He is driven out of human society and lives like an animal in the fields. After the passage of an indeterminate period of time, Nebuchadnezzar's human reason returns. He suddenly realizes and acknowledges the sovereignty of the Most High God as the true "King of Heaven". Indeed, as in Daniel 2, the chapter climaxes with a focus on the everlasting kingdom of God:

> At the end of the days I, Nebuchadnezzar, lifted my eyes to heaven, and my reason returned to me, and I blessed the Most High, and praised and honored him who lives for ever;
>
> > *for his dominion is an everlasting dominion,*
> > *and his kingdom endures from generation to generation.* (Dan 4:34)

Wordplay in the Writing on the Wall

The cryptic message "*mene mene tekel u-pharsin*" delivered to Belshazzar is an example of complex Aramaic wordplay. On the face of it, the message seems to be a phrase about money: "a mina, a mina, a shekel and half-shekels." *Tekel* is Aramaic for "shekel", the basic unit of silver currency. A mina was worth fifty or sixty shekels. *Upharsin* translates as "and halves"—that is, half-shekels, since the root *paras* means "divide in half, split" in Semitic languages.

The words also have non-monetary connotations. *Mene* sounds like the Aramaic verb meaning "to number". Likewise, *tekel* shares the same consonants as the verb "to weigh". Finally, *pharsin*, "halves", not only comes from the root *paras*, "divide", but is also very close to Aramaic *pārās*, "Persia".

Thus Daniel's interpretation:

Mene: "God has *numbered* your days."

Tekel: "God has *weighed* you in the balance."

Pharsin: "God has *divided* your kingdom and given it to *Persia*."

With this hymn of praise, the king's "reason" returns to him, his courtiers seek him out once more, and he is restored to his position as king.

Belshazzar's Feast and the Writing on the Wall (Daniel 5)

Without segue, the narrative of Daniel shifts abruptly to the last days of Belshazzar, son of King Nabonidus (ca. 556–539 B.C.), who ruled Babylon as co-regent with his father in the mid-sixth century (ca. 553–539 B.C.).

In this narrative, Belshazzar gives a great feast for his entire court and foolishly brings out the sacred vessels from the Jerusalem Temple confiscated by Nebuchadnezzar (cf. Dan 1:2). While Belshazzar and his courtiers are feasting and drinking from the sacred vessels and praising their own gods, a man's hand appears and writes the message "MENE, MENE, TEKEL, and PARSIN" (Dan 5:25).

Needless to say, Belshazzar is gravely frightened, but the queen (that is, the queen mother) enters the banquet hall and recommends he call for Daniel, who had interpreted dreams and visions for the king's predecessors. Daniel is summoned, arrives, rebukes the king for his pride and offenses against the God of Israel, and interprets the handwritten message: God has judged and weighed the king and found him wanting; therefore his kingdom has been divided and given to "the Medes and Persians" (Dan 5:28). Despite the ominous interpretation, Belshazzar rewards Daniel by making him the third ruler of the kingdom (that is, after his father Nabonidus and himself). That same night, Daniel's oracle is fulfilled when Belshazzar is slain as the Medes and Persians capture Babylon and Darius the Mede becomes king (Dan 5:30–31).

The Historical Belshazzar

Because no ancient pagan historians mention him, Bible scholars long considered Belshazzar a fictitious character until 1854, when his name was found on the Nabonidus Cylinder—a clay barrel inscribed with an account of the reign of King Nabonidus of Babylon (556–539 B.C.). For most of Nabonidus' reign, his son Belshazzar ruled as his co-regent in Babylon, while the king devoted himself to the worship of the moon-god in the desert oasis of Tema.

Since Belshazzar was never formally installed as king, many have suggested the book of Daniel errs in calling him "King (Aramaic *melek*) Belshazzar". However, the Nabonidus Cylinder says Nabonidus "entrusted the *kingship*" (Akk. *sharrutu*) to him, and the Aramaic *melek* could be used loosely to describe a governor or ruler of a city.

Several times Nebuchadnezzar is called Belshazzar's "father". Since, as far as we know, Nebuchadnezzar was not his biological father, this probably represents a claim to dynastic legitimacy. Belshazzar's father, Nabonidus, was a usurper, but he and his son asserted the legitimacy of their succession from the founder of the Babylonian Empire, Nebuchadnezzar, by calling him their "father", i.e., legal ancestor and predecessor. In a similar way, a ninth-century B.C. Assyrian text (the Black Obelisk) calls Omri the "father" of the usurper Jehu, who assassinated Omri's grandson Joram to take the throne (see 1 Kings 16; 2 Kings 9). For all that, Jehu still claimed to be the "son" (i.e., legitimate heir) of Omri.[a]

[a] See Ernest C. Lucas, "Daniel", in *Isaiah, Jeremiah, Lamentations, Ezekiel, Daniel*, vol. 4 of *Zondervan Illustrated Bible Backgrounds Commentary*, ed. John H. Walton (Grand Rapids, Mich.: Zondervan, 2009), 542.

The sacred author recounts this narrative in such a way as to suggest it is the profanation of the sacred vessels of the Jerusalem Temple (cf. Dan 1:4) that provokes the final judgment of God on Babylon and Belshazzar's reign. Belshazzar and his courtiers use the Lord's vessels in the worship of their own gods, but the Lord vindicates his cult through the Persian destruction of Babylon and its empire.

Daniel in the Lions' Den (Daniel 6)

Immediately after assuming control of Babylon, Darius sets about appointing 120 new "administrators" (Greek *satraps*) over his realm (Dan 6:1). He places Daniel, the (now aged) courtier and prophet who had predicted the Persian victory, among the top three administrators and plans in the future to make him into a sort of prime minister. Jealousy prompts Daniel's fellow courtiers to urge Darius to pass a law forbidding prayer to any god or man but himself (Darius) for thirty days. This is, of course, a trap: the courtiers know that, since Daniel is a faithful Jew, his conscience will not allow him to follow this law, and, indeed, shortly thereafter they discover him in prayer to the Lord. They bring the matter to the attention of the king and compel him to enforce the penalty of death by lions. With great reluctance, Darius complies, and Daniel is thrown into the lions' den (Dan 6:16). Overnight, however, the Lord sends an angel to calm the lions' hunger, and Daniel is still alive in the morning when the king rushes to the den to inquire after his fate. In great relief,

> #### How Many Satraps?
>
> The book of Daniel speaks of Darius wishing to establish "one hundred and twenty" satraps over the empire (Dan 6:1), whereas external historical sources indicate that the Persian Empire had only twenty satrapies. Some see this as hyperbole on the sacred author's part. Others suggest the word "hundred" may be a scribal insertion to a text that originally read "twenty", or else Darius' intention was to increase greatly the administrative districts of the empire, but the plan was never carried out due to his untimely death. Furthermore, since satrapies were usually subdivided into smaller territories, and the rulers of these subunits were also sometimes called "satraps", it is difficult to know exactly how many persons may have borne this title at any one time during the Medo-Persian Empire.

Darius has Daniel raised up from the pit and his accusers cast in. Then he issues a decree to the kingdom demanding that all persons reverence Daniel's God, and, like Nebuchadnezzar before him, he utters a hymn about the kingdom of the true God:

> I make a decree, that in all my royal dominion men tremble and fear before the God of Daniel,
>
> > for he is the living God,
> > enduring for ever;
> > *his kingdom shall never be destroyed,*
> > *and his dominion shall be to the end.*
> > He delivers and rescues,
> > he works signs and wonders
> > in heaven and on earth. (Dan 6:26–27)

Who Is "Darius the Mede"?

The book of Daniel says that the same night Belshazzar was slain, "Darius the Mede received the kingdom" (Dan 5:31). Furthermore, the account of Daniel in the lions' den takes place during Darius' reign (Dan 6:1–28). However, extra-biblical sources do not record a person by this name, and it is generally understood that Cyrus of Persia became king of Babylon upon the death of Belshazzar. Therefore, scholars have suggested that "Darius the Mede" is

1. *unhistorical*, a simple confusion on the part of the biblical author with later rulers with this name (e.g., Darius I "the Great", fl. 522–486 B.C.);

2. just another name for *Cyrus the Great* himself (fl. 559–530 B.C.)—from this point of view, the key text may be translated: "Daniel prospered during the reign of Darius, that is, the reign of Cyrus the Persian" (cf. Dan 6:28); or

3. an alternate name for *Gubaru* (Greek *Gobryas*), Cyrus' general, who actually invaded and captured Babylon, was installed as its governor, appointed administrators over the realm, and died shortly thereafter. Some object that Gubaru was never "king" (Aramaic *melek*), as he is called throughout Daniel 6. However, the Aramaic *melek* is attested elsewhere for governors of cities.[a]

[a] For further discussion, see Edwin M. Yamauchi, *Persia and the Bible* (Grand Rapids, Mich.: Baker, 1996), 58–59; Ernest C. Lucas, "Daniel", in *Isaiah, Jeremiah, Lamentations, Ezekiel, Daniel*, vol. 4 of *Zondervan Illustrated Bible Backgrounds Commentary*, ed. John H. Walton (Grand Rapids, Mich.: Zondervan, 2009), 544; H.H. Rowley, *Darius the Mede and the Four World Empires in the Book of Daniel* (Eugene, Ore.: Wipf & Stock, 2006).

The message of this narrative is very similar to the account of the three young men in the fiery furnace. Daniel refuses to comply with the demand for false worship. He continues to pray "toward Jerusalem"—"three times a day", in fact—apparently at the times when the daily sacrifices and prayers would ordinarily be offered (Dan 6:10).[4] Though the Temple no longer stands and he is unable to worship and sacrifice, nonetheless he consents to *become* a sacrifice at the teeth of the lions. Yet once again God vindicates those who worship him against their enemies and through "signs and wonders" shows that he is the true king and his the true kingdom.

The Four Beasts, the Son of Man, and the Kingdom of God (Daniel 7)

Whereas Daniel 1–6 was dominated by accounts of adventures in the royal court, Daniel 7–12 consists of a series of visions and oracles about the course of future world events, from the time of Daniel to the advent of the kingdom of God. Nonetheless, there is continuity with Daniel 1–6, because the initial vision of Daniel 7 runs largely parallel to the interpreted dream of Nebuchadnezzar in Daniel 2.

In the "first year of Belshazzar", Daniel dreams at night and sees "four great beasts" rise from the sea (Dan 7:1–2). The first is a winged lion; the second, a lopsided bear; the third, a leopard with four wings and four heads; the fourth, a great dragon-like beast. These animals each appear and dominate for a while,

[4] Cf. *1QSRule of the Community* 10:1–2; Mishnah, *Berakoth* 4:1; John J. Collins, *Daniel*, Hermeneia (Minneapolis: Fortress Press, 1993), 268–69.

The Meaning of the Four Beasts (Daniel 7–12)

The most ancient interpretation of the sequence of beasts is that they represent the four kingdoms:

1. *Winged Lion*: Babylon
2. *Lopsided Bear*: Medo-Persia
3. *Winged Leopard*: Greece
4. *Great Beast*: Rome

The winged lion was a common symbol of Babylon. The lopsided bear represents the unequal partnership of the Medes and Persians (compare the lopsided ram of Dan 8:3). The leopard with four wings and heads represents the Greek Empire of Alexander, which took over the world with incredible speed (four wings) only to be split roughly in four parts among Alexander's generals (four heads). The fourth beast is Rome, whose power and origins were unlike the others. Approximately ten Roman emperors reigned between Julius Caesar and Tiberius, who conquered Jerusalem and razed the Temple.

In modern times, many scholars have proposed an alternative interpretation of the four beasts:

1. Winged Lion: Babylon
2. Lopsided Bear: Media
3. Winged Leopard: Persia
4. Great Beast: Greece

From this point of view, the boastful horn is identified with Antiochus IV Epiphanes (175–164 B.C.), the persecuting Seleucid ruler and villain of the books of Maccabees.

---

only to be followed by the next. The fourth and last, the great dragon, is remarkable for its ten horns, one of which speaks boastfully and displaces three others (Dan 7:3–8).

While Daniel watches, the "ancient of days" appears and sets up his throne, surrounded by myriads of angelic servants and worshippers (Dan 7:9–14). He convenes his court, passes judgment on the beasts, destroys the dragon, and strips the others of their authority. Then one "like a son of man" is presented before the "ancient of days" and receives all world authority in a climax where once again the kingdom of God stands front and center:

> I saw in the night visions,
>   and behold, *with the clouds of heaven*
>   *there came one like a son of man,*
>   and he came to the Ancient of Days
>   and was presented before him.
>   *And to him was given dominion*
>   *and glory and kingdom,*
>   that all peoples, nations, and languages
>   should serve him;
>   his dominion is an everlasting dominion,
>   which shall not pass away,
>   and his kingdom one
>   that shall not be destroyed.
>   (Dan 7:13–14)

As might be expected, interpreters continue to debate: Who is the "one like a son of man"? Most ancient interpreters saw him as (1) the future king and deliverer—namely, *the Messiah*; some contemporary commentators argue that that he is instead (2) a *corporate symbol* for the "people of the saints of the most high"; (3) still others identify him as *an angel*, specifically Michael.[5]

Significantly, the most plausible solution to the identification of the Danielic "son of man" can be found by interpreting the text in the broader context of Daniel's question to the angel about the meaning of the vision (Dan 7:15–18). The angel declares that the four beasts are not just four kingdoms, but four "kings" (Aramaic *malkin*) (Dan 7:17): in other words, the beasts are both *corporate* and *individual* symbols of the kings and their kingdoms. In the words of John Collins:

> If the MT reading [of "kings" in Dan 7:17] is correct, it has some significance for the interpretation of the "one like a human being", insofar as the beasts are not simply collective symbols but can also be understood to represent the rulers.[6]

This suggestion makes the best sense of the ancient *messianic* interpretations of the "son of man" in early Jewish writings like *4 Ezra* and *1 Enoch* as well as the New Testament: if "one like a son of man" is both a corporate and individual symbol for the kingdom of the "saints of the most high", then it is both the saints *and* the future king who will receive the "kingdom for ever, for ever and ever" (cf. Dan 7:18, 25). This son of man will "arise" during the time of the fourth kingdom on earth, different from the previous three. This kingdom will produce ten kings and then another who is particularly boastful and will persecute the "saints of the Most High", but only until he is judged by God. Then the saints will receive the kingdom. Daniel is alarmed, but he ponders what the vision means.

This vision parallels the earlier dream of the image of four metals and the kingdom of God in Daniel 2. The four metals correspond to the four animals. The metal image signified the idolatry of the pagan kingdoms; the sequence of beasts represents their subhuman morality and worship of gods in the form of animals. The "one like a son of man" (Dan 7:13) is the "stone ... cut out by no human hand" (2:34–35, 45); and the "kingdom of the saints of the Most High" (7:18, 22) is the temple-mountain that fills the whole earth (2:35, 45).

The Vision of the Ram and the Goat (Daniel 8)

Two years later, in the third year of the reign of Belshazzar, Daniel is in the capital, Susa, and sees a similarly "beastly" vision on the banks of the river Ulai (Dan 8:1). A ram with two horns, one larger than the other, prances along the banks, and no man or beast is able to oppose him. From the west comes a goat at great speed, not touching the ground. The goat has a single horn, with which he smashes the ram and tramples him to the ground. The goat magnifies himself, but his great horn is broken and replaced with four others. From one horn grows a small horn that becomes greater and greater: it rises up to heaven,

---

[5] See Collins, *Daniel*, 304–10.
[6] Ibid., 312.

The Ram, the Goat, and the Small Horn

Unlike the visions of Daniel 2 and 7, the vision of Daniel 8 is transparent in its meaning, in part because much of it is interpreted within the chapter itself. The goat's large central horn is Alexander the Great (356–323 B.C.), who conquered the Persian Empire in a mere four years (334–331 B.C.) and died as master of the known world. After his death, four of his successors (Greek *diadochoi*) prevailed in the ensuing power struggle and set up independent kingdoms: Cassander in Macedonia and Greece, Lysimachus in Asia Minor and Thrace, Seleucus in the Levant to India, and Ptolemy in Egypt. These are the "four horns" that replace the one great "horn" (Dan 8:5–8). The small horn that grows from one of the four is almost certainly Antiochus IV Epiphanes (175–164 B.C.), a successor to the throne of the Seleucid Empire who desecrated the Jerusalem Temple and attempted to suppress Judaism within its native land (cf. 1 Mac 1–2).

---

encircles "the glorious land", and overthrows the sanctuary and the "continual burnt offering" for 2,300 evenings and mornings (cf. Dan 8:9–14).

Once again, Daniel seeks the interpretation of the vision from the angel, who is in this case explicitly named "Gabriel" (Dan 8:16). The ram is the kingdom of Media and Persia (Dan 8:20); the goat is the king of Greece (Dan 8:21). The four horns are the four successor kingdoms (of Alexander's empire) (Dan 8:22). The small horn is a boastful king who will arise, prosper, and persecute the "people of the saints", but he will meet his end without human intervention ("by no human hand") (Dan 8:25). Daniel is overcome and made ill by the vision, and even when he recovers, he does not understand it.

The Seventy Weeks of Years until "the Messiah" (Daniel 9)

The next vision is somewhat different, insofar as it comes, not through a dream, but through Daniel's meditation on Scripture: in the first year of "Darius" the "Mede", Daniel "perceived (Hebrew *bînotî*) in the books the number of years which, according to the word of the LORD to Jeremiah the prophet, must pass before the end of the desolations of Jerusalem, namely, seventy years" (Dan 9:2).

In this line, the author is referring to oracles in the book of Jeremiah that predict seventy years during which "the nations" shall serve Babylon and after which Babylon will be punished, and the Lord will "visit" the Judeans and bring them back to their land (see Jer 25:11–12 and 29:10). However, as the date reference to the "first year of Darius ... a Mede" makes clear (Dan 9:1), at the time that Daniel is reading this Scripture, the "seventy years for Babylon" are already over (cf. Jer 29:10). Yet where is the promised "visitation" of Israel and return of the Jews to their land? Apparently, Daniel "understands" or "perceives" (for the first time) that the prophecy of Jeremiah was *conditional upon the repentance of the people*. Compare the key text:

> Then you will call upon me and come and pray to me, and I will hear you. You will seek me and find me. *If you seek me with all your heart*, I will be found by you, says the LORD, and *I will restore your fortunes and gather you from all the nations and all the places where I have driven you*, says the LORD, and I will bring you back to the place from which I sent you into exile. (Jer 29:12–14 [author's trans.])

According to Jeremiah, the restoration from exile will take place "if" (Hebrew *ki*) the people of God repent; but Daniel recognizes that the exiles have not yet sought the Lord with "all" their "heart". Indeed, in the immediately subsequent prayer, Daniel declares: "All this calamity has come upon us, yet we have not entreated the favor of the LORD our God, turning from our iniquities and giving heed to your truth" (Dan 9:13).

That Jeremiah's prophecy was conditioned on repentance, and Daniel's perception that the repentance has not taken place, explains the dynamic of the rest of this chapter. After perceiving that seventy years were prophesied, but the fulfillment has not yet arrived, Daniel prays an intense prayer of repentance and intercession (Dan 9:3–19). Very much like Moses before him (see Ex 32:11–13, 31–32; Num 14:13–19), Daniel repents *on behalf of* the people of Israel, pleading for God to have mercy on them and the "holy city".

In answer to Daniel's prayer, the angel Gabriel arrives from God's presence with a mixed message (Dan 9:20–27). On the one hand, Daniel's repentance and prayer for the restoration of his city and people have been heard and will be answered. On the other hand, the time of fulfillment has been delayed by a factor of seven, presumably because the people themselves have not sought the Lord with "all [their] heart" (Jer 29:13). The increase by a factor of seven is a principle articulated by the book of Leviticus, in which YHWH says: "If by this discipline you are not turned to me.... I myself will strike you *sevenfold* for your sins" (Lev 26:23; cf. Lev 23:18, 21, 27). The discipline of the exile has not led to repentance, so the exile is prolonged by a factor of seven. Therefore Gabriel informs Daniel:

> *Seventy weeks of years* are decreed concerning your people and your holy city, to finish the transgression, to put an end to sin, and to atone for iniquity, to bring in everlasting righteousness, to seal both vision and prophet, and to anoint a most holy place. (Dan 9:24)

How Many Messiahs? And When?

The traditional Hebrew punctuation (Masoretic Text) of Daniel 9:25–26 reads as follows:

> From the going forth of the word to restore and build Jerusalem to the coming of messiah prince, there shall be seven weeks. Then for sixty-two weeks it shall be built again with squares and moat, but in a troubled time. And after the sixty-two weeks, messiah shall be cut off.

Apparently, one messiah arrives after seven weeks of years, and another is cut off after a further sixty-two weeks.

However, the Masoretic punctuation was not inserted until the early medieval period. All ancient translations (Vulgate, LXX, Syriac, etc.) interpreted the chronology in the Hebrew text as follows:

> From the going forth ... to messiah prince, there shall be *seven weeks and sixty-two weeks*. (Dan 9:25 LXX [author's trans.])

This places the coming of "messiah" after a total of sixty-nine weeks, and shortly thereafter he is "cut off". This seems to have been the consensus interpretation of the passage in antiquity.

In what is the only oracle in the Old Testament in which a future king is explicitly called an "anointed one" or "messiah" (Hebrew *mashiah*), Gabriel then describes the coming of this "messiah" after seven (or sixty-nine, see inset) weeks, the rebuilding of the Temple, the cutting off (= killing) of the "messiah", the destruction of the city and sanctuary, the making of a "strong covenant" with many, the cessation of sacrifice and offering, and the end of the "desolator" (Dan 9:25–27). In this way, the oracle of Gabriel connects a number of key eschatological expectations: the forgiveness of sins, the restoration of the Temple, the coming of the messianic king, and the establishment of a New Covenant.

Interpreting the Seventy Weeks of Daniel

The prophecy of Daniel 9:24–27 is cryptic, and caution should be exercised when interpreting it.

Traditionally, these verses have been understood as a description of events leading up to the coming of "a messiah prince" (Dan 9:25 [author's trans.]) and his death (the "cutting off" of the messiah, cf. Dan 9:26), the destruction of Jerusalem and the Temple that took place under Tiberius Caesar (A.D. 70), the establishment of a New Covenant (the "strong covenant with many" [Dan 9:27]), and the cessation of Old Covenant sacrifices.[a] A similar reading seems to be implied by Josephus when he says that "Daniel also wrote about the empire of the Romans and that Jerusalem would be taken by them and the temple laid waste."[b] The chronology of the text, however, does not always fit comfortably into this scheme.

Among contemporary scholars, it has become common to understand the passage as a description of the persecution of the Jews under Antiochus IV Epiphanes, who would be the "desolator" (Dan 9:27). The major difficulty with this interpretation, however, is that *Antiochus did not actually destroy the city and the sanctuary as described in Daniel 9:26*, and the time frame of his reign does not quite fit the chronology of the prophecy, either.[c] This is somewhat difficult to explain if, as many contemporary scholars suppose, Daniel was written after the death of Antiochus Epiphanes.

[a] See Eusebius of Caesarea, *Proof of the Gospel*, 8.2.389.
[b] Josephus, *Antiquities* 10.276, in Josephus, *Jewish Antiquities Book 9–11*, trans. Ralph Marcus, Loeb Classical Library 326 (Cambridge, Mass.: Harvard University Press, 1937), 311.
[c] Cf. Collins, *Daniel*, 36–57.

The Tribulation, the Resurrection, and the End of Days (Daniel 10–12)

The last vision of Daniel comprises the final three chapters of the Hebrew form of the book. In the "third year of Cyrus King of Persia", Daniel is fasting and praying when he sees a "man clothed in linen", beaming with light, coming to him as he stands on the banks of the Tigris River (Dan 10:1, 5). He faints in the man's presence, but the man revives him and gives him encouragement. He has come from God to reveal to Daniel what is about to take place.

In a lengthy oracle, the "man" describes, without the use of specific names, the ebb and flow of the struggle over the land of Israel that will be waged by the two successor empires of Alexander the Great: "the king of the north" (the Seleucid Empire based in Syria) and "the king of the south" (the Ptolemaic Empire based in Egypt) (see Dan 11:2–45). The "man" traces this conflict fairly accurately up through the reign of a certain "contemptible person" (Dan 11:21), who is almost certainly Antiochus IV Epiphanes. The oppressive reign of

Antiochus is described in great detail (Dan 11:21–45). After the end of his reign, the heavenly "man" informs Daniel about the final tribulation and the general resurrection of the dead (Dan 12:1–4). Daniel wishes to know when these things will take place, but he receives only cryptic answers (Dan 12:5–13).

As in earlier chapters, liturgical themes prevail throughout Daniel 10–12. The "man clothed with linen" is an angelic-priestly figure, since linen was the clothing of priests (see Lev 16:4; Ezek 44:17–18), and the primary concern of the account of future events is the fate of the sanctuary, particularly the *tamid*, or continual burnt offering (Dan 11:31; 12:11), sacrificed in the morning and evening (Num 28:2–7).

Susanna and Bel and the Dragon (Daniel 13–14 LXX)

As mentioned above, the last two chapters of Daniel in its canonical form are only extant in the longer, Greek edition of the book: (1) the story of Susanna's deliverance from death by Daniel's wisdom (Dan 13) and (2) the story of Darius' deliverance from idolatry by Daniel's shrewdness (Dan 14). The distinctive character of these narratives is highlighted by the fact that they are located in different places in different ancient manuscripts. For example, in the Greek version, Susanna is actually a *preface* to the book of Daniel, since the events occur while Daniel is a young man. In the Latin Vulgate, Susanna is the first of two *appendices* or narrative epilogues to the canonical book.

1. *Susanna's Deliverance from Death (Daniel 13)*: The story of Susanna is relatively simple. Susanna is a beautiful young wife of a wealthy and important member of the Jewish exilic community. Two Jewish elders are overcome with lust for her. They connive to enter her private garden while she is alone and bathing and urge her to have sexual relations with them, or else they will accuse her publicly of adultery with a young man. Susanna refuses their advances and screams for help. The threesome are discovered, and the two elders claim they caught Susanna in the very act of committing adultery. She is promptly tried and condemned. But before the sentence is carried out, the young Daniel steps forward. He insists that the two elders be separated for interrogation. Once isolated from each other, their stories about exactly what kind of tree they saw Susanna committing adultery beneath do not agree. As a result, Susanna is exonerated, and, in keeping with "the law of Moses" according to which false witness in a capital case is a grave offense, the two elders are put to death (cf. Deut 19:18–21).[7]

A couple of puns in Daniel 13:52–59 that only work in Greek have led some to conclude that the story of Susanna was composed in that language. However, most of the other linguistic characteristics of this narrative suggest it was translated from Hebrew or Aramaic. The puns may have been introduced by the translator: many Jewish scholars in antiquity were proficient enough in Greek to engage in wordplay.[8]

---

[7] Moore, *Daniel, Esther*, 113.
[8] Daniel Sperber, *Greek in Talmudic Palestine* (Ramat Gan: Bar Ilan University, 2012).

2. *Cyrus' Deliverance from Idolatry (Daniel 14)*: The account commonly known as "Bel and the Dragon" actually comprises two narratives. In the first, Daniel discusses idolatry with King Cyrus of Persia (Dan 14:1–22 LXX). Cyrus insists that the idol of the god Bel (= Baal) is alive, because it consumes the food offered to it. Daniel urges the king to spread dust on the floor of Bel's temple. In the morning, the footprints of Bel's priests and their families are visible in the dust. They are the ones who have really been consuming the sacrifices. Cyrus executes the priests, and the idol is destroyed.

In the second story, Daniel slays a sacred Babylonian dragon by feeding it cakes of pitch, fat, and hair until it bursts (Dan 14:23–42). The enraged Babylonians insist that the king punish Daniel, so he is again thrown to the lions for the period of a week. Curiously, during this time, he is sustained by soup brought to him by "the prophet Habakkuk", who was "in Judea"—one of the twelve "minor prophets"—who is transported to Babylon by an angel (Dan 14:33). At the end of the week, the lions have still not consumed Daniel, so the king withdraws him and casts in his accusers.

These two stories of Daniel's struggle against the pagan cults of Babylon constitute a fitting final word to the canonical book, which, as we have seen, has been from beginning to end an account of liturgical conflict between paganism and the cult of the Lord, between the pagan kingdoms of men and the everlasting kingdom of God.

Historical Issues in Daniel

The Origins of the Book of Daniel

Unlike certain other books of the Old Testament, the question of the date and authorship of the book of Daniel has been debated at least since the time of the pagan anti-Christian writer Porphyry. The pagan philosopher Celsus also famously attacked the authenticity of the book, and Origen devoted part of his work *Contra Celsum* to refuting his assertions. Like the book itself, the issues involved in its origins are somewhat complex and will take a few moments to unpack.

On the one hand, ancient Jewish and Christian tradition unanimously understood the book of Daniel to be the composition of the Judean exile and prophet of the same name, who was taken into exile in Babylon as a young man in the first deportation from Judah and lived from the reign of King Nebuchadnezzar (ca. 605 B.C.) down to the time of King Cyrus of Persia (ca. 536 B.C.). The internal reasons for such conclusions were several: throughout the second half of the book, Daniel speaks in the first person and repeatedly identifies himself as the source of the oracles (Dan 7:1–6, 8:1–6; 9:2–9; 10:2–12; 11:2; cf. 12:1–9). In the case of the dream about the four beasts and the son of man, the narrator even state: "In the first year of Belshazzar king of Babylon, Daniel had a dream and visions of his head as he lay in his bed. Then *he wrote down the* dream, and told the sum of the matter" (Dan 7:1). Likewise, the final oracle is described as being sealed in a "book" until the time of the end (Dan 12:4).

Outside the book of Daniel, Jews and Christians alike understood the narratives in the book of Daniel as history and the oracles as predictive of future events. For example, by the second century A.D., the books of Maccabees recall the story of Daniel and the three young men in the lions' den as examples to be followed (1 Mac 2:59–60; cf. 3 Mac 6:6–7). Along similar lines, in the Gospel of Matthew, Jesus refers to the "desolating sacrilege spoken of by the prophet Daniel" (Mt 24:15), apparently referring to the oracle regarding the seventy weeks and the abomination of desolation (Dan 9:25–27). Finally, and of great importance, in the first century A.D., Josephus clearly identifies the book of Daniel with the exilic prophet and wise man and says the following about Daniel:

> Now it is fitting to relate certain things about this man (Daniel) which one may greatly wonder at hearing . . . as to *one of the greatest prophets*, and during his lifetime he received honor and esteem from kings and people, and, since his death, his memory lives on eternally. *For the books which he wrote and left behind are still read by us even now, and we are convinced by them that Daniel spoke with God, for he was not only wont to prophesy future things, as did the other prophets, but he also fixed the time at which these would come to pass.* And, whereas the other prophets foretold disasters and for that reason were in disfavor with kings and people, Daniel was a prophet of good tidings to them, so that through the auspiciousness of his predictions he attracted the goodwill of all, while from their realization he gained credit among the multitude for his truthfulness and at the same time won their esteem for his divine power. And he left behind writings in which he has made plain to us the accuracy and faithfulness of the truth of his prophecies.[9]

Notice here that Josephus clearly regards both the narratives about Daniel's vindication and honoring by kings (Dan 1–2, 6, and so on) and the oracle about the "seventy weeks of years" (Dan 9:24–27) as being written by Daniel himself. In fact, in another place, Josephus reports that the Jerusalem priests showed Alexander the Great a copy of the book of Daniel with the oracles about the Greeks overthrowing the Persians, and Alexander "believed himself to be the one indicated".[10]

If we fast-forward to twentieth-century biblical scholarship, however, the attribution of the oracles to the prophet Daniel (to say nothing of the narratives) has been almost universally rejected. Instead, it is generally assumed that the book of Daniel was composed, not in the sixth-century B.C., but in the second century B.C., near the end of the oppressive reign of the Seleucid ruler Antiochus IV Epiphanes (ca. 175–164 B.C.). However, it is allowed that some of the narratives in the first half of the book (Dan 1–6) may stem from the Persian period (ca. 537–333 B.C.). Like the contrary view, the second-century dating of Daniel's oracles has ancient roots; it was first proposed by the third-century A.D. pagan philosopher Porphyry, in his famous treatise *Against the Christians*.[11] Although complete copies of the treatise have been lost, Jerome begins the preface to his *Commentary on Daniel* by referring to Porphyry's arguments:

---

[9] Josephus, *Antiquities* 10.266–68, in Josephus, *Jewish Antiquities Book 9–11*, trans. Ralph Marcus, Loeb Classical Library 326 (Cambridge, Mass.: Harvard University Press, 1937), 305–7.

[10] Ibid., 11.336–37, p. 477.

[11] See R. Joseph Hoffman, *Porphyry's Against the Christians* (Amherst, N.Y.: Prometheus Books, 1994).

Porphyry wrote his twelfth book against the prophecy of Daniel, denying that it was composed by the person to whom it is ascribed in its title, but rather by some individual living in Judaea at the time of Antiochus who was surnamed Epiphanes. *He furthermore alleged that "Daniel" did not foretell the future so much as he related the past*, and lastly that whatever he spoke of up till the time of Antiochus contained authentic history, whereas anything he may have conjectured beyond that point was false, inasmuch as he would not have foreseen the future.[12]

In modern times, scholars have expanded Porphyry's original arguments against the Danielic authorship of the Hebrew version. Although the issues are extremely complex, three principal arguments can be singled out as supporting the late, non-Danielic date of composition:

1. *Detailed Prophecies of the Reign of Antiochus*: The prophecies of the book, particularly Daniel 10–11, are considered too detailed and too accurate truly to have been composed prior to the events leading up to and including the reign of Antiochus Epiphanes. Instead, they are identified as *ex eventu* prophecies— prophecy after the fact—in the manner of extra-biblical Jewish apocalypses composed after the events prophetically described and tied to the names of great figures (for example, *2 Baruch*, *4 Ezra*).

2. *Apparent Historical Errors in the Book of Daniel*: There are apparent historical errors concerning the reigns of the Babylonian and Persian emperors in the opening narratives of the book (especially Dan 1–6). For example, Nebuchadnezzar is described as going mad (Dan 4:28–37), whereas some sources indicate that a later Babylonian king, Nabonidus, suffered mental illness. Moreover, Belshazzar is described as "king" (Dan 5:1; 8:1) and son of Nebuchadnezzar (Dan 5:11), although he was the son of Nabonidus and never formally installed as king. Finally, according to extra-biblical evidence, there were only about twenty known satrapies in the Persian Empire, so the 120 satraps of Darius seem exaggerated (Dan 6:1) (see insets on pp. 883–84). Taken together, problems such as these lead many modern scholars to the conclusion that the author was not familiar with the Babylonian and Persian period, but lived later.

3. *The Lack of Evidence for the Figure of "Darius the Mede"*: By far the most famous argument against the historical reliability (and, thus, authenticity) of the book of Daniel is that "Darius the Mede", the "son of Ahasuerus" whom Daniel describes as conquering Babylon and reigning over it (Dan 6:1–28; 9:1), is unknown to external historical sources. Some scholars take this as a deliberate attempt by the author of Daniel to "alert" the reader to its non-historical character.

In light of such evidence, most modern scholars on Daniel do not even feel the need to argue for the pseudonymous, second-century origins of the book. They are widely accepted as a given.

---

[12] Jerome, *Commentary on Daniel*, prologue, trans. Gleason L. Archer (1958; repr., Eugene, Ore.: Wipf & Stock, 2006), 15.

The Second-Century Origins of Daniel

With that said, as recent scholarship has also demonstrated, there are difficulties faced by the theory that the book of Daniel originated entirely in the second-century A.D. as an *ex eventu* prophecy written during the reign of Antiochus IV Epiphanes. These difficulties can be outlined as follows.

First, if the book of Daniel was in fact intended by the author to be understood as a non-historical account and *ex eventu* prophecies, then all of the known ancient interpreters of the book missed the point. Indeed, as we saw above, the first-century Jewish historian Josephus, writing only a couple of centuries after Antiochus IV Epiphanes not only interpreted the book as an actual account of a historical prophet, but he also emphasized that Daniel was renowned for the fact that he, unlike other prophets, not only told the future but did so with exactitude.[13] In other words, for ancient Jews and Christians who believed in the omniscience of God and the divine ability to reveal the future accurately, the argument from *ex eventu* prophecy is not conclusive. If the book is to be dated to the second century, it must be on other grounds.

Second, it may be that the apparent historical errors in Daniel are due to our misunderstanding of the text or incomplete or inaccurate external historical sources. As we noted above, critics used to consider the figure of Belshazzar (Dan 5) to be fictitious, because he was not mentioned in any extant extra-biblical literature. That changed in 1854, however, when Belshazzar's name was found on the Nabonidus Cylinder—a clay barrel inscribed with an account of the reign of King Nabonidus of Babylon (ca. 556–539 B.C.). Moreover, although Belshazzar was never formally installed as king, the Nabonidus Cylinder tells us that Nabonidus "entrusted the kingship" (Akk. *sharrutu*) to him, and we now know that the Aramaic word for "king" (*melek*) can be used loosely to describe a governor or ruler of a city.[14] In the same way, other apparent historical errors or our current inability to identify "Darius the Mede" may in fact be due to the extremely fragmentary state of our knowledge of ancient Babylon, Persia, and Media.

Third, in favor of a sixth-century date of composition, some scholars have pointed out that the Aramaic of the book is appropriate to that time period.[15] Moreover, several of the narratives reflect goodwill, cooperation, and/or reconciliation between devout Jews and the pagan emperor (Dan 1–6), something very unlikely to have been penned during the second century, when hostility and bloodshed were the rule of the day between the Jews and their pagan Greek overlords.

Fourth and finally, there are significant literary issues with interpreting all of the oracles in the book of Daniel (especially Dan 2, 7, and 9), with reference to the second-century B.C. persecution of the Jewish people by the Seleucid emperor Antiochus IV Epiphanes (ca. 165 B.C.). To be sure, some oracles—such as those regarding the "little horn" of the goat (Dan 8:9–14, 23–25) and the

[13] Josephus, *Antiquities* 10.266–68, pp. 305–7.
[14] Yamauchi, *Persia and the Bible*, 85–87; Lucas, "Daniel", 542.
[15] Kenneth A. Kitchen, "The Aramaic of Daniel", in *Notes on Some Problems in the Book of Daniel*, ed. D.J. Wiseman (London: Tyndale Press, 1965), 31–79.

"contemptible person" who rules as king (Dan 11:21–45)—are clearly about the reign of Antiochus, down to the details. On the other hand, there are difficulties with interpreting the vision of the fourth beast (Dan 7) with the kingdom of the Greeks and the vision of the "prince who is to come" (Dan 9:26–27) with the figure of Antiochus:

1. *Splitting the Medes and Persians into Two Empires*: In order to make the second-century interpretation of Daniel 2 and 7 work, scholars have to split the Medes and Persians into *two* different empires in order to have the fourth metal and the fourth beast be that of the Greeks.[16] But as we saw above, the book of Daniel itself repeatedly speaks of the one kingdom of "Medes and Persians" (Dan 5:28; cf. 6:8, 12, 15; 8:20). Hence, if we interpret the present form of the text according to its literary features, the third beast must be the Greeks, and the fourth the empire that followed: in retrospect, the Romans.

2. *The Internal Parallels between Daniel 7 and 8*: Furthermore, although the "little horn" of the beast (Dan 7:8) is described in ways that are similar to the "little horn" of the goat (Dan 8:9), there are also important differences between the two. Most importantly, it is difficult to correlate the beast of Daniel 7 with the goat of Daniel 8. The *lopsided* ram (Medo-Persia) and *four-horned, flying* goat (Greece) of Daniel 8 seem best to correlate with the *lopsided* bear and *four-winged, four-headed flying* leopard of Daniel 7, respectively. Thus, the "beast" of Daniel 7, which replaces the four-headed leopard (the Hellenistic empires of the *Diadochoi*), would have to be the successor empire of the Hellenistic empires: again, in hindsight, Rome. The "little horn" in the vision of the four beasts (Dan 7:8), then, could not be correlated with Antiochus, but must be a Roman ruler.

3. *Antiochus Did Not Destroy Jerusalem or the Temple*: According to the second-century interpretation of Daniel 9, Antiochus IV Epiphanes is the "prince who is to come [and] destroy the city and the sanctuary" (Dan 9:26). However, Antiochus Epiphanes did not destroy Jerusalem or the Temple; he only defiled them (cf. 1 Mac 1–2). As one prominent commentator on Daniel remarks: "The Syrians did not demolish Jerusalem."[17]

The difficulty all of this raises for the second-century dating of Daniel is that if these central oracles—Daniel 2, 7, and 9—are referring to a post-Hellenistic empire that would actually destroy the Jerusalem Temple, then—to be consistent in the interpretation of the book as *ex eventu* prophecy—the date of the book of Daniel should not be placed in the Greek period (second century B.C.) but needs to be moved forward into the *Roman period* (ca. first century A.D.). But this is, of course, impossible, since the book of Daniel is already being quoted in books written before and during the first century A.D. (for example, 1 Mac 2:59–60; *Sib. Or.* 3:397; Mt 24:15; Josephus, *Ant.* 10.266–68; 3 Mac 6:6–7). So one ends up with a certain inconsistency and a selective use of prophecies to demonstrate the *ex eventu* dating of the book.

---

[16] For example, Collins, *Daniel*, 166.
[17] Ibid., 357.

In sum, no interpretation of the date of composition of Daniel is without difficulties, and scholarship will likely continue to wrestle with these issues unless and until more data come to light.

Theological Issues in Daniel

Kingdom, Cult, and Martyrdom as Liturgy

The dominant theological concern of the book of Daniel is the (re)establishment of true worship of God. The book is concerned with current and future disruptions of the true liturgy associated with Jerusalem and the final, eschatological restoration of that liturgy.

Indeed, almost all the major conflicts of the first half of the book arise from the clash of two mutually exclusive liturgical empires or cultic kingdoms: the kingdom of man, embodied in the current monarch, and the kingdom of God, embodied in his chosen people. Several of the most colorful narratives of the book follow the experiences of the true worshippers of the Lord as they negotiate the conflicts between living in the kingdom of men and still maintaining citizenship in the kingdom of God. On more than one occasion, this balancing act requires of the worshipper of the Lord that he consent to his own death by agents of the earthly kingdoms in order to preserve his participation in the kingdom of God. This consent to self-sacrifice is given a liturgical coloring in Daniel 3 and, to a lesser extent, in Daniel 6; self-sacrifice replaces Temple sacrifices as the form of the "liturgy" of God's people.

One of the central questions of Daniel is: How does the faithful worshipper of the Lord cope when there is no longer any political expression of the kingdom of God (that is, the kingdom of Israel) or access to the true cult (the Temple liturgy) and he is compelled to participate in the earthly kingdom and its liturgy? The answers provided by the book are complex and sometimes surprising.

First, it is notable that both Daniel and his companions serve the king of Babylon with great skill and fidelity; in fact, the text commends them for their loyal and valuable service and never suggests that such service is in conflict with their commitment to God (Dan 1–2). One could imagine a devout author adopting a different approach. Would not any cooperation or loyalty to a pagan regime and a pagan ruler necessarily involve support of paganism?

However, the sacred author of Daniel does not adopt this paradigm of total nonparticipation in the kingdom of man. Instead, it is permissible and even laudatory for Daniel and his companions to participate in the civil service of the Babylonian Empire; they show loyalty (Dan 6:22) and, at times, even affection (Dan 4:19) for the civil ruler—all the more remarkable since one of the monarchs, Nebuchadnezzar, was responsible for the destruction of Jerusalem, the confiscation of the Temple vessels, and the razing of the Temple itself. Nonetheless, Daniel serves him faithfully and offers him counsel in his best interest (especially Dan 4:19–27). It is not the civil service but the state cult in which Daniel and his companions refuse to participate.

With Daniel and his companions, conflict arises over the issue of *worship*. Cut off from the Temple liturgy, exiled in a foreign land under a totalitarian regime, the Judean youths find that fidelity and obedience to God involve their consent to their own deaths. We have seen that, read canonically, the three young men in Daniel 3 essentially become holocausts in "substitute" for the Temple holocausts that have been cut off (Dan 3:15–16). So, in a sense, cut off from the Temple, the youths become incorporated into the "real" liturgy, or, expressed differently, they undergo a profound experience of the reality represented symbolically in the Temple liturgy, the reality of a worship of God that involves the total self-gift of the worshipper. In the two primary instances of this worship-through-self-gift (Dan 3 and 6), God acts in an extraordinary fashion for the deliverance of his worshippers, with the result that knowledge and praise of the Lord—one of the goals or *teloi* of the Temple and its liturgy—are spread among all the nations.

Therefore, Daniel is a book of hope, showing with some irony that in the midst of what appears to be the bleakest of times for the people of God— with no political expression of God's kingdom and no opportunity to celebrate the true liturgy—nonetheless, true worship is still offered in a more profound form, and the purpose for which both the people of God (Gen 12:3; 22:18; Ex 19:6) and the Temple itself (1 Kings 8:43) were established—namely, to spread the knowledge and worship of the Lord among the nations—is indeed being accomplished more successfully even than when the Temple stood and the Davidic king sat on the throne.

Daniel in the Living Tradition

Given its status as the last of the four "major prophets" and the fact that Daniel is heavily utilized by Jesus in the Gospels in his repeated emphasis on the "kingdom of God" and the "son of man", it is no surprise that Daniel became the object of intense study in the living tradition of the Church, especially in the early centuries in which Christians were defending the messianic identity and divinity of Jesus against pagan as well as Jewish critics. In this polemical context, Daniel was repeatedly used to demonstrate that the Old Testament prophesied not only the coming of the Messiah, but the time of his arrival, his death, and the ultimate destruction of the Temple.

The Stone and the Mountain and Christ and the Church

For example, Christian writers early on recognized the central significance of Daniel's interpretation of Nebuchadnezzar's dream. The metallic image is destroyed by the "stone cut out by no human hand" that grew and became a "great mountain" that spread throughout the earth (Dan 2). For the early Church Fathers, this was indeed a prophecy of the coming of Christ (the stone) and the Church universal (the mountain). Consider, for example, the words of Augustine of Hippo:

> We know that the stone cut from the mountain without hands is Christ, who
> came from the kingdom of the Jews without human father: the stone that shattered

all the kingdoms of the earth, all the tyrannies of idols and devils; the stone that grew and became a great mountain and filled the whole world.[18]

"His holy Hill" [Ps 3:4] is His holy church. It is that mountain which, according to Daniel's vision, grew from a very small "stone," till it crushed the kingdoms of the earth; and grew to such a size, that it "filled the face of the earth".[19]

Notice here that for Augustine, as for many of the Church Fathers, the victory of Christ and the Church over the universal worship of idols in the pagan world was always regarded as a visible motive of credibility for the truth of the Gospel as a fulfillment of prophecy for the Jewish people and a sign of the power of God to the pagans.

The "Son of God" in the Furnace and Christ's Descent into Hell

In addition to prophetic interpretation of the oracles in Daniel, the Church Fathers also engaged in typological interpretation of the narratives in the book. Perhaps the most striking of these is Jerome's interpretation of King Nebuchadnezzar's ability to see the one "like a son of the gods" in the furnace with Shadrach, Meshach, and Abednego (Dan 3:25). Although some Church Fathers made a simple equation between the son of God in Daniel and Christ, Jerome gave a more nuanced interpretation:

As for the appearance of the fourth man [in the furnace], which he asserts to be like that of a son of God ... we are to think of angels here, who after all are very frequently called gods as well as sons of God. So much for the story itself. But as for its *typical* significance, *this angel or son of God foreshadows our Lord Jesus Christ, who descended into the furnace of hell*, in which the souls of both sinners and of the righteous were imprisoned, in order that He might without suffering any scorching by fire or injury to His person deliver those who were held imprisoned by chains of death.[20]

For Jerome, then, the account of the three men is far more than just a moral example of fortitude in the face of persecution. Rather, the suffering of the righteous Jews in the furnace of Nebuchadnezzar and their deliverance from the flames by the angelic son of God is a foreshadowing of the same deliverance the righteous dead will experience in the paschal descent of Jesus into the realm of Hades.

The Son of Man and the Eternal Kingdom, Not the Maccabean Revolt

Given the importance of the Danielic son of man in the teaching of Jesus, it is unsurprising that the Church Fathers produced a wealth of material discussing Daniel's vision of the coming of "one like a son of man" on the clouds of heaven (Dan 7:13–14). For our purposes here, two points are worth highlighting.

[18] Augustine, *Homilies on 1 John* 1.13, in *NPNF1* 7:467.
[19] Augustine, *Explanations of the Psalms* 43.4, in *NPNF1* 8:139.
[20] Jerome, *Commentary on Daniel* 3.92 [25], pp. 43–44.

First and foremost, this passage was almost universally interpreted by the Church Fathers as an *eschatological* prophecy about both (1) the Second Advent of Christ at the end of time and (2) the rise of the Antichrist in the latter days. In this regard, the catechetical lectures of Cyril of Jerusalem are quite representative:

> What we proclaim is not one single coming of Christ but a second as well, much fairer than the first. For the first presented a demonstration of long-suffering, but the second wears the crown of the kingdom of God.... *These doctrines are not the fruit of ingenuity but are derived from the sacred scriptures read in the church, particularly as gathered out of the prophecy of Daniel,* in today's lection, and according to the interpretation given by the archangel Gabriel, who spoke as follows, "the fourth beast shall be the fourth kingdom on earth, which shall surpass all kingdoms." Ecclesiastical commentators have traditionally taking this kingdom to be the Roman Empire.... Further on Gabriel continues his interpreting and says, "... Another king shall rise up, and he shall surpass in wickedness all who were before him...." Antichrist is a blasphemer and flouter of all law.[21]

Second, not only was the eschatological interpretation of Daniel 7 taught as common doctrine, but the Maccabean interpretation (forwarded by Porphyry, for example) was rejected by Theodoret of Cyrus, who writes in his commentary:

> This is the end of all affairs of this life, all the empires of the earth coming to a close and the eternal kingdom being given to the holy ones of the Most High ... (Dan 7:25). This cannot be applied to the Maccabees; instead of being entrusted with kingship, they led troops and conquered and met a rapid end.[22]

Theodoret has a point here: if Daniel 7 really was written in order to give the promise of an eternal kingdom to the Jewish people at the time of the Maccabean revolt, then he would have quickly been proven wrong by the turning tide of historical events, in which the Maccabean family was given anything but an "everlasting" kingdom.

The 490 Years and the Time of Christ's Coming

Finally, as noted above, although the text and interpretation of the oracle regarding the coming of the "messiah" (Dan 9:24–27) are complex and debated, in the living tradition, it was widely regarded as one of the greatest prophecies in the Old Testament because it not only told what would happen (the coming and death of the messiah) but when it would happen. In the words of Jerome's preface to his commentary:

---

[21] Cyril of Jerusalem, *Catechetical Lectures* 15.1, 13, in Kenneth Stevenson and Michael Glerup, *Ezekiel, Daniel*, Old Testament 13, Ancient Christian Commentary on Scripture, ed. Thomas C. Oden (Downers Grove, Ill.: InterVarsity Press, 2008), 244.

[22] Theodoret of Cyrus, *Commentary on Daniel* 7.27–28, in Stevenson and Glerup, *Ezekiel, Daniel*, 246.

I wish to stress in my preface this fact, that none of the prophets has so clearly spoken concerning Christ as has this prophet Daniel. For not only did he assert that He would come, a prediction common to the other prophets as well, but also he set forth the very time at which He would come.[23]

[W]e must count the numbers, that is to say the seventy weeks, which are 490 years, from the going forth of the word of answer and from the building of Jerusalem.... For Nehemiah his cup-bearer made the request, and received the answer that Jerusalem should be rebuilt, and the order went forth to carry it out.... *And from that date to the coming of Christ is seventy weeks.*[24]

In short, for both Jerome and Eusebius—two giants among ancient Christian writers—the "seventy weeks of years"—that is, 490 years—between the "going forth of the word to restore and build Jerusalem" (Dan 9:25) and the coming of an "anointed one" (Dan 9:26) refers to the 490 years that elapsed between the time of King Artaxerxes of Persia's decree to rebuild the Temple in the fifth century B.C. (see Ezra 7:11–26) and the coming of Christ in the first century A.D.[25] Consider the following timeline of events:

The Prophecy of the Messiah's Death (Daniel 9:25–27)		
Daniel's Prophecy	*Historical Events*	*Dates*
Word to restore Jerusalem	Artaxerxes' decree: Rebuild the Temple	ca. 457 B.C.
Seventy weeks of years	70 × 7 Years = 490 Years	457 B.C.–33 A.D.
"Messiah" will be "cut off"	Jesus is crucified	ca. A.D. 33
"City and sanctuary" destroyed	Jerusalem & Temple destroyed	A.D. 70

The Book of Daniel in the Liturgy

We have noted the strong liturgical themes and concern for the Temple sanctuary that run throughout Daniel, even calling Daniel a story of struggle between two "liturgical empires", the kingdom of God and the kingdom of man.

In the proclamation of Daniel in the contemporary liturgy of God's people, the most treasured passages are from the longer Greek version: the Prayer of Azariah and the Song of the Three Young Men (Dan 3 LXX). These texts are liturgical in their very nature and may, in fact, be adaptations of texts recited in worship at the sanctuary in Jerusalem from the First or Second Temple periods. They continue to serve admirably as expressions of communal repentance and petition (Prayer of Azariah) or universal, jubilant exaltation of God (Song of the Three Young Men). The Prayer is employed in some weekday Masses of Lent

---

[23] Jerome, *Commentary on Daniel*, prologue, p. 15.

[24] Eusebius of Caesarea, *Proof of the Gospel* 8.2.389, trans. W.J. Ferrar (1920; repr., Eugene, Ore.: Wipf & Stock, 2001), 124–25.

[25] Jerome, *Commentary on Daniel*, 9.24–27, p. 96.

and for special Masses for situations of duress. The Song functions as a response
for the Solemnity of the Holy Trinity and during all the ferial Masses of the last
week in Ordinary Time (Thirty-Fourth) in Year 1. In this way, the people of
God complete the liturgical year calling on the entire cosmos to join in praise
of God, in light of his act of deliverance. In the Liturgy of the Hours, selections
from the Song comprise the Canticle for every Sunday, thus beginning each
weekly cycle of prayer with a call for cosmic praise.

Other passages of Daniel that have honored places in the liturgical calendar include the vision of the "son of man" presented to the "ancient of days"
(Dan 7:9–14) and the arising of Saint Michael and the general resurrection (Dan
12:1–3). In Daniel's vision of the "son of man", read for the Feast of the Transfiguration and of Christ the King, the Church perceives a prophecy of the glorification of Jesus Christ and his role as king over all creation. Daniel 12:1–3 is
one of the most succinct scriptural descriptions of the general resurrection at the
end of the age, so the Church meditates on it near the very end of the liturgical
year (Thirty-Third Sunday, Year B).

Readings from Daniel in the Lectionary and Liturgy of the Hours on Sundays, Feast Days, Liturgical Seasons, and Other Occasions *MSO*= Masses for Special Occasions; *OM*= Optional Memorial; *VM*= Votive Mass; *Rit*= Ritual; *LH*= Liturgy of the Hours			
Passage	Description	Occasion	Explanation
3:14–20, 91–92, 95	The basic story of the three men in the fiery furnace	Wed., 5th Week of Lent	The first readings of Lent highlight accounts of the persecution of Old Testament saints in order to prepare the faithful to understand Christ's Passion in continuity with the experience of the heroes of Israel's faith.
3:25, 34–43	Azariah prays in lament and repen- tance, pleading to God on the basis of the covenant with Abraham to accept their lives as a pleasing sacrifice.	Tues., 3rd Week of Lent; *MSO*: For Persecuted Christians; For Good Weather or Any Need	Azariah's prayer superbly articulates the attitude of communal repentance adopted by the Church during the penitential season of Lent. It also expresses the sentiments of local churches undergoing persecution or any other form of duress.
3:26–41 (excerpts)	Lament portion of the Prayer of Azariah	*LH*: Canticle for Morn. Prayer Tues., Week IV	Week IV of the *LH* focuses on peni- tence, employing classic penitential prayers from the Old Testament.
3:52–55	Excerpt from the Song of the Three Young Men, calling on the earth to praise God	*Holy Trinity (A)* (resp.); Wed., Week V of Lent (resp.)	The Holy Trinity deserves praise for its own sake; the song of the young men calls on all nature to praise the true God.

(continued)

Readings from Daniel in the Lectionary and Liturgy of the Hours on Sundays, Feast Days, Liturgical Seasons, and Other Occasions (*continued*)			
MSO = Masses for Special Occasions; *OM* = Optional Memorial; *VM* = Votive Mass; *Rit* = Ritual; *LH* = Liturgy of the Hours			
Passage	Description	Occasion	Explanation
3:52–57	Excerpt of praises from the Song of the Three Young Men	*LH*: Canticle for Morn. Prayer, Sun., Weeks II & IV	Sunday, as the particular day of worship and the start of each weekly cycle of the *LH*, is especially appropriate for the recitation of the universal call to praise expressed in the Song of the Three Young Men.
3:56–88	Extensive section of praises from the Song of the Three Young Men	*LH*: Canticle for Morn. Prayer, Sun., Weeks I & III	See above. This longer selection of praise begins the entire four-week cycle in Week I.
7:9–10, 13–14	The Ancient of Days sits upon his heavenly throne; the "son of man" is presented and receives the kingdom of heaven.	Feast of the Transfiguration (Aug. 6)	This account of Daniel's vision of the glorification of the "son of man" sheds light on the identity of Jesus Christ and the significance of his appearance in glory on top of the Mount of Transfiguration.
7:13–14	Daniel sees the one "like a son of man" coming on clouds to receive the kingdom.	*Christ the King (B) (34th Sun. in OT)*	Jesus is the "Son of Man" who receives the universal kingdom. Daniel 7:13–14 reminds us that the mission of Christ was prophesied of old, and in the future all things will be visibly under his authority.
9:4b–10	Daniel's prayer of repentance on behalf of Israel and Jerusalem	Mon., 2nd Week of Lent	The first readings of Lent make generous use of the classic prayers of repentance embedded in the narrative of the Old Testament.
12:1–3	The arising of Michael and the general resurrection	*33rd Sun. in OT (B)*; Mass for the Dead, opt. 7	The last weeks of Ordinary Time (occurring in November) are given over to meditation on the Last Things. Daniel 12:1–3 is a classic vision of the resurrection from the Old Testament.
13:1–62 (excerpts)	The story of Susannah, condensed	Mon., 5th Week of Lent	Susannah is an example to believers of faithfulness while suffering unjust persecution and defamation, appropriate to Lent as the Church ponders the mystery of suffering in the life of holiness.

In Year 1, the Church reads the first half of Daniel semi-continuously in the last week in Ordinary Time (Thirty-Fourth Week). In Year 2, the Church reads Revelation at this time, and the parallel is instructive. The Church perceives Daniel as the quintessential "eschatological" book of the Old Testament, which foresees the culmination of human history. The perseverance of Daniel and his companions through their various trials under the oppressive Babylonian regime is a type of the perseverance of the saints through the coming final tribulation. The vision of Daniel 7, with which the ferial calendar comes to an end, foresees and summarizes the climax of salvation history, in which the authority of all human kingdoms will pass into the hands of Jesus of Nazareth, the Son of Man.

Reading of Daniel for Daily Mass: Ordinary Time, Year I: Week 34			
Week	Day	Passage Read	Description
34	M	1:1–20; 3:52–56 (resp.)	Daniel and his three companions are exiled, trained, refuse the king's food, and rise in the king's service.
34	Tu	2:31–45; 3:57–61 (resp.)	Daniel recounts and interprets Nebuchadnezzar's dream of the metallic image and its destruction.
34	W	5:1–28 (sel.); 3:62–67 (resp.)	Belshazzar sees the handwriting on the wall; Daniel interprets and is rewarded with high office.
34	Th	6:12–28; 3:68–74 (resp.)	Daniel in the lions' den: Daniel prays in defiance of the king's ordinance, is cast to the lions, survives, is vindicated.
34	F	7:2–14; 3:75–81 (resp.)	Daniel's vision of the four beasts from the sea; the son of man receives the kingdom from the Ancient of Days.
34	Sa	7:15–27; 3:82–87 (resp.)	An angel explains the vision of the four beasts, the fifth beast, and the one "like a son of man".

The role of Daniel in the Office of Readings of the Liturgy of the Hours is similar, if less pronounced. Semi-continuous reading of chapters 1–12 commences in the Thirty-Second Week in Ordinary Time, during the contemplation of the Last Things characteristic of November.

In sum, then, the liturgical use of Daniel shows that the Church values this text primarily as a source of encouragement to persevere through persecution until the culmination of human history in the kingdom of the Christ.

Conclusion

The book of Daniel is a collection of biographical narratives and prophecies concerning the figure of Daniel, a Jewish exile, courtier, and prophet in Babylon. The book circulated in longer and shorter editions in antiquity, but the longer edition was canonized by the Church. The book roughly divides into narratives about the adventures of Daniel and his Jewish companions in the service of the Babylonian and Persian courts (Dan 1–6) and prophecies about the sequence of kingdoms, events, and chronology until the coming of the kingdom of God (Dan 7–12). Three dischronologized narratives of Daniel's life form an epilogue (Dan 13–14).

The book has a pronounced liturgical focus and presents, in essence, an understanding of world history as that of conflict between two mutually

			Daniel in the Office of Readings for the Liturgy of the Hours, Ordinary Time, Week 32
Week	Day	Passage	Description
32	Su	1:1–21	Daniel and his three companions are exiled, trained, refuse the king's food, and rise in the king's service.
32	M	2:26–47	Daniel recounts and interprets Nebuchadnezzar's dream of the metallic image and its destruction.
32	Tu	3:8–12, 19–24, 91–97	The account of the three young men cast into the fiery furnace
32	W	5:1–6:1 excerpts	Belshazzar sees the handwriting on the wall; Daniel interprets and is rewarded with high office. Babylon is captured by Darius the Mede.
32	Th	9:1–4a, 18–27	Daniel ponders Jeremiah's prophecy and prays in repentance; Gabriel arrives and reveals the seventy-week chronology until the arrival of the Messiah and destruction of the sanctuary.
32	F	10:1–21	The "man clothed in linen" appears to Daniel to reveal the course of events in the latter days.
32	Sa	12:1–13	The angel reveals to Daniel the final resurrection and the cryptic chronology until all things are fulfilled.

exclusive sacral-liturgical kingdoms: the kingdom of man and the kingdom of God, with the eventual triumph of the latter. The Temple and its liturgy are central concerns, and several narratives explore the dilemma of faithful worshippers who lack access to participation in the liturgy of the Lord, suggesting that the embrace of martyrdom may constitute a substitute for sacrificial worship. The Church's Lectionary most values Daniel as a book of eschatological vision and reads from it at or near the end of the Church year as part of her anticipation of the Second Advent.

For Further Reading

Commentaries and Studies on Daniel

Chisholm, Robert B. *Handbook on the Prophets.* Grand Rapids, Mich.: Baker Academic, 2002. (See pp. 291–333.)

Collins, John J. *Daniel: A Commentary on the Book of Daniel.* Hermeneia. Minneapolis: Fortress Press, 1993.

DeSilva, David A. *Introducing the Apocrypha: Message, Context, and Significance.* Grand Rapids, Mich.: Baker Academic, 2002. (See pp. 222–43.)

Goldingay, John. *Daniel.* Word Biblical Commentary 30. Dallas: Word, 1989.

Hartman, Louis F., and Alexander A. Di Lella. *The Book of Daniel.* Anchor Bible 23. New York: Doubleday, 1978.

Moore, Carey A. *Daniel, Esther, and Jeremiah: The Additions.* Anchor Bible 44. New York: Doubleday, 1977. (See pp. 1–147.)

Historical Issues in Daniel

Collins, John J., and Peter W. Flint, eds. *The Book of Daniel: Composition and Reception.* 2 vols. Leiden and Boston: Brill, 2001.

Kitchen, Kenneth A. "The Aramaic of Daniel". Pages 31–79 in *Notes on Some Problems in the Book of Daniel.* Edited by D.J. Wiseman. London: The Tyndale Press, 1965.

Lucas, Ernest C. "Daniel". Pages 518–75 in *Isaiah, Jeremiah, Lamentations, Ezekiel, Daniel.* Vol. 4 of *Zondervan Illustrated Bible Backgrounds Commentary.* Edited by John H. Walton. Grand Rapids, Mich.: Zondervan, 2009.

Rowley, Harold Henry. *Darius the Mede and the Four World Empires in the Book of Daniel.* Repr., Eugene, Ore.: Wipf & Stock, 2006.

Sperber, Daniel. *Greek in Talmudic Palestine.* Ramat Gan: Bar-Ilan University Press, 2012.

Yamauchi, Edwin M. *Persia and the Bible.* Grand Rapids, Mich.: Baker Book House, 1990.

Daniel in the Living Tradition

Hippolytus, Saint. "Commentary on Daniel". Pages 177–94 in vol. 5 of *Ante-Nicene Fathers.* Edited by Alexander Roberts and James Donaldson. 1886. Repr., Peabody, Mass.: Hendrickson, 1994.

Jerome, Saint. *Commentary on Daniel.* Translated by Gleason L. Archer. Grand Rapids, Mich.: Baker Book House, 1958. Repr., Eugene, Ore.: Wipf & Stock, 2006.

McDonald, Lee Martin. *The Biblical Canon: Its Origin, Transmission, and Authority.* Grand Rapids, Mich.: Baker Academic, 2007. (See pp. 439–44.)

Stevenson, Kenneth, and Michael Glerup. *Ezekiel, Daniel.* Ancient Christian Commentary on Scripture. Edited by Thomas C. Oden. Old Testament 13. Downers Grove, Ill.: InterVarsity Press, 2008. (See pp. 149–313.)

Theodoret of Cyrus. *Commentary on Daniel.* Translated by Robert C. Hill. Writings from the Greco-Roman World 7. Leiden and Boston: Brill, 2006.

Voicu, Sever J. *Apocrypha.* Old Testament 15 of Ancient Christian Commentary on Scripture. Edited by Thomas C. Oden. Downers Grove, Ill.: InterVarsity Press, 2010. (See pp. 443–74.)

36. THE BOOK OF THE TWELVE MINOR PROPHETS

In contrast to contemporary Bibles, in which the twelve "minor prophets"—Hosea through Malachi—are printed as twelve separate books, in antiquity they were written on a single scroll and treated as one book, the "Book of the Twelve". This practice was already established at least as early as the second century B.C., as can be seen from the Dead Sea Scrolls, which include the oldest extant copies of the Book of the Twelve.[1] With the transition from scrolls to codices and the rise of Christianity, the Book of the Twelve began to be treated more frequently as a series of individual books, but they have continued to form a distinct unit within the canon with a fairly rigid traditional order among themselves.

In this chapter, we will treat the twelve both as a unit and as individual compositions. For reasons of space, historical and theological issues will be dealt with in the overview itself and in the sidebars. The chapter will conclude with a brief look at some of the key passages from the Book of the Twelve that have left their mark on the living tradition.

The Book of the Twelve as a Canonical Unit

Even when the twelve minor prophets are treated as a single unit, they consist of about 20,000 Hebrew words, which is still significantly shorter than the shortest of the three major prophets of the Hebrew tradition, Ezekiel (~26,000 Hebrew words). In this regard, the chapter divisions in current editions can be somewhat deceptive. For example, the longest of the minor prophets, Zechariah, is about *half* the length of the book of Daniel, even though they both have fourteen chapters (~8800 vs. ~4400 words). The shortness of the twelve compositions, combined with their many similarities in theme and perspective, motivated ancient scribes to treat them as a composite unit.

The Twelve by Length		
1. Zechariah	Words ~4400	Chaps. 14
2. Hosea	~3100	14
3. Amos	~2800	9
4. Micah	~1900	7
5. Joel	~1300	3 or 4
6. Malachi	~1200	4
7. Zephaniah	~1025	3
8. Jonah	~980	4
9. Habakkuk	~890	3
10. Haggai	~870	2
11. Nahum	~730	3
12. Obadiah	~400	1

The traditional order of the twelve familiar to contemporary readers (Hosea through Malachi) is that of the Latin Vulgate, which in this instance follows

---

[1] See Martin G. Abegg Jr., Peter Flint, and Eugene Ulrich, *The Dead Sea Scrolls Bible: The Oldest Known Bible Translated for the First Time into English* (San Francisco: HarperOne, 1999), 415.

| Different Orders of the Twelve ||
Masoretic Text & Vulgate	Septuagint
Hosea	Hosea
Joel	Amos
Amos	Micah
Obadiah	Joel
Jonah	Obadiah
Micah	Jonah
Nahum	Nahum
Habakkuk	Habakkuk
Zephaniah	Zephaniah
Haggai	Haggai
Zechariah	Zechariah
Malachi	Malachi

exactly the traditional Hebrew text (Masoretic Text) and is also attested in seven of the eight manuscripts of the twelve from Qumran. The Greek Septuagint employs a slightly different order, beginning with Hosea–Amos–Micah and then the rest of the books following in their usual order. A single manuscript from Qumran places Jonah at the end of the twelve, but this arrangement was not adopted in the tradition of any religious community.

The traditional order of the twelve intends to be approximately historical. It begins with prophets who were understood to have ministered in the eighth century B.C. (Hosea, Joel, Amos, Jonah, Micah), then prophets of the seventh century B.C. (Nahum, Habakkuk, Zephaniah), of the sixth century B.C. (Haggai, Zechariah), and then, finally, of the fifth century B.C. (Malachi). Obadiah and Joel may be exceptions to this pattern, but neither has explicit indications of date in its heading, and both were probably considered to be older in antiquity than most critical scholarship holds them to be today. The Septuagint order is more strongly historical, beginning with the three prophets who clearly ministered in the eighth century (Hosea, Amos, Micah), followed by three believed to have done so (Joel, Obadiah, Jonah), and then the rest in approximate historical order.

Approximate Dates for the Ministries of the Twelve	
Hosea	ca. 750–725 B.C.
Joel	ca. 760 B.C.?
Amos	ca. 770–760 B.C.
Obadiah	ca. 585 B.C.?
Jonah	ca. 782–745 B.C.
Micah	ca. 740–705 B.C.
Nahum	ca. 650 B.C.
Habakkuk	ca. 626–590 B.C.
Zephaniah	ca. 640–610 B.C.
Haggai	ca. 520 B.C.
Zechariah	ca. 520–516 B.C.
Malachi	ca. 450

In the rabbinic Jewish tradition, the Book of the Twelve is placed after the three great prophets (Isaiah, Jeremiah, Ezekiel), forming the conclusion of the second canonical division, the Prophets (Hebrew *nevi'im*). In this way, the message of the twelve is highlighted as God's "last word" to Israel, especially Malachi, which concludes with what appear to be last instructions to the people of God as they await the eschatological judgment (Mal 3:19–23 [= Mal 4:1–5]):[2] Stay faithful to the Mosaic covenant until the return of Elijah, who will precede the "great and awesome day of the LORD" (Mal 3:23 [4:5]). In the Greek Septuagint tradition, the twelve actually *precede* the four major prophets (Isaiah, Jeremiah, Ezekiel, Daniel), which tends to reduce their significance somewhat to the level of theological "appetizers" prior to the greater prophetic works.

---

[2] When two verse references are given for a minor prophet, the first is to the Hebrew text (e.g., NAB), the second is to the Latin text (e.g., RSV). See p. 972.

Why Begin with Hosea?

Hosea was probably placed first among the twelve because the opening chapters reveal the nuptial mystery of the relationship between YHWH and Israel so strongly: Israel (or Judah or Jerusalem) is the Lord's bride who has become a harlot but will be espoused once again (Hos 1–3). This theme runs through several of the minor prophets and culminates in a sense in the word given through Malachi: "I hate divorce, says the LORD" (Mal 2:16). In this way, Hosea and Malachi form a kind of *inclusio* around the twelve, with Hosea introducing the nuptial allegory of the Lord and Israel and Malachi insisting that the Lord does not divorce. In this way, the twelve are construed as a composite document concerned with the nuptial-covenantal relationship between the Lord and his people, and the readers have the assurance from Malachi that this relationship will never be repudiated.

The Vulgate follows the Hebrew tradition in placing the twelve at the end of the prophets. In this way, Malachi provides the last prophetic word—keep the law and wait for Elijah!—and the books of Maccabees provide a historical narrative bridge to the New Testament, in which John the Baptist (the new Elijah) will burst onto the stage of history (Mt 3:1–17).

Finally, as a close study of the Hebrew names shows, the majority of the names of the twelve minor prophets have meanings that can often be tied to the message of that particular prophet (see chart):

The Names of the Twelve Minor Prophets				
English	Hebrew	Meaning	Greek	Latin
Hosea	*hoshēa'*	"save!"	*Ōsēè*	*Osee*
Joel	*yô'ēl*	"The LORD is God"	*Iōēl*	*Ioel*
Amos	*'āmôs*	"burdened"	*Amōs*	*Amos*
Obadiah	*'obadyāh*	"servant of the LORD"	*Abdioù*	*Abdias*
Jonah	*yônāh*	"dove"	*Iōnās*	*Ionas*
Micah	*mîkhāh*	"who is like [God]?"	*Michaías*	*Micha*
Nahum	*nahûm*	"comforted", "relieved"	*Naoùm*	*Naum*
Habakkuk	*hăbaqqûq*	"embraced"	*Abakoùm*	*Abacuc*
Zephaniah	*tsĕphanyāh*	"the LORD has hidden"	*Sophonías*	*Sofonias*
Haggai	*haggay*	"feast of the LORD"	*Aggaîos*	*Aggeus*
Zechariah	*zekharyāh*	"the LORD remembers"	*Zacharías*	*Zaccharias*
Malachi	*mal'ākhî*	"my messenger"	*Malachías*	*Malachi*

Overview of the Book of the Twelve

I. Hosea: The Lord's Romance with Israel

1. *The Context of Hosea*: According to the opening lines of the book, the prophet "Hosea, the son of Beeri" was active during the reigns of King "Uzziah, Jotham,

Ahaz, and Hezekiah, kings of Judah, and in the days of Jeroboam the son of
Joash, king of Israel" (Hos 1:1), that is, in the eighth century B.C. Hosea himself
was probably active from 750–725 B.C., and his written prophecies seem all to
have preceded the destruction of northern Israel in 722 B.C.

Significantly, Hosea is the only northern Israelite among the twelve minor
prophets, and he directs his ministry toward his homeland. He frequently calls
northern Israel "Ephraim" because that tribe was the largest and most central
and provided the kings for the federation of ten tribes (Hos 6:4). Indeed, perhaps more than any other major or minor prophet, Hosea stresses the enduring
love of God for Israel, specifically *northern* Israel. Hosea reminds us that God has
not forgotten these tribes of Israel or narrowed his concern only to the southern
tribes of Judah (cf. Hos 2:1–2 [1:10–11]).

Nothing is known about Hosea other than the information he provides in his
book, which primarily concerns his marriage to his promiscuous and unfaithful
wife, Gomer, which he undertook by command of the Lord in order to provide a vivid depiction to Israel of her spiritual state in relationship to God (Hos
1–3). By Gomer, Hosea had three children, to whom he gave names symbolizing the fractured relationship between YHWH and Israel. Afterward, Gomer
abandoned him for a time, ending up as a slave, at which point Hosea went to
purchase her back and made her live with him in continence for an indefinite
period (Hos 3).

2. *The Structure of the Book of Hosea*: The book of Hosea divides clearly into
two parts: (1) Hosea's symbolic marriage to Gomer (Hos 1–3) and (2) the Lord's
covenant-lawsuit against Israel (Hos 4–14). Although subunits can be difficult to
identify, the book can be outlined as follows:

Outline of the Book of Hosea

I. Hosea and Gomer and YHWH and Israel (Hos 1–3)
  A. Hosea's Early Marriage to Gomer (1)
    B. The Lord's Marriage to Unfaithful Israel (2)
  A'. Hosea Resumes His Marriage to Gomer after Infidelity (3)

II. The Lord's Covenant-Lawsuit against Israel (Hos 4–14)
  A. The Lord's Prosecution (4:1—14:1 [4:1—13:16])
  B. Hosea's Appeal for Repentance (14:2–10 [14:1–9])

As form-critical analyses have shown, part 2 of Hosea is shaped as a "dispute"
or "covenant-lawsuit" (Hebrew *rib*) that the Lord brings against Israel, based
on analogy with ancient judicial procedures, in which one citizen would take
another to court for breaking a covenant ("breach of contract"). From this point
of view, the Mosaic covenant formed a legal bond between the Lord and Israel,
which Israel has broken. Now the Lord calls Israel into court to answer for her
crimes. Mixed into the Lord's *rib* are literary units of different genres, appeals
from the prophet for the people's repentance, and oracles of judgment. There
are frequent reminiscences of Israel's sacred history, from the patriarchs through

the period of the early monarchy. The prophet seems well aware of the story line of Genesis through Samuel.

3. *The Message of Hosea*: Hosea's theological outlook is strongly covenantal, being firmly grounded on the covenant structure of the primary Old Testament historical narrative (Genesis–Samuel), to which he makes frequent and generous reference. As the opening narrative about his marriage to Gomer makes clear, he understands the Mosaic covenant as a kind of *betrothal* between the Lord and Israel, and this nuptial mystery dominates the rhetoric of his book (Hos 1–3). Indeed, God repeatedly accuses Israel of "harlotry" in both a spiritual and a literal sense. The crimes of Ephraim include (1) trusting in covenants with Egypt and Assyria rather than in the covenant with the Lord, (2) idolatry and paganism, especially directed to the calf idols in Bethel and Samaria, (3) sexual immorality, and (4) general social injustice ("swearing, lying, killing, stealing"; Hos 4:2).

Indeed, the heart of Hosea's understanding of the covenant is expressed in the oracle in which the prophet, speaking in the name of the Lord, not only talks of the spiritual adultery committed by Israel in the past but also promises a new marriage covenant in days to come:

> And in that day, says the LORD, *you will call me, "My husband," and no longer will you call me, "My Baal."* For I will remove the names of the Baals from her mouth, and they shall be mentioned by name no more. *And I will make for you a covenant on that day* with the beasts of the field, the birds of the air, and the creeping things of the ground; and I will abolish the bow, the sword, and war from the land; and I will make you lie down in safety. *And I will espouse you for ever; I will espouse you in righteousness and in justice, in steadfast love, and in mercy.* I will espouse you in faithfulness; and you shall know the LORD. (Hos 2:16–20 RSVCE 2)

Several aspects of this central oracle are worth highlighting. First, notice the striking wordplay here on the Hebrew term *ba'al*, which can mean "master", "lord", or "husband" (in a domineering sense). The pagan gods were called *ba'alim*, "lords", and the chief Canaanite deity was known as "Baal" as a proper name. By stark contrast, YHWH speaks of a future time in which the nuptial relationship between himself and Israel will be resumed on a basis of intimacy: "you will call me, 'My husband'" (Hebrew *'ishî*), and not on the basis of the master-servant dynamic ("no longer will you call me, 'My Baal'" [master]). Second, notice also that this New Covenant will include the beasts, birds, and creeping things, suggesting a renewal of the *shalom* or peace characteristic of the initial Adamic or creation covenant, while the abolishment of the "bow" evokes the memory of the Noahic covenant; the sign of which was God's bow hung up in the sky (that is, retired from battle, Gen 9:13). Finally, the promise to "espouse" or "betroth" Israel is repeated three times as way of stressing the solemnity of the promise— and perhaps reflecting ritual repetition of promises in ancient marriage ceremonies. The promise "you shall know the LORD" has the connotation of marital intimacy, not simply intellectual knowledge, based on the use of the Hebrew *yada'* ("know") to refer to marital relations (for example, Gen 4:1, 17, 25).

Although the Mosaic covenant conceived as betrothal predominates throughout the book, Hosea does not lack references to the other pivotal covenants of salvation history or to other images of the relationship between God and his people. To the contrary, the book is replete with allusions to the various covenants of salvation history: the Adamic, Abrahamic, Mosaic, and Davidic. For example, Hosea compares Israel's covenant infidelity to that of Adam, in a passage that reads literally in the Hebrew: "Like Adam, they transgressed the covenant" (Hos 6:7 [author's trans.]). Hosea also hearkens back to the exodus when he includes oracles that make heavy use of *filial* (sonship) *imagery*, such as in the famous "Out of Egypt I called my son" passage (Hos 11:1; cf. Ex 4:22). Thus, Israel can be portrayed both as bride of YHWH and as son of God throughout the book. Finally, the prophet also makes indirect references to the promises of the covenant with Abraham (for example, Hos 1:10; cf. Gen 22:17), and he foresees the restoration of the covenant with the house of David (Hos 1:11; 3:5).

II. Joel: The Prophet of the "Day of the Lord"

1. *The Context of Joel*: Nothing is known of the life and ministry of the prophet Joel aside from the very little that can be gleaned from indications in the book: for example, that he was the son of an unknown man named Pethu'el (Joel 1:1). Nor does the book contain any clear references to datable events.

However, because (1) the king is never mentioned, (2) the Temple is functioning (Joel 1:16), (3) other nations have misused the Judeans and divided their land (Joel 4:1–8; 19 [3:1–8; 19]), and (4) some passages appear influenced by other prophets (for example, Ezekiel, Zechariah), most contemporary scholars imagine a postexilic date for the prophet's ministry and the writing of his book (ca. 450–400 B.C.), after the Temple had been rebuilt. However, none of the evidence above is conclusive, and, as we saw above, ancient Jewish tradition remembered the book as an early work, placing it among the older eighth-century prophets in the structure of the twelve (Hosea, Amos, Micah). In the history of modern scholarship, dozens of plausible proposals for the book's date have been advanced, from the ninth through the third centuries B.C. It has been accurately said that the book "resists dating". This may be, in part, because it is a liturgical document that was reused in the Temple cult and, thus, became generalized to fit changing historical circumstances.

2. *The Structure of the Book of Joel*: The book of Joel divides rather easily into two major sections: (1) a lament to God and response from God occasioned by a plague of locusts on Judah (Joel 1–2), and (2) a collection of oracles about the coming "day of the LORD" (Joel 3). Thus, the literary structure of the book can be outlined as follows:

Outline of the Book of Joel

I. The Plague of Locusts on Judah (Joel 1–2)
    A. Description of the Plague and Calls for Repentance (1)
    B. Oracle of a Coming Locust-Like Military Invasion (2:1–17)
        1. The Coming Invasion (2:1–11)
        2. The Call to Repentance (2:12–17)
    C. Oracle of Salvation and Restoration from the Lord (2:18–27)

II. The Coming Day of the Lord (Joel 3–4 [2:28—4:13])
    A. Signs, Wonders, and Salvation on Mount Zion (3:1–5 [2:28–32])
    B. Judgment on the Nations in the Valley of Jehoshaphat (4:1–6 [3:1–6])
    C. Signs, Wonders, and Salvation on Mount Zion (4:17–21 [3:17–21])

3. *The Message of the Book of Joel*: The message of the book of Joel can be summed up as a call to repentance in the face of the coming judgment, which the prophet refers to ominously as "the day of the LORD" (Hebrew *yom YHWH*):

> Blow the trumpet in Zion;
>   sound the alarm on my holy mountain!
> Let all the inhabitants of the land tremble,
>   for the day of the LORD is coming, it is near,
> a day of darkness and gloom,
>   a day of clouds and thick darkness!
>   (Joel 2:1–2)

This call to repentance begins in the first half of the book, in which the prophet delivers a long poem that combines vivid descriptions (Joel 2:25–32) of the devastation of the locust plague on Judah with calls for nationwide repentance (Joel 1). This is followed by a prophetic oracle in which Joel employs the imagery of a locust plague—something that would have been both terrifying and economically devastating to any ancient Near Eastern people—to describe a coming invasion of Judah by a northern power, and then renews his call for national repentance, in the form of "fasting", "weeping", and "mourning", in which the people rend their "hearts" and not their "garments" (Joel 2:12–17). Finally, there is an oracle of salvation and restoration in which the Lord heeds the repentance of his people (Joel 2:18–27).

In the second half of the book, the prophet delivers two memorable oracles about the signs and salvation of the day of the Lord (Joel 3:1–5 [2:25–32] and 4:17–21 [3:17–21]). These oracles stress that supernatural signs among the heavenly bodies and on earth—such as the darkening of the sun, the turning of the moon to "blood", the coming of supernatural streams, rivers, and agricultural abundance (Joel 3:3–4; 4:18 [2:30–31; 3:18])—will accompany the coming of the Lord and lead to the salvation of a remnant of Judah on Mount Zion. Between these two oracles, there is a lengthy description of the eschatological battle of the Lord against the nations in the valley of "Jehoshaphat" (Hebrew for "the Lord has judged!"), when all their crimes against his people will be avenged (Joel 4:1–16 [3:1–21]). The book ends with a promise that "Judah shall be inhabited forever, and Jerusalem to all generations", when the Lord brings his judgment and comes to dwell in Zion (Joel 4:20–21 [3:20–21]).

III. Amos: The Southern Prophet to the Northern Kingdom

1. *The Context of Amos*: Amos is often thought to be the earliest of all the literary (writing) prophets, since his relatively short ministry probably fell in the decade 770–760 B.C. The opening lines date his prophecy to "two years before

the earthquake" during the reigns of Uzziah of Judah and Jeroboam II of Israel (Amos 1:1). Archaeologists now estimate that this event took place around 760 B.C. (± 25 years). This would probably place his ministry just prior to Hosea's longer career (ca. 750–725 B.C.).

Amos, like Hosea, prophesied to northern Israel; but, unlike Hosea, Amos was not a northerner himself. He was a Judean from Tekoa, a village to the south of Jerusalem, an agricultural worker who raised sheep and tended an orchard of sycamore-figs (Amos 7:14). He was called by God to preach judgment to northern Israel at a time when that nation was wealthy, arrogant, and oppressive to its southern neighbors. Amos clearly distances himself from the professional prophets who learned prophesying from their fathers and practiced it as a kind of family trade (see Amos 7:12–14). He was not motivated by a desire to earn a living, but he was impelled by a commission from God (Amos 7:15).

Amos is probably grouped with Hosea and Joel at the beginning of the minor prophets because of ties between the books. Like Hosea, Amos ministers to the north during the reigns of Uzziah and Jeroboam II (cf. Hos 1:1; Amos 1:1). Like Joel, Amos lays stress on the theme, "The LORD roars from Zion" (Amos 1:2; cf. Joel 4:16), and both books end with a similar eschatological vision of fertility and abundance in the Promised Land in which "the mountains shall drip sweet wine" (Amos 9:13; cf. Joel 4:18).

Amos and Source Criticism of the Pentateuch

Julius Wellhausen, who popularized the Documentary Hypothesis of the composition of the Pentateuch (JEDP), became convinced at a young age, probably for theological reasons, that "the prophets preceded the law"; that is, the literary history of the religion of Israel is not truly as it appears to be in the Old Testament, in which Moses precedes the prophets. Rather, the literary prophets, starting with Amos, represent the "original" religion of Israel, and later, when Israel was in an advanced state of cultural and religious decay after the exile, the bulk of the laws and liturgy of the Pentateuch (the "Priestly source") were invented and retrojected into the mouth of Moses.

One of the problems with this theory is that several prophets presuppose knowledge of the "Priestly" portions of the Pentateuch. The most notable of these is Ezekiel, but the list includes Amos, who is often regarded as the oldest literary prophet. The prophecies of Amos reveal that the northern Israelites in the eighth century B.C. were performing sacrificial worship largely in line with the Mosaic regulations, even if their sanctuaries were illicit from a Judean perspective. This has now been confirmed by archaeological evidence as well.[a] Amos also presupposes (as does Hosea) the essential story of Israel's origin as presented in the Pentateuch and Joshua, particularly the exodus from Egypt and conquest of the land. In short, the earliest literary prophets reflect a picture of Israelite religion consistent with the narrative story line of the Pentateuch.

The response of some critics has been to isolate those passages of Amos (and other prophets) inconsistent with Wellhausen's reconstruction of Israelite religion and attribute them to later "redactors". In other words, the textual data is rearranged to fit the theory of the development of Israel's religion.

[a] Jonathan Samuel Greer, *Dinner at Dan: Biblical and Archaeological Evidence for Sacred Feasts at Iron Age II Tel Dan and Their Significance*, Culture and History of the Ancient Near East 66 (Leiden and Boston: Brill, 2013).

While scholars are comfortable attributing the origin of most of the book of Amos to the prophet himself, doubt is often expressed about the originality of some passages, particularly the ones that stress God's faithfulness to Zion and the Davidic kingdom (Amos 1:2; 9:11–12). Many contemporary scholars think these are later editorial additions, though they are not missing from any ancient Hebrew manuscripts we possess.

2. *The Structure of the Book of Amos*: Either Amos himself or his scribal heirs made a concerted effort to arrange his literary legacy in an accessible form. Amos exhibits one of the clearest literary structures of any of the prophets. After a short introductory section introducing the prophet, the book consists of a series of oracles, all topically arranged, and a concluding epilogue looking forward to the future restoration of the Davidic kingdom. In this way, the book can be easily outlined as follows:

Outline of the Book of Amos

I. Prologue: Amos' Ministry and Message (Amos 1:1–2)

II. Oracles against the Nations (Amos 1:3—2:16)
    A. Against Aram (1:4–5)
    B. Against Philistia (1:6–8)
    C. Against Tyre (1:9–10)
    D. Against Edom (1:11–12)
    E. Against Ammon (1:13–15)
    F. Against Moab (2:1–3)
    G. Against Judah (2:4–5)
    H. Against Israel (2:6–16)

III. Three Calls to Hear the Word of the Lord (Amos 3:1—5:9)
    A. To the Israelites (3:1–15)
    B. To the "Cows of Bashan" (4:1–13)
    C. To the "House of Israel" (5:1–9)

IV. Three Woes on Israel (Amos 5:7—6:14)
    A. Woe on Those Who Pervert Justice (5:7–17)
    B. Woe on Those Who Seek the Day of the Lord (5:18–27)
    C. Woe on Those at Ease in Zion and Samaria (6:1–14)

V. Five Visions of Judgment (Amos 7:1—9:8)
    A. Vision One: The Swarm of Locusts (7:1–3)
    B. Vision Two: The Rain of Fire (7:4–6)
    C. Vision Three: The Plummet in the Hand of the Lord (7:7–9)
    X. *The Conflict of Amos and Amaziah the Priest (7:10–17)*
    D. Vision Four: The Summer Fruit (8:1–14)
    E. Vision Five: The Lord Destroys the Sanctuary (9:1–8)

VI. Epilogue: The Davidic Kingdom Restored (Amos 9:11–15)

3. *The Message of Amos*: After a brief historical/biographical introduction (Amos 1:2), the prophet states his thesis: "The LORD roars from Zion." The city of Zion is associated with the Davidic covenant; thus, "roaring from Zion" means acting in such a way as to defend and vindicate Zion and all it stands for—that is, the Davidic covenant and the kingdom established upon it (Amos 1:2). In the same way, the book will end with an oracle about the restoration of the Davidic kingdom and covenant (Amos 9:11–15).

Following the introduction and statement of the thesis, Amos continues with a series of oracles against nations: Damascus, Gaza, Tyre, Edom, Ammon, Moab, Judah, and Israel (Amos 1:3—2:16). What do these nations have in common? They were all once members of the Davidic empire ruled from Jerusalem by David and Solomon. Accordingly, they were all parties to the Davidic covenant and owed covenantal fidelity to one another (Hebrew *hesed*). Yet these nations "did not remember the covenant of brotherhood" (Amos 1:9) and have committed atrocities against each other. Notice here that the sequence of oracles against the nations is arranged for psychological effect upon Amos' northern audience. Northern Israelites would delight to hear judgment pronounced on all their neighbors round about, from Damascus to Moab (Amos 1:3—2:3), and especially on their southern cousins in Judah (Amos 2:4–5). But Amos holds his longest condemnation in reserve for the Israelites *themselves* at the end (Amos 2:6–16), showing where the gravest fault lies. How surprised they would have been, when their *schadenfreude* for other nations turned to shocked indignation to hear the prophet's rebuke of themselves!

After the oracles against the nations, Amos proceeds with three summons to "Hear this word [Hebrew *dabar*]" of the Lord (Amos 3:1; 4:1; 5:1). The first summons is to all the "sons of Israel" (Amos 3): Assyria and/or Egypt will be used by God to bring judgment on them for their oppressive self-indulgence and false worship. The second summons is to the "cows of Bashan"—that is, the wealthy, aristocratic women of Samaria (the northern capital), whose self-indulgent life-style leads to social injustice against the poor (Amos 4:1). They will be taken into exile, despite YHWH's many warnings (Amos 4:2–13). The third summons is again addressed to the "house of Israel" (Amos 5:1). It takes up an anticipatory dirge over the death of "virgin Israel", followed by an impassioned plea for repentance so that this "death" may be averted (Amos 5:2–17).

Amos' three summons to "hear this word" are followed by the pronouncement of three "woes", first on those who "turn justice to wormwood" (Amos 5:7–17), second on those who "desire the day of the LORD" (Amos 5:18–27), finally on "those who are at ease in Zion and ... feel secure on the mountain of Samaria" (Amos 6:1–14). In response to their hypocritical worship and oppression of the poor, the cultural elite of Israel will experience oppression and exile.

After Amos' three "woes", there follow a series of five visions: First, the prophet sees a locust swarm sent to consume all Israel's remaining crops, but he pleads for mercy to the Lord, and the Lord relents (Amos 7:1–3). Second, a rain of fire arrives, but again Amos intercedes and the Lord relents (Amos 7:4–6). Third, Amos sees the Lord himself, standing with plummet in hand, inspecting a wall. The Lord has assessed Israel as with a plummet; he will forgive no longer but will judge them (Amos 7:7–9).

Is Amos Criticizing All Liturgical Worship?

Because of the influence of Protestantism on the development of modern biblical studies, the conflict between Amos the prophet and Amaziah the priest (7:10–17) has been seen through the lens of Protestant critiques of the Catholic Church, with Amos representing the purity of "prophetic" religion (i.e., Protestantism) against the recrudescence of "priestly" religion (i.e., Catholicism) represented by Amaziah. Obviously this reading misunderstands both the dynamics of Amos 7:10–17 and the true nature of the conflict between the Protestant reformers and the Catholic Church.

The Old Testament does not recognize a distinction between "prophetic" and "priestly" religion. Some of the prophets were also priests or Levites: notably Ezekiel, Jeremiah, Zechariah, possibly Isaiah, and others. Ezekiel, Haggai, Zechariah, and Malachi were all very concerned about the proper function of the Temple, the priesthood, and the liturgy. The prophets do not critique public ritual worship *per se* but, rather, schismatic, syncretistic, hypocritical, and pagan forms of ritual.

The sequence of visions is interrupted by a narrative about Amos' conflict with the priestly authorities of the Bethel temple in Israel (Amos 7:10–17). Amaziah, the chief priest in charge of the sanctuary, drives Amos out of the Temple precincts for prophesying against the royal house of King Jeroboam, ruler of the northern tribes. In response, Amos gives his classic defense of his ministry:

> Then Amos answered Amaziah, "*I am no prophet, nor a prophet's son; but I am a herdsman, and a dresser of sycamore trees, and the LORD took me from following the flock, and the LORD said to me, 'Go, prophesy to my people Israel.'*
> "Now therefore hear the word of the LORD." (Amos 7:14–16)

By this, Amos means he is no professional prophet, who learned how to prophesy in his youth and plies the trade as a career. Rather, his prophetic ministry was completely initiated by God through a supernatural vocation and unexpected commissioning.

After an oracle of judgment against Amaziah (Amos 7:16–17), the visions continue with Amos beholding a "basket of summer fruit [Hebrew *qāyîtz*]", which indicates that the "end (Hebrew *qētz*) has come upon my people Israel" (Amos 8:1–3). Significantly, wailing, mourning, death, and a famine of God's word will come on the Israelites because of their failure both to love their neighbor rightly in their abuse of the poor (Amos 8:4–7) and to love YHWH rightly in their worship of false gods (Amos 8:13–14). In the fifth and final vision, Amos sees the Lord standing in the temple (probably in the northern sanctuary at Bethel), commanding its destruction as well as the slaughter of the inhabitants of the land (Amos 9:1). Wherever the sinners in Israel flee, the Lord will hunt them down and bring upon them the judgment they fear (Amos 9:2–10).

Significantly, the book does not end on a note of judgment but on one of hope: after all this judgment has come to pass, the Lord will raise up the fallen "booth of David", which will once more reign over all the nations once incorporated into the Davidic empire (Amos 9:11–12). Even more, the peace and fertility characteristic of Eden shall be restored to the land of Israel (Amos 9:13–15).

IV. Obadiah: Doom to Mount Esau, Salvation to Mount Zion

1. *The Context of Obadiah*: We know little to nothing from internal evidence about the prophet Obadiah, apart from the fact that his name means "Servant of YHWH" (Hebrew *'obadyahû*) (Obad 1:1). Although this could be a proper name—Hebrew names ordinarily have such theophoric meaning—it could also be a prophetic appellation.

According to ancient Jewish tradition, as reflected by the first-century book on the *Lives of the Prophets*, Obadiah was "a disciple of Elijah" who had formerly served King Ahaziah but left to take up a life of prophecy.[3] This tradition thus connects the prophetic book with the figure of "Obadiah" from the book of Kings, in which a man named Obadiah, who was chief steward in the kingdom of Ahab, protected the prophets of the Lord from Jezebel by hiding them in a cave, and later encountered Elijah (1 Kings 18:1–16). Indeed, some scholars have held that the book is quite ancient, dating to the preexilic period, sometime in the ninth century B.C., around the time of the invasion of Judah by various tribes that took place during the kingship of Joram (see 2 Kings 8:20–22; 2 Chron 21:8–10).

On the other hand, most scholars date the book to the postexilic period, based on the apparent references to the destruction of Jerusalem in 586 B.C. (Obad 11–14), in which Edom certainly played a role (cf. Lam 4:21–22; Ezek 25:12–14; 35:1–15), and to a series of parallels between Obadiah and the book of Jeremiah (cf. Obad 1–4; Jer 49:14–16; Obad 5–6; Jer 49:9–10; Obad 8; Jer 49:7; Obad 16; Jer 49:12).[4]

2. *The Structure of the Book of Obadiah*: Obadiah is by far the shortest of the twelve minor prophets. In fact, consisting of a mere twenty-two verses (about four hundred Hebrew words), it is the shortest book of the Old Testament! Obadiah is barely over half the length of Nahum, the next shortest prophet, and consists of a single oracle directed against the land of Edom. A basic outline of this oracle is as follows:

Outline of the Book of Obadiah

Mount Esau vs. Mount Zion
1. Heading: Vision of Obadiah (1a)
2. Judgment Is Coming to Edom (Mount Esau) (1b–10)
3. Mount Esau (Edom) Gloated over Mount Zion (Judah) (11–14)
4. The Day of the Lord Is Coming upon the Nations (15–16)
5. Salvation Will Come to Mount Zion (17–21)

3. *The Message of Obadiah*: The oracle of Obadiah is relatively easy to summarize: the nation of Edom—also referred to as "Mount Esau" (Obad 8)—has fallen under the judgment of God because the Edomites took advantage of Judah and Jerusalem during the recent military invasion, defeat, and exile of the

---

[3] *Lives of the Prophets* 9.1–5, in D.R. Hare, "Lives of the Prophets", in *The Old Testament Pseudepigrapha*, vol. 2, ed. James H. Charlesworth, Anchor Bible Reference Library (New York: Doubleday, 1985), 392.

[4] Robert B. Chisholm, *Handbook on the Prophets* (Grand Rapids, Mich.: Baker Academic, 2002), 403.

Judeans (Obad 10–14). The cruel opportunism of the Edomites will be punished at some time in the future, when Jerusalem and Judea will again be inhabited and will dominate the land of Edom (Obad 15–21). Once again, exactly which invasion, defeat, and exile of Judah occasioned the book of Obadiah is not entirely clear, but most scholars see it as a reference to the Babylonian triumph in 587 B.C. and would date Obadiah sometime shortly thereafter.

The climactic prophecy of the book, that "Saviors shall go up to Mount Zion to rule Mount Esau" (Obad 21), found a historical fulfillment during the reign of the Maccabees, who annexed Idumea (Edom) to Judea and forcibly circumcised the Idumean population, thus assimilating them within the Judean nation.[5] However, after the Maccabees, Herod the Great, whose father was an Idumean, succeeded in having himself appointed king of the Jews by the Romans in 37 B.C., and his dynasty ruled until A.D. 66.

Edom tends to be overlooked historically and theologically in treatments of the Old Testament, but it is, significantly, "the subject of more separate oracles against foreign nations and more brief or passing hostile references in the prophetical books than any other nation".[6] This goes back, of course, to the prominence of the figure of Esau himself in the book of Genesis, brother of Jacob the patriarch (Gen 25–28). From the persecution of Jacob by Esau, to the persecution of Judah by the Edomites, to the persecution of Jesus the Judean by Herod the Edomite—throughout salvation history, Edom stands as a type of the opposition to the people of God from those who should be closest to them, from their own family. The Book of Obadiah stands in judgment on Edom and all who are like Edom, assuring the people of God that the justice of God will finally triumph and that they will be vindicated over against their enemies.

V. Jonah: Reluctant Prophet to the Gentiles

The book of Jonah is clearly an exception among the twelve minor prophets. While the other books record the oracles of this or that prophet, the book of Jonah consists almost entirely of a prose narrative about the prophet's mission to Nineveh and its aftermath. It records only one prophetic oracle, a half-verse in length: "Yet forty days, and Nineveh shall be overthrown!" (Jon 3:4). The story of Jonah has captured the imagination of popular piety through the ages because of the fantastic account of the prophet being swallowed by a great fish and subsequently vomited up. However, the account of the fish is only supplemental to the main theological thrust of the book, which concerns God's grace and forgiveness toward the Gentiles (that is, toward all mankind).

1. *The Context of Jonah*: The central figure in the narrative, "Jonah, the son of Amittai" (Jon 1:1), is a historical figure who engaged in prophetic activity during the reign of Jeroboam II of Israel (783–743 B.C.), during which time he prophesied the expansion of the northern kingdom to its Solomonic boundaries

---

[5] Josephus, *Antiquities* 13.257.

[6] Tremper Longman III and Raymond B. Dillard, *An Introduction to the Old Testament* (Grand Rapids, Mich.: Zondervan, 2006), 439.

(2 Kings 14:25). Jonah seems to have been identified with Israelite nationalism; thus, his commission from God to preach repentance to northern Israel's greatest foe (Nineveh) provokes a strong negative reaction from the prophet (Jon 1:3).

None of the details of the book of Jonah itself permit a very specific dating of his mission to Nineveh. Second Kings associates Jonah with the lengthy reign of Jeroboam II (783–743 B.C.). The narrative of the book assumes that northern Israel is still in existence, and the prophet has enough freedom of movement to be able easily to book a passage to Tarshish from Joppa—thus the nation does not seem to be occupied or under siege. Therefore, the events of the book are presented as taking place sometime in the eighth century B.C., probably prior to 732 B.C., when the Assyrian destruction of northern Israel began.

2. *The Genre and Historical Character of the Book of Jonah*: Although there is no reason to doubt Jonah as a historical figure *per se*, scholars continue to debate the literary genre of the book and the related question of its historical character.

On the one hand, ancient Jewish and Christian tradition is unanimous in regarding the book as a historical narrative of miraculous events (cf. Tob 14:4; 3 Mac 6:8). A notable example of this may be the saying of Jesus in the Gospel of Matthew, in which he prophesies the historical event of his Resurrection by reference to a previous event: "For as Jonah was three days and three nights in the belly of the whale, so will the Son of man be three days and three nights in the heart of the earth" (Mt 12:40). Along similar lines, the Jewish historian Josephus—despite his occasional embarrassment about miraculous events—treats the book of Jonah as history: "Since I have promised to give an exact account of our history, I have thought it necessary to recount what I have found written in the Hebrew books concerning this prophet [Jonah]" and proceeds to relate the events described in the book of Jonah as part of the history of the reign of King Jeroboam.[7]

Jonah and Historical Nineveh

Jonah 3:3 states literally, "Nineveh was an exceedingly great city to God; *three days' journey in breadth*." What does "three days' journey in breadth" mean? Some have taken it to mean three days were necessary to travel the circumference of the city. If so, this is an exaggeration: the historical Nineveh was not that large. However, if it means three days were necessary for a messenger to travel through all the neighborhoods of the city, as Jonah would have done, the expression is historically plausible.

The repentance of Nineveh (Jon 3:5–9) is not recorded in external historical records, but extant records are far from complete, and accounts of the event may have been suppressed subsequently. On the other hand, it is important to stress that what the book recounts is temporary repentance in the face of destruction, not a permanent conversion to the worship of the God of Israel. About a generation after Jonah's lifetime, Nineveh invaded and destroyed the northern kingdom of Israel (722 B.C.; 2 Kings 17).

On the other hand, most contemporary scholars argue that the literary genre of the book is not history but some other genre, such as a parable, allegory, or short

---

[7] See Josephus, *Antiquities* 9.208–14, trans. Ralph Martin, Loeb Classical Library (Cambridge, Mass.: Harvard University Press, 1937), 109, 111.

story.[8] The primary reason for adopting this view is that the events described in the book are thought to be too outlandish; the prophet surviving in the belly of a fish (Jon 2:1 [1:17]), the sudden and complete repentance of Nineveh (Jon 3:5), the appearance of the vine that grows overnight and vanishes as quickly (Jon 4:10). Moreover, other aspects of the book are regarded as historical errors or are undocumented: such as the reported great size of Nineveh, "three days' journey in breadth" (Jon 3:3), and the otherwise-unknown complete repentance and conversion of the Gentile city (Jon 3:5–9). In light of such data, many scholars in modern times take the position that the book of Jonah, although perhaps based on a historical figure, was not meant be read as history. As noted, however, the earliest interpreters of the work apparently did not understand this. Jack Sasson's summary of the debate is apropos: "Whether Jonah is history or fiction … is likely to be debated as long as Jonah is read."[9]

3. *The Structure of the Book of Jonah*: As a piece of literature, Jonah is elegant, succinct, clever, artistic, and even humorous. It ranks with the book of Ruth as an example of the high art of the Hebrew narrative. The literary structure of Jonah is as follows:

Outline of the Book of Jonah

I. Jonah's Disobedient Flight to Tarshish (Jon 1–2)
   A. Jonah's Adventures Aboard Ship (1)
   B. Jonah's "Prayer" from the Belly of the Fish (2)

II. Jonah's Obedient Preaching Mission to Nineveh (Jon 3–4)
   A. Jonah's Preaching and Nineveh's Repentance (3)
   B. Jonah's Dispute with God (4)

4. *The Message of Jonah*: The message of the book of Jonah can be gleaned directly from its two major sections: Jonah's abortive voyage to Tarshish (Jon 1–2) and Jonah's journey to Nineveh (Jon 3–4).

In the first section, the narrative opens with the famous northern Israelite prophet Jonah being commissioned by God to preach to Nineveh, the capital of Israel's archenemy Assyria. Attempting to avoid the divine commission, Jonah books passage to Tarshish (Jon 1:2; possibly Tartessos in Spain, at the far end of the Mediterranean). As a result, YHWH, the God of Israel, sends a storm to impede Jonah's progress. The sailors in the ship eventually elicit the truth from the prophet, reluctantly cast him overboard, and in the process come to acknowledge YHWH as the true "God of heaven" and offer sacrifice and make vows to him (Jon 1:9–16).

In the meantime, a "great fish" swallows Jonah, and he is said to pray in the belly of the fish (Jon 2:1–10 [1:17—2:9]). Significantly, from a form-critical

[8] See John J. Collins, *Introduction to the Hebrew Bible* (Minneapolis: Fortress Press, 2004), 534–36; Chisholm, *Handbook on the Prophets*, 406–8.

[9] Jack M. Sasson, *Jonah*, Anchor Bible 24B (New York: Doubleday, 1990), 328.

Jonah Alive in the Belly of the Whale?

Whether it was possible for Jonah to survive in the belly of a whale or other great fish has been much debated. In 1896, the *New York Times* reported a sailor surviving after being swallowed by a sperm whale that was subsequently harpooned and opened up, but the story is difficult to confirm. Furthermore, it is not clear that the book of Jonah actually affirms that the prophet was physically alive in the fish. The "prayer" of Jonah 2, which is a retrospective *todah* psalm written later, affirms that the prophet descended to "Sheol" and the "Pit" (Jon 2:3, 7 [2:2, 6])—that is, *the place of the dead*. Perhaps we are to understand the prophet as *dying* in the fish, later to be expelled and resurrected. If so, then Jesus' comparison of his own death and Resurrection to "the sign of Jonah" becomes completely explicable (cf. Mt 12:38–41).

---

perspective, Jonah's prayer is actually a *todah*, or thanksgiving, psalm reflecting back on the prophet's experience of death and salvation from a vantage point later in time. (The reader is probably meant to understand this as a composition penned by the prophet later but inserted here in the narrative because it describes his descent into Sheol and subsequent deliverance.) Given the long-standing debate over whether or not it would be possible for a human being to live inside the belly of a fish for three days, it is important to emphasize that the prayer of Jonah actually suggests that he does *not* remain alive for three days but rather *dies* and descends into Sheol, the realm of the dead:

> The waters closed in over me,
>   the deep was round about me;
> weeds were wrapped about my head
>   at the roots of the mountains.
> *I went down to the land*
>   *whose bars closed upon me for ever;*
> *yet you brought up my life from the Pit,*
>   O LORD my God.
> *When my soul fainted within me,*
>   I remembered the LORD;
> and my prayer came to you,
>   into your holy temple.
>   (Jon 2:5–7 RSVCE 2)

From this point of view, the story of Jonah and the whale is not so much a "miraculous survival" story as a death-and-resurrection story. Indeed, in ancient Near Eastern literature outside the Bible, the descent into the realm of the dead was often depicted as a three-day journey.[10] After spewing the corpse of Jonah onto the dry land, YHWH declares: "Arise, go to Nineveh" (Jon 3:2)—and this time, the prophet does it. At the very least, this interpretation would explain why Jesus in the Gospels uses Jonah's "three days and three nights in the belly of the whale" as a prefiguration of his own death, burial, and Resurrection (Mt 12:40). In any case, the message of this section of Jonah is both the importance

---

[10] Chisholm, *Handbook on the Prophets*, 411; George M. Landes, "The 'Three Days and Three Nights' Motif in Jonah 2:1", *Journal of Biblical Literature* 86 (1967): 246–50.

of fidelity to YHWH's prophetic mission and the mercy of God to those who cry out to him in prayer and distress.

The second part of the book opens with Jonah once more being commissioned to preach to Nineveh (Jon 3:1–3). Despite making no attempt whatsoever to offer hope to the populace or persuade them to repentance—his "message" is merely "Yet forty days, and Nineveh shall be overthrown!" (Jon 3:4)—his "mission" is wildly successful, as the whole city from king to animals puts on sackcloth and turns to God in repentance. In response, God relents of his intended punishment. Somewhat surprisingly, Jonah is angered by God's mercy, since he had hoped to witness the destruction of Israel's enemy (Jon 4:1–2). He departs the city to the east, where he makes himself a shelter to observe the city's fate. God causes a vine to grow quickly to shelter Jonah from the heat of the sun, for which the prophet is grateful. The next day, however, God causes the vine to wither, and Jonah is enraged with God to the point of death. There ensues a dialogue between the prophet and God, in which the Lord insists he has much more cause to be concerned about the fate of the people and animals of Nineveh than Jonah did about the fate of the vine. As God declares

> ### The Striking Contrast between Jonah and the Gentiles
>
> Particularly notable throughout the book is the contrast between Jonah and the Gentiles in their response to God. Jonah, the Israelite prophet, intentionally defies God's express will for his life. The Gentile sailors, on the other hand, actively seek to find out the will of God. They have to wake the prophet and urge him to pray. Even when they discover that he has thoughtlessly endangered the entire crew and cargo by making them complicit in his defiance against the Divinity, the sailors show humanitarian concern for Jonah's welfare and attempt to row ashore to save the cursed man's life. Only with great reluctance do they cast him overboard, and then they piously offer sacrifice to the God of Israel in gratitude for their salvation. Again, the response of the Ninevites is similar. Though given no reason for hope by the prophet himself, they engage in a mass repentance the like of which was scarcely ever seen in Israel itself. They throw themselves on the mercy of the Lord God of Israel, while the prophet himself becomes enraged with God and pleads for death.

in the book's famous final lines: "And should not I pity Nineveh, that great city, in which there are more than a hundred and twenty thousand persons who do not know their right hand from their left, and also much cattle?" (Jon 4:11).

This seemingly strange ending points us to the central theological message of the book: YHWH is the God of the Gentiles, too, and indeed of all creation. Throughout the narrative, God demonstrates his sovereignty over both human and natural affairs, both within and without the land of Israel. The Lord shows absolute control over the weather, the sea, the monsters of the deep, the vine, and the course of history in foreign lands. All these arenas were the domains of specific gods in pagan thought: the weather was controlled by Baal (Jupiter/ Zeus), the sea by Yam (Neptune/Poseidon), the depths by Tiamat or Mot (Pluto/Hades), and so on. In the book of Jonah, however, there is no hint of the existence of any of these deities, much less of their opposition to God. Rather, all nature and human history follows the will of the Lord with docility, who sovereignly "appoints" (Hebrew *manah*) creatures to do his bidding (Jon

2:1 [1:17]; 4:6, 7, 8). Moreover, men far outside the orbit of Israel—pagan sailors and Assyrian commoners—respond to the Lord with repentance and worship. In sum, Israel as a people has a prophetic mission to the Gentiles, to all the nations. Whether willingly or unwillingly, God will ensure that they communicate his saving word to the nations, and that word will be effective.

VI. Micah: God's Prosecuting Attorney against Israel

The book of Micah forms a stark contrast to Jonah. Whereas Jonah is a well-ordered, elegantly structured narrative with little prophetic oracle, Micah consists mostly of prophetic oracles with no narrative and little in the way of obvious structure or design.

1. *The Context of Micah*: The prophet Micah himself has the singular distinction of being mentioned in another prophetic book: the book of Jeremiah records that in his day, "Micah of Moresheth" was still remembered for having led a successful religious reform during the reign of Hezekiah (ca. 715–686 B.C.; see Jer 26:18–19). This reference agrees with the heading of the book of Micah, which dates the ministry of the prophet during the reigns of the Judean kings Jotham (ca. 740–735 B.C.), Ahaz (735–715 B.C.), and Hezekiah (ca. 715–686 B.C.). This would make Micah a contemporary of Isaiah, and, indeed, the book shows similarity to Isaiah in language, perspective, and historical references. In fact, the two books contain virtually identical oracles about the restoration of Zion (cf. Is 2:2–5 and Mic 4:1–5).

Most scholars hold the early chapters to reflect the words of the prophet himself (Mic 1–3), but there is debate about the date and authorship of the subsequent chapters. Many hold that certain passages or oracles reflect an attitude or perspective from the period of the Babylonian exile or the postexilic restoration, but this is difficult to demonstrate (see Mic 4–7). Most of this material could fit the context of eighth-century Israel and Judah (that is, within the lifetime of the prophet), during which Assyria constituted the perennial threat to the two Hebrew kingdoms (see Mic 5:4–5 [5:5–6]; 7:12) and when there were rampant economic abuses of the poor by the wealthy elites in both nations (see Mic 6:9–12; cf. Amos 8:4–10). The sins for which Micah reproaches Israel and Judah are the same as those mentioned by the eighth-century prophets Hosea and Amos: abuse of the poor by the wealthy elite (Mic 6:9–12), corruption within the leadership classes (Mic 7:2–4), and false and/or hypocritical cultic practice (Mic 5:11–13 [5:12–14]; 6:6–7). There is, however, one clear mention of the future Babylonian exile (Mic 4:9–10), but even this oracle may be authentic if the possibility of predictive prophecy is granted.

Basic Structure of Micah
I. First Oracle Cycle (chaps. 1–2)
A. Judgment (1:2–9)
B. Lament (1:10—2:11)
C. Salvation (2:12–13)
II. Second Oracle Cycle (chaps. 3–5)
A. Judgment (3:1–12)
B. Salvation (4:1—5:14 [5:15])
III. Third Oracle Cycle (chaps. 6–7)
A. Judgment (6:1–16)
B. Lament (7:1–6)
C. Salvation (7:7–20)

2. *The Structure of the Book of Micah*: The structure of Micah is notoriously obscure. However, many recognize three prophetic cycles in the book, each moving from oracles of judgment to oracles of salvation, usually with a lament sandwiched between. With this basic structure in mind, a more detailed outline of the book of Micah can be given as follows:

Outline of the Book of Micah

Heading (Mic 1:1)
   I. First Cycle of Oracles: Judgment on Jerusalem and Samaria (Mic 1:2—2:13)
     A. An Oracle of Judgment on Jerusalem and Samaria (1:2–7)
       1. Summons of the Peoples of the Earth as "Jury" (1:2)
       2. The Lord's Accusations against Jerusalem and Samaria (1:3–5)
       3. The Proclamation of the Verdict and Sentence (1:6–7)
     B. A Lament of the Prophet (1:8–2:11)
       1. Micah Laments for the Towns to Be Destroyed in the Assyrian Invasion (1:10–16)
       2. Micah Predicts that the Evildoers Will Soon Lament (2:1–5)
       3. Micah Disputes with the People Who Reject His Preaching of Lament (2:6–11)
     C. An Oracle of Salvation: Jerusalem Regathered under Its Shepherd-King (2:12–13)

  II. Second Cycle of Oracles: Judgment on the Leadership of Israel (Mic 3–5)
     A. A Tripartite Oracle against the Rulers and Prophets (3:1–12)
       1. Summons, Accusation, and Sentence against the "Leaders of Jacob" (3:1–4)
       2. Accusation and Sentence against the False Prophets (3:5–8)
       3. Summons, Accusation, and Sentence against the "Leaders of the House of Jacob" (3:9–12)
     B. Two Oracles of Salvation (4–5)
       1. Zion Exalted above All Mountains "in Days to Come" (4:1–8)
       2. A Contrast between "Now" and "Then" (4:9—5:15)
         a. "Now" the Daughter of Zion Grieves under Siege (4:9–14 [4:9—5:1])
         b. "Then" the Davidic Shepherd-King Will Lead Israel (5:1–14 [5:2–15])

 III. Third Cycle of Oracles: The Lord's Court Case against Israel (Mic 6–7)
     A. An Oracle of Judgment on the "People of the LORD" (6:1–16)
       1. A Summons for the Mountains to Serve as "Jury" (6:1–2a)
       2. The Lord States His Case against Israel (6:2b–5)
       3. *Israel Interrupts to Ask for Terms of Acquittal (6:6–8)*
       4. The Lord Continues His Case against Israel (6:9–12)
       5. The Lord Pronounces Sentence against Israel (6:13–16)
     B. A Lament of the Prophet over the Evil of His Day (7:1–6)
     C. Personified Jerusalem Utters a Psalm of Confidence in the Lord's Salvation (7:7–20)

3. *The Message of Micah*: In the first oracle cycle, the Lord calls the peoples of the earth to heed his case against Jerusalem and Samaria, upon which he passes the sentence of destruction on account of their sin of idolatry (Mic 1:7). The prophet responds with a lament over all the cities to be destroyed along the path of the Assyrian army to Jerusalem (ca. 701 B.C.), employing untranslatable puns on the names of the various towns (Mic 1:10–16). Then he predicts that the wealthy oppressors of Israel themselves will soon lament because of the Lord's punishment; they respond by telling him to shut his mouth, but the prophet will not stop preaching (Mic 2:7–11). The cycle ends with an abrupt glimpse of hope for the future, when Israel will be regathered under a restored shepherd-king (Mic 2:12–13).

In the second oracle cycle, the Lord summons the leaders and rulers of Israel to take the "defense stand", as it were, and hear his accusation against them (Mic 3:1–2). This is the accusation: they consume the common people like meat, so the Lord will not hear their prayers in time of distress (Mic 3:2–4). The prophets join their evildoing and so will share the punishment of silence from heaven, a cutting off of revelation except for Micah the true prophet (Mic 3:5–8). Again, the Lord summons princes, priests, and prophets, accuses them of bloodshed, wickedness, bribery, and money-grubbing, and declares the sentence of destruction on Jerusalem (Mic 3:9–12).

> ### The "Courtroom Language" of Micah
>
> The vocabulary of Micah is marked by the rhetoric of the courtroom. Each prophetic cycle (Mic 1–2; 3–5; 6–7) begins with a summons ("Hear!"; 1:2; 3:1; 6:1) to some aspect of reality—the "peoples" and the "earth"; the "heads of Jacob" and "rulers of the house of Israel"; or the "mountains" and the "hills"—to listen to the court case that the Lord either brings against them or argues before them (Mic 1:2; 3:1; 6:1–2). Legal terms recur especially in the accusatory passages of the book: "witness", "justice", "[court] case", "acquit", "(legal) cause", "judgment", "pardon" (Mic 1:2; 3:1, 8, 9; 6:1–2, 11; 7:9, 18). The legal terminology of the book rests on a foundation of covenant theology: Israel and Judah are in covenant relationship with the Lord and have breached the terms of the covenant as summarized in the law of Moses (Mic 6:4).

This second cycle lacks a lament but, instead, has two oracles of salvation. First, in a passage almost identical to Isaiah 2:1–5, the prophet promises the future restoration of Mount Zion, the revelation of the law of the Lord from Jerusalem to all the world, and the regathering of the pitiful remnant of his people (Mic 4:1–8). Second, the prophet composes a skillful oracle based on a contrast between "now" and "then". The present situation of Zion "now" (Hebrew *'attāh*; Heb 4:9, 10, 11, 14 [= 5:1 RSV]) is dire, but her future situation "then" (Hebrew *wĕhāyāh*, lit. "and [then] it shall be"; Heb 5:4, 6, 7, 9) will be glorious. The change in mood falls in Micah 5:1 (5:2 in the RSV), where the phrase "but you!" (Hebrew *wĕ'attāh*), addressed to Bethlehem, sounds almost the same as "and now!" (Hebrew *wĕ'attāh*). "Now" Jerusalem is besieged and surrounded by enemies, but "then" the Davidic shepherd-king will arise from Bethlehem, deliver them from

> ### Versification of Micah
>
> Micah 4:14 in the Hebrew Masoretic Text corresponds to Micah 5:1 in the Vulgate and most English translations (e.g., RSVCE). In Micah 5, the number of the English verses is one higher than the Hebrew, so Hebrew Micah 5:1 = English 5:2, through the end of the chapter. (Heb. 5:14 = Eng. 5:15). The versification coincides again beginning with chapter 6. The New American Bible follows the Hebrew versification.

Assyria, and lead the remnant in victory over the nations, and the Lord will purify his people of idolatry and sorcery (Mic 5:1–8 [5:2–9]).

In the third oracle cycle, the Lord calls the mountains and hills to serve as "jury" as he presents his court case (Hebrew *rib*) against Israel. The Lord has been blameless in his covenant conduct toward Israel (Mic 6:3–5). The voice of the people interrupts abruptly here, asking what terms the Lord will accept for reconciliation (Mic 6:6–7). After reminding the people of the basic moral law in a famous summary—"do justice,... love kindness,... walk humbly with your God" (Mic 6:8)—the Lord continues with his accusations. The wealthy have cheated the poor in the marketplace, spread violence, and given false testimony (Mic 6:9–12). The sentence is destruction by sword and famine (Mic 6:13–16). The prophet responds by lamenting the evil times in which he lives, when all are violent, dishonest, overbearing, prone to bribes, and unfaithful (Mic 7:1–6). But the book ends on a note of hope: the prophet, perhaps speaking as the personification of the remnant of Jerusalem, sings a psalm of confidence (Mic 7:7–19), in which he looks beyond his current distress to future vindication against the enemies of the righteous and the forgiveness of the sins of God's people on the basis of the Abrahamic covenant (Mic 7:18–20).

The theological perspective of Micah is based on a firm covenantal understanding of God's relationship with Israel. The Lord's *rib* or "dispute" with Israel at the beginning of each oracular cycle can be translated "covenant-lawsuit". It is a legal case brought for a kind of "breach of contract" between two parties. The "contract" between the Lord and Israel is the Mosaic covenant, whose laws against idolatry and abuse of the poor have been violated by Israel and Judah. The oracles of salvation, by contrast, are based on the promises of the Davidic covenant, which assures the restoration of David's city Zion, with David's heir on its throne (Mic 2:13; 4:1–8; 5:1–5 [5:2–6]), and on the covenant with Abraham, which assures God's mercy and loyalty to his descendants forever (Mic 7:19).

As with most of the prophets, the issue of true worship is a central theme in Micah. Jerusalem and Samaria are condemned for participating in false cults of pagan idols, which is spiritual prostitution (Mic 1:7). The Lord will root this idolatry and paganism out of his people by force (Mic 11–13 [5:12–14]). At the same time, even excessive practice of the true cult is worthless without attention to the ethical demands of the law of God (Mic 6:6–8). The grand double oracle of Micah 4–5, forming the center of the book and synthesizing the prophet's view of the eschatological age, foresees the restoration of the Temple-city Jerusalem (the "mountain of the house of the LORD") as a place of instruction in divine law for all the world, with the Lord's own people purified of all false worship under the leadership of the son of David (Mic 4:1–4, 5:1–14 [5:2–15]).

In sum, the themes and content of Micah's message are very similar to those of his fellow eighth-century prophets (Isaiah, Hosea, Amos). The people of Israel and Judah will experience judgment for violations of the Mosaic covenant, but God's mercy (Hebrew *hesed*) toward his people, based on his covenant-oath to Abraham, will be expressed in the restoration of the house of David and David's kingdom. While delivering this same basic message, the book of Micah distinguishes itself by the beauty of its rhetoric, so that its great messianic prophecy (Mic 1:9—2:1 [1:9–15]) and summary of God's law (Mic 6:6–8) are some of the best-known passages of the Old Testament.

VII. Nahum: The Destruction of Nineveh

1. *The Context of Nahum*: The short book of Nahum consists of a psalm extoling the power and justice of God, followed by a single oracle announcing the imminent destruction of Nineveh, the capital of the Assyrian Empire, which had terrorized and subjugated the smaller nations of the Near East for three hundred years, until it was overthrown by Babylon in 612 B.C.

Nahum's name means "comfort" (Hebrew *nahhum*), and his oracle of Nineveh's destruction surely brought comfort to Judah, which had lived in fear of that great city for generations. Nothing more is known about the prophet apart from the scant information pro-

> **The Versification of Nahum**
>
> The Vulgate tradition, followed by the RSV and related translations, ends the first chapter of Nahum with Nahum 1:15: "Behold, on the mountains the feet of him who brings good tidings." However, this verse is counted as Nahum 2:1 in the Hebrew Masoretic Text (MT) and the Septuagint (LXX). The NAB follows the MT and LXX. Therefore, the versification of Nahum 2 differs by one verse between the RSVCE and the NAB (i.e., 2:1 RSV = 2:2 NAB).

vided in the book, which identifies him as "of Elkosh", either a clan or town of Judah (Nahum 1:1). Because Nahum refers to the fall of the Egyptian city No-Amon (= Thebes) as a past event (Nahum 3:8–10), but the fall of Nineveh is still in the future, the book must have been composed between the dates of the destructions of those two cities—that is, sometime between 663 B.C. and 612 B.C.

2. *The Structure of the Book of Nahum*: After introducing the prophet (Nahum 1:1), the book opens with a psalm or poem describing a theophany of the Lord as he comes to judge his enemies (Nahum 1:2–8). After the psalm comes a single complex oracle about the destruction of Nineveh with a chiastic structure, the contents of which can be outlined as follows (the chiasm is indicated by the letters to the right):

Outline of the Book of Nahum

I. Heading (Nahum 1:1)

II. Psalm of the Lord God, Powerful, Just, and Merciful (Nahum 1:2–7)

III. Prophecy of Nineveh's Destruction (Nahum 1:8—3:19)
1. Rebuke of Assyria's King and Comfort to Judah (1:9—2:1 [1:9–15])　　A
2. A Call to Arms for Nineveh: Guard the Rampart! (2:2–11 [2:1–10])　　B
3. A Taunt of Nineveh: Where Is the Lioness? (2:12–13 [2:11–12])　　C
4. Oracle of the Lord's Judgment (2:14 [2:13])　　D
5. Dirge for Nineveh (3:1–4)　　E
6. Oracle of the Lord's Judgment (3:5–7)　　D'
7. A Taunt: Are You Better than No-Amon? (3:8–13)　　C'
8. A Call to Arms for Nineveh: Draw Water for Siege! (3:14–17)　B'
9. Rebuke of Assyria's King and Comfort to His Victims (3:18–19)　A'

3. *The Message of Nahum*: The opening poem summarizes the basic theological message of the book: the Lord's power is incomparable; he displays his justice by judging his enemies and his mercy by showing compassion to those who seek his protection (Nahum 1:2–8).

The message of this opening psalm is then illustrated in the elaborate oracle against the city of Nineveh, the enemy of Israel (Nahum 1:9—3:19). This oracle begins and ends with rebukes addressed to the king of Assyria (Nahum 1:9–14; 3:18–19) intermixed with words of comfort to Judah (Nahum 1:12b–13, 2:1 [1:15]; 3:19bc). Within this frame are two solemn "calls to arms" that command Nineveh to prepare (in vain) for its imminent siege (Nahum 2:2–11 [2:1–10]; 3:14–17). These calls to arms surround two "taunts" (Nahum 1:11–12; 3:8–13), each beginning with a rhetorical question: "Where is the lions' den?" and "Are you better than Thebes?" (Nahum 2:11 [2:12]; 3:8). Two "oracles" (Hebrew *Ne'um*) of the Lord's imminent judgment (Nahum 1:13; 3:5–7) bracket a central dirge for Nineveh, in which the image of a prostitute being publicly shamed is used to describe the overthrow and destruction of the city:

> And all for the countless harlotries of the harlot,
>   graceful and of deadly charms,
> who betrays nations with her harlotries,
>   and peoples with her charms.
>
> Behold, I am against you,
>   says the LORD of hosts,
>   and will lift up your skirts over your face;
> and I will let nations look on your nakedness
>   and kingdoms on your shame.
> I will throw filth at you
>   and treat you with contempt,
>   and make you an object of scorn.
> And all who look on you will shrink from you and say,
> Wasted is Nineveh; who will moan over her?
>   from where shall I seek comforters for her?
>   (Nahum 3:4–7)

Contemporary readers may wonder why an entire biblical book is devoted to prophesying the destruction of Assyria, and why such shocking imagery is utilized. In order to put Nahum's oracle in context, it is critical to recall that for the people of Israel in the seventh century B.C., the fall of Nineveh was an epochal event, the ancient Israelite equivalent of the Battle of Lepanto, V-E Day, or the fall of the Berlin Wall. Ever since Ahab and his allies had been defeated by Shalmaneser III in 853 B.C., the kings of northern Israel had been vassals of Assyria. King Shalmaneser V and Sargon II of Assyria had besieged and destroyed the northern kingdom altogether in the Assyrian exile of 722 B.C. (see 2 Kings 17), and only a miracle stopped King Sennacherib's destruction of Judah at the very gates of Jerusalem itself in 701 B.C. (see 2 Kings 19). Assyria was the "Evil Empire" of the Near East for three centuries and still seemed invincible just decades before its fall. Yet the capture and sacking of Nineveh in 612 B.C. by Babylonian and Median forces demonstrated that no human power is eternal and that the course of history lies in the hands of YHWH. This is the enduring message of the book of Nahum to the people of God: no persecuting enemy will stand forever. The day of God's judgment will come, bringing punishment on those who have done evil and consolation to those who have sought refuge in the Lord.

As one of the twelve, Nahum is best read in tandem with the book of Jonah. Both books are concerned with the destruction of Nineveh. In Jonah, this wicked city repents; in Nahum, the city experiences the destruction that did not fall in Jonah's lifetime. Jonah reminds us that God's mercy and forgiveness are available even to hardened sinners. Nahum reminds us that the window of opportunity to avail ourselves of this mercy can indeed come to a close, both for individuals and for nations.

VIII. Habakkuk: The Righteous Shall Live by Faith

Like the book of Jonah, Habakkuk is an anomaly among the twelve minor prophets. The other ten relate oracles that the various prophets delivered on behalf of the Lord to Israel and/or the nations. In Jonah and Habakkuk, however, the focus is largely on the spiritual struggle between the prophet and YHWH concerning the wisdom and righteousness of God's providence over world history. Both Jonah and Habakkuk struggle with the justice of God's ways. The book of Jonah explores this question largely through narrative, whereas Habakkuk addresses it through dialogue between the prophet and the Lord. Habakkuk resolves doubts about God's justice by urging God's people to live by faith in God's promises, even if contemporary events seem contradictory or inexplicable.

1. *The Context of Habakkuk:* As is the case with so many of the minor prophets, no biographical information is available for Habakkuk. The form of his name is unusual, and its meaning uncertain. It may be a passive form derived from the Hebrew root *h-b-q*, "to embrace"—that is, "one who is embraced" (Hebrew *habaquq*). The date of the book is likewise uncertain. At least Judah, if not Israel, still seems to be in existence as the prophet writes, so it must be sometime before the exile in 587 B.C. Beyond that, the mention of the "Chaldeans" (=Babylonians) as a rising threat is the best piece of evidence for dating (Hab 1:6). The prophet's words indicate that people will be surprised to hear that Babylon will be the agent of God's judgment (Hab 1:5–6). This would certainly not be the case in the early sixth century B.C. (ca. 590s–580s), when Babylon was a dominant and feared world power, so Habakkuk should probably be placed sometime in the late eighth or (as is more likely) seventh century B.C., when Assyria was still dominant in the Levant but Babylon was growing in power (cf. Is 39).

2. *The Structure of the Book of Habakkuk:* The basic units of the book of Habakkuk are fairly clear: there are two complaints addressed by the prophet to the Lord (Hab 1:2–4; 1:13–17), two responses from God (Hab 1:5–11; 2:1–4),

a set of five woes against one or more oppressors (Hab 2:6–20), and a psalm of confidence composed by the prophet (Hab 3). One way to understand how these different units work together is to arrange them in two cycles of dialogue in which (1) the prophet questions God, (2) God answers, and (3) the prophet accepts God's response. Thus, we understand the woes section (Hab 2:6–10) as part of God's answer to Habakkuk's second complaint. With these points in mind, the book can be outlined as follows:

Outline of the Book of Habakkuk

I. Heading (Hab 1:1)

II. First Cycle of Dialogue (Hab 1:2–12)
   A. Habakkuk's First Complaint: Why Do the Wicked Prosper? (1:2–4)
   B. God's Answer: Chaldeans Are Coming in Judgment! (1:5–11)
   C. Habakkuk's Acquiescence (1:12)

III. Second Cycle of Dialogue (Hab 1:13—3)
   A. Habakkuk's Second Complaint: Shall the More Wicked Judge the Less? (1:13—2:1)
   B. God's Answer: In Time, Justice Will Come to All (2:2–20).
   C. Habakkuk's Acquiescence: A Psalm of Confidence (3)

3. *The Message of Habakkuk*: Habakkuk begins his book by complaining to the Lord: Why does God seem to do nothing about the violence and injustice the prophet sees all around him (Hab 1:2–4)? God replies that he is preparing the Babylonians to come and destroy the evildoers, and Habakkuk acknowledges this divine judgment (Hab 1:5–12). However, sending the Babylonians as executors of justice raises another theological problem: How can God judge wicked persons by others who are yet more wicked (Hab 1:13)? The prophet goes on to describe the wickedness of the wealthy man who consumes others and "slays the nations", perhaps referring to the king of Assyria or Babylon (Hab 1:14–17).

The Lord's response to this second, more sharply focused complaint from Habakkuk is much longer and more detailed. First, the Lord counsels the prophet and all the righteous to have patience, even if it seems like the oracles of God are slow in fulfillment (Hab 2:2–4). Second, the Lord pronounces five woes on the "arrogant man" whose "greed is as wide as Sheol" and "gathers for himself all nations" (Hab 2:5–8; cf. 9–11; 12–14; 15–17; 18–20). This may be simultaneously (1) a hyperbolic description of any wealthy oppressor and (2) a specific description of the king of Babylon (or Assyria). The message of these woes is that the wickedness of the wicked man will come back on his head: those he oppresses will one day suddenly turn on him, and he will experience the destruction to which he subjugated others (Hab 2:7, 8, 10, 17).

The book of Habakkuk ends with a psalm attributed to the prophet, which appears in its present context to be a response to the woes against the evildoer just pronounced by the Lord (Hab 2:6–20). This psalm, which bears a strong resemblance to Psalm 68 and others, recounts a theophany of the Lord in which he marches north to Israel from the south (the region around Sinai), accompanied by a violent storm and earthquake (Hab 3:3–12). Having arrived, he vindicates his "anointed" (Hebrew *mashiah*)—a reference either to the Davidic king or to the people—by destroying the wicked enemies of his people (Hab 3:13–15). This entire poetic composition, colored with figurative imagery, may be a description of the exodus, the conquest of the land, or one or more other of God's great saving acts of his people in Israel's history. Essentially, it is a poetic description of God's power over the forces of evil as the divine warrior, which is manifested in various ways throughout history. In response to his vision of God manifesting his power and justice, the prophet resolves to "quietly wait" for the day of judgment on those "who invade us" and to rejoice in the Lord even though there is, as yet, no sign of the consolations and blessing that God has promised his people (Hab 3:16–19).

The book of Habakkuk is of perennial theological and spiritual interest because it struggles with the ever-pertinent question of *theodicy*, the justice of God. If God is good and all-powerful, why do the wicked seem to prosper? Of course, many other biblical books, notably Job and the Psalms, also deal with this issue. The answer offered by the book of Habakkuk is that God will, in the end, deliver justice to all. In the meantime, it is necessary for the righteous to exercise trust in the goodness, justice, and promises of God. This practical advice is summed up well in the best-known lines from the book:

> If it seem slow, wait for it;
>   it will surely come, it will not delay.
> Behold, he whose soul is not upright in him shall fail,
>   but *the righteous shall live by his faith*.
>
>   (Hab 2:3–4)

The word translated "faith" (Hebrew *'emunah*) is more precisely rendered "faithfulness", "integrity", or "fidelity". It derives from the same Hebrew root meaning "true" (*'-m-n*) that gives us "Amen"—that is, "so be it!" or "it is true!" In the New Testament, Paul quotes this verse but follows the Greek Septuagint in rendering the Hebrew word *'emunah* as "faith" (Greek *pistis*) (Rom 1:17). Although the Greek *pistis* ("faith") is not the exact equivalent of the Hebrew *'emunah* ("faithfulness"), it certainly is the case that the book of Habakkuk, taken as a whole, counsels the follower of the Lord to exercise *trust* or *faith* in God during the present tribulation while he awaits the fulfillment of God's promises in the future.

In fact, the conclusion of Habakkuk's psalm (Hab 3:16–19) is one of the more powerful statements of faith in the Lord God of Israel—despite all evidence to the contrary—in all the Old Testament:

> Though the fig tree does not blossom,
>   nor fruit be on the vines,
> the produce of the olive fail
>   and the fields yield no food,

the flock be cut off from the fold
  and there be no herd in the stalls,
yet I will rejoice in the Lord,
  I will joy in the God of my salvation.
GOD, the Lord, is my strength;
  he makes my feet like deer's feet,
  he makes me tread upon my high places.
  (Hab 3:17–19)

Therefore, the book of Habakkuk is truly evidence that, already in the Old Testament, the life of righteousness required the exercise of faith, and not merely observance of the ceremonies of the Mosaic law.

IX. Zephaniah: The Day of the Lord and the Restoration of Israel

1. *The Context of Zephaniah*: As with several of the other minor prophets, nothing more can be determined about the life of the prophet or his dates of ministry beyond the information given in the book's superscription (Zeph 1:1). However, what we do learn there is interesting: Zephaniah is unique among the biblical prophets in that he descended, apparently, from the royal house of David, being a great-great-grandson of King Hezekiah (Zeph 1:1). Sometime in the seventh century, during the reign of King Josiah (ca. 641–609 B.C.), Zephaniah announced, in bold and colorful rhetoric, the imminent arrival of the "day of the Lord", which he described as a day of definitive judgment on all the people of the earth, including and especially the people of Judah.

2. *The Structure of the Book of Zephaniah*: The book of Zephaniah divides easily into three major units: (1) an announcement of the coming day of the Lord (Zeph 1:2–18); (2) a series of oracles against nations and cities, beginning and ending with Judah and Jerusalem (Zeph 2:1–3:8); and (3) oracles of restoration for the nations and Jerusalem (Zeph 3:9–20). Its structure can be outlined in more detail as follows:

Outline of the Book of Zephaniah

I. Superscription (Zeph 1:1)

II. The "Day of the Lord" Is at Hand (Zeph 1:2–18)
  A. Proclamation of Judgment on All the Earth and on Judah/Jerusalem (1:2–6)
  B. Proclamation of the Coming Wrathful "Day of the Lord" (1:7–18)

III. Oracles of Judgment on Judah/Jerusalem and the Nations (Zeph 2:1—3:8)
  A. On Judah (2:1–3)
  B. On Philistia (2:4–7)
  C. On Moab and Ammon (2:8–11)
  D. On Ethiopia (2:12)
  E. On Assyria and Nineveh (2:13–15)
  F. On Jerusalem (3:1–7)
  G. On the Whole Earth (3:8)

3. *The Message of Zephaniah*: The book of Zephaniah begins with a statement of universal, cosmic judgment that quickly turns its focus to Judah and Jerusalem as punishment for their idolatry and paganism (Zeph 1:2–3, 4–6). A description of the imminent "day of the Lord" ensues (Zeph 1:7–18).

In order to understand the heart of this oracle, it is important to remember that the "day of the Lord" was a Judean phrase applied to any holy day or period of holy days in the Temple calendar, such as those associated with the feasts of Passover, First Fruits, Weeks, Trumpets, Yom Kippur, and Tabernacles (see Lev 23). Thus, the "day of the Lord" had positive and festive connotations of social and liturgical celebration. Zephaniah reverses this image: the coming "day of the Lord" he foresees will not be a time of feasting and celebration, but a day of "distress and anguish ... ruin and devastation ... darkness and gloom" (Zeph 1:15–16), during which YHWH will pour out his wrath on a people given to syncretism and paganism. The people of Jerusalem will find that they themselves are the sacrifices on the coming "day of the LORD" (Zeph 1:7–8).

After the description of the day of the Lord, Zephaniah, like other prophets we have surveyed (Isaiah, Jeremiah, and so on), delivers a series of interrelated oracles of judgment on the nations of the earth, beginning with Judah, then Philistia, Moab and Ammon, Ethiopia, and Assyria (Zeph 2:1–15). From describing Assyria's wicked capital, Nineveh (Zeph 2:13–15), the prophet slides seamlessly to describing Jerusalem and its sins (Zeph 3:1–7) and then concludes his entire series of oracles against nations with a final statement of cosmic judgment (Zeph 3:8) reminiscent of the opening proclamation of the book.

Like many prophetic books, Zephaniah ends on a note of hope. In the future, all nations will call on the name of the Lord using a "pure speech", and the exiles of Israel will return to the land (Zeph 3:9–10). The humble remnant of Israel that survives the wrathful "day of the Lord" will find refuge in the Lord, who will comfort them (Zeph 3:11–13). The book concludes with an exuberant song addressed to the "daughter of Zion"—that is, Jerusalem. Like a warrior renewing his affections for a maiden, the Lord will renew his love for Jerusalem and come into its "midst" (Zeph 3:14–18). The Lord will gather his humble ones into the holy city and restore its fortunes (Zeph 3:14–20).

There is a strong liturgical theme throughout Zephaniah. The coming time of God's judgment is described as if it were a liturgical feast (a "day of the Lord"), and the pouring out of God's wrath upon the earth, and especially Jerusalem, is presented as a heavenly liturgy in which the evildoers are transformed into sacrifices. In the coming age of salvation, the nations will be prepared for authentic worship by being made able to "call on the name of the Lord" and "serve him" and by being granted a "pure speech"—that is, a language suitable for the celebration of the liturgy (Zeph 3:9). The humble and lowly remnant of God is saved, not just by being gathered out of exile, but by being gathered

Important Dates of the Exile and Postexilic Period	
605 B.C.	Nebuchadnezzar the Great of Babylon establishes hegemony over the Levant and reduces Judah to a vassal state. Some Jerusalem aristocracy are taken as hostages into exile (Dan 1:1–7).
597 B.C.	Judah revolts; Nebuchadnezzar conquers Jerusalem for the first time and exiles the middle and upper classes of Judean society (2 Kings 24:10–17). Ezekiel is exiled (cf. Ezek 1:1–3).
587 B.C.	Judah revolts again; Babylon captures Jerusalem a second time, exiles the remaining populace, and razes Jerusalem and the Temple (2 Kings 25:1–26).
585 B.C.	Jeremiah is last seen in Egypt (Jer 44).
572 B.C.	Ezekiel sees his last vision (Ezek 40:1).
550 B.C.	Cyrus II the Great becomes king of the Medes and Persians.
537 B.C.	Cyrus conquers Babylon and issues a decree allowing Jews to return to Judah (2 Chr 36:22–23; Ezra 1:1–2).
529 B.C.	Cyrus is succeeded by his son Cambyses II.
521 B.C.	Darius I the Great, son-in-law of Cyrus, becomes king of Persia (Ezra 4:5).
520 B.C.	Date of the oracles of Haggai and Zechariah 1–6
518 B.C.	Date of Zechariah 7–8
516/17	The Second Temple is completed (Ezra 6).

to the place of *worship*: the "holy mountain" (Zeph 3:11–12). The renewal of God's love for Jerusalem will involve joy suitable for a sacred festival (Zeph 3:17). Thus, Zephaniah's eschatological hope focuses on the restoration of communion between God and his people through the celebration of the liturgy, in the proper place of its celebration (Zion/Jerusalem), and the tribulations leading up to this restoration of communion are in fact the earthly manifestations of a heavenly liturgy.

X. Haggai: Rebuild My House!

The book of Haggai begins a three-book collection of clearly postexilic prophets: Haggai, Zechariah, Malachi. These works appear to have been edited together as an intentional conclusion to the book of the Twelve. All three books are strongly marked by a concern for the reestablishment of a purified Temple and liturgy after the Babylonian exile, and the eschatological restoration of the remnant of God's people.

1. *The Context of Haggai*: Unlike most of the minor prophets, the figure of Haggai is mentioned elsewhere in the Bible. Ezra records him preaching to the exiles who returned from Babylon in the late sixth century, around 537–510 B.C. (Ezra 5:1; 6:14). His name derives from the Hebrew word "sacred festival" (Hebrew *hag*). Providentially, the meaning of his name nicely coincides with his concern for the reestablishment of the Temple and its cult. Saint Jerome records a tradition—probably received from the rabbis who taught him Hebrew—that

Haggai was a priest. While the tradition cannot be verified, it is plausible. Haggai's concern for the Temple and for cultic law suggest a priestly mind-set, and his meticulous recording of dates on which he received oracles (Hag 1:1; 2:1, 10, 20) is comparable with that of the priest-prophet Ezekiel (Ezek 1:1, 8:1, 20:1 and so on) and may reflect the scribal training in record-keeping given to priests in the ancient Near East.

The book of Haggai consists of four oracles (Hag 1:1–11; 2:1–9; 2:10–19; 2:20–23), each introduced by a date formula specifying the day on which Haggai received "the word of the LORD" (Hag 1:1; 2:1, 10, 20). The first oracle is followed by a brief historical narration describing the response of Judah's leaders and people to the prophet's message (Hag 1:12–15). The other three oracles have no such historical supplement. All four oracles are dated between the sixth and ninth months (by the Jewish calendar) of "the second year of Darius the king" (Hag 1:1). This would be Darius I "the Great" of Persia, who reigned about 522–486 B.C. Thus, by modern reckoning, Haggai prophesied between August and December of 520 B.C.

2. *The Structure of the Book of Haggai*: The book of Haggai consists of four oracles, each introduced by a date formula specifying the day on which Haggai received "the word of the LORD" (Hag 1:1; 2:1, 10, 20). The first oracle is followed by a brief historical narration describing the response of Judah's leaders and people to the prophet's message (Hag 1:12–15); the other three oracles have no such historical supplement and can be outlined as follows:

Outline of the Book of Haggai

I. The Prophetic Call to Rebuild the Temple (Hag 1:1–15)
   A. Oracle: Judah Not Blessed Because Temple Not Built (1:1–11)
   B. Response: The People Renew the Temple Building (1:12–15)

II. The Latter Glory of This House Will Exceed the Former (Hag 2:1–9)

III. Rebuilding the Temple Renders the People Clean Again (Hag 2:10–19)

IV. Zerubbabel Shall Be the Lord's Signet Ring (Hag 2:20–23)

3. *The Message of Haggai*: Cyrus the Great of Persia conquered Babylon in ca. 537 B.C. and shortly thereafter issued decrees permitting exiled peoples—including the Jews—to return to their homelands and rebuild their temples. Many Jews took advantage of this opportunity and began to return to Judah in waves, probably beginning around 535 B.C. Cyrus' generous policy toward displaced peoples was continued by his son Cambyses (530–522 B.C.) and Darius I (522–486 B.C.), a Persian aristocrat who took the throne when Cambyses died childless.

The first priority for Jews returning to Jerusalem was to rebuild homes and restore farmland that had been lying fallow, so the effort to rebuild the Temple generated lukewarm support and eventually stalled. This is the historical situation at the beginning of Haggai's preaching ministry (520 B.C.) and the overall context of his four oracles: (1) In Haggai's first oracle, he rebukes the people of Judah for living in "paneled houses" while the Temple lies in ruins, and he blames the poor economic conditions of Judah on the fact that the people fail to honor God properly (Hag 1:1–11). Haggai's rebuke has its intended result, and the people are stirred to action under the leadership of Zerubbabel, the governor, and Jehozadak, the high priest. (2) Haggai's second oracle is a word of encouragement to the Temple builders: although the Second Temple is not much compared to Solomon's of old (Hag 2:3–4), nonetheless, one day, the splendor of the future Temple of the Lord will exceed even that of Solomon's Temple in all its glory:

> For thus says the LORD of hosts: Once again, in a little while, I will shake the heavens and the earth and the sea and the dry land; and I will shake all nations, so that the treasures of all nations shall come in, and I will fill this house with splendor, says the LORD of hosts. The silver is mine, and the gold is mine, says the LORD of hosts. *The latter splendor of this house shall be greater than the former, says the LORD of hosts*; and in this place I will give prosperity, says the Lord of hosts. (Hag 2:6–9)

(3) In his third oracle, Haggai states that the people of Judah have been ritually "unclean" up to the present time, due to their failure to build the Temple. But now that they have become obedient, God will restore his blessing upon them (Hag 2:10–19). (4) Haggai's fourth and final word is directed to Zerubbabel, the governor and a descendant of David. In the future, God will shake the nations and wield Zerubbabel as his "signet ring", for God has "chosen" him (Hag 2:20–23).

Theologically, Haggai may be considered an exploration of the theme of seeking first the will of the Lord. The people of Judah in Haggai's day had prioritized their own wealth and comfort over their religious obligations to worship God and honor him with the first portion of their wealth. As a result, they had lost the blessing of God and (ironically) were failing to achieve the wealth they sought. By returning God to first place in their personal and communal life, the people also began to receive the material blessings they had been pursuing. This principle needs to be kept in tension with another articulated in several other prophets: God cannot be bought. At other times in their history, the people of Israel had made the opposite error from the one Haggai denounces: they sought to guarantee their material prosperity by lavish and assiduous attention to ritual worship, even while neglecting the moral requirements of God's law (Is 1:10–20). Thus, on the one hand, prioritizing the worship of God can be a means of returning to God's favor and experiencing his tangible blessings. On the other hand, dutiful attention to formal worship does not compensate for a neglect of the moral law.

XI. Zechariah: The Gentiles Will Gather to Worship in Jerusalem

1. *The Context of Zechariah*: The book of Zechariah, whose Hebrew name means "The Lord remembers" (Hebrew *zekaryah*), is attributed to "Zechariah, the son of Berechiah, son of Iddo, the prophet" (Zech 1:1). In addition to being the

descendant of a prophet, he also appears to have been a member of an important priestly family (cf. Ezra 8:17; Neh 12:1–16). As a result, it is unsurprising
that his oracles, much like those of Ezekiel, are shot through with images and
motifs taken from the Temple and its liturgy. Significantly, the book of Ezra
describes Zechariah's ministry as contemporary with that of Haggai (Ezra 5:1;
6:14). Significantly, the book contains exact dates for certain oracles delivered
by Zechariah:[11]

1. "Second year, eighth month of Darius"   = 520 B.C.
(Zech 1:1–6)

2. "Twenty fourth day of the eleventh month in the second year of Darius" = 519 B.C.
(Zech 1:7)

3. "Fourth year of King Darius ... fourth day of the ninth month."   = 518 B.C.
(Zech 7:1)

On the basis of such data, scholars conclude that Zechariah was probably a
young man in the early postexilic period when his dated oracles were delivered. His main mission—to see the Temple rebuilt—was successful (Ezra
6:14), but he may well have lived long enough into the postexilic period to
see the beginnings of the pessimism, disillusionment, and lukewarmness in
Judean society that Nehemiah later witnessed (ca. 445 B.C.) The oracles of the
second part of his book may reflect these changed circumstances (Zech 9–14)
and are often regarded as the work of a later prophet, referred to by scholars
as "Second Zechariah".[12]

2. *The Structure of the Book of Zechariah*: Zechariah is the longest of the minor
prophets, about half the length (by Hebrew word count) of Daniel. The book
divides into two major parts: (1) the first half contains explicitly dated prophecies
from the early postexilic period (ca. 520–518 B.C.) concerning the rebuilding of
the Temple and Judean society (Zech 1–8); and (2) the second half contains
undated, cryptic oracles of apocalyptic, messianic, and eschatological character
(Zech 9–14). With this overarching twofold structure in mind, the book can be
outlined as follows:

Outline of the Book of Zechariah

I. The Restoration of the Temple, the High Priest, and the King (Zech 1–8)
  A. The Visions of Zechariah (1:1—6:15)
    1. The Four Horsemen (1:1–17)
    2. The Four Horns (2:1–4 [1:18–21])
    3. The Man Measuring Jerusalem (2:5–9 [2:1–5])
    4. Joshua the High Priest and Satan (3:1–10)
    5. The Lampstand and the Olive Trees (4:1–14)
    6. The Flying Scroll (5:1–4)
    7. The Woman in the Basket (5:5–11)

---

[11] See Chisholm, *Handbook on the Prophets*, 456.
[12] Carol L. Meyers and Eric M. Meyers, *Zechariah 9–14*, Anchor Bible 25C (New York: Doubleday,
1993), 13–60; see sidebar below on p. 941 for discussion.

   3. The Message of Part 1: Restoration of the Temple, Priest, and King (Zechariah 1–8): As mentioned above, Zechariah divides into two major parts (Zech 1–8 and 9–14) very different in tone and character. Further, the first part of the book consists of two subsections: (a) a set of seven or eight mystic visions closely concerned with the restoration of the Temple and the leadership of God's people ca. 520 B.C. (Zech 1–6) and (b) a series of straightforward prophetic exhortations dated two years later (518 B.C.; Zech 7–8). Although the visions of the prophet are cryptic by nature, given what we know of Zechariah's postexilic context, interpretations for each of them can be suggested in the form of a chart:

Table of the Eight "Night Visions" of Zechariah and Epilogue			
Vision	Verses	Description	Possible Interpretation
1	1:1–17	Four heavenly horsemen patrol the earth and find it in peace. The Lord proclaims the restoration of favor to Jerusalem and Judah.	The international situation is ripe for the rebuilding of the Temple and restoration of Judean society.
2	2:1–4 [1:18–21]	A set of four horns is destroyed by four smiths.	The forces that destroyed Judah will themselves be destroyed.
3	2:5–9 [2:1–5]	A man measures Jerusalem with a measuring cord. The Lord promises to be a wall of fire around the city.	Jerusalem will grow too large for walls, but the Lord will be the defense of his city.
4	3:1–10	Joshua the high priest stands in filthy garments and accused by Satan in God's presence; the Lord orders him stripped and re-vested in the vestments of the high priest.	Joshua bears divine favor and authority for priestly leadership in his own day and symbolizes a greater "servant" yet to come, who will inaugurate messianic peace.
5	4:1–14	A lampstand like that of the Holy Place is fed with oil directly from two mysterious olive trees.	Zechariah and Joshua, the two "anointed ones" of the houses of David and Aaron respectively, will restore the Temple and its worship.

(continued)

Table of the Eight "Night Visions" of Zechariah and Epilogue (*continued*)			
Vision	Verses	Description	Possible Interpretation
6	5:1–4	A large flying scroll traverses the land, visiting judgment on thieves and liars.	The scroll may represent the law of God (the Ten Commandments) being divinely enforced within postexilic Judah.
7	5:5–11	A woman representing "wicked-ness" is seen in a basket, covered with a leaden lid. The basket is taken away by angels to Babylon.	The Lord is removing wickedness from Judah and restricting it to Babylon.
8	6:1–8	Four chariots pulled by horses of different color depart in the four cardinal directions to patrol the earth. God's spirit will find rest with the chariot that heads to the north.	Perhaps this means divine judgment on Israel's foes "to the north"?
Epilogue	6:9–15	Zechariah makes two crowns; one is placed on Joshua the high priest; the other is reserved in the Temple for the coming "Branch", a royal figure who will rebuild the Temple.	God will yet raise up the houses of Levi and David, to which the covenants of priesthood and kingship have been given.

As can be seen by surveying the table, Zechariah's visions focus on the following themes: divine judgment on Judah's enemies and divine restoration of Jerusalem; the removal of sin from Judah and its leadership; and the restoration of the royal and priestly houses (David and Levi), as represented by their contemporary heads: the Davidic governor Zerubbabel son of Shealtiel, and the high priest Joshua son of Jehozadak the high priest. The oracles concerning these two men emphasize not only their significance in their own generation but also their symbolic role as types of priestly and/or royal figure(s) yet to come.

After the accounts of Zechariah's visions (Zech 1–6), we find a narrative account of a question sent to the Jerusalem priests from leaders of the Jewish community in Babylon about 518 B.C. concerning whether Jews in the diaspora should continue to observe fasts in the fifth and seven month. (These fasts commemorated the events connected with the destruction of Jerusalem and the Temple in 587 B.C. and no longer seemed relevant in light of the progress that had been made on rebuilding the Temple.) This question prompts the delivery of a series of oracles from Zechariah, in which he reviews the history of the unfaithfulness of Judah to the words of the prophets, reaffirms the Lord's good intentions for the future prosperity of Judah and Jerusalem, and finally answers the query about fasting indirectly by assuring Judah that the days of fasting for the Temple will be turned into days of feasting and rejoicing in the future (Zech 7:1—8:19). At the end of this series of oracles, the prophet describes a coming time when not only Judah and Israel but the *Gentile nations* will go up to worship the Lord at the Temple in Jerusalem:

Thus says the LORD of hosts: Peoples shall yet come, even the inhabitants of many cities; the inhabitants of one city shall go to another, saying, "Let us go at once to entreat the favor of the LORD, and to seek the LORD of hosts; I am going." Many peoples and strong nations shall come to seek the LORD of hosts in Jerusalem, and to entreat the favor of the LORD. *Thus says the LORD of hosts: In those days ten men from the nations of every tongue shall take hold of the robe of a Jew, saying, "Let us go with you, for we have heard that God is with you."* (Zech 8:20–23)

Second Zechariah (Zechariah 9–14)

It is common to attribute Zechariah 9–14 to a different, later author referred to as "Second Zechariah" due to (1) differences in grammar and diction, (2) the apocalyptic character of some of the visions, and (3) possible allusions to historical events after the lifetime of the prophet.[a]

These data could be explained in several ways: (1) by positing a different author; (2) by suggesting that chapters may have been written by the same author at a much later period in his lifetime or career, when his theological perspective and linguistic preferences had changed; (3) as the product of redaction: an editor placed dated materials from the prophet first (Zech 1–8), followed by a loosely organized collection of his undated literary remains (Zech 9–14).

The possible allusions to events after the lifetime of Zechariah are not completely compelling. The most important is the reference to the "sons of Greece" (Zech 9:13), which some scholars conclude points to authorship in the Hellenistic or Maccabean periods (333–63 B.C.). However, the Greeks were a world power from the time of their defeat of Persia at Marathon (490 B.C., within Zechariah's lifetime). Other literary data in Zechariah 9–14 point to a time much earlier in Judah's history: references to "Ephraim" as a separate political entity (Zech 9:10) and to the pair "Assyria and Egypt" as the main enemies of Israel (Zech 10:10–12) seem more appropriate to the eighth or seventh century B.C. than to the postexilic period.

[a] See Meyers and Meyers, *Zechariah 9–14*, 13–60.

In this remarkable text, we see clearly expressed the prophetic expectation of a coming era of *international* salvation, in which the promises and the worship first given to Israel will be sought by the Gentiles.

2. *The Message of Part 2: Visions of the Future of Judah and Jerusalem (Zechariah 9–14):* This second part has a different literary character from the earlier chapters of the book. While the oracles of the first half (Zech 1-8) are explicitly dated and fit recognizably into the context of postexilic Judah in the late sixth century B.C., the oracles of the second half (Zech 9-14) are not dated, and their particular details resist identification with any certain time period in the history of Judah. Therefore, Zechariah 9–14 is frequently called "Second Zechariah" and associated with a different, unknown prophetic author living long after Zechariah himself, perhaps in the Hellenistic period (330–166 B.C.) or even the Maccabean period (164–63 B.C.). However, the evidence for dating these chapters so much later and to a different author than the rest of the book is inconclusive (see inset).

In the first oracle, the prophet foresees an age when all the vassal kingdoms of the old Davidic empire will once more be subsumed into the kingdom of Israel (Zech 9:1–8), and the Davidic king will ride into Jerusalem in the manner of Solomon (Zech 9:9–10). Significantly, the coming of the future king—who will later come to be identified as the Messiah—is tied to the outpouring of the "blood" of a future "covenant":

> Rejoice greatly, O daughter of Zion!
>   Shout aloud, O daughter of Jerusalem!
> *Behold, your king comes to you;*
>   *triumphant and victorious is he,*
> *humble and riding on a donkey,*
>   on a colt the foal of a donkey.
> I will cut off the chariot from Ephraim
>   and the war horse from Jerusalem;
> and the battle bow shall be cut off,
>   and he shall command peace to the nations;
> his dominion shall be from sea to sea,
>   and from the River to the ends of the earth.
>
> As for you also, *because of the blood of my covenant with you,*
>   *I will set your captives free from the waterless pit.*
>   (Zech 9:9–11)

Notice here that the triumphal arrival of the future king riding on a donkey is directly tied to the ingathering of God's people, not just from exile, but from the realm of the dead—"the pit"—by means of the "blood of the covenant". Thus, the prophet combines both new Solomon and new exodus imagery in his description of the future age of salvation, seemingly going beyond the mere vision of a geographical return from exile.

Then follows a series of cryptic oracles loosely unified by the theme of shepherding God's people (Zech 10–12). After an initial rebuke of God's people for the practice of paganism, the Lord threatens to punish the "shepherds of his people" but grant victory in battle and restoration of land to the people themselves, especially "Ephraim"—that is, northern Israel (Zech 10:1–12). God commissions the prophet to shepherd the people, but "shepherd" and "sheep" dislike each other, and the prophet breaks two staffs symbolizing covenants: the one between God and the peoples, the other between Israel and Judah (Zech 11:4–14). Yet after this, God again commissions Zechariah to portray a "worthless shepherd" who will come under divine judgment (Zech 11:15–17).

Finally, the book ends with a diverse collection of short oracles describing a future battle between Jerusalem and all the nations, one in which Judah itself at times wars against its capital city (Zech 12–14). This battle will take place on the "day of the LORD" (Zech 14:1)—that is, an eschatological period of judgment. Indeed, although there are a number of individual oracles, they typically begin with the phrase "On that day" (Zech 12:3, 4, 6, 8, 11; 13:1, 2, 4; 14:4, 6, 8, 9, 13, 20, 21), suggesting that they should be interpreted as various aspects or facets of the same eschatological event. "On that day" the Lord will strengthen Jerusalem and Judah to defeat all the nations that have gathered against them (Zech 12:1–9), but curiously there will also be national mourning for "him whom they have pierced" (Zech 12:10–14). There will be a fountain that cleanses from sin (Zech 13:1) and the removal of false prophets and idols (Zech 13:2–6). The oracles about "the day of the Lord" are then interrupted by a prophecy about striking "the shepherd" so that "the sheep may be scattered", which seems to hearken back to the oracles about the wicked shepherds (Zech 13:7–9; cf. Zech 10–11).

After this, the oracles about "the day of the Lord" resume: the Mount of Olives will be split; cold and frost will cease; a river of "living waters" will flow from Jerusalem; God's universal kingship will be established; Jerusalem will be exalted; and a plague will fall on all Gentile enemies of Jerusalem (Zech 14:1–15). Afterward, the surviving nations will make annual pilgrimage on the Feast of Tabernacles (Zech 14:16–19), and the sanctity of the Temple will encompass all of Jerusalem (Zech 14:20–21).

In sum, the sustained concern throughout the book of Zechariah is the purification, rehabilitation, and glorification of the Temple in Jerusalem, the place of liturgical worship and sacrifice. Even Zechariah's concern for Zerubbabel and the Davidic line is ultimately oriented toward the Temple, because the role of the son of David was to provide the political and material conditions that would allow the sanctuary to flourish. The narrative shape of Zechariah begins with no Temple and no worship even in Judah (Zech 1:16–17) and ends with every nation of the earth making pilgrimage to Zion to observe the Feast of Tabernacles, which was the great celebration of God's habitation among his people in various sanctuaries through history. Zechariah's vision of the eschaton culminates in all mankind celebrating and worshipping in God's Temple.

> ### The Feast of Tabernacles
>
> The Feast of Tabernacles was the Jewish celebration of God "tabernacling" or dwelling with his people—in other words, the celebration of God's presence in the Temple. The analogue to Tabernacles in Christianity is the Feast of the Incarnation—in other words, Christmas, in which we celebrate God's Word becoming flesh and "tabernacling" among us (see Greek of Jn 1:14).

XII. Malachi: Fidelity to the Covenants and the Coming of Elijah

As the last of the twelve, the book of Malachi occupies a decisive position in shaping the interpretation of the minor prophets. Writing sometime between the ministries of Haggai and Zechariah in the late sixth century B.C. and the reforms of Nehemiah in the mid-fifth century B.C., Malachi was remembered in the Jewish and Christian traditions as the last of the classical writing prophets and, thus, the one to give the final divine instructions to Israel as she awaited the "day of the Lord" and the coming of the Messiah.

1. *The Context of Malachi:* There is little doubt that the book of Malachi was written during the Persian period (ca. 537–334 B.C.). Based on internal evidence, the Second Temple seems to be reconstructed and functioning (Mal 1:6–2:9), which would place the ministry of Malachi after Haggai and Zechariah, sometime after 520 B.C. On the other hand, there is no mention of Nehemiah (ca. 444–420 B.C.), and his reforms seem not to have been implemented

Versification of Malachi

The Masoretic Text and Septuagint both divide Malachi into three chapters, whereas the Vulgate adopts Malachi 3:19–24 as a fourth chapter (Mal 4:1–6). Thus, English translations that follow the Hebrew versification (NAB, JPS) end with Malachi 3:19–24, whereas those following the Vulgate tradition (KJV, RSV, etc.) end with Malachi 4:1–6.

yet, because mixed marriages with Gentiles (among other issues) are still a pressing problem (Mal 2:11; cf. Neh 13). Therefore, Malachi is almost universally held by scholars to have been written sometime between 500 B.C. and 450 B.C.[13] Those who are impressed with Malachi's similarity in language and concepts with Haggai-Zechariah tend to date the book toward 500 B.C., while those who place more weight on the similarity of the social pathologies addressed in Malachi and Nehemiah tend toward 450 B.C.

As is the case with some others of the twelve (Joel, Obadiah, Habakkuk), the superscription of Malachi provides no other information about the prophet than his name. Moreover, since "Malachi" means "my messenger" (Hebrew *mal'ākî*), it is not clear whether it is a personal name or a title (Mal 1:1). The Septuagint, for example, translates the superscription as a title: "The oracle of the word of the Lord to Israel by the hand of his angel/messenger [Greek *angelos*]" (Mal 1:1 LXX [author's trans.]). Therefore, some scholars see the book as anonymous and "Malachi" simply a title given to an unknown prophet. One ancient Jewish writing from the first century A.D. states that he was known as an "angel" because he "led a virtuous life" and was "beautiful to behold",[14] whereas Jerome held that the unknown "messenger" was Ezra. In more recent times, some scholars have proposed that Malachi was once the third of three sets of anonymous "oracles" (Hebrew *massā'*) appended to the end of Zechariah: (1) Zechariah 9–11; (2) Zechariah 13–14, and (3) Malachi 1–3 [1–4]. According to this hypothesis, scribes later separated Malachi and made it an independent book in order to produce the round number of twelve minor prophets. However, there is no textual evidence for this theory, and the literary character of Malachi—with its unique dialogues between God, the prophet, and the people—is singular and quite unlike anything in Zechariah. Finally, the mainstream of Jewish and Christian interpretation has understood "Malachi" to be the name of the prophetic author, whether or not it was his given name. The book lends itself most naturally to being understood as recording, in abbreviated form, the prophet's dialogical preaching and rebuke of the people of Judah and Jerusalem in a specific time period (ca. 500–450 B.C.), which resulted in a communal repentance on the part of the more religiously faithful members of the populace (Mal 3:16). Thus, it appears to be rooted in the historical events of a largely unknown prophet's ministry, and not simply a literary creation.

2. *The Structure of the Book of Malachi*: The main body of Malachi consists of six *disputations* between the Lord and Israel (Mal 1:2—3:15). Typically, a

---

[13] See Andrew E. Hill, "Malachi", in vol. 5 of *Zondervan Illustrated Bible Backgrounds Commentary*, ed. John H. Walton (Grand Rapids, Ill.: Zondervan, 2009), 15–18.

[14] *Lives of the Prophets* 16.1–3, in D. R. Hare, "Lives of the Prophets", in *The Old Testament Apocrypha*, vol. 2, ed. James H. Charlesworth, Anchor Bible Reference Library (New York: Doubleday, 1985), 394.

disputation begins with (a) an initial statement of theological truth from the Lord (Mal 1:2a: "I have loved you"), followed by (b) an objection raised by the people (Mal 1:2b: "How have you loved us?"), and continuing with (c) the Lord's response to the objection (Mal 1:2–5: "Yet I have loved Jacob but I have hated Esau"). Yet the form of the disputation is flexible: the length varies a great deal (eighteen verses [1:6—2:9] vs. three [3:13–15]), and sometimes there are multiple objections (for example, 1:6–7; 3:7–8) and responses as well as variations in the way the initial statement is phrased (for example, either as a proposition [1:2a; 2:17a; 3:6, 13] or as a question [1:6; 2:10]). In one case, the Lord's response to the people's objection is omitted (cf. Mal 3:13–15). In this way, the book can be outlined as follows:

Outline of the Book of Malachi

I. Superscription (Mal 1:1)

II. Six Disputations between God and Israel (Mal 1:2—3:15)
    A. On God's Love for Israel (1:2–5)
    B. On Offering Unblemished Sacrifices (1:6—2:9)
    C. On Faithfulness to the Wife of One's Youth (2:10–16)
    D. On the Apparent Delay of God's Justice (2:17—3:5)
    E. On Offering the Full Tithe to God (3:6–12)
    F. On the Apparent Vanity of Serving God (3:13–15)

III. The Repentance of a Remnant (Mal 3:16)

IV. Words of Comfort and Instruction to the Remnant (Mal 3:17–24 [3:17—4:6])

3. *The Message of Malachi*: In order to understand the message of Malachi, contemporary exegesis has shown us that we must pay close attention to its form. In this regard, many scholars have noted that Malachi seems to employ the rhetoric of the legal court. Some have suggested that the disputations are in the form of the covenant "lawsuit", or *rib*, similar to Micah. Covenant certainly is a dominating concept in Malachi, as the prophet mentions four of them:

    1. the "covenant" with Levi (Mal 2:4–8);
    2. the "covenant" with "our fathers" (Mal 2:10: cf. Abrahamic);
    3. the "covenant" with one's spouse in marriage (Mal 2:14: cf. Adamic);
    4. the "covenant" associated with a divine messenger (Mal 3:1: Mosaic?).

In general, we may say that the literary dynamic of Malachi presents the prophet as the "attorney" for the Lord, who is prosecuting Israel for various interrelated breaches of covenant.

With this covenantal framework in mind, the topics of the six disputations between God and Israel may be stated as questions: (1) Does God really love Israel? (Mal 1:2–5); (2) Do priests and people do well to offer blemished sacrifices? (Mal 1:6—2:9); (3) Do Israelite men do well to divorce their wives and marry Gentiles? (Mal 2:10–16); (4) Will God ever execute justice on the wicked? (Mal 2:17—3:5); (5) Should the people shortchange the Lord in tithes and offerings? (Mal 3:6–12); (6) Is it truly vain to serve God? (Mal 3:13–15).

Of these questions, the two that have long caught interpreters' attention are Malachi's teachings about divorce and almsgiving. With regard to the former, Malachi's declaration that the Lord "hate[s] divorce!" is the strongest repudiation of the breach of the marital bond in the entire Old Testament:

> You cover the LORD's altar with tears, with weeping and groaning because he no longer regards the offering or accepts it with favor at your hand. You ask, "Why does he not?" Because the LORD was witness to *the covenant between you and the wife of your youth, to whom you have been faithless, though she is your companion and your wife by covenant.* Has not the one God made and sustained for us the spirit of life? And what does he desire? Godly offspring. So take heed to yourselves, and let none be faithless to the wife of his youth. "*For I hate divorce, says the LORD the God of Israel*, and covering one's garment with violence, says the LORD of hosts. So take heed to yourselves and do not be faithless." (Mal 2:13–16)

It should be noted here that the exact translation of the verse regarding divorce continues to be hotly debated, with some translations eliminating all reference to divorce.[15] Taken in context, however, it appears that Malachi was addressing a situation in which wealthier Israelite men were divorcing their Israelite wives whom they had betrothed as young men (the "wife of your youth") in order to marry younger Gentile women, either for reasons of physical attraction or socioeconomic gain. The prophet roundly condemns this injustice against women who have borne children and heirs for their husbands, only to be cast off when older. The biblical ideal, even in the Old Testament, was monogamous fidelity to the "wife of your youth", as can be seen in the introduction to Proverbs (for example, Prov 5:1–23).

With regard to almsgiving, Malachi's great stress on offering the best of one's possessions to the Lord (Mal 1:6–2:9) and being generous in the gift of the "*tithe*"—the tenth of one's income due to the Lord as a gift to the sanctuary and those who maintain it (cf. Lev 27:30; Num 18:21; Deut 14:22–28)—is striking (Mal 3:6–12). In fact, the practice of tithing to the Lord is one of the few instances in the Hebrew Bible where the believer is encouraged to "test" the Lord:

> *Bring the full tithes into the storehouse*, that there may be food in my house; *and thereby put me to the test*, says the LORD of hosts, if I will not open the windows of heaven for you and pour down for you an overflowing blessing. (Mal 3:10; cf. Deut 6:16)

After the disputations, there is a very short historical narrative about a group of pious Jews ("those who feared the LORD") who took heed of the prophet's message and wrote a kind of covenant-renewal document entitled "a book of remembrance" (Mal 3:16).

---

[15] See Hill, "Malachi", 221–24, who translates it as "Surely [The] One Who made everything!"

The remainder of the book consists of four words of consolation and instruction to this repentant remnant: (1) They will be God's possession (Mal 3:17–18) and (2) will be vindicated on the day of the Lord (Mal 3:19–21 [4:1–3]). In the meantime, (3) they should diligently observe the law of Moses (Mal 3:22 [4:4]) and (4) watch vigilantly for Elijah's arrival as harbinger of the day of the Lord:

> Behold, I will send you Elijah the prophet before the great and awesome day of the LORD comes. And he will turn the hearts of fathers to their children and the hearts of children to their fathers, lest I come and strike the land with a curse. (Mal 3:23–24 [4:5–6])

Being the last of the literary prophets, Malachi significantly shaped the messianic and eschatological hopes of Second Temple Judaism, especially by means of the epilogue of the book. The exhortation to "remember the law of my servant Moses" during the period of waiting served to summarize the message of the twelve and, in a sense, the whole prophetic corpus, thus aligning it with the teaching of the Torah (Mal 3:22 [4:4]). In this way, the two divisions of the ancient Jewish canon, the Law and Prophets, are read as complementary rather than competing. Diligent observance of the Mosaic law became the religious agenda for pious Jews up to the coming of the Messiah and remains the agenda for observant branches of Judaism to this day. The communities of Jews from which John the Baptist and Jesus came took seriously the concluding exhortations of Malachi.

The Message of the Book of the Twelve

Having reviewed the twelve as individual books, we are now in a position to summarize the message of the twelve as a composite unity. We have already observed that Hosea's allegory of God and Israel as Bridegroom and Bride (Hos 1–3) forms an *inclusio* with Malachi's divine repudiation of divorce (Mal 2:10–16), thereby establishing a nuptial, covenantal frame around the twelve, assuring God's people of his faithfulness toward them despite their infidelities. Furthermore, the last three postexilic prophets—Haggai, Zechariah, Malachi—pound home the importance of prioritizing the Temple and the worship of God above anything else that might compete for the interest of God's people (Hag 1:2–11; Zech 8:9–13; Mal 3:6–12). This *liturgical* stress complements the nuptial frame of the twelve, since the liturgy in the Temple is the means by which the nuptial intimacy between God and his people is achieved and maintained.

Finally, the coming "day of the Lord" forms perhaps the major theme throughout the twelve, present in a remarkable number of passages (Hos 2:18, 23 [2:16, 21]; 9:5; Joel 1:15, 2:1, 11, 31; 4:14, 18 [3:14–18]; Amos 5:18; 8:3, 9; Obad 15; Mic 4:6; Zeph 1:7, 10, 14, 18; 2:2–3; 3:8; Hag 2:23; Zech 2:15 [2:11]; 3:9–10; 12:4, 8; 13:2; 14:1–21; Mal 3:17–23 [3:17—4:5]). As we have seen, the "day of the Lord" becomes a term referring to the Lord's final intervention into history, at which the twelve expected the following: (1) the restoration of the Davidic king and his rule over all the nations; (2) the judgment on all Israel's enemies; (3) the vindication of the faithful remnant of Israel; (4) the purification and restoration of the Temple, liturgy, and priesthood; and (5) the establishment of the Temple-city as a place of universal pilgrimage for the nations. These expectations form the backdrop against which the hope for the Jewish Messiah emerged in the Second Temple period.

The Book of the Twelve in the Living Tradition

Despite its comparative brevity and the traditional identification of this unit as the "minor" prophets, the Book of the Twelve, as prophetic literature, has played a significant role in the living tradition of the Church. For reasons of space, in what follows, we will for the most part offer a single example of how each of the twelve minor prophets has been interpreted in the living tradition of the Church.

Hosea and the New Marriage Covenant

In the early Church, following the New Testament itself, the idea of the nuptial mystery of YHWH's relationship with Israel and Christ's relationship with the Church played a central role in explaining the gospel (for example, Eph 5:21–35). Along similar lines, the nuptial imagery in Hosea was seen as revealing the various stages of God's betrothal to mankind—a kind of divine "love story" that would culminate in the wedding of Christ and the Church. In the words of Jerome:

> First, he [God] betrothed her [Israel] in Abraham (or rather, in Egypt), so that he may have an everlasting spouse. Second, on Mount Sinai in the betrothal.... By his crucifixion and resurrection from the dead, he [Jesus] betroths [her] not in the equity of the law but rather in faith and the grace of the gospel.[16]

Notice here that Jerome is commenting on Hosea's oracle about a future "covenant" between YHWH and his faithless bride (Hos 2:18–22 [2:16–20]), which is the functional equivalent of Jeremiah's great promise of the New Covenant (Jer 31:31–34). Significantly, an abbreviated form of the oracle in Hosea 2 is the most commonly read passage of Hosea in the contemporary Lectionary.

Joel and the Call to Repentance during Lent

The short book of Joel is best remembered in the living tradition of the Church for the prophet's stirring call for sincere, interior conversion on the part of God's people (Joel 2:12–18)—proclaimed each Ash Wednesday in the Roman rite—and his vivid depiction of the eschatological outpouring of the Spirit of God (Joel 3:1–5 [2:25–32]), a text that the apostle Peter declared fulfilled on Pentecost (Acts 2:14–21).

---

[16] Jerome, *Commentary on Hosea* 1.2, in Alberto Ferreiro, *The Twelve Prophets*, Old Testament 14, Ancient Christian Commentary on Scripture, ed. Thomas C. Oden (Downers Grove, Ill.: InterVarsity Press, 2003), 12.

Remarkably, the first of these texts, which is proclaimed in the contemporary Lectionary each Ash Wednesday, was from ancient times associated with the Christian custom of fasting during the season of Lent. Consider the words of the fourth-fifth century Caesarius, bishop of Arles, who writes:

> "Return to me with your whole heart, with fasting, and weeping and mourning" [Joel 2:12]. *If we notice carefully, dearest brethren, the holy days of Lent signify the life of the present world, just as Easter prefigures eternal bliss.* Now just as we have a kind of sadness in Lent in order that we may rightly rejoice at Easter, so as long as we live in this world we ought to do penance in order that we may be able to receive pardon for our sins in the future and arrive at eternal joy. Each one ought to sigh over his own sins, shed tears, and give alms in such a way that with God's help he may always try to avoid the same faults as long as he lives.[17]

In this way, the Church has continued to use Joel's stirring calls for communal repentance—with their particular emphasis on interior conversion rather than merely external acts of self-denial—as models and articulations of the continuing call for repentance within his Church.

Amos: The Kingdom of David and the Inclusion of the Gentiles

Amos is best remembered in the Jewish and Christian tradition as a preacher of justice who was unafraid to rebuke publicly the wealthy elite of his day, whose hypocritical and syncretistic religious practices did nothing to alleviate the guilt of their social and economic abuse of the poor: "Let justice roll down like waters, and righteousness like an ever-flowing stream" (Amos 5:21–24). To this very day, Amos' words remind Christian believers that external observance of the Church's rituals does not excuse or justify life-styles of self-indulgence and indifference to the poor and needy.

In addition to this moral component, Amos had a monumental impact on the life of the Church from her very earliest days. In the wake of the controversy over whether Gentiles must be circumcised to be saved (Acts 15:1–4), it is Amos' prophecy of the restoration of the Davidic kingdom (Amos 9:11–12) that is quoted by James the brother of Jesus as prophetic demonstration of the inclusion of the Gentiles:

> After they finished speaking, James replied, "Brethren, listen to me. Symeon has related how God first visited the Gentiles, to take out of them a people for his name. And with this the words of the prophets agree, as it is written,
>
>> After this I will return,
>> and I will rebuild the dwelling of David, which has fallen;
>> I will rebuild its ruins,
>> and I will set it up,
>> that the rest of men may seek the Lord,
>> and all the Gentiles who are called by my name,
>> says the Lord, who has made these things known from of old.

---

[17] Caesarius of Arles, *Sermon* 198.1, in Caesarius, *Sermons*, vol. 3, *187–238*, trans. Mary Magdeleine Mueller, O.S.F., The Fathers of the Church 66 (Washington, D.C.: Catholic University of America Press, 1964), 48–49.

Therefore my judgment is that we should not trouble those of the Gentiles who turn to God, but should write to them to abstain from the pollutions of idols and from unchastity and from what is strangled and from blood." (Acts 15:13–20)

Notice here that James sees the prophecy of the restoration of the Davidic empire—which had always incorporated several of the Gentile nations that surrounded the territory of Israel (see 2 Sam 8–9; 1 Kings 4)—as being fulfilled in the growth of the early Church through the inclusion of Gentiles. In other words, the testimony of James demonstrates that from the very beginning, *the living tradition of the Church, as expressed in the teaching of the apostles, understood the Church to be the manifestation and fulfillment of the kingdom of David.* This theological understanding of the relationship of the kingdom of David and the Church is important to grasp, because it provides the biblical basis for many of the external and hierarchical aspects of the Church's structure—for example, the exercise of authority in a Church council by Church leaders, as at the Council of Jerusalem.

Obadiah: Mount Zion and the Kingdom of God

Although the book of Obadiah is not read in the contemporary Roman Lectionary for Mass or in the Liturgy of the Hours, it was the object of a remarkable amount of commentary in the early Church. In particular, its potent typology of the battle between Mount Esau and Mount Zion and its closing reference to the "kingdom" of the Lord were seen as prefiguring the mystery of the Church. Consider, for example, the striking exposition of Obadiah by Augustine:

> Obadiah, so far as his writings are concerned the briefest of all the prophets, speaks against Edom, that is, the nation of Esau, that reprobate elder of the twin sons of Isaac.... Now by that form of speech in which a part is understood for the whole, we understand Edom as referring to the nations.... [And] Mount Zion signifies Judea, where it is predicted that there shall be safety and a holy one, that is, Jesus Christ. But Mount Esau is Edom. *It signifies the church of the Gentiles, which is defended by the redeemed from Mount Zion, so that it should become a kingdom to the Lord.* This was obscure before it took place, but what believer does not understand it now that it has happened?[18]

In contrast to some contemporary readers, who might be tempted to dismiss Obadiah as an irrelevant oracle against a forgotten pagan rival to Israel, Augustine sees in it a prophecy of the universal kingdom of God, by which the descendants of both Esau (the Gentiles) and Jacob (the Israelites) will at last be reunited.

Jonah: Descent into Hell followed by Resurrection

As we have already noted above, the primary significance of the book of Jonah for Christianity was in Jesus' use of Jonah's time in the "belly of the whale" as a

---

[18] Augustine, *City of God* 18.31, in Ferrerio, *Twelve Prophets*, 126.

type of his own death and Resurrection (Mt 12:38–41). This typological significance was not lost on the early Church Fathers, who picked up on the imagery of Jonah's descent into "the Pit" and "the belly of Sheol" (Jon 2:2, 6 RSVCE 2) as a type of Christ's descent into hell, followed by his Resurrection. Such typological exegesis was a basic part of the catechetical teaching of Cyril of Jerusalem:

> Jona fulfilled a type of our Savior when he prayed from the belly of the fish and said, "I cried for help from the midst of the nether world." He was in fact in the fish, yet he says that he is in the nether world. In a later verse he manifestly prophesies in the person of Christ: "My head went down into the chasms of the mountains" [Jonah 2:6]. Yet he was still in the belly of the fish. What mountains encompass you? But I know, he says, that I am a type of Him who is to be laid in the sepulchre hewn out of rock. While he was in the sea Jona says, "I went down into the earth"; for he typified Christ, who went down into the heart of the earth.[19]

In addition to such typological interpretation, the book of Jonah continues to play a role in the Church's liturgy. In particular, selections from Jonah's call to repentance (Jon 3) are read in the Liturgy of the Word on a handful of occasions in which the themes of repentance, forgiveness of sin, and conversion of the Gentiles are appropriate, such as on the Third Sunday in Ordinary Time in Year B to set up a parallel with the opening of Jesus' preaching (Jon 3:1–5, 10; cf. Mk 1:14–20). Between Jonah and Jesus we see both comparisons and contrasts: they share a prophetic role, and their message(s) elicit repentance. But Jonah's message is one of pure threat, whereas Jesus calls his hearers to enter the "kingdom of God". A longer reading of the same passage (Jon 3:1–10) is proclaimed during the First Week of Lent (Wednesday) and is an option for special Masses for the remission of sins. In addition, the end of Jonah forms an optional first reading for special Masses for the Evangelization of Peoples, thus reminding the Church that God's desire for the salvation of all people was present already in the Old Covenant era (Jon 3:11—4:10).

Micah and the Birth of the Eternally Begotten Messiah

Micah is best remembered in the living tradition for the prophecy of the origin of a ruler from Bethlehem (Mic 2:4–6), which is cited in the Gospel of Matthew by the scribes in their famous response to Herod's query about the birthplace of the Messiah (Mt 2:6). Indeed, the prophecy of the birth of the future king was not merely used as a motive of credibility for belief in Jesus' identity as Messiah. Micah's declaration that his "origin is from of old, from ancient days" (Mic 5:2 RSVCE 2) was seen as pointing to the preexistence of Christ before he was conceived:

> It is enough for piety for you to know ... that God has One Only Son, One naturally begotten; who did not begin to be when He was born in Bethlehem,

---

[19] Cyril of Jerusalem, *Catechetical Lectures* 14.20, in *The Works of Saint Cyril of Jerusalem*, vol. 2, trans. Leo P. McCauley, S.J., and Anthony A. Stephenson, The Fathers of the Church 64 (Washington, D.C.: Catholic University of America Press, 1970), 45.

but is before all ages. For listen to the Prophet Michea: "And you, Bethlehem, house of Ephratha ... from you shall come forth for me a leader who shall feed my people Israel; and his goings forth are from the beginning, from the days of eternity" [Micah 5:2]. *Therefore do not fix your attention on Him as coming from Bethlehem simply, but worship Him as begotten eternally of the Father.* Admit no one who speaks of a beginning of the Son in time, but acknowledge His timeless Beginning, the Father.[20]

Notice here once again how the Church Fathers derive key Christological doctrines—such as the eternal nature of Christ as divine Son, against the Arian view that there was "a time when he was not"—not only from the books of the New Testament, but also from the Old Testament prophets.

In the contemporary Lectionary, the Bethlehem oracle and the condensation of the moral law of God (Mic 6:6–8) to "justice" (Hebrew *mishpāt*), "kindness" (Hebrew *hesed*, lit. "covenant fidelity"), and "humility" (Hebrew *tzānā'*) (Mic 6:6–8) are the passages of this small book that are proclaimed most frequently. The prophecy of the rule from Bethlehem is proclaimed on the Fourth Sunday of Advent (Year C) and is the first option for the first reading on the Feast of the Nativity of the Blessed Virgin (September 8). In addition to these well-known texts, it is also significant that the Church has always seen a Marian reference in the description of "she who has labor pains and has brought forth" (Mic 5:3 RSVCE 2) and, so, typically reads this passage in conjunction with a Marian Gospel selection (for example, Lk 1:39–45, the Visitation) or on a feast in her honor. On the other hand, Micah's summary of the moral law is proper to the memorial of Saint Henry (July 13), who exemplified these virtues, and is also an option for the first reading for the Common of Holy Men and Women. Two other passages of Micah find a place in the liturgy on more somber occasions: The vision of the Word of the Lord going forth from Zion to establish peace (Mic 4:1–4) is an option for the first reading for Masses on the occasion of war or civil disturbance. Also, portions of Micah's psalm of confidence in the eventual mercy of God, despite present sufferings (Mic 7:7–20), serves to encourage the faithful during daily Masses in Lent (see table on pp. 961–62).

Nahum: The Overthrow of Assyria and the Defeat of Satan

As with other cities who persecuted the people of Israel without mercy in the Old Testament period, the kingdom of Assyria and its destruction came to be seen in the living tradition as a prefiguration of the ultimate overthrow of the true enemy of God's people, Satan. In his commentary on Nahum's image of one who comes up "blowing in your face, rescuing you from tribulation" (Nahum 2:2 LXX), Theodoret of Cyrus writes:

Since Adam lost what he had received by way of image through the divine blowing, it was right that Christ the Lord should renew the image and restore it to

---

[20] Cyril of Jerusalem, *Catechetical Lectures* 11.20; in *The Works of Saint Cyril of Jerusalem*, vol. 1, trans. Leo P. McCauley, S.J., The Fathers of the Church 61 (Washington, D.C.: Catholic University of America Press, 1969), 222.

the sacred apostles and through them to all the believers, blowing on them and saying, "Receive the Holy Spirit" [John 20:22]. Since former things are a type of the new, therefore, *let us take the Assyrians' kingdom that was destroyed as the devil's tyranny brought to an end through Christ the Lord.*[21]

The book of Nahum is not read in the contemporary Lectionary or Liturgy of the Hours except on Friday of the Eighteenth Week in Ordinary Time in Year II, when selections from the book are read at Mass in order to give a sense for the prophet's basic message (Nahum 2:1, 3; 3:1–3, 6–7).

Habakkuk: Justification by Faith apart from Works of the Law

The central significance of Habakkuk's oracle about the righteous living by "faith" (Hab 2:4) in the living tradition of the Church begins with the New Testament itself, in which it stands as one of the most-quoted verses of the Old Testament in the New:

> For I am not ashamed of the gospel: it is the power of God for salvation to every one who has faith, to the Jew first and also to the Greek. For in it the righteousness of God is revealed through faith for faith; as it is written, "He who through faith is righteous shall live" [Hab 2:4]. (Rom 1:16–17)

> Now it is evident that no man is justified before God by the law; for "The righteous shall live by faith" [Hab 2:4]; but the law does not rest on faith, for "He who does them shall live by them" [Lev 18:5]. (Gal 3:11)[22]

>> For you have need of endurance, so that you may do the will of God and
>>   receive what is promised.
>> "For yet a little while,
>> and the coming one shall come and shall not tarry;
>> but my righteous one shall live by faith,
>> and if he shrinks back,
>> my soul has no pleasure in him" [Hab 2:3–4]. (Heb 10:36–38)

The seed planted in the little book of Habakkuk has borne great fruit: from it, the New Testament derives the teachings of justification by faith apart from the works of the law as well as the call to patient endurance in the face of trials and tribulations. As a result, Habakkuk has powerfully influenced Christian piety, prayer, and theology.

In the contemporary Lectionary, the Church proclaims Habakkuk on the Twenty-Seventh Sunday in Ordinary Time (Year C), on which the first reading consists of Habakkuk's first complaint (Hab 1:2–3) followed by the Lord's second response (Hab 2:2–4). Together, these passages suffice to summarize the message of the book. It is paired with the Gospel account of the apostles' request "Increase our faith!" and Jesus' teaching on "faith as a grain of mustard seed" (Lk 17:5–10). In this way, the Church emphasizes the continuity of the prophetic

---

[21] Theodoret of Cyrus, *Commentary on Nahum* 2.1, in Ferrerio, *Twelve Prophets*, 184.
[22] Using the alternate translation provided by the RSVCE2 footnote.

tradition and of the Scriptures in teaching the importance of faith to the daily life of the one who follows the God of Israel.

In the Liturgy of the Hours, the Church employs the beautiful psalm of Habakkuk stressing his faith in God despite a lack of all external consolation as the psalm for Morning Prayer on Fridays of Week II and on Good Friday itself (Hab 3:2–4, 13a, 15–19). Thus the Church makes her own Habakkuk's powerful statement of faith on her liturgical day of greatest sorrow, when she recalls the apparent divine abandonment and collapse of all external consolation at the Cross.

Habakkuk 1–2 is also read in the Office of Readings in the Twenty-Third Week in Ordinary Time, where it follows Jeremiah and thus forms, together with Lamentations, a meditation on the decline, fall, and exile of Jerusalem at the hand of the Babylonians recorded in Jeremiah.

Taken together, the Church remembers Habakkuk as a great prophet of faith, whose small book beautifully expresses both the dynamic struggle of life in relationship to God in a world marked by rampant and visible injustice, and the stance of total trust or faith in God that the worshipper must adopt in order successfully to weather the trials of this life.

Zephaniah: The Pure Speech of the Liturgy and the Incarnation

In the living tradition of the Church, two oracles from the book of Zephaniah stand out as significant. First, Zephaniah's prophecy of a future time when the Lord would "change the speech of the peoples" so that they might "call on the name of the LORD and serve him with one accord" (Zeph 3:9) was widely interpreted by the early Church Fathers as fulfilled in the fact that the Gentile nations no longer worshipped in Jerusalem but throughout the world in the liturgy of the Eucharist. For example, Fulgentius of Ruspe writes:

> They [the prophets] predicted with a certain and most faithful prophecy, that in the time of the New Testament, spiritual sacrifices were to be offered not to the Father only but also to the Son by the faithful. For Zephaniah says, "Therefore, wait for me, says the Lord.... For my decision is to gather nations, to assemble kingdoms.... At the time I will change the speech of the peoples to a pure speech, that all of them may call on the name of the Lord and serve him with one accord" [Zeph 3:9].[23]

Hence, for Fulgentius, the "pure speech" of Zephaniah is nothing other than the language of the Christian liturgy, sung as one throughout the world.

Second, the oracle of the Lord coming to dwell in "the midst" of the daughter of Jerusalem was from early times interpreted as a prophecy of the Incarnation.[24] Building on the typological identification of Mary with the daughter

---

[23] Fulgentius of Ruspe, *To Monimus* 2.5.1, in Fulgentius, *Selected Works*, trans. Robert B. Eno, The Fathers of the Church 95 (Washington, D.C.: Catholic University of America Press, 1996), 239.

[24] See Ferreiro, *Twelve Prophets*, 217–18.

of Zion in the tradition, the 1992 *Catechism of the Church* takes the oracle of Zephaniah and sees in it a foreshadowing of the mystery of the Incarnation, insofar as Mary is the one in whom God himself makes his "dwelling" as "the daughter of Zion in person" (*CCC* 2676). Along these lines, the contemporary Roman Lectionary chooses all of its readings from Zephaniah from the oracles of restoration (Zeph 3:9–20), especially from the song of the daughter of Zion (3:14–18). The Church sees the "daughter of Zion" as an image of the Church, the Bride of Christ. Accordingly, portions of Zephaniah's song are proclaimed during Advent (for example, Tuesday, Week 3; December 21), notably on the Third or "Laetare" Sunday (Year C), when the Church is called to relive the time of anticipation of her Bridegroom King coming to her in the Incarnation, when he wedded her nature to his own (Zeph 3:14–18). The same oracle from Zephaniah is proclaimed on the Feast of the Visitation.

Zephaniah's oracles about the "humble of the land" and the "lowly" (Zeph 2:3; 3:12–13) are proclaimed on the Fourth Sunday in Ordinary Time (Year A). Paired with the Beatitudes (Mt 5:1–12a), they function to show that Jesus' concept of the "poor in spirit" who will receive the "kingdom of heaven" (Mt 5:3) is not a theological *novum*, but a development of the prophetic theme of the humble and righteous remnant. The community of disciples gathered around Jesus *is* this "people humble and lowly" prophesied by Zephaniah, and this community *becomes* the Church.

Haggai: The New Temple of the Lord

In the living tradition of the Church, Haggai's oracle concerning the future Temple, that the "latter glory of this house will be greater than the former" (Hag 2:8–9), has played perhaps the most significant role. Indeed, from the time of the New Testament itself, this oracle was interpreted as being fulfilled in the inauguration of the heavenly "kingdom" that "cannot be shaken" (Heb 12:26–29). The Church Fathers, picking up on this typological interpretation, applied this fulfillment to the Church as the New Temple of God:

> Surely the glory of the house of the New Testament is greater than that of the Old because it was built of better materials, namely, those living stones which are human beings renewed by faith and grace. Yet, precisely because Solomon's Temple was renovated—was made new—it was a prophetic symbol of the second Testament which is called New. Accordingly we must understand the words God spoke by Aggeus' mouth, "And I will give peace in that place" [Hag 2:9 LXX], as referring to the place for which the Temple stood.[25]

Notice once again how Augustine emphasizes that the coming of a new Temple that not only fulfills but *exceeds* the glory of the old is not a novelty

---

[25] Augustine, *City of God* 18.48, in Augustine, *The City of God, Books XVII–XXII*, trans. Gerald G. Walsh and Daniel J. Honan, The Fathers of the Church 24 (Washington, D.C.: Catholic University of America Press, 1964), 167–68.

proposed by Christians, but something foretold by the Old Testament prophets themselves.

Unfortunately, Haggai is never proclaimed in a Sunday liturgy. The prophet's
message is only proclaimed during daily Mass on Thursday (Hag 1:1–8) and
Friday (2:1–9) of the Twenty-Fifth Week in Ordinary Time (Year I). Haggai
follows Ezra as the first reading in the Twenty-Fifth Week and, in so doing,
fills out the history of Judah's return from exile. In the Office of Readings,
the entire book is read on Sunday and Monday of the Twenty-Eighth Week
in Ordinary Time, the week given over to reading the three postexilic minor
prophets (Haggai, Zechariah, Malachi).

Zechariah: The High Priest "Jesus" and the Passion of Christ

Although Zechariah belongs to the "minor" prophets, its influence upon the
living tradition of the Church was anything but. For one thing, all four Gospels
record the fact that Jesus deliberately enacted the fulfillment of the oracle of the
coming king to Jerusalem in the second half of the book when he rode into
Jerusalem on a donkey in the "triumphal entry" (Mt 21:1–11; Mk 11:1–10;
Lk 19:29–38; Jn 12:12–18; cf. Zech 9:9–10). Along similar lines, during his
Passion in Gethsemane (Mt 26:30–31; Mk 14:27–28), Jesus applies to himself
Zechariah's oracle of the "shepherd" who is "struck" and whose sheep scatter.
Finally, both the Gospel of John and the book of Revelation apply the vision
of the people of Judea looking upon "the one whom they pierced" (Zech
12:10) to the Passion and return of Jesus (Jn 19:37; Rev 1:7). Indeed, by some
measures, the Gospels quote or allude to Zechariah 9–14 in the Passion narratives more than any other section of the Old Testament.

In addition to these well-known uses of the prophecies of Zechariah in the
New Testament, perhaps the most popular and influential passage among the
Church Fathers was Zechariah's vision of "Joshua the high priest" clothed in
"filthy garments" standing with "Satan ... at his right hand to accuse him"
(Zech 3:1–5). In the Greek Septuagint of Zechariah, the high priest's name is
"Jesus" (Greek *Iesous*), and multiple early Fathers—Gregory of Nyssa, Cyprian
of Carthage, Ambrose of Milan, and Theodoret of Cyrus, to mention but a
few—saw in this a prefiguration of the "clothing" of Jesus in our sins during his
Passion, and his subsequent vindication:

> As for the words 'to accuse him,' the devil was His adversary, just as we said,
> because Jesus was clothed in garments that were filthy with our sins; but after
> Satan heard the command, 'May the Lord who has chosen Jerusalem rebuke you!'
> [Zech 3:2] he stood no longer on the right but retired behind Him and crawled
> under His feet. Without delay Jesus the High Priest dons the long garment and
> is clothed in shining raiment, and in harmony with kingly authority—with the
> hands of Zorobabel—[he] lays the foundations of the Church and erects the spir-
> itual Jerusalem.[26]

---

[26]Jerome, *Homilies on the Psalms*, Alternate Series 61, in Jerome, *Homilies*, vol. 2, trans. Marie Liguori
Ewald, The Fathers of the Church 57 (Washington, D.C.: Catholic University of America Press, 1966), 31.

This is a marvelous example of spiritual exegesis by Jerome: in Zechariah's oracle, he sees the prefiguration of both Jesus' priestly mission of becoming a "sin-bearer" and his royal mission of building the New Temple of the Church.

In the contemporary Lectionary, two passages of Zechariah, both from the second half of the book, are proclaimed regularly: the triumphal entry of the messianic king on a donkey (Zech 9:9–10; Fourteenth Sunday in Ordinary Time [Year A]) and the eschatological outpouring of Spirit and water upon those who mourn for the pierced one (Zech 12:10–11, 13:1; Twelfth Sunday in Ordinary Time [Year C]). These complement Gospel readings that emphasize the gentleness and humility of Christ (Mt 11:25–30) and his inevitable crucifixion (Lk 9:18–24).

In the Liturgy of the Hours, Zechariah 1–8 is read semi-continuously in historical sequence with other postexilic books in Week 28 (for daily Mass, in Weeks 25–26), but Zechariah 9–14 holds a privileged place as the biblical book read in Week 33 leading up to the Solemnity of Christ the King, the great feast of expectation of the final judgment and Second Coming. Thus, as in antiquity, Zechariah continues to function in the modern liturgy as book of messianic and eschatological oracles.

Malachi: The "Pure Sacrifice" Offered from the Rising of the Sun

When we turn to the living tradition of the Church, there are two major aspects of the book that left an indelible mark on the Christian faith.

The first is already present in the New Testament, insofar as Malachi's exhortation to watch for the coming of Elijah before the day of the Lord (Mal 3:23–24 [4:5–6]) is interpreted by Jesus himself with reference to the coming of John the Baptist as "Elijah who is to come" (Mt 11:14; cf. Mt 17:10–13; Mk 9:11–13; Lk 1:17). In this way the evangelists point out the fulfillment of Malachi's prophecy in the figure of John the Baptist.

The second, though perhaps less well known, was very widely utilized in the early Church Fathers: the interpretation of Malachi's oracle describing a time when "from the rising of the sun to its setting my name is great among the nations [= Gentiles]" and "in every place ... a pure offering" offered in YHWH's name (Mal 1:11). Now, insofar as the oracle describes an actual "bread offering" (Hebrew *minhah*)—which could only be offered under Mosaic law in the Tabernacle or Temple (Deut 12)—a stunning string of Church Fathers, such as Augustine, Chrysostom, Justin Martyr, Origen, and others—saw this as an oracle of the offering of the sacrifice of the Eucharist throughout the world by the Church.[27] For example, Augustine cites this oracle as a demonstration to the Jewish people that Jesus was in fact the Messiah:

> Now I turn to Malachias.... *Now if we see that everywhere in our time, 'from the rising of the sun to the going down thereof'* [Mal 1:11], *this sacrifice is being offered by Christ's priests according to the order of Melchisedeh*, and if the Jews are in no position to deny that their sacrifices, rejected in the first verse, have come to an end—how is

---

[27] See Ferreiro, *Twelve Prophets*, 288–93.

it that they can be looking for another Christ? They read the prophecy; they see its fulfillment before their very eyes. Why can they not realize that He must have been the Christ to fulfil it, since nobody else could?[28]

Significantly, in more recent times, the third Eucharistic Prayer of the contemporary *Roman Missal* employs the very words of Malachi as part of the Epiclesis over the bread and wine:

> You give life to all things and make them holy,
> and you never cease to gather a people to yourself,
> *so that from the rising of the sun to its setting,*
> *a pure sacrifice may be offered to your name.*[29]

In short: the Church sees the Eucharist as the "pure offering" offered to God from "the rising of the sun to its setting"—that is, in all places (from east to west) and at all times (from dawn to dusk). In this way, the one eternal sacrifice of Christ's Body and Blood assimilates to itself and fulfills all the sacrifices of the old liturgy, fulfilling Malachi's longing for a perfection of worship that is universal in time and space.

Other passages of Malachi used as Lectionary readings summarize the book's moral, messianic, and eschatological themes. Near the end of the Church year, on the Thirty-First Sunday in Ordinary Time, a passage summing up the prophet's rebuke of priest and people for their hypocrisy in worship (by offering blemished animals) (Mal 1:14—2:2, 8–10) complements Jesus' pointed rebuke of the Pharisees for their hypocrisy in manipulating the interpretation of the Mosaic law (Mt 15:1–13). This shows the consistency of Jesus' prophetic message with the classical prophets of Israel.

The Church also proclaims the dramatic oracle of the sudden coming of the "messenger of the covenant" to the Temple (Mal 3:1–4) on the Feast of the Presentation of the Lord, suggesting that this first arrival of the child Jesus to the Temple was a premonition of his mission to purify the Temple and those who served there. The same passage is also proclaimed the day before Christmas Eve (December 23), allowing the "last" of the canonical prophets to voice his vision of the coming of the Messiah on this "last" day before the birth of Christ.

Finally, on almost the last Sunday of Year C (Thirty-Third Sunday in Ordinary Time), the Church proclaims an abbreviated form of Malachi's vision of the day of the Lord (Mal 3:19–20a [= Mal 4:1–2b]) in conjunction with a portion of Jesus' eschatological discourse in Luke 21:5–19. Again, this "last" of the canonical prophets finds a place near the end of the liturgical year, this time providing scriptural background for understanding that, according to Jesus, the prophetic expectations of the "day of the Lord" are not fully realized in his first coming: the definitive universal judgment remains to be actualized when he comes again.

---

[28] Augustine, *City of God* 18.35, pp. 139–40.

[29] Eucharistic Prayer III, trans. Walsh and Honan, from *Daily Roman Missal*, ed. James Socias, 3rd ed. (Woodridge, Ill.: Midwest Theological Forum, 2010), 791.

Readings from the Minor Prophets in the Lectionary and Liturgy of the Hours on Sundays, Feast Days, Liturgical Seasons, and Other Occasions			
MSO = Masses for Special Occasions; *OM* = Optional Memorial; *VM* = Votive Mass; *Rit* = Ritual; *LH* = Liturgy of the Hours			
Passage	Description	Occasion	Explanation
Hos 2:16b, 17b, 21–22 (= 2:14b, 15b, 19–20, RSVCE 2)	Israel will call the LORD "My Husband", not "my Ba'al", and God will restore fertility to the land.	*8th Sun. in OT (B)*; St. Cecilia (Nov. 22); Common of Virgins (opt. 2); *Rit*: Consecration of Virgins & Religious Profession (opt. 10); *MSO*: For the Church (opt. 4)	Combined with Mk 2:18–22, Jesus' teaching on fasting when he says, "Can the wedding guests fast while the bridegroom is with them?", Hosea helps us identify Jesus as the God of Israel, who promised to return and resume his nuptial relationship with his people. In other contexts, the nuptial language of Hosea applies personally to virgins and women religious, or to the Church as a whole as Bride of Christ.
Hos 6:1–6	The LORD urges repentance, for "he will revive us after two days, on the third he will raise us up", and he "desires mercy, not sacrifice".	Opt. Cant. II for Vigils in Easter; Sat., 3rd Week of Lent	In Easter, this passage is understood as a mystical prophecy of the Resurrection, in which we all participate through Baptism and the other sacraments. During Lent, it reminds us to practice the works of mercy, not simply cultic observances.
Hos 6:3–6	As above, abbreviated.	*10th Sun. in OT (A)*	Jesus quotes Hos 6:6 ("I desire mercy, not sacrifice") in the Gospel (Mt 9:9–13) when Jesus is challenged for eating with sinners and tax collectors.
Hos 11:1, 3–4, 8c–9	God recalls "out of Egypt I called my son" and his tender upbringing of "Ephraim". God will yet have compassion on Ephraim.	Sacred Heart (B); *Rit*: Presentation of Lord's Prayer; *VM*: Most Sacred Heart of Jesus (opt. 7)	On liturgical celebrations of the Sacred Heart, this movingly tender poetry of Hosea serves as one of the best expressions of God's love for his people in the Old Testament, enabling us to see the crucifixion (Jn 19:31–37) as an act of love by the LORD of Israel.
Hos 14:2–10	Israel will repent and return to the LORD; he will bless them and make them flourish like a garden or vine under his shade.	Fri., 3rd Week of Lent	During Lent, these words of Hosea remind us of God's promises of compassion and blessing for those who repent and turn to seek him.
Joel 2:12–18	Joel's great call to repentance: "Return to	Ash Wednesday (1st Reading); *MSO*:	The Church uses Joel's famous line "Rend your hearts, not your garments" to remind her children

(continued)

Readings from the Minor Prophets in the Lectionary and Liturgy of the Hours on Sundays, Feast Days, Liturgical Seasons, and Other Occasions (*continued*)

MSO = Masses for Special Occasions; *OM* = Optional Memorial;
VM = Votive Mass; *Rit* = Ritual; *LH* = Liturgy of the Hours

Passage	Description	Occasion	Explanation
	me with your whole heart ... fasting, weeping, mourning. Rend your hearts, not your garments."	Remission of Sins (opt. 3)	of the spiritual nature of the great Lenten fast. Lenten mortifications are meant to express interior sorrow for sin and genuine repentance, not merely externals.
Joel 2:21–24, 26–27	The LORD has abundantly blessed the harvest; let Israel rejoice in him!	*MSO*: After the Harvest (opt. 2)	This passage is one of the most direct expressions of thanks for God's blessing of the land with fertility.
Joel 2:23–3:3a (sel.)	Rejoice, Israel, for the LORD sends rain and you will eat till satisfied. He will pour out his Spirit on all flesh.	*Rit*: Confirmation (opt. 5)	In the ritual of Confirmation, this text speaks mystically of the sacraments of Eucharist ("eat till satisfied") and Confirmation ("pour out my Spirit on all flesh"). The sacraments are seen as fulfillment of God's promises to Israel.
Joel 3:1–5 (= 2:25–32 RSVCE 2)	In the latter days, the LORD will pour out his Spirit on all people, make signs in the heavens, and all who call on him will be saved.	Pentecost Vigil (opt. 4); *MSO*: For the Laity	This is the text St. Peter quotes in his inaugural sermon during the first Pentecost (Acts 2:17–21). The outpouring of the Spirit in the New Covenant era fulfills what was "spoken through the prophets". All Christians share this Spirit: the laity are spirit-filled, sharing the prophetic charism of Christ.
Amos 5:4, 14–15, 21–24	Let Israel seek good and hate evil, that the LORD may have pity. False worship is worthless; instead, let justice surge like waters.	*MSO*: For Reconciliation (opt. 3)	Amos reminds God's people of the actions and behaviors that lead to reconciliation with God.
Amos 6:1a, 4–7	Woe to the leaders of Israel who live in indulgent luxury; they shall be the first to go into exile.	*26th Sun. in OT (C)*	Together with the parable of the rich man and Lazarus, the people of God get double testimony—from each Testament—to God's concern for the poor and opposition to selfish indulgence.
Amos 7:12–15	Amos is told to leave Bethel and flee to Judah; he denies being a	*15th Sun. in OT (B)*	There is a parallel between Amos—unlearned farm worker—commissioned as a prophet, and the apostles—unlearned fishermen—

(*continued*)

Readings from the Minor Prophets in the Lectionary and Liturgy of the Hours on Sundays, Feast Days, Liturgical Seasons, and Other Occasions (*continued*)

MSO = Masses for Special Occasions; *OM* = Optional Memorial;
VM = Votive Mass; *Rit* = Ritual; *LH* = Liturgy of the Hours

Passage	Description	Occasion	Explanation
	prophet, but claims divine commission.		commissioned by Jesus (Mk 6:7–13) to go out and preach, even if the reaction is hostile.
Amos 8:4–7	Those who trample on the needy take warning: Never will the Lord forget what they have done!	*25th Sun. in OT (C)*	Juxtaposed with the parable of the dishonest steward (Lk 16:1–3), the key theme is: "Make friends for yourselves by unrighteous mammon", and "You cannot serve God and mammon." God's people must live in detachment and generosity.
Jon 3:1–5, 10	Jonah preaches judgment in Nineveh; the people repent, and the LORD spares them.	*3rd Sun. in OT (B);* +vv. 6–9: Wed., 1st Week of Lent; *MSO*: Remission of Sins (opt. 4)	A parallel is set up between Jonah and Jesus, who preaches, "Repent, for the kingdom of God is at hand", in the Gospel (Mk 1:14–20). This passage is also used on other liturgical occasions where the theme of repentance is prominent.
Jon 3:10—4:11	Jonah fumes at the repentance of Ninevah; God teaches him a lesson in compassion by giving and then taking away his shady vine.	*MSO*: For Evangelization of Peoples (opt. 4)	This passage reminds the Church of God's compassion for the unrighteous nations, even such a place as Nineveh. We are called to look beyond the violence of governments to see the plight of the common people.
Mic 4:1–4	The LORD will raise up Mount Zion. The Word of the LORD shall go forth to judge the nations and establish peace.	*MSO*: War or Civil Disturbance (opt. 2)	Those suffering from war and rampant violence are encouraged to hope in the eschatological salvation of God. Justice and peace will triumph in God's time.
Mic 5:1–4a	From Bethlehem shall come forth a shepherd for Israel who shall establish peace.	*4th Sun. of Advent (C);* Nativity of BVM (opt. 1)	The obvious Christmas themes of this passage are highlighted by its prominent placement near the end of Advent. The mention of "she who has labor pains" (Mic 5:3) gives a Marian dimension to this prophecy.
Mic 6:6–8	What shall I sacrifice to atone for sin? "Only do justice, and love goodness, and walk humbly with your God."	St. Henry (July 13); Common of Holy Men and Women (opt. 17)	The saints, particulary St. Henry, set an example of those who followed the tripartite formula of Mic 6:8: justice, goodness, humility.

(*continued*)

Readings from the Minor Prophets in the Lectionary and Liturgy of the Hours on Sundays, Feast Days, Liturgical Seasons, and Other Occasions (*continued*)

MSO = Masses for Special Occasions; *OM* = Optional Memorial;
VM = Votive Mass; *Rit* = Ritual; *LH* = Liturgy of the Hours

Passage	Description	Occasion	Explanation
Mic 7:7–9	"As for me, I will look to the LORD … and endure his wrath … until he pleads my case."	4th Week of Lent, opt. Mass	Micah encourages the people of God to endure punishment—during Lent, self-inflicted in the form of mortifications—until the forgiveness of the LORD is made manifest.
Mic 7:14–15, 18–20	A prayer that God will shepherd his people once again and "cast into the depths of the sea all our sins" out of "loyalty to Abraham"	Sat., 2nd Week of Lent	This text comforts the hearts of the faithful during Lent by reminding them of God's faithfulness to his covenant and his abundant mercy and forgiveness.
Hab 1:2–3; 2:2–4	Habakkuk complains to the LORD; the LORD responds: Wait patiently, for the righteous "shall live by faith".	*27th Sun. in OT (C)*	Combined with Luke 17:5–10, including the Lord's statement on "faith as a grain of mustard seed", this passage emphasizes the essential role of faith in the life of the believer and shows the unity of the Testaments in pointing to the way of faith.
Hab 3:2–4, 13a, 15–19	Habakkuk sees the LORD coming up from the South in judgment and trembles; though at present all seems bleak, he confesses faith in God's salvation.	Canticle for Morn. Prayer, Fri., Wk II, and Good Friday	On Fridays, a traditional day of mourning for sin, Habakkuk reminds the people of God of the reality of God's judgment and also the hope of future forgiveness and salvation.
Zeph 2:3; 3:12–13	The humble should seek shelter in the LORD; he will leave them as a righteous remnant in Zion.	*4th Sun. in OT (A)*; Common of Holy Men and Women (opt. 18)	The Gospel is the Beatitudes (Mt 5:1–12a), a description of the poor, meek, hungry, persecuted remnant prophesied by Zephaniah: "I will leave in the midst of you a people humble and lowly."
Zeph 3:1–2, 9–13	Jerusalem is rebellious, but in days to come the nations will come to the LORD, and he will purify his people, leaving the "humble and lowly" remnant in Zion.	Tues., 3rd Week of Advent	In the Advent season, we learn to recognize the holy community of the early saints (Mary, Joseph, Zechariah, Elizabeth, Simeon, Anna), from whom John and Jesus came forth, as the "humble and lowly" remnant in Zion foreseen by the prophets.

(*continued*)

Readings from the Minor Prophets in the Lectionary and Liturgy of the Hours on Sundays, Feast Days, Liturgical Seasons, and Other Occasions (*continued*)

MSO = Masses for Special Occasions; *OM* = Optional Memorial;
VM = Votive Mass; *Rit* = Ritual; *LH* = Liturgy of the Hours

Passage	Description	Occasion	Explanation
Zeph 3:8–13	The LORD will come on his Day, to judge the nations and purify a remnant of his people: humble and lowly, they will be disturbed by no one.	Optional Canticle III for Vigils in the Easter Season	In the season of Easter, we recognize ourselves as the new "humble and lowly" community of the Risen Christ, who, through the Holy Spirit, will "not be disturbed" despite the persecutions of the nations.
Zeph 3:14–15	Shout and rejoice, O Zion, for the LORD has come to dwell in your midst.	*MSO*: Thanksgiving to God (opt. 4)	Zephaniah's poem of praise expresses the sentiments of the people of God gathered on occasions of public thanksgiving.
Zeph 3:14–18a	As above; further, the LORD will rejoice over Zion like a bridegroom over a bride.	*3rd Sun. of Advent (C)*; Dec. 21 (opt. 2); Visitation of BVM (opt. 1); *MSO*: For the Church (opt. 5)	Mary is the "daughter of Zion" (3:14) who can rejoice because "the LORD is in [her] midst." Mary is spouse of the Holy Spirit, but Zephaniah's nuptial language can also be applied to the Church, the Bride of Christ; and to the nuptial nature of the Incarnation, through which human and divine natures are wed in "one flesh".
Zeph 3:16–20	The LORD will rejoice over Zion, gathering her lame and oppressed, restoring her renown and praise in all the earth.	*MSO*: For Unity of Christians (opt. 4)	Typologically, divided and scattered Israel is a symbol of Christianity divided and rent by many sects. Yet the promise of God is restoration and renewal.
Zech 2:14–17	Rejoice! The LORD is coming to dwell in Israel; many nations will bind themselves to him, and the LORD will choose Zion.	Presentation of BVM; Our Lady of Guadalupe (opt. 1)	Again, Mary is the embodiment of the "daughter of Zion" to whom the LORD is coming "to dwell in the midst" of her; therefore, this text is appropriate for Marian feast days.
Zech 8:20–23	In the latter days, the nations shall go up to Jerusalem to seek the LORD.	*MSO*: For Evangelization of Peoples (opt. 5)	The incoming of the Gentiles to Jerusalem is fulfilled in the missionary efforts of the Church to bring the Gospel to all people.
Zech 9:9–10	Rejoice, O Daughter of Zion! Your king comes	*14th Sun. in OT (A)*; *MSO*: War or Civil	In the Gospel (Mt 11:25–30), Jesus says, "Take my yoke upon you ... for I am gentle and lowly in heart."

(*continued*)

Readings from the Minor Prophets in the Lectionary and Liturgy of the Hours on Sundays, Feast Days, Liturgical Seasons, and Other Occasions (*continued*)

MSO= Masses for Special Occasions; *OM*= Optional Memorial;
VM= Votive Mass; *Rit*= Ritual; *LH*= Liturgy of the Hours

Passage	Description	Occasion	Explanation
	to you humble and seated on a donkey, to establish peace.	Disturbance (opt. 3)	Jesus is revealed as the humble, peaceful king foreseen by the prophets. He is the king of peace able to put an end to wars.
Zech 12:10–11; 13:1	God will pour out a Spirit of mercy and open a fountain for David and Jerusalem, as they mourn the one they have pierced.	*12th Sun. in OT* (C)	In the Gospel (Lk 9:18–24), Jesus predicts his Passion and warns his disciples: "If any man would come after me … let him take up his cross daily." Zechariah's prophecy focuses on the Cross ("the one they have pierced") and its cleansing effects ("a fountain opened").
Zech 12:10–11; 13:6–7	As above; further, the LORD will strike the shepherd, and the sheep will be scattered.	*VM*: Mystery of the Holy Cross (opt. 5)	Zechariah's prophecies about the "pierced one" and the "shepherd struck down" focus our thoughts on the mystery of the Cross, foreseen in shadows by the prophets.
Mal 1:14b—2:2b, 8–10	The LORD condemns cheating worshippers and corrupt priests.	*31st Sun. in OT* (A)	In the Gospel (Mt 15:1–13), Jesus upbraids the scribes and Pharisees for their hypocrisy, pride, and scandalous behavior. Jesus is seen to stand in the prophetic tradition of calling for reform of piety.
Mal 3:1–4	The LORD will send his messenger, who will suddenly enter the Temple and purify the priesthood.	Presentation of the Lord; Advent, Dec. 23 (+vv. 23–24)	This passage is employed on liturgical occasions anticipating the arrival of the child Jesus, understood to be the LORD's messenger who will enter the Temple and purify the priesthood of God's people.
Mal 3:19–20a (= 4:1–2b RSV)	The day of the LORD is coming, to burn up the evildoers like chaff, but a Sun of Justice will arise for those who fear his name.	*33rd Sun. in OT* (C)	The Gospel is similarly apocalyptic (Lk 21:5–19), describing the eschatological tribulation. Yet both passages encourage perseverance of the righteous through the persecution to come, until the Sun of Justice rises.

			Reading of the Minor Prophets for Daily Mass: Ordinary Time, Year I: Weeks 25–27
Week	Day	Passage Read	Description
25	M–W	*Ezra*	
25	Th	Hag 1:1–8	The people dwell in paneled houses while the House of the LORD lies in ruins. Haggai calls the people to rebuild the Temple, that the LORD may restore blessing to them.
25	F	Hag 2:1–9	Though the Temple seems like nothing, let Zerubbabel and Jehozadak take courage: the latter splendor of this house shall be greater than the former.
25	Sa	Zech 2:5–9, 14–15a	Zechariah sees a man measure Jerusalem. God will be a wall of fire around it. He will dwell in its midst, and many nations shall join themselves to the LORD.
26	M	Zech 8:1–8	The LORD will return to Zion; the city shall be filled with old people and playing children. The LORD will bring his people back to Zion from the nations.
26	Tu	Zech 8:20–23	"Many peoples and strong nations shall come to seek the LORD of hosts in Jerusalem, and to entreat the favor of the LORD."
26	W–Th	*Nehemiah*	
26	F–Sa	*Baruch*	
27	M	Jon 1:1—2:2, 11; 2:3–8 (resp.)	God commands Jonah to preach to Nineveh. He flees on a ship to Tarshish. A storm arises, and the sailors throw him into the sea, and he is swallowed by a fish. He prays, and the fish vomits him on dry land.
27	Tu	Jon 3:1–10	Jonah preaches to Nineveh, and the whole city repents. The LORD relents from punishing them.
27	W	Jon 4:1–11	Jonah is very angry with the LORD's mercy. God teaches him a lesson in mercy by granting, then removing, a shady vine that comforts him.
27	Th	Mal 3:13–20b	The LORD rebukes those who say it is vain to serve the LORD. Those who feared God came together and wrote a Book of Remembrance. The LORD promises mercy to them.
27	Fr	Joel 1:13–15; 2:1–2	Lament and call a fast, for the terrible day of the LORD is coming, a day of judgment on all flesh.
27	Sa	Joel 4:12–21	The LORD will call all the nations to the valley of Jehoshaphat and judge them there, while he restores and avenges Jerusalem.
			Readings for Year II: Weeks 13–20
13	M	Amos 2:6–10, 13–16	The LORD condemns the Israelites for their abuse of the poor and for sexual sins, though God had destroyed the Canaanites before them and brought them up from Egypt.
13	Tu	Amos 3:1–8; 4:11–12	Because the LORD chose Israel from all the nations, yet it spurned him, so he will enter into judgment against it.

(continued)

Readings for Year II (*continued*)			
Week	Day	Passage Read	Description
13	W	Amos 5:14–15, 21–24	"Hate evil, love good, establish justice", and God may be gracious; he hates Israel's false worship, but desires that it "let justice roll down like the waters."
13	Th	Amos 7:10–17	The king and priest of Bethel tell Amos to flee to the land of Judah; Amos denies being a professional prophet, but he claims divine inspiration while calling a curse on his persecutors.
13	F	Amos 8:4–6, 9–12	The Lord condemns traders who rush the Sabbath and holy days to sell goods at unfair prices. They will be judged. A famine of the word of the Lord is coming on Israel.
13	Sa	Amos 9:11–15	In the future, God will restore the house of David and Edenic fertility to Israel.
14	M	Hos 2:16, 17c–18, 21–22	The Lord will renew his marriage to Israel, making a New Covenant of peace with it, and blessing the land.
14	Tu	Hos 8:4–7, 11–13	The Lord condemns the false altars, calf worship, and idolatry of Ephraim.
14	W	Hos 10:1–3, 7–8, 12	The Lord will tear down the altars, sacred pillars, and royal house of Samaria; the people should seek the Lord that he may "rain salvation" upon them.
14	Th	Hos 11:1–4, 8e–9	"When Israel was a child ... out of Egypt I called my son." The Lord recalls his paternal love for Israel and intention to restore that filial relationship.
14	F	Hos 14:2–10	The Lord will heal the "faithlessness" of Israel; it shall "blossom as the lily" and "flourish as a garden". Let the wise ponder these things.
14, 15	Sa–F	*Isaiah*	
15	Sa	Mic 2:1–5	Micah rebukes wealthy oppressors who "devise wickedness ... on their beds.... When the morning dawns, they perform it." The Lord will bring ruin upon them.
16	M	Mic 6:1–4, 6–8	The Lord brings a covenant-lawsuit against the people of Israel. He does not desire sacrifice, but that they "do justice, love kindness, and walk humbly" with their God.
16	Tu	Mic 7:14–15, 18–20	God will again shepherd his people Israel, and "cast all [their] sins into the depths of the sea" for the sake of his covenant love with Abraham.
16, 17, 18	W–Th	*Jeremiah*	
18	F	Nah 2:1, 3; 3:1–3, 6–7	Nineveh, full of blood and booty, will be destroyed, with none to save it.
18	Sa	Hab 1:12—2:4	Habakkuk queries: Why does the Lord allow the wicked to swallow up one more righteous than he? The Lord responds: Wait patiently for my judgment, for the righteous shall live by faith.
19, 20	M–Sa	*Ezekiel*	

Week	Day	Passage	Description
The Minor Prophets in the Office of Readings for the Liturgy of the Hours, Ordinary Time, Weeks 18–33			
18	Su	Amos 1:1—2:3	The words of Amos: "The LORD roars from Zion" and decries the crimes of Damascus, Gaza, Tyre, Edom, Ammon, and Moab.
18	M	Amos 2:4–16	The LORD decries the sins of Judah and Israel last of all. They shall surely be destroyed for their iniquities.
18	Tu	Amos 7:1–17	Amos pleads for Israel, but the LORD will send judgment nonetheless. Amaziah the priest ejects Amos from the Bethel temple for speaking against the king and sanctuary; Amos claims a divine commission to proclaim judgment.
18	W	Amos 9:1–15	The LORD promises fierce judgment on Israel and Judah, except for a remnant; nonetheless, in the future he will "raise up the tent of David" and restore Edenic fertility to the land.
18	Th	Hos 1:1–9; 3:1–5	God commands Hosea to marry Gomer, who bears children given symbolic names. She goes astray; Hosea buys her back. They live in continence, like the people of God deprived of king, priest, and Temple. Yet David will return.
18	F	Hos 2:4a, 10–25	Israel is a bride who has gone astray and forgotten the favors of her husband. Yet after she is brought low, the LORD will woo her back, renew his covenant with her, and espouse her to himself, together with the land.
18	Sa	Hos 6:1—7:2	In their affliction, the people of Israel shall return to the LORD to find mercy; nonetheless, in the present, the people are morally hopeless and headed for destruction.
19	Su	Hos 11:1–11	Out of Egypt the LORD called his son, but the Israelites strayed farther and farther from him. They will be consumed in exile; yet the LORD will restore them once more, calling them from Egypt and Assyria to resettle their land.
19	M	Hos 14:2–10	The LORD calls Israel to repentance, promising free and full forgiveness and restoration of peace and prosperity.
19	Tu	Mic 3:1–12	The prophet decries the princes, priests, and prophets of Israel, who seek only money and consume the people like a piece of meat. Because of them, Jerusalem will be reduced to rubble.
19	W	Mic 4:1–7	The mountain of the LORD shall be raised above all mountains, and the word of the LORD shall go forth from Jerusalem to judge the nations and establish peace.
19	Th	Mic 4:14—5:7	From Bethlehem shall come forth a ruler to shepherd the people of Israel. The remnant of Judah shall dwell among the nations in power and might.
19	F	Mic 6:1–15	The LORD takes Israel to court in the presence of the mountains and all nature: Israel has broken its covenant with the LORD for no reason. Yet "you have been told, O man, what is good, and what the LORD requires of you: Only to do the right and love goodness, and walk humbly with your God."

(continued)

The Minor Prophets in the Office of Readings for the Liturgy of the Hours, Ordinary Time, Weeks 18–33 *(continued)*			
Week	Day	Passage	Description
19	Sa	Mic 7:7–20	The prophet, acting in the person of Israel, bemoans his sin and pleads for God's mercy. God will remove guilt and pardon sin, in keeping with his sworn covenant with Abraham.
20	Su–Sa	*Isaiah*	
21	Su	Zeph 1:1–7;14 —2:3	The "great day of the LORD" is coming, when God will sweep away man and beast, bird and fish. Jerusalem will be wiped clean, all idolaters and wicked exterminated. Let the humble seek refuge in the LORD on the day of judgment.
21	M	Zeph 3:8–20	The LORD will gather and judge the nations, and purify them that they may worship the LORD. The remnant of Israel will be forgiven. The LORD will dwell with them and care for their poor and lame.
21, 22, 23	T–M	*Jeremiah*	
23	Tu	Hab 1:1— 2:4	Habakkuk queries God: Why do the wicked prosper? The LORD responds: I am bringing the Chaldeans to judge them. Habakkuk queries: Why judge Israel with a more wicked nation? The LORD responds: You must have faith.
23	W	Hab 2:5–20	The LORD pronounces woe on wicked nations and wicked persons alike. All shall come into judgment, for the LORD is in his holy Temple; let all mortal flesh keep silence!
23	Th–Sa	*Lamentations*	
24, 25	Su–Sa	*Ezekiel*	
26, 27		*Philippians, Timothy*	
28	Su	Hag 1:1— 2:10	Haggai rebukes the people for building their own houses and neglecting the house of the LORD. The people respond and resume construction of the Temple. Though it is humble when completed, the LORD promises future glory for it.
28	M	Hag 2:11–24	While the Temple stood in ruins, the people were unclean and struggled to survive; but now God will bless them with abundance, and Zerubbabel will be the LORD's signet ring.
28	Tu	Zech 1:1— 2:4	Zechariah sees night visions: four horseman patrolling the earth; four horns destroyed by four blacksmiths. The LORD will again have compassion on Jerusalem and Judah and rebuild his house.
28	W	Zech 3:1—4:14	Zechariah sees Joshua the high priest in dirty rags, accused by Satan before God, but God pronounces judgment in his favor and clothes him in garments of dignity. Joshua and Zerubbabel will be glorified by the LORD; they are the two "olive trees" from which the holy lampstands draw their oil and light.

(continued)

Week	Day	Passage	Description
28	Th	Zech 8:1–17, 20–23	The LORD will come and return to Zion; the city shall be filled with old people and children. Those building the Temple should take heart; the LORD will watch over them for blessing, and the Gentiles shall come to worship.
28	F	Mal 1:1–14; 2:13–16	The LORD promises his love for Jacob; yet he rebukes the people for offering marred sacrificial animals and divorcing their wives.
28	Sa	Mal 3:1–24	The end of Malachi: The LORD will send his messenger ahead of him who will come suddenly to purify the Temple. The LORD rebukes Israel for withholding tithes and grumbling against the LORD. Elijah the prophet will precede the great day of the LORD.
29–32		*Esther, Baruch, Wisdom, Maccabees, Daniel*	
33	Su	Joel 2:21—3:5	The LORD promises a restoration of fertility to the land; in the latter days, he will pour out his Spirit on all flesh, men and women, young and old. He will work signs in the heavens, and the remnant on Zion shall be saved.
33	M	Joel 4:1–3, 9–21	The LORD will enter into apocalyptic judgment against the nations in the valley of Jehoshaphat; Jerusalem will drip with wine and milk; the river of life shall spring from the Temple, and Judah and Jerusalem will abide for all generations.
33	Tu	Zech 9:1—10:2	All Judah's traditional enemies will be subdued and assimilated within it. Jerusalem will rejoice as its king arrives humbly, seated on a donkey. God will honor his covenant with his people and restore peace, prosperity, and fertility to the land.
33	W	Zech 10:3—11:3	God proclaims judgment on the "shepherds" and promises to strengthen Judah and Joseph for battle. He will call his people back from all the far places to which they have been scattered and humble their enemies.
33	Th	Zech 11:4—12:8	The LORD commands the prophet to "shepherd" his people with two staffs, "Grace" (Davidic covenant) and "Union" (bond of Israel with Judah). He breaks both staffs, showing the breach of the covenants. Yet the LORD will return and strengthen Judah and Jerusalem for the eschatological struggle.
33	F	Zech 12:9–12a; 13:1–9	The house of David and Jerusalem shall look on the one they have pierced and mourn for him. A fountain shall be opened for the cleansing of David's house and the city. False prophets shall be eradicated, and the remnant of the LORD's flock shall be saved and renew the covenant.

(continued)

Week	Day	Passage	Description
33	Sa	Zech 14:1–21	Zechariah's final apocalyptic vision: The nations will besiege and capture Jerusalem and exile half the population. Yet the LORD will come down to fight and split the Mount of Olives. The River of Life shall flow from the Temple, and there shall be no more night. The enemies will be struck with plague; those who survive among the Gentiles shall come up year after year for the Feast of Booths, and all Jerusalem shall be as holy as the Temple.

The Minor Prophets in the Office of Readings for the Liturgy of the Hours, Ordinary Time, Weeks 18–33 (*continued*)

For Further Reading

Commentaries and Studies on the Twelve Minor Prophets

Andersen, Francis I. *Habakkuk*. Anchor Yale Bible 25. New York: Doubleday, 2001.

———, and David Noel Freedman. *Amos*. Anchor Bible 24A. New York: Doubleday, 1989.

———, and David Noel Freedman. *Hosea*. Anchor Bible 24. New York: Doubleday, 1980.

Berlin, Adele. *Zephaniah*. Anchor Bible 25A. New York: Doubleday, 1994.

Chisholm, Robert B. *Handbook on the Prophets*. Grand Rapids, Mich.: Baker Academic, 2002. (See pp. 335–501.)

Christensen, Duane L. *Nahum*. Anchor Yale Bible 24f. New Haven, Conn.: Yale University Press, 2009.

Crenshaw, James L. *Joel*. Anchor Bible 24C. New York: Doubleday, 1995.

Dearman, J. Andrew. *Hosea*. New International Commentary on the Old Testament 22. Grand Rapids, Mich.: Eerdmans, 2010.

Hill, Andrew E. *Malachi*. Anchor Bible 25D. New York: Doubleday, 1998.

Landes, George M. "The 'Three Days and Three Nights' Motif in Jonah 2:1". *Journal of Biblical Literature* 86 (1967): 246–50.

Meyers, Carol L., and Eric M. Meyers. *Haggai, Zechariah 1–8*. Anchor Bible 25B. New York: Doubleday, 1987.

———. *Zechariah 9–14*. Anchor Bible 25C. New York: Doubleday, 1993.

Raabe, Paul R. *Obadiah*. Anchor Bible 24D. New York: Doubleday, 1996.

Sasson, Jack M. *Jonah*. Anchor Bible 24B. New York: Doubleday, 1990.

Sweeney, Marvin A. *Zephaniah*. Hermeneia. Minneapolis: Fortress Press, 2003.

Wolff, Hans Walter. *Joel and Amos*. Translated by Waldemar Janzen, S. Dean McBride Jr., and Charles A. Muenchow. Hermeneia. Philadelphia: Fortress Press, 1977.

———. *Micah*. Translated by Gary Stansell. Minneapolis: Augsburg, 1990.

Historical Issues in the Twelve Minor Prophets

Chavalas, Mark W. "Joel". Pages 42–53 in *The Minor Prophets, Psalms, Proverbs, Ecclesiastes, Song of Songs*. Vol. 5 of *Zondervan Illustrated Bible Backgrounds Commentary*. Volume 5. Edited by John H. Walton. Grand Rapids, Mich.: Zondervan, 2009.

———. "Zephaniah". Pages 178–91 in *The Minor Prophets, Psalms, Proverbs, Ecclesiastes, Song of Songs*. Vol. 5 of *Zondervan Illustrated Bible Backgrounds Commentary*. Edited by John H. Walton. Grand Rapids, Mich.: Zondervan, 2009.

Greer, Jonathan S. *Dinner at Dan: Biblical and Archaeological Evidence for Sacred Feasts at Iron Age II Tel Dan and Their Significance.* Culture and History of the Ancient Near East 66. Leiden and Boston: Brill, 2013.

Hill, Andrew E. "Malachi". Pages 232–45 in *The Minor Prophets, Psalms, Proverbs, Ecclesiastes, Song of Songs.* Vol. 5 of *Zondervan Illustrated Bible Backgrounds Commentary.* Edited by John H. Walton. Grand Rapids, Mich.: Zondervan, 2009.

Hoglund, Kenneth G. "Haggai". Pages 192–201 in *The Minor Prophets, Psalms, Proverbs, Ecclesiastes, Song of Songs.* Vol. 5 of *Zondervan Illustrated Bible Backgrounds Commentary.* Edited by John H. Walton. Grand Rapids, Mich.: Zondervan, 2009.

———, and John H. Walton. "Zechariah". Pages 202–31 in *The Minor Prophets, Psalms, Proverbs, Ecclesiastes, Song of Songs.* Vol. 5 of *Zondervan Illustrated Bible Backgrounds Commentary.* Edited by John H. Walton. Grand Rapids, Mich.: Zondervan, 2009.

Johnston, Philip S. "Amos". Pages 54–89 in *The Minor Prophets, Psalms, Proverbs, Ecclesiastes, Song of Songs.* Vol. 5 of *Zondervan Illustrated Bible Backgrounds Commentary.* Edited by John H. Walton. Grand Rapids, Mich.: Zondervan, 2009.

Master, Daniel M. "Micah". Pages 120–47 in *The Minor Prophets, Psalms, Proverbs, Ecclesiastes, Song of Songs.* Vol. 5 of *Zondervan Illustrated Bible Backgrounds Commentary.* Edited by John H. Walton. Grand Rapids, Mich.: Zondervan, 2009.

Matthews, Victor H. "Habakkuk". Pages 164–77 in *The Minor Prophets, Psalms, Proverbs, Ecclesiastes, Song of Songs.* Vol. 5 of *Zondervan Illustrated Bible Backgrounds Commentary.* Edited by John H. Walton. Grand Rapids, Mich.: Zondervan, 2009.

Millard, Alan R. "Nahum". Pages 148–67 in *The Minor Prophets, Psalms, Proverbs, Ecclesiastes, Song of Songs.* Vol. 5 of *Zondervan Illustrated Bible Backgrounds Commentary.* Edited by John H. Walton. Grand Rapids, Mich.: Zondervan, 2009.

———. "Obadiah". Pages 90–99 in *The Minor Prophets, Psalms, Proverbs, Ecclesiastes, Song of Songs.* Vol. 5 of *Zondervan Illustrated Bible Backgrounds Commentary.* Edited by John H. Walton. Grand Rapids, Mich.: Zondervan, 2009.

Taylor, J. Glen. "Hosea". Pages 2–41 in *The Minor Prophets, Psalms, Proverbs, Ecclesiastes, Song of Songs.* Vol. 5 of *Zondervan Illustrated Bible Backgrounds Commentary.* Edited by John H. Walton. Grand Rapids, Mich.: Zondervan, 2009.

Walton, John H. "Jonah". Pages 100–119 in *The Minor Prophets, Psalms, Proverbs, Ecclesiastes, Song of Songs.* Vol. 5 of *Zondervan Illustrated Bible Backgrounds Commentary.* Edited by John H. Walton. Grand Rapids, Mich.: Zondervan, 2009.

The Twelve Minor Prophets in the Living Tradition

Augustine, Saint. *The City of God, Books XVII–XXII.* Translated by Gerald G. Walsh and Daniel J. Honan. The Fathers of the Church 24. Washington, D.C.: Catholic University of America Press, 1964.

Caesarius of Arles, Saint. *Sermons.* Vol. 3. *187–238.* Translated by Mary Magdeleine Mueller O.S.F. The Fathers of the Church 66. Washington, D.C.: Catholic University of America Press, 1964.

Cyril of Alexandria, Saint. *Commentary on the Twelve Minor Prophets.* Vol. 1. Translated by Robert C. Hill. The Fathers of the Church 115. Washington, D.C.: Catholic University of America Press, 2007.

Cyril of Jerusalem, Saint. *The Works of Saint Cyril of Jerusalem.* Vol. 1. Translated by Leo P. McCauley, S.J. The Fathers of the Church 61. Washington, D.C.: Catholic University of America Press, 1969.

————. *Works*. Vol. 2. Translated by Leo P. McCauley, S.J., and Anthony A. Stephenson. The Fathers of the Church 64. Washington, D.C.: Catholic University of America Press, 1970.

Ferreiro, Alberto. *The Twelve Prophets*. Old Testament 14 of Ancient Christian Commentary on Scripture. Edited by Thomas C. Oden. Downers Grove, Ill.: InterVarsity Press, 2003.

Fulgentius. *Selected Works*. Translated by Robert B. Eno. The Fathers of the Church 95. Washington, D.C.: Catholic University of America Press, 1996.

Jerome, Saint. *Homilies*. Vol. 2. *Homilies 60–96*. Translated Marie Liguori Ewald. The Fathers of the Church 57. Washington, D.C.: Catholic University of America, 1966.

Theodore of Mopsuestia. *Commentary on the Twelve Minor Prophets*. Translated by Robert C. Hill. The Fathers of the Church 108. Washington, D.C.: Catholic University of America Press, 2004.

Versification of the Minor Prophets

The versification of the Hebrew Masoretic Text (MT) differs slightly from the Latin Vulgate (Vg.). Traditionally, English translations have followed the Vulgate (so KJV, ASV, RSV, RSVCE, RSVCE2, NRSV, NRSVCE, NIV, NKJV), but some recent translations follow the Masoretic Text (JPS, NJPS, NAB, NABRE). In American Catholicism, confusion may arise between the popular NAB/NABRE, which follows the MT, and translations based on the RSV tradition (RSVCE, RSVCE2, NRSVCE). Seven minor prophets are affected. The following table gives the verse equivalences:

	Hebrew MT (NAB, NABRE)	Latin Vulgate (RSV, etc.)
Hosea	2:1–2	1:10–11
	2:3–25	2:1–23
	12:1	11:12
	12:2–15	12:1–14
	14:1	13:16
	14:2–10	14:1–9
Joel	3:1–5	2:25–32
	4:1–21	3:1–21
Jonah	2:1	1:17
	2:2–11	2:1–10
Micah	4:14	5:1
	5:1–14	5:2–15
Nahum	2:1	1:15
	2:2–14	2:1–13
Zechariah	2:1–4	1:18–21
	2:5–17	2:1–13
Malachi	3:19–24	4:1–6

SUBJECT INDEX

Page numbers in *italics* indicate illustrations. Page numbers appended with an italic *b*, *m*, or *t* indicate box features, maps, or tables.

SCRIPTURE INDEX